D0924329

Essentials of FEDERAL INCOME TAXATION For Individuals and Business

LINDA M. JOHNSON, Ph.D., CPA
Accounting Professor (retired), and
CEO, LNV Services Inc.

Wolters Kluwer

EDITORIAL STAFF
Production: Jennifer Schencker, Geraldine Lally
Cover Design: Laila Gaidulis

ISBN: 978-0-8080-4156-6

4025 W. Peterson Ave.
Chicago, IL 60646-6085
800 248 3248
CCHGroup.com

Printed in the United States of America

MIX
Paper from responsible sources
FSC
www.fsc.org
FSC® C101537

List of acronyms used:

AAA—Accumulated Adjustments Account
ABLE—Achieving a Better Life Experience
ACA—(Patient Protection and) Affordable Care Act
ACRS—Accelerated Cost Recovery System
ACV—Amortized Carrying Value
ADS—Alternate Depreciation System
AFR—Applicable Federal Rate
AGI—Adjusted Gross Income
AMT—Alternative Minimum Tax
AMTI—Alternative Minimum Tax Income
AVD—Alternative Valuation Date
CD—Certificate of Deposit
CDE—Community Development Entity
CPA— Certified Public Accountant
CPE—Continuing Professional Education
CPI—Consumer Price Index
CTC—Child Tax Credit
DB—Declining Balance
DOMA—Defense of Marriage Act
DRD—Dividend Received Deduction
E&P—Earnings and Profits
EIC—Earned Income Credit
EIN—Employer Identification Number
FICA—Federal Insurance Contributions Act
FMV—Fair Market Value
FSA—Flexible Spending Account
FTE—Full-time Equivalent
FUTA—Federal Unemployment Tax Act
HI—Hospital Insurance
HOH—Head of Household
HSA—Health Savings Account
IRA—Individual Retirement Arrangement
IRS—Internal Revenue Service
LLC—Limited Liability Company
LLP—Limited Liability Partnership
MACRS—Modified Accelerated Cost Recovery System
MFJ—Married Filing Jointly
MFS—Married Filing Separately
NII—Net Investment Income
NOL—Net Operating Loss
OASDI—Old Age, Survivors, and Disability Insurance
OID—Original Issue Discount
PSC—Personal Service Corporation
PTC —Premium Tax Credit
PTIN—Preparer Tax Identification Number
QPAI—Qualified Production Activity Income
SEP—Simplified Employee Pension
SIMPLE—Savings Incentive Match Plan for Employees
SL—Straight-line
SSN—Social Security Number
TI—Taxable Income
TIN—Taxpayer Identification Number
WOTC—Work Opportunity Tax Credit

Preface

WHY STUDY FEDERAL INCOME TAXATION?

Essentials of Federal Income Taxation for Individuals and Business, 2016 Edition, covers the taxation of individuals for the 2015 tax year. It provides complete coverage in an easy-to-read and easy-to-understand format for your first course in taxation. This practical text helps you understand the tax laws and improve the reporting quality of your tax returns. The coverage does not assume that you have had an introductory accounting course. If you are interested in learning how to prepare tax returns, including your own, studying this text and mastering its content will help you solve actual tax problems and succeed in preparing your own tax returns. At press time, the *2016 Edition* contains the latest information and tax forms available for the 2015 tax year. It also contains the latest information for the 2016 tax planning process.

LOADED WITH OUTSTANDING FEATURES

Many outstanding features make the new *2016 Edition* the main reference for completing 2015 federal income tax returns. Before you start reading *Essentials of Federal Income Taxation for Individuals and Business, 2016 Edition,* you are encouraged to spend a little time looking over the next few pages. The *2016 Edition* benefits from the helpful comments and suggestions contributed by instructors and students who have taught and learned federal income taxation from previous editions.

BUSINESS ENTITY OPTION

While this text focuses on the income taxation of individuals, it is also makes available an optional course of study that examines the taxation of income earned by corporations and partnerships, as well as sole proprietorships. This option is included in response to the growing number of instructors who believe that an introductory tax course should compare and contrast the tax challenges facing the different forms of business organizations.

Those who choose to place more attention on the taxation of business entities are encouraged to study the chapters in the following sequence: 1, 2, 14, 15, 16, 3, 4, 5, 6, 7, 8, 9, 10, 11, 12, and 13. Chapters 1 and 2 cover the basic tax structure for individuals. Chapters 14, 15 and 16 introduce the students to the taxation of C corporations, S corporations, and partnerships. All subsequent chapters (3–13) include at least one special business entity problem. These problems require students to relate material covered in the chapter to the different forms of business.

The business entity problems are located near the end of each chapter's QUESTIONS AND PROBLEMS. The solutions to the business entity problems generally require information from Chapters 14, 15 and 16. Consequently, students will be reviewing these chapters on a regular basis throughout the course. The business entity problems are indicated by the business folder icon (shown here in the left margin).

OTHER SPECIAL FEATURES

- The information icon (shown here in the left margin) next to a shaded box, highlights tax tips, planning opportunities, general observations and fun facts designed to enrich the learning experience.

- The computer mouse icon (shown here in the left margin) indicates homework problems suitable for completion using tax preparation software.

- Since the last edition of *Essentials of Federal Income Taxation for Individuals and Businesses*, several tax provisions were allowed to expire at the end of 2014. At the time this textbook was sent to the printer in October, 2015, efforts to extend these provisions had not been successful. However, many believe that Congress will pass tax legislation late in 2015 or early in 2016 that will retroactively reinstate most, if not all, of these provisions. The potential changes to the tax law that may affect the 2015 tax year are discussed in shaded boxes and are identified with the new developments icon shown here in the left margin.
  Feature: This textbook presents the tax laws that will assist you in preparing tax returns for the 2015 tax year. Additional information about possible tax legislation that may affect the current tax year is discussed separately in a legislative developments box identified with the icon shown here to the left of the shaded box.
  Benefit: Although there is never any way of knowing for certain what the tax laws will be from year to year, some of the provisions presented in the textbook are expected to change in the near future. The material presented in the legislative developments box will provide you with that information, which, in turn, will assist you in tax planning for the current and future tax years.

- Line-by-line instructions describing how to complete tax forms and schedules are illustrated throughout the chapters. These illustrations are found next to the filled-in forms icon shown here in the left margin.
  Feature: Each filled-in tax form is supported by information provided from the taxpayer's records and receipts. References to specific line numbers where the taxpayer's information is entered has been provided for each filled-in form and schedule presented in the chapter. The line number references shown in the textbook correspond to the line numbers on the tax forms and schedules included in the textbook, including draft versions of the 2015 tax forms, when necessary.
  Benefit: This concise presentation makes it easier for you to relate tax data to the tax form. The format presents information supplied by the taxpayer highlighted in bold. Once this data has been entered on the apropriate line(s) of the tax form, the rest of the lines on the form can be completed by following the instructions provided on the form. This approach helps you see how information is used to complete each tax form and schedule introduced in the chapter.

- COMPREHENSIVE PROBLEMS are included in most chapters; many include two versions of the problem.
  Feature: These problems incorporate many concepts introduced in the chapter. Many of these involve completing a tax return or portions of a tax return.
  Benefit: This learning application integrates and summarizes the concepts covered in the chapter. Completing the comprehensive problems will help you see how the concepts from the chapter are reported on the tax return. By including multiple versions of the problem, students have more opportunities to solve real-world tax problems, as well as complete real-world tax returns.

- Eleven CUMULATIVE PROBLEMS are included in this textbook.
  Feature: Comprehensive problems focus primarily on the concepts introduced in the chapter. Cumulative problems, on the other hand, not only incorporate the concepts from the current chapter, but also include concepts studied in prior chapters. Many of these involve using the taxpayer's information to complete the entire income tax return.
  Benefit: These learning applications integrate and summarize concepts from multiple chapters to give students the opportunity to step back and see the big picture. Also, by completing the Cumulative Problems presented at the end-of-chapter homework materials for Chapters 2, 4, 6, 7, 9, and 12, you will gain a greater sense of what all is involved in preparing a real-world income tax return.

- Tax questions and problems requiring use of the IRS website are included at the end of the chapter. These problems are identified by the icon shown to the left here.
  Feature: The answers to these questions and problems are found in the information contained in IRS tax forms and schedules, the instructions to IRS forms and schedules, or IRS publications.
  Benefit: You will learn how to find answers to tax questions from IRS publications available on the Internet. You will also learn how to find needed tax forms, fill them out while on the Internet, and print out copies of the completed forms. These learning applications provide you the opportunity to obtain knowledge about tax law using information outside of the textbook.

HELPFUL INFORMATION INCLUDED IN THE 2016 EDITION!!

- Frequently used tax facts are provided.
  Feature: Handy Tax Facts appear on the inside front cover. Included are the 2015 tax rate schedules and standard mileage rates; standard deduction and exemption deduction amounts for 2015 and 2016; and OASDI base amounts for 2015 and 2016.
  Benefit: This helpful page provides a quick and easy reference source for frequently used tax facts.

- Commonly used AGI threshold amounts and phaseout ranges are provided.
  Feature: These amounts and ranges appear on the inside back cover.
  Benefit: This helpful page provides a quick and easy reference to some of the more commonly-used AGI thresholds and phase-out ranges.

- Paragraph referencing system.
  Feature: All major headings and subheadings in the chapter have been referenced using a paragraph referencing system.
  Benefit: Paragraph references provide an additional method of indexing the material in each chapter. When referring to information in a chapter, students and instructors can refer to either the page number on the page or the paragraph number where the material can be found. Paragraph references also are used throughout the chapters to cross-reference material discussed elsewhere in the textbook.

- Learning objectives provided at the beginning of each chapter.
  Feature: The major learning objectives for each chapter have been provided and referenced in the homework problems.
  Benefit: Each homework problem is linked to a learning objective. This helps students make sure that they have mastered all major learning objectives before proceeding to the next chapter.

- Numerous examples are provided.
  Feature: Every chapter includes numerous easy-to-follow examples.
  Benefit: These examples show you how the tax laws are applied to a variety of real-life situations.

- Step-by-step instructions on how to access IRS forms and publications from the IRS website is given.
  Feature: Information on how to obtain forms and publications from the IRS through the Internet appears in Appendix A after Chapter 16.
  Benefit: This information will help you access the most up-to-date forms, instructions to forms, and IRS publications referenced in the text.

- Appendix of commonly-used blank tax forms.
  Feature: Blank copies of selected tax forms and schedules are provided in Appendix B.
  Benefit: The selected forms and schedules provided are some of the more commonly-used forms and schedules. Having these forms and schedules in one place will help students visualize the flow of tax information on the tax return. The tax forms and schedules included in Appendix B are the most recent ones available at the time the *2016 Edition* was sent to the printer.

OTHER SUCCESSFUL FEATURES OF ESSENTIALS OF FEDERAL INCOME TAXATION FOR INDIVIDUALS AND BUSINESS, 2016 EDITION

- Comprehensive coverage of self-employed taxpayers (Chapter 7)
- Detailed coverage of business entities, including C corporations, partnerships, and S corporations
- Almost 50 filled-in forms, schedules, and worksheets are illustrated, each including details regarding the line numbers where data is initially entered by the taxpayer or tax preparer
- Multiple versions (a./b.) for many comprehensive problems, allowing students the opportunity to work two different problems using the same tax forms
- A table referencing the filled-in tax forms, schedules, and worksheets follows the Table of Contents
- A detailed Table of Contents of headings and subheadings for each chapter is located at the end of this Preface
- Tax tips are provided throughout the textbook to assist with tax planning and tax reduction
- Problems at end of chapters designated for tax software solution
- Assignments that provide actual application and check students' understanding
- Acronym list on copyright page (that precedes this Preface) provides actual words to the acronyms used in this textbook

SPECIAL NOTE REGARDING FINAL TAX FORMS AND SCHEDULES FOR THE 2015 TAX YEAR

One of the user-friendly features of *Essentials of Federal Taxation for Individuals and Business*, is the filled-in forms that follow the discussion of the tax topic. To illustrate how the relevant tax form is completed, the information needed to complete the form is provided. Line number references and calculations are then provided to help you see how to prepare the form. This technique enhances your learning experience, and gives you the tools necessary to prepare the real-world tax return problems found at the end of the chapter. To this end, the *2016 Edition* includes the most up-to-date tax forms and schedules available at the time the textbook was sent to the printer in October, 2015. When final forms were not available, draft versions of the form were included in the textbook. When a draft version of the current year's tax form had not been released, the final version of the prior year's form was used. Usually, the use of draft forms or the prior year's tax forms does not pose much of a problem, as many tax forms do not change much from year to year.

When completing tax return problems at the end of the chapters, it is recommended that the final version of each form and schedule be used. However, please keep in mind that the line number references might change should the final version of the form differ in any way from the form that appears in the textbook. Final tax forms and schedules can be downloaded from the IRS website. Appendix A includes step-by-step instructions on how to use the IRS website to download tax forms and IRS Publications.

CURRENT LEGISLATIVE DEVELOPMENTS

For well over a decade, several tax provisions have been allowed to expire time and again, only to be temporarily extended at a later date. Often these provisions are renewed retroactively. Most recently, several tax "extenders" expired at the end of 2014. At the time this textbook was sent to the printer, Congress had not passed legislation to extend them. Although many feel that some sort of tax legislation will be passed by Congress late in 2015 or early in 2016, there is no way of knowing with any certainty what that final tax bill will include.

With that in mind, the *2016 Edition* contains all of the current tax law in effect as of the time this textbook was sent to the printer in October, 2015. It also includes a discussion of possible (retroactive) changes to the tax laws in shaded text (next to the New Developments icon). In the event that Congress passes tax legislation late in 2015 or early in 2016 that affects the 2015 tax year, a summary of the tax bill can be found at: **CCHGroup.com/Legislation.**

For the latest developments and updates please visit **CCHGroup.com/Resources.**

About the Author

LINDA M. JOHNSON, PH.D., C.P.A.

Professor Johnson received her Bachelor of Science degree in Accountancy from the University of Illinois, Urbana-Champaign and her doctorate from Arizona State University. In her over 20 years of collegiate teaching of graduate and undergraduate tax courses, Professor Johnson received over a dozen departmental, college, and university teaching awards, including the university's top teaching award while on the faculty at Northern Illinois University and as a teaching assistant at Arizona State University. Her professional experience includes working in the tax department for three years at Arthur Young & Company in Houston, Texas (now part of Ernst & Young) and as a faculty intern with Crowe Chizek & Company, LLC at the Oakbrook, Illinois office (now part of Crowe Horwath, LLP). Professor Johnson has published several articles on topics in taxation at various professional journals, including the *Journal of Accountancy*, *Taxes – The Tax Magazine*, *The CPA Journal*, and *The Tax Adviser*.

Acknowledgments

We express our appreciation to the many instructors and students who have contributed suggestions to make this textbook more interesting, understandable, and practical to those who study federal income taxation. Because of their very helpful recommendations, the *2016 Edition* will better satisfy the learning needs of students and the teaching needs of instructors. Our goal is to continue to make improvements with each edition. In this regard, we welcome and appreciate any comments, criticisms or suggestions you may have about this textbook.

Linda M. Johnson

Contents

FILLED-IN TAX FORMS AND SCHEDULES

Table of Contents

Chapter

1

Overview of the Tax Structure

CHAPTER CONTENTS

LEARNING OBJECTIVES

After completing Chapter 1, you should be able to:

1. Describe how taxable income is computed.
2. Distinguish between the concepts of gross income, deductions, and tax credits.
3. Compute a taxpayer's total standard deduction.
4. Determine the number of persons the taxpayer can claim as a dependent, and compute the taxpayer's exemption deduction.
5. Determine a taxpayer's filing status.
6. Understand a taxpayer's filing requirements and responsibilities.
7. Understand how Congress uses the tax laws to meet certain objectives and how taxpayers can use tax planning to their advantage.

CHAPTER OVERVIEW

This textbook provides an introduction of the U.S. income tax system as it pertains to individuals and their businesses. Prior to the Civil War, government revenues came mainly from sales taxes and tariffs. In 1862, Congress enacted the first income tax to pay for the costs of the Civil War. After 10 years, the war was paid for and the income tax went away. In 1894, the government found itself in need of more revenue, prompting Congress to re-enact the income tax. A year later, the U.S. Supreme Court ruled that the individual income tax was unconstitutional, as the Constitution required a direct tax to be "apportioned according to the population of each state." Thus, the only way to impose an individual income tax was for Congress to amend the Constitution. In 1913, Congress passed the 16th Amendment to the Constitution, which allowed the income tax to become a permanent part of the U.S. tax system.

The federal government uses a progressive tax rate structure to tax income. This means that as income rises, the tax rate increases. Back in 1913, an individual's income was taxed at a 1% rate. When income reached $20,000, a surtax was imposed. This surtax started at 1% and gradually increased to 6% for taxable income above $500,000. Today, tax rates range from 10% to 39.6%. The current rate schedules appear on the Handy Tax Facts page on the inside front cover of this textbook.

Our current tax system, like the original one, requires taxpayers to determine their own taxes. It also requires that each taxpayer file a tax return and pay any tax due the government by certain deadlines. Taxpayers that fail to meet these requirements face possible fines, penalties, and in extreme cases, jail time. In addition, the Internal Revenue Service (IRS) charges interest on unpaid taxes.

Many taxpayers seek help from tax professionals, who prepare about half of all filed tax returns. Although many taxpayers hire tax preparers to prepare their tax returns, every taxpayer should have a basic understanding of the tax laws. This understanding will help them prepare their own returns or anticipate the information tax professionals need to prepare their clients' returns. This basic knowledge also will help them review a professionally prepared return before filing it with the IRS. Finally, an understanding of the tax laws can help taxpayers recognize potential problems before taxable events take place. Through proper planning, taxpayers can reduce the amount of taxes they owe.

The first part of this chapter provides an overview of our current income tax system. The last section presents basic tax planning guidelines.

¶101 Income Tax Objectives

The federal income tax system raises money (tax revenues) to help cover the government's annual operating costs. The U.S. Constitution gives Congress the power to enact and change federal tax laws. Thus, it is Congress that decides what amount to tax and what tax rates to use in raising tax revenues. However, Congress also uses tax laws to achieve various economic, political, and social goals. These include redistributing the country's wealth, encouraging economic growth and full employment, and modifying certain behaviors.

For example, if the government's goal is to increase employment, Congress can lower taxes, thereby giving taxpayers more money to spend. Increased spending by taxpayers would create more demand for products and services, and result in a need for an increased number of workers to make the products and provide the services. An example of Congress's use of the tax laws to discourage certain behavior is the excise tax added to the cost of cigarettes. With an added cost, the desired result is a decrease in demand for tobacco.

¶102 Basic Tax Formula

Governments levy taxes by assessing a tax rate to a tax base. In the income tax system, the tax base is taxable income. Simply put, "taxable income" is the difference between the amount of income the government decides to tax and the deductions it allows to be subtracted from this income.

Anything that causes wealth to increase generally is regarded as income. However, not all items that increase one's wealth are taxed. Income that the government taxes is called "gross income." Most deductions involve expenses that the government allows to reduce gross income. However, some deductions are not tied to expenditures. Gross income is discussed in Chapters 3 and 4. Tax deductions are discussed later in this chapter and in Chapters 4 through 11.

Basic Taxable Income Formula

	Income from all sources
–	Exempt income
=	Gross income
–	Deductions
=	Taxable income

For purposes of this textbook, a "taxpayer" is any person or entity required to file an income tax return with the Internal Revenue Service (IRS). Regular corporations (called "C corporations") are business entities that pay tax each year on their taxable income. In this regard, they are similar to individual taxpayers. Corporations are the focus of Chapter 14.

However, not all taxpayers pay income taxes. Flow-through entities report their gross income and tax deductions to the IRS. However, it is the owners of these entities that pay taxes on their respective shares of the entity's taxable income. Partnerships and S corporations are examples of flow-through entities. They are the focus of Chapters 15 and 16.

Although the focus of this textbook begins with the individual taxpayer, the taxation of businesses is presented in this textbook as well. Many of the tax laws described in this textbook apply equally to all types of taxpayers. However, special rules sometimes apply only to one group of taxpayers. For example, the basic formula for computing taxable income presented above is the same for both corporations and individuals. However, individuals are entitled to more types of deductions and thus use an expanded taxable income formula (described in ¶103).

For purposes of this textbook, unless from the discussion it is clear that use of the term "taxpayer" refers to a particular type of taxpayer (for example, an individual or a corporation), when the term "taxpayer" is used when discussing a tax law, such law applies to all types of taxpayers, including corporations, individuals, and flow-through entities. If a tax law is unique to one type of taxpayer, then the title of the section or the discussion itself will state the type of taxpayer to which that particular tax law applies.

After C corporations and individuals compute taxable income, they compute their tax liability using the tax rates set by Congress. Although different tax rates may apply, the federal income tax rates are progressive, which means that as taxable income increases, so too does the tax rate.

Taxpayers may owe other taxes in addition to income taxes. Individuals may owe self-employment taxes, penalties for early distributions from retirement accounts, or alternative minimum tax (AMT). Corporations also may be subject to AMT. Many of these other taxes are discussed in this textbook.

Individuals and C corporations may also be entitled to subtract tax credits from these taxes to arrive at their taxes owed (or refund due) at the end of the year. Tax credits can be business-related or personal in nature. The former applies to all types of businesses. The latter applies only to individual taxpayers. Tax credits generated by flow-through entities are passed through to the owners, who then report the tax credits on their income tax returns.

Calculation of Taxes Owed (To Be Refunded)

	Taxable income
×	Tax rate
=	Income tax liability
+	Additional taxes
–	Tax credits and prepayments
=	Final tax due (refund)

¶102.01 DEDUCTIONS VERSUS CREDITS

The distinction between a deduction and a credit is important. Tax credits reduce tax liability. Tax deductions reduce taxable income. Tax credits reduce the taxpayer's taxes by the amount of the tax credit. Deductions reduce the taxpayer's taxes by the amount of the deduction times the taxpayer's tax rate. For example, a $100 deduction reduces taxable income by $100. This saves $15 in taxes if the tax rate is 15% ($100 × 15%), but saves $35 if the tax rate is 35% ($100 × 35%). A $100 tax credit, on the other hand, reduces taxes by $100 regardless of the taxpayer's tax rate.

¶103 Individual Taxpayers

Although there are a variety of types of income, the concept of gross income is the same for all taxpayers. That is, the government taxes some income, while other types of income are not subject to income tax. The tax laws also allow a variety of deductions in the calculation of taxable income. Individual taxpayers can reduce their taxable income by a mix of business and personal deductions. Accordingly, the tax laws separate the deductions available to individuals into two categories: deductions for adjusted gross income (AGI) and deductions from AGI. Deductions from AGI are more personal in nature. They are introduced in this chapter and are the focus of Chapters 5 and 6.

The tax rate that individual taxpayers apply to taxable income depends on their filing status. A person's filing status depends on whether he or she is married on the last day of the tax year, along with other factors. More about the rules for each filing status will be presented later in the chapter at ¶112. The five filing statuses are: (1) married filing jointly (MFJ); (2) married filing separately (MFS); (3) qualifying widow(er); (4) head of household (HOH); and (5) single.

Tax Formula for Individuals

	Income from all sources
–	Exempt income
=	Gross income
–	Deductions for AGI (adjusted gross income)
=	AGI
–	Deductions from AGI
	Itemized deductions or standard deduction
	Exemption deduction (personal and dependency)
=	Taxable income
×	Tax rate
=	Income tax liability
+	Additional taxes
–	Tax credits and prepayments
=	Final tax due (refund)

Individuals who are required to file an income tax return file one of the following tax returns:

1. Form 1040EZ, Income Tax Return for Single and Joint Filers with No Dependents
2. Form 1040A, U.S. Individual Income Tax Return
3. Form 1040, U.S. Individual Income Tax Return

As its title suggests, Form 1040EZ is the easiest of the tax forms to complete. However, only certain taxpayers can use Form 1040EZ, as will be explained in Chapter 2. Form 1040A is introduced in Chapters 3 and 4. Although many individual taxpayers can use either Form 1040EZ or 1040A, many must file Form 1040 (often referred to as the "long form").

¶104 Gross Income

Taxpayers must be able to compute their gross income. The Internal Revenue Code (the Code) is the source of tax law written by Congress. The Code defines gross income as all wealth that flows to a taxpayer from whatever source derived. It then exempts some income from taxation. The Code lists the following different gross income sources (and implies that others exist):

1. Compensation for services, including salary, wages, fees, commissions, fringe benefits, etc.
2. Gross income from a business
3. Gains from the disposal of property
4. Interest
5. Rents
6. Royalties
7. Dividends
8. Alimony and separate maintenance payments
9. Annuities
10. Income generated from life insurance proceeds
11. Pensions
12. Income from forgiveness of debt
13. Share of distributive partnership income and prorata share of S Corporation income
14. Income in respect of a decedent
15. Income from an interest in an estate or trust

To determine gross income, taxpayers generally examine their various sources of income (items that increase their wealth) and subtract out exempt income. Regardless of the form or name of an income item, proper authority must exist to exclude the item from gross income. Taxpayers may find such authority in the tax laws, which include the Code, Treasury Regulations, IRS rulings, or case law. From gross income, taxpayers subtract allowed deductions to arrive at taxable income.

¶104.01 IMPORTANCE OF GROSS INCOME

It is important that taxpayers correctly compute their gross income. When gross income exceeds a certain amount, taxpayers must file an income tax return (see ¶113.02). Failure to file a proper return on time can result in tax penalties. Also, when a taxpayer accidentally understates gross income by more than 25%, the IRS is given more time to audit the taxpayer's return (see ¶115.01). Finally, individuals may be allowed or denied a deduction for claiming another person as a dependent based on the amount of that other person's gross income (discussed at ¶109.03).

¶105 Deductions for Individual Taxpayers

Individual taxpayers have two broad groups of deductions: deductions for AGI and deductions from AGI. Taxpayers subtract deductions for AGI from gross income to arrive at AGI. They then subtract deductions from AGI to arrive at taxable income.

There are two types of deductions from AGI. One is the *greater of* a taxpayer's itemized deductions or standard deduction. The other is a (personal and dependency) exemption deduction. Corporations, partnerships, estates, and trusts do not compute AGI.

¶105.01 DEDUCTIONS FOR AGI

The Code defines an individual's AGI as gross income less certain deductions. Deductions for AGI are covered in Chapters 4, and 7–11. Some of the major deductions include:

1. Trade and business deductions for business owners
2. Losses on the disposal of business or investment property
3. Deductions related to rental and royalty income
4. Certain contributions to retirement plans of self-employed individuals
5. Certain contributions to traditional Individual Retirement Accounts (IRAs)
6. Penalties for early withdrawals from certificates of deposits
7. Alimony paid
8. Qualified moving expenses
9. One-half of self-employment tax
10. Health insurance premiums paid by self-employed persons
11. Individual contributions to a medical savings or health savings accounts
12. Interest paid on student loans
13. Domestic production activities deduction

¶105.02 DEDUCTIONS FROM AGI

After computing AGI, individuals subtract out the greater of their itemized deductions or their total standard deduction. They then subtract out their exemption deduction. Relative to deductions for AGI, itemized deductions are expenses that typically are more personal in nature. Itemized deductions are the focus of Chapters 5 and 6. They include:

1. Medical expenses
2. Taxes
3. Interest
4. Charitable contributions
5. Casualty and theft losses
6. Employee business (job) expenses and some miscellaneous deductions
7. Other miscellaneous deductions

¶106 Standard Deduction

The standard deduction is a deduction from AGI that only applies to individual taxpayers. It consists of two amounts: the basic standard deduction and the additional standard deduction. Both amounts are adjusted for inflation each year (a process described in ¶202). Taxpayers filing Form 1040EZ or Form 1040A must use the standard deduction. Also, when spouses file separate returns, both spouses must either itemize deductions or take the standard deduction. Thus, if one spouse itemizes, the other spouse's standard deduction is $0. This forces the other spouse to itemize as well.

¶106.01 BASIC STANDARD DEDUCTION

There are four basic standard deduction amounts. Filing status determines which amount applies. A special rule applies to persons who are claimed as a dependent of another taxpayer (as discussed later in ¶106.03, Standard Deduction for Dependents).

Basic Standard Deduction Amounts for 2015

Filing Status	Amount
Married filing jointly (MFJ)	$12,600
Qualifying widow(er)	12,600
Head of household (HOH)	9,250
Single	6,300
Married filing separately (MFS)	6,300

¶106.02 ADDITIONAL STANDARD DEDUCTION

Blind and elderly taxpayers claim an additional standard deduction amount. This additional deduction is available only for the taxpayer, which includes both spouses when a joint return is filed. A taxpayer cannot claim an additional standard deduction for an elderly or blind dependent. There are two additional standard deduction amounts. The taxpayer's filing status determines which amount is used.

Additional Standard Deduction Amounts for 2015

MFJ, MFS and qualifying widow(er)	$1,250
Single and head of household	1,550

For a taxpayer to get an additional standard deduction, his or her status as elderly or blind must exist at the end of the tax year (or at death). For tax purposes, individuals age the day before their calendar birthday, and elderly is defined as having reached age 65. Thus, a taxpayer who turns 65 on January 1 is 65 for tax purposes as of December 31 of the preceding year.

A taxpayer may claim the additional deduction for blindness either by failing a visual ability or field of vision test. For the visual ability test, sight in either eye cannot exceed 20/200 with a corrective lens. For the field of vision test, the person's field of vision cannot exceed 20 degrees. The taxpayer supports the additional deduction for blindness with a certified statement from an eye doctor.

Each incidence of age and blindness carries with it an additional deduction. In the case of married taxpayers, each spouse is eligible for both deductions. Thus, if both spouses are age 65, the total additional standard deduction is $2,500 (2 × $1,250). If both spouses are age 65 and one is blind, the extra deduction is $3,750 (3 × $1,250). For a single person, age 65 and blind, the extra deduction is $3,100 (2 × $1,550).

EXAMPLE 1

Pam is 70 and blind. Her filing status is single. Pam's 2015 total standard deduction equals $9,400 ($6,300 + ($1,550 × 2)).

EXAMPLE 2

Don and Dina Miner are married and file a joint return (MFJ) in 2015. As of December 31, 2015, Don is 67 and Dina is 64. Neither have any problems with their vision. The Miners add to their $12,600 basic standard deduction for MFJ an additional $1,250 for Don's age. Their total standard deduction equals $13,850. If the Miners' itemized deductions exceed this amount, they will itemize. Otherwise they will subtract $13,850 from their AGI when computing their 2015 taxable income.

¶106.03 STANDARD DEDUCTION FOR DEPENDENTS

For 2015, a person who qualifies as a dependent of another taxpayer computes the basic standard deduction as the *greater of* (i) $1,050 or (ii) earned income plus $350. The deduction cannot exceed the basic standard deduction for the dependent's filing status. Any additional standard deduction for which the dependent qualifies is added to the basic standard deduction.

Special rules apply to married persons who file separate returns. If either spouse is claimed as a dependent by another taxpayer, each spouse's basic standard deduction is limited to the *greater of* (i) $1,050 or (ii) the spouse's earned income plus $350. However, if one spouse itemizes deductions, the total standard deduction for the other spouse is $0.

For purposes of computing a dependent's basic standard deduction, earned income includes salaries, tips, professional fees, and other compensation received for personal services rendered. It also includes taxable scholarships and net profit from self-employment activities.

EXAMPLE 3

Sue, age 74, has no earned income and is claimed as a dependent on her son's tax return. Her 2015 basic standard deduction is limited to $1,050 (the *greater of* (i) $1,050 or (ii) $0 earned income + $350). Her additional standard deduction is $1,550. Sue deducts $2,600 ($1,050 + $1,550) from AGI when computing her 2015 taxable income.

¶106.04 STANDARD DEDUCTION WORKSHEET FOR DEPENDENTS

INFORMATION FOR FIGURE 1-1:

Figure 1-1 presents a filled-in Standard Deduction Worksheet for 16-year-old Gloria Moore. Gloria's parents claim her as a dependent. Gloria has perfect vision. She earned $1,400 working part-time during the year. Her standard deduction of $1,750 is computed as follows.

Figure 1-1: Standard Deduction Worksheet For Dependents		
1. Enter your earned income plus $350.	1.	1,750
2. Enter $1,050 (minimum amount).	2.	1,050
3. Enter the larger of line 1 or line 2.	3.	1,750
4. Enter $6,300 for single or MFS; $12,600 for MFJ or qualifying widow(er); $9,250 for HOH.	4.	6,300
5. a. Enter the lesser of line 3 or line 4.	5a.	1,750
b. If 65 or older or blind, multiply $1,550 ($1,250 if MFJ, MFS, or qualifying widow(er)) by the number of incidences of age and blindness.	5b.	0
c. Add lines 5a and 5b. This is your standard deduction.	5c.	1,750

¶107 Exemptions

The exemption deduction, like the standard deduction, reduces AGI. For 2015, this reduction is $4,000 for each exemption claimed. Like the standard deduction amount, the exemption amount is adjusted each year for inflation. Generally, the taxpayer may claim an exemption for one's self and each person who qualifies as a dependent. If a married couple files a joint tax return, each spouse can claim a personal exemption. Exemptions provide many taxpayers with their biggest tax deduction. For example, a married taxpayer with two dependent children reduces AGI by $16,000 (4 × $4,000).

¶107.01 PHASE-OUT OF EXEMPTIONS

The tax law phases out the exemption deduction for higher income taxpayers. Figure 1-2 shows the AGI amounts where both the phase-out begins and ends for each filing status.

Figure 1-2: AGI Phase-Out Range for the 2015 Exemption Deduction	Phase-Out Begins	Phase-Out Ends
Married filing jointly (MFJ) and qualifying widow(er)	$309,900	$432,400
Head of household (HOH)	284,050	406,550
Single	258,250	380,750
Married filing separately (MFS)	154,950	216,200

For every $2,500 of AGI ($1,250 for MFS), or fraction thereof, over the lower threshold amount, the taxpayer's exemption deduction is reduced by 2%. Figure 1-3 presents a worksheet used to compute the reduced deduction.

¶107.02 FILLED-IN PERSONAL AND DEPENDENCY EXEMPTION WORKSHEET

INFORMATION FOR FIGURE 1-3:

Using the worksheet below, Jack and Lauren Tanner calculate their exemption deduction. The Tanners file a joint return and claim their four children as dependents. Their AGI for 2015 is $333,460, which falls in the $309,900–$432,400 phase-out range for MFJ taxpayers (from Figure 1-2).

Figure 1-3: Filled-In Personal and Dependency Exemption Worksheet

1.	Multiply $4,000 by the number of exemptions claimed.			1.	24,000
2.	Enter the amount of AGI.	2.	333,460		
3.	Enter the AGI threshold for your filing status. a. Single, $258,250. b. Married filing jointly or qualifying widow(er), $309,900. c. Head of household, $284,050. d. Married filing separately, $154,950.	3.	309,900		
4.	Subtract line 3 from line 2. This is your excess AGI.	4.	23,560		
5.	Divide line 4 by $2,500 ($1,250 if MFS). If the result is not a whole number, round up to the next whole number. For example, round 6.0004 up to 7.	5.	10		
6.	Multiply line 5 by 2% and enter the result as a decimal amount.	6.	.20		
7.	Multiply line 1 by line 6.			7.	4,800
8.	Subtract line 7 from line 1. This is your exemption deduction.			8.	19,200

The worksheet in Figure 1-3 is used to compute the reduced exemption deduction for taxpayers whose AGI falls between the amounts shown in the two columns of Figure 1-2. If AGI is lower than the lesser amount, the taxpayer's deduction is $4,000 times the total number of exemptions claimed. If AGI exceeds the higher amount, the exemption deduction is $0.

EXAMPLE 4

Nelly's AGI for 2015 is $323,734. Nelly is divorced and files as head of household. She claims one personal exemption and her two children as dependents. Nelly's AGI falls in the $284,050–$406,550 phase-out range for head of household (from Figure 1-2). Thus, her exemption deduction is reduced.

Full exemption amount ($4,000 × 3)		$12,000
AGI	$ 323,734	
AGI threshold for HOH	(284,050)	
Excess AGI	$ 39,684	
Divide by $2,500 for HOH	÷ $2,500	
	15.87	
Rounded up to a whole number	16	
	× .02	
	.32	
	× $12,000	(3,840)
Nelly's exemption deduction		$ 8,160

CCH StudyMATE™

Your Personal Online Tax "Tutor"—24/7!

If you find taxes difficult, you're not alone!

Now you have CCH StudyMATE™, a personal online "tutor." With StudyMATE you can plug into online learning any time of day or night. CCH StudyMATE walks you through the most important concepts covered in your textbook using individual learning sessions designed to make learning as easy as possible.

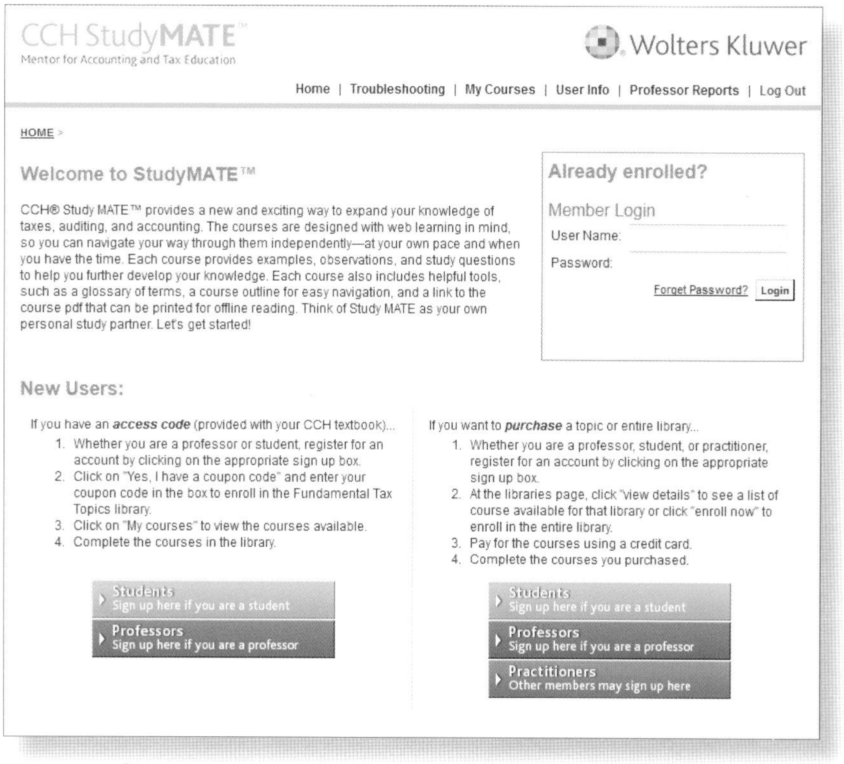

CCH Study MATE is easy to use, and since you've bought our book, you have free access to our Fundamental Tax Topics Library for a full year! CCH StudyMATE courses are designed with web learning in mind, so you can navigate your way through them independently. They are relatively short, but each course covers a substantial amount of material—including the top concepts covered in your textbook. These are student-centered courses with presentations that are different than those found in the text, so they give you another voice—another opportunity for concepts to sink in.

How Many Courses Do I Take?

Your instructor may want you to access all the courses in the fundamental series, you may be asked to take selective courses on certain topics, or your instructor may leave it up to you to use StudyMATE as you choose.

Access CCH Study MATE at www.cchstudymate.com

For your records, print your User ID and Password below:

User ID: ______________________________

Password: ______________________________

So, How Do I Get In?

Getting started is easy.

1. Go to www.cchstudymate.com and follow the instructions for New Users with an ACCESS CODE to sign up for a free account. Fill in the information on the registration page including a user ID and password of your choice.
2. Continue following the online instructions to enter your access code (provided below).
3. Click on MY COURSES to view the list of online courses, then click on the course title to begin.

ACCESS CODE:

CCHSM_15_EFIT16_1_379007

Technical Support: 866-798-5897 • support@learning.net

Wolters Kluwer

Wolters Kluwer • 4025 West Peterson Ave. • Chicago, IL 60646-6085

EXAMPLE 5

Jack's AGI for 2015 is $180,052. Jack is married at the end of 2015, but files separately from his wife. He claims one personal exemption. Jack's AGI falls within the $154,950–$216,200 phase-out range for MFS. Thus, his exemption deduction is reduced.

Full exemption amount ($4,000 × 1)		$4,000
AGI	$ 180,052	
AGI threshold for MFS	(154,950)	
Excess AGI	$ 25,102	
Divide by $1,250 for MFS	÷ $1,250	
	20.08	
Rounded up to a whole number	21	
	× .02	
	.42	
	× $4,000	(1,680)
Jack's exemption deduction		$2,320

¶107.03 PERSONAL EXEMPTIONS

Normally, a taxpayer deducts a personal exemption for him or herself. When a married couple files a joint tax return, two exemptions are allowed. However, a person who is claimed as a dependent on another taxpayer's return cannot take a personal exemption. The death of a taxpayer does not affect the amount of the personal exemption. The full exemption is allowed on a decedent's final return. No prorating is necessary.

¶107.04 EXEMPTIONS FOR DEPENDENTS

The taxpayer may claim an exemption for each person who qualifies as a "dependent." While minor children and elderly parents generally make up the taxpayer's list of dependents, others may qualify. To claim an exemption, the tax law requires that each dependent's social security number (SSN) be shown on the tax return. Without a SSN, no dependency exemption will be allowed.

Three groups of persons may qualify as the taxpayer's dependent: a qualifying child, a qualifying relative, or a qualifying nonrelative. The next sections examine the rules for each of these three groups. A dependent must meet all requirements listed for the applicable group. The taxpayer may claim an exemption for a qualified dependent, even if the dependent files a tax return. However, the dependent cannot claim a personal exemption on his or her own return. The taxpayer may also claim a full exemption for a dependent who either was born or died during the year. An exemption cannot be claimed for a stillborn child.

¶108 Qualifying Child

One group of persons who may qualify as a dependent includes those who meet the rules of a qualifying child. The first rule is that a qualifying child must be younger than the taxpayer. On a joint return, the qualifying child need only be younger than one of the spouses. In addition, a **qualifying child** must pass each of the following six tests.

1. Relationship test for qualifying child
2. Age test
3. Residency test
4. Support test for qualifying child
5. Joint return test
6. Citizenship test

¶108.01 RELATIONSHIP TEST FOR QUALIFYING CHILD

Each of the following persons passes the relationship test for a qualifying child:

- Taxpayer's natural child, stepchild, adopted child, eligible foster child, or descendants of any of these children (the taxpayer's grandchildren, great-grandchildren, etc.). An eligible foster child is a child placed with the taxpayer by an authorized agency or by a court order.
- Taxpayer's brothers and sisters, half-brothers and half-sisters, stepbrothers and stepsisters, or descendants of these siblings (the taxpayer's nieces and nephews).

EXAMPLE 6 Marie's household includes her son, her son's daughter (Marie's granddaughter), her younger sister, her sister's son (Marie's nephew), her younger stepbrother, and her stepbrother's daughter (her stepniece). Each of these persons is younger than Marie and passes the relationship test with respect to Marie. Thus, if the other five tests are passed, these persons would qualify as Marie's dependents using the qualifying child rules.

¶108.02 AGE TEST

The age test does not apply to persons who are permanently and totally disabled. For all others, a qualifying child must be either under the age of 19, or a full-time student under the age of 24. A full-time student is a person who meets the institution's full-time enrollment standard and attends classes during some part of each of five calendar months during the year. The institution must have a full-time faculty and course offerings plus a regular body of attending students. A qualifying child who has a full-time day job and attends night school cannot be a full-time student. Enrollment in correspondence or employment training courses will not qualify a person as a full-time student.

¶108.03 RESIDENCY TEST

A qualifying child must have the same residence as the taxpayer for more than half of the year. Temporary absences, such as those due to illness, education, business, military service, or vacations, are ignored. Also, special rules apply to children of divorced or separated parents (see ¶108.07).

¶108.04 SUPPORT TEST FOR QUALIFYING CHILD

A qualifying child must not provide over 50% of his or her own support. Support includes amounts paid for food, clothing, education, medical and dental care, entertainment, transportation, and lodging. It does not include funeral costs or payments of life insurance premiums.

Support also does not include scholarships received from educational institutions. For example, take a child who receives a $4,500 college scholarship in a year in which the taxpayer provides $3,800 for the child's support. If no other sources of support exist, the taxpayer meets the support requirements to claim the child as a dependent because the tax law ignores the $4,500. Thus, the taxpayer is treated as having provided all $3,800 of the child's total support.

Usually the status and source of support funds make no difference. Social security income, student loans and welfare payments count if the dependent uses them to buy support items. However, the definition of support excludes amounts a state pays for training and educating a handicapped or mentally ill child.

¶108.05 JOINT RETURN TEST

To qualify as the dependent of another taxpayer, a married person cannot file a joint return. However, an exception applies when the IRS treats a married couple's joint return as strictly means for claiming a refund of all prepaid taxes during the year. This occurs when all three of the following conditions are met:

1. Neither spouse is required to file a tax return (see discussion at ¶113),
2. A separate return filed by either spouse would not result in any tax liability, and
3. The only reason for filing a return is to get a refund of all federal income taxes withheld.

EXAMPLE 7

Amy provides 75% of her married daughter's support. For the year, her daughter earns $3,100 working part-time. Amy's son-in-law receives $4,000 of nontaxable interest. The couple lives with Amy for over half of the year. To get a refund of the income taxes withheld from the daughter's wages, the couple files a joint return. Because their combined gross income is only $3,100, the tax law does not require them to file a tax return (see ¶113). Also, both the daughter and son-in-law would have a zero tax liability if they filed separate tax returns. Thus, both the daughter and son-in-law pass the joint return test.

¶108.06 CITIZENSHIP TEST

A dependent must be a citizen of the United States, or resident of Canada or Mexico. However, an exception exists for foreign-born children adopted by U.S. citizens living abroad. These children may qualify as dependents, but only if they live with the taxpayer the entire year.

i

Children not classified as a "qualifying child" because they fail to meet one or more of the rules described at ¶108, may still qualify as dependents under the "qualifying relative" rules (see ¶109).

¶108.07 CHILDREN OF DIVORCED OR SEPARATED PARENTS

When a couple gets divorced or separates, one parent can claim an exemption for a child (son or daughter) who passes all of the tests for a qualifying child if together, the parents have custody of the child for more than half of the year. The tax law gives the exemption to the parent with the longer actual custody (**custodial parent**). However, the custodial parent may give away the exemption to the noncustodial parent. This is done by having the custodial parent complete and sign Form 8332 (or similar statement), and giving it to the noncustodial parent. The release may cover one or several years. For each year in effect, the noncustodial parent must attach the release statement to his or her tax return.

Figure 1-4 illustrates a filled-in Form 8332 for Joyce C. Black, the noncustodial parent. By completing and signing Part II of Form 8332, the custodial parent, Anthony B. Black, has agreed to allow Joyce to claim their daughter, Janet, as a dependent for the 2015-2017 tax years.

Part I of Form 8332 is completed if the custodial parent wants to give away the dependency exemption for only one year. Part III is completed if the custodial parent wants to revoke a previously granted right given to the noncustodial parent to claim the child as a dependent. For all years in which a revocation is in effect, Form 8332 is attached to the custodial parent's tax return.

Figure 1-4: Filled-In Form 8332

Form **8332**
(Rev. January 2010)
Department of the Treasury
Internal Revenue Service

Release/Revocation of Release of Claim to Exemption for Child by Custodial Parent

▶ Attach a separate form for each child.

OMB No. 1545-0074
Attachment Sequence No. **115**

Name of noncustodial parent: **Joyce C. Black**
Noncustodial parent's social security number (SSN) ▶ **693 : 24 : 6802**

Part I Release of Claim to Exemption for Current Year

I agree not to claim an exemption for ____________________
Name of child

for the tax year 20____.

____________________ Signature of custodial parent releasing claim to exemption
____________________ Custodial parent's SSN
____________________ Date

Note. If you choose not to claim an exemption for this child for future tax years, also complete Part II.

Part II Release of Claim to Exemption for Future Years (If completed, see **Noncustodial Parent** on page 2.)

I agree not to claim an exemption for **Janet A. Black**
Name of child

for the tax year(s) **2015, 2016, 2017**.
(Specify. See instructions.)

Anthony B. Black — Signature of custodial parent releasing claim to exemption
280 : 64 : 2396 — Custodial parent's SSN
12-5-15 — Date

Part III Revocation of Release of Claim to Exemption for Future Year(s)

I revoke the release of claim to an exemption for ____________________
Name of child

for the tax year(s)____________________.
(Specify. See instructions.)

____________________ Signature of custodial parent revoking the release of claim to exemption
____________________ Custodial parent's SSN
____________________ Date

¶108.08 TIE-BREAK RULES FOR CLAIMING A DEPENDENCY EXEMPTION

In situations where multiple taxpayers qualify to claim a qualifying child as a dependent, only one person can claim the child. Usually the eligible parties can decide amongst themselves which one will claim the qualifying child. However, when one of the eligible persons is the child's parent, a non-parent can claim the qualifying child only if the non-parent's AGI is higher than the AGI of the parent with the highest AGI. If the parties cannot agree as to which one will claim the qualifying child, the Code provides the following "tie-break" rules.

- When only one of the child's parents is among the group of persons who qualifies to claim the child as a dependent, the dependency exemption goes to the parent.
- When both parents qualify to claim the child as a dependent, the exemption goes to the custodial parent (or the noncustodial parent if the custodial parent has signed over the dependency exemption to the noncustodial parent, as described in ¶108.07).
- When both parents qualify to claim the child as a dependent and the child spends equal amounts of time with each parent (there is no custodial parent), the exemption goes to the parent with the highest AGI.
- When neither parent qualifies to claim the child as a dependent, the dependency exemption goes to the (non-parent) eligible person who has the highest AGI.

EXAMPLE 8

Hanna and her son, Jeffrey, live with Hanna's father. Hanna's AGI is $20,000; her father's AGI is $60,000. Jeffrey is a qualifying child to both Hanna and her father. If Hanna and her father cannot agree on who gets to claim Jeffrey as a qualifying child, under the tie-break rules, Hanna (the parent) gets to claim Jeffrey as her dependent.

EXAMPLE 9

Roy and Karen divorced in 2014. Their 10-year-old son spends half of his time with each parent. Since there is no custodial parent, the tie-break rules give the dependency exemption to the parent with the higher AGI.

i

Taxpayers use the qualifying child rules in ¶108 to determine their eligibility for: head of household filing status (discussed at ¶112.04); the earned income credit (discussed at ¶204.11); the child tax credit (discussed at ¶204.07); and the child and dependent care credit (discussed at ¶204.02).

¶109 Qualifying Relatives

A second group of persons who can be claimed as a dependent are qualifying relatives of the taxpayer. A qualifying relative is anyone who meets the following five tests, but does not meet the requirements to be a qualifying child.

1. Relationship test for qualifying relatives
2. Support test for qualifying relatives
3. Gross income test
4. Joint return test
5. Citizenship test

The rules for the joint return and citizenship tests are the same as those for a qualifying child (¶108.05 and ¶108.06). The three remaining tests are discussed in the sections that follow.

¶109.01 RELATIONSHIP TEST FOR QUALIFYING RELATIVES

The relationship test for qualifying relatives requires that the person be a relative of the taxpayer. It is not necessary that a relative live with the taxpayer to qualify as a dependent. For income tax purposes, the Code specifies that the following persons qualify as a taxpayer's relatives.

- Brother, sister, half-brother, half-sister, stepbrother, or stepsister
- Child, grandchild or other descendant of the taxpayer, including a legally adopted child
- Stepchild of the taxpayer, but not the stepchild's descendants
- Parent, grandparent, or other direct ancestor (but not a foster parent, foster grandparent, etc.)
- Stepparent
- Father-in-law, mother-in-law, son-in-law, daughter-in-law, brother-in-law, or sister-in-law
- Nephew or niece (but only if related by blood, not by marriage)
- Uncle or aunt (but only if related by blood, not by marriage)

At the time of a couple's marriage, the tax law sets up permanent legal relationships with the in-laws that continue after the couple divorces or a spouse's death. Thus, a husband may claim an exemption for his mother-in-law after his wife's death (provided the other four tests for qualifying relatives are met). Aunts, uncles, nieces, and nephews are relatives only if their relationship to the taxpayer is established by blood (not through marriage). On a joint return, relatives of either spouse may qualify as dependents. Thus, even though the aunt of one's spouse does not qualify as one's relative, on a joint return the aunt is a relative of the spouse and may qualify as the couple's dependent.

EXAMPLE 10

Linda's mother has two sisters, Linda's Aunt Jane and her Aunt Reva. Jane's husband is Linda's Uncle Jim. Jane and Jim have a son, Bruce, who is Linda's cousin. For tax purposes, Linda's aunts qualify as her relatives since they are related to her by blood. Her Uncle Jim is not a relative since his relationship to Linda was established by his marriage to her Aunt Jane. Cousins are not included in the definition of a relative; thus, the Code does not count Bruce as Linda's relative.

EXAMPLE 11

Margaret and Ken adopted Rachel in 2000. Rachel and her lineal descendants (children, grandchildren, etc.) are forever relatives of both Margaret and Ken.

EXAMPLE 12

Dan and April were married in 1998. At the time of their marriage, April's parents permanently became Dan's mother-in-law and a father-in-law. Thus, they will always be Dan's relatives, even if he and April divorce or should April die.

¶109.02 SUPPORT TEST FOR QUALIFYING RELATIVES

The support test for a qualifying relative is different than for a qualifying child. For a qualifying relative to pass the support test, the taxpayer usually must provide more than 50% of the person's total support during the tax year. On a joint return, support coming from either spouse counts. Support includes food, clothing, education, medical and dental care, entertainment, transportation, and lodging.

When a taxpayer furnishes a relative's lodging, the IRS treats the fair rental value of the lodging as support. Fair rental value is the rent a taxpayer could expect to receive from a stranger for the same lodging. Fair rental value covers the use of one room or a proportionate share of a house. Capital items such as cars and furniture count as support if given to (or bought for) a relative. Support also includes costs paid for a relative's wedding.

Support does not include scholarships received from educational institutions, and the status and source of support funds generally makes no difference. Also, payments for life insurance premiums and funeral costs do not count as support. These rules are the same as used to define support for a qualifying child (¶108.04).

To determine if a taxpayer provides over 50% of a relative's support, the taxpayer calculates the relative's total support, which consists of three amounts:

1. Fair rental value of lodging provided to the relative
2. The relative's share of household expenses (such as food, but not lodging) unrelated to any specific household members
3. Other support-related expenses incurred or paid directly to or for the relative

EXAMPLE 13

Martha's parents live with her. Martha's parents do not pay any rent. The fair rental value of the lodging she provides is $4,200 for each parent. Martha's father receives nontaxable social security income of $9,600, which he spent equally on support items for himself and for his wife. Dental expenses for Martha's mother total $3,200. Martha paid $700 of these expenses; Martha's brother paid $2,500. Martha's parents eat all of their meals in her home. The cost of all meals consumed in the home was $5,400 ($1,800 per person). Support for Martha's parents for the year is as follows:

	Mother	Father	Total
Lodging (provided by Martha)	$4,200	$4,200	$8,400
Social security spent by parents	4,800	4,800	9,600
Dental expense	3,200	0	3,200
Share of food provided by Martha	1,800	1,800	3,600
Total	$14,000	$10,800	$24,800

In order for Martha to claim her mother as a dependent, she must provide more than half of her mother's total support. Martha provided $6,700 towards her mother's support during the year ($4,200 lodging + $700 dental + $1,800 for food). Since this amount does not exceed $7,000 ($14,000 of the mother's total support × 50%), the support test has not been met with respect to the mother. However, Martha provided $6,600 towards her father's support during the year ($4,800 lodging + $1,800 for food). Since this amount exceeds $5,400 ($10,800 of the father's total support × 50%), the support test has been met with respect to the father.

Multiple Support Agreements

Sometimes, a group of people (e.g., children) together provide for a dependent's (e.g., parent) support, but no one person (including the dependent) provides over 50% of the support. A special rule allows one member of the group to claim the exemption. The group member claiming the exemption may change from year to year. To qualify for the exemption, the group member must:

1. Provide more than 10% of the dependent's support,
2. Provide, with the other group members, more than 50% of the dependent's support, and
3. Be able to otherwise claim the person as a dependent.

In addition, the eligible group members must agree on the member who is to receive the exemption. It is not uncommon to rotate the exemption among group members from year to year. Once the group reaches this agreement:

1. Eligible group members who do not claim the exemption need to complete and give to the claiming member a signed statement waiving their rights to claim the exemption. The statement must include: (a) the applicable tax year, (b) the name of dependent, and (c) the name, address, and social security number of person waiving the exemption. The claiming member then holds on to this statement to support the exemption. It is not filed with the tax return.
2. The claiming member completes and files Form 2120, Multiple Support Declaration, with his or her tax return. This form lists out the names of the persons waiving their rights to claim an exemption for the dependent in question.

EXAMPLE 14

Elaine, a U.S. citizen, lives with Logan for the entire year. Elaine is single and has no gross income. Logan, Marty, Nan, Michael, and Lilly provide 100% of Elaine's support. Each person's relationship to Elaine, plus the amounts of support they provided are as follows.

	Amounts	Percentage
Logan (Elaine's son)	$1,000	10%
Marty (Elaine's son-in-law)	2,500	25%
Nan (Elaine's stepdaughter)	2,500	25%
Michael (Elaine's brother)	2,500	25%
Lilly (Elaine's friend)	1,500	15%
Total	$10,000	100%

Eligible group members include Marty, Nan, and Michael. Logan and Lilly cannot be eligible group members. Since Elaine is not one of Lilly's relatives, for Elaine to pass the relationship test, she would have to live with Lilly the entire year (discussed later in the test for qualifying nonrelatives, ¶110). Instead, Elaine lives with Logan. Logan cannot be an eligible group member because he does not provide more than 10% of Elaine's support. Elaine qualifies as a relative to Marty, Nan, and Michael. Thus, each passes the relationship test. Marty, Nan, and Michael must decide which of them will claim Elaine as a dependent.

¶109.03 GROSS INCOME TEST

To pass the gross income test, the person's gross income must be less than the exemption amount ($4,000 for 2015). In addition to wages, dividends, and taxable interest, gross income includes gross receipts from rental property before expenses are deducted. To compute the gross income of a business, cost of goods sold is subtracted from net sales and any miscellaneous income is added to the difference. Gross income includes only the income that the government taxes. The calculation of gross income is the focus of Chapters 3 and 4.

¶110 Qualifying Nonrelatives

An unrelated person may qualify as the taxpayer's dependent. To qualify, a nonrelative must meet the following tests that apply to relatives.

1. Citizenship test (see discussion at ¶108.06)
2. Support test (see discussion at ¶109.02)
3. Gross income test (see discussion at ¶109.03)
4. Joint return test (see discussion at ¶108.05)

In addition, the person must live with the taxpayer the entire year. The death or birth of these persons will shorten the "entire year" requirement to that period during which they were alive. Also, temporary absences due to illness, school, vacation, work, or military service continue to count as time living with the taxpayer. Indefinite nursing home stays to receive constant medical care may be considered temporary.

EXAMPLE 15

For the past two years, Darcy lived with her younger cousin Mary. In January, Darcy moved to a nursing home. The doctor informed Mary that Darcy will stay in the nursing home indefinitely so that she can receive required medical care. For tax purposes, Darcy still lives with Mary. Thus, if the other dependency tests are met, Mary can claim Darcy as a dependent. The fact that Darcy is older than Mary is irrelevant. The rule that the dependent be younger than the taxpayer only applies to a qualifying child.

¶111 Tax Base Formula—Another View

Below is another view of the tax base formula. It should enhance the meaning of new tax terms and concepts.

Income from all sources:		
Rent from tenants	$12,400	
Salary	16,200	
Dividends on common stock	720	
Interest from savings account	80	
Tax-exempt bond interest	30	$29,430
Gross income exclusions:		
Tax-exempt bond interest		(30)
Gross income		$29,400
Deductions for AGI:		
Expenses of apartment (rental property)		(1,400)
AGI		$28,000
Deductions from AGI:		
Standard deduction (single person)	$6,300	
Exemptions (one personal exemption)	4,000	(10,300)
Taxable Income		$17,700

¶112 Filing Status

Any individual who files a return falls into one of five filing status groups. In some cases, filing status determines which tax return the taxpayer must file. The filing status also determines the standard deduction amount used in computing taxable income and the tax rates used in calculating the tax liability.

Married couples generally have two filing options: married filing jointly or married filing separately. Head of household status is available to married taxpayers in certain cases (see the Abandoned Spouse rules at ¶112.04). The filing statuses available to unmarried persons include qualifying widow(er), head of household, and single. Both married filing jointly and qualifying widow(er) share the most favorable tax rates, followed by head of household, and then single. The least favorable of the tax rates apply to taxpayers who file married filing separately. Whenever possible, taxpayers would like to qualify for the most favorable tax rate possible for their marital status.

¶112.01 MARRIED FILING JOINTLY

For tax purposes, a taxpayer's marital status is determined on the last day of the tax year. Thus, a person who is married on the last day of the tax year may file a joint return with his or her spouse. Likewise, a person who is legally divorced or separated before the end of the year may not file a joint return. When the divorce or legal separation has not been finalized at year-end, the couple is still legally married for tax purposes, and as such, may file a joint return.

A married couple can file a joint return even if only one spouse has income. Both spouses must sign a jointly filed tax return, thereby making each spouse liable for the entire tax liability. The IRS's authority to collect any taxes owed against either spouse continues should the couple divorce.

The Defense of Marriage Act (DOMA) is a federal law enacted in 1996. One part of DOMA defined marriage as a legal union between a man and a woman. For this reason, the IRS (a federal agency) did not recognize legal unions between same-sex couples. Thus, same-sex spouses were treated as unmarried taxpayers under federal tax law. In December 2012, the Supreme Court ruled that this part of DOMA was unconstitutional. Accordingly, spouses legally married in a state that recognizes same-sex marriages are treated as married taxpayers. It does not matter whether the state the couple lives in is one that recognizes same-sex marriage.

Year of Death

Marital status is also determined at the date of death in the event that a spouse dies. The tax law requires a final income tax return to be filed on behalf of the decedent. A widow(er) may file a joint return with the deceased spouse in the year the spouse dies. When the widow(er) files a joint return, two personal exemptions are allowed in the year of death. The surviving spouse should enter the word *deceased,* the name of the deceased spouse, and the date of death across the top of the return. When signing the return, the survivor should enter *filing as surviving spouse* on the spouse's signature line. When someone other than the widow(er) is the personal representative of the deceased, that person's signature should appear in the deceased's signature line along with the words *personal representative.*

If a widowed person remarries before the end of the year, the widow(er) may file a joint return with the new spouse. A remarried widow(er) cannot file a joint return with the deceased spouse, even if the survivor's new spouse files as married filing separately.

¶112.02 MARRIED FILING SEPARATELY

When spouses have their own income, they may pay less taxes as a couple by filing separate returns. Taxpayers should compute their tax liabilities using both the joint and separate return statuses to see which one yields the least tax liability.

Several factors may work against filing separate returns. Several tax credits, like the child and dependent care credit, education credits, and the earned income credit, are not available to taxpayers who file married filing separately.

Filing Separate Returns in Community Property States

The laws of the state where the taxpayer lives control whether property is considered community property or separate property. There are currently nine community property states. In a community property state, all property acquired during a marriage (other than gifts or inheritances) is considered jointly-owned property, regardless of which spouse legally owns the property. Community property laws can be complex, and vary by state.

Election to File Joint or Separate Return

An election to file a joint or separate return for one year does not carry over to future years. Each year stands alone. After a couple files a joint return, they cannot change to separate returns after the due date of the tax return. However, spouses who file separately may change to a joint return even after the due date passes. An amended return must be filed within three years. Chapter 13 (at ¶1313) covers the filing of amended returns.

¶112.03 QUALIFYING WIDOW(ER)

For two tax years following the year of a spouse's death, special status as a qualifying widow(er) may apply to the survivor. Persons filing as a qualifying widow(er) use the married filing jointly tax rates to compute their tax liability. They also use the married filing jointly basic and additional standard deduction amounts. It is important to note that even though qualifying widows(ers) use the joint return tax rates and other amounts, they do not file a joint return. Thus, a person filing as a qualifying widow(er) claims only one personal exemption. Qualifying widow(er) status is not available to a spouse who remarries. A widow(er) who remarries files a joint or separate return with the new spouse.

To qualify for qualifying widow(er) status, a widow(er) must pay over 50% of the household costs where the widow(er) and a dependent son or daughter live for the entire year. This child may be the taxpayer's qualifying foster, adopted, natural, or stepchild. Temporary absences from the household do not affect the ability to file as a qualifying widow(er). Thus, a son or daughter who attends a boarding school and returns home during vacation periods remains a member of the widow(er)'s household. Hospital stays receive the same treatment.

EXAMPLE 16 Ron maintains a household where he and his 12-year-old dependent daughter live. Ron's wife died in 2014. Ron filed a joint return in 2014. Assuming Ron does not remarry and continues to claim his daughter as a dependent, he files his tax returns for 2015 and 2016 using qualifying widow(er) filing status.

¶112.04 HEAD OF HOUSEHOLD

Head of household status can be used by certain unmarried persons. The tax rates for head of household are lower than for single taxpayers, but are higher than for those who file married filing jointly. Head of household status does not apply to persons who can file as a qualifying widow(er), as these taxpayers should file using the more favorable filing status.

To qualify for head of household status, the taxpayer must pay more than half the cost of maintaining a household where a "qualifying child" (see ¶108) or a relative or nonrelative the taxpayer claims as a dependent (see ¶109 and ¶110) lives with the taxpayer for more than half of the year. A dependent parent need not live with the taxpayer. However, the taxpayer must pay over 50% of the parent's household costs for the year. Also,

1. A married "qualifying child" or a married child who is not a qualifying child must pass each of the five dependency tests for a "qualifying relative" (see ¶109).
2. When a dependent child is used to obtain head of household status, custodial parents do not lose head of household status when they give away their right to claim their child as a dependent (¶108.07).
3. Head of household status is not available if the dependency exemption is obtained through a multiple support agreement (¶109.02).

Maintaining a household means that the taxpayer pays more than 50% of the household costs for the year, which usually covers payments for the mutual benefit of household occupants. These costs include amounts paid for food, utilities, and repairs. They do not include the value of services provided by the taxpayer or household members.

EXAMPLE 17

Candy is single and maintains a household where she and her 25-year-old unmarried son live. Candy provides all of her son's support during the year. The son is a full-time student and has no gross income. Because of his age, the son is not a qualifying child. He does, however, pass all five tests for a qualifying relative. Thus, Candy claims her son as a dependent and files as head of household.

EXAMPLE 18

Same facts as in Example 17, except that the son's gross income for the year is $5,000. Candy cannot claim her son as a dependent. The dependency tests for qualifying relatives require that the person's gross income not exceed the exemption amount ($4,000 in 2015). Candy's filing status is single.

EXAMPLE 19

Tom and Drew divorced in 2010. Together they share custody of their 9-year-old son, Mark, for more than six months of the year and provide over half of his support. Tom has custody of Mark; however, he has given away his right to claim Mark as a dependent. Even though Drew is entitled to the dependency exemption for Mark, for purposes of filing as head of household, Mark is a qualifying child for Tom, but not for Drew. Thus, Tom files as head of household. Drew's filing status is single.

EXAMPLE 20

Pat's husband died in 2014. Pat maintains a household where she lives with her married son and his wife. Neither the son nor the daughter-in-law qualifies as Pat's dependent. Thus, neither the son nor his wife qualify Pat for head of household filing status. However, Pat also pays over half of the costs to maintain a separate home for her aging mother, who qualifies as Pat's dependent. Pat files as head of household because she maintains a household for her dependent mother. A dependent parent is the only person who can qualify Pat for head of household filing status without having to live with her.

EXAMPLE 21

Same facts as in Example 20, except that Pat lives with her unmarried son, who is 18 and a full-time student. The son is a qualifying child to Pat, and accordingly, she is entitled to claim him as a dependent. Assuming Pat can continue to claim her son as a dependent, she will file as a qualifying widow(er) in 2015 and 2016, the two tax years that follow the year of her husband's death.

Abandoned Spouses (Married Persons Who Live Apart)

Married persons who do not live with their spouses during the last six months of the year may qualify as abandoned spouses. For tax purposes, abandoned spouses are treated as not married and thus can qualify for head of household filing status. To qualify as an abandoned spouse, a married taxpayer must meet these five requirements.

1. The taxpayer does not file a joint return.
2. For more than six months of the year, the taxpayer lives with a son or daughter who is the taxpayer's natural, step, adopted, or qualifying foster child.
3. During the year, the taxpayer pays more than 50% of the costs of maintaining the home.
4. At least one son or daughter qualifies as a dependent of the taxpayer. This rule does not apply if the taxpayer passes each of the tests to claim the exemption but has agreed to give the exemption to the noncustodial parent.
5. The taxpayer did not live with his or her spouse at any time during the last six months of the tax year.

EXAMPLE 22

Jim and Danielle Nova are legally separated. They have not lived together since March, 2015. In 2015, Danielle pays more than half of the costs to maintain the home where she and her two children live. However, Danielle has agreed to allow Jim to claim the children as dependents. As of the end of 2015, the Novas' divorce had not been finalized. Even though Danielle cannot claim the children as dependents, she qualifies as an abandoned spouse. Her filing status for 2015 is head of household. Jim will claim the two children as his dependents, but he must file as married filing separately.

¶112.05 SINGLE

An unmarried person who does not qualify to file as qualifying widow(er) or as head of household must file as a single taxpayer. A person legally separated, but not yet divorced, files as a single taxpayer unless head of household filing status applies. Likewise, in the years following a spouse's death, a widow(er) who has not remarried files as a single taxpayer unless the rules for filing as qualifying widow(er) or as head of household are met.

¶113 Filing Requirements for Individuals

Under our self-reporting tax system, persons who meet certain conditions must file an income tax return. Current filing requirements depend primarily on the taxpayer's:

1. Net earnings from self-employment, or
2. Gross income and filing status.

The filing requirements apply to all U.S. citizens and resident aliens. Resident aliens are non-U.S. citizens who pay U.S. tax on their worldwide income. These requirements can apply to nonresident aliens married to U.S. citizens. Nonresident aliens are non-U.S. citizens who only pay U.S. tax on their U.S. income.

¶113.01 SELF-EMPLOYMENT INCOME THRESHOLD

Persons with self-employment income must file a tax return when net earnings from self-employment is $400 or more. Net earnings from self-employment is 92.35% of the self-employment profits.

EXAMPLE 23

Antoine's only source of income is $1,000 of gross income from self-employment. His business deductions total $580. Self-employment profit is $420 ($1,000 – $580), and net earnings from self-employment is $388 ($420 × 92.35%). Since this amount does not exceed $400, Antoine is not required to file a tax return.

¶113.02 GROSS INCOME THRESHOLD

Persons who are claimed as a dependent on another taxpayer's return must file a 2015 tax return when their gross income exceeds *greater of* (i) $1,050 or (ii) their earned income plus $350 (not to exceed $6,300). Any additional standard deductions for age and blindness that apply increase this threshold. However, dependents who have unearned income (interest, dividends, etc.), must file a tax return when the amount of their unearned income exceeds $1,050 plus any amounts for additional standard deductions. A married dependent whose spouse files separately and deducts itemized deductions must file a tax return when gross income is $5 or more.

EXAMPLE 24

Toddra is claimed as a dependent on her son's tax return. Toddra is widowed and 68 years old. She earned $2,800 during the year from a part-time job and has $300 of interest income. Toddra's $300 of unearned income does not exceed the $2,600 threshold ($1,050 + $1,550 additional standard deduction). Likewise, her $3,100 of gross income ($2,800 + $300) does not exceed the $4,700 threshold ($2,800 earned income + $350 + $1,550). Thus, Toddra is not required to file a return for 2015.

Higher thresholds generally apply to persons who are not claimed as dependents on another's return. Married persons filing separately must file a return when gross income exceeds the exemption amount ($4,000 for 2015). All other persons must file a return when their gross income exceeds the sum of the amounts for taxpayer's personal exemption, basic standard deduction, and additional standard deduction for age. On a joint tax return, the deductions for both spouses count. Neither the additional standard deduction for blindness nor any exemption deductions for dependents are taken into account. Thus, for a married couple filing jointly, where one spouse is 65 and the other is blind, the filing requirement is $21,850. This represents a combination of the personal exemption amount, $8,000 (2 × $4,000); the basic standard deduction, $12,600; and the $1,250 additional standard deduction for age.

Figure 1-5: Who Must File a Tax Return—Rules for Nondependents

Gross income thresholds for 2015:

1.	Single	$10,300	($6,300 + $4,000)
	65 or over	11,850	($6,300 + $1,550 + $4,000)
2.	Married filing jointly	20,600	($12,600 + $8,000)
	One 65 or over	21,850	($12,600 + $1,250 + $8,000)
	Both 65 or over	23,100	($12,600 + $2,500 + $8,000)
3.	Married filing separately	4,000	(2015 exemption amount)
4.	Head of household	13,250	($9,250 + $4,000)
	65 or over	14,800	($9,250 + $1,550 + $4,000)
5.	Qualifying widow(er)	16,600	($12,600 + $4,000)
	65 or over	17,850	($12,600 + $1,250 + $4,000)

i

Note that in determining whether a dependent must file a tax return, the additional standard deduction for both age and blindness increases the gross income threshold. For example, the threshold for a blind, 65-year-old, single person claimed as a dependent on another's return is $4,150 in 2015 if the dependent has no earned income ($1,050 basic standard deduction + $1,550 for age + $1,550 for blindness). Because the personal exemption for a dependent is $0, it does not affect a dependent's gross income threshold.

¶114 Tax Year

Although most individuals use the calendar year for tax reporting, a few use a fiscal year. Some corporations and partnerships use a fiscal year. A **fiscal year** consists of any 12-month period that ends on the last day of a calendar month other than December. Unless otherwise stated, this textbook assumes that all taxpayers use the calendar year.

Tax returns for individuals are due on or before the 15th day of the fourth month following the close of the tax year. For calendar year taxpayers, this is would be April 15 of the following year. However, if this date falls on Saturday, Sunday, or a legal holiday, the due date is the next business day. A taxpayer files a timely return when the return is postmarked on or before the due date and it is properly addressed and has the correct amount of postage.

¶115 Taxpayer Responsibilities

Under our self-reporting tax system, the law requires taxpayers to compute their tax liabilities, file proper returns on time, and pay the taxes when due. Taxpayers who do not meet these responsibilities face possible fines, penalties, and imprisonment. In addition, the IRS charges interest on unpaid taxes. The IRS wants taxpayers to file their returns electronically but they have the option of mailing them to the proper IRS service center.

¶115.01 MAINTAINING GOOD RECORDS

Taxpayers need to keep good records to support all items reported on the tax return. Taxpayers should develop and maintain an organized tax record system. This system should allow easy access to the nature, purpose, and amount of old transactions. The underlying files should contain invoices, canceled checks, payment receipts, property titles, and copies of old tax returns. An orderly indexing system helps taxpayers find stored documents. A good record-keeping system helps prevent taxpayers from overlooking deductions at tax time. These records and receipts need to be kept until the closing date of the tax return.

The normal closing date (last chance for the IRS to initiate an audit) is three years after the *later of* (i) the return's due date (including extensions) or (ii) the date when the return was filed. For example, if the taxpayer files a return for the 20x0 tax year before its April 15, 20x1 due date, then the 20x0 tax year closes on April 15, 20x4.

The closing date for a tax return that includes an omission of more than 25% of the gross income reported on the return is six years after the *later of* (i) the return's due date (including extensions) or (ii) the actual filing date. Thus, if a taxpayer files a return for the year 20x0 before its April 15, 20x1 due date, and the inadvertent omission rule for gross income applies, the taxpayer's 20x0 tax year closes on April 15, 20x7. There is no statutory limit for assessing the additional taxes on a fraudulent return.

Taxpayers should keep records showing the cost of property longer. This includes items like stocks, homes, and other investments. Taxpayers must report gain (and sometimes loss) when they dispose of property. Thus, all documents used in computing cost basis should be kept until the closing date of the tax return on which the disposal is reported. A copy of the tax return and tax calculations should also be retained.

¶116 Reducing the Tax Bite

All taxpayers have the right to use all legal means to avoid or postpone paying taxes. Through proper tax planning, taxpayers may be able to reduce the tax bite. As a basic goal, taxpayers should try to reduce current and future taxes. Often, it is a good idea to defer taxes to future years, if possible.

¶116.01 ACQUIRE A WORKING KNOWLEDGE OF THE TAX LAWS

The tax laws contain an overwhelming number of rules covering a multitude of personal, business, and investment situations. The average taxpayer should not expect to develop even a general familiarity with all aspects of these laws. However, the "game of life" happens to involve taxation, and it is difficult to play the game without a working knowledge of the basic rules. Taxpayers should focus on those laws that impact their particular personal and business situations. Developing a working knowledge of these rules is most beneficial in reducing current and future taxes. It will improve tax problem recognition skills. It will also lead to improved record keeping and reduced time for tax return preparation. For taxpayers who use computer tax software, knowledge of the tax laws will provide some assurance that the software produces proper results.

Although taxpayers may hire tax advisers to prepare their returns, knowledge of the tax laws should help minimize the adviser's fee. Most advisers base their fees on the time spent preparing the client's tax return and the time spent advising the client. With a more knowledgeable taxpayer, the adviser will not have to charge for explaining basic tax rules.

¶116.02 ADVANCED PLANNING TO REDUCE TAXES

The way the law taxes most completed events or transactions is fairly clear. Consequently, it is important for taxpayers to plan their transactions in advance. Once an action is taken, the tax consequences are usually locked in. Proper planning of the action can produce desirable tax results.

Taxpayers need to be aware of those available deductions and tax credits that will benefit their particular situations. To facilitate planning, taxpayers should become familiar with methods that will:

1. Accelerate or postpone the recognition of revenue.
2. Accelerate or postpone the recognition of expenses.

Taxpayers whose total itemized deductions are about the same as their standard deduction amount can use the bunching process to slow down or speed up their itemized deduction payments. By using the bunching process, taxpayers influence the year in which an itemized deduction falls. Taxpayers who use this process itemize their deductions in one year and take the standard deduction in the next. The timing of payments for charitable contributions, medical expenses, property taxes, and state income taxes are among the easiest to control.

Couples might arrange their wedding date (December versus January) to reduce the tax bite. Taxpayers with dependents under the multiple support rules (¶109.02) can use the bunching process. By controlling the amount they pay to support other persons, they can control the number of dependents they can claim. To some degree, taxpayers can control their tax credits. Usually, taxpayers want to claim their credits as early as possible to generate cash (tax) savings sooner rather than later.

EXAMPLE 25 Bruno files as a single taxpayer. Bruno's total itemized deductions are usually around $6,000 (less than the standard deduction amount). However, the $6,000 includes $1,500 of charitable contributions he makes to his church each December. For 2015, the *greater of* Bruno's standard deduction or itemized deductions would be the $6,300 standard deduction for single taxpayers. If Bruno were to delay making the $1,500 charitable contribution for 2015 until early 2016, he would still deduct $6,300 in 2015. However, his 2016 itemized deductions of $7,500 ($6,000 + $1,500 held over from 2015) would exceed his 2016 standard deduction. By using this bunching strategy, Bruno would get a greater deduction from AGI in 2016.

Although tax planning is advantageous for everyone, most tax benefits favor business owners and taxpayers who itemize. People who have their own businesses stand to gain the most through tax planning. Current trends show an increasing number of people starting their own businesses. Thus, a greater number of taxpayers will benefit from comprehensive tax planning. For business owners, greater deduction possibilities exist. They can convert many expenses that are normally itemized deductions or nondeductible items into deductions from gross income. Knowledge of these situations is highly beneficial, and many are presented in this textbook.

Timing the recognition of revenues and expenses is more easily done in a business setting. For example, taxpayers in service businesses who use the cash method of accounting can control end-of-year income. They might increase income by accelerating billings or postpone it by delaying them. Other taxpayers who use the cash method of accounting (most persons) can control end-of-year gains and losses by advancing or delaying the closing dates on the sales of property they own. Taxpayers who control the timing of their transactions can adjust their income and deductions to take full advantage of the tax laws.

As indicated before, taxpayers can reduce their taxes through careful planning. Some tax plans cover a short-term period, while others cover a long-term period. A short-term plan tries to reduce taxes over the next few years; a long-term plan tries to reduce them over a longer time span. Long-term plans usually involve complex techniques beyond the scope of this textbook. They include selecting retirement plans and developing estate, gift, and trust strategies. A taxpayer with stable income, deductions, exemptions, and credits usually develops a short-term tax plan covering one to three years. When uncertainty exists, the taxpayer should consider aggressive, conservative, and middle-of-the-road assumptions. In all cases, the plan should be updated annually.

¶116.03 MAXIMIZE UNREALIZED INCOME

Some taxpayers want more after-tax dollars so they can spend it on consumable items. Others prefer to accumulate wealth. For those who want the latter, maximizing unrealized income is important. Taxpayers can generally accumulate more wealth by investing in assets that produce income that is not currently taxable. Such income can then grow without being taxed each year. Making contributions to tax-free or tax-deferred retirement accounts is one way to meet this goal. The tax advantages of contributing to retirement accounts are discussed in Chapters 3, 4, and 7 (see ¶305, ¶402.11, and ¶707).

The tax laws operate under the **realization principle**, where gains from property are not taxed until realized (the property is disposed of). Thus, taxpayers that invest in property that appreciates in value (e.g. stocks or real estate) can defer (delay) the tax on the unrealized gain (i.e., the appreciation).

Watch for Tax Opportunities

As taxpayers learn more about the tax laws, they can spot planning opportunities more quickly. Remember the basic goal: reduce current and future taxes. As you study each chapter, keep this goal in mind and watch for tax-reducing suggestions.

1

Name:

Section:

Date:

QUESTIONS AND PROBLEMS

1. **Income Tax Objectives.** (Obj. 7) The primary objective of the U.S. income tax system is to raise revenues to cover government spending. Name some of the other objectives of our income tax system.

2. **Taxable Income Formula.** (Obj. 1) Is the basic taxable income formula the same for all taxpayers? What is the difference between the basic formula and the expanded formula used by individuals?

3. **Gross Income.** (Obj. 2) The Code lists a number of different gross income sources. When a taxpayer receives something that is not one of the listed items, is it exempt from tax? Explain your answer.

4. **Itemized Deductions.** (Obj. 2) Itemized deductions fall into one of seven groups. Two of the groups are (1) job expenses and most other miscellaneous itemized deductions and (2) other miscellaneous deductions. What are the other five groups?

5. **Standard Deduction.** (Obj. 3) Under what circumstances is a person's standard deduction $0?

6. **Itemized Deductions.** (Obj. 2) Explain when itemized deductions are used in computing taxable income.

7. **Standard Deduction.** (Obj. 3) Who qualifies for the additional standard deduction? What additional amount is available?

8. **Standard Deduction.** (Obj. 3) Compute each taxpayer's 2015 total standard deduction.

   a. Bryce, age 20, is a full-time student. His parents claim him as a dependent. Bryce has interest income of $320 and wages from a part-time job of $3,800.

   b. Same as in Part a., except that Bryce's wages are $6,500.

   c. Heather, age 66, is married and files a separate return. Her husband also uses the standard deduction on his return.

   d. Juliet, age 19, is blind and claimed as a dependent by her parents. Her only income is $5,200 of taxable interest.

9. **Exemptions.** (Obj. 4) How many exemptions can be claimed on a joint income tax return by an employed taxpayer who is married and has two unmarried children? One child, a daughter age 17, has no income. The other child, a son age 22, is a part-time college student. The son earned $4,170 during the year. The taxpayer provides over half of each child's support. The taxpayer's spouse is not employed.

10. Exemptions. (Obj. 4) Kevin Kirby, age 67 and blind, is married to Susan Kirby, age 56 with good vision. Their 37-year-old divorced daughter, along with her 18-year-old son, lives with them. The Kirbys provided more than half the support of their daughter and grandson. The daughter earned wages of $4,800 during the year; the grandson, a part-time college student, earned wages of $5,000. How many exemptions can the Kirbys claim on their 2015 joint tax return? Explain your answer.

11. Exemptions. (Obj. 4) Vera and Billy were divorced during the year. Vera was awarded custody of the children, ages 6 and 9. There was no agreement about who would receive the dependency exemptions for the children. Billy provides all of the support for the children.

a. Who receives the dependency exemptions?

b. Might the other parent receive the exemptions under certain conditions? Explain.

12. Exemption Deduction. (Obj. 4)

a. Shirley's child is born at 10 P.M. on December 31 of the taxable year. Can Shirley claim a full exemption for this child for the year or must she prorate her exemption?

b. A qualifying dependent of a taxpayer dies on January 4 of the taxable year. Can the taxpayer claim a full exemption for the dependent for the year?

13. Exemptions. (Obj. 4) Henry and Margaret were married on December 28. Henry, age 22 and a full-time student, had no gross income during the year. He lived with his parents and was supported by them prior to his marriage. Margaret's gross salary for the year was $35,000. Describe the circumstances under which Henry's parents can claim him as a dependent.

14. **Exemption Deduction.** (Obj. 4) Jenna claims one personal exemption and three dependents on her 2015 tax return. Her filing status is head of household. Compute Jenna's exemption deduction if her AGI is $319,650.

15. **Exemption Deduction.** (Obj. 4) Anthony files as single and claims one personal exemption in 2015. Compute Anthony's exemption deduction if his AGI is $325,050.

16. **Exemption Deduction.** (Obj. 4) Isabel is married, but files separately from her husband in 2015. She claims one personal exemption and two dependents on her tax return. Compute Isabel's exemption deduction if her AGI is $197,310.

17. **Exemption Deduction.** (Obj. 4) Megan files as a single taxpayer. She claims one personal exemption and one dependent. Compute Megan's 2015 exemption deduction if her AGI is:

   a. $288,550.

   b. $392,600.

   c. $182,950.

18. **Exemptions and Taxable Income.** (Objs. 1 and 4) John and Jamie Kerr (ages 67 and 64, respectively) do not claim any dependents on their joint tax return. Both have good vision. Compute their 2015 taxable income if the Kerrs use the standard deduction and their AGI is $361,980.

phase out exemptions

19. **Exemptions and Taxable Income.** (Objs. 1 and 4) In 2015, Terry (age 48 with good vision) uses qualifying widow(er) as his filing status. Terry claims one personal exemption and three dependents. Compute Terry's taxable income if his AGI is $326,640 and he uses the standard deduction.

20. **Dependents.** (Obj. 4) Indicate by inserting an **X** in the proper column which of the following persons pass, with respect to the taxpayer, (1) the relationship test for a qualifying child or (2) the relationship test for a qualifying relative. The taxpayer is 46 years old and unmarried.

	Qualifying Child?	*Qualifying Relative?*
a. Taxpayer's 31-year-old cousin		X
b. Taxpayer's father		X
c. Taxpayer's 67-year-old foster mother		X
d. Taxpayer's 50-year-old stepsister		X
e. Taxpayer's 45-year-old brother-in-law		X
f. Taxpayer's grandchild	X	
g. Taxpayer's 42-year-old half-brother		X
h. Taxpayer's 21-year-old nephew (sister's son)		X
i. Father (age 62) of taxpayer's former spouse		X
j. Uncle (age 59) of taxpayer's deceased spouse		X
k. Taxpayer's 29-year-old son-in-law		X
l. Taxpayer's grandfather		X
m. Taxpayer's mother-in-law (taxpayer's spouse deceased)		X

21. Filing Status. (Obj. 5) Indicate the proper filing status for each of the following taxpayers.

a. Unmarried; divorced last year; no dependents

b. Married; spouse has been properly claimed as a dependent on another taxpayer's return

c. Married on December 31, no dependents

d. Widower; spouse died last year; has a dependent 6-year-old child; has not remarried

e. Divorce finalized on December 30; has no dependents

f. Married; maintains a household for more than six months of the year for self and an adopted 4-year-old child who qualifies as a dependent; spouse left home on February 15 of current year and has not been seen since

g. Unmarried; maintains a home for entire year for self and his 8-year-old grandchild, whom the taxpayer claims as a dependent

h. Married; has $15,000 of gross income; spouse has filed a separate return

i. Widower; spouse died January 16 last year; has not remarried; maintained parent's home for the entire year; parent qualifies as a dependent

22. **Filing Status.** (Obj. 5) Grace provides 52% of the household costs for her widowed mother during the year. Grace claims her mother as a dependent. Can Grace file a return as head of household if her mother does not live with her? Explain the reason for your answer.

23. **Filing Requirements.** (Obj. 6) For each of the following situations, determine whether the taxpayer must file a tax return for 2015. Provide a full explanation for your answer, including which threshold was used in making your determination.

    a. Andy, age 17, is claimed as a dependent on his parents' tax return. He earned $3,190 from his paper route and other after-school jobs. Andy deposits most of his earnings in a savings account at the local bank. His interest income was $400.

    b. Marla, age 25, is claimed as a dependent on her parents' tax return. She received a $5,000 tax-free academic scholarship during the year. Marla had interest income of $125 and $415 of net earnings from self-employment.

    c. Todd, age 22 and single, graduated from college last year. He has not been able to find a full-time job. Todd had wages from a part-time job of $5,000 and no other income. Although he used some of his earned income for support items, the majority of Todd's support came from his parents.

24. **Fiscal Year.** (Obj. 6) Most individual taxpayers use the calendar year for reporting their taxable income. However, a few use the fiscal year. What is a fiscal year?

25. Tax Years. (Obj. 6) The date a tax year closes is an important date from a taxpayer's point of view because it stops the IRS from assessing a tax deficiency on a closed tax year. It is an important date from the government's point of view because it stops a taxpayer from making a refund claim on a closed tax year.

a. If a taxpayer files her tax return for 2015 on April 1, 2016, on what specific date does her 2015 tax year close under the normal closing rule?

b. If a taxpayer inadvertently (mistakenly) omits too much gross income from his or her income tax return, the normal closing of a tax year is extended by three years. What percentage of the taxpayer's gross income must be omitted from his or her income tax return in order for the closing year to be extended? As part of your answer, explain exactly how this percentage is applied.

26. Standard Deduction and Filing Requirements. (Obj. 6) For each of the following individuals, determine (1) their total standard deduction and (2) the amount of their gross income threshold (and unearned income threshold for dependents) they use to determine whether they must file an income tax return for 2015.

a. Steve is 36 years old. His filing status is single and he has 20/20 vision.

b. Maggie is a 70 years old widow. Her son claims her as a dependent. Maggie is permanently blind. Her gross income includes investment income, but no earned income.

c. Same as in Part b., except that Maggie is not claimed a dependent on her son's return.

d. Jeannie and Tom file a joint tax return. Jennie turned 65 on January 1, 2016; Tom turned 69 on March 8, 2016. Neither have any vision problems.

e. Sally files a separate tax return from her husband. She is 40 years old and blind.

f. Joe's wife died in 2015. Joe is 70 years old and has good eyesight. At the time of her death, Joe's wife was 60 and had good eyesight. Joe does not itemize.

27. **Tax Laws.** (Obj. 7) Wendy engages a local tax professional to prepare her tax return each year. She sees no reason to learn more about the tax laws. After she files her return each year, she just wants to forget the whole thing. Explain to Wendy why it would be her advantage to know more about the tax laws.

28. **Tax Planning.** (Obj. 7)

a. Define the concept of tax planning and distinguish between short-term and long-term tax planning.

b. What is the primary reason for tax planning?

c. Identify three tax-planning principles that will help a taxpayer achieve a tax-planning objective.

d. Under what circumstances should a taxpayer plan to control the timing of payments that are deductible as itemized deductions?

29. **Internet problem: Filling out Form 8332.** (Obj. 4)

James R. Greene (SSN 846-87-1660) is the custodial parent of his daughter, Jackie A. Greene. The divorce decree grants the 2015 exemption for Jackie to Colette C. Royce (SSN 662-79-5500), who is Jackie's mother. Go to the IRS website and locate Form 8332, Release/Revocation of Release of Claim to Exemption for Child by Custodial Parent. Fill out the form for Colette C. Royce. James R. Greene signs the form on December 5, 2015.

See Appendix A for instructions on use of the IRS website.

30. Internet problem: Filling out Form 2120. (Obj. 4)

With the exception of the support test, Agnes B. Jones (SSN 995-73-3446) and Robert A. Brown (SSN 199-46-6677) can each claim their father, Kenneth J. Brown, as a dependent. Agnes and Robert each contribute 45% of Kenneth's support. Robert gave Agnes a signed statement giving away his right to the dependency exemption for Kenneth in 2015. Robert lives at 321 Highland Ave., Kettering, Ohio, 45429. Go to the IRS website and locate Form 2120, Multiple Support Declaration. Fill out the form that Agnes B. Jones will attach to her 2015 tax return.

See Appendix A for instructions on use of the IRS website.

Chapter 2

Tax Determination, Payments, and Reporting Procedures

CHAPTER CONTENTS

LEARNING OBJECTIVES

After completing Chapter 2, you should be able to:

1. Compute a taxpayer's tax liability using the appropriate tax table or tax rate schedule.
2. List out the various personal tax credits and compute the amount of each credit.
3. Learn about the impact of the Affordable Care Act (ACA) on filing an individual income tax return.
4. Determine whether a taxpayer is able to file Form 1040EZ.
5. Complete the various tax forms and schedules introduced in the chapter, including Form 2441, Schedule 8812, Form 8863, Schedule EIC, Form 8962, and Form 1040EZ.

CHAPTER OVERVIEW

Chapter 1 presented the tax structure and the process for computing taxable income. Chapter 2 shows how individual taxpayers compute the amount of their tax liability. It reviews the role of tax payments and personal tax credits in determining the final amount due to or from the government. It also introduces the impact that the Patient Protection and Affordable Care Act (ACA) can have on a taxpayer's tax liability and tax reporting responsibilities. The chapter shows how to complete Form 1040EZ, Individual Tax Return for Single and Joint Filers with No Dependents.

¶201 Individual Income Tax Rates

The Internal Revenue Code (Code) dictates the tax rates taxpayers apply to taxable income to compute their tax liability. The current income tax rate structure is a progressive structure — the higher the income, the higher the tax rate that applies. For individual taxpayers, the seven rates currently used are 10%, 15%, 25%, 28%, 33%, 35%, and 39.6%. The Internal Revenue Service (IRS) presents these rates in **Tax Rate Schedules** and a **Tax Table**.

To determine their tax, taxpayers first must know their taxable income and filing status. Taxpayers with $100,000 or more of taxable income must use the Tax Rate Schedules. The tax rate schedules are found on the inside front cover of this textbook. Those with less than $100,000 of taxable income must use the Tax Table. All Form 1040EZ and Form 1040A filers must find their tax using the Tax Table. The Tax Tables can be found in Appendix T at the back of the textbook.

¶201.01 TAX RATE SCHEDULES

Four tax rate schedules apply—one for each filing status (married filing jointly and qualifying widow(er) use the same tax rates). The tax rate schedules are harder to use than the Tax Table. Taxpayers using a tax rate schedule must actually compute their tax. The Tax Table requires no tax calculations.

Example 1 shows how to use the tax rate schedules. Those using the tax rate schedule to compute their tax follow these steps:

1. Select the correct rate schedule (based on filing status).
2. Locate the proper income range and take note of both the dollar amount and the tax rate applicable to taxable income in that range.
3. Subtract the lowest amount in that income range from taxable income.
4. Multiply the difference from Step 3 by the tax rate noted in Step 2.
5. Add the amount from Step 4 to the dollar amount noted in Step 2 to arrive at the tax on taxable income.

EXAMPLE 1

Four taxpayers each have $100,000 of taxable income. The following list shows their filing status and income tax for 2015 as computed using Schedules X, Y-1, Y-2, and Z, which can be found on the inside front cover of the textbook.

Filing Status	Tax Liability
Married filing jointly	$16,587.50
Head of household	19,322.50
Single	21,071.25
Married filing separately	21,525.75

Using Schedule Y-1, the tax calculation for married couples that file jointly is shown below.

Taxable income (TI)	$100,000	
Less	– 74,900*	$10,312.50
TI taxed at 25% rate	$ 25,100	
Multiply by rate	× 25%	6,275.00
Tax on TI of $100,000		$16,587.50

* Note that the 10% rate and the 15% rate combined produce a tax of $10,312.50 on $74,900 of TI [($18,450 × 10%) + ($56,450 × 15%)]. The 25% rate applies only to the last $25,100 of TI. Total tax on $100,000 of TI equals the sum of the taxes on these two amounts.

¶201.02 TAX TABLE

The tax law requires that taxpayers with less than $100,000 of taxable income use the Tax Table to determine their tax. The Tax Table is easier to use than the tax rate schedules. Taxpayers simply locate their tax from the table using their taxable income and filing status.

The Tax Table contains separate columns for each filing status. A qualifying widow(er) uses the same column as married filing jointly. Taxpayers filing Form 1040EZ, Form 1040A, and Form 1040 all can use the Tax Table in this textbook to find their tax.

If taxable income is --		**And you are:**			
At least	But less than	Single	Married filing jointly*	Married filing separately	Head of Household
		Your tax is --			
23,000					
23,000	23,050	2,993	2,531	2,993	2,796
23,050	23,100	3,000	2,539	3,000	2,804
23,100	23,150	3,008	2,546	3,008	2,811
23,150	23,200	3,015	2,554	3,015	2,819

* and Qualifying widow(er)

To determine the Tax Table amounts, the IRS uses the tax rate schedules to compute the tax on the midpoint of each income range. For a single taxpayer with $23,000 of taxable income, the Tax Table shows a tax of $2,993. This amount represents the tax on $23,025 – the midpoint of $23,000 and $23,050. The table shows this amount on the line that includes taxable income of at least $23,000, but less than $23,050. Since the taxpayer is single, the proper tax appears at the intersection of the row for the income range and the "Single" column.

¶201.03 REDUCED TAX RATE ON QUALIFIED DIVIDENDS AND NET CAPITAL GAIN

A reduced tax rate applies to qualified dividends and net capital gain included in individual taxpayers' taxable income. The reduced rate is 0% for taxpayers whose taxable income falls in income range for the two lowest tax brackets (10% and 15%). It is 20% for taxpayers in the highest tax bracket (39.6%), and 15% for all other taxpayers. Dividends are distributions of earnings and profits (E&P) that corporations pay to their owners (called shareholders). Not all dividends paid to shareholders are qualified dividends, and only qualified dividends are taxed at the reduced rate. Dividend income is covered in Chapter 3 (¶309).

When taxpayers sell property that they own, they realize a gain or loss measured by the difference between the amount realized from the sale and their adjusted basis (net investment) in the property sold. The three types of property taxpayers can own include business property, investment property, and personal-use property (the taxpayer's personal belongings). Investment property and personal-use property are called capital assets.

The tax laws usually tax all gains from the sale of capital assets, but only allow taxpayers to offset capital gains with capital losses from the sale of investment property. Net capital gain results when the net gains from the sale of capital assets held for more than a year (net long-term capital gains) exceed the net losses on the sale of capital assets held for less than one year (short-term capital losses). Chapter 11 (¶1101.03) describes the calculation of net capital gain in greater detail, and explains how a taxpayer's tax liability is computed when net capital gain or qualified dividends are included in taxable income.

¶201.04 ADDITIONAL TAX ON INVESTMENT INCOME

Certain taxpayers may be subject to a higher tax rate on their investment income, which includes interest, dividends, capital gains, rents and royalties (topics discussed in ¶¶308-311). First, dependent children with investment (unearned) income may find some of their unearned income taxed at their parents' higher tax rates. Second, taxpayers in the highest 39.6% tax bracket whose taxable income includes net investment income (NII) will be subject to an additional tax on at least some, if not all, of their NII. Both the "kiddie tax" and the NII tax are discussed in Chapter 3 (see ¶¶314-315).

¶202 Indexing for Inflation

The tax laws specify that certain amounts be adjusted each year for inflation. These include the basic and additional standard deduction amounts, the (personal and dependency) exemption deduction, and the brackets (taxable income ranges) in the tax rate schedules. Various other amounts introduced in this textbook are also subject to annual inflation adjustments. The IRS adjusts these amounts annually using Consumer Price Index (CPI) data for the previous 12-month period ending on August 31. For example, the inflation-adjusted amounts for the 2016 tax year are based on the CPI for the period September 1, 2014 – August 31, 2015.

¶203 Paying the Tax Liability

When it comes to paying the tax liability, taxpayers generally pay their taxes through the tax withholding system imposed on them by their employers. They also may make estimated tax payments. Other factors that can reduce tax liability include tax credits, prior year overpayments, excess payroll taxes withheld, and payments mailed with taxpayers' requests to extend the filing deadline of their tax returns. Taxpayers subtract these items from their tax liability to determine the net amount due to or from the government.

¶203.01 FEDERAL TAXES WITHHELD

The tax law requires employers to withhold income, social security, and Medicare taxes from wages they pay their employees. To help employers determine the correct amount of federal income tax to withhold, the IRS publishes tax withholding tables. Employers use these tables in conjunction with personal data provided by their employees on Form W-4, Employee's Withholding Allowance Certificate (discussed in Chapter 13). By cross-referencing the information on the two documents, employers determine the proper amount of federal income tax to withhold.

Before February 1 of each year, employers inform employees of their previous year's earnings and tax withholdings. They use Form W-2, Wage and Tax Statement, to communicate this information to employees. When preparing their federal income tax returns, employees enter their federal income tax withholdings in the "Payments" section on their tax returns.

¶203.02 ESTIMATED TAX PAYMENTS

The tax withholding system only applies to certain types of income. In addition to wages, those paying interest, dividends and pensions are able to withhold taxes on the payee's behalf if the payee requests it. The taxes associated with all other types of income must be paid to the IRS through quarterly estimated tax payments. Like federal income tax withheld, estimated payments are reported in the "Payments" section. Estimated payments are discussed in Chapter 13.

¶203.03 EXCESS FICA WITHHOLDING

In addition to withholding income taxes, employers withhold FICA taxes from their employees' wages. FICA taxes consist of (1) social security taxes (also called OASDI taxes) and (2) Medicare taxes. The amount of FICA taxes employers are required to withhold is set by law. When an employee ends up with having too much FICA tax withheld, the excess is returned to the employee.

In 2015, employers must withhold 6.2% of the first $118,500 of each employee's social security (OASDI) wages. When an employee works for more than one employer during the year and total OASDI wages exceed $118,500, the employee will end up having too much OASDI taxes withheld. In 2015, the maximum OASDI tax an employee is required to pay is $7,347 ($118,500 × 6.2%). If the employee ends up paying more than this amount because FICA tax is withheld from multiple employers, the excess is returned by reporting the excess in the "Payments" section on the employee's tax return (Form 1040).

The second part of FICA tax is the Medicare tax. For unmarried taxpayers, a 1.45% tax rate applies to the first $200,000 of Medicare wages, and a 2.35% rate applies to Medicare wages in excess of $200,000. For married taxpayers who file a joint tax return, the 2.35% tax rate applies once the couple's combined Medicare wages exceed $250,000. For married taxpayers who file separately from their spouses, the higher rate applies to Medicare wages in excess of $125,000.

The tax laws require employers to withhold 1.45% of the first $200,000 of each employee's Medicare wages, and 2.35% of Medicare wages in excess of $200,000. This rule applies to all employees, regardless of the employee's marital status or whether the employee is employed elsewhere during the year. Consequently, it is possible that an employee's Medicare taxes withheld may differ from the employee's actual Medicare tax liability. Employees who end up having too much Medicare taxes withheld report the excess in the "Payments" section on Form 1040. FICA taxes are discussed in greater detail in Chapter 13 (see ¶1302).

¶203.04 TAX CREDITS

Tax credits reduce a taxpayer's tax liability dollar-for-dollar. Some tax credits are refundable, but most are nonrefundable. **Refundable credits** not only offset income tax liability, but also entitle the taxpayer to a payment from the government when the amount of these credits exceeds the taxpayer's tax liability. **Nonrefundable credits**, in contrast, can only offset the taxpayer's total income tax liability. A taxpayer's total income tax liability is the sum of the taxpayer's regular income tax liability (¶201) and alternative minimum tax (discussed in Chapter 12).

Calculation of Taxes Owed (To Be Refunded)

	Total income tax liability (regular income tax and alternative minimum tax)
–	Nonrefundable tax credits (not to exceed total income tax liability)
+	Additional taxes (for example, self-employment tax)
=	Remaining tax liability
–	Refundable tax credits, prepaid income taxes, and overwithheld FICA taxes
=	Final tax due to (or refund from) the government

¶204 Personal Tax Credits

Some tax credits are personal in nature. Others relate to business activities. This chapter covers personal tax credits. Chapter 12 covers the business tax credits. Many personal tax credits can be taken on Form 1040A; however, a few can only be reported on Form 1040. The only personal tax credit allowed on Form 1040EZ is the earned income credit.

¶204.01 FOREIGN TAX CREDIT

The foreign tax credit applies to both individuals and corporations. U.S. citizens, U.S. residents, and domestic corporations are taxed on their worldwide income. Thus, foreign income may be taxed twice—once by the foreign country and again by the United States government. The foreign tax credit reduces the U.S. income tax by the taxes paid to foreign countries. Thus, it prevents foreign income from being taxed twice. The foreign tax credit cannot exceed the portion of U.S. taxes related to the foreign income reported in taxable income. Form 1116, Foreign Tax Credit, is used to compute the amount of foreign tax credit. As an alternative, individuals can deduct foreign taxes paid as an itemized deduction (discussed at ¶504.04 in Chapter 5).

¶204.02 CHILD AND DEPENDENT CARE CREDIT

A nonrefundable child and dependent care credit is available to individual taxpayers who pay someone to care for a qualifying person while they work. The credit equals a percentage of the qualified expenses incurred for the care of one or more qualifying persons. The percentage used in computing the credit ranges from 20% to 35%, depending on the taxpayer's AGI. Taxpayers with AGI up to $15,000 compute their credit by multiplying their qualified expenses by 35%. For each $2,000 of AGI over $15,000, this percentage drops by 1% until it reaches 20% for taxpayers with AGI in excess of $43,000. Figure 2-1 shows the percentages that apply for each level of AGI.

Figure 2-1: Child and Dependent Care Credit

Amount of AGI	Applicable Percentage	Amount of AGI	Applicable Percentage
Up to $15,000	35%	$29,001 – 31,000	27%
$15,001 – 17,000	34%	31,001 – 33,000	26%
17,001 – 19,000	33%	33,001 – 35,000	25%
19,001 – 21,000	32%	35,001 – 37,000	24%
21,001 – 23,000	31%	37,001 – 39,000	23%
23,001 – 25,000	30%	39,001 – 41,000	22%
25,001 – 27,000	29%	41,001 – 43,000	21%
27,001 – 29,000	28%	43,001 and over	20%

Qualifying Person

To claim the child and dependent care credit, at least one qualifying person must live with the taxpayer for more than half of the year. For purposes of this credit, a *qualifying person* includes:

1. A "qualifying child" (defined at ¶108) under age 13 whom the taxpayer can claim as a dependent,
2. A dependent (of any age) physically or mentally unable to provide self-care, or
3. A spouse physically or mentally unable to provide self-care.

For parents who are divorced or separated, only the custodial parent can claim the child as a qualifying person. Even when the custodial parent allows the noncustodial parent to claim the dependency exemption, the noncustodial parent cannot claim the child as a qualifying person (since the child will not have lived with the parent for more than half of the year). When both parents share custody of a child, the parent having custody for the longer period during the year can claim the child as a qualifying person.

Qualified Expenses

For purposes of the child and dependent care credit, qualified expenses are the amounts taxpayers spend for child and dependent care so that they can work, look for work, or go to school. The costs can include payments for household services such as cooking and housekeeping, as long as the main reason for the cost was to provide care for a qualifying person.

The qualified expenses can be for services provided in the taxpayer's home or for out-of-home care. Payments to a relative count towards the credit unless the taxpayer claims the relative as a dependent. However, payments to the taxpayer's child who will not reach the age of 19 by the end of the year, never count as qualified expenses. Likewise, payments to the taxpayer's spouse are not qualified expenses.

EXAMPLE 2

While Jerry works, he pays his 22-year-old daughter, Francis, to watch his 4-year-old son, Adam. Jerry claims Adam, but not Francis, as a dependent. Payments to Francis for Adam's care are qualified expenses. Had Francis not reached the age of 19 by December 31, or had Jerry been able to claim Francis as a dependent, the payments would not count as qualified expenses.

Qualified expenses must be reduced by nontaxable reimbursements the taxpayer receives from an employer's dependent care assistance plan. Dependent care assistance plans are a fringe benefit discussed in Chapter 4 (see ¶401.03).

EXAMPLE 3

During the year, Al and Lisa Sherman paid a childcare provider $6,000 to look after their sons (ages 4 and 6) while they worked. Al received a $2,500 nontaxable reimbursement from his employer's dependent care assistance plan. The Shermans' qualified expenses are $3,500 ($6,000 – $2,500).

Limitations on Qualified Expenses

The Code initially limits the amount of qualified expenses to $3,000 for one qualifying person ($6,000 for two or more qualifying persons). These dollar amounts are reduced by nontaxable reimbursements that the taxpayer receives from an employer's dependent care assistance plan. The Code further limits these amounts to the taxpayer's earned income. If the taxpayer is married, the maximum qualified expenses are limited to the earned income of the spouse with the lower amount of earned income. Thus, the **maximum qualified expenses** are the *lesser of* (i) the taxpayer's qualified expenses reduced by nontaxable reimbursements from a dependent care assistance plan, (ii) the dollar limits ($3,000/$6,000) reduced by the nontaxable reimbursements, or (iii) the taxpayer's earned income.

EXAMPLE 4

Marlin paid $2,100 in qualified expenses for the care of his 7-year-old son. Marlin's earned income is $15,500. His maximum qualified expenses are $2,100 [the *lesser of* (i) qualified expenses of $2,100, (ii) $3,000 limit for one qualifying person, or (iii) earned income of $15,500].

EXAMPLE 5

Same facts as in Example 4, except that during the year Marlin received a $1,700 nontaxable reimbursement from his employer's dependent care assistance plan. Marlin's maximum qualified expenses are $400 [the *lesser of* (i) $400 of qualified expenses ($2,100 – $1,700), (ii) $1,300 limit for one qualifying person ($3,000 – $1,700), or (iii) earned income of $15,500].

A married couple must file a joint return to be able to take the child and dependent care credit. Usually a taxpayer's spouse must be gainfully employed for the couple to be eligible for the child and dependent care credit. However, a special rule applies to spouses who are either disabled or full-time students. This rule assumes the spouse has some earned income for purposes of the earned income limitation. The amount "deemed" earned is $250 per month when the couple has one qualifying person and $500 when the couple has two or more qualifying persons. The amount is "deemed" earned only for those months that the spouse is a full-time student or incapable of self-care.

EXAMPLE 6

Paul and Kim Foxx have two children, ages 3 and 5. During the year, Paul worked full-time. Kim did not work, but she attended college full-time 10 months out of the year. The Foxxes paid $6,600 in qualified childcare expenses. Since the Foxxes' childcare expenses exceed the $6,000 limit for two or more qualifying persons, the Foxxes' qualified expenses are initially limited to $6,000. Even though Kim does not work, she is "deemed" to be employed for 10 months of the year with earnings of $5,000 ($500 × 10 months). Since Kim's "deemed" earnings of $5,000 are less than $6,000, the Foxxes' maximum qualified expenses for purposes of computing the child and dependent care credit are $5,000.

Giving a full-time student spouse who does not work "deemed" earned income allows the couple to claim the child and dependent care credit. Without this special rule, the lesser of qualified expenses, the dollar limit, and earned income would be $0 in situations where the full-time student spouse did not work. However, these "deemed" earnings are not taxable income and are not included in the calculation of the couple's taxable income.

To compute the child and dependent care credit, taxpayers multiply their maximum qualified expenses by the applicable percentage (from Figure 2-1).

EXAMPLE 7

Assume that in Example 6, the Foxxes' only source of gross income is Paul's wages of $29,500. Taxpayers with AGI between $29,001 and $31,000 multiply their maximum qualified expenses by 27% (Figure 2-1). Thus, the Foxxes' nonrefundable child and dependent care credit would equal $1,350 ($5,000 × 27%). Although Kim's "deemed" wages of $5,000 were used in determining the couple's maximum qualified expenses, they are not real wages. Accordingly, they are not used in computing the couple's $29,500 of AGI.

Claiming the Credit

Taxpayers who file Form 1040 or Form 1040A claim their credit on Form 2441, Child and Dependent Care Expenses. Form 2441 is illustrated in Figure 2-2. The child and dependent care credit is a nonrefundable credit. The amount of the credit is limited to the taxpayer's total tax liability, minus any foreign tax credit taken by the taxpayer. Any unused amounts cannot be used in any other tax year.

¶204.03 FILLED-IN FORM 2441

To assist your learning on how to complete the various forms and schedules illustrated in this textbook, amounts in bold come from either the taxpayer's tax records or from other tax forms, schedules, or worksheets that already have been completed. Once the information in bold has been entered on the form, all that is left is to follow the instructions provided for the rest of the lines on the tax form.

INFORMATION FOR FIGURE 2-2:

Patricia and Clyde Smith live and work in Chicago. Patricia works full-time and earns **$30,000**. Clyde works part time during the year and earns **$10,500**. The Smiths have no other sources of income and have no deductions for AGI. They claim their 6-year-old son as a dependent. For the year, the Smiths paid **Lucy Burke $3,200** to care for their son after school until the Smiths got home from work.

Line #

3: The **$3,000** limit for one qualifying person applies
7: AGI, **$40,500** ($30,000 + $10,500)
8: Decimal amount from table, **.22** (based on AGI of $40,500)
10: Tax liability limit, **$1,593** (source: Credit Limit Worksheet, found in the instructions to Form 2441)

Figure 2-2: Filled-In Form 2441

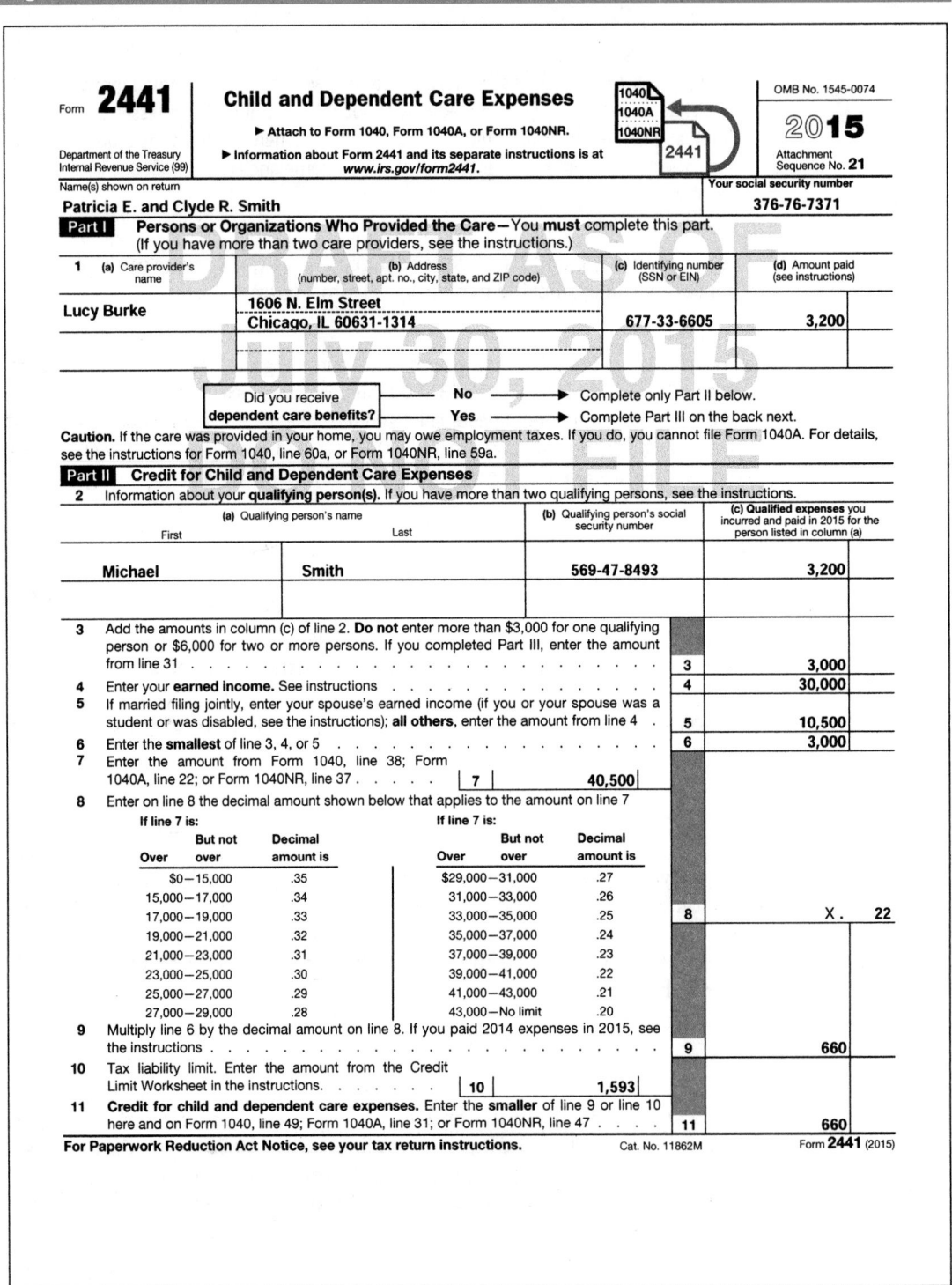

Form **2441** — Department of the Treasury, Internal Revenue Service (99)

Child and Dependent Care Expenses

► Attach to Form 1040, Form 1040A, or Form 1040NR.

► Information about Form 2441 and its separate instructions is at *www.irs.gov/form2441*.

1040 / 1040A / 1040NR — 2441

OMB No. 1545-0074 — **2015** — Attachment Sequence No. **21**

Name(s) shown on return	Your social security number
Patricia E. and Clyde R. Smith	**376-76-7371**

Part I **Persons or Organizations Who Provided the Care**—You **must** complete this part. (If you have more than two care providers, see the instructions.)

1 (a) Care provider's name	(b) Address (number, street, apt. no., city, state, and ZIP code)	(c) Identifying number (SSN or EIN)	(d) Amount paid (see instructions)
Lucy Burke	1606 N. Elm Street Chicago, IL 60631-1314	677-33-6605	3,200

Did you receive dependent care benefits? — **No** ──► Complete only Part II below. — **Yes** ──► Complete Part III on the back next.

Caution. If the care was provided in your home, you may owe employment taxes. If you do, you cannot file Form 1040A. For details, see the instructions for Form 1040, line 60a, or Form 1040NR, line 59a.

Part II **Credit for Child and Dependent Care Expenses**

2 Information about your **qualifying person(s).** If you have more than two qualifying persons, see the instructions.

(a) Qualifying person's name — First	Last	(b) Qualifying person's social security number	(c) **Qualified expenses** you incurred and paid in 2015 for the person listed in column (a)
Michael	Smith	569-47-8493	3,200

3	Add the amounts in column (c) of line 2. **Do not** enter more than $3,000 for one qualifying person or $6,000 for two or more persons. If you completed Part III, enter the amount from line 31	3	3,000
4	Enter your **earned income.** See instructions	4	30,000
5	If married filing jointly, enter your spouse's earned income (if you or your spouse was a student or was disabled, see the instructions); **all others,** enter the amount from line 4	5	10,500
6	Enter the **smallest** of line 3, 4, or 5	6	3,000
7	Enter the amount from Form 1040, line 38; Form 1040A, line 22; or Form 1040NR, line 37 — 7: 40,500		
8	Enter on line 8 the decimal amount shown below that applies to the amount on line 7	8	X. 22

If line 7 is: Over	But not over	Decimal amount is	If line 7 is: Over	But not over	Decimal amount is
$0	15,000	.35	$29,000	31,000	.27
15,000	17,000	.34	31,000	33,000	.26
17,000	19,000	.33	33,000	35,000	.25
19,000	21,000	.32	35,000	37,000	.24
21,000	23,000	.31	37,000	39,000	.23
23,000	25,000	.30	39,000	41,000	.22
25,000	27,000	.29	41,000	43,000	.21
27,000	29,000	.28	43,000	No limit	.20

9	Multiply line 6 by the decimal amount on line 8. If you paid 2014 expenses in 2015, see the instructions	9	660
10	Tax liability limit. Enter the amount from the Credit Limit Worksheet in the instructions — 10: 1,593		
11	**Credit for child and dependent care expenses.** Enter the **smaller** of line 9 or line 10 here and on Form 1040, line 49; Form 1040A, line 31; or Form 1040NR, line 47	11	660

For Paperwork Reduction Act Notice, see your tax return instructions. Cat. No. 11862M Form **2441** (2015)

¶204.04 HIGHER EDUCATION CREDITS

Education credits are available for persons who pay qualified education expenses during the year on behalf of themselves or eligible students. There are two types of education credits. One is the American opportunity credit; the second is the lifetime learning credit. Taxpayers cannot claim both credits in the same year for the same student. However, they can claim both credits in the same year, but for different students. These credits are not available once a taxpayer's AGI exceeds a certain level. Married persons that file separately are not allowed to claim the education credits.

To qualify for the credit, the tuition normally must be paid in the same year as the year in which the semester or quarter begins. However, tuition paid in one year for a course that starts within three months of the next year, qualifies for the credit in the year it is paid. Thus, tuition paid in 2015 for classes that begin before April 1, 2016, count towards the 2015 education credit.

Only "adjusted qualified education expenses" are used to compute either education credit. These are the taxpayer's out-of-pocket amounts paid for tuition, fees, and course-related books, supplies, and equipment. Thus, any costs paid for with nontaxable scholarships and other tax-free educational benefits cannot be used to compute the credit. This includes amounts received from an employer's educational assistance plan (a type of fringe benefit discussed in Chapter 4, see ¶401.03).

American Opportunity Credit

The American opportunity credit provides for a maximum $2,500 tax credit for *each* eligible student. *Eligible students* for purposes of this credit are students enrolled in their first four years of post-secondary education. The student must also be enrolled at least half of full-time credit hours during one semester or quarter during the year.

> Post-secondary education is the stage of learning that takes place after high school. Students receive a post-secondary education when they attend universities, academies, colleges, seminaries, technical institutes, vocational or trade schools, and other institutions that award academic degrees or professional certifications.

To compute the amount of the credit, taxpayers add 100% of the first $2,000 of adjusted qualified education expenses to 25% of the *lesser of* (i) $2,000 or (ii) those expenses in excess of $2,000. The maximum credit is $2,500 [(100% × $2,000) + (25% × $2,000)].

EXAMPLE 8

> On December 22, 2014, Brad paid $800 for his son's tuition for the Spring 2015 semester. The son attends college full-time and is a freshman during the Spring semester. On August 15, 2015, Brad paid $840 for his son's Fall 2015 tuition. Brad's American opportunity credit for 2015 equals $840. The $800 paid in 2014 for classes that began before April 1, 2015 qualified for the American opportunity credit in 2014.

Taxpayers whose filing status is single, head of household, or qualifying widow(er), and whose AGI exceeds $80,000, must reduce their American opportunity credit. Married couples who file a joint return must reduce their credit if AGI exceeds $160,000. (Married taxpayers who file separately (MFS) cannot take the education credit.) The reduction in the credit equals:

$$\text{American opportunity credit} \times \frac{[\text{AGI} - \$80{,}000^{*}]}{\$10{,}000^{**}}$$

*** $160,000 for married couples filing a joint return**
**** $20,000 for married couples filing a joint return**

The phase-out range is $10,000 for taxpayers filing as single, head of household or qualifying widow(er). Thus, when AGI for these taxpayers exceeds $90,000 ($80,000 + $10,000), the

American opportunity credit is reduced to $0. The phase-out range is $20,000 for married couples filing a joint return. Thus, when the couple's AGI exceeds $180,000 ($160,000 + $20,000), their American opportunity credit is fully phased-out.

EXAMPLE 9

Betty reports AGI of $82,330 on her tax return. During the year, Betty paid $3,000 in tuition and fees for her dependent son, who is a full-time student attending his fourth year of college. Betty's initial American opportunity credit is $2,250 [($2,000 × 100%) + ($1,000 × 25%)]. However, because AGI exceeds the $80,000 threshold for unmarried taxpayers, Betty must reduce her credit by $524 [$2,250 × ($82,330 – $80,000)/$10,000)]. Betty's American opportunity credit is $1,726 ($2,250 – $524).

For most taxpayers, 40% of their American opportunity credit is a refundable tax credit. The remaining 60% is a nonrefundable credit, which only can be used to offset a taxpayer's total income tax liability. For example, in Example 9, Betty would report $690 as a refundable credit ($1,726 × 40%), and $1,036 as a nonrefundable credit ($1,726 – $690).

Lifetime Learning Credit

The lifetime learning credit provides for a maximum tax credit of $2,000 each year. This differs from the American opportunity credit where the maximum credit is $2,500 for each eligible student. Other differences between the two credits are as follows.

1. A student can attend less than half-time and qualify for the lifetime learning credit.
2. Tuition and course-related items paid for education that extends beyond the first four years of college qualify for the lifetime learning credit.
3. The lifetime learning credit is 100% nonrefundable.
4. Lower AGI thresholds apply to reduce the lifetime learning credit for higher-income taxpayers.

To compute the lifetime learning credit, taxpayers multiply 20% by the *lesser of* (i) $10,000 or (ii) adjusted qualified education expenses for the year.

EXAMPLE 10

On August 10, 2015, Becky paid $3,000 to cover her tuition for the Fall semester. Becky is a graduate student in the nursing program at Arizona State University. Becky's lifetime learning credit for 2015 equals $600 ($3,000 × 20%).

EXAMPLE 11

On December 16, 2015, the Johnsons paid $6,000 for their daughter's and $7,000 for their son's Spring 2016 tuition. The Spring semester began on January 20, 2016. Both children attend college less than half-time. The Johnsons' lifetime learning credit for 2015 equals $2,000 [(*lesser of* $10,000 or $13,000) × 20%]. The maximum lifetime learning credit is $2,000 per taxpayer each year.

Taxpayers whose filing status is single, head of household, or qualifying widow(er), and whose AGI in 2015 exceeds $55,000, must reduce the amount of their lifetime learning credit. The AGI threshold is $110,000 for couples filing a joint return. (The education credit is not allowed if a married taxpayer files MFS.) For 2015, the reduction in the credit equals:

$$\text{Lifetime learning tax credit} \times \frac{[\text{AGI} - \$55{,}000^{*}]}{\$10{,}000^{**}}$$

*** $110,000 for married couples filing a joint return**
**** $20,000 for married couples filing a joint return**

As with the American opportunity credit, the phase-out range for the lifetime learning credit is $10,000 for taxpayers whose filing status is single, head of household or qualifying widow(er). Thus, when these taxpayers' AGI in 2015 exceeds $65,000 ($55,000 + $10,000), their lifetime learning credit is $0. The phase-out range for married couples filing a joint return (MFJ) is $20,000. Thus, when a couple's AGI in 2015 exceeds $130,000 ($110,000 + $20,000), their lifetime learning credit is fully phased-out.

EXAMPLE 12

The Steins' AGI is $124,000. In 2015, the Steins paid $8,000 for their son's tuition. Their son is in his first year of college, but he does not attend college at least half time, so the Steins cannot claim the American opportunity credit. The Steins' initial lifetime learning credit is $1,600 ($8,000 × 20%). Because AGI exceeds the $110,000 threshold for MFJ, their lifetime learning credit is reduced to $480.

Initial lifetime learning credit		$1,600
AGI	$ 124,000	
Less AGI threshold	(110,000)	
Excess AGI	$ 14,000	
	÷ $20,000	
	70%	
	× $1,600	(1,120)
Lifetime learning credit		$ 480

i

The AGI thresholds for the lifetime learning credit are adjusted annually for inflation, using the method described earlier in the chapter (see ¶202). This differs from the AGI thresholds for the American opportunity credit, which are fixed in amount and never change.

Claiming the Credit

Taxpayers claim the education credit on Form 8863, Education Credits (American Opportunity and Lifetime Learning Credits). They start by completing a separate Part III (found on page 2 of the form) for each student for whom the taxpayer is claiming an education credit. In Part III, taxpayers provide the student's name (line 20) and social security number (line 21). They also provide information about the educational institution the student attended and whether the student received a scholarship that was reported to the IRS by the institution on Form 1098-T (line 22). They then answer questions (lines 23-26) that determine whether the taxpayer can claim the American opportunity credit or the lifetime learning credit for the student.

If the student identified in Part III qualifies the taxpayer for the American opportunity credit, the adjusted qualified education expenses are entered on line 27, and the initial credit (before any reduction due to excess AGI) is computed by following the instructions on lines 28-30. If the student qualifies the taxpayer for the lifetime learning credit, adjusted qualified education expenses are entered on line 31.

Once page 2 of Form 8863 has been completed for each student, the taxpayer adds up all adjusted qualified expenses for each credit and enters the total for the American opportunity credit on Part I (line 1). The total for the lifetime learning credit is then entered on Part II (line 10). On line 11, the initial lifetime learning credit is limited to the lesser of the total adjusted qualified expenses or $10,000. Twenty percent of the amount from line 11 is entered on line 12. This amount represents the taxpayer's initial lifetime learning credit.

If the taxpayer is claiming the American opportunity credit, the taxpayer follows the directions on lines 2 through 7 to reduce the amount of the credit when AGI exceeds $80,000 ($160,000 if married filing jointly). Any credit remaining on line 7 is multiplied by 40%. This is the refundable portion of the taxpayer's education credit. The nonrefundable portion (60%) is entered in Part II (line 9), and gets added to the taxpayer's nonrefundable lifetime learning credit.

If the taxpayer is claiming the lifetime learning credit, the taxpayer follows the directions on lines 13 through 18 to reduce the amount of the credit when AGI exceeds $55,000 ($110,000 if married filing jointly). The taxpayer's nonrefundable education credit is the lesser of (i) the taxpayer's tax liability, minus the foreign tax credit, child and dependent care credit, and elderly or disabled credit, or (ii) the taxpayer's total nonrefundable education credits. This determination is done on a Credit Limit Worksheet found in the instructions for Form 8863. The final step is to transfer any refundable credit (from line 8) and nonrefundable credit (from line 19) to their respective lines on the taxpayer's tax return (Form 1040A or Form 1040).

EXAMPLE 13

In 2015, Ed and Sue Reese pay $3,500 for their daughter, Mary's, tuition at Flathead Community College, in Kalispell, MT. Mary is a freshman attending college full-time. Mary did not receive any scholarship income, and the Reeses' 2015 AGI is $174,660. The Reeses' initial American opportunity credit is $2,375 [($2,000 × 100%) + ($1,500 × 25%)]. Because their AGI exceeds $160,000, they must reduce their credit by $1,741 [$2,375 × ($14,660 excess AGI/$20,000 for MFJ)]. The Reeses' education credit for 2015 is $634 ($2,375 – $1,741), of which 40%, or $254, is refundable and the rest ($380) is nonrefundable.

¶204.05 FILLED-IN FORM 8863

INFORMATION FOR FIGURE 2-3:

Figure 2-3 shows a completed Form 8863, Education Credits (American Opportunity and Lifetime Learning Credits), for the Reeses from Example 13. The Reeses first complete Part III (lines 20–26). It is here that they answer questions about Mary and her educational institution. They then enter the amounts shown below in bold on the designated lines.

Line #

3: AGI, **$174,660**

19: Nonrefundable education credits (from the Credit Limit Worksheet, which makes sure the nonrefundable portion of the credit does not exceed the taxpayer's tax liability minus any foreign tax credit, child and dependent care credit and elderly or disabled credit), **$380**.

27: Adjusted qualified education expenses, up to $4,000, **$3,500**

Starting with lines 27-30, the Reeses compute their initial American opportunity credit. The Reeses transfer the amount from line 30 to Part I (line 1). They then follow the instructions for the remaining lines on the form to compute the refundable and nonrefundable portions of their education credit. These amounts are transferred to the Reeses' Form 1040.

Before there was an American opportunity credit, the Hope scholarship credit provided taxpayers with a nonrefundable tax credit up to $1,800 per eligible student. Eligible students were those attending their first two years of college. In 2009, Congress replaced the Hope scholarship credit with the American opportunity credit. The American opportunity credit increased the amount of the credit to $2,500, expanded the credit to include students attending their first four years of college, and provided taxpayers with a partially refundable tax credit. The American opportunity credit was originally scheduled to be around through 2010. However, Congress has extended it through 2017. Unless Congress extends the American opportunity credit beyond 2017, starting in 2018, the original Hope scholarship credit will take its place.

Figure 2-3: Filled-In Form 8863 (Page 1)

Form **8863** | Department of the Treasury Internal Revenue Service (99)

Education Credits
(American Opportunity and Lifetime Learning Credits)
▶ Attach to Form 1040 or Form 1040A.
▶ Information about Form 8863 and its separate instructions is at *www.irs.gov/form8863.*

OMB No. 1545-0074 | **2015** | Attachment Sequence No. **50**

Name(s) shown on return: **Edward L. and Susan L. Reese** | Your social security number: **839 | 74 | 2576**

CAUTION: *Complete a separate Part III on page 2 for each student for whom you are claiming either credit before you complete Parts I and II.*

Part I Refundable American Opportunity Credit

1	After completing Part III for each student, enter the total of all amounts from all Parts III, line 30			1	2,375
2	Enter: $180,000 if married filing jointly; $90,000 if single, head of household, or qualifying widow(er)	2	180,000		
3	Enter the amount from Form 1040, line 38, or Form 1040A, line 22. If you are filing Form 2555, 2555-EZ, or 4563, or you are excluding income from Puerto Rico, see Pub. 970 for the amount to enter	3	174,660		
4	Subtract line 3 from line 2. If zero or less, **stop**; you cannot take any education credit	4	5,340		
5	Enter: $20,000 if married filing jointly; $10,000 if single, head of household, or qualifying widow(er)	5	20,000		
6	If line 4 is: • Equal to or more than line 5, enter 1.000 on line 6 • Less than line 5, divide line 4 by line 5. Enter the result as a decimal (rounded to at least three places)			6	.267
7	Multiply line 1 by line 6. **Caution:** If you were under age 24 at the end of the year **and** meet the conditions described in the instructions, you **cannot** take the refundable American opportunity credit; skip line 8, enter the amount from line 7 on line 9, and check this box ▶ ☐			7	634
8	**Refundable American opportunity credit.** Multiply line 7 by 40% (.40). Enter the amount here and on Form 1040, line 68, or Form 1040A, line 44. Then go to line 9 below.			8	254

Part II Nonrefundable Education Credits

9	Subtract line 8 from line 7. Enter here and on line 2 of the Credit Limit Worksheet (see instructions)			9	380
10	After completing Part III for each student, enter the total of all amounts from all Parts III, line 31. If zero, skip lines 11 through 17, enter -0- on line 18, and go to line 19			10	0
11	Enter the smaller of line 10 or $10,000			11	
12	Multiply line 11 by 20% (.20)			12	
13	Enter: $130,000 if married filing jointly; $65,000 if single, head of household, or qualifying widow(er)	13			
14	Enter the amount from Form 1040, line 38, or Form 1040A, line 22. If you are filing Form 2555, 2555-EZ, or 4563, or you are excluding income from Puerto Rico, see Pub. 970 for the amount to enter	14			
15	Subtract line 14 from line 13. If zero or less, skip lines 16 and 17, enter -0- on line 18, and go to line 19	15			
16	Enter: $20,000 if married filing jointly; $10,000 if single, head of household, or qualifying widow(er)	16			
17	If line 15 is: • Equal to or more than line 16, enter 1.000 on line 17 and go to line 18 • Less than line 16, divide line 15 by line 16. Enter the result as a decimal (rounded to at least three places)			17	.
18	Multiply line 12 by line 17. Enter here and on line 1 of the Credit Limit Worksheet (see instructions) ▶			18	0
19	**Nonrefundable education credits.** Enter the amount from line 7 of the Credit Limit Worksheet (see instructions) here and on Form 1040, line 50, or Form 1040A, line 33			19	380

For Paperwork Reduction Act Notice, see your tax return instructions. Cat. No. 25379M Form **8863** (2015)

Figure 2-3: Filled-In Form 8863 (Page 2)

Form 8863 (2015) Page **2**

Name(s) shown on return: Edward L. and Susan L. Reese

Your social security number: 839 | 74 | 2576

CAUTION ***Complete Part III for each student for whom you are claiming either the American opportunity credit or lifetime learning credit. Use additional copies of page 2 as needed for each student.***

Part III **Student and Educational Institution Information** See instructions.

20 Student name (as shown on page 1 of your tax return): **Mary Reese**

21 Student social security number (as shown on page 1 of your tax return): **641 | 14 | 8330**

22 Educational institution information (see instructions)

a. Name of first educational institution	b. Name of second educational institution (if any)
Flathead Community College	
(1) Address. Number and street (or P.O. box). City, town or post office, state, and ZIP code. If a foreign address, see instructions. **777 Grandview Drive, Kalispell, MT 59901**	**(1)** Address. Number and street (or P.O. box). City, town or post office, state, and ZIP code. If a foreign address, see instructions.
(2) Did the student receive Form 1098-T from this institution for 2015? ☐ Yes ☑ No	**(2)** Did the student receive Form 1098-T from this institution for 2015? ☐ Yes ☐ No
(3) Did the student receive Form 1098-T from this institution for 2014 with Box 2 filled in and Box 7 checked? ☐ Yes ☑ No	**(3)** Did the student receive Form 1098-T from this institution for 2014 with Box 2 filled in and Box 7 checked? ☐ Yes ☐ No
If you checked "No" in **both (2) and (3)**, skip **(4)**.	If you checked "No" in **both (2) and (3)**, skip **(4)**.
(4) If you checked "Yes" in **(2) or (3)**, enter the institution's federal identification number (from Form 1098-T). __ __ - __ __ __ __ __ __ __	**(4)** If you checked "Yes" in **(2) or (3)**, enter the institution's federal identification number (from Form 1098-T). __ __ - __ __ __ __ __ __ __

23 Has the Hope Scholarship Credit or American opportunity credit been claimed for this student for any 4 tax years before 2015? ☐ Yes — **Stop!** Go to line 31 for this student. ☑ No — Go to line 24.

24 Was the student enrolled at least half-time for at least one academic period that began or is treated as having begun in 2015 at an eligible educational institution in a program leading towards a postsecondary degree, certificate, or other recognized postsecondary educational credential? (see instructions) ☑ Yes — Go to line 25. ☐ No — **Stop!** Go to line 31 for this student.

25 Did the student complete the first 4 years of postsecondary education before 2015 (see instructions)? ☐ Yes — **Stop!** Go to line 31 for this student. ☑ No — Go to line 26.

26 Was the student convicted, before the end of 2015, of a felony for possession or distribution of a controlled substance? ☐ Yes — **Stop!** Go to line 31 for this student. ☑ No — Complete lines 27 through 30 for this student.

CAUTION *You **cannot** take the American opportunity credit and the lifetime learning credit for the **same student** in the same year. If you complete lines 27 through 30 for this student, do not complete line 31.*

American Opportunity Credit

27	Adjusted qualified education expenses (see instructions). **Do not enter more than $4,000**	27	3,500
28	Subtract $2,000 from line 27. If zero or less, enter -0-	28	1,500
29	Multiply line 28 by 25% (.25)	29	375
30	If line 28 is zero, enter the amount from line 27. Otherwise, add $2,000 to the amount on line 29 and enter the result. Skip line 31. Include the total of all amounts from all Parts III, line 30, on Part I, line 1	30	2,375

Lifetime Learning Credit

31	Adjusted qualified education expenses (see instructions). Include the total of all amounts from all Parts III, line 31, on Part II, line 10	31	0

Form **8863** (2015)

¶204.06 RETIREMENT SAVINGS CONTRIBUTIONS CREDIT

Certain taxpayers may take a nonrefundable tax credit for contributions (including amounts withheld from their paychecks) to retirement savings plans. The credit is in addition to any deduction or exclusion relating to the retirement plan contributions. The credit applies to contributions made to traditional and Roth IRAs and other qualified retirement plans such as 401(k) plans, 403(b) annuities, 457 plans, SIMPLE and SEP plans.

The credit for 2015 is determined by multiplying the contributions (not to exceed $2,000 per taxpayer) by a percentage taken from Figure 2-4. On a joint tax return, the credit can be based on a $4,000 maximum contribution, provided both spouses make at least a $2,000 contribution to a retirement plan during the year. The percentages used to compute the credit depend on the taxpayer's filing status and AGI.

Figure 2-4: Retirement Savings Contributions Credit

Married Filing Jointly		Head of Household		All Others		Applicable
AGI Over	Not Over	AGI Over	Not Over	AGI Over	Not Over	%
$0	$36,500	$0	$27,375	$0	$18,250	50%
36,500	39,500	27,375	29,625	18,250	19,750	20
39,500	61,000	29,625	45,750	19,750	30,500	10
61,000	—	45,750	—	30,500	—	0

Taxpayers must be at least 18 years old to qualify for the credit. Also, no credit is available for persons claimed as dependents or those who are full-time students. As Figure 2-4 shows, no credit is available in 2015 for joint filers with AGI in excess of $61,000; head of households filers with AGI over $45,750, or for all other filers with AGI in excess of $30,500 (which includes taxpayers whose filing status is single, married filing separately, or qualifying widow(er)).

Claiming the Credit

The retirement savings contributions credit is computed on Form 8880, Credit for Qualified Retirement Savings Contributions. The credit is then reported on Form 1040A or Form 1040 along with the taxpayer's other nonrefundable tax credits. The amount of the credit is limited to the taxpayer's total tax liability after subtracting out the following nonrefundable tax credits: foreign tax credit, child and dependent care credit, elderly or disabled credit, and education credit.

EXAMPLE 14

Dave and Sue Orr report $37,200 of AGI on their 2015 joint return. During the year Dave contributed $5,000 to his Roth IRA. Sue did not make any contributions during the year. The Orrs' retirement savings contributions credit equals $400 ($2,000 per taxpayer maximum × 20% from the table in Figure 2-4). Assuming the Orrs do not have any other nonrefundable tax credits for the year, they report this amount on Form 1040 or Form 1040A.

EXAMPLE 15

Same facts as in Example 14, except that in addition to the retirement savings contributions credit, the Orrs claim a $1,000 education credit. The Orrs' total tax liability for 2015 is $1,263. Once the Orrs reduce their tax liability by the $1,000 education credit, only $263 of tax liability remains. Their retirement savings contributions credit will be limited to $263. Since the retirement savings contributions credit is nonrefundable, the Orrs receive no tax benefit from the $137 ($400 – $263) unused portion of the credit.

¶204.07 CHILD TAX CREDIT (CTC)

Taxpayers may be able to claim a $1,000 tax credit for each “qualifying child” (defined at ¶108). The child must be under the age of 17 as of the end of the tax year and claimed as a dependent on the taxpayer’s tax return. For divorced or separated parents, the child tax credit (CTC) can be taken only by the parent who claims the child as a dependent.

The full CTC is available to unmarried taxpayers whose AGI does not exceed $75,000. A married taxpayer who files head of household under the abandoned spouse rules is considered unmarried. The AGI threshold is $110,000 for married couples that file jointly (MFJ); and is $55,000 for couples that file married filing separately (MFS). The taxpayer loses $50 of the credit for each $1,000 (or portion thereof) that AGI exceeds the threshold amount.

EXAMPLE 16

Tom and Carol Normand file a joint tax return. They claim their two children, ages 8 and 9, as dependents. Because the Normands’ AGI of $116,400 exceeds the $110,000 threshold for MFJ, they are not entitled to the full $2,000 CTC. Their $1,650 CTC is calculated below.

Initial CTC ($1,000 × 2 qualifying children)		$2,000
AGI	$116,400	
Less: AGI threshold for MFJ	(110,000)	
Excess AGI	$ 6,400	
	÷ $1,000	
	6.4	
Number of $1,000 intervals (or portion thereof)	7	
	× $50	(350)
Child tax credit		$1,650

EXAMPLE 17

John files as head of household and claims his 10-year-old nephew as a dependent. John’s AGI is $77,430. Since a nephew is a qualifying child, John computes the $850 CTC as follows.

Initial CTC ($1,000 × 1 qualifying child)		$1,000
AGI	$77,430	
Less: AGI threshold for unmarried taxpayers	(75,000)	
Excess AGI	$ 2,430	
	÷ $1,000	
	2.43	
Number of $1,000 intervals (or portion thereof)	3	
	× $50	(150)
Child tax credit		$ 850

The phase out of the CTC is $50 per $1,000 of excess AGI (or portion thereof). How quickly the taxpayer’s CTC is phased out depends on the amount of AGI, the taxpayer’s filing status, and the number of qualifying children.

Claiming the Credit

While the CTC is generally nonrefundable, it may be a refundable credit for certain taxpayers. However, before computing the refundable portion of the CTC, taxpayers first compute the amount of the CTC that is nonrefundable. This is done on the Child Tax Credit Worksheet found in the instructions for Form 1040. This worksheet subtracts from the taxpayer's total tax liability the following nonrefundable personal credits: foreign tax credit, child and dependent care credit, nonrefundable education credit, elderly or disabled credit, and retirement savings contributions credit. The *lesser of* (i) the remaining tax liability or (ii) the taxpayer's CTC represents the nonrefundable portion of the credit. Taxpayers report their nonrefundable CTC with their other nonrefundable tax credits on Form 1040A or Form 1040.

EXAMPLE 18

The Stewarts file a joint return. They claim their three children (all under age 17) as dependents. The Stewarts' AGI is $65,970 and their total tax liability is $4,084. They are only entitled to one tax credit—the CTC. Since the Stewarts' AGI is less than $110,000, they do not lose any of their $3,000 CTC ($1,000 × 3 qualifying children) due to excess AGI. The Stewarts report the entire $3,000 CTC as a nonrefundable credit.

Calculation of Additional Child Tax Credit

In 2015, the amount of the taxpayer's CTC that cannot be taken as a nonrefundable credit is refundable up to 15% of the taxpayer's earned income in excess of $3,000. Taxpayers compute the refundable portion of the CTC on Schedule 8812, Child Tax Credit, and report this amount with their other refundable tax credits on Form 1040A or Form 1040.

EXAMPLE 19

Joel and Ruth Floyd file a joint return. They claim their two children, ages 8 and 10, as dependents. The Floyds' 2015 AGI is $43,530, which includes their combined wages of $41,200. The Floyds' tax liability before credits is $1,493, and they are entitled to a $642 child and dependent care credit. After subtracting this credit from their taxes, the Floyds' remaining tax liability is $851 ($1,493 – $642). Since their AGI is less than $110,000, the $2,000 CTC ($1,000 × 2) is not reduced due to excess AGI. Therefore, they report $851 as their nonrefundable CTC on Form 1040. They then complete Form 8812, Additional Child Tax Credit, to compute the refundable portion of their CTC.

Because of the rest of the CTC of $1,149 ($2,000 – $851) does not exceed 15% of the Floyds' earned income in excess $3,000 (15% × ($41,200 – $3,000) = $5,730), the Floyds report a $1,149 as a refundable CTC.

In situations where the refundable credit is limited, a special rule for calculating the refundable CTC exists for taxpayers with three or more qualifying children. Those interested in learning more about the calculation of the refundable CTC for taxpayers in this special situation should refer to IRS Publication 972.

¶204.08 FILLED-IN SCHEDULE 8812

INFORMATION FOR FIGURE 2-5:

Figure 2-5 shows a completed Schedule 8812, Child Tax Credit, for the Floyds from Example 19. Amounts shown in bold below are entered on the lines indicated. The form is then completed by following the instructions provided for the rest of the lines on the form.

Line #

1: CTC to be claimed ($1,000 × 2 children), **$2,000**
2: Nonrefundable CTC from Form 1040, **$851**
4a: Total earned income, **$41,200**

Figure 2-5: Filled-In Schedule 8812 (Page 1)

SCHEDULE 8812
(Form 1040A or 1040)

Department of the Treasury
Internal Revenue Service (99)

Child Tax Credit

▶ **Attach to Form 1040, Form 1040A, or Form 1040NR.**
▶ **Information about Schedule 8812 and its separate instructions is at *www.irs.gov/schedule8812*.**

1040 / 1040A / 1040NR → 8812

OMB No. 1545-0074
2015
Attachment Sequence No. 47

Name(s) shown on return: **Joel and Ruth Floyd**
Your social security number: **861-22-9418**

Part I Filers Who Have Certain Child Dependent(s) with an ITIN (Individual Taxpayer Identification Number)

CAUTION

Complete this part only for each dependent who has an ITIN and for whom you are claiming the child tax credit. If your dependent is not a qualifying child for the credit, you cannot include that dependent in the calculation of this credit.

Answer the following questions for each dependent listed on Form 1040, line 6c; Form 1040A, line 6c; or Form 1040NR, line 7c, who has an ITIN (Individual Taxpayer Identification Number) and that you indicated is a qualifying child for the child tax credit by checking column (4) for that dependent.

A For the first dependent identified with an ITIN and listed as a qualifying child for the child tax credit, did this child meet the substantial presence test? See separate instructions.

☑ **Yes** ☐ **No**

B For the second dependent identified with an ITIN and listed as a qualifying child for the child tax credit, did this child meet the substantial presence test? See separate instructions.

☑ **Yes** ☐ **No**

C For the third dependent identified with an ITIN and listed as a qualifying child for the child tax credit, did this child meet the substantial presence test? See separate instructions.

☐ **Yes** ☐ **No**

D For the fourth dependent identified with an ITIN and listed as a qualifying child for the child tax credit, did this child meet the substantial presence test? See separate instructions.

☐ **Yes** ☐ **No**

Note: If you have more than four dependents identified with an ITIN and listed as a qualifying child for the child tax credit, see separate instructions and check here . . . ▶ ☐

Part II Additional Child Tax Credit Filers

1 **1040 filers:** Enter the amount from line 6 of your Child Tax Credit Worksheet (see the Instructions for Form 1040, line 52).
1040A filers: Enter the amount from line 6 of your Child Tax Credit Worksheet (see the Instructions for Form 1040A, line 35).
1040NR filers: Enter the amount from line 6 of your Child Tax Credit Worksheet (see the Instructions for Form 1040NR, line 49).
If you used **Pub. 972,** enter the amount from line 8 of the Child Tax Credit Worksheet in the publication. — **1** — **2,000**

2 Enter the amount from Form 1040, line 52; Form 1040A, line 35; or Form 1040NR, line 49 . . . — **2** — **851**

3 Subtract line 2 from line 1. If zero, **stop;** you cannot take this credit . . . — **3** — **1,149**

4a Earned income (see separate instructions) . . . — **4a** — **41,200**

b Nontaxable combat pay (see separate instructions) . . . — **4b** —

5 Is the amount on line 4a more than $3,000?
☐ **No.** Leave line 5 blank and enter -0- on line 6.
☑ **Yes.** Subtract $3,000 from the amount on line 4a. Enter the result . . . — **5** — **38,200**

6 Multiply the amount on line 5 by 15% (.15) and enter the result . . . — **6** — **5,730**

Next. Do you have three or more qualifying children?
☑ **No.** If line 6 is zero, stop; you cannot take this credit. Otherwise, skip Part III and enter the **smaller** of line 3 or line 6 on line 13.
☐ **Yes.** If line 6 is equal to or more than line 3, skip Part III and enter the amount from line 3 on line 13. Otherwise, go to line 7.

For Paperwork Reduction Act Notice, see your tax return instructions. Cat. No. 59761M **Schedule 8812 (Form 1040A or 1040) 2015**

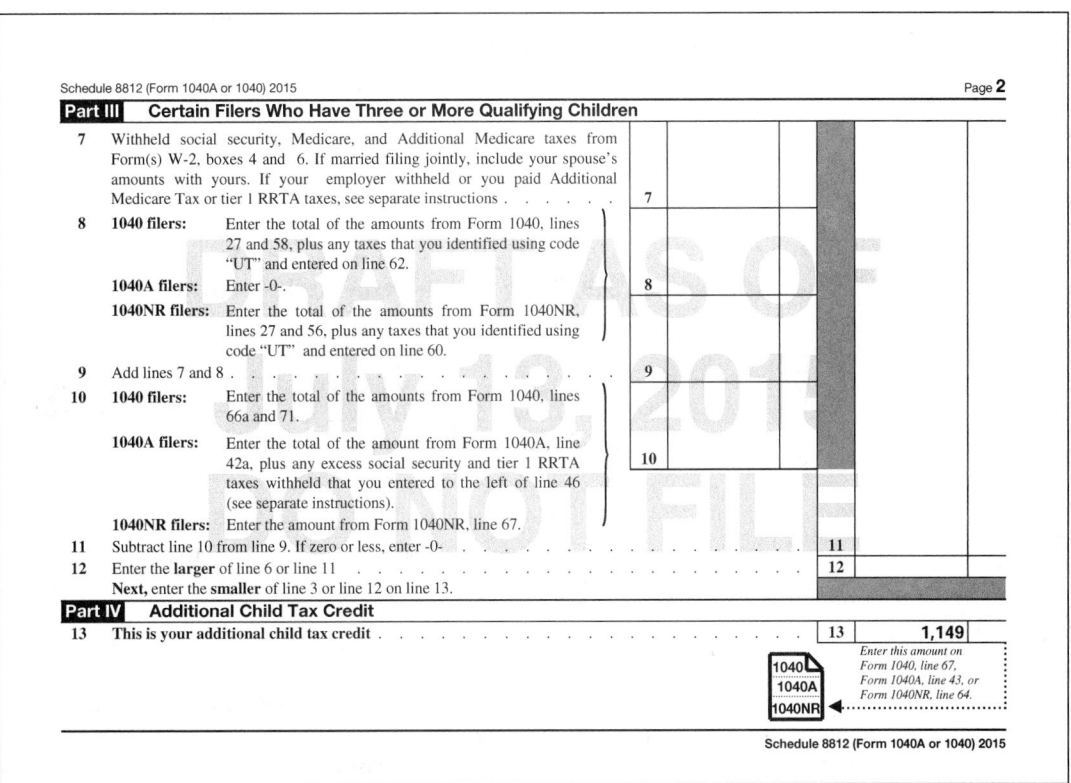

Figure 2-5: Filled-In Schedule 8812 (Page 2)

Schedule 8812 (Form 1040A or 1040) 2015 Page **2**

Part III Certain Filers Who Have Three or More Qualifying Children

7	Withheld social security, Medicare, and Additional Medicare taxes from Form(s) W-2, boxes 4 and 6. If married filing jointly, include your spouse's amounts with yours. If your employer withheld or you paid Additional Medicare Tax or tier 1 RRTA taxes, see separate instructions	7	
8	**1040 filers:** Enter the total of the amounts from Form 1040, lines 27 and 58, plus any taxes that you identified using code "UT" and entered on line 62. **1040A filers:** Enter -0-. **1040NR filers:** Enter the total of the amounts from Form 1040NR, lines 27 and 56, plus any taxes that you identified using code "UT" and entered on line 60.	8	
9	Add lines 7 and 8	9	
10	**1040 filers:** Enter the total of the amounts from Form 1040, lines 66a and 71. **1040A filers:** Enter the total of the amount from Form 1040A, line 42a, plus any excess social security and tier 1 RRTA taxes withheld that you entered to the left of line 46 (see separate instructions). **1040NR filers:** Enter the amount from Form 1040NR, line 67.	10	
11	Subtract line 10 from line 9. If zero or less, enter -0-	11	
12	Enter the **larger** of line 6 or line 11 **Next,** enter the **smaller** of line 3 or line 12 on line 13.	12	

Part IV Additional Child Tax Credit

13	**This is your additional child tax credit**	13	1,149

1040 / 1040A / 1040NR — *Enter this amount on Form 1040, line 67, Form 1040A, line 43, or Form 1040NR, line 64.*

Schedule 8812 (Form 1040A or 1040) 2015

¶204.09 RESIDENTIAL ENERGY CREDIT

The **residential energy efficient property credit** allows taxpayers a tax credit for installing alternative energy equipment in any home located in the U.S. that they own. Thus, the credit can be used for installations made to the taxpayer's main home and any vacation home the taxpayer owns. Qualified property includes solar hot water heaters, solar electric equipment and wind turbines. The amount of the credit equals 30% of the cost of the alternative energy equipment. No dollar limit applies to this credit. Furthermore, a unique feature of this nonrefundable credit is that should the amount of the credit exceed the taxpayer's remaining tax liability, the excess can be carried over to the next tax year. Computing the remaining tax liability involves subtracting all other nonrefundable credits from the taxpayer's total tax liability.

> Taxpayers claim the residential energy efficient property credit on Form 5695, Residential Energy Credits. This credit is available through 2016.

¶204.10 ADOPTION CREDIT

Taxpayers can take a nonrefundable tax credit for qualified adoption expenses. For adoptions of U.S. citizens or residents, the credit is taken in the year the expenses are paid only if the adoption is finalized in that year or was finalized in a prior year. Otherwise the credit is taken in the year after the year in which the expenses are paid. This is often called the one-year delay rule. When the adoption expenses are spread over more than one year, the limits in effect in the year the adoption is finalized are used in computing the credit. For adoptions of U.S. citizens or residents, the adoption credit can be taken even if the adoption is never finalized. For adoptions of a foreign child, the adoption credit can only be taken if the adoption is finalized.

For 2015, the amount of the adoption credit is limited to the first $13,400 of qualified adoption expenses. The amount of the credit is cumulative. Thus, if expenses are paid over 2014 and 2015 for an adoption finalized in 2015, the $13,400 limit would apply. The amount of the 2015 adoption credit is further limited for taxpayers with modified AGI in excess of $201,010. Those with excess modified AGI (AGI plus any foreign earned income exclusion, discussed at ¶401.02) reduce their credit by:

(the *lesser of* $13,400 or qualified expenses) × (excess modified AGI ÷ $40,000)

EXAMPLE 20

In 2014, the Holdens paid $14,000 in qualified adoption expenses. The adoption was finalized in 2015. The Holdens' modified AGI in 2014 was $169,450. It was $219,124 in 2015. Since the adoption was not finalized in 2014, the Holdens claim a $7,332 adoption credit in 2015 (under the one-year delay rule).

Lesser of (i) $13,400 or (ii) $14,000 of qualified adoption expenses	$13,400
Less phase-out of credit [$13,400 × (($219,124 – $201,010) ÷ $40,000)]	(6,068)
Adoption credit	$ 7,332

Qualified adoption expenses include the expenses directly related to the legal adoption of a child who is either under the age of 18 at the time of the adoption, or physically or mentally incapable of self-care. Such costs include reasonable and necessary adoption fees, court costs, and attorney's fees. Both the qualified adoption expenses and the $13,400 limit must be reduced by nontaxable reimbursements that the taxpayer receives from an employer's adoption assistance plan (another nontaxable fringe benefit discussed in Chapter 4, see ¶401.03).

EXAMPLE 21

Same facts as in Example 20, except that the Holdens receive a $2,000 nontaxable reimbursement from an employer adoption assistance plan. The Holdens' credit would be $6,238.

Initial credit, lesser of ($13,400 – $2,000) or ($14,000 – $2,000)	$11,400
Less phase-out of credit [$11,400 × (($219,124 – $201,010) ÷ $40,000)]	(5,162)
Adoption credit	$ 6,238

The full $13,400 initial credit is allowed for the adoption of a special needs child regardless of the amount actually paid for qualified adoption expenses. This amount is reduced by nontaxable amounts received from an employer adoption assistance plan or when the taxpayer's modified AGI exceeds the stated threshold ($201,010 in 2015).

Claiming the Credit

Taxpayers claiming the adoption credit complete Form 8839, Qualified Adoption Expenses. They then include their adoption credit on Form 1040, along with their other nonrefundable credits. They also must attach proof documenting their expenses paid. Taxpayers unable to benefit from the full amount of their adoption credit (due to the fact it is a nonrefundable credit) can carry over the unused credit for five years.

¶204.11 EARNED INCOME CREDIT

The earned income credit (EIC) is a refundable tax credit that provides tax relief to lower-paid workers. Taxpayers reporting a small amount of earned income may actually receive money back from the government by claiming the EIC. This happens when the amount of their EIC exceeds their tax liability.

Congress designed the EIC to encourage people to become part of the workforce. Within limits, as a person's earned income (wages) goes up, the amount of the EIC increases. The purpose of the EIC is to encourage people to seek employment (see discussion of income tax objectives in ¶101).

Taxpayers Qualifying for the Credit

The EIC is not available to married persons using married filing separately filing status, or to anyone claimed as a dependent. Also, taxpayers with disqualified income in excess of $3,400 in 2015 cannot take the EIC. Disqualified income includes dividends, taxable and tax-exempt interest, net rental income, and capital gains. Taxpayers who qualify for the EIC must either:

1. Be between the ages of 25 and 64 as of the end of the tax year and have lived in the U.S. over half of the year, or
2. Have a "qualifying child."

A qualifying child must be younger than the taxpayer. Taxpayers claiming the EIC for a qualifying child must provide the child's name, age and social security number (SSN). If any of these are not provided, the EIC will be denied with respect to that child. In Chapter 1, a qualifying child was defined as a person that passes six tests: relationship, age, residency, support, joint return, and citizenship (see ¶108). For purposes of the EIC, a "qualifying child" must meet only the first three of these tests (relationship, age, and residency).

To be a qualifying child for purposes of the EIC, an unmarried person does not have to be the taxpayer's dependent, but a married person does. However, the custodial parent may claim a married child as a qualifying child (and claim the EIC for that child) when the dependency exemption for a married child has been given to the noncustodial parent.

If the parents are divorced or separated and the child is a qualifying child for both parents, the child is treated as a qualifying child of the custodial parent. If there is no custodial parent, then the parent with the highest AGI gets to claim the EIC for the child. In other situations where the child may be a qualifying child for more than one taxpayer, the credit goes to the child's parent. If neither person is the child's parent, then the taxpayer with the highest AGI gets to claim the EIC for the child. These tie-break rules are the same as those used in determining which person can claim the dependency exemption for a qualifying child (¶108.08).

EXAMPLE 22 Jake and his 5-year-old son live with Jake's father, Frank, for the whole year. Jake's AGI is $15,000, and Frank's AGI is $20,000. The son is a qualifying child to both Jake and Frank. Since Jake is the parent, he claims the EIC.

Credit Rates and Dollar Amounts

Generally, as taxable earned income increases, the EIC increases. However, the credit is phased out when income exceeds a certain level. This phase-down is based on the higher of earned income or AGI. Taxpayers use the Earned Income Credit Worksheet (shown in ¶204.12) to compute the proper EIC using the Earned Income Credit tables (found in Appendix E at the back of this textbook). Taxpayers keep this worksheet for their records. However, those with qualifying children must also complete and attach Schedule EIC, Earned Income Credit, to their tax returns.

For purposes of the EIC, earned income includes all types of taxable compensation, as well as net earnings from self-employment. It does not include nontaxable employee compensation such as salary deferrals under retirement plans, salary reductions under cafeteria plans, or any dependent care, adoption or educational assistance benefits. Earned income also does not include retirement income, social security or unemployment benefits, or alimony.

¶204.12 FILLED-IN EIC WORKSHEET

INFORMATION FOR FIGURE 2-6:

James Williams earned $19,665 in wages in 2015. His employer withheld no income taxes from his pay. Sarah Williams earned $12,100 in wages. Her employer withheld no income taxes. The Williamses also earned $150 of interest on their joint savings account.

The Williamses file a joint tax return. They claim their two qualifying children as dependents. Figure 2-7 shows the Williamses' filled-in Schedule EIC. They claim a $3,801 EIC on their tax return and attach Schedule EIC to their return.

Figure 2-6: Filled-In EIC Worksheet

1. Enter your earned income. ($19,665 + $12,100)	1.	31,765
2. Look up the EIC on the amount on line 1 above in the EIC Table. Enter the credit here.	2.	3,833
3. Enter your AGI. ($31,765 + $150)	3.	31,915
4. Are the amounts on lines 1 and 3 the same?		
Yes. Skip line 5; enter the amount from line 2 on line 6		
No. Go to line 5.		
5. If you have:		
a. No qualifying children, is the amount on line 3 less than $8,250 ($13,750 if married filed jointly)?		
b. One or more qualifying children, is the amount on line 3 less than $18,150 ($23,650 if married filed jointly)?		
Yes. Leave line 5 blank; enter the amount from line 2 on line 6		
No. Look up the EIC on the amount on line 3 above in the EIC Table. Enter the credit here.	5.	3,801
6. Your earned income credit (the smaller of line 2 or line 5).	6.	3,801

As the EIC worksheet shows, the earned income credit is the smaller of two amounts from the EIC Table. The first amount is found using the taxpayer's earned income; the second amount using the taxpayer's AGI. For 2015, taxpayers will have at least $1 of earned income credit as long as they have earned income and their earned income or AGI (whichever is greater) does not exceed the following amounts.

	Married Filing Jointly	All Other Taxpayers
No children	$20,330	$14,820
One qualifying child	44,651	39,131
Two qualifying children	49,974	44,454
Three or more qualifying children	53,267	47,747

Figure 2-7: Filled-In Schedule EIC

SCHEDULE EIC
(Form 1040A or 1040)

Department of the Treasury
Internal Revenue Service (99)

Earned Income Credit
Qualifying Child Information

▶ **Complete and attach to Form 1040A or 1040 only if you have a qualifying child.**
▶ **Information about Schedule EIC (Form 1040A or 1040) and its instructions is at *www.irs.gov/scheduleeic.***

1040A 1040 EIC

OMB No. 1545-0074
2015
Attachment Sequence No. **43**

Name(s) shown on return	Your social security number
James R. and Sarah O. Williams	**282-56-9320**

Before you begin:
- See the instructions for Form 1040A, lines 42a and 42b, or Form 1040, lines 66a and 66b, to make sure that **(a)** you can take the EIC, and **(b)** you have a qualifying child.
- Be sure the child's name on line 1 and social security number (SSN) on line 2 agree with the child's social security card. Otherwise, at the time we process your return, we may reduce or disallow your EIC. If the name or SSN on the child's social security card is not correct, call the Social Security Administration at 1-800-772-1213.

CAUTION
- *If you take the EIC even though you are not eligible, you may not be allowed to take the credit for up to 10 years. See the instructions for details.*
- *It will take us longer to process your return and issue your refund if you do not fill in all lines that apply for each qualifying child.*

Qualifying Child Information	Child 1	Child 2	Child 3
1 Child's name If you have more than three qualifying children, you have to list only three to get the maximum credit.	First name: **Martha** Last name: **Williams**	First name: **Kyle** Last name: **Williams**	First name Last name
2 Child's SSN The child must have an SSN as defined in the instructions for Form 1040A, lines 42a and 42b, or Form 1040, lines 66a and 66b, unless the child was born and died in 2015. If your child was born and died in 2015 and did not have an SSN, enter "Died" on this line and attach a copy of the child's birth certificate, death certificate, or hospital medical records.	**826-34-3710**	**850-21-5263**	
3 Child's year of birth	Year **2 0 0 8** *If born after 1996* ***and*** *the child is younger than you (or your spouse, if filing jointly), skip lines 4a and 4b; go to line 5.*	Year **2 0 1 2** *If born after 1996* ***and*** *the child is younger than you (or your spouse, if filing jointly), skip lines 4a and 4b; go to line 5.*	Year ____ *If born after 1996* ***and*** *the child is younger than you (or your spouse, if filing jointly), skip lines 4a and 4b; go to line 5.*
4 a Was the child under age 24 at the end of 2015, a student, and younger than you (or your spouse, if filing jointly)?	☐ **Yes.** *Go to line 5.* ☐ **No.** *Go to line 4b.*	☐ **Yes.** *Go to line 5.* ☐ **No.** *Go to line 4b.*	☐ **Yes.** *Go to line 5.* ☐ **No.** *Go to line 4b.*
b Was the child permanently and totally disabled during any part of 2015?	☐ **Yes.** *Go to line 5.* ☐ **No.** The child is not a qualifying child.	☐ **Yes.** *Go to line 5.* ☐ **No.** The child is not a qualifying child.	☐ **Yes.** *Go to line 5.* ☐ **No.** The child is not a qualifying child.
5 Child's relationship to you (for example, son, daughter, grandchild, niece, nephew, foster child, etc.)	**daughter**	**son**	
6 Number of months child lived with you in the United States during 2015 • If the child lived with you for more than half of 2015 but less than 7 months, enter "7." • If the child was born or died in 2015 and your home was the child's home for more than half the time he or she was alive during 2015, enter "12."	**12** months *Do not enter more than 12 months.*	**12** months *Do not enter more than 12 months.*	____ months *Do not enter more than 12 months.*

For Paperwork Reduction Act Notice, see your tax return instructions. Cat. No. 13339M **Schedule EIC (Form 1040A or 1040) 2015**

¶204.13 PREMIUM TAX CREDIT (PTC)

The Patient Protection and Affordable Care Act (ACA) mandates that individuals carry minimum essential health insurance coverage or qualify for an exemption from carrying such coverage. As a result of the ACA mandate, individual taxpayers need to be aware of the tax implications when filing their tax returns. Taxpayers who fail to comply with the mandate must make a shared responsibility payment that they report on their tax returns. This payment acts as a penalty in that it increases the amount of taxes they will owe, or reduces their tax refund. The penalty for failing to comply with the mandate is discussed at ¶205.

Taxpayers who comply with the ACA mandate get their insurance at work, or they buy it from an insurance company or from a government exchange (Marketplace). Taxpayers who buy their insurance through the government's health insurance "Marketplace" may be eligible for federal government assistance to subsidize (help pay for) a portion of their premiums. For some taxpayers, this subsidy may be in the form of reduced monthly payments. For others, this assistance comes in the form of a refundable tax credit, called the premium tax credit (PTC).

The amount of the premium reduction (advance subsidy) is based on household income and family size reported by the taxpayer at the time of enrollment. Since the taxpayer's actual household income for the year will likely differ from the self-reported amount provided at the time of enrollment, taxpayers who receive assistance during the year need to reconcile their advanced subsidies (total premium reduction) with the amounts to which they were entitled based on actual household income. Taxpayers whose actual subsidies they received during the year were greater than their entitled assistance must repay the excess by reporting additional tax on their tax returns. Taxpayers who did not receive the assistance they were entitled to during the year claim a refundable PTC for the difference.

Taxpayers Who Qualify for the PTC

Only taxpayers whose household income is at least 100%, but no more than 400%, of the federal poverty line can claim the PTC. Taxpayers who qualify for Medicare or Medicaid, or who are eligible to get insurance under an employer-sponsored plan, self-funded student health plan, or through high-risk pools offered by the state government, cannot claim the PTC. Married taxpayers must file a joint tax return in order to claim the PTC, and taxpayers claimed as a dependent on another person's return are not eligible for this credit.

Computing the PTC

Using the taxpayer's total household income and family size, the government determines the maximum amount each taxpayer should have to pay for health insurance. The term the IRS uses to describe this amount is "annual contribution for health care." The government also determines what the taxpayer's annual premiums would be for its silver plan (the second lowest cost plan offered by the Marketplace). The taxpayer's PTC is the *lesser of* (i) the taxpayer's actual premiums (prior to any subsidy), or (ii) the difference between the cost of the silver plan and the taxpayer's annual contribution for health care.

> Form 1095-A, Health Insurance Marketplace Statement, is an information return sent out to Marketplace participants after the end of each year. This form informs participants of the cost of the premiums (prior to any subsidies) for the policy in which they enrolled, as well as what their cost would have been had they chosen the silver plan.

EXAMPLE 23

Duke purchases his health insurance through the federal Marketplace. Duke selects a bronze plan, which is the least costly of the four types of plans offered by the Marketplace. Total annual premiums for his plan are $3,000. Had Duke selected the silver plan, his premiums would have been $5,600. Based on Duke's household income and family size, the government has determined that Duke's annual contribution for health care is $1,700. Duke's PTC is $3,000, which is the *lesser of* (i) $3,000 total premiums for the plan Duke enrolled in, or (ii) $3,900 ($5,600 premiums under the silver plan – $1,700 annual contribution for health care).

EXAMPLE 24

Same facts as in Example 23, except that Duke selects a platinum (most expensive) plan, and his premiums are $8,000. Duke's PTC is $3,900, which is the *lesser of* (i) $8,000, or (ii) $3,900 ($5,600 – $1,700).

From looking at how the PTC is calculated, the government has concluded that every individual is entitled to receive the benefits offered by the Marketplace's silver plan. For taxpayers whom the government does not believe have enough household income to pay for these benefits (based on the ratio of household income to the federal poverty line), it is willing to provide assistance up to the difference between the silver plan premiums and the taxpayer's annual contribution limit (as shown in Example 24). Taxpayers who decide to go with a less expensive (bronze) plan will find their PTC limited to the cost of premiums under that plan (as shown in Example 23).

The taxpayer's annual contribution for health care represents what the government has determined should be the maximum amount that the taxpayer should have to pay for health insurance premiums. It is based on total household income and the number of exemptions the taxpayer claims. Household income is the sum of the modified AGI for all exemptions (personal and dependency) claimed on the taxpayer's return. For purposes of the PTC, "modified AGI" is AGI plus any tax-exempt interest income (¶401.06), nontaxable social security benefits (¶307), and foreign earned income exclusion (¶401.02).

EXAMPLE 25

Jim and Cathy Thompson live in Missouri. They file a joint tax return and claim their three children as dependents. The Thompsons are not eligible for health insurance through their work, so they purchase their insurance through the Marketplace. On their joint tax return, the Thompsons report $500 of tax-exempt interest income and $52,000 of AGI. The Thompsons' son earned $2,000 working part-time during the year. The Thompsons' household income equals $54,500. This amount is the sum of the couples' $52,500 of modified AGI ($52,000 + $500) and their dependent child's $2,000 of modified AGI.

Once the taxpayer's household income has been computed, the taxpayer uses an IRS-provided table to find the federal poverty line that corresponds to the total number of (personal and dependency) exemptions the taxpayer claimed. The 2015 poverty line thresholds for most taxpayers are provided in Figure 2-8. There are different amounts for taxpayers living in Alaska and Hawaii. This information can be found in the Instructions to Form 8962.

Figure 2-8: Federal Poverty Line Thresholds for 2015

Total Exemptions Claimed	Threshold
1	$11,770
2	15,930
3	20,090
4	24,250
5	28,410
6	32,570
7	36,730
8	40,890

EXAMPLE 26 Continuing with Example 25, the Thompsons use Table 1 to look up the federal poverty amount for taxpayers claiming five total exemptions. This amount is $28,410.

The next step in the process of determining the taxpayer's annual contribution for health care is to divide household income by the federal poverty line threshold. Only taxpayers whose household income falls between 100% and 400% of the threshold qualify for the PTC.

EXAMPLE 27 Continuing with Example 26, the Thompsons divide their $54,500 of household income by $28,410. The 1.92 result means that the Thompsons' household income is 192% above the federal poverty line. Because this percentage falls between 100% and 400%, the Thompsons qualify for the PTC.

Once it has been determine that the taxpayer qualifies for the PTC, the taxpayer's annual contribution for health care can be computed. This is done by multiplying the taxpayer's household income by the taxpayer's "applicable figure" from an IRS-provided table (reproduced in Appendix C at the back of the textbook). The applicable figure is the number from the table that corresponds to the percentage previous calculated (household income divided by the federal poverty line).

EXAMPLE 28 Continuing with Example 27, the Thompsons go to the table in Appendix C and find that the applicable figure for 192 is .0593. They multiply this number by their $54,500 of household income to arrive at their annual contribution for health care ($54,500 × .0593 = $3,232). This amount represents the maximum amount the government has determined the Thompsons should have to pay for health insurance premiums.

After the annual contribution for health care has been computed, taxpayers can use the information reported to them on Form 1095-A to compute their PTC. This amount is the *lesser of* (i) the taxpayer's actual premiums (prior to any subsidy), or (ii) the difference between the cost of the silver plan and the taxpayer's annual contribution for health care.

EXAMPLE 29 Continuing with Example 28, the Thompsons' Form 1095-A shows that their annual premiums for the policy they enrolled in was $7,000, and that their premiums would have been $6,600 had they enrolled in the silver plan. The Thompsons' PTC equals $3,368. This is the *lesser of* (i) the $7,000 cost of premiums for the plan they enrolled in, or (ii) $3,368 (the $6,600 cost for premiums under the silver plan minus their $3,232 annual contribution for health care).

For taxpayers who did not receive any premium reductions during the year, the PTC is reported as a refundable tax credit on Form 1040A (line 45) or Form 1040 (line 69). Form 1040EZ cannot be used to report the PTC. Taxpayers receiving premium reductions (advance payment of PTC) need to reconcile the difference between their advance payment and their PTC.

Reconciling Advance Payment of PTC and Actual PTC

In addition to providing taxpayers with the cost of their insurance premiums under both the plan they enrolled in and the silver plan, Form 1095-A also provides taxpayers with the amount of premium reductions they received during the year. This amount represents their advance payment of PTC. Taxpayers compare their PTC to their advance payment of PTC. If the taxpayer's PTC exceeds their advance payment, the difference ("net PTC") is reported as a refundable tax credit on Form 1040A or Form 1040.

EXAMPLE 30 June and Jim Rosen compute their PTC to be $4,500. The Rosens' Form 1095-A shows that they received advance payments totaling $3,850 during the year. The Rosens reduce their PTC by their advance payments and report the $650 net PTC ($4,500 – $3,850) as a refundable tax credit on Form 1040A or Form 1040.

Excess Advance PTC Repayment

When the taxpayer's advance payment of PTC exceeds their PTC, at least some of the excess must be paid back to the government. This is done by having the taxpayer report an additional tax on Form 1040A (line 29) or Form 1040 (line 46). The amount that must be repaid is the *lesser of* (i) the excess of the advance payment over the PTC, or (ii) the amount from the table below that corresponds to the taxpayer's filing status. Thus, the amounts in the table serve as a maximum repayment for taxpayers receiving advanced payments.

Taxpayer's Household Income as a Percentage of Federal Poverty Line:	Taxpayer's Filing Status	
	Single	**All Others**
Less than 200%	$ 300	$ 600
At least 200% but less than 300%	750	1,500
At least 300% but less than 400%	1,250	2,500

EXAMPLE 31 Continuing with Example 29, assume that the Thompsons' Form 1095-A shows that they received $4,000 of advanced payment of PTC. This amount exceeds the Thompsons' PTC by $632 ($4,000 – $3,368). From the above table, the amount that corresponds to MFJ taxpayers whose household income as a percentage of the federal poverty line is 192% is $600. Since the $632 of excess exceeds this amount, the Thompsons report the $600 as an additional tax on their Form 1040A or Form 1040.

Form 8962

Form 8962, Premium Tax Credit (PTC), is a two-page tax form that calculates the taxpayer's PTC. For taxpayers who received advanced payment of PTC (through reduced premiums), the taxpayer's net PTC (not enough subsidies) or excess advance PTC repayment (too much subsidy) is also calculated on this form. These calculations are performed in Parts I-III of Form 8962 (page 1). Parts IV and V involve complex situations that are beyond the scope of this discussion.

In Part I, taxpayers compute their annual contribution for health care. In Part II, taxpayers report the information provided to them on Form 1095-A and calculate their PTC. Net PTC is also calculated in Part II. Taxpayers receiving advanced payment of PTC during the year in excess of their PTC compute their required repayment in Part III.

¶204.14 FILLED-IN FORM 8962

INFORMATION FOR FIGURE 2-9:

The Thompsons (from Examples 25-29, and Example 31) compute their net PTC or repayment amount by entering on the form the information provided below in bold font. The Thompsons then follow the instructions on Form 8962 to compute their $600 excess advance premium tax credit repayment. They report this amount as an additional tax on Form 1040 (line 46).

Line #

1: Family size, **5** (2 personal + 3 dependency exemptions)
2a: Modified AGI reported on the Thompsons' tax return, **$52,500** ($52,000 + $500, provided in Example 25)
2b: Modified AGI of the Thompsons' dependents, **$2,000** (provided in Example 25)
4: Federal poverty line, **$28,410** (source: Figure 2-8, see Example 26)
6: The Thompsons check **No**. because the 192% reported on line 5 does not exceed 400%.
7: Applicable Figure, **.0593** (source: Appendix C, see Example 28)
11(a): Premium Amount, **$7,000** (source: Form 1095-A, line 33A. This is the total cost of the premiums (before subsidies) of the insurance plan the Thompsons enrolled in).
11(b): Annual Premium Amount of SLCSP, **$6,600** (source: Form 1095-A, line 33B. This is the total cost of the premiums for the second lowest cost silver plan).
11(f): Annual Advance Payment of PTC, **$4,000** (source: Form 1095-A, line 33C. This is the amount of the Thompsons' health care premiums that the government paid on their behalf.)

¶205 Shared Responsibility Payment

Taxpayers who fail to comply with the ACA mandate during any portion of the year must include a shared responsibility payment on their income tax returns. The mandate to carry minimum essential health care coverage extends not only to the taxpayer, but to the taxpayer's spouse (when filing a joint return) as well as to all dependents listed on the taxpayer's return. In essence, this payment acts as a penalty, as it increases the taxpayer's taxes owed for the year, or reduces the amount of their tax refunds. The ACA penalty is reported on Form 1040EZ (line 11), Form 1040A (line 38), or Form 1040 (line 61) on the line designated, "Health care: individual responsibility."

For 2015, the amount of the ACA penalty is the *greater of* (i) $325 for each uninsured adult plus $162.50 for each uninsured child under the age of 18 that is reported on the taxpayer's tax return (up to a maximum of $975), or (ii) 2% of household income over the taxpayer's filing threshold (see Figure 1-5, ¶113.02). For this calculation, household income is defined as AGI plus the taxpayer's tax-exempt interest and any foreign earned income exclusion.

EXAMPLE 32

Dena (ages 22) files as a single taxpayer. Dena fails to comply with the ACA mandate for 2015. Her household income is $25,000, and her filing threshold is $10,300. Dena's penalty for failing to comply with the ACA mandate is $325. This is the *greater of* (i) $325 for one uninsured adult, or (ii) $294 (2% × ($25,000 – $10,300)). Dena reports this amount on Form 1040EZ.

Figure 2-9: Filled-In Form 8962

Form **8962** | **Premium Tax Credit (PTC)** | OMB No. 1545-0074

Department of the Treasury
Internal Revenue Service

▶ Attach to Form 1040, 1040A, or 1040NR.
▶ Information about Form 8962 and its separate instructions is at *www.irs.gov/form8962*.

2015
Attachment Sequence No. **73**

Name shown on your return	Your social security number
James and Cathy Thompson	**859-76-4466**

You cannot claim the PTC if your filing status is married filing separately unless you are eligible for an exception (see instructions). If you qualify, check the box. ☐

Part I Annual and Monthly Contribution Amount

1	Tax family size. Enter the number of exemptions from Form 1040 or Form 1040A, line 6d, or Form 1040NR, line 7d	1	5
2a	Modified AGI. Enter your modified AGI (see instructions) . . . . . 2a 52,500 — **b** Enter the total of your dependents' modified AGI (see instructions) . . .	2b	2,000
3	Household income. Add the amounts on lines 2a and 2b . . .	3	54,500
4	Federal poverty line. Enter the federal poverty line amount from Table 1-1, 1-2, or 1-3 (see instructions). Check the appropriate box for the federal poverty table used. **a** ☐ Alaska **b** ☐ Hawaii **c** ☑ Other 48 states and DC	4	28,410
5	Household income as a percentage of federal poverty line (see instructions) . . .	5	192 %
6	Did you enter 401% on line 5? (See instructions if you entered less than 100%.) ☑ **No.** Continue to line 7. ☐ **Yes.** You are not eligible to receive PTC. If advance payment of the PTC was made, see the instructions for how to report your excess advance PTC repayment amount.		
7	Applicable Figure. Using your line 5 percentage, locate your "applicable figure" on the table in the instructions . .	7	.0593
8a	Annual contribution amount. Multiply line 3 by line 7 . . . . 8a 3,232 — **b** Monthly contribution amount. Divide line 8a by 12. Round to whole dollar amount . .	8b	269

Part II Premium Tax Credit Claim and Reconciliation of Advance Payment of Premium Tax Credit

9 Are you allocating policy amounts with another taxpayer or do you want to use the alternative calculation for year of marriage (see instructions)?
☐ **Yes.** Skip to Part IV, Shared Policy Allocation, or Part V, Alternative Calculation for Year of Marriage. ☑ **No.** Continue to line 10.

10 See the instructions to determine if you can use line 11 or must complete lines 12 through 23.
☑ **Yes.** Continue to line 11. Compute your annual PTC. Then skip lines 12–23 and continue to line 24. ☐ **No.** Continue to lines 12–23. Compute your monthly PTC and continue to line 24.

Annual Calculation	(a) Annual enrollment premiums (Form(s) 1095-A, line 33a)	(b) Annual applicable SLCSP premium (Form(s) 1095-A, line 33b)	(c) Annual contribution amount (line 8a)	(d) Annual maximum premium assistance (subtract (c) from (b), if zero or less, enter -0-)	(e) Annual premium tax credit allowed (smaller of (a) or (d))	(f) Annual advance payment of PTC (Form (s) 1095-A, line 33c)
11 Annual Totals	7,000	6,600	3,232	3,368	3,368	4,000

Monthly Calculation	(a) Monthly enrollment premiums (Form(s) 1095-A, lines 21–32, column a)	(b) Monthly applicable SLCSP premium (Form (s) 1095-A, lines 21–32, column b)	(c) Monthly contribution amount (amount from line 8b or alternative marriage monthly contribution)	(d) Monthly maximum premium assistance (subtract (c) from (b), if zero or less, enter -0-)	(e) Monthly premium tax credit allowed (smaller of (a) or (d))	(f) Monthly advance payment of PTC (Form(s) 1095-A, lines 21–32, column c)
12 January						
13 February						
14 March						
15 April						
16 May						
17 June						
18 July						
19 August						
20 September						
21 October						
22 November						
23 December						

24	Total premium tax credit. Enter the amount from line 11(e) or add lines 12(e) through 23(e) and enter the total here	24	3,368
25	Advance payment of PTC. Enter the amount from line 11(f) or add lines 12(f) through 23(f) and enter the total here	25	4,000
26	Net premium tax credit. If line 24 is greater than line 25, subtract line 25 from line 24. Enter the difference here and on Form 1040, line 69; Form 1040A, line 45; or Form 1040NR, line 65. If you elected the alternative calculation for marriage, enter zero. If line 24 equals line 25, enter zero. Stop here. If line 25 is greater than line 24, leave this line blank and continue to line 27 .	26	

Part III Repayment of Excess Advance Payment of the Premium Tax Credit

27	Excess advance payment of PTC. If line 25 is greater than line 24, subtract line 24 from line 25. Enter the difference here	27	632
28	Repayment limitation (see instructions)	28	600
29	Excess advance premium tax credit repayment. Enter the smaller of line 27 or line 28 here and on Form 1040, line 46; Form 1040A, line 29; or Form 1040NR, line 44	29	600

For Paperwork Reduction Act Notice, see your tax return instructions. Cat. No. 37784Z Form **8962** (2015)

EXAMPLE 33

Paul and Jean Hunt (ages 44 and 42, respectively) file a joint return and claim their three young children as dependents. The Hunts fail to comply with the ACA mandate for 2015. Their household income is $75,000; their filing threshold is $20,600. The Hunts' penalty for failing to comply with the mandate is $1,088. This is the *greater of* (i) $975 maximum amount (since $325 × 2 uninsured adults + $162.50 × 3 uninsured children exceeds the $975 maximum amount), or (ii) $1,088 (2% × ($75,000 – $20,600)).

EXAMPLE 34

Ben (age 34) files as head of household and claims his son and mother as dependents. Ben fails to comply with the ACA mandate for 2015. His household income is $35,000; his filing threshold is $13,250. Ben's penalty for failing to carry minimum essential coverage is $812.50, which is the *greater of* (i) $812.50 ($650 for two adults + $162.50 for one uninsured child), or (ii) $435 (2% × ($35,000 – $13,250)). Ben enters this amount on his Form 1040A or Form 1040.

Certain taxpayers are exempt from the penalty. Among the exempt group are taxpayers whose costs of getting minimum essential coverage exceed 8% of their household income. The group also includes taxpayers whose household income or gross income falls below their thresholds for filing a tax return (see ¶113, ¶113.02). Taxpayers whose lapse in minimum essential coverage during the year does not exceed three months are also exempt from the penalty. A complete list of exemptions can be found in the Instructions to Form 8965, Health Coverage Exemptions. Noncompliant taxpayers exempt from coverage complete Form 8965 and attach it to their tax returns to support their exemption from the penalty.

Taxpayers who are compliant only part of the year compute their prorated penalty on the Shared Responsibility Payment Worksheet and enter the prorated amount on their tax returns. This worksheet can be found in the Instructions to Form 8965.

¶206 Form 1040EZ

Form 1040EZ, Income Tax Return for Single and Joint Filers with No Dependents, is a one-page form that is fairly simple to complete. Taxpayers using this form may report only certain types of income: wages, salaries, tips, taxable scholarships/fellowships (treated as additional wages), unemployment compensation, taxable interest totaling $1,500 or less, and Alaska Permanent Fund dividends. They have only two possible deductions: the standard deduction and the exemption deduction. Taxpayers who are dependents, however, receive no exemption deduction, and their standard deduction may be limited (see Standard Deduction for Dependents at ¶106.03).

Taxpayers claiming dependents cannot file Form 1040EZ. Taxpayers who do not have a "qualifying child" may use Form 1040EZ to claim the EIC. This credit plus federal income tax withheld from Forms W-2 and 1099 are the only items that can reduce the taxpayer's tax liability on Form 1040EZ.

Form 1040EZ Tests—Users Must:

- Use single or married filing jointly filing status
- Claim the standard deduction
- Be under age 65 and not claim the additional standard deduction for blindness
- Not claim any dependents
- Have gross income only from wages, salaries, tips, taxable scholarship or fellowship grants, interest, unemployment compensation, and Alaska Permanent Fund dividends
- Have taxable interest income of $1,500 or less
- Have taxable income of less than $100,000
- Not have received any advance payments of the premium tax credit

On all tax returns, taxpayers must clearly identify themselves. They must place their name, address, and social security number at the top of the form. Also at the top of the tax form, taxpayers can instruct the IRS whether or not they want $3 of their tax payments to go to the Presidential election campaign fund. If so, they simply place an **X** in the proper box located under the taxpayer's social security number. This election does not affect the amount of taxes owed or refunded.

¶206.01 REPORTING TAXABLE INCOME

Taxpayers filing Form 1040EZ use lines 1 through 4 to report their income. They then subtract out their standard deduction and any exemption deduction that may apply (line 5). The remainder is taxable income (line 6).

All taxpayers receive a standard deduction. However, persons who are dependents may not claim an exemption deduction for themselves. **Nondependents** deduct $10,300 ($6,300 + $4,000) if single and $20,600 ($12,600 + $4,000 + $4,000) if married filing jointly. **Dependents** use a worksheet to determine their standard deduction, which is the *greater of* (i) $1,050 or (ii) earned income plus $350. This amount cannot exceed $6,300 if single or $12,600 if married filing jointly (see worksheet at ¶106.03).

¶206.02 COMPUTING THE TAX, REFUND, OR AMOUNT DUE

After computing taxable income, taxpayers report on Form 1040EZ all federal income taxes withheld (line 7) plus any earned income credit (line 8a). The sum of these two amounts is the taxpayer's total payments and credits (line 9). Form 1040EZ filers then determine the amount of tax on taxable income using the Tax Table and enter this amount on the tax return (line 10). Taxpayers subject to a penalty for not having minimum essential insurance add their penalty (reported on line 11) to their tax (from line 10) to arrive at their total tax (line 12). If the taxpayer's total tax (line 12) exceeds the total payments and credits (line 9), the difference is reported as the amount owed (line 14). However, if total payments and credits (line 9) exceed the total tax (line 12), the difference represents a refund owed the taxpayer from the IRS (line 13a).

Taxpayers who comply with the ACA mandate during all 12 months of the year indicate this on their tax returns by checking the "Full-year coverage" box on the line designated, "Health care: individual responsibility." On Form 1040EZ, this box is located on line 11. This box also appears on Form 1040A (line 38) and Form 1040 (line 61). For purposes of complying with the ACA mandate, if the taxpayer had minimum essential coverage for any day of a month, the taxpayer is considered to have complied with the ACA mandate for that entire month.

¶206.03 SIGNATURE AND FILING THE RETURN

Taxpayers sign, date, and enter their occupation at the bottom of Form 1040EZ. Taxpayers normally file their return no later than April 15, the due date for calendar year filers. If this date falls on Saturday, Sunday, or a legal holiday, the law extends the filing deadline to the next business day. After attaching Copy B of Form W-2 to the return, the return is ready for filing.

Taxpayers receiving a refund may choose to receive it in the form of a check or a direct deposit. Direct deposit refunds are faster, more secure, and more convenient for the taxpayer than refunds by check. They are also less expensive for the government to issue. To receive a direct deposit refund, the taxpayer must include the bank's routing number on line 13(b), and the taxpayer's bank account number on line 13(d). This information is found on the taxpayer's check, but one should verify these numbers with the bank to make sure the correct numbers are used. The taxpayer must also check the appropriate box on line 13(c) to report the type of account to which the deposit will be made (checking or savings).

If an amount is owed, the taxpayer should also enclose a check for the balance due. Taxpayers may incur a penalty for not paying enough tax during the year. Those in this situation who file Form 1040EZ must let the IRS compute the penalty and send them a bill. If they choose to compute the penalty themselves, they must use either Form 1040A or Form 1040.

All checks should be made payable to the United States Treasury, not the IRS. Never leave the payee line blank. Also, include the following information on each payment:

1. Taxpayer's name and current address
2. Taxpayer's social security number (SSN)
3. Taxpayer's daytime phone number
4. Year (2015) and name of form (Form 1040EZ, Form 1040A, or Form 1040) in the memo line

¶206.04 FILLED-IN FORM 1040EZ

INFORMATION FOR FIGURE 2-10:

Amelia Z. Sanchez (SSN **295-24-1408**) works as a **sales clerk.** She lives at **8290 Edgewater Drive, Chula Vista, CA 91911.** Amelia does not have health insurance through her work and she did not purchase minimum essential coverage during 2015. Thus, Amelia is subject to a penalty that she reports on Form 1040EZ (line 11). In addition to her wages, Amelia received interest earned on her savings account. She has no other sources of income, and no other taxpayer can claim her as a dependent. Amelia wants $3 to go to the Presidential election campaign fund. She enters the amounts highlighted in bold on the lines indicated and then completes Form 1040EZ by following the instructions provided for the remaining lines on the form.

Line #

1: Total wages, salaries, and tips, **$22,920** (source: Form W-2)
2: Taxable interest, **$395** (source: Form 1099-INT)
5: Standard deduction and exemption deduction for nondependents, **$10,300** ($6,300 + $4,000)
7: Federal income tax withheld, **$1,619** (source: Form W-2)
10: Tax, **$1,493** (source: Single column in the Tax Table for $13,015 of taxable income)
11: Health care, individual responsibility, **$325** (*greater of* (i) $325 for one uninsured adult, or (ii) $260 (2% × ($23,315 household income – $10,300 filing status threshold for a single taxpayer)))

Amelia signs and dates her return. She makes a photocopy for her files. She then attaches Copy B of her W-2 to the original return, before mailing it to the IRS.

Figure 2-10: Filled-In Form 1040EZ

Form **1040EZ** — Department of the Treasury—Internal Revenue Service
Income Tax Return for Single and Joint Filers With No Dependents (99) **2015** OMB No. 1545-0074

Your first name and initial	Last name	Your social security number
Amelia Z.	Sanchez	295 24 1408
If a joint return, spouse's first name and initial	Last name	Spouse's social security number

Home address (number and street). If you have a P.O. box, see instructions.	Apt. no.	▲ Make sure the SSN(s) above are correct.
8290 Edgewater Drive		

City, town or post office, state, and ZIP code. If you have a foreign address, also complete spaces below (see instructions).
Chula Vista, CA 91911

Foreign country name	Foreign province/state/county	Foreign postal code

Presidential Election Campaign Check here if you, or your spouse if filing jointly, want $3 to go to this fund. Checking a box below will not change your tax or refund. ☑ You ☐ Spouse

Income	1	Wages, salaries, and tips. This should be shown in box 1 of your Form(s) W-2. Attach your Form(s) W-2.	1	22,920
Attach Form(s) W-2 here.	2	Taxable interest. If the total is over $1,500, you cannot use Form 1040EZ.	2	395
Enclose, but do not attach, any payment.	3	Unemployment compensation and Alaska Permanent Fund dividends (see instructions).	3	
	4	Add lines 1, 2, and 3. This is your **adjusted gross income.**	4	23,315
	5	If someone can claim you (or your spouse if a joint return) as a dependent, check the applicable box(es) below and enter the amount from the worksheet on back. ☐ **You** ☐ **Spouse** If no one can claim you (or your spouse if a joint return), enter $10,300 if **single;** $20,600 if **married filing jointly.** See back for explanation.	5	10,300
	6	Subtract line 5 from line 4. If line 5 is larger than line 4, enter -0-. This is your **taxable income.** ▶	6	13,015
Payments, Credits, and Tax	7	Federal income tax withheld from Form(s) W-2 and 1099.	7	1,619
	8a	**Earned income credit (EIC)** (see instructions)	8a	
	b	Nontaxable combat pay election. 8b		
	9	Add lines 7 and 8a. These are your **total payments and credits.** ▶	9	1,619
	10	**Tax.** Use the amount on **line 6 above** to find your tax in the tax table in the instructions. Then, enter the tax from the table on this line.	10	1,493
	11	Health care: individual responsibility (see instructions) Full-year coverage ☐	11	325
	12	Add lines 10 and 11. This is your **total tax.**	12	1,818
Refund	13a	If line 9 is larger than line 12, subtract line 12 from line 9. This is your **refund.** If Form 8888 is attached, check here ▶ ☐	13a	
Have it directly deposited! See instructions and fill in 13b, 13c, and 13d, or Form 8888.	▶ b	Routing number ▶ c Type: ☐ Checking ☐ Savings		
	▶ d	Account number		
Amount You Owe	14	If line 12 is larger than line 9, subtract line 9 from line 12. This is the **amount you owe.** For details on how to pay, see instructions. ▶	14	199

Third Party Designee — Do you want to allow another person to discuss this return with the IRS (see instructions)? ☐ **Yes.** Complete below. ☐ **No**
Designee's name ▶ Phone no. ▶ Personal identification number (PIN) ▶

Sign Here — Under penalties of perjury, I declare that I have examined this return and, to the best of my knowledge and belief, it is true, correct, and accurately lists all amounts and sources of income I received during the tax year. Declaration of preparer (other than the taxpayer) is based on all information of which the preparer has any knowledge.

Joint return? See instructions. Keep a copy for your records.

Your signature	Date	Your occupation	Daytime phone number
Amelia Z. Sanchez	4-5-16	Sales clerk	
Spouse's signature. If a joint return, **both** must sign.	Date	Spouse's occupation	If the IRS sent you an Identity Protection PIN, enter it here (see inst.)

Paid Preparer Use Only

Print/Type preparer's name	Preparer's signature	Date	Check ☐ if self-employed	PTIN
Firm's name ▶		Firm's EIN ▶		
Firm's address ▶		Phone no.		

For Disclosure, Privacy Act, and Paperwork Reduction Act Notice, see instructions. Cat. No. 11329W Form **1040EZ** (2015)

¶207 Electronic Filing

The IRS encourages electronic filing of tax returns. Electronic filing reduces the IRS's processing costs and speeds up the time it takes taxpayers to get their refunds. Taxpayers who file their returns electronically and have their refunds deposited directly into their bank accounts can receive their refunds much faster than returns filed by mail. According to the IRS, 91% of all 2014 individual income tax returns filed in the Spring of 2015 were electronically filed.

Persons who e-file their tax returns and have their refunds deposited directly to their checking or savings accounts should expect to receive their refunds within 1-3 weeks. The processing of refunds takes a little longer during peak tax filing season. Taxpayers interested in checking on the status of their federal income tax refunds can call 1-800-829-4477, where they will reach an automated information line. Alternatively, taxpayers can check online the status of their federal tax refunds (as well as the state tax refunds for many states) at:

http://www.efile.com/tax-refund/where-is-my-refund/

¶208 IRS Website

The IRS provides lots of useful information through its Internet home page (*http://www.irs .gov*). This is a good source of forms, publications, and other material that may be downloaded. Appendix A (located at the back of this textbook) provides instructions on how to use the IRS website.

In 2013, the IRS website was accessed over 430 million times. This was 24% more than the previous year, and suggests that more people may be using the IRS website to get answers to their tax questions and help with filing their tax returns.

¶209 Extension of Time to File

Individuals and corporations may obtain an automatic six-month extension of time to file their income tax returns. The automatic extension period for partnerships is five months. This provides taxpayers with more time to file their tax returns but does not give them more time to pay their taxes. Taxpayers must pay their taxes by original due date for their returns even when they file an extension. Amounts paid to the IRS when filing an extension are reported in the "Payments" section when the tax return is prepared at a later date. Interest is charged on any unpaid amounts and penalties may be assessed as well.

Type of Taxpayer	File for Extension on:
Individual (Form 1040, Form 1040A, or Form 1040EZ)	Form 4868
Partnership (Form 1065)	Form 7004
S Corporation (Form 1120S)	Form 7004
C Corporation (Form 1120)	Form 7004

2

Name:

Section:

Date:

QUESTIONS AND PROBLEMS

1. **Using the Tax Rate Schedules.** (Obj. 1) The IRS publishes tax rate schedules and a Tax Table. When must taxpayers use the tax rate schedules instead of the Tax Table to compute their income tax liability?

2. **Comparison of Tax Tables and Tax Rate Schedules.** (Obj. 1) Matteo (unmarried) files his tax return using head of household filing status. His taxable income is $60,550.

   a. What is Matteo's tax liability using the Tax Table?

   b. Compute Matteo's tax liability using the tax rate schedule. Explain any difference in your answers to Parts a. and b.

3. **Tax Computation.** (Obj. 1) Barb, age 25, files as a single taxpayer. She is employed at a monthly salary of $2,150. She claims no dependents. Her employer withheld $1,600 from her wages for income taxes for 12 months of work. Compute Barb's taxable income and income tax due to or from the IRS.

4. **Tax Computations.** (Obj. 1) Compute the taxable income and income tax liability (before credits) for each of the following taxpayers. Each taxpayer uses the standard deduction.

   a. A widowed taxpayer, age 30, has one dependent. Her filing status is qualifying widow(er); AGI is $46,400.

   b. An unmarried taxpayer, age 74, has no dependents and AGI of $19,590.

   c. A taxpayer, age 40, is married but files a separate return from his spouse. The taxpayer is the noncustodial parent of his 8-year-old child. His wife has signed Form 8832 giving him the right to claim their daughter as a dependent. AGI is $130,580.

   d. An unmarried taxpayer, age 72, is claimed as a dependent on her son's return. Her AGI consists solely of $3,150 of taxable interest.

   e. A married couple, ages 67 and 66, file a joint return. They claim one dependent. AGI is $161,555.

5. **Tax Credits vs. Tax Deductions.** (Obj. 1) What is the difference between a tax credit and a tax deduction? If a taxpayer with a marginal tax rate of 15% has a $1,000 deduction, how much tax will she save? How much tax will she save with a $1,000 tax credit?

6. **Child and Dependent Care Credit.** (Obj. 2) Bud and Katie Milner file a joint return. During the year, they paid $11,000 to their nanny to look after their three children, ages 2, 9, and 11. Bud and Katie both work and earned $24,000 and $31,000, respectively. The wages are the Milners' only source of income, and they have no deductions for AGI.

   a. Compute the Milners' child and dependent care credit.

   b. Compute the Milners' child and dependent care credit assuming Katie received a $4,000 nontaxable reimbursement from her employer's dependent care assistance plan.

7. **Child and Dependent Care Credit.** (Obj. 2) Todd and Jo Mendin pay their 17-year-old daughter, Erin, $5,000 to look after their 10-year-old son, TJ. The Mendins file a joint return and claim Erin and TJ as their dependents. The Mendlins' AGI is $84,000. Both spouses work and each has wages in excess of $30,000.

   a. Compute the Mendlins' child and dependent care credit.

   b. How, if at all, would your answer to Part a. change if Erin were 22-years-old, but still claimed as a dependent on her parents' return?

   c. How, if at all, would your answer to Part a. change if the Mendins paid Todd's mother to look after TJ?

8. **Child and Dependent Care Credit and Form 2441.** (Objs. 2 and 5) Denise (SSN 182-90-0113) and Marcus Anders claim their two children, David (SSN 392-40-7417, age 7) and Stacy (SSN 813-20-4444, age 11), as dependents. During the year, Denise worked full-time and earned $38,200. Marcus was a full-time student at the local college for 9 months during the year. The Anders paid Tanya McCully (SSN 921-44-0122) $5,500 for qualified childcare expenses that allowed Denise to work and Marcus to attend college. Tanya lives at 130 N. Main Street, Unit B, Memphis, TN 37501.

   a. Compute the Anders's child and dependent care credit if their AGI is $38,710.

   b. How, if at all, would your answer to Part a. change if Marcus attended college full-time for five months during the spring semester, but only took classes part-time in the fall?

   c. Prepare Form 2441 for the Anders from Part b. The Anders's tax liability limit is $1,013.

(Use for Problem 8.)

Form **2441** — Department of the Treasury, Internal Revenue Service (99)

Child and Dependent Care Expenses

▶ Attach to Form 1040, Form 1040A, or Form 1040NR.

▶ Information about Form 2441 and its separate instructions is at *www.irs.gov/form2441*.

OMB No. 1545-0074 — **2015** — Attachment Sequence No. **21**

1040 / 1040A / 1040NR — 2441

Name(s) shown on return | Your social security number

Part I — Persons or Organizations Who Provided the Care—You **must** complete this part. (If you have more than two care providers, see the instructions.)

1 (a) Care provider's name	(b) Address (number, street, apt. no., city, state, and ZIP code)	(c) Identifying number (SSN or EIN)	(d) Amount paid (see instructions)

Did you receive **dependent care benefits?** — **No** ——▶ Complete only Part II below. **Yes** ——▶ Complete Part III on the back next.

Caution. If the care was provided in your home, you may owe employment taxes. If you do, you cannot file Form 1040A. For details, see the instructions for Form 1040, line 60a, or Form 1040NR, line 59a.

Part II — Credit for Child and Dependent Care Expenses

2 Information about your **qualifying person(s).** If you have more than two qualifying persons, see the instructions.

(a) Qualifying person's name — First	Last	(b) Qualifying person's social security number	(c) **Qualified expenses** you incurred and paid in 2015 for the person listed in column (a)

3 Add the amounts in column (c) of line 2. **Do not** enter more than $3,000 for one qualifying person or $6,000 for two or more persons. If you completed Part III, enter the amount from line 31 . . . . . **3**

4 Enter your **earned income.** See instructions **4**

5 If married filing jointly, enter your spouse's earned income (if you or your spouse was a student or was disabled, see the instructions); **all others**, enter the amount from line 4 . **5**

6 Enter the **smallest** of line 3, 4, or 5 . . . . . **6**

7 Enter the amount from Form 1040, line 38; Form 1040A, line 22; or Form 1040NR, line 37 . . . . . **7**

8 Enter on line 8 the decimal amount shown below that applies to the amount on line 7

If line 7 is: Over	But not over	Decimal amount is	If line 7 is: Over	But not over	Decimal amount is
$0	15,000	.35	$29,000	31,000	.27
15,000	17,000	.34	31,000	33,000	.26
17,000	19,000	.33	33,000	35,000	.25
19,000	21,000	.32	35,000	37,000	.24
21,000	23,000	.31	37,000	39,000	.23
23,000	25,000	.30	39,000	41,000	.22
25,000	27,000	.29	41,000	43,000	.21
27,000	29,000	.28	43,000	No limit	.20

8 X.

9 Multiply line 6 by the decimal amount on line 8. If you paid 2014 expenses in 2015, see the instructions **9**

10 Tax liability limit. Enter the amount from the Credit Limit Worksheet in the instructions. **10**

11 **Credit for child and dependent care expenses.** Enter the **smaller** of line 9 or line 10 here and on Form 1040, line 49; Form 1040A, line 31; or Form 1040NR, line 47 . . . . **11**

For Paperwork Reduction Act Notice, see your tax return instructions. Cat. No. 11862M Form **2441** (2015)

9. **Education Tax Credit and Form 8863.** (Objs. 2 and 5) In 2015, Jean Loptein (SSN 169-34-2903) paid $3,300 for her son's fall tuition. Her son, Robert Loptein (SSN 399-40-1120), is a full-time student and a freshman at the University of Georgia (212 Carlton Street, Athens, GA 30602). Jean files as head of household.

   a. Compute Jean's education tax credit if her AGI is $32,800. How much of her credit is refundable versus nonrefundable?

   b. Same as in Part a., except that Jean's AGI is $84,700.

   c. Prepare Form 8863 for Jean in Part b. Robert did not receive a Form 1098-T from the University of Georgia, nor has he been convicted of a felony.

10. **Education Tax Credit.** (Obj. 2) Curt and Kathy Norton paid $3,200 of tuition for their son, who attends college less than half-time. Of this amount, $1,500 was paid on December 28, 2014, for the Spring 2015 semester, and $1,700 was paid on August 4, 2015, for the Fall 2015 semester.

    a. Compute the Nortons' 2015 education tax credit if their AGI is $71,900. How much of their credit is refundable versus nonrefundable?

    b. Same as in Part a., except that the Nortons' AGI is $118,816.

11. **Education Tax Credit.** (Obj. 2) In 2015, Paul and Karen Mitchell pay $12,000 for their daughter's tuition for the Spring and Fall semesters. Their daughter is a full-time graduate student. The Mitchells also paid $3,800 for their son's tuition for the Spring and Fall semesters. In the Fall of 2015, their son, Ron began his sophomore year of college. The son attends college full-time.

    a. Compute the Mitchells' 2015 education tax credit if their AGI is $120,600. How much of their credit is refundable versus nonrefundable?

    b. Same as in Part a., except that the Mitchells' AGI is $174,360.

(Use for Problem 9.)

Form **8863**

Department of the Treasury
Internal Revenue Service (99)

Education Credits
(American Opportunity and Lifetime Learning Credits)

▶ Attach to Form 1040 or Form 1040A.

▶ Information about Form 8863 and its separate instructions is at *www.irs.gov/form8863.*

OMB No. 1545-0074

2015

Attachment Sequence No. **50**

Name(s) shown on return | Your social security number

CAUTION

Complete a separate Part III on page 2 for each student for whom you are claiming either credit before you complete Parts I and II.

Part I Refundable American Opportunity Credit

1	After completing Part III for each student, enter the total of all amounts from all Parts III, line 30	1	
2	Enter: $180,000 if married filing jointly; $90,000 if single, head of household, or qualifying widow(er)	2	
3	Enter the amount from Form 1040, line 38, or Form 1040A, line 22. If you are filing Form 2555, 2555-EZ, or 4563, or you are excluding income from Puerto Rico, see Pub. 970 for the amount to enter	3	
4	Subtract line 3 from line 2. If zero or less, **stop**; you cannot take any education credit	4	
5	Enter: $20,000 if married filing jointly; $10,000 if single, head of household, or qualifying widow(er)	5	
6	If line 4 is: • Equal to or more than line 5, enter 1.000 on line 6 • Less than line 5, divide line 4 by line 5. Enter the result as a decimal (rounded to at least three places)	6	.
7	Multiply line 1 by line 6. **Caution:** If you were under age 24 at the end of the year **and** meet the conditions described in the instructions, you **cannot** take the refundable American opportunity credit; skip line 8, enter the amount from line 7 on line 9, and check this box ▶ ☐	7	
8	**Refundable American opportunity credit.** Multiply line 7 by 40% (.40). Enter the amount here and on Form 1040, line 68, or Form 1040A, line 44. Then go to line 9 below.	8	

Part II Nonrefundable Education Credits

9	Subtract line 8 from line 7. Enter here and on line 2 of the Credit Limit Worksheet (see instructions)	9	
10	After completing Part III for each student, enter the total of all amounts from all Parts III, line 31. If zero, skip lines 11 through 17, enter -0- on line 18, and go to line 19	10	
11	Enter the smaller of line 10 or $10,000	11	
12	Multiply line 11 by 20% (.20)	12	
13	Enter: $130,000 if married filing jointly; $65,000 if single, head of household, or qualifying widow(er)	13	
14	Enter the amount from Form 1040, line 38, or Form 1040A, line 22. If you are filing Form 2555, 2555-EZ, or 4563, or you are excluding income from Puerto Rico, see Pub. 970 for the amount to enter	14	
15	Subtract line 14 from line 13. If zero or less, skip lines 16 and 17, enter -0- on line 18, and go to line 19	15	
16	Enter: $20,000 if married filing jointly; $10,000 if single, head of household, or qualifying widow(er)	16	
17	If line 15 is: • Equal to or more than line 16, enter 1.000 on line 17 and go to line 18 • Less than line 16, divide line 15 by line 16. Enter the result as a decimal (rounded to at least three places)	17	.
18	Multiply line 12 by line 17. Enter here and on line 1 of the Credit Limit Worksheet (see instructions) ▶	18	
19	**Nonrefundable education credits.** Enter the amount from line 7 of the Credit Limit Worksheet (see instructions) here and on Form 1040, line 50, or Form 1040A, line 33	19	

For Paperwork Reduction Act Notice, see your tax return instructions. Cat. No. 25379M Form **8863** (2015)

(Use for Problem 9.)

Form 8863 (2015) Page **2**

Name(s) shown on return | **Your social security number**

CAUTION ***Complete Part III for each student for whom you are claiming either the American opportunity credit or lifetime learning credit. Use additional copies of page 2 as needed for each student.***

Part III **Student and Educational Institution Information** See instructions.

20 Student name (as shown on page 1 of your tax return)	**21** Student social security number (as shown on page 1 of your tax return)
22 Educational institution information (see instructions)	
a. Name of first educational institution	**b.** Name of second educational institution (if any)
(1) Address. Number and street (or P.O. box). City, town or post office, state, and ZIP code. If a foreign address, see instructions.	**(1)** Address. Number and street (or P.O. box). City, town or post office, state, and ZIP code. If a foreign address, see instructions.
(2) Did the student receive Form 1098-T from this institution for 2015? ☐ Yes ☐ No	**(2)** Did the student receive Form 1098-T from this institution for 2015? ☐ Yes ☐ No
(3) Did the student receive Form 1098-T from this institution for 2014 with Box 2 filled in and Box 7 checked? ☐ Yes ☐ No	**(3)** Did the student receive Form 1098-T from this institution for 2014 with Box 2 filled in and Box 7 checked? ☐ Yes ☐ No
If you checked "No" in **both (2) and (3)**, skip **(4)**.	If you checked "No" in **both (2) and (3)**, skip **(4)**.
(4) If you checked "Yes" in **(2) or (3)**, enter the institution's federal identification number (from Form 1098-T). __ __ - __ __ __ __ __ __ __	**(4)** If you checked "Yes" in **(2) or (3)**, enter the institution's federal identification number (from Form 1098-T). __ __ - __ __ __ __ __ __ __

23	Has the Hope Scholarship Credit or American opportunity credit been claimed for this student for any 4 tax years before 2015?	☐ Yes — **Stop!** Go to line 31 for this student.	☐ No — Go to line 24.
24	Was the student enrolled at least half-time for at least one academic period that began or is treated as having begun in 2015 at an eligible educational institution in a program leading towards a postsecondary degree, certificate, or other recognized postsecondary educational credential? (see instructions)	☐ Yes — Go to line 25.	☐ No — **Stop!** Go to line 31 for this student.
25	Did the student complete the first 4 years of postsecondary education before 2015 (see instructions)?	☐ Yes — **Stop!** Go to line 31 for this student.	☐ No — Go to line 26.
26	Was the student convicted, before the end of 2015, of a felony for possession or distribution of a controlled substance?	☐ Yes — **Stop!** Go to line 31 for this student.	☐ No — Complete lines 27 through 30 for this student.

CAUTION *You **cannot** take the American opportunity credit and the lifetime learning credit for the **same student** in the same year. If you complete lines 27 through 30 for this student, do not complete line 31.*

American Opportunity Credit

27	Adjusted qualified education expenses (see instructions). **Do not enter more than $4,000**	**27**	
28	Subtract $2,000 from line 27. If zero or less, enter -0-	**28**	
29	Multiply line 28 by 25% (.25)	**29**	
30	If line 28 is zero, enter the amount from line 27. Otherwise, add $2,000 to the amount on line 29 and enter the result. Skip line 31. Include the total of all amounts from all Parts III, line 30, on Part I, line 1	**30**	

Lifetime Learning Credit

31	Adjusted qualified education expenses (see instructions). Include the total of all amounts from all Parts III, line 31, on Part II, line 10	**31**	

Form **8863** (2015)

12. **Retirement Savings Contributions Credit.** (Obj. 2) Tom and Meg Wherry's joint tax return for 2015 shows $46,000 of AGI. During the year, Tom contributed $3,000 to his IRA and Meg contributed $1,500 to her IRA. What amount of tax credit is available for these contributions?

13. **Child Tax Credit.** (Obj. 2) Compute the child tax credit for each of the following taxpayers.

    a. Jett is married but does not file a joint return with his spouse. Jett claims his 6-year-old son as a dependent and files as head of household under the abandoned spouse rules. Jett's AGI is $85,440.

    b. Eren is divorced. She and her ex-husband share custody of their four children, ages 2-8, but Eren is the custodial parent. She has not signed away her right to claim the children as dependents. Her AGI is $95,694.

    c. Michelle is 43-years old and a single parent. She claims her three children, ages 9, 14 and 17, as dependents. Her AGI is $123,639.

    d. Randy and Tammy O'Brien file a joint return. Tammy's 16-year-old sister lives with them the entire year. They claim the sister and their 2-year-old daughter as dependents. The O'Briens' AGI is $145,800.

14. **Child Tax Credit.** (Obj. 2) Compute the child tax credit for each of the following taxpayers.

    a. Jay and Marie Stockton file a joint return and claim their three children, all under age 17, as dependents. The Stocktons' AGI is $121,400.

    b. DJ files as head of household. He claims his twin sons, age 4, as dependents. DJ's AGI is $80,340.

    c. Jenn files as head of household. She claims her 12-year-old daughter as a dependent. Jenn's AGI is $78,450.

15. **Refundable Child Tax Credit.** (Obj. 2) Pat and Diedra Dobson file a joint tax return for 2015. The Dobsons' AGI is $30,700, of which $27,300 is taxable wages. The Dobsons take the standard deduction and claim as dependents their two teenage children, ages 13 and 15. Other than the child tax credit, the Dobsons do not claim any nonrefundable personal tax credits. Compute the Dobsons' nonrefundable and refundable child tax credit.

16. **Residential Energy Credit.** (Obj. 2) During 2015, Maureen installed a solar hot water heater and energy efficient exterior windows to improve her main home. The cost for these items was $2,350 and $5,500, respectively. Compute Maureen's residential energy efficient property credit.

17. **Adoption Credit.** (Obj. 2) Jon and Mary Hoppe paid $15,000 in qualified adoption expenses of a healthy child. The adoption was finalized in 2015. The Hoppes' modified AGI is $223,332. In addition, Jon received $3,000 from an employer adoption assistance plan. Compute the Hoppes' adoption credit.

18. **Adoption Credit.** (Obj. 2) In 2014, a married couple paid $6,000 in qualified adoption expenses to adopt a child that is a U.S. citizen. In 2015, they paid an additional $4,200 in qualified adoption expenses. The adoption was finalized in 2015.

    a. Compute the couples' adoption credit if their modified AGI in both years is $115,000. In what year(s) is the credit taken?

    b. How would your answer to Part a. change if the couples' modified AGI was $218,910 in both years?

    c. How would your answer to Part a. change if the couple adopted a child with special needs?

    d. How would your answer to Part a. change if the adoption fell through?

19. Adoption Credit. (Obj. 2) In 2014, a married couple paid $14,000 in qualified adoption expenses to adopt a child that is a U.S. citizen. The adoption was finalized in 2015.

a. Compute the adoption credit if the couple's modified AGI is $200,000 in 2014 and $212,000 in 2015. In what year(s) is the credit taken?

b. How, if at all, would your answer to Part a. change if the couple adopted a foreign child?

c. How, if at all, would your answer to Part b. change if the adoption fell through?

20. Earned Income Credit. (Obj. 2) For each of the following situations, compute the taxpayer's 2015 earned income credit.

a. Patty and Ron Barnett file a joint return, claiming their two sons, ages 3 and 5, as dependents. The Barnetts' AGI is $14,400, which consists entirely of Ron's wages.

b. Joseph is a 25-year-old graduate student. His gross income consists of $5,000 of wages, and $80 in interest from a savings account. Joseph files as single and claims no dependents.

c. Suzanne and Vernon Zimmerman file a joint return, claiming their 6-year-old daughter as a dependent. The Zimmermans' AGI consists of Vernon's $26,375 in wages, and $400 in dividend income.

d. Sarah files as head of household, claiming her 2-year-old son as a dependent. Sarah's AGI consists of $18,000 in wages and $3,520 in interest income.

21. Earned Income Credit. (Obj. 2) For each of the following situations, determine under the tie-break rules the person entitled to claim the qualifying child for purpose of the earned income credit.

a. Kate (age 30) and her son, Jimmy (age 3), live with Kate's father, Fred, the entire year. Jimmy is a qualifying child to both Kate and Fred. Kate's AGI is $20,000; Fred's is $64,000.

b. Ned and Tammy are divorced. They share custody of their twin sons, age 13. The boys live with Ned half of the year and with Tammy the other half of the year. Tammy lives with her parents. The twins are qualifying children to Ned, Tammy, and Tammy's parents. Ned's AGI is $45,000, Tammy's AGI is $20,200, and the parents' AGI is $36,900.

c. Same as in Part b., except that the boys spend more days with Tammy during the year.

d. Same as in Part b., except that the boys spend more days with Ned during the year.

e. Darcy's parents are both deceased. Darcy is 15 and is being raised by her aunt. Her grandparents also participate in her upbringing and support. Darcy is a qualifying child for both her aunt and her grandparents. The aunt's AGI is $21,500. The grandparents' AGI is $45,300.

22. Premium Tax Credit. (Objs. 2 and 3) During all of 2015, each of the following taxpayers fully comply with the ACA mandate to carry minimum essential (health care) coverage. Compute each taxpayer's premium tax credit.

a. John is married, but files separately from his wife. John purchases his health insurance through the federal Marketplace. He selects the bronze plan, and his premiums for the year are $2,500. Had John selected the silver plan, his premiums would have been $4,000. Based on his household income and family size, the government has determined that John's annual contribution for health care is $1,400.

b. Same as in part a., except that John's premiums under the bronze plan were $3,000.

c. The Wagners purchase a bronze plan through the federal Marketplace. The Wagners file a joint tax return, and their premiums for 2015 were $5,000. Had the Wagners selected the silver plan, their premiums would have been $8,000. Based on their household income and family size, the government has determined that the Wagners' annual contribution for health care is $6,400.

d. Same as in part c., except that the Wagners' annual contribution for health care is $2,200.

23. Shared Responsibility Payment. (Obj. 3) Each of the taxpayers below fails to comply with the ACA mandate to carry minimum essential (health care) coverage during 2015. Compute each taxpayer's ACA penalty.

a. Megan (age 40) files as a qualifying widow(er). She claims her two children (age 12 and 14) as dependents. Megan's household income is $58,000.

b. Ryan (age 45) files as head of household. He claims his 19-year-old daughter and 17-year old son as dependents. Ryan's household income is $40,000.

c. Denis and Bunny Sewell (ages 35 and 37) file a joint tax return. They claim their three young children as dependents. The Sewells' household income is $65,000.

24. 1040EZ Requirements. (Obj. 4) The taxpayers described in Parts a. through f. want to file Form 1040EZ. For these taxpayers, state whether they can file Form 1040EZ. If not, provide a reason for your answer.

a. A single taxpayer has tax-exempt interest income of $1,400 and taxable income of $99,900 from wages.

b. A married taxpayer filing a separate return has taxable income of $47,290, including interest income of $100.

c. A single taxpayer has taxable income of $35,683, including $1,700 of interest income. The taxpayer also has $200 of tax-exempt interest.

d. A taxpayer filing as head of household has taxable income of $30,400, including interest income of $250. The taxpayer claims two dependents.

e. A single taxpayer has taxable income of $47,800, including dividend income of $300.

f. A married taxpayer filing jointly has taxable income of $47,290, including interest income of $100. Both the taxpayer and spouse are elderly and blind. They do not claim any dependents.

25. Form 1040EZ. (Obj. 5)

a. Jeanne M. Searson (SSN 369-48-5783), a 28-year-old unmarried clerk, lives at 4502 Lakeside Drive, Sunrise, FL 33920. Jeanne's employers do not offer health care, and Jeanne decided against buying minimum essential coverage on her own. Her Forms W-2 contain the following information:

	Taxable Wages	*Federal Income Tax Withheld*	*OASDI Tax Withheld*	*Medicare Tax Withheld*
Interlake Co.	$ 5,240	$169	$325	$ 76
Data-Mate Co.	6,280	206	389	91
Totals	$11,520	$375	$714	$167

In addition to her wages, Jeanne received $175 in interest on her account at the Echo Savings and Loan Bank. She wants $3 to go to the Presidential election campaign fund. Prepare Jeanne's Form 1040EZ. She signs the return on February 6, 2016.

b. Cele P. (SSN 268-40-8455) and Marvin K. (SSN 248-40-7834) Goldman, ages 36 and 38, received interest income of $390 on their savings account at the Portage Bank. Cele and Marvin are both employed by Portage Hardware. Cele is a cashier; Marvin is a sales representative. Through their employers, the Goldmans are able to purchase minimum essential health care coverage. Their home address is 248 Maple Street, Portage, MO 49067. The Goldmans have no other sources of income and they take the standard deduction. Neither Cele nor Marvin is blind or claimed as a dependent. They choose to file a joint return. Both want $3 to go to the Presidential election campaign fund. Using the following Form W-2 data, prepare the Goldmans' 2015 Form 1040EZ. They sign and file their return on January 20, 2016.

	Taxable Wages	*Federal Income Tax Withheld*	*OASDI Tax Withheld*	*Medicare Tax Withheld*	*State Income Tax Withheld*
Cele	$13,400	$ 657	$ 831	$194	$ 402
Marvin	21,900	918	1,358	318	657
Totals	$35,300	$1,575	$2,189	$512	$1,059

(Use for Problem 25.)

Form **1040EZ** Department of the Treasury—Internal Revenue Service
Income Tax Return for Single and Joint Filers With No Dependents (99) **2015** OMB No. 1545-0074

Your first name and initial	Last name		**Your social security number**
If a joint return, spouse's first name and initial	Last name		**Spouse's social security number**
Home address (number and street). If you have a P.O. box, see instructions.		Apt. no.	▲ Make sure the SSN(s) above are correct.
City, town or post office, state, and ZIP code. If you have a foreign address, also complete spaces below (see instructions).			**Presidential Election Campaign** Check here if you, or your spouse if filing jointly, want $3 to go to this fund. Checking a box below will not change your tax or refund. ☐ You ☐ Spouse
Foreign country name	Foreign province/state/county	Foreign postal code	

Income

Attach Form(s) W-2 here.

Enclose, but do not attach, any payment.

1	Wages, salaries, and tips. This should be shown in box 1 of your Form(s) W-2. Attach your Form(s) W-2.	1	
2	Taxable interest. If the total is over $1,500, you cannot use Form 1040EZ.	2	
3	Unemployment compensation and Alaska Permanent Fund dividends (see instructions).	3	
4	Add lines 1, 2, and 3. This is your **adjusted gross income.**	4	
5	If someone can claim you (or your spouse if a joint return) as a dependent, check the applicable box(es) below and enter the amount from the worksheet on back. ☐ **You** ☐ **Spouse** If no one can claim you (or your spouse if a joint return), enter $10,300 if **single;** $20,600 if **married filing jointly.** See back for explanation.	5	
6	Subtract line 5 from line 4. If line 5 is larger than line 4, enter -0-. This is your **taxable income.** ▶	6	

Payments, Credits, and Tax

7	Federal income tax withheld from Form(s) W-2 and 1099.	7	
8a	**Earned income credit (EIC)** (see instructions)	8a	
b	Nontaxable combat pay election. 8b		
9	Add lines 7 and 8a. These are your **total payments and credits.** ▶	9	
10	**Tax.** Use the amount on **line 6 above** to find your tax in the tax table in the instructions. Then, enter the tax from the table on this line.	10	
11	Health care: individual responsibility (see instructions) Full-year coverage ☐	11	
12	Add lines 10 and 11. This is your **total tax.**	12	

Refund

Have it directly deposited! See instructions and fill in 13b, 13c, and 13d, or Form 8888.

13a	If line 9 is larger than line 12, subtract line 12 from line 9. This is your **refund.** If Form 8888 is attached, check here ▶ ☐	13a	
▶ b	Routing number ☐☐☐☐☐☐☐☐☐ ▶ c Type: ☐ Checking ☐ Savings		
▶ d	Account number ☐☐☐☐☐☐☐☐☐☐☐☐☐☐☐☐☐		

Amount You Owe

14	If line 12 is larger than line 9, subtract line 9 from line 12. This is the **amount you owe.** For details on how to pay, see instructions. ▶	14	

Third Party Designee

Do you want to allow another person to discuss this return with the IRS (see instructions)? ☐ **Yes.** Complete below. ☐ **No**

Designee's name ▶ Phone no. ▶ Personal identification number (PIN) ▶ ☐☐☐☐☐

Sign Here

Joint return? See instructions.

Keep a copy for your records.

Under penalties of perjury, I declare that I have examined this return and, to the best of my knowledge and belief, it is true, correct, and accurately lists all amounts and sources of income I received during the tax year. Declaration of preparer (other than the taxpayer) is based on all information of which the preparer has any knowledge.

Your signature	Date	Your occupation	Daytime phone number
Spouse's signature. If a joint return, **both** must sign.	Date	Spouse's occupation	If the IRS sent you an Identity Protection PIN, enter it here (see inst.) ☐☐☐☐☐☐

Paid Preparer Use Only

Print/Type preparer's name	Preparer's signature	Date	Check ☐ if self-employed	PTIN
Firm's name ▶		Firm's EIN ▶		
Firm's address ▶		Phone no.		

For Disclosure, Privacy Act, and Paperwork Reduction Act Notice, see instructions. Cat. No. 11329W Form **1040EZ** (2015)

26. **Tax Planning.** (Obj. 1) Mary and Chuck, unmarried individuals, are both 29 years of age. For 2015, Mary and Chuck will earn wages of $60,000 and $35,000, respectively. This will be their only source of income. They are considering getting married in either December 2015 or January 2016. Before setting a wedding date, they want to know how much they will save in federal income taxes if they get married in December and file a joint return. They ask you to compare their combined federal income taxes as single individuals with their taxes as a married couple filing jointly. Neither taxpayer has any dependents. Also, no other taxpayer can claim either of them as a dependent. Regardless of their marital status, they will claim the standard deduction.

27. **Internet Problem: Filling out Form 4868.** (Obj. 5)

Cheryl Bier needs more time to file her 2015 tax return. Cheryl expects her total tax liability to be $16,500. She had $15,800 withheld from her wages. Cheryl (SSN 678-59-1234) lives at 829 North Broadway, Garden Grove, CA 92842.

Go to the IRS website and locate Form 4868, Application for Automatic Extension of Time To File U.S. Individual Income Tax Return. Using the computer, fill in the form for Cheryl and print out a completed copy.

See Appendix A for instructions on use of the IRS website.

COMPREHENSIVE PROBLEM

28. Toni Tornan is a single parent. During 2015 she earned wages $26,550. Her employer did not withhold federal income taxes from her pay. Toni claims her two children, age 5 and 8, as dependents. The wages are Toni's only source of gross income. Compute Toni's taxable income and her taxes due to (or from) the government when she files her 2015 tax return.

CUMULATIVE PROBLEM 1 (CHAPTERS 1-2)

Jack Bennett is married but does not file a joint return with his spouse. He is 36 years of age and has excellent vision. Jack and his wife share custody of their 10-year-old son. They have lived in separate households since May 2015. Jack is not the custodial parent, but his wife has signed Form 8332, allowing Jack to claim their son as a dependent. Jack's AGI is $63,440 (all from wages) and he uses the standard deduction. His employer withheld $8,000 for federal income taxes during the year. Through his employer, Jack purchases his health insurance. He complies with the ACA mandate for the entire year. Compute Jack's 2015 taxable income and taxes owed (to be refunded).

CUMULATIVE PROBLEM 2 (CHAPTERS 1-2)

Emily and David Chen claim their three children, ages 5-10, as dependents. During 2015, Emily worked full-time and earned $39,600. Emily's employer provides her with family health care coverage that complies with the ACA mandate. Her employer withheld nothing for federal income taxes. David attended college full-time for the entire year. Other than Emily's wages, the couple's only other source of earned income is $800 of taxable interest. (David received a tax-free scholarship that paid for his college tuition, book, and fees.) The Chens paid $2,500 in qualified childcare expenses so that Emily could work and David could attend college. Compute the couple's taxable income and taxes owed (to be refunded) on their 2015 joint tax return. The couple uses the standard deduction. They are both under age 65 and have no problems with their vision.

Chapter

3

Gross Income Inclusions

CHAPTER CONTENTS

LEARNING OBJECTIVES

After completing Chapter 3, you should be able to:

1. Recognize the various types of income and determine in what tax year income should be reported.
2. Describe how pensions, annuities, IRA distributions, and social security benefits are taxed.
3. Discuss how the tax laws treat the income from original issue discount (OID) bonds, market discount bonds, and below market loans.
4. Understand the tax treatment of distributions from corporations and mutual funds, including ordinary dividends, return of capital distributions, and capital gain distributions.
5. Determine how investment income is taxed to certain children and higher-income taxpayers.
6. Prepare the forms and schedules introduced in the chapter, including Schedule B, Form 8615, and Form 1040A.

CHAPTER OVERVIEW

Chapters 1 and 2 presented an overview of the basic tax and reporting structure. They illustrated several tax forms, schedules, and worksheets, including the simplest tax return, Form 1040EZ. The next few chapters focus on particular segments of the taxable income formula, starting with gross income.

As was discussed in Chapter 1, the amount of gross income determines whether an individual must file a tax return and whether a person qualifies as a dependent. Strangely, though, nowhere on Form 1040EZ, Form 1040A, or Form 1040 do taxpayers report their gross income.

Chapter 3 and the first half of Chapter 4 examine the two components of gross income, namely "income" and "exclusions" from gross income. Chapter 3 starts off the discussion of gross income by examining items of income that, with few exceptions, remain in gross income. This includes sources of earned income (like wages and business income), retirement income (like social security and pension benefits), and investment income (like interest, dividends, and rental income). Chapter 4 continues the discussion of gross income by examining the most common types of exclusions, which are items of income subtracted from total income in arriving at gross income. Chapter 3 concludes by introducing and showing a completed Form 1040A.

¶301 General Recognition Guidelines

Gross income is all income from every source, except those sources specifically excluded by tax law. Thus, taxpayers face two problems:

1. Recognizing income, and
2. Identifying exclusions (income that is not taxed).

Although the Internal Revenue Code (Code) does not define income, it generally includes any increase in wealth (assets minus liabilities). Taxpayers usually report income only in the year it is realized as determined by their accounting method.

Cash basis taxpayers report income in the year money, property, or services are actually or constructively received in an income-producing event. **Constructive receipt** takes place when assets are credited or made available to the taxpayer without restriction (e.g., interest credited to the taxpayer's bank account.) Taxpayers report as income the amount of money or the value of property and services they receive.

Accrual basis taxpayers normally report income in the year they earn it, regardless of when they receive the cash. They report service revenue in income in the year they perform the services. They report interest in income in the year the interest accrues. They report the revenues from the sale of goods in the year the sale occurs.

Although appreciation in property values may cause an increase in wealth, the tax law does not recognize mere appreciation of assets as income. Instead, taxpayers must convert the property into cash or other property before realizing a gain. Furthermore, only the excess of the amount realized over the taxpayer's investment in the property (known as "basis") counts as income.

¶301.01 EXCEPTIONS

Accrual basis taxpayers normally report income in the year they earn it. However, certain advanced payments are taxed in the year received. This includes payments for interest income and for warranty services offered by third parties. It also includes most prepaid rent. The Code taxes most other types of advanced payments over two tax years. Income earned in the year the payment is received is reported as income in that year. The rest is reported as income in the next year. This rule holds even if the payment is for goods and services that extend beyond the second year.

EXAMPLE 1

On November 2, 20x1, Jenny buys an appliance from ASE, a local retailer. She pays ASE $900 for a warranty that will cover all repair costs for the first two years. ASE uses a calendar tax year and the accrual method. Since the seller (not a third party) offered the warranty, ASE prorates the income over two years. In 20x1, ASE reports income of $75 ($900/24 × 2 months). ASE reports the rest ($900 – $75 = $825) in 20x2. Even though the warranty extends into 20x3, ASE cannot defer (delay) the income beyond the second tax year.

EXAMPLE 2

Same facts as in Example 1, except that Jenny purchases the warranty from a third party. The third party must include the $900 in income in 20x1. The rule that allows the deferral of income to the next tax year does not apply to warranties offered by third parties.

EXAMPLE 3

On August 1, 20x1, an accrual basis taxpayer, Dance Studio, received $1,800 for 36 dance lessons. Eight lessons are given in 20x1. On its 20x1 tax return, Dance Studio reports $400 ($1,800/36 × 8). It reports the rest ($1,800 – $400 = $1,400) in 20x2.

EXAMPLE 4

On April 6, 20x1, accrual basis taxpayer, Golf World, received $2,400 for 48 golf lessons under a two-year contract. Ten lessons are given in 20x1, 20 were given in 20x2, and 15 were given in 20x3. The customer forfeited the last three lessons. On its 20x1 tax return, Golf World reports income of $500 ($2,400/48 × 10). It reports the rest ($2,400 – $500 = $1,900) in 20x2. The fact that some of the services were provided in 20x3 (or never provided at all) does not affect the timing of when the $2,400 is reported in gross income.

¶302 Employee Compensation

Employee compensation includes wages, salaries, commissions, bonuses, and tips. Employers inform their employees of their taxable compensation for the year on Form W-2. Employees include the amount reported in the box labeled "Wages, tips, other compensation" from Form W-2 on their tax returns. Employees can report compensation on Form 1040EZ, Form 1040A, or Form 1040. Students who receive scholarships add the taxable amount to their wages. Thus, these too can be reported on any of the three tax returns. The tax laws that govern scholarship income are discussed in ¶401.05. Form W-2 is illustrated in Figure 13-3 (¶1303.03).

¶302.01 FEES, BONUSES, COMMISSIONS, SALARIES, AND WAGES

Compensation is something received in exchange for services rendered. Most compensation is taxable, regardless of the form it takes. When a person receives compensation in the form of property, the Code taxes its fair market value (FMV). For example, when a person speaks at a conference and is paid by being given free merchandise, the speaker includes the FMV of the merchandise in gross income.

Fair market value (FMV) is the price that a willing buyer will pay and a willing seller will accept. FMV assumes that neither the buyer nor the seller must buy or sell. It also assumes that the buyer and the seller have reasonable knowledge of all necessary facts. In the absence of an actual sale or exchange, FMV can be determined by an expert appraisal or other supporting evidence.

Unless an exclusion applies, an employee who provides services and receives something of value in return has taxable compensation. Taxpayers include as compensation amounts withheld from their pay for social security, Medicare, and income taxes. Compensation also includes amounts withheld to pay insurance premiums, union dues, etc. Unless specifically exempt by the tax laws, compensation includes all employee fringe benefits (noncash compensation provided by employers, discussed in the next chapter at ¶401.03).

¶302.02 TIPS

The Code taxes tips as other compensation. This includes cash tips and credit card tips received from customers or other employees. Taxpayers who receive tips must follow special reporting rules.

Reporting Tips to the Employer

Employees are expected to file tip reports with their employers by the 10th day of the month that follows the month in which they receive the tips. However, employers may require more frequent reporting. Employers add reported tip income to wages on the employee's Form W-2. Thus, employees who receive tips in December 20x1 and report the tips to their employers in January 20x2 will have these tips added to the wages reported on their 20x2 Form W-2. When employees fail to turn in tip reports, they must add their unreported tips to their wages in the year they receive the tips.

Tips of Less than $20

Employees who receive less than $20 in tips during the month while working for one employer do not need to tell the employer about that month's tips. Although employees must add these tips to their wages on their tax returns, they do not pay social security or Medicare taxes on these tips.

EXAMPLE 5

Rodney works for a hotel. Sometimes hotel guests give him tips. However, his total tips are always less than $20 a month. Rodney's tips for the year total $165. He adds this amount to his taxable wages when he files his tax return. Although Rodney pays income tax on his tip income, he does not pay social security or Medicare taxes on the $165.

Tips of $20 or More

An employee who receives $20 or more in tips during the month while working for one employer must report that month's tips to the employer. The employer adds reported tips to the employee's wages and withholds social security and Medicare taxes, as well as income taxes on the reported amounts.

Employees who have monthly tips of $20 or more but fail to report them to their employers add the unreported tips to their wages on Form 1040. Employees then compute social security and Medicare taxes on their unreported tips on Form 4137, Social Security and Medicare Tax on Unreported Tip Income. These social security and Medicare taxes are added to the employee's other taxes on page 2 of Form 1040. Employees must attach Form 4137 to their tax returns.

Allocating Tips to Employees

The government assumes that food and beverage servers earn tips equal to at least 8% of gross sales. When employees of certain large restaurants and bars report less than this amount to their employers, the employers must pay their employees the difference and report it as additional income on the employees' Form W-2. These "allocated tips" appear on Form W-2 as a separate item. Employers do not report them with wages and reported tips. Thus, employers do not withhold income, social security, or Medicare taxes on these amounts. Employees add their allocated tips to their taxable wages on Form 1040. They then complete and attach Form 4137 to their tax return to pay social security and Medicare taxes on their allocated tip income.

Allocating tips usually applies to businesses that employ more than ten persons on a typical business day. Only businesses that serve food or beverages on the premises and have regular tipping customers are subject to this rule. Cafeterias and fast-food restaurants are exempt from this rule.

¶303 Business Activities

Amounts independent contractors and business owners receive for their goods and services are reported as business income on Schedule C, Profit or Loss From Business (Sole Proprietorship). Deductible business expenses are also reported on Schedule C. Schedule C is the focus of Chapter 7. Special rules apply to farming because of the unique activities associated with growing crops, raising animals, and maintaining land and other resources. Thus, income and expenses from farming activities are reported on Schedule F, Profit or Loss From Farming, rather than Schedule C.

¶304 Divorce and Separation Agreements

When a married couple gets a divorce or becomes legally separated, three financial issues arise:

1. Division of marital property (property settlement)
2. Spousal support (alimony)
3. Support of the children (child support)

¶304.01 PROPERTY SETTLEMENT

A property settlement involves the transfer of cash and other property between spouses or former spouses during the process of splitting up marital assets. Neither party reports income or deductions on these transfers. The transferee's investment ("tax basis") in the property received is the same as that of the transferor.

EXAMPLE 6

Tim and Cher Hudsen's divorce was finalized during the year. As part of the divorce decree, Tim transfers to Cher title to the couple's vacation home. At the time of the transfer the home is worth $250,000. Tim bought the home prior to their marriage. He paid $110,000 for the home. Cher does not report gross income on the transfer. Her tax basis in the home is $110,000. Cher uses this to determine her taxable gain when she later sells the home.

¶304.02 ALIMONY

Spousal support (alimony) is taxable to the recipient and deductible by the payer. A person receiving spousal support reports it as "Alimony received" on Form 1040. The payer deducts the same amount for AGI and provides the IRS with the recipient's social security number (SSN). The IRS charges the taxpayer $50 for failure to report the recipient's SSN. Taxpayers cannot use Form 1040EZ or Form 1040A to report either the receipt or payment of alimony.

For separations and divorces that occur after 1984, payments to a spouse or former spouse must meet several conditions in order to qualify as alimony:

1. The payment must be made in cash.
2. The payment cannot be for child support.
3. The payment must be required under a legal divorce decree or a separate maintenance or divorce instrument.
4. The governing decree or instrument must not label payments as something other than alimony.
5. The payer must not be required to make payments after the recipient's death.
6. The parties cannot be living in the same household at the time of the payment.

A different set of rules applies to divorces and separations occurring before 1985. These rules can be found in IRS Publication 504.

¶304.03 CHILD SUPPORT

The Code excludes child support payments from gross income. The exclusion applies to payments clearly labeled as child support as well as those that can be implied as child support. For example, if payments to a former spouse decline when the child reaches age 18, the tax law treats the amount of the reduction as child support. When the total alimony and child support payments are less than the required amount, payments first apply toward child support. For a divorce or separation before 1985, child support must be clearly labeled in the agreement. Otherwise, the payments are treated as alimony.

EXAMPLE 7

Bud and Suzie divorced in 2014. As part of the divorce decree, Bud is to pay Suzie $1,600 each month. The agreement states that $700 represents support for their 8-year-old son. During the year, Bud pays Suzie $19,200 ($1,600 × 12). Suzie reports in gross income the $10,800 she received that represents alimony ($1,600 – $700 = $900 × 12). Bud deducts this same amount for AGI on his tax return and gives the IRS Suzie's SSN.

EXAMPLE 8

Same facts as in Example 7, except that the divorce decree states that the entire $1,600 payment represents alimony. However, Bud's payments drop to $900 once the son turns 18. The tax laws treat the $700 reduction in payments as child support. Since $8,400 of the total payments ($700 × 12) is considered nontaxable child support, Suzie reports $10,800 ($19,200 – $8,400) in gross income as alimony. Bud deducts this same $10,800 for AGI.

EXAMPLE 9

Same facts as in Example 7, except that Bud fails to make two of his required payments during the year. Suzie receives $16,000 ($1,600 × 10 monthly payments) during the year. Of this amount, $8,400 is considered to be child support ($700 × 12). Suzie reports $7,600 ($16,000 – $8,400) in gross income as alimony. Bud deducts this same $7,600 for AGI.

¶305 Distributions from Traditional IRAs

Persons who stop working often pay their expenses during their retirement years from a variety of sources, including amounts saved and invested during their working years. Common sources of income retirees may receive include social security benefits, distributions from retirement plans, and earnings from investments. The tax laws regarding these types of income are discussed in ¶¶305-311.

Individual retirement arrangements (IRAs) are a type of retirement account. Unlike pension plans that are offered through and often funded by an employer, IRAs are set up and funded by the worker. There are two types of IRAs: traditional IRAs and Roth IRAs. The most attractive feature of IRAs is that earnings from these accounts are not taxed when earned. Instead, these earnings are either taxed when taken out (traditional IRAs) or never taxed at all (Roth IRAs).

Persons with earned income can contribute to an IRA. Earned income includes wages, net income from self-employment, and alimony. Some people can deduct amounts they contribute to a traditional IRA, whereas contributions to a Roth IRA are never deductible. Those who cannot make deductible contributions to their traditional IRAs can still make nondeductible contributions. The rules regarding the deductibility of contributions to traditional IRAs are discussed in Chapter 4 (¶402.11). Because the earnings taken out of Roth IRAs are excluded from gross income, the tax laws regarding contributions to and distributions from Roth IRAs are discussed along with other gross income exclusions in Chapter 4 (¶401.09). The discussion that follows pertains solely to distributions from traditional IRAs.

Deductible contributions to an IRA are made with "pre-tax" dollars, which means that these amounts have yet to be taxed. Nondeductible contributions, on the other hand, are made with "after-tax" dollars. To illustrate this distinction, assume a person with $10,000 of wages contributes $2,000 to an IRA. If the $2,000 is deducted for AGI, the person's AGI only increases by $8,000 ($10,000 – $2,000). Deductible contributions are made with what is called "pre-tax" dollars, as only $8,000 of the $10,000 has been taxed at this point. In contrast, AGI would include the entire $10,000 if the $2,000 contribution were not deductible. Hence, nondeductible contributions are made with previously taxed, or "after-tax" dollars.

When a taxpayer withdrawals amounts from a traditional IRA, only the amount that has not been previously taxed is included in gross income. If no nondeductible contributions were ever made, then the entire distribution came entirely from a combination of deductible contributions and earnings. Thus, all amounts withdrawn would be taxable. However, if nondeductible contributions were made, then the portion of the distribution that represents nondeductible contributions is not taxed again. Taxpayers use the following formula to compute the nontaxable portion of their distributions.

$$\frac{\textbf{Balance of nondeductible contributions}}{\textbf{Value of the IRA}} \times \textbf{Distribution} = \textbf{Nontaxable distribution}$$

The numerator in the fraction represents the amount of nondeductible contributions that remain in the IRA account. Right before the very first distribution from the account is made, this amount is the total of all nondeductible contributions the taxpayer made over the years. Once distributions begin, this amount is reduced each year by the nontaxable portion of the distribution (as computed using the formula above). Thus, it is up to the taxpayer to keep track of the nondeductible contributions that are still left in the IRA account. The denominator in the fraction is the value in the IRA account, which is measured as account balance at the end of the year plus the withdrawals made during the year.

EXAMPLE 10

Over the years, Peter made nondeductible contributions to his traditional IRA. At the beginning of the year, he had yet to withdraw $40,000 of his nondeductible contributions. At the end of the year, the value of the assets in the IRA was $120,000. During the year, Peter withdrew $30,000 from the account. Using the above formula, Peter computes his $8,000 nontaxable distribution ($40,000/($120,000 + $30,000) × $30,000). Only $22,000 of the distribution is included in Peter's gross income ($30,000 – $8,000).

EXAMPLE 11

Same facts as in Example 10, except that all of Peter's contributions were deductible. Peter includes the entire $30,000 distribution in his gross income.

¶305.01 AVOIDING PENALTIES

The timing of when distributions from a traditional IRA are made is important, as penalties are imposed on withdrawals taken either too early or too late. A 10% penalty is imposed on taxpayers who take a distribution before reaching age 59½. This penalty can be avoided if the early distribution is:

1. Due to the IRA owner's death or disability,
2. Made as part of a series of equal periodic payments over the owner's life expectancy (or the joint life expectancies of the owner and the owner's spouse),
3. Used to pay unreimbursed qualified medical expenses in excess of the AGI floor,
4. Used by an unemployed IRA owner to buy health insurance for the owner, the owner's spouse, or the owner's dependents,
5. Used to pay qualified higher education expenses,
6. Used to pay expenses as a qualified first-time homebuyer ($10,000 lifetime limit), or
7. Made as part of a qualified distribution by a military reservist called up to active duty.

A penalty is also imposed if the taxpayer waits too long before starting to take (and paying taxes on) distributions. Taxpayers are required to start taking distributions from their traditional IRAs in the year they turn 70½. However, the first distribution can be delayed until as late as April 1 of the next year. This exception only applies to the first distribution, and if selected, in the year after the taxpayer turns 70½, the taxpayer must make both the first and second year distributions. For example, a taxpayer who reaches age 70½ in 20x1 has until April 1, 20x2 to make the first required distribution. The taxpayer then has until December 31, 20x2 to make the second required distribution. Alternatively, the taxpayer can take the first distribution prior to the end of 20x1 and spread out the first two distributions over two tax years. At the time distributions are required to start, the taxpayer may choose to withdraw the entire balance in the account, or start receiving periodical distributions over the taxpayer's life expectancy. Failure to make the required minimum distributions results in a penalty equal to 50% of the shortage.

¶305.02 REPORTING TRADITIONAL IRA DISTRIBUTIONS

Persons who receive distributions from IRAs receive Form 1099-R, Distributions from Pensions, Annuities, Retirement or Profit-Sharing Plans, IRAs, Insurance Contracts, etc. This form shows the total distributions received during the year, and sometimes provides the taxable amount. The taxable amount is the total distribution minus the nontaxable amount computed using the formula from ¶305.

Taxpayers can use Form 1040 or Form 1040A to report their distributions from traditional IRAs. However, if the 10% early withdrawal penalty is imposed, the taxpayer must use Form 1040 and report both the distribution and the penalty. Form 1040EZ cannot be used by persons who receive a distribution from a traditional IRA. Taxpayers report on the tax return both their total distribution and the taxable amount.

¶306 Pensions and Annuities

Two other common sources of a retiree's income are pension benefits and annuity income. Each of these is discussed in the sections that follow.

¶306.01 PENSIONS

Retired workers receive a pension if they participated in their employer's pension plan during their working years. Persons receiving a pension get a series of cash payments (benefits) that last for the rest of their lives. Many pensions pay benefits for the lives of the retiree's spouse as well. Often, contributions to the employee's pension plan were made either by the employee with pre-tax amounts or by the employer. The pension benefits from these plans have never been taxed and are 100% taxable when paid to the retiree. However, if any of the employee's contributions were made with after-tax dollars, a formula similar to that used to compute the nontaxable portion of IRA withdrawals must be used to determine the nontaxable pension benefits.

Each year, employers send retirees a Form 1099-R. This form shows the total benefits paid during the year. Often the employer is able to provide the retiree with both the taxable and non-taxable portions of those benefits. Persons who started receiving their pensions from a qualified retirement plan after November 18, 1996 use the following formula to compute the nontaxable portion of their monthly pension benefits.

$$\frac{\textbf{After-tax contributions}}{\textbf{Number of monthly payments}} = \textbf{Nontaxable amount}$$

If the number of payments is fixed, the number of payments is used as the denominator. However, most pension benefits are paid for the rest of the retiree's life, and thus, the number of expected monthly payments is used in the denominator. The number of expected monthly payments is based on the retiree's age when payments begin and determined from the following table:

Age as of the Starting Date	Number of Expected Monthly Payments
55 and under	360
56–60	310
61–65	260
66–70	210
71 and over	160

When benefits are paid over the lives of both the retiree and the retiree's spouse, the number of expected monthly payments is determined by the couple's combined ages using the following table.

Combined Age as of the Starting Date	Number of Expected Monthly Payments
110 and under	410
111–120	360
121–130	310
131–140	260
141 and over	210

When the payments are not made on a monthly basis, the numbers from these tables must be adjusted. For example, if the payments are quarterly, the number of payments from the table is divided by four.

These procedures apply only to qualified pension plans where some or all of the taxpayer's contributions have already been taxed. If no taxes have been paid on any of the contributions into the plan, all payments (benefits) are taxed.

EXAMPLE 12

On July 1, 20x1, Jason (age 65) retired and started receiving $4,000 a month from his employer's pension plan. Based on his age, Jason is expected to receive 260 payments over his lifetime. Over the years, Jason had contributed $124,800 to the plan with after-tax dollars. Each month, the nontaxable portion of Jason's payment is $480 ($124,800/260 payments). Thus, for 20x1 his total benefits are $24,000 ($4,000 × 6). His taxable amount is $21,120 ($24,000 – ($480 × 6)). He includes the $21,120 in gross income. For 20x2, Jason's total benefits are $48,000 ($4,000 × 12). His taxable amount is $42,240 ($48,000 – ($480 × 12)). He includes the $42,240 in his gross income for 20x2.

EXAMPLE 13

Same facts as in Example 12, except that Jason is married and his wife is age 62 at the time he begins receiving his pension. The pension benefits will continue for both Jason and his wife's lives. Based on their combined age of 127, this is expected to be 310 months. Each month, the nontaxable portion of the payment is $402.58 ($124,800/310). Thus, for 20x1 taxable amount of their pension benefits is $21,585 ($24,000 – ($402.58 × 6)). For 20x2, the taxable amount is $43,169 ($48,000 – ($402.58 × 12)).

Taxpayers report both the total and taxable pension benefits on Form 1040A or Form 1040. Form 1040EZ cannot be used by taxpayers who receive pension benefits.

Because the formula for determining the nontaxable pension payments uses life expectancy tables, it is possible that the payments will continue beyond the expected number of payments. Likewise, they could stop before the full amount of the after-tax contributions has been recovered. For pensions starting after November 18, 1996, any payments received beyond the number of payments used in the formula are fully taxable. If payments stop before the last of the number of payments used in the formula, any unrecovered contribution amounts are taken as an itemized deduction on the final income tax return of the deceased.

EXAMPLE 14

Going back to the facts in Example 12, assume that Jason dies on April 9, 20x9. At the time of his death, Jason had received 94 of the 260 payments he was expected to receive over his lifetime. For 20x9, Jason's final income tax return shows total pension benefits of $16,000 ($4,000 × 4) and taxable benefits of $14,080 ($16,000 – ($480 × 4)). The $14,080 is included in gross income. The unrecovered contributions of $79,680 ($124,800 – ($480 × 94)) are taken as an itemized deduction on Jason's 20x9 final tax return.

¶306.02 ANNUITIES

Recipients of annuity payments pay for the right to receive cash payments for the rest of their lives (life annuity) or for a set period of time (term annuity). The amount paid for this right is typically made with after-tax dollars. Thus, the portion of each annuity payment that comes from these previously taxed amounts is not taxed again. These amounts are a return of the recipient's previously taxed investment in the annuity. The formula used to determine the nontaxable portion of the annuity payments is as follows:

$$\frac{\textbf{Amount paid for the annuity}}{\textbf{Total expected return}} \times \textbf{Amount received} = \textbf{Nontaxable proceeds}$$

When computing the total expected return for a life annuity, life expectancy tables are used to estimate how long the recipient is expected to live (and how many payments are estimated to be made). For a term annuity, the term of the annuity is used to compute the expected return. Once determined, the ratio in the formula does not change. For annuities starting after 1986, this ratio is used each year until the recipient has recovered the entire investment in the annuity. After that, all payments are subject to tax. If the payments are based on the recipient's life expectancy, and the recipient dies before recovering his or her entire investment, the tax laws allow the unrecovered amounts to be deducted as an itemized deduction on the deceased's final tax return. For annuities that started before 1987, the formula is used until the payments cease, and no deduction is allowed for any unrecovered amounts.

EXAMPLE 15

Late last year, Sally purchased a life annuity for $72,000. The annuity pays equal annual installments of $8,000 beginning January 1 of the current year. Sally's life expectancy is 12 years. She computes the taxable portion of each payment as follows:

Investment in contract	$72,000
Expected return ($8,000 × 12 years)	÷ $96,000
Exclusion percentage	75%
Amount received during a year	$8,000
Less: Exclusion ($8,000 × 75%)	(6,000)
Taxable portion	$2,000

For the first 12 years, Sally includes $2,000 in gross income from the annuity. After the 12th year, she includes all $8,000 in gross income each year. If Sally should die before receiving the 12th payment, she would deduct the unrecovered portion of her $72,000 investment in the annuity as an itemized deduction on her final tax return.

¶307 Social Security Benefits

Nine out of every 10 persons age 65 or older receive social security benefits. Dependents of these persons also receive social security benefits until they turn 18. Other persons who receive social security benefits are disabled workers and dependents of disabled workers until they turn 18.

Many social security recipients are not taxed on the benefits they receive. Some, however, must include a portion of their social security benefits in gross income. Depending on the amount of the taxpayer's "revised AGI," they can be taxed on 50% to 85% of their social security benefits. Examples 16–18 show how the taxable portion of social security benefits is computed.

EXAMPLE 16

Derrick May is unmarried. His adjusted gross income (AGI) is $31,500, not including $13,500 of social security benefits. Derrick also has $3,500 of tax-exempt interest.

1. AGI before social security	$31,500
2. Plus: 50% of social security benefits (50% × $13,500)	6,750
3. Plus: Tax-exempt interest	3,500
4. Revised AGI	$41,750
5. Less: Base amount*	(25,000)
** $32,000 MFJ; $0 MFS and lived with spouse during part of the year; $25,000 all others*	
6. Excess Revised AGI	$16,750
7. 50% of excess Revised AGI (from line 6)	$ 8,375
8. Tentative taxable social security benefits (lesser of line 2 or line 7)	$ 6,750

If Revised AGI (line 4) does not exceed the threshold amount ($44,000 for MFJ; $0 for MFS taxpayers who lived with spouse during part of the year; $34,000 for all others), the amount on line 8 equals the taxable social security benefits. If Revised AGI exceeds the threshold amount, the following calculations are required.

9. The lesser of the amount from line 8 or a set amount ($6,000 for MFJ; $0 for MFS and lived with spouse any part of the year; $4,500 for all others)	$ 4,500
10. Plus: 85% × ($41,750 Revised AGI – $34,000 threshold for unmarried taxpayers)	6,588
11. Sum of lines 9 and 10	$11,088
12. 85% of social security benefits (85% × $13,500)	$ 11,475
13. Taxable social security benefits (lesser of line 11 or line 12)	$11,088

EXAMPLE 17

Same facts as in Example 16, except Derrick is married and files a joint return with his wife.

1. AGI before social security	$31,500
2. Plus: 50% of social security benefits	6,750
3. Plus: Tax-exempt interest	3,500
4. Revised AGI	$41,750
5. Less: Base amount ($32,000 for MFJ)	(32,000)
6. Excess Revised AGI	$ 9,750
7. 50% of excess Revised AGI (from line 6)	$ 4,875
8. Tentative taxable social security benefits (lesser of line 2 or line 7)	$ 4,875

Since the Mays' Revised AGI (line 4) does not exceed the $44,000 threshold for MFJ taxpayers, the Mays' taxable social security benefits equal the $4,875 from line 8.

EXAMPLE 18

Same facts as in Example 17, except that Derrick files separately from his wife, whom he lived with during part of the year. Derrick computes his $11,475 of taxable social security benefits as follows.

1. AGI before social security	$31,500
2. Plus: 50% of social security benefits	6,750
3. Plus: Tax-exempt interest	3,500
4. Revised AGI	$41,750
5. Less: Base amount ($0 since MFS and lived with spouse part of the year)	(0)
6. Excess Revised AGI	$41,750
7. 50% of excess Revised AGI (from line 4)	$20,875
8. Tentative taxable social security benefits (lesser of line 2 or line 7)	$ 6,750

Since Derrick's Revised AGI (line 4) exceeds the $0 threshold for MFS taxpayers who lived with spouse during part of the year, he must complete lines 9–13.

9. The lesser of line 8 or $0 threshold	$ 0
10. Plus: 85% × ($41,750 Revised AGI – $0 threshold)	35,488
11. Sum of lines 9 and 10	$35,488
12. 85% of social security benefits	$ 11,475
13. Taxable social security benefits (lesser of line 11 or line 12)	$ 11,475

Taxpayers who receive social security benefits report both gross and taxable amounts on either Form 1040A or Form 1040. Form 1040EZ cannot be used by taxpayers who receive social security benefits.

¶308 Interest Income

Interest represents a charge for the use of money. Gross income includes interest received on bank deposits, notes, mortgages, corporate bonds, and U.S. savings bonds. Gross income also includes interest on income tax refunds. In some cases, the IRS requires taxpayers to impute interest income on low interest or no interest loans. Unless an exception applies, all interest is included in gross income. One example of an exception is the interest from municipal bonds, which the tax laws exempt from gross income. Other exclusions are discussed in Chapter 4.

¶308.01 SAVINGS ACCOUNTS AND CERTIFICATES

Gross income includes interest depositors receive from banks. This includes interest received on certificates of deposit (CDs). When a bank credits a depositor's account with interest, a cash basis depositor includes the interest in gross income under the constructive receipt rule (¶301). Once the interest has been credited to the account, it belongs to the taxpayer and is taxable at that time.

¶308.02 U.S. SAVINGS BONDS

The federal government issues U.S. savings bonds. Investors can buy Series EE savings bonds by paying a fraction of their face value (amount paid at maturity). They then redeem the bonds for full face value at maturity. The difference between the cost of the bond and its face value represents interest (the amount paid to investors for the use of their money). Investors can also buy Series I savings bonds from the government. These bonds are purchased at face value. Interest on Series I bonds accrues every three months. The accrued interest is added to the redemption value of the bond.

The tax laws allow cash-basis investors two options for reporting the interest on U.S. savings bonds. The first option is to wait until they redeem the bonds to report all accrued (accumulated) interest. Under this option, the difference between the redemption amount (which includes accrued interest) and the amount paid for the bonds would be included in gross income. Under the second option, investors can elect to report the interest in gross income as it accrues each year. The accrued interest is the difference between in the bond's redemption value at end and the start of the year. If the taxpayer elects to report the accrued interest each year, the taxpayer's investment in the bonds increases by the amounts reported in income. Whichever method is selected, it must be used for all U.S. savings bonds the taxpayer owns.

EXAMPLE 19

Carl purchases Series EE U.S. savings bonds for $500 during 20x1. The face value of the bonds is $1,000. At the end of 20x1, the redemption value of the bonds is $520; at the end of 20x2, it is $543. Carl has two options for reporting the interest on the bonds. He can wait until he redeems the bonds to report the interest. For example, if Carl waits to redeem the bonds for their $1,000 face value, he will report $500 ($1,000 – $500 purchase price) of interest in gross income in the redemption year. Alternatively, if he elects report the accrued interest each year, Carl will include $20 in gross income ($520 – $500) in 20x1 and $23 ($543 – $520) in gross income in 20x2. Carl increases his basis in the bonds by the amounts he includes in gross income.

¶308.03 U.S. TREASURY BILLS, NOTES, AND BONDS

In addition to savings bonds, the U.S. government also issues Treasury bills, Treasury notes and Treasury bonds. Treasury bills are short-term and mature in 4-, 13-, or 26-weeks. They are issued at a discount (for less than face value) in multiples of $1,000. The difference between the discounted price investors pay and the face value is interest income. Investors report the interest in gross income in the year the Treasury bill matures.

Treasury notes have maturity periods ranging from one to 10 years. Treasury bonds have maturity periods of more than 10 years. Both Treasury notes and bonds are issued in multiples of $1,000. Both pay interest every six months (semiannually). Cash basis investors report interest in gross income in the year it is paid to them. When the notes or bonds mature, investors redeem them for face value.

Sometimes Treasury notes and bonds are issued at a discount (less than face value). The difference between issue price and face value is called **original issue discount.** This amount represents additional interest income the investor earns over the life of the bond. Unless the discount is *de minimis* (small in amount), the investor reports the OID in gross income as it accrues over the life of the bond (see discussion on OID at ¶308.05). The OID reported in income is then added to the investor's basis (investment) in the bond. When the bond matures, the investor will have reported all OID in gross income and the investor's basis in the bond will equal its face value.

¶308.04 ACCRUED INTEREST

When a taxpayer purchases a bond between interest dates, the accrued interest up to the purchase date belongs to the seller. The buyer pays this interest to the seller at the time of purchase and subtracts it from the first interest payment received. The buyer then includes all future interest on the bond in gross income.

EXAMPLE 20

On October 1, 20x3, a cash basis investor pays $10,134 for bonds. The bonds were originally issued on December 1, 20x1 at their $10,000 face value. The bonds pay $200 interest on June 1 and December 1. Included in the purchase price is $134 of interest that had accrued from June 1, 20x3 – October 1, 20x3. The seller includes this amount in gross income in 20x3. On December 1, 20x3 the corporation (issuer of the bonds) pays the investor $200. The investor reports $66 ($200 – $134) in gross income on his 20x3 tax return.

¶308.05 ORIGINAL ISSUE DISCOUNT (OID) BONDS

Taxpayers that use the cash method include the interest from bonds in gross income when they receive it. However, when a corporation issues its bonds at a discount, a different situation arises for the purchasing bondholder. Because bondholders receive the full face value at maturity, they must recognize the discount (face value minus issue price) as income. One issue that arises is when this income should be reported. Another issue is whether to treat the income as ordinary interest or capital gain.

To answer these questions, the taxpayer must first determine the amount of original issue discount (OID). The Code defines OID as the difference between a bond's face value and its (original) issue price.

EXAMPLE 21

A corporation issues a 20-year, $100,000 bond for $12,861. Thus, an investor pays the corporation $12,861 for the right to receive $100,000 20 years from now. The OID equals $87,139 ($100,000 – $12,861).

The Code treats the amount of OID as $0 when the amount is de minimis (a small amount). The Code defines **de minimis OID** as less than one-fourth of 1% (0.0025) of the face value times the number of full years to maturity. When the de minimis rule applies, the holder includes the discount in income when the bond is sold or redeemed. If the bond is held as an investment (i.e., capital asset), the bondholder reports the income as a capital gain.

EXAMPLE 22

A corporation issues a 10-year, $100,000 bond for $98,000. Although the true amount of OID equals $2,000, the Code treats it as $0. The $2,000 discount falls below the OID threshold of $2,500 (.0025 × $100,000 face value of bond × 10 full years to maturity). The investor's tax basis (investment) in the bond stays at $98,000. If the investor holds the bond to maturity, at that time the $2,000 will be reported as capital gain ($100,000 face value – $98,000 basis in the bond).

When the amount of the discount exceeds the de minimis threshold, the taxpayer recognizes the OID as income over the life of the bond by including a portion of it in gross income each year. For OID bonds issued after April 3, 1993, taxpayers use the *effective interest rate method* to determine the interest earned. In making this computation, a taxpayer multiplies his investment (basis) in the bond by the interest rate, which is the rate needed to produce the desired yield. The interest must be compounded semiannually (twice a year). The taxpayer reports the difference between the resulting product and the interest actually paid on the bond as ordinary income. This amount reduces the remaining OID and increases the taxpayer's basis in the bonds. Note that this is an exception to the cash basis method of accounting because the taxpayer must recognize income long before receiving the cash.

EXAMPLE 23

On January 1, 20x1, a corporation issues a 30-year, $1,000,000 zero-coupon bond for $169,700. The annual yield to maturity equals 6%. Interest is compounded semiannually (June 30 and December 31). The bond's original issue discount equals $830,300 ($1,000,000 – $169,700). Earned interest for 20x1 is as follows:

January 1, 20x1 through June 30, 20x1 ([6% × $169,700] × 6/12)	$ 5,091
July 1, 20x1 through December 31, 20x1 ([6% × ($169,700 + $5,091 accrued interest)] × 6/12)	5,244
	$10,335

At the end of 20x1, the investor's basis in the bond is $180,035 ($169,700 + $10,335). Over the 30 years, the investor writes off the discount and recognizes interest income of $830,300. At the end of 30 years, the carrying value of the bond will equal its $1,000,000 face value ($169,700 + $830,300).

Using the method shown in Example 23, companies that issue OID bonds compute for investors the amount of OID to be included in income each year. They report this amount on Form 1099-OID, Original Issue Discount. In Example 23, the corporation issues to the investor of the $1,000,000 bond a Form 1099-OID for 20x1. On this form, the investor is told of the $10,335 of OID. This amount is reported as interest income on the investor's 20x1 tax return.

For OID bonds issued before April 4, 1993, different write-off rules apply. Also, original issue discount rules do not apply to U.S. Savings Bonds.

¶308.06 MARKET DISCOUNT BONDS

A market discount arises when an investor purchases a bond from an existing bondholder (rather than from the issuing corporation) for less than its amortized carrying value. **Amortized carrying value (ACV)** equals a bond's (original) issue price plus all OID previously included in gross income. Taxpayers purchasing a market discount bond may elect to include some of the discount as interest income each year, or wait until the bond is sold/redeemed and recognize the entire market discount as interest income at that time.

Some bondholders must deal with both OID and market discount. It is important to note that an investor must accrue the OID income over the life of the bond using the effective interest rate method. Bondholders with market discount who elect to amortize the interest may choose either the effective rate method or the straight-line method to accrue the interest.

EXAMPLE 24

On January 1, 2015, Ron pays $9,320 for 30-year corporate bonds. The bonds were originally issued on January 1, 1999 for $9,200 and have a $10,000 face value. They mature on January 1, 2029. At the time the bonds were issued, the OID was $800 ($10,000 – $9,200). This amount exceeds the $750 threshold for de minimis OID ($10,000 × .0025 × 30 years to maturity). Thus, the prior owner(s) included some of the OID in gross income each year. The amortized OID was added to the bond's ACV. As of January 1, 2015, the ACV of the bond is $9,410.

Ron purchased the bonds at a $90 market discount ($9,320 – $9,410 ACV). Ron can elect to include a share of this amount in gross income each year from 2015-2028. The amount would be taxed as interest income and would increase his basis in the bonds. His other choice is to wait until he sells the bonds or until they mature to report the $90 as interest income. As of January 1, 2015, the bond had remaining OID of $590 ($10,000 – $9,410). Each year, the corporation will issue Ron a Form 1099-OID to let him know how much of this OID he must include in gross income. Ron will increase his tax basis (investment) in the bonds by the amount of OID he includes in gross income.

¶308.07 BOND PREMIUMS ON TAXABLE BONDS

Taxpayers who purchase taxable bonds at a premium (an amount in excess of face value) can choose to offset interest income by a portion of the bond's premium each year and decrease the basis of the bond by the premium written off. Taxpayers may also choose not to write off bond premiums and report more interest income each year. This would result in a higher basis in the bonds upon sale or redemption, which translates into less gain or more loss when the bonds are sold or redeemed. The taxpayer's choice must be applied to all bonds the taxpayer owns.

EXAMPLE 25

Donna pays $102,000 for bonds that have a face value of $100,000. Donna has two options for dealing with the $2,000 premium she paid for these bonds. She can amortize the premium over the life of the bonds and reduce the amount of interest income she reports in gross income each year. If she does this, Donna will decrease her basis in the bonds by the amortized amount. At maturity, her basis would equal the face value of the bonds. Her second option is to not reduce the amount of interest she reports in gross income and keep her basis in the bonds at $102,000. If Donna holds the bonds to maturity she will report a long-term capital loss when the bonds are redeemed. If she sells the bonds prior to maturity, the difference between the amount realized from the sale and $102,000 will result in a gain or loss.

¶308.08 IMPUTED INTEREST ON BELOW-MARKET LOANS

The IRS may impute interest on loans made with no or too low of an interest rate. This means the lender must recognize interest income equal to the imputed interest, and the borrower has an implied interest payment to the lender. To impute the interest, the IRS uses the applicable federal rate (AFR) at the time the loan is made, compounded semiannually. The difference between the interest using the AFR and the interest actually paid on the loan is the amount of imputed interest.

Published Applicable Federal Rates (AFRs)

Each month the IRS publishes AFRs for short-term, mid-term, and long-term loans. Taxpayers use the short-term rates for demand loans (loans that are due upon the lender's demand) and loans with a maturity date of three years or less. They use the mid-term rates for loans with three to nine-year maturities, and long-term rates for loans maturing in more than nine years.

Potential Below-Market Loan Situations

1. Tax-avoidance loans
2. Gift loans (for example, a loan from a parent to a child)
3. Compensation-related loans between employer and employee
4. Loans between a corporation and its shareholder

Gift Loans

Loans to family members and friends (gift loans) fall under the imputed interest rules. Unless an exception applies, the IRS imputes interest on a gift loan when the interest charged is less than the AFR. The lender includes the imputed interest in gross income. Under certain conditions, the borrower may deduct the imputed interest payment as investment interest expense (discussed at ¶505.04). In addition, since the lender never actually takes possession of this interest, the tax laws assume that the lender makes annual gifts to the borrower equal to the imputed interest. Depending on the amount of the gifts, the lender may have to a file a gift tax return.

Interest is always imputed on gift loans made for tax avoidance reasons. However, for all other gift loans, the amount of imputed interest may be limited or be $0 in certain situations. The three exceptions to the imputed interest rule on gift loans are as follows.

1. No interest is imputed on gift loans of $10,000 or less, as long as the loan proceeds are not used to purchase income-producing property (like stocks, bonds, and similar property).
2. No interest is imputed on a gift loan of $100,000 or less if the borrower's net investment income for the year does not exceed $1,000. Net investment income includes taxable interest, dividends and capital gains from investments minus any deductible investment-related expenses.
3. The amount of imputed interest on a gift loan cannot exceed the borrower's net investment income for the year when the borrower's net investment income exceeds $1,000 and the amount of the loan between the individuals does not exceed $100,000.

EXAMPLE 26

Bob and Sandra Grady are saving to buy a house. Sandra's parents offer them a $10,000 interest-free loan, provided Bob and Sandra sign a ten-year note. Bob and Sandra agree to these terms. If the Gradys use the loan proceeds to make the down payment (and not to buy income-producing property), the IRS will not impute interest on the $10,000 gift loan (see Exception 1).

EXAMPLE 27

Marilyn and Rod Lange are having trouble saving enough for a down payment on a home. Marilyn's parents offer to loan them $10,000. No interest would be charged on the loan. The $10,000 would be due at the end of 10 years. The Langes intend to use the proceeds to invest in stock and bonds. They plan is to let the balance grow until they have enough for a down payment. Normally, gift loans of $10,000 or less are not subject to the imputed interest rules. However, since the proceeds were used to buy income-producing property, this exception does not apply (see Exception 1). The amount of the gift loan does not exceed $100,000. Thus, no imputed interest will be charged as long as the Langes' net investment income (NII) does not exceed $1,000 (Exception 2). If their NII exceeds $1,000, then the imputed interest is limited to the amount of the Langes' NII (Exception 3).

For example, if the Langes' NII for the year is $900, no imputed interest would be charged (see Exception 2). If, however, their NII is $1,100, then the amount of imputed interest could not exceed $1,100 (see Exception 3). Imputed interest would be the interest charged using the long-term AFR (for loans longer than nine years) less the $0 of interest the Langes are paying Marilyn's parents. Should the imputed interest rules apply, the IRS treats the Langes as having paid Marilyn's parents this amount as interest. The parents report the imputed interest in gross income. Because the proceeds were used to purchase investments, the Langes may be able to deduct this amount as investment interest expense (an itemized deduction, see ¶505.04). The parents are then deemed to make a gift to the Langes for the amount of imputed interest.

EXAMPLE 28

Same facts as in Example 27, except that the Langes do not buy income-producing property with the $10,000. Since the amount of the loan does not exceed $10,000, no interest would be imputed (see Exception 1).

EXAMPLE 29

Same facts as in Example 28, except that the parents loan the Langes $10,001. The exception for gift loans of $10,000 or less does not apply. The same reasoning as presented in Example 27 holds. Thus, as long as the Langes' NII does not exceed $1,000, no interest would be imputed (see Exception 2). However, if their NII exceeds $1,000, the amount of imputed interest cannot exceed their NII since the loan amount does not exceed $100,000 (see Exception 3).

Compensation-Related Loans

When an employer loans money to one of its employees and charges no interest or too low of an interest rate, the imputed interest rules apply if either the loan exceeds $10,000, or the loan was made for tax avoidance reasons. As with all below-market loans, the amount of imputed interest is the difference between the amount of interest computed semiannually using the AFR at the time of the loan and the actual interest paid.

In a compensation-related loan, the employee is deemed to pay the imputed interest to the employer. The employer reports the interest in gross income. Since the employee does not actually pay interest to the employer, to square things up, the employer is deemed to pay wages to the employee for the same amount. These deemed wages are included in the employee's gross income, and are deducted as wage expense on the employer's tax return. If the proceeds from the loan were used for personal reasons, the interest would be nondeductible personal interest to the employee. However, if the proceeds were used to purchase an investment, the employee may be able to deduct the interest as an itemized deduction (see discussion at ¶505.04).

EXAMPLE 30

On January 1, Backe & Co. loans $20,000 to its employee, Ross. The terms of the note require no interest to be paid and for the $20,000 to be repaid at the end of five years. At the time the loan was made, the current annual mid-term AFR (for loans between three and nine years) was 9% (4.5% semiannually). Imputed interest for the first year is $1,840.50 [($20,000 × 4.5%) + ($20,900 × 4.5%) – $0 interest paid]. Backe & Co. includes the $1,840.50 of interest in gross income. Whether Ross will be able to deduct the $1,840.50 depends on how he used the loan proceeds. Backe & Co. is then deemed to pay wages to Ross for $1,840.50 and deducts this amount as wage expense on its tax return. Ross includes the additional $1,840.50 of wages in his gross income.

Corporation-Shareholder Loans

When an employer makes a loan to one of its shareholders and charges interest below the AFR, the imputed interest rules apply if either the loan exceeds $10,000, or the loan was made for tax avoidance reasons. When the imputed interest rules apply, the shareholder is deemed to pay the imputed interest to the corporation. The corporation includes the interest in gross income. The shareholder may or may not deduct the interest expense depending on how the proceeds from the loan are used. To even things up, the corporation is deemed to pay a dividend to the shareholder for the same amount. The deemed dividends are reported as dividend income on the shareholder's tax return. There is no deduction to the corporation for dividends paid.

EXAMPLE 31

Same facts as in Example 30, except that Ross is a shareholder, instead of an employee, of Backe & Co. At the end of the year, Ross is deemed to have paid $1,840.50 of interest to Backe & Co. In turn, Backe & Co. is deemed to pay a $1,840.50 dividend to Ross. Backe & Co. includes the deemed interest in its gross income. Ross reports the deemed dividend on his tax return.

EXAMPLE 32

Same facts as in Example 31, except that the terms of the loan required Ross to pay 4% simple interest annually. Ross now pays $800 interest to Backe & Co. annually ($20,000 × 4%). At the end of the first year, Ross is deemed to have paid additional interest to Backe & Co. of $1,040.50 ($1,840.50 – $800). The imputed amount is taxed as interest income to Backe & Co. and as dividend income to Ross.

Summary of Below Market Loans

Type of Loan	Tax Consequences to the Lender	Tax Consequences to the Borrower
Gift loan	Interest income Gift tax (perhaps)	Interest expense (perhaps)
Employer-employee loan	Interest income Wage expense	Interest expense (perhaps) Wage income
Corporation-shareholder loan	Interest income	Interest expense (perhaps) Dividend income

¶308.09 REPORTING INTEREST INCOME

Taxpayers may report taxable interest income on Form 1040EZ, Form 1040A, or Form 1040. The IRS also wants to see the amount of tax-exempt interest on these forms. Normally, a taxpayer receiving interest income of $10 or more receives a Form 1099-INT, Interest Income, from the payer. This form identifies taxable interest and any state or federal tax withholding that might have taken place. Copies of Form 1099-INT go to the payee and the IRS. Taxpayers do not file this form with their returns unless tax was withheld that they are claiming as a tax payment on their tax returns. Taxpayer should keep copies of Form 1099-INT with their tax records.

Taxpayers who withdraw certificate of deposit (CD) funds before the due date pay a penalty. This penalty is a deduction for AGI (see discussion at ¶402.09). Taxpayers with an early withdraw penalty will want to file Form 1040 to deduct the penalty.

Almost all taxable interest can be reported on Form 1040A. However, Form 1040 must be used to report the following types of taxable interest.

1. When the taxpayer includes in gross income OID other than the amount reported on Form 1099-OID.
2. When the taxpayer has accrued interest on bonds bought between interest dates.
3. When the taxpayer elects to reduce interest income by writing off a bond premium.

Form 1040EZ

Form 1040EZ can only be used to report taxable interest income of $1,500 or less. If taxable interest exceeds $1,500, the taxpayer must file Form 1040A or Form 1040. Tax-exempt is reported, regardless of the amount. Form 1040EZ filers report tax-exempt interest income in the blank space after the words "Taxable interest." They write **TEI =**, followed by the amount of tax-exempt interest. However, taxpayers who exclude Educational Savings Bond interest from gross income cannot use Form 1040EZ (discussed at ¶401.06).

Form 1040A

Form 1040A filers with taxable interest income of $1,500 or less report it on the "Taxable interest" line and do not prepare a separate reporting schedule. If they have taxable interest income of more than $1,500, they complete Schedule B, Part I. Figure 3-1 shows the filled-in Schedule B interest income section. On this schedule, interest (both taxable and nontaxable) from all payers is listed separately. The taxpayer adds these amounts together and enters the total of all interest received. The taxpayer then subtracts out the total amount of tax-exempt interest and enters the difference on line 2. Note that Schedule B does not have special lines for the total and subtotals. Instead, the subtotal for total interest should be labeled as such on Schedule B. Likewise, the amount of tax-exempt interest subtracted from this subtotal should be shown with "( )" around the amount. The amount of tax-exempt interest is also reported on Form 1040A (line 8b).

Schedule B handles the exclusion for interest from educational savings bonds interest on a separate line. The interest earned from these savings bonds is listed on Schedule B (line 1). The excluded interest is computed on Form 8815, Exclusion of Interest From Series EE and I U.S. Savings Bonds Issued After 1989 (discussed at ¶401.06) before it is entered (and subtracted out) on Schedule B (line 3).

Form 1040

There are no restrictions on the amount or type of interest income that a person may report on Form 1040. When taxable interest income exceeds $1,500, the taxpayer lists each item of interest income (taxable and tax-exempt) separately on Schedule B, Part I. Tax-exempt interest is backed out on Schedule B (line 1) and reported on Form 1040 (line 8b).

¶308.10 FILLED-IN SCHEDULE B, PART I

INFORMATION FOR FIGURE 3-1:

Ruth Baker uses Part I on Schedule B to report her interest income. Ruth receives **$700** from **Erie Lake Distributing Company**, **$250** from **Buckeye Lake Brewing Company**, **$1,505** from **Franklin Company**, and **$1,010** of tax-exempt interest from **City of Madison bonds**. Ruth transfers the $2,455 of taxable interest ($3,465 total interest – $1,010 tax-exempt interest) to Form 1040A or Form 1040 (line 8a). She reports the $1,010 of tax-exempt interest on Form 1040A or Form 1040 (line 8b).

Figure 3-1: Filled-In Schedule B, Part I

SCHEDULE B (Form 1040A or 1040)
Department of the Treasury Internal Revenue Service (99)

Interest and Ordinary Dividends

▶ Attach to Form 1040A or 1040.
▶ Information about Schedule B and its instructions is at *www.irs.gov/scheduleb.*

OMB No. 1545-0074
2015
Attachment Sequence No. 08

Name(s) shown on return: Ruth O. Baker
Your social security number: 727-69-3205

				Amount
Part I Interest	1	List name of payer. If any interest is from a seller-financed mortgage and the buyer used the property as a personal residence, see instructions on back and list this interest first. Also, show that buyer's social security number and address ▶		
		Erie Lake Distributing Company		700
		Buckeye Lake Brewing Company		250
(See instructions on back and the instructions for Form 1040A, or Form 1040, line 8a.)		Franklin Company		1,505
		City of Madison bonds		1,010
		Total interest	1	3,465
		Less: Tax-exempt interest		(1,010)
Note: If you received a Form 1099-INT, Form 1099-OID, or substitute statement from a brokerage firm, list the firm's name as the payer and enter the total interest shown on that form.	2	Add the amounts on line 1	2	2,455
	3	Excludable interest on series EE and I U.S. savings bonds issued after 1989. Attach Form 8815	3	
	4	Subtract line 3 from line 2. Enter the result here and on Form 1040A, or Form 1040, line 8a . . . . ▶	4	2,455

¶309 Dividend Income

Corporations can distribute to their shareholders cash and noncash property, as well as rights to purchase more of the corporation's stock. Each year, corporations report the value of these distributions to shareholders on Form 1099-DIV, Dividends and Distributions. Distributions of a corporation's earnings and profits (E&P) are taxed to the shareholders as ordinary dividends. Any distribution in excess of E&P is treated as a return of capital to the shareholders. Mutual funds that generate income pass along each investor's share of income on Form 1099-DIV. Such income may include ordinary dividends, qualified dividends included in ordinary dividends, as well as capital gain distributions.

By definition, dividends represent a distribution of a corporation's profits to its owners (shareholders). E&P keeps a running total of a corporation's undistributed profits. When a corporation distributes cash or property in excess of its E&P, the excess is treated as a return of the shareholder's investment (basis) in the stock of the corporation (known as a return of capital distribution).

¶309.01 ORDINARY DIVIDENDS

Both cash and accrual basis shareholders include ordinary dividends in gross income in the year received. When a corporation distributes noncash property to its shareholders from its E&P, the shareholder increases gross income by the FMV of the distributed property.

Most ordinary dividends received by individual taxpayers are taxed at a reduced rate. A 0% rate applies to taxpayers in the 10% and 15% tax brackets. A 20% rate applies to those in the top 39.6% bracket, and a 15% rate applies to all other taxpayers. These dividends, called **qualified dividends**, are taxed using the same rates that apply to net capital gains. Some dividends (nonqualified dividends) are not eligible for these reduced rates. Shortly after the end of the year, corporations issue a Form 1099-DIV to each of its shareholders. On that form, the corporation reports the shareholder's total ordinary dividends and the amount of ordinary dividends that are qualified dividends.

EXAMPLE 33 James is single. His taxable income is $49,000, which includes $5,000 of qualified dividends. This level of taxable income places James in the 25% tax bracket. James's qualified dividends will be taxed at a 15% tax rate.

¶309.02 DIVIDEND REINVESTMENT PLANS

Some corporations offer shareholders dividend reinvestment plans. Under these plans, the dividends paid to the shareholder are used to buy more shares of stock in the same corporation. After the dividend, the shareholder owns more shares of stock in the corporation. The taxpayer's investment (basis) in the new shares is the amount of the taxable dividend.

EXAMPLE 34 Mona owns 300 shares of stock in ABX. Mona participates in ABX's dividend reinvestment plan. During the year, ABX pays its shareholders a $.50 dividend at a time when the stock was selling for $40 a share. Mona includes the $150 of dividends paid (300 shares owned × $.50) in her gross income. This $150 is then used to purchase 3.75 more shares of stock in ABX ($150/$40). After the dividend, Mona owns 303.75 shares of ABX stock. The $150 of qualified dividends is reported to Mona on Form 1099-DIV.

¶309.03 RETURN OF CAPITAL DISTRIBUTIONS

Distributions of cash or noncash property in excess of E&P are treated as a return of shareholders' basis in the stock. These "return-of-capital" distributions are not taxed as dividends. Instead they reduce a shareholder's tax basis in the stock until it reaches zero. Once the stock's basis has been reduced to zero, the Code taxes any additional distribution as a capital gain. The gain is long-term or short-term, depending on how long the taxpayer has owned the stock.

EXAMPLE 35

Doc Hinder is the sole shareholder in DH Corporation. Doc has owned the stock for two years. At the beginning of the year, DH has E&P of $22,000 and Doc's basis in his shares of DH was $5,000. During the year, DH distributes $30,000 to Doc. The first $22,000 is taxed as ordinary dividends (to the extent of E&P). The next $5,000 (to the extent of Doc's tax basis) is treated as a nontaxable return of capital. The last $3,000 ($30,000 – $22,000 – $5,000) is taxed as long-term capital gain.

¶309.04 REPORTING DIVIDEND INCOME

Individual taxpayers may use Form 1040A or Form 1040 to report dividend income. Both Form 1040A and Form 1040 have separate lines for ordinary dividends (those included in gross income) and for qualified dividends (those taxed at a reduced rate). When the taxpayer's taxable dividends exceed $1,500, Schedule B must be completed. Figure 3-2 illustrates Schedule B, Part II, where dividend income is reported. Capital gains distributions are usually reported on Schedule D (Form 1040), Capital Gain or Loss.

¶309.05 FILLED-IN SCHEDULE B, PART II

INFORMATION FOR FIGURE 3-2:

Jackie Heard uses Part II on Schedule B to report the ordinary dividends she received during the year. Jackie received dividends of **$530** from **Bay Weaving Company** and **$1,340** from **Pike Moving Company**. She transfers the $1,870 of ordinary dividends to her tax return (Form 1040A or Form 1040 (line 9a)). She then enters the amount of qualified dividends included in the $1,870 on her tax return (Form 1040A or Form 1040 (line 9b)). This amount is reported to her on Form 1099-DIV, Dividends and Distributions.

Figure 3-2: Filled-In Schedule B, Part II

Part II	5	List name of payer ▶		
		Bay Weaving Company		530
Ordinary Dividends		Pike Moving Company		1,340
(See instructions on back and the instructions for Form 1040A, or Form 1040, line 9a.)			5	
Note. If you received a Form 1099-DIV or substitute statement from a brokerage firm, list the firm's name as the payer and enter the ordinary dividends shown on that form.	6	Add the amounts on line 5. Enter the total here and on Form 1040A, or Form 1040, line 9a . . . . ▶	6	1,870
	Note.	If line 6 is over $1,500, you must complete Part III.		

¶310 Gains and Losses

When taxpayers sell or exchange property, a gain or loss results. As a rule, taxpayers report on their tax returns all gains, but they report losses only from sales or exchanges of investment or business property.

In theory, recognized gains are included in gross income and recognized losses are deducted for AGI. On the tax return, gain and losses are netted against one another and only the net gain or loss appears on the tax return. However, an individual can only deduct up to $3,000 of capital losses in excess of capital gains each year. Chapters 10 and 11 describe the calculation of gains and losses, as well as the tax forms where they appear.

¶311 Rents and Royalties

Gross income includes rent and royalty income. The tax law allows ordinary, necessary, and reasonable rental expenses to offset rental income on the tax return. However, limits on the deductions may apply. The rules governing rental property are discussed in Chapter 9.

¶312 Unemployment Compensation

Unemployed workers may receive unemployment compensation. Unemployment compensation is taxable and reported on Form 1040A or Form 1040. It cannot be reported on Form 1040EZ.

¶313 Other Sources of Income

The topics discussed thus far in the chapter are not an exhaustive list of income items. Recall that income is any item that increases the taxpayer's net worth. Examples of other items of income include certain state and local refunds, illegal income, and gambling winnings.

¶313.01 STATE AND LOCAL INCOME TAX REFUNDS

When taxpayers get back amounts they deducted in a prior tax year, the amounts they are refunded may be subject to tax. The **tax benefit rule** gets its name because the amounts refunded are included in gross income if the taxpayer benefited from deducting these amounts in a prior tax year. A "benefit" results if the deduction reduced the taxpayer's taxes in that year. In years in which taxpayers report negative taxable income, normally there is no tax benefit. When the deduction involves an itemized deduction, the amount recovered is not taxable if the taxpayer took the standard deduction in the prior year. Even when the taxpayer itemized, the recovered amounts are taxable only to the extent that they resulted in less taxes paid.

The tax benefit rule applies to refunds of state and local income taxes. Taxpayers deduct as an itemized deduction amounts they pay during the year for state or local income taxes. This includes amounts employers withhold from their pay, as well as any other payments for state and local income taxes that they make during the year. Amounts withheld from employees' paychecks in 20x1 to cover their state and local income taxes owed for the 20x1 tax year are deducted as itemized deductions on their 20x1 federal income tax return.

Like the federal income tax return, taxpayers file their state and local tax returns in the next tax year. Thus, a taxpayer's 20x1 state income tax return is not due until 20x2. As a result, taxpayers that overpay their 20x1 income taxes do not receive their refunds until the next tax year. The tax benefit rule requires that a refund of state or local income taxes be included in gross income in the year received if the taxpayer "benefited" from taking a deduction for the amount in a prior tax year. In the year a taxpayer receives a state or local income tax refund, the amount included in gross income is the *lesser of* (i) the amount refunded or (ii) the taxpayer's excess itemized deductions.

EXAMPLE 36

Rory, age 46 and single, deducted $4,260 for state income taxes on his 2014 federal income tax return. Rory has excellent vision. In 2015, he received a state income tax refund of $700. On his 2014 tax return, Rory deducted itemized deductions of $9,313. His excess itemized deductions were $3,113 ($9,313 – $6,200 standard deduction for single taxpayers in 2014). Thus, he includes in gross income the *lesser of* (i) the $700 refunded amount, or (ii) his $3,113 of excess itemized deductions. Rory includes $700 in gross income in 2015.

¶313.02 ILLEGAL INCOME

Income from illegal activities is included in gross income. Taxpayers may deduct the ordinary and necessary business expenses (rents, wages, utilities, etc.) required to produce this income. However, illegal payments (bribes to police and judges) are not deductible. In the case of illegal drug trafficking, the cost of goods sold reduces gross receipts to yield gross income, but no other costs are deductible.

EXAMPLE 37

Riley operates an illegal gambling business. During the year, he generated $93,000 of income. His ordinary and necessary expenses related to his business totaled $32,000. Riley is required to report the $61,000 of profits from his business on his tax return. If he fails to report this amount to the IRS, he faces stiff penalties imposed on tax evaders.

¶313.03 GAMBLING WINNINGS

Gross income includes gambling winnings. Casual gamblers may claim an itemized deduction for gambling losses up to the amounts of their winnings. Professional gamblers can deduct their gambling losses (to the extent of their winnings) for AGI.

EXAMPLE 38

An amateur poker player wins $1.2 million at a poker event in Las Vegas. During the same year, the taxpayer can document $230,000 of gambling losses. On his tax return, the taxpayer includes the $1.2 million on Form 1040 as "Other income." He then deducts $230,000 of gambling losses as an itemized deduction.

EXAMPLE 39

Same facts as in Example 38, except that the taxpayer's documented gambling losses total $1.5 million. The taxpayer still includes the $1.2 million on Form 1040 as "Other income." He deducts $1.2 million as an itemized deduction.

¶313.04 OTHER INCOME

Gross income includes amounts taxpayers receive from contests, raffles, and similar promotions. It also includes the value of door prizes and employee awards. A limited exclusion (up to $400) exists for awards employees receive for length of service and safety achievement. These awards must be in the form of personal property (not cash). Unless de minimis rules apply (see ¶401.03), gross income includes all other awards or prizes from employers. Taxpayers include noncash prizes and awards in gross income at their FMV.

Gross income includes awards in recognition of past religious, charitable, scientific, educational, artistic, literary, or civic achievements. Such awards include the Pulitzer Prize and the Nobel Peace Prize. The only way these types of prizes can avoid being taxed is if the recipient immediately assigns the award to a qualified governmental unit or tax-exempt charity.

Taxpayers who enter into a business with the intent to make a profit usually report the activities from the business on Schedule C (¶303). However, sometimes the activity does not rise to the level of a bona fide business, and is instead treated as a hobby. Since all sources of income are taxable unless the tax laws state otherwise, hobby income must be reported in gross income. Hobby income is reported on the line designated as "Other income" on Form 1040 (page 1). The tax treatment of the expenses related to hobby activities are discussion in Chapter 6 (¶603.01).

¶314 "Kiddie Tax"

Certain children with unearned income may find some of that income taxed at their parents' higher tax rate. Unearned income is basically investment income from sources such as dividends, interest, capital gains, rents, royalties, and annuities. The parent's higher tax rate applies only to the child's **net unearned income.** The child's tax rate (from the Tax Tables) determines the tax on the child's remaining taxable income.

Total unearned income		
Less: $1,050		
Less: The *greater of*	**(i)**	**$1,050 standard deduction or**
	(ii)	**Itemized deductions directly related to the production of the unearned income**
Equals: Net Unearned Income		

The child's total tax for the year is the sum of (i) net unearned income taxed at the parent's higher tax rate and (ii) remaining taxable income taxed at the child's tax rate. Any qualified dividends and net capital gain are taxed at the parent's reduced tax rate (0%, 15% or 20%).

This "kiddie tax" does not apply to children who do not have at least one living parent or stepparent. It also does not apply to married children who file a joint tax return with their spouse. For all others, the kiddie tax applies in 2015 to children under age 18 who have unearned income of more than $2,100. It also applies to children who are 18 years old or full-time students between the ages of 19 and 23 who have unearned income in excess of $2,100 and whose earned income does not exceed 50% of their total support for the year. The kiddie tax is calculated on Form 8615, Tax for Certain Children Who Have Unearned Income (see Figure 3-3).

EXAMPLE 40

During 2015, Betsy, age 17, has interest income of $3,200 and wages of $4,000. Betsy's parents are in the 35% tax bracket and claim Betsy as a dependent on their joint tax return. Total support for Betsy during the year was $7,600. Betsy's taxable income is $2,850 ($3,200 + $4,000 = $7,200 AGI – $4,350 standard deduction for dependents – $0 personal exemption). Since Betsy is under the age of 18 and has unearned income in excess of $2,100, she is subject to the kiddie tax. She will pay tax on her $1,100 of net unearned income ($3,200 – $1,050 – $1,050) using her parents' 35% tax rate. The tax on the rest of her taxable income ($2,850 – $1,100) will be computed using the tax table and the column for single taxpayers.

EXAMPLE 41

Same facts as Example 40, except that Betsy is 18 years old. Although Betsy's unearned income exceeds $2,100, her earned income ($4,000) exceeds one-half of her total support for the year ($7,600 × 50% = $3,800). Therefore, Betsy is not subject to the kiddie tax. She will pay tax on her $2,850 taxable income using the column in the tax table for single taxpayers.

EXAMPLE 42

During 2015, Tim, age 21, has interest income of $3,600 and wages of $3,000. Tim was a full-time student during the year. His parents are in the 35% tax bracket and claim Tim as a dependent on their joint tax return. Support from all sources during the year for Tim was $7,000. Tim's taxable income is $3,250 ($6,600 AGI – $3,350 standard deduction for dependents – $0 personal exemption). Tim is between the ages of 19 and 24 and a full-time student with unearned income in excess of $2,100. His earned income ($3,000) does not exceed one-half of his total support for the year ($7,000 × 50% = $3,500). Thus, Tim is subject to the kiddie tax. He will pay tax on his $1,500 of net unearned income ($3,600 – $1,050 – $1,050) using his parents' 35% tax rate. The tax on the remaining $1,750 ($3,250 – $1,500) will be found in the tax table (using the column for single taxpayers).

EXAMPLE 43

During 2015, Ray, age 13, has interest income of $3,700 and no earned income. Ray's parents are deceased. He lives with his grandmother, who claims Ray as a dependent on her tax return. Since Ray does not have at least one living parent or stepparent, he is not subject to the kiddie tax. He will file a tax return and use the tax table to compute tax on his $2,650 of taxable income ($3,700 – $1,050 standard deduction for dependents – $0 personal exemption).

Under certain conditions, parents can choose to report their child's income on their tax returns. For this reporting, parents must file Form 1040. When parents choose this reporting option, the child does not file a return. However, any unearned income of the child reported on the parents' tax return is considered to be the parents' investment income for purposes of the net investment income tax (see ¶315).

¶314.01 FILLED-IN FORM 8615

INFORMATION FOR FIGURE 3-3:

Helen Wong, age 16, receives $3,600 of interest from her investments. Helen has no other income and no itemized deductions. Thus, Helen's net unearned income is $1,500 ($3,600 – $1,050 – $1,050). This amount is taxed at the parents' higher tax rate. Helen has no brothers or sisters. Her parents file a joint return and have taxable income of $94,200. Helen's $481 tax liability is computed on Form 8615 by entering the following information on the appropriate lines and then following the instructions on the form.

Line #

1: Child's unearned income, **$3,600**
4: Child's taxable income ($3,600 – $1,050 standard deduction for dependents – $0 personal exemption), **$2,550**
6: Parent's taxable income, **$94,200**
7: Net unearned income reported on Form 8615 filed for the parents' other children, **$0** (Helen is an only child)
9: Tax on $95,700 (parents' taxable income of $94,200 + Helen's $1,500 of net unearned income), **$15,519**
10: Tax on parents' taxable income of $94,200, **$15,144**
15: Tax on amount taxed at child's rate ($1,050), **$106**
17: Tax on child's taxable income of $2,550, **$256**

Figure 3-3: Filled-In Form 8615

Form **8615**

Department of the Treasury
Internal Revenue Service (99)

Tax for Certain Children Who Have Unearned Income

▶ Attach only to the child's Form 1040, Form 1040A, or Form 1040NR.
▶ Information about Form 8615 and its separate instructions is at *www.irs.gov/form8615*.

OMB No. 1545-0074
2015
Attachment Sequence No. **33**

Child's name shown on return: **Helen I. Wong**
Child's social security number: **344-72-0156**

Before you begin: If the child, the parent, or any of the parent's other children for whom Form 8615 must be filed must use the Schedule D Tax Worksheet or has income from farming or fishing, see **Pub. 929,** Tax Rules for Children and Dependents. It explains how to figure the child's tax using the **Schedule D Tax Worksheet** or **Schedule J** (Form 1040).

A Parent's name (first, initial, and last). **Caution:** *See instructions before completing.* **Kenneth A. Wong**
B Parent's social security number: **374-51-9234**

C Parent's filing status (check one):
☐ Single ☑ Married filing jointly ☐ Married filing separately ☐ Head of household ☐ Qualifying widow(er)

Part I Child's Net Unearned Income

1	Enter the child's unearned income (see instructions)	1	3,600
2	If the child **did not** itemize deductions on **Schedule A** (Form 1040 or Form 1040NR), enter $2,100. Otherwise, see instructions	2	2,100
3	Subtract line 2 from line 1. If zero or less, **stop;** do not complete the rest of this form but **do** attach it to the child's return	3	1,500
4	Enter the child's **taxable income** from Form 1040, line 43; Form 1040A, line 27; or Form 1040NR, line 41. If the child files Form 2555 or 2555-EZ, see the instructions	4	2,550
5	Enter the **smaller** of line 3 or line 4. If zero, **stop;** do not complete the rest of this form but **do** attach it to the child's return	5	1,500

Part II Tentative Tax Based on the Tax Rate of the Parent

6	Enter the parent's **taxable income** from Form 1040, line 43; Form 1040A, line 27; Form 1040EZ, line 6; Form 1040NR, line 41; or Form 1040NR-EZ, line 14. If zero or less, enter -0-. If the parent files Form 2555 or 2555-EZ, see the instructions	6	94,200
7	Enter the total, if any, from Forms 8615, line 5, of **all other** children of the parent named above. **Do not** include the amount from line 5 above	7	0
8	Add lines 5, 6, and 7 (see instructions)	8	95,700
9	Enter the tax on the amount on line 8 based on the **parent's** filing status above (see instructions). If the Qualified Dividends and Capital Gain Tax Worksheet, Schedule D Tax Worksheet, or Schedule J (Form 1040) is used to figure the tax, check here ▶ ☐	9	15,519
10	Enter the parent's tax from Form 1040, line 44; Form 1040A, line 28, minus any alternative minimum tax; Form 1040EZ, line 10; Form 1040NR, line 42; or Form 1040NR-EZ, line 15. **Do not** include any tax from **Form 4972** or **8814** or any tax from recapture of an education credit. If the parent files Form 2555 or 2555-EZ, see the instructions. If the Qualified Dividends and Capital Gain Tax Worksheet, Schedule D Tax Worksheet, or Schedule J (Form 1040) was used to figure the tax, check here ▶ ☐	10	15,144
11	Subtract line 10 from line 9 and enter the result. If line 7 is blank, also enter this amount on line 13 and go to **Part III**	11	375
12a	Add lines 5 and 7 — 12a: 1,500		
b	Divide line 5 by line 12a. Enter the result as a decimal (rounded to at least three places)	12b	× 1.00
13	Multiply line 11 by line 12b	13	375

Part III Child's Tax—If lines 4 and 5 above are the same, enter -0- on line 15 and go to line 16.

14	Subtract line 5 from line 4 — 14: 1,050		
15	Enter the tax on the amount on line 14 based on the **child's** filing status (see instructions). If the Qualified Dividends and Capital Gain Tax Worksheet, Schedule D Tax Worksheet, or Schedule J (Form 1040) is used to figure the tax, check here ▶ ☐	15	106
16	Add lines 13 and 15	16	481
17	Enter the tax on the amount on line 4 based on the **child's** filing status (see instructions). If the Qualified Dividends and Capital Gain Tax Worksheet, Schedule D Tax Worksheet, or Schedule J (Form 1040) is used to figure the tax, check here ▶ ☐	17	256
18	Enter the **larger** of line 16 or line 17 here and on the **child's** Form 1040, line 44; Form 1040A, line 28; or Form 1040NR, line 42. If the child files Form 2555 or 2555-EZ, see the instructions	18	481

For Paperwork Reduction Act Notice, see your tax return instructions. Cat. No. 64113U Form **8615** (2015)

¶315 Net Investment Income (NII) Tax

Higher-income taxpayers must pay an additional tax on some, if not all, of their net investment income (NII). Investment income includes taxable interest (¶308), dividends (¶309), taxable gains on the sale of investment property (¶310, ¶1101), rents and royalties (¶311), and the earnings portion of amounts withdrawn from nonqualified annuities (annuities purchased with after-tax dollars, ¶306.02). NII is investment income minus expenses properly allocated to items included in investment income. Examples include rental expenses, investment interest expense, and various investment expenses.

The amount subject to the 3.8% additional tax is the *lesser of* (i) NII, or (ii) modified AGI in excess of the amounts shown in Figure 3-4. Modified AGI is AGI with any foreign earned income exclusion (¶401.01) added back. Taxpayers compute their NII tax on Form 8960, Net Investment Income Tax–Individuals, Estates, and Trusts. The NII tax is then reported in the section with "Other Taxes" on Form 1040 (page 2).

Figure 3-4: Modified AGI Thresholds for Additional 3.8% NII Tax	
Married filing jointly (MFJ) and qualifying widow(er)	$250,000
Single and head of household (HOH)	200,000
Married filing separately (MFS)	125,000

EXAMPLE 44 Suzy and Marv Dion file a joint tax return. Their modified AGI is $278,776. Included in this amount is $39,505 of NII. The Dion's modified AGI exceeds the $250,000 threshold for MFJ taxpayers. Their NII tax is $1,093 (3.8% × (*lesser of* (i) $39,505 NII or (ii) $28,776 excess modified AGI)). This tax is owed in addition to the income taxes owed on taxable income.

EXAMPLE 45 Karol files her tax return using head of household filing status. Karol's modified AGI is $203,883. Included in this amount is $9,960 of NII. Karol's modified AGI exceeds the $200,000 threshold for taxpayers who file as head of household. She computes her NII tax on Form 8960 (3.8% × (*lesser of* (i) $9,960 NII or (ii) $3,883 excess modified AGI) = $148). She reports her $148 NII tax in the Other Taxes section of her Form 1040 and attaches Form 8960 to her tax return.

¶316 Form 1040A

Form 1040A, U.S. Individual Income Tax Return, is a two-page return. It is more challenging than Form 1040EZ, but less complex than Form 1040. It allows for more types of income than Form 1040EZ. It also allows more types of deductions and personal tax credits.

Page 1 lists the taxpayer's income items. It also allows four deductions to arrive at adjusted gross income. Page 2 provides for the standard deduction and allowable exemptions to produce taxable income. After computing the amount of tax, the form allows for reductions for tax credits, withheld taxes, and other payments. The taxpayer then computes the refund or the amount due.

¶316.01 TAXPAYERS WHO MAY USE FORM 1040A

Only taxpayers with taxable incomes of less than $100,000 can use Form 1040A. The income of Form 1040A filers can include only wages, salaries, tips, taxable scholarships and fellowships (these are added to taxable wages), interest, dividends, capital gain distributions, distributions from Individual retirement accounts (IRAs), pensions and annuities, social security benefits, unemployment compensation and Alaska Permanent Fund dividends.

Form 1040A differs from Form 1040EZ in that no deductions for AGI are allowed on Form 1040EZ. However, only four deductions for AGI are allowed on Form 1040A. Taxpayers wanting to take deductions for AGI other than the four allowed on Form 1040A must file Form 1040. Like Form 1040EZ, the only deductions from AGI allowed on Form 1040A are the standard deduction and exemption deduction. Taxpayers wanting to claim itemized deductions in lieu of the standard deduction must file Form 1040.

Although not all personal tax credits can be claimed on Form 1040A, many more are allowed on Form 1040A than on Form 1040EZ. The credits allowed on Form 1040A include the child and dependent care credit, the elderly or disabled credit, the education credits, the retirement savings contributions credit, the child tax credit, the net premium tax credit, and the earned income credit. Similar to what was discussed in Chapter 2 (¶206), taxpayers filing Form 1040A either indicate their compliance with the ACA mandate or pay a penalty on Form 1040A (line 38).

Two of the four deductions for AGI previously allowed on Form 1040A expired at the end of 2014. When the IRS released the draft of Form 1040A in the summer of 2015, it had not decided which two other deductions for AGI to allow on the Form 1040A for 2015. Thus, lines 16 and 19 on the draft version of the form are marked "Reserved." These two deductions will be identified when the final version of Form 1040A is released.

¶316.02 FILLED-IN FORM 1040A

INFORMATION FOR FIGURE 3-5:

Jesse and Sue Tate have two dependent children, both under age 17. The Tates file a joint tax return for 2015. They complete lines 1–6 and enter the amounts shown in bold below on the lines indicated. They complete the rest of Form 1040A by following the instructions for the other lines on the form.

Line #

7: Wages, **$38,630** (source: Form W-2)
8a: Taxable interest, **$150** (source: Form 1099-INT)
8b: Tax-exempt interest, **$550** (source: Form 1099-INT)
13: Unemployment compensation, **$2,800** (source: Form 1099-G)
17: IRA deduction, **$4,000** ($2,000 for each spouse)
24: Standard deduction for MFJ, **$12,600**
26: Exemptions, **$16,000** ($4,000 × 4)
28: Tax, **$898** (source: tax rate Schedule Y-1 for MFJ taxpayers)
34: Retirement savings contributions credit, **$800** (source: Form 8880)
35: (Nonrefundable) child tax credit, **$98** (source: $2,000 child tax credit (two qualifying children × $1,000), limited to remaining tax after subtracting out the retirement savings contributions credit ($898 – $800 = $98)). The rest of the credit qualifies as a refundable child tax credit (see line 43).
38: Health care individual responsibility, check box to indicate Full-year coverage (Jesse's employer provides full-time health care coverage for the Tate family)
40: Tax withheld, **$0** (source: Form W-2)
42a: Earned income credit, **$2,390** (source: Schedule EIC Worksheet, the lesser of the amounts from the EIC Tables for $38,630 wages or $37,580 AGI for MFJ with two children, see ¶204.11).
43: Additional (refundable) child tax credit, **$1,902** (source: Schedule 8812)

Figure 3-5: Filled-In Form 1040A (Page 1)

Form **1040A** Department of the Treasury—Internal Revenue Service
U.S. Individual Income Tax Return (99) **2015** IRS Use Only—Do not write or staple in this space.

OMB No. 1545-0074

Your first name and initial	Last name	Your social security number
Jesse R.	Tate	282 56 9320
If a joint return, spouse's first name and initial	Last name	Spouse's social security number
Susan E.	Tate	271 04 7926

Home address (number and street). If you have a P.O. box, see instructions. Apt. no.
1624 West Third Street

▲ Make sure the SSN(s) above and on line 6c are correct.

City, town or post office, state, and ZIP code. If you have a foreign address, also complete spaces below (see instructions).
Muskegon, MO 45441

Foreign country name | Foreign province/state/county | Foreign postal code

Presidential Election Campaign
Check here if you, or your spouse if filing jointly, want $3 to go to this fund. Checking a box below will not change your tax or refund. ☐ You ☐ Spouse

Filing status
Check only one box.
1 ☐ Single
2 ☑ Married filing jointly (even if only one had income)
3 ☐ Married filing separately. Enter spouse's SSN above and full name here. ▶
4 ☐ Head of household (with qualifying person). (See instructions.) If the qualifying person is a child but not your dependent, enter this child's name here. ▶
5 ☐ Qualifying widow(er) with dependent child (see instructions)

Exemptions
6a ☑ **Yourself.** If someone can claim you as a dependent, **do not** check box 6a.
b ☑ **Spouse**
Boxes checked on 6a and 6b: 2

c **Dependents:**
If more than six dependents, see instructions.

(1) First name	Last name	(2) Dependent's social security number	(3) Dependent's relationship to you	(4) ✓ if child under age 17 qualifying for child tax credit (see instructions)
Martha	Tate	826-34-3716	daughter	☑
Kyle	Tate	850-21-5213	son	☑
				☐
				☐
				☐
				☐

No. of children on 6c who:
• lived with you: 2
• did not live with you due to divorce or separation (see instructions):
Dependents on 6c not entered above:

d Total number of exemptions claimed. Add numbers on lines above ▶ 4

Income

Attach Form(s) W-2 here. Also attach Form(s) 1099-R if tax was withheld.

If you did not get a W-2, see instructions.

7	Wages, salaries, tips, etc. Attach Form(s) W-2.	7	38,630
8a	**Taxable** interest. Attach Schedule B if required.	8a	150
b	**Tax-exempt** interest. **Do not** include on line 8a. 8b 550		
9a	Ordinary dividends. Attach Schedule B if required.	9a	
b	Qualified dividends (see instructions). 9b		
10	Capital gain distributions (see instructions).	10	
11a	IRA distributions. 11a — **11b** Taxable amount (see instructions).	11b	
12a	Pensions and annuities. 12a — **12b** Taxable amount (see instructions).	12b	
13	Unemployment compensation and Alaska Permanent Fund dividends.	13	2,800
14a	Social security benefits. 14a — **14b** Taxable amount (see instructions).	14b	
15	Add lines 7 through 14b (far right column). This is your **total income.** ▶	15	41,580

Adjusted gross income

Line	Description		Amount		Amount
16	Reserved	16			
17	IRA deduction (see instructions).	17	4,000		
18	Student loan interest deduction (see instructions).	18			
19	Reserved	19			
20	Add lines 16 through 19. These are your **total adjustments.**			20	4,000
21	Subtract line 20 from line 15. This is your **adjusted gross income.** ▶			21	37,580

For Disclosure, Privacy Act, and Paperwork Reduction Act Notice, see separate instructions. Cat. No. 11327A Form **1040A** (2015)

Figure 3-5: Filled-in Form 1040A (Page 2)

Form 1040A (2015) Page **2**

Tax, credits, and payments

Line	Description	Sub-line	Sub-amount	Line	Amount
22	Enter the amount from line 21 (adjusted gross income).			22	37,580
23a	Check if: ☐ **You** were born before January 2, 1951, ☐ Blind; ☐ **Spouse** was born before January 2, 1951, ☐ Blind. **Total boxes checked** ▶ 23a ☐				
b	If you are married filing separately and your spouse itemizes deductions, check here ▶ 23b ☐				
24	Enter your **standard deduction**.			24	12,600
25	Subtract line 24 from line 22. If line 24 is more than line 22, enter -0-.			25	24,980
26	**Exemptions.** Multiply $4,000 by the number on line 6d.			26	16,000
27	Subtract line 26 from line 25. If line 26 is more than line 25, enter -0-. This is your **taxable income.**			▶ 27	8,980
28	**Tax,** including any alternative minimum tax (see instructions).	28	898		
29	Excess advance premium tax credit repayment. Attach Form 8962.	29			
30	Add lines 28 and 29.			30	898
31	Credit for child and dependent care expenses. Attach Form 2441.	31			
32	Credit for the elderly or the disabled. Attach Schedule R.	32			
33	Education credits from Form 8863, line 19.	33			
34	Retirement savings contributions credit. Attach Form 8880.	34	800		
35	Child tax credit. Attach Schedule 8812, if required.	35	98		
36	Add lines 31 through 35. These are your **total credits.**			36	898
37	Subtract line 36 from line 30. If line 36 is more than line 30, enter -0-.			37	0
38	Health care: individual responsibility (see instructions). Full-year coverage ☑			38	
39	Add line 37 and line 38. This is your **total tax.**			39	0
40	Federal income tax withheld from Forms W-2 and 1099.	40	0		
41	2015 estimated tax payments and amount applied from 2014 return.	41			
42a	**Earned income credit (EIC).**	42a	2,390		
b	Nontaxable combat pay election. 42b				
43	Additional child tax credit. Attach Schedule 8812.	43	1,902		
44	American opportunity credit from Form 8863, line 8.	44			
45	Net premium tax credit. Attach Form 8962.	45			
46	Add lines 40, 41, 42a, 43, 44, and 45. These are your **total payments.**			▶ 46	4,292

Standard Deduction for—
• People who check any box on line 23a or 23b **or** who can be claimed as a dependent, see instructions.
• All others:
Single or Married filing separately, $6,300
Married filing jointly or Qualifying widow(er), $12,600
Head of household, $9,250

If you have a qualifying child, attach Schedule EIC.

Refund

Line	Description	Sub-line	Sub-amount	Line	Amount
47	If line 46 is more than line 39, subtract line 39 from line 46. This is the amount you **overpaid.**			47	4,292
48a	Amount of line 47 you want **refunded to you.** If Form 8888 is attached, check here ▶ ☐			48a	4,292
▶ b	Routing number ☐☐☐☐☐☐☐☐☐ ▶ c Type: ☐ Checking ☐ Savings				
▶ d	Account number ☐☐☐☐☐☐☐☐☐☐☐☐☐☐☐☐☐				
49	Amount of line 47 you want **applied to your 2016 estimated tax.**	49			

Direct deposit? See instructions and fill in 48b, 48c, and 48d or Form 8888.

Amount you owe

Line	Description	Sub-line	Sub-amount	Line	Amount
50	**Amount you owe.** Subtract line 46 from line 39. For details on how to pay, see instructions.			▶ 50	
51	Estimated tax penalty (see instructions).	51			

Third party designee

Do you want to allow another person to discuss this return with the IRS (see instructions)? ☐ **Yes.** Complete the following. ☐ **No**

Designee's name ▶ Phone no. ▶ Personal identification number (PIN) ▶ ☐☐☐☐☐

Sign here

Under penalties of perjury, I declare that I have examined this return and accompanying schedules and statements, and to the best of my knowledge and belief, they are true, correct, and accurately list all amounts and sources of income I received during the tax year. Declaration of preparer (other than the taxpayer) is based on all information of which the preparer has any knowledge.

Joint return? See instructions. Keep a copy for your records.

Your signature	Date	Your occupation	Daytime phone number
Jesse R. Tate	2-26-16	Sales	
Spouse's signature. If a joint return, **both** must sign.	Date	Spouse's occupation	If the IRS sent you an Identity Protection PIN, enter it here (see inst.)
Susan E. Tate	2-26-16	Chef	

Paid preparer use only

Print/type preparer's name	Preparer's signature	Date	Check ▶ ☐ if self-employed	PTIN
Firm's name ▶			Firm's EIN ▶	
Firm's address ▶			Phone no.	

Form **1040A** (2015)

3

Name:
Section:
Date:

QUESTIONS AND PROBLEMS

1. **Receipt of advanced payments.** (Obj. 1) On May 1, 20x1, an insurance company sells a three-year insurance policy to one of its customers. The cost of the premiums is $1,200. The insurance company uses the accrual basis and a calendar year.

   a. What amount of the $1,200 must the company include in its gross income over the term of the policy (20x1 – 20x4)?

   b. Would your answer change if the company used the cash basis? Explain.

2. **Compensation.** (Obj. 1) Mark Wellaby, M.D., practices medicine. During the year he received the following items in payment for his services: cash of $48,000; farm produce worth $1,000; common stock with a total par value of $500; and a $485, 90-day noninterest-bearing note dated December 1. The stock at the time of receipt had a fair market value of $1,000. At December 31, the fair market value of the stock had dropped to $900. Compute Dr. Wellaby's gross income.

3. Tips. (Obj. 1) The following questions involve tip income. Answer each question by inserting an **X** in the proper column.

	True	*False*
a. Employees receiving less than $20 in monthly tips while working for one employer need not report them to the employer.	_____	_____
b. Employees receiving less than $20 in monthly tips do not pay social security and Medicare taxes on their tips.	_____	_____
c. Employees receiving less than $20 in monthly tips do not pay income taxes on their tips.	_____	_____
d. The IRS normally assumes that food and beverage servers make at least 10% of gross sales in tips.	_____	_____
e. When tips reported to employers are less than the IRS's assumed tipping rate, some employers must report the difference as additional income on the employee's Form W-2.	_____	_____
f. "Allocated tips" are subject to withholding for income, social security, and Medicare taxes.	_____	_____

4. Tips. (Obj. 1) Marge is a hostess at a local diner. As a hostess, Marge normally does not receive tips. However, on occasion she will help out with an order and the waitress will give Marge part of her tips. During the current year, Marge's total tips were $200.

a. Discuss the tax consequences of the tip income if Marge did not receive more than $20 in tips in any one month during the year.

b. How would your answer to Part a. differ if she received more than $20 in tips during the month of May?

5. Property Settlements, Alimony, and Child Support. (Obj. 1) Distinguish between the three types of payments former spouses may make to one another and discuss the tax treatment to both the paying spouse and the recipient spouse of each type of payment.

6. **Alimony.** (Obj. 1) For a divorce or legal separation after 1984, alimony payments are deducted by the payer and included in the payee's gross income. However, to be considered alimony, the payments must meet six conditions. What are these conditions?

    1. ______________________________
    2. ______________________________
    3. ______________________________
    4. ______________________________
    5. ______________________________
    6. ______________________________

7. **Alimony and Child Support.** (Obj. 1) Under the terms of their divorce, Henry is to pay Winona $1,000 a month. The terms of the agreement specify that $550 of each payment is to be for child support.

    a. If Henry makes all of his required payments during the current year, how much must Winona include in gross income? What amount can Henry deduct?

    b. How, if at all, would your answer to Part a. change if the agreement were silent as to how much of each payment constituted child support?

    c. How, if at all, would your answer to Part a. change if Henry only makes 8 of the 12 required payments during the year?

8. **Property Settlements, Alimony, and Child Support.** (Obj. 1) Under the terms of a divorce agreement, Gary is to pay $300 per month as child support to Judy who has custody of their 12-year-old child. Judy is also to receive $1,200 per month for 12 years, but this payment will change to $1,000 per month when the child reaches age 18. Gary is also to transfer stock to Judy. The stock cost $20,000 and has a fair market value of $50,000. The divorce is finalized on May 1. In the first year under the agreement, Judy receives the stock and 8 months of cash payments.

   a. How do these transfers affect Judy's gross income and Gary's AGI?

   b. How, if at all, would your answer to Part a. change if during the first year Gary only made 6 of the 8 required cash payments?

9. **Traditional IRA Distributions.** (Obj. 2) Over the years, Jen made nondeductible contributions to her traditional IRA. At the beginning of the year, she had yet to withdraw $56,420 of her nondeductible contributions. At the end of the year, the value of the assets in the IRA was $225,850. During the year, Jen withdrew $42,000 from the account.

   a. Describe the tax consequences to Jen assuming Jen is 61 years old at the time of the distribution.

   b. Same as in Part a., except that Jen is 56 years old, and does not meet one of the penalty-free exceptions for making early withdrawals from her IRA.

10. **Pension Benefits.** (Obj. 2) On August 10, 2015, Don turned 65 and received his first pension payment. Over the years, he had contributed $68,900 to his employer's qualified retirement plan. Taxes were paid on $24,700 of this amount. The remaining $44,200 was contributed after the law was changed to permit pre-tax contributions to the plan. Don is to receive monthly benefits of $425 on the same day every month for the remainder of his life.

    a. From the 5 monthly payments Don receives in 2015, what amount is included in gross income?

    b. If Don receives 12 payments in 2016, what amount does he include in gross income?

    c. If Don lives longer than his expected 260 payments, how much of each month's $425 payment will be included in his gross income?

    d. How would your answer to Parts a. - c. change if Don were married and his pension benefits were to continue for both his and his wife's lives? Don's wife is 61 as on August 10, 2015.

11. **Annuity Income.** (Obj. 2) Gregg purchased an annuity contract for $92,400. The contract stated that he would receive $550 a month for life, starting on January 1, 2010. On that date, Gregg's remaining life expectancy was 20 years. For 2015, how much of the $6,600 of annuity payments can Gregg exclude from gross income?

12. Social Security Benefits. (Obj. 2) Taxpayers A through C received social security (SS) benefits during the year. Taxpayer C lived with his spouse part of the year. Follow the instructions and fill in the blank lines in the table below for each taxpayer. On line p. show the amount of taxable social security benefits for each taxpayer.

		A *Single*	*B* *MFJ*	*C* *MFS*
	Social Security benefits received	$ 7,800	$12,900	$11,000
	First-Tier Formula			
a.	AGI before SS	$50,000	$48,000	$ 5,000
b.	50% SS benefits	3,900	6,450	5,500
c.	Tax-exempt interest	500	400	400
d.	Revised AGI	$ _____	$ _____	$ _____
e.	Less: Base amount	(25,000)	(32,000)	(0)
f.	Excess revised AGI	$ _____	$ _____	$ _____
g.	50% of line f.	$ _____	$ _____	$ _____
h.	Tentative taxable SS benefits (lesser of line g. or b.)	$ _____	$ _____	$ _____
	Second-Tier Formula			
i.	Revised AGI (line d.)	$ _____	$ _____	$ _____
j.	Less: Threshold amount	(34,000)	(44,000)	(0)
k.	Excess	$ _____	$ _____	$ _____
l.	Line k. × 85%	$ _____	$ _____	$ _____
m.	Lesser of line h. or q.	$ _____	$ _____	$ _____
n.	Line l. + line m.	$ _____	$ _____	$ _____
o.	SS benefits × 85%	$ _____	$ _____	$ _____
p.	Taxable benefits (lesser of line n. or o.)	$ _____	$ _____	$ _____
	Threshold amount (line j)	$34,000	$44,000	$ 0
	Less base amount (line e.)	(25,000)	(32,000)	(0)
	Difference	$ 9,000	$12,000	$ 0
q.	50% of the difference	$ 4,500	$ 6,000	$ 0

13. Social Security Benefits. (Obj. 2) Taxpayers D through G receive social security (SS) benefits during the year. Taxpayer F did not live with his spouse at all during the year. Information used to determine the taxable amount of their benefits is provided below. Fill in blank lines e. through h. for each taxpayer. On line h., determine the amount of the taxable social security benefits included in gross income for each taxpayer.

		D	E	F	G
	Taxpayer status	*Single*	*MFJ*	*MFS*	*MFJ*
a.	Social security benefits	$ 7,800	$ 9,400	$ 6,200	$11,000
b.	AGI before SS benefits	25,000	32,300	12,000	24,000
c.	50% SS benefits	3,900	4,700	3,100	5,500
d.	Tax-exempt interest	500	0	0	400
e.	Revised AGI	$ _____	$ _____	$ _____	$ _____
f.	Less base amount	(_____)	(_____)	(_____)	(_____)
g.	Excess revised AGI	$ _____	$ _____	$ _____	$ _____
h.	Taxable SS benefits (lesser of line c. or 50% of g.)	$ _____	$ _____	$ _____	$ _____

14. Series EE U.S. Savings Bonds. (Obj. 3) Norma, age 30 and single, is considering investing $2,000 in Series EE U.S. Savings Bonds. Discuss the options Norma has with respect to reporting the interest income from these bonds.

15. Series EE U.S. Savings Bonds. (Obj. 3) Following are the issue (purchase) price, original face (maturity) value, and selected redemption values of Series EE bonds purchased by Grady in 2015.

Issue (Purchase) Price	*Face (Maturity) Value*	*Redemption Value As of 12/31/15*	*Redemption Value As of 12/31/16*
$ 600	$ 1,200	$ 638	$ 673
200	400	233	261
1,000	2,000	1,025	1,051
50	100	54	58
150	300	156	162

Grady elects to report the increase in redemption value each year on Series EE bonds. At the election date he owned no other U.S. savings bonds. What amount does Grady include in gross income from these bonds in 2015 and 2016?

16. **Accrued Interest on Bonds.** (Obj. 3) Ramona purchased a $40,000 par value bond of DPQ Corporation. She paid the seller $40,533 ($40,000 par value + $533 accrued interest). The 8% bond pays interest semiannually on June 30 and December 31. Ramona received the first semiannual interest payment of $1,600 on December 31, 2015. Discuss how much interest income Ramona must include in gross income in 2015.

17. **Original Issue Discount.** (Obj. 3) On January 1, 2015, a cash basis taxpayer paid $32,870 for a 25-year, zero-coupon bond with a face value of $100,000. The annual yield to maturity is 4.5%.

    a. What is the OID on the bond?

    b. What portion of the OID would be included in taxable interest income for 2015?

    c. What portion of the OID would be included in taxable interest income for 2016?

18. **Original Issue Discount.** (Obj. 3) A 30-year bond with a face value of $100,000 is issued at a discount. How large can the discount be and still be treated as de minimis OID? Discuss the tax consequences to the purchaser of a bond with de minimis OID.

19. **Market Discount.** (Obj. 3) On January 1, 2015, Dolly pays $9,380 for corporate bonds. The bonds were originally issued on January 1, 2010 for $9,330 and have a $10,000 face value. They mature on January 1, 2035. The bond's amortized carrying value (ACV) on January 1, 2015 was $9,450. What portion of the $620 difference between the $9,380 Dolly paid for the bonds and their $10,000 face value is OID? What portion is market discount? Discuss how Dolly treats these amounts on her tax return.

20. **Bond Premium.** (Obj. 3) Dean pays $104,700 for bonds with a face value of $100,000. Describe the tax consequences to Dean of buying bonds at a premium.

21. **Below Market Loans.** (Obj. 3) Under what circumstances do the below market loan rules apply? Describe the tax consequences of making a below market loan. Be sure to discuss the consequences to both the borrower and the lender.

22. **Imputed Interest.** (Obj. 3)

    a. What are Applicable Federal Rates (AFRs)? What purpose do they serve?

    b. How is the imputed interest on a below market loan computed?

23. **Gift Loans.** (Obj. 3) Janet's parents lend Janet and her husband $125,000 to buy a new home. The loan is for ten years with no interest.

    a. Must interest be imputed on the loan? If so, how would the amount of imputed interest be determined?

    b. If the loan amount were $100,000, would interest have to be imputed? If so, how would the amount of imputed interest be determined?

    c. If the loan amount were $10,000, would interest have to be imputed?

24. **Compensation-Related Loans.** (Obj. 3) On January 1, a company loans its employee, Liz Kittner, $50,000. The terms of the note require that Liz pay interest annually based on a 1.5% annual rate of interest. In addition, Liz is to repay the $50,000 at the end of three years. At the time the loan was made, the current annual AFR short-term, mid-term and long-term rates were 4%, 5% and 6%, respectively. Determine the tax consequences of this loan to both the company and to Liz in the first year.

25. **Corporation-Shareholder Loans.** (Obj. 3) On January 1, a corporation loans its shareholder, Lynda Matsen, $120,000. The terms of the loan require that Lynda pay interest annually based on a 2.5% annual rate of interest. In addition, Lynda is to repay the $120,000 at the end of six years. At the time the loan was made, the current annual AFR short-term, mid-term and long-term rates were 4.5%, 5.5% and 6.5%, respectively. Determine the tax consequences of this loan to both the corporation and to Lynda in the first year.

26. **Dividend Income.** (Obj. 4) What are dividends and how are qualified dividends taxed differently from nonqualified dividends?

27. **Dividend Income.** (Obj. 4) Susan owns shares of stock in a corporation. In January 2016, she received a 1099-DIV reporting the following:

Total ordinary dividends	$526
Qualified dividends included in total dividends	450

How are these dividends reported on Susan's tax return?

28. **Kiddie Tax.** (Obj. 5) Dee Evans (SSN 842-11-6940), age 10, received taxable interest of $4,500 during 2015. She has no other income, and no itemized deductions related to investment income. Dee's parents, Robert and Lee Ann Evans, have $85,000 of taxable income. Compute the amount of Dee's income that will be taxed at her parents' tax rate. Then compute Dee's tax liability by completing Dee's Form 8615. Robert's SSN is 490-44-9919.

(Use for Problem 28.)

Form **8615**

Department of the Treasury
Internal Revenue Service (99)

Tax for Certain Children Who Have Unearned Income

▶ Attach only to the child's Form 1040, Form 1040A, or Form 1040NR.
▶ Information about Form 8615 and its separate instructions is at *www.irs.gov/form8615*.

OMB No. 1545-0074
2015
Attachment Sequence No. **33**

Child's name shown on return | **Child's social security number**

Before you begin: If the child, the parent, or any of the parent's other children for whom Form 8615 must be filed must use the Schedule D Tax Worksheet or has income from farming or fishing, see **Pub. 929,** Tax Rules for Children and Dependents. It explains how to figure the child's tax using the **Schedule D Tax Worksheet** or **Schedule J** (Form 1040).

A Parent's name (first, initial, and last). **Caution:** *See instructions before completing.* | **B Parent's social security number**

C Parent's filing status (check one):
☐ Single ☐ Married filing jointly ☐ Married filing separately ☐ Head of household ☐ Qualifying widow(er)

Part I Child's Net Unearned Income

1	Enter the child's unearned income (see instructions)	1	
2	If the child **did not** itemize deductions on **Schedule A** (Form 1040 or Form 1040NR), enter $2,100. Otherwise, see instructions	2	
3	Subtract line 2 from line 1. If zero or less, **stop;** do not complete the rest of this form but **do** attach it to the child's return	3	
4	Enter the child's **taxable income** from Form 1040, line 43; Form 1040A, line 27; or Form 1040NR, line 41. If the child files Form 2555 or 2555-EZ, see the instructions	4	
5	Enter the **smaller** of line 3 or line 4. If zero, **stop;** do not complete the rest of this form but **do** attach it to the child's return	5	

Part II Tentative Tax Based on the Tax Rate of the Parent

6	Enter the parent's **taxable income** from Form 1040, line 43; Form 1040A, line 27; Form 1040EZ, line 6; Form 1040NR, line 41; or Form 1040NR-EZ, line 14. If zero or less, enter -0-. If the parent files Form 2555 or 2555-EZ, see the instructions	6	
7	Enter the total, if any, from Forms 8615, line 5, of **all other** children of the parent named above. **Do not** include the amount from line 5 above	7	
8	Add lines 5, 6, and 7 (see instructions)	8	
9	Enter the tax on the amount on line 8 based on the **parent's** filing status above (see instructions). If the Qualified Dividends and Capital Gain Tax Worksheet, Schedule D Tax Worksheet, or Schedule J (Form 1040) is used to figure the tax, check here ▶ ☐	9	
10	Enter the parent's tax from Form 1040, line 44; Form 1040A, line 28, minus any alternative minimum tax; Form 1040EZ, line 10; Form 1040NR, line 42; or Form 1040NR-EZ, line 15. **Do not** include any tax from **Form 4972** or **8814** or any tax from recapture of an education credit. If the parent files Form 2555 or 2555-EZ, see the instructions. If the Qualified Dividends and Capital Gain Tax Worksheet, Schedule D Tax Worksheet, or Schedule J (Form 1040) was used to figure the tax, check here ▶ ☐	10	
11	Subtract line 10 from line 9 and enter the result. If line 7 is blank, also enter this amount on line 13 and go to **Part III**	11	
12a	Add lines 5 and 7 ... 12a		
b	Divide line 5 by line 12a. Enter the result as a decimal (rounded to at least three places)	12b	× .
13	Multiply line 11 by line 12b	13	

Part III Child's Tax—If lines 4 and 5 above are the same, enter -0- on line 15 and go to line 16.

14	Subtract line 5 from line 4 ... 14		
15	Enter the tax on the amount on line 14 based on the **child's** filing status (see instructions). If the Qualified Dividends and Capital Gain Tax Worksheet, Schedule D Tax Worksheet, or Schedule J (Form 1040) is used to figure the tax, check here ▶ ☐	15	
16	Add lines 13 and 15	16	
17	Enter the tax on the amount on line 4 based on the **child's** filing status (see instructions). If the Qualified Dividends and Capital Gain Tax Worksheet, Schedule D Tax Worksheet, or Schedule J (Form 1040) is used to figure the tax, check here ▶ ☐	17	
18	Enter the **larger** of line 16 or line 17 here and on the **child's** Form 1040, line 44; Form 1040A, line 28; or Form 1040NR, line 42. If the child files Form 2555 or 2555-EZ, see the instructions	18	

For Paperwork Reduction Act Notice, see your tax return instructions. Cat. No. 64113U Form **8615** (2015)

29. **Net Investment Income (NII) Tax.** (Obj. 5) Compute the net investment income (NII) tax for each of the following taxpayers.

a. A married couple files a joint return. Their modified AGI is $316,990, and they have net investment income of $19,965.

b. A taxpayer files as head of household. His modified AGI is $270,888, and he has net investment income of $60,640.

c. A married taxpayer files separately from his spouse. His modified AGI is $306,408, and he has net investment income of $213,049.

d. An unmarried taxpayer files as single. Her modified AGI is $189,640, and she has net investment income of $14,233.

e. A taxpayer files his tax return using qualified widow(er) filing status. His modified AGI is $263,815, and he has net investment income of $34,588.

30. **Tax Benefit Rule.** (Obj. 1) Explain the tax benefit rule as it applies to refunds of state and local income taxes, as well as federal income taxes.

31. **Tax Benefit Rule.** (Obj. 1) In 2014, Lou, age 35 and single, deducted $5,325 on his federal income tax return for state income taxes withheld during the year. Lou has excellent vision. In 2015, Lou received an $875 refund from the state. For 2014, Lou deducted $11,504 in itemized deductions. After these deductions, Lou's taxable income was $100,000. The 2014 standard deduction for a single taxpayer was $6,200. How much of the refund must Lou include in his 2015 gross income?

32. Internet Problem: Filling out Schedule B. (Obj. 6)

Joyce Mayer (SSN 234-56-7891) receives two 1099s for the year. Form 1099-DIV from Fidelity Investments reports $10,290 of ordinary dividends. Form 1099-INT from State Bank reports interest income of $2,655. Joyce files as single and does not have any foreign bank accounts.

Go to the IRS website and locate Schedule B. Using the computer, fill in Schedule B for Joyce Mayer and print out a completed copy.

See Appendix A for instructions on use of the IRS website.

33. Business Entity Problem: This problem is designed for those using the "business entity" approach. **The solution may require information from Chapters 14–16.** Please answer the following true and false questions in the space provided.

	True	*False*
a. Corporations owning less than 80% of another corporation are generally taxed on at least a portion of the dividends they receive from that company.	______	______
b. Corporations receiving dividends from another corporation are taxed on 70% of the dividend income if they own 10% of the other company.	______	______
c. S corporations receiving a dividend from another corporation do not pay taxes on the dividend.	______	______
d. Partnerships receiving dividends from a corporation must include the dividends in the calculation of "ordinary income."	______	______
e. A shareholder receiving a property distribution from a corporation must recognize the property distribution at its fair market value (FMV) on the distribution date.	______	______
f. A partner receiving a property distribution from the partnership must recognize the property distribution at its fair market value (FMV) on the distribution date.	______	______

34. Business Entity Problem: This problem is designed for those using the "business entity" approach. **The solution may require information from Chapter 14.**

Jason owns 100% of the stock in a C corporation. At December 31, the end of the corporation's tax year, the company has earnings and profits of $20,000 before consideration of any distribution to the owner. On December 31, the company distributes property with a market value of $50,000 to Jason. The basis of the property is $30,000.

a. If the corporation is in the 25% tax bracket, what are the tax implications to the corporation?

b. What are the tax implications to Jason if his basis in the stock prior to the distribution is $27,000?

COMPREHENSIVE PROBLEMS

35. Schedule B. (Obj. 6)

a. Neale D. (SSN 394-57-7584) and Judith L. (SSN 746-38-4457) Hamilton file a joint Form 1040. The Hamiltons have no foreign accounts or trusts. During the year, they received interest and dividends. Using the information provided below, prepare the Hamiltons' Schedule B (Form 1040A or 1040), Interest and Ordinary Dividends.

Amounts Reported on Form 1099-INT	*Amount*
U.S. Treasury bond	$ 600
Ace Manufacturing Company note	50
AT&T debenture bond	60
Bank of America	90
State of Michigan municipal (tax-exempt) bond	75
City of Meadowood municipal (tax-exempt) bond	160

Interest Not Reported on Form 1099-INT	*Amount*
Interest on the mortgage of Mr. and Mrs. K. J. Roe	$ 732
K. R. Smith, personal note	115

Amounts Reported on Form 1099-DIV	*Amount*
Red Corporation dividend on preferred stock	$ 280
USX Corporation dividend on common stock	1,341
Dow Chemical Company dividend on common stock	185

b. Albert B. Kennedy (SSN 664-73-7857) receives various Form 1099s during the year. He has no foreign accounts or trusts. From the information provided below, prepare Albert's Schedule B (Form 1040A or 1040), Interest and Ordinary Dividends.

Amounts Reported on Form 1099-INT	*Amount*
Bryce Corporation bonds	$3,830
Canyon Enterprises corporate bonds	490
State of Illinois municipal (tax-exempt) bonds	1,750

Amounts Reported on Form 1099-DIV	*Amount*
Exxon Mobil common stock	$ 975
UCB Corporation dividend on preferred stock	280
GE dividend reinvested in common stock through GE's dividend reinvestment plan	108

36. Form 1040A. (Obj. 6)

a. Robert A. Harrington (SSN 509-93-8830), a 66-year-old widower, is recently retired. He currently lives at 3487 S. Center, Salt Lake City, UT 84101-9876. During 2015, Robert received $6,000, from his IRA, of which 86.9% is taxable. He received $36,000 from his pension, of which 65% is taxable. He also received $9,200 in social security benefits. Through Medicare, Robert receives health care coverage that complies with the ACA mandate. Robert made estimated payments totaling $3,000 during 2015, which he reports in the Tax, credits, and payments section on Form 1040A. Prepare Robert's 2015 Form 1040A. He does not want $3 to go to the Presidential election campaign fund. He signs and files his tax return on April 14, 2016.

b. John J. (SSN 291-27-4631) and Madilyn (SSN 293-41-7032) Jackson are ages 66 and 65, respectively. Both are retired and have good vision. The Jacksons live at 4622 Beaver Lake Road, Blooming Grove, MN 55164. They file a joint tax return and claim no dependents. During 2015, the Jacksons received $3,517 from their traditional IRAs, all of which is taxable. They also received $30,000 from John's pension. John's exclusion ratio is 16%. The only other item of income for the Jacksons is $13,540 of social security benefits. Through Medicare, the Jacksons each receive health care coverage that complies with the ACA mandate. Prepare the Jacksons' Form 1040A. Both want $3 to go to the Presidential election campaign fund. They sign and date their return on February 7, 2016.

(Use for Problem 35.)

SCHEDULE B (Form 1040A or 1040)
Department of the Treasury Internal Revenue Service (99)

Interest and Ordinary Dividends

▶ Attach to Form 1040A or 1040.
▶ Information about Schedule B and its instructions is at *www.irs.gov/scheduleb*.

OMB No. 1545-0074
2015
Attachment Sequence No. 08

Name(s) shown on return | Your social security number

Part I Interest

(See instructions on back and the instructions for Form 1040A, or Form 1040, line 8a.)

Note: If you received a Form 1099-INT, Form 1099-OID, or substitute statement from a brokerage firm, list the firm's name as the payer and enter the total interest shown on that form.

			Amount
1	List name of payer. If any interest is from a seller-financed mortgage and the buyer used the property as a personal residence, see instructions on back and list this interest first. Also, show that buyer's social security number and address ▶	1	
2	Add the amounts on line 1	2	
3	Excludable interest on series EE and I U.S. savings bonds issued after 1989. Attach Form 8815	3	
4	Subtract line 3 from line 2. Enter the result here and on Form 1040A, or Form 1040, line 8a ▶	4	

Note: If line 4 is over $1,500, you must complete Part III.

Part II Ordinary Dividends

(See instructions on back and the instructions for Form 1040A, or Form 1040, line 9a.)

Note: If you received a Form 1099-DIV or substitute statement from a brokerage firm, list the firm's name as the payer and enter the ordinary dividends shown on that form.

			Amount
5	List name of payer ▶	5	
6	Add the amounts on line 5. Enter the total here and on Form 1040A, or Form 1040, line 9a ▶	6	

Note: If line 6 is over $1,500, you must complete Part III.

Part III Foreign Accounts and Trusts

(See instructions on back.)

You must complete this part if you **(a)** had over $1,500 of taxable interest or ordinary dividends; **(b)** had a foreign account; or **(c)** received a distribution from, or were a grantor of, or a transferor to, a foreign trust.

		Yes	No
7a	At any time during 2015, did you have a financial interest in or signature authority over a financial account (such as a bank account, securities account, or brokerage account) located in a foreign country? See instructions		
	If "Yes," are you required to file FinCEN Form 114, Report of Foreign Bank and Financial Accounts (FBAR), to report that financial interest or signature authority? See FinCEN Form 114 and its instructions for filing requirements and exceptions to those requirements		
b	If you are required to file FinCEN Form 114, enter the name of the foreign country where the financial account is located ▶		
8	During 2015, did you receive a distribution from, or were you the grantor of, or transferor to, a foreign trust? If "Yes," you may have to file Form 3520. See instructions on back		

For Paperwork Reduction Act Notice, see your tax return instructions. Cat. No. 17146N **Schedule B (Form 1040A or 1040) 2015**

(Use for Problem 36.)

Form **1040A** Department of the Treasury—Internal Revenue Service
U.S. Individual Income Tax Return (99) **2015** IRS Use Only—Do not write or staple in this space.

Your first name and initial	Last name		OMB No. 1545-0074 **Your social security number**
If a joint return, spouse's first name and initial	Last name		**Spouse's social security number**
Home address (number and street). If you have a P.O. box, see instructions.		Apt. no.	▲ Make sure the SSN(s) above and on line 6c are correct.
City, town or post office, state, and ZIP code. If you have a foreign address, also complete spaces below (see instructions).			**Presidential Election Campaign** Check here if you, or your spouse if filing jointly, want $3 to go to this fund. Checking a box below will not change your tax or refund. ☐ You ☐ Spouse
Foreign country name	Foreign province/state/county	Foreign postal code	

Filing status
Check only one box.

1 ☐ Single
2 ☐ Married filing jointly (even if only one had income)
3 ☐ Married filing separately. Enter spouse's SSN above and full name here. ▶
4 ☐ Head of household (with qualifying person). (See instructions.) If the qualifying person is a child but not your dependent, enter this child's name here. ▶
5 ☐ Qualifying widow(er) with dependent child (see instructions)

Exemptions

6a ☐ **Yourself.** If someone can claim you as a dependent, **do not** check box 6a.
b ☐ **Spouse**

Boxes checked on 6a and 6b
No. of children on 6c who:
• lived with you
• did not live with you due to divorce or separation (see instructions)
Dependents on 6c not entered above

If more than six dependents, see instructions.

c **Dependents:**

(1) First name	Last name	(2) Dependent's social security number	(3) Dependent's relationship to you	(4) ✓ if child under age 17 qualifying for child tax credit (see instructions)
				☐
				☐
				☐
				☐
				☐
				☐

d Total number of exemptions claimed. **Add numbers on lines above ▶**

Income

Attach Form(s) W-2 here. Also attach Form(s) 1099-R if tax was withheld.

If you did not get a W-2, see instructions.

7	Wages, salaries, tips, etc. Attach Form(s) W-2.		7
8a	**Taxable** interest. Attach Schedule B if required.		8a
b	**Tax-exempt** interest. **Do not** include on line 8a.	8b	
9a	Ordinary dividends. Attach Schedule B if required.		9a
b	Qualified dividends (see instructions).	9b	
10	Capital gain distributions (see instructions).		10
11a	IRA distributions. 11a	11b Taxable amount (see instructions).	11b
12a	Pensions and annuities. 12a	12b Taxable amount (see instructions).	12b
13	Unemployment compensation and Alaska Permanent Fund dividends.		13
14a	Social security benefits. 14a	14b Taxable amount (see instructions).	14b
15	Add lines 7 through 14b (far right column). This is your **total income.** ▶		15

Adjusted gross income

16	Reserved	16	
17	IRA deduction (see instructions).	17	
18	Student loan interest deduction (see instructions).	18	
19	Reserved	19	
20	Add lines 16 through 19. These are your **total adjustments.**		20
21	Subtract line 20 from line 15. This is your **adjusted gross income.** ▶		21

For Disclosure, Privacy Act, and Paperwork Reduction Act Notice, see separate instructions. Cat. No. 11327A Form **1040A** (2015)

(Use for Problem 36.)

Form 1040A (2015) Page **2**

Tax, credits, and payments

22	Enter the amount from line 21 (adjusted gross income).	22
23a	Check if: ☐ **You** were born before January 2, 1951, ☐ Blind; ☐ **Spouse** was born before January 2, 1951, ☐ Blind } **Total boxes checked** ▶ 23a ☐	
b	If you are married filing separately and your spouse itemizes deductions, check here ▶ 23b ☐	
24	Enter your **standard deduction.**	24
25	Subtract line 24 from line 22. If line 24 is more than line 22, enter -0-.	25
26	**Exemptions.** Multiply $4,000 by the number on line 6d.	26
27	Subtract line 26 from line 25. If line 26 is more than line 25, enter -0-. This is your **taxable income.**	▶ 27
28	**Tax,** including any alternative minimum tax (see instructions). 28	
29	Excess advance premium tax credit repayment. Attach Form 8962. 29	
30	Add lines 28 and 29.	30
31	Credit for child and dependent care expenses. Attach Form 2441. 31	
32	Credit for the elderly or the disabled. Attach Schedule R. 32	
33	Education credits from Form 8863, line 19. 33	
34	Retirement savings contributions credit. Attach Form 8880. 34	
35	Child tax credit. Attach Schedule 8812, if required. 35	
36	Add lines 31 through 35. These are your **total credits.**	36
37	Subtract line 36 from line 30. If line 36 is more than line 30, enter -0-.	37
38	Health care: individual responsibility (see instructions). Full-year coverage ☐	38
39	Add line 37 and line 38. This is your **total tax.**	39
40	Federal income tax withheld from Forms W-2 and 1099. 40	
41	2015 estimated tax payments and amount applied from 2014 return. 41	
42a	**Earned income credit (EIC).** 42a	
b	Nontaxable combat pay election. 42b	
43	Additional child tax credit. Attach Schedule 8812. 43	
44	American opportunity credit from Form 8863, line 8. 44	
45	Net premium tax credit. Attach Form 8962. 45	
46	Add lines 40, 41, 42a, 43, 44, and 45. These are your **total payments.**	▶ 46

Standard Deduction for—
- People who check any box on line 23a or 23b **or** who can be claimed as a dependent, see instructions.
- All others:

Single or Married filing separately, $6,300

Married filing jointly or Qualifying widow(er), $12,600

Head of household, $9,250

If you have a qualifying child, attach Schedule EIC.

Refund

47	If line 46 is more than line 39, subtract line 39 from line 46. This is the amount you **overpaid.**	47
48a	Amount of line 47 you want **refunded to you.** If Form 8888 is attached, check here ▶ ☐	48a
▶ b	Routing number ☐☐☐☐☐☐☐☐☐ ▶ c Type: ☐ Checking ☐ Savings	
▶ d	Account number ☐☐☐☐☐☐☐☐☐☐☐☐☐☐☐☐☐	
49	Amount of line 47 you want **applied to your 2016 estimated tax.** 49	

Direct deposit? See instructions and fill in 48b, 48c, and 48d or Form 8888.

Amount you owe

50	**Amount you owe.** Subtract line 46 from line 39. For details on how to pay, see instructions.	▶ 50
51	Estimated tax penalty (see instructions). 51	

Third party designee

Do you want to allow another person to discuss this return with the IRS (see instructions)? ☐ **Yes.** Complete the following. ☐ **No**

Designee's name ▶ Phone no. ▶ Personal identification number (PIN) ▶ ☐☐☐☐☐

Sign here

Joint return? See instructions. Keep a copy for your records.

Under penalties of perjury, I declare that I have examined this return and accompanying schedules and statements, and to the best of my knowledge and belief, they are true, correct, and accurately list all amounts and sources of income I received during the tax year. Declaration of preparer (other than the taxpayer) is based on all information of which the preparer has any knowledge.

Your signature	Date	Your occupation	Daytime phone number
Spouse's signature. If a joint return, **both** must sign.	Date	Spouse's occupation	If the IRS sent you an Identity Protection PIN, enter it here (see inst.)

Paid preparer use only

Print/type preparer's name	Preparer's signature	Date	Check ▶ ☐ if self-employed	PTIN
Firm's name ▶			Firm's EIN ▶	
Firm's address ▶			Phone no.	

Form **1040A** (2015)

Chapter

4

Gross Income Exclusions and Deductions for AGI

CHAPTER CONTENTS

LEARNING OBJECTIVES

After completing Chapter 4, you should be able to:

1. Describe the items of income that can be excluded from gross income and compute the amount of the exclusion.
2. Recognize the various types of fringe benefits that employees might receive from their employers.
3. Describe the deductions for AGI specifically listed on Form 1040 and compute the amount of the deduction.
4. Compare and contrast Roth IRAs and traditional IRAs, including the limits imposed on contributions to each type of IRA and the rules that govern distributions from these two types of IRAs.
5. Understand the various tax deductions and exclusions available for education-related expenses.
6. Prepare the tax forms and schedules introduced in the chapter, including Form 8815, Form 3903, and Form 1040.

CHAPTER OVERVIEW

Chapter 3 started the discussion of the calculation of gross income by describing some of the more common types of gross income inclusions. The first part of Chapter 4 continues that discussion by introducing items included in income that are specifically excluded from gross income. The latter part of the chapter introduces the details behind the deductions from gross income (commonly called "deductions for AGI") that are reported directly on the tax return. The chapter concludes with an illustration of Form 1040.

¶401 Exclusions from Gross Income

Income includes all wealth that flows to a taxpayer. Gross income is all income that the government taxes. Exclusions are amounts of income not subject to tax. This section describes several items of income that are entirely or partially exempt from gross income.

¶401.01 GIFTS AND INHERITANCES

The recipient of a gift or inheritance excludes from gross income the value of the gifted or inherited property. The donor of gifted property may be subject to gift tax. However, the recipient is not taxed on these transfers. After the transfer, any subsequent income the property earns is taxed to the recipient under the normal tax laws described in this textbook.

¶401.02 FOREIGN-EARNED INCOME EXCLUSION

For 2015, U.S. citizens and residents may elect to exclude up to $100,800 of income earned while working in foreign countries. To qualify for this exclusion, the taxpayer must either (1) be a bona fide resident of a foreign country for the entire tax year or (2) be physically present in a foreign country for 330 full days during a 12-month period.

When the taxpayer qualifies for the exclusion, but resides in a foreign country only part of the year, the exclusion must be prorated. For example, if a taxpayer resides in France for the last 210 days of 2015 and the first 300 days in 2016, the taxpayer's 510 days of physical presence easily meets the 330-days in a 12-month period requirement. Thus, the taxpayer qualifies for the foreign-earned income exclusion in each year. Assuming the maximum exclusion in both years is $100,800, the maximum exclusion must be prorated as shown below:

2015: (210/365) × $100,800 = $57,995 maximum exclusion

2016: (300/366) × $100,800 = $82,623 maximum exclusion

As an alternative to the exclusion, taxpayers may elect to include all foreign income in gross income and take a tax credit for the income taxes paid to foreign countries. The foreign tax credit is discussed in ¶204.01.

EXAMPLE 1

On June 5, 2015, Jane's employer sends her to work in the Paris office. She is there until October 26, 2016. Jane's annual pay is $90,000. Her earnings while working in France were $52,500 in 2015 and $75,000 in 2016. Jane was not present in France for the entire year in 2015 and 2016, but lived there at least 330 days during a 12-month period. (She lived in France 210 days during 2015 and 300 days during 2016, a leap year). Assuming the maximum exclusion in both years is $100,800, she can reduce her AGI by $57,995 in 2015 and $82,623 in 2016 (see calculations above). Her other option is to include the $90,000 in AGI and use the rules from Chapter 2 to take a foreign tax credit for the income taxes she pays to the French government.

EXAMPLE 2

Same facts as in Example 1, except that Jane works in France until February 15, 2017. Her annual pay remains at $90,000, with $10,000 earned while working in Paris in 2017. Assuming the maximum exclusion stays at $100,800 through 2017, the maximum foreign-earned income exclusion for 2016 would be $100,800. Because Janet's foreign earnings were $90,000 in 2016, her foreign-earned income exclusion is limited to $90,000. In 2017, her maximum foreign-earned income exclusion is $12,704 (46 days/365 × $100,800). However, her foreign earnings that year were $10,000, so her 2017 exclusion is limited to $10,000.

The purpose of the foreign-earned income exclusion and the foreign tax credit is to give tax relief to U.S. citizens and residents of the U.S. who might end up paying income taxes to both the U.S. and the foreign country where they work. In Examples 1 and 2, the maximum exclusion in each of the years was assumed to be $100,800. In reality, the maximum exclusion is adjusted each year to reflect changes in the cost of living (see ¶202 for discussion of indexing for inflation).

¶401.03 FRINGE BENEFITS

A fringe benefit is a type of pay employees receive. It is often in the form of goods or services given to them by their employers. When an employer provides fringe benefits, the employee often avoids paying the costs for these goods or services themselves. Thus, fringe benefits are a source of wealth to employees, and as such, are income. A fringe benefit is taxable unless the tax laws exclude it from gross income. Many tax laws exist that exclude fringe benefits. In the discussion that follows, some of the more common nontaxable fringe benefits are discussed.

Fringe Benefits Discussed in this Chapter

- Accident and health insurance
- Adoption assistance
- Athletic facilities
- Dependent care assistance
- De minimis benefits
- Educational assistance
- Employee discounts
- Group-term life insurance
- Meals and lodging provided on the employer's premises
- Moving expense reimbursement
- No-additional-cost services
- Retirement planning services
- Transportation benefits
- Tuition reduction
- Working condition fringe benefits

Although fringe benefits may be excluded from an employee's gross income, the discrimination rule taxes key and highly paid employees on the value of most fringe benefits they receive when the benefit plan favors them. The discrimination rule applies to all fringe benefits discussed in this chapter, except for de minimis benefits, transportation benefits, and working condition fringe benefits. However, any benefits included as part of a collective bargaining agreement (union contract) are not considered to favor key or highly paid employees (and therefore, not subject to the discrimination rule).

For 2015, a **key employee** is (1) an officer of the company whose annual pay exceeds $170,000; (2) an employee who owns at least 5% of the company; or (3) an employee who owns at least 1% of the company and whose pay exceeds $150,000. **Highly paid employees** are employees, their spouses and dependents who (1) are an officer of the company; (2) own more than 5% of the voting stock in the company; or (3) are highly paid. The tax laws for defining what is considered "highly paid" vary depending on the type of fringe benefit. These rules are beyond the scope of this discussion and can be found in IRS Publication 15-B, Employer's Guide to Fringe Benefits.

The Internal Revenue Code (Code) denies an exclusion to both key and highly paid employees when the benefit plan favors them. However, it continues to allow all other employees to exclude the benefits from gross income. The discrimination rule is intended to encourage employers to provide benefits to all of their employees, not just those who are officers, shareholders, or highly paid.

Accident and Health Insurance

Employers often offer their employees health insurance coverage. Employees exclude from gross income the premiums employers pay on their behalf. Employees also exclude any insurance reimbursements they receive for medical care. However, the discrimination rule denies this exclusion to key and highly paid employees if the employer's plan favors them.

EXAMPLE 3

Santex, Inc. provides its employees with health insurance coverage. During the year, it pays $8,000 of insurance premiums for each of its employees. As long as Santex's plan does not favor key or highly paid employees, none of the employees are taxed on the $8,000 of insurance premiums. However, if the plan discriminates in favor of these employees, then the employer adds $8,000 to the taxable wages of its key and highly paid employees (but not its other employees).

Dependent Care Assistance

An employee can exclude from gross income up to $5,000 of amounts employers pay to provide dependent care for their employees under a dependent care assistance program. Only an employee's children and dependents can receive such care. Also, the care must be provided so that the employee can work. Instead of making payments to outsiders, an employer can provide care at the work site.

The annual exclusion cannot exceed the *lesser of* (i) $5,000 ($2,500 for married persons filing separately) or (ii) the employee's earned income. If the employee is married, then the earned income of the spouse with the lesser earnings is used. Special rules (similar to those discussed in ¶204.02) apply if the taxpayer or the taxpayer's spouse is either a full-time student or incapable of self-care. Taxpayers who use the exclusion must reduce their child and dependent care payments by the excluded amount when computing the child and dependent care credit (¶204.02).

Instead of providing dependent care for their employees, employers can set up plans that allow employees to be reimbursed for their dependent care costs from accounts that employees fund with their own wages. These accounts are commonly known as dependent care flexible spending accounts (FSAs). A dependent care FSA allows employees to set aside each year up to $5,000 of their wages from which they can pay qualified dependent care costs. Employers withhold FSA contribution amounts from employees' pay. Amounts withheld are excluded from employees' taxable wages. Thus, contributions to FSAs are made with pre-tax dollars. As employees pay for qualified dependent care costs, they submit receipts to their plan administrator for reimbursement from their FSA accounts.

EXAMPLE 4

Janet's employer offers a dependent care FSA. This year, Janet contributes $5,000 of her $45,000 wages to her FSA. As Janet pays for dependent care, she will submit her receipts to the plan administrator for reimbursement from her account. The $5,000 Janet uses to fund her FSA is excluded from gross income. This will be reflected on her W-2, which will report $40,000 of taxable wages. Because of her FSA contribution (and reduced taxable wages), Janet will pay less taxes this year. Hence, Janet's total out-of-pocket costs for dependent care are actually less than the $5,000 she paid to the child care provider.

Adoption Assistance

Under an adoption assistance program, employers pay or reimburse employees for qualified adoption costs. For 2015, employees exclude from gross income up to $13,400 of such costs. This amount is phased-out when the employee's AGI falls between $201,010 and $241,010. These amounts are the same as those used in computing the adoption credit (¶204.10). Amounts excluded from gross income reduce the amount eligible for the adoption credit.

EXAMPLE 5

Joe's employer offers an adoption assistance program. During 2015, Joe is reimbursed $8,000 for adoption costs incurred during the year. Joe's AGI is $120,000. Since this amount is less than the $201,010 AGI threshold, the entire $8,000 is excluded from Joe's gross income.

Educational Assistance

Under an educational assistance plan, employers pay or reimburse employees for qualified education costs. Each year, employees can exclude up to $5,250. The exclusion covers amounts paid for tuition, fees, books and supplies. Both graduate and undergraduate courses are included.

EXAMPLE 6

Leon's employer offers an educational assistance program. During the year, Leon was reimbursed $4,000 for tuition, books and fees for courses he took at the local college. Since this amount is less than the $5,250 maximum exclusion, the $4,000 is excluded from Leon's gross income.

Tuition Reduction

Colleges and universities can exclude from their employees' wages the value of a qualified tuition reduction they give their employees. A tuition reduction for graduate education qualifies for the exclusion if it is for the education of a graduate student who performs teaching or research activities for the institution. For undergraduate courses, the exclusion is allowed if the education is for of one of the following persons.

1. A current employee.
2. A former employee who retired or left on disability.
3. A widow(er) of a person who died while working as an employee.
4. A widow(er) of a former employee who retired or left on disability.
5. A dependent child or spouse of any person listed above.

Group-Term Life Insurance

Sometimes an employer buys life insurance for employees under a group-term plan, where the employees name their beneficiaries. For each employee, the employer can purchase up to $50,000 of insurance without increasing the employee's gross income. When the coverage exceeds $50,000, the employee adds to gross income the cost associated with the excess insurance coverage. To determine this cost, the employer uses a uniform premium table (Figure 4-1).

Figure 4-1: Uniform Premium Table

Age at Year-End	Taxable Amount Each Month for $1,000 of Excess Coverage
Under 25	$.05
25–29	.06
30–34	.08
35–39	.09
40–44	.10
45–49	.15
50–54	.23
55–59	.43
60–64	.66
65–69	1.27
70 and over	2.06

To compute the employee's taxable amount, first determine the excess coverage under the plan. Next, divide the excess by $1,000, and round the result to the nearest tenth. The uniform premium table (Figure 4-1) lists the insurance rates by age. The employer determines an employee's age on the last day of the year and looks up the monthly rate for the employee's age. The employer then multiplies the monthly rate by the number of $1,000 increments. Finally, the employer multiplies this amount by the number of months of insurance coverage. The formula used is as follows:

Taxable Amount = **Monthly Rate from Figure 4-1** × **Number of $1,000 Increments of Excess Coverage (rounded to the nearest tenth)** × **Number of Months of Coverage**

When the employee pays part of the premiums, the employer subtracts all of the employee's payments from the (calculated) cost of the excess insurance. When the cost exceeds an employee's payments, the excess is included in the employee's gross income as additional taxable wages on Form W-2. When an employee's payments exceed the cost of the excess insurance, the employee has no additional gross income.

EXAMPLE 7

Bow Company pays an annual premium for $94,700 of life insurance for Harry Socket, age 56. Bow shares the cost with Harry, who pays Bow $12.50 a month through payroll deductions. With these payments, Harry gets 12 months of group-term life insurance protection. For Harry's age, the table in Figure 4-1 shows a monthly cost of $0.43. Bow adds $80.65 to Harry's taxable wages, as computed below.

Group-term life insurance coverage	$94,700
Less exempt coverage	(50,000)
Taxable coverage	$44,700
Cost subject to gross income inclusion [$44,700/$1,000 = 44.7; 44.7 × $0.43 × 12]	$230.65
Less payments by Harry ($12.50 × 12)	(150.00)
Gross income	$80.65

Employers whose plan favors key or highly paid employees must include in these favored employees' gross income the full cost of group-term life insurance provided to them (not just the excess over $50,000). The taxable amount for these favored employees is the *greater of* (i) the actual premiums paid, or (ii) the amount computed using the table in Figure 4-1.

EXAMPLE 8

Tom is 45 years old and a key employee at his firm. The employer provides Tom with $200,000 of group life insurance coverage. The employer's actual cost for this coverage is $800; Tom pays nothing. If the employer's plan favors key or highly paid employees, Tom's employer would add $800 to Tom's taxable wages on Form W-2. This amount is the *greater of* (i) the employer's $800 actual cost, or (ii) $360, as determined using the monthly amounts in Figure 4-1 ($.15 × 200 increments based on $200,000 of coverage × 12 months). If the plan does not favor key or highly paid employees, the employer adds $270 to Tom's taxable wages ($150,000 excess coverage ÷ $1,000 = 150 increments × $.15 × 12).

Other Fringe Benefits

Employers may also offer a number of other fringe benefits. The discrimination rule applies to each of these benefits, except for transportation (6.), working condition (7.), and de minimis benefits (9.).

1. **Athletic facilities.** Employees exclude from gross income the value of the use of athletic facilities provided on the employer's property. These services include tennis courts, swimming pools, weight rooms, etc. To qualify for the exclusion, substantially all of the facility's use must be by employees, their spouses, and their dependent children.
2. **Qualified employee discounts.** Employees may exclude from gross income discounts they receive from their employers on goods and services. To qualify for the exclusion, the employee must work in the part of the employer's business giving the discount. For example, airline employees cannot exclude discounts they receive at a hotel owned by the airline company. For services, the amount of the discount cannot exceed 20% of the price charged to nonemployees. For goods, the discount cannot exceed the employer's gross profit percentage times the price charged to nonemployees.

EXAMPLE 9

A department store's gross profit percentage is 40%. The store's policy is to offer all its employees a 60% discount. The 20% excess discount times the sales price charged to nonemployees would be taxed as additional wages to employees who take advantage of the employee discount.

EXAMPLE 10

A clothing store offers a 15% discount to regular employees. It gives a 25% discount to highly paid employees. The store's gross profit percentage is 35%. Although neither discount exceeds the store's 35% gross profit percentage, the difference in discounts shows that the plan favors highly paid employees. Thus, the entire 25% discount to employees in the favored group is added to their gross income. Regular employees are not affected. They still exclude their 15% discount.

3. **No-additional-cost services.** Employees exclude from gross income the value of services that do not cause large added costs or lost revenues to the employer. Examples of no-additional-cost services are the use of vacant hotel rooms, as well as unsold seats on airlines, buses and trains. To get the exclusion, the employee must work in the line of business providing the services.
4. **Meals and lodging.** Employees exclude the value of meals and lodging provided by their employer when provided on the employer's premises for the convenience of the employer as a condition of employment. For example, nurses and doctors may be allowed to eat in the hospital cafeteria free-of-charge so that they can be reached, if needed in an emergency. Likewise, resident advisors of college dorms may exclude the value of the room and board provided to them free-of-charge if the college requires them to live in the dorm as a condition of their employment.

5. **Moving reimbursements.** Employees can exclude from gross income amounts their employers pay or reimburse to them for qualified moving expenses. To qualify for the exclusion, the costs covered by the employer must be those that the employee would have been able to deduct for AGI. Deductible moving expenses are discussed later in this chapter at ¶402.04.
6. **Transportation (commuting) benefits.** In 2015, employees exclude from gross income up to $250 a month for employer-provided qualified parking. They also can exclude up to $130 a month for employer-provided qualified transportation. **Qualified parking** includes parking provided near the employer's business or near the place where the employee commutes to work using mass transit or carpools. **Qualified transportation** includes transit passes and transportation to the employer's workplace in a commuter vehicle. Employees can also exclude up to $20 a month paid to them for using a bike to commute to work. Unlike many of the other fringe benefits, the discrimination rule does not apply to transportation benefits. Thus, key employees and highly paid employees can exclude the value of these benefits, even when the benefit plan favors them.

EXAMPLE 11

Quinn's employer provides free monthly parking to its employees. The parking is valued at $300. The maximum monthly benefit for 2015 is $250. Thus, the employer includes an additional $600 ($50 excess × 12 months) in Quinn's 2015 taxable wages.

7. **Working condition fringe benefits.** Usually employees deduct their job-related expenses as an itemized deduction. When an employer pays for these costs, employees exclude their value from gross income. This includes amounts that qualify as deductible education costs that exceed the $5,250 fringe benefit under an employer's educational assistance plan. The discrimination rule does not apply to working condition fringe benefits. Thus, key employees and highly paid employees can exclude the value of working condition fringe benefits, even when the benefit plan favors them.

EXAMPLE 12

Lenny's employer offers a qualifying educational assistance program. Lenny is reimbursed $8,400 for tuition, books and fees for courses he took at the local college. If not reimbursed, the $8,400 would have been deductible as an employee business expense. Lenny excludes $5,250 under the educational assistance program. He excludes the rest ($8,400 – $5,250 = $3,150) as a working condition fringe benefit.

8. **Qualified retirement plan services.** Employees exclude from gross income the value of any qualified retirement plan services provided to them or their spouses by their employers.
9. ***De minimis* fringe benefits.** Employees exclude from gross income benefits of a small (de minimis) value that they receive from employers. Examples include occasional personal use of copy machines and office supplies. They also may include occasional tickets to entertainment and sporting events and office parties. Employees also exclude small holiday gifts, such as turkeys and hams. The discrimination rule does not apply to *de minimis* fringe benefits. Thus, key employees can exclude the value of occasional tickets to a sporting event, even if such tickets are only offered to key employees.

¶401.04 LIFE INSURANCE PROCEEDS

Usually, life insurance proceeds paid because of the insured's death are tax-free. However, gross income results when an insurance company holds on to the proceeds of the policy and pays out the interest to the beneficiary. Under such an arrangement, gross income includes the interest when it becomes available to the beneficiary (e.g. credited to the beneficiary's account).

¶401.05 SCHOLARSHIPS AND FELLOWSHIPS

A student excludes from gross income the portion of scholarships and fellowship grants used to pay tuition and course-required fees, books, supplies, and equipment. Only degree candidates get this exclusion. Degree candidates include undergraduate and graduate students who pursue studies aimed at getting an academic or professional degree. Postdoctoral fellowship students do not get this exclusion.

Graduate students who get paid to teach or do research at their degree-granting institutions can exclude tuition waivers they receive. They cannot reduce their taxable wages by amounts spent on books, supplies, and equipment.

The exclusion for scholarships does not apply to compensation for services rendered, even if all candidates for the degree are required to perform the services.

Students with taxable scholarships report this amount as additional wages on Form 1040EZ, Form 1040A or Form 1040. The student writes in the words **SCH =** and the taxable amount in the space to the left of where taxable wages are reported. Thus, these amounts count as earned income for purposes of computing the standard deduction for those claimed as a dependent on another's return (¶106.03).

EXAMPLE 13

Mandy is awarded a $10,000 scholarship to attend State College. Mandy is claimed as a dependent on her parents' return. Her tuition and course-required books and fees for the year are $6,000. The rest of the scholarship is used to cover room and board. Mandy excludes $6,000 of the scholarship from gross income. On her tax return she writes in "SCH = $4,000" and adds the $4,000 to her taxable wages. This amount is used to compute her limited standard deduction (the *lesser of* (i) $1,050 or (ii) earned income + $350; see ¶106.03).

¶401.06 TAX-EXEMPT INTEREST

Interest on general obligation bonds of a state, territory, or the District of Columbia is not taxable. This exclusion also applies to bonds issued by cities, counties, and school districts. Although it is not taxable, taxpayers report the amount of tax-exempt interest separately on their returns as an information item.

Educational Savings Bonds, Series EE and I

You may recall from Chapter 3 that the interest on savings bonds is not taxed until the bonds are redeemed (see ¶308.02). Under certain conditions, taxpayers can exclude the interest on Series EE and I U.S. Savings Bonds they redeem during the year. The exclusion applies when the taxpayer uses the proceeds to pay for qualified educational expenses at an eligible institution. When there are proceeds left over after the educational expenses are paid, some of the interest is taxed. Also, when the taxpayer's income rises above a certain level, the exclusion is phased out. This exclusion applies only to bonds purchased after 1989.

To qualify for the exclusion, the taxpayer (or spouse, if filing jointly) must be the registered owner of the bond. Married taxpayers must file a joint return to qualify for the exclusion. Bonds issued to persons under age 24 do not qualify for the exclusion, unless they received the bonds upon the death of the registered owner. Taxpayers use Form 8815, Exclusion of Interest From Series EE and I U.S. Savings Bonds Issued After 1989, to compute the excluded interest.

Eligible institutions include public and nonprofit higher education schools, as well as post-secondary institutions. They do not include proprietary schools. **Qualified educational expenses** include tuition and fees paid to an eligible institution for the taxpayer, the taxpayer's spouse, and the taxpayer's dependents. Such expenses do not include payments for room and board. They also do not include payments for courses involving sports, games, or hobbies, unless the courses are taken as part of a degree- or certificate-granting program in sports. The taxpayer must reduce qualified expenses by certain nontaxable benefits received during the year. These benefits include scholarships awarded to the student and amounts received from an employer-provided educational assistance plan. Expenses used in computing the education tax credit for the student also reduce qualified expenses.

Taxpayers use the following formula to determine the interest exclusion before applying the phase-out rules.

Bonds Interest Exclusion Before Phase-Out

$$\text{Initial Exclusion} = \text{Interest Portion of the Proceeds} \times \frac{\text{Qualified Education Expenses} - \text{Nontaxable Benefits} - \text{Expenses Used in Computing Education Credits}}{\text{Redemption Proceeds}}$$

After using the above formula to determine the initial exclusion amount, taxpayers compute their modified AGI. This amount is AGI computed without the educational savings bond interest exclusion (currently being calculated) and the foreign earned income exclusion (¶401.02). They then compare this amount with the $77,200 threshold ($115,750 for MFJ or qualifying widow(er)). If modified AGI exceeds this threshold, the phase-out applies. The interest exclusion phases out proportionately over a range of $15,000 ($30,000 for MFJ or qualifying widow(er)). The phase-out threshold is adjusted each year for inflation (see ¶202).

Phase-Out of Bond Interest Exclusion

$$\text{Initial Exclusion} \times \frac{\text{Modified AGI} - \$77{,}200^{*}}{\$15{,}000^{**}} = \text{Reduction in Interest Exclusion}$$

* $115,750 for MFJ or qualifying widow(er)
** $30,000 for MFJ or qualifying widow(er)

EXAMPLE 14 Fred and Ida Smith file a joint return. They claim their daughter, Inez, as a dependent. During the year, the Smiths paid $5,000 for Inez's tuition at Kent State University, where Inez is a full-time student. During the year, Inez received a $1,000 nontaxable scholarship. In September, the Smiths redeemed $10,000 of Series EE bonds. Of the cash received, $1,500 is interest and $8,500 is principal. The Smiths' modified AGI is $120,400.

Qualified education expenses for the year were $4,000 ($5,000 – $1,000 nontaxable scholarship). Because the Smiths did not use the entire $10,000 of proceeds on qualified education expenses, a portion of the $1,500 of interest income does not qualify for the exclusion. Their initial exclusion is $600 ($1,500 × $4,000/$10,000). However, since the Smiths' modified AGI exceeds the $115,750 MFJ threshold, they must further reduce the amount of their exclusion. The amount of the reduction is $93 ($600 initial exclusion × ($120,400 modified AGI – $115,750 MFJ)/$30,000). Thus, $507 ($600 – $93) of the interest is excluded from gross income.

¶401.07 FILLED-IN FORM 8815

INFORMATION FOR FIGURE 4-2:

The Smiths (from Example 14) complete Form 8815 to compute their educational savings bond interest exclusion. They enter the amounts in bold from below on the appropriate lines on the form. They then follow the instructions on the form to complete the rest of the form. After the Smiths report all $1,500 as interest income on Schedule B (line 1), they enter $507 on Schedule B (line 3) to subtract out their "Excludable interest on series EE and I U.S. savings bonds."

Line #

2: Qualified higher education expenses paid in 2015, **$5,000**
3: Inez's nontaxable scholarship, **$1,000**
5: Proceeds from Series EE bonds, **$10,000**
6: Interest associated with EE bonds, **$1,500**
9: Modified AGI, **$120,400**

Figure 4-2: Filled-In Form 8815

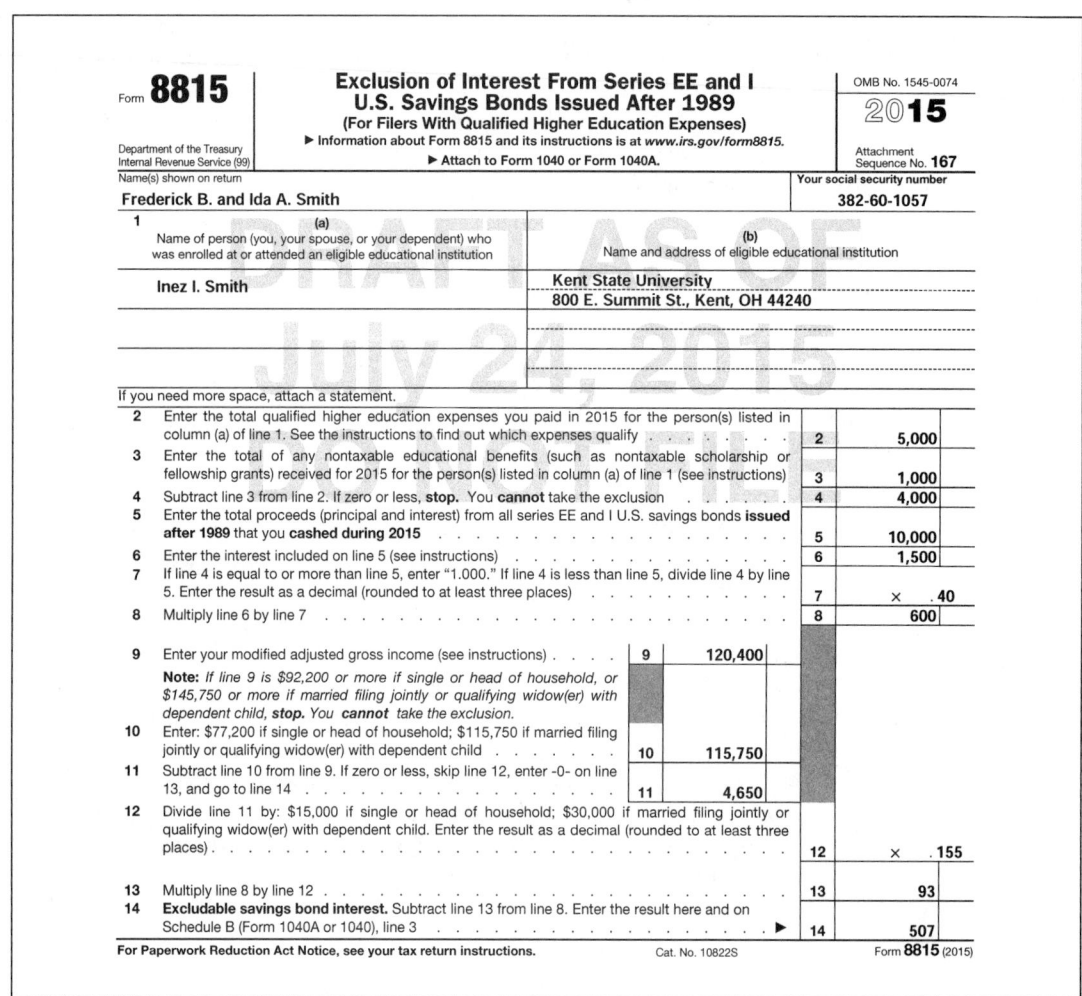

Form **8815**

Department of the Treasury
Internal Revenue Service (99)

Exclusion of Interest From Series EE and I U.S. Savings Bonds Issued After 1989
(For Filers With Qualified Higher Education Expenses)
▶ Information about Form 8815 and its instructions is at *www.irs.gov/form8815.*
▶ Attach to Form 1040 or Form 1040A.

OMB No. 1545-0074
2015
Attachment Sequence No. **167**

Name(s) shown on return	Your social security number
Frederick B. and Ida A. Smith	382-60-1057

1 (a) Name of person (you, your spouse, or your dependent) who was enrolled at or attended an eligible educational institution	(b) Name and address of eligible educational institution
Inez I. Smith	Kent State University 800 E. Summit St., Kent, OH 44240

If you need more space, attach a statement.

2	Enter the total qualified higher education expenses you paid in 2015 for the person(s) listed in column (a) of line 1. See the instructions to find out which expenses qualify			2	5,000
3	Enter the total of any nontaxable educational benefits (such as nontaxable scholarship or fellowship grants) received for 2015 for the person(s) listed in column (a) of line 1 (see instructions)			3	1,000
4	Subtract line 3 from line 2. If zero or less, **stop.** You **cannot** take the exclusion			4	4,000
5	Enter the total proceeds (principal and interest) from all series EE and I U.S. savings bonds **issued after 1989** that you **cashed during 2015**			5	10,000
6	Enter the interest included on line 5 (see instructions)			6	1,500
7	If line 4 is equal to or more than line 5, enter "1.000." If line 4 is less than line 5, divide line 4 by line 5. Enter the result as a decimal (rounded to at least three places)			7	× .40
8	Multiply line 6 by line 7			8	600
9	Enter your modified adjusted gross income (see instructions)	9	120,400		
	Note: *If line 9 is $92,200 or more if single or head of household, or $145,750 or more if married filing jointly or qualifying widow(er) with dependent child,* ***stop.*** *You* ***cannot*** *take the exclusion.*				
10	Enter: $77,200 if single or head of household; $115,750 if married filing jointly or qualifying widow(er) with dependent child	10	115,750		
11	Subtract line 10 from line 9. If zero or less, skip line 12, enter -0- on line 13, and go to line 14	11	4,650		
12	Divide line 11 by: $15,000 if single or head of household; $30,000 if married filing jointly or qualifying widow(er) with dependent child. Enter the result as a decimal (rounded to at least three places)			12	× .155
13	Multiply line 8 by line 12			13	93
14	**Excludable savings bond interest.** Subtract line 13 from line 8. Enter the result here and on Schedule B (Form 1040A or 1040), line 3 ▶			14	507

For Paperwork Reduction Act Notice, see your tax return instructions. Cat. No. 10822S Form **8815** (2015)

¶401.08 COMPENSATION FOR PHYSICAL INJURY AND SICKNESS

Persons who are harmed on or off the job will sometimes receive payments related to their injuries. These payments can vary from workers' compensation, damage awards, and payments from an accident or health plan. Under the general rule, these payments are all types of income to the recipient. Whether any of these payments can be excluded from gross income depends on the type of payment, and in some cases, the type of injury.

WORKERS' COMPENSATION

Workers' compensation is payments made to an injured employee to cover lost wages and pay the employee's medical expenses. In exchange, the employee gives up the right to sue the employer for negligence. Taxpayers who receive workers' compensation exclude it from gross income, even though the payments are meant to replace wages that would have been taxed if earned on the job.

COMPENSATORY PAYMENTS AND MEDICAL REIMBURSEMENTS

Payments a person receives to compensate them for a physical injury or sickness are excluded from gross income. Such payments are awarded to injured parties to make them whole again. Compensatory payments may cover lost wages or profits, which normally would be taxed had they been earned. Although emotional distress is not a physical injury, when payments for emotional distress are received as a result of a physical injury or sickness, they too are excluded from gross income. The reasoning is that the emotional distress is considered a part of the physical injury or sickness.

Also excluded from gross income are reimbursements for medical expenses stemming from a physical injury or sickness. However, if in a prior tax year the taxpayer had deducted and received a tax benefit for the medical expenses being reimbursed, then to the extent of the tax benefit received, the taxpayer reports that amount as "Other income" on Form 1040. (See ¶313.01 for a discussion of the tax benefit rule).

Compensatory payments awarded for nonphysical injuries are always taxable. Examples of nonphysical injuries for which someone might be awarded payments include harassment, discrimination, wrongful termination, libel, slander, and invasion of privacy. Even though these compensatory payments are made to make the injured person whole again, payments received for nonphysical injuries are taxable to the person receiving them.

> As a rule, it does not matter if the amounts awarded stem from a lawsuit or an out-of-court settlement. It also does not matter if the amount awarded is received in a lump sum or a series of payments.

PUNITIVE DAMAGES

Amounts awarded by the courts for punitive damages are taxable, even if they stem from a physical injury or sickness. Punitive damages are meant to punish the wrongdoer, rather than to compensate the victim. They often are awarded when the party that caused the harm was negligent or did something illegal.

PAYMENTS FROM AN ACCIDENT OR HEALTH PLAN

When the injured person receives payments from an accident or health plan, whether those payments are excluded from gross income depends on who paid the premiums. However, if any part of the payment received is a reimbursement for medical costs, the rules discussed earlier in this section (for compensatory payments) apply. Non-medical payments received from the plan are included in the employee's gross income to the extent that the employer paid the premiums. Thus, if 75% of the premiums are paid by the employer and 25% by the employee, only 25% the payments received will be excluded from gross income. If the employee pays the entire premiums, then all payments are excluded from gross income. If the employer pays all of the premiums, then the employee is taxed on all payments received.

¶401.09 ROTH IRAS

Another source of tax-free income comes from investing in a Roth IRA. Taxpayers make non-deductible contributions to Roth IRAs and in return, the earnings grow tax-free. Taxpayers make withdrawals tax- and penalty-free if the distribution is made after the Roth IRA has been open for five tax years and any one of the following conditions is met.

1. The distribution is made after the taxpayer reaches age 59½.
2. The distribution is made to a beneficiary as a result of the taxpayer's death.
3. The distribution is made on account of the taxpayer's disability.
4. The distribution is used to pay first-time homebuyer expenses (subject to a $10,000 lifetime limit).

Amounts withdrawn from a Roth IRA are considered to come first from contributions, and then earnings. When distributions do not meet at least one of the above criteria, amounts received in excess of the taxpayer's contributions are included in gross income. A 10% early withdrawal penalty also applies to the amount taxed. However, taxpayers can withdraw their contributions at any time and for any reason without tax or penalty. Since contributions to a Roth IRA are not deductible, there is never any tax when only the taxpayer's contributions are taken from a Roth IRA. However, once the taxpayer has withdrawn amounts from a Roth IRA, they cannot be returned to the IRA to grow tax-free.

EXAMPLE 15 After making contributions of $4,500 over a three-year period, Ben (age 35) withdraws the $5,400 from his Roth IRA to buy a new car. Of this amount, $4,500 is a tax-free withdrawal of his contributions. Ben must pay income tax on the earnings of $900. He also pays a nondeductible early withdrawal penalty of $90 (10% × $900).

For 2015, the maximum contribution to a Roth IRA is the *lesser of* (i) $5,500 or (ii) 100% of the taxpayer's earned income. Taxpayers at least 50 years old may contribute another $1,000. When a married couple files a joint tax return, the amount increases to $11,000 (plus $1,000 for each spouse who is 50 or older). However, the couple must have enough combined earnings to match the total contribution. Each spouse must establish a separate Roth IRA. Also, the amount that can be contributed to either spouse's Roth IRA cannot exceed $5,500 ($6,500 if age 50 or older). The taxpayer's maximum contribution is proportionally phased out when AGI falls within the following ranges:

Single, head of household, and MFS but did not live with spouse at any time during the year: $116,000–$131,000 [$15,000 range]
MFJ and qualifying widow(er): $183,000–$193,000 [$10,000 range]
MFS and lived with spouse at some point during the year: $0–$10,000 [$10,000 range]

Taxpayers round their reduced contribution up to the nearest $10. If their reduced contribution is more than $0, but less than $200, they increase the amount to $200. Examples 16 and 17 show how the reduced contribution is computed for taxpayers whose AGI falls in the phase-out range.

EXAMPLE 16

Grace is single and 43 years old. She wants to contribute the most she can to a Roth IRA. Her AGI is $118,181. For 2015, Grace may contribute $4,700. She computes her maximum contribution as follows:

Reduction in maximum contribution:

[($118,181 – $116,000) / $15,000 phase-out range for unmarried taxpayers] × $5,500 = $800

Contribution limit:

$5,500 – $800 = $4,700 (no rounding needed)

EXAMPLE 17

Kathy and Adam Keck are both age 60. Since both are age 50 or older, their initial Roth IRA limit increases to $6,500 ($5,500 + $1,000). However, their AGI is $191,482 (most of which comes from taxable wages), so the maximum each of them can contribute to their respective Roth IRA for 2015 is $990.

Reduction in maximum contribution:

[($191,482 – $183,000)/$10,000 phase-out range for MFJ] × $6,500 = $5,513

Contribution limit:

$6,500 – $5,513 = $987, rounded up to nearest $10: $990

Taxpayers filing MFJ with over $193,000 of AGI ($10,000 for MFS and living with their spouse; $131,000 for all others) cannot contribute to a Roth IRA for 2015. They may, however, contribute to a traditional IRA (discussed at ¶402.11).

The deadline for making contributions to a Roth IRA for 2015 is April 15, 2016. The IRS charges a 6% penalty on excess contributions made to an IRA. In addition to the penalty, when the excess amounts are withdrawn, the earnings withdrawn are subject to income tax and a 10% early withdrawal penalty.

¶401.10 ROTH 401(k) PLANS

An employer's 401(k) plan may let employees make designated Roth 401(k) contributions. **Designated Roth contributions** are made with post-tax wages. This means that that amounts designated as Roth contributions do not reduce the employee's taxable wages. However, as with Roth IRAs, qualified distributions from Roth 401(k) plans are tax-free once the account has been around for five years. Like with Roth IRAs, the part of a nonqualified distribution that is earnings is included in gross income and subject to a 10% early withdrawal penalty. Although Roth 401(k) plans are similar to Roth IRAs, the two differ in several ways.

1. There is no income limit on who can make designated Roth contributions. [Contributions allowed to a Roth IRA are phased out once unmarried taxpayer's AGI in 2015 exceeds $131,000 ($193,000 for MFJ taxpayers; $10,000 for most MFS taxpayers)].
2. In 2015, employees can contribute up to $18,000 of their wages (plus $6,000 if age 50 or older) to a Roth 401(k). [The 2015 limits for Roth IRAs are $5,500 and $6,500, respectively].
3. Qualified distributions are the same as those used for Roth IRAs. However, withdrawing amounts for first-time home purchases is a nonqualified distribution from a Roth 401(k).

¶401.11 COVERDELL EDUCATION SAVINGS ACCOUNTS

An education savings account (ESA) is a tax-advantaged way to save for a child's education. The contributor opens an ESA and names the child as the beneficiary. Often the contributor is the child's parent or grandparent. However, there is no rule that contributor be related to the child.

Contributions to an ESA are not deductible and must be made prior to the child's 18th birthday. Otherwise a 6% penalty is assessed. There is no age restriction for a child with special needs.

An annual $2,000 contribution limit applies to all ESAs where the child is the named the beneficiary. A 6% penalty is assessed if combined contributions for a child during any year exceed $2,000. Since $2,000 is a per beneficiary limit, a taxpayer can contribute to multiple ESAs for different children, as long as the $2,000 per beneficiary limit (by all contributors) is not exceeded.

EXAMPLE 18 Three years ago, Grandpa Joe opened up an ESA for his grandson, Kyle. The next year, Kyle's father opened up a second ESA in his son's name. These are the only two ESAs where Kyle is the beneficiary. If in the current year Grandpa Joe contributes $700 to the first ESA, the most Kyle's father can contribute to the second ESA is $1,300 ($2,000 per beneficiary limit – $700). If Kyle's father mistakenly contributes $2,000 during the year, a 6% penalty will be assessed on the $700 excess.

Married taxpayers who file MFJ and have modified AGI in excess of $220,000 ($110,000 for all other taxpayers) cannot contribute to an ESA. A reduced contribution is allowed for MFJ taxpayers with modified AGI that falls between $190,000–$220,000 ($95,000–$110,000 for all other taxpayers). For most taxpayers, modified AGI is the same as their AGI.

EXAMPLE 19 Same as in Example 18, except that Grandpa Joe, who is widowed, has modified AGI of $115,000. Since Grandpa Joe's modified AGI exceeds $110,000, he is not allowed to make any ESA contributions this year. If he mistakenly contributes to an ESA, a 6% penalty will be assessed on his contribution.

The tax-advantaged feature of these accounts is that earnings distributed from an ESA are excluded from the child's gross income as long as the child uses the amounts to pay for qualified education expenses before the child's 30th birthday. When distributions during the year exceed the amount of qualified higher education expenses, the law treats some of the excess as a distribution of earnings and taxes it.

Qualified education expenses include tuition, fees, books, supplies, equipment, and room and board. For room and board to qualify, the student must attend school on at least a half-time basis in a program leading to a recognized educational credential. It does not matter whether the qualified expenses are paid for the student's elementary (grade school), secondary (junior high and high school), or post-secondary (college) education.

When the beneficiary reaches age 30, any unused amount in the account must be distributed to the beneficiary. Any earnings included in the distribution will be added to the beneficiary's gross income and taxed. A 10% penalty on the earnings will also be assessed. To avoid this situation, the unused amount may be rolled over into an ESA of a sibling or child of the beneficiary and escape both income taxes and the 10% penalty.

i

The beneficiary can make a tax-free distribution from a Coverdell ESA in the same year part of the beneficiary's education costs are paid for with tax-free educational assistance. A tax-free distribution can also be made in a year in which an education tax credit is claimed on behalf of the beneficiary. However, the same educational expenses cannot be used for more than one purpose. Thus, in computing qualified education expenses from the ESA, the beneficiary must first reduce the education costs by amounts paid for with tax-free educational assistance from an employer's fringe benefit plan. Any remaining costs then must be reduced by expenses taken into account in computing the American opportunity or lifetime learning tax credit.

¶401.12 529 PLANS

Many states, colleges, and brokerage firms have set up qualified tuition programs from which taxpayers can later pay a beneficiary's college expenses. In most cases, the beneficiary is the taxpayer's child or grandchild; however, there is no rule that the beneficiary be related to the taxpayer (contributor). The more common name for these accounts is **529 plans**.

Contributions to 529 plans are not deductible, but the earnings from these accounts remain tax free if the funds are later used to pay qualified education expenses for the beneficiary. Qualified expenses include tuition, fees, books, and supplies, as well as room and board. However, these amounts must be reduced by any tax-free assistance the student uses to pay for these costs. For example, if the student receives a nontaxable scholarship, qualified expenses are computed net of the scholarship. Likewise, if a parent is reimbursed amounts from an employer's educational assistance plan, qualified expenses are computed net of the reimbursement.

EXAMPLE 20

Starting in 2007, Paul has contributed each year to a 529 plan for his daughter, Susan. At the end of last year, the balance in the plan is $30,000. In the fall of this year, $6,000 is withdrawn from the account to pay for Susan's tuition and fees at Northwest College. None of the $6,000 is taxable. The balance left in the account can be used in the future to pay more of Susan's qualified education expenses.

If amounts withdrawn from a 529 plan are not used to pay the beneficiary's qualified education expenses, a portion of the earnings withdrawn are included in the beneficiary's gross income. The taxable earnings equal the earnings withdrawn times the ratio of the nonqualified distribution to the total amount withdrawn from the 529 plan.

EXAMPLE 21

Same facts as in Example 20, except that Susan received a $4,500 scholarship to cover her tuition. Qualified expenses would be reduced to $1,500 ($6,000 – $4,500), leaving the excess of $4,500 withdrawn as a nonqualified distribution. If $1,000 of the $6,000 withdrawn is earnings, then 75% ($4,500 nonqualified distribution ÷ $6,000 withdrawn) of the $1,000, or $750, would be included in Susan's gross income.

If the beneficiary ends up not going to college, the plan refunds the amount in the account to the contributor. Any portion returned that is earnings is taxed to the contributor as interest income.

The earnings on amounts withdrawn from a 529 plan that are not used for qualified education expenses are taxed to the beneficiary. However, when the beneficiary does not attend college, the 529 plan funds revert back to the contributor and the earnings are taxed to the contributor. This is different from the way education savings accounts (ESAs) work. With an ESA, if the beneficiary does not attend college, the earnings from the account are taxed to the beneficiary, unless they are rolled over into an ESA of the beneficiary's sibling or child.

¶401.13 ABLE ACCOUNTS

ABLE accounts were enacted by Congress late in 2014 as part of the Achieving a Better Life Experience (ABLE) Act. ABLE accounts are similar to 529 plans in that contributions are not deductible (made with after-tax dollars). Likewise, the earnings are never taxed as long as the amounts from the account are used to pay for qualified expenses.

The account owner and beneficiary of an ABLE account is a person who became disabled before turning 26 and who receives social security benefits as a result of that disability. Eligible persons can have only one ABLE account, and the account must be one offered by the state where the disabled person lives. Total contributions to an ABLE account (from all contributors) are limited each year. The limit for 2015 is $14,000. Excess contributions are subject to a 6% penalty.

Distributions from ABLE accounts are tax-free as long as the amounts are used to pay the beneficiary's "qualified disability expenses." Earnings withdrawn as part of a nonqualified distribution are included in the beneficiary's gross income and subject to a 10% penalty. Qualified disability expenses are those related to the beneficiary's blindness or disability, as well as those that help the disabled person maintain or improve health, independence, and quality of life. Examples include costs related to housing, education, transportation, health care, job training, and personal support services.

¶401.14 DISCHARGE OF DEBT

When a taxpayer's debt is forgiven, the decrease in debt causes the taxpayer's net worth to increase, thereby resulting in income. Usually the amount of forgiven debt is included in gross income; however, if the taxpayer is bankrupt or insolvent at the time that debt is forgiven, the forgiven debt is excluded from gross income.

From 2007-2014, up to $2 million of income resulting from the discharge of debt on the taxpayer's principal residence (main home) was excluded from gross income ($1 million for MFS). Although this exclusion expired at the end of 2014, some believe that it may be renewed before the end of 2015.

¶402 Deductions for AGI

Not all deductions for AGI are deducted directly on Form 1040. Some deductions offset gross income on supporting forms and schedules, with the net result shown in the income section of Form 1040. For example, a sole proprietor's deductible business expenses reduce gross income from the business on Schedule C. Only the net profit (or loss) appears on Form 1040 and is included in calculation of the taxpayer's AGI.

Common Deductions Reported Elsewhere

1. Trade or business deductions, Schedule C (Chapter 7)
2. Losses from property sales, Schedule D (Chapter 11)
3. Rent and royalty expenses, Schedule E (Chapter 9)

Figure 4-3 lists out all deductions for which there are separate lines on Form 1040, page 1. The taxpayer can also write in the foreign-earned income exclusion (¶401.02) on the dotted portion of the last line before entering the total deductions.

Figure 4-3: Deductions Listed on Form 1040

1.	Certain business expenses of reservists, performing artists, and fee-basis government officials
2.	Health savings account deduction
3.	Moving expenses
4.	Deductible part of self-employment tax
5.	Self-employed SEP, SIMPLE, and qualified plans
6.	Self-employed health insurance deduction
7.	Penalty on early withdrawal of savings
8.	Alimony paid
9.	IRA deduction
10.	Student loan interest deduction
11.	Domestic production activities deduction

¶402.01 EDUCATOR EXPENSES

Educators can deduct their out-of-pocket classroom expenses as an employee business expense (miscellaneous itemized deduction on Schedule A). Prior to 2015, a deduction for AGI of up to $250 was available to elementary through high school educational workers for their out-of-pocket classroom expenses. On a joint return, a deduction up to $500 was allowed if both spouses were eligible for the deduction and each spouse spent at least $250 on classroom expenses. Although the deduction for AGI expired at the end of 2014, some believe that it may be reinstated prior to the end of 2015.

Should Congress be successful in reinstating the educators expense deduction for 2014, the deduction would be claimed on Form 1040A (line 16) or Form 1040 (line 23), in the space currently marked "Reserved" on the draft version of these tax forms.

¶402.02 CERTAIN BUSINESS EXPENSES OF RESERVISTS, PERFORMING ARTISTS, AND FEE-BASIS GOVERNMENT OFFICIALS

Normally, taxpayers deduct employee business expenses as a miscellaneous itemized deduction subject to the 2% AGI floor. An exception exists for reservists, performing artists, and fee-basis government officials. Like all employees, these taxpayers compute the amount of their deduction on Form 2106, Employee Business Expenses. However, these taxpayers report their employee business expense deduction as a deduction for AGI on Form 1040, instead of as a miscellaneous itemized deduction on Schedule A. Chapter 6 shows how to complete Form 2106.

Members of a reserve component of the Armed Forces who travel more than 100 miles away from home to perform services as a member of the reserves can deduct their travel expenses as a deduction for AGI. Travel expenses that do not take reservists more than 100 miles from home are deducted as a miscellaneous itemized deduction.

State and local government officials who are paid on a fee basis may also deduct their related employee business expenses as a deduction for AGI.

Certain performing artists may qualify to deduct their employee business expenses as deduction for AGI. Artists who fail to meet any one of the following three requirements deduct their business expenses as a miscellaneous itemized deduction on Schedule A. To claim a deduction for AGI, married taxpayers must file jointly unless the spouses lived apart at all times during the year. The three requirements are:

1. During the year, the artist performs services in the performing arts for at least two employers, each of whom pay the artist at least $200,
2. Business expenses must exceed 10% of gross income from the performing arts, and
3. AGI (before deducting these expenses) does not exceed $16,000.

¶402.03 HEALTH SAVINGS ACCOUNT DEDUCTION

Taxpayers deduct for AGI contributions they make to their **health savings accounts** (HSAs). HSAs can be used by individuals who have high-deductible health care plans. They allow taxpayers to save money to pay for their medical costs. In 2015, the maximum that can be contributed to an HSA is $3,350 for single coverage ($6,650 for family coverage). Taxpayers 55 and older can contribute an additional $1,000. Unlike IRAs, there is no rule that HSAs be funded with earned income. All contributions for the current year must be made by April 15 of the next tax year. Once a taxpayer turns 65, contributions to an HSA must stop. Amounts contributed to HSAs in excess of the allowed amounts are subject to a 6% excise tax. Taxpayers claiming HSA deductions complete Form 8889, Health Savings Accounts (HSA), and attach it to their tax returns.

For 2015, a **high-deductible health plan** is one that has at least a $1,300 deductible for single coverage and a $2,600 deductible for family coverage. Maximum out-of-pocket costs are $6,450 for single coverage ($12,900 for family coverage). Eligible taxpayers cannot also be covered under a health care plan offering the same coverage that does not qualify as a high-deductible plan.

Amounts withdrawn from an HSA to pay for medical costs are excluded from gross income. Any balance in an HSA at the end of the year stays in the account to pay medical costs in future years. Amounts withdrawn and not used to pay medical expenses are included in gross income and subject to a 20% penalty. However, when withdrawn after the taxpayer turns 65, the amounts are included in gross income but avoid the penalty. Since the earnings on amounts put in an HSA are not taxed until withdrawn (if ever), taxpayers can accumulate a sizeable sum in their HSAs over the years.

EXAMPLE 22

During 2015, Hope contributes the maximum $6,650 to her employer's health care plan at work. The deductible for her family plan is $2,600, which makes it a high-deductible plan. During the year, Hope withdraws $1,000 from the HSA to pay unreimbursed medical costs for her family. At the end of the year, the balance in the account is $5,700 ($6,650 contributed – $1,000 withdrawn + $50 earnings). Hope is not taxed on either the $1,000 withdrawn or the $50 of earnings. The $5,700 balance carries forward to 2016 where it can be used to pay medical costs in that year or continue to earn tax-free income.

¶402.04 MOVING EXPENSES

Deductible moving expenses include costs paid to move the taxpayer's family and personal belongings to the new location so the taxpayer can start work. Self-employed persons and employees who pay unreimbursed qualified moving expenses deduct them for AGI.

Timing the Move

Usually, a taxpayer moves to a new location near the time the new job starts. However, the move may be delayed if the family waits for a child to finish out the school year or until the old house is sold. Moving expenses qualify for the deduction if they are incurred within one year of when the taxpayer starts work. To be able to deduct moving expenses incurred later than one year after that date, the taxpayer must prove that something prevented an earlier move. The IRS views waiting for a child to graduate from high school as an acceptable reason for delaying a move. However, failing to sell one's home is not.

Qualified Moving Expenses

Qualified moving expenses include the reasonable costs of transportation and lodging (but not meals) for the taxpayer and members of the taxpayer's household (including expenses on the arrival day). However, costs of moving a nurse or personal assistant generally are not deductible. Although only one trip is deductible, all household members need not travel together or at the same time. Qualified moving expenses also include the costs of packing, crating, in-transit storage, and moving of household goods and personal effects. They include expenses for special handling of pets.

EXAMPLE 23

A taxpayer pays $4,200 in moving costs so that he could start work at his new job in another state. This included the cost of a moving van, $3,500; transportation, $550; and meals $150. The taxpayer can deduct $4,050 ($3,500 + $550). The meals are not deductible.

A taxpayer using a personal car to move to the new job location can deduct out-of-pocket expenses like gasoline, oil, etc. To deduct those expenses, the taxpayer must maintain adequate expense records. However, for moves that take place in 2015, a taxpayer can instead deduct $.23 per mile. Here, the taxpayer needs only to verify the mileage. Parking fees and tolls are added to the expenses under either method.

Nondeductible Expenses

In addition to post-transit storage and the cost of meals during the move, other nondeductible expenses include mortgage prepayment penalties, costs to refit rugs and curtains, and losses arising from getting rid of property. Nondeductible expenses also include commissions paid to sell a former home or acquire a new one, and amounts paid to break a lease or get a new one. House hunting expenses and temporary living expenses are also not deductible.

Reimbursements

Employees only deduct the unreimbursed portion of their qualified moving expenses. They exclude from gross income reimbursements they receive from their employers for qualified moving expenses. They also exclude amounts employers pay directly to third parties for qualified moving expenses. Amounts an employer pays for moving costs that do not qualify for the moving expense deduction are taxable to the employee as additional wages on Form W-2.

EXAMPLE 24

John took a new job in Atlanta, Georgia. His new job is 509 miles away. John pays a moving company $2,800 to move his personal belongings. While driving himself and his family to their new home in April, John paid $90 in gas, $220 in lodging and $60 for meals. He also paid $9 in tolls. Because John's new home was not ready when he arrived in Atlanta, he paid $1,200 in temporary living expenses and $300 to store his personal belongings. John's employer reimbursed him $1,500 of his qualified moving costs.

John's qualified moving expenses total $3,146. This includes the $2,800 for moving his personal effects, $117 for mileage (509 × $.23), $9 for tolls, and $220 for lodging. The cost for meals and post-transit storage are not qualified moving expenses. John reduces this amount by the $1,500 reimbursement he receives from his employer and deducts the rest ($1,646) as a deduction for AGI on Form 1040. John takes the deduction for his mileage because this amount exceeds his actual costs for gasoline during the move.

Mileage and Employment Tests

Taxpayers can deduct moving expenses only if they meet both the mileage and employment tests. These tests help ensure that the deduction is allowed for work-related moves, and not for those made for personal reasons.

Mileage Test. A taxpayer can deduct moving expenses only if the new job site is 50 or more miles farther from the former residence than was the old job site. If an old job location does not exist, the distance between the new place of work and the former residence must be at least 50 miles.

EXAMPLE 25

The distance between a taxpayer's old residence and former workplace was 12 miles. This was the taxpayer's former commute to work. To qualify as a deductible move, the location of the new workplace must be at least 62 miles from the old residence (50 miles + 12 miles).

To qualify for the deduction, the taxpayer must live in the old and new residences, treating both as the taxpayer's main home. Here, *home* may be a house, a condominium, or an apartment. A second home, such as a vacation home, does not qualify as the taxpayer's main home. The need for a main home can create problems for a new college graduate starting a first job. Persons starting work for the first time can deduct moving expenses as long as they move from one main home to another. A college dorm room does not qualify as the taxpayer's main home.

Employment Test. An employee who deducts moving expenses must be employed full-time in the area of the new job site for 39 weeks during the 12 months right after the move. This test does not apply if the employee fails this test due to disability, death, discharge not due to willful misconduct, or transfer for the employer's benefit. The employee can deduct moving expenses in the year they are paid even though the 39-week employment test has not been met by the due date of the tax return. However, the employee must have a reasonable expectation of meeting this test in the future.

EXAMPLE 26

A taxpayer moved to a new job on September 1, 20x1, and expects to work indefinitely at the new job site. Deductible moving expenses are $3,450. On the 20x1 tax return, the taxpayer deducts these expenses even though the employment test will not be met until June of 20x2.

A taxpayer may deduct moving expenses in the year of payment. However, if at a later date the taxpayer fails to meet the employment test, two choices exist. The taxpayer can include the deducted expenses in gross income of the year the test is failed. The other option involves filing an amended return for the deduction year and removing the deduction.

Self-Employed Persons

Self-employed persons can deduct the same types of moving costs as employees if they meet the mileage test and a stricter employment test. During the 24-month period right after the move, a self-employed person must provide services on a full-time basis for 78 weeks (as either a self-employed person or an employee). Thirty-nine of those weeks must fall within 12 months of the move. Like an employee, a self-employed person can take the moving expense deduction even though the 78-week employment test has not been met by the due date of the tax return. If the self-employed taxpayer later fails the employment test, the taxpayer can either include the deducted amounts in gross income in the year the test is failed, or file an amended return for the year the deduction was taken.

¶402.05 FILLED-IN FORM 3903

Taxpayers compute their moving expense deduction on Form 3903, Moving Expenses. They attach Form 3903 to their tax returns to support their deduction for AGI on Form 1040.

INFORMATION FOR FIGURE 4-4:

Lois Clarke is employed as an accountant. A promotion earlier this year required her to move to New York (743 miles away). Her employer reimbursed her $2,000 for her move. The reimbursement is not included in taxable wages on Lois's W-2. Lois's actual moving costs include $2,675 paid to a moving company to move her belongings, $53 for lodging, and $92 for gasoline. She enters the amounts highlighted below in bold on the appropriate line numbers on the form, and follows the instructions on the form to compute her moving expense deduction. Lois uses the mileage method (instead of actual costs) for her travel expense because it results in a greater deduction. She enters her $899 deduction on the "Moving expense" line on page 1 of Form 1040.

Line #

1: Cost of moving personal effects, **$2,675**

2: Travel and lodging, **$224** ($53 for lodging + (743 × $.23 for travel))

4: Employer reimbursement, **$2,000** (source: Form W-2, box 12)

Figure 4-4: Filled-In Form 3903

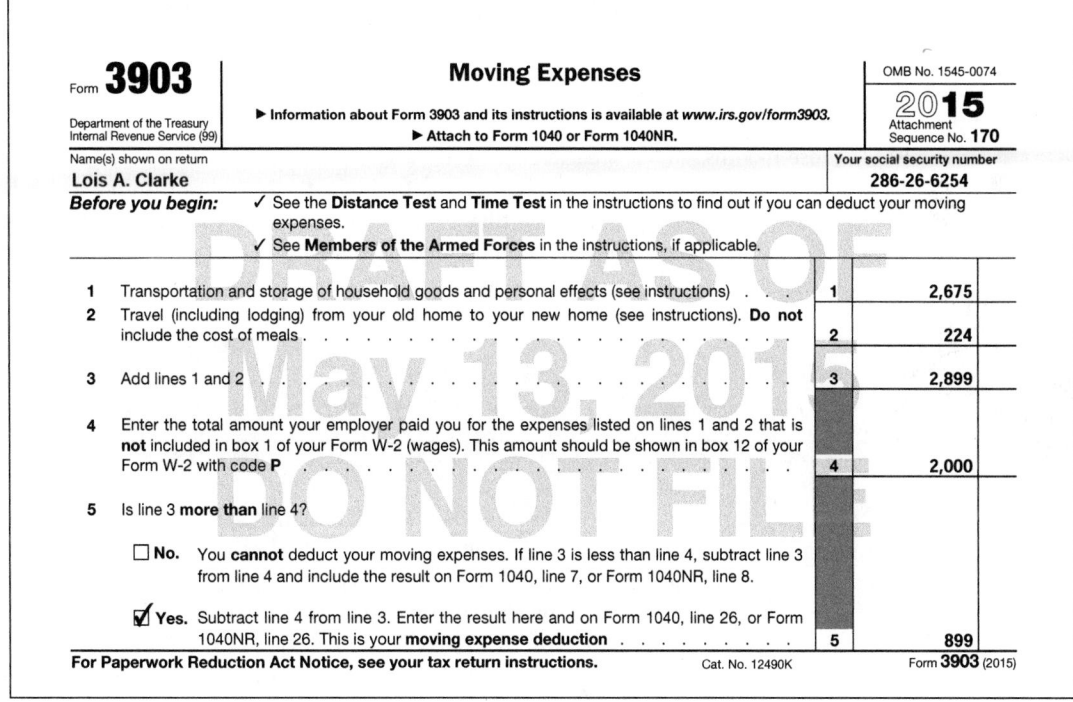

Form **3903** | **Moving Expenses** | OMB No. 1545-0074

Department of the Treasury
Internal Revenue Service (99)

► Information about Form 3903 and its instructions is available at *www.irs.gov/form3903.*
► Attach to Form 1040 or Form 1040NR.

2015 Attachment Sequence No. **170**

Name(s) shown on return: **Lois A. Clarke** | **Your social security number:** **286-26-6254**

Before you begin: ✓ See the **Distance Test** and **Time Test** in the instructions to find out if you can deduct your moving expenses.
✓ See **Members of the Armed Forces** in the instructions, if applicable.

1	Transportation and storage of household goods and personal effects (see instructions) . . .	1	2,675
2	Travel (including lodging) from your old home to your new home (see instructions). **Do not** include the cost of meals . . .	2	224
3	Add lines 1 and 2 . . .	3	2,899
4	Enter the total amount your employer paid you for the expenses listed on lines 1 and 2 that is **not** included in box 1 of your Form W-2 (wages). This amount should be shown in box 12 of your Form W-2 with code **P** . . .	4	2,000
5	Is line 3 **more than** line 4?		
	☐ **No.** You **cannot** deduct your moving expenses. If line 3 is less than line 4, subtract line 3 from line 4 and include the result on Form 1040, line 7, or Form 1040NR, line 8.		
	☑ **Yes.** Subtract line 4 from line 3. Enter the result here and on Form 1040, line 26, or Form 1040NR, line 26. This is your **moving expense deduction** . . .	5	899

For Paperwork Reduction Act Notice, see your tax return instructions. Cat. No. 12490K Form **3903** (2015)

¶402.06 DEDUCTIBLE PART OF SELF-EMPLOYMENT TAX

Self-employed persons pay self-employment tax on their net earnings from self-employment. The self-employment tax consists of the employer and employee shares of FICA taxes (see discussion in ¶203.03). Self-employed persons deduct the employer's (one-half) share of this tax for AGI on Form 1040. The self-employment tax is covered in Chapter 7.

¶402.07 KEOGH, SIMPLE, AND SEP PLANS

Keogh, SIMPLE, and simplified employee pension (SEP) plans allow self-employed persons to make deductible contributions to retirement plans for themselves. A taxpayer deducts the contributions as a deduction for AGI on Form 1040, page 1. Chapter 7 describes the rules for contributing to these plans.

¶402.08 SELF-EMPLOYED HEALTH INSURANCE DEDUCTION

Self-employed taxpayers deduct their health insurance premiums for AGI. The deduction equals the *lesser of* (i) 100% of the eligible health insurance premiums or (ii) net profit from the taxpayer's business reduced by any retirement plan contributions. The taxpayer treats any nondeductible premiums for health insurance as a medical expense (see ¶503.02 in Chapter 5).

Eligible health insurance premiums include amounts paid to insure the taxpayer, the taxpayer's spouse, the taxpayer's dependents, and the taxpayer's children under the age of 27. Self-employed persons cannot take this deduction for any month in which they (or their spouses) are eligible to participate in an employer's health care plan. Also, a self-employed taxpayer with employees cannot take the deduction when the plan favors the taxpayer.

EXAMPLE 27

Pete Douglas is self-employed. His wife, Emma, works full-time for five months during the year. During those months, Emma is eligible for health insurance coverage through her employer. However, due to Emma's unsteady work, the Douglases chose to pay for their own health insurance coverage through Pete's business. During the current year, they paid $1,200 a month for family coverage ($14,400 for the year). Since Emma was eligible for health insurance through her employer for five months during the year, the Douglases can only deduct $8,400 in the current year ($1,200 × 7 months). They deduct this amount for AGI on Form 1040, page 1.

¶402.09 PENALTY ON EARLY WITHDRAWAL OF SAVINGS

Money invested in certificates of deposit (CDs) usually earns a higher rate of interest than normal savings accounts. Banks offer higher rates for funds that remain on deposit until maturity. CDs can have maturities ranging anywhere from 1-month to 10-years. Usually, the longer the term, the higher the interest rate. In return for these higher rates, banks impose a large penalty if the investor cashes in the CD early. A taxpayer who cashes in the CD early includes the full interest income in gross income and then deducts the lost interest as a deduction for AGI on the line, "Penalty on early withdrawal of savings."

EXAMPLE 28

In 2011, Arthur invested $50,000 in a 5-year CD. In return, the bank promised to pay him an annual interest rate of 3% on his $50,000 investment. In 2015, Arthur decides to cash in his CD. He receives a check from the bank for $53,606, even though at the time of the withdrawal, the balance in his account was $55,231. The difference between these two amounts was the penalty for early withdrawal. After the end of the year, the bank will issue Arthur a Form 1099-INT reporting interest paid to him in the amount of $5,231 ($55,231 – $50,000) and his $1,625 early withdrawal penalty ($55,231 – $53,606). Arthur will report the full amount of interest income on Schedule B. He will then deduct the penalty as a deduction for AGI on Form 1040, page 1. Only the net of these two amounts ($5,231 – $1,625 = $3,606) will increase his AGI in 2015.

¶402.10 ALIMONY PAID

As discussed in Chapter 3 (¶304.02), a person who pays alimony deducts it for AGI, and the recipient includes the same amount in gross income.

¶402.11 INDIVIDUAL RETIREMENT ARRANGEMENT (IRA) DEDUCTION

Working taxpayers can contribute to a traditional Individual Retirement Arrangement (IRA). Like the Roth IRA, this savings program allows the earnings to accumulate tax-free. However, unlike Roth IRAs, the earnings from a traditional IRA are taxed when withdrawn (as discussed in ¶305). Certain taxpayers can also deduct from gross income their contributions to a traditional IRA. For these people, the contributions and the earnings are tax-free until funds are withdrawn from the account.

IRA Contribution Limits

Contributions to an IRA must come from earned income. The tax law treats alimony as earned income. However, interest, dividends, and other types of investment income are not earned income.

For 2015, the maximum contribution to an IRA is the *lesser of* (i) $5,500 or (ii) 100% of the taxpayer's earned income. Taxpayers at least 50 years old may contribute another $1,000. When a married couple files a joint tax return, the amount increases to $11,000 (plus $1,000 for each spouse who is 50 or older), as long as the couple has enough combined earnings to match the contribution. Each spouse must establish a separate (traditional) IRA. Also, the amount that can be contributed to either spouse's IRA cannot exceed $5,500 ($6,500 if age 50 or older).

The maximum contribution rules for (traditional) IRAs are the same as those for contributing to Roth IRAs (¶401.09). All taxpayers with enough earned income can contribute to a traditional IRA, regardless of their level of AGI. The maximum contribution to a Roth IRA is reduced for certain higher income taxpayers (see ¶401.09).

The deadline for contributing to an IRA for the current year is April 15 of the next year. If April 15 falls on a weekend day or legal holiday, the taxpayer has until the next business day to make the contribution. In the year a taxpayer reaches age 70½, no further contributions usually are allowed.

EXAMPLE 29

Jim and Jeanette (both age 45) file a joint return. During 2015, Jim earns $50,000 at his job. Jeanette does not work. Jim and Jeanette can each contribute up to $5,500 to their respective IRAs. They have until April 15, 2016 to make their respective contributions.

EXAMPLE 30

Same facts as in Example 29, except that Jim is age 50. Jim can contribute up to $6,500 to his IRA. He can contribute up to $5,500 to Jeanette's IRA.

IRA contributions made between January 1 and April 15 could be considered contributions for either the current or previous tax year. Most IRA trustees assume a contribution made in this time frame is for the current year. If the taxpayer wants the contribution to count towards the prior year, then the taxpayer should inform the IRA trustee of this (preferably in writing) at the time the contribution is made.

Excess Contributions to IRAs

When contributions to all IRAs (Roth and traditional combined) exceed the allowed limit, the IRS assesses a 6% excise tax on the excess. This excise tax is not assessed if the taxpayer withdraws the excess (plus any related earnings) before the due date of the taxpayer's tax return. Withdrawn earnings are taxable and may be assessed a 10% early withdrawal penalty.

The maximum contribution taxpayers under age 50 can make to all IRAs during the year (includes both Roth and traditional) is the lesser of $5,500 or the taxpayer's earned income. Thus, qualifying taxpayers cannot contribute $5,500 to a traditional IRA and another $5,500 to a Roth IRA. Doing this will result in a 6% excise tax on the excess $5,500 contribution.

Limitation on IRA Deductions

Taxpayers who are not active participants in an employer-sponsored retirement plan can deduct up to $5,500 ($6,500 if 50 or older) for contributions made to a traditional IRA for 2015. Anyone participating in an employer-sponsored retirement plan may see their deduction reduced if "modified AGI" exceeds a certain amount. However, a nonparticipating taxpayer (filing MFJ) whose spouse is a participant in an employer plan can still receive a full IRA deduction as long as the couple's modified AGI does not exceed $183,000.

For participants in an employer-sponsored retirement plan, the reduction takes place proportionally when modified AGI falls within the following ranges:

Single and head of household	$61,000–$71,000
Married filing jointly and qualifying widow(er)	$98,000–$118,000
Married filing separately and not living with spouse any part of the year	$61,000–$71,000
Married filing separately and living with spouse part of the year	$0–$10,000
Nonparticipating spouse who files MFJ with participating spouse	$183,000–$193,000

When modified AGI exceeds the upper amounts in these ranges, no deduction is allowed. For purposes of the IRA deduction, "modified AGI" is AGI without any deduction for IRAs (currently being computed), student loan interest (see ¶402.12), or domestic production activities (¶402.14). Also, any amounts the taxpayer excluded for interest from series EE and I educational savings bonds (¶401.06), foreign-earned income (¶401.02), or adoption assistance (¶401.03) are added back in computing modified AGI.

A participant in a qualified plan whose modified AGI is within the phase-out range must compute a reduced IRA deduction. The maximum deduction is reduced proportionately for each dollar of modified AGI that falls within the phase out range ($20,000 for MFJ and qualifying widow(er); $10,000 for all others). Taxpayers round their reduced deductions up to the nearest $10. If their deduction is more than $0, but less than $200, they increase the deduction to $200.

EXAMPLE 31

Stan Decker, age 48, is married and files a joint return with his wife, Dorothy, age 52. They both want to make the largest possible deductible contributions to their IRAs. Their modified AGI is $103,000. Stan is an active participant in his employer's retirement plan. Dorothy does not have a retirement plan at work. Because the Deckers' modified AGI is $5,000 above the $98,000 threshold for MFJ and Stan is in a retirement plan at work, his maximum deductible contribution is $4,125 [$5,500 – ($5,000 excess/$20,000 phase out range × $5,500)]. In contrast, Dorothy does not participate in an employer-sponsored retirement plan, and because the Deckers' modified AGI does not exceed $183,000, she can contribute and deduct $6,500 (includes $1,000 for being age 50 or older).

EXAMPLE 32

Same facts as in Example 31, except that the Deckers' modified AGI is $190,000. Stan may contribute up to $5,500 but he cannot deduct any of his contribution because modified AGI exceeds the $118,000 ceiling for MFJ active participants. Because Dorothy is not an active participant, her modified AGI threshold is $183,000. Thus, Dorothy's maximum deduction is $1,950 [$6,500 – ($7,000 excess/$10,000 phase out range × $6,500)]. If she contributes the maximum $6,500, she will only be able to deduct $1,950.

EXAMPLE 33

Laura, age 38, is single and has modified AGI of $64,434. Included in this amount is $50,000 of wage income. Laura can contribute up to $5,500 to an IRA for 2015. However, the maximum that she can deduct is $3,620 (as computed below). If Laura contributes more than $3,620 (but less than $5,500) to her IRA for 2015, the excess over $3,620 will be a nondeductible contribution.

Reduction factor:

[($64,434 – $61,000)/$10,000] × $5,500 = $1,889

Contribution limit:

$5,500 – $1,889 = $3,611, rounded up to nearest $10: $3,620

EXAMPLE 34

Same facts as in Example 33, except that Laura's modified AGI is $70,820. She can still contribute up to $5,500 to an IRA for 2015, but will only be able to deduct $200.

Reduction factor:

[($70,820 – $61,000)/$10,000] × $5,500 = $5,401

Contribution limit:

$5,500 – $5,401 = $99, rounded up to $200

Employer Plans

The AGI phase-out limits come into play only when the taxpayer (or the taxpayer's spouse for MFJ taxpayers) is a participant in an employer-sponsored retirement plan. Employer plans include qualifying pension plans, profit-sharing plans, 401(k) plans, SIMPLE plans, and simplified employee pension (SEP) plans. Keoghs and other retirement plans of self-employed taxpayers also count as employer plans.

Nondeductible Contributions

Taxpayers who do not qualify to deduct their contributions to an IRA can still make nondeductible contributions to their IRAs. Taxpayers who make both deductible and nondeductible contributions to the same IRA should keep good records to show the amount of their nondeductible contributions, which are tax-free when withdrawn (as discussed in ¶305). To help with this task, the IRS provides Form 8606, Nondeductible IRAs. Taxpayers who make nondeductible IRA contributions should file Form 8606 with the IRS, even if they do not file a tax return.

¶402.12 STUDENT LOAN INTEREST DEDUCTION

Each year, taxpayers may deduct for AGI up to $2,500 of interest they paid on money borrowed to pay qualified higher education expenses for themselves, their spouses, and dependents. No deduction is allowed for persons who are claimed as a dependent on another person's tax return. Qualified education expenses include tuition, books, supplies, and room and board. These expenses must be paid on behalf of a student enrolled at least half-time in a program leading to a recognized credential at a qualified institution of higher education.

Several limitations on the deduction exist. First, the interest deduction is phased out evenly as "modified AGI" increases from $65,000 to $80,000 ($130,000 to $160,000 for MFJ taxpayers). For purposes of this deduction, "modified AGI" is AGI plus any foreign-earned income exclusion (¶401.02) and without the deductions for student loan interest (currently being computed) or domestic production activities (¶402.14). Second, taxpayers may not take the student loan interest deduction if the interest is deductible under another section of the Code (e.g., home equity loan). Third, married taxpayers must file a joint return to claim the deduction.

EXAMPLE 35

Danny paid $800 interest on a qualified student loan. Danny files a joint return with his wife. Their modified AGI is $155,000. Danny and his wife deduct $133 for AGI on their joint tax return.

Reduction amount:

[($155,000 – $130,000)/$30,000 phase-out range] × $800 = $667

Student loan interest deduction:

$800 – $667 = $133

EXAMPLE 36

Avery paid interest of $2,620 on a qualified student loan. Avery is not married. His modified AGI is $76,400. Avery deducts $600 for AGI on his tax return.

Reduction amount:

[($76,400 – $65,000)/$15,000 phase-out range] × $2,500 maximum deduction = $1,900

Student loan interest deduction:

$2,500 – $1,900 = $600

¶402.13 TUITION AND FEES DEDUCTION

A number of tax breaks exist for taxpayers who pay education-related costs. These include education tax credits (¶204.04), tax-free distributions from Coverdell education savings accounts (¶401.11), and tax-free interest income from series EE and I U.S. savings bonds (¶401.06). Prior to 2015, taxpayers also had the option of taking a deduction for AGI for tuition and fees (but not books, supplies, or room and board). The tuition and fees deduction expired at the end of 2014, but there is a chance that it could be retroactively reinstated prior to the end of 2014. Thus, a brief discussion of the deduction is included in the paragraph that follows.

The tuition and fees deduction allowed taxpayers to deduct up to $4,000 of these expenses paid to allow the taxpayer, the taxpayer's spouse, or the taxpayer's dependents to attend an eligible institution of higher education (universities, colleges, etc.). The deduction was reduced to $2,000 once the taxpayer's modified AGI reached a certain level ($65,000 for unmarried taxpayers; $130,000 for couples filing MFJ). It was further reduced to $0 once modified AGI reached $80,000 for unmarried taxpayers ($160,000 MFJ). The deduction was not allowed to anyone claimed as a dependent on another person's tax return, or to married couples who file MFS. Also, any amounts used in computing the tuition and fees deduction could not also be used in computing the education tax credit.

Should Congress be successful in reenacting the tuition and fees deduction for 2015, taxpayers qualifying for the deduction would claim it on Form 1040A (line 19) or Form 1040 (line 34), in the space currently marked "Reserved" on the draft version of these tax forms.

¶402.14 DOMESTIC PRODUCTION ACTIVITIES DEDUCTION

Taxpayers can deduct for AGI 9% of the *lesser of* (i) qualified production activity income or (ii) taxable income. The rate is 6% for oil and gas businesses. This deduction is available to taxpayers that manufacture, grow, or extract products in the United States. The amount deductible cannot exceed 50% of the W-2 wages paid during the year for these activities. Thus, to increase their W-2 wages, companies can hire more employees instead of independent contractors.

Qualified production activity income (QPAI) is basically "net income" computed on receipts from the sale of products produced in the U.S. This amount is compared with the company's taxable income, and the lower of the two amounts is used in calculating the deduction. For individual taxpayers, AGI is substituted for taxable income.

EXAMPLE 37 A company's taxable income is $150,000. Included in this amount is $95,000 of QPAI. The company's W-2 wages for the year were $220,000. The lesser of QPAI or taxable income is $95,000. The company's domestic production activities (DPA) deduction is $8,550 ($95,000 × 9%), since this amount does not exceed 50% of the company's W-2 wages.

EXAMPLE 38 Same facts as in Example 37, except that the company's taxable income is $78,000. The company's DPA deduction is $7,020 ($78,000 × 9%).

¶403 Form 1040

Form 1040, U.S. Individual Income Tax Return, is a 2-page tax form filed by most taxpayers. The format of Form 1040 is similar to Form 1040A. Page 1 focuses on calculating AGI. Page 2 calculates taxable income, tax liability and the amount owed to (or due from) the IRS. However, Form 1040 differs from Form 1040A in that there are no limits on the types of income, deductions, credits or additional taxes that can be reported on Form 1040. Taxpayers filing Form 1040 may be required to prepare and file numerous forms and schedules to support the amounts reported on the tax return.

Taxpayers must use Form 1040 when they do not qualify to use either Form 1040EZ or Form 1040A. Others may elect to use Form 1040 over Form 1040EZ or Form 1040A to save taxes, as more types of deductions and credits are allowed on Form 1040. Similar to what was discussed in Chapter 2 (¶205.02), taxpayers filing Form 1040 either indicate their compliance with the ACA healthcare mandate or pay a penalty on Form 1040 (line 61). Figure 4-5 shows the completed Form 1040 for Karl and Jill Cook.

¶403.01 FILLED-IN FORM 1040

INFORMATION FOR FIGURE 4-5:

Karl and Jill Cook (ages 40 and 39, respectively) file a joint tax return. They claim their 7-year-old daughter, Nan, as a dependent. The payroll data from their Forms W-2 is shown below.

	Taxable Wages	Federal Income Tax Withheld	FICA Taxes Withheld	Net Pay
Karl E. Cook	$ 96,200	$ 17,316	$ 7,359	$ 71,525
Jillian R. Cook	45,950	3,569	3,515	38,866
Totals	$142,150	$20,885	$10,874	$110,391

Although the Cooks' take-home pay was $110,391, they include their gross wages of $142,150 on Form 1040. FICA taxes are withheld from an employee's pay, but are not deductible on the tax return.

Prior to April 15, 2016, Karl and Jill contribute to their respective IRAs the maximum allowed for 2015 ($5,500 for persons under the age of 50). Karl has a pension plan at work; Jill does not. Because the Cooks' AGI exceeds $118,000, Karl (an active participant) cannot deduct any of his IRA contribution. However, because AGI does not exceed $183,000, Jill (who is not an active participant, but files a joint return with Karl, who is an active participant) will be allowed to deduct her entire $5,500 IRA contribution (¶402.11).

Line #

6c: The box in column (4) is checked to indicate that Nan is a qualifying child for purposes of the child tax credit

7: Taxable wages, **$142,150** (source: Karl and Jill's W-2s)

8a: Taxable interest, **$3,640** (source: Schedule B)

32: IRA deduction, **$5,500** (Jill's contribution)

40: Standard deduction for MFJ, **$12,600**

42: Exemptions, **$12,000** ($4,000 × 3)

44: Tax, **$20,510** (source: tax rate Schedule Y-1 for MFJ taxpayers)

49: Credit for child and dependent care expenses, **$600** (source: Form 2441)

52: Child tax credit, **$450** (source: since the Cooks' AGI exceeds the $110,000 AGI threshold for MFJ, the Cooks reduce their initial $2,000 CTC using the method presented in ¶204.07 and shown in Example 16 in Chapter 2)

61: Healthcare: individual responsibility, check box to indicate Full-year coverage. (Karl's employer provides full health care coverage for the Cook family.)

64: Federal income tax withheld, **$20,885** (source: Karl and Jill's W-2s)

76a: Amount refunded to the Cooks, **$1,425** (the Cooks chose to receive a refund for their overpayment, rather than apply the excess to their 2016 tax liability)

By not providing information about their bank or bank account on Form 1040 (lines 76b-76d), the Cooks have decided to have the IRS mail them their refund check.

Figure 4-5: Filled-In Form 1040 (Page 1)

Form **1040** Department of the Treasury—Internal Revenue Service (99) **U.S. Individual Income Tax Return** **2015** OMB No. 1545-0074 IRS Use Only—Do not write or staple in this space.

For the year Jan. 1–Dec. 31, 2015, or other tax year beginning , 2015, ending , 20 See separate instructions.

Your first name and initial: **Karl E.**	Last name: **Cook**	Your social security number: **269 09 9092**
If a joint return, spouse's first name and initial: **Jillian R.**	Last name: **Cook**	Spouse's social security number: **390 16 2222**
Home address (number and street). If you have a P.O. box, see instructions. **400 South Elm Street**	Apt. no.	▲ Make sure the SSN(s) above and on line 6c are correct.
City, town or post office, state, and ZIP code. If you have a foreign address, also complete spaces below (see instructions). **Chicago, IL 60631-1314**		**Presidential Election Campaign** Check here if you, or your spouse if filing jointly, want $3 to go to this fund. Checking a box below will not change your tax or refund. ☐ You ☐ Spouse
Foreign country name	Foreign province/state/county	Foreign postal code

Filing Status

Check only one box.

1 ☐ Single
2 ☑ Married filing jointly (even if only one had income)
3 ☐ Married filing separately. Enter spouse's SSN above and full name here.
4 ☐ Head of household (with qualifying person). (See instructions.) If the qualifying person is a child but not your dependent, enter this child's name here.
5 ☐ Qualifying widow(er) with dependent child

Exemptions

6a ☑ **Yourself.** If someone can claim you as a dependent, **do not** check box 6a — Boxes checked on 6a and 6b: **2**
b ☑ **Spouse**
c **Dependents:**

(1) First name	Last name	(2) Dependent's social security number	(3) Dependent's relationship to you	(4) ✓ if child under age 17 qualifying for child tax credit (see instructions)
Nan	Cook	624 18 1111	daughter	☑
				☐
				☐
				☐

No. of children on 6c who: • lived with you **1** • did not live with you due to divorce or separation (see instructions) — Dependents on 6c not entered above —

If more than four dependents, see instructions and check here ▶ ☐

d Total number of exemptions claimed — Add numbers on lines above ▶ **3**

Income

Attach Form(s) W-2 here. Also attach Forms W-2G and 1099-R if tax was withheld.

If you did not get a W-2, see instructions.

7	Wages, salaries, tips, etc. Attach Form(s) W-2	7	142,150
8a	**Taxable** interest. Attach Schedule B if required	8a	3,640
b	**Tax-exempt** interest. **Do not** include on line 8a — 8b		
9a	Ordinary dividends. Attach Schedule B if required	9a	
b	Qualified dividends — 9b		
10	Taxable refunds, credits, or offsets of state and local income taxes	10	
11	Alimony received	11	
12	Business income or (loss). Attach Schedule C or C-EZ	12	
13	Capital gain or (loss). Attach Schedule D if required. If not required, check here ▶ ☐	13	
14	Other gains or (losses). Attach Form 4797	14	
15a	IRA distributions 15a — b Taxable amount	15b	
16a	Pensions and annuities 16a — b Taxable amount	16b	
17	Rental real estate, royalties, partnerships, S corporations, trusts, etc. Attach Schedule E	17	
18	Farm income or (loss). Attach Schedule F	18	
19	Unemployment compensation	19	
20a	Social security benefits 20a — b Taxable amount	20b	
21	Other income. List type and amount	21	
22	Combine the amounts in the far right column for lines 7 through 21. This is your **total income** ▶	22	145,790

Adjusted Gross Income

23	Reserved	23			
24	Certain business expenses of reservists, performing artists, and fee-basis government officials. Attach Form 2106 or 2106-EZ	24			
25	Health savings account deduction. Attach Form 8889	25			
26	Moving expenses. Attach Form 3903	26			
27	Deductible part of self-employment tax. Attach Schedule SE	27			
28	Self-employed SEP, SIMPLE, and qualified plans	28			
29	Self-employed health insurance deduction	29			
30	Penalty on early withdrawal of savings	30			
31a	Alimony paid b Recipient's SSN ▶	31a			
32	IRA deduction	32	5,500		
33	Student loan interest deduction	33			
34	Reserved	34			
35	Domestic production activities deduction. Attach Form 8903	35			
36	Add lines 23 through 35			36	5,500
37	Subtract line 36 from line 22. This is your **adjusted gross income** ▶			37	140,290

For Disclosure, Privacy Act, and Paperwork Reduction Act Notice, see separate instructions. Cat. No. 11320B Form **1040** (2015)

Figure 4-5: Filled-In Form 1040 (Page 2)

Form 1040 (2015) Page **2**

Tax and Credits	38	Amount from line 37 (adjusted gross income)			38	140,290
	39a	Check if: ☐ **You** were born before January 2, 1951, ☐ Blind. ☐ **Spouse** was born before January 2, 1951, ☐ Blind. } **Total boxes checked ▶ 39a**				
	b	If your spouse itemizes on a separate return or you were a dual-status alien, check here ▶ 39b☐				
	40	**Itemized deductions** (from Schedule A) **or** your **standard deduction** (see left margin)			40	12,600
	41	Subtract line 40 from line 38			41	127,690
	42	**Exemptions.** If line 38 is $154,950 or less, multiply $4,000 by the number on line 6d. Otherwise, see instructions			42	12,000
	43	**Taxable income.** Subtract line 42 from line 41. If line 42 is more than line 41, enter -0-			43	115,690
	44	**Tax** (see instructions). Check if any from: **a** ☐ Form(s) 8814 **b** ☐ Form 4972 **c** ☐			44	20,510
	45	**Alternative minimum tax** (see instructions). Attach Form 6251			45	
	46	Excess advance premium tax credit repayment. Attach Form 8962			46	
	47	Add lines 44, 45, and 46 ▶			47	20,510
	48	Foreign tax credit. Attach Form 1116 if required	48			
	49	Credit for child and dependent care expenses. Attach Form 2441	49	600		
	50	Education credits from Form 8863, line 19	50			
	51	Retirement savings contributions credit. Attach Form 8880	51			
	52	Child tax credit. Attach Schedule 8812, if required	52	450		
	53	Residential energy credit. Attach Form 5695	53			
	54	Other credits from Form: **a** ☐ 3800 **b** ☐ 8801 **c** ☐	54			
	55	Add lines 48 through 54. These are your **total credits**			55	1,050
	56	Subtract line 55 from line 47. If line 55 is more than line 47, enter -0- ▶			56	19,460
Other Taxes	57	Self-employment tax. Attach Schedule SE			57	
	58	Unreported social security and Medicare tax from Form: **a** ☐ 4137 **b** ☐ 8919			58	
	59	Additional tax on IRAs, other qualified retirement plans, etc. Attach Form 5329 if required			59	
	60a	Household employment taxes from Schedule H			60a	
	b	First-time homebuyer credit repayment. Attach Form 5405 if required			60b	
	61	Health care: individual responsibility (see instructions) Full-year coverage ☑			61	
	62	Taxes from: **a** ☐ Form 8959 **b** ☐ Form 8960 **c** ☐ Instructions; enter code(s)			62	
	63	Add lines 56 through 62. This is your **total tax** ▶			63	19,460
Payments	64	Federal income tax withheld from Forms W-2 and 1099	64	20,885		
	65	2015 estimated tax payments and amount applied from 2014 return	65			
	66a	**Earned income credit (EIC)**	66a			
	b	Nontaxable combat pay election 66b				
	67	Additional child tax credit. Attach Schedule 8812	67			
	68	American opportunity credit from Form 8863, line 8	68			
	69	Net premium tax credit. Attach Form 8962	69			
	70	Amount paid with request for extension to file	70			
	71	Excess social security and tier 1 RRTA tax withheld	71			
	72	Credit for federal tax on fuels. Attach Form 4136	72			
	73	Credits from Form: **a** ☐ 2439 **b** Reserved **c** ☐ 8885 **d** ☐	73			
	74	Add lines 64, 65, 66a, and 67 through 73. These are your **total payments** ▶			74	20,885
Refund	75	If line 74 is more than line 63, subtract line 63 from line 74. This is the amount you **overpaid**			75	1,425
	76a	Amount of line 75 you want **refunded to you.** If Form 8888 is attached, check here ▶☐			76a	1,425
	▶ b	Routing number ▶ c Type: ☐ Checking ☐ Savings				
	▶ d	Account number				
	77	Amount of line 75 you want **applied to your 2016 estimated tax** ▶	77			
Amount You Owe	78	**Amount you owe.** Subtract line 74 from line 63. For details on how to pay, see instructions ▶			78	
	79	Estimated tax penalty (see instructions)	79			

Standard Deduction for—
- People who check any box on line 39a or 39b **or** who can be claimed as a dependent, see instructions.
- All others:

Single or Married filing separately, $6,300

Married filing jointly or Qualifying widow(er), $12,600

Head of household, $9,250

If you have a qualifying child, attach Schedule EIC.

Direct deposit? See instructions.

Third Party Designee — Do you want to allow another person to discuss this return with the IRS (see instructions)? ☐ **Yes.** Complete below. ☐ **No**
Designee's name ▶ Phone no. ▶ Personal identification number (PIN) ▶

Sign Here — Under penalties of perjury, I declare that I have examined this return and accompanying schedules and statements, and to the best of my knowledge and belief, they are true, correct, and complete. Declaration of preparer (other than taxpayer) is based on all information of which preparer has any knowledge.

Joint return? See instructions. Keep a copy for your records.

Your signature	Date	Your occupation	Daytime phone number
Karl E. Cook	2-26-16	Clerk	
Spouse's signature. If a joint return, **both** must sign.	Date	Spouse's occupation	If the IRS sent you an Identity Protection PIN, enter it here (see inst.)
Jillian R. Cook	2-26-16	Bank Teller	

Paid Preparer Use Only

Print/Type preparer's name	Preparer's signature	Date	Check ☐ if self-employed	PTIN

Firm's name ▶ Firm's EIN ▶
Firm's address ▶ Phone no.

www.irs.gov/form1040 Form **1040** (2015)

4

Name:

Section:

Date:

QUESTIONS AND PROBLEMS

1. **Foreign Earned Income Exclusion.** (Obj. 1) From March 9, 2015 until August 14, 2016 Eva is sent to London, England on a temporary work assignment. Eva's salary during 2015 is $100,000, of which $84,000 is earned while working in London. Her salary during 2016 (a leap year) is $125,000, of which $77,000 is earned while working in London.

   a. How much of Eva's salary is taxed in 2015 and 2016? Assume the maximum foreign earned income exclusion for 2016 remains at $100,800.

   b. Besides taking the exclusion for foreign earned income, what other options are available to Eva?

2. **Foreign Earned Income Exclusion.** (Obj. 1) From October 6, 2015 until September 5, 2016, Jack was sent to work at his employer's office in Rome, Italy. Jack's salary during 2015 was $72,000. Of this amount, $18,000 was earned while working in Rome.

   a. How much of Jack's salary can be excluded from gross income in 2015?

   b. How, if at all, would your answer to Part a. differ if Jack's assignment lasted until August 7, 2016?

3. **Fringe Benefits.** (Obj. 2) The discrimination rule applies to certain fringe benefits, but not to others.

   a. For each category of fringe benefits given, state whether the discrimination rule applies, and give two examples of specific fringe benefits in that category.

Fringe Benefit Category	*Discrimination Rule Applies?*	*Examples of Specific Benefits in Each Category*
De minimis fringe benefits	________	________________
		________________
Qualified employee discounts	________	________________
		________________
Working condition fringe benefits	________	________________
		________________
No-additional-cost services	________	________________
		________________
On-premise athletic facilities	________	________________
		________________

   b. What are the tax consequences of violating the discrimination rule?

4. **Group-Term Life Insurance.** (Obj. 2) Paine Distributing pays an annual premium for $90,000 for nondiscriminatory group-term life insurance coverage on its president, Fred J. Noble. Fred is 44 years of age. His wife, Melanie, is the policy's beneficiary. For this group-term life insurance, Fred pays the company $0.20 per year for each $1,000 of coverage. His share of the insurance premium is deducted from his gross salary under Paine's payroll deduction plan. What portion of the group-term life insurance cost is included in Fred's gross income for the year?

5. **Group-Term Life Insurance.** (Obj. 2) Remix, Inc. provides group-term life insurance coverage for each of its employees. The amount of coverage is equal to one year's salary. Remix pays 100% of the cost for the premiums. Tony and Ruth are employees of Remix. Tony is 46 years old; his salary for the year is $85,000. Ruth is 52 years old; her salary for the year is $120,000. Ruth is a key employee of Remix; Tony is not.

   a. Discuss the consequences to Tony and Ruth if Remix's plan does not favor key and highly paid employees.

   b. Discuss the consequences to Tony and Ruth if Remix's plan favors key or highly paid employees.

6. **Employer-Provided Health Insurance.** (Obj. 2) Monix Enterprises provides its employees with health insurance coverage. During the year, it pays $7,500 of insurance premiums for each of its employees. Randy is a highly paid employee of Monix. Jon is not one of Monix's highly paid employees.

   a. Discuss the consequences to Randy and Jon if the plan favors highly paid employees.

   b. Discuss the consequences to Randy and Jon if the plan does not favor key or highly paid employees.

7. **Fringe Benefits.** (Obj. 2) A retailer gives a 20% discount to its full-time employees; key employees are entitled to a 30% discount. The retailer's gross profit percentage on the goods it sells is 35%. During the year, two full-time employees, Fritz and Tad, each buy goods that sell for $2,000. Fritz is a key employee; Tad is not. Discuss the tax consequences to Fritz and Tad of the discounts they each received during the year.

8. **Bond Interest.** (Obj. 1) A single taxpayer owns five different bonds listed below. During the current year she received the interest amounts shown. In the space provided for each bond, state the amount of interest to be included in or excluded from gross income. If excluded, state why.

Bond	*Issuer*	*Date Purchased*	*Interest*
A	Racer Tannery	12–10–05	$ 276
B	City of Austin	7–1–08	800
C	U.S. Treasury	2–1–11	600
D	Matured Series EE U.S. Savings	11–1–13	1,000
E	Kingsville School District	7–10–14	500

Bond	*Interest Includable*	*Interest Excludable and Why*
A		
B		
C		
D		
E		

9. **Form 8815.** (Obj. 6) Michael J. Dugan (SSN 372-90-6729) and his wife, Rachel, received $15,000 ($12,000 principal and $3,000 interest) from the redemption of a Series EE U.S. Savings Bond. They used the proceeds to pay university tuition and fees totaling $8,250 for their two dependent children, Colleen R. Dugan and Patrick T. Dugan. Colleen is 21 years of age; Patrick is 20. With the exception of temporary absences from home to attend the University of Michigan in Ann Arbor, MI 48104 full-time, they live with their parents. During the year, Colleen and Patrick each received a tax-exempt university scholarship of $2,250. Michael's salary is $125,500. The salary and interest from the bonds are the Dugans' only sources of income. Prepare Form 8815 to be attached to the Dugans' 2015 joint tax return.

10. **Exclusion for Series EE and I U.S. Savings Bonds.** (Obj. 5) Irina cashes in Series I Savings Bonds during 2015. She receives $18,755, of which $15,000 was principal and the rest interest. Irina uses the proceeds to pay out-of-state tuition and fees totaling $16,500 for her son, who is a full-time student during the year. She uses the rest of the proceeds to pay for her son's room and board. Irina's filing status is head of household. Irina's only other source of income is her $76,100 salary. Compute Irina's exclusion for Series EE and I interest and her AGI.

(Use for Problem 9.)

Form **8815**

Department of the Treasury
Internal Revenue Service (99)

Exclusion of Interest From Series EE and I U.S. Savings Bonds Issued After 1989
(For Filers With Qualified Higher Education Expenses)
▶ **Information about Form 8815 and its instructions is at *www.irs.gov/form8815*.**
▶ **Attach to Form 1040 or Form 1040A.**

OMB No. 1545-0074
2015
Attachment Sequence No. **167**

Name(s) shown on return	**Your social security number**

1 (a) Name of person (you, your spouse, or your dependent) who was enrolled at or attended an eligible educational institution	(b) Name and address of eligible educational institution

If you need more space, attach a statement.

2	Enter the total qualified higher education expenses you paid in 2015 for the person(s) listed in column (a) of line 1. See the instructions to find out which expenses qualify	**2**	
3	Enter the total of any nontaxable educational benefits (such as nontaxable scholarship or fellowship grants) received for 2015 for the person(s) listed in column (a) of line 1 (see instructions)	**3**	
4	Subtract line 3 from line 2. If zero or less, **stop.** You **cannot** take the exclusion	**4**	
5	Enter the total proceeds (principal and interest) from all series EE and I U.S. savings bonds **issued after 1989** that you **cashed during 2015**	**5**	
6	Enter the interest included on line 5 (see instructions)	**6**	
7	If line 4 is equal to or more than line 5, enter "1.000." If line 4 is less than line 5, divide line 4 by line 5. Enter the result as a decimal (rounded to at least three places)	**7**	× .
8	Multiply line 6 by line 7	**8**	
9	Enter your modified adjusted gross income (see instructions) . . . . **9** ______ **Note:** *If line 9 is $92,200 or more if single or head of household, or $145,750 or more if married filing jointly or qualifying widow(er) with dependent child,* ***stop.*** *You* ***cannot*** *take the exclusion.*		
10	Enter: $77,200 if single or head of household; $115,750 if married filing jointly or qualifying widow(er) with dependent child . . . . **10** ______		
11	Subtract line 10 from line 9. If zero or less, skip line 12, enter -0- on line 13, and go to line 14 . . . . **11** ______		
12	Divide line 11 by: $15,000 if single or head of household; $30,000 if married filing jointly or qualifying widow(er) with dependent child. Enter the result as a decimal (rounded to at least three places)	**12**	× .
13	Multiply line 8 by line 12	**13**	
14	**Excludable savings bond interest.** Subtract line 13 from line 8. Enter the result here and on Schedule B (Form 1040A or 1040), line 3 . . . . ▶	**14**	

For Paperwork Reduction Act Notice, see your tax return instructions. Cat. No. 10822S Form **8815** (2015)

11. **Scholarships.** (Obj. 5) On August 1, 2015, Rob was granted a $5,400 scholarship for each of four academic years (nine months each year) to earn a degree from Birdhaven University. The scholarship grant includes $3,600 for tuition, fees, and books and $1,800 for room and board. Payment is one-ninth each month, starting September 10, 2015, and is made on the tenth of each month thereafter.

    a. How much of the scholarship payments can Rob exclude from gross income in 2015? Why?

    b. If Rob is not a degree candidate, is there any limitation to the amount of his exclusion? Explain.

12. **Gross Income Exclusions.** (Obj. 1) Indicate, by placing an **X** in the proper column, whether each of the following items is includable in or excludable from gross income.

Item	*Includable*	*Excludable*
a. Life insurance proceeds paid because of insured's death	_____	_____
b. Workers' compensation for a physical injury	_____	_____
c. Employer-paid health insurance premiums paid to a non-key, non-highly paid employee	_____	_____
d. FMV of automobile won on television game show	_____	_____
e. Free parking in employer's lot (valued at $100/month)	_____	_____
f. A nonbankrupt taxpayer is forgiven of $1,000 of credit card debt	_____	_____
g. Gold necklace received as a gift	_____	_____
h. Health resort fee paid for taxpayer by employer	_____	_____

13. **Physical Injury and Sickness Payments.** (Obj. 1) For each taxpayer, discuss how much (if any) of the payments received during the year are included in gross income.

a. Anne sued her employer for discrimination and was awarded $50,000.

b. Todd was physically injured on the job. He is reimbursed $16,400 for medical expenses he paid as a result of his injuries. Todd's employer paid 100% of the premiums on his health insurance policy.

c. Meg was physically injured on the job. She received $12,000 of workers' compensation.

d. Sandra had an adverse reaction to the drug her doctor prescribed. She sued the drug company and was awarded $12 million. Of this amount, $11.5 million was for punitive damages.

14. **Roth IRAs.** (Obj. 4) Kenya and Carl Reed are ages 48 and 50, respectively. Their 2015 AGI is $190,520, most of which stems from taxable wages. Compute the maximum amounts Kenya and Carl can contribute to their respective Roth IRAs for 2015.

15. **Roth IRA.** (Obj. 4) Kathy, age 40, is single and wants to contribute to a Roth IRA in 2015. Her AGI is $118,500. Compute the maximum contribution that Kathy may make to her Roth IRA. Where does she deduct this amount on her tax return?

16. Deductions for AGI. (Obj. 3) For each statement, check *true* or *false*.

	True	*False*
a. Reservists who travel 100 miles or less from home to perform services as a member of the reserves deduct their travel expenses as a miscellaneous itemized deduction.	_____	_____
b. Qualified performing artists may deduct their business expenses from gross income to arrive at AGI.	_____	_____
c. To receive the tax benefits of a "performing artist," the individual's AGI cannot exceed $14,000 before deducting business expenses.	_____	_____
d. State and local government officials paid on a fee basis report their business expenses on Form 2106.	_____	_____
e. Taxpayers 55-years-old may contribute an additional $1,000 to their health savings accounts.	_____	_____
f. Retired taxpayers may continue to make deductible contributions to a health savings account.	_____	_____
g. Withdrawals from a health savings account that are not used for medical expenses may be subject to a 6% penalty tax.	_____	_____

17. Health Savings Accounts. (Obj. 3) Mari's employer offers an HSA plan.

a. Discuss the tax consequences to Mari if she participates in the plan. Mari is 44-years-old, unmarried, and does not claim any dependents on her tax return.

b. Same as in Part a., except that Mari is 56 years old.

18. Moving Expenses. (Obj. 3) Trey Wilson accepted a new job in Baltimore, Maryland, which is 804 miles from his old home. In April he flew out to Baltimore to start his new job. His wife, Veronica remained at their old home so that the children could finish out the school year. In July, the Wilsons paid a moving company $6,200 to move their belongings to Baltimore. Veronica then drove the family out to their new home. Trey's airfare to Baltimore was $450. Veronica paid $151 for gas, $260 for lodging, and $110 for meals while en route to Baltimore. Trey's employer reimbursed him $5,000 for the cost of the moving company.

a. Compute the Wilsons' moving expense deduction.

b. Where is this amount reported on their return?

19. Moving Expenses. (Obj. 3) Jimmy incurs the following moving expenses as a result of a change in job location. Compute Jimmy's moving expense deduction.

Expenses of moving household goods	$ 4,500
Travel and lodging for family in moving to new home	345
Meals en route	72
Pre-move house hunting trips	925
Temporary living expenses in new location	700
Real estate commission on sale of the former home	12,000
Total moving expenses	$18,542

20. Self-Employed Health Insurance Deduction. (Obj. 3) Ashley is a self-employed artist. She pays $650 a month for health insurance coverage through her business. From August 1 through October 31, Ashley worked 30 hours a week for an ad agency. During that period, she was eligible for her employer's health insurance, but opted not to enroll in it.

a. How much of the $7,800 in health insurance premiums can Ashley deduct?

b. Where on her tax return does she take this deduction?

21. Self-Employed Health Insurance Deduction. (Obj. 3)

a. What is the maximum self-employed health insurance deduction that can be claimed as a deduction for AGI?

b. Under what conditions would a taxpayer not be eligible for the self-employed health insurance deduction?

22. IRA Contributions. (Obj. 4) Joyce and Barry Bright are both employed and 56 years of age. In 2015 Barry earned wages of $2,500; Joyce earned wages of $86,530. Joyce is an active participant in her employer-maintained pension plan. The Brights plan to file a joint tax return. Their modified AGI is $108,782.

a. What is the latest date by which an IRA contribution must be made in order for it to be claimed on the Brights' 2015 return?

b. Can the payments be claimed on Form 1040EZ? On Form 1040A?

c. What is the maximum amount Joyce and Barry can each contribute to an IRA and be able to deduct for 2015?

d. Are the earnings from the IRA subject to federal income taxes in 2015? Explain.

23. IRA Deduction. (Obj. 4) Fred and Diane Workman file a joint return. Neither taxpayer is covered by a retirement plan at work. Fred's wages are $37,900; Diane's are $31,500. Between January 1, 2015 and April 15, 2016, Diane and Fred contributed the following amounts to their respective traditional IRAs:

Diane:	April 26, 2015	$ 750
	July 1, 2015	750
	October 3, 2015	750
	January 4, 2016	750
Fred:	June 16, 2015	$1,500
	February 3, 2016	1,500

Earnings credited to their IRAs during 2015 were $890 for Diane and $340 for Fred. Discuss the tax implications of the contributions to and the earnings from the IRAs as they pertain to the Workmans' 2015 tax return.

24. Traditional IRA Characteristics. (Obj. 4) For each statement, check *true* or *false*.

	True	*False*
a. Contributions to a nonworking spouse's IRA must be equal to the IRA contributions of the working spouse.	_____	_____
b. Contributions to a traditional IRA are deductible in the computation of AGI for a single employee whose only income is wages of $25,000.	_____	_____
c. Contributions to a traditional IRA generally must stop in the year the IRA account owner reaches age 70½.	_____	_____
d. The earnings of a traditional IRA are taxed to the employee in the year earned.	_____	_____
e. The income earned on nondeductible traditional IRA contributions is not taxable until it is withdrawn.	_____	_____
f. The maximum deductible IRA contributions in 2015 is $5,500 for a married couple of which only one spouse works and earns $25,000.	_____	_____

25. Nondeductible IRA Contributions. (Obj. 4) Mike and Marg Sweeney, both age 42, each want to set aside the maximum amount for their retirement using an individual retirement account. They prefer to make deductible contributions. Mike and Marg have $75,000 and $48,000 of earned income, respectively. Their modified AGI is $127,000. Marg is covered by an employer-maintained retirement plan. Mike's employer has no such plan.

a. Discuss the tax consequences if the Sweeneys use traditional IRAs to save for retirement.

b. Can you suggest a better plan? If so, what would it be?

c. How would your responses to Parts a. and b. change if Marg's earned income was $106,000, Mike's was $88,000, and the Sweeney's modified AGI was $200,000?

26. Student Loan Interest. (Obj. 5) Larry paid $580 interest on a qualified student loan. Larry files his tax return as a single taxpayer. His modified AGI is $69,810. Compute Larry's deduction for AGI for the interest paid on his student loan.

27. Miscellaneous Questions. (Obj. 3) For each statement, check *true* or *false*.

	True	*False*
a. Withdrawals from a Roth IRA may be subject to a 6% early withdrawal penalty.	_____	_____
b. Regardless of the number of children, a taxpayer may contribute only $2,000 each year to a Coverdell Education Savings Account.	_____	_____
c. Contributions to an ABLE account are deductible for AGI.	_____	_____
d. Contributions to a Coverdell Education Savings Account (ESA) must be for a person under age 18.	_____	_____
e. The student loan interest deduction is available only for the first 60 months of interest payments.	_____	_____

	True	*False*
f. In 2015, employees may exclude up to $130 a month for parking provided by the employer, even if the parking privilege is discriminatory.	_____	_____
g. Under a qualified tuition program (529 plan), if the child does not go to college, a refund is made to the child who must pay taxes on the interest income included in the refund.	_____	_____
h. Some employers provide meals to their employees. For the value of the meals to be tax-free, the meals must be served on the premises of the employer for the employer's convenience.	_____	_____

28. Miscellaneous Questions. (Obj. 3)

a. Explain the deduction for the penalty on early withdrawal of savings.

b. What are the tax consequences of purchasing a new truck with funds from a Roth IRA for a taxpayer of age 50?

c. What are the tax consequences of purchasing a new truck with funds from a traditional IRA for a taxpayer of age 50?

29. Internet Problem: Filling out Form 3903. (Obj. 6)

Charles Randall (SSN 567-89-1234) took a new job that required him to move from Cleveland, Ohio, to Kansas City, Missouri. As part of the move, Charles drove his car 717 miles and paid the following amounts. Charles' new employer reimbursed Charles for 75% of his qualified moving expenses.

House hunting trip expenses	$1,600
Moving van	3,300
Cost of meals en route	85
Lodging en route	120

Go to the IRS website and locate Form 3903. Using the computer, fill in the form for Charles Randall and print out a completed copy.

See Appendix A for instructions on use of the IRS website.

30. Business Entity Problem: This problem is designed for those using the "business entity" approach. **The solution may require information from Chapters 14–16.** For each statement, check *true* or *false.*

	True	*False*
a. Self-employed persons may deduct 50% of their self-employment tax for AGI.	______	______
b. Companies reimbursing their employees for house hunting and temporary living expenses do not report these reimbursements as income on the employee's W-2.	______	______
c. When a company provides "free meals" as part of the employee's compensation package, the company includes the value of the meals as taxable wages on the employee's W-2.	______	______
d. In 2015, a company pays $300 per month to provide its CEO with a parking space. The company must include $600 on the CEO's W-2 as taxable wages.	______	______
e. When a company reimburses an employee for deductible moving expenses, it must report the reimbursement as additional taxable wages on the employee's W-2.	______	______
f. Employers may annually provide up to $5,250 of tax-free educational assistance to their employees to pursue a Master's Degree.	______	______
g. When a company provides over $50,000 of group-term life insurance to an employee, it must add the taxable portion of the premiums to wages on the employee's W-2.	______	______
h. A self-employed person who provides health insurance for himself, but not his three full-time employees, may deduct the premiums for AGI.	______	______
i. The domestic production activities deduction is limited to 100% of the W-2 wages paid during the year.	______	______

COMPREHENSIVE PROBLEM

31. Use the information below to compute the 2015 taxable income and tax liability for an unmarried taxpayer (age 52 with no dependents). Prepare an analysis showing each item and amount under the appropriate headings of (1) income, (2) gross income exclusions, (3) total gross income, (4) deductions for AGI, (5) AGI, (6) deductions from AGI, and (7) taxable income.

Cash Received	
Interest on savings account	$ 1,728
Gift of money from parent	1,000
Rent from farmland owned	30,000
Proceeds of life insurance policy received upon parent's death	40,000
Nondegree candidate fellowship, granted 8/20/15, of $450 per month for four months	1,800
Net pay received (Gross salary of $33,000 less $7,440 state and federal income taxes, $2,046 social security taxes, and $479 Medicare taxes)	23,035
Employer's share of health insurance premiums, $4,260	0
De minimis employee fringe benefits valued at $25	0
Company provided parking costing employer $300/month for 12 months	0
Total cash received	$97,563
Cash Payments	
Expenses of farmland rental (real estate taxes)	$ 1,750
Personal living expenses	26,600
Total cash payments	$28,350

CUMULATIVE PROBLEM 1 (CHAPTERS 1–4)

Use the following information to prepare Erica Hansen's tax return. Use Form 1040A, Schedule EIC, and Schedule 8812. This problem is suitable for manual preparation or computer software application.

Erica L. Hansen (SSN 376-38-4930), age 42, is a single parent with three children. She resides at 19 Sunset Road, Normal, Illinois 61761. She chooses to support the Presidential campaign fund.

Her household includes Randall L. Hansen, her 19-year-old son (SSN 369-62-3418), Tiffany A. Hansen, her 12-year-old daughter (SSN 396-30-6439), and Donna M. Hansen, her 14-year-old daughter (SSN 653-29-8177). Erica provides over half of the support of each child.

Donna has no income of her own, but Randall earns $4,200 during the year delivering papers and mowing lawns. All children lived in the household for 12 months. Randall is a full-time student at Heartland College in Normal, Illinois.

Erica works as an office manager for Universal Development Corporation. Information from her W-2, as well as other relevant information follows.

Gross wages	$39,500
Social security tax withheld	2,449
Medicare tax withheld	573
Federal income tax withheld	0
State income tax withheld	819
Interest received:	
First Federal Savings Bank	$775
Olympic Savings—certificate of deposit cashed in	175
State of Maryland bonds	300

Erica gets her family health care coverage through her work. Erica is a participant in an employer-sponsored retirement plan. However, she wants to make the largest possible deductible contribution to her traditional IRA. If Erica has overpaid her taxes, she prefers to receive a refund. She signs and dates her return on April 5, 2016.

Retirement Savings Contributions Credit:

Compute the amount of the credit using the information presented in ¶204.06. Enter the credit on Form 1040A, page 2.

EIC Calculation:

Look up the amount in the EIC Tables for both earned income and AGI. The smaller of these two amounts is the EIC reported on Form 1040A, page 2.

Additional Child Tax Credit:

Enter on Schedule 8812 (line 1) $1,000 for each qualifying child.

CUMULATIVE PROBLEM 2 (CHAPTERS 1–4)

Use the following information to prepare the tax return for Bryan Connel. Use Form 1040, Schedule B, Form 3903, and Form 8863. This problem is suitable for manual preparation or computer software application.

Bryan Connel (SSN 573-99-5878) works as a manager for an oil company. In October 2015, he was relocated by his employer from Houston, Texas to Wichita Falls, Kansas. His moving costs include $230 for an airline ticket and $5,300 that he paid to a local moving company. His employer reimbursed him $3,000 for the move. This amount was not included in his W-2 wages. His taxable wages for 2015 were $132,900, from which his employer withheld $9,450 and $1,900, respectively for federal and state income taxes.

During 2015, Bryan paid $6,000 for tuition for his dependent daughter, April Connel (SSN 549-43-5584). April (age 20) attends the University of Houston full-time. She entered her sophomore year during 2015. April lives with Bryan when she is not in school. The University of Houston is located at 4800 Calhoun Road, Houston, Texas 77004.

Bryan is divorced. During 2015, he paid alimony totaling $50,000 to his ex-wife, Anne Connel (SSN 558-99-5377). His only other income includes $4,250 of interest from a Texas Commerce Bank certificate of deposit and $1,840 of interest from State of Iowa government bonds. He does not have an interest in any foreign accounts or trusts. Bryan lives at 1143 W. Adams Ave., Wichita Falls, KS 76300. Bryan uses the standard deduction, is under age 65, and has good eyesight. Bryan receives full health care benefits through his employer. He does not want $3 to go to the Presidential election campaign fund. Bryan signs and dates his return on April 10, 2016.

(Use for Cumulative Problem 1.)

Form **1040A** Department of the Treasury—Internal Revenue Service
U.S. Individual Income Tax Return (99) **2015** IRS Use Only—Do not write or staple in this space.

Your first name and initial	Last name	OMB No. 1545-0074 **Your social security number**
If a joint return, spouse's first name and initial	Last name	**Spouse's social security number**
Home address (number and street). If you have a P.O. box, see instructions.	Apt. no.	▲ Make sure the SSN(s) above and on line 6c are correct.
City, town or post office, state, and ZIP code. If you have a foreign address, also complete spaces below (see instructions).		**Presidential Election Campaign** Check here if you, or your spouse if filing jointly, want $3 to go to this fund. Checking a box below will not change your tax or refund. ☐ You ☐ Spouse
Foreign country name	Foreign province/state/county	Foreign postal code

Filing status
Check only one box.

1 ☐ Single
2 ☐ Married filing jointly (even if only one had income)
3 ☐ Married filing separately. Enter spouse's SSN above and full name here. ▶
4 ☐ Head of household (with qualifying person). (See instructions.) If the qualifying person is a child but not your dependent, enter this child's name here. ▶
5 ☐ Qualifying widow(er) with dependent child (see instructions)

Exemptions

6a ☐ **Yourself.** If someone can claim you as a dependent, **do not** check box 6a.
b ☐ **Spouse**

Boxes checked on 6a and 6b

c **Dependents:**

If more than six dependents, see instructions.

(1) First name Last name	(2) Dependent's social security number	(3) Dependent's relationship to you	(4) ✓ if child under age 17 qualifying for child tax credit (see instructions)
			☐
			☐
			☐
			☐
			☐
			☐

No. of children on 6c who:
- **lived with you**
- **did not live with you due to divorce or separation (see instructions)**

Dependents on 6c not entered above

d Total number of exemptions claimed. **Add numbers on lines above ▶**

Income

Attach Form(s) W-2 here. Also attach Form(s) 1099-R if tax was withheld.

If you did not get a W-2, see instructions.

7	Wages, salaries, tips, etc. Attach Form(s) W-2.		7
8a	**Taxable** interest. Attach Schedule B if required.		8a
b	**Tax-exempt** interest. **Do not** include on line 8a.	8b	
9a	Ordinary dividends. Attach Schedule B if required.		9a
b	Qualified dividends (see instructions).	9b	
10	Capital gain distributions (see instructions).		10
11a	IRA distributions. 11a	**11b** Taxable amount (see instructions).	11b
12a	Pensions and annuities. 12a	**12b** Taxable amount (see instructions).	12b
13	Unemployment compensation and Alaska Permanent Fund dividends.		13
14a	Social security benefits. 14a	**14b** Taxable amount (see instructions).	14b
15	Add lines 7 through 14b (far right column). This is your **total income.** ▶		15

Adjusted gross income

16	Reserved	16	
17	IRA deduction (see instructions).	17	
18	Student loan interest deduction (see instructions).	18	
19	Reserved	19	
20	Add lines 16 through 19. These are your **total adjustments.**		20
21	Subtract line 20 from line 15. This is your **adjusted gross income.** ▶		21

For Disclosure, Privacy Act, and Paperwork Reduction Act Notice, see separate instructions. Cat. No. 11327A Form **1040A** (2015)

(Use for Cumulative Problem 1.)

Form 1040A (2015) Page **2**

Tax, credits, and payments

22	Enter the amount from line 21 (adjusted gross income).		22
23a	Check if: { ☐ **You** were born before January 2, 1951, ☐ Blind } { ☐ **Spouse** was born before January 2, 1951, ☐ Blind } **Total boxes checked** ▶ 23a ☐		
b	If you are married filing separately and your spouse itemizes deductions, check here ▶ 23b ☐		
24	Enter your **standard deduction.**		24
25	Subtract line 24 from line 22. If line 24 is more than line 22, enter -0-.		25
26	**Exemptions.** Multiply $4,000 by the number on line 6d.		26
27	Subtract line 26 from line 25. If line 26 is more than line 25, enter -0-. This is your **taxable income.** ▶		27
28	**Tax,** including any alternative minimum tax (see instructions).	28	
29	Excess advance premium tax credit repayment. Attach Form 8962.	29	
30	Add lines 28 and 29.		30
31	Credit for child and dependent care expenses. Attach Form 2441.	31	
32	Credit for the elderly or the disabled. Attach Schedule R.	32	
33	Education credits from Form 8863, line 19.	33	
34	Retirement savings contributions credit. Attach Form 8880.	34	
35	Child tax credit. Attach Schedule 8812, if required.	35	
36	Add lines 31 through 35. These are your **total credits.**		36
37	Subtract line 36 from line 30. If line 36 is more than line 30, enter -0-.		37
38	Health care: individual responsibility (see instructions). Full-year coverage ☐		38
39	Add line 37 and line 38. This is your **total tax.**		39
40	Federal income tax withheld from Forms W-2 and 1099.	40	
41	2015 estimated tax payments and amount applied from 2014 return.	41	
42a	**Earned income credit (EIC).**	42a	
b	Nontaxable combat pay election. 42b		
43	Additional child tax credit. Attach Schedule 8812.	43	
44	American opportunity credit from Form 8863, line 8.	44	
45	Net premium tax credit. Attach Form 8962.	45	
46	Add lines 40, 41, 42a, 43, 44, and 45. These are your **total payments.** ▶		46

Standard Deduction for—
- People who check any box on line 23a or 23b **or** who can be claimed as a dependent, see instructions.
- All others:

Single or Married filing separately, $6,300

Married filing jointly or Qualifying widow(er), $12,600

Head of household, $9,250

If you have a qualifying child, attach Schedule EIC.

Refund

47	If line 46 is more than line 39, subtract line 39 from line 46. This is the amount you **overpaid.**		47
48a	Amount of line 47 you want **refunded to you.** If Form 8888 is attached, check here ▶ ☐		48a
▶ b	Routing number ☐☐☐☐☐☐☐☐☐ ▶ c Type: ☐ Checking ☐ Savings		
▶ d	Account number ☐☐☐☐☐☐☐☐☐☐☐☐☐☐☐☐☐		
49	Amount of line 47 you want **applied to your 2016 estimated tax.**	49	

Direct deposit? See instructions and fill in 48b, 48c, and 48d or Form 8888.

Amount you owe

50	**Amount you owe.** Subtract line 46 from line 39. For details on how to pay, see instructions. ▶		50
51	Estimated tax penalty (see instructions).	51	

Third party designee

Do you want to allow another person to discuss this return with the IRS (see instructions)? ☐ **Yes.** Complete the following. ☐ **No**

Designee's name ▶ Phone no. ▶ Personal identification number (PIN) ▶

Sign here

Joint return? See instructions. Keep a copy for your records.

Under penalties of perjury, I declare that I have examined this return and accompanying schedules and statements, and to the best of my knowledge and belief, they are true, correct, and accurately list all amounts and sources of income I received during the tax year. Declaration of preparer (other than the taxpayer) is based on all information of which the preparer has any knowledge.

Your signature	Date	Your occupation	Daytime phone number
Spouse's signature. If a joint return, **both** must sign.	Date	Spouse's occupation	If the IRS sent you an Identity Protection PIN, enter it here (see inst.)

Paid preparer use only

Print/type preparer's name	Preparer's signature	Date	Check ▶ ☐ if self-employed	PTIN
Firm's name ▶			Firm's EIN ▶	
Firm's address ▶			Phone no.	

Form **1040A** (2015)

(Use for Cumulative Problem 1.)

SCHEDULE EIC
(Form 1040A or 1040)

Department of the Treasury
Internal Revenue Service (99)

Earned Income Credit

Qualifying Child Information

▶ **Complete and attach to Form 1040A or 1040 only if you have a qualifying child.**

▶ **Information about Schedule EIC (Form 1040A or 1040) and its instructions is at *www.irs.gov/scheduleeic*.**

1040A
1040
EIC

OMB No. 1545-0074

2015

Attachment
Sequence No. **43**

Name(s) shown on return | **Your social security number**

Before you begin:

- See the instructions for Form 1040A, lines 42a and 42b, or Form 1040, lines 66a and 66b, to make sure that **(a)** you can take the EIC, and **(b)** you have a qualifying child.
- Be sure the child's name on line 1 and social security number (SSN) on line 2 agree with the child's social security card. Otherwise, at the time we process your return, we may reduce or disallow your EIC. If the name or SSN on the child's social security card is not correct, call the Social Security Administration at 1-800-772-1213.

CAUTION

- *If you take the EIC even though you are not eligible, you may not be allowed to take the credit for up to 10 years. See the instructions for details.*
- *It will take us longer to process your return and issue your refund if you do not fill in all lines that apply for each qualifying child.*

Qualifying Child Information	**Child 1**	**Child 2**	**Child 3**
1 Child's name If you have more than three qualifying children, you have to list only three to get the maximum credit.	First name Last name	First name Last name	First name Last name
2 Child's SSN The child must have an SSN as defined in the instructions for Form 1040A, lines 42a and 42b, or Form 1040, lines 66a and 66b, unless the child was born and died in 2015. If your child was born and died in 2015 and did not have an SSN, enter "Died" on this line and attach a copy of the child's birth certificate, death certificate, or hospital medical records.			
3 Child's year of birth	Year __ __ __ __ *If born after 1996 **and** the child is younger than you (or your spouse, if filing jointly), skip lines 4a and 4b; go to line 5.*	Year __ __ __ __ *If born after 1996 **and** the child is younger than you (or your spouse, if filing jointly), skip lines 4a and 4b; go to line 5.*	Year __ __ __ __ *If born after 1996 **and** the child is younger than you (or your spouse, if filing jointly), skip lines 4a and 4b; go to line 5.*
4 a Was the child under age 24 at the end of 2015, a student, and younger than you (or your spouse, if filing jointly)?	☐ **Yes.** *Go to line 5.* ☐ **No.** *Go to line 4b.*	☐ **Yes.** *Go to line 5.* ☐ **No.** *Go to line 4b.*	☐ **Yes.** *Go to line 5.* ☐ **No.** *Go to line 4b.*
b Was the child permanently and totally disabled during any part of 2015?	☐ **Yes.** *Go to line 5.* ☐ **No.** The child is not a qualifying child.	☐ **Yes.** *Go to line 5.* ☐ **No.** The child is not a qualifying child.	☐ **Yes.** *Go to line 5.* ☐ **No.** The child is not a qualifying child.
5 Child's relationship to you (for example, son, daughter, grandchild, niece, nephew, foster child, etc.)			
6 Number of months child lived with you in the United States during 2015 • If the child lived with you for more than half of 2015 but less than 7 months, enter "7." • If the child was born or died in 2015 and your home was the child's home for more than half the time he or she was alive during 2015, enter "12."	______ months *Do not enter more than 12 months.*	______ months *Do not enter more than 12 months.*	______ months *Do not enter more than 12 months.*

For Paperwork Reduction Act Notice, see your tax return instructions. Cat. No. 13339M **Schedule EIC (Form 1040A or 1040) 2015**

(Use for Cumulative Problem 1.)

SCHEDULE 8812 (Form 1040A or 1040)

Department of the Treasury Internal Revenue Service (99)

Child Tax Credit

▶ Attach to Form 1040, Form 1040A, or Form 1040NR.
▶ Information about Schedule 8812 and its separate instructions is at *www.irs.gov/schedule8812*.

1040 1040A 1040NR 8812

OMB No. 1545-0074

2015

Attachment Sequence No. 47

Name(s) shown on return | Your social security number

Part I Filers Who Have Certain Child Dependent(s) with an ITIN (Individual Taxpayer Identification Number)

CAUTION

Complete this part only for each dependent who has an ITIN and for whom you are claiming the child tax credit. If your dependent is not a qualifying child for the credit, you cannot include that dependent in the calculation of this credit.

Answer the following questions for each dependent listed on Form 1040, line 6c; Form 1040A, line 6c; or Form 1040NR, line 7c, who has an ITIN (Individual Taxpayer Identification Number) and that you indicated is a qualifying child for the child tax credit by checking column (4) for that dependent.

A For the first dependent identified with an ITIN and listed as a qualifying child for the child tax credit, did this child meet the substantial presence test? See separate instructions.

☐ **Yes** ☐ **No**

B For the second dependent identified with an ITIN and listed as a qualifying child for the child tax credit, did this child meet the substantial presence test? See separate instructions.

☐ **Yes** ☐ **No**

C For the third dependent identified with an ITIN and listed as a qualifying child for the child tax credit, did this child meet the substantial presence test? See separate instructions.

☐ **Yes** ☐ **No**

D For the fourth dependent identified with an ITIN and listed as a qualifying child for the child tax credit, did this child meet the substantial presence test? See separate instructions.

☐ **Yes** ☐ **No**

Note: If you have more than four dependents identified with an ITIN and listed as a qualifying child for the child tax credit, see separate instructions and check here . . . . . ▶ ☐

Part II Additional Child Tax Credit Filers

1	**1040 filers:** Enter the amount from line 6 of your Child Tax Credit Worksheet (see the Instructions for Form 1040, line 52). **1040A filers:** Enter the amount from line 6 of your Child Tax Credit Worksheet (see the Instructions for Form 1040A, line 35). **1040NR filers:** Enter the amount from line 6 of your Child Tax Credit Worksheet (see the Instructions for Form 1040NR, line 49). If you used **Pub. 972,** enter the amount from line 8 of the Child Tax Credit Worksheet in the publication.			1	
2	Enter the amount from Form 1040, line 52; Form 1040A, line 35; or Form 1040NR, line 49			2	
3	Subtract line 2 from line 1. If zero, **stop;** you cannot take this credit			3	
4a	Earned income (see separate instructions)	4a			
b	Nontaxable combat pay (see separate instructions) 4b				
5	Is the amount on line 4a more than $3,000? ☐ **No.** Leave line 5 blank and enter -0- on line 6. ☐ **Yes.** Subtract $3,000 from the amount on line 4a. Enter the result . . .	5			
6	Multiply the amount on line 5 by 15% (.15) and enter the result			6	

Next. Do you have three or more qualifying children?

☐ **No.** If line 6 is zero, stop; you cannot take this credit. Otherwise, skip Part III and enter the **smaller** of line 3 or line 6 on line 13.

☐ **Yes.** If line 6 is equal to or more than line 3, skip Part III and enter the amount from line 3 on line 13. Otherwise, go to line 7.

For Paperwork Reduction Act Notice, see your tax return instructions. Cat. No. 59761M **Schedule 8812 (Form 1040A or 1040) 2015**

(Use for Cumulative Problem 1.)

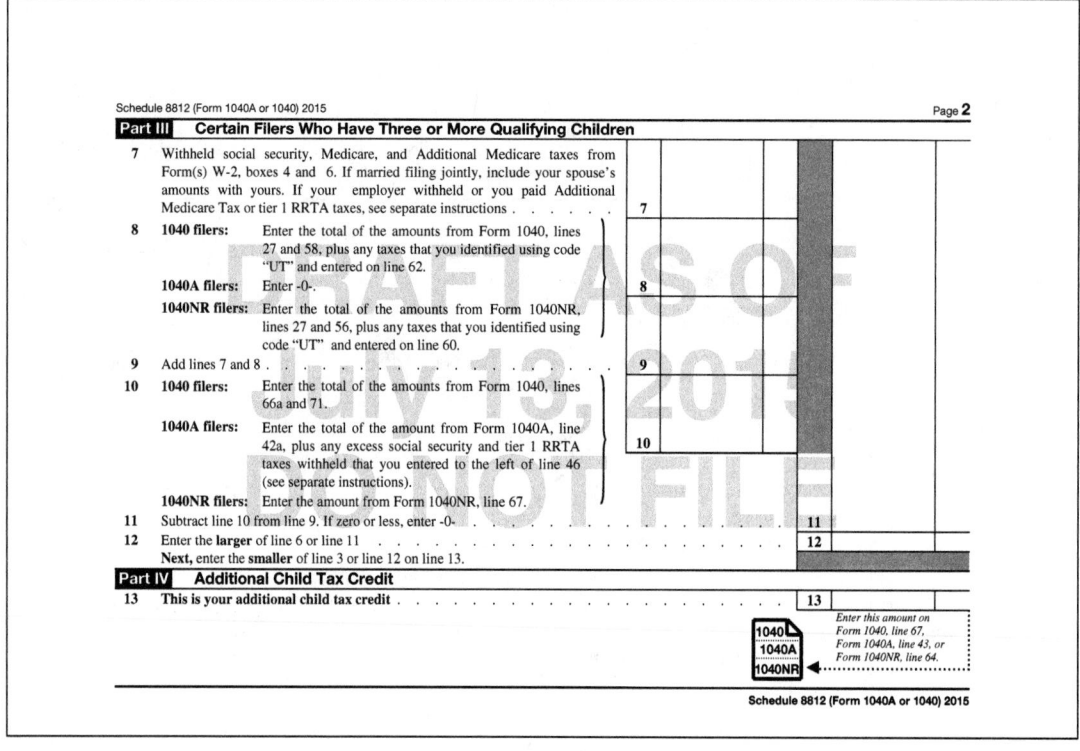

Schedule 8812 (Form 1040A or 1040) 2015 Page **2**

Part III Certain Filers Who Have Three or More Qualifying Children

7	Withheld social security, Medicare, and Additional Medicare taxes from Form(s) W-2, boxes 4 and 6. If married filing jointly, include your spouse's amounts with yours. If your employer withheld or you paid Additional Medicare Tax or tier 1 RRTA taxes, see separate instructions	7	
8	**1040 filers:** Enter the total of the amounts from Form 1040, lines 27 and 58, plus any taxes that you identified using code "UT" and entered on line 62. **1040A filers:** Enter -0-. **1040NR filers:** Enter the total of the amounts from Form 1040NR, lines 27 and 56, plus any taxes that you identified using code "UT" and entered on line 60.	8	
9	Add lines 7 and 8	9	
10	**1040 filers:** Enter the total of the amounts from Form 1040, lines 66a and 71. **1040A filers:** Enter the total of the amount from Form 1040A, line 42a, plus any excess social security and tier 1 RRTA taxes withheld that you entered to the left of line 46 (see separate instructions). **1040NR filers:** Enter the amount from Form 1040NR, line 67.	10	
11	Subtract line 10 from line 9. If zero or less, enter -0-	11	
12	Enter the **larger** of line 6 or line 11 **Next,** enter the **smaller** of line 3 or line 12 on line 13.	12	

Part IV Additional Child Tax Credit

13	**This is your additional child tax credit**	13	

1040 / 1040A / 1040NR ◄ *Enter this amount on Form 1040, line 67, Form 1040A, line 43, or Form 1040NR, line 64.*

Schedule 8812 (Form 1040A or 1040) 2015

(Use for Cumulative Problem 2.)

Form **1040** Department of the Treasury—Internal Revenue Service (99)
U.S. Individual Income Tax Return **2015** OMB No. 1545-0074 IRS Use Only—Do not write or staple in this space.

For the year Jan. 1–Dec. 31, 2015, or other tax year beginning , 2015, ending , 20 See separate instructions.

Your first name and initial	Last name	**Your social security number**
If a joint return, spouse's first name and initial	Last name	**Spouse's social security number**
Home address (number and street). If you have a P.O. box, see instructions.	Apt. no.	▲ Make sure the SSN(s) above and on line 6c are correct.
City, town or post office, state, and ZIP code. If you have a foreign address, also complete spaces below (see instructions).		**Presidential Election Campaign** Check here if you, or your spouse if filing jointly, want $3 to go to this fund. Checking a box below will not change your tax or refund. ☐ You ☐ Spouse
Foreign country name	Foreign province/state/county / Foreign postal code	

Filing Status

Check only one box.

1 ☐ Single
2 ☐ Married filing jointly (even if only one had income)
3 ☐ Married filing separately. Enter spouse's SSN above and full name here.
4 ☐ Head of household (with qualifying person). (See instructions.) If the qualifying person is a child but not your dependent, enter this child's name here.
5 ☐ Qualifying widow(er) with dependent child

Exemptions

6a ☐ **Yourself.** If someone can claim you as a dependent, **do not** check box 6a
b ☐ **Spouse**
c **Dependents:**

(1) First name Last name	(2) Dependent's social security number	(3) Dependent's relationship to you	(4) ✓ if child under age 17 qualifying for child tax credit (see instructions)
			☐
			☐
			☐
			☐

If more than four dependents, see instructions and check here ▶☐

d Total number of exemptions claimed

Boxes checked on 6a and 6b
No. of children on 6c who:
• lived with you
• did not live with you due to divorce or separation (see instructions)
Dependents on 6c not entered above
Add numbers on lines above ▶

Income

Attach Form(s) W-2 here. Also attach Forms W-2G and 1099-R if tax was withheld.

If you did not get a W-2, see instructions.

7	Wages, salaries, tips, etc. Attach Form(s) W-2		7
8a	**Taxable** interest. Attach Schedule B if required		8a
b	**Tax-exempt** interest. **Do not** include on line 8a	8b	
9a	Ordinary dividends. Attach Schedule B if required		9a
b	Qualified dividends	9b	
10	Taxable refunds, credits, or offsets of state and local income taxes		10
11	Alimony received		11
12	Business income or (loss). Attach Schedule C or C-EZ		12
13	Capital gain or (loss). Attach Schedule D if required. If not required, check here ▶ ☐		13
14	Other gains or (losses). Attach Form 4797		14
15a	IRA distributions 15a	b Taxable amount	15b
16a	Pensions and annuities 16a	b Taxable amount	16b
17	Rental real estate, royalties, partnerships, S corporations, trusts, etc. Attach Schedule E		17
18	Farm income or (loss). Attach Schedule F		18
19	Unemployment compensation		19
20a	Social security benefits 20a	b Taxable amount	20b
21	Other income. List type and amount		21
22	Combine the amounts in the far right column for lines 7 through 21. This is your **total income** ▶		22

Adjusted Gross Income

23	Reserved	23	
24	Certain business expenses of reservists, performing artists, and fee-basis government officials. Attach Form 2106 or 2106-EZ	24	
25	Health savings account deduction. Attach Form 8889	25	
26	Moving expenses. Attach Form 3903	26	
27	Deductible part of self-employment tax. Attach Schedule SE	27	
28	Self-employed SEP, SIMPLE, and qualified plans	28	
29	Self-employed health insurance deduction	29	
30	Penalty on early withdrawal of savings	30	
31a	Alimony paid b Recipient's SSN ▶	31a	
32	IRA deduction	32	
33	Student loan interest deduction	33	
34	Reserved	34	
35	Domestic production activities deduction. Attach Form 8903	35	
36	Add lines 23 through 35		36
37	Subtract line 36 from line 22. This is your **adjusted gross income** ▶		37

For Disclosure, Privacy Act, and Paperwork Reduction Act Notice, see separate instructions. Cat. No. 11320B Form **1040** (2015)

(Use for Cumulative Problem 2.)

Form 1040 (2015) Page **2**

Tax and Credits

38	Amount from line 37 (adjusted gross income)		38
39a	Check if: ☐ **You** were born before January 2, 1951, ☐ Blind. ☐ **Spouse** was born before January 2, 1951, ☐ Blind. **Total boxes checked ▶ 39a**		
b	If your spouse itemizes on a separate return or you were a dual-status alien, check here ▶ 39b☐		
40	**Itemized deductions** (from Schedule A) **or** your **standard deduction** (see left margin)		40
41	Subtract line 40 from line 38		41
42	**Exemptions.** If line 38 is $154,950 or less, multiply $4,000 by the number on line 6d. Otherwise, see instructions		42
43	**Taxable income.** Subtract line 42 from line 41. If line 42 is more than line 41, enter -0-		43
44	**Tax** (see instructions). Check if any from: a ☐ Form(s) 8814 b ☐ Form 4972 c ☐		44
45	**Alternative minimum tax** (see instructions). Attach Form 6251		45
46	Excess advance premium tax credit repayment. Attach Form 8962		46
47	Add lines 44, 45, and 46 ▶		47
48	Foreign tax credit. Attach Form 1116 if required	48	
49	Credit for child and dependent care expenses. Attach Form 2441	49	
50	Education credits from Form 8863, line 19	50	
51	Retirement savings contributions credit. Attach Form 8880	51	
52	Child tax credit. Attach Schedule 8812, if required	52	
53	Residential energy credit. Attach Form 5695	53	
54	Other credits from Form: a ☐ 3800 b ☐ 8801 c ☐	54	
55	Add lines 48 through 54. These are your **total credits**		55
56	Subtract line 55 from line 47. If line 55 is more than line 47, enter -0- ▶		56

Standard Deduction for—
• People who check any box on line 39a or 39b **or** who can be claimed as a dependent, see instructions.
• All others:
Single or Married filing separately, $6,300
Married filing jointly or Qualifying widow(er), $12,600
Head of household, $9,250

Other Taxes

57	Self-employment tax. Attach Schedule SE		57
58	Unreported social security and Medicare tax from Form: a ☐ 4137 b ☐ 8919		58
59	Additional tax on IRAs, other qualified retirement plans, etc. Attach Form 5329 if required		59
60a	Household employment taxes from Schedule H		60a
b	First-time homebuyer credit repayment. Attach Form 5405 if required		60b
61	Health care: individual responsibility (see instructions) Full-year coverage ☐		61
62	Taxes from: a ☐ Form 8959 b ☐ Form 8960 c ☐ Instructions; enter code(s)		62
63	Add lines 56 through 62. This is your **total tax** ▶		63

Payments

If you have a qualifying child, attach Schedule EIC.

64	Federal income tax withheld from Forms W-2 and 1099	64	
65	2015 estimated tax payments and amount applied from 2014 return	65	
66a	**Earned income credit (EIC)**	66a	
b	Nontaxable combat pay election 66b		
67	Additional child tax credit. Attach Schedule 8812	67	
68	American opportunity credit from Form 8863, line 8	68	
69	Net premium tax credit. Attach Form 8962	69	
70	Amount paid with request for extension to file	70	
71	Excess social security and tier 1 RRTA tax withheld	71	
72	Credit for federal tax on fuels. Attach Form 4136	72	
73	Credits from Form: a ☐ 2439 b ☐ Reserved c ☐ 8885 d ☐	73	
74	Add lines 64, 65, 66a, and 67 through 73. These are your **total payments** ▶		74

Refund

75	If line 74 is more than line 63, subtract line 63 from line 74. This is the amount you **overpaid**		75
76a	Amount of line 75 you want **refunded to you.** If Form 8888 is attached, check here ▶ ☐		76a
▶ b	Routing number ▶ c Type: ☐ Checking ☐ Savings		
▶ d	Account number		
77	Amount of line 75 you want **applied to your 2016 estimated tax** ▶	77	

Direct deposit? See instructions.

Amount You Owe

78	**Amount you owe.** Subtract line 74 from line 63. For details on how to pay, see instructions ▶		78
79	Estimated tax penalty (see instructions)	79	

Third Party Designee Do you want to allow another person to discuss this return with the IRS (see instructions)? ☐ **Yes.** Complete below. ☐ **No**

Designee's name ▶ Phone no. ▶ Personal identification number (PIN) ▶

Sign Here

Under penalties of perjury, I declare that I have examined this return and accompanying schedules and statements, and to the best of my knowledge and belief, they are true, correct, and complete. Declaration of preparer (other than taxpayer) is based on all information of which preparer has any knowledge.

Joint return? See instructions. Keep a copy for your records.

Your signature	Date	Your occupation	Daytime phone number
Spouse's signature. If a joint return, **both** must sign.	Date	Spouse's occupation	If the IRS sent you an Identity Protection PIN, enter it here (see inst.)

Paid Preparer Use Only

Print/Type preparer's name	Preparer's signature	Date	Check ☐ if self-employed	PTIN
Firm's name ▶			Firm's EIN ▶	
Firm's address ▶			Phone no.	

www.irs.gov/form1040 Form **1040** (2015)

(Use for Cumulative Problem 2.)

SCHEDULE B (Form 1040A or 1040)
Department of the Treasury Internal Revenue Service (99)

Interest and Ordinary Dividends

▶ Attach to Form 1040A or 1040.
▶ Information about Schedule B and its instructions is at *www.irs.gov/scheduleb*.

OMB No. 1545-0074
2015
Attachment Sequence No. 08

Name(s) shown on return | Your social security number

				Amount
Part I Interest (See instructions on back and the instructions for Form 1040A, or Form 1040, line 8a.) **Note:** If you received a Form 1099-INT, Form 1099-OID, or substitute statement from a brokerage firm, list the firm's name as the payer and enter the total interest shown on that form.	1	List name of payer. If any interest is from a seller-financed mortgage and the buyer used the property as a personal residence, see instructions on back and list this interest first. Also, show that buyer's social security number and address ▶	1	
	2	Add the amounts on line 1	2	
	3	Excludable interest on series EE and I U.S. savings bonds issued after 1989. Attach Form 8815	3	
	4	Subtract line 3 from line 2. Enter the result here and on Form 1040A, or Form 1040, line 8a ▶	4	

Note: If line 4 is over $1,500, you must complete Part III.

				Amount
Part II Ordinary Dividends (See instructions on back and the instructions for Form 1040A, or Form 1040, line 9a.) **Note:** If you received a Form 1099-DIV or substitute statement from a brokerage firm, list the firm's name as the payer and enter the ordinary dividends shown on that form.	5	List name of payer ▶	5	
	6	Add the amounts on line 5. Enter the total here and on Form 1040A, or Form 1040, line 9a ▶	6	

Note: If line 6 is over $1,500, you must complete Part III.

			Yes	No
Part III Foreign Accounts and Trusts (See instructions on back.)		You must complete this part if you **(a)** had over $1,500 of taxable interest or ordinary dividends; **(b)** had a foreign account; or **(c)** received a distribution from, or were a grantor of, or a transferor to, a foreign trust.		
	7a	At any time during 2015, did you have a financial interest in or signature authority over a financial account (such as a bank account, securities account, or brokerage account) located in a foreign country? See instructions		
		If "Yes," are you required to file FinCEN Form 114, Report of Foreign Bank and Financial Accounts (FBAR), to report that financial interest or signature authority? See FinCEN Form 114 and its instructions for filing requirements and exceptions to those requirements		
	b	If you are required to file FinCEN Form 114, enter the name of the foreign country where the financial account is located ▶		
	8	During 2015, did you receive a distribution from, or were you the grantor of, or transferor to, a foreign trust? If "Yes," you may have to file Form 3520. See instructions on back		

For Paperwork Reduction Act Notice, see your tax return instructions. Cat. No. 17146N **Schedule B (Form 1040A or 1040) 2015**

(Use for Cumulative Problem 2.)

Form **3903**

Department of the Treasury
Internal Revenue Service (99)

Moving Expenses

▶ Information about Form 3903 and its instructions is available at *www.irs.gov/form3903.*
▶ Attach to Form 1040 or Form 1040NR.

OMB No. 1545-0074
2015
Attachment
Sequence No. 170

Name(s) shown on return | **Your social security number**

Before you begin: ✓ See the **Distance Test** and **Time Test** in the instructions to find out if you can deduct your moving expenses.
✓ See **Members of the Armed Forces** in the instructions, if applicable.

1	Transportation and storage of household goods and personal effects (see instructions) . . .	1	
2	Travel (including lodging) from your old home to your new home (see instructions). **Do not** include the cost of meals	2	
3	Add lines 1 and 2	3	
4	Enter the total amount your employer paid you for the expenses listed on lines 1 and 2 that is **not** included in box 1 of your Form W-2 (wages). This amount should be shown in box 12 of your Form W-2 with code **P**	4	
5	Is line 3 **more than** line 4? ☐ **No.** You **cannot** deduct your moving expenses. If line 3 is less than line 4, subtract line 3 from line 4 and include the result on Form 1040, line 7, or Form 1040NR, line 8. ☐ **Yes.** Subtract line 4 from line 3. Enter the result here and on Form 1040, line 26, or Form 1040NR, line 26. This is your **moving expense deduction**	5	

For Paperwork Reduction Act Notice, see your tax return instructions. Cat. No. 12490K Form **3903** (2015)

(Use for Cumulative Problem 2.)

Form **8863**

Department of the Treasury
Internal Revenue Service (99)

Education Credits
(American Opportunity and Lifetime Learning Credits)

▶ **Attach to Form 1040 or Form 1040A.**
▶ **Information about Form 8863 and its separate instructions is at *www.irs.gov/form8863.***

OMB No. 1545-0074
2015
Attachment Sequence No. **50**

Name(s) shown on return | **Your social security number**

CAUTION *Complete a separate Part III on page 2 for each student for whom you are claiming either credit before you complete Parts I and II.*

Part I Refundable American Opportunity Credit

1	After completing Part III for each student, enter the total of all amounts from all Parts III, line 30		1
2	Enter: $180,000 if married filing jointly; $90,000 if single, head of household, or qualifying widow(er)	2	
3	Enter the amount from Form 1040, line 38, or Form 1040A, line 22. If you are filing Form 2555, 2555-EZ, or 4563, or you are excluding income from Puerto Rico, see Pub. 970 for the amount to enter	3	
4	Subtract line 3 from line 2. If zero or less, **stop**; you cannot take any education credit	4	
5	Enter: $20,000 if married filing jointly; $10,000 if single, head of household, or qualifying widow(er)	5	
6	If line 4 is: • Equal to or more than line 5, enter 1.000 on line 6 • Less than line 5, divide line 4 by line 5. Enter the result as a decimal (rounded to at least three places)		6 .
7	Multiply line 1 by line 6. **Caution:** If you were under age 24 at the end of the year **and** meet the conditions described in the instructions, you **cannot** take the refundable American opportunity credit; skip line 8, enter the amount from line 7 on line 9, and check this box ▶ ☐		7
8	**Refundable American opportunity credit.** Multiply line 7 by 40% (.40). Enter the amount here and on Form 1040, line 68, or Form 1040A, line 44. Then go to line 9 below		8

Part II Nonrefundable Education Credits

9	Subtract line 8 from line 7. Enter here and on line 2 of the Credit Limit Worksheet (see instructions)		9
10	After completing Part III for each student, enter the total of all amounts from all Parts III, line 31. If zero, skip lines 11 through 17, enter -0- on line 18, and go to line 19		10
11	Enter the smaller of line 10 or $10,000		11
12	Multiply line 11 by 20% (.20)		12
13	Enter: $130,000 if married filing jointly; $65,000 if single, head of household, or qualifying widow(er)	13	
14	Enter the amount from Form 1040, line 38, or Form 1040A, line 22. If you are filing Form 2555, 2555-EZ, or 4563, or you are excluding income from Puerto Rico, see Pub. 970 for the amount to enter	14	
15	Subtract line 14 from line 13. If zero or less, skip lines 16 and 17, enter -0- on line 18, and go to line 19	15	
16	Enter: $20,000 if married filing jointly; $10,000 if single, head of household, or qualifying widow(er)	16	
17	If line 15 is: • Equal to or more than line 16, enter 1.000 on line 17 and go to line 18 • Less than line 16, divide line 15 by line 16. Enter the result as a decimal (rounded to at least three places)		17 .
18	Multiply line 12 by line 17. Enter here and on line 1 of the Credit Limit Worksheet (see instructions) ▶		18
19	**Nonrefundable education credits.** Enter the amount from line 7 of the Credit Limit Worksheet (see instructions) here and on Form 1040, line 50, or Form 1040A, line 33		19

For Paperwork Reduction Act Notice, see your tax return instructions. Cat. No. 25379M Form **8863** (2015)

(Use for Cumulative Problem 2.)

Form 8863 (2015) Page **2**

Name(s) shown on return | **Your social security number**

CAUTION ***Complete Part III for each student for whom you are claiming either the American opportunity credit or lifetime learning credit. Use additional copies of page 2 as needed for each student.***

Part III **Student and Educational Institution Information**
See instructions.

20 Student name (as shown on page 1 of your tax return)	21 Student social security number (as shown on page 1 of your tax return)

22 Educational institution information (see instructions)

a. Name of first educational institution	**b.** Name of second educational institution (if any)
(1) Address. Number and street (or P.O. box). City, town or post office, state, and ZIP code. If a foreign address, see instructions.	**(1)** Address. Number and street (or P.O. box). City, town or post office, state, and ZIP code. If a foreign address, see instructions.
(2) Did the student receive Form 1098-T from this institution for 2015? ☐ Yes ☐ No	**(2)** Did the student receive Form 1098-T from this institution for 2015? ☐ Yes ☐ No
(3) Did the student receive Form 1098-T from this institution for 2014 with Box 2 filled in and Box 7 checked? ☐ Yes ☐ No	**(3)** Did the student receive Form 1098-T from this institution for 2014 with Box 2 filled in and Box 7 checked? ☐ Yes ☐ No
If you checked "No" in **both (2) and (3)**, skip **(4)**.	If you checked "No" in **both (2) and (3)**, skip **(4)**.
(4) If you checked "Yes" in **(2) or (3)**, enter the institution's federal identification number (from Form 1098-T). __ __ - __ __ __ __ __ __ __	**(4)** If you checked "Yes" in **(2) or (3)**, enter the institution's federal identification number (from Form 1098-T). __ __ - __ __ __ __ __ __ __

23	Has the Hope Scholarship Credit or American opportunity credit been claimed for this student for any 4 tax years before 2015?	☐ Yes — **Stop!** Go to line 31 for this student.	☐ No — Go to line 24.
24	Was the student enrolled at least half-time for at least one academic period that began or is treated as having begun in 2015 at an eligible educational institution in a program leading towards a postsecondary degree, certificate, or other recognized postsecondary educational credential? (see instructions)	☐ Yes — Go to line 25.	☐ No — **Stop!** Go to line 31 for this student.
25	Did the student complete the first 4 years of postsecondary education before 2015 (see instructions)?	☐ Yes — **Stop!** Go to line 31 for this student.	☐ No — Go to line 26.
26	Was the student convicted, before the end of 2015, of a felony for possession or distribution of a controlled substance?	☐ Yes — **Stop!** Go to line 31 for this student.	☐ No — Complete lines 27 through 30 for this student.

CAUTION *You **cannot** take the American opportunity credit and the lifetime learning credit for the **same student** in the same year. If you complete lines 27 through 30 for this student, do not complete line 31.*

American Opportunity Credit

27	Adjusted qualified education expenses (see instructions). **Do not enter more than $4,000**	**27**	
28	Subtract $2,000 from line 27. If zero or less, enter -0-	**28**	
29	Multiply line 28 by 25% (.25)	**29**	
30	If line 28 is zero, enter the amount from line 27. Otherwise, add $2,000 to the amount on line 29 and enter the result. Skip line 31. Include the total of all amounts from all Parts III, line 30, on Part I, line 1 .	**30**	

Lifetime Learning Credit

31	Adjusted qualified education expenses (see instructions). Include the total of all amounts from all Parts III, line 31, on Part II, line 10	**31**	

Form **8863** (2015)

Chapter 5

Personal Itemized Deductions

CHAPTER CONTENTS

LEARNING OBJECTIVES

After completing Chapter 5, you should be able to:

1. Identify and describe the five types of itemized deductions that are the focus of this chapter.
2. Describe the various types of expenses deductible as medical and dental expenses.
3. List out the various types of taxes taxpayers pay during the year and distinguish between those that are and are not deductible as itemized deductions.
4. Identify the types of interest expense that taxpayers can deduct as itemized deductions.
5. Understand how to compute a taxpayer's charitable contribution deduction, including the deduction for gifts of ordinary income property and capital gain property.
6. Compute a taxpayer's personal casualty and theft loss deduction.
7. Compute the reduction in itemized deductions for higher-income taxpayers.
8. Prepare Schedule A.

CHAPTER OVERVIEW

The tax laws usually do not allow individuals to deduct personal expenses on their tax returns. There are, however, exceptions. Several types of personal expenses can be deducted as **itemized deductions.** As an alternative to itemizing, taxpayers may choose to take the standard deduction if that amount is greater.

Individuals have two basic types of deductions. One type reduces gross income to yield adjusted gross income (AGI). Expenses incurred in a trade or business are examples of this type of deduction. Deductions for AGI were discussed in the last chapter. The other type of deduction (which includes itemized deductions) reduces AGI.

Deductions for AGI are the most desirable deduction. One reason for this is that the tax law uses AGI as a base to limit some deductions from AGI. As examples, medical expenses and personal casualty losses are deductible only to the extent they exceed 10% of AGI. Thus, the lesser the AGI, the better the chances of deducting these types of itemized deductions. Another reason deductions for AGI are preferred is that over 60% of all taxpayers use the standard deduction in lieu of itemizing deductions. Taxpayers deducting the (higher) standard deduction do not benefit from having expenses that are deductible as itemized deductions. Thus, taxpayers should look for ways to maximize their deductions for AGI.

Chapters 5 and 6 present itemized deductions, which taxpayers report on Schedule A. These two chapters explain when these deductions can be taken and how the deduction is calculated. Chapter 5 describes the most common personal deductions available on Schedule A, which includes medical expenses, taxes, interest, charitable contributions, and casualty or theft losses. The chapter also describes the reduction in total itemized deductions that higher-income taxpayers face. Chapter 6 expands the details of the miscellaneous and job-related deductions, which this chapter covers briefly.

For those who itemize, the tax laws generally allow taxpayers only to deduct their own expenses that they pay from their own funds. Only in limited cases is it possible for taxpayers to take deductions for expenses they pay on behalf of other people. These exceptions are pointed out in the chapter.

¶501 Reporting Itemized Deductions

Taxpayers usually deduct the larger of either the standard deduction or the total amount of itemized deductions. However, recall from Chapter 1 that when spouses file separately and one spouse itemizes deductions, the other spouse must also itemize, even if that amount is $0 (see ¶106).

Taxpayers that itemize show their deductions on Schedule A. For some deductions, an extra form must be completed to support the amount reported on Schedule A. Examples include Form 4952 (Investment Interest), Form 8283 (Noncash Charitable Contributions), Form 4684 (Casualty and Theft Losses), and Form 2106 (Employee Business Expenses).

Itemized Deductions Reported on Schedule A

Medical and Dental Expenses
Taxes You Paid
Interest You Paid
Gifts to Charity
Casualty and Theft Losses
Job Expenses and Certain Miscellaneous Deductions
Other Miscellaneous Deductions

¶502 Filled-In Schedule A

INFORMATION FOR FIGURE 5-1:

Steven T. and Laurie R. Neal report AGI of $374,864 on their joint tax return. The Neals compute their itemized deductions on Schedule A (Figure 5-1) by entering the amounts shown below in bold font on the appropriate lines. They then follow the instructions on the form to complete Schedule A. They transfer their total itemized deductions to the "Itemized Deductions" line on Form 1040, page 2. How the Neals came up with each deduction reported on Schedule A is explained in numerous examples throughout the chapter.

Line #

1: Medical and dental expenses, **$16,952** (Example 5)
2: AGI, **$374,864** (source: Form 1040, page 1)
5: State and local income taxes, **$13,050** (Example 7)
6: Real estate taxes, **$10,483** (Example 10)
7: Personal property taxes, **$667** (Example 11)
10: Home mortgage interest, **$16,435** (Example 12)
14: Investment interest expense, **$5,457** (Example 21)
16: Gifts by cash or check, **$3,725** (Example 22)
17: Noncash gifts, **$4,220** (Example 27)
23: Investment expenses, **$9,640** (given in Example 21)
25: AGI, **$374,864** (source: Form 1040, page 1)
29: Total itemized deductions, **$54,231** (Example 39)

Figure 5-1: Filled-In Schedule A

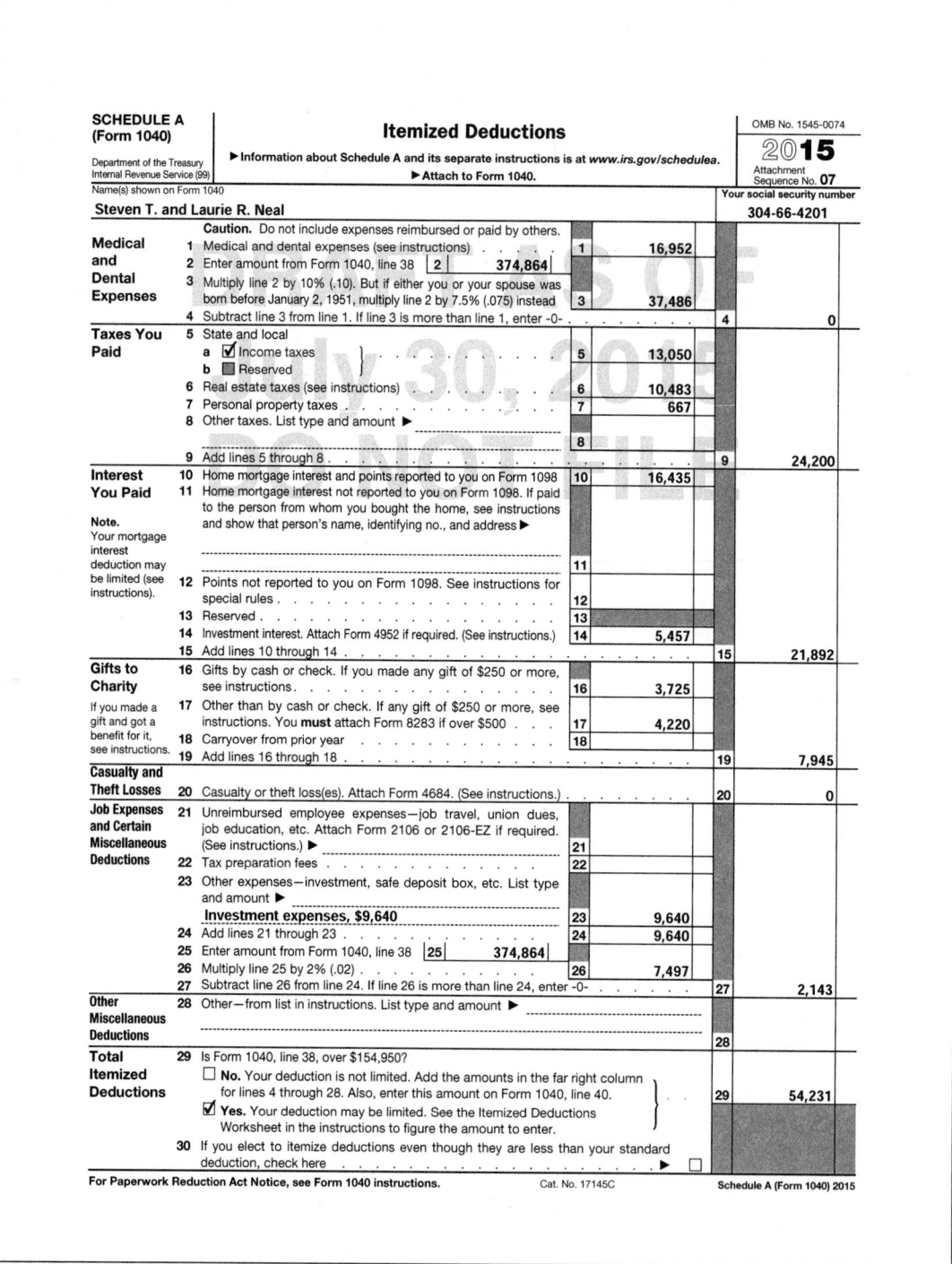

SCHEDULE A (Form 1040)
Department of the Treasury
Internal Revenue Service (99)

Itemized Deductions

▶ Information about Schedule A and its separate instructions is at *www.irs.gov/schedulea*.
▶ Attach to Form 1040.

OMB No. 1545-0074
2015
Attachment Sequence No. **07**

Name(s) shown on Form 1040	Your social security number
Steven T. and Laurie R. Neal	**304-66-4201**

Section	Line	Description	Line no.	Amount	Line no.	Total
Medical and Dental Expenses		**Caution.** Do not include expenses reimbursed or paid by others.				
	1	Medical and dental expenses (see instructions)	1	16,952		
	2	Enter amount from Form 1040, line 38 [2] 374,864				
	3	Multiply line 2 by 10% (.10). But if either you or your spouse was born before January 2, 1951, multiply line 2 by 7.5% (.075) instead	3	37,486		
	4	Subtract line 3 from line 1. If line 3 is more than line 1, enter -0-			4	0
Taxes You Paid	5	State and local				
		a ☑ Income taxes b ■ Reserved	5	13,050		
	6	Real estate taxes (see instructions)	6	10,483		
	7	Personal property taxes	7	667		
	8	Other taxes. List type and amount ▶	8			
	9	Add lines 5 through 8			9	24,200
Interest You Paid	10	Home mortgage interest and points reported to you on Form 1098	10	16,435		
Note. Your mortgage interest deduction may be limited (see instructions).	11	Home mortgage interest not reported to you on Form 1098. If paid to the person from whom you bought the home, see instructions and show that person's name, identifying no., and address ▶	11			
	12	Points not reported to you on Form 1098. See instructions for special rules	12			
	13	Reserved	13			
	14	Investment interest. Attach Form 4952 if required. (See instructions.)	14	5,457		
	15	Add lines 10 through 14			15	21,892
Gifts to Charity	16	Gifts by cash or check. If you made any gift of $250 or more, see instructions	16	3,725		
If you made a gift and got a benefit for it, see instructions.	17	Other than by cash or check. If any gift of $250 or more, see instructions. You **must** attach Form 8283 if over $500	17	4,220		
	18	Carryover from prior year	18			
	19	Add lines 16 through 18			19	7,945
Casualty and Theft Losses	20	Casualty or theft loss(es). Attach Form 4684. (See instructions.)			20	0
Job Expenses and Certain Miscellaneous Deductions	21	Unreimbursed employee expenses—job travel, union dues, job education, etc. Attach Form 2106 or 2106-EZ if required. (See instructions.) ▶	21			
	22	Tax preparation fees	22			
	23	Other expenses—investment, safe deposit box, etc. List type and amount ▶ **Investment expenses, $9,640**	23	9,640		
	24	Add lines 21 through 23	24	9,640		
	25	Enter amount from Form 1040, line 38 [25] 374,864				
	26	Multiply line 25 by 2% (.02)	26	7,497		
	27	Subtract line 26 from line 24. If line 26 is more than line 24, enter -0-			27	2,143
Other Miscellaneous Deductions	28	Other—from list in instructions. List type and amount ▶			28	
Total Itemized Deductions	29	Is Form 1040, line 38, over $154,950? ☐ **No.** Your deduction is not limited. Add the amounts in the far right column for lines 4 through 28. Also, enter this amount on Form 1040, line 40. ☑ **Yes.** Your deduction may be limited. See the Itemized Deductions Worksheet in the instructions to figure the amount to enter.			29	54,231
	30	If you elect to itemize deductions even though they are less than your standard deduction, check here ▶ ☐				

For Paperwork Reduction Act Notice, see Form 1040 instructions. Cat. No. 17145C **Schedule A (Form 1040) 2015**

¶503 Medical and Dental Expenses

Most taxpayers cannot take advantage of the medical and dental deduction. To be deductible, unreimbursed medical expenses normally must exceed 10% of the taxpayer's AGI. However, from 2013–2016, the "floor" for taxpayers age 65 and older is 7.5% of AGI. On a joint tax return, only one spouse needs to qualify to use the 7.5% AGI floor.

Taxpayers normally cannot deduct expenses they pay on behalf of others. However, the Internal Revenue Code (Code) allows taxpayers to deduct medical and dental expenses they pay on behalf of their dependents (as defined in ¶108–¶110). They also can deduct medical and dental expenses they pay for other persons whom they do not claim as dependents, provided that the person either (1) passes the citizenship, relationship, and support tests (as described in ¶109.01–¶109.03), or (2) passes the citizenship and relationship tests for a qualifying child (see ¶108.01, ¶108.06). Thus, a taxpayer can deduct amounts paid for her father's prescription drugs whom the taxpayer supports, but cannot claim as a dependent because the father's gross income exceeds $4,000. Likewise, a taxpayer can deduct the medical bills paid on behalf of the taxpayer's sister, whom the taxpayer cannot claim as a dependent because the sister provides over half of her own support for the year. (Recall from ¶108.01, that siblings pass the relationship test for a qualifying child).

> When one spouse receives extensive medical care, the couple should consider filing separate returns. The 10% (or 7.5%) AGI floor applies to a lower AGI amount when only one spouse's income is reported on the return.

¶503.01 PRESCRIPTION DRUGS AND INSULIN

Only prescription drugs are deductible as medical expenses. Even when prescribed, over-the-counter items do not qualify as a deductible medical expense. Some commonly used over-the-counter (nondeductible) prescribed items include iron and calcium supplements, gluten-free foods, birth control devices, cold medicines, aspirin, allergy medications, and antacid tablets.

EXAMPLE 1 For Steven Neal's cold and fever, a doctor prescribed an antibiotic and an over-the-counter cold remedy. Steven's co-pay for the antibiotic was $25. The insurance company paid the rest. The cold remedy cost $5. Only the $25 Steven paid for the antibiotic may be deducted.

¶503.02 MEDICAL AND DENTAL INSURANCE PREMIUMS

Medical expenses include insurance premiums paid for medical and dental care, including amounts paid through payroll deductions at work. Also deductible are Medicare premiums withheld from the taxpayer's monthly social security checks, as well as amounts social security recipients pay to supplement their Medicare coverage. Long-term care insurance premiums are also deductible. Self-employed taxpayers deduct for AGI insurance premiums paid for months when the taxpayer (and the taxpayer's spouse, if married) is not eligible for an employer's medical plan (¶402.08). Any premiums paid by self-employed taxpayers not deductible for AGI are deductible as a medical expense on Schedule A (line 1).

Amounts that are not deductible as a medical expense include premiums paid on the medical portion of auto insurance, life insurance premiums, and premiums paid for insurance that covers lost earnings or loss of a limb or sight. Taxpayers also cannot deduct insurance premiums employers pay on their behalf.

EXAMPLE 2

The Neals' medical and dental insurance premiums for the year total $24,930. Steven paid $9,972 of this amount through payroll deductions. His employer paid the rest. During the year, the Neals also paid $1,200 for life insurance and $600 for disability insurance. Only the $9,972 of health insurance premiums Steven paid counts as a medical deduction. The $14,958 of premiums paid by the employer is a tax-free fringe benefit (¶401.03).

¶503.03 OTHER MEDICAL EXPENSES

Taxpayers can deduct payments made directly to medical providers, such as doctors, dentists, nurses, hospitals, and clinics. Deductible payments also include those made to authorized Christian Science practitioners, chiropractors, osteopaths, and therapists. Deductible forms of medical care include lab work, medical procedures, X-rays, CAT scans, and MRIs.

Some treatments designed to help patients stop smoking also qualify as a medical expense deduction. This includes participation in a stop-smoking program. It also includes the purchase of drugs requiring a physician's prescription to lessen the effects of nicotine withdrawal. Taxpayers can deduct the cost of a weight-loss program if weight loss is the treatment for a specific disease diagnosed by a doctor (e.g. obesity, hypertension, or heart disease). They cannot deduct the cost of a weight-loss program when the reason for the weight loss is the improvement of appearance, general health, or sense of well-being.

Cosmetic surgery is deductible only when it is necessary for medical reasons, such as correction of a birth defect or to repair of damage from injury or disease. The cost of cosmetic surgery undergone for personal (vanity) reasons is not deductible.

Nursing Home Care

Depending on the condition of a nursing home resident and the types of services offered by the home, the entire amount paid to the facility may be deductible. When the main purpose of the stay relates to a medical condition, the taxpayer deducts all expenses, even the cost of food and lodging. Some conditions that qualify for 100% medical treatment include Alzheimer's disease, paralysis, alcoholism, drug rehabilitation, and a physical injury or handicap. If the main reason for living in the home relates to personal care or family convenience, the taxpayer deducts only the specific medical expenses. However, amounts paid for qualified long-term care are deductible when such services are required by a chronically ill person.

School for the Handicapped

Amounts paid to send a mentally or physically handicapped spouse or disabled dependent to a special school or facility are deductible medical costs. The school's main focus must be to help the student compensate or overcome problems in order to function better.

Employee Physicals

Many employees involved with hazardous materials or dangerous jobs get annual physicals. When the employer requires physicals, the costs are deducted as miscellaneous employee business expenses (see ¶602.07). Employees getting physicals on their own deduct their out-of-pocket costs as a medical expense.

Travel and Transportation

Taxpayers can deduct the costs of traveling to seek medical care. This includes the cost for bus, train, and airline tickets, as well as taxi fares, and the costs for rental cars and ambulance services. The travel costs for a nurse also are deductible when paid to accompany a sick person who is unable to travel alone. This rule also applies to the travel costs for a parent when accompanying a child seeking medical care. When overnight travel is required, the Code limits the deduction for lodging to $50 per night for each person. The cost of meals while traveling for medical reasons is not deductible.

Taxpayers who use their personal car in seeking medical care may use either a standard mileage rate or their actual costs to compute their medical deduction. For 2015, the standard mileage rate for medical expenses is $.23 per mile. The costs of tolls and parking are added to this amount. Although individuals may deduct their actual expenses, the standard mileage rate is easier to use. When choosing to use the actual expense method, taxpayers may deduct only out-of-pocket expenses. Taxpayers must keep a log showing the mileage and expenses, as well as receipts for all items paid.

Capital Expenditures

Home improvements and special equipment installed in a home may be deducted when prescribed by a medical provider as part of a specific treatment. Three common improvements are swimming pools, air conditioners, and elevators. When the improvement increases the value of the home by more than the cost of the improvement, no medical deduction is allowed. The reasoning is that the taxpayer will be repaid when the home is later sold for more money. However, when the cost exceeds the increase in value of the home, the excess is deducted as a medical expense.

EXAMPLE 3

Under a doctor's prescription for a medical condition, the Neals (from Figure 5-1) pay $7,000 for a hot tub. The hot tub increases the value of the home by $4,000. The Neals can deduct the $3,000 difference. They add this amount to their other unreimbursed medical expenses on Schedule A (line 1).

An exception exists for improvements that make it possible for a physically handicapped individual to live independently. Examples include constructing ramps, widening hallways and doorways for wheelchair use, installing support bars and railings, and adjusting outlets and fixtures. The IRS treats the costs of these types of improvements as adding no value to the home for tax purposes. Thus, the entire cost of the improvement is deductible.

EXAMPLE 4

Robin (age 36) is confined to a wheelchair. In order to live alone, Robin pays $10,000 to have entrance ramps, bars and railings installed in her home. Although these features are estimated to add as much as $2,000 to the value of her home, the IRS treats their added value as $0. This allows Robin to deduct the full $10,000 as a medical expense deduction. She adds this to her other unreimbursed medical expenses. She then reduces the total by 10% of her AGI.

Other Expenditures

Other commonly deductible medical expenses include eye exams, eyeglasses, contact lenses, noncosmetic dental work (crowns, dentures, braces, etc.), crutches, canes, wheelchairs, and guide dogs. Common nondeductible medical items include health club memberships, massages, burial and funeral costs, and illegal drugs or operations.

¶503.04 REIMBURSEMENTS

A taxpayer's medical and dental expense deduction equals the sum of all qualified medical expenses minus any reimbursements received during the year related to those expenses. This net amount is reported on Schedule A (line 1).

EXAMPLE 5

In addition to the $25 prescription medicine (Example 1), $9,972 of health insurance premiums (Example 2), and $3,000 for the (doctor-prescribed) hot tub (Example 3), the Neals (from Figure 5-1) also paid $28,375 of deductible medical costs during the year. The Neals were reimbursed $24,420 by their insurance company. The Neals enter the $16,952 difference ($25 + $9,972 + $3,000 + $28,375 – $24,420) on Schedule A (line 1). They reduce this amount by $37,486 ($374,864 AGI × 10%), leaving them with a $0 medical expense deduction on Schedule A (line 4).

Two situations occur that make medical reimbursements taxable. First, when an employer-paid insurance policy provides reimbursements greater than the medical expenses actually paid, the excess is taxable. (When the employee pays the premium, the excess is not taxable.) Second, when the taxpayer takes a medical deduction and receives a reimbursement in the following year, all or part of that reimbursement may be taxable under the tax benefit rule described in Chapter 3. This rule requires that taxpayers report the reimbursement in gross income only when they benefited from deducting medical expenses in an earlier year (see discussion of the tax benefit rule in ¶313.01).

EXAMPLE 6

Terri pays $5,000 of medical expenses in 20x1. Although this amount exceeds the AGI floor, Terri's standard deduction is higher than her total itemized deductions in 20x1. Early in 20x2, Terri's insurance company reimburses her $2,000 for medical costs paid in 20x1. Terri does not include any of the $2,000 in gross income in 20x2. Because Terri's income taxes were not lowered by the $5,000 of medical costs in 20x1, she did not receive a tax benefit from the amounts reimbursed.

¶504 Taxes You Paid

The tax law limits the types of taxes that are deductible. Income taxes and property taxes qualify as itemized deductions, but only when levied by an agency other than the federal government. Qualifying taxes must meet two conditions before a deduction is available. First, the taxpayer must actually pay the taxes. Second, the taxes paid must be those owed by the taxpayer. Amounts the taxpayer pays for someone else's taxes cannot be deducted.

Other nondeductible taxes include federal income taxes; FICA (social security and Medicare) taxes; federal and state estate, gift or inheritance taxes; use and excise taxes (taxes imposed on gasoline, tobacco, and alcohol). Although sales taxes have been deductible in prior years, they are not deductible in the current Code (see note in the New Developments box later in this section). The remainder of this section describes the types of taxes that can be deducted as an itemized deduction on Schedule A.

¶504.01 STATE AND LOCAL TAXES

Taxpayers can deduct on Schedule A state and local income taxes paid during 2015. There are three ways of paying state and local income taxes. These are: (1) through W-2 (paycheck) withholdings, (2) by making estimated tax payments in the current tax year, and (3) by paying additional taxes (but not interest or penalties) for the current or previous years.

EXAMPLE 7

The Neals (from Figure 5-1) paid the following state income taxes in 2015. They enter $13,050 on Schedule A (line 5).

State income tax withheld during 2015	$10,420
Estimated state income tax paid during 2015	2,400
State income tax paid with 2014 return filed in April 2015	175
Additional tax assessed on 2013 state income tax paid in May 2015	55
Total deduction for state income taxes in 2015	$13,050

Taxpayers who live in a state that does not impose a state income tax do not benefit from the deduction for state and local income taxes. A provision in the Code from 2005-2014 allowed taxpayers to deduct the *greater of* (i) state and local income taxes, or (ii) general sales taxes paid during the year. The general sales tax deduction was based on either actual sales tax receipts or an estimated amount from an IRS-provided table. Many believe Congress may reinstate this deduction prior to the end of 2015. However, at the time this textbook was sent to the printer, Congress had not been successful at extending this provision. If re-enacted by Congress, taxpayers who itemize will have the option of (i) checking box 5a on Schedule A and deducting their state and local income taxes, or (ii) checking box 5b (currently marked "Reserved") and deducting their general sales tax deduction on Schedule A (line 5).

Refund of State and Local Income Taxes

A refund of prior year's state or local income taxes does not reduce the amount of taxes paid during the year. Instead, when the refund stems from taxes deducted in a prior tax year, the amount is reported on Form 1040 (page 1) as "Taxable refunds, etc." in accordance with the tax benefit rule (discussed at ¶313.01).

EXAMPLE 8

During 20x1, Jason's employer withheld $3,600 for state income taxes from his wages. Jason's itemized deductions in 20x1 exceeded his standard deduction by $8,000. In April of 20x2, Jason files his state income tax return. Two months later he receives a $700 refund. Since Jason's tax liability was lowered in 20x1 when he deducted the $3,600 as an itemized deduction, he reports the $700 in gross income in 20x2. The tax benefit rule taxes Jason on the *lesser of* (i) the $700 refund, or (ii) the $8,000 excess of his 20x1 itemized deductions over his standard deduction amount.

¶504.02 REAL ESTATE TAXES

The tax laws allow individuals to deduct from AGI ad valorem taxes they pay to state and local governments. **Ad valorem taxes** are taxes imposed on the value of the property. Local governments levy real estate taxes on the owners of real property based on the property's value. Thus, the owners can deduct state and local real estate taxes as an itemized deduction. They also can deduct real estate taxes paid to foreign governments.

When real estate is sold during the year, the seller is responsible for the real estate taxes up until the day of the sale. The buyer's responsibility starts on the day of the sale. Real estate taxes are normally assessed once a year. The tax bill is sent to the property owner. The tax laws allow taxpayers to deduct expenses that they both pay and are responsible for. When real estate is sold during the year, the party that pays the real estate tax bill may not be the one responsible for all of the taxes being paid. In these situations, only the portion of the taxes that the owner is responsible for can be deducted. To ensure no deductions are lost, at the time real estate is sold, sellers need to remit to the buyers their share of real estate taxes up to the date of the sale. Standard language to this effect is found in most sales contracts.

EXAMPLE 9 On May 11, 20x1, Jill sells her home to the Ryans for $200,000. Real estate taxes on the home are expected to be $3,000 for 20x1. At the closing, Jill pays the Ryans $1,068 ($3,000 × 130/365). This amount is her share of the real estate taxes for the 130 days she owned the home during 20x1. In turn, Jill deducts this amount as real estate taxes on Schedule A in 20x1. At the end of the year, the local government sends the Ryans the tax bill for 20x1. Although they will pay the entire amount due, the Ryans' out-of-pocket costs will be the amount paid minus the $1,068 they received from Jill at the closing. This net amount is the Ryans' share of the real estate taxes. They deduct this amount as real estate taxes on Schedule A in 20x1.

Condominium and cooperative housing owners may deduct their shares of real estate taxes paid on these properties. When the homeowners association pays real estate taxes, it must identify the actual pass-through of property taxes to provide owners with the documentation for the tax deduction. "Special assessments" added to the property tax bill for local improvements like streets, sidewalks, and sewers do not qualify as deductible taxes. Instead, these amounts are added to the owner's basis (investment) in the property.

EXAMPLE 10 During the year, the Neals (from Figure 5-1) paid real estate taxes on their main home ($6,405), their vacation home ($3,322), and on a vacant lot they own as an investment ($756). They report the $10,483 total real estate taxes paid on Schedule A (line 6). The tax law does not limit the number of properties on which real estate taxes can be deducted.

¶504.03 PERSONAL PROPERTY TAXES

Real estate is not the only type of property where a property tax is imposed. Some states levy taxes on personal property. For tax purposes, "personal property" is all property that is not real estate. This means that all property that is neither land nor buildings is called personal property. Individuals and businesses can own personal property. Individuals can own personal property that they use in their personal lives or hold for investment. This would include clothing, home furnishings, artwork, and shares of stock. Examples of personal property businesses might own include trucks, office furniture, and machinery.

Personal property should not be confused with the property that individuals own and use in their personal lives. This type of property is personal-use property. Other uses of property include business and investment-use. State and local personal property taxes are deductible if the tax base used is the value of the personal property. Also, the tax must be charged on an annual basis, even if it is collected more or less often.

Personal property can be tangible or intangible. Tangible property has physical characteristics. Intangible property does not. Examples of tangible personal property include automobiles, books, clothing, and equipment. Examples of intangible property include patents, copyrights, goodwill, trademarks, etc. The tax law also considers stocks, bonds, mutual funds, and money market accounts to be intangible property. Almost all states that impose a tax on intangible property impose a tax on these latter intangibles. If the amount of tax depends on the property's value, the tax is deductible.

States that impose a tax on tangible personal property generally tax property that the owners register with the state (e.g. motor vehicles, boats, and aircraft). This allows the tax to be included as part of the annual registration fee charged to owners. In states where the annual registration fee is based on the property's value, individuals can deduct that portion of the fee as an itemized deduction. Any added fees not based on the property's value cannot be deducted.

EXAMPLE 11

The Neals (from Figure 5-1) paid the Department of Motor Vehicles $717 for the annual cost to register their two cars. The fee includes a $50 tag renewal fee. The rest of the fee is based on the value of the car. The Neals deduct $667 ($717 – $50) as personal property tax on Schedule A (line 7).

¶504.04 OTHER TAXES

Taxpayers with foreign sources of income may pay foreign income taxes. Individual taxpayers have two options on how to handle foreign income taxes paid during the year. First, they can take the taxes as a foreign tax credit (¶204.01). Second, they can deduct the foreign taxes as an itemized deduction. When deducting foreign taxes, taxpayers write "Foreign income taxes" and the amount on the "Other taxes" line on Schedule A.

¶505 Interest You Paid

Most personal interest is not deductible. However, home mortgage interest, points, and investment interest may qualify as itemized deductions. In contrast, interest on student loans is not an itemized deduction. Taxpayers deduct student loan interest for AGI on Form 1040, page 1 (¶402.12).

¶505.01 HOME MORTGAGE INTEREST

Taxpayers deduct interest paid on qualified home loans, which include debt on the taxpayer's principal residence (main home) plus a second home. A vacation home qualifies as a second home. Houses, condos, and mobile homes all count as personal homes. Sometimes boats and motor homes qualify as well. To take the mortgage interest deduction, the one paying the interest must also own the home.

Persons who own three or more homes can deduct the mortgage interest paid on only their main home plus one other home of their choosing. When allowing others to use a home, the home will qualify as a second home if the taxpayer uses the home during the year for more than the *greater of* (i) 14 days or (ii) 10% of the total days rented.

EXAMPLE 12

The Neals (from Figure 5-1) make mortgage payments on their main home and their vacation home. The interest paid on these properties was $13,215 and $3,220, respectively. The Neals deduct $16,435 ($13,215 + $3,220) as home mortgage interest on Schedule A.

EXAMPLE 13

The Friedlands live most of the year in Dallas, Texas. They vacation in Phoenix, Arizona and Park City, Utah. They own homes in all three locations and have mortgages on all three homes. In the current year, the Friedlands paid interest expense on the Dallas, Phoenix, and Park City mortgages of $6,000, $10,000, and $18,500, respectively. When preparing Schedule A, the Friedlands can deduct the $6,000 interest paid on the loan used to finance their main home (in Dallas). They also can deduct the $18,500 paid on the mortgage of their Park City home. The $10,000 paid on their other vacation home is nondeductible personal interest.

Acquisition Indebtedness

One type of qualifying home interest is **acquisition indebtedness** (acquisition debt). This includes money borrowed to buy, build, or substantially improve the taxpayer's main or second home. Only the interest paid on up to $1,000,000 of acquisition debt can be deducted ($500,000 for married couples filing MFS). However, no interest deduction limits exist on debt incurred before October 13, 1987. Still, a sizable loan on the main home may limit the interest deduction on a second home acquired after this date.

Special rules limit the deduction when refinancing the original debt. If the new loan has a balance higher than the old loan, the amount of new debt that replaces the old debt qualifies as acquisition debt. Also, any portion of the excess debt used to buy or improve the taxpayer's main or second home qualifies as acquisition debt. Any remaining new debt is not acquisition debt, but may qualify as home equity debt.

EXAMPLE 14

The Tremlins own a home in Evanston, Illinois. They paid $1.5 million for the home many years ago. When the mortgage on the home was $750,000, and the value of their home was $1.7 million, the Tremlins refinanced their mortgage. Their new mortgage is for $1.3 million. The Tremlins did not use any of the loan proceeds to improve their home. Interest paid on $750,000 of the new loan is deductible as acquisition debt. Some of the interest paid on the rest of the debt may qualify as home equity debt (see discussion to follow). Any interest paid on the excess borrowed that is not home equity debt is nondeductible personal interest.

EXAMPLE 15

Same facts as in Example 14, except that the Tremlins used $120,000 of the loan proceeds to remodel their kitchen. The Tremlins can deduct interest on $870,000 ($750,000 + $120,000) of the $1.3 million mortgage as acquisition debt. Interest on some of the $430,000 excess debt may be deductible as home equity debt.

EXAMPLE 16

Same facts as in Example 15, except that in addition to using $120,000 to improve their home, the Tremlins spent $200,000 to buy a second home. The Tremlins can deduct interest on $1 million of the mortgage as acquisition debt. Interest on some of the $300,000 excess debt may be deductible as home equity debt.

Home Equity Debt

Within limits, taxpayers may deduct interest on any loan secured by their homes. These include home equity loans and bill consolidation loans. Such debt, plus the balance of any acquisition debt, cannot exceed the fair market value (FMV) of the home. Total home equity debt cannot exceed $100,000 ($50,000 for married couples who file MFS). The deduction for the interest on home equity debt allows homeowners to borrow up to $100,000 on their homes without any restrictions on how the money is spent.

EXAMPLE 17

Continuing with Example 16, $300,000 of the $1.3 million mortgage that did not count as acquisition debt qualifies as home equity debt. However, the Code limits the Tremlins' deduction to interest on $100,000 of such debt. Thus, they will be allowed to deduct interest related to $1.1 million of their debt as home mortgage interest on Schedule A. Once the Tremlins' loan balance falls below $1.1 million, their interest deduction will not be limited.

EXAMPLE 18

Back in 1996, the Hoffmans bought a home for $60,000 and took out $40,000 of acquisition debt. By February 10, 2015, the loan had a balance of $18,000, and the FMV of the home was $100,000. The Hoffmans took out a second mortgage of $20,000 and used the money to buy a car and take a trip. Since this money was not used to improve the home, it falls under the rules for home equity debt.

On August 15, 2015, the Hoffmans decided to add a pool and a patio, which cost $15,000. The builder financed the work. The property secures the builder's loan, along with the other loans. This loan to finance improvements to the Hoffmans' main home qualifies as acquisition debt. Total interest associated with their house payments is $2,500 ($1,700 on their acquisition debt + $800 on their home equity debt). The Hoffmans deduct $2,500 as home mortgage interest.

Reporting Home Mortgage Interest

Most taxpayers who have a mortgage receive from their lender Form 1098, Mortgage Interest Statement. This form reports to taxpayers the amount of mortgage interest paid during the year. Mortgage interest reported on Form 1098 is shown on a different line on Schedule A, from any home mortgage interest paid during the year not reported on Form 1098.

¶505.02 POINTS

Also called "loan origination fees" or "loan fees," **points** are a type of prepaid interest. In exchange for paying points (interest) up front, the borrower gets a lower interest rate over the term of the loan. One point equals 1% of the loan amount. The more points paid, the lower the interest rate. Taxpayers may deduct points as interest. However, not all loan costs qualify as deductible points. For example, fees charged for loan services provided by the lender are not deductible. To be deductible, the points must meet these three conditions:

1. Paying points on borrowed money is an established business practice in the area.
2. The amount charged does not exceed the amount usually charged in the area.
3. Funds to pay the points must come from the borrower's own money, not from the lender's funds.

As a rule, taxpayers deduct prepaid expenses over the periods to which they apply. Since points are the same as prepaying interest, they usually must be deducted (amortized) evenly over the life of the loan. However, when the proceeds of the loan are used to buy or improve the taxpayer's main home, cash basis taxpayers can deduct points in the year paid. This special rule only applies to cash basis taxpayers who take out loans to buy or improve their main homes. It does not extend to vacation homes, second homes or to refinancing of loans. It also does not apply to accrual basis taxpayers.

A special situation arises when the property is sold or the loan is refinanced. If the property is sold, any unamortized (not yet deducted) points are deducted in the year of the sale. If the loan is refinanced, then the unamortized points plus any new points paid with the refinancing are deducted over the life of the new loan. However, if a part of the proceeds from refinancing a main home are used to improve the home, cash basis taxpayers can deduct a portion of the points in the year paid. The rest are deducted evenly over the term of the loan.

EXAMPLE 19

In 20x0, Carrey (cash basis taxpayer) took out a mortgage to buy his main home. In 20x4, Carrey refinanced his mortgage with a 30-year, $150,000 loan. To get a lower interest rate, he paid three points ($150,000 × 3% = $4,500). Two points ($3,000) were for prepaid interest. One point ($1,500) was charged for services provided by the lender. The payment of points is an established practice in the area. The 2% charged is not more than the amount typically charged for points. Carrey's first payment on the new loan was due May 1, 20x4.

Since the proceeds from the new loan were not used to buy or improve his main home, Carrey cannot deduct all of the points in 20x4. Instead, he deducts the $3,000 evenly over the life of the loan. The $1,500 for the other one point cannot be deducted. In 20x4, Carrey's deduction is $67 [($3,000/360 months in a 30-year loan) × 8 payments made in 20x4].

Reporting Points

When points are paid on the purchase of a main home, the amount of points paid should be reported on Form 1098. The points are fully deductible in the year paid and are added to any home mortgage interest reported on Form 1098. The deductible portion of points not reported on Form 1098 are reported on the line designated "Points not reported to you on Form 1098," on Schedule A.

¶505.03 MORTGAGE INSURANCE PREMIUMS

Taxpayers who do not put at least a 20% down payment on the purchase of a home usually must take out mortgage insurance. From 2007-2014, taxpayers whose AGI did not exceed $100,000 ($50,000 for married couples who file MFS) could deduct premiums paid on qualified mortgage insurance policies taken out on the purchase or improvement of the taxpayer's main home or second home. This deduction did not apply to premiums paid on the purchase of any other home or on the refinancing of any loan. A reduced deduction was available for taxpayers whose AGI did not exceed $109,000 ($54,500 for married couples who file MFS).

"Qualified mortgage insurance" included mortgage insurance provided by the Department of Veterans affairs, the Federal Housing Administration, or the Rural Housing Service. It also included private mortgage insurance. Although the deduction for mortgage insurance premiums expired at the end of 2014, there is a chance it could be reinstated for 2015. However, at the time this textbook went to the printer, no such legislation had been passed.

Should Congress pass tax legislation to retroactively reinstate the deduction for qualified mortgage insurance premiums for 2015, the deduction would be taken on Schedule A (line 13), currently marked RESERVED.

¶505.04 INVESTMENT INTEREST

Investment interest includes interest paid on a loan to buy or hold on to taxable investments, which include stocks, taxable bonds, vacant land, gemstones, and artwork. The tax law does not allow deductions for expenses related to nontaxable income. Therefore, interest paid on amounts borrowed to buy or hold onto nontaxable investments (like municipal bonds) is not deductible. Some investments are considered "passive" investments. The tax law does not treat interest expense related to a passive investment as investment interest. This interest is deducted elsewhere on the tax return. For instance, interest expense on rental property (a passive investment) belongs on Schedule E, not on Schedule A. Passive investments are discussed in Chapter 9.

The **investment interest limitation** limits the deduction of investment interest to the amount of the taxpayer's net investment income. Any investment interest not deducted because of this limit may be carried over and used in future years. When carried to the next year, it acts just like that year's investment interest and faces the same limits.

Investment income includes taxable interest, nonqualified dividends, and some royalties. It may also include qualified dividends and the gain from the sale of investments. If the taxpayer chooses to tax qualified dividends and net capital gains at the lower tax rates (¶201.03, ¶1101.03), then these amounts cannot count as investment income. However, if the taxpayer elects to pay the normal tax rates on qualified dividends and net capital gains, then these amounts count as investment income. This second option may allow the taxpayer to take a higher deduction for investment interest in the current year.

EXAMPLE 20

Joel borrows $30,000 to purchase taxable investments. He pays $2,800 of interest on the loan during the year. Joel is in the 31% tax bracket. During the year his investments produce $1,600 in taxable interest, $600 in qualified dividends, $240 in nonqualified dividends, and $1,600 in net capital gains. The $1,840 of taxable interest and nonqualified dividends counts as investment income. However, the $2,200 of qualified dividends and net capital gains only counts as investment income if Joel elects to tax these amounts at his normal (31%) tax rate.

Joel's options regarding the investment interest are as follows. First, he can choose to tax the $2,200 of qualified dividends and net capital gains at the lower 15% tax rate. This will result in his investment interest expense being limited to his $1,840 of investment income. He would carry over the $960 excess ($2,800 – $1,840) to the next tax year. Joel's second option is to elect to tax $960 of the qualified dividends and net capital gains at the 31% tax rate. If he does this, then his investment income will increase to $2,800 ($1,840 + $960). This will allow him to deduct the entire $2,800 of investment interest in the current year. He will then be allowed to tax the remaining $1,240 of qualified dividends and net capital gains ($2,200 – $960) at the lower 15% tax rate.

Net investment income is the excess of the taxpayer's investment income over the amount of investment expenses actually included in the taxpayer's total itemized deductions (i.e., those that exceed the 2% AGI floor). These expenses include fees paid to an investment advisor, safe deposit box rental fees, and the costs of investment publications. Taxpayers file Form 4952, Investment Interest, to support their investment interest deduction on Schedule A.

EXAMPLE 21

During 2015, the Neals (from Figure 5-1) paid investment interest of $6,300 and reported $9,640 of investment expenses as a miscellaneous deduction subject to the 2% AGI floor. Taxable investment income for the year was $7,600. The Neals' investment interest expense deduction on Schedule A is limited to their $5,457 of net investment income. They carry forward to 2016 the $843 ($6,300 – $5,457) of investment interest expense not deducted in 2015.

Taxable investment income		$7,600
Investment expenses reported on Schedule A	$9,640	
Less 2% of AGI ($374,864 × 2%)	(7,497)	
Less investment expenses actually deducted		(2,143)
Net investment income		$5,457

¶506 Gifts to Charity

Individuals can deduct as an itemized deduction both cash and noncash property they donate to a qualified charity. The most that can be deducted in any one year depends on the amount of the taxpayer's AGI. Any deductions limited due to AGI carry over to the next five tax years.

¶506.01 GIFTS BY CASH OR CHECK

Deductible gifts (donations) must be made to qualified charitable organizations. To deduct gifts to foreign countries for disaster relief and other causes, taxpayers must make the donation to qualified U.S. nonprofit organizations.

Gifts may be made by cash, check, or credit card. When taxpayers use their car for charitable purposes, they may deduct actual car expenses or a standard rate of $.14 per mile. Car expenses are treated as cash gifts. As a rule, donations are deducted in the year that they are made, regardless of whether the taxpayer uses the cash or accrual method. Taxpayers must keep receipts to support their deduction. If the charity gave the taxpayer any gifts or services in return for the donation, the amount of the deduction must be reduced by the value of what the taxpayer received in return for their donation.

EXAMPLE 22 The Neals (from Figure 5-1) paid $400 a plate for a YMCA benefit and made a cash donation of $3,000 at the banquet. The YMCA's cost for the dinner was $20 per person. The Neals could have bought the same two meals at a bistro for $75. The charitable contribution deduction is $3,725, the difference between the amount donated and the value of the dinner ($3,000 cash donation + $800 meals – $75 value). The Neals do not take the YMCA's cost into account. The Neals enter $3,725 on the "Gifts by cash or check" line on Schedule A.

Taxpayers may only deduct gifts made to qualified non-profit organizations. All other gifts are not deductible. Handouts to needy people may be generous, but they are not deductible.

EXAMPLE 23 The Neals have a widowed neighbor to whom they gave $200 each month for groceries over a four-month period. The Neals' gifts to the widow are not deductible.

Qualified charities are nonprofit organizations that are exempt from tax under Section 501(c)(3) of the Internal Revenue Code. They include organizations that operate solely for religious, scientific, charitable, literary, or educational purposes. They also include organizations that promote the arts or to prevent cruelty to children or animals. This is only a partial list of the types of organizations that qualify as 501(c)(3) organizations. A complete list of qualified charities can be found on the IRS website.

Donations with the Right to Buy Colligate Athletic Tickets

A special rule applies to certain donations to a college or university. When the taxpayer's donation provides the taxpayer with the right to buy tickets to athletic events, 80% of the gift is considered a charitable contribution. The other 20% is a nondeductible right to buy the tickets.

EXAMPLE 24 Waylon donates $1,000 to his alma mater. His gift allows him to buy season tickets to the university's football and basketball games. The tax law treats $800 ($1,000 × 80%) as a charitable contribution. The rest ($200) is treated as a nondeductible payment for the right to purchase athletic tickets.

¶506.02 NONCASH GIFTS

Special rules apply to donations of property that fall in either of these two categories: (1) ordinary income property (includes all property held for one year or less) or (2) capital gain property held more than one year. Donations in both categories may include real estate, tangible personal property, or intangible personal property.

Tangible personal property consists of most tangible property that a taxpayer owns that is not real estate. The usual items contributed under this category include clothing, toys, furniture, appliances, and books. Normally, the FMV of these items is less than the taxpayer's basis. The FMV of household goods and clothing is their thrift shop or garage sale value. "Blue book" value is a common source for valuing vehicles.

Intangible assets most commonly donated include stocks, bonds, and mutual funds. For the most part, these assets are widely traded and their FMV is easy to determine.

Generally, the deduction for noncash gifts is equal to the FMV of the property at the time of donation. This holds true when the FMV is less than the taxpayer's basis (investment) in the property. However, when the FMV is greater than the basis, the amount of the deduction depends on whether the item takes the form of (1) ordinary income property or long-term capital gain property and (2) how the charity uses the property.

When the total deduction for noncash items exceeds $500, the donor provides information about each noncash donation on Form 8283, Noncash Charitable Contributions. For any noncash donation, a receipt from the qualifying organization must specify how the organization uses the property.

Taxpayers who donate vehicles to charities that then sell the vehicles can only deduct what the charity gets from the sale. The charity may incur penalties if it does not report the sales price to both the donor and the IRS.

EXAMPLE 25

The Neals (from Figure 5-1) make several noncash donations during the year. Even though the amounts paid for the donated items were far greater than their value at the time of the donations, their deduction is limited to the FMV of the donated items. The Neals got receipts from the charities for each of their donations, and use thrift store value to arrive at their $720 deduction.

Ordinary Income Property

Ordinary income property is property that, if sold, would generate income taxed at the regular (ordinary) tax rates. It includes such items as business inventory and investments held for one year or less. When a taxpayer donates ordinary income property, the tax law limits the value of the contribution to the taxpayer's basis (investment) in the property. Most often, this is the amount the taxpayer paid for the property. As a result, no deduction is allowed for the value of personal services rendered to a charity.

EXAMPLE 26

Steven Neal (from Figure 5-1) built a bookcase and donated it to the local public high school. The bookcase was appraised at $800. Steven spent $125 on materials. The Neals deduct only the $125 cost of materials, as the bookcase would be ordinary income property if they had sold it. They receive no deduction for the value of Stephen's time in constructing the bookcase.

Capital Gain Property

Capital gain property consists of certain appreciated assets held for more than one year that, if sold, would produce long-term capital gain. This category includes stocks, bonds, and real estate. It also includes most investments and an individual's personal belongings. FMV at the time of the donation determines the value of the gift. Taxpayers can get written appraisals or stock market quotes to establish the value. Taxpayers who have decided to make donations to qualifying charities have a tax incentive when the FMV of the item exceeds the taxpayer's basis. The donor avoids reporting the increased value as income. In addition to avoiding paying taxes on the increase in the asset's value, the donor gets to deduct the higher FMV amount.

EXAMPLE 27

The Neals (from Figure 5-1) donated shares of IBM stock to their church. They paid $2,000 for the stock many years ago. On the date of the donation, the stock was worth $3,500. The Neals' deduction for noncash contributions total $4,220 ($720 from Example 25 + $3,500 FMV of the stock). Since this amount exceeds $500, the Neals complete Form 8283 to provide details of their noncash donations. They attach Form 8283 to their tax return and enter $4,220 on the "Other than cash or check" line on Schedule A.

The Code allows taxpayers to deduct only their basis in appreciated tangible personal property when such property is not used by the charity directly for its tax exempt purpose. This rule only applies to gifts of appreciated tangible personal property. Thus, the reduced deduction does not apply to gifts of capital gain property that is intangible property or real estate.

EXAMPLE 28

Ray, an art collector, donates a painting worth $25,000 to the local hospital. Ray paid $3,000 for the painting years ago. The painting is tangible personal property held long-term. Thus, it is capital gain property. However, since the hospital cannot use the painting in relation to its exempt purpose (treating patients), Ray's charitable deduction is limited to $3,000.

EXAMPLE 29

Same facts as in Example 28, except that Ray donates the painting to a local art museum. Since the painting will be put to use in the museum's tax-exempt purpose, Ray can deduct the full $25,000 FMV of the painting.

EXAMPLE 30

Same facts as in Example 28, except that Ray purchased the painting nine months earlier. Since the painting was not held for more than one year at the time it was donated, if it had been sold it would have produced short-term capital gain taxed at Ray's regular (ordinary) tax rate. Thus, the painting is ordinary income property. The Code limits the deduction of such property to Ray's $3,000 basis.

EXAMPLE 31

Same facts as in Example 28, except that the donated property was stock in a corporation. Stock is intangible property and Ray held it for more than one year prior to donating it. Thus, the stock is capital gain property, and the Code allows Ray to deduct the $25,000 FMV of the stock.

EXAMPLE 32

Same facts as in Example 28, except that the property donated was land held as an investment. Since land is real property that Ray held it for more than one year, it is capital gain property and Ray deducts the $25,000 FMV of the land.

EXAMPLE 33

Same facts as in Example 28, except that Ray paid $25,000 for the painting and at the time it was donated, it was worth $3,000. Since the painting declined in value since Ray bought it, it is not capital gain (appreciated) property. The general rule allows Ray to deduct the ($3,000) FMV of the property.

¶506.03 NONDEDUCTIBLE GIFTS

Taxpayers should verify a charity's status as a 501(c)(3) organization prior to making a gift. This information can be found on the IRS website. Many fund-raising groups may look like qualified charities, but are not. Donations to lobbying or political action groups of qualified organizations may not be deductible. Other contributions that cannot be deducted include dues to clubs or lodges and tuition paid to private or religious schools. Also, the cost of raffle tickets is not deductible.

¶506.04 LIMITATIONS

The Code limits a taxpayer's total charitable contribution deduction each year to 50%, 30%, or 20% of the taxpayer's AGI. The percentage limitation that applies depends on the type of contribution being made and the nature of the charity. The deduction of contributions of cash and property to most organizations may never exceed 50% of AGI. The deduction for appreciated capital gain property when the (higher) FMV is deducted can never exceed 30% of AGI. Taxpayers can avoid the 30% AGI limit on the contribution of appreciated capital gain property by reducing the amount of the donation of the appreciated capital gain property to the taxpayer's basis. Then, the taxpayer's limitation increases to 50% of AGI. The 30% limit also applies to donations of cash and ordinary income property to certain private nonoperating foundations. When taxpayers contribute capital gain property to certain private foundations not operating for the benefit of the public at large, the contribution is limited to 20% of AGI.

EXAMPLE 34

In 20x1, Jackie donates stock worth $35,000 to the local university. Jackie paid $25,000 for the stock three years ago. In 20x1, Jackie's AGI is $60,000. If Jackie reports a $35,000 FMV donation for the stock, she will only be able to deduct $18,000 in 20x1 ($60,000 × 30%). She carries over the $17,000 excess to 20x2-20x6. When preparing her tax returns for 20x2-20x6, the same 30% AGI limit will apply to the $17,000 deduction.

EXAMPLE 35

Same facts as in Example 34, except that Jackie elects to report her donation using her $25,000 basis in the stock, and apply the 50% AGI limit. Jackie will be able to deduct the full $25,000 on Schedule A in 20x1. Since she elected to reduce the amount of her deduction, the $10,000 difference between FMV and her basis in the stock will never be deducted. This is the "price" Jackie paid to be able to use the higher 50% AGI limit.

Reporting Carryovers

The 50%, 30%, and 20% AGI limits sometimes reduce a taxpayer's contribution deduction. Taxpayers carry forward the unused contributions for up to five years. When carried forward, the same 50%, 30%, and 20% AGI limits apply to the contributions. For example, an unused contribution subject to the 30% AGI limit in 20x1 is subject to the same 30% AGI limit when carried over to 20x2. Taxpayers report the deductible amount of contributions carried over from a prior tax year on the "Carryover from prior year" line on Schedule A.

¶507 Casualty and Theft Losses

Individuals are allowed to deduct losses they incur when their personal belongings are stolen or damaged in a casualty. They measure each casualty (or theft) loss as the *lesser of* (i) the difference between the FMV before and after the casualty (or theft) or (ii) the basis of the property. They reduce this amount first, by any insurance or other reimbursements they receive, and then, by $100 per event (not per item). Taxpayers then total the net loss from each casualty event that occurs during the year. From this total they subtract 10% of AGI. Only the remaining amount is deductible.

Loans taken out to cover the loss do not count as reimbursements. When an individual has insurance coverage but declines to report the incident in order to avoid raising insurance premiums, no personal casualty loss deduction results for the amount of insurance benefits given up.

All of these rules make losses from personal casualties hard to deduct. Personal casualty deductions rarely take place without a major uninsured disaster. Lesser casualties generally result in losses below the 10% of AGI threshold and result in no tax benefits. Taxpayers compute their casualty loss deduction on Form 4684, Casualties and Thefts, and then enter the net loss in excess of 10% of AGI on Schedule A. If more than one casualty takes place during the year, the IRS requires that taxpayers fill out a separate Form 4684 for each event.

EXAMPLE 36

Roy wrecked his personal automobile that originally cost $30,000. This was his only casualty for the year. The vehicle had a FMV of $25,855 before the accident. The estimated FMV after the accident was $1,000, resulting in a $24,855 change in value ($25,855 – $1,000). Roy collected $16,355 of insurance proceeds. His AGI of $52,090 reduces the casualty loss deduction to $3,191.

Lesser of (i) $24,855 change in FMV or (ii) $30,000 basis	$24,855
Less insurance proceeds	(16,355)
Less $100 reduction	(100)
Less 10% of AGI	(5,209)
Net casualty loss deduction, not less than $0	$ 3,191

Taxpayers may be able to exclude from gross income reimbursements they receive to cover additional living expenses they incur as a result of a casualty. Such amounts are nontaxable to the extent that they compensate the taxpayer for a temporary increase in living expenses. Reimbursements in excess of actual costs are taxable, as are reimbursements that cover normal expenses. While often associated with casualties, these reimbursements do not affect the casualty loss deduction.

EXAMPLE 37

A casualty damages a couple's home. While repairing the home, the couple lives in another house, costing them $3,500 per month. The couple's normal living expenses before the storm were $1,500 per month. They continue to pay all of their normal living expenses in addition to the $3,500 each month. The insurance company reimburses the couple $4,000 per month. They include $500 per month in gross income for the reimbursement they receive in excess of the $3,500 increase in living expenses. This amount is reported as "Other income" on Form 1040 (page 1).

¶507.01 CASUALTY EVENTS

The IRS defines a **casualty** as a sudden, unexpected, or unusual event. Events creating casualty losses include accidents, fires, storms, earthquakes, floods, hurricanes, thefts, and other disasters. Many irritating events, although expensive and inconvenient, do not qualify as casualties because they are not considered sudden, unexpected, or unusual. Some examples include long-term termite or moth damage, plant disease, property value reduction due to a landslide on a nearby lot, or loss of a diamond ring dropped down a drain. No deduction is allowed for items deliberately destroyed or damaged by willful neglect. Also, deductions are allowed only for damage to the taxpayer's own property. Therefore, if a driver hits and destroys the neighbor's fence, the cost of repairing the neighbor's fence cannot be deducted as a casualty loss on the driver's tax return.

¶507.02 PROOF

The mere loss of an item does not create a casualty. The taxpayer must prove that a theft, accident, or disaster took place. Taxpayers should report any loss to the police or other government authority to get a written report for their files. The taxpayer must also establish the amount of the casualty loss. "Before" and "after" pictures can help prove the extent of the damage. Objective appraisals of the property both before and after the event provide evidence of the loss suffered. The IRS generally will accept the cost of repairing the property as the amount of the loss. However, the cost of repairs cannot be used if the repairs restore the property to a better condition and a higher value than before the loss.

¶507.03 YEAR OF DEDUCTION

The general rule allows a casualty loss deduction only in the year the casualty occurs. A theft loss is deducted in the year the taxpayer discovers the theft. However, the taxpayer can elect to deduct a loss occurring in a federally-declared disaster area in the year of the disaster or in the previous tax year. This special rule makes it possible for taxpayers to get disaster-based tax refunds sooner.

¶508 Reduction in Itemized Deductions for Higher-Income Taxpayers

Higher-income taxpayers must reduce their total itemized deductions by up to 3% of AGI in excess of a specified threshold. The threshold amounts vary by filing status. They are the same amounts used in computing the phase-out of the exemption deduction (¶107.01).

Figure 5-2: 2015 AGI Thresholds for Reducing Itemized Deductions for Higher-Income Taxpayers	
Married filing jointly (MFJ) and qualifying widow(er)	$309,900
Head of household (HOH)	284,050
Single	258,250
Married filing separately (MFS)	154,950

However, unlike the phase-out of the exemption deduction, where with enough AGI the taxpayer's exemption deduction can be reduced to $0, the reduction in itemized deductions is limited to 80% of all itemized deductions other than medical, investment interest, gambling losses and casualty and theft losses. The calculation of the reduction in itemized deductions is illustrated in Examples 38 and 39.

EXAMPLE 38

Pete is unmarried and files as single. His AGI is $373,920, and his itemized deductions include:

State and local income tax deduction	$12,374
Mortgage interest expense	22,500
Investment interest expense	15,325
Charitable contributions	6,200
Miscellaneous deductions (after the 2% AGI floor)	3,121
	$59,520

Because Pete's AGI exceeds the $258,250 threshold for single taxpayers, he must reduce his itemized deductions by $3,470 [the *lesser of* (i) $3,470 (3% × ($373,920 – $258,250)), or (ii) $35,356 (80% × ($59,520 total itemized deduction – $15,325 investment interest – $0 for medical, casualty and theft loss, and gambling losses))]. Pete reports on Schedule A (line 29) his total itemized deductions of $56,050 ($59,520 – $3,470).

EXAMPLE 39

Because the Neals (from Figure 5-1) have AGI in excess of $154,950, they check the YES box on Schedule A (line 29). They then compute their reduction in itemized deductions using the AGI threshold amount for MFJ. The Neals reduce their itemized deductions by $1,949 [the *lesser of* (i) $1,949 (3% × ($374,864 – $309,900 threshold for MFJ)), or (ii) $40,578 (80% × ($56,180 – $5,457 investment interest))]. The Neals enter their total itemized deductions (after reduction) of $54,231 ($56,180 – $1,949) on Schedule A (line 29). They transfer this amount to the "Itemized Deduction" line on Form 1040, page 2.

5

Name:

Section:

Date:

QUESTIONS AND PROBLEMS

1. **Medical Expense Deduction.** (Obj. 2) Ian and Bella Brown (ages 55 and 54, respectively) maintain a home where they live with their disabled daughter, Brenda, who is 24. The Browns' AGI is $60,000. Unreimbursed amounts paid for medical and dental expenses during the year follow.

	Brenda	*The Browns*
R. J. Stone, M.D.	$ 260	$ 250
G. O. Wright, D.D.S.	220	200
Hearing aid		525
Premium on health insurance		1,240
Eyeglasses		130
Toothpaste	20	35
Prescription drugs	3,275	125
Total	$3,775	$2,505

a. Compute the Browns' medical and dental expense deduction on their 2015 joint tax return.

b. How would your answer to Part a. change if Ian was 65 (instead of 55)?

2. **Medical Expense Deduction.** (Obj. 2) Mei (age 40, unmarried, no dependents) paid various expenses during the year.

a. In the space after each unreimbursed item, indicate whether or not the item is deductible as a medical expense, and if so, enter the deductible amount (without regard to the AGI floor).

Item	*Deductible?*	*Deductible Amount*
1. Premium on health insurance, $386	________	________
2. Premium on life insurance, $275	________	________
3. Premium on automobile accident insurance, $610	________	________
4. Acne cream, $30	________	________
5. Prescription medication, $300	________	________
6. Prescribed vitamins, $60	________	________
7. Cosmetics, $150	________	________
8. Dr. Wall, dentist, $120	________	________
9. Dues to health spa, $325	________	________
10. X-ray examination, $60	________	________
11. City Hospital, room and services, $375	________	________
12. Eyeglasses, $125	________	________
13. Cemetery plot, $600	________	________
14. Miles driven for medical in May—1,000	________	________
15. Illegal drugs, $135	________	________
16. Vacation recommended by doctor to improve general health, $875	________	________
17. Dr. Root, minor surgery, $350	________	________
18. Used wheelchair, $275	________	________
19. Dr. Spencer for false teeth, $480, and fittings, $100	________	________

b. If Mei's AGI is $24,290, compute her medical and dental expense deduction.

3. **Medical Reimbursements.** (Obj. 2) A taxpayer receives a reimbursement for a medical expense of $455 in the current year. What is the proper tax treatment of the $455 if:

   a. The reimbursed expense was paid in the current year.

   b. The reimbursed expense was paid last year. The taxpayer took the standard deduction last year.

   c. The reimbursed expense was paid last year, and last year the taxpayer's total itemized deductions exceeded the standard deduction by $2,000 and medical expenses in excess of the AGI floor were $840.

   d. Same as in Part c. except that medical expenses in excess of the AGI floor were $350.

   e. The total reimbursement includes $75 in excess of the taxpayer's medical expenses for the current year. The taxpayer paid the premiums on the policy.

   f. Same as in Part e., except that the employer paid the premiums on the policy, which were treated as a tax-free fringe benefit to the taxpayer.

4. **Physical Exams.** (Obj. 2) If an employee pays for a periodic medical checkup required by an employer, can the amount paid be deducted, and if so, is there any limitation? Explain.

5. **Medical Deduction.** (Obj. 2) Tracey suffers from severe arthritis. His doctor has prescribed that he install a hot tub at his home to help relieve the pain. Tracey pays $7,500 to have a hot tub installed. The hot tub is expected to increase the value of his home by $3,000. What amount, if any, can Tracey deduct as a medical expense on his tax return?

6. **State and Local Income Taxes.** (Obj. 3) In April, 2015, Jose filed his 2014 federal and state income tax returns. He paid $800 with his federal return and $450 when he filed his state income tax return. During 2015, Jose's employer withheld $6,600 and $3,100, respectively for federal and state income taxes. Jose files as single.

   a. What amount can Jose deduct as an itemized deduction on his 2015 tax return?

   b. When Jose files his 2015 tax returns early in 2016, he receives a $90 refund from the federal government and $120 back from the state. Discuss the tax consequences to Jose of receiving refunds totaling $210. Jose's other itemized deductions in 2015 totaled $3,150.

   c. Same as in Part b. except that Jose's other itemized deductions total $1,000.

7. **Estimated State and Local Income Taxes.** (Obj. 3) Ivy is self-employed and a cash basis taxpayer. For the 2014 and 2015 tax years, she makes quarterly estimated tax payments to the state, as shown below. When she files her 2014 tax return in April 2015, she receives a $300 refund from the state. When she files her 2015 tax return in April 2016, she owes $650 to the state. Compute Ivy's 2015 state and local income tax deduction.

	Date Paid	*Amount Paid*
1st installment	April 15, 2014	$220
2nd installment	June 15, 2014	220
3rd installment	September 15, 2014	250
4th installment	January 15, 2015	250
1st installment	April 15, 2015	$300
2nd installment	June 15, 2015	300
3rd installment	September 15, 2015	275
4th installment	January 15, 2016	250

8. **Personal Property Taxes.** (Obj. 3) Jan lives in a state that imposes a property tax on the value on motor vehicles. Karl lives in a state that imposes a flat $55 renewal fee for license tags. Jan pays the state $430 to renew her license tags. Included in this amount is a $25 license plate fee. The rest is an ad valorem tax. Discuss the tax consequences to each of these taxpayers on their federal income tax returns.

9. **Home Mortgage Interest.** (Obj. 4) The Hemphills own three homes. Their main home is located in Pittsburg. They also own condos in Las Vegas and Tampa. The amount of acquisition debt and interest paid on each property is shown below.

Location of Home	*Acquisition Debt*	*Interest Paid*
Pittsburg	$140,000	$ 8,330
Las Vegas	440,000	21,555
Tampa	400,000	23,443

a. Compute the Hemphills' home mortgage interest deduction.

b. How would your answer to Part a. change if the Pittsburg home were fully paid for, and the Hemphills only had mortgages on the two vacation homes?

10. **Home Mortgage Interest.** (Obj. 4) The Stephens own a home in Boston. They paid $780,000 for the home three years ago. Their current balance on their mortgage is $660,000. At the time that their home was worth $900,000, they refinanced their mortgage. Their new mortgage is for $800,000. In addition to the home in Boston, the Stephens also own a vacation home in Florida. They paid $350,000 for the home several years ago, and the current mortgage on the second home is $295,000.

a. Discuss how much interest the Stephens are allowed to deduct if the excess proceeds from the refinancing are used to buy or improve their main home.

b. Same as in Part a. except that the excess proceeds from the loan are used to buy a new car.

11. **Points.** (Obj. 4) During 2015, Lee borrowed money on two different occasions from the local bank. She took out the first loan on March 1, 2015 to purchase land for a place to graze horses and livestock as an investment activity. Lee paid $33,000 for the land, making a down payment of $6,000 and borrowing $27,000 for 10 years at 9% interest. To obtain a lower interest rate on the loan, she was required to pay two points, totaling $540 (2% × $27,000). In August, 2015, Lee bought a new house that she uses as her main home. Her mortgage was $48,000 at 8% for 20 years. Lee paid the lender one point, or $480 (1% × $48,000) to get a lower interest rate.

    a. Determine the amount of points Lee may use as a 2015 interest deduction in connection with the two loans.

    b. What happens to any amount of points not deducted in 2015?

12. **Points.** (Obj. 4) Years ago, the Devons took out a 30-year mortgage on their vacation home. When they originally took out the loan, they paid the lender $24,000 in points. On September 1 of the current year, the Devons refinanced their $650,000 balance of the mortgage with another 30-year mortgage. To get a lower interest rate, the Devons paid the lender points totaling $13,000. At the time of the refinancing, the Devons had unamortized points from the first loan of $18,000. How much can the Devons deduct as points on their tax return for the current year?

13. **Investment Interest.** (Obj. 4) In 2013, the Edlins borrowed money to purchase stocks and taxable corporate bonds. During 2015, the Edlins paid $11,900 of interest in conjunction with this loan. Their investment income for 2015 consists of $5,000 of qualified dividend income, $2,400 of taxable interest income, and $3,300 of net capital gain. How much of the $11,900 can the Edlins deduct on their 2015 Schedule A? Be sure to discuss all options available to the Edlins.

14. Interest Deduction. (Obj. 4) Indicate the correct treatment for each listed item by placing an **X** in the appropriate column.

Description	*Deductible*	*Nondeductible*
a. Al took out a $20,000 home equity loan to buy an airplane. Al paid interest of $1,750.	________	________
b. Betty paid $300 in credit card interest, including $30 in late fees.	________	________
c. Charles borrowed $50,000 to buy City of Austin bonds. The interest he paid was $3,000. His net investment interest income was $2,500.	________	________
d. David constructed a new home for $175,000. He borrowed $157,500 as a construction loan. The interest on the new mortgage was $8,500.	________	________
e. Ed paid $80 in interest on back state taxes due.	________	________
f. Fred took out a loan to buy a vacation home. The lender charged Fred $350 to process his loan.	________	________
g. Gabe borrowed $60,000 to buy corporate bonds. He paid $4,000 interest on this loan. The corporation paid Gabe $5,000 of interest.	________	________

15. Interest Deduction. (Obj. 4) The Greenfields' 2015 AGI is $98,500, which includes $620 of taxable interest income. They incurred the following interest expenses during the year.

Credit card interest	$ 79
Automobile loan interest (on their older car)	337
Mortgage interest on their main home prior to refinancing	6,300
Mortgage interest on their main home after refinancing	7,200
Points paid on main home refinancing ($190,000 × 3%)	5,700
Mortgage interest on vacation home	13,080
Investment interest expense on a loan to purchase corporate stocks	543
Investment interest expense on a loan to purchase tax-exempt bonds	381

The Greenfields originally paid $260,000 for their main home. At the beginning of 2015, the home was worth $300,000 and the balance on the mortgage on their main home was $138,000. On May 1, 2015, the Greenfields refinanced the mortgage on their main home with a $190,000, 10-year loan. They used the extra proceeds to buy a new car, take a vacation, and consolidate other loans. Compute the Greenfields' 2015 interest expense deduction on Schedule A.

16. Charitable Contribution Deduction. (Obj. 5) Place an **X** in the proper column to indicate whether each of the following gifts or other expenditures is (i) deductible as a charitable contribution, (ii) deductible but not as a charitable contribution, or (iii) not deductible. Assume that the taxpayer has a receipt from the charity for the donation.

Item	*Deductible Contribution*	*Deductible, Not a Contribution*	*Not Deductible*
a. Cash to American Red Cross	________	________	________
b. Pledge to make a gift to one's church	________	________	________
c. Auto expense of church employee	________	________	________
d. Cash to Girl Scouts of America	________	________	________
e. Inherited land to American Legion	________	________	________
f. Cash to political party	________	________	________
g. Cash to public library	________	________	________
h. Clothing to Salvation Army	________	________	________
i. Common stock to St. Mary's Church	________	________	________
j. Cash to Brigham Young University	________	________	________
k. U.S. bonds to Mayo Clinic	________	________	________
l. Reading at The Braille Institute (value of services rendered, $35)	________	________	________
m. Auto expense of a volunteer worker while running errands for a local food bank	________	________	________

17. Charitable Contribution—Benefit Event. (Obj. 5) A professional football team plays a game for the benefit of the American Heart Association each year. The admission charge is $32 per ticket, which is also the usual admission price for a professional football game. One-half of the purchase price goes directly to the American Heart Association. Clark purchases four tickets at a total cost of $128. Clark itemizes deductions.

a. How much can Clark deduct per ticket as a charitable contribution?

b. How would your answer to Part a. differ if Clark had no intention of going to the football game and in fact did not go, leaving the tickets unused?

c. How would your answer be different if Clark paid $32 for each ticket, when the usual admission charge per ticket was $20?

18. **Charitable Contribution Deduction.** (Obj. 5) A single taxpayer has AGI of $60,000. During the year the taxpayer makes the following contributions. Compute the taxpayer's charitable contribution deduction.

Item	*FMV*	*Cost*
Check to the Greek Orthodox Church		$4,000
Used clothing to Children's Hospital	$100	380
Cash to University of Cal State Fullerton		1,200
Check to Mayor Fred's election campaign		300
Used camping equipment to the Boy Scouts of America	300	1,200
Cash to homeless father for his children's clothing		150

19. **Charitable Contribution—Appreciated Property.** (Obj. 5) A taxpayer contributed land worth $190,000 to the City General Hospital. The land has been held for five years and had a basis of $72,000. The taxpayer's AGI is $389,200.

a. What amount can the taxpayer deduct as a charitable gift?

b. How would your answer change the property were artwork, rather than land?

20. **Charitable Contribution—Appreciated Property.** (Obj. 5) An individual with AGI of $49,000 transfers common stock with a market value of $15,000 to an educational institution to be sold and used for scholarships. The basis in the stock is $3,575, and it was purchased six years ago.

a. What amount may be claimed as an itemized deduction resulting from this contribution?

b. How would your answer to Part a. change if the stock had been purchased 6 months ago?

21. **Charitable Contributions.** (Obj. 5) Toni occasionally donates her services as an attorney to a qualified charitable organization. During the current year, Toni spent 45 hours working for the charity. Her normal billing rate is $250 an hour. Toni drove 115 miles going to and from the offices for the charity. She also spent $160 for supplies necessary in conjunction with providing her services. Compute Toni's charitable deduction.

22. **Casualty Loss.** (Obj. 6) The Wildes' home was damaged by a severe storm. The home had been purchased in 2000 for $73,000, excluding the cost of the land. The building's FMV just before the storm was $97,000, and its FMV after the storm was estimated at $79,000. The Wildes collected $15,000 in insurance proceeds, and their AGI is $22,000. This was their only casualty loss during the year.

    a. Determine the amount that the Wildes can report as a casualty loss deduction.

    b. The Wildes lived in a motel while their home was being repaired. The cost of living at the motel was $2,000 each month. Their normal living expenses are $900 per month, but only $500 of these expenses continued during the repair period. They were reimbursed at the rate of $1,900 per month for the three months they lived in the motel. How much of the reimbursement, if any, must they include in gross income?

23. **Personal Casualty Loss.** (Obj. 6) The Tavels left for vacation on December 18, 2014. When they returned home on January 4, 2015, they found their home had been burglarized. Taken from their home were a high definition TV worth $4,000 and artwork worth $22,500. The Tavels had purchased the TV a few months ago for $5,600. They had purchased the artwork for $8,400 in 2005. Unfortunately, the Tavels allowed their homeowners' insurance to lapse last year. The Tavels' AGI in 2014 and 2015 is $83,000 and $92,000, respectively.

    a. In which year can the Tavels claim a casualty and theft loss deduction?

    b. Compute the Tavels' casualty and theft loss deduction.

    c. How would your answer to Part b. change if the Tavels had insured the artwork and received $7,500 from the insurance company for their loss?

24. Casualty Loss Deduction. (Obj. 6) The Steels file a joint return each year. During 2015 their house was burglarized, and the following items were taken. Their AGI for 2015 is $20,000.

Item	*Cost*	*FMV*
Television	$ 595	$ 375
Microwave	575	400
DVR	850	700
Jewelry	2,200	2,500

The Steels collected $500 from the insurance company. Compute the Steels' casualty and theft loss deduction.

25. Itemized Deductions. (Obj. 1) State whether each of the following payments can be deducted as an itemized deduction by placing an "X" in the appropriate *Yes* or *No* column. Assume that the amount is within any limit that applies.

Item	*Yes*	*No*
a. Payment to a nursing home for a person in need of help with self-care:		
(1) Meals	___	___
(2) Lodging	___	___
(3) Nursing care	___	___
b. Interest on amounts borrowed to buy municipal bonds	___	___
c. Supplemental Medicare insurance premiums	___	___
d. Credit card interest	___	___
e. Interest on a student loan	___	___
f. Canadian income taxes paid	___	___
g. Interest paid on past due state income taxes	___	___
h. Long-term care insurance premiums	___	___

26. Total Itemized Deductions. (Obj. 7 and 8)

a. Brian Pido (SSN 476-93-3477) is 42 years old and files his tax return as a single taxpayer. Brian's AGI is $172,552, including $15,000 of taxable interest. Brian has the following itemized deductions for 2015. Compute Brian's total itemized deductions and complete his Schedule A.

Amount paid to the state with 2014 income tax return	$ 425
Charitable contributions	5,000
Investment interest expense	12,000
Unreimbursed employee business expenses (from Form 2106)	2,749
Mortgage interest	11,880
Real estate taxes	6,898
State and local income taxes withheld from wages	3,583
Unreimbursed medical	3,200

b. Same as in Part a., except that Brian's AGI is $272,552 (instead of $172,552).

c. Randy (SSN 937-46-8266) and Misty Moore file a joint tax return. Randy and Misty are ages 39 and 40, respectively. Their AGI for 2015 is $184,583, including $1,800 of taxable interest income. They report the following itemized deductions for 2015. Compute the Moores' total itemized deductions and complete their Schedule A.

Amount paid to the state with 2014 income tax return	$ 888
Charitable contributions	13,540
Investment interest expense	2,600
Unreimbursed employee business expenses (from Form 2106)	3,950
Mortgage interest	17,559
Real estate taxes	4,582
State and local income taxes withheld from wages	6,682
Unreimbursed medical	20,414

d. Same as in Part c., except that the Moores are ages 69 and 63, respectively.

e. Same as in Part c., except that the Moores' AGI is $384,583 (instead of $184,583).

(Use for Problem 26.)

SCHEDULE A (Form 1040)

Department of the Treasury
Internal Revenue Service (99)

Itemized Deductions

▶ Information about Schedule A and its separate instructions is at *www.irs.gov/schedulea.*

▶ Attach to Form 1040.

OMB No. 1545-0074

2015

Attachment Sequence No. **07**

Name(s) shown on Form 1040 | Your social security number

Medical and Dental Expenses		**Caution.** Do not include expenses reimbursed or paid by others.		
	1	Medical and dental expenses (see instructions)	1	
	2	Enter amount from Form 1040, line 38 [2]		
	3	Multiply line 2 by 10% (.10). But if either you or your spouse was born before January 2, 1951, multiply line 2 by 7.5% (.075) instead	3	
	4	Subtract line 3 from line 1. If line 3 is more than line 1, enter -0-		4
Taxes You Paid	5	State and local		
		a ☐ Income taxes b ■ Reserved }	5	
	6	Real estate taxes (see instructions)	6	
	7	Personal property taxes	7	
	8	Other taxes. List type and amount ▶	8	
	9	Add lines 5 through 8		9
Interest You Paid **Note.** Your mortgage interest deduction may be limited (see instructions).	10	Home mortgage interest and points reported to you on Form 1098	10	
	11	Home mortgage interest not reported to you on Form 1098. If paid to the person from whom you bought the home, see instructions and show that person's name, identifying no., and address ▶	11	
	12	Points not reported to you on Form 1098. See instructions for special rules	12	
	13	Reserved	13	
	14	Investment interest. Attach Form 4952 if required. (See instructions.)	14	
	15	Add lines 10 through 14		15
Gifts to Charity If you made a gift and got a benefit for it, see instructions.	16	Gifts by cash or check. If you made any gift of $250 or more, see instructions.	16	
	17	Other than by cash or check. If any gift of $250 or more, see instructions. You **must** attach Form 8283 if over $500 . . .	17	
	18	Carryover from prior year	18	
	19	Add lines 16 through 18		19
Casualty and Theft Losses	20	Casualty or theft loss(es). Attach Form 4684. (See instructions.)		20
Job Expenses and Certain Miscellaneous Deductions	21	Unreimbursed employee expenses—job travel, union dues, job education, etc. Attach Form 2106 or 2106-EZ if required. (See instructions.) ▶	21	
	22	Tax preparation fees	22	
	23	Other expenses—investment, safe deposit box, etc. List type and amount ▶	23	
	24	Add lines 21 through 23	24	
	25	Enter amount from Form 1040, line 38 [25]		
	26	Multiply line 25 by 2% (.02)	26	
	27	Subtract line 26 from line 24. If line 26 is more than line 24, enter -0-		27
Other Miscellaneous Deductions	28	Other—from list in instructions. List type and amount ▶		28
Total Itemized Deductions	29	Is Form 1040, line 38, over $154,950? ☐ **No.** Your deduction is not limited. Add the amounts in the far right column for lines 4 through 28. Also, enter this amount on Form 1040, line 40. ☐ **Yes.** Your deduction may be limited. See the Itemized Deductions Worksheet in the instructions to figure the amount to enter. } . .		29
	30	If you elect to itemize deductions even though they are less than your standard deduction, check here . . . . ▶ ☐		

For Paperwork Reduction Act Notice, see Form 1040 instructions. Cat. No. 17145C **Schedule A (Form 1040) 2015**

27. **Tax Planning for Itemized Deductions.** Individuals can deduct the *greater of* their standard deduction or itemized deductions.

    a. Under what circumstances can a taxpayer control the timing of payments that are deductible as itemized deductions?

    b. Identify some specific ways in which the current tax law allows for tax planning with regard to itemized deductions.

28. **Internet Problem: Researching Instructions to Form 4684.** (Obj. 6)

    If a taxpayer experiences a loss from a deposit in a credit union that became financially insolvent, what options are available for recognizing this loss on the tax return?

    Go to the IRS website. Locate the Instructions for Form 4684 and find the solution to the above question.

    See Appendix A for instructions on use of the IRS website.

29. **Internet Problem: Filling out Form 8283.** (Obj. 5)

    Jacob R. (SSN 846-66-7922) and Brenda Tyler made the following noncash contributions during 2015. On May 5, they donated two bags of clothing (consisting of 22 items) valued at $120. On July 8, they donated a TV worth $50. On October 5, they donated a 5-piece queen bedroom set valued at $440. All items were donated to Goodwill, Industries (147 W. 53rd Street, Mesa, AZ 85203). The Tylers used thrift store value to value their items.

    Go to the IRS website and locate Form 8283, Noncash Charitable Contributions. Fill out Form 8283 for the Tylers that they will attach to their 2015 tax return.

    See Appendix A for instructions on use of the IRS website.

30. **Business Entity Problem:** This problem is designed for those using the "business entity" approach. **The solution may require information from Chapters 14–16.**

    a. A corporation has $350,000 of taxable income before consideration of charitable contributions. If the corporation donates $50,000 to a qualified charity, what amount can it deduct in the current year?

    b. By what date must the corporation make its donation?

c. Same as in Part a., except that the business is an S corporation.

d. Same as in Part a., except that the business is a partnership.

COMPREHENSIVE PROBLEMS

31. Schedule A. (Obj. 8)

a. Marcus (SSN 397-73-8399) and Debra Cross own three homes. Information regarding the amount of acquisition debt, as well as interest and taxes paid on each home during the year is as follows.

	Acquisition Debt	*Interest Paid*	*Taxes Paid*
Main home	$240,000	$18,330	$2,400
Vacation home #1	300,000	18,583	2,800
Vacation home #2	350,000	19,044	3,400

During 2015, the Crosses made cash gifts totaling $12,000 to various qualified public charities. The Crosses gifted 150 shares of stock to their church during 2015. They purchased 100 shares of the stock for $10 a share in 2010. The other 50 shares were purchased earlier in 2015 for $18 a share. At the time the shares were donated to the church, their fair market value was $24 a share. The Crosses' only other itemized deductions for 2015 were $4,240 that their employers withheld from their paychecks for state income taxes. The Crosses' AGI for 2015 is $216,952. Compute the Crosses' total itemized deductions and prepare their Schedule A.

b. Maurice Prior (SSN 839-44-9222) is married, but files separately from his spouse. Below is a summary of expenditures that Maurice has made. In addition, Maurice's employer withheld $3,967 and $13,550 in state and federal income taxes in 2015. His employer also withheld $6,300 in social security and Medicare taxes. Maurice's AGI for 2015 is $166,417. Maurice made the following quarterly estimated payments taxes for 2014 and 2015.

Date Paid	*Amount Paid to the State*	*Amount Paid to the IRS*
April 15, 2014	$ 700	$3,500
June 15, 2014	700	3,500
September 15, 2014	800	3,500
January 15, 2015	800	3,500
April 15, 2015	1,200	5,000
June 15, 2015	1,200	5,000
September 15, 2015	1,200	5,000
January 15, 2016	1,200	5,000

Other taxes Maurice paid during 2015 include $3,290 in real estate taxes; $296 for ad valorem taxes on his boat; and $800 for a special assessment for a new sidewalk. Maurice paid home mortgage interest totaling $16,940 during 2015, and he gave cash totaling $1,500 to his church. Compute Maurice's total itemized deductions and prepare his Schedule A.

c. Daniel Saad (SSN 432-61-7809) and his wife Marion (ages 52 and 51, respectively) file a joint return. Their 2015 AGI is $167,900, consisting of wages of $164,200 and interest income of $3,700. The Saads put together the following list of expenses. Compute the Saads' total itemized deductions and prepare their Schedule A.

Unreimbursed medical expenses	$27,743
Jacuzzi for John's aching back (not prescribed)	2,500
Real estate taxes	4,400
Homeowners association assessment for street repairs	1,200
State and local income taxes withheld	4,800
Federal income tax	22,300
General sales tax	785
Mortgage interest	15,200
Credit card interest	945
Investment interest	5,000
Charitable contributions (cash)	6,400
Uninsured damage to auto from accident	3,300

(Use for Problem 31.)

SCHEDULE A (Form 1040)

Department of the Treasury Internal Revenue Service (99)

Itemized Deductions

▶ Information about Schedule A and its separate instructions is at *www.irs.gov/schedulea*.

▶ Attach to Form 1040.

OMB No. 1545-0074

2015

Attachment Sequence No. **07**

Name(s) shown on Form 1040 | **Your social security number**

Medical and Dental Expenses		**Caution.** Do not include expenses reimbursed or paid by others.		
	1	Medical and dental expenses (see instructions)	1	
	2	Enter amount from Form 1040, line 38 [2]		
	3	Multiply line 2 by 10% (.10). But if either you or your spouse was born before January 2, 1951, multiply line 2 by 7.5% (.075) instead	3	
	4	Subtract line 3 from line 1. If line 3 is more than line 1, enter -0-		4
Taxes You Paid	5	State and local		
		a ☐ Income taxes b ■ Reserved }	5	
	6	Real estate taxes (see instructions)	6	
	7	Personal property taxes	7	
	8	Other taxes. List type and amount ▶ ________________	8	
	9	Add lines 5 through 8		9
Interest You Paid **Note.** Your mortgage interest deduction may be limited (see instructions).	10	Home mortgage interest and points reported to you on Form 1098	10	
	11	Home mortgage interest not reported to you on Form 1098. If paid to the person from whom you bought the home, see instructions and show that person's name, identifying no., and address ▶ ________________	11	
	12	Points not reported to you on Form 1098. See instructions for special rules	12	
	13	Reserved	13	
	14	Investment interest. Attach Form 4952 if required. (See instructions.)	14	
	15	Add lines 10 through 14		15
Gifts to Charity If you made a gift and got a benefit for it, see instructions.	16	Gifts by cash or check. If you made any gift of $250 or more, see instructions	16	
	17	Other than by cash or check. If any gift of $250 or more, see instructions. You **must** attach Form 8283 if over $500 . . .	17	
	18	Carryover from prior year	18	
	19	Add lines 16 through 18		19
Casualty and Theft Losses	20	Casualty or theft loss(es). Attach Form 4684. (See instructions.)		20
Job Expenses and Certain Miscellaneous Deductions	21	Unreimbursed employee expenses—job travel, union dues, job education, etc. Attach Form 2106 or 2106-EZ if required. (See instructions.) ▶ ________________	21	
	22	Tax preparation fees	22	
	23	Other expenses—investment, safe deposit box, etc. List type and amount ▶ ________________	23	
	24	Add lines 21 through 23	24	
	25	Enter amount from Form 1040, line 38 [25]		
	26	Multiply line 25 by 2% (.02)	26	
	27	Subtract line 26 from line 24. If line 26 is more than line 24, enter -0-		27
Other Miscellaneous Deductions	28	Other—from list in instructions. List type and amount ▶ ________________		28
Total Itemized Deductions	29	Is Form 1040, line 38, over $154,950? ☐ **No.** Your deduction is not limited. Add the amounts in the far right column for lines 4 through 28. Also, enter this amount on Form 1040, line 40. ☐ **Yes.** Your deduction may be limited. See the Itemized Deductions Worksheet in the instructions to figure the amount to enter.		29
	30	If you elect to itemize deductions even though they are less than your standard deduction, check here . . . . ▶ ☐		

For Paperwork Reduction Act Notice, see Form 1040 instructions. Cat. No. 17145C **Schedule A (Form 1040) 2015**

Chapter

6

Other Itemized Deductions

CHAPTER CONTENTS

LEARNING OBJECTIVES

After completing Chapter 6, you should be able to:

1. Understand the difference between accountable and nonaccountable reimbursement plans and determine how employee business expenses reimbursed under each of these plans are handled on the tax returns of both the employer and the employee.
2. Describe the various types of deductible business expenses and compute an employee's business expense deduction.
3. Distinguish between expenditures that are deductible for AGI from those that are deductible from AGI and from those that are not deductible.
4. List out the factors that may classify an activity as a hobby instead of a trade or business, and describe how the expenses of each are treated on the taxpayer's tax return.
5. Complete Form 2106, and understand how the information reported on this form is reported on Schedule A, and then Form 1040.

CHAPTER OVERVIEW

Chapter 5 examined itemized deductions that are somewhat personal in nature: medical expenses, taxes, interest, charitable contributions, and casualty and theft losses. This chapter focuses on the remaining itemized deductions: job-related expenses and miscellaneous deductions. It illustrates the flow of data from Form 2106, Employee Business Expenses, to Schedule A and finally, to Form 1040.

¶601 Job Expenses and Certain Miscellaneous Deductions

Two types of miscellaneous deductions can be taken on Schedule A. One type is subject to a 2% AGI floor; the other is not. "Job Expenses and Certain Miscellaneous Deductions" allows a deduction for tax preparation fees, investment expenses, and an employee's unreimbursed business expenses. The taxpayer reduces the sum of these three types of expenses by 2% of AGI and deducts the net amount on Schedule A.

While most employees report the total amount of their job-related expenses on Schedule A, they use Form 2106 to compute their total expenses. A notable exception is the "statutory employee." **Statutory employees** include full-time employees in the following occupations: outside salespersons, life insurance sales agents, some agent/commission-drivers, and home-based piece-goods workers. As for all employees, the wages of these workers are reported to them on Form W-2. However, the tax law treats statutory employees as self-employed for purposes of reporting their income and expenses. Thus, statutory employees report their W-2 wages and deduct all work-related expenses on Schedule C. However, self-employment taxes do not apply to statutory employees, as both the employer and the employee each pay FICA taxes through the tax withholding system. The employer alerts the IRS of this situation by checking the "Statutory Employee" box on Form W-2.

¶602 Unreimbursed Employee Expenses

Regular (other than statutory) employees who have deductible job-related expenses may or may not be reimbursed by their employers. They report their unreimbursed expenses from AGI on Form 2106. Treatment of reimbursed expenses depends on whether the reimbursement comes from an "accountable" or "nonaccountable" plan.

¶602.01 ACCOUNTABLE REIMBURSEMENT PLANS

Employees receiving reimbursements under an accountable plan do not report them in gross income. Likewise, employers do not report them on the employee's Form W-2. On the expense side, employees do not deduct reimbursed expenses on their tax returns. However, when the deductible expenses exceed the amounts reimbursed, the employee reports all expenses and reimbursements on Form 2106 in order to deduct the excess on Schedule A.

Reimbursements from an accountable plan must meet the following requirements:

1. Employees must account for (substantiate) their expenses to the employer.
2. The plan must require employees to return any reimbursement in excess of substantiated expenses.

To satisfy the substantiation requirement, employees must keep good records. Employee business expense records must include six elements: amount, date, place, business purpose, business relationship, and identity of the persons in attendance.

The IRS will accept date books, logs, and trip sheets to verify travel and mileage. To support other expenses, the employee must keep receipts and paid bills, canceled checks, expense reports, etc. However, for all expenses other than lodging, the IRS does not require a receipt for expenses less than $75. All reimbursements for lodging require a receipt, regardless of the amount. If the taxpayer loses any records, the IRS may accept written statements from witnesses.

¶602.02 NONACCOUNTABLE REIMBURSEMENT PLANS

If an employer's reimbursement plan does not require employees to substantiate their expenses or allows them to keep excess reimbursements, the arrangement is not an accountable plan. Under a nonaccountable plan, employers report reimbursements as additional wages on the employee's Form W-2. Employees then report their documented expenses on Form 2106, which then flows through to Schedule A. Even though these plans are "nonaccountable," employees must still substantiate their expense deduction.

Reimbursements under a nonaccountable plan are subject to income and FICA taxes. After paying these taxes, the employee is left with less reimbursement than the amount of the expense. Also, some or all of the expense may be disallowed as a result of the 2% AGI floor. Accountable plans avoid all of this.

EXAMPLE 1

Sark Industries pays its sales staff a $1,000 a month to cover their travel expenses. Sark does not require its workers to submit any receipts for their expenses. Lonny is one of Sark's salesmen. Lonny's annual salary is $60,000. During the year, Lonny receives $12,000 in travel allowances from Sark. According to Lonny's receipts, his deductible travel expenses total $15,420. Because Sark runs a nonaccountable reimbursement plan, it must add the travel allowances as taxable wages on its employees' W-2s. Thus, Lonny's taxable wages will be $72,000 ($60,000 + $12,000). Lonny can deduct the entire $15,420 on Schedule A as a miscellaneous itemized deduction (subject to the 2% AGI floor). If Lonny does not itemize, he will be taxed on the $12,000 with no offsetting deduction for his travel expenses.

EXAMPLE 2

Same facts as in Example 1, except that Sark requires that its employees submit receipts to support their travel expenses and requires that any excess amounts be returned. Since Sark now runs an accountable reimbursement plan, Lonny's taxable wages will show up on his W-2 as $60,000. He will report the $15,420 of deduction travel expenses and the $12,000 reimbursement on Form 2106. He will then be allowed to deduct the $3,420 excess as a miscellaneous itemized deduction on Schedule A. Even if Lonny does not itemize, or if his total miscellaneous itemized deductions do not exceed 2% of AGI, he will avoid being taxed on the $12,000 reimbursement he received during the year.

¶602.03 VEHICLE EXPENSES

Taxpayers use either the standard mileage rate or actual expenses to deduct the business use of a vehicle. Under both methods, taxpayers keep track of:

- Date the vehicle was first used for work
- Total miles driven during the year
- Total work-related miles driven during the year
- Commuting miles driven during the year

Taxpayers provide this information for each vehicle driven for business. The IRS also requires employees to answer to four specific questions on Form 2106. Responding "No" to the third or fourth question may trigger an audit. Also, the lack of written evidence can result in the loss of deductions.

1. Was the vehicle available for personal use?
2. Does the taxpayer (or the taxpayer's spouse) have another vehicle available for personal use?
3. Does the taxpayer have evidence to support the deduction?
4. Is the evidence written?

Employee Transportation

Employees may deduct the cost of getting from one job location to another in the course of their employment. Commuting costs are not deductible. These costs include getting to and from work as well as parking while at work. However, when an employee has two jobs, the cost of getting from one job to the other is deductible. When an employee goes home before going to the second job, the deduction is based on the distance between the two jobs. To claim a deduction, employees must keep detailed records of their business mileage.

EXAMPLE 3

Tyra works two jobs. Each morning, Tyra drives 25 miles to her first job. After work, she drives 15 miles to her second job. At the end of the day, she drives 22 miles home. The 25 miles Tyra drives to her first job and the 22 miles she drives home from her second job are nondeductible commuting miles. The 15 miles she drives between the two jobs are work-related miles. As an employee, Tyra deducts her work-related transportation costs as a miscellaneous itemized deduction (subject to the 2% AGI floor).

EXAMPLE 4

Same facts as in Example 3, except that Tyra drives home between the two jobs to change clothes. Tyra must base her deduction on the mileage between the two jobs. Therefore, the Trya's deduction would not change.

Actual Expenses

When using the actual expenses method, taxpayers must keep records of their car expenses, total miles, and total business miles driven during the year. The deductible amount equals the total car expenses times the percentage of business use during the year. Car expenses include amounts paid for gas, insurance, repairs, maintenance, tags and licenses, garage rent, and depreciation.

Taxpayers compute depreciation using the depreciation methods described later in the textbook in Chapter 8. These methods include accelerated depreciation methods, which allow taxpayers to take more depreciation in the earlier years of the vehicle's life. However, once taxpayers take depreciation on a car using an accelerated method, they can no longer use the standard mileage rate method for that car in later years. Instead, they must use the actual expenses method to compute their car expense deduction.

Standard Mileage Rate

For 2015, the standard mileage rate is $.575 per mile. The taxpayer must prove the business miles driven for all vehicles by keeping a detailed log. When an employer reimburses an employee for business miles at a rate in excess of this amount, the employee reports the excess in gross income.

EXAMPLE 5

Gina uses her personal car to make deliveries for her employer. During 2015, Gina drove 3,668 work-related miles. Gina deducts $2,109 (3,668 × $.575) as vehicle expenses. She reports this amount on Form 2106, which supports her employee business expense deduction on Schedule A.

EXAMPLE 6

Same facts as in Example 5, except that Gina's employer reimburses her $.40 a mile for the 3,668 of business miles she drove during the year. Gina can deduct as an employee business expense the excess of the $2,109 over the $1,467 (3,668 × $.40) that she was reimbursed during the year.

Leasing

When leasing a car, employees may elect to use the standard mileage rate, or they may elect to deduct the entire business portion of the monthly lease payments. When using the actual expense method, employees enter these amounts on Form 2106 as "Vehicle rentals" (line 24a). For more expensive cars, the IRS reduces the deduction by an inclusion amount (reported on line 24b). The deduction for leased cars is covered in Chapter 8 (¶802.09).

¶602.04 PARKING FEES, TOLLS, AND TRANSPORTATION THAT DO NOT INVOLVE OVERNIGHT TRAVEL

In addition to expenses directly-related to the car, employees can deduct business-related parking, tolls, and other transportation expenses, regardless of whether the standard rate or the actual expenses method is used. Deductible transportation expenses include cab, bus, and train fares.

EXAMPLE 7

Harvey uses his personal car for his work as an employee. In 2015, Harvey drove 8,300 work-related miles and 21,430 total miles. His car expenses are as follows. In addition to these amounts, Harvey paid $253 in business-related parking and tolls.

Depreciation	$1,875
Gas	2,670
Insurance	1,540
License tags	75
Repairs and maintenance	850
Total	$7,010

Under the actual expenses method, Harvey deducts $2,968 [($7,010 × 8,300/21,430) + $253]. Using the standard mileage method, his deduction would be $5,026 [(8,300 × $.575) + $253]. Under both methods, the business parking and tolls are deducted in addition to the deduction for other car-related expenses. Based on these calculations, Harvey would be better off using the standard mileage method to deduct his car expenses. He can use this method as long as he has not depreciated the car using an accelerated depreciation method in a previous tax year.

¶602.05 TRAVEL EXPENSES

Employee travel expenses include amounts paid when an employee is temporarily away from home overnight for work-related reasons. "Temporary" absences from home are those not exceeding one year. Travel expenses usually cannot be deducted when the absence exceeds one year. The IRS defines "home" as an employee's workplace, regardless of where the employee lives. Travel expenses include all transportation costs, plus lodging and the incidental costs incurred while away from home. Employees can deduct meals purchased while traveling (subject to the 50% limit that applies to meals and entertainment). A spouse's travel expenses are deducted only when the spouse actually works during the bulk of the trip and the spouse works for the same employer.

EXAMPLE 8

Kathy's travel expenses include airfare, $120; hotel, $75; car rental, $35; and meals, $150. Kathy's deductible travel equals $230 ($120 + $75 + $35). She also includes the $150 cost of meals with her other meals and entertainment, but can only deduct 50%.

Per Diem Option

The IRS allows employers to reimburse their employees using a flat daily amount that covers the costs of meals, lodging, and incidentals. This flat daily amount is called a **per diem**. When a per diem rate is used, the employer must use it with respect to that employee for all travel during the year. The IRS announces federal per diem rates for various cities and counties. The per diem rates can change every few months. These rates can be found on the IRS website (see Appendix A for instructions on how to use the IRS website). Separate rates apply to lodging and for meals and incidentals. Since the per diem rates include the value of meals, employees using Form 2106 must separately report the daily rate for travel (line 3) from the rate for meals and entertainment (line 5). Only 50% of the meal allowance is deductible.

When the employer's daily allowance does not exceed the allowable federal per diem rate, nothing is reported on the employee's W-2. This is true even if the employee's actual expenses are less than the allowance received. Not only is the excess not taxable, but the employee does not have to return the excess. However, when the employer's daily allowance exceeds the federal per diem rate, the employer adds the excess to the employee's wages on Form W-2.

When the reimbursement does not exceed the federal per diem amount and the actual expenses do not exceed the reimbursement, employees do not report the reimbursement or the expenses on their tax returns. If the actual expenses exceed the reimbursement, employees may deduct the excess on Schedule A by reporting both the expenses and reimbursements on Form 2106. In this situation, employees must be able to prove the amounts of their expenses.

Employees who are not reimbursed for work-related meals may take a deduction on Form 2106 for the federal per diem for meals instead of deducting their actual meal costs. This amount must be reduced by 50%, along with all meals and entertainment. Employees cannot deduct the per diem rate for lodging. Employees can only deduct their actual costs for lodging.

EXAMPLE 9

Brad's employer sends him on a business trip to New York City. He is gone for 3 days, and is reimbursed for his airfare, transportation to and from the airport and hotel, and a per diem for meals and lodging. At the time of his travels, the federal per diem rate for New York City is $332 ($64 for meals and $268 for lodging). Brad's actual costs for meals and lodging for his trip were $820. Although the $996 reimbursement ($332 × 3) exceeds his $820 of actual expenses, the tax laws do not require Brad to return the $176 excess to his employer. Moreover, Brad is not taxed on the excess.

EXAMPLE 10

Same facts as in Example 9, except that Brad's actual costs of meals and lodging were $1,154. Brad reports both the expenses and reimbursement on Form 2106. He deducts the excess (after subtracting out 50% of the meals) as an employee business expense on Schedule A.

Combined Business and Pleasure Trips

Employees who combine business and pleasure on the same trip face limits on the amount they can deduct. Different rules apply to trips within the United States and foreign travel. When traveling in the United States on a trip primarily for business (more than 50% work-related), employees deduct 100% of the expenses traveling to and from the destination. Once at their destination, they deduct only their work-related expenses (lodging, meals, entertainment, and local transportation for work days only). For domestic travel that is 50% or less work-related, employees can only deduct their work-related expenses while at the business destination. They cannot deduct any airfare or other costs of traveling to and from their destination (like cab fare to and from the airport).

EXAMPLE 11

Blake attends a three-day seminar in Boston. After the seminar he stays five more days in Boston to visit friends. Blake spent $450 on airfare, $250 a night for lodging, and $100 a day for meals. Because Blake's (domestic) trip was not primarily for business, the cost of his airfare is not deductible. He can, however, deduct the hotel expenses and 50% of the cost of his meals for the three days he spent conducting business.

On trips involving travel outside the United States, the employee must separate the costs for the business and personal portions of the trip. The employee divides the business and personal costs based on the time devoted to each activity. For instance, trips comprised of 40% personal activities permit the employee to deduct only 60% of the total travel expenses. However, any of the following three conditions eliminates the need to allocate the cost of traveling to and from the destination: (1) the employee has no control over arranging the trip and there is no significant element of vacation present; (2) the employee is away from home for less than eight days; or (3) the personal portion of the trip is less than 25% of the total days away from home.

For purposes of determining whether an employee's trip lasts for less than eight days (see (2) above), the day the employee returns home from the trip is counted, but the day of departure is not. Thus, if an employee leaves on a business trip on a Saturday, and returns home the following Saturday, the employee is considered to have been away from home for seven days (Sunday through Saturday). Since the trip is deemed to have lasted for less than eight days, the employee would be able to deduct all costs of traveling to and from the foreign destination. Ignoring the day of departure only applies for purposes of determining whether the employee's trip last for eight days or less. When counting business versus personal days for purposes of allocating the costs of a business trip between business and nonbusiness, both the day of departure and day the employee returns home count as business days (see discussion that follows).

Allocating expenses between business and nonbusiness activities requires separating the days spent away from home between business and personal days. When separating business days from personal days, both travel days count as business days. Weekends and holidays on which no significant business is conducted count as business days if a business day precedes and follows the weekend or holiday. Otherwise, the weekend or holiday counts as a personal day.

EXAMPLE 12

Edward attends a trade show in Paris, France that begins on Tuesday and ends on Friday, with no meetings on Wednesday or Thursday. Edward travels to the trade show on Monday and returns home on Saturday. The trip lasts less than eight days. Therefore, for this (outside the U.S.) trip, all qualified travel expenses to and from his home and the trade show are deductible. The rest of the expenses must be allocated between the four business days (Monday, Tuesday, Friday, Saturday) and the two personal days (Wednesday, Thursday). Monday and Saturday count as business days because for purposes of allocating expenses between business and personal activities, both days spent traveling count as business days. Neither Wednesday or Thursday count as business days because Wednesday is not followed by a business day, and Thursday is not preceded by a business day.

EXAMPLE 13

Toddra is sent by her employer to a training seminar in London, England. She is gone for a total of 11 days, of which 8 count as business days. Since none of the three exceptions apply, Toddra must allocate all of her travel costs between business and personal days. Of her travel costs, 72.73% (8/11) are deductible; 27.27% are nondeductible personal expenses. If Toddra's employer reimburses her for her trip, she subtracts the amount of the reimbursement from the deductible portion of her travel costs.

Special rules apply for travel outside of North America (which includes the United States and its possessions, the Trust Territories, Canada, and Mexico). For an employee to deduct expenses for traveling to conventions outside North America, the meeting must satisfy the following two conditions:

1. The convention must be directly related to the employee's job, and
2. It must be as reasonable to hold the meeting outside North America as it would be to hold it in North America.

¶602.06 MEALS AND ENTERTAINMENT EXPENSES

Taxpayers may deduct 50% of all qualified meals and entertainment expenses. Two categories of meals and entertainment are: (1) those incurred while conducting business with clients and associates and (2) those incurred while traveling for business. In the first instance, only costs either directly related to or associated with the taxpayer's business can be deducted. **Directly related to** means that the meal or entertainment takes place during a business discussion. **Associated with** means that the event takes place immediately before or after a business meeting.

For meals to be deductible, the taxpayer must be present. Paying for a dinner meeting and not attending it does not qualify as a deductible expense. This rule does not apply to other forms of entertainment (e.g., tickets to the theater or sporting events). Here, the taxpayer does not need to be present to take the deduction. However, only the business portion of meals and entertainment is deductible. Also, no deduction is allowed for lavish costs.

EXAMPLE 14

Janet spent $250 on meals and entertainment while away from home overnight on a business trip. Included in that amount is $100 she spent on meals with family members. Janet reports $150 ($250 – $100) as a business meals and entertainment expense. After applying the 50% limitation, Janet deducts $75 for meals on Form 2106.

EXAMPLE 15

Fisher pays $200 for four tickets to a Yankees game. Fisher gives the tickets to a client. He does not attend the event. Fisher's entertainment expense deduction equals $100 ($200 × 50%).

Employees often receive supper money when required to work overtime. Supper money is not considered a reimbursement or gross income. However, when paid as a disguised form of compensation, supper money becomes taxable.

Taxpayers can deduct dues they pay to the Chamber of Commerce, or to civic and public service organizations, like the Lions, Kiwanis, or Rotary clubs. They also can deduct dues to professional organizations, provided the dues are an ordinary and necessary expense of the taxpayer's business or employment. Examples would include dues a certified public accountant (CPA) pays to the American Institute of CPAs, or dues a doctor pays to belong to the American Medical Association. However, the IRS does not allow taxpayers to deduct dues they pay to various business, social, athletic, sporting, or airline clubs. This rule applies, even if the taxpayer joined the club solely as a means to meet or entertain clients or customers. Although club dues are never deductible, taxpayers can deduct the cost of meals charged while dining with business clients at the club (subject to the 50% limit).

EXAMPLE 16

Ralph keeps receipts for his employee business expenses. The total consists of $150 for meals and entertainment, $522 for car expenses, $35 of transportation costs, and $230 for travel. None of these amounts were reimbursed by his employer. Ralph's employee business deduction on Form 2106 consists of the following amounts:

Total meals and entertainment	$150	
Less 50% limit	(75)	
Deductible meals and entertainment		$ 75
Travel		230
Transportation		35
Car expenses		522
Total employee business expenses		$862

¶602.07 OTHER BUSINESS EXPENSES NOT INCLUDED ELSEWHERE ON FORM 2106

A number of other work-related expenses can be deducted by employees as miscellaneous itemized deductions subject to the 2% AGI floor. These expenses are reported on Form 2106 along with unreimbursed employee travel, transportation, meals and entertainment. A brief discussion of these other expenses follows.

Union Dues

Employees may deduct union dues and initiation fees paid either directly or through payroll deductions. If the payroll deduction includes specific retirement or savings plan contributions paid to the union by the employee, these amounts are not deductible as union dues.

Licenses and Insurance

Employees deduct malpractice and other professional insurance. Nursing licenses, hair stylist licenses, health department certifications, and any other professional licenses are also deductible.

Uniforms and Safety Equipment

Employees deduct the costs of special protective clothing and devices required for safety purposes. Hard hats, gloves, goggles, back supports, and steel-toed shoes not provided by the employer all qualify. Employees may also deduct the costs of uniforms specifically designed for the job or industry when the employer requires clothing not suitable for everyday wear. Uniforms suitable for street wear cannot be deducted.

Employee Physicals

Some employers require their employees to undergo an annual physical. The employee deducts the cost as an employee business expense, not as a medical expense. Only the costs not covered by insurance (the employee's out-of-pocket costs) are deductible.

EXAMPLE 17

Dillon's employer required that he undergo an annual physical as a condition of his employment. In the current year, $550 of the cost of his physical was not covered by insurance. Dillon deducts this amount as an employee business expenses on Schedule A. This amount will be included along with his other miscellaneous itemized deductions subject to the 2% AGI floor.

Equipment, Telephones, and Computers

For an employee to deduct the cost of equipment, the employer must have a written policy requiring the items as standard job tools. All other employees of the same company doing the same or similar work must have the same equipment requirements. Employees must depreciate equipment with a useful life in excess of one year.

Employees do not deduct the costs of equipment directly on Form 2106. They use Form 4562, Depreciation and Amortization, to compute depreciation expense on the equipment. The depreciation expense is then transferred to Form 2106 (line 4), as another business expense. Items falling in this category include cell phones, tools, fax machines, and the like. Depreciation methods are discussed in Chapter 8.

EXAMPLE 18

Amir prefers not to stay late at the office, so he buys a home computer for the convenience of working at home at night. Amir may not deduct depreciation on the computer. In this situation, the IRS will consider the purchase of the computer as simply for the employee's convenience.

Supplies

Employees may deduct office supplies and other business supplies. This category also includes calculators and briefcases, depending on the job requirements. Each industry has its own version of supplies. For instance, supplies for construction workers include disposable masks, work gloves, and small tools. For school teachers, it would include chalk, red ink pens, and notebooks.

Education

Only already employed or self-employed taxpayers can claim a deduction for education expenses. To qualify as an employee business expense, an employee's education must first meet one of two conditions:

1. The employer, the law, or the employee's profession must require the education, or
2. The education must maintain or improve the employee's skills for the employee's present job.

Even if the education is not required by the employer, the law, or the employee's profession, employees are often able to show that the education was taken to keep or improve the skills required at their current jobs. Thus, it is not too hard to meet one of the two conditions listed above. However, even after clearing this hurdle, two situations will always cause the deduction to be disallowed. The first is when the employee uses the courses to meet the minimum education requirements of the employee's present job. The second is when the education leads to a degree that qualifies the employee for a *new* trade or business.

EXAMPLE 19

Seth is a junior accountant with an associate's degree in accounting. Seth works for a CPA firm as a tax preparer while he attends State College and earns a bachelor's degree in accounting. With this degree, Seth can now take the CPA exam and become a CPA. Although Seth will continue doing the same work for his current employer, he now will qualify for a new line of work as a certified public accountant (CPA). Therefore, Seth may not deduct any of the costs associated with the courses taken at State College.

EXAMPLE 20

Scarlett works as a tax accountant for a CPA firm. Scarlett holds a Bachelor's of Science degree in accounting. She is currently taking night classes towards a Master's in Taxation degree. Scarlett has already met the minimum educational requirements of her current position. Furthermore, the degree she is pursuing will not enable her to enter a new profession. Instead, the courses Scarlett is taking will help her improve her current skills as a tax accountant. Thus, her educational costs are deductible as an employee business expense.

As these two examples show, education that is part of a program of study that either helps the employee meet the minimum education requirements of the current job or allows the employee to seek employment in a new line of business are not qualified education expenses. Thus, the education costs would not be deductible as an employee business expense. Being able to conclude whether the education costs qualify as a deductible employee business expense is important should the employer provide its employees with fringe benefits in the form of educational assistance or working condition fringe benefits. Under the fringe benefit rules, only amounts paid for qualified education costs are excluded from employees' gross income (¶401.03). If the education costs are not deductible as an employee business expense, the employer-paid amounts are taxed to the employee as additional wages.

Deductible education costs include unreimbursed amounts paid for tuition, books, supplies, lab fees, transportation costs, and costs of traveling to seminars. However, no amounts paid for travel as a form of education (like a trip to France to study the culture) are eligible for the deduction. Also, any amounts used in computing another deduction or credit (like the education credit (¶204.04)) cannot be included in the education expense deduction.

Unless the taxpayer is self-employed or an employee, education expenses are nondeductible personal expenses. People who use a "temporary leave of absence" to pursue their education on a full-time basis are treated as maintaining their employee or business status. This holds true even if they take another job after completing their courses.

Job or Employment Search

Taxpayers may deduct the costs of looking for work in a comparable position or in the same line of employment. Costs incurred to look for work in a different line of business are not deductible. Also, neither first-time job seekers nor someone returning to the work force after a long absence can deduct their job-hunting costs. The job search deduction includes the cost of career counseling when used to find employment in the same trade or business. Even if the search is unsuccessful, qualified job search expenses are still deductible. Costs that can be deducted include travel, postage, office supplies, printing, employment agency fees, and job counseling.

EXAMPLE 21

Manny is currently employed as a sales person. During the year he spends $3,500 for qualified job search expenses in his pursuit of a new sales position. His efforts are not successful. Manny can deduct the $3,500 as an employee business expense.

EXAMPLE 22

Several years ago, Dana was employed as a consultant. Dana left the workforce six years ago when she was pregnant with her first child. Now that her children are in school, Dana would like to return to work. During the year she spends $350 in job-hunting expenses. Since Dana is not currently working and has not recently worked as a consultant, she cannot deduct these costs.

Office in the Home

Under very limited circumstances, employees may qualify to take a deduction for working at home. The employee must use a specific portion of the home exclusively and on a regular basis for work. The employee must maintain an office area as either the principal place of work or the place where the employee regularly meets with clients. In addition, the employee must work at home for the convenience of the employer. The office-in-the-home deduction would apply if an employee worked for a company that did not have an office in the employee's home town but needed a representative in that area. (See ¶705.03 in Chapter 7 for more on this topic.)

EXAMPLE 23

Kim teaches at the local high school 25 hours a week. She spends another 35 hours a week in her office at home grading tests, writing assignments, and developing lesson plans. Although the work Kim does at home is essential to her job as a teacher and very time-consuming, Kim cannot deduct her home office costs. Working at home is simply more convenient for her.

¶602.08 FILLED-IN FORM 2106

INFORMATION FOR FIGURE 6-1:

Arthur McBurney is a district manager for the Drake Corporation. Arthur took a five-day business trip for his employer in November. Drake has an accountable reimbursement plan. However, it did not reimburse all expenses of Arthur's job-related costs. It reimbursed Arthur only for a business meal with a client ($190) and his air travel ($210). Arthur was expected to pay his own meals ($140) and lodging ($250). He also paid $12 to take a cab to meet with a client across town (unrelated to the business trip).

Arthur drove his personal car **34,204** total miles during the year, of which **22,709** were work-related. Drake reimbursed Arthur $10,219 (22,709 × $.45) for his business miles. Arthur's daily round trip commute is **10** miles, and his total commuting miles were **2,500.** He began using his car for business on **January 2, 2013.** Arthur elects to claim the standard mileage deduction rather than use actual expenses. Parking and tolls paid for business totaled $445. The $445 was not reimbursed.

The $10,619 of reimbursements ($10,219 + $210 + $190) was not reported on Arthur's W-2. Since the reimbursements were made from an accountable plan, the excess of Arthur's employee expenses of $3,616 from Form 2106 are reported as miscellaneous itemized deductions subject to the 2% AGI floor on Schedule A.

Line #

- 2A: Parking fees, tolls, and transportation unrelated to overnight travel, **$457** ($445 parking + $12 cab fare)
- 3A: Travel expense, **$460** ($210 airfare + $250 lodging)
- 5B: Meals and entertainment, **$330** ($190 + $140)
- 7A: Reimbursed travel and transportation, **$10,429** ($210 airfare + $10,219 auto)
- 7B: Reimbursed meals and entertainment, **$190** (business meal with client)
- 22: Standard mileage rate, **$13,058** (22,709 × $.575), which is transferred to line 1

Figure 6-1: Filled-In Form 2106 (Page 1)

Form **2106** — **Employee Business Expenses** — OMB No. 1545-0074 — **2015**

Department of the Treasury Internal Revenue Service (99)

▶ Attach to Form 1040 or Form 1040NR.

▶ Information about Form 2106 and its separate instructions is available at *www.irs.gov/form2106*.

Attachment Sequence No. **129**

Your name	Occupation in which you incurred expenses	Social security number
Arthur McBurney	Management	272 11 8245

Part I **Employee Business Expenses and Reimbursements**

Step 1 Enter Your Expenses		**Column A** Other Than Meals and Entertainment	**Column B** Meals and Entertainment
1 Vehicle expense from line 22 or line 29. (Rural mail carriers: See instructions.)	1	13,058	
2 Parking fees, tolls, and transportation, including train, bus, etc., that **did not** involve overnight travel or commuting to and from work	2	457	
3 Travel expense while away from home overnight, including lodging, airplane, car rental, etc. **Do not** include meals and entertainment	3	460	
4 Business expenses not included on lines 1 through 3. **Do not** include meals and entertainment	4		
5 Meals and entertainment expenses (see instructions)	5		330
6 Total expenses. In Column A, add lines 1 through 4 and enter the result. In Column B, enter the amount from line 5	6	13,975	330

Note. *If you were not reimbursed for any expenses in Step 1, skip line 7 and enter the amount from line 6 on line 8.*

Step 2 Enter Reimbursements Received From Your Employer for Expenses Listed in Step 1			
7 Enter reimbursements received from your employer that were **not** reported to you in box 1 of Form W-2. Include any reimbursements reported under code "L" in box 12 of your Form W-2 (see instructions)	7	10,429	190

Step 3 Figure Expenses To Deduct on Schedule A (Form 1040 or Form 1040NR)			
8 Subtract line 7 from line 6. If zero or less, enter -0-. However, if line 7 is greater than line 6 in Column A, report the excess as income on Form 1040, line 7 (or on Form 1040NR, line 8)	8	3,546	140
Note. *If* ***both columns*** *of line 8 are zero, you cannot deduct employee business expenses. Stop here and attach Form 2106 to your return.*			
9 In Column A, enter the amount from line 8. In Column B, multiply line 8 by 50% (.50). (Employees subject to Department of Transportation (DOT) hours of service limits: Multiply meal expenses incurred while away from home on business by 80% (.80) instead of 50%. For details, see instructions.)	9	3,546	70
10 Add the amounts on line 9 of both columns and enter the total here. **Also, enter the total on Schedule A (Form 1040), line 21** (or on **Schedule A (Form 1040NR), line 7**). (Armed Forces reservists, qualified performing artists, fee-basis state or local government officials, and individuals with disabilities: See the instructions for special rules on where to enter the total.) ▶		10	3,616

For Paperwork Reduction Act Notice, see your tax return instructions. Cat. No. 11700N Form **2106** (2015)

Figure 6-1: Filled-In Form 2106 (Page 2)

Form 2106 (2015) Page **2**

Part II **Vehicle Expenses**

Section A—General Information (You must complete this section if you are claiming vehicle expenses.)		**(a)** Vehicle 1	**(b)** Vehicle 2
11 Enter the date the vehicle was placed in service	**11**	1 / 2 / 13	/ /
12 Total miles the vehicle was driven during 2015	**12**	34,204 miles	miles
13 Business miles included on line 12	**13**	22,709 miles	miles
14 Percent of business use. Divide line 13 by line 12	**14**	66.39 %	%
15 Average daily roundtrip commuting distance	**15**	10 miles	miles
16 Commuting miles included on line 12	**16**	2,500 miles	miles
17 Other miles. Add lines 13 and 16 and subtract the total from line 12	**17**	8,995 miles	miles

18 Was your vehicle available for personal use during off-duty hours?	☑ **Yes** ☐ **No**
19 Do you (or your spouse) have another vehicle available for personal use?	☑ **Yes** ☐ **No**
20 Do you have evidence to support your deduction?	☑ **Yes** ☐ **No**
21 If "Yes," is the evidence written?	☑ **Yes** ☐ **No**

Section B—Standard Mileage Rate (See the instructions for Part II to find out whether to complete this section or Section C.)

22 Multiply line 13 by 57.5¢ (.575). Enter the result here and on line 1	**22**	13,058

Section C—Actual Expenses		**(a)** Vehicle 1	**(b)** Vehicle 2
23 Gasoline, oil, repairs, vehicle insurance, etc.	**23**		
24a Vehicle rentals	**24a**		
b Inclusion amount (see instructions)	**24b**		
c Subtract line 24b from line 24a	**24c**		
25 Value of employer-provided vehicle (applies only if 100% of annual lease value was included on Form W-2—see instructions)	**25**		
26 Add lines 23, 24c, and 25.	**26**		
27 Multiply line 26 by the percentage on line 14	**27**		
28 Depreciation (see instructions)	**28**		
29 Add lines 27 and 28. Enter total here and on line 1	**29**		

Section D—Depreciation of Vehicles (Use this section only if you owned the vehicle and are completing Section C for the vehicle.)

		(a) Vehicle 1	**(b)** Vehicle 2
30 Enter cost or other basis (see instructions)	**30**		
31 Enter section 179 deduction (see instructions)	**31**		
32 Multiply line 30 by line 14 (see instructions if you claimed the section 179 deduction or special allowance)	**32**		
33 Enter depreciation method and percentage (see instructions)	**33**		
34 Multiply line 32 by the percentage on line 33 (see instructions)	**34**		
35 Add lines 31 and 34	**35**		
36 Enter the applicable limit explained in the line 36 instructions	**36**		
37 Multiply line 36 by the percentage on line 14	**37**		
38 Enter the **smaller** of line 35 or line 37. If you skipped lines 36 and 37, enter the amount from line 35. Also enter this amount on line 28 above	**38**		

Form **2106** (2015)

¶603 Miscellaneous Deductions Reported on Schedule A

Schedule A also provides a place to deduct various other allowable expenses. These expenses are added to unreimbursed employee business expenses. The taxpayer then reduces total miscellaneous deductions by 2% of AGI. The three primary categories of other deductible nonbusiness expenses include the following:

1. Costs paid to produce or collect taxable income
2. Costs paid to manage or protect income-producing (investment) property
3. Amounts spent to determine, contest, pay, or claim a refund of any tax

Taxpayers can deduct expenses relating to the production of taxable income on investment property they own. These "investment expenses" do not include investment interest expense, which is interest paid on loans where the loan proceeds were used to buy or hold investment property. Investment interest expense is a type of deductible interest and is reported elsewhere on Schedule A (see ¶505.04).

In recent years, many areas of the United States have experienced disasters. Ensuring the deductibility of casualty losses requires objective verification of the asset's value. When taxpayers incur appraisal and other evaluation expenses, they deduct these costs as miscellaneous expenses on Schedule A, and not as a part of the casualty loss deduction.

Because casualty losses are reduced by 10% AGI, allowing appraisal costs to be deducted as a miscellaneous deduction (subject to a 2% AGI floor) makes it more likely that taxpayers can deduct these amounts.

Taxpayers often hire tax professionals to prepare their tax returns, respond to IRS or other tax agency inquiries, or represent them in audits. Tax professionals also deal with refund claims and contested tax bills. Taxpayers include all costs associated with tax preparation, representation, and advice as miscellaneous itemized deductions. Other deductible amounts include the costs of electronic filing, certified postage for the tax return, and tax preparation software.

EXAMPLE 24

Leroy buys Quicken for $60 to help him keep track of his investments. He buys Turbo Tax for $50 to help him prepare his own tax return. Leroy also subscribes to *Money Magazine*, the *Wall Street Journal*, and *Value Line* for a total cost of $400. His deductible investment expenses total $510. He adds these amounts to his other miscellaneous itemized deductions subject to the 2% AGI floor.

Examples of Other Expenses

Other expenses from a hobby activity (see ¶603.01)
Safe deposit box fees
Investment advice and fees paid to a financial planner, bank, or trustee
Subscriptions to financial newspapers, newsletters, magazines, etc.
Investment fees
Costs associated with attending investment seminars and conventions
Legal, accounting, and related software
Depreciation on computer used for investment (subject to limitations)
Appraisal fees for casualty loss or charitable contributions
Convenience fees charged by credit card companies when paying Federal income taxes via credit card

¶603.01 HOBBY LOSSES

When an activity has elements of both personal pleasure and profit, the question often arises as to whether the taxpayer had a profit motive. The presence of a profit motive affects the amount of expenses taxpayers deduct as well as where on the tax return they deduct them. Taxpayers who enter into an activity expecting to make a profit can deduct all expenses from the activity as a deduction for AGI. In contrast, expenses from an activity in which the taxpayer did not have a profit motive (a hobby) can be deducted to the extent of income from the activity as a miscellaneous itemized deduction (subject to the 2% AGI floor).

Of the expenses related to the hobby activity, taxpayers continue to deduct expenses that they would otherwise be able to deduct even if the activity did not exist. These include home mortgage interest, property taxes, and casualty losses. Other expenses, like supplies, utilities, insurance, and depreciation, are deductible only because of tax laws that allow taxpayers to deduct them against hobby income. The hobby loss rules limit the taxpayer's deduction for these otherwise nondeductible expenses to the gross income from the hobby activity minus the expenses deductible elsewhere on the return. Any disallowed expenses are lost and cannot be carried over to future years.

EXAMPLE 25 Rob paints as a hobby. Rob does his painting in a separate studio located in his home. During the year, Rob sold some paintings for $2,300. His expenses totaled $3,025 and consisted of $400 for real estate taxes on the studio, $1,125 for utilities, and $1,500 for painting supplies.

Gross income		$2,300
Less real estate taxes deductible elsewhere on Schedule A		(400)
Limit on deduction for "other expenses"		$1,900
"Other expenses" related to the hobby:		
Utilities	$1,125	
Painting supplies	1,500	
Total "other expenses"	$2,625	
Deductible "other expenses"		(1,900)
Net hobby income		$0

Rob reports $2,300 of gross income from the hobby as "Other income" on Form 1040. On Schedule A, Rob deducts $400 as real estate taxes and the remaining $1,900 of "other expenses" as a miscellaneous itemized deduction. He adds the $1,900 to his other miscellaneous deductions, and reduces the total by 2% of AGI. Rob cannot deduct the $725 of painting supplies and utilities that exceed $1,900 ($2,625 – $1,900 = $725).

EXAMPLE 26 Same facts as in Example 25, except that Rob's activity has a profit motive. Rob would report $2,300 as income and deduct the entire $3,025 of expenses on Schedule C. He would carry the net loss of $725 to Form 1040, page 1 to offset other income items. Schedule C is the focus of Chapter 7.

Unlike hobby losses, losses from a profit activity can be used to offset other income. The drawback of having an activity treated as a hobby should help explain why taxpayers should make every effort to be able to treat an activity as a business. The fact that a taxpayer enjoys an activity does not prevent it from being profitable. The burden of proving whether an activity is engaged in for profit generally rests with the taxpayer. However, the burden of proof shifts to the IRS for an activity that shows a profit in any three of five consecutive years (two of seven for activities involving horses). When this happens, it is assumed that a profit motive exists, and it is up to the IRS to prove that the activity is a hobby.

Taxpayers involved in an activity for less than three years may elect to postpone any challenge from the IRS until after the first five years. This gives taxpayers the opportunity to show a profit in three of those years and shift the burden of proof to the IRS. However, filing such an election may alert the IRS to a possible hobby activity. Factors used to decide whether an activity is a business or a hobby include:

1. The taxpayer's expertise in the area
2. Whether the taxpayer keeps separate books and records for the activity
3. Whether the activity showed profits in some years and losses in others
4. The amount of occasional profits the taxpayer earned from the activity
5. The relative amount of pleasure the taxpayer derives from the activity
6. The extent to which the taxpayer depends on the activity for financial support
7. The time and effort the taxpayer devotes to the activity
8. The taxpayer's past success with other activities
9. The taxpayer's expectation that the property used in the activity will rise in value

When the taxpayer uses the standard deduction or when the taxpayer's miscellaneous deductions do not exceed 2% of AGI, all of the gross income from the hobby is taxed, with no offsetting deductions.

¶604 Other Miscellaneous Deductions

Taxpayers report the following expenses as "Other Miscellaneous Deductions" on Schedule A (line 28). These deductions are not reduced by 2% of AGI.

- Gambling losses to the extent of gambling income (see ¶604.01 below)
- Casualty losses from investment property (¶507)
- Federal estate taxes on income in respect of a decedent
- Repayment under the claim of right doctrine
- Unrecovered costs in pensions and annuities (¶306.01, ¶306.02)
- Impairment-related work expenses of disabled persons (see ¶604.02 below)

¶604.01 GAMBLING LOSSES

Taxpayers report all gambling winnings on Form 1040, page 1, as "Other income." They may deduct their gambling losses up to the amount of their reported winnings as an itemized deduction. Thus, taxpayers who do not itemize lose the gambling deduction, but are still taxed on their gambling winnings.

EXAMPLE 27 In several trips to Las Vegas, Newman lost $8,000 playing blackjack and poker. However, he won $4,500 from the state lottery. Newman reports the $4,500 lottery winnings as "Other income" on Form 1040. He reports only $4,500 as gambling losses as "Other miscellaneous deductions" on Schedule A (line 28). He cannot deduct the other $3,500 of gambling losses. Newman cannot take advantage of any deduction for the gambling loss unless his total itemized deductions exceed his total standard deduction amount.

¶604.02 IMPAIRMENT-RELATED WORK EXPENSES

An impairment is a physical or mental disability when it limits a taxpayer's employment. Impairments include those limiting vision, hearing, or movement. When impaired taxpayers purchase special tools or devices to make it possible to work as an employee, they deduct the costs directly on Schedule A. They are not required to depreciate these special purchases or subject them to the 2% AGI floor. Deductible expenses include modifications to computers, special listening devices, and reading devices. Self-employed persons deduct their impairment-related work expenses on Schedule C.

¶604.03 NONDEDUCTIBLE EXPENSES

Over the years, some taxpayers have become accustomed to taking deductions for certain expenses that are not deductible. Below is a non-exhaustive list of nondeductible expenses.

- Funeral costs, including the lot
- Political contributions, illegal bribes and kickbacks
- Parking tickets and fines, even if related to business
- Personal living expenses, like rent, insurance, utilities and life insurance

¶605 Schedule A and Form 1040 Revisited

Form 2106 is used to compute an employee's business expense deduction. The deductible amount from Form 2106 is then transferred to Schedule A and is added to other miscellaneous itemized deductions subject to the 2% AGI floor. Figures 6-2 and 6-3 fill in the missing information for the McBurneys' (from Figure 6-1) to show how the information flows from Form 2106, to Schedule A, and finally to Form 1040.

¶605.01 FILLED-IN SCHEDULE A

INFORMATION FOR FIGURE 6-2:

Arthur and Drea McBurney (from Figure 6-1) have **$91,517** of AGI. Neither Arthur nor Drea are 65 or older. The McBurneys use the deduction computed on Form 2106 and the information shown below to compute their itemized deductions on Schedule A.

Line #

1: Unreimbursed medical and dental expenses, **$9,754**
2: AGI, **$91,517** (given)
5: State of Wisconsin income taxes, **$2,730**
6: Real estate taxes, **$2,224**
7: Personal (ad valorem) property taxes, **$96**
10: Home mortgage interest, **$4,426**
16: Gifts by cash or check, **$1,287**
17: Noncash gifts, **$181** (used clothing ($160) + (150 miles × $.14 = $21))
18: Charitable contribution carryover from a prior year, **$200**
21: Unreimbursed employee expenses, **$3,616** (source: Form 2106, see Figure 6-1)
22: Tax preparation fees, **$250** (for 2014 income tax return)
23: Other expenses, **$1,689** (**safe deposit box rental, $50** + **investment expenses, $1,639**)
25: AGI, **$91,517** (given)

Figure 6-2: Filled-In Schedule A

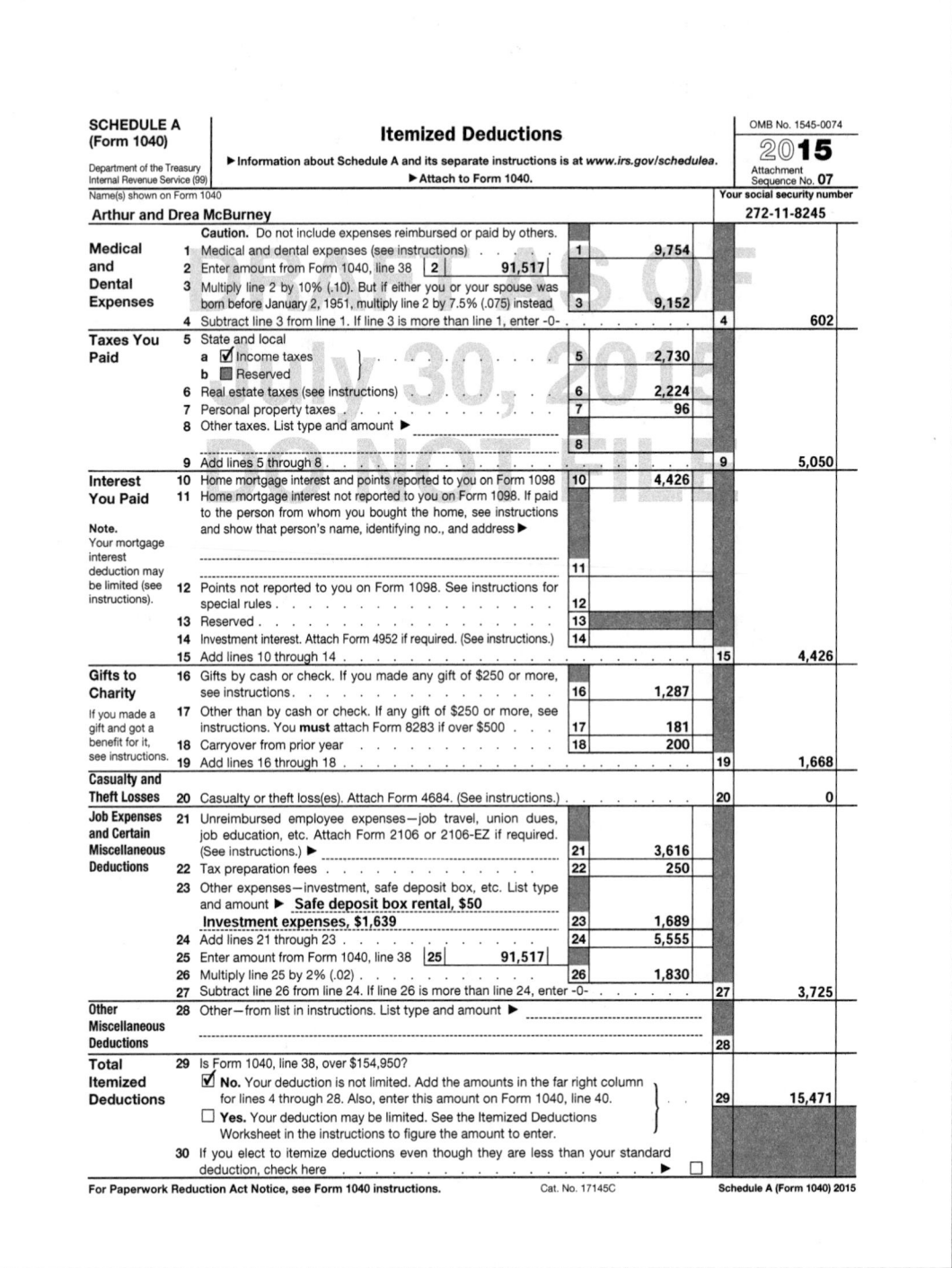

SCHEDULE A (Form 1040) — **Itemized Deductions** — OMB No. 1545-0074 — **2015**

Department of the Treasury Internal Revenue Service (99) — ▶ **Information about Schedule A and its separate instructions is at *www.irs.gov/schedulea*.** ▶ **Attach to Form 1040.** — Attachment Sequence No. **07**

Name(s) shown on Form 1040: **Arthur and Drea McBurney** — **Your social security number: 272-11-8245**

Section	Line	Description	Line box	Amount	Line box	Total
Medical and Dental Expenses		**Caution.** Do not include expenses reimbursed or paid by others.				
	1	Medical and dental expenses (see instructions)	1	9,754		
	2	Enter amount from Form 1040, line 38 [2] 91,517				
	3	Multiply line 2 by 10% (.10). But if either you or your spouse was born before January 2, 1951, multiply line 2 by 7.5% (.075) instead	3	9,152		
	4	Subtract line 3 from line 1. If line 3 is more than line 1, enter -0-			4	602
Taxes You Paid	5	State and local: a ☑ Income taxes; b ■ Reserved	5	2,730		
	6	Real estate taxes (see instructions)	6	2,224		
	7	Personal property taxes	7	96		
	8	Other taxes. List type and amount ▶	8			
	9	Add lines 5 through 8			9	5,050
Interest You Paid	10	Home mortgage interest and points reported to you on Form 1098	10	4,426		
Note. Your mortgage interest deduction may be limited (see instructions).	11	Home mortgage interest not reported to you on Form 1098. If paid to the person from whom you bought the home, see instructions and show that person's name, identifying no., and address ▶	11			
	12	Points not reported to you on Form 1098. See instructions for special rules	12			
	13	Reserved	13			
	14	Investment interest. Attach Form 4952 if required. (See instructions.)	14			
	15	Add lines 10 through 14			15	4,426
Gifts to Charity	16	Gifts by cash or check. If you made any gift of $250 or more, see instructions	16	1,287		
If you made a gift and got a benefit for it, see instructions.	17	Other than by cash or check. If any gift of $250 or more, see instructions. You **must** attach Form 8283 if over $500	17	181		
	18	Carryover from prior year	18	200		
	19	Add lines 16 through 18			19	1,668
Casualty and Theft Losses	20	Casualty or theft loss(es). Attach Form 4684. (See instructions.)			20	0
Job Expenses and Certain Miscellaneous Deductions	21	Unreimbursed employee expenses—job travel, union dues, job education, etc. Attach Form 2106 or 2106-EZ if required. (See instructions.) ▶	21	3,616		
	22	Tax preparation fees	22	250		
	23	Other expenses—investment, safe deposit box, etc. List type and amount ▶ **Safe deposit box rental, $50** **Investment expenses, $1,639**	23	1,689		
	24	Add lines 21 through 23	24	5,555		
	25	Enter amount from Form 1040, line 38 [25] 91,517				
	26	Multiply line 25 by 2% (.02)	26	1,830		
	27	Subtract line 26 from line 24. If line 26 is more than line 24, enter -0-			27	3,725
Other Miscellaneous Deductions	28	Other—from list in instructions. List type and amount ▶			28	
Total Itemized Deductions	29	Is Form 1040, line 38, over $154,950? ☑ **No.** Your deduction is not limited. Add the amounts in the far right column for lines 4 through 28. Also, enter this amount on Form 1040, line 40. ☐ **Yes.** Your deduction may be limited. See the Itemized Deductions Worksheet in the instructions to figure the amount to enter.			29	15,471
	30	If you elect to itemize deductions even though they are less than your standard deduction, check here ▶ ☐				

For Paperwork Reduction Act Notice, see Form 1040 instructions. Cat. No. 17145C **Schedule A (Form 1040) 2015**

¶605.02 FILLED-IN FORM 1040

INFORMATION FOR FIGURE 6-3:

Arthur and Drea McBurney (from Figures 6-1 and 6-2) claim their two minor children and Arthur's mother as dependents. Neither Arthur nor Drea is a participant in an employer's pension program. Figure 6-3 shows the McBurneys' completed Form 1040 which is based on the information shown below, as well as Form 2106 and Schedule A from Figures 6-1 and 6-2.

Line #

7: Wages, **$94,000** (Arthur, $55,000 + Drea, $39,000, source: Form W-2)
8a: Taxable interest, **$1,913** (source: Schedule B)
10: Taxable state income tax refund, **$342** (source: Form 1099-G from 2014 state income tax return)
13: Short-term capital gain, **$250** (source: Schedule D)
17: Net rent from apartments, **$5,212** (source: Schedule E)
21: Door prize, **$800** (source: Form 1099-MISC)
32: IRA deduction, **$11,000** (neither taxpayer is an active participant)
40: Itemized deductions, **$15,471** (source: Schedule A, see Figure 6-2)
42: Exemptions, **$20,000** ($4,000 × 5 exemptions)
44: Tax, **$7,481** (source: MFJ tax table)
49: Child and dependent care credit, **$1,200** (source: Form 2441)
52: Child tax credit, **$2,000** (2 qualifying children × $1,000)
61: Health care: individual responsibility, check box to indicate Full-year coverage. (Arthur's employer provides full health care coverage for the McBurney family)
64: Federal income tax withheld, **$4,200** (source: Form W-2)

Figure 6-3: Filled-In Form 1040 (Page 1)

Form **1040** Department of the Treasury—Internal Revenue Service (99) **U.S. Individual Income Tax Return** **2015** OMB No. 1545-0074 IRS Use Only—Do not write or staple in this space.

For the year Jan. 1–Dec. 31, 2015, or other tax year beginning , 2015, ending , 20 See separate instructions.

Your first name and initial: Arthur	Last name: McBurney	Your social security number: 272 11 8245
If a joint return, spouse's first name and initial: Drea	Last name: McBurney	Spouse's social security number: 369 41 3822
Home address (number and street). If you have a P.O. box, see instructions.: 1438 East Second Street	Apt. no.	▲ Make sure the SSN(s) above and on line 6c are correct.
City, town or post office, state, and ZIP code. If you have a foreign address, also complete spaces below (see instructions).: Verona, WI 53593-9088		**Presidential Election Campaign** Check here if you, or your spouse if filing jointly, want $3 to go to this fund. Checking a box below will not change your tax or refund. ☐ You ☐ Spouse
Foreign country name	Foreign province/state/county	Foreign postal code

Filing Status

Check only one box.

1 ☐ Single
2 ☑ Married filing jointly (even if only one had income)
3 ☐ Married filing separately. Enter spouse's SSN above and full name here.
4 ☐ Head of household (with qualifying person). (See instructions.) If the qualifying person is a child but not your dependent, enter this child's name here.
5 ☐ Qualifying widow(er) with dependent child

Exemptions

6a ☑ **Yourself.** If someone can claim you as a dependent, **do not** check box 6a
b ☑ **Spouse**

Boxes checked on 6a and 6b: 2

c **Dependents:**

(1) First name	Last name	(2) Dependent's social security number	(3) Dependent's relationship to you	(4) ✓ if child under age 17 qualifying for child tax credit (see instructions)
Mary	McBurney	453 26 8109	daughter	☑
Douglas	McBurney	453 26 8189	son	☑
Mildred	McBurney	168 29 4501	mother	☐
				☐

If more than four dependents, see instructions and check here ▶ ☐

No. of children on 6c who: • lived with you: 2
• did not live with you due to divorce or separation (see instructions):
Dependents on 6c not entered above: 1

d Total number of exemptions claimed — Add numbers on lines above ▶ 5

Income

Attach Form(s) W-2 here. Also attach Forms W-2G and 1099-R if tax was withheld.

If you did not get a W-2, see instructions.

7	Wages, salaries, tips, etc. Attach Form(s) W-2	7	94,000
8a	**Taxable** interest. Attach Schedule B if required	8a	1,913
b	**Tax-exempt** interest. **Do not** include on line 8a — 8b		
9a	Ordinary dividends. Attach Schedule B if required	9a	
b	Qualified dividends — 9b		
10	Taxable refunds, credits, or offsets of state and local income taxes	10	342
11	Alimony received	11	
12	Business income or (loss). Attach Schedule C or C-EZ	12	
13	Capital gain or (loss). Attach Schedule D if required. If not required, check here ▶ ☐	13	250
14	Other gains or (losses). Attach Form 4797	14	
15a	IRA distributions — 15a; b Taxable amount	15b	
16a	Pensions and annuities — 16a; b Taxable amount	16b	
17	Rental real estate, royalties, partnerships, S corporations, trusts, etc. Attach Schedule E	17	5,212
18	Farm income or (loss). Attach Schedule F	18	
19	Unemployment compensation	19	
20a	Social security benefits — 20a; b Taxable amount	20b	
21	Other income. List type and amount: Door prize	21	800
22	Combine the amounts in the far right column for lines 7 through 21. This is your **total income** ▶	22	102,517

Adjusted Gross Income

23	Reserved	23			
24	Certain business expenses of reservists, performing artists, and fee-basis government officials. Attach Form 2106 or 2106-EZ	24			
25	Health savings account deduction. Attach Form 8889	25			
26	Moving expenses. Attach Form 3903	26			
27	Deductible part of self-employment tax. Attach Schedule SE	27			
28	Self-employed SEP, SIMPLE, and qualified plans	28			
29	Self-employed health insurance deduction	29			
30	Penalty on early withdrawal of savings	30			
31a	Alimony paid b Recipient's SSN ▶	31a			
32	IRA deduction	32	11,000		
33	Student loan interest deduction	33			
34	Reserved	34			
35	Domestic production activities deduction. Attach Form 8903	35			
36	Add lines 23 through 35			36	11,000
37	Subtract line 36 from line 22. This is your **adjusted gross income** ▶			37	91,517

For Disclosure, Privacy Act, and Paperwork Reduction Act Notice, see separate instructions. Cat. No. 11320B Form **1040** (2015)

Figure 6-3: Filled-In Form 1040 (Page 2)

Form 1040 (2015) Page **2**

Tax and Credits

Line	Description		Amount
38	Amount from line 37 (adjusted gross income)	38	91,517
39a	Check if: ☐ **You** were born before January 2, 1951, ☐ Blind. ☐ **Spouse** was born before January 2, 1951, ☐ Blind. **Total boxes checked ▶ 39a**		
b	If your spouse itemizes on a separate return or you were a dual-status alien, check here ▶ 39b ☐		
40	**Itemized deductions** (from Schedule A) **or** your **standard deduction** (see left margin)	40	15,471
41	Subtract line 40 from line 38	41	76,046
42	**Exemptions.** If line 38 is $154,950 or less, multiply $4,000 by the number on line 6d. Otherwise, see instructions	42	20,000
43	**Taxable income.** Subtract line 42 from line 41. If line 42 is more than line 41, enter -0-	43	56,046
44	**Tax** (see instructions). Check if any from: **a** ☐ Form(s) 8814 **b** ☐ Form 4972 **c** ☐	44	7,481
45	**Alternative minimum tax** (see instructions). Attach Form 6251	45	
46	Excess advance premium tax credit repayment. Attach Form 8962	46	
47	Add lines 44, 45, and 46 ▶	47	7,481
48	Foreign tax credit. Attach Form 1116 if required	48	
49	Credit for child and dependent care expenses. Attach Form 2441	49: 1,200	
50	Education credits from Form 8863, line 19	50	
51	Retirement savings contributions credit. Attach Form 8880	51	
52	Child tax credit. Attach Schedule 8812, if required	52: 2,000	
53	Residential energy credit. Attach Form 5695	53	
54	Other credits from Form: **a** ☐ 3800 **b** ☐ 8801 **c** ☐	54	
55	Add lines 48 through 54. These are your **total credits**	55	3,200
56	Subtract line 55 from line 47. If line 55 is more than line 47, enter -0- ▶	56	4,281

Standard Deduction for—
- People who check any box on line 39a or 39b **or** who can be claimed as a dependent, see instructions.
- All others:

Single or Married filing separately, $6,300

Married filing jointly or Qualifying widow(er), $12,600

Head of household, $9,250

Other Taxes

Line	Description		Amount
57	Self-employment tax. Attach Schedule SE	57	
58	Unreported social security and Medicare tax from Form: **a** ☐ 4137 **b** ☐ 8919	58	
59	Additional tax on IRAs, other qualified retirement plans, etc. Attach Form 5329 if required	59	
60a	Household employment taxes from Schedule H	60a	
b	First-time homebuyer credit repayment. Attach Form 5405 if required	60b	
61	Health care: individual responsibility (see instructions) Full-year coverage ☑	61	
62	Taxes from: **a** ☐ Form 8959 **b** ☐ Form 8960 **c** ☐ Instructions; enter code(s)	62	
63	Add lines 56 through 62. This is your **total tax** ▶	63	4,281

Payments

If you have a qualifying child, attach Schedule EIC.

Line	Description		Amount
64	Federal income tax withheld from Forms W-2 and 1099	64: 4,200	
65	2015 estimated tax payments and amount applied from 2014 return	65	
66a	**Earned income credit (EIC)**	66a	
b	Nontaxable combat pay election	66b	
67	Additional child tax credit. Attach Schedule 8812	67	
68	American opportunity credit from Form 8863, line 8	68	
69	Net premium tax credit. Attach Form 8962	69	
70	Amount paid with request for extension to file	70	
71	Excess social security and tier 1 RRTA tax withheld	71	
72	Credit for federal tax on fuels. Attach Form 4136	72	
73	Credits from Form: **a** ☐ 2439 **b** Reserved **c** ☐ 8885 **d** ☐	73	
74	Add lines 64, 65, 66a, and 67 through 73. These are your **total payments** ▶	74	4,200

Refund

Line	Description		Amount
75	If line 74 is more than line 63, subtract line 63 from line 74. This is the amount you **overpaid**	75	
76a	Amount of line 75 you want **refunded to you.** If Form 8888 is attached, check here ▶ ☐	76a	
▶ b	Routing number ▶ c Type: ☐ Checking ☐ Savings		
▶ d	Account number		
77	Amount of line 75 you want **applied to your 2016 estimated tax** ▶	77	

Direct deposit? See instructions.

Amount You Owe

Line	Description		Amount
78	**Amount you owe.** Subtract line 74 from line 63. For details on how to pay, see instructions ▶	78	81
79	Estimated tax penalty (see instructions)	79	

Third Party Designee Do you want to allow another person to discuss this return with the IRS (see instructions)? ☐ **Yes.** Complete below. ☐ **No**

Designee's name ▶ Phone no. ▶ Personal identification number (PIN) ▶

Sign Here

Under penalties of perjury, I declare that I have examined this return and accompanying schedules and statements, and to the best of my knowledge and belief, they are true, correct, and complete. Declaration of preparer (other than taxpayer) is based on all information of which preparer has any knowledge.

Joint return? See instructions. Keep a copy for your records.

Your signature	Date	Your occupation	Daytime phone number
Arthur McBurney	4-12-16	Manager	
Spouse's signature. If a joint return, **both** must sign.	**Date**	**Spouse's occupation**	**If the IRS sent you an Identity Protection PIN, enter it here (see inst.)**
Drea McBurney	4-12-16	Nurse	

Paid Preparer Use Only

Print/Type preparer's name	Preparer's signature	Date	Check ☐ if self-employed	PTIN

Firm's name ▶ Firm's EIN ▶

Firm's address ▶ Phone no.

www.irs.gov/form1040 Form **1040** (2015)

6

Name:

Section:

Date:

QUESTIONS AND PROBLEMS

1. **Substantiation.** (Obj. 1) Describe the six elements that are required to properly substantiate an employee's business expense deduction.

2. **Accountable vs. Nonaccountable Reimbursement Plans.** (Obj. 1) Martin works as a delivery person for a local restaurant. His job requires that he use his own personal car to deliver food to customers' homes. During 2015, Martin drives 4,300 business miles. His employer reimburses him $.35 a mile for each business mile.

   a. Discuss the tax consequences of the $1,505 (4,300 × $.35) reimbursement Martin receives if his employer has an accountable reimbursement plan.

   b. Same as Part a., except that the employer has a nonaccountable reimbursement plan.

   c. What are the characteristics of an accountable reimbursement plan and what distinguishes it from a nonaccountable plan?

3. Vehicle Expenses. (Obj. 2) Shaun uses his personal car for work. Shaun is employed as a messenger. In 2015, he drove 12,400 work-related miles and 18,340 total miles. His employer reimburses him $.30 a mile for his documented business miles under an accountable reimbursement plan. Shaun's car expenses for the year were as follows. In addition, Shaun paid $398 in business-related parking.

Depreciation	$2,498
Gas	2,347
Insurance	1,840
License tags	120
Repairs and maintenance	122
	$6,927

a. Compute Shaun's car expense deduction using the standard mileage method.

b. Compute his car expense deduction using the actual expenses method.

c. Based on your answers to Parts a. and b., under what conditions should Shaun use the standard mileage method?

d. Based on your answers to Parts a. and b., under what conditions must Shaun use the actual expenses method?

4. **Vehicle Expenses.** (Obj. 2) Ginger uses her personal car for work as an employee. In 2015, Ginger drove 2,235 work-related miles and 15,544 total miles. Ginger's expenses for the car are as follows.

Depreciation	$4,800
Gas	2,224
Insurance	790
License tags	60
Repairs and maintenance	210
	$8,084

An accelerated depreciation method was used to compute the $4,800 depreciation expense. Last year was the first year Ginger used her car for business. Last year she used the standard mileage deduction. Her employer reimburses her $.40 a mile under an accountable reimbursement plan for each documented business mile.

a. Discuss the alternatives Ginger has for computing her car expense deduction. What amount should Ginger deduct for car expenses for 2015?

b. Discuss where Ginger reports the reimbursement and car expense deduction on her tax return.

5. **Transportation Expense.** (Obj. 2) Ricardo works two jobs each day, Monday through Friday. He works eight hours at his first job and three hours at his second job. He drives the following miles each day:

Home to first job	20 miles
First job to second job	12 miles
Second job to home	30 miles

a. If Ricardo follows this routine for 250 days during 2015, how many miles qualify for the mileage deduction?

b. Compute Ricardo's mileage deduction using the standard mileage method.

6. **Travel Expense.** (Obj. 2) Josh went on a business trip lasting ten days. He spent six days on business (includes his travel days). He spent four days playing golf and visiting with a friend. He incurred the following unreimbursed expenses:

Lodging	$1,250
Meals	500
Entertainment of clients	130
Airfare	1,500

a. If the trip was within the United States, how much can Josh deduct?

b. If the trip involved foreign travel, how much can Josh deduct?

7. **Travel Expenses.** (Obj. 2) Katie attends a convention related to her employment. Her employer does not reimburse her for any of her expenses. After the convention, Katie takes a vacation in the area and stays an additional week. Katie is gone a total of 14 days, seven of which are spent conducting business. Her travel costs include:

Airfare	$ 650
Transportation to and from the airport	180
Hotel ($200 a night for 13 nights – 6 business, 7 personal)	2,600
Meals ($40 a day for 14 days – 7 business, 7 personal)	560

a. Compute Katie's travel expense deduction assuming the convention was held in the United States.

b. Same as in Part a., except that the convention was held in Canada.

c. How, if at all, would your answer to Part a. change if Katie stayed one less personal day?

d. How, if at all, would your answer to Part b. change if she stayed one less personal day?

8. **Meals and Entertainment.** (Obj. 2) Courtney is employed as a sales person. During the year, Courtney pays $250 for tickets to a concert that she gives to a client. Courtney does not attend the concert with the client. Also during the year, she picks up the $210 tab for a dinner for one of her customers. She was in the restaurant at the time the customer was dining, but did not dine with the customer. Courtney was not reimbursed for either of these amounts. Compute Courtney's meals and entertainment deduction and discuss where she reports this amount on her tax return.

9. **Education Expenses.** (Obj. 2) For each situation described in Parts a. through d., determine whether the taxpayer meets the criteria for the education expense deduction.

   a. An accountant pays $525 for accounting courses to meet the state's continuing professional education (CPE) requirement. The accountant is employed as a CPA.

   b. A CPA pays $3,500 for tuition and books for courses he is enrolled in at law school. The courses count in meeting the state's CPE requirements.

   c. A high school teacher pays tuition of $2,700. The teacher is enrolled in graduate school and is taking classes in order to meet the state law requirements that will allow her to renew her teaching certificate.

   d. A company executive pays $8,000 for tuition, books, and transportation to attend an executive MBA program to improve his business management and employee relations skills.

10. **Job Search Expenses.** (Obj. 2) During the year, Kris spends $1,700 on qualified job search expenses in his pursuit of a job as a manager.

a. Can Kris deduct the $1,700 if he is currently employed as a manager and as a result of his efforts, he finds a new managerial position? Where would he report his deduction?

b. Same as in Part a. except that his efforts are unsuccessful.

c. Same as in Part a., except that Kris is not currently employed as a manager.

d. Same as in Part a. except that Kris is not currently employed as a manager and his efforts are unsuccessful.

11. **Deductions.** (Obj. 3) Use the knowledge you have acquired from Chapters 1 through 6 to identify each of the following expenditures as **(A)** deductible for AGI, **(B)** deductible from AGI, or **(C)** not deductible. Ignore any AGI limitations.

a. State inheritance taxes __________

b. Commuting costs __________

c. Safe deposit box rental (used to store stock investments) __________

d. CPA examination registration fee __________

e. IRS penalty for late filing __________

f. Fee paid to an accountant to prepare the personal property tax return on rental property __________

g. Loss on bookstore operations (Schedule C is used) __________

h. Auto registration for business vehicle __________

12. **Deductions.** (Obj. 3) Use the knowledge you have acquired from Chapters 1 through 6 to identify each of the following expenditures as **(A)** deductible for AGI, **(B)** deductible from AGI, or **(C)** not deductible. Ignore any AGI limitations.

a. Purchase of uniforms for work suitable for street wear ____________

b. Homeowner's insurance on the taxpayer's main home ____________

c. Union dues paid by a steelworker ____________

d. Unreimbursed employee business travel expense ____________

e. Mortgage interest on rental property ____________

f. Unreimbursed storm damage to trees in main home's yard ____________

g. Loss on sale of the taxpayer's personal car ____________

h. Repairs to friend's car for damage caused when taxpayer's car hit friend's car ____________

13. **Deductions.** (Obj. 3) Use the knowledge you have acquired from Chapters 1 through 6 to identify each of the following expenditures as **(A)** deductible for AGI, **(B)** deductible from AGI, or **(C)** not deductible. Ignore any AGI limitations.

a. Loss on sale of stock held as an investment ____________

b. Interest on loan to pay for family vacation ____________

c. Statutory employee's travel expenses ____________

d. Depreciation on rental property ____________

e. Charitable contributions to a university ____________

f. Sole proprietor's cost for continuing education seminar ____________

g. Storm damage to rental property ____________

14. **Hobby Criteria.** (Obj. 4)

a. What are the criteria for determining whether an activity is a legitimate business or a hobby?

b. If a doctor operates a farm that is used to graze cattle, will showing a profit automatically keep the IRS from considering the activity a hobby? Explain.

15. **Hobby Losses.** (Obj. 4) Russ is retired from his regular work and now spends his time painting landscapes in a studio set up in his home. The studio occupies 12% of the living space in his home. During the year, Russ sold some of his paintings for the first time. Russ is not certain whether he is required to file a tax return and, if so, whether he will be required to pay any taxes on his painting as a business. The revenue from sales of paintings was $2,300. Russ's expenses were as follows: property taxes on his home, $3,600; interest on a loan for painting supplies, $140; painting supplies, $1,750; electricity for the home, $2,400; and gas heat for the home, $2,900.

    a. How much can Russ deduct of the above expenses if his painting activity is treated as a business? Show your calculations.

    b. Same as in Part a., except that the painting activity is treated as a hobby.

    c. Explain what Russ might do in the way of tax planning to further support a claim that his painting is a business activity.

16. **Employee Business Expenses.** (Obj. 2) Roger, a single taxpayer, is a plumber employed by a company in the city where he lives. Roger attends the monthly dinner meetings of the local union. During the year, he paid $120 for dinners at the meetings and drove 259 miles to attend the meetings. Roger paid union dues of $110 and a plumbing license fee of $35.

    a. Compute Roger's itemized deductions for the work-related expenses.

    b. Explain where Roger deducts his employee business expenses.

17. **Gambling Losses.** (Obj. 3) During the year, Mark won $1,400 from football bets. He lost $750 from basketball wagering. Mark also lost $1,150 at the track.

    a. How do these gambling activities affect Mark's gross income and his deductible expenses?

    b. Where would the appropriate income and expenses be entered on Mark's income tax return?

18. Form 2106. (Obj. 5) Use the following information to prepare Form 2106 for Nancy Lopez (SSN 234–56–7891). Nancy incurs the following work-related expenses:

Travel expenses (not including meals, entertainment, or car expenses)	$3,750
Parking	180
Toll charges	30
Meals (while away overnight)	1,500
Entertainment of clients	426
Miscellaneous	135

Nancy's employer provides a business expense allowance of $750 per month to cover all expenses. The $9,000 reimbursement was paid from her employer's nonaccountable plan. Thus, the $9,000 was reported as additional taxable wages on Nancy's W-2. Nancy does not account to her employer for expenses, but she keeps detailed records of her business expenses and mileage. During the year she drove 25,200 miles, of which 14,922 were work-related. The miles do not include Nancy's 10-mile round-trip commuting distance when she is not traveling. Her total commuting miles for the year are 2,200. Nancy uses the standard mileage rate to determine the tax deduction for the use of her automobile, which she acquired on November 10, 2014.

19. Internet Problem: Researching IRS Publication 463. (Obj. 2)

The Alpha-Beta Company rents a 12-seat luxury skybox at a football stadium for the entire season. The season consists of eight home games. Alpha-Beta uses the skybox exclusively for entertaining clients. The cost of renting the skybox for the season is $20,000. In contrast, nonluxury box seats sell for $50 for each game. How much can Alpha-Beta deduct for its rental of a luxury skybox?

Go to the IRS website. Locate IRS Publication 463, and find an answer to the above question involving luxury skyboxes. Print out a copy of the page where you found your answer. Underline or highlight the pertinent information.

See Appendix A for instructions on use of the IRS website.

20. Business Entity Problem: This problem is designed for those using the "business entity" approach. **The solution may require information from Chapters 14–16.** For each statement, check *true* or *false*.

	True	*False*
a. Statutory employees use Form 2106 to report their deductible travel expenses.	______	______
b. An employee may deduct 50% of the federal per diem rate for meals instead of deducting 50% of the actual meal costs.	______	______
c. Employers that reimburse their employees using an accountable reimbursement plan are able to deduct the entire cost of meal reimbursements paid to their employees.	______	______
d. When an employee pays his own deductible education expenses, the expenses are deductible as a miscellaneous itemized deduction subject to the 2% AGI floor.	______	______

(Use for Problem 18.)

Form **2106**

Department of the Treasury
Internal Revenue Service (99)

Employee Business Expenses

▶ Attach to Form 1040 or Form 1040NR.

▶ Information about Form 2106 and its separate instructions is available at *www.irs.gov/form2106.*

OMB No. 1545-0074

2015

Attachment Sequence No. **129**

Your name	Occupation in which you incurred expenses	Social security number

Part I **Employee Business Expenses and Reimbursements**

Step 1 Enter Your Expenses		**Column A** Other Than Meals and Entertainment	**Column B** Meals and Entertainment
1 Vehicle expense from line 22 or line 29. (Rural mail carriers: See instructions.)	1		
2 Parking fees, tolls, and transportation, including train, bus, etc., that **did not** involve overnight travel or commuting to and from work	2		
3 Travel expense while away from home overnight, including lodging, airplane, car rental, etc. **Do not** include meals and entertainment	3		
4 Business expenses not included on lines 1 through 3. **Do not** include meals and entertainment	4		
5 Meals and entertainment expenses (see instructions)	5		
6 **Total expenses.** In Column A, add lines 1 through 4 and enter the result. In Column B, enter the amount from line 5	6		

Note. *If you were not reimbursed for any expenses in Step 1, skip line 7 and enter the amount from line 6 on line 8.*

Step 2 Enter Reimbursements Received From Your Employer for Expenses Listed in Step 1			
7 Enter reimbursements received from your employer that were **not** reported to you in box 1 of Form W-2. Include any reimbursements reported under code "L" in box 12 of your Form W-2 (see instructions)	7		

Step 3 Figure Expenses To Deduct on Schedule A (Form 1040 or Form 1040NR)			
8 Subtract line 7 from line 6. If zero or less, enter -0-. However, if line 7 is greater than line 6 in Column A, report the excess as income on Form 1040, line 7 (or on Form 1040NR, line 8)	8		
Note. *If **both columns** of line 8 are zero, you cannot deduct employee business expenses. Stop here and attach Form 2106 to your return.*			
9 In Column A, enter the amount from line 8. In Column B, multiply line 8 by 50% (.50). (Employees subject to Department of Transportation (DOT) hours of service limits: Multiply meal expenses incurred while away from home on business by 80% (.80) instead of 50%. For details, see instructions.)	9		

10 Add the amounts on line 9 of both columns and enter the total here. **Also, enter the total on Schedule A (Form 1040), line 21** (or on **Schedule A (Form 1040NR), line 7**). (Armed Forces reservists, qualified performing artists, fee-basis state or local government officials, and individuals with disabilities: See the instructions for special rules on where to enter the total.) ▶ **10**

For Paperwork Reduction Act Notice, see your tax return instructions. Cat. No. 11700N Form **2106** (2015)

(Use for Problem 18.)

Form 2106 (2015) Page **2**

Part II Vehicle Expenses

Section A—General Information (You must complete this section if you are claiming vehicle expenses.)		**(a)** Vehicle 1	**(b)** Vehicle 2
11 Enter the date the vehicle was placed in service	11	/ /	/ /
12 Total miles the vehicle was driven during 2015	12	miles	miles
13 Business miles included on line 12	13	miles	miles
14 Percent of business use. Divide line 13 by line 12	14	%	%
15 Average daily roundtrip commuting distance	15	miles	miles
16 Commuting miles included on line 12	16	miles	miles
17 Other miles. Add lines 13 and 16 and subtract the total from line 12	17	miles	miles

18 Was your vehicle available for personal use during off-duty hours?	☐ **Yes** ☐ **No**
19 Do you (or your spouse) have another vehicle available for personal use?	☐ **Yes** ☐ **No**
20 Do you have evidence to support your deduction?	☐ **Yes** ☐ **No**
21 If "Yes," is the evidence written?	☐ **Yes** ☐ **No**

Section B—Standard Mileage Rate (See the instructions for Part II to find out whether to complete this section or Section C.)

22 Multiply line 13 by 57.5¢ (.575). Enter the result here and on line 1	22	

Section C—Actual Expenses		**(a)** Vehicle 1	**(b)** Vehicle 2
23 Gasoline, oil, repairs, vehicle insurance, etc.	23		
24a Vehicle rentals	24a		
b Inclusion amount (see instructions)	24b		
c Subtract line 24b from line 24a	24c		
25 Value of employer-provided vehicle (applies only if 100% of annual lease value was included on Form W-2—see instructions)	25		
26 Add lines 23, 24c, and 25	26		
27 Multiply line 26 by the percentage on line 14	27		
28 Depreciation (see instructions)	28		
29 Add lines 27 and 28. Enter total here and on line 1	29		

Section D—Depreciation of Vehicles (Use this section only if you owned the vehicle and are completing Section C for the vehicle.)

		(a) Vehicle 1	**(b)** Vehicle 2
30 Enter cost or other basis (see instructions)	30		
31 Enter section 179 deduction (see instructions)	31		
32 Multiply line 30 by line 14 (see instructions if you claimed the section 179 deduction or special allowance)	32		
33 Enter depreciation method and percentage (see instructions)	33		
34 Multiply line 32 by the percentage on line 33 (see instructions)	34		
35 Add lines 31 and 34	35		
36 Enter the applicable limit explained in the line 36 instructions	36		
37 Multiply line 36 by the percentage on line 14	37		
38 Enter the **smaller** of line 35 or line 37. If you skipped lines 36 and 37, enter the amount from line 35. Also enter this amount on line 28 above	38		

Form **2106** (2015)

COMPREHENSIVE PROBLEMS

21. Miscellaneous Deductions. (Obj. 5) The Pierres' AGI is $47,400. During the year they pay the following expenses. Using this information, compute the amounts that the Pierres should enter on the various lines of Schedule A as miscellaneous deductions.

Mr. Pierre:	
Employee business expenses:	
Airfare	$569
Meals while away from home overnight	90
Hotels	185
Miscellaneous travel expenses	18
	$862
Travel expenses (including all $90 of meals) reimbursed under an accountable plan	(486)
Net travel expenses paid out of pocket	$376
Other business expenses:	
Subscriptions to professional journals	$115
Unreimbursed meals and entertainment	256
Other expenses:	
Tax return preparation fee	$175
Gambling losses (gambling winnings were $65)	120
Mrs. Pierre:	
Safe deposit box rent (where investments are stored)	$45
Investment publications	120
Cost of nurse's uniform	340
Professional liability insurance	85

Job Expenses and Most Other Miscellaneous Deductions:

1. Unreimbursed employee expenses ________
2. Tax preparation fees ________
3. Other expenses subject to the 2% AGI floor ________
4. Total expenses ________
5. Less 2% of AGI ________
6. Deductible expenses ________

Other Miscellaneous Deductions:

7. Misc. expenses not subject to the 2% AGI floor ________

22. **Schedule A.** (Obj. 5) Charlie P. (SSN 367-83-9403) and Maggie S. Church (ages 32 and 33, respectively) file a joint tax return. Their AGI is $74,105. The Churchs' expenses follow. Unless otherwise stated, they have canceled checks or receipts for each item. Prepare the Churchs' Schedule A.

Mortgage interest on main home	$6,200
Cash contributions to church	1,500
Hunting license	90
Marriage license	16
Cash to homeless person begging for money (no receipt)	50
Cash contribution to American Red Cross	30
Paid to United Way (no canceled check or receipt)	310
Property tax on main home	2,450
R. K. Snell, physician (unreimbursed by insurance)	980
E. I. Newman, dentist (unreimbursed by insurance)	290
G. R. Gross, veterinarian (unreimbursed by insurance)	125
Medical insurance premiums	556
Safe deposit box rental (storing securities)	22
Paid to Evanston Drug for over-the-counter medications	160
State income taxes withheld	3,890

23. **Schedule A.** (Obj. 5) Roberto (SSN 123-45-6789) and Lena Gomez, both engineers, and both 53 years old, file a joint return reporting AGI of $381,031. This amount includes $326,500 in wages, $38,051 in interest income, and $16,480 in nonqualified dividends. They have receipts for the following deductions.

Unreimbursed medical expenses	$12,000
Unreimbursed employee job expenses (from Form 2106)	10,610
State income taxes	14,500
Real estate taxes on main home	8,000
Mortgage interest on main home	17,000
Investment interest expense	2,000
Investment fees and expenses	2,800
Tax preparation fees	500
Charitable contributions (all cash)	6,400

a. Prepare the Gomez's Schedule A.

b. Assuming Roberto and Lena claim their son as a dependent, compute the Gomez's taxable income.

(Use for Problem 22.)

SCHEDULE A (Form 1040)

Department of the Treasury
Internal Revenue Service (99)

Itemized Deductions

▶ Information about Schedule A and its separate instructions is at *www.irs.gov/schedulea.*
▶ Attach to Form 1040.

OMB No. 1545-0074
2015
Attachment Sequence No. **07**

Name(s) shown on Form 1040 | **Your social security number**

Medical and Dental Expenses		**Caution.** Do not include expenses reimbursed or paid by others.		
	1	Medical and dental expenses (see instructions)	1	
	2	Enter amount from Form 1040, line 38 [2]		
	3	Multiply line 2 by 10% (.10). But if either you or your spouse was born before January 2, 1951, multiply line 2 by 7.5% (.075) instead	3	
	4	Subtract line 3 from line 1. If line 3 is more than line 1, enter -0-		4
Taxes You Paid	5	State and local		
		a ☐ Income taxes b ▩ Reserved }	5	
	6	Real estate taxes (see instructions)	6	
	7	Personal property taxes	7	
	8	Other taxes. List type and amount ▶	8	
	9	Add lines 5 through 8		9
Interest You Paid	10	Home mortgage interest and points reported to you on Form 1098	10	
Note. Your mortgage interest deduction may be limited (see instructions).	11	Home mortgage interest not reported to you on Form 1098. If paid to the person from whom you bought the home, see instructions and show that person's name, identifying no., and address ▶	11	
	12	Points not reported to you on Form 1098. See instructions for special rules	12	
	13	Reserved	13	
	14	Investment interest. Attach Form 4952 if required. (See instructions.)	14	
	15	Add lines 10 through 14		15
Gifts to Charity	16	Gifts by cash or check. If you made any gift of $250 or more, see instructions.	16	
If you made a gift and got a benefit for it, see instructions.	17	Other than by cash or check. If any gift of $250 or more, see instructions. You **must** attach Form 8283 if over $500 . . .	17	
	18	Carryover from prior year	18	
	19	Add lines 16 through 18		19
Casualty and Theft Losses	20	Casualty or theft loss(es). Attach Form 4684. (See instructions.)		20
Job Expenses and Certain Miscellaneous Deductions	21	Unreimbursed employee expenses—job travel, union dues, job education, etc. Attach Form 2106 or 2106-EZ if required. (See instructions.) ▶	21	
	22	Tax preparation fees	22	
	23	Other expenses—investment, safe deposit box, etc. List type and amount ▶	23	
	24	Add lines 21 through 23	24	
	25	Enter amount from Form 1040, line 38 [25]		
	26	Multiply line 25 by 2% (.02)	26	
	27	Subtract line 26 from line 24. If line 26 is more than line 24, enter -0-		27
Other Miscellaneous Deductions	28	Other—from list in instructions. List type and amount ▶		28
Total Itemized Deductions	29	Is Form 1040, line 38, over $154,950? ☐ **No.** Your deduction is not limited. Add the amounts in the far right column for lines 4 through 28. Also, enter this amount on Form 1040, line 40. ☐ **Yes.** Your deduction may be limited. See the Itemized Deductions Worksheet in the instructions to figure the amount to enter.		29
	30	If you elect to itemize deductions even though they are less than your standard deduction, check here . . . . ▶ ☐		

For Paperwork Reduction Act Notice, see Form 1040 instructions. Cat. No. 17145C **Schedule A (Form 1040) 2015**

(Use for Problem 23.)

SCHEDULE A (Form 1040)
Department of the Treasury
Internal Revenue Service (99)

Itemized Deductions

► Information about Schedule A and its separate instructions is at *www.irs.gov/schedulea*.
► Attach to Form 1040.

OMB No. 1545-0074
2015
Attachment Sequence No. **07**

Name(s) shown on Form 1040 | **Your social security number**

Medical and Dental Expenses		**Caution.** Do not include expenses reimbursed or paid by others.		
	1	Medical and dental expenses (see instructions)	1	
	2	Enter amount from Form 1040, line 38 [2]		
	3	Multiply line 2 by 10% (.10). But if either you or your spouse was born before January 2, 1951, multiply line 2 by 7.5% (.075) instead	3	
	4	Subtract line 3 from line 1. If line 3 is more than line 1, enter -0-		4
Taxes You Paid	5	State and local		
		a ☐ Income taxes b ■ Reserved }	5	
	6	Real estate taxes (see instructions)	6	
	7	Personal property taxes	7	
	8	Other taxes. List type and amount ► ____________	8	
	9	Add lines 5 through 8		9
Interest You Paid **Note.** Your mortgage interest deduction may be limited (see instructions).	10	Home mortgage interest and points reported to you on Form 1098	10	
	11	Home mortgage interest not reported to you on Form 1098. If paid to the person from whom you bought the home, see instructions and show that person's name, identifying no., and address ► ____________	11	
	12	Points not reported to you on Form 1098. See instructions for special rules	12	
	13	Reserved	13	
	14	Investment interest. Attach Form 4952 if required. (See instructions.)	14	
	15	Add lines 10 through 14		15
Gifts to Charity If you made a gift and got a benefit for it, see instructions.	16	Gifts by cash or check. If you made any gift of $250 or more, see instructions.	16	
	17	Other than by cash or check. If any gift of $250 or more, see instructions. You **must** attach Form 8283 if over $500 . . .	17	
	18	Carryover from prior year	18	
	19	Add lines 16 through 18		19
Casualty and Theft Losses	20	Casualty or theft loss(es). Attach Form 4684. (See instructions.)		20
Job Expenses and Certain Miscellaneous Deductions	21	Unreimbursed employee expenses—job travel, union dues, job education, etc. Attach Form 2106 or 2106-EZ if required. (See instructions.) ► ____________	21	
	22	Tax preparation fees	22	
	23	Other expenses—investment, safe deposit box, etc. List type and amount ► ____________	23	
	24	Add lines 21 through 23	24	
	25	Enter amount from Form 1040, line 38 [25]		
	26	Multiply line 25 by 2% (.02)	26	
	27	Subtract line 26 from line 24. If line 26 is more than line 24, enter -0-		27
Other Miscellaneous Deductions	28	Other—from list in instructions. List type and amount ► ____________		28
Total Itemized Deductions	29	Is Form 1040, line 38, over $154,950? ☐ **No.** Your deduction is not limited. Add the amounts in the far right column for lines 4 through 28. Also, enter this amount on Form 1040, line 40. ☐ **Yes.** Your deduction may be limited. See the Itemized Deductions Worksheet in the instructions to figure the amount to enter. } . .		29
	30	If you elect to itemize deductions even though they are less than your standard deduction, check here . . . . ► ☐		

For Paperwork Reduction Act Notice, see Form 1040 instructions. Cat. No. 17145C **Schedule A (Form 1040) 2015**

CUMULATIVE PROBLEM (CHAPTERS 1–6)

Use the following information to prepare the joint income tax return of Frank and Sandra Anderson. Use Form 1040, Schedule A, Form 2106 and Form 2441. All parties sign and date the return on April 1, 2016. This problem is suitable for manual preparation or computer software application.

Frank A. (SSN 811-26-3717) and Sandra K. (SSN 820-47-9231) Anderson (ages 48 and 51, respectively) reside at 2121 Century Avenue, Middleton, CA 92657, with their three children whom they fully support: Mandy (age 9, SSN 998-21-5246), Charles (age 11, SSN 998-21-5247), and Carol (age 14, SSN 998-21-1827).

The Andersons file a joint return, and neither elects to have $3 go to the Presidential election campaign fund. Frank is employed as a customer service representative. Sandra is employed as a computer operator. Details of their salaries and withholdings, are as follows:

	Gross Wages	*State Income Tax Withheld*	*Federal Income Tax Withheld*	*Social Security Tax Withheld*	*Medicare Tax Withheld*
Frank	$56,500	$1,792	$2,100	$3,503	$819
Sandra	40,343	1,087	980	2,501	585

Frank's employer provides him with full family health care coverage as a tax-free employee benefit. Part of Frank's compensation package also includes group-term life insurance equal to 75% of his annual salary. The cost to the company for the premium was $240.

During the year, Frank received a $6,600 business travel expense reimbursement from his employer, which was not included on his Form W-2. By agreement with his employer, none of the allowance was for meals or entertainment. Frank must make an adequate accounting of his expenses to his employer and return any excess reimbursements. His daily business journal disclosed that from January 2 (the date of purchase) through December 31, he drove his own automobile 29,151 miles, of which 13,515 were work-related. Frank's average roundtrip commuting distance is 6 miles, and his commuting miles total 1,440 for the year. Sandra belongs to a car pool and drives to work every fourth week. The family uses her car on vacations. Since Frank dislikes keeping records, he uses the standard mileage rate to determine his car expense deduction. His substantiated business expenses are as follows:

Travel expenses, excluding meals, entertainment, and car expenses	$2,168
Parking fees	210
Meals and entertainment	560
Miscellaneous expenses	91

In August, Sandra earned $400 of interest when she cashed in a certificate of deposit from State Bank. The Middleton Farmers Bank credited $300 of interest to the Andersons' joint savings account during the year. The Andersons overpaid their 2015 state income taxes by $142. They received their refund in June. The Andersons' itemized deductions exceeded the standard deduction by $2,300 last year.

Since they both work outside the home, they are unable to be there when their children return home from school. This year the Andersons paid a neighbor, Gloria Dryden (SSN 992-31-4270), $4,100 to care for Mandy and Charles in her home after school hours and during the summer vacation period while the Andersons were at work. Gloria's address is 2132 Century Avenue, Middleton, CA 92657.

During the year, Sandra received unemployment compensation of $5,000. Frank is covered by a qualified pension plan at work; Sandra is not. The Andersons are interested in contributing to their respective traditional IRAs the maximum that they can deduct on their 2015 tax return. Both contributions take place before April 15, 2016.

Cancelled checks, receipts, and paid bills support the following expenditures:

Orlo T. Miller, M.D. (not covered by insurance)	$ 818
Qualified stop smoking program for Sandra	175
Alex B. Kramer, D.V.M. (treatment of Fritz, the Andersons' dog)	168
Life insurance premiums on Frank's life (Sandra is the beneficiary)	1,200
Kathryn R. Smith, dentist (not covered by insurance)	459
Weight loss program for Frank (cosmetic purposes)	180
Martin R. Jones, optometrist (not covered by insurance)	50
Eyeglasses for Mandy (not covered by insurance)	175
Driver's license renewal for Sandra	32
Fishing license for Frank	12
Credit card interest	275
Home mortgage interest on the main home	5,690
Real estate taxes on the main home	2,851
Trash pickup fees	120
Home repairs and improvements	620
Homeowner's insurance	500
General sales taxes paid during the year	572
State excise taxes	98
Cash gift to First Unity Church (with receipt)	2,200
Value of Frank's time volunteered to the Girl Scouts	300
Political contributions	50
Bingo and lottery tickets	260
Rental for safe deposit box to store investment items	47
Legal fees paid for preparation of the Andersons' personal wills	875

In addition, on April 24, 2015, the Andersons paid $600 to Homer P. Gill for preparation of their 2014 tax return.

When Frank's father died on Christmas day, Frank inherited his father's savings account. The account balance was $20,000.

In March, Sandra's best friend, Nancy, moved to Sweden. Nancy's 17-year-old daughter, Inga, stayed with the Andersons for the rest of the year. Inga had a part-time job after school and earned $4,120. The Andersons provided over half of Inga's support.

(Use for Cumulative Problem.)

Form **1040** Department of the Treasury—Internal Revenue Service (99)
U.S. Individual Income Tax Return **2015** OMB No. 1545-0074 IRS Use Only—Do not write or staple in this space.

For the year Jan. 1–Dec. 31, 2015, or other tax year beginning , 2015, ending , 20 See separate instructions.

Your first name and initial	Last name	Your social security number
If a joint return, spouse's first name and initial	Last name	Spouse's social security number
Home address (number and street). If you have a P.O. box, see instructions.	Apt. no.	▲ Make sure the SSN(s) above and on line 6c are correct.
City, town or post office, state, and ZIP code. If you have a foreign address, also complete spaces below (see instructions).		**Presidential Election Campaign** Check here if you, or your spouse if filing jointly, want $3 to go to this fund. Checking a box below will not change your tax or refund. ☐ You ☐ Spouse
Foreign country name	Foreign province/state/county	Foreign postal code

Filing Status

Check only one box.

1 ☐ Single
2 ☐ Married filing jointly (even if only one had income)
3 ☐ Married filing separately. Enter spouse's SSN above and full name here.
4 ☐ Head of household (with qualifying person). (See instructions.) If the qualifying person is a child but not your dependent, enter this child's name here.
5 ☐ Qualifying widow(er) with dependent child

Exemptions

6a ☐ **Yourself.** If someone can claim you as a dependent, **do not** check box 6a
b ☐ **Spouse**

Boxes checked on 6a and 6b

c **Dependents:**

(1) First name Last name	(2) Dependent's social security number	(3) Dependent's relationship to you	(4) ✓ if child under age 17 qualifying for child tax credit (see instructions)
			☐
			☐
			☐
			☐

No. of children on 6c who:
• lived with you
• did not live with you due to divorce or separation (see instructions)
Dependents on 6c not entered above

If more than four dependents, see instructions and check here ▶☐

d Total number of exemptions claimed

Add numbers on lines above ▶

Income

Attach Form(s) W-2 here. Also attach Forms W-2G and 1099-R if tax was withheld.

If you did not get a W-2, see instructions.

7	Wages, salaries, tips, etc. Attach Form(s) W-2		7
8a	**Taxable** interest. Attach Schedule B if required		8a
b	**Tax-exempt** interest. **Do not** include on line 8a	8b	
9a	Ordinary dividends. Attach Schedule B if required		9a
b	Qualified dividends	9b	
10	Taxable refunds, credits, or offsets of state and local income taxes		10
11	Alimony received		11
12	Business income or (loss). Attach Schedule C or C-EZ		12
13	Capital gain or (loss). Attach Schedule D if required. If not required, check here ▶ ☐		13
14	Other gains or (losses). Attach Form 4797		14
15a	IRA distributions	15a	b Taxable amount 15b
16a	Pensions and annuities	16a	b Taxable amount 16b
17	Rental real estate, royalties, partnerships, S corporations, trusts, etc. Attach Schedule E		17
18	Farm income or (loss). Attach Schedule F		18
19	Unemployment compensation		19
20a	Social security benefits	20a	b Taxable amount 20b
21	Other income. List type and amount		21
22	Combine the amounts in the far right column for lines 7 through 21. This is your **total income** ▶		22

Adjusted Gross Income

23	Reserved	23	
24	Certain business expenses of reservists, performing artists, and fee-basis government officials. Attach Form 2106 or 2106-EZ	24	
25	Health savings account deduction. Attach Form 8889	25	
26	Moving expenses. Attach Form 3903	26	
27	Deductible part of self-employment tax. Attach Schedule SE	27	
28	Self-employed SEP, SIMPLE, and qualified plans	28	
29	Self-employed health insurance deduction	29	
30	Penalty on early withdrawal of savings	30	
31a	Alimony paid b Recipient's SSN ▶	31a	
32	IRA deduction	32	
33	Student loan interest deduction	33	
34	Reserved	34	
35	Domestic production activities deduction. Attach Form 8903	35	
36	Add lines 23 through 35		36
37	Subtract line 36 from line 22. This is your **adjusted gross income** ▶		37

For Disclosure, Privacy Act, and Paperwork Reduction Act Notice, see separate instructions. Cat. No. 11320B Form **1040** (2015)

(Use for Cumulative Problem.)

Form 1040 (2015) Page **2**

Tax and Credits	38	Amount from line 37 (adjusted gross income)		38
	39a	Check if: { ☐ **You** were born before January 2, 1951, ☐ Blind. } **Total boxes** ☐ **Spouse** was born before January 2, 1951, ☐ Blind. } **checked ▶ 39a**		
	b	If your spouse itemizes on a separate return or you were a dual-status alien, check here ▶ **39b**☐		
Standard Deduction for—	40	**Itemized deductions** (from Schedule A) **or** your **standard deduction** (see left margin)		40
• People who check any box on line 39a or 39b **or** who can be claimed as a dependent, see instructions.	41	Subtract line 40 from line 38		41
• All others:	42	**Exemptions.** If line 38 is $154,950 or less, multiply $4,000 by the number on line 6d. Otherwise, see instructions		42
Single or Married filing separately, $6,300	43	**Taxable income.** Subtract line 42 from line 41. If line 42 is more than line 41, enter -0-		43
Married filing jointly or Qualifying widow(er), $12,600	44	**Tax** (see instructions). Check if any from: **a** ☐ Form(s) 8814 **b** ☐ Form 4972 **c** ☐		44
Head of household, $9,250	45	**Alternative minimum tax** (see instructions). Attach Form 6251		45
	46	Excess advance premium tax credit repayment. Attach Form 8962		46
	47	Add lines 44, 45, and 46 ▶		47
	48	Foreign tax credit. Attach Form 1116 if required	48	
	49	Credit for child and dependent care expenses. Attach Form 2441	49	
	50	Education credits from Form 8863, line 19	50	
	51	Retirement savings contributions credit. Attach Form 8880	51	
	52	Child tax credit. Attach Schedule 8812, if required	52	
	53	Residential energy credit. Attach Form 5695	53	
	54	Other credits from Form: **a** ☐ 3800 **b** ☐ 8801 **c** ☐	54	
	55	Add lines 48 through 54. These are your **total credits**		55
	56	Subtract line 55 from line 47. If line 55 is more than line 47, enter -0- ▶		56
Other Taxes	57	Self-employment tax. Attach Schedule SE		57
	58	Unreported social security and Medicare tax from Form: **a** ☐ 4137 **b** ☐ 8919		58
	59	Additional tax on IRAs, other qualified retirement plans, etc. Attach Form 5329 if required		59
	60a	Household employment taxes from Schedule H		60a
	b	First-time homebuyer credit repayment. Attach Form 5405 if required		60b
	61	Health care: individual responsibility (see instructions) Full-year coverage ☐		61
	62	Taxes from: **a** ☐ Form 8959 **b** ☐ Form 8960 **c** ☐ Instructions; enter code(s)		62
	63	Add lines 56 through 62. This is your **total tax** ▶		63
Payments	64	Federal income tax withheld from Forms W-2 and 1099	64	
	65	2015 estimated tax payments and amount applied from 2014 return	65	
If you have a qualifying child, attach Schedule EIC.	66a	**Earned income credit (EIC)**	66a	
	b	Nontaxable combat pay election 66b		
	67	Additional child tax credit. Attach Schedule 8812	67	
	68	American opportunity credit from Form 8863, line 8	68	
	69	Net premium tax credit. Attach Form 8962	69	
	70	Amount paid with request for extension to file	70	
	71	Excess social security and tier 1 RRTA tax withheld	71	
	72	Credit for federal tax on fuels. Attach Form 4136	72	
	73	Credits from Form: **a** ☐ 2439 **b** ■ Reserved **c** ☐ 8885 **d** ☐	73	
	74	Add lines 64, 65, 66a, and 67 through 73. These are your **total payments** ▶		74
Refund	75	If line 74 is more than line 63, subtract line 63 from line 74. This is the amount you **overpaid**		75
	76a	Amount of line 75 you want **refunded to you.** If Form 8888 is attached, check here ▶ ☐		76a
Direct deposit? See instructions.	▶ b	Routing number ▶ **c** Type: ☐ Checking ☐ Savings		
	▶ d	Account number		
	77	Amount of line 75 you want **applied to your 2016 estimated tax** ▶	77	
Amount You Owe	78	**Amount you owe.** Subtract line 74 from line 63. For details on how to pay, see instructions ▶		78
	79	Estimated tax penalty (see instructions)	79	

Third Party Designee Do you want to allow another person to discuss this return with the IRS (see instructions)? ☐ **Yes.** Complete below. ☐ **No**

Designee's name ▶ Phone no. ▶ Personal identification number (PIN) ▶

Sign Here Under penalties of perjury, I declare that I have examined this return and accompanying schedules and statements, and to the best of my knowledge and belief, they are true, correct, and complete. Declaration of preparer (other than taxpayer) is based on all information of which preparer has any knowledge.

Joint return? See instructions. Keep a copy for your records.

Your signature	Date	Your occupation	Daytime phone number
Spouse's signature. If a joint return, **both** must sign.	Date	Spouse's occupation	If the IRS sent you an Identity Protection PIN, enter it here (see inst.)

Paid Preparer Use Only

Print/Type preparer's name	Preparer's signature	Date	Check ☐ if self-employed	PTIN
Firm's name ▶			Firm's EIN ▶	
Firm's address ▶			Phone no.	

www.irs.gov/form1040 Form **1040** (2015)

(Use for Cumulative Problem.)

SCHEDULE A (Form 1040) | **Itemized Deductions** | OMB No. 1545-0074 | **2015**

Department of the Treasury
Internal Revenue Service (99)

▶ Information about Schedule A and its separate instructions is at *www.irs.gov/schedulea*.
▶ **Attach to Form 1040.**

Attachment Sequence No. **07**

Name(s) shown on Form 1040 | **Your social security number**

Medical and Dental Expenses		**Caution.** Do not include expenses reimbursed or paid by others.		
	1	Medical and dental expenses (see instructions)	1	
	2	Enter amount from Form 1040, line 38 [2]		
	3	Multiply line 2 by 10% (.10). But if either you or your spouse was born before January 2, 1951, multiply line 2 by 7.5% (.075) instead	3	
	4	Subtract line 3 from line 1. If line 3 is more than line 1, enter -0-		4
Taxes You Paid	5	State and local		
		a ☐ Income taxes b ■ Reserved	5	
	6	Real estate taxes (see instructions)	6	
	7	Personal property taxes	7	
	8	Other taxes. List type and amount ▶	8	
	9	Add lines 5 through 8		9
Interest You Paid **Note.** Your mortgage interest deduction may be limited (see instructions).	10	Home mortgage interest and points reported to you on Form 1098	10	
	11	Home mortgage interest not reported to you on Form 1098. If paid to the person from whom you bought the home, see instructions and show that person's name, identifying no., and address ▶	11	
	12	Points not reported to you on Form 1098. See instructions for special rules	12	
	13	Reserved	13	
	14	Investment interest. Attach Form 4952 if required. (See instructions.)	14	
	15	Add lines 10 through 14		15
Gifts to Charity If you made a gift and got a benefit for it, see instructions.	16	Gifts by cash or check. If you made any gift of $250 or more, see instructions	16	
	17	Other than by cash or check. If any gift of $250 or more, see instructions. You **must** attach Form 8283 if over $500	17	
	18	Carryover from prior year	18	
	19	Add lines 16 through 18		19
Casualty and Theft Losses	20	Casualty or theft loss(es). Attach Form 4684. (See instructions.)		20
Job Expenses and Certain Miscellaneous Deductions	21	Unreimbursed employee expenses—job travel, union dues, job education, etc. Attach Form 2106 or 2106-EZ if required. (See instructions.) ▶	21	
	22	Tax preparation fees	22	
	23	Other expenses—investment, safe deposit box, etc. List type and amount ▶	23	
	24	Add lines 21 through 23	24	
	25	Enter amount from Form 1040, line 38 [25]		
	26	Multiply line 25 by 2% (.02)	26	
	27	Subtract line 26 from line 24. If line 26 is more than line 24, enter -0-		27
Other Miscellaneous Deductions	28	Other—from list in instructions. List type and amount ▶		28
Total Itemized Deductions	29	Is Form 1040, line 38, over $154,950? ☐ **No.** Your deduction is not limited. Add the amounts in the far right column for lines 4 through 28. Also, enter this amount on Form 1040, line 40. ☐ **Yes.** Your deduction may be limited. See the Itemized Deductions Worksheet in the instructions to figure the amount to enter.		29
	30	If you elect to itemize deductions even though they are less than your standard deduction, check here ▶ ☐		

For Paperwork Reduction Act Notice, see Form 1040 instructions. Cat. No. 17145C **Schedule A (Form 1040) 2015**

(Use for Cumulative Problem.)

Form **2106** — **Employee Business Expenses**

Department of the Treasury Internal Revenue Service (99)

▶ Attach to Form 1040 or Form 1040NR.

▶ Information about Form 2106 and its separate instructions is available at *www.irs.gov/form2106.*

OMB No. 1545-0074 **2015** Attachment Sequence No. **129**

Your name	Occupation in which you incurred expenses	Social security number

Part I **Employee Business Expenses and Reimbursements**

Step 1 Enter Your Expenses		**Column A** Other Than Meals and Entertainment	**Column B** Meals and Entertainment
1 Vehicle expense from line 22 or line 29. (Rural mail carriers: See instructions.)	1		
2 Parking fees, tolls, and transportation, including train, bus, etc., that **did not** involve overnight travel or commuting to and from work	2		
3 Travel expense while away from home overnight, including lodging, airplane, car rental, etc. **Do not** include meals and entertainment	3		
4 Business expenses not included on lines 1 through 3. **Do not** include meals and entertainment	4		
5 Meals and entertainment expenses (see instructions)	5		
6 **Total expenses.** In Column A, add lines 1 through 4 and enter the result. In Column B, enter the amount from line 5	6		

Note. *If you were not reimbursed for any expenses in Step 1, skip line 7 and enter the amount from line 6 on line 8.*

Step 2 Enter Reimbursements Received From Your Employer for Expenses Listed in Step 1

7 Enter reimbursements received from your employer that were **not** reported to you in box 1 of Form W-2. Include any reimbursements reported under code "L" in box 12 of your Form W-2 (see instructions)	7		

Step 3 Figure Expenses To Deduct on Schedule A (Form 1040 or Form 1040NR)

8 Subtract line 7 from line 6. If zero or less, enter -0-. However, if line 7 is greater than line 6 in Column A, report the excess as income on Form 1040, line 7 (or on Form 1040NR, line 8)	8		
Note. *If **both columns** of line 8 are zero, you cannot deduct employee business expenses. Stop here and attach Form 2106 to your return.*			
9 In Column A, enter the amount from line 8. In Column B, multiply line 8 by 50% (.50). (Employees subject to Department of Transportation (DOT) hours of service limits: Multiply meal expenses incurred while away from home on business by 80% (.80) instead of 50%. For details, see instructions.)	9		
10 Add the amounts on line 9 of both columns and enter the total here. **Also, enter the total on Schedule A (Form 1040), line 21** (or on **Schedule A (Form 1040NR), line 7**). (Armed Forces reservists, qualified performing artists, fee-basis state or local government officials, and individuals with disabilities: See the instructions for special rules on where to enter the total.) ▶	10		

For Paperwork Reduction Act Notice, see your tax return instructions. Cat. No. 11700N Form **2106** (2015)

(Use for Cumulative Problem.)

Form 2106 (2015) Page **2**

Part II Vehicle Expenses

Section A—General Information (You must complete this section if you are claiming vehicle expenses.)		**(a)** Vehicle 1	**(b)** Vehicle 2
11 Enter the date the vehicle was placed in service	**11**	/ /	/ /
12 Total miles the vehicle was driven during 2015	**12**	miles	miles
13 Business miles included on line 12	**13**	miles	miles
14 Percent of business use. Divide line 13 by line 12	**14**	%	%
15 Average daily roundtrip commuting distance	**15**	miles	miles
16 Commuting miles included on line 12	**16**	miles	miles
17 Other miles. Add lines 13 and 16 and subtract the total from line 12	**17**	miles	miles

18 Was your vehicle available for personal use during off-duty hours? ☐ **Yes** ☐ **No**

19 Do you (or your spouse) have another vehicle available for personal use? ☐ **Yes** ☐ **No**

20 Do you have evidence to support your deduction? ☐ **Yes** ☐ **No**

21 If "Yes," is the evidence written? ☐ **Yes** ☐ **No**

Section B—Standard Mileage Rate (See the instructions for Part II to find out whether to complete this section or Section C.)

22 Multiply line 13 by 57.5¢ (.575). Enter the result here and on line 1 . . . **22** ______

Section C—Actual Expenses		**(a)** Vehicle 1	**(b)** Vehicle 2
23 Gasoline, oil, repairs, vehicle insurance, etc.	**23**		
24a Vehicle rentals	**24a**		
b Inclusion amount (see instructions)	**24b**		
c Subtract line 24b from line 24a	**24c**		
25 Value of employer-provided vehicle (applies only if 100% of annual lease value was included on Form W-2—see instructions)	**25**		
26 Add lines 23, 24c, and 25	**26**		
27 Multiply line 26 by the percentage on line 14	**27**		
28 Depreciation (see instructions)	**28**		
29 Add lines 27 and 28. Enter total here and on line 1	**29**		

Section D—Depreciation of Vehicles (Use this section only if you owned the vehicle and are completing Section C for the vehicle.)		**(a)** Vehicle 1	**(b)** Vehicle 2
30 Enter cost or other basis (see instructions)	**30**		
31 Enter section 179 deduction (see instructions)	**31**		
32 Multiply line 30 by line 14 (see instructions if you claimed the section 179 deduction or special allowance)	**32**		
33 Enter depreciation method and percentage (see instructions)	**33**		
34 Multiply line 32 by the percentage on line 33 (see instructions)	**34**		
35 Add lines 31 and 34	**35**		
36 Enter the applicable limit explained in the line 36 instructions	**36**		
37 Multiply line 36 by the percentage on line 14	**37**		
38 Enter the **smaller** of line 35 or line 37. If you skipped lines 36 and 37, enter the amount from line 35. Also enter this amount on line 28 above	**38**		

Form **2106** (2015)

(Use for Cumulative Problem.)

Form **2441**

Department of the Treasury
Internal Revenue Service (99)

Child and Dependent Care Expenses

► Attach to Form 1040, Form 1040A, or Form 1040NR.

► Information about Form 2441 and its separate instructions is at *www.irs.gov/form2441*.

1040
1040A
1040NR
2441

OMB No. 1545-0074

2015

Attachment Sequence No. **21**

Name(s) shown on return | Your social security number

Part I **Persons or Organizations Who Provided the Care—**You **must** complete this part. (If you have more than two care providers, see the instructions.)

1 (a) Care provider's name	(b) Address (number, street, apt. no., city, state, and ZIP code)	(c) Identifying number (SSN or EIN)	(d) Amount paid (see instructions)

Did you receive **dependent care benefits?** No ⟶ Complete only Part II below. Yes ⟶ Complete Part III on the back next.

Caution. If the care was provided in your home, you may owe employment taxes. If you do, you cannot file Form 1040A. For details, see the instructions for Form 1040, line 60a, or Form 1040NR, line 59a.

Part II **Credit for Child and Dependent Care Expenses**

2 Information about your **qualifying person(s).** If you have more than two qualifying persons, see the instructions.

(a) Qualifying person's name — First	Last	(b) Qualifying person's social security number	(c) **Qualified expenses** you incurred and paid in 2015 for the person listed in column (a)

3 Add the amounts in column (c) of line 2. **Do not** enter more than $3,000 for one qualifying person or $6,000 for two or more persons. If you completed Part III, enter the amount from line 31 . . . . . **3**

4 Enter your **earned income.** See instructions **4**

5 If married filing jointly, enter your spouse's earned income (if you or your spouse was a student or was disabled, see the instructions); **all others**, enter the amount from line 4 . **5**

6 Enter the **smallest** of line 3, 4, or 5 . . . . . **6**

7 Enter the amount from Form 1040, line 38; Form 1040A, line 22; or Form 1040NR, line 37 . . . . . **7**

8 Enter on line 8 the decimal amount shown below that applies to the amount on line 7

If line 7 is: Over	But not over	Decimal amount is	If line 7 is: Over	But not over	Decimal amount is
$0	15,000	.35	$29,000	31,000	.27
15,000	17,000	.34	31,000	33,000	.26
17,000	19,000	.33	33,000	35,000	.25
19,000	21,000	.32	35,000	37,000	.24
21,000	23,000	.31	37,000	39,000	.23
23,000	25,000	.30	39,000	41,000	.22
25,000	27,000	.29	41,000	43,000	.21
27,000	29,000	.28	43,000	No limit	.20

8 X.

9 Multiply line 6 by the decimal amount on line 8. If you paid 2014 expenses in 2015, see the instructions **9**

10 Tax liability limit. Enter the amount from the Credit Limit Worksheet in the instructions. **10**

11 **Credit for child and dependent care expenses.** Enter the **smaller** of line 9 or line 10 here and on Form 1040, line 49; Form 1040A, line 31; or Form 1040NR, line 47 . . . . **11**

For Paperwork Reduction Act Notice, see your tax return instructions. Cat. No. 11862M Form **2441** (2015)

Chapter 7

Self-Employment

CHAPTER CONTENTS

LEARNING OBJECTIVES

After completing Chapter 7, you should be able to:

1. Compare and contrast the reporting of income and deductions for cash vs. accrual basis taxpayers.
2. Distinguish between self-employment income and income not from self-employment.
3. Recognize the expenses deducted on Schedule C and compute the amount of the deduction.
4. Understand when the home office deduction can be taken and compute the amount of the deduction.
5. Compute a sole proprietor's self-employment tax.
6. Understand the various types of retirement plans available to self-employed persons.
7. Prepare the forms and schedules introduced in this chapter, including Schedule C, Schedule SE, and Form 8829.

CHAPTER OVERVIEW

Chapters 1 through 6 presented the basic structure for reporting income and deductions. This chapter focuses on the tax reporting for self-employed taxpayers. It shows how they compute their self-employment profits or losses and self-employment taxes. This chapter also covers retirement plans available to self-employed persons.

Sole proprietors report income and expenses on Schedule C, Profit or Loss From Business. They then compute the self-employment tax on their profits on Schedule SE, Self-Employment Tax. After they complete Schedules C and SE, they can compute the amount they can contribute (and deduct for AGI) to their retirement plans.

To understand the reporting process for self-employed taxpayers, it is important to realize that tax and financial accounting rules may differ. Thus, profits reported on Schedule C may not be the same as the net income reflected on the "books" of the business. For example, self-employed taxpayers who sell business property do not report the gain or loss on Schedule C. Instead, they report it on Form 4797, Sales of Business Property. However, for financial accounting purposes, they include the gain or loss in computing "book" net income. With the exception of the section on self-employment tax and retirement plans for self-employed taxpayers, the scope of this chapter is limited to income and expense items reported on Schedule C.

¶701 Accounting Methods

All businesses must keep records to support the calculation of taxable income. Most taxpayers use either the cash or accrual method of accounting. Taxpayers using the cash method to report income must use it to deduct expenses. Likewise, those who deduct expenses using the accrual method must use the accrual method to report income. Some taxpayers use one method for tax purposes and another for their financial statements.

Taxpayers may use the accrual method to compute business profits and the cash method for their nonbusiness items. Those with more than one business may use different accounting methods for each separate and distinct business. Most businesses with gross receipts in excess of $5 million must use the accrual method.

¶701.01 CASH METHOD

Under the cash method, taxpayers report income when they actually or constructively receive it. Taxpayers constructively receive income when it is credited to their accounts or made available to them without restrictions. Constructive receipt has nothing to do with when the taxpayer actually takes possession of the cash. Instead, it has to do with when the taxpayer is entitled to the cash.

EXAMPLE 1

On December 31, 20x1, Carson receives a check for $200 in payment of fees earned. Carson constructively receives the $200 in 20x1, even if the check cannot be cashed until January 2, 20x2. Thus, Carson reports the $200 as income in 20x1.

EXAMPLE 2

On December 30, 20x1, Jamie receives a check for $500 as payment for services rendered. The customer informs Jamie that the check will bounce if cashed before January 2, 20x2. Because the funds are not available until 20x2, Jamie has not constructively received the $500 in 20x1. Jamie reports the $500 as income in 20x2.

Taxpayers who sell services rather than merchandise often use the cash method of accounting. For example, lawyers who use the cash method will keep logs of fees charged to clients but record the fees as income only upon receipt of the cash. Taxpayers who receive income other than cash report as income the fair market value (FMV) of the property or services received.

EXAMPLE 3

Scott receives ten shares of stock in exchange for services rendered. The market value of a share of stock is $28. Scott reports income of $280 ($28 × 10 shares).

Under the cash method, taxpayers deduct expenses when they pay the cash, but only if the expenses relate to the current or a previous tax year. Taxpayers usually deduct prepaid amounts in the year the prepaid item is used in their businesses. Thus, cash basis taxpayers who prepay rent, insurance, etc., must wait until it is used in their businesses before they deduct it.

EXAMPLE 4

On September 23, 20x1, Ming pays $36,000 for two years' insurance coverage that begins on October 1, 20x1. Although Ming is a cash basis taxpayer, she cannot deduct the $36,000 payment in 20x1. Instead she deducts $4,500 ($36,000/24 × 3) in 20x1. Ming will deduct $18,000 ($36,000/24 × 12) in 20x2 and the rest ($36,000/24 × 9 = $13,500) in 20x3.

¶701.02 ACCRUAL METHOD

Under the accrual method, income includes amounts earned or accrued but not received. Expenses include liabilities incurred but not paid. The accrual method acts on the right to receive the revenue rather than the actual receipt of cash. It acts on the use of the asset or service rather than the actual cash payment.

EXAMPLE 5

On January 3, 20x2, an employer pays salaries that its employees earned for the week ended December 31, 20x1. Under the accrual method, the employer reports the salaries as an expense in 20x1. Under the cash method, the employer reports the expense in 20x2.

Taxpayers account for prepaid expenses the same way under both the cash and accrual methods. That is, they deduct only the amounts properly allocable to a given year and carry forward the rest to the next year. In Example 4, the amount deducted each year would be the same had Ming used the accrual method of accounting.

The tax law generally requires taxpayers using the accrual method to recognize prepaid income in the year they receive it. However, when the taxpayer sells goods or performs services that extend beyond the current tax year, most prepaid income can be spread over the current year and the next tax year. Also, many accrual-method taxpayers do not have to accrue service revenue that experience indicates will not be collectible. These taxpayers include those who perform certain services (like health, law, consulting) and those whose businesses had average annual gross receipts of $5 million or less for the last three years.

EXAMPLE 6

Kent is in the business of selling and repairing televisions. On April 1, 20x1, Kent receives $1,200 from one of his customers for a 2-year warranty contract. Kent spreads his prepaid income over two tax years. He reports $450 ($1,200 × 9 months/24 months) on his 20x1 tax return, and the rest ($1,200 – $450 = $750) on his 20x2 tax return. Kent must report the entire $1,200 on his 20x1 and 20x2 tax returns, even though some of the services extend into 20x3.

The exception that allows accrual method taxpayers to spread out prepaid income over two tax years, does not extend to prepaid interest and most prepaid rent. It also does not extend to prepaid warranty income received by third parties. A third-party provider is one who did not sell the goods being warranted to the customer to whom the warranty is sold. Taxpayers who receive these types of prepaid items report the full amounts in income in the year they receive it.

EXAMPLE 7

Same facts as in Example 6, except that Kent offers the warranty contract as a third-party provider. Kent must report the entire $1,200 in gross income in 20x1.

¶702 Reporting Business Profit or Loss

There are several forms in which businesses can operate. One of the most popular and easiest to start is the sole proprietorship. As the name implies, this type of business can only have a single owner, who must be an individual. When a business is operated as a sole proprietorship, all activities of the business are reported on the owner's tax return. The details of reporting the profit and loss of self-employed persons (sole proprietors) is the focus of this chapter.

Partnerships and corporations are other means through which businesses can operate. Partnerships and corporations are entities separate from their owners and must file separate income tax returns. The details of these businesses' tax returns are discussed in Chapters 14–16.

A self-employed taxpayer who owns a business reports net profit or (loss) on Form 1040. Schedule C, Profit or Loss From Business, summarizes the revenues and expenses of sole proprietors. Only self-employment income and related expenses are reported on Schedule C.

Income reported on Schedule C comes from revenues earned while operating a business as a sole proprietorship. It can result from part-time or full-time activities. Self-employment income includes gross receipts from sales (for businesses that sell goods), as well as fees earned by service providers, clergymen, and Christian Science practitioners. Also reported on Schedule C are royalties authors receive, fees earned by serving on the Board of Directors for a corporation (director's fees), fees earned by professional executors (those whose business is managing estates), and commissions earned by real estate agents.

Sometimes determining whether earnings are reported as self-employment income depends on where the services are rendered. For example, fees charged by a childcare provider (babysitter) are reported on Schedule C only if the services are provided outside of the parent's home. Other times it is the party who employs the worker that determines whether the earnings are reported on Schedule C. For instance, when a registered nurse or licensed practicing nurse is employed directly by the patient, the earnings are reported on the nurse's Schedule C. However, if the nurse is employed by an agency, doctor, or a hospital to care for a patient, the nurse's earnings are considered wages.

In the case of newspaper vendors and carriers, the worker's age determines whether the earnings are self-employment income or wages. The earnings of a newspaper vendor or carrier over the age of 17 are reported on Schedule C; whereas the earnings of a vendor or carrier under the age of 18 are treated as wages.

There are many items of income that are not reported on Schedule C. For instance, interest earned on the taxpayer's investments is not business income. Instead, it is reported as a separate line item on the tax return (see discussion at ¶308.09). However, interest earned on business accounts (like from customer balances or the business bank account) is reported as other income on Schedule C.

Rental income from real estate holdings is not reported on Schedule C, unless the taxpayer's business involves rental real estate. Most rental activities are considered passive activities, and are reported on Schedule E, Supplemental Income or Loss. Rental activities and Schedule E are the focus of Chapter 9.

Gains and losses from the sale of business property (other than inventory) are not reported as part of business profit or loss on Schedule C. These gains and losses are reported on Form 4797, Sales of Business Property, and appear on a separate line item from business profits on page 1 of Form 1040. The sale of business property is discussed in Chapter 11.

¶703 Reporting Net Profit (or Loss) by Sole Proprietorships

Net profit derived from a business operated as a sole proprietorship is taxable. A net loss is deducted in arriving at adjusted gross income. In computing the amount of net profit (or loss), sole proprietors subtract from business income the cost of goods sold and all deductible business expenses. To be deductible, expenses from a business must be *ordinary and necessary* for its operation. Also, the expenses must be *reasonable* in amount. An expense is ordinary if it is customary or usual in the taxpayer's line of business. An expense is necessary if it helps the taxpayer's business. The costs of capital expenditures (assets lasting more than one year), such as trucks, office machinery, and buildings, are deducted over several years through annual depreciation deductions. Depreciation is the focus of Chapter 8.

Sole proprietorships report net profit on either Schedule C-EZ, Net Profit From Business, or Schedule C, Profit or Loss From Business. Sole proprietorship reporting a net loss must file Schedule C. Furthermore, only certain businesses can file Schedule C-EZ. This chapter focuses on completing Schedule C.

Requirements for Using Schedule C-EZ

- Cash method of accounting is used
- Taxpayer operated only one business as a sole proprietor
- No employees during the year
- No inventory at any time during the year
- Business expenses of $5,000 or less
- No net loss from the business
- No unallowed prior year passive activity loss from the business
- No deduction for business use of the home
- Not required to file Form 4562, Depreciation and Amortization, for the business

¶704 Structure of Schedule C

Schedule C, Profit or Loss From Business, is a two-page schedule that reports the net profit or (loss) from a business operated as a sole proprietorship. A sole proprietor must pay self-employment tax on Schedule C profits. When a married couple files a joint return and each spouse owns a business, each spouse must file a Schedule C. If only one spouse owns a business, only the owner's name appears on Schedule C. If a proprietor owns more than one business, a separate Schedule C must be filed for each business.

Schedule C (Figure 7-1) supports the amount shown on Form 1040, page 1 (line 12). Page 1 of Schedule C focuses on the calculation of net profit (or loss). It also requests general information about the business. Page 2 provides the supporting data for cost of goods sold, vehicle expenses, and Other Expenses reported on page 1.

¶704.01 FILLED-IN SCHEDULE C

INFORMATION FOR FIGURE 7-1:

Monroe Peters is the owner of Monroe L. Peters, Consulting (line C). Monroe operates the business out of his home, which is located at 1712 Market Street, Cincinnati, Ohio 45227-3193 (line E). He uses the cash method (line F) and materially participates in the operation of his consulting business (line G). The principal business code for consulting is 541600 (line B), which is found in instructions to Schedule C. Because Monroe is required to withhold and pay payroll taxes on behalf of his employees, he has an Employer ID number, which he reports on Schedule C (line D).

Figure 7-1: Filled-In Schedule C (Page 1)

SCHEDULE C (Form 1040)
Department of the Treasury
Internal Revenue Service (99)

Profit or Loss From Business
(Sole Proprietorship)
▶ **Information about Schedule C and its separate instructions is at *www.irs.gov/schedulec.***
▶ **Attach to Form 1040, 1040NR, or 1041; partnerships generally must file Form 1065.**

OMB No. 1545-0074
2015
Attachment Sequence No. **09**

Name of proprietor: **Monroe L. Peters**
Social security number (SSN): **139-24-6860**

A Principal business or profession, including product or service (see instructions): **Management Consultant**
B Enter code from instructions ▶ **5 4 1 6 0 0**

C Business name. If no separate business name, leave blank.: **Monroe L. Peters, Consulting**
D Employer ID number (EIN), (see instr.): **3 9 6 4 2 0 7 9 7**

E Business address (including suite or room no.) ▶ **1712 Market Street**
City, town or post office, state, and ZIP code: **Cincinnati, Ohio 45227-3193**

F Accounting method: **(1)** ☑ Cash **(2)** ☐ Accrual **(3)** ☐ Other (specify) ▶

G Did you "materially participate" in the operation of this business during 2015? If "No," see instructions for limit on losses . ☑ **Yes** ☐ **No**

H If you started or acquired this business during 2015, check here . . . ▶ ☐

I Did you make any payments in 2015 that would require you to file Form(s) 1099? (see instructions) . . . ☐ **Yes** ☑ **No**

J If "Yes," did you or will you file required Forms 1099? . . . ☐ **Yes** ☐ **No**

Part I Income

1	Gross receipts or sales. See instructions for line 1 and check the box if this income was reported to you on Form W-2 and the "Statutory employee" box on that form was checked . . . ▶ ☐	1	156,921
2	Returns and allowances . . .	2	
3	Subtract line 2 from line 1 . . .	3	156,921
4	Cost of goods sold (from line 42) . . .	4	
5	**Gross profit.** Subtract line 4 from line 3 . . .	5	156,921
6	Other income, including federal and state gasoline or fuel tax credit or refund (see instructions) . . .	6	
7	**Gross income.** Add lines 5 and 6 . . . ▶	7	156,921

Part II Expenses. Enter expenses for business use of your home **only** on line 30.

8	Advertising . . .	8	492	18	Office expense (see instructions)	18	1,640
9	Car and truck expenses (see instructions) . . .	9	2,940	19	Pension and profit-sharing plans .	19	
				20	Rent or lease (see instructions):		
10	Commissions and fees .	10		a	Vehicles, machinery, and equipment	20a	1,200
11	Contract labor (see instructions)	11		b	Other business property . . .	20b	
12	Depletion . . .	12		21	Repairs and maintenance . . .	21	1,389
13	Depreciation and section 179 expense deduction (not included in Part III) (see instructions) . . .	13	1,619	22	Supplies (not included in Part III) .	22	1,642
				23	Taxes and licenses . . .	23	7,210
				24	Travel, meals, and entertainment:		
14	Employee benefit programs (other than on line 19) . .	14		a	Travel . . .	24a	842
15	Insurance (other than health)	15	742	b	Deductible meals and entertainment (see instructions) .	24b	215
16	Interest:			25	Utilities . . .	25	3,600
a	Mortgage (paid to banks, etc.)	16a		26	Wages (less employment credits) .	26	40,616
b	Other . . .	16b		27a	Other expenses (from line 48) . .	27a	780
17	Legal and professional services	17	310	b	**Reserved for future use** . . .	27b	

28	**Total expenses** before expenses for business use of home. Add lines 8 through 27a . . . ▶	28	65,237
29	Tentative profit or (loss). Subtract line 28 from line 7 . . .	29	91,684
30	Expenses for business use of your home. Do not report these expenses elsewhere. Attach Form 8829 unless using the simplified method (see instructions). **Simplified method filers only:** enter the total square footage of: (a) your home: ______ and (b) the part of your home used for business: ______ . Use the Simplified Method Worksheet in the instructions to figure the amount to enter on line 30 . . .	30	1,084
31	**Net profit or (loss).** Subtract line 30 from line 29. • If a profit, enter on both **Form 1040, line 12** (or **Form 1040NR, line 13**) and on **Schedule SE, line 2.** (If you checked the box on line 1, see instructions). Estates and trusts, enter on **Form 1041, line 3.** • If a loss, you **must** go to line 32.	31	90,600

32 If you have a loss, check the box that describes your investment in this activity (see instructions).
• If you checked 32a, enter the loss on both **Form 1040, line 12,** (or **Form 1040NR, line 13**) and on **Schedule SE, line 2.** (If you checked the box on line 1, see the line 31 instructions). Estates and trusts, enter on **Form 1041, line 3.**
• If you checked 32b, you **must** attach **Form 6198.** Your loss may be limited.

32a ☐ All investment is at risk.
32b ☐ Some investment is not at risk.

For Paperwork Reduction Act Notice, see the separate instructions. Cat. No. 11334P **Schedule C (Form 1040) 2015**

Figure 7-1: Filled-In Schedule C (Page 2)

Schedule C (Form 1040) 2015 Page 2

Part III Cost of Goods Sold (see instructions)

33 Method(s) used to value closing inventory: a ☐ Cost b ☐ Lower of cost or market c ☐ Other (attach explanation)

34 Was there any change in determining quantities, costs, or valuations between opening and closing inventory? If "Yes," attach explanation . . . ☐ Yes ☐ No

35 Inventory at beginning of year. If different from last year's closing inventory, attach explanation	35	
36 Purchases less cost of items withdrawn for personal use	36	
37 Cost of labor. Do not include any amounts paid to yourself	37	
38 Materials and supplies	38	
39 Other costs	39	
40 Add lines 35 through 39	40	
41 Inventory at end of year	41	
42 **Cost of goods sold.** Subtract line 41 from line 40. Enter the result here and on line 4	42	

Part IV Information on Your Vehicle. Complete this part **only** if you are claiming car or truck expenses on line 9 and are not required to file Form 4562 for this business. See the instructions for line 13 to find out if you must file Form 4562.

43 When did you place your vehicle in service for business purposes? (month, day, year) ▶ / /

44 Of the total number of miles you drove your vehicle during 2015, enter the number of miles you used your vehicle for:

a Business ______ b Commuting (see instructions) ______ c Other ______

45 Was your vehicle available for personal use during off-duty hours? . . . ☐ Yes ☐ No

46 Do you (or your spouse) have another vehicle available for personal use? . . . ☐ Yes ☐ No

47a Do you have evidence to support your deduction? . . . ☐ Yes ☐ No

b If "Yes," is the evidence written? . . . ☐ Yes ☐ No

Part V Other Expenses. List below business expenses not included on lines 8–26 or line 30.

Education expense		780
48 **Total other expenses.** Enter here and on line 27a	48	780

Schedule C (Form 1040) 2015

¶705 Item-by-Item Reporting on Schedule C

This section explains each line item shown on Schedule C. The amounts reported relate to Monroe Peters's filled-in Schedule C from Figure 7-1.

¶705.01 SCHEDULE C, PART I: INCOME

Total Gross Receipts, $156,921 (Line 1)

In addition to gross receipts from the business, statutory employees report their W-2 wages on Schedule C (line 1). [Recall that statutory employees are a type of worker that report their W-2 wages and job-related expenses on Schedule C (¶601)]. Monroe uses the cash method. He reports the $156,921 actually and constructively received during the year.

Returns and Allowances, $0 (Line 2)

Taxpayers subtract returns and allowances from total gross receipts. Since Monroe operates a service business, he had no returns or allowances.

Cost of Goods Sold, $0 (Line 4)

Taxpayers report their cost of goods sold on Schedule C (line 4) and subtract it from the amount on Schedule C (line 3) to arrive at their gross profit (line 5). Taxpayers calculate cost of goods sold on Schedule C, Part III (covered later in the chapter). Since Monroe's business does not involve selling products, he does not complete Part III. Monroe's gross profit (reported on line 5) is $156,921.

Gross Income, $156,921 (Line 7)

Gross income equals other income (line 6) plus gross profit (line 5). Other income includes interest income earned by the business.

¶705.02 SCHEDULE C, PART II: EXPENSES

Sole proprietors generally deduct all ordinary, necessary, and reasonable expenses of operating a business. Schedule C, Part II lists 19 separate expenses that sole proprietors can deduct.

Advertising, $492 (Line 8)

Taxpayers generally can deduct advertising expenses related to their businesses. They cannot, however, deduct advertising for purposes of influencing legislation.

Car and Truck Expenses, $2,940 (Line 9)

The tax laws for computing an employee's transportation expense deduction (see ¶602.03) are the same ones self-employed taxpayers use to compute their car and truck expense deduction on Schedule C (line 9). Taxpayers use either the standard mileage rate ($.575 per business mile in 2015) or the business portion of their actual costs, and add to that amount their business parking and tolls. Self-employed taxpayers not required to file Form 4562, Depreciation and Amortization, must complete Schedule C, Part IV to support their deductions. Monroe uses the standard mileage rate method. Monroe drove a total of 5,113 business miles in 2015. His car and truck expense deduction equals $2,940 (5,113 × $.575).

EXAMPLE 8

In 2015, Terry drove 6,000 business miles and 20,000 total miles. In 2014, Terry used the actual cost method and accelerated depreciation to deduct expenses related to the business use of his car. Terry's expenses for the car are as follows.

Business parking and tolls	$ 100
Depreciation	4,000
Gas	1,000
Insurance	450
License tags	50
Oil change	20
Total	$5,620

Under the actual cost method, Terry deducts $1,756 [($5,520 × 6,000/20,000) + $100 business parking and tolls]. Since Terry used an accelerated depreciation method in 2014, he must use the actual cost method in 2015 (see discussion at ¶602.03). Had Terry been able to use the standard mileage rate method, his deduction would have been $3,550 [(6,000 × $.575) + $100]

Commissions and Fees, $0 (Line 10)

Taxpayers can deduct commissions and fees paid for business purposes.

Contract Labor, $0 (Line 11)

Taxpayers deduct amounts paid for contract labor on Schedule C (line 11). Contract labor includes amounts paid to workers who are independent contractors. It does not include wages paid to employees. Wages paid to employees are reported on Schedule C (line 26).

Depletion, $0 (Line 12)

Taxpayers operating a business that owns a natural resource, such as an oil well, a coal mine or a gold mine, may claim a depletion deduction. **Depletion** is the process that allows taxpayers to deduct the cost of natural resources as units from the resource are sold (under the accrual method) or sold and payment is received (under the cash method). The two methods for computing the depletion deduction are the cost method and the percentage depletion method. Each year the taxpayer may use whichever method produces the greatest deduction.

The *cost method* allows taxpayers to deduct the costs of natural resources as the resource units are recovered and sold. The cost of the natural resource is divided by the number of units expected to be recovered. This provides depletion per unit. The per unit cost is then multiplied by the number of units sold during the year.

Under the *percentage depletion method,* taxpayers multiply a set percentage by the gross income generated by the resource during the year. The government specifies the percentages used, which range from 5% for sand and gravel to 22% for lead, zinc, tin, and sulfur. A 15% rate applies to copper, gold, silver, iron, oil, and gas. The percentage depletion method has a distinct advantage over cost depletion in that the taxpayer can continue to take the percentage depletion deduction even after the entire cost invested in the natural resource has been fully recovered through annual depletion deductions.

Depreciation and Section 179 Expense Deduction, $1,619 (Line 13)

Monroe completes and attaches Form 4562, Depreciation and Amortization, to support the depreciation and section 179 expense deduction. Depreciation expense is the focus of Chapter 8.

Employee Benefit Programs, $0 (Line 14)

Employers generally can deduct the costs of benefits they provide for their employees. For example, employers can deduct life insurance premiums paid for policies on employees' lives, but only for policies that do not list the employer as the beneficiary. Employers also deduct the cost of health insurance premiums paid on behalf of their employees. Other examples include the costs of adoption assistance, childcare, parking, and transportation provided to employees.

Insurance, $742 (Line 15)

Taxpayers deduct insurance premiums on business property, including real estate, furniture, machinery, and equipment. Employers deduct premiums paid for medical and life insurance for their employees as employee benefits (line 14). As mentioned earlier in the chapter (¶701.01), cash method taxpayers cannot deduct advance payments on policies that cover more than one tax year. They can deduct only the premiums that apply to the current or previous years.

Interest, $0 (Lines 16a and 16b)

Business interest includes interest on mortgages (line 16a) and other business loans (line 16b). If the taxpayer borrows money and uses the loan proceeds partly for nonbusiness purposes, then only the interest related to the business-use portion of the borrowed funds can be deducted.

EXAMPLE 9

Jay borrows funds secured by business property. Jay uses 25% of the funds to buy a personal car. He uses the rest in his business. Jay deducts 75% of the interest on Schedule C. Personal interest is not deductible.

Legal and Professional Services, $310 (Line 17)

Taxpayers can deduct legal and professional fees, including the portion of tax preparation fees that relate to the preparation of Schedule C. They cannot deduct legal fees incurred to acquire business property. Instead, these amounts are added to the amount the taxpayer pays for the property.

Office Expense, $1,640 (Line 18)

Office expense includes postage, stationery, and other general expenses of operating a business office.

Pension and Profit-Sharing Plans, $0 (Line 19)

Sole proprietors deduct on Schedule C amounts they contribute to their employees' qualified pension and profit-sharing plans. Under a qualified plan, the employer must offer the plan to all eligible full-time employees. Two common qualified plans are defined benefit and defined contribution plans.

A **defined benefit plan** focuses on the annual benefits at retirement. Employers must contribute annually to the plan so that the promised benefits will be available at retirement. The benefit formula used in computing the annual contribution considers employees' compensation levels and years of service. This calculation usually requires professional help.

In contrast, a **defined contribution plan** focuses on annual contributions. The amount contributed is usually a percentage of the employee's compensation. Unlike a defined benefit plan, this type of plan promises no predetermined benefits. Instead, annual contributions are made to individual employee accounts. Employees then receive whatever benefits accumulate in their respective accounts.

A **simplified employee pension (SEP) plan** is a defined contribution plan employers can establish for their employees. In 2015, the maximum contribution an employer can make to an employee's SEP is the *lesser of* (i) $53,000 or (ii) 25% of the employee's compensation. For SEP plans established after 1986, only employers (not employees) can make contributions to an employee's SEP.

An alternative to a SEP is a 401(k). The main advantage to a 401(k) over a SEP is that employees can make pre-tax contributions to their 401(k)s, thereby reducing their taxable wages. In 2015, employees can contribute up to $18,000 to a 401(k). Employees age 50 and older can contribute up to $24,000. Employers may contribute to their employees' 401(k)s, but are not required to do so. A common practice for employers is to match 50% of the employee's contributions, up to a certain percentage of the employee's wages. Employers deduct only the matching contributions they make on Schedule C (line 19).

In recent years, some employers have begun offering Roth 401(k)s to their employees. Employees' contributions to a Roth 401(k) are made with after-tax funds. This means that the wages used to contribute to a Roth 401(k) are reported as taxable wages on the employee's Form W-2. Only the employee can contribute to a Roth 401(k). Employer contributions are not allowed. Although contributions to a Roth 401(k) are made with after-tax dollars, all amounts in a Roth 401(k) grow tax-free. Thus, when qualified distributions are eventually made from a Roth 401(k), both employee contributions and the accumulated earnings are exempt from tax. Roth 401(k)s are subject to the same contribution limits that apply to 401(k) plans, including catch up provisions for participants age 50 or older. The $18,000 limit ($24,000 for age 50 and older) applies to all 401(k) contributions made during 2015.

EXAMPLE 10

Bobby is 42 years old. He participates in a 401(k) plan at work. His employer offers both a standard 401(k) and a Roth 401(k). In 2015, Bobby designates that $13,000 of his pre-tax wages be designated to his 401(k). This allows him to designate up to another $5,000 as an after-tax contribution to his Roth 401(k). His taxable wages will be reduced by the $13,000 that he contributes to his (standard) 401(k).

EXAMPLE 11

Same facts as in Example 10, except that Bobby is 51 years old. Bobby can contribute up to $11,000 ($24,000 maximum contribution – $13,000) of his after-tax wages to his Roth 401(k).

Employers that have 100 or fewer employees who earned $5,000 or more in the prior year can adopt a **savings incentive match plan for employees (SIMPLE)**. Employers can set up SIMPLE plans using either IRAs or 401(k)s. Employees who earned at least $5,000 in any two prior years and expect to earn at least $5,000 in the current year would be allowed to contribute up to $12,500 of their salaries to the plan for 2015. Employees age 50 and older can contribute up to $15,500. Employers generally are required to make matching contributions up to 3% of the employee's compensation. Only the employer's contribution is deductible on Schedule C.

Rent or Lease, $1,200 (Line 20a) and $0 (Line 20b)

Rent or lease expense is the amount paid for the use of property not owned by the taxpayer. If the taxpayer will receive title to the property at the end of the lease, then the amount paid is not rent expense. Instead, these payments are included in the purchase price of the property.

Taxpayers can deduct rent on property used in their trade or business. Those that pay rent in advance only deduct the amount that applies to the current or a previous tax year. They deduct the rest in the year or years to which the rent applies.

EXAMPLE 12

> Katy leases property for three years beginning June 1, 20x1. On June 1, 20x1, Katy pays $12,000 for 12 months' rent, but can deduct only $7,000 in 20x1 ($12,000/12 × 7) under both the cash and the accrual methods. On June 1, 20x2, she pays $13,200 for another 12 months' rent. In 20x2, Katy will deduct the remaining $5,000 paid in 20x1, and $7,700 ($13,200/12 × 7) of the $13,200 paid on June 1, 20x2.

Taxpayers who lease a car deduct the costs related to the business-use portion of the lease. Taxpayers must spread any advance lease payments over the entire term of the lease. Payments made to buy a car are not deductible as rent, even if they are described as lease payments. Chapter 8 describes the rules for leased cars.

Repairs and Maintenance, $1,389 (Line 21)

Taxpayers can deduct the costs of keeping business property in its normal operating condition. Repair costs must be distinguished from capital expenditures. Taxpayers capitalize (increase their basis in the property) any costs that either add to the value or usefulness of the property, or significantly extend its useful life. Repairs and maintenance allocable to the cost of goods sold are deducted on Schedule C, Part III when calculating cost of goods sold, not in Part II.

Supplies, $1,642 (Line 22)

Taxpayers can deduct the cost of supplies that they normally use within one year. The cost of supplies not expected to be used within one year are deducted in the year the supplies are used.

Taxes and Licenses, $7,210 (Line 23)

Sole proprietors can deduct property taxes paid on business property. They also can deduct their (the employer's) share of social security and Medicare taxes paid for employees plus amounts paid for state and federal unemployment taxes. Deductible licenses include business licenses required by state and local governments for operating the taxpayer's trade or business.

Travel, $842 (Line 24a), Deductible Meals and Entertainment, $215 (Line 24b)

Chapter 6 presented the rules employees use for deducting travel, meals, and entertainment (¶602.05, ¶602.06). For the most part, the same rules govern the amount sole proprietors can deduct. Amounts owners pay for business-related travel, meals, and entertainment on behalf of themselves or their employees are deductible on Schedule C. When an owner reimburses an employee for work-related expenses, how much of and where on Schedule C the reimbursement is reported, depends on whether the reimbursement was paid from an "accountable" or "nonaccountable" plan.

An accountable plan requires the employee to, (1) adequately report the expenses to the employer, and (2) return any excess reimbursements to the employer (¶602.01). Owners with an accountable plan deduct the reimbursements under "Travel, meals, and entertainment," but can deduct only 50% of the amounts reimbursed for meals and entertainment.

When the reimbursement is made from a nonaccountable plan (one that does not meet both criteria for an accountable plan), the reimbursement is treated as "Wages" and is deductible as such on Schedule C. Employees are taxed on these additional wages and can deduct their work-related expenses (but only 50% of meals and entertainment) as miscellaneous itemized deductions subject to the 2% AGI floor (see discussion at ¶602.02).

EXAMPLE 13

Gene is self-employed. He reimburses an employee $10,000 for travel expenses and $2,000 for meals and entertainment under an accountable plan. Gene deducts $10,000 as travel on Schedule C (line 24a) and $1,000 (50% × $2,000) as deductible meals and entertainment (line 24b).

EXAMPLE 14

Same facts as in Example 13, except that Gene has a nonaccountable plan. Gene deducts all $12,000 as wages on Schedule C (line 26). The employee is taxed on the $12,000, and can deduct $11,000 (only 50% of meals and entertainment) as a miscellaneous itemized deduction subject to the 2% AGI floor.

Deductible Travel Expenses

- Air, rail, and bus transportation, including transportation to and from the airport and the hotel
- Baggage handling charges
- Dry cleaning and laundry
- Lodging
- Meals and entertainment (subject to limitations)
- Car expenses, including car rental
- Telephone, internet, and fax costs
- Tips related to travel

As was mentioned in Chapter 6, some employers use the "per diem" approach to reimburse employees for the costs of meals and lodging. Employers deduct a reimbursement based on a per diem amount as "Travel, meals, and entertainment," but deduct only 50% of the per diem meal allowance. The rules regarding the use of per diems in lieu of actual expenses for meals also apply to sole proprietors. However, the per diem for lodging can only be used for purposes of reimbursing employees. When the owner of the business is away from home overnight on business, the owner must deduct the actual costs for lodging.

When a person's travels combine business and pleasure, only the business portion of the trip can be deducted. The rules described for employees in ¶602.05 also apply to sole proprietors. Thus, when taking a business trip in the U.S., the costs of traveling to and from the destination are only allowed if the trip is primarily (more than 50%) for business. When the trip involves travel outside of the U.S., the costs of traveling to and from the destination must be prorated unless one of the three exceptions described in ¶602.05 applies. For all travels, the business portion of all other expenses is deductible.

EXAMPLE 15

Mandy is self-employed. During the year, Mandy takes a business trip to Boston. She is gone a total of six days (five nights), four of which were spent conducting business. Her travel costs include $600 for airfare, $220 for transportation to and from the airport, $150 a night for lodging, and $60 a day for meals. The per diem for Boston was $270, which includes $203 for lodging, and $67 for meals and incidentals.

Because her trip is primarily for business (4/6 > 50%), Mandy can deduct the $820 she spent for traveling to and from the destination ($600 + $220). The $67 daily per diem rate for meals exceeds her actual costs for meals. Thus, she is allowed to deduct $134 ($67 × 4 days × 50%) for business meals. She also can deduct $450 for lodging ($150 × 3 nights). Although the nightly per diem for lodging ($203) exceeds her actual daily lodging costs ($150), sole proprietors cannot use the per diem rates for lodging. They must deduct their actual lodging costs.

EXAMPLE 16

Lucas is self-employed. During the year, Lucas sends his employee on a business trip to Boston. The employee is gone four days (three nights), all of which were spent conducting business. The employee's actual travel costs include $600 for airfare, $220 for transportation to and from the airport, $150 a night for lodging, and $60 a day for meals. The per diem for Boston was $270, which includes $203 for lodging, and $67 for meals and incidentals.

Lucas reimburses the employee $1,697 under an accountable reimbursement plan. This amount includes $820 for traveling to and from the destination ($600 + $220), $609 for lodging ($203 × 3), and $268 ($67 × 4) for meals. The employee is not taxed on the $1,697 reimbursement. On his Schedule C, Lucas deducts $1,429 ($820 + $609) for travel (line 24a) and $134 ($268 × 50%) for meals (line 24b).

EXAMPLE 17

Same facts as Example 16, except that Lucas advances the employee $1,500 before the trip and does not require the employee to turn in receipts for amounts spent on the trip. Lucas now has made a reimbursement from a nonaccountable plan. He adds the $1,500 to the employee's taxable wages on Form W-2. He then deducts the $1,500 as wage expense on Schedule C (line 26). It is up to the employee to report his deductible travel expenses on Form 2106. These amounts will then be deducted as miscellaneous itemized deductions (subject to the 2% AGI floor) on the employee's Schedule A.

Utilities, $3,600 (Line 25)

Utilities include the costs for heat, power, water, and telephone. Taxpayers can deduct the costs for utilities to the extent the costs are not incurred for personal use. Taxpayers deduct utilities for an office located in their home on Form 8829, Business Use of the Home (covered later in the chapter at ¶705.03).

Wages, $40,616 (Line 26)

Employers deduct amounts paid as wages to employees. They also deduct amounts paid to employees as bonuses, vacation pay, taxable employee achievement awards, and reimbursements under nonaccountable plans. The amount shown for wages on Schedule C (line 26) does not include wages included in cost of goods sold or withdrawals the owner makes from the business.

Other Expenses, $780 (Line 27)

Other expenses are amounts not deductible elsewhere on Schedule C. Sole proprietors deducting other expenses list the type and amount of each expense on Schedule C, page 2, Part V. Total other expenses from Part V are transferred to Schedule C, Part II (line 27). Four common other expenses sole proprietors may have are education expenses, business gifts, dues and subscriptions, and bad debts.

Self-employed taxpayers can deduct professional dues and subscriptions related to their line of business. They also can deduct the ordinary and necessary costs incurred to educate and train employees in operating the business. Deductible education expenses include tuition, books, transportation, meals (subject to the 50% rule), and lodging. In addition, sole proprietors can deduct amounts spent on their own education as long as it does not (1) prepare them to meet the minimum education requirements of their present profession or (2) qualify them for a new trade or business. Assuming neither of these situations apply, to deduct these costs, sole proprietors must show that the education (1) maintains or improves the skills required in their business or (2) is required by law to keep their status in the profession. The rules for deducting education expenses for self-employed taxpayers are essentially the same as those presented in Chapter 6 for employees (see ¶602.07). Monroe deducts $780 for educational courses taken in during the year.

EXAMPLE 18

Raines is a self-employed tax accountant. Raines holds a Bachelor of Science degree in accounting. He is currently taking night classes in pursuit of his law degree. During the year, his education costs include $2,500 for tuition, $620 for books and $220 for transportation. Since getting a law degree will allow him to enter a new profession (the practice of law), the costs of his education are not deductible on Schedule C. The fact that the content of the courses will enable him to be a better tax accountant are irrelevant if the courses are part of a program of study that will enable him to enter into a new (different) profession.

EXAMPLE 19

Same facts as in Example 18, except that the classes Raines is taking are in pursuit of a Masters of Taxation degree. Since completion of this degree prepares Raines to be a tax accountant (which he already is), the education is not preparing him to enter into a new profession. Instead, the courses help him improve his skills at his existing profession. Thus, Raines can deduct $3,340 ($2,500 + $620 + $220) as an other expense on Schedule C, Part V.

Sole proprietors can deduct the costs of business gifts to customers and clients. The maximum deduction cannot exceed $25 for business gifts given to any one person during the tax year. Gifts not subject to the $25 limit include:

1. A widely distributed item costing $4 or less on which the donor's company name is permanently imprinted. Examples include pens and key chains.
2. Signs, display racks, and other promotional material used on the recipient's business premises.
3. Incidental costs, such as engraving, packaging, insuring, and mailing the gift.

i

Employees can deduct the costs of business gifts to clients and customers using these same rules. They can deduct the cost of gifts they make to people who work for them. They cannot deduct the cost of gifts to people they work for (their bosses). Employees deduct these costs as miscellaneous itemized deductions subject to the 2% AGI floor.

Any item that can be considered either a gift or entertainment generally is considered entertainment. A taxpayer who gives a business client tickets to an event but does not attend the event with the client can treat the tickets either as a gift or as entertainment. However, if the taxpayer goes with the client to the event, the tickets must be treated as entertainment. Employers also may deduct property valued at up to $400 given to employees for their length of service or safety achievement.

EXAMPLE 20

Tori is self-employed. During the current year Tori pays $35 for a ticket to a sporting event. She gives the ticket to a client. She does not attend the event with her client. Tori can choose between treating the $35 as either a business gift or as entertainment. If she includes the $35 as entertainment, she will deduct $17.50 ($35 × 50%). Tori would be better off deducting $25 (maximum deduction for business gifts) as a business gift on Schedule C, Part V.

EXAMPLE 21

Same facts as in Example 20, except that the ticket costs $75. Since the deduction for business gifts is limited to $25, Tori would be better off taking the cost of the tickets as entertainment expense. She will deduct $37.50 ($75 × 50%) on Schedule C (line 24b).

EXAMPLE 22

Same facts as in Example 20, except that Tori attends the event with her client. Tori must treat the cost of the ticket as entertainment expense. Thus, she will be able to deduct 50% of the costs of the tickets for her client and herself.

Taxpayers deduct bad debts that result from business operations. Bad debts may result from credit sales to customers. They also may result from loans to suppliers, clients, employees, or distributors. Sole proprietors deduct bad debts when a receivable, or a portion of a receivable, becomes uncollectible (known as the direct write-off method). The tax law does not permit the use of the "reserve" method, which is an acceptable financial accounting practice. For a bad debt to be deductible, a true creditor-debtor relationship must exist between the taxpayer (creditor) and the debtor. Also, the taxpayer must incur an actual loss of money or have previously reported the amount owed in gross income. Thus, a cash basis taxpayer who renders services cannot take a bad debt deduction when a customer's receivable becomes uncollectible because no income was ever reported.

To deduct a business bad debt, the taxpayer must show a valid business reason for making the loan or sale. Only the uncollectible portion of a receivable qualifies as a business bad debt. A business bad debt is deductible in the year it becomes partially or completely worthless. Should the IRS challenge the bad debt deduction, the taxpayer must prove that the debt is worthless and will remain worthless. Doing so may involve going to court, which taxpayers can avoid by showing that the court would rule that the receivable was uncollectible. This usually occurs in the case of a bankrupt debtor.

EXAMPLE 23

Tucker is self-employed. During 20x1, Tucker loans his friend $5,000 so that his friend can start his own business. In 20x3, the friend files for bankruptcy and Tucker is told that he should expect to receive $.15 on the dollar. Since the purpose of the loan was not related to Tucker's business, the bad debt is a nonbusiness bad debt. The tax treatment for nonbusiness bad debts is discussed in Chapter 10.

EXAMPLE 24

Same facts as in Example 23, except that Tucker's loan is to his business supplier. The reason for the loan is to keep the supplier in business and prevent delivery of Tucker's inventory from being delayed. Because the purpose of the loan is related to Tucker's business, Tucker can begin taking a bad debt deduction in 20x3 when the debt becomes partially worthless. He reports $4,250 ($5,000 – ($5,000 × $.15)) as an other expense on Schedule C, Part V.

EXAMPLE 25

Continuing with Example 24, assume that in 20x4, the bankruptcy proceedings are finalized and Tucker receives $300 for his $5,000 loan. Tucker's total bad debt deduction is $4,700 ($5,000 – $300). Since Tucker deducted $4,250 in 20x3, he deducts $450 ($4,700 – $4,250) as an other expense on his 20x4 Schedule C.

EXAMPLE 26

Same facts as in Example 25, except that Tucker receives $1,000 (instead of $300) from the bankruptcy court. Tucker's total bad debt deduction is now $4,000 ($5,000 – $1,000). Because Tucker deducted $4,250 in 20x3, the tax benefit rule (see ¶313) requires that he include $250 as other income on his 20x4 Schedule C (line 6).

Total Expenses, $65,237 (Line 28)

Monroe subtracts total expenses from gross income (line 7) to arrive at tentative profit (loss) of $91,684 (line 29).

¶705.03 BUSINESS USE OF THE HOME

Sole proprietors normally can deduct expenses related to an office located in the home only if they use that part of the home regularly and exclusively as either (1) the principal place of business, or (2) a place to meet or deal with patients, clients, or customers in the normal course of business. However, they are allowed to deduct expenses for using part of the home as a day-care facility or as a place to store inventory, even if sometimes that part of the home is used for personal purposes.

To claim a home office deduction, the taxpayer usually must be able to demonstrate that, relative to the work done outside the office, the work done in the office is more important to the business. However, this rule does not apply to those who use their home office exclusively and regularly for administrative or management activities and have no other location to perform these duties. For example, a self-employed plumber who spends several hours each week scheduling appointments and preparing invoices qualifies for the home office deduction, provided that the office is used regularly and exclusively for administrative and management activities.

EXAMPLE 27

Stan, a self-employed writer, uses an office located in his home exclusively and regularly to write. Stan conducts most of his interviews outside of the office. He also spends many hours doing research at the library. Although doing research and conducting interviews are important to the business, the most important part is the actual writing. Since Stan does his writing at the office located in his home, he qualifies for the home office deduction.

EXAMPLE 28

Robyn is a self-employed physical therapist who works at three different hospitals. Robyn uses one room in her two bedroom apartment exclusively as a home office. She uses the office to schedule and confirm appointments. She also uses it prepare and file medical insurance claims for her patients. None of the hospitals provide her with an office to perform these tasks. Although the most important aspect to her job is treating patients (which is done at the hospital), she must perform these administrative tasks in order to make a living. Since the home office is used regularly and exclusively to perform these administrative tasks and there is no other place for her to do this, Robyn qualifies for the home office deduction.

EXAMPLE 29

Same facts as in Example 28, except that one of the hospitals provides its contractors with an office to perform their administrative tasks. Robyn, however, prefers to do these tasks in the comfort of her own home. Because she has been given another place to perform her administrative duties, Robyn cannot take the home office deduction.

Sole proprietors who qualify to take the home office deduction can choose each year between one of two methods allowed to compute the deduction. The first method uses the actual costs of operating the home. Some of the more common operating costs are home mortgage interest, real estate taxes, insurance, utilities, repairs, and depreciation. Only the business-use portion of these costs is used in computing the deduction.

To allocate expenses to the home office, taxpayers divide the square feet of the home office by the total square feet of the home. Taxpayers who use part of their home exclusively as a childcare facility also use this method to allocate a portion of their expenses of the home to the childcare business. However, for areas of the home not used on an exclusive basis, the deductible costs must be reduced by the ratio of hours the area is used for day care to the total hours in the year. Total hours in 2015 are 8,760 (24 hours × 365 days).

EXAMPLE 30 Jennifer provides childcare in her home. The area of the home used in her childcare business is 40% of the total area of the home. For 50 weeks, Jennifer provides childcare services 10 hours a day, 5 days a week, for a total of 2,500 hours (10 × 5 × 50). Jennifer can deduct 11.42% (40% × 2,500/8,760) of the expenses of her home against the income she earns providing childcare in 2015.

The second method for computing the home office deduction is the safe harbor method. Taxpayers using this method multiply the square footage of the home office (up to 300 square feet) by $5. The safe harbor method can be used by renters, as well as home owners. Sole proprietors using the safe harbor method enter the square footage of both the home office and the entire home, plus the amount of the deduction, on Schedule C (line 30).

¶705.04 FILLED-IN FORM 8829

Sole proprietors who use their actual operating costs of the home to compute their home office deduction, must complete Form 8829, Expenses for Business Use of Your Home, to support their deduction. On Form 8829, Part I, proprietors determine the business percentage of the home. Using this percentage, in Part II they compute their home office deduction. The depreciation expense deduction reported on Form 8829 (line 29) is computed in Form 8829, Part III. It is here in Part III that only the business portion of the home itself (excluding the land) is depreciated using the depreciation methods described in Chapter 8 (see ¶803.03). Figure 7-2 shows a completed Form 8829 for Monroe Peters (from Figure 7-1).

INFORMATION FOR FIGURE 7-2:

Monroe Peters (from Figure 7-1) enters the amounts shown below in bold on the appropriate lines of Form 8829. He then follows the instructions on the form to compute his home office deduction. Monroe enters the deduction from Form 8829 (line 35) on Schedule C (line 30).

Line #
1: Area used regularly and exclusively for business, **240**
2: Total area of home, **2,400**
8: Tentative profit from Schedule C, line 29, **$91,684** (from Figure 7-1)
10(b): Mortgage interest, **$4,300**
11(b): Real estate taxes, **$1,500**
17(b): Insurance, **$280**
19(b): Repairs and maintenance, **$950**
20(b): Utilities, **$1,810**
36: Smaller of the home's adjusted basis ($90,000) or its FMV ($128,000), **$90,000**
37: Value of land included on line 36, **$12,000**
40: Depreciation percentage, **2.564** (1/39 years, explained in Chapter 8)

Figure 7-2: Filled-In Form 8829

Form **8829** — **Expenses for Business Use of Your Home**

▶ File only with Schedule C (Form 1040). Use a separate Form 8829 for each home you used for business during the year.

▶ Information about Form 8829 and its separate instructions is at *www.irs.gov/form8829*.

Department of the Treasury
Internal Revenue Service (99)

OMB No. 1545-0074
2015
Attachment Sequence No. 176

Name(s) of proprietor(s): Monroe L. Peters

Your social security number: 139-24-6860

Part I — Part of Your Home Used for Business

1	Area used regularly and exclusively for business, regularly for daycare, or for storage of inventory or product samples (see instructions)			1	240
2	Total area of home			2	2,400
3	Divide line 1 by line 2. Enter the result as a percentage			3	10 %
	For daycare facilities not used exclusively for business, go to line 4. All others, go to line 7.				
4	Multiply days used for daycare during year by hours used per day	4	hr.		
5	Total hours available for use during the year (365 days x 24 hours) (see instructions)	5	8,760 hr.		
6	Divide line 4 by line 5. Enter the result as a decimal amount	6			
7	Business percentage. For daycare facilities not used exclusively for business, multiply line 6 by line 3 (enter the result as a percentage). All others, enter the amount from line 3 ▶			7	10 %

Part II — Figure Your Allowable Deduction

			(a) Direct expenses		(b) Indirect expenses		
8	Enter the amount from Schedule C, line 29, **plus** any gain derived from the business use of your home, **minus** any loss from the trade or business not derived from the business use of your home (see instructions)					8	91,684
	See instructions for columns (a) and (b) before completing lines 9–21.						
9	Casualty losses (see instructions)	9					
10	Deductible mortgage interest (see instructions)	10			4,300		
11	Real estate taxes (see instructions)	11			1,500		
12	Add lines 9, 10, and 11	12			5,800		
13	Multiply line 12, column (b) by line 7			13	580		
14	Add line 12, column (a) and line 13					14	580
15	Subtract line 14 from line 8. If zero or less, enter -0-					15	91,104
16	Excess mortgage interest (see instructions)	16					
17	Insurance	17			280		
18	Rent	18					
19	Repairs and maintenance	19			950		
20	Utilities	20			1,810		
21	Other expenses (see instructions)	21					
22	Add lines 16 through 21	22			3,040		
23	Multiply line 22, column (b) by line 7			23	304		
24	Carryover of prior year operating expenses (see instructions)			24			
25	Add line 22, column (a), line 23, and line 24					25	304
26	Allowable operating expenses. Enter the **smaller** of line 15 or line 25					26	304
27	Limit on excess casualty losses and depreciation. Subtract line 26 from line 15					27	90,800
28	Excess casualty losses (see instructions)			28			
29	Depreciation of your home from line 41 below			29	200		
30	Carryover of prior year excess casualty losses and depreciation (see instructions)			30			
31	Add lines 28 through 30					31	200
32	Allowable excess casualty losses and depreciation. Enter the **smaller** of line 27 or line 31					32	200
33	Add lines 14, 26, and 32					33	1,084
34	Casualty loss portion, if any, from lines 14 and 32. Carry amount to **Form 4684** (see instructions)					34	
35	**Allowable expenses for business use of your home.** Subtract line 34 from line 33. Enter here and on Schedule C, line 30. If your home was used for more than one business, see instructions ▶					35	1,084

Part III — Depreciation of Your Home

36	Enter the **smaller** of your home's adjusted basis or its fair market value (see instructions)	36	90,000
37	Value of land included on line 36	37	12,000
38	Basis of building. Subtract line 37 from line 36	38	78,000
39	Business basis of building. Multiply line 38 by line 7	39	7,800
40	Depreciation percentage (see instructions)	40	2.564 %
41	Depreciation allowable (see instructions). Multiply line 39 by line 40. Enter here and on line 29 above	41	200

Part IV — Carryover of Unallowed Expenses to 2016

42	Operating expenses. Subtract line 26 from line 25. If less than zero, enter -0-	42	
43	Excess casualty losses and depreciation. Subtract line 32 from line 31. If less than zero, enter -0-	43	

For Paperwork Reduction Act Notice, see your tax return instructions. Cat. No. 13232M Form **8829** (2015)

In Figure 7-2, the income from the business activity exceeded both the business expenses reported on Schedule C, Part II, and the expenses related to the office in the home. With the exception of the business portion of home mortgage interest, real estate taxes, and casualty losses, home office expenses cannot create a loss on Schedule C. Specifically, taxpayers can deduct these other types of home office expenses only to the extent of net income derived from the business. **Net income derived from the business** equals tentative profit shown on Schedule C (line 29) minus the home office expenses for home mortgage interest, real estate taxes, and casualty losses. Any disallowed expenses carry over to the next year.

EXAMPLE 31

Morgan conducts a business in his home. The business portion equals 20% of the total square footage of the home. Expenses of operating the home include utilities, $3,500; real estate taxes, $5,000; mortgage interest, $6,000; insurance, $800; general home repairs, $2,000; and depreciation, $4,500. Tentative profit from the business is $3,300. Morgan computes net income derived from the business as follows.

Tentative profit	$3,300
Less business portion of mortgage interest and real estate taxes [20% × ($6,000 + $5,000)]	(2,200)
Net income derived from the business	$1,100

After deducting the business portion of mortgage interest, real estate taxes, and casualty losses, taxpayers deduct the other home office expenses (to the extent of net income derived from the business) in the following order:

1. The business portion of expenses (other than depreciation) incurred in operating the business in the home. These expenses include repairs, maintenance, insurance, and utilities.
2. The depreciation on the business portion of the home.

Any home office expenses in excess of net income derived from the business carry over to the next year.

EXAMPLE 32

Continuing with Example 31, Morgan computes the rest of the home office deduction and the expenses carried over to the next year as follows.

Utilities, insurance, repairs (20% × $6,300)	$1,260
Depreciation on the home office (20% × $4,500)	900
Total other home office expenses	$2,160
Deductible expenses limited to net income derived from the business	(1,100)
Home office expenses carried forward to next year	$1,060

The $1,100 of deductible home office expenses comes from the home office portion of expenses for utilities, insurance, and repairs. The $1,060 of expenses carried over consists of $160 ($1,260 – $1,100) of utilities, insurance, and repairs, and $900 of depreciation (since depreciation is the last home office expense that is deducted).

Although the one drawback of the safe harbor method is the $1,500 limit placed on the deduction, the safe harbor method has its advantages. In addition to being an easier deduction to compute, taxpayers who use the safe harbor method do not have to complete Form 8829. Instead, they report their home office deduction directly on Schedule C (line 30). Second, in the years the safe harbor method is used, taxpayers do not have to keep receipts for the various expenses related to the home. Third, the depreciation component in the $5 per square foot amount is assumed to be $0. Thus, in years in which the safe harbor method is used, taxpayers do not reduce the basis in their homes by any depreciation taken for the home office.

¶705.05 SCHEDULE C, PART III: COST OF GOODS SOLD

Inventory is a major part of manufacturing, wholesale, and retail businesses. For sole proprietors, the calculation of cost of goods sold is done on Schedule C, Part III. Cost of goods sold equals beginning inventory plus the cost of net purchases, labor, materials, and other costs for the year minus ending inventory. Cost of goods sold should include only expenses directly related to getting or producing the goods sold.

For merchants, beginning inventory consists of products held for sale. For manufacturers, beginning inventory is the sum of raw materials, work in process, and finished goods. Beginning inventory of one year should be the same as ending inventory of the prior year.

For merchants, purchases include all goods bought for sale during the year. For manufacturers, purchases of raw materials include all materials bought during the year to be used in making the finished products. Any freight paid is added to the costs of purchases. The cost of goods returned reduce total purchases. Cash discounts either can be credited to separate discount accounts (as other income) or deducted from total purchases. The method for handling cash discounts must be used consistently from year to year. Figure 7-4 shows a filled-in Schedule C for a taxpayer in the retail business.

¶705.06 FILLED-IN SCHEDULE C

INFORMATION FOR FIGURE 7-4:

Harold R. Wilson is the owner of Harold's Hardware Store. Harold operates his business as a sole proprietorship. Figure 7-3 shows Harold's income statement. He completes Schedule C using this information. His business code is 444130. This code can be found in the instructions to Schedule C. Harold enters this code on line B. Harold materially participates in the business, so he checks the Yes box on line G. He uses the accrual method of accounting (box 2, line F) and the cost method to value inventory (box a, line 33). Because Harold has employees, he has an Employer ID number (EIN) that he reports on line D.

Net income from Harold's income statement is $60,496. Schedule C, however, shows a net profit of $61,131. Part of the $635 difference ($61,131 – $60,496) relates to the $460 of charitable contributions. Although the business paid this amount, the tax laws require charitable contributions of a sole proprietor to be deducted as an itemized deduction on Schedule A. The rest of the $175 difference is due to reducing meals and entertainment by 50% on Schedule C.

Figure 7-3: Income Statement for Harold's Hardware Store

HAROLD'S HARDWARE STORE
Income Statement
For Year Ended December 31, 2015

Operating revenue:			
Sales		$284,280	
Less: Sales returns and allowances		(2,751)	
Net sales			$281,529
Cost of merchandise sold:			
Merchandise inventory, beginning of period		$ 131,216	
Purchases	$180,716		
Less: Purchases discount	(3,614)		
Net purchases	$ 177,102		
Less: Merchandise withdrawn for personal use	(400)	176,702	
Merchandise available for sale		$ 307,918	
Less: Merchandise inventory end of period		(167,546)	
Cost of merchandise sold			(140,372)
Gross profit on sales			$ 141,157
Operating expenses:			
Advertising expense		$ 5,437	
Charitable contributions		460	
Depreciation expense		1,133	
Entertainment expense		350	
Insurance expense		2,250	
Legal and professional services		6,693	
Miscellaneous expense		15	
Payroll taxes		8,845	
Personal property taxes		960	
Rent expense		10,200	
Repairs to store equipment		2,125	
Supplies expense		3,400	
Telephone expense		1,258	
Travel		184	
Truck rental expense		2,498	
Utilities expense		3,908	
Wage expense		31,297	
Total operating expenses			(81,013)
Operating income			$ 60,144
Other income:			
Interest income			584
			$ 60,728
Other expenses:			
Interest expense			(232)
Net income			$ 60,496

Figure 7-4: Filled-In Schedule C (Page 1)

SCHEDULE C (Form 1040)
Department of the Treasury Internal Revenue Service (99)

Profit or Loss From Business
(Sole Proprietorship)
▶ Information about Schedule C and its separate instructions is at *www.irs.gov/schedulec.*
▶ Attach to Form 1040, 1040NR, or 1041; partnerships generally must file Form 1065.

OMB No. 1545-0074
2015
Attachment Sequence No. **09**

Name of proprietor	Social security number (SSN)
Harold R. Wilson	272-11-8855

A	Principal business or profession, including product or service (see instructions): Retail Hardware	B Enter code from instructions ▶ 4 4 4 1 3 0
C	Business name. If no separate business name, leave blank.: Harold's Hardware Store	D Employer ID number (EIN), (see instr.) 9 1 0 6 2 4 4 3 1
E	Business address (including suite or room no.) ▶ 27 Main Street	
	City, town or post office, state, and ZIP code: Madison, WI 53593-1344	
F	Accounting method: (1) ☐ Cash (2) ☑ Accrual (3) ☐ Other (specify) ▶	
G	Did you "materially participate" in the operation of this business during 2015? If "No," see instructions for limit on losses	☑ Yes ☐ No
H	If you started or acquired this business during 2015, check here	▶ ☐
I	Did you make any payments in 2015 that would require you to file Form(s) 1099? (see instructions)	☐ Yes ☑ No
J	If "Yes," did you or will you file required Forms 1099?	☐ Yes ☐ No

Part I Income

1	Gross receipts or sales. See instructions for line 1 and check the box if this income was reported to you on Form W-2 and the "Statutory employee" box on that form was checked ▶ ☐	1	284,280
2	Returns and allowances	2	2,751
3	Subtract line 2 from line 1	3	281,529
4	Cost of goods sold (from line 42)	4	140,372
5	**Gross profit.** Subtract line 4 from line 3	5	141,157
6	Other income, including federal and state gasoline or fuel tax credit or refund (see instructions)	6	584
7	**Gross income.** Add lines 5 and 6 ▶	7	141,741

Part II Expenses. Enter expenses for business use of your home **only** on line 30.

8	Advertising	8	5,437	18	Office expense (see instructions)	18	
9	Car and truck expenses (see instructions)	9		19	Pension and profit-sharing plans	19	
10	Commissions and fees	10		20	Rent or lease (see instructions):		
11	Contract labor (see instructions)	11		a	Vehicles, machinery, and equipment	20a	2,498
12	Depletion	12		b	Other business property	20b	10,200
13	Depreciation and section 179 expense deduction (not included in Part III) (see instructions)	13	1,133	21	Repairs and maintenance	21	2,125
				22	Supplies (not included in Part III)	22	3,400
				23	Taxes and licenses	23	9,805
				24	Travel, meals, and entertainment:		
14	Employee benefit programs (other than on line 19)	14		a	Travel	24a	184
15	Insurance (other than health)	15	2,250	b	Deductible meals and entertainment (see instructions)	24b	175
16	Interest:			25	Utilities	25	5,166
a	Mortgage (paid to banks, etc.)	16a		26	Wages (less employment credits)	26	31,297
b	Other	16b	232	27a	Other expenses (from line 48)	27a	15
17	Legal and professional services	17	6,693	b	**Reserved for future use**	27b	

28	**Total expenses** before expenses for business use of home. Add lines 8 through 27a ▶	28	80,610
29	Tentative profit or (loss). Subtract line 28 from line 7	29	61,131
30	Expenses for business use of your home. Do not report these expenses elsewhere. Attach Form 8829 unless using the simplified method (see instructions). **Simplified method filers only:** enter the total square footage of: (a) your home: ______ and (b) the part of your home used for business: ______ . Use the Simplified Method Worksheet in the instructions to figure the amount to enter on line 30	30	
31	**Net profit or (loss).** Subtract line 30 from line 29. • If a profit, enter on both **Form 1040, line 12** (or **Form 1040NR, line 13**) and on **Schedule SE, line 2.** (If you checked the box on line 1, see instructions). Estates and trusts, enter on **Form 1041, line 3.** • If a loss, you **must** go to line 32.	31	61,131
32	If you have a loss, check the box that describes your investment in this activity (see instructions). • If you checked 32a, enter the loss on both **Form 1040, line 12,** (or **Form 1040NR, line 13**) and on **Schedule SE, line 2.** (If you checked the box on line 1, see the line 31 instructions). Estates and trusts, enter on **Form 1041, line 3.** • If you checked 32b, you **must** attach **Form 6198.** Your loss may be limited.		32a ☐ All investment is at risk. 32b ☐ Some investment is not at risk.

For Paperwork Reduction Act Notice, see the separate instructions. Cat. No. 11334P **Schedule C (Form 1040) 2015**

Figure 7-4: Filled-In Schedule C (Page 2)

Schedule C (Form 1040) 2015 Page **2**

Part III **Cost of Goods Sold** (see instructions)

33 Method(s) used to value closing inventory: **a** ☑ Cost **b** ☐ Lower of cost or market **c** ☐ Other (attach explanation)

34 Was there any change in determining quantities, costs, or valuations between opening and closing inventory? If "Yes," attach explanation . . . ☐ **Yes** ☑ **No**

35	Inventory at beginning of year. If different from last year's closing inventory, attach explanation	35	131,216
36	Purchases less cost of items withdrawn for personal use	36	176,702
37	Cost of labor. Do not include any amounts paid to yourself	37	
38	Materials and supplies	38	
39	Other costs	39	
40	Add lines 35 through 39	40	307,918
41	Inventory at end of year	41	167,546
42	**Cost of goods sold.** Subtract line 41 from line 40. Enter the result here and on line 4	42	140,372

Part IV **Information on Your Vehicle.** Complete this part **only** if you are claiming car or truck expenses on line 9 and are not required to file Form 4562 for this business. See the instructions for line 13 to find out if you must file Form 4562.

43 When did you place your vehicle in service for business purposes? (month, day, year) ▶ ___ / ___ / ___

44 Of the total number of miles you drove your vehicle during 2015, enter the number of miles you used your vehicle for:

a Business ______ **b** Commuting (see instructions) ______ **c** Other ______

45 Was your vehicle available for personal use during off-duty hours? . . . ☐ **Yes** ☐ **No**

46 Do you (or your spouse) have another vehicle available for personal use? . . . ☐ **Yes** ☐ **No**

47a Do you have evidence to support your deduction? . . . ☐ **Yes** ☐ **No**

b If "Yes," is the evidence written? . . . ☐ **Yes** ☐ **No**

Part V **Other Expenses.** List below business expenses not included on lines 8–26 or line 30.

Miscellaneous expense			15
48	**Total other expenses.** Enter here and on line 27a	48	15

Schedule C (Form 1040) 2015

¶706 Self-Employment Tax for the Self-Employed

For the government to generate enough funds to pay social security and Medicare benefits, taxpayers who work must pay social security and Medicare taxes (FICA). Employees pay FICA taxes through withholdings from their wages. Employers make matching FICA contributions on behalf of their employees. Employers then send all FICA contributions to the government. Employers deduct as a payroll tax expense their share of FICA taxes paid.

FICA consists of two parts: (1) social security or OASDI (Old-Age, Survivors, and Disability Insurance) and (2) Medicare or HI (Hospital Insurance). The OASDI tax rate is 6.2% for employees (12.4% after employer matching). The Medicare rate is 1.45% (2.9% after employer matching). For 2015, the first $118,500 of a taxpayer's earnings is subject to OASDI taxes. All earnings are subject to Medicare taxes.

The self-employment tax is similar to FICA taxes withheld from employees' wages. However, instead of having the tax withheld from their wages, self-employed taxpayers pay the tax with their (quarterly) estimated payments. They make up any balance due when they file their tax return. Because there is no employer to make matching contributions, self-employed taxpayers must pay both the employee's and the employer's shares of the FICA tax. These two shares combined make up the 15.3% self-employment tax. Self-employed taxpayers deduct the employer's (one-half) share of self-employment taxes paid. This deduction is taken on Form 1040, page 1, not on Schedule C.

Self-employed taxpayers pay self-employment tax on their *net earnings from self-employment.* Net earnings from self-employment is 92.35% of self-employment net profit (reported on Schedule C, line 31). This calculation provides a substitute for the sole proprietor's net earnings after deducting the employer's share of the OASDI and Medicare taxes (100% – 6.2% OASDI tax – 1.45% Medicare tax = 92.35%).

Only taxpayers with $400 or more of net earnings from self-employment owe self-employment tax. Taxpayers with a net loss from self-employment do not pay self-employment tax. Computing self-employment net profit involves combining net profit (or loss) from all activities.

EXAMPLE 33

Jessica owns two businesses. Jessica uses a separate Schedule C to report the net profit (or loss) from each business. Net profit from the first business is $45,000; net profit from the second business is $5,000. Jessica's self-employment net profit is $50,000.

EXAMPLE 34

Same facts as in Example 33, except that Jessica reports a net loss of $5,000 from the second business. Jessica's self-employment net profit is $40,000.

EXAMPLE 35

Same facts as in Example 34, except that Jessica is married and her spouse owns the second business. Jessica's self-employment net profit is $45,000. Because her spouse reports a net loss, he pays no self-employment tax. Jessica pays self-employment tax on her $41,558 of net earnings from self-employment ($45,000 × 92.35%).

The full self-employment tax rate is 15.3% (12.4% for OASDI taxes + 2.9% for Medicare taxes). The full rate applies until the taxpayer's OASDI earnings reach the limit for the year ($118,500 for 2015). After that, the OASDI component goes away, and the self-employment tax rate drops to the 2.9% Medicare tax component.

EXAMPLE 36

Avery reports $10,000 of self-employment net profit. Avery's net earnings from self-employment equals $9,235 ($10,000 × 92.35%). His self-employment tax is $1,413 ($9,235 × 15.3%). The employer's share of the tax is $707 ($1,413 × ½). Avery deducts this amount on Form 1040, page 1.

For self-employed taxpayers who are also employees, their wages subject to social security (OASDI) tax reduce the maximum earnings subject to the 12.4% OASDI tax.

EXAMPLE 37

Same facts as in Example 36, except that in addition to the $10,000 of self-employment net profit, Avery has FICA taxes withheld on $111,900 of wages earned as an employee in 2015. The first $118,500 of earnings is subject to OASDI taxes. Through withholding on wages, Avery has paid OASDI taxes on $111,900. All $9,235 of net earnings from self-employment is subject to Medicare taxes, but only $6,600 ($118,500 – $111,900) is subject to the OASDI tax. Avery's self-employment tax equals $1,086 [($6,600 × 12.4%) + ($9,235 × 2.9%)]. Avery deducts $543 ($1,086 × ½) for AGI on Form 1040, page 1.

The employee portion of the Medicare tax rate is normally 1.45% of Medicare earnings (which include net earnings from self-employment). The employee's Medicare tax rate increases to 2.35% once a taxpayer's Medicare earnings reach a certain threshold (the employer's Medicare rate remains at 1.45%). This additional .9% Medicare tax is not part of the self-employment tax calculation. Instead, taxpayers whose Medicare earnings exceed the specified threshold complete Form 8959, Additional Medicare Tax. They then report their additional Medicare tax separately on Form 1040, page 2. The additional Medicare tax is discussed in Chapter 13 (¶1302.02)

¶706.01 SHORT SCHEDULE SE

Taxpayers compute self-employment tax on Schedule SE. Self-employed taxpayers who do not have wages use the short schedule (Section A) to compute their self-employment tax. Taxpayers whose net earnings from self-employment plus their wages and tips subject to social security tax do not exceed the OASDI limit ($118,500 in 2015) also use the short schedule. Taxpayers using the short schedule report their self-employment net profit (lines 1, 2, and 3). They compute their net earnings from self-employment (line 4) by multiplying self-employment net profit (line 3) by 92.35%. They compute self-employment tax (line 5) by multiplying the first $118,500 of net earnings from self-employment by 15.3% and the rest by 2.9%. Self-employment tax is reported as an additional tax on Form 1040, page 2. One-half of the tax (the employer's share) is reported on Schedule SE (line 6) and then deducted for AGI on Form 1040, page 1.

¶706.02 FILLED-IN SCHEDULE SE (SECTION A)

INFORMATION FOR FIGURE 7-5:

Harold R. Wilson (from Figure 7-4) computes his self-employment tax on Schedule SE (Section A). On a joint return, only the name and social security number of the person with self-employment income is shown on Schedule SE.

Line #

2: Net profit from Schedule C, line 31, **$61,131**
5: Self-employment tax, **$8,637** ($56,454 net earnings from self-employment from line 4 × 15.3%, since $56,454 ≤ $118,500)
6: Deduction for one-half of self-employment tax, **$4,319** ($8,637 × ½)

Figure 7-5: Filled-In Schedule SE (Section A)

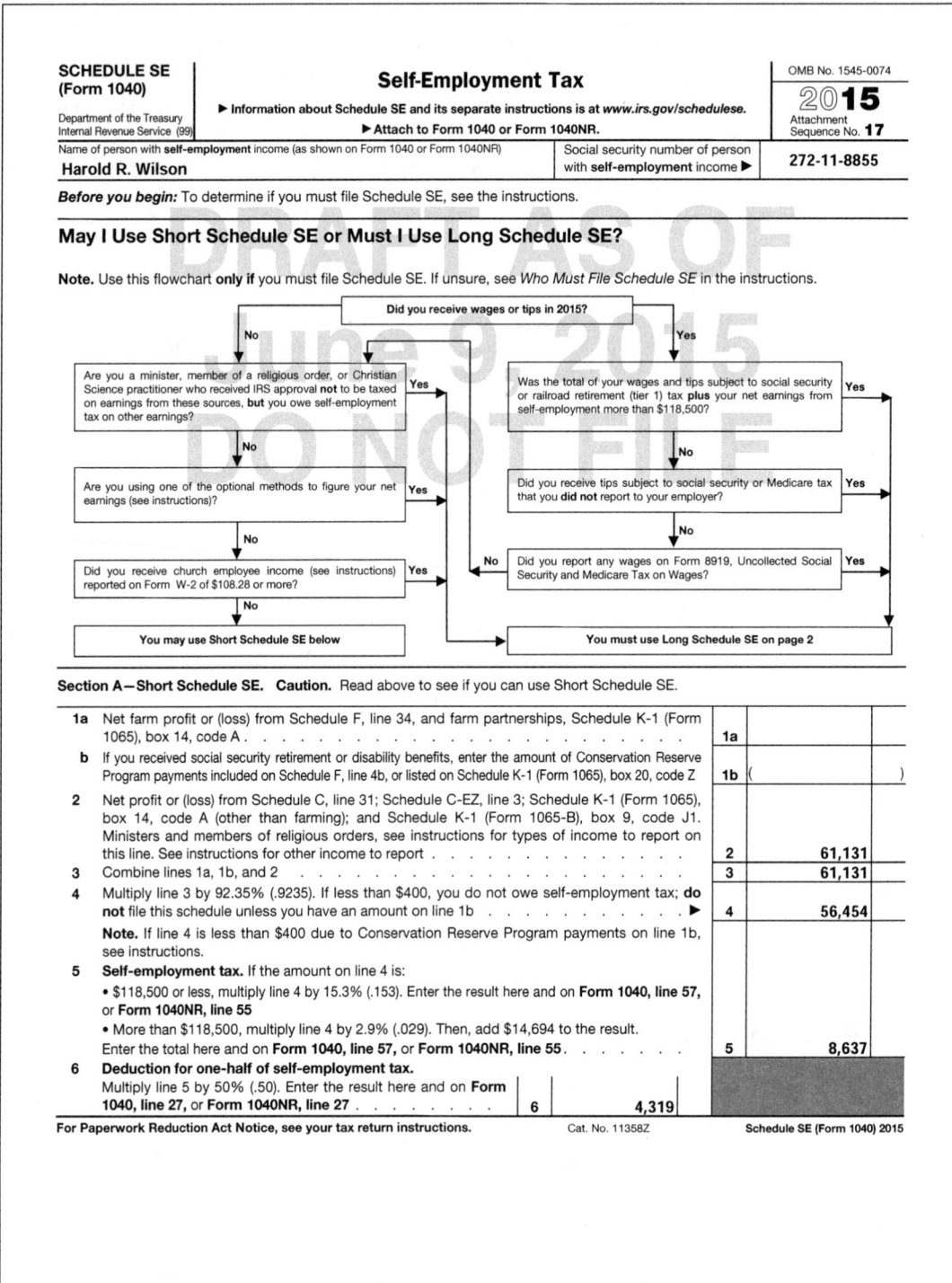

SCHEDULE SE (Form 1040)
Department of the Treasury
Internal Revenue Service (99)

Self-Employment Tax

► Information about Schedule SE and its separate instructions is at *www.irs.gov/schedulese.*
► Attach to Form 1040 or Form 1040NR.

OMB No. 1545-0074
2015
Attachment Sequence No. **17**

Name of person with **self-employment** income (as shown on Form 1040 or Form 1040NR)	Social security number of person with **self-employment** income ►
Harold R. Wilson	272-11-8855

Before you begin: To determine if you must file Schedule SE, see the instructions.

May I Use Short Schedule SE or Must I Use Long Schedule SE?

Note. Use this flowchart **only if** you must file Schedule SE. If unsure, see *Who Must File Schedule SE* in the instructions.

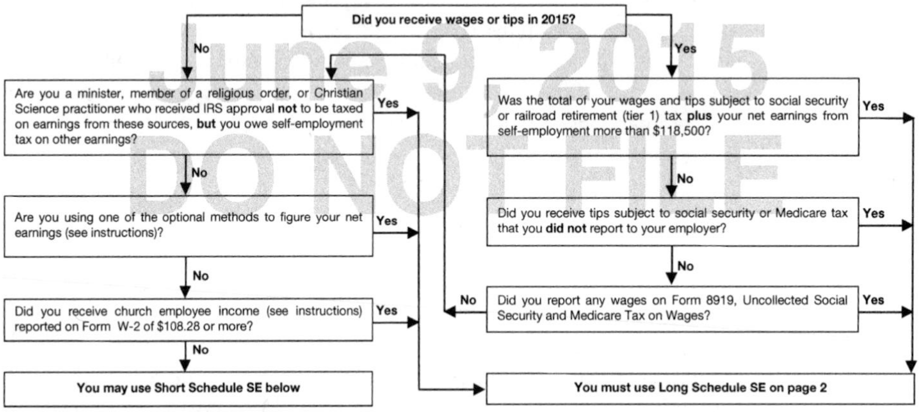
Did you receive wages or tips in 2015?
No
Yes
Are you a minister, member of a religious order, or Christian Science practitioner who received IRS approval not to be taxed on earnings from these sources, but you owe self-employment tax on other earnings?
Yes
No
Are you using one of the optional methods to figure your net earnings (see instructions)?
Yes
No
Did you receive church employee income (see instructions) reported on Form W-2 of $108.28 or more?
Yes
No
You may use Short Schedule SE below
Was the total of your wages and tips subject to social security or railroad retirement (tier 1) tax plus your net earnings from self-employment more than $118,500?
Yes
No
Did you receive tips subject to social security or Medicare tax that you did not report to your employer?
Yes
No
Did you report any wages on Form 8919, Uncollected Social Security and Medicare Tax on Wages?
Yes
No
You must use Long Schedule SE on page 2

Section A—Short Schedule SE. Caution. Read above to see if you can use Short Schedule SE.

1a	Net farm profit or (loss) from Schedule F, line 34, and farm partnerships, Schedule K-1 (Form 1065), box 14, code A	**1a**	
b	If you received social security retirement or disability benefits, enter the amount of Conservation Reserve Program payments included on Schedule F, line 4b, or listed on Schedule K-1 (Form 1065), box 20, code Z	**1b**	( )
2	Net profit or (loss) from Schedule C, line 31; Schedule C-EZ, line 3; Schedule K-1 (Form 1065), box 14, code A (other than farming); and Schedule K-1 (Form 1065-B), box 9, code J1. Ministers and members of religious orders, see instructions for types of income to report on this line. See instructions for other income to report	**2**	61,131
3	Combine lines 1a, 1b, and 2	**3**	61,131
4	Multiply line 3 by 92.35% (.9235). If less than $400, you do not owe self-employment tax; **do not** file this schedule unless you have an amount on line 1b . . . . . ►	**4**	56,454
	Note. If line 4 is less than $400 due to Conservation Reserve Program payments on line 1b, see instructions.		
5	**Self-employment tax.** If the amount on line 4 is: • $118,500 or less, multiply line 4 by 15.3% (.153). Enter the result here and on **Form 1040, line 57,** or **Form 1040NR, line 55** • More than $118,500, multiply line 4 by 2.9% (.029). Then, add $14,694 to the result. Enter the total here and on **Form 1040, line 57,** or **Form 1040NR, line 55**	**5**	8,637
6	**Deduction for one-half of self-employment tax.** Multiply line 5 by 50% (.50). Enter the result here and on **Form 1040, line 27,** or **Form 1040NR, line 27** **6** 4,319		

For Paperwork Reduction Act Notice, see your tax return instructions. Cat. No. 11358Z **Schedule SE (Form 1040) 2015**

¶706.03 LONG SCHEDULE SE

Taxpayers whose net earnings from self-employment plus their wages and tips subject to social security tax exceed the OASDI limit cannot use the Short Schedule SE. They instead must use Section B—Long Schedule SE. As in Section A, taxpayers first compute their self-employment net profit (lines 1 through 3) and their net earnings from self-employment (lines 4 through 6). They then report the amount of their wages for the year subject to social security tax withholding (line 8). If this amount exceeds the OASDI limit ($118,500 in 2015), the taxpayer is not subject to the 12.4% OASDI on the net earnings from self-employment. If the amount does not exceed the OASDI limit, then the taxpayer multiplies 12.4% by the *lesser of* the difference (line 9) or net earnings from self-employment (line 6). The taxpayer adds this amount to 2.9% of net earnings from self-employment (computed on line 11) to compute the self-employment tax (line 12). The taxpayer then calculates the employer's (one-half) share of the tax on line 13 and enters the amount as a deduction for AGI on Form 1040, page 1.

¶706.04 FILLED-IN SCHEDULE SE (SECTION B)

INFORMATION FOR FIGURE 7-6:

Avery Garza from Example 37 completes Section B of Schedule SE to compute his self-employment tax. He transfers the $1,086 of self-employment tax to Form 1040, page 2. He computes the employer's share (one-half) of this amount on Schedule SE (line 13) and enters the amount as a deduction for AGI on Form 1040, page 1.

Line #

2: Net profit from Schedule C, line 31, **$10,000**
8a: Total social security wages, **$111,900** (Source: box 3 on Form W-2)
10: Total OASDI taxes, **$818** (smaller of line 6 ($9,235) or line 9 ($6,600) multiplied by 12.4% OASDI rate, $6,600 × 12.4% = $818)
13: Deduction for one-half of the self-employment tax, **$543** ($1,086 from line 12 × ½)

¶707 Retirement Plans for the Self-Employed

Sole proprietors can establish retirement plans for themselves and deduct the contributions from their gross income on Form 1040, page 1. Any contributions sole proprietors make to their own retirement plans do not reduce their Schedule C net profits, but will reduce their AGI. Only deductions reported on Schedule C reduce a sole proprietor's self-employment tax. Thus, sole proprietors' contributions to their own retirement plans will reduce their income tax liability, but have no impact on their self-employment tax. Sole proprietors who set up retirement plans for themselves also may have to provide retirement plans for eligible employees. They deduct any contributions they make to their employees' retirement plans on Schedule C (line 19).

Self-employed taxpayers have several retirement plan options. They can set up defined benefit and defined contribution plans. When set up for self-employed taxpayers, these plans are commonly referred to as Keoghs. They can also set up SEP, 401(k), and SIMPLE plans. Whichever retirement plan they choose, they must also make it available to all eligible employees.

Figure 7-6: Filled-In Schedule SE (Section B)

Schedule SE (Form 1040) 2015 — Attachment Sequence No. **17** — Page **2**

Name of person with **self-employment** income (as shown on Form 1040 or Form 1040NR): **Avery Garzia**

Social security number of person with **self-employment** income ▶ **692-43-1922**

Section B—Long Schedule SE

Part I Self-Employment Tax

Note. If your only income subject to self-employment tax is **church employee income,** see instructions. Also see instructions for the definition of church employee income.

A	If you are a minister, member of a religious order, or Christian Science practitioner **and** you filed Form 4361, but you had $400 or more of **other** net earnings from self-employment, check here and continue with Part I ▶ ☐		
1a	Net farm profit or (loss) from Schedule F, line 34, and farm partnerships, Schedule K-1 (Form 1065), box 14, code A. **Note.** Skip lines 1a and 1b if you use the farm optional method (see instructions)	1a	
b	If you received social security retirement or disability benefits, enter the amount of Conservation Reserve Program payments included on Schedule F, line 4b, or listed on Schedule K-1 (Form 1065), box 20, code Z	1b	( )
2	Net profit or (loss) from Schedule C, line 31; Schedule C-EZ, line 3; Schedule K-1 (Form 1065), box 14, code A (other than farming); and Schedule K-1 (Form 1065-B), box 9, code J1. Ministers and members of religious orders, see instructions for types of income to report on this line. See instructions for other income to report. **Note.** Skip this line if you use the nonfarm optional method (see instructions)	2	10,000
3	Combine lines 1a, 1b, and 2	3	10,000
4a	If line 3 is more than zero, multiply line 3 by 92.35% (.9235). Otherwise, enter amount from line 3. **Note.** If line 4a is less than $400 due to Conservation Reserve Program payments on line 1b, see instructions.	4a	9,235
b	If you elect one or both of the optional methods, enter the total of lines 15 and 17 here	4b	
c	Combine lines 4a and 4b. If less than $400, **stop;** you do not owe self-employment tax. **Exception.** If less than $400 and you had **church employee income,** enter -0- and continue ▶	4c	9,235
5a	Enter your **church employee income** from Form W-2. See instructions for definition of church employee income — 5a:		
b	Multiply line 5a by 92.35% (.9235). If less than $100, enter -0-	5b	
6	Add lines 4c and 5b	6	9,235
7	Maximum amount of combined wages and self-employment earnings subject to social security tax or the 6.2% portion of the 7.65% railroad retirement (tier 1) tax for 2015	7	118,500 00
8a	Total social security wages and tips (total of boxes 3 and 7 on Form(s) W-2) and railroad retirement (tier 1) compensation. If $118,500 or more, skip lines 8b through 10, and go to line 11 — 8a: 111,900		
b	Unreported tips subject to social security tax (from Form 4137, line 10) — 8b:		
c	Wages subject to social security tax (from Form 8919, line 10) — 8c:		
d	Add lines 8a, 8b, and 8c	8d	111,900
9	Subtract line 8d from line 7. If zero or less, enter -0- here and on line 10 and go to line 11 ▶	9	6,600
10	Multiply the **smaller** of line 6 or line 9 by 12.4% (.124)	10	818
11	Multiply line 6 by 2.9% (.029)	11	268
12	**Self-employment tax.** Add lines 10 and 11. Enter here and on **Form 1040, line 57,** or **Form 1040NR, line 55**	12	1,086
13	**Deduction for one-half of self-employment tax.** Multiply line 12 by 50% (.50). Enter the result here and on **Form 1040, line 27,** or **Form 1040NR, line 27** — 13: 543		

Part II Optional Methods To Figure Net Earnings (see instructions)

Farm Optional Method. You may use this method **only** if **(a)** your gross farm income[1] was not more than $7,320, **or (b)** your net farm profits[2] were less than $5,284.

14	Maximum income for optional methods	14	4,880 00
15	Enter the **smaller** of: two-thirds (2/3) of gross farm income[1] (not less than zero) **or** $4,880. Also include this amount on line 4b above	15	

Nonfarm Optional Method. You may use this method **only** if **(a)** your net nonfarm profits[3] were less than $5,284 and also less than 72.189% of your gross nonfarm income,[4] **and (b)** you had net earnings from self-employment of at least $400 in 2 of the prior 3 years. **Caution.** You may use this method no more than five times.

16	Subtract line 15 from line 14	16	
17	Enter the **smaller** of: two-thirds (2/3) of gross nonfarm income[4] (not less than zero) **or** the amount on line 16. Also include this amount on line 4b above	17	

[1] From Sch. F, line 9, and Sch. K-1 (Form 1065), box 14, code B.

[2] From Sch. F, line 34, and Sch. K-1 (Form 1065), box 14, code A—minus the amount you would have entered on line 1b had you not used the optional method.

[3] From Sch. C, line 31; Sch. C-EZ, line 3; Sch. K-1 (Form 1065), box 14, code A; and Sch. K-1 (Form 1065-B), box 9, code J1.

[4] From Sch. C, line 7; Sch. C-EZ, line 1; Sch. K-1 (Form 1065), box 14, code C; and Sch. K-1 (Form 1065-B), box 9, code J2.

Schedule SE (Form 1040) 2015

¶707.01 KEOGH PLANS

The same contribution limits that apply to employees apply to sole proprietors. For defined contribution plans, the maximum contribution for 2015 is the *lesser of* (i) $53,000 or (ii) 25% of the participant's compensation. **Compensation** for a self-employed taxpayer equals self-employment net profit minus both the deduction for one-half of the self-employment tax and the contribution made to the retirement plan.

In computing their maximum allowable contribution, self-employed taxpayers first complete Schedule C to determine net profit. They then compute their self-employment tax on Schedule SE and deduct one-half of this tax from their net profit. Self-employed taxpayers may contribute up to 20% of the remaining amount to a defined contribution plan. This percentage is less than the 25% maximum contribution limit that is allowed for employees because of how a sole proprietor's "compensation" is computed. Example 38 shows how the 20% is determined.

EXAMPLE 38

Lloyd, a self-employed taxpayer, has Schedule C net profit of $60,000. His Keogh plan requires a 25% contribution each year. Net earnings from self-employment is $55,410 ($60,000 × 92.35%). Self-employment tax is $8,478 ($55,410 × 15.3%). Lloyd deducts $4,239 ($8,478 × ½), on Form 1040, page 1.

Using the required percentage of 25% of his compensation, Lloyd sets up a formula to solve for the required contribution (C): **25% × (Schedule C net profit – ½ of SE tax – C) = C**

For Lloyd, this equation is: **25% × ($60,000 – $4,239 – C) = C**

Solving for C: **25% × ($55,761 – C) = C**
$13,940 = 125% × C
$11,152 = C

Lloyd contributes $11,152 to his Keogh. He deducts this amount for AGI on Form 1040, page 1.

As shown in Example 38, 20% of the Schedule C net profit minus the employer's share of the self-employment tax [20% × ($60,000 – $4,239) = $11,152] is the same as 25% of the Schedule C net profit minus one-half of the self-employment tax and the contribution [25% × ($60,000 – $4,239 – $11,152) = $11,152]. Another way to compute the 20% is to divide the required percentage by the sum of 100% and the required percentage (25%/125% = 20%). This short cut is used in Example 39.

EXAMPLE 39

Same facts as in Example 38, except that the plan requires a 10% contribution. Using the short cut approach, Lloyd computes his deductible contribution: **10%/110% = .0909 × $55,761 = $5,069.**

Keogh Requirements

1. The plan must be established before the end of the tax year.
2. The plan must be in writing and employees must be provided a summary description, including the rules on discrimination and vesting.
3. The plan should be intended as a permanent plan.
4. The plan must have a designated trustee.
5. The contribution must be made by the due date of the tax return (including extensions).

Taxpayers can make contributions to qualified retirement plans until the due date of the tax return (including extensions). The big benefit of a Keogh plan is the ability to deduct the contributions each year plus postpone paying taxes on the accrued earnings until the funds are withdrawn. For this reason, the sooner the taxpayer contributes to the plan, the sooner the contributions begin earning tax-deferred (postponed) income.

To illustrate, on January 2, 20x1, a self-employed taxpayer makes a $30,000 contribution to a Keogh plan. During 20x1, $2,000 of earnings accrue on the $30,000. The income tax on that $2,000 is postponed until the funds are withdrawn after retirement. Had the taxpayer held the $30,000 in a taxable investment account and waited until December 31, 20x1, to make the Keogh contribution, the $2,000 earned by the taxable investment during 20x1 would be included in gross income on the taxpayer's 20x1 tax return.

¶707.02 SIMPLIFIED EMPLOYEE PENSION (SEP) PLANS

Another retirement plan option for sole proprietors is a SEP. A SEP is a defined contribution plan, so the maximum contribution self-employed taxpayers can make to a SEP in 2015 is the *lesser of* (i) $53,000 or (ii) 25% of the participant's compensation. This is the same as the *lesser of* (i) $53,000 or (ii) 20% of self-employment net profit after it is reduced by one-half of the self-employment tax.

As with a Keogh, self-employed taxpayers may contribute to a SEP until the due date of the return, including extensions. However, unlike a Keogh, a SEP does not need to be set up before the end of the tax year. Self-employed taxpayers have until the due date of their tax returns (including extensions) to set up a SEP plan. SEP plans have another advantage—they have no annual reporting requirements. Keoghs have annual reporting requirements, even if the taxpayer is the only participant. (These requirements are beyond the scope of this textbook).

EXAMPLE 40

Vince is self-employed and has a SEP. During 2015, he reports Schedule C net profits of $49,520. His self-employment tax is $6,997 ($49,520 × 92.35% × 15.3%), and his deduction for one-half of the self-employment tax is $3,499 ($6,997 × ½). Vince's maximum SEP contribution is $9,204.

25%/125% = 20% × ($49,520 – $3,499 deduction for SE tax) = $9,204

EXAMPLE 41

Kallie is self-employed and has a SEP. During 2015, she reports Schedule C net profits of $334,559. Her self-employment tax on this amount is $23,654 [($118,500 × 12.4%) + ($334,559 × 92.35% × 2.9%)]. The deduction for one-half of this amount is $11,827 ($23,654 × ½). Although the formula shows a maximum contribution of $64,546 (20% × ($334,559 – $11,827), her contribution is limited to $53,000 in 2015.

SEP Requirements

1. Each employee has an individual account.
2. Contributions must be made for all full-time employees who are at least age 21, have worked for the employer for three of the last five years, and have received at least $600 of wages during 2015.
3. Contributions are made under a written allocation formula.
4. The SEP cannot discriminate in favor of highly paid employees.
5. Employees must be able to withdraw the employer's contributions without restriction.

¶707.03 SAVINGS INCENTIVE MATCH PLAN FOR EMPLOYEES (SIMPLE)

Sole proprietors can set up a SIMPLE plan for themselves and their employees. The maximum that sole proprietors can contribute to their own SIMPLE plan in 2015 is the *lesser of* (i) $12,500 or (ii) 100% of their compensation. Sole proprietors age 50 and older can contribute up to $3,000 more, or $15,500 (assuming they have at least $15,500 of compensation). An advantage to having a SIMPLE plan is that it is not subject to the nondiscrimination and top-heavy rules associated with other retirement plans. A disadvantage is that employer matching is required with a SIMPLE plan. Neither of these are issues for sole proprietors with no employees. Due to the $12,500 ($15,500) limit, sole proprietors with no employees may want to consider a SEP plan, which has a higher contribution limit.

Simple Requirements

1. There must be 100 or fewer employees in the previous year.
2. The SIMPLE plan is the only retirement plan offered.
3. All employees who had at least $5,000 of compensation in the previous year and expect to have at least $5,000 of compensation in the current year must be allowed to participate.

The choice of a retirement plan will depend on the extent of compliance requirements, administrative and other costs, contribution limits, and flexibility. Sole proprietors considering setting up a retirement plan should carefully review the requirements and limitations of each type of plan and determine the type of plan best suited to their needs. Since most plans require that all eligible employees be allowed to participate, sole proprietors with employees may want to consider the potential costs of required employer (matching) contributions when deciding on a retirement plan for themselves.

7

Name:
Section:
Date:

QUESTIONS AND PROBLEMS

1. **Cash vs. Accrual Method.** (Obj. 1) Torres is a self-employed attorney. He wants to know how reporting each of the following items would differ under the cash method versus the accrual method. In the space provided, enter the correct amount that would be reported on Schedule C under each method. If there is no amount to be reported, enter **0**.

			Cash Method	*Accrual Method*
a.	Cash received from last year's fees	$ 7,200	$_______	$_______
b.	Cash received from current year's fees	49,000	_______	_______
c.	Fees billed for current year for which cash has not been received	10,200	_______	_______
d.	Cash received for computer with a tax basis of $200	200	_______	_______
e.	Cash received from bank loan	2,500	_______	_______
f.	Cash received from client to repay loan made last year	500	_______	_______
g.	Cash received for retainer from client for whom work is to be done next year	3,800	_______	_______

2. **Cash vs. Accrual Method.** (Obj. 1) Lis is a self-employed CPA. She wants to know how reporting each of the following items would differ under the cash method versus the accrual method. In the space provided, enter the correct amount that would be reported on Schedule C under each method. If there is no amount to be reported, enter **0**.

		Cash Method	*Accrual Method*
a. Repaid loan at bank:			
Principal	$1,000	$______	$______
Interest	60	______	______
b. Paid contribution pledged to church	1,000	______	______
c. Paid for supplies used last year	150	______	______
d. Paid for supplies used during current year	850	______	______
e. Paid two-year subscription for professional journals on January 1	200	______	______
f. Supplies not used during current year and not yet paid for	40	______	______
g. Paid for a new computer	1,564	______	______

3. **Cash vs. Accrual Method.** (Obj. 1) Taylor is a self-employed dentist. He wants to know how reporting each of the following items would differ under the cash method versus the accrual method. In the space provided, enter the correct amount that would be reported on Schedule C under each method. If there is no amount to be reported, enter **0**.

		Cash Method	*Accrual Method*
a. Salary paid to receptionist	$12,500	$______	$______
b. Paid for long-distance phone charges made during last year	4	______	______
c. Written-off client billing for fees; work performed in current year	150	______	______
d. Written-off client billing for fees; work performed last year	135	______	______
e. Paid annual subscription to magazines for the office waiting room	50	______	______
f. Paid life insurance premium on the owner's life	516	______	______

4. **Prepaid Income.** (Obj. 1) Scott operates a fitness center as a sole proprietorship. On May 1, 2015, Scott sells a 24-month membership for $1,200.

   a. How much of the $1,200 must Scott report on his 2015-2017 tax returns if he uses the accrual method of accounting?

   b. How would your answer to Part a. change if Scott uses the cash method?

5. **Prepaid Income.** (Obj. 1) Cliff uses the accrual method for his business he runs as a sole proprietorship. Cliff fixes and sells major appliances. He also sells warranty contracts. On April 1, 2015, Cliff collects $480 for a 36-month warranty contract. How much of the $480 must he include in gross income in 2015-2018?

6. **Prepaid Expenses.** (Obj. 1) On August 1, 2015, a sole proprietor pays $24,000 for two years' rent.

   a. How much of the $24,000 can be deducted in 2015 if the cash method is used?

   b. How much of the $24,000 can be deducted in 2015 if the accrual method is used?

7. **Prepaid Expenses.** (Obj. 1) A sole proprietor who operates a warehouse purchases insurance for his building and equipment in three-year increments to get a good insurance premium rate. The insurance policy was acquired on October 1, 2013, for $4,800 and will be in effect until September 30, 2016. The premium on this policy was paid on July 1, 2013.

   a. Compute the amount of insurance premium that can be deducted on Schedule C in 2013–2016, assuming the taxpayer uses the cash method of accounting.

   b. Same as Part a., except that the taxpayer uses the accrual method.

8. **Self-Employment Income.** (Obj. 2) Indicate with **Y** (yes) or **N** (no) if the following items are amounts subject to self-employment tax.

______ a. Net rentals from an apartment building

______ b. Net profit from an accounting practice

______ c. Interest income on a loan to a friend

______ d. Consulting fees

______ e. Fees earned for services as a minister

______ f. Dividends from U.S. corporations

9. **Self-Employment Income.** (Obj. 2) Indicate with **Y** (yes) or **N** (no) if the following items are amounts subject to self-employment tax.

______ a. Gross rent received on an office building

______ b. Net profit from a doctor's practice

______ c. Prize for winning an essay contest

______ d. Salary for a secretary

______ e. Net gain on the sale of business property

______ f. Director's fees

10. **Self-Employment Income.** (Obj. 2) Indicate whether each statement is *true* or *false*.

______ a. Interest on accounts receivable received by a trade or business is treated as self-employment income.

______ b. Babysitters who provide childcare in the parents' homes treat their earnings as self-employment income.

______ c. Registered nurses who are hired directly by patients to provide private nursing services are treated as self-employed.

______ d. Real estate agents' commissions are considered self-employment income.

______ e. A 16-year-old newspaper delivery boy's earnings are not considered self-employment income.

______ f. All executors of estates are treated as self-employed.

11. **Car and Truck Expense.** (Obj. 3) Keith is self-employed. During 2015, he drove his car a total of 9,169 miles for work. He drove a total of 21,468 miles during the year. His car expenses for the year were as follows.

Business parking and tolls	$ 360
Depreciation	1,475
Gas	2,557
Insurance	940
License tags	50
Repairs and maintenance	52
	$5,434

a. Compute Keith's car expense deduction using the standard mileage rate.

b. Compute Keith's car expense deduction using the actual cost method.

12. **Pension Plans.** (Obj. 3) Three common pension plans employers can provide to their employees are SEP, 401(k), and SIMPLE plans. For each of the following statements, identify the plan or plans having the described characteristics.

______ a. This plan allows employees under age 50 to contribute up to $12,500 of their wages to their plan in 2015.

______ b. This plan allows only employers to make contributions to employees' plans.

______ c. Employers are required to make matching contributions to this plan.

______ d. The maximum contribution to this plan is the *lesser of* $53,000 or 25% of the employee's compensation.

______ e. Employees can contribute pre-tax earnings to this plan.

13. **Travel Expense.** (Obj. 3) Andre is self-employed. In October, he attends a three-day seminar. Andre is out of town for 5 days and 4 nights. He spends the two extra days visiting friends and sightseeing. His travel costs are as follows.

Airfare	$ 850
Transportation to and from the airport	150
Hotel ($170 a night for 4 nights — 2 for business)	680
Meals ($42 a day for 5 days — 3 for business)	210
	$1,890

a. Compute Andre's travel expense deduction assuming the seminar was held in Texas.

b. Compute his travel expense deduction assuming the seminar was held in Germany.

14. Accountable vs. Nonaccountable Plans. (Obj. 3) Amanda operates her business as a sole proprietorship. Amanda has two full-time employees. She reimburses each employee $250 per month for meals and entertainment ($6,000 per year) without any specific accounting. Assuming that the employees incur meal expenses of $2,000 and entertainment expenses of $4,900, answer the following questions about the way the $6,000 should be reported on Amanda's tax return.

a. How much and where on Schedule C should Amanda deduct the reimbursements?

b. How would your answer to Part a. differ if Amanda required her employees to make an adequate accounting of their meals and entertainment expenses and also required them to return any excess reimbursement?

15. Education Expense. (Obj. 3) Aimee is a self-employed CPA. She holds both a bachelor's and a master's degree in accounting. Each year she takes two graduate courses at the local university to satisfy her continuing education requirements, as required by state law to keep her CPA license. Her coursework will not lead to her getting another degree. During 2015, Aimee spent $2,400 for tuition and $600 for books. She also drove her personal car 600 miles getting to and from her classes. What amount can Aimee deduct as an education expense on Schedule C?

16. Business Gifts. (Obj. 3) Dabny operates his business as a sole proprietorship. During the year, he sends holiday gifts to 20 of his clients. Each gift cost $55. What amount can Dabny deduct as business gifts on Schedule C?

17. Business Gifts and Entertainment. (Obj. 3) Stu is self-employed. During the year, Stu paid $60 for a concert ticket. He gave the ticket to a client.

a. What amount can Stu deduct on Schedule C if he did not attend the event with the client?

b. What amount can Stu deduct if he were to attend the event with his client?

18. **Bad Debt Expense.** (Obj. 3) Mickey is self-employed. In 2014, Mickey loaned a business associate $10,000 so that the associate could stay in business. Mickey's business would suffer if his associate went out of business. In 2015, the business associate filed for bankruptcy and Mickey was told that he might not receive more than $1,000 back from the loan. In 2016, Mickey receives $800 from the bankruptcy court. Discuss the tax consequences of the loan to Mickey, including the amount and year in which he can take a bad debt deduction.

19. **Schedule C.** (Obj. 3) Robert works as a cost accountant. He also works nights and weekends preparing tax returns for some regular clients. He does not have a regular office in his home, so he does not take a deduction for a home office. However, he prepares Schedule C to reflect the income from his tax practice. Robert has asked you to review his Schedule C to determine whether he is properly reporting the operating expenses of his business in relation to other aspects of his tax return. Robert has included the following expenses on Schedule C.

Supplies and postage	$ 72
Professional dues paid to AICPA tax division	120
Professional dues to the Institute of Management Accountants (IMA)	175
Meals ($80) and entertainment ($120) of tax clients	200
Automobile expenses for tax clients (using the standard mileage rate)	110
Contribution to New York State Society's Political Action Committee	100
CPE course fees to meet the annual requirements to be a member of the AICPA and the New York State society of CPAs	600
Cost of new printer for use with tax clients (shown as a repair)	650
Interest paid on bank loan used to buy computer for tax and personal use (used for tax clients 60% of the time during the tax year)	400

Of these expenses, indicate what amounts, if any, cannot be deducted on Schedule C, and explain why in each case.

20. **Home Office Expense.** (Obj. 4) Rita operates a childcare service in her home. The rooms used for this purpose constitute 30% of the total living space of the home. Expenses of operating the home during the year included electricity, $3,600; water, $340; gas heating, $480; property taxes, $4,000; and home repairs, $800. The depreciation on the rooms used for childcare was $1,800. What is the total amount of expenses that Rita can deduct for using her own home to provide the childcare services if she uses these rooms 2,000 hours in 2015 for her childcare business?

21. **Form 8829.** (Obj. 7) Elaine Gerber conducts a business in her home. Tentative profit from Schedule C (line 29) was $9,600.

a. Follow the instructions on Form 8829 on the following page to compute Elaine's home office deduction.

b. How, if at all, would your answer to Part a. change if Elaine elects to use the safe harbor method to compute her home office deduction?

c. How, if at all, would your answer to Part b. change if the square footage of the areas used for business was 340, instead of 240 square feet?

22. **Schedule C, Part III, Cost of Goods Sold.** (Obj. 7) Roger operates a novelty shop as a sole proprietor. You have been asked to compute the Cost of Goods Sold section of Schedule C for his 2015 income tax return since he is unfamiliar with detailed accounting concepts. You have been given the following information from his records to help meet his request:

Sales revenue	$200,000
Purchases	80,000
Cash operating expenses	40,000
Depreciation expense	15,000
Beginning inventory	60,000
Ending inventory	54,000
Bad debts written off	3,200

Using the appropriate information from Roger's books, prepare the Cost of Goods Sold section of Schedule C. Roger uses the cost method to value inventory.

Schedule C (Form 1040) 2015 Page **2**

Part III **Cost of Goods Sold** (see instructions)

33	Method(s) used to value closing inventory: **a** ☐ Cost **b** ☐ Lower of cost or market **c** ☐ Other (attach explanation)		
34	Was there any change in determining quantities, costs, or valuations between opening and closing inventory? If "Yes," attach explanation . . . ☐ **Yes** ☐ **No**		
35	Inventory at beginning of year. If different from last year's closing inventory, attach explanation	35	
36	Purchases less cost of items withdrawn for personal use	36	
37	Cost of labor. Do not include any amounts paid to yourself	37	
38	Materials and supplies	38	
39	Other costs	39	
40	Add lines 35 through 39	40	
41	Inventory at end of year	41	
42	**Cost of goods sold.** Subtract line 41 from line 40. Enter the result here and on line 4	42	

(Use for Problem 21.a.)

Form **8829** — Department of the Treasury, Internal Revenue Service (99)

Expenses for Business Use of Your Home

▶ File only with Schedule C (Form 1040). Use a separate Form 8829 for each home you used for business during the year.

▶ Information about Form 8829 and its separate instructions is at *www.irs.gov/form8829.*

OMB No. 1545-0074 — **2015** — Attachment Sequence No. **176**

Name(s) of proprietor(s)	Your social security number
Elaine Gerber	243-56-7182

Part I Part of Your Home Used for Business

1	Area used regularly and exclusively for business, regularly for daycare, or for storage of inventory or product samples (see instructions)	1	240
2	Total area of home	2	3,000
3	Divide line 1 by line 2. Enter the result as a percentage	3	%
	For daycare facilities not used exclusively for business, go to line 4. All others, go to line 7.		
4	Multiply days used for daycare during year by hours used per day	4	hr.
5	Total hours available for use during the year (365 days x 24 hours) (see instructions)	5	8,760 hr.
6	Divide line 4 by line 5. Enter the result as a decimal amount	6	
7	Business percentage. For daycare facilities not used exclusively for business, multiply line 6 by line 3 (enter the result as a percentage). All others, enter the amount from line 3 ▶	7	%

Part II Figure Your Allowable Deduction

			(a) Direct expenses	(b) Indirect expenses		
8	Enter the amount from Schedule C, line 29, **plus** any gain derived from the business use of your home, **minus** any loss from the trade or business not derived from the business use of your home (see instructions)				8	
	See instructions for columns (a) and (b) before completing lines 9–21.					
9	Casualty losses (see instructions)	9				
10	Deductible mortgage interest (see instructions)	10		11,800		
11	Real estate taxes (see instructions)	11		2,500		
12	Add lines 9, 10, and 11	12				
13	Multiply line 12, column (b) by line 7		13			
14	Add line 12, column (a) and line 13				14	
15	Subtract line 14 from line 8. If zero or less, enter -0-				15	
16	Excess mortgage interest (see instructions)	16				
17	Insurance	17		500		
18	Rent	18				
19	Repairs and maintenance	19				
20	Utilities	20		1,750		
21	Other expenses (see instructions)	21				
22	Add lines 16 through 21	22				
23	Multiply line 22, column (b) by line 7		23			
24	Carryover of prior year operating expenses (see instructions)		24			
25	Add line 22, column (a), line 23, and line 24				25	
26	Allowable operating expenses. Enter the **smaller** of line 15 or line 25				26	
27	Limit on excess casualty losses and depreciation. Subtract line 26 from line 15				27	
28	Excess casualty losses (see instructions)		28			
29	Depreciation of your home from line 41 below		29			
30	Carryover of prior year excess casualty losses and depreciation (see instructions)		30			
31	Add lines 28 through 30				31	
32	Allowable excess casualty losses and depreciation. Enter the **smaller** of line 27 or line 31				32	
33	Add lines 14, 26, and 32				33	
34	Casualty loss portion, if any, from lines 14 and 32. Carry amount to **Form 4684** (see instructions)				34	
35	**Allowable expenses for business use of your home.** Subtract line 34 from line 33. Enter here and on Schedule C, line 30. If your home was used for more than one business, see instructions ▶				35	

Part III Depreciation of Your Home

36	Enter the **smaller** of your home's adjusted basis or its fair market value (see instructions)	36	160,000
37	Value of land included on line 36	37	30,000
38	Basis of building. Subtract line 37 from line 36	38	
39	Business basis of building. Multiply line 38 by line 7	39	
40	Depreciation percentage (see instructions)	40	2.564 %
41	Depreciation allowable (see instructions). Multiply line 39 by line 40. Enter here and on line 29 above	41	

Part IV Carryover of Unallowed Expenses to 2016

42	Operating expenses. Subtract line 26 from line 25. If less than zero, enter -0-	42	
43	Excess casualty losses and depreciation. Subtract line 32 from line 31. If less than zero, enter -0-	43	

For Paperwork Reduction Act Notice, see your tax return instructions. Cat. No. 13232M Form **8829** (2015)

23. **Self-Employment Tax.** (Obj. 5) Determine the self-employment tax that would be paid for 2015 by each of the following taxpayers. If there is no self-employment tax, explain why.

a. Net business profit, $39,000; dividend income, $300; wages subject to social security, $5,000; gross rental income, $6,000; net rental income, $1,500.

b. Net business profit, $29,000; dividend income, $500; wages subject to social security, $60,000.

c. Net business profit, $70,000; dividend income, $200.

d. Net business profit, $15,000; dividend income, $100; wages subject to social security, $114,500.

e. Net business profit, $3,000; dividend income, $450; net rental loss, $500.

f. Net business profit, $420; dividend income, $50; wages subject to social security, $400.

24. **Self-Employment Tax.** (Obj. 5) Rosemary is employed as an attorney and also operates a consulting business on the side. If her net profit reported on Schedule C was $425, how much self-employment tax would Rosemary pay?

25. **Self-Employment Tax.** (Obj. 5) Connor has Schedule C net profit of $10,000. Compute Connor's 2015 self-employment tax if his salary as a CPA was $136,200.

26. **Self-Employment Tax.** (Obj. 5) Theodore Williams (SSN 327-59-8119) reports $130,000 of net profit on Schedule C. Complete Theodore's 2015 Schedule SE if his salary subject to social security taxes for the year was $76,000.

27. **Retirement Plans.** (Objs. 5 and 6).

a. Assume that Liz Bell (SSN 304-16-1059) had $14,000 of net profit from self-employment in 2015 and wants to make the maximum contribution to a SEP. Prepare Schedule SE to determine the amount of self-employment tax that Liz owes on her self-employment profits.

b. What is the maximum Liz can contribute to a SEP plan that would be fully deducted from gross income on her 2015 income tax return? Where on the tax return is the deduction claimed?

c. If Liz wants to contribute to a SEP plan, by what date must she make a contribution for 2015?

28. **Retirement Plans.** (Obj. 6) Diana has a consulting practice. She has no employees. For the 2015 tax year, Diana's gross consulting revenue was $155,000, and her operating expenses, not including retirement plan contributions, were $30,000. In addition to her consulting income, Diana also received $5,000 in 2015 for writing a chapter in a book about management consulting. During 2015, Diana established a defined contribution (Keogh) plan. The plan stipulates a fixed percentage of 10% of compensation as the amount of the required annual contribution.

a. What is the amount of self-employment tax that Diana must pay in 2015?

b. What is the required dollar contribution that Diana must make to her Keogh for 2015?

c. By what date must the Keogh be established in order for Diana to take a deduction for the contributions on her 2015 tax return?

d. By what date must the contributions be paid into the Keogh plan in order for Diana to take a deduction on her 2015 tax return?

(Use for Problem 26.)

Schedule SE (Form 1040) 2015 — Attachment Sequence No. **17** — Page **2**

Name of person with **self-employment** income (as shown on Form 1040 or Form 1040NR)	Social security number of person with **self-employment** income ▶	

Section B—Long Schedule SE

Part I Self-Employment Tax

Note. If your only income subject to self-employment tax is **church employee income,** see instructions. Also see instructions for the definition of church employee income.

A If you are a minister, member of a religious order, or Christian Science practitioner **and** you filed Form 4361, but you had $400 or more of **other** net earnings from self-employment, check here and continue with Part I . . . . . . ▶ ☐

1a	Net farm profit or (loss) from Schedule F, line 34, and farm partnerships, Schedule K-1 (Form 1065), box 14, code A. **Note.** Skip lines 1a and 1b if you use the farm optional method (see instructions)	**1a**		
b	If you received social security retirement or disability benefits, enter the amount of Conservation Reserve Program payments included on Schedule F, line 4b, or listed on Schedule K-1 (Form 1065), box 20, code Z	**1b**	(	)
2	Net profit or (loss) from Schedule C, line 31; Schedule C-EZ, line 3; Schedule K-1 (Form 1065), box 14, code A (other than farming); and Schedule K-1 (Form 1065-B), box 9, code J1. Ministers and members of religious orders, see instructions for types of income to report on this line. See instructions for other income to report. **Note.** Skip this line if you use the nonfarm optional method (see instructions)	**2**		
3	Combine lines 1a, 1b, and 2	**3**		
4a	If line 3 is more than zero, multiply line 3 by 92.35% (.9235). Otherwise, enter amount from line 3 **Note.** If line 4a is less than $400 due to Conservation Reserve Program payments on line 1b, see instructions.	**4a**		
b	If you elect one or both of the optional methods, enter the total of lines 15 and 17 here	**4b**		
c	Combine lines 4a and 4b. If less than $400, **stop;** you do not owe self-employment tax. **Exception.** If less than $400 and you had **church employee income,** enter -0- and continue ▶	**4c**		
5a	Enter your **church employee income** from Form W-2. See instructions for definition of church employee income . . . **5a**			
b	Multiply line 5a by 92.35% (.9235). If less than $100, enter -0-	**5b**		
6	Add lines 4c and 5b	**6**		
7	Maximum amount of combined wages and self-employment earnings subject to social security tax or the 6.2% portion of the 7.65% railroad retirement (tier 1) tax for 2015	**7**	118,500	00
8a	Total social security wages and tips (total of boxes 3 and 7 on Form(s) W-2) and railroad retirement (tier 1) compensation. If $118,500 or more, skip lines 8b through 10, and go to line 11 . . . **8a**			
b	Unreported tips subject to social security tax (from Form 4137, line 10) **8b**			
c	Wages subject to social security tax (from Form 8919, line 10) **8c**			
d	Add lines 8a, 8b, and 8c	**8d**		
9	Subtract line 8d from line 7. If zero or less, enter -0- here and on line 10 and go to line 11 . ▶	**9**		
10	Multiply the **smaller** of line 6 or line 9 by 12.4% (.124)	**10**		
11	Multiply line 6 by 2.9% (.029)	**11**		
12	**Self-employment tax.** Add lines 10 and 11. Enter here and on **Form 1040, line 57,** or **Form 1040NR, line 55**	**12**		
13	**Deduction for one-half of self-employment tax.** Multiply line 12 by 50% (.50). Enter the result here and on **Form 1040, line 27,** or **Form 1040NR, line 27** **13**			

Part II Optional Methods To Figure Net Earnings (see instructions)

Farm Optional Method. You may use this method **only** if **(a)** your gross farm income[1] was not more than $7,320, **or (b)** your net farm profits[2] were less than $5,284.

14	Maximum income for optional methods	**14**	4,880	00
15	Enter the **smaller** of: two-thirds (2/3) of gross farm income[1] (not less than zero) **or** $4,880. Also include this amount on line 4b above	**15**		

Nonfarm Optional Method. You may use this method **only** if **(a)** your net nonfarm profits[3] were less than $5,284 and also less than 72.189% of your gross nonfarm income,[4] **and (b)** you had net earnings from self-employment of at least $400 in 2 of the prior 3 years. **Caution.** You may use this method no more than five times.

16	Subtract line 15 from line 14	**16**		
17	Enter the **smaller** of: two-thirds (2/3) of gross nonfarm income[4] (not less than zero) **or** the amount on line 16. Also include this amount on line 4b above	**17**		

[1] From Sch. F, line 9, and Sch. K-1 (Form 1065), box 14, code B.

[2] From Sch. F, line 34, and Sch. K-1 (Form 1065), box 14, code A—minus the amount you would have entered on line 1b had you not used the optional method.

[3] From Sch. C, line 31; Sch. C-EZ, line 3; Sch. K-1 (Form 1065), box 14, code A; and Sch. K-1 (Form 1065-B), box 9, code J1.

[4] From Sch. C, line 7; Sch. C-EZ, line 1; Sch. K-1 (Form 1065), box 14, code C; and Sch. K-1 (Form 1065-B), box 9, code J2.

Schedule SE (Form 1040) 2015

(Use for Problem 27.)

SCHEDULE SE (Form 1040)

Department of the Treasury Internal Revenue Service (99)

Self-Employment Tax

▶ Information about Schedule SE and its separate instructions is at *www.irs.gov/schedulese*.

▶ Attach to Form 1040 or Form 1040NR.

OMB No. 1545-0074

2015

Attachment Sequence No. **17**

Name of person with **self-employment** income (as shown on Form 1040 or Form 1040NR)	Social security number of person with **self-employment** income ▶

Before you begin: To determine if you must file Schedule SE, see the instructions.

May I Use Short Schedule SE or Must I Use Long Schedule SE?

Note. Use this flowchart **only if** you must file Schedule SE. If unsure, see *Who Must File Schedule SE* in the instructions.

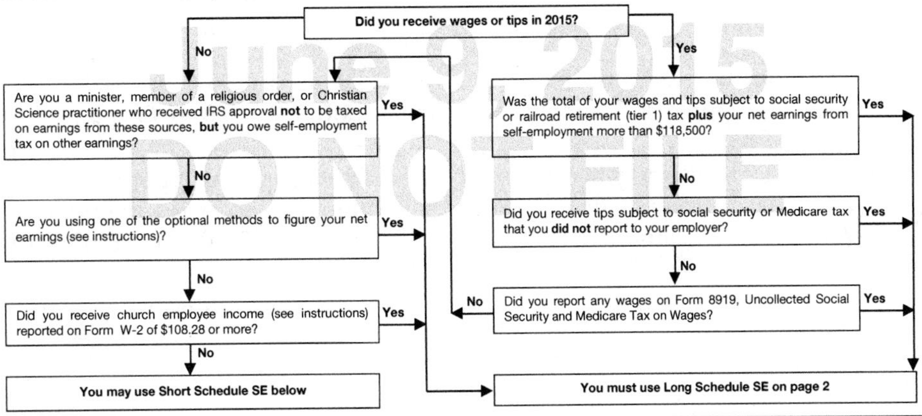
Did you receive wages or tips in 2015?
No
Yes
Are you a minister, member of a religious order, or Christian Science practitioner who received IRS approval not to be taxed on earnings from these sources, but you owe self-employment tax on other earnings?
Yes
No
Are you using one of the optional methods to figure your net earnings (see instructions)?
Yes
No
Did you receive church employee income (see instructions) reported on Form W-2 of $108.28 or more?
Yes
No
You may use Short Schedule SE below
Was the total of your wages and tips subject to social security or railroad retirement (tier 1) tax plus your net earnings from self-employment more than $118,500?
Yes
No
Did you receive tips subject to social security or Medicare tax that you did not report to your employer?
Yes
No
Did you report any wages on Form 8919, Uncollected Social Security and Medicare Tax on Wages?
Yes
No
You must use Long Schedule SE on page 2

Section A—Short Schedule SE. Caution. Read above to see if you can use Short Schedule SE.

1a	Net farm profit or (loss) from Schedule F, line 34, and farm partnerships, Schedule K-1 (Form 1065), box 14, code A	**1a**	
b	If you received social security retirement or disability benefits, enter the amount of Conservation Reserve Program payments included on Schedule F, line 4b, or listed on Schedule K-1 (Form 1065), box 20, code Z	**1b**	( )
2	Net profit or (loss) from Schedule C, line 31; Schedule C-EZ, line 3; Schedule K-1 (Form 1065), box 14, code A (other than farming); and Schedule K-1 (Form 1065-B), box 9, code J1. Ministers and members of religious orders, see instructions for types of income to report on this line. See instructions for other income to report	**2**	
3	Combine lines 1a, 1b, and 2	**3**	
4	Multiply line 3 by 92.35% (.9235). If less than $400, you do not owe self-employment tax; **do not** file this schedule unless you have an amount on line 1b . . . . . ▶	**4**	
	Note. If line 4 is less than $400 due to Conservation Reserve Program payments on line 1b, see instructions.		
5	**Self-employment tax.** If the amount on line 4 is: • $118,500 or less, multiply line 4 by 15.3% (.153). Enter the result here and on **Form 1040, line 57,** or **Form 1040NR, line 55** • More than $118,500, multiply line 4 by 2.9% (.029). Then, add $14,694 to the result. Enter the total here and on **Form 1040, line 57,** or **Form 1040NR, line 55**	**5**	
6	**Deduction for one-half of self-employment tax.** Multiply line 5 by 50% (.50). Enter the result here and on **Form 1040, line 27,** or **Form 1040NR, line 27** **6**		

For Paperwork Reduction Act Notice, see your tax return instructions. Cat. No. 11358Z **Schedule SE (Form 1040) 2015**

29. Internet Problem: Researching the Instructions to Form 5329. (Obj. 6)

Normally a 10% penalty is assessed when employees and self-employed taxpayers take distributions from a retirement plan before reaching age 59½. However, exceptions do exist. Describe the various circumstances under which individuals can take early distributions from the various retirement plans discussed in Chapter 7 and not have to pay the 10% penalty.

Go to the IRS website. Locate the Instructions for Form 5329, and find the answer to the above question regarding exceptions to the 10% penalty. Print out a copy of the page(s) where you found your answer. Underline or highlight the pertinent information.

See Appendix A for instructions on use of the IRS website.

30. Business Entity Problem: This problem is designed for those using the "business entity" approach. **The solution may require information from Chapters 15 and 16.**

Tom is a general partner in a partnership that reports ordinary income of $80,000. His distributive share of partnership ordinary income is $40,000. During the year his guaranteed payments were $30,000 and he withdrew $25,000 from the partnership.

a. What amount would be subject to social security and Medicare taxes? Explain.

b. Is the partnership responsible for withholding income taxes and FICA taxes on the partner's earnings? Explain how these taxes are paid to the government.

c. How would your answers to Parts a. and b. change if the business was operated as an S corporation?

31. Tax Ethics Case.* The date is April 14, and Helen Baldwin, CPA tax practitioner, sits at her desk, pondering the tax return before her. Helen has spent plenty of time pondering during the past year since moving from her home in a large eastern city to set up her new tax practice in a small western town. Clients in this small town have not exactly beaten a path to Helen's door to take advantage of her services. Building a client base has proven much more difficult than she had anticipated.

The return in front of Helen was completed on behalf of her newest client, Billy Joe Carter, who owns Honest Bill's Used Car Lot. He is a cousin of half of the members of the town council and is very influential in the local business community. Establishing a client relationship with Billy is the break that Helen has been looking for. In fact, Billy has made it clear that if Helen can complete and file his return before the April 15 deadline, Helen will receive his tax return business, as well as that of his family, for years to come.

Of concern to Helen, however, are several items on Billy's return. Billy insists that he is entitled to a business deduction for his new four-wheel-drive truck, since he uses it 100% of the time for business errands (such as traveling to car auctions, picking up parts, etc.). Helen thinks she has seen Billy driving the truck a number of times on what appeared to be personal trips. Also, Billy insists that the expenses associated with several trips to Las Vegas are deductible since the trips were "primarily of a business nature." Billy also claims several other large deductions without offering what Helen would consider to be "substantial documentation." As if anticipating Helen's skepticism, Billy said, "I don't know how things were in the big city where you came from, but around here people believe that a person's word is worth something. You'll just have to trust good old 'Honest Bill' this year, and next year I'll try to keep some better records."

a. What are the ethical issues in this case?

b. Who and what are the stakeholders who will be affected directly or indirectly by an inappropriate decision on Helen's part?

c. What are Helen's options in this situation?

d. What do you recommend that Helen do?

* *Case adapted from ethics cases prepared for publication by the American Accounting Association.*

COMPREHENSIVE PROBLEM

32. Maria A. Solo (SSN 318-01-6921) lives at 190 Glenn Drive, Grand Rapids, Michigan 49527-2005. Maria (age 45 and single) claims her aunt, Selda Ray (SSN 282-61-4011), as a dependent. Selda lives with Maria. Maria owns and operates the Reliable Drug Company at 1816 First Street in Grand Rapids, Michigan 49503-1902, in which she materially participates the entire year. Her EIN is 38-9654321. Employer quarterly payroll tax returns were filed as required, and Maria values her inventory at cost. The income statement for 2015 is reproduced on the next page. Maria reports on the accrual method, but uses the "direct write-off" method to compute bad debt expense. Her business code is 446110. She does not deduct expenses for an office in her home.

An examination of Maria's business records reveals that the depreciable property includes furniture and fixtures, a delivery truck, and store equipment. The depreciation expense shown on the 2015 income statement meets the income tax requirements for depreciation for using the mentioned assets during 2015. Maria rounds calculations to the nearest dollar. Miscellaneous expenses include the following:

Reimbursement to Maria for actual expenses of a business trip ($256 for airfare and lodging, $70 for meals)	$326
Contributions to the Red Cross and United Way	350
Chamber of Commerce dues	125
Personal electric bill for August	80
Total miscellaneous expenses	$881

Other income for Maria includes a salary of $100 each month for her services as a member of a working committee of the Drug Association. Her Form W-2 from the association shows gross wages of $1,200 and federal income tax withheld of $296. Through her work as an employee of the Drug Association, Maria is able to purchase her own full-year health insurance coverage. Thus, Maria is compliant with the ACA mandate.

Maria also earned $320 in taxable interest. Maria made federal estimated tax payments totaling $5,000 during 2015. This amount is reported in the Payments section on Form 1040, page 2.

Prepare Form 1040, and Schedules C, and SE for Maria Solo using the forms provided on the pages that follow. Maria does not want $3 to go to the Presidential election campaign fund. She signs her return on April 15, 2016.

RELIABLE DRUG COMPANY
Income Statement
For the Year Ended December 31, 2015

Operating revenue:		
Sales		$324,200
Less sales returns and allowances		(3,390)
Net sales		$320,810
Cost of merchandise sold:		
Merchandise inventory, beginning	$ 68,920	
Purchases	$198,240	
Less purchases returns and allowances	(8,100)	
Net purchases	$190,140	
Merchandise available for sale	$259,060	
Less merchandise inventory, ending	(69,185)	
Cost of merchandise sold		(189,875)
Gross profit on sales		$130,935
Operating expenses:		
Advertising expense	$ 6,541	
Bad debt expense (direct write off method)	850	
Car and truck expense	7,967[1]	
Depreciation expense	3,396	
Insurance expense (other than health)	644	
Miscellaneous expense	881	
Payroll taxes	3,471	
Rent expense (other business property)	12,000	
Telephone and utilities expense	2,395	
Wages expense	62,500	
Total operating expenses		(100,645)
Net income		$ 30,290

[1] *Maria drove her personal automobile for 13,856 business miles during the year. Total miles for the year were 32,815. There were 1,300 commuting miles. This is Maria's only car. She has kept a written log documenting her business miles. Maria first used the car in her business on May 4, 2013. She uses the standard mileage method.*

(Use for Problem 32.)

Form **1040** Department of the Treasury—Internal Revenue Service (99)
U.S. Individual Income Tax Return **2015** OMB No. 1545-0074 IRS Use Only—Do not write or staple in this space.

For the year Jan. 1–Dec. 31, 2015, or other tax year beginning , 2015, ending , 20 | See separate instructions.

Your first name and initial	Last name	**Your social security number**
If a joint return, spouse's first name and initial	Last name	**Spouse's social security number**
Home address (number and street). If you have a P.O. box, see instructions.	Apt. no.	▲ Make sure the SSN(s) above and on line 6c are correct.
City, town or post office, state, and ZIP code. If you have a foreign address, also complete spaces below (see instructions).		**Presidential Election Campaign** Check here if you, or your spouse if filing jointly, want $3 to go to this fund. Checking a box below will not change your tax or refund. ☐ You ☐ Spouse
Foreign country name	Foreign province/state/county	Foreign postal code

Filing Status

Check only one box.

1 ☐ Single
2 ☐ Married filing jointly (even if only one had income)
3 ☐ Married filing separately. Enter spouse's SSN above and full name here.
4 ☐ Head of household (with qualifying person). (See instructions.) If the qualifying person is a child but not your dependent, enter this child's name here.
5 ☐ Qualifying widow(er) with dependent child

Exemptions

6a ☐ **Yourself.** If someone can claim you as a dependent, **do not** check box 6a
b ☐ **Spouse**

Boxes checked on 6a and 6b

c **Dependents:**

(1) First name Last name	(2) Dependent's social security number	(3) Dependent's relationship to you	(4) ✓ if child under age 17 qualifying for child tax credit (see instructions)
			☐
			☐
			☐
			☐

If more than four dependents, see instructions and check here ► ☐

No. of children on 6c who:
• lived with you
• did not live with you due to divorce or separation (see instructions)

Dependents on 6c not entered above

d Total number of exemptions claimed

Add numbers on lines above ►

Income

Attach Form(s) W-2 here. Also attach Forms W-2G and 1099-R if tax was withheld.

If you did not get a W-2, see instructions.

7	Wages, salaries, tips, etc. Attach Form(s) W-2		7
8a	**Taxable** interest. Attach Schedule B if required		8a
b	**Tax-exempt** interest. **Do not** include on line 8a	8b	
9a	Ordinary dividends. Attach Schedule B if required		9a
b	Qualified dividends	9b	
10	Taxable refunds, credits, or offsets of state and local income taxes		10
11	Alimony received		11
12	Business income or (loss). Attach Schedule C or C-EZ		12
13	Capital gain or (loss). Attach Schedule D if required. If not required, check here ► ☐		13
14	Other gains or (losses). Attach Form 4797		14
15a	IRA distributions	15a	b Taxable amount 15b
16a	Pensions and annuities	16a	b Taxable amount 16b
17	Rental real estate, royalties, partnerships, S corporations, trusts, etc. Attach Schedule E		17
18	Farm income or (loss). Attach Schedule F		18
19	Unemployment compensation		19
20a	Social security benefits	20a	b Taxable amount 20b
21	Other income. List type and amount		21
22	Combine the amounts in the far right column for lines 7 through 21. This is your **total income** ►		22

Adjusted Gross Income

23	Reserved	23	
24	Certain business expenses of reservists, performing artists, and fee-basis government officials. Attach Form 2106 or 2106-EZ	24	
25	Health savings account deduction. Attach Form 8889	25	
26	Moving expenses. Attach Form 3903	26	
27	Deductible part of self-employment tax. Attach Schedule SE	27	
28	Self-employed SEP, SIMPLE, and qualified plans	28	
29	Self-employed health insurance deduction	29	
30	Penalty on early withdrawal of savings	30	
31a	Alimony paid b Recipient's SSN ►	31a	
32	IRA deduction	32	
33	Student loan interest deduction	33	
34	Reserved	34	
35	Domestic production activities deduction. Attach Form 8903	35	
36	Add lines 23 through 35		36
37	Subtract line 36 from line 22. This is your **adjusted gross income** ►		37

For Disclosure, Privacy Act, and Paperwork Reduction Act Notice, see separate instructions. Cat. No. 11320B Form **1040** (2015)

(Use for Problem 32.)

Form 1040 (2015) Page **2**

Tax and Credits

38	Amount from line 37 (adjusted gross income)	38	
39a	Check if: ☐ **You** were born before January 2, 1951, ☐ Blind. ☐ **Spouse** was born before January 2, 1951, ☐ Blind. } **Total boxes checked** ▶ **39a**		
b	If your spouse itemizes on a separate return or you were a dual-status alien, check here ▶ **39b** ☐		
40	**Itemized deductions** (from Schedule A) **or** your **standard deduction** (see left margin)	40	
41	Subtract line 40 from line 38	41	
42	**Exemptions.** If line 38 is $154,950 or less, multiply $4,000 by the number on line 6d. Otherwise, see instructions	42	
43	**Taxable income.** Subtract line 42 from line 41. If line 42 is more than line 41, enter -0-	43	
44	**Tax** (see instructions). Check if any from: **a** ☐ Form(s) 8814 **b** ☐ Form 4972 **c** ☐	44	
45	**Alternative minimum tax** (see instructions). Attach Form 6251	45	
46	Excess advance premium tax credit repayment. Attach Form 8962	46	
47	Add lines 44, 45, and 46 ▶	47	
48	Foreign tax credit. Attach Form 1116 if required — 48		
49	Credit for child and dependent care expenses. Attach Form 2441 — 49		
50	Education credits from Form 8863, line 19 — 50		
51	Retirement savings contributions credit. Attach Form 8880 — 51		
52	Child tax credit. Attach Schedule 8812, if required — 52		
53	Residential energy credit. Attach Form 5695 — 53		
54	Other credits from Form: **a** ☐ 3800 **b** ☐ 8801 **c** ☐ — 54		
55	Add lines 48 through 54. These are your **total credits**	55	
56	Subtract line 55 from line 47. If line 55 is more than line 47, enter -0- ▶	56	

Standard Deduction for—
- People who check any box on line 39a or 39b **or** who can be claimed as a dependent, see instructions.
- All others:

Single or Married filing separately, $6,300

Married filing jointly or Qualifying widow(er), $12,600

Head of household, $9,250

Other Taxes

57	Self-employment tax. Attach Schedule SE	57	
58	Unreported social security and Medicare tax from Form: **a** ☐ 4137 **b** ☐ 8919	58	
59	Additional tax on IRAs, other qualified retirement plans, etc. Attach Form 5329 if required	59	
60a	Household employment taxes from Schedule H	60a	
b	First-time homebuyer credit repayment. Attach Form 5405 if required	60b	
61	Health care: individual responsibility (see instructions) Full-year coverage ☐	61	
62	Taxes from: **a** ☐ Form 8959 **b** ☐ Form 8960 **c** ☐ Instructions; enter code(s)	62	
63	Add lines 56 through 62. This is your **total tax** ▶	63	

Payments

If you have a qualifying child, attach Schedule EIC.

64	Federal income tax withheld from Forms W-2 and 1099 — 64		
65	2015 estimated tax payments and amount applied from 2014 return — 65		
66a	**Earned income credit (EIC)** — 66a		
b	Nontaxable combat pay election — 66b		
67	Additional child tax credit. Attach Schedule 8812 — 67		
68	American opportunity credit from Form 8863, line 8 — 68		
69	Net premium tax credit. Attach Form 8962 — 69		
70	Amount paid with request for extension to file — 70		
71	Excess social security and tier 1 RRTA tax withheld — 71		
72	Credit for federal tax on fuels. Attach Form 4136 — 72		
73	Credits from Form: **a** ☐ 2439 **b** ▪ Reserved **c** ☐ 8885 **d** ☐ — 73		
74	Add lines 64, 65, 66a, and 67 through 73. These are your **total payments** ▶	74	

Refund

75	If line 74 is more than line 63, subtract line 63 from line 74. This is the amount you **overpaid**	75	
76a	Amount of line 75 you want **refunded to you.** If Form 8888 is attached, check here ▶ ☐	76a	
▶ b	Routing number ▶ **c** Type: ☐ Checking ☐ Savings		
▶ d	Account number		
77	Amount of line 75 you want **applied to your 2016 estimated tax** ▶ — 77		

Direct deposit? See instructions.

Amount You Owe

78	**Amount you owe.** Subtract line 74 from line 63. For details on how to pay, see instructions ▶	78	
79	Estimated tax penalty (see instructions) — 79		

Third Party Designee

Do you want to allow another person to discuss this return with the IRS (see instructions)? ☐ **Yes.** Complete below. ☐ **No**

Designee's name ▶ Phone no. ▶ Personal identification number (PIN) ▶

Sign Here

Joint return? See instructions. Keep a copy for your records.

Under penalties of perjury, I declare that I have examined this return and accompanying schedules and statements, and to the best of my knowledge and belief, they are true, correct, and complete. Declaration of preparer (other than taxpayer) is based on all information of which preparer has any knowledge.

Your signature	Date	Your occupation	Daytime phone number
Spouse's signature. If a joint return, **both** must sign.	Date	Spouse's occupation	If the IRS sent you an Identity Protection PIN, enter it here (see inst.)

Paid Preparer Use Only

Print/Type preparer's name	Preparer's signature	Date	Check ☐ if self-employed	PTIN
Firm's name ▶			Firm's EIN ▶	
Firm's address ▶			Phone no.	

www.irs.gov/form1040 Form **1040** (2015)

(Use for Problem 32.)

SCHEDULE C (Form 1040)
Department of the Treasury
Internal Revenue Service (99)

Profit or Loss From Business
(Sole Proprietorship)

▶ Information about Schedule C and its separate instructions is at *www.irs.gov/schedulec.*
▶ Attach to Form 1040, 1040NR, or 1041; partnerships generally must file Form 1065.

OMB No. 1545-0074
2015
Attachment Sequence No. 09

Name of proprietor | **Social security number (SSN)**

A Principal business or profession, including product or service (see instructions) | **B Enter code from instructions** ▶

C Business name. If no separate business name, leave blank. | **D Employer ID number (EIN),** (see instr.)

E Business address (including suite or room no.) ▶
City, town or post office, state, and ZIP code

F Accounting method: **(1)** ☐ Cash **(2)** ☐ Accrual **(3)** ☐ Other (specify) ▶

G Did you "materially participate" in the operation of this business during 2015? If "No," see instructions for limit on losses . ☐ Yes ☐ No

H If you started or acquired this business during 2015, check here . . . . . ▶ ☐

I Did you make any payments in 2015 that would require you to file Form(s) 1099? (see instructions) . . . ☐ Yes ☐ No

J If "Yes," did you or will you file required Forms 1099? . . . ☐ Yes ☐ No

Part I Income

1	Gross receipts or sales. See instructions for line 1 and check the box if this income was reported to you on Form W-2 and the "Statutory employee" box on that form was checked . . . ▶ ☐	1	
2	Returns and allowances . . .	2	
3	Subtract line 2 from line 1 . . .	3	
4	Cost of goods sold (from line 42) . . .	4	
5	**Gross profit.** Subtract line 4 from line 3 . . .	5	
6	Other income, including federal and state gasoline or fuel tax credit or refund (see instructions) . . .	6	
7	**Gross income.** Add lines 5 and 6 . . . ▶	7	

Part II Expenses. Enter expenses for business use of your home only on line 30.

8	Advertising . . .	8		18	Office expense (see instructions)	18	
9	Car and truck expenses (see instructions) . . .	9		19	Pension and profit-sharing plans .	19	
				20	Rent or lease (see instructions):		
10	Commissions and fees .	10		a	Vehicles, machinery, and equipment	20a	
11	Contract labor (see instructions)	11		b	Other business property . . .	20b	
12	Depletion . . .	12		21	Repairs and maintenance . . .	21	
13	Depreciation and section 179 expense deduction (not included in Part III) (see instructions) . . .	13		22	Supplies (not included in Part III) .	22	
				23	Taxes and licenses . . .	23	
				24	Travel, meals, and entertainment:		
14	Employee benefit programs (other than on line 19) . .	14		a	Travel . . .	24a	
15	Insurance (other than health)	15		b	Deductible meals and entertainment (see instructions) .	24b	
16	Interest:			25	Utilities . . .	25	
a	Mortgage (paid to banks, etc.)	16a		26	Wages (less employment credits) .	26	
b	Other . . .	16b		27a	Other expenses (from line 48) . .	27a	
17	Legal and professional services	17		b	**Reserved for future use** . . .	27b	

28	**Total expenses** before expenses for business use of home. Add lines 8 through 27a . . . ▶	28	
29	Tentative profit or (loss). Subtract line 28 from line 7 . . .	29	
30	Expenses for business use of your home. Do not report these expenses elsewhere. Attach Form 8829 unless using the simplified method (see instructions). **Simplified method filers only:** enter the total square footage of: (a) your home: ______ and (b) the part of your home used for business: ______ . Use the Simplified Method Worksheet in the instructions to figure the amount to enter on line 30 . . .	30	
31	**Net profit or (loss).** Subtract line 30 from line 29. • If a profit, enter on both **Form 1040, line 12** (or **Form 1040NR, line 13**) and on **Schedule SE, line 2.** (If you checked the box on line 1, see instructions). Estates and trusts, enter on **Form 1041, line 3.** • If a loss, you **must** go to line 32.	31	

32 If you have a loss, check the box that describes your investment in this activity (see instructions).

• If you checked 32a, enter the loss on both **Form 1040, line 12,** (or **Form 1040NR, line 13**) and on **Schedule SE, line 2.** (If you checked the box on line 1, see the line 31 instructions). Estates and trusts, enter on **Form 1041, line 3.**

• If you checked 32b, you **must** attach **Form 6198.** Your loss may be limited.

32a ☐ All investment is at risk.
32b ☐ Some investment is not at risk.

For Paperwork Reduction Act Notice, see the separate instructions. Cat. No. 11334P **Schedule C (Form 1040) 2015**

(Use for Problem 32.)

Schedule C (Form 1040) 2015 Page **2**

Part III **Cost of Goods Sold** (see instructions)

33	Method(s) used to value closing inventory: a ☐ Cost b ☐ Lower of cost or market c ☐ Other (attach explanation)		
34	Was there any change in determining quantities, costs, or valuations between opening and closing inventory? If "Yes," attach explanation . . . ☐ Yes ☐ No		
35	Inventory at beginning of year. If different from last year's closing inventory, attach explanation . . .	35	
36	Purchases less cost of items withdrawn for personal use . . .	36	
37	Cost of labor. Do not include any amounts paid to yourself . . .	37	
38	Materials and supplies . . .	38	
39	Other costs . . .	39	
40	Add lines 35 through 39 . . .	40	
41	Inventory at end of year . . .	41	
42	**Cost of goods sold.** Subtract line 41 from line 40. Enter the result here and on line 4 . . .	42	

Part IV **Information on Your Vehicle.** Complete this part **only** if you are claiming car or truck expenses on line 9 and are not required to file Form 4562 for this business. See the instructions for line 13 to find out if you must file Form 4562.

43 When did you place your vehicle in service for business purposes? (month, day, year) ▶ ____/____/____

44 Of the total number of miles you drove your vehicle during 2015, enter the number of miles you used your vehicle for:

a Business ______________ b Commuting (see instructions) ______________ c Other ______________

45 Was your vehicle available for personal use during off-duty hours? . . . ☐ Yes ☐ No

46 Do you (or your spouse) have another vehicle available for personal use?. . . ☐ Yes ☐ No

47a Do you have evidence to support your deduction? . . . ☐ Yes ☐ No

b If "Yes," is the evidence written? . . . ☐ Yes ☐ No

Part V **Other Expenses.** List below business expenses not included on lines 8–26 or line 30.

48 Total other expenses. Enter here and on line 27a . . .	48	

Schedule C (Form 1040) 2015

(Use for Problem 32.)

SCHEDULE SE (Form 1040)
Department of the Treasury
Internal Revenue Service (99)

Self-Employment Tax

▶ Information about Schedule SE and its separate instructions is at *www.irs.gov/schedulese*.
▶ Attach to Form 1040 or Form 1040NR.

OMB No. 1545-0074
2015
Attachment Sequence No. **17**

Name of person with **self-employment** income (as shown on Form 1040 or Form 1040NR)	Social security number of person with **self-employment** income ▶	

Before you begin: To determine if you must file Schedule SE, see the instructions.

May I Use Short Schedule SE or Must I Use Long Schedule SE?

Note. Use this flowchart **only if** you must file Schedule SE. If unsure, see *Who Must File Schedule SE* in the instructions.

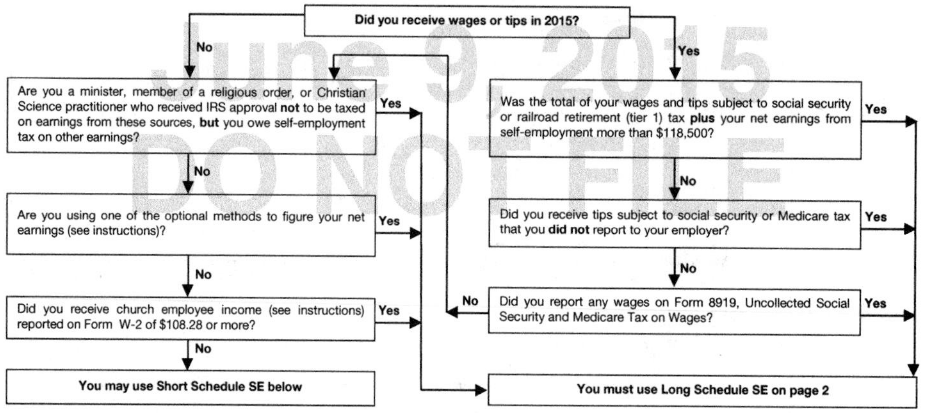
Did you receive wages or tips in 2015?
No
Yes
Are you a minister, member of a religious order, or Christian Science practitioner who received IRS approval not to be taxed on earnings from these sources, but you owe self-employment tax on other earnings?
Yes
No
Are you using one of the optional methods to figure your net earnings (see instructions)?
Yes
No
Did you receive church employee income (see instructions) reported on Form W-2 of $108.28 or more?
Yes
No
You may use Short Schedule SE below
Was the total of your wages and tips subject to social security or railroad retirement (tier 1) tax plus your net earnings from self-employment more than $118,500?
Yes
No
Did you receive tips subject to social security or Medicare tax that you did not report to your employer?
Yes
No
Did you report any wages on Form 8919, Uncollected Social Security and Medicare Tax on Wages?
No
Yes
You must use Long Schedule SE on page 2

Section A—Short Schedule SE. Caution. Read above to see if you can use Short Schedule SE.

1a	Net farm profit or (loss) from Schedule F, line 34, and farm partnerships, Schedule K-1 (Form 1065), box 14, code A	**1a**	
b	If you received social security retirement or disability benefits, enter the amount of Conservation Reserve Program payments included on Schedule F, line 4b, or listed on Schedule K-1 (Form 1065), box 20, code Z	**1b**	( )
2	Net profit or (loss) from Schedule C, line 31; Schedule C-EZ, line 3; Schedule K-1 (Form 1065), box 14, code A (other than farming); and Schedule K-1 (Form 1065-B), box 9, code J1. Ministers and members of religious orders, see instructions for types of income to report on this line. See instructions for other income to report	**2**	
3	Combine lines 1a, 1b, and 2	**3**	
4	Multiply line 3 by 92.35% (.9235). If less than $400, you do not owe self-employment tax; **do not** file this schedule unless you have an amount on line 1b . . . . . ▶	**4**	
	Note. If line 4 is less than $400 due to Conservation Reserve Program payments on line 1b, see instructions.		
5	**Self-employment tax.** If the amount on line 4 is: • $118,500 or less, multiply line 4 by 15.3% (.153). Enter the result here and on **Form 1040, line 57,** or **Form 1040NR, line 55** • More than $118,500, multiply line 4 by 2.9% (.029). Then, add $14,694 to the result. Enter the total here and on **Form 1040, line 57,** or **Form 1040NR, line 55**.	**5**	
6	**Deduction for one-half of self-employment tax.** Multiply line 5 by 50% (.50). Enter the result here and on **Form 1040, line 27,** or **Form 1040NR, line 27** **6**		

For Paperwork Reduction Act Notice, see your tax return instructions. Cat. No. 11358Z **Schedule SE (Form 1040) 2015**

CUMULATIVE PROBLEM (CHAPTERS 1–7)

Use the following information to prepare the tax return of Robert E. Dunkin using Form 1040, Schedule A, Schedule C, Schedule SE, and Form 8829. This problem is suitable for manual preparation or computer software application.

Robert E. Dunkin (SSN 392-48-6844) operates a consulting business out of his home located at 293 E. Main Street, Lafayette, LA 70503. The IRS business code (Schedule C, line B) is 541600. He uses the cash basis and materially participates in the business. During 2015, his business generated income of $55,088 and he had the following expenses: advertising, $150; depreciation expense, $1,630; office expense, $695; and supplies, $450. Rob drove his personal automobile 504 business miles during 2015. He uses the standard mileage rate method.

Rob uses one of the rooms in his house regularly and exclusively as a home office. The size of the room used as an office is 224 square feet. The total square footage of his home is 2,800 square feet. The expenses of operating the home during the year included utilities, $3,500; insurance, $250; home mortgage interest, $8,500; and real estate taxes, $3,205. The depreciable basis in the home is $110,840 ($130,840 minus $20,000 for the land). His depreciation percentage (Form 8829, line 40) is 2.564%.

a. Complete Schedule C and Form 8829 for Rob Dunkin. Then complete Rob's Schedule SE.

b. Based on your answers to Part a., what is the maximum amount Rob can contribute to a SEP plan for 2015?

c. How long does Rob have to set up a SEP and make his 2015 SEP contribution?

d. Complete Rob's Form 1040 assuming that he makes the maximum contribution allowed to his SEP for 2015. Rob files as single with no dependents. He is 47 years old and made $10,000 of estimated federal income tax payments for the 2015 tax year. This amount is reported in the Payments section on Form 1040. Rob's only other source of gross income is $1,120 of taxable interest and his only other deduction for AGI is $3,600 that he pays during the year for health insurance. Rob's health insurance covers the full-year. Thus, he is compliant with the ACA mandate.

   In addition to the non-home office portion of the interest and taxes on his home, his other itemized deductions include $2,000 of state income taxes paid during the year, $1,300 of cash contributions to his alma mater, and $150 of noncash contributions to Goodwill. Rob does not want $3 to go to the Presidential election campaign. He signs and dates his return on April 11, 2016.

(Use for Cumulative Problem.)

Form **1040** Department of the Treasury—Internal Revenue Service (99) **U.S. Individual Income Tax Return** **2015** OMB No. 1545-0074 IRS Use Only—Do not write or staple in this space.

For the year Jan. 1–Dec. 31, 2015, or other tax year beginning , 2015, ending , 20 See separate instructions.

Your first name and initial | Last name | **Your social security number**

If a joint return, spouse's first name and initial | Last name | **Spouse's social security number**

Home address (number and street). If you have a P.O. box, see instructions. | Apt. no. | ▲ Make sure the SSN(s) above and on line 6c are correct.

City, town or post office, state, and ZIP code. If you have a foreign address, also complete spaces below (see instructions).

Foreign country name | Foreign province/state/county | Foreign postal code

Presidential Election Campaign Check here if you, or your spouse if filing jointly, want $3 to go to this fund. Checking a box below will not change your tax or refund. ☐ You ☐ Spouse

Filing Status

Check only one box.

1 ☐ Single
2 ☐ Married filing jointly (even if only one had income)
3 ☐ Married filing separately. Enter spouse's SSN above and full name here.
4 ☐ Head of household (with qualifying person). (See instructions.) If the qualifying person is a child but not your dependent, enter this child's name here.
5 ☐ Qualifying widow(er) with dependent child

Exemptions

6a ☐ **Yourself.** If someone can claim you as a dependent, **do not** check box 6a
b ☐ **Spouse**

Boxes checked on 6a and 6b

c **Dependents:**

(1) First name Last name	(2) Dependent's social security number	(3) Dependent's relationship to you	(4) ✓ if child under age 17 qualifying for child tax credit (see instructions)
			☐
			☐
			☐
			☐

If more than four dependents, see instructions and check here ▶☐

No. of children on 6c who:
• lived with you
• did not live with you due to divorce or separation (see instructions)
Dependents on 6c not entered above
Add numbers on lines above ▶

d Total number of exemptions claimed

Income

Attach Form(s) W-2 here. Also attach Forms W-2G and 1099-R if tax was withheld.

If you did not get a W-2, see instructions.

7	Wages, salaries, tips, etc. Attach Form(s) W-2		7
8a	**Taxable** interest. Attach Schedule B if required		8a
b	**Tax-exempt** interest. **Do not** include on line 8a	8b	
9a	Ordinary dividends. Attach Schedule B if required		9a
b	Qualified dividends	9b	
10	Taxable refunds, credits, or offsets of state and local income taxes		10
11	Alimony received		11
12	Business income or (loss). Attach Schedule C or C-EZ		12
13	Capital gain or (loss). Attach Schedule D if required. If not required, check here ▶ ☐		13
14	Other gains or (losses). Attach Form 4797		14
15a	IRA distributions	15a	b Taxable amount 15b
16a	Pensions and annuities	16a	b Taxable amount 16b
17	Rental real estate, royalties, partnerships, S corporations, trusts, etc. Attach Schedule E		17
18	Farm income or (loss). Attach Schedule F		18
19	Unemployment compensation		19
20a	Social security benefits	20a	b Taxable amount 20b
21	Other income. List type and amount		21
22	Combine the amounts in the far right column for lines 7 through 21. This is your **total income** ▶		22

Adjusted Gross Income

23	Reserved	23	
24	Certain business expenses of reservists, performing artists, and fee-basis government officials. Attach Form 2106 or 2106-EZ	24	
25	Health savings account deduction. Attach Form 8889	25	
26	Moving expenses. Attach Form 3903	26	
27	Deductible part of self-employment tax. Attach Schedule SE	27	
28	Self-employed SEP, SIMPLE, and qualified plans	28	
29	Self-employed health insurance deduction	29	
30	Penalty on early withdrawal of savings	30	
31a	Alimony paid **b** Recipient's SSN ▶	31a	
32	IRA deduction	32	
33	Student loan interest deduction	33	
34	Reserved	34	
35	Domestic production activities deduction. Attach Form 8903	35	
36	Add lines 23 through 35		36
37	Subtract line 36 from line 22. This is your **adjusted gross income** ▶		37

For Disclosure, Privacy Act, and Paperwork Reduction Act Notice, see separate instructions. Cat. No. 11320B Form **1040** (2015)

(Use for Cumulative Problem.)

Form 1040 (2015) Page 2

Tax and Credits

38	Amount from line 37 (adjusted gross income)	38	
39a	Check if: ☐ **You** were born before January 2, 1951, ☐ Blind. ☐ **Spouse** was born before January 2, 1951, ☐ Blind. **Total boxes checked ▶ 39a**		
b	If your spouse itemizes on a separate return or you were a dual-status alien, check here ▶ 39b☐		
40	**Itemized deductions** (from Schedule A) **or** your **standard deduction** (see left margin)	40	
41	Subtract line 40 from line 38	41	
42	**Exemptions.** If line 38 is $154,950 or less, multiply $4,000 by the number on line 6d. Otherwise, see instructions	42	
43	**Taxable income.** Subtract line 42 from line 41. If line 42 is more than line 41, enter -0-	43	
44	**Tax** (see instructions). Check if any from: **a** ☐ Form(s) 8814 **b** ☐ Form 4972 **c** ☐	44	
45	**Alternative minimum tax** (see instructions). Attach Form 6251	45	
46	Excess advance premium tax credit repayment. Attach Form 8962	46	
47	Add lines 44, 45, and 46 ▶	47	
48	Foreign tax credit. Attach Form 1116 if required	48	
49	Credit for child and dependent care expenses. Attach Form 2441	49	
50	Education credits from Form 8863, line 19	50	
51	Retirement savings contributions credit. Attach Form 8880	51	
52	Child tax credit. Attach Schedule 8812, if required	52	
53	Residential energy credit. Attach Form 5695	53	
54	Other credits from Form: **a** ☐ 3800 **b** ☐ 8801 **c** ☐	54	
55	Add lines 48 through 54. These are your **total credits**	55	
56	Subtract line 55 from line 47. If line 55 is more than line 47, enter -0- ▶	56	

Standard Deduction for—
- People who check any box on line 39a or 39b **or** who can be claimed as a dependent, see instructions.
- All others:

Single or Married filing separately, $6,300

Married filing jointly or Qualifying widow(er), $12,600

Head of household, $9,250

Other Taxes

57	Self-employment tax. Attach Schedule SE	57	
58	Unreported social security and Medicare tax from Form: **a** ☐ 4137 **b** ☐ 8919	58	
59	Additional tax on IRAs, other qualified retirement plans, etc. Attach Form 5329 if required	59	
60a	Household employment taxes from Schedule H	60a	
b	First-time homebuyer credit repayment. Attach Form 5405 if required	60b	
61	Health care: individual responsibility (see instructions) Full-year coverage ☐	61	
62	Taxes from: **a** ☐ Form 8959 **b** ☐ Form 8960 **c** ☐ Instructions; enter code(s)	62	
63	Add lines 56 through 62. This is your **total tax** ▶	63	

Payments

If you have a qualifying child, attach Schedule EIC.

64	Federal income tax withheld from Forms W-2 and 1099	64	
65	2015 estimated tax payments and amount applied from 2014 return	65	
66a	**Earned income credit (EIC)**	66a	
b	Nontaxable combat pay election	66b	
67	Additional child tax credit. Attach Schedule 8812	67	
68	American opportunity credit from Form 8863, line 8	68	
69	Net premium tax credit. Attach Form 8962	69	
70	Amount paid with request for extension to file	70	
71	Excess social security and tier 1 RRTA tax withheld	71	
72	Credit for federal tax on fuels. Attach Form 4136	72	
73	Credits from Form: **a** ☐ 2439 **b** ■ Reserved **c** ☐ 8885 **d** ☐	73	
74	Add lines 64, 65, 66a, and 67 through 73. These are your **total payments** ▶	74	

Refund

75	If line 74 is more than line 63, subtract line 63 from line 74. This is the amount you **overpaid**	75	
76a	Amount of line 75 you want **refunded to you.** If Form 8888 is attached, check here ▶☐	76a	
▶ b	Routing number ▶ **c** Type: ☐ Checking ☐ Savings		
▶ d	Account number		
77	Amount of line 75 you want **applied to your 2016 estimated tax** ▶	77	

Direct deposit? See instructions.

Amount You Owe

78	**Amount you owe.** Subtract line 74 from line 63. For details on how to pay, see instructions ▶	78	
79	Estimated tax penalty (see instructions)	79	

Third Party Designee

Do you want to allow another person to discuss this return with the IRS (see instructions)? ☐ **Yes.** Complete below. ☐ **No**

Designee's name ▶ Phone no. ▶ Personal identification number (PIN) ▶

Sign Here

Joint return? See instructions. Keep a copy for your records.

Under penalties of perjury, I declare that I have examined this return and accompanying schedules and statements, and to the best of my knowledge and belief, they are true, correct, and complete. Declaration of preparer (other than taxpayer) is based on all information of which preparer has any knowledge.

Your signature	Date	Your occupation	Daytime phone number
Spouse's signature. If a joint return, **both** must sign.	Date	Spouse's occupation	If the IRS sent you an Identity Protection PIN, enter it here (see inst.)

Paid Preparer Use Only

Print/Type preparer's name	Preparer's signature	Date	Check ☐ if self-employed	PTIN
Firm's name ▶			Firm's EIN ▶	
Firm's address ▶			Phone no.	

www.irs.gov/form1040 Form **1040** (2015)

(Use for Cumulative Problem.)

SCHEDULE A (Form 1040)

Department of the Treasury Internal Revenue Service (99)

Itemized Deductions

▶ Information about Schedule A and its separate instructions is at *www.irs.gov/schedulea*.
▶ Attach to Form 1040.

OMB No. 1545-0074
2015
Attachment Sequence No. 07

Name(s) shown on Form 1040 | Your social security number

Medical and Dental Expenses		**Caution.** Do not include expenses reimbursed or paid by others.		
	1	Medical and dental expenses (see instructions)	1	
	2	Enter amount from Form 1040, line 38 [2]		
	3	Multiply line 2 by 10% (.10). But if either you or your spouse was born before January 2, 1951, multiply line 2 by 7.5% (.075) instead	3	
	4	Subtract line 3 from line 1. If line 3 is more than line 1, enter -0-	4	
Taxes You Paid	5	State and local		
		a ☐ Income taxes b ■ Reserved	5	
	6	Real estate taxes (see instructions)	6	
	7	Personal property taxes	7	
	8	Other taxes. List type and amount ▶	8	
	9	Add lines 5 through 8	9	
Interest You Paid **Note.** Your mortgage interest deduction may be limited (see instructions).	10	Home mortgage interest and points reported to you on Form 1098	10	
	11	Home mortgage interest not reported to you on Form 1098. If paid to the person from whom you bought the home, see instructions and show that person's name, identifying no., and address ▶	11	
	12	Points not reported to you on Form 1098. See instructions for special rules	12	
	13	Reserved	13	
	14	Investment interest. Attach Form 4952 if required. (See instructions.)	14	
	15	Add lines 10 through 14	15	
Gifts to Charity If you made a gift and got a benefit for it, see instructions.	16	Gifts by cash or check. If you made any gift of $250 or more, see instructions.	16	
	17	Other than by cash or check. If any gift of $250 or more, see instructions. You **must** attach Form 8283 if over $500 . . .	17	
	18	Carryover from prior year	18	
	19	Add lines 16 through 18	19	
Casualty and Theft Losses	20	Casualty or theft loss(es). Attach Form 4684. (See instructions.)	20	
Job Expenses and Certain Miscellaneous Deductions	21	Unreimbursed employee expenses—job travel, union dues, job education, etc. Attach Form 2106 or 2106-EZ if required. (See instructions.) ▶	21	
	22	Tax preparation fees	22	
	23	Other expenses—investment, safe deposit box, etc. List type and amount ▶	23	
	24	Add lines 21 through 23	24	
	25	Enter amount from Form 1040, line 38 [25]		
	26	Multiply line 25 by 2% (.02)	26	
	27	Subtract line 26 from line 24. If line 26 is more than line 24, enter -0-	27	
Other Miscellaneous Deductions	28	Other—from list in instructions. List type and amount ▶	28	
Total Itemized Deductions	29	Is Form 1040, line 38, over $154,950? ☐ **No.** Your deduction is not limited. Add the amounts in the far right column for lines 4 through 28. Also, enter this amount on Form 1040, line 40. ☐ **Yes.** Your deduction may be limited. See the Itemized Deductions Worksheet in the instructions to figure the amount to enter.	29	
	30	If you elect to itemize deductions even though they are less than your standard deduction, check here . . . . ▶ ☐		

For Paperwork Reduction Act Notice, see Form 1040 instructions. Cat. No. 17145C **Schedule A (Form 1040) 2015**

(Use for Cumulative Problem.)

SCHEDULE C (Form 1040)
Department of the Treasury
Internal Revenue Service (99)

Profit or Loss From Business
(Sole Proprietorship)

▶ Information about Schedule C and its separate instructions is at *www.irs.gov/schedulec.*
▶ Attach to Form 1040, 1040NR, or 1041; partnerships generally must file Form 1065.

OMB No. 1545-0074
2015
Attachment Sequence No. 09

Name of proprietor | **Social security number (SSN)**

A Principal business or profession, including product or service (see instructions) | **B Enter code from instructions** ▶

C Business name. If no separate business name, leave blank. | **D Employer ID number (EIN),** (see instr.)

E Business address (including suite or room no.) ▶
City, town or post office, state, and ZIP code

F Accounting method: (1) ☐ Cash (2) ☐ Accrual (3) ☐ Other (specify) ▶

G Did you "materially participate" in the operation of this business during 2015? If "No," see instructions for limit on losses . ☐ Yes ☐ No

H If you started or acquired this business during 2015, check here . . . ▶ ☐

I Did you make any payments in 2015 that would require you to file Form(s) 1099? (see instructions) . . . ☐ Yes ☐ No

J If "Yes," did you or will you file required Forms 1099? . . . ☐ Yes ☐ No

Part I Income

1	Gross receipts or sales. See instructions for line 1 and check the box if this income was reported to you on Form W-2 and the "Statutory employee" box on that form was checked . . . ▶☐	1	
2	Returns and allowances . . .	2	
3	Subtract line 2 from line 1 . . .	3	
4	Cost of goods sold (from line 42) . . .	4	
5	**Gross profit.** Subtract line 4 from line 3 . . .	5	
6	Other income, including federal and state gasoline or fuel tax credit or refund (see instructions) . . .	6	
7	**Gross income.** Add lines 5 and 6 . . . ▶	7	

Part II Expenses. Enter expenses for business use of your home **only** on line 30.

8	Advertising . . .	8		18	Office expense (see instructions)	18	
9	Car and truck expenses (see instructions) . . .	9		19	Pension and profit-sharing plans .	19	
				20	Rent or lease (see instructions):		
10	Commissions and fees .	10		a	Vehicles, machinery, and equipment	20a	
11	Contract labor (see instructions)	11		b	Other business property . . .	20b	
12	Depletion . . .	12		21	Repairs and maintenance . . .	21	
13	Depreciation and section 179 expense deduction (not included in Part III) (see instructions) . . .	13		22	Supplies (not included in Part III) .	22	
				23	Taxes and licenses . . .	23	
				24	Travel, meals, and entertainment:		
14	Employee benefit programs (other than on line 19) . .	14		a	Travel . . .	24a	
15	Insurance (other than health)	15		b	Deductible meals and entertainment (see instructions) .	24b	
16	Interest:			25	Utilities . . .	25	
a	Mortgage (paid to banks, etc.)	16a		26	Wages (less employment credits) .	26	
b	Other . . .	16b		27a	Other expenses (from line 48) . .	27a	
17	Legal and professional services	17		b	**Reserved for future use** . . .	27b	

28	**Total expenses** before expenses for business use of home. Add lines 8 through 27a . . . ▶	28	
29	Tentative profit or (loss). Subtract line 28 from line 7 . . .	29	
30	Expenses for business use of your home. Do not report these expenses elsewhere. Attach Form 8829 unless using the simplified method (see instructions). **Simplified method filers only:** enter the total square footage of: (a) your home: ______ and (b) the part of your home used for business: ______. Use the Simplified Method Worksheet in the instructions to figure the amount to enter on line 30 . . .	30	
31	**Net profit or (loss).** Subtract line 30 from line 29. • If a profit, enter on both **Form 1040, line 12** (or **Form 1040NR, line 13**) and on **Schedule SE, line 2.** (If you checked the box on line 1, see instructions). Estates and trusts, enter on **Form 1041, line 3.** • If a loss, you **must** go to line 32.	31	
32	If you have a loss, check the box that describes your investment in this activity (see instructions). • If you checked 32a, enter the loss on both **Form 1040, line 12,** (or **Form 1040NR, line 13**) and on **Schedule SE, line 2.** (If you checked the box on line 1, see the line 31 instructions). Estates and trusts, enter on **Form 1041, line 3.** • If you checked 32b, you **must** attach **Form 6198.** Your loss may be limited.	32a ☐ All investment is at risk. 32b ☐ Some investment is not at risk.	

For Paperwork Reduction Act Notice, see the separate instructions. Cat. No. 11334P **Schedule C (Form 1040) 2015**

(Use for Cumulative Problem.)

SCHEDULE SE (Form 1040)

Department of the Treasury
Internal Revenue Service (99)

Self-Employment Tax

▶ Information about Schedule SE and its separate instructions is at *www.irs.gov/schedulese.*
▶ Attach to Form 1040 or Form 1040NR.

OMB No. 1545-0074
2015
Attachment Sequence No. **17**

Name of person with **self-employment** income (as shown on Form 1040 or Form 1040NR) | Social security number of person with **self-employment** income ▶

Before you begin: To determine if you must file Schedule SE, see the instructions.

May I Use Short Schedule SE or Must I Use Long Schedule SE?

Note. Use this flowchart **only if** you must file Schedule SE. If unsure, see *Who Must File Schedule SE* in the instructions.

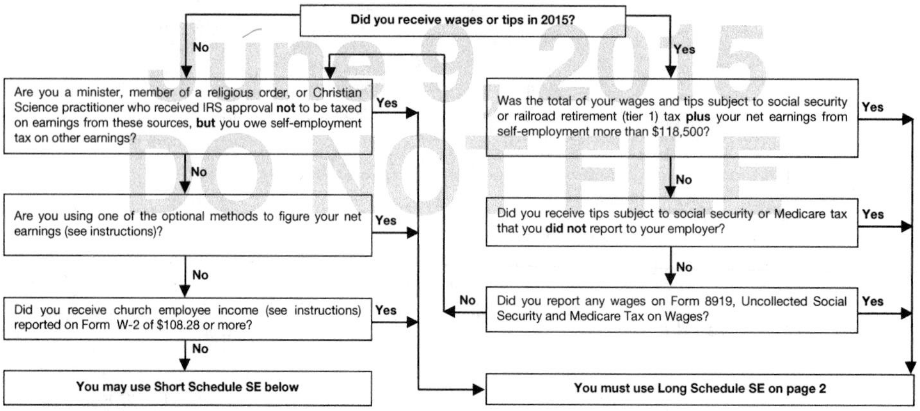

Did you receive wages or tips in 2015?
No
Yes
Are you a minister, member of a religious order, or Christian Science practitioner who received IRS approval not to be taxed on earnings from these sources, but you owe self-employment tax on other earnings?
Yes
Was the total of your wages and tips subject to social security or railroad retirement (tier 1) tax plus your net earnings from self-employment more than $118,500?
Yes
No
No
Are you using one of the optional methods to figure your net earnings (see instructions)?
Yes
Did you receive tips subject to social security or Medicare tax that you did not report to your employer?
Yes
No
No
No
Did you receive church employee income (see instructions) reported on Form W-2 of $108.28 or more?
Yes
Did you report any wages on Form 8919, Uncollected Social Security and Medicare Tax on Wages?
Yes
No
You may use Short Schedule SE below
You must use Long Schedule SE on page 2

Section A—Short Schedule SE. Caution. Read above to see if you can use Short Schedule SE.

1a	Net farm profit or (loss) from Schedule F, line 34, and farm partnerships, Schedule K-1 (Form 1065), box 14, code A . . .	**1a**	
b	If you received social security retirement or disability benefits, enter the amount of Conservation Reserve Program payments included on Schedule F, line 4b, or listed on Schedule K-1 (Form 1065), box 20, code Z	**1b**	( )
2	Net profit or (loss) from Schedule C, line 31; Schedule C-EZ, line 3; Schedule K-1 (Form 1065), box 14, code A (other than farming); and Schedule K-1 (Form 1065-B), box 9, code J1. Ministers and members of religious orders, see instructions for types of income to report on this line. See instructions for other income to report . . .	**2**	
3	Combine lines 1a, 1b, and 2 . . .	**3**	
4	Multiply line 3 by 92.35% (.9235). If less than $400, you do not owe self-employment tax; **do not** file this schedule unless you have an amount on line 1b . . . ▶	**4**	
	Note. If line 4 is less than $400 due to Conservation Reserve Program payments on line 1b, see instructions.		
5	**Self-employment tax.** If the amount on line 4 is: • $118,500 or less, multiply line 4 by 15.3% (.153). Enter the result here and on **Form 1040, line 57,** or **Form 1040NR, line 55** • More than $118,500, multiply line 4 by 2.9% (.029). Then, add $14,694 to the result. Enter the total here and on **Form 1040, line 57,** or **Form 1040NR, line 55** . . .	**5**	
6	**Deduction for one-half of self-employment tax.** Multiply line 5 by 50% (.50). Enter the result here and on **Form 1040, line 27,** or **Form 1040NR, line 27** . . . **6**		

For Paperwork Reduction Act Notice, see your tax return instructions. Cat. No. 11358Z **Schedule SE (Form 1040) 2015**

(Use for Cumulative Problem.)

Form **8829** Department of the Treasury Internal Revenue Service (99)	**Expenses for Business Use of Your Home** ▶ File only with Schedule C (Form 1040). Use a separate Form 8829 for each home you used for business during the year. ▶ Information about Form 8829 and its separate instructions is at *www.irs.gov/form8829*.	OMB No. 1545-0074 **2015** Attachment Sequence No. **176**
Name(s) of proprietor(s)		**Your social security number**

Part I — Part of Your Home Used for Business

Line	Description			Box	Amount
1	Area used regularly and exclusively for business, regularly for daycare, or for storage of inventory or product samples (see instructions)			1	
2	Total area of home			2	
3	Divide line 1 by line 2. Enter the result as a percentage			3	%
	For daycare facilities not used exclusively for business, go to line 4. All others, go to line 7.				
4	Multiply days used for daycare during year by hours used per day	4	hr.		
5	Total hours available for use during the year (365 days x 24 hours) (see instructions)	5	8,760 hr.		
6	Divide line 4 by line 5. Enter the result as a decimal amount	6			
7	Business percentage. For daycare facilities not used exclusively for business, multiply line 6 by line 3 (enter the result as a percentage). All others, enter the amount from line 3 ▶			7	%

Part II — Figure Your Allowable Deduction

			(a) Direct expenses	(b) Indirect expenses		
8	Enter the amount from Schedule C, line 29, **plus** any gain derived from the business use of your home, **minus** any loss from the trade or business not derived from the business use of your home (see instructions)				8	
	See instructions for columns (a) and (b) before completing lines 9–21.		(a) Direct expenses	(b) Indirect expenses		
9	Casualty losses (see instructions)	9				
10	Deductible mortgage interest (see instructions)	10				
11	Real estate taxes (see instructions)	11				
12	Add lines 9, 10, and 11	12				
13	Multiply line 12, column (b) by line 7			13		
14	Add line 12, column (a) and line 13				14	
15	Subtract line 14 from line 8. If zero or less, enter -0-				15	
16	Excess mortgage interest (see instructions)	16				
17	Insurance	17				
18	Rent	18				
19	Repairs and maintenance	19				
20	Utilities	20				
21	Other expenses (see instructions)	21				
22	Add lines 16 through 21	22				
23	Multiply line 22, column (b) by line 7			23		
24	Carryover of prior year operating expenses (see instructions)			24		
25	Add line 22, column (a), line 23, and line 24				25	
26	Allowable operating expenses. Enter the **smaller** of line 15 or line 25				26	
27	Limit on excess casualty losses and depreciation. Subtract line 26 from line 15				27	
28	Excess casualty losses (see instructions)			28		
29	Depreciation of your home from line 41 below			29		
30	Carryover of prior year excess casualty losses and depreciation (see instructions)			30		
31	Add lines 28 through 30				31	
32	Allowable excess casualty losses and depreciation. Enter the **smaller** of line 27 or line 31				32	
33	Add lines 14, 26, and 32				33	
34	Casualty loss portion, if any, from lines 14 and 32. Carry amount to **Form 4684** (see instructions)				34	
35	**Allowable expenses for business use of your home.** Subtract line 34 from line 33. Enter here and on Schedule C, line 30. If your home was used for more than one business, see instructions ▶				35	

Part III — Depreciation of Your Home

36	Enter the **smaller** of your home's adjusted basis or its fair market value (see instructions)	36	
37	Value of land included on line 36	37	
38	Basis of building. Subtract line 37 from line 36	38	
39	Business basis of building. Multiply line 38 by line 7	39	
40	Depreciation percentage (see instructions)	40	%
41	Depreciation allowable (see instructions). Multiply line 39 by line 40. Enter here and on line 29 above	41	

Part IV — Carryover of Unallowed Expenses to 2016

42	Operating expenses. Subtract line 26 from line 25. If less than zero, enter -0-	42	
43	Excess casualty losses and depreciation. Subtract line 32 from line 31. If less than zero, enter -0-	43	

For Paperwork Reduction Act Notice, see your tax return instructions. Cat. No. 13232M Form **8829** (2015)

Chapter

8

Depreciation and Amortization

CHAPTER CONTENTS

LEARNING OBJECTIVES

After completing Chapter 8, you should be able to:

1. Compute a taxpayer's depreciation expense deduction for personal and real property.
2. Determine how much Section 179 a taxpayer can elect to expense for the year and how that affects the taxpayer's total depreciation expense for the year.
3. Understand the special tax rules that govern the amount of depreciation allowed on luxury automobiles, leased vehicles, and listed property.
4. Understand which intangible assets are subject to amortization and how to calculate the amount of a taxpayer's amortization expense deduction.
5. Prepare Form 4562.

CHAPTER OVERVIEW

Chapter 7 covered the reporting requirements for sole proprietors. Sole proprietors report most of their business activities on Schedule C. The filled-in Schedule Cs shown in Chapter 7 (Figures 7–1 and 7–4) reported amounts for depreciation expense but did not explain where those amounts came from. This chapter presents the depreciation rules for business property and shows how to compute the depreciation expense deduction. This chapter also introduces Form 4562, Depreciation and Amortization, which supports the amount deducted for depreciation and amortization on Schedule C. The same Form 4562 is also used by corporations and partnerships to support their deductions for depreciation and amortization expense.

¶801 Depreciation of Business Property

When taxpayers buy business property with a useful life of more than one year, they recover the cost over several years by taking annual deductions from gross income. These annual deductions, called **depreciation expense,** represent the portion of the property's cost written off each year because of wear and tear, deterioration, and normal obsolescence. How quickly taxpayers depreciate business property depends on (1) whether the property is real property or tangible personal property and (2) when the property is placed in service.

Taxpayers recover the costs of tangible personal property more quickly than the costs of real property. Also, they can use more accelerated methods to depreciate tangible personal property. **Real property** includes all real estate, such as office buildings, apartment buildings, manufacturing plants, and warehouses. Land is not depreciated, even though it is real property. **Tangible personal property** includes tangible property other than real estate, such as furniture, machinery, equipment, and vehicles. The depreciation methods taxpayers can use depend on when the property was placed in service.

The depreciation rules in effect when the asset is placed in service continue to apply during the entire time the taxpayer owns the property. For example, to compute the 2015 depreciation expense on a building placed in service in 2011, the taxpayer uses the rules that applied to property placed in service in 2011.

Taxpayers need to understand how to depreciate property correctly. Depreciation expense reduces a property's adjusted basis, even if the taxpayer fails to deduct it on the tax return. Thus, the adjusted basis must be reduced by the *greater of* depreciation "allowed or allowable." This refers to depreciation that is deducted or that which the taxpayer is entitled to deduct. A taxpayer can claim overlooked depreciation expense by filing an amended return within three years of the due date of the tax return on which the expense went unclaimed. After three years, overlooked depreciation cannot be claimed, but it still reduces the taxpayer's basis in the property. (See ¶1313 for more discussion on how to file an amended tax return.)

This chapter focuses on the rules that apply to the depreciation of property placed in service after 1986, since property placed in service before 1987 has been fully depreciated. Those interested in learning more about pre-1986 depreciation rules should refer to IRS Publication 534. The depreciation rules for tangible personal property are presented first, followed by the rules for real property.

> Sole proprietors deduct depreciation expense on their business property on Schedule C. Depreciation expense taken on rental property is reported on Schedule E. Depreciation expense on other types of investment property is taken as a deduction on Schedule A as a miscellaneous itemized deduction (subject to the 2% AGI floor).

¶802 Depreciation of Tangible Personal Property

Normally taxpayers deduct the cost of long-lived assets over several years, thereby requiring them to wait several years to recognize the full tax benefits from taking depreciation deductions. Occasionally, tax laws are passed that speed up the recovery process by allowing taxpayers to deduct extra amounts (and get greater tax benefits) in the first year. These practices are done to encourage taxpayers to buy more business property, often in hopes of stimulating the economy. Section 179 immediate expensing (discussed later in the chapter at ¶802.05) is one such method. Another method used is first-year "bonus" depreciation.

¶802.01 "BONUS" FIRST-YEAR DEPRECIATION

In an effort to jump-start a sluggish economy after the events of 9-11, Congress enacted first-year **bonus depreciation** for purchases of new personal property used for business or investment acquired after September 10, 2001 and placed in service by December 31, 2004. Taxpayers were required to deduct bonus depreciation for all eligible purchases unless they made an election not to take it. After deducting bonus depreciation from the cost of the property, taxpayers depreciated the remaining cost (known as "MACRS basis") using the MACRS rules presented in ¶802.02. For property placed in service between September 11, 2001 and May 5, 2003, the bonus percentage was 30% of the cost of the property. After May 5, 2003, the percentage increased to 50%.

More recently, Congress enacted bonus depreciation on purchases of new personal property placed in service for business or investment use from 2008–2014. Only new property purchased with a recovery period of 20 years or less (personal property) was eligible for bonus depreciation. The cost of new computer software was eligible as well. The bonus percentage rate remained at 50% from 2008-2014, with the exception of property placed in service from September 9, 2010 and December 31, 2011, when bonus percentage increased to 100% of the cost of the property.

EXAMPLE 1

On August 1, 2014, Victor paid $20,000 for new personal property to be used in his business. Victor deducted $10,000 ($20,000 × 50%) of bonus depreciation in 2014. He uses MACRS to depreciate the remaining $10,000, starting in 2014 using the rules described in ¶802.02–¶802.04.

EXAMPLE 2

Same facts as in Example 1, except that Victor purchased used personal property in 2014. Victor could not deduct bonus depreciation in 2014 because bonus depreciation can only be taken on purchases of new personal property.

The provision allowing taxpayers to deduct bonus depreciation equal to 50% of the cost of new tangible personal property expired at the end of 2014. Many believe that bonus depreciation will be retroactively reinstated for 2015. However, at the time this textbook went to the printer, Congress had not been able to extend it. Since no action had been taken at the time this textbook was sent to the printer, the discussion of this topic in the chapter assumes no bonus depreciation allowed on property placed in service after 2014. In the event that Congress passes legislation that affects bonus depreciation, a summary of the tax bill can be found at: *CCHGroup.com/Legislation.*

¶802.02 MODIFIED ACCELERATED COST RECOVERY SYSTEM (MACRS)

To calculate depreciation expense using MACRS, taxpayers multiply the MACRS basis of the property by a percentage taken from an IRS-provided table. Under MACRS, personal property is assigned a life of 3, 5, 7, 10, or 15 years, regardless of its actual useful life. MACRS assigns the more common properties a 5-year or 7-year life. The 5-year-life class includes vehicles, office equipment, and cell phones. Office equipment includes copiers, fax machines, computers, printers, and the like. The 7-year-life class includes furniture and fixtures, machinery, and equipment other than office equipment.

MACRS uses the 200% declining balance method to recover the costs of 3-, 5-, 7-, and 10-year property. The 150% declining balance method is used for 15-year property. MACRS switches to the straight-line method when straight-line depreciation yields a greater deduction.

MACRS ignores salvage value. Instead, taxpayers multiply the percentage from the table by the property's MACRS basis to compute their MACRS deduction. Computing MACRS basis begins with the unadjusted basis in the property, which is the taxpayer's total cost of the property for use at its operating location. It includes the purchase price, sales tax, plus any delivery and installation costs. Any Section 179 expense or bonus depreciation taken in the first year is subtracted from the unadjusted basis to compute the taxpayer's MACRS basis.

The unadjusted basis of nonbusiness property that a taxpayer converts to business or investment use equals the *lesser of* (i) the taxpayer's adjusted basis in the property, or (ii) its fair market value (FMV) on the conversion date. Special rules also apply to property acquired by exchange, gift, or inheritance. These rules are discussed in Chapter 10.

¶802.03 AVERAGING CONVENTIONS

Two averaging conventions determine the date on which taxpayers can begin depreciating personal property. These two conventions are the half-year convention and the mid-quarter convention. The half-year convention applies when at least 60% of the basis of personal property placed in service during the year is placed in service during the first nine months of the year. The mid-quarter convention applies when more than 40% of the basis of personal property placed in service during the year is placed in service during the last three months of the year.

Half-Year Convention

When at least 60% of all personal property placed in service during the year is placed in service during the first nine months of the year, all personal property placed in service during that year is depreciated using the half-year convention. When using the half-year convention, the actual date on which personal property is placed in service is ignored. Instead, the **half-year convention** assumes that taxpayers place personal property in service halfway through the tax year. The half-year convention also assumes that taxpayers dispose of (e.g., sell) property halfway through the tax year. Thus, under the half-year convention, taxpayers get one-half year's depreciation in the first and last years, regardless of how long the taxpayer actually owned the property in those years.

Figure 8-1 shows the MACRS percentages for 5- and 7-year classes under the half-year convention. To compute MACRS on property depreciated under the half-year convention, taxpayers multiply these percentages by the MACRS basis of the property (as described in ¶802.02).

Figure 8-1: MACRS Table for 5- and 7-Year Classes Using the Half-Year Convention

	Recovery Period	
Year	5-Year	7-Year
1	20.00%	14.29%
2	32.00	24.49
3	19.20	17.49
4	11.52*	12.49
5	11.52	8.93*
6	5.76	8.92
7		8.93
8		4.46

*Switching to straight-line results in the maximum depreciation deduction

2022

The Year 1 percentages from Figure 8-1 reflect a half year of depreciation. Using the 200% declining balance method, taxpayers should deduct 40% of the cost of 5-year property in the first year (1/5 × 200%). However, because the half-year convention assumes taxpayers place property in service halfway through the year, the MACRS percentage for Year 1 is one-half of the full-year percentage, or 20% for 5-year property. Starting in Year 2, the percentages shown in Figure 8-1 reflect a full year of depreciation under the 200% declining balance method. An asterisk shows the switch to the straight-line method when straight-line yields a greater deduction. Figure 8-1 also shows that the rest of the first year's depreciation is deducted in the year after the recovery period ends. This is the sixth year for 5-year property and the eighth year for 7-year property.

EXAMPLE 3

On March 2, 2014, new 5-year property costing $10,000 is placed in service. After deducting $5,000 for bonus depreciation ($10,000 × 50%), the remaining $5,000 of MACRS basis is depreciated using the rates from the 5-year column in Figure 8-1. Depreciation using the half-year convention is shown below. In 2014, the taxpayer deducted $5,000 bonus depreciation and $1,000 MACRS ($5,000 MACRS basis × 20% year 1 percentage for 5-year property). At the end of 2015, the taxpayer's adjusted basis in the property is $2,400 ($10,000 – $7,600 accumulated depreciation).

Year	Depreciation	Calculation
2014	$6,000	$5,000 bonus depreciation + $1,000 MACRS
2015	1,600	$5,000 × 32% (year 2 percentage for 5-year property)
Total	$7,600	

Except in the last year of the recovery period, when using the half-year convention, taxpayers multiply the MACRS percentage from the table by one-half in the year they dispose of the property. In the last year of the recovery period (for example, year 6 for 5-year property), taxpayers use the full MACRS percentage to compute depreciation expense on the property, even if they dispose of the property in that year.

EXAMPLE 4

On April 10, 2012, Kate placed in service used 5-year property costing $10,000. On November 30, 2015, Kate sells the property. Under the half-year convention, the annual depreciation for the property is shown below.

Year	MACRS	Calculation
2012	$2,000	$10,000 × 20%
2013	3,200	$10,000 × 32%
2014	1,920	$10,000 × 19.2%
2015	576	$10,000 × 11.52% × ½
Total	$7,696	

No bonus depreciation was taken in 2012 since bonus depreciation does not apply to purchases of used property. It does not matter when in 2015 Kate actually sells the property. The half-year convention assumes that she sells the property on June 30, 2015, halfway through the tax year.

Mid-Quarter Convention

During the first few years after the half-year convention was enacted, many taxpayers took advantage of it by purchasing assets near the end of the year. This allowed them to take a half-year's depreciation in the first year, even though they owned the property for less than half of the year. To counter this strategy, the government now imposes a mid-quarter convention on all personal property placed in service during the year for taxpayers that purchase over 40% of their depreciable personal property (non real-estate) during the last quarter of the year.

Like the half-year convention, the mid-quarter convention ignores the actual date personal property is placed in service. Instead, the **mid-quarter convention** assumes that taxpayers placed their personal property in service in the middle of the quarter. Thus, taxpayers that place personal property in service between January 1 and March 31 are assumed to place it in service on February 15. This means that, in the first year, they can depreciate the property from February 15 until December 31 (10.5 months). Figure 8-2 shows the four mid-quarter tables for 5- and 7-year classes.

Figure 8-2: MACRS Table for 5- and 7-Year Classes Using the Mid-Quarter Convention

Placed in Service in	Years							
1st quarter	**1**	**2**	**3**	**4**	**5**	**6**	**7**	**8**
5-year	35.00%	26.00%	15.60%	11.01%	11.01%	1.38%		
7-year	25.00	21.43	15.31	10.93	8.75	8.74	8.75%	1.09%
2nd quarter								
5-year	25.00	30.00	18.00	11.37	11.37	4.26		
7-year	17.85	23.47	16.76	11.97	8.87	8.87	8.87	3.34
3rd quarter								
5-year	15.00	34.00	20.40	12.24	11.30	7.06		
7-year	10.71	25.51	18.22	13.02	9.30	8.85	8.86	5.53
4th quarter								
5-year	5.00	38.00	22.80	13.68	10.94	9.58		
7-year	3.57	27.55	19.68	14.06	10.04	8.73	8.73	7.64

The Year 1 percentages in Figure 8-2 reflect the portion of the year in which the property is assumed to be in service. For property placed in service in the first quarter, depreciation on the property begins on February 15. For 5-year property, the first-year percentage equals 35% (1/5 × 200% × 10.5/12). For 7-year property placed in service in the fourth quarter (deemed placed in service on November 15), the first-year percentage equals 3.57% (1/7 × 200% × 1.5/12). Starting in Year 2, the percentages reflect a full year of depreciation under the 200% declining balance method, switching to straight-line when straight-line results in a greater deduction.

When property is being depreciated using the mid-quarter convention, the tax laws assume that taxpayers dispose of property halfway through the quarter. Thus, all personal property sold during October, November, and December is deemed to have been sold on November 15, regardless of the quarter in which the property was purchased. Likewise, all personal property sold during April, May, and June is deemed sold on May 15. Except in the last year of the recovery period, in the year taxpayers dispose of personal property, the percentage from the table must be reduced to reflect the portion of the year the property was assumed to be in service. When using the mid-quarter convention, this would be from January 1 until the middle of the quarter in which the property is sold.

EXAMPLE 5

In March 2013, Ed placed in service new 7-year property that cost $20,000. Ed sold the property in June 2015. Under the mid-quarter convention, depreciation taken on the property is as follows.

Year	Depreciation	Calculation
2013	$12,500	($20,000 × 50%) bonus depreciation + ($10,000 MACRS basis × 25%)
2014	2,143	$10,000 MACRS basis × 21.43%
2015	574	$10,000 MACRS basis × 15.31% × 4.5/12
Total	$15,217	

The MACRS first-quarter percentages apply since Ed placed the property in service during the first quarter. Although Ed actually sold the property in June, the property is deemed sold halfway through the second quarter (May 15). Ed multiplies the Year 3 MACRS percentage by 4.5/12 to reflect the property's depreciation from January 1 through May 15. Notice that Ed uses the percentages for 7-year property placed in service in the 1st quarter for all years that he depreciates the property.

Each year taxpayers must determine whether the half-year or mid-quarter convention applies to personal property placed in service that year. If the mid-quarter convention applies, taxpayers may need to use four different tables to compute depreciation on personal property placed in service that year. (Under the half-year convention, taxpayers use one table to depreciate all personal property placed in service during the year.) The mid-quarter convention applies when the taxpayer placed in service in the fourth quarter more than 40% of the total depreciable personal property placed in service that year. Otherwise, the half-year convention applies. Thus, the relevant percentage is fourth quarter depreciable personal property placed in service divided by total depreciable personal property placed in service during the year. Only the cost of personal property after subtracting out all Section 179 expenses elected on the properties is used in this calculation. Neither the cost of real property placed in service during the year, nor bonus depreciation taken on personal property, are considered in making this calculation.

EXAMPLE 6

On June 21, 20x1, Nelson placed in service 7-year property that costs $40,000. On October 10, 20x1, he placed in service 5-year property that costs $30,000. These are the only properties placed in service in 20x1. Section 179 was not taken on either property. Nelson is considered to have placed in service 42.9% ($30,000/$70,000) of the personal property in the fourth quarter. Thus, the mid-quarter convention applies to all personal property placed in service in 20x1. Nelson uses the mid-quarter tables to compute depreciation on the MACRS basis. He continues to use the same mid-quarter tables to depreciate these properties in future tax years.

EXAMPLE 7

Same facts as in Example 6, except that Nelson placed the 5-year property in service on September 30, 20x1. Since at least 60% of the personal property placed in service in 20x1 was placed in service in the first three quarters, the half-year convention applies to both properties.

¶802.04 ELECTION CHOICES

Taxpayers that do not wish to use the regular MACRS (accelerated) method can elect to use either straight-line MACRS or the Alternative Depreciation System (ADS).

Straight-line MACRS

Straight-line MACRS uses the straight-line method instead of the accelerated method. Straight-line depreciation spreads the cost evenly over the MACRS recovery period. When the taxpayer elects the straight-line method, the recovery periods and averaging conventions continue to apply.

EXAMPLE 8

On June 5, 20x1, a taxpayer places in service used 5-year property costing $10,000. The half-year convention applies to all personal property placed in service that year. The taxpayer sells the property on January 14, 20x4. A comparison of regular (accelerated) MACRS and straight-line MACRS follows. Since the property purchased was used property, bonus depreciation was not taken on the property.

Year	**Regular MACRS**		**Straight-line MACRS**	
20x1	$10,000 × 20%	$2,000	$10,000 × 1/5 × ½	$1,000
20x2	$10,000 × 32%	3,200	$10,000 × 1/5	2,000
20x3	$10,000 × 19.2%	1,920	$10,000 × 1/5	2,000
20x4	$10,000 × 11.52% × ½	576	$10,000 × 1/5 × ½	1,000
Total		$7,696		$6,000

EXAMPLE 9

Same facts as in Example 8, except that the mid-quarter convention applies to all personal property placed in service during 20x1.

Year	**Regular MACRS**		**Straight-line MACRS**	
20x1	$10,000 × 25%	$2,500	$10,000 × 1/5 × 7.5/12	$1,250
20x2	$10,000 × 30%	3,000	$10,000 × 1/5	2,000
20x3	$10,000 × 18%	1,800	$10,000 × 1/5	2,000
20x4	$10,000 × 11.37% × 1.5/12	142	$10,000 × 1/5 × 1.5/12	250
Total		$7,442		$5,500

Under the mid-quarter convention, the taxpayer begins depreciating the property in the middle of the quarter in which it is placed in service. In this case, that would be on May 15 (the middle of the second quarter). Thus, in the first year, depreciation is allowed for 7.5 months (built into the MACRS tables). This property was sold in the first quarter. Thus, depreciation in 20x4 is allowed until the middle of the first quarter (February 15, or 1.5 months (not built into the MACRS tables)).

The election to use the straight-line method can be made annually for each class of property. For example, a taxpayer that elects the straight-line method in 2015 for 5-year property must use the straight-line method to depreciate all 5-year property placed in service in 2015. However, the taxpayer can use the regular (accelerated) MACRS for 7-year property purchased in 2015. This is called an election on a **class-by-class basis**. A taxpayer that uses the straight-line method to depreciate 5-year property placed in service in one year does not have to use it to depreciate 5-year property placed in service in any other year.

EXAMPLE 10

Jones Company placed in service the following properties during 20x1.

- Equipment (7-year personal property)
- Furniture (7-year personal property)
- Delivery van (5-year personal property)
- Warehouse (commercial real property)
- Office building (commercial real property)

If Jones wants to use straight-line MACRS to depreciate the equipment, it must use the straight-line method to depreciate all 7-year property placed in service during 20x1 (i.e., the furniture). Jones's decision to use straight-line MACRS to depreciate the 7-year property placed in service during 20x1 does not affect the depreciation method it uses to depreciate the 5-year property or any real property placed in service during 20x1. Also, its decision to use straight-line MACRS to depreciate the 7-year property placed in service during in 20x1 does not affect the depreciation method it uses to depreciate 7-year property placed in service in 20x2 or any future tax year.

Alternative Depreciation System (ADS)

The **Alternative Depreciation System (ADS)** differs from MACRS in that most properties have longer recovery periods. For most property, the taxpayer can choose between the straight-line method and the 150% declining balance method. The half-year and mid-quarter conventions apply to personal property depreciated under the ADS method. Separate tables are available for this method. These tables can be found in IRS Publication 946. The following table compares the recovery periods under MACRS and ADS.

	MACRS	ADS
Office furniture, fixtures, and equipment	7 years	10 years
Automobiles, light general-purpose trucks, computers, and printers	5 years	5 years
Copiers, calculators, and typewriters	5 years	6 years
Heavy general purpose trucks	5 years	6 years

Personal property with no designated class life has a recovery period of 12 years under ADS. The taxpayer makes the election to use ADS annually on a class-by-class basis. Once a taxpayer elects to depreciate a specific class of property using ADS, that election for that class of property cannot be revoked. Straight-line ADS must be used to depreciate property used 50% or less for business. It also is used to compute a corporation's "earnings and profits." Example 11 shows the four different options available for depreciating personal property.

EXAMPLE 11

Natalie places in service a desk. To recover the cost of the desk and all other 7-year property placed in service during the year, Natalie can choose from the following methods:

MACRS:
- 200% declining balance over 7 years (regular MACRS)
- Straight-line over 7 years (straight-line MACRS)

ADS:
- Straight-line over 10 years
- 150% declining balance over 10 years

No matter which method Natalie selects, the percentage of all personal property placed in service in the fourth quarter will determine whether the half-year or mid-quarter convention applies. Also, the method Natalie selects will apply to all 7-year property placed in service during the year. Regardless of which depreciation method Natalie selects, she must continue to depreciate the desk (plus all other 7-year property placed in service during the year) using that method in all future years.

It is often assumed that the taxpayer should take the maximum deduction allowed at the earliest possible time. However, a taxpayer currently in a low tax bracket may expect to be in a higher tax bracket in future years. This particular taxpayer may benefit more by delaying depreciation deductions until the higher tax bracket years. This can be accomplished by electing straight-line MACRS or ADS to depreciate property.

¶802.05 SECTION 179 EXPENSE ELECTION

Taxpayers that qualify can elect to take an up-front deduction in the year certain personal property is placed in service. Under current tax law for 2015, taxpayers can expense up to $25,000 of Section 179 property placed in service during 2015. The Internal Revenue Code (Code) defines **Section 179 property** as *tangible personal property purchased* by the taxpayer and *used in a trade or business.* Thus, real property and property acquired by means other than a purchase are not Section 179 property. Likewise, depreciable personal property used for investment is not Section 179 property. However, used property that the taxpayer purchases for use in the taxpayer's business is eligible for Section 179 expensing.

The amount of Section 179 property that taxpayers can expense in the first year is reduced dollar-for-dollar when more than $200,000 of Section 179 property is placed in service during 2015. For example, taxpayers who place in service $216,000 of Section 179 property during 2015 would be allowed to expense up to $9,000 [$25,000 – ($216,000 – $200,000)] of the Section 179 property in that year. Married couples who file married filing separately can each claim one-half of the couples' allowed Section 179 amount, or they can agree to split the allowed amount in any other manner. Taxpayers compute the maximum Section 179 expense they can take each year on Form 4562, Part I (lines 1 to 5).

Taxpayers can elect Section 179 expense only in the year they place the property in service. Once taxpayers determine the amount of Section 179 expense they wish to elect, they allocate it amongst one or more of the Section 179 properties placed in service during the year. Taxpayers must identify on the tax return the property (or properties) they elect to expense under Section 179. Taxpayers make this election on Form 4562, Part I (line 6). After selecting the property (or properties) to expense under Section 179, they can recover the rest of the unadjusted basis of the property (or properties) using bonus depreciation (when allowed), MACRS (regular or straight-line), or ADS (straight-line or 150% declining balance).

EXAMPLE 12

On February 10, 2015, Lowe Enterprises placed in service used personal property that costs $204,000, which includes $80,000 of used equipment (7-year property). The half-year convention applies to personal property placed in service in 2015. Lowe elects to expense part of the equipment under Section 179. Since Lowe placed in service more than $200,000 of Section 179 property, it can elect to expense up to $21,000 under Section 179 [$25,000 – ($204,000 – $200,000)]. Lowe can then deduct regular MACRS on the remaining $59,000 ($80,000 – $21,000). In 2015, total depreciation on the equipment equals $29,431 [$21,000 Section 179 expense + $8,431 MACRS ($59,000 × 14.29%)].

Section 179 expense cannot exceed a taxpayer's taxable income from any trade or business after all other depreciation has been taken. Taxpayers can carry over to the next tax year any Section 179 expense disallowed because of the taxable income limit. However, this carryover is subject to the Section 179 limit that applies to the next year(s). For purposes of MACRS, taxpayers must reduce the basis in the property by the total amount they *elect* to expense under Section 179.

EXAMPLE 13

Same facts as in Example 12, except that Lowe's taxable income from the business (after regular depreciation) is $5,000. Although Lowe can elect up to $21,000 of Section 179 expense, only $5,000 can be deducted in 2015. The $16,000 of disallowed expense can be carried over to 2016 and later years.

For purposes of computing MACRS on the equipment, Lowe reduces its basis by the amount it elects to expense under Section 179, even though part of the expense must be postponed. If Lowe does not do this, over the next eight years Lowe will deduct $21,000 under Section 179 ($5,000 in 2015 and $16,000 in a future year) and $75,000 ($80,000 – $5,000) as MACRS depreciation. The total deductions of $96,000 would exceed the $80,000 cost of the equipment.

¶802.06 FILLED-IN FORM 4562, PART I

INFORMATION FOR FIGURE 8-3:

Lowe Enterprises from Example 13 computes the maximum amount it can elect to expense under Section 179. Lowe enters the amounts shown below in bold on Form 4562 and then follows the instructions on the form to determine that $5,000 of Section 179 expense that can be deducted in the current year and $16,000 must be carried over to next year.

Line #

1: Maximum amount, **$25,000**
2: Total cost of section 179 property placed in service, **$204,000**
3: Threshold cost of section 179 property before reduction in limitation, **$200,000**
4: Reduction in limitation, **$4,000** ($204,000 – $200,000)
5: Dollar limit (maximum Section 179 that can be elected), **$21,000** ($25,000 – $4,000)
6(a): Description of property, **Equipment**
6(b): Cost (business use only), **$80,000**
6(c): Elected cost (to be expensed under Section 179), **$21,000**
11: Smaller of business income ($5,000) or line 5 ($21,000), **$5,000**

Figure 8-3: Filled-In Form 4562, Part I

Form **4562** | **Depreciation and Amortization** | OMB No. 1545-0172

(Including Information on Listed Property)

▶ **Attach to your tax return.**

Department of the Treasury Internal Revenue Service (99) | ▶ **Information about Form 4562 and its separate instructions is at *www.irs.gov/form4562.*** | **2015** Attachment Sequence No. **179**

Name(s) shown on return	Business or activity to which this form relates	Identifying number
Lowe Enterprises	**Retail Sales**	**71-6928490**

Part I Election To Expense Certain Property Under Section 179

Note: If you have any listed property, complete Part V before you complete Part I.

1	Maximum amount (see instructions)	1	25,000
2	Total cost of section 179 property placed in service (see instructions)	2	204,000
3	Threshold cost of section 179 property before reduction in limitation (see instructions)	3	200,000
4	Reduction in limitation. Subtract line 3 from line 2. If zero or less, enter -0-	4	4,000
5	Dollar limitation for tax year. Subtract line 4 from line 1. If zero or less, enter -0-. If married filing separately, see instructions	5	21,000

6	(a) Description of property	(b) Cost (business use only)	(c) Elected cost
	Equipment	80,000	21,000

7	Listed property. Enter the amount from line 29	7	
8	Total elected cost of section 179 property. Add amounts in column (c), lines 6 and 7	8	21,000
9	Tentative deduction. Enter the **smaller** of line 5 or line 8	9	21,000
10	Carryover of disallowed deduction from line 13 of your 2014 Form 4562	10	
11	Business income limitation. Enter the smaller of business income (not less than zero) or line 5 (see instructions)	11	5,000
12	Section 179 expense deduction. Add lines 9 and 10, but do not enter more than line 11	12	5,000
13	Carryover of disallowed deduction to 2016. Add lines 9 and 10, less line 12 ▶ 13	16,000	

Section 179 expense was first introduced in 1986. The maximum amount that could be immediately expensed that year was $5,000. From 1987-2002, Congress gradually increased the amount that could be expensed. Then, in 2003, Congress significantly increased the amount of the deduction and placed in service limits to give businesses an extra incentive to spend more on new equipment and other new tangible personal property. The hope was that this could provide a boost to the economy (see discussion of tax incentives at ¶101). From 2011-2014, these amounts were at their highest ($500,000 and $2 million, respectively). However, when Congress failed to extend the higher limits for 2015, the amounts reverted back to their 2002 levels. Although many believe that the enhanced Section 179 expensing will be retroactively reinstated for 2015, like bonus depreciation, no such legislation had been passed at the time this textbook was sent to the printer. Thus, the discussion of this topic in this textbook includes the Section 179 limits in effect at the time the textbook was sent to the printer ($25,000 and $200,000, respectively). In the event that Congress passes legislation that affects Section 179, a summary of the tax bill can be found at: *CCHGroup.com/Legislation.*

¶802.07 LISTED PROPERTY LIMITATIONS

Special rules apply to property *suitable for personal use.* Such property, referred to as **listed property,** commonly includes vehicles, computers, and printers. Listed property that the taxpayer does not use more than 50% of the time for business does not qualify for regular (accelerated) MACRS, bonus depreciation, or Section 179 first-year expense. Instead, such property must be depreciated under ADS using the straight-line method. The half-year and mid-quarter provisions apply to listed property.

Property Suitable for Personal Use

Property used for transportation

- Passenger automobiles and motorcycles
- Trucks, buses, boats, and airplanes

Property used for entertainment, recreation, or amusement

- Cameras and VCRs
- Communication and stereo equipment

Computers and related equipment (but not if used only at the taxpayer's regular business establishment, including a qualified home office)

For property used for transportation (like automobiles), the 50% test should be based on *miles used for business* in relation to total miles used. For other types of listed property, taxpayers should use the appropriate *units of time* (hours) to allocate between business use and other use. Although any investment use of the property is not considered in meeting the more-than-50% business use test, taxpayers can depreciate the portion of the property's cost that involves investment use. Whichever depreciation method (regular MACRS or ADS) is chosen, that method is used to depreciate both the business and the investment use portions of the property.

Taxpayers must be able to substantiate the amount, time, place, and business purpose of transportation expenses. For automobiles and other vehicles, they must establish both the business/investment miles and total miles the vehicle was driven during the year. They do this by keeping adequate records or by producing evidence that supports statements they prepare.

Part V of Form 4562 is where taxpayers report the depreciation of listed property. In Part V, taxpayers confirm that they have written evidence to support the business or investment use of the property. They then separate the listed property used more than 50% of the time for business from property used 50% or less for business. Only property used more than 50% for business can be expensed under Section 179 and depreciated using bonus depreciation (when applicable) and regular (accelerated) MACRS. When Section 179 or bonus depreciation is taken on listed property placed in service during the year, taxpayers report Section 179 expense on line 26(i) and bonus depreciation on line 25(h). Only the remaining (MACRS) basis is reported on line 26(e).

EXAMPLE 14

On August 9, 2014, Tom placed in service a new computer that costs $4,000. This is the only property Tom placed in service in 2014, so the half-year convention applies. Tom uses the computer 60% of the time for business, 15% of the time for investment purposes, and 25% of the time for personal use. Since the business use of the computer exceeds 50%, accelerated depreciation methods can be used to depreciate the 75% combined business and investment use ($4,000 × 75% = $3,000 business/investment basis). Bonus depreciation of $1,500 ($3,000 × 50%) was taken in 2014, along with $300 of MACRS ($1,500 MACRS basis × 20%). MACRS for 2015 is $480 ($1,500 MACRS basis × 32%).

Since business use exceeds 50%, Tom could have elected to expense $2,400 ($4,000 × 60%) under Section 179 and used bonus depreciation and MACRS to depreciate the $600 investment basis ($4,000 × 15%).

EXAMPLE 15

Same facts as in Example 14, except that Tom uses the computer 40% for business, 15% for investment purposes, and 45% for personal use. Because business use does not exceed 50%, Section 179 cannot be elected and Tom cannot take bonus depreciation in 2014. Instead, he must use straight-line ADS and the half-year convention to depreciate the 55% combined business/investment basis. Tom's 2014 depreciation on computer would be $220 ($2,200 basis × 1/5 × ½). His 2015 depreciation would be $440 ($2,200 × 1/5).

If the business usage of listed property drops at or below 50% in a future year and the taxpayer has used Section 179, bonus depreciation, or regular (accelerated) MACRS to depreciate the property, the taxpayer must permanently switch to the straight-line ADS method. Also, the taxpayer must recompute what depreciation would have been in all prior years for that property using only straight-line ADS to depreciate the listed property. The difference between accumulated depreciation taken on the property (including any bonus depreciation and Section 179 expense) and what accumulated depreciation would have been using straight-line ADS must be included in the taxpayer's income in the year business usage drops at or below 50%. "Recapture" is the term used to describe the inclusion of the excess amount in gross income.

EXAMPLE 16

Fred paid $3,000 for a computer on April 3, 20x1. He used the computer 60% for business and 40% for personal use during both 20x1 and 20x2. Fred used regular (accelerated) MACRS and the half-year convention to depreciate the computer. On his 20x1 and 20x2 tax returns, Fred deducted $360 ($3,000 × 60% × 20%) and $576 ($3,000 × 60% × 32%), respectively. In 20x3, Fred's business usage drops to 45%.

Beginning in 20x3, Fred must permanently switch to straight-line ADS. His 20x3 depreciation expense deduction is $270 ($3,000 × 45% × 1/5). In addition, Fred must compute what his depreciation expense would have been in 20x1 and 20x2 using straight-line ADS. His depreciation would have been $180 ($3,000 × 60% × 1/5 × ½) in 20x1 and $360 ($3,000 × 60% × 1/5) in 20x2. Fred must include in his 20x3 gross income the $396 difference between the $936 ($360 + $576) he deducted in 20x1 and 20x2 and the $540 ($180 + $360) that he have deducted had he used straight-line ADS from the beginning.

¶802.08 FILLED-IN FORM 4562, PART V

INFORMATION FOR FIGURE 8-4:

Tom from Example 15 uses Form 4562, Part V to report the depreciation on his computer. Tom has written evidence to support his 40% business use and 15% investment use so he marks **YES** on lines 24a and 24b. He enters the information for the computer on line 27 because his business use alone does not exceed 50%. The depreciation deduction on line 27(h) reflects straight-line ADS depreciation using the half-year convention.

Line #
27(a): Type of property, **Computer**
27(b): Date placed in service, **8-9-14**
27(c): Business/investment use percentage, **55%**
27(d): Cost or other basis, **$4,000**
27(e): Basis for depreciation, **$2,200** ($4,000 cost × 55% business/investment percentage)
27(f): Recovery period, **5 yr.**
27(g): Convention, **HY**, half-year convention applies
27(h): Depreciation deduction, **$440** ($2,200 basis × 1/5)

Figure 8-4: Filled-In Form 4562, Part V

Form 4562 (2015) Page **2**

Part V **Listed Property** (Include automobiles, certain other vehicles, certain aircraft, certain computers, and property used for entertainment, recreation, or amusement.)

Note: For any vehicle for which you are using the standard mileage rate or deducting lease expense, complete **only** 24a, 24b, columns (a) through (c) of Section A, all of Section B, and Section C if applicable.

Section A—Depreciation and Other Information (Caution: See the instructions for limits for passenger automobiles.)

24a Do you have evidence to support the business/investment use claimed? ☑ **Yes** ☐ **No** **24b** If "Yes," is the evidence written? ☑ **Yes** ☐ **No**

(a) Type of property (list vehicles first)	(b) Date placed in service	(c) Business/ investment use percentage	(d) Cost or other basis	(e) Basis for depreciation (business/investment use only)	(f) Recovery period	(g) Method/ Convention	(h) Depreciation deduction	(i) Elected section 179 cost
25 Special depreciation allowance for qualified listed property placed in service during the tax year and used more than 50% in a qualified business use (see instructions) .						**25**		
26 Property used more than 50% in a qualified business use:								
		%						
		%						
		%						
27 Property used 50% or less in a qualified business use:								
Computer	**8-9-14**	**55** %	**4,000**	**2,200**	**5 yr.**	S/L – **HY**	**440**	
		%				S/L –		
		%				S/L –		
28 Add amounts in column (h), lines 25 through 27. Enter here and on line 21, page 1 .						**28**	**440**	
29 Add amounts in column (i), line 26. Enter here and on line 7, page 1							**29**	

¶802.09 LUXURY AUTOMOBILE LIMITS

The tax laws limit the depreciation of vehicles used for business, even those used 100% for business. These limits apply to all types of depreciation, including Section 179 expenses and bonus depreciation. Figure 8-5 shows the depreciation limits for cars (other than trucks or vans) placed in service from 2008–2015. Slightly higher limits apply to trucks and vans.

Figure 8-5: Luxury Car Depreciation Limits for the Years 2008–2015

	Placed in Service During			
Year	**2008 or 2009**	**2010 or 2011**	**2012–2014**	**2015**
1	$2,960/$10,960*	$3,060/$11,060*	$3,160/$11,160*	$3,160
2	4,800	4,900	5,100	5,100
3	2,850	2,950	3,050	3,050
4	1,775	1,775	1,875	1,875

* For 2008 and 2009, the limit for used cars and cars used 50% or less for business was $2,960. For 2010 and 2011, this amount was $3,060. For 2012–2014, it was $3,160. The higher amounts for these years represent the limits for new cars used more than 50% for business (due to bonus depreciation allowed in those years).

The limits in Figure 8-5 apply only to passenger automobiles. A passenger automobile is any four-wheeled vehicle made primarily for use on public streets, roads, and highways and whose unloaded gross vehicle weight is 6,000 pounds or less. Ambulances, hearses, taxis, and limousines are not subject to the luxury automobile rules. Neither are trucks and vans placed in service after July 6, 2003, if they have been modified so that they are not likely to be used for personal use.

When the luxury automobile rules were first enacted, the rules applied to "passenger automobiles" that did not weigh over 6,000 pounds. Since then, many sports utility vehicles (SUVs) weigh over 6,000 pounds, and taxpayers found they could avoid the luxury automobile limits by purchasing these heavier SUVs and using them in their businesses. This allowed them to expense the SUV's cost under Section 179 (assuming 100% business use).

Congress addressed this issue by enacting tax rules that now limit the amount of Section 179 expense allowed on SUVs weighing between 6,000 and 14,000 pounds to a maximum of $25,000 (based on 100% business use). Amounts not expensed under Section 179 are depreciated using the MACRS rules discussed in this chapter. Under current tax law, only SUVs weighing more than 14,000 pounds are exempt from the $25,000 Section 179 limit.

The luxury automobile limits, like those shown for cars in Figure 8-5, are the limits imposed for vehicles used 100% of the time for business. Taxpayers must reduce the limits when the vehicle is used less than 100% for business. For vehicles used partially for business, taxpayers must combine the rules for listed property with those for luxury automobiles.

EXAMPLE 17

On August 2, 2013, Paula placed in service a new car that cost $40,000. The half-year convention applies to personal property Paula placed in service in 2013. Paula uses the car 70% of the time for business. Thus, her business-use cost of the car is $28,000 ($40,000 × 70%). Since business use exceeds 50%, bonus depreciation and regular MACRS were taken on the car. Paula uses the "2012–2014" column from Figure 8-5 to compute her luxury car limits. In 2013, Paula deducted $7,812 [the *lesser of* (i) $16,800 (($28,000 business-use cost × 50% bonus depreciation rate) + ($14,000 MACRS basis × 20%)) or (ii) $7,812 ($11,160 × 70%)]. In 2015 (year 3), she deducts $2,135 [the *lesser of* (i) $2,688 ($14,000 MACRS basis × 19.2%) or (ii) $2,135 ($3,050 × 70%)].

EXAMPLE 18

On July 15, 2011, Anne placed in service a used car that cost $30,000. The half-year convention applies to personal property Anne placed in service in 2011. Anne uses the car 80% of the time for business. She uses the "2010 or 2011" column from Figure 8-5 to compute her luxury car limits. Anne was limited to $2,448 ($3,060 × 80%) of depreciation in 2011, since it is less than $4,800 ($30,000 × 80% × 20% MACRS). (Bonus depreciation was not taken in 2011, since Anne purchased a used car.) In 2015 (year 5), Anne's depreciation deduction is limited to $1,420 [*lesser of* (i) $2,765 ($30,000 × 80% × 11.52%) or (ii) $1,420 ($1,775 × 80%)].

EXAMPLE 19

On April 5, 2015, Phil placed in service a car costing $45,000. Phil uses the car 100% for business. He elected to use straight-line ADS to depreciate the car. The half-year convention applied to all personal property placed in service during 2015. Phil computes his first year ADS depreciation on the car to be $4,500 ($45,000 × 1/5 × ½). However, this amount exceeds the $3,160 first year limit for cars placed in service during 2015. Thus, Phil's deduction is limited to $3,160. In 2016, ADS depreciation would be $9,000 ($45,000 × 1/5). However, this amount exceeds the $5,100 year 2 limit for cars placed in service during 2015. Thus, Phil's 2016 depreciation deduction will be limited to $5,100.

Leased Vehicles

Taxpayers leasing cars and other vehicles can either use the standard mileage rate or deduct the business portion of their lease payments. To prevent taxpayers from getting around the luxury automobile limits by leasing (rather than buying) expensive cars, the government reduces the amount taxpayers can deduct for their lease payments. They do this by reducing the taxpayer's car expense deduction by an "inclusion amount." The inclusion amount is based on the FMV of the vehicle. Taxpayers multiply the inclusion amount from the IRS table by the business-use percentage. In the first and last years of the lease, the amount is further reduced to reflect the portion of the year the car was leased.

The inclusion amounts for leased cars can be found in IRS Publication 463. Figure 8-6 shows the portion of the table for cars with a FMV between $35,000 and $40,000 that were first leased during 2015. Inclusion amounts for trucks and vans are slightly lower. These amounts, along with inclusion amounts for car values not listed in Figure 8-6, can be found in IRS Publication 463, Appendix A.

Figure 8-6: Inclusion Amounts for Cars First Leased in 2015

Fair Market Value		Tax Year of Lease				
Over	**Not Over**	**1st**	**2nd**	**3rd**	**4th**	**5th and later**
$35,000	$36,000	$28	$62	$92	$110	$126
36,000	37,000	30	65	96	116	133
37,000	38,000	31	68	102	121	139
38,000	39,000	33	71	106	127	146
39,000	40,000	34	75	110	132	153

EXAMPLE 20

On September 1, 2015, Lane began leasing a car for $400 a month. Lane leased the car for 122 days during 2015 (September 1 to December 31). The FMV of the car was $37,200 and Lane's business usage is 70%. In 2015, Lane's initial deduction equals 70% of her lease payments, or $1,120 ($400 × 4 × 70%). From Figure 8-6, the inclusion amount for 2015 (1st year of the lease) for a car valued at $37,200, is $31. Lane reduces her 2015 lease expense deduction by $7 ($31 × 70% × 122/365) and deducts $1,113 ($1,120 – $7) on Schedule C (line 20a). In 2016, Lane's lease expense deduction is $3,312 [$3,360 for her lease payments ($400 × 12 × 70%) – $48 ($68 inclusion amount × 70%)]

EXAMPLE 21

On March 2, 2015, Michelle entered into a 36-month lease. The FMV of the car she leased is $39,430. Michelle drives the car 75% for business each year. To compute her inclusion amount in 2015, Michelle multiplies the $34 first year inclusion amount from Figure 8-6 by 75% and then by 305/365 (the portion of 2015 that she leased the car). For 2016 and 2017, she multiplies the $75 and $110 inclusion amounts by 75% to compute her inclusion amount in those years. In 2018 (the last year of the lease), Michelle multiplies the $132 fourth year inclusion amount by both 75% and 60/365 (the portion of the fourth year that she leased the car during 2018).

¶803 Depreciation of Real Property

¶803.01 MODIFIED ACRS (MACRS)

Under MACRS, taxpayers depreciate real property using the straight-line method. The recovery period for real property under MACRS depends on whether the property is residential or nonresidential real property. Taxpayers recover the cost of residential rental property over 27.5 years. Real property is residential rental realty if the building is used as a place where people live. Examples of residential realty include apartment buildings and rental vacation homes. The recovery period for nonresidential (commercial and industrial) real estate, such as office buildings, manufacturing plants, and warehouses, is 31.5 years if placed in service before May 13, 1993. For nonresidential property placed in service after May 12, 1993, the recovery period is 39 years. Although land is real property, it is not depreciated.

The **mid-month convention** applies to real property depreciated under MACRS. The mid-month convention assumes taxpayers place real property in service in the middle of the month they actually place it in service. The mid-month convention also assumes that taxpayers dispose of real property in the middle of a month.

EXAMPLE 22

On March 1, 1993, Vicky placed in service residential real property that cost $100,000. Vicky sells the property on December 5, 2015. Vicky's annual cost recovery for the property follows.

Year	Calculation	MACRS
1993	$100,000 × 1/27.5 = $3,636 × 9.5/12 =	$ 2,879
1994–2014	$100,000 × 1/27.5 = $3,636 × 21 years =	76,356
2015	$100,000 × 1/27.5 = $3,636 × 11.5/12 =	3,485
Total		$82,720

EXAMPLE 23

Same facts as in Example 22, except that on March 1, 1993, Vicky placed in service nonresidential real property. In this scenario, the recovery period Vicky uses is 31.5 years for nonresidential real property placed in service before May 13, 1993.

Year	Calculation	MACRS
1993	$100,000 × 1/31.5 = $3,175 × 9.5/12 =	$ 2,514
1994–2014	$100,000 × 1/31.5 = $3,175 × 21 years =	66,675
2015	$100,000 × 1/31.5 = $3,175 × 11.5/12 =	3,043
Total		$72,232

EXAMPLE 24

Same facts as in Example 23, except that Vicky placed the nonresidential real property in service on July 1, 1993. In this scenario, nonresidential real property is place in service after May 12, 1993, so a 39-year recovery period applies. Also, the property is now placed in service in July, so Vicky starts depreciating the building on July 15.

Year	Calculation	MACRS
1993	$100,000 × 1/39 = $2,564 × 5.5/12 =	$ 1,175
1994–2014	$100,000 × 1/39 = $2,564 × 21 years =	53,844
2015	$100,000 × 1/39 = $2,564 × 11.5/12 =	2,457
Total		$57,476

EXAMPLE 25

Chuck operates a business out of his home. In the current year, Chuck began using one room in his home exclusive as an office where he regularly meets with clients. Although the rest of the home is where Chuck lives, the room where Chuck conducts his business is used solely for work. Thus, the home office is nonresidential realty. Under MACRS, the home office is depreciated over 39 years using the straight-line method.

¶803.02 ALTERNATIVE DEPRECIATION SYSTEM (ADS)

Instead of using MACRS recovery periods of 27.5 (for residential realty) or 31.5 or 39 years (for nonresidential realty), taxpayers can elect under the Alternative Depreciation System (ADS) to depreciate both residential and nonresidential realty over 40 years. Those who elect ADS continue to use the straight-line method and the mid-month convention. Taxpayers can elect to use the 40-year recovery period on a **property-by-property** basis. This allows them to depreciate one piece of real property over 40 years and another over the regular MACRS recovery period.

EXAMPLE 26

During the year, a taxpayer places in service an office building and a warehouse. The taxpayer can elect to use MACRS to depreciate one of the buildings and ADS to depreciate the other. Regardless of which depreciation method is used to depreciate the buildings, the mid-month convention applies to both the first and last years.

¶803.03 DEPRECIATION FOR BUSINESS USE OF A HOME

Persons who use part of their home for business purposes can depreciate the business portion of the home. Chapter 7 discussed the rules regarding deductions for the business use of the home (¶705.03). To compute the depreciation deduction, taxpayers first determine the percentage of the total square footage of the home used for business. If the rooms are all of approximately equal size, they can divide the number of rooms used for business by the total number of rooms in the home. The business-use percentage of the home is used to compute depreciation on the home.

The depreciable basis for the home is the *lesser of* (i) the home's adjusted basis or (ii) its FMV at the time the home office was placed in service. In determining the depreciable basis, the cost of the land must be removed from the adjusted basis. Likewise, the value of the land cannot be included when computing the FMV of the home. Taxpayers report the allowable depreciation deduction for a business in the home for a sole proprietor on Form 8829, Expenses for Business Use of Your Home, Part III. Figure 8-7 shows the calculation of the depreciation deduction.

Chapter 7 (¶705.03) discussed the order in which taxpayers deduct home office expenses:

1. All non–home office expenses from Schedule C. This amount includes depreciation on personal and real property (other than the home office).
2. The portion of mortgage interest, real estate taxes, and casualty losses taken on Form 8829 that relates to the home office.
3. The portion of operating expenses that relates to the business use of the home. These amounts include repairs, maintenance, utilities, and insurance.
4. The business portion of depreciation on the home.

Expenses listed in items 3 and 4 cannot create or increase a business loss. The disallowed expenses may be carried forward and included on Form 8829 in the following year. Home office expenses that carry over to the next year are reported on Form 8829, Part IV. Form 8829 (line 24) reports the disallowed operating expenses (insurance, utilities, etc.) from prior years. Form 8829 (line 30) reports the disallowed depreciation and casualty loss from prior years.

EXAMPLE 27

In 2015 Mack reports $1,600 as tentative profit on Schedule C. He uses 10% of his home exclusively as an office. Expenses for the 10% business portion of the home include mortgage interest and real estate taxes of $420, operating expenses (insurance, maintenance, and utilities) of $1,000, and depreciation of $650. Mack's deduction on Form 8829 for the business use of his home follows:

Tentative profit (line 8)	$ 1,600
Less interest and taxes (line 14)	(420)
Net income derived from the business (line 15)	$ 1,180
Less allowable operating expenses (line 26)	(1,000)
Limit placed on depreciation expense (line 27)	$ 180
Depreciation expense (line 29)	(650)
Depreciation expense not deductible in 2015 (show on line 43 and carry forward to 2016)	($ 470)

All business expenses except the $470 of depreciation offset 2015 income. Since Mack cannot deduct the entire depreciation in 2015, he reduces the basis of the home office by the $180 deducted in 2015. The basis in the home will be reduced for the rest of the depreciation in the year he deducts it.

¶803.04 FILLED-IN FORM 8829

INFORMATION FOR FIGURE 8-7:

In 2005 Darryl Collins bought a home for $320,000 (includes $80,000 for the land). On March 1, 2009, when the FMV of the home was $340,000 (includes $80,000 for the land), Darryl began using one room exclusively as a business office. The square footage of the office is **200**; the total square footage of the home is **4,000**. Since Darryl uses the business portion of the home as an office, it meets the definition of nonresidential real property. A 2.564% depreciation percentage is used (straight-line over 39 years applies to nonresidential realty placed in service after May 12, 1993).

Darryl computes the depreciation on the home office in Part III (lines 36-41). He then enters this amount on line 29 to include it as part of his deduction for the business use of his home.

Line #

36: Smaller of home's adjusted basis or fair market value, **$320,000**
37: Value of land included on line 36, **$80,000**
40: Depreciation percentage, **2.564** (1/39)

Figure 8-7: Filled-In Form 8829

Form **8829** — **Expenses for Business Use of Your Home**

Department of the Treasury
Internal Revenue Service (99)

▶ File only with Schedule C (Form 1040). Use a separate Form 8829 for each home you used for business during the year.
▶ Information about Form 8829 and its separate instructions is at *www.irs.gov/form8829.*

OMB No. 1545-0074
2015
Attachment Sequence No. **176**

Name(s) of proprietor(s)	Your social security number
Darryl Collins	531-64-9923

Part I — Part of Your Home Used for Business

1	Area used regularly and exclusively for business, regularly for daycare, or for storage of inventory or product samples (see instructions)	1	200
2	Total area of home	2	4,000
3	Divide line 1 by line 2. Enter the result as a percentage	3	5 %
	For daycare facilities not used exclusively for business, go to line 4. All others, go to line 7.		
4	Multiply days used for daycare during year by hours used per day	4	hr.
5	Total hours available for use during the year (365 days x 24 hours) (see instructions)	5	8,760 hr.
6	Divide line 4 by line 5. Enter the result as a decimal amount	6	
7	Business percentage. For daycare facilities not used exclusively for business, multiply line 6 by line 3 (enter the result as a percentage). All others, enter the amount from line 3 ▶	7	5 %

Part II — Figure Your Allowable Deduction

		(a) Direct expenses	(b) Indirect expenses		
8	Enter the amount from Schedule C, line 29, **plus** any gain derived from the business use of your home, **minus** any loss from the trade or business not derived from the business use of your home (see instructions)			8	
	See instructions for columns (a) and (b) before completing lines 9–21.				
9	Casualty losses (see instructions)				
10	Deductible mortgage interest (see instructions)				
11	Real estate taxes (see instructions)				
12	Add lines 9, 10, and 11				
13	Multiply line 12, column (b) by line 7		13		
14	Add line 12, column (a) and line 13			14	
15	Subtract line 14 from line 8. If zero or less, enter -0-			15	
16	Excess mortgage interest (see instructions)				
17	Insurance				
18	Rent				
19	Repairs and maintenance				
20	Utilities				
21	Other expenses (see instructions)				
22	Add lines 16 through 21				
23	Multiply line 22, column (b) by line 7		23		
24	Carryover of prior year operating expenses (see instructions)		24		
25	Add line 22, column (a), line 23, and line 24			25	
26	Allowable operating expenses. Enter the **smaller** of line 15 or line 25			26	
27	Limit on excess casualty losses and depreciation. Subtract line 26 from line 15			27	
28	Excess casualty losses (see instructions)		28		
29	Depreciation of your home from line 41 below		29: 308		
30	Carryover of prior year excess casualty losses and depreciation (see instructions)		30		
31	Add lines 28 through 30			31	
32	Allowable excess casualty losses and depreciation. Enter the **smaller** of line 27 or line 31			32	
33	Add lines 14, 26, and 32			33	
34	Casualty loss portion, if any, from lines 14 and 32. Carry amount to **Form 4684** (see instructions)			34	
35	**Allowable expenses for business use of your home.** Subtract line 34 from line 33. Enter here and on Schedule C, line 30. If your home was used for more than one business, see instructions ▶			35	

Part III — Depreciation of Your Home

36	Enter the **smaller** of your home's adjusted basis or its fair market value (see instructions)	36	320,000
37	Value of land included on line 36	37	80,000
38	Basis of building. Subtract line 37 from line 36	38	240,000
39	Business basis of building. Multiply line 38 by line 7	39	12,000
40	Depreciation percentage (see instructions)	40	2.564 %
41	Depreciation allowable (see instructions). Multiply line 39 by line 40. Enter here and on line 29 above	41	308

Part IV — Carryover of Unallowed Expenses to 2016

42	Operating expenses. Subtract line 26 from line 25. If less than zero, enter -0-	42	
43	Excess casualty losses and depreciation. Subtract line 32 from line 31. If less than zero, enter -0-	43	

For Paperwork Reduction Act Notice, see your tax return instructions. Cat. No. 13232M Form **8829** (2015)

¶804

Filled-In Form 4562

INFORMATION FOR FIGURE 8-9:

Figure 7-3 in Chapter 7 (¶705.06), the income statement from Harold's Hardware Store gave an amount of $1,133 for depreciation expense. Figure 8-8 shows how Harold's depreciation expense was computed. The amounts in the third column are the cost (for 2015 purchases) or MACRS basis (for pre-2015 purchases) of the property. The half-year convention applies to all personal property. Harold has written evidence to support the business use of the computer. The tools purchased in 2015 are used property. All other properties were purchased new.

Figure 8-8: Depreciation for Harold's Hardware Store

Property	Date Acquired	Cost or MACRS Basis	Recovery Period	% or Method	Depreciation in 2015
Computer (80% business)	8-01-13	$ 480[1]	5	200% DB	92[2]
Paint mixer	3-01-13	1,930	7	200% DB	338[3]
Tool cabinet	3-14-13	1,865	7	200% DB	326[4]
Tools	7-16-15	454	7	200% DB	65[5]
Table saw	1-15-09	216	12*	ADS/SL	18
Jointer/planer	6-29-09	316	12*	ADS/SL	26
Storage shed	12-06-09	10,450	39	SL	268
Total cost recovery					$1,133

*Since no designated class life applies to the equipment, the recovery period is 12 years.

[1] $600 (cost minus 50% bonus depreciation taken in 2013) × 80% = $480 MACRS basis

[2] $480 MACRS basis × 19.2% (year 3 percentage)

[3] $1,930 MACRS basis (after 50% bonus depreciation taken in 2013) × 17.49% (year 3 percentage)

[4] $1,865 MACRS basis (after 50% bonus depreciation taken in 2013) × 17.49% (year 3 percentage)

[5] $454 × 14.29% year 1 percentage

Because computers are listed property, the depreciation deduction is first recorded in Part V, and then is entered on Part IV (line 21). See Figure 8-9.

Line #

26(a): Type of property used more than 50% for business, **Computer**
26(b): Date placed in service, **8-01-13**
26(c): Business/investment use percentage, **80%**
26(d): Cost or other basis, **$600** (cost minus 50% bonus depreciation)
26(e): Basis for depreciation, **$480** ($600 × 80%)
26(f): Recovery period, **5 yr.**
26(g): Method/convention, **DDB/HY** (double declining balance method; half-year convention)
26(h): Depreciation deduction, **$92** ($480 × 19.2% year 3 percentage from the 5-year column in Figure 8-1)
17: MACRS on pre-2015 assets (includes regular and straight-line MACRS, as well as ADS), **$976** (paint mixer, $338 + tool cabinet, $326 + table saw, $18 + jointer/planer, $26 + storage shed, $268)
19c(c): Basis for depreciation, **$454**
19c(d): Recovery period, **7 yr.**
19c(e): Convention, **HY** (half-year)
19c(f): Method, **DDB** (double declining balance)
19c(g): Depreciation deduction, **$65** ($454 × 14.29% year 1 percentage from the 7-year column in Figure 8-1)

Figure 8-9: Filled-In Form 4562 (Page 1)

Form **4562** — Department of the Treasury, Internal Revenue Service (99)

Depreciation and Amortization
(Including Information on Listed Property)
▶ Attach to your tax return.
▶ Information about Form 4562 and its separate instructions is at *www.irs.gov/form4562*.

OMB No. 1545-0172 — **2015** — Attachment Sequence No. **179**

Name(s) shown on return	Business or activity to which this form relates	Identifying number
Harold R. Wilson	Harold's Hardware Store	272-11-8855

Part I Election To Expense Certain Property Under Section 179
Note: If you have any listed property, complete Part V before you complete Part I.

1	Maximum amount (see instructions)	1	
2	Total cost of section 179 property placed in service (see instructions)	2	
3	Threshold cost of section 179 property before reduction in limitation (see instructions)	3	
4	Reduction in limitation. Subtract line 3 from line 2. If zero or less, enter -0-	4	
5	Dollar limitation for tax year. Subtract line 4 from line 1. If zero or less, enter -0-. If married filing separately, see instructions	5	

6 (a) Description of property	(b) Cost (business use only)	(c) Elected cost

7	Listed property. Enter the amount from line 29 (7)		
8	Total elected cost of section 179 property. Add amounts in column (c), lines 6 and 7	8	
9	Tentative deduction. Enter the **smaller** of line 5 or line 8	9	
10	Carryover of disallowed deduction from line 13 of your 2014 Form 4562	10	
11	Business income limitation. Enter the smaller of business income (not less than zero) or line 5 (see instructions)	11	
12	Section 179 expense deduction. Add lines 9 and 10, but do not enter more than line 11	12	
13	Carryover of disallowed deduction to 2016. Add lines 9 and 10, less line 12 ▶ (13)		

Note: Do not use Part II or Part III below for listed property. Instead, use Part V.

Part II Special Depreciation Allowance and Other Depreciation (Do not include listed property.) (See instructions.)

14	Special depreciation allowance for qualified property (other than listed property) placed in service during the tax year (see instructions)	14	
15	Property subject to section 168(f)(1) election	15	
16	Other depreciation (including ACRS)	16	

Part III MACRS Depreciation (Do not include listed property.) (See instructions.)

Section A

17	MACRS deductions for assets placed in service in tax years beginning before 2015	17	976
18	If you are electing to group any assets placed in service during the tax year into one or more general asset accounts, check here ▶ ☐		

Section B—Assets Placed in Service During 2015 Tax Year Using the General Depreciation System

(a) Classification of property	(b) Month and year placed in service	(c) Basis for depreciation (business/investment use only—see instructions)	(d) Recovery period	(e) Convention	(f) Method	(g) Depreciation deduction
19a 3-year property						
b 5-year property						
c 7-year property		454	7 yr.	HY	DDB	65
d 10-year property						
e 15-year property						
f 20-year property						
g 25-year property			25 yrs.		S/L	
h Residential rental property			27.5 yrs.	MM	S/L	
			27.5 yrs.	MM	S/L	
i Nonresidential real property			39 yrs.	MM	S/L	
				MM	S/L	

Section C—Assets Placed in Service During 2015 Tax Year Using the Alternative Depreciation System

20a Class life					S/L	
b 12-year			12 yrs.		S/L	
c 40-year			40 yrs.	MM	S/L	

Part IV Summary (See instructions.)

21	Listed property. Enter amount from line 28	21	92
22	**Total.** Add amounts from line 12, lines 14 through 17, lines 19 and 20 in column (g), and line 21. Enter here and on the appropriate lines of your return. Partnerships and S corporations—see instructions	22	1,133
23	For assets shown above and placed in service during the current year, enter the portion of the basis attributable to section 263A costs (23)		

For Paperwork Reduction Act Notice, see separate instructions. Cat. No. 12906N Form **4562** (2015)

Figure 8-9: Filled-In Form 4562 (Page 2)

Form 4562 (2015) Page **2**

Part V **Listed Property** (Include automobiles, certain other vehicles, certain aircraft, certain computers, and property used for entertainment, recreation, or amusement.)

Note: For any vehicle for which you are using the standard mileage rate or deducting lease expense, complete **only** 24a, 24b, columns (a) through (c) of Section A, all of Section B, and Section C if applicable.

Section A—Depreciation and Other Information (Caution: See the instructions for limits for passenger automobiles.**)**

24a Do you have evidence to support the business/investment use claimed? ☑ **Yes** ☐ **No** **24b** If "Yes," is the evidence written? ☑ **Yes** ☐ **No**

(a) Type of property (list vehicles first)	(b) Date placed in service	(c) Business/ investment use percentage	(d) Cost or other basis	(e) Basis for depreciation (business/investment use only)	(f) Recovery period	(g) Method/ Convention	(h) Depreciation deduction	(i) Elected section 179 cost
25 Special depreciation allowance for qualified listed property placed in service during the tax year and used more than 50% in a qualified business use (see instructions) . **25**								
26 Property used more than 50% in a qualified business use:								
Computer	**8-1-13**	**80** %	**600**	**480**	**5 yr.**	**DDB/HY**	**92**	
		%						
		%						
27 Property used 50% or less in a qualified business use:								
		%				S/L –		
		%				S/L –		
		%				S/L –		
28 Add amounts in column (h), lines 25 through 27. Enter here and on line 21, page 1 . **28**							**92**	
29 Add amounts in column (i), line 26. Enter here and on line 7, page 1 . . . . **29**								

Section B—Information on Use of Vehicles

Complete this section for vehicles used by a sole proprietor, partner, or other "more than 5% owner," or related person. If you provided vehicles to your employees, first answer the questions in Section C to see if you meet an exception to completing this section for those vehicles.

	(a) Vehicle 1		(b) Vehicle 2		(c) Vehicle 3		(d) Vehicle 4		(e) Vehicle 5		(f) Vehicle 6	
30 Total business/investment miles driven during the year (**do not** include commuting miles) .												
31 Total commuting miles driven during the year												
32 Total other personal (noncommuting) miles driven												
33 Total miles driven during the year. Add lines 30 through 32												
	Yes	**No**	**Yes**	**No**	**Yes**	**No**	**Yes**	**No**	**Yes**	**No**	**Yes**	**No**
34 Was the vehicle available for personal use during off-duty hours?												
35 Was the vehicle used primarily by a more than 5% owner or related person? . .												
36 Is another vehicle available for personal use?												

Section C—Questions for Employers Who Provide Vehicles for Use by Their Employees

Answer these questions to determine if you meet an exception to completing Section B for vehicles used by employees who **are not** more than 5% owners or related persons (see instructions).

	Yes	**No**
37 Do you maintain a written policy statement that prohibits all personal use of vehicles, including commuting, by your employees?		
38 Do you maintain a written policy statement that prohibits personal use of vehicles, except commuting, by your employees? See the instructions for vehicles used by corporate officers, directors, or 1% or more owners . .		
39 Do you treat all use of vehicles by employees as personal use?		
40 Do you provide more than five vehicles to your employees, obtain information from your employees about the use of the vehicles, and retain the information received?		
41 Do you meet the requirements concerning qualified automobile demonstration use? (See instructions.) . . .		

Note: If your answer to 37, 38, 39, 40, or 41 is "Yes," do not complete Section B for the covered vehicles.

Part VI **Amortization**

(a) Description of costs	(b) Date amortization begins	(c) Amortizable amount	(d) Code section	(e) Amortization period or percentage	(f) Amortization for this year
42 Amortization of costs that begins during your 2015 tax year (see instructions):					
43 Amortization of costs that began before your 2015 tax year				**43**	
44 **Total.** Add amounts in column (f). See the instructions for where to report				**44**	

Form **4562** (2015)

¶805 Amortization of Intangible Property

Depreciation applies to the cost recovery of tangible personal and real property. Amortization applies to the cost recovery of intangible personal property. Tangible property differs from intangible property in that the former has physical traits, whereas the latter does not. Amortization recovers the cost of intangible property through annual deductions over a fixed period of time (similar to the straight-line method).

The Code requires that Section 197 intangibles used in a trade or business or for the production of income be amortized over 15 years (180 months). The 15-year amortization period applies to all Section 197 intangibles, even those that have shorter or longer actual useful lives. Franchises, trademarks, and trade names are always Section 197 intangibles, regardless of how they are acquired. Also, amounts paid for licenses, permits, or other rights granted by a government agency are Section 197 intangibles. All other Section 197 intangibles are acquired when the taxpayer buys a business and pays more than the value of its tangible property (minus any debt owed by the business). The excess paid is to purchase Section 197 intangibles, which may include:

- Goodwill, going concern, and the business's existing work force,
- Business books and records, operating systems, or any other data base (including customer lists),
- Patents, copyrights, formulas, designs, computer software, or similar items,
- Customer-based or supplier-based intangibles, and
- Covenants not to compete.

The Code allows taxpayers to write off the cost of other intangible property (those that are not Section 197 intangibles) that have an ascertainable value and a limited life that can be determined with reasonable accuracy. Patents, copyrights, and covenants not-to-compete acquired separately (not as part of the purchase of a business) are examples of intangibles other than Section 197 intangibles. The cost of intangibles other than those covered under Section 197 is amortized over their useful lives. In the case of computer software, the Code specifies that its useful life is 36 months.

The amortization only applies to purchased intangibles. Although self-created goodwill provides value to the business, there is no cost to amortize.

EXAMPLE 28

Kataran Corporation pays $75,000 to a departing executive in exchange for his promise not to compete with the corporation for the next four years. The covenant not to compete is not a Section 197 intangible (it was not acquired in connection with the acquisition of a business). Thus, Kataran will write-off (expense) the $75,000 over the next four years.

EXAMPLE 29

On June 1, 2015, Blake Industries acquired all of the assets of Fontaine, Inc. Of the $10 million purchase price, $2 million is allocated to goodwill. Since purchased goodwill is a Section 197 intangible (it was acquired in a purchase of a business), the $2 million cost basis for the goodwill must be amortized using the straight-line method over 15 years beginning on June 1, 2015. If Blake uses a calendar year-end, it can deduct $77,778 ($2,000,000/180 months × 7 months) on its 2015 tax return. From 2016-2029 it will deduct $133,333 ($2,000,000/180 × 12 months). In 2030, Blake will deduct the last of the goodwill ($55,560).

EXAMPLE 30

On February 1, 2015, Amicable Company paid $12,000 for off-the-shelf computer software. Because the software was not part of the purchase of a business, Amicable deducts $3,667 ($12,000/36 × 11 months) in 2015. It will deduct $4,000 ($12,000/36 × 12) in both 2016 and 2017, and $333 ($12,000/36 × 1 month) in 2018.

8

Name:
Section:
Date:

QUESTIONS AND PROBLEMS

1. **MACRS Recovery Periods.** (Obj. 1) For each of the following types of properties, state the MACRS recovery period, depreciation method, and averaging convention(s) that are used to depreciate the property under regular MACRS.

	Recovery Period	*Depreciation Method*	*Averaging Convention*
Automobiles	________	________	________
Light trucks	________	________	________
Computers	________	________	________
Furniture and fixtures	________	________	________
Machinery and equipment	________	________	________
Commercial buildings	________	________	________
Residential buildings	________	________	________

2. **Mid-Quarter vs. Half-Year Convention.** (Obj. 1) A calendar-year taxpayer acquired four new machines in 2015 on the dates shown below. Section 179 is not elected, but regular MACRS is used to depreciate the machines.

February 1	$25,000
April 1	35,000
October 1	30,000
December 1	40,000

a. Compute total depreciation expense for 2015 that would be reported on Schedule C, using the appropriate averaging convention.

b. Same as in Part a., except that the third machine was acquired on September 30 (instead of October 1). Comment on the significance of the difference between this amount and your answer to Part a.

3. **MACRS.** (Obj. 1) Florence placed in service the following properties during 2014. Compute Florence's total depreciation expense for 2014 and 2015, assuming that she does not elect Section 179 expensing, but did take bonus depreciation, when applicable. The machine, equipment, and furniture were all purchased new.

Type of Property	*Cost*	*Date Placed in Service*
Machine	$130,000	March 3, 2014
Equipment	110,000	June 8, 2014
Furniture	48,000	August 15, 2014
Office building	200,000	October 4, 2014

4. **MACRS, Year of Sale.** (Obj. 1) Bradford Company sold the following properties. Compute the allowable depreciation deduction for 2015 for each property.

Property	*Date Acquired*	*MACRS Basis**	*Depreciation Method*	*Averaging Convention*	*Date of Sale*
Computer	7-1-13	$ 4,200	DDB	HY	9-5-15
Automobile	4-1-12	12,000	DDB	MQ	3-1-15
Furniture	7-10-10	24,000	DDB	MQ	7-1-15

**After subtracting bonus depreciation from the original cost*

5. **MACRS, Year of Sale.** (Obj. 1) Judson Company sold the following properties. Compute the allowable depreciation deduction for 2015 for each property.

Property	*Date Acquired*	*MACRS Basis**	*Depreciation Method*	*Averaging Convention*	*Date of Sale*
Machine	6-1-10	$44,000	DDB	MQ	12-9-15
Furniture	8-8-14	12,000	DDB	HY	3-21-15
Computer	1-6-13	24,000	DDB	MQ	9-30-15

**After subtracting bonus depreciation from the original cost*

6. **ADS and MACRS.** (Obj. 1) Peter purchased the following new properties to use in his business.

Equipment:	Acquired in April, 2007 at a cost of $72,000
Furniture:	Acquired in March, 2012 at a cost of $84,000
Computer:	Acquired in July, 2014 at a cost of $10,000

a. Compute Peter's 2015 depreciation expense. Peter has never elected Section 179, nor has he ever elected out of taking bonus depreciation. Peter uses ADS straight-line method with a ten-year life to depreciate the equipment. He uses regular (accelerated) MACRS to depreciation the furniture and computer. The half-year convention applies to all three properties.

b. Same as in Part a., except that the mid-quarter convention applied to all personal property placed in service in 2012.

c. Same as in Part a. except that Peter purchased each of these properties in 2015. Compute depreciation for each of these properties for 2015 using the maximum depreciation allowed for each property without electing Section 179.

7. **MACRS.** (Obj. 1) Marv uses the following properties in his business.

Computer:	Acquired new in August 24, 2014 at a cost of $32,000
Machine:	Acquired new in October 11, 2010 at a cost of $120,000
Furniture:	Acquired new in January 16, 2008 at a cost of $42,000

a. Compute Marv's 2015 depreciation expense. Marv has never elected Section 179, but took bonus depreciation. He uses regular (accelerated) MACRS to depreciate these properties. The mid-quarter convention applies to property placed in service during 2008 and 2010. The half-year convention applied to property placed in service in 2014.

b. Same as in Part a., except that Marv purchased each of these properties in 2015. Compute depreciation for each of these properties for 2015 using regular MACRS depreciation. Assume Marv does not elect to take Section 179 on any of the three properties. Also assume these were the only properties placed in service during the year.

8. **Section 179.** (Obj. 2) Sand Corporation purchases one asset in 2015—used machinery costing $209,000. The machine was placed in service on June 2, 2015. Sand wants to elect the maximum Section 179 possible, even if some must be carried over to 2016. Sand's 2015 taxable income before Section 179 expense (but after all other expenses, including depreciation) is $3,000.

   a. Compute the maximum Section 179 Sand can elect in 2015 and the Section 179 carryover to 2016.

   b. Compute the maximum total depreciation on the machine for 2015.

9. **Section 179.** (Obj. 2) In May 2015, Riddick Enterprises placed in service new 7-year property costing $100,000 and new 5-year property costing $100,000. These are the only two properties Riddick placed in service during the year. Riddick's taxable income before deducting Section 179 expense (but after all other expenses, including depreciation expense) is $1,000,000.

   a. Compute Riddick's total depreciation expense deduction assuming Riddick uses regular MACRS and elects to take the maximum Section 179 expense on the 5-year property.

   b. Compute Riddick's total depreciation expense deduction assuming Riddick uses regular MACRS and elects to take the maximum Section 179 expense on the 7-year property.

   c. Which choice results in the largest total depreciation deduction? Comment on your answers to Parts a. and b.

10. **MACRS, Section 179.** (Objs. 1 and 2) The Redwood Company, a calendar-year corporation, acquired the following new properties.

Item	*Cost*	*Date Acquired*
Copier	$ 4,000	March 1, 2015
Furniture	42,000	June 1, 2015
Equipment	160,000	June 30, 2015
Warehouse	110,250	July 9, 2015

a. Compute the maximum depreciation deduction that Redwood can take in 2015 and 2016 on each of these properties assuming Section 179 is not elected.

b. Assume that Redwood elects to take the maximum allowed Section 179 expense on the equipment acquired on June 30, 2015. The company uses regular MACRS to depreciate the rest of the cost. Redwood's taxable income before Section 179 expense (but after all other expenses, including depreciation) is $950,000. Compute the maximum total depreciation deduction for the equipment for 2015 and 2016.

c. Same facts as in Part b. except that Redwood elects Section 179 expense first on the copier, then the furniture, and finally the equipment. Compute Redwood's maximum total depreciation deduction for the furniture for 2015 and 2016.

11. Listed Property, Section 179. (Objs. 2 and 3) Terrell is a self-employed personal financial adviser. In March 2015, Terrell purchased a computer for $2,800. This was his only purchase of depreciable property in 2015. He uses the computer 60% of the time in providing financial advice to clients, 15% of the time managing his own investments, and the rest of the time for personal use.

a. Compute Terrell's maximum depreciation expense deduction in 2015 for the computer assuming he does not elect Section 179 in 2015.

b. Same as in Part a., except that Terrell elects the maximum Section 179 expense.

c. Where on his tax return does Terrell deduct this depreciation expense?

12. Listed Property. (Obj. 3) During 2015, Simon (self-employed) pays $14,500 for a new car that he uses 45% of the time for business, 25% of the time for investment purposes, and 30% of the time for personal use. The half-year convention applies to the car. How much depreciation is Simon entitled to deduct in 2015?

13. **Luxury Automobiles.** (Obj. 3) Charlotte purchased a new car on March 1, 2010, for $40,000 and uses it 80% of the time for business purposes. Prepare a schedule that shows the maximum depreciation she will be entitled to take in each of the years 2010 through 2015, assuming that she uses the automobile 80% of the time for business each year.

14. **Luxury Automobiles.** (Obj. 3) On September 13, 2015, Debi places in service a new car costing $25,000 (her only acquisition during the year). She uses the car 90% of the time for business. Compute Debi's maximum depreciation expense for 2015.

15. **Leased Vehicles.** (Obj. 3) On March 1, 2015, Casey enters into a 36-month lease for a car valued at $36,400. Her monthly lease payment is $470, and she uses the car 75% for business. What amount will Casey deduct in 2015 and 2016?

16. **Leased Vehicles.** (Obj. 3) Bart operates his business as a sole proprietorship. On October 1, 2015, Bart enters into a 24-month lease on a car valued at $39,900. His monthly payments are $800. Bart uses the car 85% for business each year. Compute Bart's lease deduction and inclusion amounts for 2015–2017.

17. **MACRS and Averaging Conventions.** (Obj. 1) Jan purchased the following properties during 2015.

Description	*Date Placed in Service*	*Cost*
New Computer	March 9, 2015	$ 3,000
Used Machinery	July 17, 2015	70,000
Used Office building	September 6, 2015	270,000
New Equipment	December 27, 2015	42,000

Compute Jan's depreciation for each of these properties for 2015 and 2016 using the maximum depreciation allowed without taking Section 179.

18. MACRS and Averaging Conventions. (Objs. 1, 3, 5) Howard Fields (SSN 748-29-4631) operates the H. B. Fields Company as a sole proprietorship. H.B. Fields has the following depreciable property. The automobile is used 100% for business. Howard has written evidence of the business use, which was 19,280 miles in 2015. He has another vehicle he uses for personal use. Using this information, prepare Howard's 2015 Form 4562, Depreciation and Amortization.

Date of Acquisition	*Item*	*Cost*	*Averaging Convention*
January 30, 2014	Used car	$24,000	HY
March 10, 2015	Garage for auto	39,000	MM
August 6, 2015	New machine	12,460	HY
December 1, 2013	Used desk	1,910	MQ

19. MACRS, Real Property. (Obj. 1) In February 2015, a taxpayer purchased an office building for $320,000 and an apartment building for $400,000. These amounts include only the buildings, not the land. Compute the 2015 MACRS expense for each building.

20. MACRS and ADS, Real Property. (Obj. 1) Drew operates a business as a sole proprietorship. On January 3, 2015, Drew placed in service a warehouse costing $650,000. On November 25, 2015, he placed in service an apartment complex costing $990,000.

a. Compute Drew's 2015 depreciation expense on each building. Drew uses MACRS to depreciate the warehouse and elects to use ADS to depreciate the apartment building.

b. Same as in Part a., except that Drew elects to depreciate the warehouse using ADS and uses MACRS to depreciate the apartment building.

c. Same as in Part a., except that Drew uses MACRS to depreciate both buildings.

d. Same as in Part a., except that Drew elects to use ADS to depreciate both buildings.

(Use for Problem 18.)

Form **4562** | **Depreciation and Amortization** | OMB No. 1545-0172

Department of the Treasury
Internal Revenue Service (99)

(Including Information on Listed Property)

▶ Attach to your tax return.

▶ Information about Form 4562 and its separate instructions is at *www.irs.gov/form4562.*

2015

Attachment Sequence No. **179**

Name(s) shown on return	Business or activity to which this form relates	Identifying number

Part I Election To Expense Certain Property Under Section 179

Note: If you have any listed property, complete Part V before you complete Part I.

1	Maximum amount (see instructions)	1	
2	Total cost of section 179 property placed in service (see instructions)	2	
3	Threshold cost of section 179 property before reduction in limitation (see instructions)	3	
4	Reduction in limitation. Subtract line 3 from line 2. If zero or less, enter -0-	4	
5	Dollar limitation for tax year. Subtract line 4 from line 1. If zero or less, enter -0-. If married filing separately, see instructions	5	

6	(a) Description of property	(b) Cost (business use only)	(c) Elected cost

7	Listed property. Enter the amount from line 29	7	
8	Total elected cost of section 179 property. Add amounts in column (c), lines 6 and 7	8	
9	Tentative deduction. Enter the **smaller** of line 5 or line 8	9	
10	Carryover of disallowed deduction from line 13 of your 2014 Form 4562	10	
11	Business income limitation. Enter the smaller of business income (not less than zero) or line 5 (see instructions)	11	
12	Section 179 expense deduction. Add lines 9 and 10, but do not enter more than line 11	12	
13	Carryover of disallowed deduction to 2016. Add lines 9 and 10, less line 12 ▶	13	

Note: Do not use Part II or Part III below for listed property. Instead, use Part V.

Part II Special Depreciation Allowance and Other Depreciation (Do not include listed property.) (See instructions.)

14	Special depreciation allowance for qualified property (other than listed property) placed in service during the tax year (see instructions)	14	
15	Property subject to section 168(f)(1) election	15	
16	Other depreciation (including ACRS)	16	

Part III MACRS Depreciation (Do not include listed property.) (See instructions.)

Section A

17	MACRS deductions for assets placed in service in tax years beginning before 2015	17	
18	If you are electing to group any assets placed in service during the tax year into one or more general asset accounts, check here ▶ ☐		

Section B—Assets Placed in Service During 2015 Tax Year Using the General Depreciation System

(a) Classification of property	(b) Month and year placed in service	(c) Basis for depreciation (business/investment use only—see instructions)	(d) Recovery period	(e) Convention	(f) Method	(g) Depreciation deduction
19a 3-year property						
b 5-year property						
c 7-year property						
d 10-year property						
e 15-year property						
f 20-year property						
g 25-year property			25 yrs.		S/L	
h Residential rental property			27.5 yrs.	MM	S/L	
			27.5 yrs.	MM	S/L	
i Nonresidential real property			39 yrs.	MM	S/L	
				MM	S/L	

Section C—Assets Placed in Service During 2015 Tax Year Using the Alternative Depreciation System

(a) Classification of property	(b) Month and year placed in service	(c) Basis for depreciation	(d) Recovery period	(e) Convention	(f) Method	(g) Depreciation deduction
20a Class life					S/L	
b 12-year			12 yrs.		S/L	
c 40-year			40 yrs.	MM	S/L	

Part IV Summary (See instructions.)

21	Listed property. Enter amount from line 28	21	
22	**Total.** Add amounts from line 12, lines 14 through 17, lines 19 and 20 in column (g), and line 21. Enter here and on the appropriate lines of your return. Partnerships and S corporations—see instructions	22	
23	For assets shown above and placed in service during the current year, enter the portion of the basis attributable to section 263A costs	23	

For Paperwork Reduction Act Notice, see separate instructions. Cat. No. 12906N Form **4562** (2015)

(Use for Problem 18.)

Form 4562 (2015) Page **2**

Part V **Listed Property** (Include automobiles, certain other vehicles, certain aircraft, certain computers, and property used for entertainment, recreation, or amusement.)

Note: For any vehicle for which you are using the standard mileage rate or deducting lease expense, complete **only** 24a, 24b, columns (a) through (c) of Section A, all of Section B, and Section C if applicable.

Section A—Depreciation and Other Information (Caution: See the instructions for limits for passenger automobiles.**)**

24a Do you have evidence to support the business/investment use claimed? ☐ **Yes** ☐ **No** | **24b** If "Yes," is the evidence written? ☐ **Yes** ☐ **No**

(a) Type of property (list vehicles first)	(b) Date placed in service	(c) Business/ investment use percentage	(d) Cost or other basis	(e) Basis for depreciation (business/investment use only)	(f) Recovery period	(g) Method/ Convention	(h) Depreciation deduction	(i) Elected section 179 cost
25 Special depreciation allowance for qualified listed property placed in service during the tax year and used more than 50% in a qualified business use (see instructions) . **25**								
26 Property used more than 50% in a qualified business use:								
		%						
		%						
		%						
27 Property used 50% or less in a qualified business use:								
		%				S/L –		
		%				S/L –		
		%				S/L –		
28 Add amounts in column (h), lines 25 through 27. Enter here and on line 21, page 1 . **28**								
29 Add amounts in column (i), line 26. Enter here and on line 7, page 1 . . . . **29**								

Section B—Information on Use of Vehicles

Complete this section for vehicles used by a sole proprietor, partner, or other "more than 5% owner," or related person. If you provided vehicles to your employees, first answer the questions in Section C to see if you meet an exception to completing this section for those vehicles.

	(a) Vehicle 1		(b) Vehicle 2		(c) Vehicle 3		(d) Vehicle 4		(e) Vehicle 5		(f) Vehicle 6	
30 Total business/investment miles driven during the year (**do not** include commuting miles) .												
31 Total commuting miles driven during the year												
32 Total other personal (noncommuting) miles driven												
33 Total miles driven during the year. Add lines 30 through 32												
	Yes	**No**	**Yes**	**No**	**Yes**	**No**	**Yes**	**No**	**Yes**	**No**	**Yes**	**No**
34 Was the vehicle available for personal use during off-duty hours?												
35 Was the vehicle used primarily by a more than 5% owner or related person? . .												
36 Is another vehicle available for personal use?												

Section C—Questions for Employers Who Provide Vehicles for Use by Their Employees

Answer these questions to determine if you meet an exception to completing Section B for vehicles used by employees who **are not** more than 5% owners or related persons (see instructions).

	Yes	**No**
37 Do you maintain a written policy statement that prohibits all personal use of vehicles, including commuting, by your employees?		
38 Do you maintain a written policy statement that prohibits personal use of vehicles, except commuting, by your employees? See the instructions for vehicles used by corporate officers, directors, or 1% or more owners . .		
39 Do you treat all use of vehicles by employees as personal use?		
40 Do you provide more than five vehicles to your employees, obtain information from your employees about the use of the vehicles, and retain the information received?		
41 Do you meet the requirements concerning qualified automobile demonstration use? (See instructions.) . . .		

Note: If your answer to 37, 38, 39, 40, or 41 is "Yes," do not complete Section B for the covered vehicles.

Part VI **Amortization**

(a) Description of costs	(b) Date amortization begins	(c) Amortizable amount	(d) Code section	(e) Amortization period or percentage	(f) Amortization for this year
42 Amortization of costs that begins during your 2015 tax year (see instructions):					
43 Amortization of costs that began before your 2015 tax year **43**					
44 **Total.** Add amounts in column (f). See the instructions for where to report **44**					

Form **4562** (2015)

21. **MACRS, Real Property.** (Obj. 1) On April 3, 1992, a taxpayer purchased land and an office building for $350,000 ($75,000 was allocated to the land). On August 2, 2015, the taxpayer sold the office building. Compute MACRS on the building for 2015, and the taxpayer's adjusted basis in the office building at the time of the sale.

22. **MACRS and ADS, Real Property.** (Obj. 1) On April 29, 2008, Conley, Inc. placed in service an office building costing $450,000. Conley depreciates the office building using ADS. It sold the building on January 4, 2015. Compute Conley's depreciation expense on the building for 2008–2015 and its adjusted basis on January 4, 2015.

23. **MACRS, Realty.** (Obj. 1) What depreciation method and useful life are used to depreciate a home office placed in service in 2015? Explain.

24. **Amortization of Intangibles.** (Obj. 4) For the intangibles listed, which can be amortized, what method should be used to amortize them, and how quickly can they be amortized?

  a. Goodwill purchased as part of a business acquired during the year.

  b. A copyright purchased separately for use in the taxpayer's business.

  c. Same as in Part b., except that the copyright is purchased as part of the acquisition of a business.

  d. Covenant not to compete entered into as part of an acquisition of a business.

  e. Same as in Part d., except that the covenant is not part of the purchase of a business.

f. Compute software not purchased as part of the acquisition of a business.

g. Same as in Part f., except that the software is part of the purchase of a business.

25. Internet Problem: Researching IRS Publication 463. (Obj. 3)

On August 29, 2012, Renee entered into a 36-month lease for a car valued at $60,220. Renee's monthly lease payment is $790. She uses the car 65% for business.

a. What affect does this lease arrangement have on the amount Renee can deduct in 2015?

b. How much of the lease payment can be deducted?

c. How is this information presented on the tax return?

Go to the IRS website. Locate IRS Publication 463 and find the appropriate page in Appendix A to answer the above question regarding Renee's inclusion amount. Print out a copy of the page where you found your answer. Underline or highlight the pertinent information.

See Appendix A for instructions on use of the IRS website.

26. Business Entity Problem. This problem is designed for those using the "business entity" approach. **The solution may require information from Chapter 14.**

MSO Corporation owns a residential apartment building that it depreciates over 27.5 years. The building originally cost $550,000.

a. How much depreciation expense can the company claim on its tax return in the fifth year of ownership?

b. Earnings and profits serve as the source of taxable dividends. By what amount does depreciation reduce the corporation's earnings and profits in the fifth year of ownership?

COMPREHENSIVE PROBLEM

27. Patrick A. and Danielle R. Beckman file a joint return for 2015. The Beckmans rent a three-bedroom apartment located at 529 W. Maywood #4, Aurora, IL 60505. They provide over half of the support for Danielle's mother, Ellen Tyler (SSN 384-58-7338), who qualifies as their dependent. Ellen lives in a nursing home in Peoria, Illinois. The Beckmans claim their 20-year-old daughter, Tara (SSN 487-58-3957) as a dependent. Tara lives with the Beckmans while attending college full-time.

Danielle (SSN 394-59-3948) works full-time for an advertising firm. Through her employer, Danielle gets full health care insurance coverage for her family. In 2015, Danielle's taxable wages were $59,000, from which her employer withheld $6,000 in federal income taxes, $3,447 in social security taxes, $806 in Medicare taxes, and $1,020 in state income taxes. Danielle is an active participant in her employer's 401(k). During the year, Danielle contributed $3,400 to her 401(k). Danielle and Patrick each contributed $1,500 to their respective traditional IRAs for 2015.

Patrick (SSN 549-82-2497) is self-employed. He began his carpet cleaning business in 2013. The business code for Schedule C (line B) is 812990. Patrick uses the spare bedroom in the apartment solely and exclusively as a home office to perform administrative tasks. The bedroom is 220 square feet in size. The square footage of the entire apartment is 1,800 square feet. Patrick elects to use the safe harbor method to compute his home office deduction. Patrick uses the cash method. During the year, his business income was $18,000, and he paid $1,828 for cleaning chemicals and supplies, $300 for advertising, and $50 for office expenses.

On November 10, 2014, Patrick purchased carpet-cleaning equipment for $17,148. This was the only depreciable property placed in service in 2014. Patrick did not elect Section 179 in 2014. He did take bonus depreciation and uses regular MACRS to depreciate the equipment. On June 8, 2015, Patrick purchased a computer for $1,600 and a printer for $400. Patrick uses the computer and printer 40% for business and 60% for personal use. Patrick has written evidence to support the 40% business use. The computer and printer were Patrick's only acquisitions in 2015.

Patrick uses his van to get to and from customers' homes. During the year Patrick drove his van 1,812 miles for business. He keeps a written log as evidence of these miles. Total miles for the year on the van were 10,540. Danielle has her own car that she uses to get to and from work. Patrick bought the van on March 5, 2011. He used the standard mileage method in 2014. Patrick incurred no business-related parking or tolls in 2015.

Prepare the Beckmans' Form 1040 and accompanying Schedules C and SE, and Form 4562. Be sure to complete lines 30–36 on Form 4562. Neither Patrick nor Danielle want $3 to go to the Presidential election campaign fund. The Beckmans sign their return on April 15, 2016.

(Use for Problem 27.)

Form **1040** Department of the Treasury—Internal Revenue Service (99)
U.S. Individual Income Tax Return **2015** OMB No. 1545-0074 IRS Use Only—Do not write or staple in this space.

For the year Jan. 1–Dec. 31, 2015, or other tax year beginning , 2015, ending , 20 See separate instructions.

Your first name and initial | Last name | **Your social security number**

If a joint return, spouse's first name and initial | Last name | **Spouse's social security number**

Home address (number and street). If you have a P.O. box, see instructions. | Apt. no. | ▲ Make sure the SSN(s) above and on line 6c are correct.

City, town or post office, state, and ZIP code. If you have a foreign address, also complete spaces below (see instructions).

Presidential Election Campaign
Check here if you, or your spouse if filing jointly, want $3 to go to this fund. Checking a box below will not change your tax or refund. ☐ **You** ☐ **Spouse**

Foreign country name | Foreign province/state/county | Foreign postal code

Filing Status

Check only one box.

1 ☐ Single
2 ☐ Married filing jointly (even if only one had income)
3 ☐ Married filing separately. Enter spouse's SSN above and full name here.
4 ☐ Head of household (with qualifying person). (See instructions.) If the qualifying person is a child but not your dependent, enter this child's name here.
5 ☐ Qualifying widow(er) with dependent child

Exemptions

6a ☐ **Yourself.** If someone can claim you as a dependent, **do not** check box 6a
b ☐ **Spouse**
Boxes checked on 6a and 6b

c **Dependents:**

(1) First name Last name	(2) Dependent's social security number	(3) Dependent's relationship to you	(4) ✓ if child under age 17 qualifying for child tax credit (see instructions)
			☐
			☐
			☐
			☐

No. of children on 6c who:
• lived with you
• did not live with you due to divorce or separation (see instructions)
Dependents on 6c not entered above

If more than four dependents, see instructions and check here ▶☐

d Total number of exemptions claimed
Add numbers on lines above ▶

Income

Attach Form(s) W-2 here. Also attach Forms W-2G and 1099-R if tax was withheld.

If you did not get a W-2, see instructions.

7	Wages, salaries, tips, etc. Attach Form(s) W-2	7	
8a	**Taxable** interest. Attach Schedule B if required	8a	
b	**Tax-exempt** interest. **Do not** include on line 8a — 8b		
9a	Ordinary dividends. Attach Schedule B if required	9a	
b	Qualified dividends — 9b		
10	Taxable refunds, credits, or offsets of state and local income taxes	10	
11	Alimony received	11	
12	Business income or (loss). Attach Schedule C or C-EZ	12	
13	Capital gain or (loss). Attach Schedule D if required. If not required, check here ▶ ☐	13	
14	Other gains or (losses). Attach Form 4797	14	
15a	IRA distributions — 15a — b Taxable amount	15b	
16a	Pensions and annuities — 16a — b Taxable amount	16b	
17	Rental real estate, royalties, partnerships, S corporations, trusts, etc. Attach Schedule E	17	
18	Farm income or (loss). Attach Schedule F	18	
19	Unemployment compensation	19	
20a	Social security benefits — 20a — b Taxable amount	20b	
21	Other income. List type and amount	21	
22	Combine the amounts in the far right column for lines 7 through 21. This is your **total income** ▶	22	

Adjusted Gross Income

23	Reserved	23	
24	Certain business expenses of reservists, performing artists, and fee-basis government officials. Attach Form 2106 or 2106-EZ	24	
25	Health savings account deduction. Attach Form 8889	25	
26	Moving expenses. Attach Form 3903	26	
27	Deductible part of self-employment tax. Attach Schedule SE	27	
28	Self-employed SEP, SIMPLE, and qualified plans	28	
29	Self-employed health insurance deduction	29	
30	Penalty on early withdrawal of savings	30	
31a	Alimony paid **b** Recipient's SSN ▶	31a	
32	IRA deduction	32	
33	Student loan interest deduction	33	
34	Reserved	34	
35	Domestic production activities deduction. Attach Form 8903	35	
36	Add lines 23 through 35	36	
37	Subtract line 36 from line 22. This is your **adjusted gross income** ▶	37	

For Disclosure, Privacy Act, and Paperwork Reduction Act Notice, see separate instructions. Cat. No. 11320B Form **1040** (2015)

(Use for Problem 27.)

Form 1040 (2015) Page **2**

Tax and Credits	38	Amount from line 37 (adjusted gross income)		38
	39a	Check if: ☐ **You** were born before January 2, 1951, ☐ Blind. ☐ **Spouse** was born before January 2, 1951, ☐ Blind. } **Total boxes checked ▶ 39a**		
	b	If your spouse itemizes on a separate return or you were a dual-status alien, check here ▶ 39b ☐		
Standard Deduction for— • People who check any box on line 39a or 39b **or** who can be claimed as a dependent, see instructions. • All others: Single or Married filing separately, $6,300 Married filing jointly or Qualifying widow(er), $12,600 Head of household, $9,250	40	**Itemized deductions** (from Schedule A) **or** your **standard deduction** (see left margin)		40
	41	Subtract line 40 from line 38		41
	42	**Exemptions.** If line 38 is $154,950 or less, multiply $4,000 by the number on line 6d. Otherwise, see instructions		42
	43	**Taxable income.** Subtract line 42 from line 41. If line 42 is more than line 41, enter -0-		43
	44	**Tax** (see instructions). Check if any from: **a** ☐ Form(s) 8814 **b** ☐ Form 4972 **c** ☐		44
	45	**Alternative minimum tax** (see instructions). Attach Form 6251		45
	46	Excess advance premium tax credit repayment. Attach Form 8962		46
	47	Add lines 44, 45, and 46 ▶		47
	48	Foreign tax credit. Attach Form 1116 if required	48	
	49	Credit for child and dependent care expenses. Attach Form 2441	49	
	50	Education credits from Form 8863, line 19	50	
	51	Retirement savings contributions credit. Attach Form 8880	51	
	52	Child tax credit. Attach Schedule 8812, if required	52	
	53	Residential energy credit. Attach Form 5695	53	
	54	Other credits from Form: **a** ☐ 3800 **b** ☐ 8801 **c** ☐	54	
	55	Add lines 48 through 54. These are your **total credits**		55
	56	Subtract line 55 from line 47. If line 55 is more than line 47, enter -0- ▶		56
Other Taxes	57	Self-employment tax. Attach Schedule SE		57
	58	Unreported social security and Medicare tax from Form: **a** ☐ 4137 **b** ☐ 8919		58
	59	Additional tax on IRAs, other qualified retirement plans, etc. Attach Form 5329 if required		59
	60a	Household employment taxes from Schedule H		60a
	b	First-time homebuyer credit repayment. Attach Form 5405 if required		60b
	61	Health care: individual responsibility (see instructions) Full-year coverage ☐		61
	62	Taxes from: **a** ☐ Form 8959 **b** ☐ Form 8960 **c** ☐ Instructions; enter code(s)		62
	63	Add lines 56 through 62. This is your **total tax** ▶		63
Payments	64	Federal income tax withheld from Forms W-2 and 1099	64	
	65	2015 estimated tax payments and amount applied from 2014 return	65	
If you have a qualifying child, attach Schedule EIC.	66a	**Earned income credit (EIC)**	66a	
	b	Nontaxable combat pay election 66b		
	67	Additional child tax credit. Attach Schedule 8812	67	
	68	American opportunity credit from Form 8863, line 8	68	
	69	Net premium tax credit. Attach Form 8962	69	
	70	Amount paid with request for extension to file	70	
	71	Excess social security and tier 1 RRTA tax withheld	71	
	72	Credit for federal tax on fuels. Attach Form 4136	72	
	73	Credits from Form: **a** ☐ 2439 **b** ■ Reserved **c** ☐ 8885 **d** ☐	73	
	74	Add lines 64, 65, 66a, and 67 through 73. These are your **total payments** ▶		74
Refund	75	If line 74 is more than line 63, subtract line 63 from line 74. This is the amount you **overpaid**		75
	76a	Amount of line 75 you want **refunded to you.** If Form 8888 is attached, check here ▶ ☐		76a
Direct deposit? See instructions.	▶ b	Routing number ▶ **c** Type: ☐ Checking ☐ Savings		
	▶ d	Account number		
	77	Amount of line 75 you want **applied to your 2016 estimated tax** ▶	77	
Amount You Owe	78	**Amount you owe.** Subtract line 74 from line 63. For details on how to pay, see instructions ▶		78
	79	Estimated tax penalty (see instructions)	79	

Third Party Designee — Do you want to allow another person to discuss this return with the IRS (see instructions)? ☐ **Yes.** Complete below. ☐ **No**

Designee's name ▶ Phone no. ▶ Personal identification number (PIN) ▶

Sign Here — Under penalties of perjury, I declare that I have examined this return and accompanying schedules and statements, and to the best of my knowledge and belief, they are true, correct, and complete. Declaration of preparer (other than taxpayer) is based on all information of which preparer has any knowledge.

Joint return? See instructions. Keep a copy for your records.

Your signature	Date	Your occupation	Daytime phone number
Spouse's signature. If a joint return, **both** must sign.	Date	Spouse's occupation	If the IRS sent you an Identity Protection PIN, enter it here (see inst.)

Paid Preparer Use Only

Print/Type preparer's name	Preparer's signature	Date	Check ☐ if self-employed	PTIN
Firm's name ▶			Firm's EIN ▶	
Firm's address ▶			Phone no.	

www.irs.gov/form1040 Form **1040** (2015)

(Use for Problem 27.)

SCHEDULE C (Form 1040)
Department of the Treasury Internal Revenue Service (99)

Profit or Loss From Business
(Sole Proprietorship)

▶ Information about Schedule C and its separate instructions is at *www.irs.gov/schedulec*.
▶ Attach to Form 1040, 1040NR, or 1041; partnerships generally must file Form 1065.

OMB No. 1545-0074
2015
Attachment Sequence No. 09

Name of proprietor | Social security number (SSN)

A Principal business or profession, including product or service (see instructions) | B Enter code from instructions ▶

C Business name. If no separate business name, leave blank. | D Employer ID number (EIN), (see instr.)

E Business address (including suite or room no.) ▶
City, town or post office, state, and ZIP code

F Accounting method: (1) ☐ Cash (2) ☐ Accrual (3) ☐ Other (specify) ▶

G Did you "materially participate" in the operation of this business during 2015? If "No," see instructions for limit on losses . ☐ Yes ☐ No

H If you started or acquired this business during 2015, check here . . . . . ▶ ☐

I Did you make any payments in 2015 that would require you to file Form(s) 1099? (see instructions) . . . ☐ Yes ☐ No

J If "Yes," did you or will you file required Forms 1099? . . . ☐ Yes ☐ No

Part I Income

1	Gross receipts or sales. See instructions for line 1 and check the box if this income was reported to you on Form W-2 and the "Statutory employee" box on that form was checked . . . ▶ ☐	1	
2	Returns and allowances . . .	2	
3	Subtract line 2 from line 1 . . .	3	
4	Cost of goods sold (from line 42) . . .	4	
5	**Gross profit.** Subtract line 4 from line 3 . . .	5	
6	Other income, including federal and state gasoline or fuel tax credit or refund (see instructions) . . .	6	
7	**Gross income.** Add lines 5 and 6 . . . ▶	7	

Part II Expenses. Enter expenses for business use of your home **only** on line 30.

8	Advertising . . .	8		18	Office expense (see instructions)	18	
9	Car and truck expenses (see instructions) . . .	9		19	Pension and profit-sharing plans .	19	
				20	Rent or lease (see instructions):		
10	Commissions and fees .	10		a	Vehicles, machinery, and equipment	20a	
11	Contract labor (see instructions)	11		b	Other business property . . .	20b	
12	Depletion . . .	12		21	Repairs and maintenance . . .	21	
13	Depreciation and section 179 expense deduction (not included in Part III) (see instructions) . . .	13		22	Supplies (not included in Part III) .	22	
				23	Taxes and licenses . . .	23	
				24	Travel, meals, and entertainment:		
14	Employee benefit programs (other than on line 19) . .	14		a	Travel . . .	24a	
15	Insurance (other than health)	15		b	Deductible meals and entertainment (see instructions) .	24b	
16	Interest:			25	Utilities . . .	25	
a	Mortgage (paid to banks, etc.)	16a		26	Wages (less employment credits) .	26	
b	Other . . .	16b		27a	Other expenses (from line 48) . .	27a	
17	Legal and professional services	17		b	**Reserved for future use** . . .	27b	

28	**Total expenses** before expenses for business use of home. Add lines 8 through 27a . . . ▶	28	
29	Tentative profit or (loss). Subtract line 28 from line 7 . . .	29	
30	Expenses for business use of your home. Do not report these expenses elsewhere. Attach Form 8829 unless using the simplified method (see instructions). **Simplified method filers only:** enter the total square footage of: (a) your home: ______ and (b) the part of your home used for business: ______ . Use the Simplified Method Worksheet in the instructions to figure the amount to enter on line 30 . . .	30	
31	**Net profit or (loss).** Subtract line 30 from line 29. • If a profit, enter on both **Form 1040, line 12** (or **Form 1040NR, line 13**) and on **Schedule SE, line 2.** (If you checked the box on line 1, see instructions). Estates and trusts, enter on **Form 1041, line 3.** • If a loss, you **must** go to line 32.	31	

32 If you have a loss, check the box that describes your investment in this activity (see instructions).
- If you checked 32a, enter the loss on both **Form 1040, line 12,** (or **Form 1040NR, line 13**) and on **Schedule SE, line 2.** (If you checked the box on line 1, see the line 31 instructions). Estates and trusts, enter on **Form 1041, line 3.**
- If you checked 32b, you **must** attach **Form 6198.** Your loss may be limited.

32a ☐ All investment is at risk.
32b ☐ Some investment is not at risk.

For Paperwork Reduction Act Notice, see the separate instructions. Cat. No. 11334P **Schedule C (Form 1040) 2015**

(Use for Problem 27.)

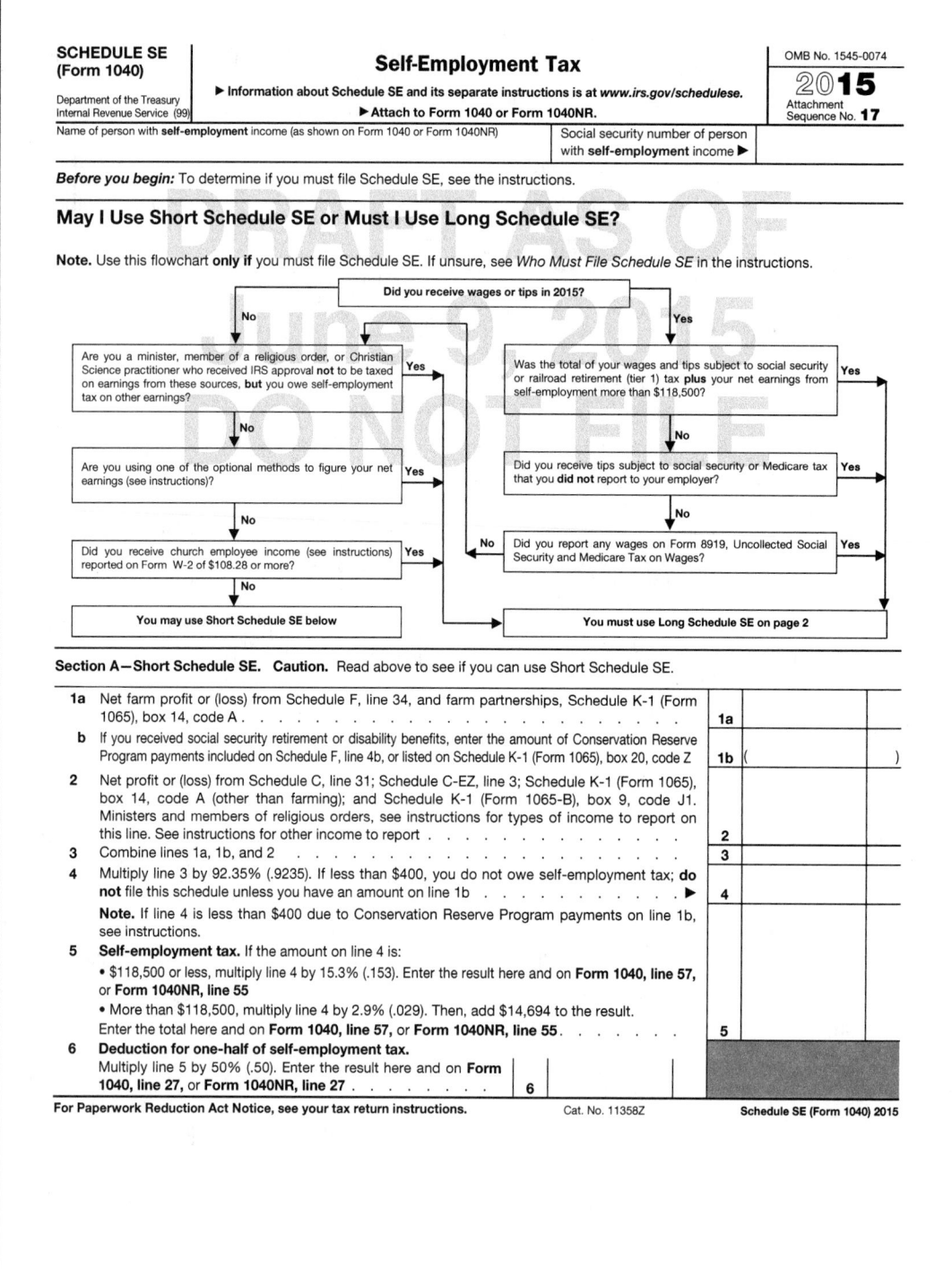

SCHEDULE SE (Form 1040)

Department of the Treasury
Internal Revenue Service (99)

Self-Employment Tax

▶ Information about Schedule SE and its separate instructions is at *www.irs.gov/schedulese.*
▶ Attach to Form 1040 or Form 1040NR.

OMB No. 1545-0074
2015
Attachment Sequence No. **17**

Name of person with **self-employment** income (as shown on Form 1040 or Form 1040NR)	Social security number of person with **self-employment** income ▶

Before you begin: To determine if you must file Schedule SE, see the instructions.

May I Use Short Schedule SE or Must I Use Long Schedule SE?

Note. Use this flowchart **only if** you must file Schedule SE. If unsure, see *Who Must File Schedule SE* in the instructions.

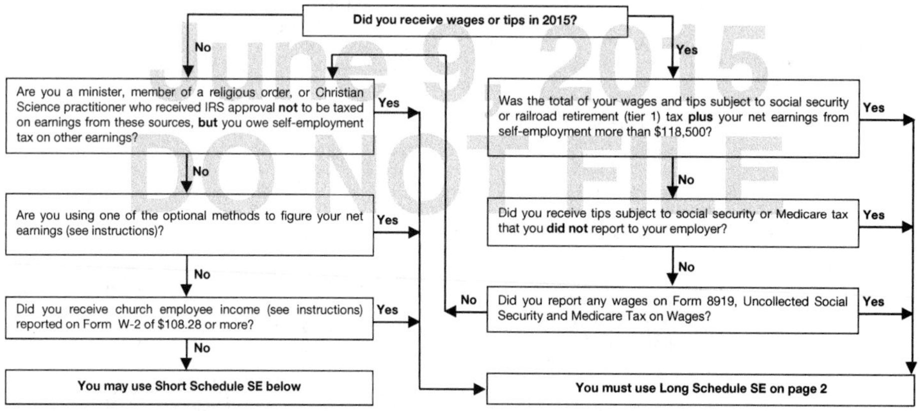
Did you receive wages or tips in 2015?
No
Yes
Are you a minister, member of a religious order, or Christian Science practitioner who received IRS approval not to be taxed on earnings from these sources, but you owe self-employment tax on other earnings?
Yes
No
Was the total of your wages and tips subject to social security or railroad retirement (tier 1) tax plus your net earnings from self-employment more than $118,500?
Yes
No
Are you using one of the optional methods to figure your net earnings (see instructions)?
Yes
No
Did you receive tips subject to social security or Medicare tax that you did not report to your employer?
Yes
No
Did you receive church employee income (see instructions) reported on Form W-2 of $108.28 or more?
Yes
No
Did you report any wages on Form 8919, Uncollected Social Security and Medicare Tax on Wages?
Yes
No
You may use Short Schedule SE below
You must use Long Schedule SE on page 2

Section A—Short Schedule SE. Caution. Read above to see if you can use Short Schedule SE.

1a	Net farm profit or (loss) from Schedule F, line 34, and farm partnerships, Schedule K-1 (Form 1065), box 14, code A	**1a**	
b	If you received social security retirement or disability benefits, enter the amount of Conservation Reserve Program payments included on Schedule F, line 4b, or listed on Schedule K-1 (Form 1065), box 20, code Z	**1b**	( )
2	Net profit or (loss) from Schedule C, line 31; Schedule C-EZ, line 3; Schedule K-1 (Form 1065), box 14, code A (other than farming); and Schedule K-1 (Form 1065-B), box 9, code J1. Ministers and members of religious orders, see instructions for types of income to report on this line. See instructions for other income to report	**2**	
3	Combine lines 1a, 1b, and 2	**3**	
4	Multiply line 3 by 92.35% (.9235). If less than $400, you do not owe self-employment tax; **do not** file this schedule unless you have an amount on line 1b . . . . ▶	**4**	
	Note. If line 4 is less than $400 due to Conservation Reserve Program payments on line 1b, see instructions.		
5	**Self-employment tax.** If the amount on line 4 is: • $118,500 or less, multiply line 4 by 15.3% (.153). Enter the result here and on **Form 1040, line 57,** or **Form 1040NR, line 55** • More than $118,500, multiply line 4 by 2.9% (.029). Then, add $14,694 to the result. Enter the total here and on **Form 1040, line 57,** or **Form 1040NR, line 55**	**5**	
6	**Deduction for one-half of self-employment tax.** Multiply line 5 by 50% (.50). Enter the result here and on **Form 1040, line 27,** or **Form 1040NR, line 27** **6**		

For Paperwork Reduction Act Notice, see your tax return instructions. Cat. No. 11358Z **Schedule SE (Form 1040) 2015**

(Use for Problem 27.)

Form **4562**

Department of the Treasury
Internal Revenue Service (99)

Depreciation and Amortization

(Including Information on Listed Property)

▶ Attach to your tax return.

▶ Information about Form 4562 and its separate instructions is at *www.irs.gov/form4562*.

OMB No. 1545-0172

2015

Attachment Sequence No. **179**

Name(s) shown on return	Business or activity to which this form relates	**Identifying number**

Part I Election To Expense Certain Property Under Section 179

Note: If you have any listed property, complete Part V before you complete Part I.

1	Maximum amount (see instructions)	1	
2	Total cost of section 179 property placed in service (see instructions)	2	
3	Threshold cost of section 179 property before reduction in limitation (see instructions)	3	
4	Reduction in limitation. Subtract line 3 from line 2. If zero or less, enter -0-	4	
5	Dollar limitation for tax year. Subtract line 4 from line 1. If zero or less, enter -0-. If married filing separately, see instructions	5	

6	**(a)** Description of property	**(b)** Cost (business use only)	**(c)** Elected cost

7	Listed property. Enter the amount from line 29	7	
8	Total elected cost of section 179 property. Add amounts in column (c), lines 6 and 7	8	
9	Tentative deduction. Enter the **smaller** of line 5 or line 8	9	
10	Carryover of disallowed deduction from line 13 of your 2014 Form 4562	10	
11	Business income limitation. Enter the smaller of business income (not less than zero) or line 5 (see instructions)	11	
12	Section 179 expense deduction. Add lines 9 and 10, but do not enter more than line 11	12	
13	Carryover of disallowed deduction to 2016. Add lines 9 and 10, less line 12 ▶	13	

Note: Do not use Part II or Part III below for listed property. Instead, use Part V.

Part II Special Depreciation Allowance and Other Depreciation (Do not include listed property.**)** (See instructions.)

14	Special depreciation allowance for qualified property (other than listed property) placed in service during the tax year (see instructions)	14	
15	Property subject to section 168(f)(1) election	15	
16	Other depreciation (including ACRS)	16	

Part III MACRS Depreciation (Do not include listed property.**)** (See instructions.)

Section A

17	MACRS deductions for assets placed in service in tax years beginning before 2015	17	
18	If you are electing to group any assets placed in service during the tax year into one or more general asset accounts, check here ▶ ☐		

Section B—Assets Placed in Service During 2015 Tax Year Using the General Depreciation System

(a) Classification of property	**(b)** Month and year placed in service	**(c)** Basis for depreciation (business/investment use only—see instructions)	**(d)** Recovery period	**(e)** Convention	**(f)** Method	**(g)** Depreciation deduction
19a 3-year property						
b 5-year property						
c 7-year property						
d 10-year property						
e 15-year property						
f 20-year property						
g 25-year property			25 yrs.		S/L	
h Residential rental property			27.5 yrs.	MM	S/L	
			27.5 yrs.	MM	S/L	
i Nonresidential real property			39 yrs.	MM	S/L	
				MM	S/L	

Section C—Assets Placed in Service During 2015 Tax Year Using the Alternative Depreciation System

20a Class life					S/L	
b 12-year			12 yrs.		S/L	
c 40-year			40 yrs.	MM	S/L	

Part IV Summary (See instructions.)

21	Listed property. Enter amount from line 28	21	
22	**Total.** Add amounts from line 12, lines 14 through 17, lines 19 and 20 in column (g), and line 21. Enter here and on the appropriate lines of your return. Partnerships and S corporations—see instructions	22	
23	For assets shown above and placed in service during the current year, enter the portion of the basis attributable to section 263A costs	23	

For Paperwork Reduction Act Notice, see separate instructions. Cat. No. 12906N Form **4562** (2015)

(Use for Problem 27.)

Form 4562 (2015) Page **2**

Part V **Listed Property** (Include automobiles, certain other vehicles, certain aircraft, certain computers, and property used for entertainment, recreation, or amusement.)

Note: For any vehicle for which you are using the standard mileage rate or deducting lease expense, complete **only** 24a, 24b, columns (a) through (c) of Section A, all of Section B, and Section C if applicable.

Section A—Depreciation and Other Information (Caution: See the instructions for limits for passenger automobiles.**)**

24a Do you have evidence to support the business/investment use claimed? ☐ **Yes** ☐ **No** **24b** If "Yes," is the evidence written? ☐ **Yes** ☐ **No**

(a) Type of property (list vehicles first)	(b) Date placed in service	(c) Business/ investment use percentage	(d) Cost or other basis	(e) Basis for depreciation (business/investment use only)	(f) Recovery period	(g) Method/ Convention	(h) Depreciation deduction	(i) Elected section 179 cost
25 Special depreciation allowance for qualified listed property placed in service during the tax year and used more than 50% in a qualified business use (see instructions) .						**25**		
26 Property used more than 50% in a qualified business use:								
		%						
		%						
		%						
27 Property used 50% or less in a qualified business use:								
		%				S/L –		
		%				S/L –		
		%				S/L –		
28 Add amounts in column (h), lines 25 through 27. Enter here and on line 21, page 1 .						**28**		
29 Add amounts in column (i), line 26. Enter here and on line 7, page 1							**29**	

Section B—Information on Use of Vehicles

Complete this section for vehicles used by a sole proprietor, partner, or other "more than 5% owner," or related person. If you provided vehicles to your employees, first answer the questions in Section C to see if you meet an exception to completing this section for those vehicles.

	(a) Vehicle 1		(b) Vehicle 2		(c) Vehicle 3		(d) Vehicle 4		(e) Vehicle 5		(f) Vehicle 6	
30 Total business/investment miles driven during the year (**do not** include commuting miles) .												
31 Total commuting miles driven during the year												
32 Total other personal (noncommuting) miles driven												
33 Total miles driven during the year. Add lines 30 through 32												
	Yes	**No**	**Yes**	**No**	**Yes**	**No**	**Yes**	**No**	**Yes**	**No**	**Yes**	**No**
34 Was the vehicle available for personal use during off-duty hours?												
35 Was the vehicle used primarily by a more than 5% owner or related person? . .												
36 Is another vehicle available for personal use?												

Section C—Questions for Employers Who Provide Vehicles for Use by Their Employees

Answer these questions to determine if you meet an exception to completing Section B for vehicles used by employees who **are not** more than 5% owners or related persons (see instructions).

	Yes	**No**
37 Do you maintain a written policy statement that prohibits all personal use of vehicles, including commuting, by your employees?		
38 Do you maintain a written policy statement that prohibits personal use of vehicles, except commuting, by your employees? See the instructions for vehicles used by corporate officers, directors, or 1% or more owners . .		
39 Do you treat all use of vehicles by employees as personal use?		
40 Do you provide more than five vehicles to your employees, obtain information from your employees about the use of the vehicles, and retain the information received?		
41 Do you meet the requirements concerning qualified automobile demonstration use? (See instructions.) . . .		
Note: If your answer to 37, 38, 39, 40, or 41 is "Yes," do not complete Section B for the covered vehicles.		

Part VI **Amortization**

(a) Description of costs	(b) Date amortization begins	(c) Amortizable amount	(d) Code section	(e) Amortization period or percentage	(f) Amortization for this year
42 Amortization of costs that begins during your 2015 tax year (see instructions):					
43 Amortization of costs that began before your 2015 tax year				**43**	
44 **Total.** Add amounts in column (f). See the instructions for where to report				**44**	

Form **4562** (2015)

Chapter 9

Rental Activities

CHAPTER CONTENTS

LEARNING OBJECTIVES

After completing Chapter 9, you should be able to:

1. Compute the amount of rental income and expenses reported in the calculation of taxable income.
2. Determine the amount of expenses taxpayers can deduct against rental income when renting out a vacation home.
3. Understand how the at-risk and passive activity loss rules may limit the taxpayer's deductions in the current year and compute any carryover to future tax years.
4. Prepare Schedule E and Form 8582.

CHAPTER OVERVIEW

In addition to earning income from their jobs, many individuals earn income from property they own. For instance, taxpayers who own stocks often earn dividend income. Likewise, those who own bonds earn interest income. Taxpayers also can earn income by renting out property that they own. Chapters 3 and 4 described the tax rules for reporting interest and dividend income. This chapter focuses on the income and expenses from rental activities. Taxpayers report rental income and expenses on Schedule E, Supplemental Income and Loss. However, in cases where rental expenses exceed rental income, the vacation home rules, at-risk rules, or passive loss rules may limit the losses taxpayers can deduct on Form 1040. The chapter begins with a discussion of rental income and expenses. The focus then shifts to the areas of the tax law that may limit deductions for losses from rental activities.

¶901 Rental Income and Expenses

Although taxpayers can rent both personal and real property, this chapter focuses on the tax aspects of owning residential rental property. **Residential rental property** is rental property where at least 80% of the income comes from the rental of dwelling units. A **dwelling unit** is property that provides the basic living accommodations—kitchen, sleeping, and toilet facilities. Examples of dwelling units include houses, apartments, condominiums, mobile homes, motor homes, yachts, and boats. Hotels, motels, and similar establishments are not considered dwelling units.

¶901.01 RENTAL INCOME

Rental income includes the payments taxpayers receive for allowing others to use or occupy their property. Usually rent payments are received in cash. However, when a tenant performs services in exchange for the use of the taxpayer's property, rental income includes the value of those services. Rental income includes payments a tenant makes to cancel a lease. It also includes the value of improvements a tenant makes to the taxpayer's property in place of rent.

EXAMPLE 1

Brent rents property he owns to a tenant for $500 a month. In November the tenant installs a ceiling fan valued at $100. Brent reduces the tenant's December rent by $100. Brent's rental income equals $6,000 ($500 × 11 months + $400 for December + $100 improvement in lieu of rent). Brent then capitalizes and depreciates the ceiling fan.

Cash basis taxpayers report rental income in the year they receive it, even when it applies to a prior or future tax year. Accrual basis taxpayers usually report rental income in the year it is due to them, but must report rent received in advance in the year they receive it. Therefore, if on December 26, 20x1, the taxpayer receives $600 from a tenant for January 20x2 rent, the $600 would be reported as rental income in 20x1 under both the cash and accrual methods.

A security deposit is considered rent received in advance when the deposit represents the tenant's final rent payment. It is not considered rent received in advance if the taxpayer intends to return the deposit at the end of the lease. However, should the tenant forfeit any part of the deposit in a future year (for example, to cover late charges), the forfeited amount is rental income to the taxpayer in the year the tenant forfeits it.

EXAMPLE 2

Connie enters into a 5-year lease to rent property she owns. On July 1, 20x1, Connie receives $6,000 for the first year's rent and $6,000 of rent in advance for the final year of the lease. Connie also receives a $1,000 security deposit that she intends to return to the tenant at the end of the lease. Connie's 20x1 rental income equals $12,000, regardless of whether she uses the cash or accrual method of accounting.

¶901.02 RENTAL EXPENSES

Taxpayers can deduct against rental income all ordinary expenses related to the rental property. Examples of common rental expenses include advertising, cleaning, utilities, real estate taxes, mortgage interest, insurance premiums, management fees, and necessary travel and transportation. Other rental expenses include repairs, maintenance, and depreciation. Accrual basis taxpayers take deductions in the year that services are received or assets are used. Cash basis taxpayers deduct rental expenses in the year the expenses are paid, except for prepaid expenses, which are spread over the periods benefited.

Repairs and maintenance keep rental property in good operating condition. Examples include painting the property (both inside and out), fixing a leak, and repairing a screen. Taxpayers deduct the costs of repairs and maintenance to rental property as a rental expense. Repairs are different from improvements, which are costs that add value to the property or prolong its useful life. Examples include adding a bathroom, installing new appliances, or replacing the roof. Taxpayers recover the cost of improvements through annual depreciation deductions.

Improvements made to residential rental property are depreciated using the straight-line method over 27.5 years (MACRS) or 40 years (ADS). Taxpayers use MACRS or ADS to depreciate rental furnishings. These include furniture, appliances, and carpeting. Section 179 is not allowed on rental furnishings. However, bonus depreciation is allowed in the first year on new rental furnishings placed in service during a year in which bonus depreciation is allowed. If MACRS is used, rental furnishings are 5-year property. If ADS is elected, the furnishings have a 9-year recovery period (see ¶802.04 for more on ADS).

Often, telling the difference between a repair and an improvement is easy. For example, fixing a leaky roof is a repair; replacing the roof is an improvement. However, sometimes it is difficult to draw the line where an expense becomes an improvement instead of a repair. For example, when a major leak in the roof results in having to replace a large portion of the roof, the question becomes whether the cost to replace part of the roof is a deductible expense or something that must be depreciated.

The IRS has recently taken some of the guesswork out of this question by issuing final "repairs regs" that can be used by smaller taxpayers. Under the repair regs, taxpayers can use a de minimis rule to expense items costing $500 or less ($5,000 if they have "applicable financial statements," which in essence, are audited financial statements). Small taxpayers are those who either (1) have assets (at the beginning of the year) that do not exceed $10 million, or (2) had no more than $10 million in annual gross receipts for each distinct business they own for the past three years.

The repair regs also allows certain landlords to use a safe harbor to deduct costs that otherwise might be considered improvements. The safe harbor rules can only be used as long as the unadjusted basis of the building (original cost plus improvements) does not exceed $1 million. The $1 million limit is applied to each rental building the landlord owns. Also, the safe harbor rules can be used only if the cost does exceed the *lesser of* (i) $10,000, or (ii) 2% of the unadjusted basis of the building. The $10,000/2% limit is applied separately to each building. Thus, if the taxpayer owns four rental properties (each with an unadjusted basis of $1 million or less), depending on the amount of expenses incurred for each building, the taxpayer may be able to use the safe harbor rule to expense all of the expenses for some of the buildings, but not others.

Taxpayers wanting to take advantage of either the de minimis or safe harbor rules must attach an election stating their intent to a timely filed tax return. Once an election is made, it cannot be revoked.

EXAMPLE 3

Vince rents out a condo that he once used as his main home. Vince's unadjusted basis in the home is $80,000. During the year, Vince paid $200 to replace a screen door and $1,000 to replace the furnace. Vince can use the safe harbor under the repair regs because his unadjusted basis in the home does not exceed $1 million, and the $1,200 he spent during the year does not exceed $1,600 ($80,000 x 2%). By attaching a statement to his return that he intends to use the safe harbor to deduct the entire $1,200 as a rental expense, Vince does not have to worry about whether any of the costs might instead be considered an improvement, rather than a repair.

¶901.03 SPECIAL RULES WHEN ONLY PART OF THE PROPERTY IS RENTED

The rules just described assume that the rental property is used exclusively by or is available for use by rent-paying tenants. Sometimes an individual rents only part of the property, as is the case when an owner of a duplex rents one unit and lives in the other. In such instances, the taxpayer must allocate expenses between rental and personal use. The taxpayer then deducts the rental portion of each expense against rental income and can deduct the personal portion of the mortgage interest and real estate taxes as itemized deductions.

Some expenses are easy to split between rental and personal use. For example, taxpayers can fully deduct the cost of repairs performed on rental units but cannot deduct the cost to repair their own personal units. Other expenses, like real estate taxes and depreciation, are harder to divide between rental and personal use. For these expenses, taxpayers can use any reasonable method to divide expenses between the two uses. The number of rooms or the relative square footage are two widely used methods for allocating these types of expenses.

EXAMPLE 4

Marvin rents one room in his home. The area of the rented room is 140 square feet. The area of the entire home is 1,400 square feet. Marvin deducts against rental income 10% (140/1,400) of the expenses related to the home during the year. Thus, if Marvin's real estate taxes are $2,000, he can deduct $200 against rental income and the rest ($1,800) as an itemized deduction.

¶901.04 CONVERTING A PERSONAL HOME TO RENTAL USE

When taxpayers convert a personal home to rental property, they must divide the expenses from the conversion year between the two uses. Rental use begins when the property is first offered for rent. Taxpayers deduct the rental portion of these expenses against rental income. They can deduct the personal portion of the mortgage interest and real estate taxes as itemized deductions.

EXAMPLE 5

In September, Sylvia moved out of her home. Sylvia listed her home for rent on October 1, and on November 1, she entered into a 2-year lease. Sylvia can deduct 25% (October–December) of the annual expenses (real estate taxes, insurance, depreciation) against the rental income she receives during the year. She also can deduct any other expenses (mortgage interest, utilities, etc.) allocated to the last three months of the year. Sylvia can deduct the personal portion (75%) of the interest and taxes as itemized deductions.

¶902 Rental of Vacation Homes

Special rules apply when taxpayers rent out their homes for part of the year and personally use the property during other parts of the year. The tax treatment of this type of rental activity depends on the number of rental and personal days during the year.

¶902.01 PROPERTY RENTED LESS THAN 15 DAYS

When individual taxpayers rent their main homes or vacation homes for less than 15 days during the year, they do not report the rental income and do not deduct any rental expenses. However, home mortgage interest (but only for the taxpayer's main home or second home), real estate taxes, and casualty losses may be deducted as itemized deductions.

EXAMPLE 6

Benton rents his vacation home for 12 days during the year and personally uses it for 80 days. The rest of the year the home sits vacant. Benton collects rents of $3,000 and incurs the following expenses.

Home mortgage interest	$ 6,000
Real estate taxes	1,800
Utilities	400
Depreciation	2,000
Total expenses	$10,200

Since Benton rents the property for less than 15 days, he does not report the $3,000 of rental income. Benton can deduct as itemized deductions the $6,000 of home mortgage interest (as his second home) and the $1,800 of real estate taxes.

¶902.02 PROPERTY RENTED MORE THAN 14 DAYS

Taxpayers who rent their main homes or vacation homes for more than 14 days during the year report the rental income on their personal tax returns. Expenses related solely to rental activities (like advertising or commissions) can be deducted against rental income. All other expenses must be allocated between rental and personal use. Taxpayers can then deduct the rental portion of these the expenses.

The Internal Revenue Code (Code) requires taxpayers to allocate expenses other than interest, taxes, and casualty losses on the basis of the days the property is used during the year. To compute the rental portion of expenses like utilities, repairs, and depreciation, taxpayers multiply the expense by the ratio of the number of days rented for a fair rental price to the number of days of use during the year.

$$\textbf{Percent allocated to rental activity} = \frac{\textbf{Number of fair rental days}}{\textbf{Number of days used during the year}}$$

The Code does not address how to allocate interest, taxes, and casualty losses between rental and personal use. In IRS Publication 527, the IRS suggests that taxpayers use the same method used to allocate other expenses. The courts, however, have allowed interest and taxes to be allocated based on the days rented to the number of days in the year. For purposes of this chapter, the same ratio (days rented/days used) is used to allocate all expenses between rental and personal use.

EXAMPLE 7

Wally rents out his vacation home for 120 days during the year. He personally uses it for 80 days. Wally collects rents of $12,000 and incurs the following expenses.

Home mortgage interest	$ 8,000
Real estate taxes	2,500
Utilities	800
Depreciation	3,000
Total expenses	$14,300

Wally allocates 60% of the expenses (120 rental days/200 total days used during the year) to rental use. He deducts $8,580 ($14,300 × 60%) as rental expense. Wally can deduct the rest of the real estate taxes ($2,500 × 40% = $1,000) as an itemized deduction. He may be able to deduct the rest of the home mortgage interest ($8,000 × 40% = $3,200) if the home is selected as Wally's second home.

A rental day is any day the taxpayer rents the property for a fair rental price, even if rented to a friend or relative. Days that the property is offered for rental, but not actually rented, do not count as days rented at a fair rental price.

What Is a Fair Rental Price?

A fair rental price is the amount of rent that an *unrelated person* would be willing to pay to use the property. If the rent charged is substantially less than the rents received on *similar* properties, it might not be considered a fair rental price. The following questions can be used to determine whether two properties are *similar:*

- Are the properties used for the same purpose?
- Are the properties about the same size?
- Are the properties in about the same condition?
- Do the properties have similar furnishings?
- Are the properties in similar locations?

Generally, answering "No" to any of these questions means that the two properties are not similar.

Expenses Limited for Certain Vacation Homes

When the property is considered a "residence," rental expenses are deductible only to the extent of rental income. Disallowed expenses carry over to offset rental income in future tax years. A vacation home qualifies as a **residence** if the number of personal days exceeds the *greater of* (i) 14 days or (ii) 10% of the fair rental days. Thus, if the taxpayer's personal days exceed *both* (i) 14 days and (ii) 10% of the number of fair rental days, then the property is considered a residence. When the property is treated as a residence, the personal portion of the mortgage interest can be deducted as an itemized deduction if the property is chosen as the taxpayer's second home. When the property does not qualify as a residence, the personal portion of the interest cannot be deducted.

In order to properly determine whether the taxpayer's home qualifies as a residence, it is important to understand what days count as personal days. Personal use includes days when the taxpayer donates use of the property to a charitable organization. Personal use also includes days when the property is used by:

1. The owner, unless the owner is working full-time to repair or maintain the property.
2. A member of an owner's family, unless the family member pays a fair rental price ***and*** the family member uses the property as his or her main home. Family members include siblings (brothers and sisters), ancestors (parents, grandparents, etc.), and lineal descendants (children, grandchildren, etc.).
3. Anyone who has a reciprocal agreement that allows the owner to use some other dwelling unit (e.g., time shares).
4. Anyone who pays less than a fair rental price to use the property.

EXAMPLE 8

Ella owns a house that she rents to her son. The son pays a fair rental price to use the house as his main home. Ella does not consider the son's use of the house personal days since the son is paying a fair rental price to use the house as his main home.

EXAMPLE 9

June and Jay Linden own a vacation home that they personally use 24 days during the year. During part of the year, the following occupants used the home. The home was vacant during the rest of the year. Fair rental price is $125 a night.

Occupant	Number of Days
June's parents, who pay no rent	32
Friends of the Lindens, who paid rent of $2,000	40
Jay's brother, who paid rent of $875	7
Unrelated persons, who paid rent of $7,500	60

The 60 days the home was used by unrelated persons are not personal days, since the tenants paid $125 a night (fair rental price). Although Jay's brother paid a fair rental price, his seven days count as personal days since he is a family member and he did not use the home as his main home. The parents did not pay a fair rental price, nor did they use the home as their main home. Thus, their 32 days count as personal days. The 40 days that the home is used by the Lindens' friends count as personal days since they did not pay a fair rental price to use the home. The Lindens' total personal days equal 103 (24 + 32 + 40 + 7). Since the 103 personal days exceed both 14 days and 6.7 days (10% of the 67 fair rental days), the vacation home qualifies as a residence. Thus, rental expenses will be limited to rental income.

EXAMPLE 10

Same facts as in Example 9, except that five of the days the Linden spent at the vacation home were spent making repairs to the property. These five days no longer count as personal days. The Lindens' personal days are reduced to 98 (103 – 5). However, the home still qualifies as a residence.

EXAMPLE 11

Bruce rents his vacation home for 200 days during the year. On 40 of the 200 days, Bruce's sister paid a fair rental price to use the house. The other 160 days also were rented at a fair rental price. Bruce treats the days his sister rents the house as personal days, since she is a relative and does not use the house as her main home. The 40 personal days exceed the *greater of* (i) 14 days, or (ii) 10% of the 200 fair rental days. Thus, the vacation home qualifies as a residence. Accordingly, even though 100% of the rental expenses are deductible (since all 200 days the home was used during the year were rented at a fair rental price), Bruce can only deduct the rental expenses to the extent of rental income.

EXAMPLE 12

From June 1 through October 31 (153 days), Denise rents her cabin (used as a vacation home) and receives a fair rental price. Denise uses the cabin five days during the year. Denise's parents stayed at the cabin for 12 days in May. In deciding whether the cabin qualifies as a residence, personal days include days the parents used the cabin (12 days). Thus, the total number of personal days equals 17 (5 + 12).

Denise treats the cabin as a residence since her 17 personal days exceed the *greater of* (i) 14 days or (ii) 15.3 days (10% of the 153 days rented at fair rental). Thus, Denise can deduct the rental portion of the expenses on the cabin only to the extent of rental income. She carries over any excess rental expense to the next year. In allocating expenses between rental and personal use, Denise allocates 90% (153 rental days/170 days used) of the expenses to the rental activity.

Denise deducts 10% of the real estate taxes on the cabin as an itemized deduction. Because the cabin qualifies as a residence, Denise can deduct the personal portion of the mortgage interest (10%) as an itemized deduction if she selects the cabin as her second home.

If the rental property qualifies as a residence and the taxpayer's rental expenses exceed rental income, the taxpayer deducts the expenses against the rental income in the following order:

1. Home mortgage interest, real estate taxes, casualty and theft losses, and rental expenses not directly related to the rental property (management fees, advertising, etc.)
2. All other rental expenses other than depreciation on the rental property
3. Depreciation of the rental property

EXAMPLE 13

Marilyn rents her vacation home at a fair rental price to an unrelated party for 35 days during the year. Marilyn personally uses the home for 15 days. The property is not used during any other time. During the year, Marilyn collects $6,000 in rents and has the following expenses:

Home mortgage interest	$ 6,000
Real estate taxes	1,500
Utilities	300
Depreciation	3,000
Total expenses	$10,800

Marilyn allocates 70% (35 rental days/50 total days used) of the expenses to the rental use. The rental portion of the expenses related to the home equals $7,560 ($10,800 × 70%). Because Marilyn's personal use (15 days) exceeds the *greater of* (i) 14 days or (ii) 10% of the fair rental days (35 × 10% = 3.5), the vacation home is treated as a residence. Thus, Marilyn's rental expenses cannot exceed rental income. Marilyn deducts the rental expenses in the following order:

Rental income	$6,000
Less rental portion of interest and taxes ($7,500 × 70%)	(5,250)
Rental income left to cover rent expenses other than interest and taxes	$ 750
Less rent expenses other than depreciation ($300 × 70%)	(210)
Rental income left to cover depreciation expense	$ 540
Less depreciation ($3,000 × 70% = $2,100)	(540)
Net rental income	$ 0

Marilyn can deduct only $540 of the $2,100 of depreciation allocated to rental use. Marilyn carries over the disallowed depreciation of $1,560 ($2,100 – $540) to the next year. She adds this amount to next year's depreciation expense.

Marilyn deducts the $450 personal portion of the real estate taxes ($1,500 × 30%) as an itemized deduction. Since the home qualifies as a residence, Marilyn can select the vacation home as her second home and deduct the $1,800 ($6,000 × 30%) personal portion of the home mortgage interest as an itemized deduction.

When renting out a vacation home, the owner's personal use of the property will determine whether the limitation rules apply. These rules cannot take effect until the owner's personal days exceed 14. Thus, to avoid having the tax law limit the deduction for rental expenses, owners might consider limiting their personal usage of the home to two weeks a year.

¶903 Reporting Rental Activities on Schedule E

Taxpayers use Schedule E (Form 1040), Supplemental Income and Loss, to report income and expenses from rental activities. In Part I (line 1), taxpayers provide the address for each property. In Part I (line 2), taxpayers provide the number of fair rental days and the number of personal use days. These numbers are used to determine whether the property qualifies as a residence. Taxpayers also report in Part I rental income and expenses used in computing their overall income or loss from the rental activity.

¶903.01 FILLED-IN SCHEDULE E

INFORMATION FOR FIGURE 9-1:

During 2015, Kurt F. and Heather M. Reding received rents of **$38,168** from an eight-unit apartment complex. The Redings paid $600,000 for the apartment building in 2007, which includes $200,000 for the land. They depreciate the building using ADS. Expenses related to the building include **$250** advertising, **$2,500** cleaning and maintenance, **$1,227** insurance, **$300** legal fees, **$14,329** mortgage interest, **$3,262** repairs, **$4,290** real estate taxes, and **$1,800** utilities.

The Redings also own a condominium in Naples, Florida that they used for 30 days in 2015. They rented the condo for 90 days and received fair rentals totaling **$15,000.** None of the tenants were members of the Redings' family. The Redings paid $295,000 for the condo in 2009 and depreciate it using MACRS. The expenses related to the condo include $9,200 for home mortgage interest, $3,400 for real estate taxes, $1,000 for utilities, $300 for insurance, $375 paid to a cleaning service (100% related to rental), and $75 for advertising the condo for rent in the local newspaper.

The Redings report their rental income and expenses on Schedule E, Supplemental Income and Loss. They enter the amounts shown in bold on the appropriate lines on the schedule. They then transfer their $210 of net rental income to Form 1040 (line 17).

Line #

1aA: Physical address: **505 West Street, Verona, WI 53593**
1bA: Type of Property, **2** (Multi-Family Residence)
1aB: Physical address: **1500 Vanderbelt Beach Road, Naples, FL 34110**
1bB: Type of Property, **3** (Vacation/Short-Term Rental)
2A: Fair rental days, **365**; Personal use days, **0**.
2B: Fair rental days, **90**; Personal use days, **30**.
5B: Advertising, **$75** (no allocation necessary since all related to rental activities)
7B: Cleaning and maintenance, **$375** (100% related to rental activities)
9B: Insurance, **$225** (90/120 × $300)
12B: Mortgage interest, **$6,900** (90/120 × $9,200)
16B: Taxes, **$2,550** (90/120 × $3,400)
17B: Utilities, **$750** (90/120 × $1,000)
18A: Depreciation expense, **$10,000** (($600,000 – $200,000)/40 years under ADS)
18B: Depreciation expense, **$4,125** ($295,000/27.5 × 90/120 = $8,045; however, property B is considered a residence. Thus, total rental expenses cannot exceed the $15,000 of rental income. Since expenses other than depreciation total $10,875, depreciation is limited to $4,125).

Figure 9-1: Filled-In Schedule E

SCHEDULE E (Form 1040)
Department of the Treasury
Internal Revenue Service (99)

Supplemental Income and Loss
(From rental real estate, royalties, partnerships, S corporations, estates, trusts, REMICs, etc.)
▶ Attach to Form 1040, 1040NR, or Form 1041.
▶ Information about Schedule E and its separate instructions is at *www.irs.gov/schedulee.*

OMB No. 1545-0074
2015
Attachment Sequence No. **13**

Name(s) shown on return	Your social security number
Kurt F. and Heather M. Reding	**895-46-5566**

Part I **Income or Loss From Rental Real Estate and Royalties** **Note:** If you are in the business of renting personal property, use **Schedule C** or **C-EZ** (see instructions). If you are an individual, report farm rental income or loss from **Form 4835** on page 2, line 40.

A Did you make any payments in 2015 that would require you to file Form(s) 1099? (see instructions) ☐ Yes ☑ No

B If "Yes," did you or will you file required Forms 1099? ☐ Yes ☐ No

1a	Physical address of each property (street, city, state, ZIP code)
A	**505 West Street, Verona WI 53593**
B	**1500 Vanderbelt Beach Road, Naples, FL 34110**
C	

1b	Type of Property (from list below)	**2** For each rental real estate property listed above, report the number of fair rental and personal use days. Check the **QJV** box only if you meet the requirements to file as a qualified joint venture. See instructions.		**Fair Rental Days**	**Personal Use Days**	**QJV**
A	2		**A**	365	0	☐
B	3		**B**	90	30	☐
C			**C**			☐

Type of Property:
1 Single Family Residence 3 Vacation/Short-Term Rental 5 Land 7 Self-Rental
2 Multi-Family Residence 4 Commercial 6 Royalties 8 Other (describe)

Income: **Properties:**		**A**	**B**	**C**
3 Rents received	3	38,168	15,000	
4 Royalties received	4			
Expenses:				
5 Advertising	5	250	75	
6 Auto and travel (see instructions)	6			
7 Cleaning and maintenance	7	2,500	375	
8 Commissions	8			
9 Insurance	9	1,227	225	
10 Legal and other professional fees	10	300		
11 Management fees	11			
12 Mortgage interest paid to banks, etc. (see instructions)	12	14,329	6,900	
13 Other interest	13			
14 Repairs	14	3,262		
15 Supplies	15			
16 Taxes	16	4,290	2,550	
17 Utilities	17	1,800	750	
18 Depreciation expense or depletion	18	10,000	4,125	
19 Other (list) ▶	19			
20 Total expenses. Add lines 5 through 19	20	37,958	15,000	
21 Subtract line 20 from line 3 (rents) and/or 4 (royalties). If result is a (loss), see instructions to find out if you must file **Form 6198**	21	210	0	
22 Deductible rental real estate loss after limitation, if any, on **Form 8582** (see instructions)	22	( )	( )	( )

23a Total of all amounts reported on line 3 for all rental properties	23a	53,168
b Total of all amounts reported on line 4 for all royalty properties	23b	
c Total of all amounts reported on line 12 for all properties	23c	21,229
d Total of all amounts reported on line 18 for all properties	23d	14,125
e Total of all amounts reported on line 20 for all properties	23e	52,958
24 **Income.** Add positive amounts shown on line 21. **Do not** include any losses	24	210
25 **Losses.** Add royalty losses from line 21 and rental real estate losses from line 22. Enter total losses here	25	( )
26 **Total rental real estate and royalty income or (loss).** Combine lines 24 and 25. Enter the result here. If Parts II, III, IV, and line 40 on page 2 do not apply to you, also enter this amount on Form 1040, line 17, or Form 1040NR, line 18. Otherwise, include this amount in the total on line 41 on page 2	26	210

For Paperwork Reduction Act Notice, see the separate instructions. Cat. No. 11344L **Schedule E (Form 1040) 2015**

¶904 At-Risk Rules

When rental expenses exceed rental income and the rental property is considered a "residence," the tax laws limit the amount of rental expenses taxpayers can deduct against rental income. For rental property not considered a "residence," two other sets of rules may affect the taxpayer's ability to deduct losses arising from rental activities: the at-risk rules and the passive activity loss rules. These rules not only affect rental activities, but also can affect losses arising from any trade, business, or income-producing activity. The at-risk rules are discussed first, followed by the passive activity loss rules (in ¶905).

The at-risk rules limit a taxpayer's loss to the amount the taxpayer could actually lose (that is, be out-of-pocket for) from the activity. This is known as the amount the taxpayer is "at-risk." The at-risk rules apply to any activity carried on as a trade or business (reported on Schedule C) or for the production of income (reported on Schedule E). A taxpayer's risk in any activity equals the following:

1. The money and adjusted basis (cost + improvements – accumulated depreciation) of any property contributed to the activity, **plus**
2. Amounts borrowed for use in the activity if the taxpayer either is personally liable for the loan or pledges personal assets to back up the loan.

Taxpayers that suffer a loss from an at-risk activity determine their deductible loss on Form 6198, At-Risk Limitations. Taxpayers can only deduct losses to the extent they have amounts at-risk. Taxpayers' amount at-risk decreases when they deduct losses from the activity on their tax returns and when they take withdrawals from the activity. In years when the taxpayer's loss is less than the amount at-risk, the taxpayer can deduct the entire loss, and the amount at-risk is reduced by the loss deducted. This (reduced) at-risk amount becomes the taxpayer's amount at-risk for the start of the next year.

EXAMPLE 14

In 20x1, William starts his own business by contributing $10,000 cash from his personal funds and by getting a $100,000 interest-only loan. William uses his personal assets to secure the loan. William's initial amount at-risk is $110,000. During 20x1, the business suffers a $60,000 loss. William can deduct the entire $60,000 loss on his tax return. His amount at-risk is reduced to $50,000.

In years when the amount of the loss exceeds the taxpayer's amount at-risk, the taxpayer's loss deduction is limited to the amount at-risk. Any disallowed loss carries over to the next year. Since the amount at-risk has been reduced to zero, no future losses will be allowed until the taxpayer gets a positive amount at-risk. This can be done through a variety of means. For example, the taxpayer could make additional investments in the activity, or have the activity take out a loan for which the taxpayer is personally responsible.

EXAMPLE 15

Continuing with Example 14, in 20x2, William's business suffers another $60,000 loss. Since William's amount at-risk is $50,000, he will only be allowed to deduct $50,000 of his 20x2 losses. He carries over the $10,000 disallowed loss to 20x3.

¶905 Passive Activity Losses

After applying the at-risk rules, taxpayers must consider the passive activity loss rules. Losses generated by activities of a passive nature can only offset income and gains generated from passive activities. Taxpayers carry over excess passive losses to offset passive income in future tax years. When the taxpayer disposes of the entire interest in a passive activity, any suspended losses left from that activity are fully deductible in that year.

¶905.01 PASSIVE ACTIVITY INCOME DEFINED

The passive activity rules classify all income and losses as coming from one of three types of activities: active, portfolio, or passive. **Active income** consists of wages, salaries, and income from material participation in a trade or business. **Portfolio income** comes from investments that generate dividends and interest. Portfolio income also includes gains from the sale of securities (stocks and bonds). **Passive income** generally comes from (1) a trade or business in which the taxpayer does not materially participate, (2) rental activities, and (3) limited partnerships.

Any of these three types of activities may produce losses. Losses from the sale of portfolio investments are capital losses. However, losses not classified as portfolio are either active or passive. The distinction is important, as taxpayers can offset losses from active activities against both portfolio and passive income. They can only offset losses from passive activities against income from other passive activities.

Material participation in a trade or business produces active income and losses. **Material participation** occurs when the taxpayer is involved in the operations of the activity on a regular, continuous, and substantial basis. Except for rental real estate activities (which must meet a stricter test, discussed later at ¶905.02), the material participation requirement can be met if the taxpayer participates in the activity for more than 500 hours during the year. (For purposes of the 500 hours test, participation by the owner's spouse is considered participation by the owner.) Another way to meet this requirement is for the taxpayer to participate in the activity for more than 100 hours during the year and for the taxpayer's participation to be at least as much as the participation of any other individual, including employees. IRS Publication 925 describes other ways to meet the material participation requirement.

EXAMPLE 16 Ginny and Barry jointly own and work for a business that does not involve rental realty. Ginny also works part-time as an employee. During the year she works 425 hours for the business, and 600 hours as an employee. Barry is not employed elsewhere and spends 40 hours a week working for the business. Because his hours of participation exceed 500, Barry materially participates in the business. Ginny does not participate in the business more than 500 hours, and although her hours exceed 100, her hours do not equal Barry's hours. Thus, unless she can meet the material participation requirements another way, the passive activity loss rules would apply to Ginny with respect to this activity.

EXAMPLE 17 Same facts as in Example 16, except that Ginny averages 10 hours a week working for the business. Since Ginny's 520 hours (10 × 52 weeks) exceed 500, she materially participates in the activity. Thus, the business would not be considered a passive activity.

The tax laws treat most rental activities as passive activities. However, exceptions do exist. One exception applies to taxpayers involved in the business of renting real property. This situation is described in ¶905.02. Three other exceptions include rental activities where: (1) the average rental period is less than eight days (e.g., a video rental store); (2) the average rental period is less than 31 days and significant personal services are provided (e.g., motels and hotels); and (3) the rental activity is incidental to the taxpayer's business. Unless one of these four exceptions applies, losses from the rental activity will be considered passive losses.

¶905.02 RENTAL REAL ESTATE LOSSES

Rental real estate activities usually are treated as passive, even if one of the seven ways for meeting the material participation requirement has been met. However, a rental real estate activity may qualify as an active trade or business if the taxpayer satisfies both of the following:

1. More than 50% of the personal services rendered during the year are performed in a trade or business involving real estate, **and**
2. At a minimum, the taxpayer performs more than 750 hours of personal service in the real property trade or business.

If the taxpayer passes both tests, then the rental real estate activity is not considered passive, and any losses from the activity would be fully deductible against ordinary income (subject to the at-risk limits described in ¶904). A married couple passes the two tests only if one spouse separately satisfies both conditions. In other words, couples cannot pool their time and efforts in meeting the two conditions for rental real estate activities. If these conditions are not met, then the rental real estate activity is considered a passive activity.

EXAMPLE 18

Same facts as in Example 17, except that Ginny and Barry's business involves rental realty. Barry performs more than 750 hours of personal services in businesses involving real property. In addition, this work is more than 50% of his total hours of personal services rendered during the year. Thus, Barry materially participates in the rental realty business. Ginny's hours, on the other hand, do not exceed 750. Thus, Ginny is not a material participant in the business. Accordingly, the business is a passive activity to Ginny.

EXAMPLE 19

A husband and wife each work 400 hours in a rental realty business. Although as a couple they work more than 750 hours in the rental realty business, the tax laws require that at least one spouse meet the two conditions for material participation. Thus, the rental activity is a passive activity to the couple.

i

The taxpayer has the burden of providing proof that any personal service tests have been met. To do this, taxpayers should keep a daily log of their hours spent on the activity to prove their hours of participation in the activity.

$25,000 Special Deduction for Active Participants

Taxpayers who are not in a "real estate trade or business" and have losses from rental real estate activities may be able to deduct up to $25,000 of rental real estate losses from active and portfolio income. The deduction limit is $12,500 for married taxpayers filing separately and living apart at all times during the year. No special deduction is allowed for married taxpayers filing separately if the couple lived together at any time during the year. To qualify for this special deduction, the taxpayer must meet both of the following requirements:

1. The taxpayer actively participates in the rental real estate activity, **and**
2. The taxpayer owns at least 10% of the value of all interests in the activity throughout the entire year.

Active participation and material participation are two different concepts. **Active participation** requires less involvement than material participation. Active participation does not require regular, continuous, and substantial involvement. However, it does require that the taxpayer participate in management decisions in a significant and real sense. Examples of this level of involvement include approving new tenants, deciding on rental terms, approving improvements or repairs, or arranging for others to provide services such as repairs.

EXAMPLE 20

Going back to Example 18, although Ginny's hours do not constitute material participation, they do indicate active participation in the rental realty business. Since Ginny owns at least 10% of the business, she qualifies for the $25,000 special deduction. Thus, in years in which the activity produces a net loss, Ginny may be able to deduct up to $25,000 of her share of the loss against her active and portfolio income.

The $25,000 annual deduction is reduced by 50% of the taxpayer's modified AGI in excess of $100,000 ($50,000 for married taxpayers who file separately). Thus, the deduction is completely phased out when modified AGI reaches $150,000 ($75,000 for married taxpayers filing separately). In computing modified AGI, passive losses cannot exceed passive income. Modified AGI is computed by adjusting AGI for the following amounts:

1. Subtracting out taxable social security and railroad retirement payments (¶307)
2. Adding back exclusions from gross income for adoption assistance (¶401.03) and interest on Series EE and I savings bonds (¶401.06)
3. Adding back deductions for one-half of the self-employment tax (¶402.06), IRA contributions (¶402.11), student loan interest (¶402.12), and domestic production activities (¶402.14)

EXAMPLE 21

Rachel, a single taxpayer, earned $110,000 from her job, $15,000 of passive income from a non–real estate activity, and $20,000 of interest income. Rachel also incurred a $50,000 loss from a rental real estate activity in which she actively participates. Rachel made a $5,500 deductible IRA contribution in 2015. Under the general rule, passive losses usually can offset only passive income. Therefore, Rachel can use $15,000 of her $50,000 rental real estate loss to offset the $15,000 of the income from the non–real estate passive activity. Because Rachel is actively involved in the rental real estate activities, she may be able to deduct more than $15,000 of her loss. Rachel computes the additional deduction and passive loss carryover as follows.

Wages	$110,000
Interest income	20,000
Passive income	15,000
Passive losses allowed under the general rule	(15,000)
Modified AGI	$130,000
Less AGI threshold for the phase-out	(100,000)
Amount subject to phase-out	$ 30,000
	× 50%
Amount of deduction lost due to phase-out	$ 15,000
Excess passive loss from rental real estate ($50,000 – $15,000)	$ 35,000
Additional passive loss deduction for active participation in rental real estate ($25,000 – $15,000 phase-out)	(10,000)
Passive loss carried forward to 2016	$ 25,000

Modified AGI does not include the $5,500 IRA deduction or the $35,000 of passive losses in excess of passive income. Rachel will deduct a total of $25,000 of passive activity losses ($15,000 under the general rule and $10,000 special deduction) against passive activity income of $15,000. The excess $20,000 loss will reduce Rachel's active and portfolio income.

¶905.03 SUSPENDED LOSSES

Passive activity losses not deducted in the current tax year carry forward to the next year. Passive losses that are carried forward must be allocated among the various activities that produced the loss. When multiple passive activities exist, taxpayers must determine the suspended loss for each separate activity using the following formula.

$$\textbf{Total disallowed loss} \times \frac{\textbf{Loss from separate activity}}{\textbf{Sum of all losses}}$$

EXAMPLE 22

Denny reports the following income and losses from his four passive activities for 20x1.

Activity A	($40,000)
Activity B	30,000
Activity C	(32,000)
Activity D	(8,000)
Net passive loss	($50,000)

Denny allocates his $50,000 net passive loss to activities A, C, and D (the activities producing a total of $80,000 of losses) as follows:

Activity A ($50,000 × $40,000/$80,000)	($25,000)
Activity C ($50,000 × $32,000/$80,000)	(20,000)
Activity D ($50,000 × $8,000/$80,000)	(5,000)
Total suspended losses	($50,000)

These suspended losses carry forward indefinitely as deductions associated with the activity to which each relates. Thus, the $25,000 passive loss carryover associated with Activity A is added to/netted against any passive income (loss) generated by Activity A in 20x2. This net amount becomes Denny's passive income (loss) from Activity A for 20x2. The same process is applied to Activities C and D.

¶905.04 DISPOSING OF A PASSIVE ACTIVITY

When taxpayers dispose of a passive activity, any suspended losses relating to that activity are deductible in full. To qualify for this treatment, taxpayers must dispose of their entire interest in the activity in a fully taxable transaction. Also, the new property owner cannot be the taxpayer's sibling (sister or brother), ancestor (parent, grandparent, etc.), or descendant (child, grandchild, etc.). Special rules apply when taxpayers dispose of a passive activity by way of gift or inheritance. These rules are beyond the scope of this textbook.

The gain or loss from the sale of a passive activity receives special treatment. If a loss results, the loss is either an ordinary loss or capital loss depending on the circumstances. The loss is not treated as a passive loss, so it is not limited to offsetting just passive income. Chapter 11 explains the difference between ordinary and capital losses in greater detail.

EXAMPLE 23

Continuing with Example 22, if Denny sells Activity A in 20x2, any part of the $25,000 passive loss carryover from 20x1 that is not utilized in 20x2 to offset passive income and gains is deducted against Denny's active and portfolio income.

¶905.05 REPORTING PASSIVE ACTIVITY LOSSES

Taxpayers with income or loss from passive activities complete Form 8582, Passive Activity Loss Limitations, to compute the amount of passive loss allowed from such activities. Taxpayers then report the passive loss allowed on the appropriate tax form or schedule. For example, taxpayers report the passive loss allowed from rental activities on Schedule E.

Regardless of the number or complexity of passive activities, taxpayers file only one Form 8582. Taxpayers prepare Form 8582 to determine whether the passive loss rules disallow any of the losses reported on those other forms and schedules.

Form 8582 consists of three parts. In Part I, taxpayers report net income (line 1a), net loss (line 1b), and prior year carryforwards (line 1c) from rental real estate activities with active participation. They also report in Part I net income (line 3a), net loss (line 3b), and prior year carryforwards (line 3c) from all other passive activities. Taxpayers then combine their passive income and losses (line 4). If net income results, taxpayers enter the net amount on the appropriate tax form or schedule to which the activity relates (for example, Schedule E for rental real estate). If a net loss results, then taxpayers proceed to Part II to see whether they can utilize any of the $25,000 special allowance for active participation in rental real estate activities.

In Part II, taxpayers determine the amount of net loss available for the $25,000 special allowance. They then compute their modified adjusted gross income and determine the amount of phase-out, if any, that applies (lines 6–9). In Part IV, taxpayers compute the passive income and loss reported on that year's tax return. Deductible passive losses (line 16) equal the total passive income (from lines 1a and 3a) plus the special allowance amount from Part II (line 10). Figure 9-2 shows a completed Form 8582 for a taxpayer who actively participates in a rental real estate activity.

¶905.06 FILLED-IN FORM 8582

INFORMATION FOR FIGURE 9-2:

Derrick Smart earned $120,000 from his job, $15,000 of interest income, $10,000 net income from a passive activity (non–real estate), and a $20,000 loss from a rental real estate activity in which he actively participates (see accompanying Schedule E). Derrick has no other income and no passive loss carryovers from prior years. Form 8582 (line 16) shows that Derrick can deduct $17,500 of his passive losses. He deducts this amount on Schedule E (line 22). Derrick's passive loss carryover to 2016 is $2,500 ($20,000 – $17,500).

Line #

1b: Activities with net loss (rental real estate activities with active participation), **$20,000**

3a: Activities with net income (all other passive activities), **$10,000**

4: Excess of total passive losses over total passive income, **($10,000)** ($20,000 passive losses – $10,000 passive income)

5: The smaller of the loss on line 1d or the loss on line 4, **$10,000** (entered as a positive amount as per the instructions for Part II)

7: Modified adjusted gross income, **$135,000** [$120,000 + $15,000 + $10,000 (non–real estate passive net income) – $10,000 (rental real estate passive loss to the extent of passive net income)]

16: Total passive losses allowed in the current year, **$17,500** ($10,000 allowed to offset passive income + $7,500 special allowance for active participation in rental real estate activities)

Figure 9-2: Filled-In Form 8582

Form **8582**
Department of the Treasury
Internal Revenue Service (99)

Passive Activity Loss Limitations

▶ See separate instructions.
▶ Attach to Form 1040 or Form 1041.
▶ Information about Form 8582 and its instructions is available at *www.irs.gov/form8582.*

OMB No. 1545-1008
2015
Attachment Sequence No. **88**

Name(s) shown on return	Identifying number
Derrick Smart	421-68-5546

Part I **2015 Passive Activity Loss**

Caution: *Complete Worksheets 1, 2, and 3 before completing Part I.*

	Rental Real Estate Activities With Active Participation (For the definition of active participation, see **Special Allowance for Rental Real Estate Activities** in the instructions.)				
1a	Activities with net income (enter the amount from Worksheet 1, column (a)) . . .	1a			
b	Activities with net loss (enter the amount from Worksheet 1, column (b)) . . .	1b	(20,000)		
c	Prior years unallowed losses (enter the amount from Worksheet 1, column (c)) . . .	1c	( )		
d	Combine lines 1a, 1b, and 1c . . .			1d	(20,000)
	Commercial Revitalization Deductions From Rental Real Estate Activities				
2a	Commercial revitalization deductions from Worksheet 2, column (a) .	2a	( )		
b	Prior year unallowed commercial revitalization deductions from Worksheet 2, column (b) . . .	2b	( )		
c	Add lines 2a and 2b . . .			2c	( )
	All Other Passive Activities				
3a	Activities with net income (enter the amount from Worksheet 3, column (a)) . . .	3a	10,000		
b	Activities with net loss (enter the amount from Worksheet 3, column (b)) . . .	3b	( )		
c	Prior years unallowed losses (enter the amount from Worksheet 3, column (c)) . . .	3c	( )		
d	Combine lines 3a, 3b, and 3c . . .			3d	10,000
4	Combine lines 1d, 2c, and 3d. If this line is zero or more, stop here and include this form with your return; all losses are allowed, including any prior year unallowed losses entered on line 1c, 2b, or 3c. Report the losses on the forms and schedules normally used . . .			4	(10,000)

If line 4 is a loss and:
- Line 1d is a loss, go to Part II.
- Line 2c is a loss (and line 1d is zero or more), skip Part II and go to Part III.
- Line 3d is a loss (and lines 1d and 2c are zero or more), skip Parts II and III and go to line 15.

Caution: *If your filing status is married filing separately and you lived with your spouse at any time during the year,* **do not** *complete Part II or Part III. Instead, go to line 15.*

Part II **Special Allowance for Rental Real Estate Activities With Active Participation**

Note: *Enter all numbers in Part II as positive amounts. See instructions for an example.*

5	Enter the **smaller** of the loss on line 1d or the loss on line 4 . . .			5	10,000
6	Enter $150,000. If married filing separately, see instructions . .	6	150,000		
7	Enter modified adjusted gross income, but not less than zero (see instructions)	7	135,000		
	Note: *If line 7 is greater than or equal to line 6, skip lines 8 and 9, enter -0- on line 10. Otherwise, go to line 8.*				
8	Subtract line 7 from line 6 . . .	8	15,000		
9	Multiply line 8 by 50% (.5). **Do not** enter more than $25,000. If married filing separately, see instructions			9	7,500
10	Enter the **smaller** of line 5 or line 9 . . .			10	7,500

If line 2c is a loss, go to Part III. Otherwise, go to line 15.

Part III **Special Allowance for Commercial Revitalization Deductions From Rental Real Estate Activities**

Note: *Enter all numbers in Part III as positive amounts. See the example for Part II in the instructions.*

11	Enter $25,000 reduced by the amount, if any, on line 10. If married filing separately, see instructions	11	
12	Enter the loss from line 4 . . .	12	
13	Reduce line 12 by the amount on line 10 . . .	13	
14	Enter the **smallest** of line 2c (treated as a positive amount), line 11, or line 13 . . .	14	

Part IV **Total Losses Allowed**

15	Add the income, if any, on lines 1a and 3a and enter the total . . .	15	10,000
16	**Total losses allowed from all passive activities for 2015.** Add lines 10, 14, and 15. See instructions to find out how to report the losses on your tax return . . .	16	17,500

For Paperwork Reduction Act Notice, see instructions. Cat. No. 63704F Form **8582** (2015)

Figure 9-2: Schedule E to Accompany Filled-In Form 8582

SCHEDULE E (Form 1040)
Department of the Treasury Internal Revenue Service (99)

Supplemental Income and Loss
(From rental real estate, royalties, partnerships, S corporations, estates, trusts, REMICs, etc.)
► Attach to Form 1040, 1040NR, or Form 1041.
► Information about Schedule E and its separate instructions is at *www.irs.gov/schedulee.*

OMB No. 1545-0074
2015
Attachment Sequence No. **13**

Name(s) shown on return: **Derrick Smart**
Your social security number: **421-68-5546**

Part I **Income or Loss From Rental Real Estate and Royalties** **Note:** If you are in the business of renting personal property, use **Schedule C** or **C-EZ** (see instructions). If you are an individual, report farm rental income or loss from **Form 4835** on page 2, line 40.

A Did you make any payments in 2015 that would require you to file Form(s) 1099? (see instructions) ☐ Yes ☑ No
B If "Yes," did you or will you file required Forms 1099? ☐ Yes ☐ No

1a	Physical address of each property (street, city, state, ZIP code)
A	**1802 Eighth Street #207, Danville, IL 60560**
B	
C	

1b	Type of Property (from list below)	**2** For each rental real estate property listed above, report the number of fair rental and personal use days. Check the **QJV** box only if you meet the requirements to file as a qualified joint venture. See instructions.		Fair Rental Days	Personal Use Days	QJV
A	2		**A**	365	0	☐
B			**B**			☐
C			**C**			☐

Type of Property:
1 Single Family Residence 3 Vacation/Short-Term Rental 5 Land 7 Self-Rental
2 Multi-Family Residence 4 Commercial 6 Royalties 8 Other (describe)

	Income: Properties:		A	B	C
3	Rents received	3	7,800		
4	Royalties received	4			
	Expenses:				
5	Advertising	5			
6	Auto and travel (see instructions)	6			
7	Cleaning and maintenance	7	1,600		
8	Commissions	8			
9	Insurance	9	140		
10	Legal and other professional fees	10			
11	Management fees	11			
12	Mortgage interest paid to banks, etc. (see instructions)	12	11,700		
13	Other interest	13			
14	Repairs	14	3,100		
15	Supplies	15			
16	Taxes	16	2,950		
17	Utilities	17	1,620		
18	Depreciation expense or depletion	18	4,810		
19	Other (list) ► Condo association fees	19	1,880		
20	Total expenses. Add lines 5 through 19	20	27,800		
21	Subtract line 20 from line 3 (rents) and/or 4 (royalties). If result is a (loss), see instructions to find out if you must file **Form 6198**	21	(20,000)		
22	Deductible rental real estate loss after limitation, if any, on **Form 8582** (see instructions)	22	(17,500)	( )	( )

23a	Total of all amounts reported on line 3 for all rental properties	23a	7,800
b	Total of all amounts reported on line 4 for all royalty properties	23b	
c	Total of all amounts reported on line 12 for all properties	23c	11,700
d	Total of all amounts reported on line 18 for all properties	23d	4,810
e	Total of all amounts reported on line 20 for all properties	23e	27,800
24	**Income.** Add positive amounts shown on line 21. **Do not** include any losses	24	
25	**Losses.** Add royalty losses from line 21 and rental real estate losses from line 22. Enter total losses here	25	(17,500)
26	**Total rental real estate and royalty income or (loss).** Combine lines 24 and 25. Enter the result here. If Parts II, III, IV, and line 40 on page 2 do not apply to you, also enter this amount on Form 1040, line 17, or Form 1040NR, line 18. Otherwise, include this amount in the total on line 41 on page 2	26	(17,500)

For Paperwork Reduction Act Notice, see the separate instructions. Cat. No. 11344L **Schedule E (Form 1040) 2015**

9

Name:

Section:

Date:

QUESTIONS AND PROBLEMS

1. **Rental Income.** (Obj. 1) State the amount of rental income that must be reported on Schedule E for 2015 by each of the following taxpayers.

Taxpayer	*Description*	*Amount*
A	On November 30, 2015, the taxpayer receives $1,500 a security deposit, $1,000 for the December rent, and an advance payment of $5,000 for an additional five months' rent.	$__________
B	The taxpayer normally receives rent of $300 per month on the first of each month. In 2015, the tenant made $600 of improvements in lieu of two months' rent.	$__________
C	Rent of $1,200 is received when the taxpayer rents a personal residence to friends for 12 days during the Mardi Gras festivities.	$__________

2. **Rental Expenses.** (Obj. 1) State the maximum amount of rental expenses attributable to the property that can be claimed by each of the following taxpayers.

Taxpayer	*Description*	*Amount*
A	A dwelling unit is rented to a friend for $100 per month for two months and to an unrelated party for $275 per month for three months. Fair rental price is $275/month.	$__________
B	A personal residence rented for 12 days during the year, for a total of $300.	$__________

3. **Net Rental Income.** (Obj. 1) Quentin owns a two-family home. He rents out the first floor and resides on the second floor. Each floor is of equal size. Quentin received $6,400 in rental income during the year, and incurred the following expenses attributable to the building.

		Expenses For	
	Entire Building	*First Floor*	*Second Floor*
Depreciation	$4,000		
Real estate taxes	2,000		
Mortgage interest	1,600		
Utilities	1,200		
Repairs		$500	
Painting			$400

a. What amount of expenses can Quentin deduct on Schedule E?

b. What amount of the expenses can Quentin deduct on Schedule A?

4. **Net Rental Income.** (Obj. 1) Sandee, a cash basis taxpayer, owns a house with two identical units. Sandee resides in one unit and rents out the other. The tenant made timely monthly rental payments of $500 for the months of January through November 2015. The tenant paid rents for December 2015 and January 2016 on January 5, 2016. During the year, Sandee paid $3,600 for utilities and $600 for insurance. These expenses were for the entire house. She paid $400 for maintenance and repairs on the rental unit. Depreciation on the entire house equals $3,000. Compute Sandee's 2015 net rental income.

5. **Vacation Homes.** (Obj. 2) Dari owns a vacation home that she personally uses 14 days during the year. The rest of the year the following occupants used the home. Fair rental price is $125 a night.

Occupant	*Number of Days*
Dari's best friend, who paid no rent	8
Dari's brother, who paid a fair rental price	21
Couple who won a charity auction	7
Unrelated persons, who paid rent of $7,500	60

Dari's expenses related to the vacation home were as follows:

Mortgage interest	$ 6,700
Real estate taxes	3,300
Utilities and repairs	2,540
Depreciation	6,650
	$19,190

a. Compute the number of (1) days the property was rented at a fair rental price; (2) total days the property was used during the year; and (3) personal days. Discuss the significance of these three numbers as they pertain to the vacation home rules.

b. Compute Dari's net rental income and any expenses that she must carry over to the next year.

6. **Vacation Homes.** (Obj. 2) Henry owns a fishing cabin in Wisconsin. Henry offered the cabin for rent from June 1 through September 30, except for 16 days in August when his family used it. Henry was unable to rent the cabin for two weeks (14 days) during the remaining rental period. At all other times, the cabin was rented at a fair rental price to unrelated persons.

a. Will Henry's cabin be treated as a residence? Explain.

b. For purposes of allocating expenses, how many fair rental days does Henry have?

7. **Vacation Homes.** (Obj. 2)

a. What is the tax advantage to having a vacation home treated as a residence?

b. What is the disadvantage to having a vacation home considered a residence?

8. **Vacation Homes.** (Obj. 2) During the year, Carlin Barone (SSN 839-62-1444) rents his vacation home for 90 days and spends 60 days there. The vacation home is a townhome located at 610 Oak St. in Boulder, Colorado 80302. Gross rental income from the property totals $6,000. Carlin's expenses for the property are shown below. Using this information, complete Carlin Barone's Schedule E.

Mortgage interest	$3,000
Real estate taxes	1,500
Utilities	800
Maintenance	900
Depreciation	4,000

9. **At-risk.** (Obj. 3)

   a. Discuss the significance of the at-risk rules.

   b. What activities are subject to the at-risk loss rules?

   c. What happens to losses that are disallowed by the at-risk rules?

10. **Passive Activities.** (Obj. 3)

   a. What types of trade or business activities are considered passive activities?

   b. Distinguish between material participation and active participation in rental activities. Explain the significance of this difference.

   c. Under the passive activity loss rules, how are dividend income and interest income treated? Can passive losses offset dividend and interest income?

(Use for Problem 8.)

SCHEDULE E (Form 1040)

Department of the Treasury Internal Revenue Service (99)

Supplemental Income and Loss

(From rental real estate, royalties, partnerships, S corporations, estates, trusts, REMICs, etc.)

▶ Attach to Form 1040, 1040NR, or Form 1041.

▶ Information about Schedule E and its separate instructions is at *www.irs.gov/schedulee*.

OMB No. 1545-0074

2015

Attachment Sequence No. **13**

Name(s) shown on return	**Your social security number**

Part I **Income or Loss From Rental Real Estate and Royalties** **Note:** If you are in the business of renting personal property, use **Schedule C** or **C-EZ** (see instructions). If you are an individual, report farm rental income or loss from **Form 4835** on page 2, line 40.

A Did you make any payments in 2015 that would require you to file Form(s) 1099? (see instructions) ☐ Yes ☐ No

B If "Yes," did you or will you file required Forms 1099? ☐ Yes ☐ No

1a	Physical address of each property (street, city, state, ZIP code)
A	
B	
C	

1b	Type of Property (from list below)	**2** For each rental real estate property listed above, report the number of fair rental and personal use days. Check the **QJV** box only if you meet the requirements to file as a qualified joint venture. See instructions.		**Fair Rental Days**	**Personal Use Days**	**QJV**
A			**A**			☐
B			**B**			☐
C			**C**			☐

Type of Property:

1 Single Family Residence 3 Vacation/Short-Term Rental 5 Land 7 Self-Rental

2 Multi-Family Residence 4 Commercial 6 Royalties 8 Other (describe)

Income:	**Properties:**		**A**	**B**	**C**
3	Rents received	**3**			
4	Royalties received	**4**			
Expenses:					
5	Advertising	**5**			
6	Auto and travel (see instructions)	**6**			
7	Cleaning and maintenance	**7**			
8	Commissions	**8**			
9	Insurance	**9**			
10	Legal and other professional fees	**10**			
11	Management fees	**11**			
12	Mortgage interest paid to banks, etc. (see instructions)	**12**			
13	Other interest	**13**			
14	Repairs	**14**			
15	Supplies	**15**			
16	Taxes	**16**			
17	Utilities	**17**			
18	Depreciation expense or depletion	**18**			
19	Other (list) ▶	**19**			
20	Total expenses. Add lines 5 through 19	**20**			
21	Subtract line 20 from line 3 (rents) and/or 4 (royalties). If result is a (loss), see instructions to find out if you must file **Form 6198**	**21**			
22	Deductible rental real estate loss after limitation, if any, on **Form 8582** (see instructions)	**22**	( )	( )	( )

23a	Total of all amounts reported on line 3 for all rental properties	**23a**	
b	Total of all amounts reported on line 4 for all royalty properties	**23b**	
c	Total of all amounts reported on line 12 for all properties	**23c**	
d	Total of all amounts reported on line 18 for all properties	**23d**	
e	Total of all amounts reported on line 20 for all properties	**23e**	
24	**Income.** Add positive amounts shown on line 21. **Do not** include any losses	**24**	
25	**Losses.** Add royalty losses from line 21 and rental real estate losses from line 22. Enter total losses here	**25**	( )
26	**Total rental real estate and royalty income or (loss).** Combine lines 24 and 25. Enter the result here. If Parts II, III, IV, and line 40 on page 2 do not apply to you, also enter this amount on Form 1040, line 17, or Form 1040NR, line 18. Otherwise, include this amount in the total on line 41 on page 2	**26**	

For Paperwork Reduction Act Notice, see the separate instructions. Cat. No. 11344L **Schedule E (Form 1040) 2015**

11. Material vs. Active Participation. (Obj. 3) For each of the following independent situations, discuss whether (**A**) the taxpayer materially participates in the activity or (**B**) the activity is a passive activity. In activities involving rental real estate, discuss whether the special deduction for active participation would apply.

a. The taxpayer works 900 hours in a nonrental real estate activity and 1,000 hours as an employee (not involving rental real estate).

b. The taxpayer works 650 hours in a rental real estate activity and 500 hours as an employee (not involving rental real estate).

c. The taxpayer works in an activity (not involving rental real estate) 150 hours during the year. The taxpayer is retired, so this is the only activity he works for during the year.

d. Both spouses participate in an activity (not involving rental real estate). The husband works 300 hours; the wife works 250 hours. Both spouses work full-time for companies that have nothing to do with rental real estate.

e. Both spouses participate in a rental real estate activity. The husband works 400 hours; the wife works 520 hours. Both spouses also work full-time as employees for companies that have nothing to do with rental real estate.

f. Same as in Part e. except that the wife's hours are 800 instead of 520.

12. Passive Activities. (Obj. 3) A taxpayer owned four passive activities. Net income (loss) for each activity is shown below.

Passive Activity	*Gross Income*	*Deductions*	*Net Income (or Loss)*
A	$12,000	$ 8,000	$ 4,000
B	20,000	32,000	(12,000)
C	3,000	6,000	(3,000)
D	14,000	12,000	2,000

a. What is the amount of passive loss that can offset passive income in the current year?

b. What is the amount of passive loss that is carried forward for each activity?

13. **Passive Activities.** (Obj. 3) A taxpayer owns three passive activities. Net income (loss) for each activity is shown below.

Passive Activity	*Net Income (or Loss)*
1	$26,000
2	(13,500)
3	(18,000)

a. Compute the amount of passive loss that can offset passive income in the current year.

b. Determine the amount of passive loss that is carried forward to each activity.

14. **Rental Real Estate.** (Obj. 3) The Warrens incur a $22,000 loss from rental real estate activities in which they actively participate. The Warrens own more than 10% of the activity. Their only other source of income for the year is $130,000 of wages. What amount of the loss can the Warrens deduct on their joint tax return?

15. **Rental Real Estate.** (Obj. 3) Martin actively participates in three different rental real estate activities. His ownership in each activity exceeds 10%. Martin's income and losses from these activities are shown below. Martin's only other source of income is $80,000 of wages. Calculate Martin's loss allowed and suspended loss.

Activity	*Income (or Loss)*
X	($10,000)
Y	(30,000)
Z	9,000

16. Passive Activities. (Obj. 3) A taxpayer owns three passive activities, none of which involve rental real estate. Suspended losses at the beginning of the year and income (or loss) generated by each activity during 2015 are shown below. Explain how the results of these activities should be reported on the taxpayer's 2015 tax return.

Activity	*Suspended Losses*	*Current Year Income (Loss)*
X	($20,000)	$10,000
Y	(30,000)	(10,000)
Z	0	20,000

17. Rental Real Estate, Active Participation. (Obj. 4)

a. In 2007, Tyler Tomey (548-55-9234) paid $135,000 for a condominium that he uses as rental property. In 2012, he spent $37,000 furnishing the condo. He uses regular (accelerated) MACRS to depreciate the furnishings. In 2012, Tyler deducted 50% of the cost of the furnishings as bonus depreciation. The half-year convention applies to the furnishings. During 2015, Tyler received $15,000 in rental income and paid the following expenses:

Association dues	$2,800
Insurance	350
Mortgage interest	7,460
Real estate taxes	1,400
Repairs	760
Utilities	360

The property is located at 5505 West End Road, #5, Farmington, IN 46883. Tyler actively participates in the rental activity. His AGI before considering the above income and expenses is $141,400. He depreciates the condominium using MACRS. Prepare Schedule E and Form 8582 for Tyler Tomey.

b. In 1999, Jeremy L. Schultz (SSN 678-88-5244) paid $90,000 for a townhouse purchased as an investment. The townhouse is located at 812 E. Locust, Springfield, MO 65807. During 2015, Jeremy received $9,600 in rental income from the tenants and paid the following expenses:

Association dues	$ 400
Insurance	130
Mortgage interest	6,200
Real estate taxes	1,100
Repairs	320
Utilities	440

Jeremy actively participates in the rental of the town home. His AGI before considering the income and expenses from the rental property is $140,000. He depreciates the townhouse using MACRS. Prepare Jeremy Schultz's Schedule E and Form 8582.

(Use for Problem 17.)

SCHEDULE E (Form 1040)
Department of the Treasury
Internal Revenue Service (99)

Supplemental Income and Loss

(From rental real estate, royalties, partnerships, S corporations, estates, trusts, REMICs, etc.)

▶ Attach to Form 1040, 1040NR, or Form 1041.

▶ Information about Schedule E and its separate instructions is at *www.irs.gov/schedulee.*

OMB No. 1545-0074
2015
Attachment Sequence No. **13**

Name(s) shown on return | **Your social security number**

Part I **Income or Loss From Rental Real Estate and Royalties** **Note:** If you are in the business of renting personal property, use **Schedule C** or **C-EZ** (see instructions). If you are an individual, report farm rental income or loss from **Form 4835** on page 2, line 40.

A Did you make any payments in 2015 that would require you to file Form(s) 1099? (see instructions) ☐ Yes ☐ No

B If "Yes," did you or will you file required Forms 1099? ☐ Yes ☐ No

1a	Physical address of each property (street, city, state, ZIP code)
A	
B	
C	

1b	Type of Property (from list below)	**2** For each rental real estate property listed above, report the number of fair rental and personal use days. Check the **QJV** box only if you meet the requirements to file as a qualified joint venture. See instructions.		**Fair Rental Days**	**Personal Use Days**	**QJV**
A			**A**			☐
B			**B**			☐
C			**C**			☐

Type of Property:
1 Single Family Residence
2 Multi-Family Residence
3 Vacation/Short-Term Rental
4 Commercial
5 Land
6 Royalties
7 Self-Rental
8 Other (describe)

Income:	**Properties:**	**A**	**B**	**C**
3 Rents received	**3**			
4 Royalties received	**4**			
Expenses:				
5 Advertising	**5**			
6 Auto and travel (see instructions)	**6**			
7 Cleaning and maintenance	**7**			
8 Commissions	**8**			
9 Insurance	**9**			
10 Legal and other professional fees	**10**			
11 Management fees	**11**			
12 Mortgage interest paid to banks, etc. (see instructions)	**12**			
13 Other interest	**13**			
14 Repairs	**14**			
15 Supplies	**15**			
16 Taxes	**16**			
17 Utilities	**17**			
18 Depreciation expense or depletion	**18**			
19 Other (list) ▶	**19**			
20 Total expenses. Add lines 5 through 19	**20**			
21 Subtract line 20 from line 3 (rents) and/or 4 (royalties). If result is a (loss), see instructions to find out if you must file **Form 6198**	**21**			
22 Deductible rental real estate loss after limitation, if any, on **Form 8582** (see instructions)	**22**	( )	( )	( )

23a Total of all amounts reported on line 3 for all rental properties	**23a**	
b Total of all amounts reported on line 4 for all royalty properties	**23b**	
c Total of all amounts reported on line 12 for all properties	**23c**	
d Total of all amounts reported on line 18 for all properties	**23d**	
e Total of all amounts reported on line 20 for all properties	**23e**	
24 **Income.** Add positive amounts shown on line 21. **Do not** include any losses	**24**	
25 **Losses.** Add royalty losses from line 21 and rental real estate losses from line 22. Enter total losses here	**25**	( )
26 **Total rental real estate and royalty income or (loss).** Combine lines 24 and 25. Enter the result here. If Parts II, III, IV, and line 40 on page 2 do not apply to you, also enter this amount on Form 1040, line 17, or Form 1040NR, line 18. Otherwise, include this amount in the total on line 41 on page 2	**26**	

For Paperwork Reduction Act Notice, see the separate instructions. Cat. No. 11344L **Schedule E (Form 1040) 2015**

(Use for Problem 17.)

Form **8582**
Department of the Treasury
Internal Revenue Service (99)

Passive Activity Loss Limitations

▶ See separate instructions.
▶ Attach to Form 1040 or Form 1041.
▶ Information about Form 8582 and its instructions is available at *www.irs.gov/form8582.*

OMB No. 1545-1008
2015
Attachment Sequence No. **88**

Name(s) shown on return	Identifying number

Part I **2015 Passive Activity Loss**
Caution: *Complete Worksheets 1, 2, and 3 before completing Part I.*

Rental Real Estate Activities With Active Participation (For the definition of active participation, see **Special Allowance for Rental Real Estate Activities** in the instructions.)

1a	Activities with net income (enter the amount from Worksheet 1, column (a))	1a			
b	Activities with net loss (enter the amount from Worksheet 1, column (b))	1b	( )		
c	Prior years unallowed losses (enter the amount from Worksheet 1, column (c))	1c	( )		
d	Combine lines 1a, 1b, and 1c			1d	

Commercial Revitalization Deductions From Rental Real Estate Activities

2a	Commercial revitalization deductions from Worksheet 2, column (a)	2a	( )		
b	Prior year unallowed commercial revitalization deductions from Worksheet 2, column (b)	2b	( )		
c	Add lines 2a and 2b			2c	( )

All Other Passive Activities

3a	Activities with net income (enter the amount from Worksheet 3, column (a))	3a			
b	Activities with net loss (enter the amount from Worksheet 3, column (b))	3b	( )		
c	Prior years unallowed losses (enter the amount from Worksheet 3, column (c))	3c	( )		
d	Combine lines 3a, 3b, and 3c			3d	
4	Combine lines 1d, 2c, and 3d. If this line is zero or more, stop here and include this form with your return; all losses are allowed, including any prior year unallowed losses entered on line 1c, 2b, or 3c. Report the losses on the forms and schedules normally used			4	

If line 4 is a loss and:
- Line 1d is a loss, go to Part II.
- Line 2c is a loss (and line 1d is zero or more), skip Part II and go to Part III.
- Line 3d is a loss (and lines 1d and 2c are zero or more), skip Parts II and III and go to line 15.

Caution: *If your filing status is married filing separately and you lived with your spouse at any time during the year,* ***do not*** *complete Part II or Part III. Instead, go to line 15.*

Part II **Special Allowance for Rental Real Estate Activities With Active Participation**
Note: *Enter all numbers in Part II as positive amounts. See instructions for an example.*

5	Enter the **smaller** of the loss on line 1d or the loss on line 4			5	
6	Enter $150,000. If married filing separately, see instructions	6			
7	Enter modified adjusted gross income, but not less than zero (see instructions)	7			
	Note: *If line 7 is greater than or equal to line 6, skip lines 8 and 9, enter -0- on line 10. Otherwise, go to line 8.*				
8	Subtract line 7 from line 6	8			
9	Multiply line 8 by 50% (.5). **Do not** enter more than $25,000. If married filing separately, see instructions			9	
10	Enter the **smaller** of line 5 or line 9			10	

If line 2c is a loss, go to Part III. Otherwise, go to line 15.

Part III **Special Allowance for Commercial Revitalization Deductions From Rental Real Estate Activities**
Note: *Enter all numbers in Part III as positive amounts. See the example for Part II in the instructions.*

11	Enter $25,000 reduced by the amount, if any, on line 10. If married filing separately, see instructions	11	
12	Enter the loss from line 4	12	
13	Reduce line 12 by the amount on line 10	13	
14	Enter the **smallest** of line 2c (treated as a positive amount), line 11, or line 13	14	

Part IV **Total Losses Allowed**

15	Add the income, if any, on lines 1a and 3a and enter the total	15	
16	**Total losses allowed from all passive activities for 2015.** Add lines 10, 14, and 15. See instructions to find out how to report the losses on your tax return	16	

For Paperwork Reduction Act Notice, see instructions. Cat. No. 63704F Form **8582** (2015)

18. Internet Problem: Researching IRS Publication 925. (Obj. 3)

The chapter discussed two ways to meet the material participation test: (1) participate in the activity for more than 500 hours during the year, and (2) participate in the activity for more than 100 hours during the year and have that participation be at least as much as the participation by all other individuals, including employees. There are five other ways in which to meet the material participation test.

Go to the IRS website. Locate IRS Publication 925 and find the appropriate page that lists all the various ways to meet the material participation test. Print out a copy of the page where you found your answer. Underline or highlight the pertinent information.

See Appendix A for instructions on use of the IRS website.

19. Business Entity Problem: This problem is designed for those using the "business entity" approach. **The solution may require information from Chapters 14–16.**

The Hampton-Lewis Partnership owns an apartment building. Gross income from the apartments was $200,000. Total deductions were $260,000. The two partners share profits and losses equally.

a. How will the partnership report the resulting $60,000 loss?

b. If Hampton-Lewis was an S corporation (with two shareholders who each own 50% of the stock), how would the loss be reported?

c. If Hampton-Lewis was a regular C corporation (with two shareholders who each own 50% of the stock), how would the loss be reported?

COMPREHENSIVE PROBLEM

20. (Obj. 4) On January 2, 2000, Janis R. Jetson (SSN 344-46-5768) purchased a two-unit apartment building at 1626 Flat Street, Detroit, Michigan 48270-8224. The costs of the land and building were $10,000 and $41,250, respectively. Both apartments are the same size, with one on the ground floor and the other upstairs. Janis has lived in the upstairs apartment since she acquired the building. The tenant in the ground-floor apartment at the time the building was purchased has continued to rent from Janis. The tenant pays $350 a month in rent. On June 30 the tenant moved out. The apartment was vacant until August 1, even though Janis advertised and attempted to rent it. On August 1, a new tenant moved in, paying rent of $400 per month. Rent is due on the first day of the month. Janis uses MACRS to depreciate the rental portion of the building. Information on the apartment follows:

Revenue	
Rent from the first tenant (6 months × $350)	$2,100
Rent from the second tenant (5 months × $400)	2,000
Total revenue	$4,100
Expenses	
Entire house:	
Real estate taxes	$1,700
Janitor and yard work	160
Electricity and water	440
Repairs	300
Heat (gas)	800
Interest on mortgage	1,100
Insurance	376
Expenses other than depreciation	$4,876
Ground-floor apartment:	
Advertising	100
Cleaning and maintenance	420
Repairs	70
	$590
Upstairs apartment:	
Repairs	$ 90
Cleaning and maintenance	480
	$570

In addition to the rental property, Janis works as an administrative assistant and earned $17,600 in wages. From this amount, $660 of federal income tax was withheld. Janis also earned $147 in interest from Bank of America. Janis is single and has no dependents. Prepare Janis Jetson's tax return. Janis is single and 68-years-old. Through Medicare, Janis receives health care coverage that complies with the ACA mandate. Janis does not want $3 to go to the Presidential election campaign fund. She signs her return on April 10, 2016.

(Use for Problem 20.)

Form **1040** Department of the Treasury—Internal Revenue Service (99)
U.S. Individual Income Tax Return **2015** OMB No. 1545-0074 | IRS Use Only—Do not write or staple in this space.

For the year Jan. 1–Dec. 31, 2015, or other tax year beginning , 2015, ending , 20 | See separate instructions.

Your first name and initial	Last name	**Your social security number**
If a joint return, spouse's first name and initial	Last name	**Spouse's social security number**
Home address (number and street). If you have a P.O. box, see instructions.	Apt. no.	▲ Make sure the SSN(s) above and on line 6c are correct.
City, town or post office, state, and ZIP code. If you have a foreign address, also complete spaces below (see instructions).		**Presidential Election Campaign** Check here if you, or your spouse if filing jointly, want $3 to go to this fund. Checking a box below will not change your tax or refund. ☐ You ☐ Spouse
Foreign country name	Foreign province/state/county / Foreign postal code	

Filing Status

Check only one box.

1 ☐ Single
2 ☐ Married filing jointly (even if only one had income)
3 ☐ Married filing separately. Enter spouse's SSN above and full name here. ▶
4 ☐ Head of household (with qualifying person). (See instructions.) If the qualifying person is a child but not your dependent, enter this child's name here. ▶
5 ☐ Qualifying widow(er) with dependent child

Exemptions

6a ☐ **Yourself.** If someone can claim you as a dependent, **do not** check box 6a
b ☐ **Spouse**

Boxes checked on 6a and 6b

c **Dependents:**

(1) First name Last name	(2) Dependent's social security number	(3) Dependent's relationship to you	(4) ✓ if child under age 17 qualifying for child tax credit (see instructions)
			☐
			☐
			☐
			☐

No. of children on 6c who:
• lived with you
• did not live with you due to divorce or separation (see instructions)
Dependents on 6c not entered above

If more than four dependents, see instructions and check here ▶☐

d Total number of exemptions claimed — Add numbers on lines above ▶

Income

Attach Form(s) W-2 here. Also attach Forms W-2G and 1099-R if tax was withheld.

If you did not get a W-2, see instructions.

7	Wages, salaries, tips, etc. Attach Form(s) W-2		7	
8a	**Taxable** interest. Attach Schedule B if required		8a	
b	**Tax-exempt** interest. **Do not** include on line 8a	8b		
9a	Ordinary dividends. Attach Schedule B if required		9a	
b	Qualified dividends	9b		
10	Taxable refunds, credits, or offsets of state and local income taxes		10	
11	Alimony received		11	
12	Business income or (loss). Attach Schedule C or C-EZ		12	
13	Capital gain or (loss). Attach Schedule D if required. If not required, check here ▶ ☐		13	
14	Other gains or (losses). Attach Form 4797		14	
15a	IRA distributions	15a	b Taxable amount 15b	
16a	Pensions and annuities	16a	b Taxable amount 16b	
17	Rental real estate, royalties, partnerships, S corporations, trusts, etc. Attach Schedule E		17	
18	Farm income or (loss). Attach Schedule F		18	
19	Unemployment compensation		19	
20a	Social security benefits	20a	b Taxable amount 20b	
21	Other income. List type and amount		21	
22	Combine the amounts in the far right column for lines 7 through 21. This is your **total income** ▶		22	

Adjusted Gross Income

23	Reserved	23	
24	Certain business expenses of reservists, performing artists, and fee-basis government officials. Attach Form 2106 or 2106-EZ	24	
25	Health savings account deduction. Attach Form 8889	25	
26	Moving expenses. Attach Form 3903	26	
27	Deductible part of self-employment tax. Attach Schedule SE	27	
28	Self-employed SEP, SIMPLE, and qualified plans	28	
29	Self-employed health insurance deduction	29	
30	Penalty on early withdrawal of savings	30	
31a	Alimony paid b Recipient's SSN ▶	31a	
32	IRA deduction	32	
33	Student loan interest deduction	33	
34	Reserved	34	
35	Domestic production activities deduction. Attach Form 8903	35	
36	Add lines 23 through 35	36	
37	Subtract line 36 from line 22. This is your **adjusted gross income** ▶	37	

For Disclosure, Privacy Act, and Paperwork Reduction Act Notice, see separate instructions. Cat. No. 11320B Form **1040** (2015)

(Use for Problem 20.)

Form 1040 (2015) Page **2**

Tax and Credits

38	Amount from line 37 (adjusted gross income)		38	
39a	Check if: ☐ **You** were born before January 2, 1951, ☐ Blind. ☐ **Spouse** was born before January 2, 1951, ☐ Blind. } **Total boxes checked ▶ 39a**			
b	If your spouse itemizes on a separate return or you were a dual-status alien, check here ▶ **39b** ☐			
40	**Itemized deductions** (from Schedule A) **or** your **standard deduction** (see left margin)		40	
41	Subtract line 40 from line 38		41	
42	**Exemptions.** If line 38 is $154,950 or less, multiply $4,000 by the number on line 6d. Otherwise, see instructions		42	
43	**Taxable income.** Subtract line 42 from line 41. If line 42 is more than line 41, enter -0-		43	
44	**Tax** (see instructions). Check if any from: **a** ☐ Form(s) 8814 **b** ☐ Form 4972 **c** ☐		44	
45	**Alternative minimum tax** (see instructions). Attach Form 6251		45	
46	Excess advance premium tax credit repayment. Attach Form 8962		46	
47	Add lines 44, 45, and 46 ▶		47	
48	Foreign tax credit. Attach Form 1116 if required	48		
49	Credit for child and dependent care expenses. Attach Form 2441	49		
50	Education credits from Form 8863, line 19	50		
51	Retirement savings contributions credit. Attach Form 8880	51		
52	Child tax credit. Attach Schedule 8812, if required	52		
53	Residential energy credit. Attach Form 5695	53		
54	Other credits from Form: **a** ☐ 3800 **b** ☐ 8801 **c** ☐	54		
55	Add lines 48 through 54. These are your **total credits**		55	
56	Subtract line 55 from line 47. If line 55 is more than line 47, enter -0- ▶		56	

Standard Deduction for—
- People who check any box on line 39a or 39b **or** who can be claimed as a dependent, see instructions.
- All others:

Single or Married filing separately, $6,300

Married filing jointly or Qualifying widow(er), $12,600

Head of household, $9,250

Other Taxes

57	Self-employment tax. Attach Schedule SE	57	
58	Unreported social security and Medicare tax from Form: **a** ☐ 4137 **b** ☐ 8919	58	
59	Additional tax on IRAs, other qualified retirement plans, etc. Attach Form 5329 if required	59	
60a	Household employment taxes from Schedule H	60a	
b	First-time homebuyer credit repayment. Attach Form 5405 if required	60b	
61	Health care: individual responsibility (see instructions) Full-year coverage ☐	61	
62	Taxes from: **a** ☐ Form 8959 **b** ☐ Form 8960 **c** ☐ Instructions; enter code(s)	62	
63	Add lines 56 through 62. This is your **total tax** ▶	63	

Payments

If you have a qualifying child, attach Schedule EIC.

64	Federal income tax withheld from Forms W-2 and 1099	64			
65	2015 estimated tax payments and amount applied from 2014 return	65			
66a	**Earned income credit (EIC)**	66a			
b	Nontaxable combat pay election **66b**				
67	Additional child tax credit. Attach Schedule 8812	67			
68	American opportunity credit from Form 8863, line 8	68			
69	Net premium tax credit. Attach Form 8962	69			
70	Amount paid with request for extension to file	70			
71	Excess social security and tier 1 RRTA tax withheld	71			
72	Credit for federal tax on fuels. Attach Form 4136	72			
73	Credits from Form: **a** ☐ 2439 **b** Reserved **c** ☐ 8885 **d** ☐	73			
74	Add lines 64, 65, 66a, and 67 through 73. These are your **total payments** ▶			74	

Refund

75	If line 74 is more than line 63, subtract line 63 from line 74. This is the amount you **overpaid**	75	
76a	Amount of line 75 you want **refunded to you.** If Form 8888 is attached, check here ▶ ☐	76a	
▶ b	Routing number ▶ **c** Type: ☐ Checking ☐ Savings		
▶ d	Account number		
77	Amount of line 75 you want **applied to your 2016 estimated tax** ▶ 77		

Direct deposit? See instructions.

Amount You Owe

78	**Amount you owe.** Subtract line 74 from line 63. For details on how to pay, see instructions ▶	78	
79	Estimated tax penalty (see instructions) 79		

Third Party Designee

Do you want to allow another person to discuss this return with the IRS (see instructions)? ☐ **Yes.** Complete below. ☐ **No**

Designee's name ▶ Phone no. ▶ Personal identification number (PIN) ▶

Sign Here

Joint return? See instructions. Keep a copy for your records.

Under penalties of perjury, I declare that I have examined this return and accompanying schedules and statements, and to the best of my knowledge and belief, they are true, correct, and complete. Declaration of preparer (other than taxpayer) is based on all information of which preparer has any knowledge.

Your signature	Date	Your occupation	Daytime phone number
Spouse's signature. If a joint return, **both** must sign.	Date	Spouse's occupation	If the IRS sent you an Identity Protection PIN, enter it here (see inst.)

Paid Preparer Use Only

Print/Type preparer's name	Preparer's signature	Date	Check ☐ if self-employed	PTIN
Firm's name ▶			Firm's EIN ▶	
Firm's address ▶			Phone no.	

www.irs.gov/form1040 Form **1040** (2015)

(Use for Problem 20.)

SCHEDULE E (Form 1040)
Department of the Treasury
Internal Revenue Service (99)

Supplemental Income and Loss
(From rental real estate, royalties, partnerships, S corporations, estates, trusts, REMICs, etc.)
▶ Attach to Form 1040, 1040NR, or Form 1041.
▶ Information about Schedule E and its separate instructions is at *www.irs.gov/schedulee.*

OMB No. 1545-0074
2015
Attachment Sequence No. **13**

Name(s) shown on return | **Your social security number**

Part I **Income or Loss From Rental Real Estate and Royalties** **Note:** If you are in the business of renting personal property, use **Schedule C** or **C-EZ** (see instructions). If you are an individual, report farm rental income or loss from **Form 4835** on page 2, line 40.

A Did you make any payments in 2015 that would require you to file Form(s) 1099? (see instructions) ☐ Yes ☐ No
B If "Yes," did you or will you file required Forms 1099? ☐ Yes ☐ No

1a	Physical address of each property (street, city, state, ZIP code)
A	
B	
C	

1b	Type of Property (from list below)	**2** For each rental real estate property listed above, report the number of fair rental and personal use days. Check the **QJV** box only if you meet the requirements to file as a qualified joint venture. See instructions.		**Fair Rental Days**	**Personal Use Days**	**QJV**
A			**A**			☐
B			**B**			☐
C			**C**			☐

Type of Property:
1 Single Family Residence
2 Multi-Family Residence
3 Vacation/Short-Term Rental
4 Commercial
5 Land
6 Royalties
7 Self-Rental
8 Other (describe)

Income:	**Properties:**	**A**	**B**	**C**
3 Rents received	**3**			
4 Royalties received	**4**			
Expenses:				
5 Advertising	**5**			
6 Auto and travel (see instructions)	**6**			
7 Cleaning and maintenance	**7**			
8 Commissions	**8**			
9 Insurance	**9**			
10 Legal and other professional fees	**10**			
11 Management fees	**11**			
12 Mortgage interest paid to banks, etc. (see instructions)	**12**			
13 Other interest	**13**			
14 Repairs	**14**			
15 Supplies	**15**			
16 Taxes	**16**			
17 Utilities	**17**			
18 Depreciation expense or depletion	**18**			
19 Other (list) ▶	**19**			
20 Total expenses. Add lines 5 through 19	**20**			
21 Subtract line 20 from line 3 (rents) and/or 4 (royalties). If result is a (loss), see instructions to find out if you must file **Form 6198**	**21**			
22 Deductible rental real estate loss after limitation, if any, on **Form 8582** (see instructions)	**22**	( )	( )	( )

23a Total of all amounts reported on line 3 for all rental properties	**23a**	
b Total of all amounts reported on line 4 for all royalty properties	**23b**	
c Total of all amounts reported on line 12 for all properties	**23c**	
d Total of all amounts reported on line 18 for all properties	**23d**	
e Total of all amounts reported on line 20 for all properties	**23e**	
24 **Income.** Add positive amounts shown on line 21. **Do not** include any losses	**24**	
25 **Losses.** Add royalty losses from line 21 and rental real estate losses from line 22. Enter total losses here	**25**	( )
26 **Total rental real estate and royalty income or (loss).** Combine lines 24 and 25. Enter the result here. If Parts II, III, IV, and line 40 on page 2 do not apply to you, also enter this amount on Form 1040, line 17, or Form 1040NR, line 18. Otherwise, include this amount in the total on line 41 on page 2	**26**	

For Paperwork Reduction Act Notice, see the separate instructions. Cat. No. 11344L **Schedule E (Form 1040) 2015**

CUMULATIVE PROBLEM (CHAPTERS 1-9)

Merv R. Baldwin (age 39, SSN 550-37-7400) and Melanie A. Baldwin (age 36, SSN 598-35-3775) live at 515 W. 35th Ave., Provo, Utah 84200. They claim their 9-year-old son, Adam (SSN 458-47-9330) as their only dependent. Merv works as a computer analyst; Melanie is employed as a manager. Details from their respective W-2s are shown below. In order to allow them both to work, the Baldwins paid Anna Furlough (Melanie's mother, SSN 583-57-9991) $3,600 during the year for after-school childcare. Anna lives down the street at 735 W. 35th Ave.

	Gross Wages	*State Income Tax Withheld*	*Federal Income Tax Withheld*	*Social Security Tax Withheld*	*Medicare Tax Withheld*
Merv	$176,500	$8,466	$36,100	$7,347	$2,559
Melanie	75,605	6,644	26,064	4,688	1,096

During 2015, the Baldwins received $33,667 from the rental of their cabin in Park City, Utah. The cabin is located at 1900 Mountain View Lane, Park City, Utah 85068. The cabin was rented out for 104 days during the year, and the Baldwins personally used the cabin for 20 days during the summer. The Baldwins paid $319,000 for the cabin in 1996, of which $50,000 was allocated to the land. They depreciate the cabin using MACRS. Expenses related to the cabin include:

Cleaning and maintenance	$ 700
Commissions*	12,400
Insurance	522
Mortgage interest	7,230
Real estate taxes	5,900
Repairs	240
Utilities	4,800

* *Paid to a leasing company to help them identify and screen potential tenants, collect rents, and schedule necessary repairs and cleaning services.*

The Baldwins also have receipts for the following income and expenses during the year.

Income:	
City of Ogden bond interest	$12,200
Key Bank CD interest	40,750
Zion Bank interest	27,294
Expenses:	
Home mortgage interest (on main home)	$15,909
Real estate taxes (on main home)	5,525
Cash contributions to qualified charity	2,000
Noncash contributions to qualified charity	150
Amount paid when filing 2014 state tax return	429
Amount paid when filing 2014 federal tax return	2,440
Tax preparation fees	275

Prepare the Baldwins' joint tax return. The Baldwins get full health care coverage thru Merv's employer. The Baldwins did not have any interest in a foreign account or trust. They sign their return on April 15, 2016 and both want to contribute $3 to the Presidential campaign fund.

(Use for Cumulative Problem.)

Form **1040** Department of the Treasury—Internal Revenue Service (99)
U.S. Individual Income Tax Return **2015** OMB No. 1545-0074 IRS Use Only—Do not write or staple in this space.

For the year Jan. 1–Dec. 31, 2015, or other tax year beginning , 2015, ending , 20 | See separate instructions.

Your first name and initial	Last name	**Your social security number**
If a joint return, spouse's first name and initial	Last name	**Spouse's social security number**
Home address (number and street). If you have a P.O. box, see instructions.	Apt. no.	▲ Make sure the SSN(s) above and on line 6c are correct.
City, town or post office, state, and ZIP code. If you have a foreign address, also complete spaces below (see instructions).		**Presidential Election Campaign** Check here if you, or your spouse if filing jointly, want $3 to go to this fund. Checking a box below will not change your tax or refund. ☐ You ☐ Spouse
Foreign country name	Foreign province/state/county / Foreign postal code	

Filing Status

Check only one box.

1 ☐ Single
2 ☐ Married filing jointly (even if only one had income)
3 ☐ Married filing separately. Enter spouse's SSN above and full name here.
4 ☐ Head of household (with qualifying person). (See instructions.) If the qualifying person is a child but not your dependent, enter this child's name here.
5 ☐ Qualifying widow(er) with dependent child

Exemptions

6a ☐ **Yourself.** If someone can claim you as a dependent, **do not** check box 6a
b ☐ **Spouse**
c **Dependents:**

(1) First name Last name	(2) Dependent's social security number	(3) Dependent's relationship to you	(4) ✓ if child under age 17 qualifying for child tax credit (see instructions)
			☐
			☐
			☐
			☐

If more than four dependents, see instructions and check here ▶☐

d Total number of exemptions claimed

Boxes checked on 6a and 6b
No. of children on 6c who:
• lived with you
• did not live with you due to divorce or separation (see instructions)
Dependents on 6c not entered above
Add numbers on lines above ▶

Income

Attach Form(s) W-2 here. Also attach Forms W-2G and 1099-R if tax was withheld.

If you did not get a W-2, see instructions.

7	Wages, salaries, tips, etc. Attach Form(s) W-2		7	
8a	**Taxable** interest. Attach Schedule B if required		8a	
b	**Tax-exempt** interest. **Do not** include on line 8a	8b		
9a	Ordinary dividends. Attach Schedule B if required		9a	
b	Qualified dividends	9b		
10	Taxable refunds, credits, or offsets of state and local income taxes		10	
11	Alimony received		11	
12	Business income or (loss). Attach Schedule C or C-EZ		12	
13	Capital gain or (loss). Attach Schedule D if required. If not required, check here ▶ ☐		13	
14	Other gains or (losses). Attach Form 4797		14	
15a	IRA distributions	15a	b Taxable amount 15b	
16a	Pensions and annuities	16a	b Taxable amount 16b	
17	Rental real estate, royalties, partnerships, S corporations, trusts, etc. Attach Schedule E		17	
18	Farm income or (loss). Attach Schedule F		18	
19	Unemployment compensation		19	
20a	Social security benefits	20a	b Taxable amount 20b	
21	Other income. List type and amount		21	
22	Combine the amounts in the far right column for lines 7 through 21. This is your **total income** ▶		22	

Adjusted Gross Income

23	Reserved	23		
24	Certain business expenses of reservists, performing artists, and fee-basis government officials. Attach Form 2106 or 2106-EZ	24		
25	Health savings account deduction. Attach Form 8889	25		
26	Moving expenses. Attach Form 3903	26		
27	Deductible part of self-employment tax. Attach Schedule SE	27		
28	Self-employed SEP, SIMPLE, and qualified plans	28		
29	Self-employed health insurance deduction	29		
30	Penalty on early withdrawal of savings	30		
31a	Alimony paid b Recipient's SSN ▶	31a		
32	IRA deduction	32		
33	Student loan interest deduction	33		
34	Reserved	34		
35	Domestic production activities deduction. Attach Form 8903	35		
36	Add lines 23 through 35		36	
37	Subtract line 36 from line 22. This is your **adjusted gross income** ▶		37	

For Disclosure, Privacy Act, and Paperwork Reduction Act Notice, see separate instructions. Cat. No. 11320B Form **1040** (2015)

(Use for Cumulative Problem.)

Form 1040 (2015) Page **2**

Tax and Credits

38	Amount from line 37 (adjusted gross income)	38	
39a	Check if: ☐ **You** were born before January 2, 1951, ☐ Blind. ☐ **Spouse** was born before January 2, 1951, ☐ Blind. } **Total boxes checked ▶ 39a** ☐		
b	If your spouse itemizes on a separate return or you were a dual-status alien, check here ▶ 39b ☐		
40	**Itemized deductions** (from Schedule A) **or** your **standard deduction** (see left margin)	40	
41	Subtract line 40 from line 38	41	
42	**Exemptions.** If line 38 is $154,950 or less, multiply $4,000 by the number on line 6d. Otherwise, see instructions	42	
43	**Taxable income.** Subtract line 42 from line 41. If line 42 is more than line 41, enter -0-	43	
44	**Tax** (see instructions). Check if any from: **a** ☐ Form(s) 8814 **b** ☐ Form 4972 **c** ☐	44	
45	**Alternative minimum tax** (see instructions). Attach Form 6251	45	
46	Excess advance premium tax credit repayment. Attach Form 8962	46	
47	Add lines 44, 45, and 46 ▶	47	
48	Foreign tax credit. Attach Form 1116 if required — 48		
49	Credit for child and dependent care expenses. Attach Form 2441 — 49		
50	Education credits from Form 8863, line 19 — 50		
51	Retirement savings contributions credit. Attach Form 8880 — 51		
52	Child tax credit. Attach Schedule 8812, if required — 52		
53	Residential energy credit. Attach Form 5695 — 53		
54	Other credits from Form: **a** ☐ 3800 **b** ☐ 8801 **c** ☐ — 54		
55	Add lines 48 through 54. These are your **total credits**	55	
56	Subtract line 55 from line 47. If line 55 is more than line 47, enter -0- ▶	56	

Standard Deduction for—
- People who check any box on line 39a or 39b **or** who can be claimed as a dependent, see instructions.
- All others:

Single or Married filing separately, $6,300

Married filing jointly or Qualifying widow(er), $12,600

Head of household, $9,250

Other Taxes

57	Self-employment tax. Attach Schedule SE	57	
58	Unreported social security and Medicare tax from Form: **a** ☐ 4137 **b** ☐ 8919	58	
59	Additional tax on IRAs, other qualified retirement plans, etc. Attach Form 5329 if required	59	
60a	Household employment taxes from Schedule H	60a	
b	First-time homebuyer credit repayment. Attach Form 5405 if required	60b	
61	Health care: individual responsibility (see instructions) Full-year coverage ☐	61	
62	Taxes from: **a** ☐ Form 8959 **b** ☐ Form 8960 **c** ☐ Instructions; enter code(s)	62	
63	Add lines 56 through 62. This is your **total tax** ▶	63	

Payments

If you have a qualifying child, attach Schedule EIC.

64	Federal income tax withheld from Forms W-2 and 1099 — 64		
65	2015 estimated tax payments and amount applied from 2014 return — 65		
66a	**Earned income credit (EIC)** — 66a		
b	Nontaxable combat pay election — 66b		
67	Additional child tax credit. Attach Schedule 8812 — 67		
68	American opportunity credit from Form 8863, line 8 — 68		
69	Net premium tax credit. Attach Form 8962 — 69		
70	Amount paid with request for extension to file — 70		
71	Excess social security and tier 1 RRTA tax withheld — 71		
72	Credit for federal tax on fuels. Attach Form 4136 — 72		
73	Credits from Form: **a** ☐ 2439 **b** Reserved **c** ☐ 8885 **d** ☐ — 73		
74	Add lines 64, 65, 66a, and 67 through 73. These are your **total payments** ▶	74	

Refund

75	If line 74 is more than line 63, subtract line 63 from line 74. This is the amount you **overpaid**	75	
76a	Amount of line 75 you want **refunded to you.** If Form 8888 is attached, check here ▶ ☐	76a	
▶ b	Routing number ▶ c Type: ☐ Checking ☐ Savings		
▶ d	Account number		
77	Amount of line 75 you want **applied to your 2016 estimated tax** ▶ — 77		

Direct deposit? See instructions.

Amount You Owe

78	**Amount you owe.** Subtract line 74 from line 63. For details on how to pay, see instructions ▶	78	
79	Estimated tax penalty (see instructions) — 79		

Third Party Designee

Do you want to allow another person to discuss this return with the IRS (see instructions)? ☐ **Yes.** Complete below. ☐ **No**

Designee's name ▶ Phone no. ▶ Personal identification number (PIN) ▶

Sign Here

Joint return? See instructions. Keep a copy for your records.

Under penalties of perjury, I declare that I have examined this return and accompanying schedules and statements, and to the best of my knowledge and belief, they are true, correct, and complete. Declaration of preparer (other than taxpayer) is based on all information of which preparer has any knowledge.

Your signature	Date	Your occupation	Daytime phone number
Spouse's signature. If a joint return, **both** must sign.	Date	Spouse's occupation	If the IRS sent you an Identity Protection PIN, enter it here (see inst.)

Paid Preparer Use Only

Print/Type preparer's name	Preparer's signature	Date	Check ☐ if self-employed	PTIN
Firm's name ▶			Firm's EIN ▶	
Firm's address ▶			Phone no.	

www.irs.gov/form1040 Form **1040** (2015)

(Use for Cumulative Problem.)

SCHEDULE A (Form 1040)

Department of the Treasury
Internal Revenue Service (99)

Itemized Deductions

▶ Information about Schedule A and its separate instructions is at *www.irs.gov/schedulea*.
▶ Attach to Form 1040.

OMB No. 1545-0074
2015
Attachment Sequence No. **07**

Name(s) shown on Form 1040 | **Your social security number**

Section	Line	Description	Box	Amount	Line	Amount
Medical and Dental Expenses		**Caution.** Do not include expenses reimbursed or paid by others.				
	1	Medical and dental expenses (see instructions)	1			
	2	Enter amount from Form 1040, line 38 [2]				
	3	Multiply line 2 by 10% (.10). But if either you or your spouse was born before January 2, 1951, multiply line 2 by 7.5% (.075) instead	3			
	4	Subtract line 3 from line 1. If line 3 is more than line 1, enter -0-			4	
Taxes You Paid	5	State and local a ☐ Income taxes b ■ Reserved	5			
	6	Real estate taxes (see instructions)	6			
	7	Personal property taxes	7			
	8	Other taxes. List type and amount ▶	8			
	9	Add lines 5 through 8			9	
Interest You Paid **Note.** Your mortgage interest deduction may be limited (see instructions).	10	Home mortgage interest and points reported to you on Form 1098	10			
	11	Home mortgage interest not reported to you on Form 1098. If paid to the person from whom you bought the home, see instructions and show that person's name, identifying no., and address ▶	11			
	12	Points not reported to you on Form 1098. See instructions for special rules	12			
	13	Reserved	13			
	14	Investment interest. Attach Form 4952 if required. (See instructions.)	14			
	15	Add lines 10 through 14			15	
Gifts to Charity If you made a gift and got a benefit for it, see instructions.	16	Gifts by cash or check. If you made any gift of $250 or more, see instructions	16			
	17	Other than by cash or check. If any gift of $250 or more, see instructions. You **must** attach Form 8283 if over $500	17			
	18	Carryover from prior year	18			
	19	Add lines 16 through 18			19	
Casualty and Theft Losses	20	Casualty or theft loss(es). Attach Form 4684. (See instructions.)			20	
Job Expenses and Certain Miscellaneous Deductions	21	Unreimbursed employee expenses—job travel, union dues, job education, etc. Attach Form 2106 or 2106-EZ if required. (See instructions.) ▶	21			
	22	Tax preparation fees	22			
	23	Other expenses—investment, safe deposit box, etc. List type and amount ▶	23			
	24	Add lines 21 through 23	24			
	25	Enter amount from Form 1040, line 38 [25]				
	26	Multiply line 25 by 2% (.02)	26			
	27	Subtract line 26 from line 24. If line 26 is more than line 24, enter -0-			27	
Other Miscellaneous Deductions	28	Other—from list in instructions. List type and amount ▶			28	
Total Itemized Deductions	29	Is Form 1040, line 38, over $154,950? ☐ **No.** Your deduction is not limited. Add the amounts in the far right column for lines 4 through 28. Also, enter this amount on Form 1040, line 40. ☐ **Yes.** Your deduction may be limited. See the Itemized Deductions Worksheet in the instructions to figure the amount to enter.			29	
	30	If you elect to itemize deductions even though they are less than your standard deduction, check here ▶ ☐				

For Paperwork Reduction Act Notice, see Form 1040 instructions. Cat. No. 17145C **Schedule A (Form 1040) 2015**

(Use for Cumulative Problem.)

SCHEDULE B (Form 1040A or 1040)

Department of the Treasury Internal Revenue Service (99)

Interest and Ordinary Dividends

▶ Attach to Form 1040A or 1040.

▶ Information about Schedule B and its instructions is at *www.irs.gov/scheduleb*.

OMB No. 1545-0074

2015

Attachment Sequence No. 08

Name(s) shown on return | Your social security number

Part I Interest

(See instructions on back and the instructions for Form 1040A, or Form 1040, line 8a.)

Note: If you received a Form 1099-INT, Form 1099-OID, or substitute statement from a brokerage firm, list the firm's name as the payer and enter the total interest shown on that form.

			Amount
1	List name of payer. If any interest is from a seller-financed mortgage and the buyer used the property as a personal residence, see instructions on back and list this interest first. Also, show that buyer's social security number and address ▶	1	
2	Add the amounts on line 1	2	
3	Excludable interest on series EE and I U.S. savings bonds issued after 1989. Attach Form 8815	3	
4	Subtract line 3 from line 2. Enter the result here and on Form 1040A, or Form 1040, line 8a ▶	4	

Note: If line 4 is over $1,500, you must complete Part III.

Part II Ordinary Dividends

(See instructions on back and the instructions for Form 1040A, or Form 1040, line 9a.)

Note: If you received a Form 1099-DIV or substitute statement from a brokerage firm, list the firm's name as the payer and enter the ordinary dividends shown on that form.

			Amount
5	List name of payer ▶	5	
6	Add the amounts on line 5. Enter the total here and on Form 1040A, or Form 1040, line 9a ▶	6	

Note: If line 6 is over $1,500, you must complete Part III.

Part III Foreign Accounts and Trusts

(See instructions on back.)

You must complete this part if you **(a)** had over $1,500 of taxable interest or ordinary dividends; **(b)** had a foreign account; or **(c)** received a distribution from, or were a grantor of, or a transferor to, a foreign trust.

		Yes	No
7a	At any time during 2015, did you have a financial interest in or signature authority over a financial account (such as a bank account, securities account, or brokerage account) located in a foreign country? See instructions		
	If "Yes," are you required to file FinCEN Form 114, Report of Foreign Bank and Financial Accounts (FBAR), to report that financial interest or signature authority? See FinCEN Form 114 and its instructions for filing requirements and exceptions to those requirements		
b	If you are required to file FinCEN Form 114, enter the name of the foreign country where the financial account is located ▶		
8	During 2015, did you receive a distribution from, or were you the grantor of, or transferor to, a foreign trust? If "Yes," you may have to file Form 3520. See instructions on back		

For Paperwork Reduction Act Notice, see your tax return instructions. Cat. No. 17146N **Schedule B (Form 1040A or 1040) 2015**

(Use for Cumulative Problem.)

SCHEDULE E (Form 1040)

Department of the Treasury
Internal Revenue Service (99)

Supplemental Income and Loss

(From rental real estate, royalties, partnerships, S corporations, estates, trusts, REMICs, etc.)

▶ Attach to Form 1040, 1040NR, or Form 1041.

▶ Information about Schedule E and its separate instructions is at *www.irs.gov/schedulee*.

OMB No. 1545-0074

2015

Attachment Sequence No. **13**

Name(s) shown on return | **Your social security number**

Part I **Income or Loss From Rental Real Estate and Royalties** **Note:** If you are in the business of renting personal property, use **Schedule C** or **C-EZ** (see instructions). If you are an individual, report farm rental income or loss from **Form 4835** on page 2, line 40.

A Did you make any payments in 2015 that would require you to file Form(s) 1099? (see instructions) ☐ Yes ☐ No

B If "Yes," did you or will you file required Forms 1099? ☐ Yes ☐ No

1a	Physical address of each property (street, city, state, ZIP code)
A	
B	
C	

1b	Type of Property (from list below)	**2** For each rental real estate property listed above, report the number of fair rental and personal use days. Check the **QJV** box only if you meet the requirements to file as a qualified joint venture. See instructions.		**Fair Rental Days**	**Personal Use Days**	**QJV**
A			**A**			☐
B			**B**			☐
C			**C**			☐

Type of Property:

1 Single Family Residence | 3 Vacation/Short-Term Rental | 5 Land | 7 Self-Rental
2 Multi-Family Residence | 4 Commercial | 6 Royalties | 8 Other (describe)

Income:	**Properties:**		**A**	**B**	**C**
3	Rents received	3			
4	Royalties received	4			
Expenses:					
5	Advertising	5			
6	Auto and travel (see instructions)	6			
7	Cleaning and maintenance	7			
8	Commissions	8			
9	Insurance	9			
10	Legal and other professional fees	10			
11	Management fees	11			
12	Mortgage interest paid to banks, etc. (see instructions)	12			
13	Other interest	13			
14	Repairs	14			
15	Supplies	15			
16	Taxes	16			
17	Utilities	17			
18	Depreciation expense or depletion	18			
19	Other (list) ▶	19			
20	Total expenses. Add lines 5 through 19	20			
21	Subtract line 20 from line 3 (rents) and/or 4 (royalties). If result is a (loss), see instructions to find out if you must file **Form 6198**	21			
22	Deductible rental real estate loss after limitation, if any, on **Form 8582** (see instructions)	22	( )	( )	( )

23a	Total of all amounts reported on line 3 for all rental properties	23a	
b	Total of all amounts reported on line 4 for all royalty properties	23b	
c	Total of all amounts reported on line 12 for all properties	23c	
d	Total of all amounts reported on line 18 for all properties	23d	
e	Total of all amounts reported on line 20 for all properties	23e	
24	**Income.** Add positive amounts shown on line 21. **Do not** include any losses	24	
25	**Losses.** Add royalty losses from line 21 and rental real estate losses from line 22. Enter total losses here	25	( )
26	**Total rental real estate and royalty income or (loss).** Combine lines 24 and 25. Enter the result here. If Parts II, III, IV, and line 40 on page 2 do not apply to you, also enter this amount on Form 1040, line 17, or Form 1040NR, line 18. Otherwise, include this amount in the total on line 41 on page 2	26	

For Paperwork Reduction Act Notice, see the separate instructions. Cat. No. 11344L **Schedule E (Form 1040) 2015**

(Use for Cumulative Problem.)

Form **2441** Department of the Treasury Internal Revenue Service (99)

Child and Dependent Care Expenses

▶ Attach to Form 1040, Form 1040A, or Form 1040NR.

▶ Information about Form 2441 and its separate instructions is at *www.irs.gov/form2441*.

1040 1040A 1040NR 2441

OMB No. 1545-0074

2015

Attachment Sequence No. **21**

Name(s) shown on return | Your social security number

Part I **Persons or Organizations Who Provided the Care**—You **must** complete this part. (If you have more than two care providers, see the instructions.)

1 (a) Care provider's name	(b) Address (number, street, apt. no., city, state, and ZIP code)	(c) Identifying number (SSN or EIN)	(d) Amount paid (see instructions)

Did you receive dependent care benefits? — **No** ⟶ Complete only Part II below. — **Yes** ⟶ Complete Part III on the back next.

Caution. If the care was provided in your home, you may owe employment taxes. If you do, you cannot file Form 1040A. For details, see the instructions for Form 1040, line 60a, or Form 1040NR, line 59a.

Part II **Credit for Child and Dependent Care Expenses**

2 Information about your **qualifying person(s).** If you have more than two qualifying persons, see the instructions.

(a) Qualifying person's name — First	Last	(b) Qualifying person's social security number	(c) **Qualified expenses** you incurred and paid in 2015 for the person listed in column (a)

3 Add the amounts in column (c) of line 2. **Do not** enter more than $3,000 for one qualifying person or $6,000 for two or more persons. If you completed Part III, enter the amount from line 31 . . . **3**

4 Enter your **earned income.** See instructions . . . **4**

5 If married filing jointly, enter your spouse's earned income (if you or your spouse was a student or was disabled, see the instructions); **all others**, enter the amount from line 4 . **5**

6 Enter the **smallest** of line 3, 4, or 5 . . . **6**

7 Enter the amount from Form 1040, line 38; Form 1040A, line 22; or Form 1040NR, line 37 . . . **7**

8 Enter on line 8 the decimal amount shown below that applies to the amount on line 7

If line 7 is: Over	But not over	Decimal amount is	If line 7 is: Over	But not over	Decimal amount is
$0	15,000	.35	$29,000	31,000	.27
15,000	17,000	.34	31,000	33,000	.26
17,000	19,000	.33	33,000	35,000	.25
19,000	21,000	.32	35,000	37,000	.24
21,000	23,000	.31	37,000	39,000	.23
23,000	25,000	.30	39,000	41,000	.22
25,000	27,000	.29	41,000	43,000	.21
27,000	29,000	.28	43,000	No limit	.20

8 X.

9 Multiply line 6 by the decimal amount on line 8. If you paid 2014 expenses in 2015, see the instructions . . . **9**

10 Tax liability limit. Enter the amount from the Credit Limit Worksheet in the instructions. . . . **10**

11 **Credit for child and dependent care expenses.** Enter the **smaller** of line 9 or line 10 here and on Form 1040, line 49; Form 1040A, line 31; or Form 1040NR, line 47 . . . **11**

For Paperwork Reduction Act Notice, see your tax return instructions. Cat. No. 11862M Form **2441** (2015)

Chapter

10

Property: Basis and Nontaxable Exchanges

CHAPTER CONTENTS

LEARNING OBJECTIVES

After completing Chapter 10, you should be able to:

1. Distinguish between realized and recognized gains and losses and calculate the realized gain or loss on the sale or exchange of property.
2. Understand when the wash sale rules apply and distinguish between realized and recognized losses on the sale of stocks and bonds involved in a wash sale.
3. Know what constitutes a related party and the rules that govern sales between related parties.
4. Understand what is involved in a like-kind exchange, and compute both the realized and recognized gain or loss resulting from a like-kind exchange, as well as the basis in the like-kind property received.
5. Recognize the various types of involuntary conversions and compute the realized and recognized gain or loss on property involved in an involuntary conversion.

CHAPTER OVERVIEW

When taxpayers sell or otherwise dispose of property, a gain or loss usually results. This chapter explains how taxpayers compute those gains and losses. It also explains which gains and losses taxpayers report on the tax return. The chapter begins by presenting the formula used to compute realized gains and losses when disposing of property. Realized gains and losses reflect the taxpayer's economic gain or loss from the transaction. They are the difference between the amount realized from the transaction and the taxpayer's adjusted basis in the property. When the amount realized exceeds the adjusted basis, a realized gain results. A realized loss occurs when the amount realized is less than the adjusted basis. The rules for computing amount realized and adjusted basis are presented in the chapter.

Although disposing of property results in a realized gain or loss, not all realized gains and losses are reported on the tax return. As a rule, taxpayers are taxed on all realized gains but can deduct only realized losses that result from disposing of investment or business property. One exception to this rule involves property destroyed in a casualty or a theft. Although the general rule does not allow taxpayers to deduct losses from the disposal of personal-use property, Chapter 5 presented the rules for the (itemized) deduction for nonbusiness casualty or theft losses. Other exceptions are introduced in this chapter.

¶1001 Realized Gain or Loss

Realized gains or losses occur when taxpayers sell, exchange, or otherwise dispose of property. They also occur when the government exercises its right to take the taxpayer's property in exchange for fair compensation (a process known as condemnation). When the amount realized from the transaction exceeds the adjusted basis in the property given up, the difference is a **realized gain.** When the adjusted basis exceeds the amount realized, the difference is a **realized loss.** Stated another way,

Realized gain (loss) = Amount realized – Adjusted basis

¶1001.01 AMOUNT REALIZED

The **amount realized** equals the sales price minus selling expenses. Selling expenses include commissions, legal fees, and other costs related to the sale. The sales price is the sum of the fair market value (FMV) of the property (which includes cash) and services received in return for the property given up. It also includes any debt of the taxpayer (seller) that the buyer assumes. (When the buyer assumes the seller's debt, it is similar to the buyer giving the seller cash that the seller uses to pay off the debt. Also, see ¶302.01 for an explanation of how to determine FMV.)

EXAMPLE 1

Howard sells stock for $12,000 cash plus a car valued at $5,000. Howard's amount realized is $17,000 ($12,000 + $5,000).

EXAMPLE 2

Marta exchanges land for a building that has a FMV of $90,000. The land is subject to a $50,000 mortgage, which the other party assumes. Marta's amount realized is $140,000 ($90,000 + $50,000).

¶1001.02 ADJUSTED BASIS

When disposing of property, the tax laws allow taxpayers to recover their investment in property tax free. **Basis** is the term used to describe the taxpayer's investment in property. Taxpayers realize a gain when the amount realized exceeds their basis in the property. If the entire basis is not recovered, taxpayers realize a loss for the unrecovered amount.

Between the time taxpayers acquire property and the time they dispose of it, events may occur that require taxpayers to adjust their basis in property. **Adjusted basis** is the term for the taxpayer's investment in property after making those adjustments. Adjusted basis can be stated as follows:

Adjusted basis = Initial basis in property + Capital additions – Capital recoveries

The initial basis of purchased property usually is its cost. However, taxpayers can acquire property in other ways, such as through gift or inheritance. The initial basis of a property depends on how the taxpayer acquired it. The rules for computing initial basis are presented later in the chapter at ¶1002.

Capital Additions

Capital additions include costs incurred in transferring or defending title to the property. Examples of such costs include commissions and legal fees. Capital additions also include the cost of improvements that increase the property's value, lengthen its useful life, or convert it to a different use. Improvements have a useful life that exceeds one year. Maintenance and repairs are not improvements since they are routine and recurring costs.

Examples of Improvements

- Installing a new furnace or roof
- Putting up a fence
- Paving a driveway
- Rebuilding a car engine
- Landscaping
- Building a recreation room in an unfinished basement
- Paying special assessments for sidewalks, roads, etc.
- Adding a room onto a house or other building

EXAMPLE 3

Years ago, Leroy paid $125,000 for a house that he uses as a vacation home. Over the years, Leroy has paid $35,000 to remodel the kitchen, $5,000 to install a wooden fence around the property, and $3,000 to reshingle the roof. He also has paid $13,800 to keep the property in good condition. Leroy's adjusted basis in the home is $168,000 ($125,000 + $35,000 + $5,000 + $3,000). Since the vacation home is a personal belonging, the $13,800 spent on repairs and maintenance are nondeductible personal expenses. If Leroy were to sell the home, his realized gain or loss would be the difference between the amount realized from the sale and his $168,000 adjusted basis in the home.

Capital Recoveries

Capital recoveries are a return of the taxpayer's investment in property. They occur when taxpayers receive money or take tax deductions in connection with the property. Any time taxpayers recover part of their investment in property prior to disposing of it, they must reduce their basis in the property accordingly. When property is damaged in a casualty, taxpayers reduce their basis in the property by amounts they receive from the insurance company. The same basis reduction rule applies to amounts taxpayers receive from the government in exchange for the government's right to use part of their property (known as an easement). The amounts taxpayers receive from the insurance company or from the government represent a return of their initial investment in the property. After receiving these amounts, the taxpayer has less invested in the property. Thus, the taxpayer's basis (investment) in the property must be reduced accordingly.

EXAMPLE 4

Several years ago, Ralph paid $120,000 for land. In the current year, Ralph receives $20,000 from the government in exchange for the right to use part of the land. Ralph must reduce his basis in the land by $20,000. Although Ralph initially paid $120,000 for the land, after receiving $20,000 from the government, his net investment in the land is $100,000. Ralph's adjusted basis in the land equals $100,000 ($120,000 initial basis – $20,000 capital recovery).

Taxpayers also reduce the basis in property by amounts deducted on their tax returns in connection with the property. This includes amounts deducted for casualty or theft losses. It also includes amounts deducted for depreciation, which includes bonus depreciation and Section 179 expense.

EXAMPLE 5

Jennie is a sole proprietor. During the year, Jennie placed in service equipment costing $24,000. She elected to expense the entire amount under Section 179. Jennie's adjusted basis in the equipment is $0. Thus, the entire amount realized on the sale of the equipment will result in realized gain.

EXAMPLE 6

In 20x1, Lee paid $62,000 for a building. Lee spent $10,000 in 20x4 for a new roof. In 20x7, a fire damaged the building. The insurance company paid Lee $20,000 for the loss. Lee claimed a $10,000 casualty loss deduction on her 20x7 tax return for the unreimbursed portion of the loss. In 20x8, Lee spent $29,000 to rebuild the part of the building destroyed in the fire. Over the years, Lee has deducted $22,000 for depreciation on the building. Lee computes the adjusted basis in the building as follows.

Initial basis in the building		$62,000
Plus capital additions		
Improvements	$10,000	
Restoration costs	29,000	39,000
Less capital recoveries		
Depreciation deductions	$22,000	
Insurance proceeds	20,000	
Casualty loss deduction	10,000	(52,000)
Adjusted basis in the building		$49,000

¶1002 Initial Basis

When computing their adjusted basis in property, taxpayers start with the initial basis. The initial basis of purchased property is its cost. However, taxpayers can acquire property through other means, such as through gifts, inheritances, and divorce settlements.

¶1002.01 PROPERTY ACQUIRED BY PURCHASE

The initial basis of purchased property is its cost (what the taxpayer gives up to buy the property). It includes amounts taxpayers borrow to buy the property. It also includes any costs incurred to obtain clear title or make the property ready for use. Examples of such costs include:

- Sales or excise taxes paid on the purchase
- Title insurance and survey costs
- Expenses paid to deliver, install, and test the property
- Recording, legal, and accounting fees

EXAMPLE 7

Burt buys real estate, paying $50,000 cash and assuming the seller's $75,000 mortgage on the property. Burt's initial basis is $125,000 ($50,000 + $75,000).

EXAMPLE 8

Kelly purchases a machine for $10,000. She pays $600 in sales tax and $400 for delivery and installation. Kelly's initial basis in the machine equals $11,000 ($10,000 + $600 + $400).

When the taxpayer performs services in exchange for property, the initial basis in the property is the value of the services the taxpayer includes in income.

EXAMPLE 9

Sal received ten shares of stock in exchange for services he rendered. The market value of the shares is $300. Sal is taxed on $300 for his services. His initial basis in the shares is $300.

Bargain Purchases

Sometimes companies sell goods or other property to their employees for less than FMV. Often, the employee is taxed on the difference between the FMV and the purchase price. In these cases, the employee's initial basis ends up the same as the FMV of the property, since the initial basis includes amounts taxed as income. If the employee does not have to report any income from the bargain purchase (as in a qualified employee discount, see ¶401.03), then the employee's initial basis equals the amount paid for the property.

EXAMPLE 10

Morgan pays $60 for property from a company where he is an employee. The FMV of the property is $100. Morgan reports the $40 difference between FMV and the purchase price on his tax return. Morgan's initial basis in the property equals $100 ($60 purchase price + $40 reported in income).

Basket Purchases

Sometimes a single purchase price buys more than one property. As we learned in Chapter 8, different depreciation rules can apply to different properties. Also, taxpayers may sell the properties at various times in the future. For these reasons, the purchase price must be allocated among the properties acquired. Taxpayers allocate the purchase price among the properties on the basis of their relative FMVs. The amount allocated to one property equals the purchase price times the ratio of the FMV of that property to the total FMV of all properties.

$$\text{Initial basis} = \text{Purchase price} \times \frac{\text{FMV of the property}}{\text{FMV of all properties}}$$

EXAMPLE 11

Devon pays $90,000 for land and a building. At the time of the purchase, the FMV of the land and building are $80,000 and $40,000, respectively. Devon's basis in the land equals $60,000 [$90,000 × ($80,000/$120,000)]. His basis in the building equals $30,000 [$90,000 × ($40,000/$120,000)].

¶1002.02 PROPERTY RECEIVED FROM A SPOUSE

When a taxpayer receives property from a spouse, the spouse's adjusted basis in the property carries over to the taxpayer. No tax consequences occur when property is transferred between spouses (or former spouses when the transfer is part of a divorce settlement).

EXAMPLE 12

As part of a divorce settlement, Drew transferred to April title to his mountain cabin. Drew paid $80,000 for the cabin six years prior to his marriage to April. Over the years, he spent $23,500 on improvements to the cabin. At the time of the transfer, the cabin was worth $240,000. April's basis in the home equals Drew's adjusted basis in the home $103,500 ($80,000 + $23,500). If April were to sell the home for its current fair market value, her realized gain would be $136,500 ($240,000 – $103,500).

¶1002.03 INHERITED PROPERTY

When a person dies, an executor is assigned to distribute the decedent's property (known as the estate). Before distributing the estate to the decedent's heirs, the executor first computes the estate tax due. Estate tax is computed on the total FMV of the decedent's estate (net of liabilities). Estate tax is due only when the value of the estate exceeds a certain amount.

In computing the estate tax, the executor usually values the estate on the date of the decedent's death (DOD). An heir's initial basis in the inherited property is the property's FMV on the DOD. However, under certain conditions, the executor can elect to value the estate six months later (known as the alternative valuation date, or AVD). When the executor values the estate on the AVD, the heir's initial basis in the inherited property is its FMV on the AVD or on the date it is distributed to the heir, whichever occurs first.

EXAMPLE 13

Rhonda inherited land from her grandfather, who died on November 5, 2015. On that day, the land was valued at $45,000. On May 5, 2016, its value was $42,000. The land was distributed to Rhonda on July 2, 2016. Rhonda's basis in the land is $45,000 if DOD is used to value the grandfather's estate. If the AVD is used, Rhonda's basis is $42,000 (since the AVD occurs before the date of distribution).

EXAMPLE 14

Same facts as in Example 13, except that the land was distributed to Rhonda on March 10, 2016, when its value was $43,000. If DOD is used to value the grandfather's estate, Rhonda's basis in the land is still $45,000. If the AVD is used, Rhonda's basis is $43,000 (since the distribution date occurs first).

In 2010, there was no estate tax and "modified carryover basis" rules could apply to property inherited from decedents dying in 2010. Under the modified carryover basis rules, the decedent's adjusted basis in the property (not its FMV) is used as the starting point in determining the heir's basis in inherited property. Those interested in learning more about the modified carryover basis rules that were in effect for 2010 only, should refer to IRS Publication 4895.

¶1002.04 GIFTED PROPERTY

Two sets of rules apply to property received as a gift. One set applies when, at the time of the gift, the FMV of the property is less than the donor's adjusted basis in the property. Another set applies when the FMV exceeds the donor's adjusted basis in the property.

FMV Less Than Donor's Basis

When at the time of the gift the FMV of the property is less than the donor's (adjusted) basis, the donee's basis in the property is not known until the donee (the person receiving the gift) disposes of the property. Upon disposal, the donee computes gain or loss first using the FMV of the property at the time of the gift as the donee's initial basis. If loss results, then the donee's initial basis is the FMV at the time of the gift. If a gain results, then the donor's basis usually is the donee's initial basis. However, if the second calculation does not result in a gain, then there is no gain or loss and the donee's adjusted basis equals the amount realized.

EXAMPLE 15

Joan receives stock valued at $15,000 as a gift. The donor paid $20,000 for the stock. Joan later sells the stock for $23,000. Since Joan sells the stock for more than the donor's basis, her basis in the stock is $20,000. Joan realizes a $3,000 gain ($23,000 amount realized – $20,000 basis).

EXAMPLE 16

Same facts as in Example 15, except that Joan sells the stock for $13,000. Joan sells the stock for less than the $15,000 FMV. Thus, her basis in the stock is $15,000, and she realizes a $2,000 loss ($13,000 amount realized – $15,000 basis).

EXAMPLE 17

Same facts as in Example 15, except that Joan sells the stock for $17,000. When Joan uses the $15,000 FMV ("loss basis") to compute her loss, a $2,000 gain results. When she uses the donor's $20,000 adjusted basis ("gain basis"), a $3,000 loss results. Thus, Joan realizes neither a gain nor a loss. Her basis in the stock equals $17,000 (the amount realized from the sale).

When the gifted property is depreciable property to the donee, the donee uses the donor's basis to compute depreciation expense.

FMV Exceeds Donor's Basis

If at the time of the gift the FMV of the property exceeds the donor's basis, the donee takes over the donor's basis. If the donor paid gift tax on the transfer, then the donee adds a portion of the gift tax to the basis. For gifts made prior to 1977, 100% of the gift tax is added to the donee's basis. For gifts made after 1976, only a fraction of the gift tax is added to the donee's basis. This fraction equals the ratio of the amount the property increased in value while owned by the donor (FMV at the time of the gift – donor's basis) to the taxable value of the gift. In both cases, the donee's basis cannot exceed the FMV of the property at the time of the gift.

EXAMPLE 18

In 1993 Millie received property from her uncle worth $75,000. The uncle paid $15,000 in gift tax on the transfer. The uncle's adjusted basis in the property was $30,000. Since the FMV exceeds the uncle's basis, Millie takes her uncle's $30,000 basis. While her uncle owned the property, it went up in value by $45,000 ($75,000 – $30,000). If the taxable value of the gift is $75,000, Millie adds 60% ($45,000 ÷ $75,000) of the gift tax to her basis. Millie's initial basis in the gifted property would be $39,000 [$30,000 + (60% × $15,000)].

EXAMPLE 19

Same facts as in Example 18, except that the gift occurred in 1973. Millie still takes her uncle's basis in the property, but adds 100% of the gift tax to arrive at her initial basis in the property. Millie's initial basis would be $45,000 ($30,000 + $15,000), as this amount is less than the $75,000 FMV of the gifted property.

Donee's Initial Basis in Gifted Property

When FMV at time of gift < donor's basis and donee disposes of the property for

- A gain: donee's initial basis = donor's basis
- A loss: donee's initial basis = FMV at time of gift
- No gain or loss: donee's adjusted basis = amount realized

When FMV at time of gift > donor's basis and no gift tax is paid, donee's initial basis = donor's basis

When FMV at time of gift > donor's basis and gift tax is paid, the donee's initial basis is the *lesser of*

- Pre-1977 gifts: FMV at time of gift or (donor's basis + 100% of the gift tax paid)
- Post-1976 gifts: FMV at time of gift or (donor's basis + the gift tax attributable to the increase in value)

¶1002.05 PROPERTY CONVERTED TO BUSINESS OR RENTAL USE

Instead of buying new property to use in a business or rental activity, taxpayers can convert their personal belongings to such use. For example, taxpayers can convert their homes to rental property, or they can start using their personal cars or computers in their businesses. As with gifted property, two sets of rules apply to the basis of converted property. The first set applies if the FMV of the property at the time of conversion exceeds the taxpayer's adjusted basis in the property. Another set applies if the FMV is less than the taxpayer's adjusted basis.

FMV Exceeds Adjusted Basis (Appreciated Property)

When taxpayers convert appreciated property, they use the general rule to compute the adjusted basis: Initial basis + Capital additions – Capital recoveries. If the converted property is depreciable property, they use the adjusted basis at the time of conversion to compute depreciation expense.

EXAMPLE 20

On May 4, 20x6, Donna converted her home into rental property. Donna paid $93,630 for the home in 20x0. Over the years she has made improvements to the home totaling $25,300. Thus, her adjusted basis in the home is $118,930 ($93,630 + $25,300). On May 4, 20x6, the home is worth $155,300. Donna's adjusted basis in the rental property is $118,930, since the FMV at the time of the conversion exceeds that amount. Donna uses this amount (minus the cost of the land) to compute her depreciation expense in 20x6.

FMV Less Than Adjusted Basis

When taxpayers convert property that has declined in value, the adjusted basis of the property is determined at the time they dispose of it. To compute realized gains, taxpayers use the general rule for computing adjusted basis: Initial basis + all capital additions – all capital recoveries. To compute realized losses, they use: FMV at conversion + postconversion capital additions – postconversion capital recoveries. If the converted property is depreciable property, taxpayers use the FMV of property at the time of the conversion to compute depreciation expense.

EXAMPLE 21

On January 1, 20x0, Emily converted her home to rental property. At the time of the conversion, the FMV of the home was $50,000. Emily paid $56,000 for the home and made $4,000 of capital improvements prior to 20x0. After converting the property, Emily deducted $6,000 for depreciation and made $3,000 in capital improvements. Emily sells the property for $59,000. Since at the time of conversion the $50,000 FMV was less than $60,000 the adjusted basis ($56,000 + $4,000 preconversion improvements), Emily computes an adjusted basis for gain and an adjusted basis for loss. Emily also uses the $50,000 FMV, minus the FMV of the land, as her basis for depreciating the home.

Initial basis	$56,000
Plus all capital additions ($4,000 + $3,000)	7,000
Less all capital recoveries	(6,000)
Adjusted basis for gain	$57,000

FMV at conversion	$50,000
Plus postconversion capital additions	3,000
Less postconversion capital recoveries	(6,000)
Adjusted basis for loss	$47,000

Because the amount realized exceeds the adjusted basis for gain, Emily sells the property for a gain. Using an adjusted basis of $57,000, Emily realizes a $2,000 gain ($59,000 – $57,000). Had Emily sold the property for a loss (an amount realized less than $47,000), her adjusted basis would have been $47,000. Had the amount realized been between $47,000 and $57,000, Emily would have realized no gain or loss, and her adjusted basis would be the amount realized.

Adjusted Basis in Converted Property

When at conversion FMV > adjusted basis,

- Adjusted basis = Initial basis + all capital additions – all capital recoveries
- Depreciable basis = Adjusted basis (minus the cost of the land, if any)

When at conversion FMV < adjusted basis,

- Adjusted basis for gains = Initial basis + all capital additions – all capital recoveries
- Adjusted basis for losses = FMV at conversion + postconversion capital additions – postconversion capital recoveries
- Depreciable basis = FMV at conversion (minus the FMV of the land, if any)

¶1002.06 SPECIAL RULES FOR STOCK OWNERSHIP

When taxpayers buy stock, their basis in the shares equals the purchase price plus commissions or transfer fees paid. If taxpayers acquire stock through other means (gift, inheritance, etc.), the rules presented earlier in the chapter for computing adjusted basis apply.

Identification of Shares

Taxpayers can acquire identical shares of stock in the same company at various times for different amounts. When taxpayers sell stock in that company, they should identify which shares they are selling at the time of the sale. If no identification is made, the Internal Revenue Code (Code) requires taxpayers to use the first-in, first-out method.

EXAMPLE 22

In 20x0 Hugh paid $10,000 for 1,000 shares of common stock in ABC corporation. In 20x2 he paid $12,500 for another 1,000 shares. During the current year, Hugh sells 1,000 of his shares in ABC for $11,000. If he does not specify which 1,000 were sold, the tax laws require him to use the $10,000 basis in the earliest shares he purchased. This would result in a $1,000 realized gain ($11,000 amount realized – $10,000 adjusted basis). However, if at the time of the sale, Hugh were to tell his stockbroker that he wanted to sell the 1,000 shares that he purchased in 20x2, he would have a realized loss of $1,500 ($11,000 – $12,500).

To identify shares sold, taxpayers should deliver the stock certificates to the broker or agent. If a broker or agent holds the stock certificates, then taxpayers should instruct the broker in writing which shares they wish to sell. Taxpayers should request confirmation from the broker as proof that the instructions were followed.

Stock Splits

Taxpayers owning stock may later acquire additional shares either through a stock split or a stock dividend. In a stock split, the corporation distributes to its shareholders a ratable portion of additional shares. This results in every shareholder getting more shares without affecting any shareholder's percentage ownership in the company. With a stock split, no income is realized. Taxpayers simply allocate their adjusted basis in the original shares to all shares held after the split.

EXAMPLE 23

Years ago, Portia paid $14,000 for 1,000 shares of stock in ABCO ($14 a share). During the current year, ABCO declared a two-for-one stock split. Each shareholder received two shares of stock for every one share they returned to ABCO. The shareholders of ABCO are not taxed on the split. After the split, Portia owns 2,000 shares of ABCO stock. Her adjusted basis in those shares is her original $14,000 adjusted basis in the stock. Thus, Portia's basis in each share of stock has been reduced to $7 ($14,000/2,000 shares).

Stock Dividends

Shareholders receive a stock dividend when the corporation pays them a dividend with shares of stock in the corporation, instead of cash. If shareholders have the option to receive either a stock or a cash dividend, then the cash or FMV of the stock (whichever they choose) must be included as income on the tax return. If they choose to receive a stock dividend, then the FMV of the stock becomes their basis in the newly acquired shares.

When the corporation pays shareholders a stock dividend without giving them the option of a cash dividend, it is a nontaxable event. As with stock splits, taxpayers must allocate some basis from the original shares to the shares acquired in the nontaxable stock dividend. When the stock dividend is of the same class, the taxpayer prorates the original basis among the total number of shares. An example of a *same class of stock* dividend would be a common stock shareholder receiving a common stock dividend. When the stock dividend is not of the same class, the taxpayer allocates the basis in the original shares using the relative FMV of the total shares. Taxpayers use the same formula used to allocate the purchase price among properties acquired in a basket purchase. An example of a stock dividend *not of the same class* would be a common stock shareholder receiving a preferred stock dividend.

EXAMPLE 24

Dean paid $1,100 for 50 shares of common stock. This year Dean received five shares of common stock as a nontaxable stock dividend. Dean's basis in 55 shares of common stock is $1,100, or $20 a share.

¶1002.07 RETURN-OF-CAPITAL

Corporations pay dividends from earnings and profits (E&P). E&P is roughly the same as retained earnings on the corporate balance sheet. When a corporation with no E&P distributes property (including cash) to its shareholders, the distribution is treated as a return of the shareholder's investment. The amount distributed is not taxable, but as with other capital recoveries, the shareholder reduces the basis in the stock by the amount distributed. If the amount distributed exceeds the shareholder's basis in the stock, then the shareholder realizes a gain for the excess amount.

Corporations report distributions to their shareholders on Form 1099-DIV. On this form, corporations report taxable dividends paid to the shareholder during the year (distributions from E&P), as well as distributions that represent a return of the shareholder's investment.

¶1003 Recognized Gains and Losses

Recognized gains and losses are realized gains and losses taxpayers report on their tax returns. Not all realized gains and losses result in taxable gains and losses. As a general rule, taxpayers recognize all realized gains but recognize losses only from the disposal of business or investment property. Chapter 5 described an exception to this rule that allows taxpayers to deduct casualty or theft losses on personal-use property. This chapter covers six more exceptions to the general rule.

- Losses involving wash sales
- Losses from sales between related parties
- Gains from the sale of qualified small business stock
- Gains and losses from like-kind exchanges
- Most gains from the sale of a principal residence
- Certain gains from involuntary conversions

¶1004 Wash Sales

Because securities (stocks and bonds) are an investment, the taxpayer usually recognizes any realized loss on the sale of securities. However, no loss is allowed when the taxpayer repurchases "substantially identical" securities within 30 days before or 30 days after the sale. The term used to describe these sales and repurchases is **wash sales.**

Substantially identical securities are securities *in the same company* that have similar features. For stocks, substantially identical would be the same class of stock with the same voting rights. For bonds, substantially identical would be bonds with similar interest rates and maturity dates. If the taxpayer repurchases only a fraction of the securities within the 61-day period surrounding the sale, then only that fraction of the loss is denied.

EXAMPLE 25

On January 5, 2015, Tom sold 1,000 shares of common stock in Omega Co. for $5,000. Tom's purchases of Omega common stock are shown below.

1,000 shares on June 6, 2012	$8,000
600 shares on November 6, 2014	4,500
250 shares on December 17, 2014	2,000
350 shares on January 10, 2015	3,000

Assuming Tom does not identify which shares were sold, he is assumed to have sold the 1,000 shares purchased on June 6, 2012 (see discussion at ¶1002.06). The sale results in a $3,000 realized loss ($5,000 – $8,000), which normally would be recognized for tax purposes. However, since Tom repurchased 600 (250 + 350) of the 1,000 shares between December 6, 2014, and February 4, 2015 (61 days surrounding January 5, 2015), 60% (600 ÷ 1,000) of the loss is disallowed ($3,000 × 60% = $1,800). Tom recognizes a $1,200 loss ($3,000 – $1,800) on the 400 shares sold and not repurchased.

Any disallowed loss due to a wash sale is merely postponed and will be allowed when the taxpayer later sells the (repurchased) shares. To postpone the loss, the taxpayer adds the disallowed loss to the basis of the repurchased shares.

EXAMPLE 26

In Example 25, Tom allocates the $1,800 disallowed loss among the 600 shares that caused the wash sale ($1,800 ÷ 600 = $3 a share). The basis in the 250 shares purchased on December 17, 2014 equals $2,750 [$2,000 + ($3 × 250)]. The basis in the 350 shares purchased on January 10, 2015, equals $4,050 [$3,000 + ($3 × 350)]. The basis in the 600 shares purchased on November 6, 2014, is their $4,500 cost since the shares were not involved in the wash sale.

¶1005 Sales Between Related Parties

Taxpayers usually can recognize a loss on the sale of investment or business property for less than its adjusted basis. However, taxpayers cannot recognize losses when they sell property to a related party. For tax purposes, individuals and their family members are considered to be related parties. **Family members** include spouses, siblings (brothers and sisters), descendants (children, grandchildren, etc.), and ancestors (parents, grandparents, etc.). Unlike wash sales, the disallowed loss does not increase the (related) buyer's basis in the property. Instead, the buyer can use the disallowed loss to offset any realized gain when the property is later sold. The buyer cannot use the disallowed loss to create or increase a loss.

EXAMPLE 27

Pete sold stock to his son, Stan, for $10,000. Pete bought the stock several years ago for $16,000. Although stock is investment property, Pete cannot recognize the $6,000 realized loss ($10,000 – $16,000) since he sold the stock to a related party. Stan's basis in the stock is $10,000, the amount he paid for it.

If Stan later sells the stock for $12,000, Stan's realized gain is $2,000 ($12,000 – $10,000). Stan can use $2,000 of Pete's disallowed loss to offset this gain. Thus, Stan's recognized gain is $0. Since the disallowed loss can only reduce realized gains and cannot create a loss, the rest of Pete's disallowed loss will never be used.

EXAMPLE 28

Same facts as in Example 27, except that Stan sells the stock for $9,000. Stan realizes a $1,000 loss ($9,000 – $10,000). Since a disallowed loss cannot create or increase a loss, Stan cannot use any of Pete's disallowed loss. Stan recognizes the $1,000 loss from the sale, and Pete's entire $6,000 disallowed loss is gone.

Besides individuals and their family members, related parties also involve individuals and corporations when an individual owns more than 50% of the voting stock in the corporation. Stock owned by family members counts as stock owned by the individual. This indirect ownership of stock is known as **constructive ownership.**

EXAMPLE 29

Henry owns 30% of Alpha Corporation. The following people own the rest of the stock:

Henry's aunt	35%
Henry's brother	25%
Henry's father	10%

Henry owns 30% of Alpha outright. He constructively owns the 25% owned by his brother and the 10% owned by his father. Henry's actual plus constructive ownership exceeds 50%.

EXAMPLE 30

Continuing on with Example 29, in current year, Henry sells land held as an investment to Alpha Corporation for its current FMV of $75,000. Henry paid $112,000 for the land. Since Henry's actual and constructive ownership in Alpha exceeds 50%, he cannot deduct the $37,000 loss he realizes on the sale ($75,000 amount realized – $112,000 basis). Alpha's basis in the land is the $75,000 it paid for the land.

EXAMPLE 31

Continuing on with Example 30, in a future tax year Alpha sells the land for $122,000. Its realized gain is $47,000 ($122,000 – $75,000). Alpha can use Henry's $37,000 disallowed loss to reduce its recognized gain to $10,000.

¶1006 Qualified Small Business Stock

Individuals can exclude a portion of the gain realized on the sale of Section 1202 qualified small business stock, provided the stock is held for more than five years. To qualify for the exclusion, the stock must have been purchased after August 10, 1993 as part of the corporation's original issuance of stock. Only certain corporations are able to issue qualified small business stock. These restrictions are beyond the scope of this discussion.

Purchases of Section 1202 qualified small business stock	Exclusion Percentage
On or before February 17, 2009	50%
Between February 18, 2009 and September 27, 2010	75%
Between September 28, 2010 and December 31, 2014	100%
After December 31, 2014	50%

EXAMPLE 32

On March 1, 2009, Marc acquires $100,000 of Section 1202 qualified small business stock. On May 1, 2015, he sells the stock for $230,000. Marc's realized gain from the sale is $130,000 ($230,000 – $100,000). However, since he bought the stock between February 18, 2009 and September 27, 2010 and held it for more than five years, Marc excludes 75% of the gain. Marc's recognized gain is $32,500 ($130,000 × 25%).

¶1007 Like-Kind Exchanges

Instead of selling property for cash, taxpayers can exchange property they own for other property. When this occurs, a realized gain or loss results from the difference between the FMV of the property received and the adjusted basis of the property given up. Under the general rule, taxpayers recognize all gains from such exchanges but recognize losses only from exchanges that involve business or investment property.

An exception to the general rule exists when the exchange involves like-kind property. In a like-kind exchange, taxpayers do not recognize gains or losses. Instead, realized gains and losses are postponed. To postpone gains and losses until such time that the property is disposed of in a non-like-kind exchange, taxpayers adjust the basis of the like-kind property they receive in the exchange. This new basis is also used to compute depreciation expense on depreciable property.

Basis of the new property = FMV of the new property + Postponed loss – Postponed gain

EXAMPLE 33

Jenn exchanges property with an adjusted basis of $100,000 for like-kind property valued at $60,000. Jenn realizes a $40,000 loss ($60,000 – $100,000) but does not recognize any of the loss. Jenn's basis in the new property equals $100,000 ($60,000 FMV of new property + $40,000 postponed loss). If the new property is depreciable property, she computes depreciation expense using her $100,000 basis in the property.

¶1007.01 LIKE-KIND PROPERTY

The rules just described apply only to exchanges involving like-kind property. To qualify as like-kind property, four conditions must be met.

1. A direct exchange must occur. Certain exchanges involving three parties can qualify as a direct exchange. Also, a direct exchange can occur if the property to be received is identified within 45 days and received within 180 days after the taxpayer transfers the property.
2. Both the property traded and the property received must be business or investment property.
3. Real property must be exchanged for other real property. Personal property (tangible property other than real estate) must be exchanged for similar personal property.
4. The property exchanged cannot be inventory, foreign real estate, securities (stocks and bonds), or partnership interests.

The like-kind rules are mandatory. When all four conditions are met, taxpayers must postpone any realized gain or loss resulting from the like-kind exchange. Thus, to deduct a loss resulting from a like-kind exchange, the taxpayer needs to not meet one or more of the four requirements. For example, the taxpayer could fail to meet the requirements for a direct exchange.

Like-Kind Exchanges of Business or Investment Personal Property

To qualify as a like-kind exchange, the taxpayer must exchange personal property held for business or investment for similar personal property to be held for business or investment. Similar personal property is that which is *nearly identical.* In addition to the exchanges involving similar functioning personal property, the following are examples of properties considered to be nearly identical (i.e., like-kind property).

- Office furniture, fixtures, and office equipment (copiers, fax machines, etc.) are all like-kind
- All automobiles are like-kind
- Computers, printers, and peripheral equipment are like-kind
- All light general-purpose trucks are like-kind (but light general-purpose trucks and heavy general-purpose trucks are not like-kind property)

EXAMPLE 34

A corporation exchanges an automobile for a light general purpose truck. Although both assets are vehicles, they are not considered to be nearly identical. Thus, the like-kind exchange rules would not apply to this exchange. The corporation would recognize gain or loss for the difference between the FMV of the property it receives and the adjusted basis of the property it gives up in the exchange.

EXAMPLE 35

A sole proprietor exchanges a computer for a new printer. The like-kind exchange rules apply to this exchange, as computers, printers, and peripheral equipment (devices that plug into a computer) are all considered to be nearly identical personal property (and therefore, like-kind).

Like-Kind Exchanges of Business or Investment Real Property

The like-kind exchange rules are more lenient for exchanges of real property. To qualify as a like-kind exchange, real property used for business or investment must be exchanged for any other real property to be used for business or investment. Thus, unimproved land held for investment can be exchanged for a warehouse used in the taxpayer's business. Likewise, an office building used in the taxpayer's business can be exchanged for an apartment building to be held as an investment.

EXAMPLE 36

An individual exchanges his vacation home for land he plans to hold as an investment. The like-kind exchange rules do not apply to this exchange. Although both properties exchanged are real property, the vacation home is a personal belonging. For the like-kind exchange rules to apply, real property held for business or investment must be exchanged for other real property held for business or investment.

¶1007.02 BOOT

Not all like-kind exchanges involve properties of equal value. When exchanging properties of unequal value, the one receiving property of lesser value will require more property from the other party. The non-like-kind property thrown in to even up the deal is known as **boot.** Often boot involves cash, but it can involve other property. Boot occurs when one party takes over the other party's debt. The party who assumes (takes over) the debt is treated as giving boot. The party relieved of debt is treated as receiving boot. When both parties assume each other's debt, only the net (excess) liability counts as boot. The amount of gain or loss recognized on like-kind exchanges involving boot depends on whether the taxpayer gave or received boot.

EXAMPLE 37

Elaine exchanges land valued at $100,000 for Bill's building valued at $80,000. Both properties qualify as like-kind. To even up the deal, Bill agrees to assume Elaine's $20,000 liability on the land. Elaine's release from debt is similar to her receiving $20,000 cash and using it to pay off the debt. Thus, Elaine receives $20,000 boot; Bill gives $20,000 boot.

EXAMPLE 38

Sam exchanges land valued at $80,000 for Diane's building valued at $100,000. Both properties qualify as like-kind. Sam owes $40,000 on the land; Diane owes $60,000 on the building. Both parties agree to assume each other's debt.

In this exchange, each party receives property worth $140,000. Sam receives a building worth $100,000 and is relieved of $40,000 of debt. Diane receives land valued at $80,000 and is relieved of $60,000 of debt. Because the parties assume each other's debt, only the net liability of $20,000 ($60,000 – $40,000) is treated as boot. Sam takes on more debt than he is relieved of; therefore, Sam gives $20,000 of boot. Diane is relieved of more debt than she assumed; therefore, Diane receives $20,000 of boot.

Receipt of Boot

Receiving boot has no effect on realized losses from the like-kind exchange. Those losses are postponed and increase the taxpayer's basis in the like-kind property received. However, the taxpayer's realized gains are recognized to the extent of the FMV of the boot received.

EXAMPLE 39

Ken exchanges a machine with an adjusted basis of $47,000 for a machine valued at $45,000 and $5,000 cash. Ken's realized gain equals $3,000 ($50,000 amount realized – $47,000 adjusted basis). Ken receives boot of $5,000; therefore, he recognizes the entire $3,000 gain. Ken's basis in the new machine is its FMV of $45,000 since there is no postponed gain.

EXAMPLE 40

Same facts as in Example 39, except that Ken's adjusted basis in the old machine is $42,000. Ken realizes an $8,000 gain ($50,000 – $42,000). He recognizes the gain to the extent of the boot received. Therefore, Ken reports a $5,000 gain on his tax return and postpones the rest. Ken reduces the basis in the new machine by the postponed gain ($45,000 FMV – $3,000 postponed gain = $42,000).

EXAMPLE 41

Same facts as in Example 39, except that Ken's adjusted basis in the old machine is $52,000. Ken realizes a $2,000 loss ($50,000 – $52,000). Since the receipt of boot has no effect on his realized losses, Ken postpones the entire loss and increases his basis in the new machine to $47,000 ($45,000 FMV + $2,000 postponed loss).

Boot Given

For the taxpayer that gives boot in a like-kind exchange, no gain or loss is recognized as long as the FMV of the boot equals the taxpayer's basis in the boot given. This occurs when the taxpayer gives cash or assumes the other party's debt. When the FMV of the boot is different from the taxpayer's basis in the boot given, the taxpayer is treated as having sold the boot to the other party and the taxpayer realizes a gain or loss for the difference between the FMV and the taxpayer's basis in the boot. Under the general rule, the taxpayer will recognize gain to the extent that the FMV of the boot exceeds its basis. However, if the FMV is less than the taxpayer's basis in the boot, the taxpayer will recognize a loss only if the boot was business or investment property.

¶1007.03 LIKE-KIND EXCHANGES BETWEEN RELATED PARTIES

Related parties can use the like-kind exchange rules. However, if either (related) party disposes of the like-kind property within two years after the exchange, any postponed gain or loss must be recognized in the disposal year. The basis of the like-kind property is increased by the recognized gain or reduced by the recognized loss.

EXAMPLE 42

On October 4, 20x1, Bach Enterprises exchanged one parcel of land for another parcel of land with Wendell Nathan, Bach Enterprises's sole shareholder. The land that Wendell exchanged was worth $200,000, and his basis in the land was $150,000. The land that Bach Enterprises exchanged was worth $190,000, and its basis in the land was $190,000. To even up the deal, the company paid Wendell $10,000 cash.

As a result of the like-kind exchange, Wendell realized a $50,000 gain ($200,000 FMV of the properties received – $150,000 basis in the land). He recognized a $10,000 gain (equal to the boot received), and postponed $40,000. Wendell's basis in his new land is $150,000 ($190,000 FMV of the new land – $40,000 postponed gain). Bach Enterprises, on the other hand, realized no gain or loss on the exchange ($200,000 FMV of the property received – $190,000 adjusted basis in the land – $10,000 cash paid). Its basis in the land received is its $200,000 FMV.

On August 5, 20x3, Bach Enterprises sells its new land in a non-like-kind exchange. Because the sale occurs within two years, Wendell must recognize the $40,000 of postponed gain on his 20x3 tax return. Wendell's basis in the land he received in the exchange increases to $190,000 ($150,000 + $40,000 recognized gain).

¶1008 Sale of a Principal Residence

The taxpayer's principal residence (main home) is personal-use property. Thus, when taxpayers sell their main home, usually they recognize a gain, but would not recognize a loss. However, the Code allows taxpayers to exclude up to $250,000 of the gain. Married couples that file a joint tax return can exclude up to $500,000. To qualify for the exclusion, taxpayers must use the home as their main home for two of the previous five years. Partial exclusions are available to taxpayers who fail to meet this requirement because of change in employment location, the taxpayer's health, or other specified unforeseen reasons.

To qualify for the full exclusion amount, homeowners need to own and live in the home as their main home for at least 2 years out of the 5 years ending on the date of sale. If the home is used other than as a main home after 2008 (for example, rented out or used as a second home), the $250,000/$500,000 exclusion must be reduced by the full exclusion amount times the ratio: period of nonqualifying use / period of ownership in the last 5 years. For example, take an unmarried homeowner who has owned a home for 12 years, including five months of nonqualifying use during the last 5 years. The homeowner's exclusion would be reduced by $20,833 ($250,000 × 5/60 months). Thus, the homeowner would be allowed to exclude up to $229,167 ($250,000 – $20,833) of the gain he realizes from the sale.

Due to the sizable exclusion ($250,000/$500,000), many taxpayers will not report gain when selling their main home. However, taxpayers still want to keep track of their basis in their home to show that the gain from the sale does not exceed the exclusion amount. This involves keeping a copy of the closing statement and receipts for all improvements made to the home. Any taxable gain from the sale is considered investment income for purposes of the 3.8% net investment income (NII) tax (see ¶315).

EXAMPLE 43

The Duncans sell their main home of 20 years for $200,000. Selling expenses are $10,000. The Duncans paid $50,000 for the home. The Duncans do not recognize any of the $140,000 ($200,000 – $10,000 – $50,000) gain, since this amount is less than $500,000.

EXAMPLE 44

Lincoln (a single taxpayer) sells his main home for $450,000. Selling expenses are $25,000. Lincoln paid $115,000 for the home 10 years ago. Seven years ago, he paid $15,000 to finish the basement, and six years ago, he paid $5,000 for landscaping. Of the $290,000 realized gain, Lincoln recognizes $40,000.

Sales price	$450,000
Less selling expenses	(25,000)
Amount realized	$425,000
Less adjusted basis ($115,000 + $15,000 + $5,000)	(135,000)
Realized gain	$290,000
Less $250,000 exclusion for single taxpayers	(250,000)
Recognized gain	$ 40,000

¶1009 Involuntary Conversions

Taxpayers realize a gain or loss on property involved in an involuntary conversion. The most common involuntary conversions are casualties, thefts, and condemnations.

¶1009.01 CONDEMNATION GAINS AND LOSSES

When the government exercises its right to take away the taxpayer's real property (known as a condemnation), the taxpayer is entitled to receive fair compensation in return. Most often, the taxpayer receives cash in exchange for the condemned property. Occasionally the taxpayer will receive property other than cash. Taxpayers realize a gain when the amount received from the government exceeds the adjusted basis in the condemned property. They realize a loss when the amount received is less than the adjusted basis of the property. Under the general rule, taxpayers would pay tax on all recognized gains resulting from condemnations, but deduct losses only on condemned business or investment property. There is no deduction for condemnation losses on personal-use property, even though it is an involuntary event.

¶1009.02 CASUALTY OR THEFT GAINS AND LOSSES

Taxpayers realize a casualty or theft loss when the amount of the loss exceeds the amount they are reimbursed by insurance. The amount of the loss for *personal-use property* and for *partially destroyed* business or investment property equals the *lesser of* (i) the property's adjusted basis or (ii) its decline in FMV. Decline in FMV is measured as the difference between the FMV before and after the casualty or theft. The amount of the loss for *completely destroyed (includes stolen)* business or investment property equals the adjusted basis in the property, even if the decline in FMV is less.

When the insurance proceeds exceed the amount of the loss, the taxpayer does not realize a casualty or theft loss. Instead, the taxpayer realizes a casualty or theft gain when the insurance proceeds exceed the taxpayer's adjusted basis in the property.

EXAMPLE 45

In March, Dirk's business auto was damaged in an accident. In June, Dirk's business computer was stolen. Information about the properties is shown below.

	FMV Before	FMV After	Adjusted Basis	Insurance Proceeds
Auto	$22,000	$8,000	$15,000	$16,000
Computer	3,000	0	1,000	2,900

The business auto was partially destroyed; therefore, Dirk computes his casualty loss using the *lesser of* (i) the decline in value ($22,000 – $8,000 = $14,000) or (ii) the adjusted basis ($15,000). However, because the insurance proceeds ($16,000) exceed the amount of the loss ($14,000), Dirk does not incur a casualty loss on the auto. Instead, he realizes a casualty gain for the amount by which the insurance proceeds exceed Dirk's adjusted basis in the auto ($16,000 – $15,000 = $1,000).

Since the computer is completely destroyed business property, the amount of the loss is measured as Dirk's adjusted basis in the property ($1,000). However, since the insurance proceeds exceed the amount of the loss, Dirk does not incur a casualty loss on the computer. Instead, he realizes a $1,900 casualty gain ($2,900 – $1,000 adjusted basis).

Generally, taxpayers recognize both gains and losses from casualty or theft events. Chapter 5 discussed the special rules for calculating the itemized deduction for casualty or theft losses on personal-use property (see ¶507). It should be noted that casualty and theft losses are the only deductible losses that an individual may claim on personal-use property.

¶1009.03 ELECTION TO POSTPONE RECOGNITION OF REALIZED GAINS

Under the general rule, taxpayers recognize gains from property involved in an involuntary conversion. However, taxpayers can postpone these gains if they invest the entire proceeds in qualified replacement property within a specified period of time. This provision is elective if the taxpayer receives cash for the converted property. If the election is made, taxpayers recognize a gain (up to the amount of realized gain) for amounts not reinvested.

EXAMPLE 46

The local government condemns Craig's property. The government pays Craig $200,000 for the property. The property has an adjusted basis of $170,000. Craig can avoid recognizing the $30,000 realized gain ($200,000 – $170,000) if he reinvests at least $200,000 in qualified replacement property within the required time period.

When the election is made to postpone gains, taxpayers reduce the basis in the new property by the amount of postponed gain. Assuming Craig from Example 46 buys qualified replacement property costing $190,000, he will recognize a $10,000 gain ($200,000 – $190,000) and can elect to postpone the rest ($30,000 – $10,000 = $20,000). Craig's basis in the qualified replacement property would equal $170,000 ($190,000 cost – $20,000 postponed gain).

¶1009.04 QUALIFIED REPLACEMENT PROPERTY

For property involved in an involuntary conversion, qualified replacement property normally is property related in service or use. Thus, taxpayers usually must replace an office building with another office building. Likewise, they must replace equipment with similar functioning equipment. There are two exceptions to this rule.

The first exception applies to taxpayers who lease out property involved in an involuntary conversion. Qualified replacement property for these taxpayers involves investing in other rental property. The rental property need not be of the same type. Thus, taxpayers that lease out an office building destroyed in a casualty can replace it with an apartment building or any other rental property that they lease out.

The second exception allows taxpayers to replace condemned business or investment realty with any other business or investment realty. Taxpayers can replace a condemned office building with land to be held for investment. Alternatively, they could replace it with an apartment building, a warehouse, or any other business or investment realty.

¶1009.05 REPLACEMENT PERIOD

Taxpayer realizing a gain from an involuntary conversion can postpone the gain by replacing the converted property within a specified period. The replacement period begins on the date the property was damaged, destroyed, or stolen. For condemned property, the period starts when the government officially threatens to condemn the property.

Taxpayers normally have two years after the close of the tax year (December 31 for calendar year taxpayers) in which they first realize any part of the gain to finish buying the qualified replacement property. Taxpayers whose business or investment real property is condemned by the government have one additional year (for a total of three years) to buy their qualified replacement property.

EXAMPLE 47

On October 19, 2014, Roland's business property was completely destroyed in a fire. At the time of the fire, the property was worth $40,000. Roland paid $80,000 for the property in 1992, and its adjusted basis at the time of the fire was $30,000. In 2015, the insurance company paid Roland $40,000. Roland's business casualty gain equals $10,000 ($40,000 – $30,000 adjusted basis). If Roland wants to postpone the entire gain, he must reinvest at least $40,000 in qualified replacement property between October 19, 2014, and December 31, 2017 (two years after 2015, the year in which Roland receives the proceeds and realizes the gain).

EXAMPLE 48

Same facts as in Example 47, except that the business property was condemned and in 2015 the government paid Roland $40,000 for the property. To avoid recognition of any of the $10,000 gain, Roland has from the date on which the government notified him of the condemnation until December 31, 2018 (three years after 2015) to buy qualified replacement property costing at least $40,000.

Taxpayers whose main home is destroyed in a casualty in a federally declared disaster area, are given an two extra years to reinvest in qualified replacement property. In essence, this gives them until December 31 of the fourth year after the year in which a gain is realized to invest in another home that they use as their main home.

EXAMPLE 49

The Hunters' main home was badly damaged by fire in a federally declared disaster area. The Hunters received $820,000 from their insurance company in 2015. The Hunters' basis in the home is $270,000. In order to postpone the entire $550,000 gain realized in 2015 ($820,000 – $270,000 adjusted basis), the Hunters have until December 31, 2019 (four years after 2015, the year the proceeds were received and the gain was first realized) to use the $820,000 proceeds to buy (or build) a new main home.

10

Name:

Section:

Date:

QUESTIONS AND PROBLEMS

1. **Amount Realized, Realized Gain or Loss.** (Obj. 1) Jamie sells land that has a $60,000 mortgage. In return for the land, Jamie receives cash of $40,000 and stock with a FMV of $30,000. The buyer also assumes the mortgage. Jamie's adjusted basis in the land is $80,000.

   a. What is Jamie's amount realized?

   b. What is Jamie's realized gain or loss?

   c. How would your answers to Parts a. and b. change if the buyer had not assumed the mortgage but instead had paid Jamie an additional $60,000 to pay off the mortgage?

2. **Adjusted Basis, Realized Gain or Loss.** (Obj. 1) Alexis sells for $200,000 rental property that she purchased in 2004 for $160,000. In 2006, Alexis spent $12,000 on landscaping and $2,200 on repairs. Over the years, Alexis has deducted a total of $18,440 for depreciation on the property. Compute Alexis's realized and recognized gain or loss on the sale.

3. **Basket Purchase.** (Obj. 1) Leo purchased an apartment building. Leo paid $300,000 in cash, assumed a $200,000 mortgage, and paid the following:

Brokerage commission	$35,000
Attorney's fee to acquire title	2,000

   What is Leo's basis for depreciation on this building if the FMV of the land and building are $100,000 and $400,000, respectively?

4. **Bargain Purchase.** (Obj. 1) Dan, president of Sugarman Corporation, was given the opportunity to buy 1,000 shares of the corporation's stock for $120 per share. The par value of the stock was $100. Dan took advantage of this offer and purchased 100 shares of stock at a time when the stock was selling for $150 per share. Dan includes as income the difference between the FMV of the stock and his cost. The company also gave Dan an additional 100 shares of stock as a bonus when the stock was selling for $160 per share.

   a. What amount of income must Dan recognize as a result of these stock acquisitions?

   b. What is Dan's per-share basis in the stock he acquired?

5. **Property Received in a Divorce.** (Obj. 1) Hal and Wendy are divorced. Under the terms of the divorce agreement, Hal transferred 100 shares of Big Rig stock (cost $30,000, fair market value $45,000) to Wendy in satisfaction of Wendy's property rights. If Wendy sells the stock for $50,000, what is her recognized gain?

6. **Inherited Property.** (Obj. 1) Terry purchased 5,000 shares of Ferrero Corporation stock in 2000 for $60,000. Terry died on December 11, 2015, leaving the stock to his daughter, Debra. Debra received the stock on April 26, 2016. The FMV of the stock for various dates follows.

December 11, 2015	$80,000
April 26, 2016	78,000
June 11, 2016	77,000

   a. Debra sold the stock for $75,000 on August 28, 2016. What is Debra's recognized gain or loss from the sale if the executor uses date of death (DOD) to value the estate?

   b. Same as in Part a. except that the executor uses the alternative valuation date (AVD).

   c. Assume instead that Debra received the stock on August 17, 2016, when the FMV of the stock was $79,000. What is Debra's recognized gain or loss if the executor uses DOD to value the estate?

   d. Same as in Part c. except that the executor uses the AVD to value the estate.

7. **Gifted Property.** (Obj. 1) Max purchased 100 shares of XQM stock in 1998 for $10,000. In 2004 Max gave the stock to his daughter, Linda, when the FMV of the stock was $8,000. No gift tax was paid.

   a. What is Linda's basis in the stock if she sells it in the current year for $11,000?

   b. What is Linda's basis in the stock if she sells it in the current year for $9,000?

   c. What is Linda's recognized gain or loss if she sells the stock in the current year for $7,000?

8. **Gifted Property.** (Obj. 1) In 1972, Tammy gave her son, Al, land worth $80,000. Tammy paid $60,000 for the land in 1970. The full $80,000 value was subject to gift tax, and Tammy paid $12,000 in gift tax on the transfer. What is Al's basis in the land?

9. **Gifted Property.** (Obj. 1) In 2015, Bruce gave Shirley a house worth $100,000. Bruce's adjusted basis in the house was $80,000. The full $100,000 value of the house was subject to gift tax, and Bruce paid $8,000 in gift tax on the transfer. What is Shirley's initial basis in the house?

10. **Gifted Property.** (Obj. 1) Darren gave stock worth $27,000 to his son. Darren paid $9,000 for the stock back in 1954. The full $27,000 value was subject to gift tax, and Darren paid $5,000 of gift tax on the transfer. In 2015, the son sold the stock for $42,000.

    a. Compute the son's recognized gain or loss assuming that the gift took place in 1970.

    b. Same as in Part a. except that the gift took place in 1985.

11. **Converted Property.** (Obj. 1) In 2007, Parker converted his personal residence to rental property. The FMV of the home at the time of conversion was $85,000, Parker paid $90,000 for the home ten years ago.

a. If Parker sells the property for $100,000 after taking depreciation deductions of $10,000, what is his recognized gain or loss?

b. Same as in Part a. except that Parker sells the property for $70,000.

c. Same as in Part a. except that Parker sells the property for $78,000.

12. **Sale of Stock.** (Obj. 1) Ima had the following purchases of common stock in the same company.

2000	400 shares at $10 per share
2003	100 shares at $20 per share
2006	300 shares at $30 per share
2008	200 shares at $40 per share

a. In 2015, Ima sold 500 shares at $35 per share. Assuming Ima did not identify which blocks of stock were sold, compute her recognized gain or loss on the sale.

b. If Ima's objective is to minimize taxes and she could adequately identify which stock she was selling, which stock should she sell, and what is the recognized gain or loss that would result?

13. **Stock Splits.** (Obj. 1) Diane owned 100 shares of common stock in the Delta Corporation when it had a two-for-one-stock split. The original 100 shares cost $50 each, for a total cost of $5,000. After the split, Diane had 200 shares that were valued at $30 each, for a total value of $6,000. As a result of the stock split, what is Diane's basis in each share of stock, and how much income must she recognize?

14. **Stock Dividends.** (Obj. 1) In 1998, Patrick paid $1,200 for 100 shares of UPI common stock. In the current year, UPI offers Patrick the choice between a $50 cash dividend or 8 additional shares of common stock valued at $9 a share. Patrick opts for the stock dividend.

    a. What is Patrick's basis in each of the 108 shares he now owns?

    b. How would your answer to Part a. change if Patrick did not have the option of a cash dividend?

15. **Wash Sales.** (Obj. 2) An individual taxpayer, not a dealer or trader in securities, completed the transactions shown below for Micro Products Company common stock.

    September 15, 2015, purchased 100 shares at a cost of $4,800
    December 10, 2015, sold the above shares for $3,200
    January 4, 2016, purchased 60 shares at a cost of $1,800

    a. Compute the recognized gain or loss from the December 10 sale and the taxpayer's basis in the stock purchased on January 4.

    b. Same as in Part a., except that the sales price of the shares sold on December 10 was $5,300.

    c. Compute the recognized gain or loss from the December 10 sale and the taxpayer's basis in the stock purchased on January 4 assuming that (i) the sales price of the shares sold on December 10 was $3,200 and (ii) the shares of stock sold on December 10 had been inherited by the taxpayer from the taxpayer's father on September 15, 2015. At the time of the father's death, the shares were valued at $2,500. The father had purchased the stock two months earlier for $2,000. No estate tax return was filed.

16. **Sale to a Related Party.** (Obj. 3) Fred sold stock ($12,000 cost basis) to his sister, Sara, for $9,000. Three years later Sara sold the stock for $14,000 to an unrelated party.

a. What was Fred's recognized loss when he sold the stock to Sara?

b. What is Sara's basis in the stock she purchased from Fred?

c. What is Sara's recognized gain or loss when she sells the stock?

d. If Sara had sold the stock for $11,000, what would be her recognized gain or loss?

e. If Sara had sold the stock for $7,000, what would be her recognized gain or loss?

17. **Sale to a Related Party.** (Obj. 3) Reed sold land to ABC company for $70,000. Reed paid $95,000 for the land 3 years ago. Reed owns 10% of the shares in ABC. The rest of the shares are owned by Reed's father (20%), Reed's uncle (15%), Reed's grandfather (30%), Reed's sister (10%), Reed's cousin (10%) and Reed's son (5%).

a. Compute Reed's realized and recognized gain or loss on the sale as well as ABC's basis in the land.

b. Compute ABC's realized and recognized gain or loss if it later sells the land for $85,000.

c. Same as in Part b., except that ABC sells the land for $115,000.

18. Qualified Small Business Stock. (Obj. 1) Jenson pays $30,000 for Section 1202 qualified small business stock on February 16, 2005. In October 2015, Jenson sells the stock for $80,000.

a. Compute Jenson's realized and recognized gain on the sale.

b. How, if at all, would your answer to Part a. change if the stock were purchased on February 16, 2012?

19. Like-Kind Exchange. (Obj. 4) Which of the following qualify as a like-kind exchange?

a. Exchanging a grocery store for a rental duplex

b. Exchanging an apartment building for a parking lot

c. Exchanging Chrysler common stock for land to be held for investment

d. Exchanging shares of Ford common stock for shares of GM common stock

e. Exchanging residential rental property for a personal residence

20. Like-Kind Exchange. (Obj. 4) Which of the following qualify as a like-kind exchange?

a. Exchanging an old computer for a new computer (both used in business)

b. Exchanging inventory for a computer (used in business)

c. Exchanging an old personal auto for a new business auto

d. Exchanging office furniture for office equipment (both used in business)

e. Exchanging an automobile for machinery (both used in business)

21. Like-Kind Exchange. (Obj. 4) Dottie exchanges investment real estate for other investment real estate. The following facts relate to the exchange.

Adjusted basis of old property	$ 75,000
FMV of new property	100,000
Cash received by Dottie	10,000
Mortgage on old property assumed by other party	30,000

a. Compute Dottie's realized and recognized gain.

b. Compute Dottie's basis in the new property.

22. **Like-Kind Exchange.** (Obj. 4) For each of the following like-kind exchanges, compute the taxpayer's realized and recognized gain or loss, as well as the basis of the new property acquired.

	Basis of Old Asset	*FMV of New Asset*	*Cash Exchanged*
a.	$ 8,000	$ 5,000	$0
b.	6,000	10,000	$5,000 paid
c.	6,000	10,000	$2,000 paid
d.	10,000	7,000	$2,000 received
e.	10,000	7,000	$5,000 received
f.	10,000	11,000	$2,000 received

23. **Like-Kind Exchange.** (Obj. 4) Bufford wants Jack's farm as a site for an amusement park and offers him $200,000 for the farm. Jack does not want to sell his farm, which has a basis to Jack of $50,000. Bufford is now considering acquiring another farm for $180,000 and then offering that farm plus $20,000 to Jack in exchange for his farm. If Jack accepts this offer, what are the tax consequences?

24. **Sale of a Principal Residence.** (Obj. 1) Adam, who is single, sold his principal residence for $440,000. He paid $28,000 in selling expenses. Adam paid $107,000 for the house 17 years ago. Over the years Adam made improvements and repairs to the house totaling $42,000 and $26,000, respectively. Compute Adam's recognized gain on the sale of his home.

25. **Involuntary Conversion.** (Obj. 5) The Wholesale Dress Shop was destroyed by fire in January. The adjusted basis of the building was $150,000. In March, the insurance company paid $140,000 to cover the loss. Shortly thereafter a new building (dress shop) was purchased for $200,000.

a. What is the Shop's recognized gain or loss?

b. What is the basis of the new building?

26. **Involuntary Conversion.** (Obj. 5) Duffy & Co.'s warehouse, which had an adjusted basis of $1,100,000, was destroyed by fire. Duffy received $2,000,000 from the insurance company. Duffy immediately invested $1,800,000 in a new warehouse and elected to postpone as much of the gain as possible.

    a. What is the amount of gain recognized for income tax purposes?

    b. What is the basis of the new warehouse?

27. **Involuntary Conversion.** (Obj. 5) On February 17, 2015, Kari was notified by the state that land she owned as an investment was needed for a state park and that the land would be condemned. The state took possession of the land on January 15, 2016, and Kari received her condemnation award on January 20, 2016.

    a. If Kari elects to postpone recognition of her gain, by what date must she purchase replacement property?

    b. What type of property could Kari purchase and still postpone recognition of her gain?

28. **Internet Problem: Researching IRS Publication 550.** (Obj. 1)

    Beta Corporation is a C Corporation whose total gross assets have never exceeded $35 million. Trish Newton purchased stock from Beta Corporation in March 2005 as part of Beta's initial issuance. Trish is interested in selling her stock in Beta Corporation and wants to know whether Beta Corporation meets the requirements of a qualified small business corporation under Section 1202.

    Go to the IRS website. Locate IRS Publication 550 and find the appropriate page that discusses the requirements for a qualified small business corporation under Section 1202. Print out a copy of the page where you found your answer. Underline or highlight the pertinent information. Comment on whether you can answer Trish's question with the information that has been provided.

    See Appendix A for instructions on use of the IRS website.

29. Business Entity Problem: This problem is designed for those using the "business entity" approach. **The solution may require information from Chapter 14.**

Davis converts his sole proprietorship into a regular C corporation. The basis of the assets he transfers into the corporation is $225,000. The fair market value is $265,000. In return for these assets, Davis received all of the corporation's stock—50,000 shares.

a. What is the basis of these assets to the corporation?

b. What is Davis's basis in stock he receives?

CUMULATIVE PROBLEM (CHAPTERS 8-10)

On September 29, 2015, Tripper sold rental property for $230,000. Five percent of the sales price was allocated to the furnishings. Tripper originally purchased the home (a condominium) in 1992, and uses it as his main home. He paid $160,000 for the home and spent $35,000 on its furnishings. From 1992-2008, Tripper made improvements to the home totaling $34,000. On March 4, 2009, he converted the home to rental property. The fair market value (FMV) of the home itself at the time of the conversion was $182,000. The FMV of the furnishings were $5,000. Tripper used MACRS to depreciate both the condo and its furnishings. This was the only depreciable property Tripper placed in service during 2009. Compute Tripper's recognized gain or loss on the sale of the home and on the sale of its furnishings.

Chapter

11

Property: Capital Gains and Losses, and Depreciation Recapture

CHAPTER CONTENTS

LEARNING OBJECTIVES

After completing Chapter 11, you should be able to:

1. Distinguish between capital assets, Section 1231 property, and ordinary income property.
2. Determine the character of recognized gains and losses.
3. Understand how the netting process works, including how to determine the amount of the taxpayer's capital loss deduction, capital loss carryover, or net capital gain.
4. Compute an individual's tax liability when taxable income includes qualified dividends or net capital gain.
5. Understand the impact of depreciation recapture and nonrecaptured 1231 losses on the taxpayer's taxable income and tax liability.
6. Compute the amount of gain to be recognized each year from an installment sale, and the character of that gain.
7. Complete the various forms and schedules introduced in this chapter, including Form 8949, Schedule D, Form 4684 (Section B), and Form 4797.

CHAPTER OVERVIEW

Chapter 10 covered the calculation of realized gains and losses from the sale, exchange, or other disposal of property. It also covered which realized gains and losses taxpayers recognize for tax purposes. This chapter examines the character of those gains and losses. Recognized gains may be capital gains or ordinary income. Recognized losses may be treated as capital losses or ordinary deductions. The distinction is important because capital gains and losses are treated differently than ordinary gains and losses. This chapter explains which gains and losses are capital and which are ordinary. It also shows where taxpayers report gains and losses on the tax return.

¶1101 Capital Gains and Losses

The tax laws treat capital gains and losses differently from ordinary gains and losses. Individual taxpayers are limited on the amount of capital losses they can deduct each year, whereas reduced tax rates may apply to capital gains. There are several ways gains and losses can be classified as capital gains and losses. The most common way is through the sale or exchange of a capital asset.

¶1101.01 CAPITAL ASSETS DEFINED

All property that taxpayers own is a capital asset unless it falls into one of the following five categories:

1. Inventory held primarily for sale to customers. This includes property that will become part of inventory, such as raw materials and work-in-process.
2. Business receivables, including accounts and notes receivable.
3. Depreciable property and land used in a trade or business.
4. Copyrights; literary, musical, or artistic compositions created by the taxpayer; or letters and memorandums created by, prepared for, or produced for the taxpayer. (However, composers of musical compositions and creators of copyrights may elect to treat their works as capital assets.)
5. U.S. government publications purchased for less than the normal sales price.

A closer look at the five categories reveals that the first three involve business property. Thus, except for items described in the last two categories, capital assets can be defined as the taxpayer's personal belongings and investment property. Common examples of capital assets include the taxpayer's clothing, residence, and automobiles (personal-use property). Other examples include stock, bonds, and land held for speculation (investment property).

Using the rules from Chapter 10, taxpayers compute the realized gains and losses that result from the sale or exchange of capital assets. Next, they determine which realized gains and losses they recognize for tax purposes. (Recall from Chapter 10 that not all realized gains and losses are recognized on the tax return.) Taxpayers then classify the recognized gains and losses as short-term or long-term capital gains and losses.

Short-term capital gains and losses result from the sale or exchange of capital assets held for one year or less. **Long-term capital gains and losses** result if the capital asset was held for more than one year. In determining whether property has been held for more than one year, the date taxpayers acquire property does not count, but the disposal date does.

EXAMPLE 1 On June 3, 20x1, Thomas buys 100 shares of common stock. Thomas's holding period begins on June 4, 20x1. On June 4, 20x2, Thomas will have held the shares for more than one year. If Thomas sells the shares after June 3, 20x2, he will recognize a long-term capital gain or loss. This, of course, assumes that neither the wash sale rules nor the related party rules from Chapter 10 prevent Thomas from recognizing a loss on the sale.

¶1101.02 HOLDING PERIODS FOR PROPERTY

Not all holding periods begin the day after the taxpayer physically acquires property. Special rules apply to inherited property and to property with a carryover basis.

Inherited Property

With the exception of property inherited from decedents dying in 2010 where the carryover basis rules applied, the holding period for property inherited from a decedent is considered to be long-term, regardless of the actual holding period.

EXAMPLE 2

Mariah inherited stock from her aunt. Mariah's basis in the stock is its $10,000 fair market value (FMV) on the date of her aunt's death on March 3, 2015. Mariah sold the stock $12,400 on November 5, 2015. Although Mariah's ownership of the property did not exceed one year, she recognizes a $2,400 long-term capital gain ($12,400 – $10,000) on the sale of inherited stock.

Carryover Basis Property

When property has a carryover basis, the holding period also carries over. A carryover basis and holding period can occur one of three ways.

1. The taxpayer uses the previous owner's basis to compute the basis in property. This occurs with transfers of property between spouses, gifted property where the taxpayer uses the donor's basis, and property inherited from decedents dying in 2010 where the carryover basis rules were used. In these cases, the previous owner's holding period carries over to the taxpayer.
2. The taxpayer allocates part of the basis in existing property to the basis of newly acquired property. This happens with nontaxable stock dividends and stock splits. When these events occur, the holding period of the original property carries over to the new property.
3. The taxpayer adjusts the basis in property to reflect a postponed gain or loss from previously owned property. This can occur with like-kind exchanges, involuntary conversions, and wash sales. In these cases, the holding period of the old property becomes the holding period of the new property.

EXAMPLE 3

On July 11, 20x9, Tara gave her nephew, Morgan, stock worth $6,000. Tara paid $7,000 for the stock on May 9, 20x2. Morgan sells the stock on December 21, 20x9, for $7,500.

Recall from Chapter 10 that when the FMV of gifted property is less than the donor's basis, the donee's basis is determined when the donee disposes of the property (¶1002.04). The donee uses the donor's basis to compute gains, and the FMV of the property at the time of the gift to compute losses. Because Morgan sells the stock for a gain (more than the donor's basis), his basis in the stock is the donor's basis. Using his aunt's basis, Morgan realizes a $500 gain ($7,500 – $7,000). Since Morgan uses the donor's basis as his basis in the stock, his holding period begins on May 10, 20x2 (the day after the day his aunt bought the stock). Therefore, Morgan recognizes a $500 long-term capital gain.

EXAMPLE 4

On May 7, 20x7, Norm received land as part of a divorce settlement. Norm holds the land as an investment. He sells the land for $72,500 on December 4, 20x7. Norm's wife paid $30,000 for the land in 20x0. Norm's holding period dates back to 20x0 – the date on which his spouse bought the land. The wife's basis carries over and becomes Norm's basis in the land (¶1002.02). Thus, Norm recognizes a $42,500 long-term capital gain ($72,500 – $30,000).

EXAMPLE 5

On March 10, 20x8, Doug exchanges land for a building in a like-kind exchange. Doug's holding period for the land dates back to August 18, 20x0. Doug's holding period in the building acquired in the like-kind exchange begins on August 18, 20x0.

¶1101.03 NETTING CAPITAL GAINS AND LOSSES

The netting process begins by separating short-term gains and losses from long-term capital gains and losses. The netting process continues by offsetting the gains and losses within each of these two groups. The result is a *net short-term capital gain or loss* and a *net long-term capital gain or loss.*

EXAMPLE 6

Mandy sold the following capital assets during the year.

Description	Gain (Loss)	Group
Stock held 6 months	$ 5,000	short-term
Stock held 8 months	(7,000)	short-term
Stock held 3 years	(14,000)	long-term
Stock held 6 years	21,000	long-term

The first step in the netting process involves separating the gains and losses into two groups (see the column **Group** above). Mandy then begins netting within each group.

Short-Term	Long-Term
$5,000	($14,000)
(7,000)	21,000
($2,000)	$ 7,000

The netting process produces a $2,000 net short-term capital loss and a $7,000 net long-term capital gain.

When a net gain results in both groups, the netting process is complete. Likewise, the netting process is complete when both groups show a net loss. Otherwise, netting losses against gains between the two groups occurs. Examples 7, 8, and 9 demonstrate netting between groups.

EXAMPLE 7

Continuing with Example 6, Mandy offsets the $2,000 net short-term loss against the $7,000 net long-term gain. This leaves Mandy with a $5,000 overall net long-term capital gain.

Short-Term	Long-Term
$5,000	($14,000)
(7,000)	21,000
($2,000)	$ 7,000
→	(2,000)
	$ 5,000

EXAMPLE 8

Brook sold four capital assets during the year. After separating the gains and losses into two groups, Brook nets the gains and losses within each group. This netting within groups produces a $2,000 net short-term loss and a $3,000 net long-term loss. Since both groups result in a loss, the netting process is complete.

Short-Term	Long-Term
$6,000	$ 1,000
(8,000)	(4,000)
($2,000)	$(3,000)

EXAMPLE 9

Ace sold five capital assets during the year. After separating the gains and losses into two groups, he nets the gains and losses within each group. This netting within groups results in a $5,000 net short-term capital gain, and a $1,000 net long-term capital loss. Ace uses the $1,000 net long-term capital loss to offset his net short-term gain. This leaves Ace with a $4,000 overall net short-term capital gain.

Short-Term	Long-Term
($13,000)	$ 3,000
7,000	(4,000)
11,000	
$ 5,000	($ 1,000)
(1,000) ←	
$ 4,000	

Once the netting process is complete, individual taxpayers with a net capital gain pay a reduced tax rate on the net capital gain. **Net capital gain** equals the excess of net long-term capital gain over net short-term capital loss. If the netting process produces a net long-term capital loss or an overall capital loss, then the taxpayer has $0 net capital gain. If the netting process produces both a net long-term capital gain and a net short-term capital gain, then net capital gain equals the net long-term capital gain.

Taxpayers with net capital gain or qualified dividends compute their tax liability by subtracting out these amounts from taxable income and computing tax on the remaining amount. They then add to this amount the tax on the net capital gain and qualified dividends. The tax rate on net capital gain and qualified dividends is 0% for taxpayers whose taxable income both with and without these items falls in the 10% or 15% tax brackets. The rate increases to 15% for taxpayers whose taxable income both with and without these items falls in the 25%, 28%, 33% or 35% tax brackets. A 20% tax rate applies to taxpayers whose taxable income both with and without these items falls in the highest (39.6%) tax bracket.

Recall from Chapter 5 (¶505.04) that taxpayers can deduct investment interest expense to the extent that they have net investment income. Taxpayers can elect to treat any amount of qualified dividends or net capital gain as investment income as long as they tax those amounts at the (higher) ordinary income tax rates. Thus, when this election is made, any amounts treated as investment income would remain in taxable income when computing the taxpayer's tax liability using the method shown in Examples 10, 11 and 12.

EXAMPLE 10

Abby's taxable income for 2015 is $135,000. Abby's filing status is single. Included in taxable income is $15,000 of net capital gain. Abby's 2015 tax liability is computed as follows.

Tax on $120,000 ($135,000 – $15,000 net capital gain)	$26,671
Plus $15,000 × 15% (Abby is in the 28% bracket)	2,250
Tax liability on $135,000	$28,921

EXAMPLE 11

Same facts as in Example 10, except that Abby's taxable income is $440,000.

Tax on $425,000 ($440,000 – $15,000)	$124,669
Plus $15,000 × 20% (Abby is in the 39.6% bracket)	3,000
Tax liability on $440,000	$127,669

For taxpayers whose taxable income with the net capital gain and qualified dividends falls in the 25%–35% tax brackets, but whose taxable income without these items drops down to the 10% or 15% tax bracket, only part of the net capital gain will be taxed at 0%. The rest will be taxed at 15%. Similarly, for taxpayers whose taxable income including these items falls in the 39.6% tax bracket, but whose taxable income without these items drops to a lower tax bracket, only part of the gain will be taxed at 20%. The rest will be taxed at a lower rate.

EXAMPLE 12

Same facts as in Example 10, except that Abby's taxable income is $50,000, which falls in the 25% tax bracket (the cutoff is $37,450 – see tax rate Schedule X on the inside front cover of this textbook). However, when you take out the qualified dividends ($0) and net capital gain ($15,000), taxable income drops to $35,000, which is in the 15% tax bracket. Thus, only $2,450 of her net capital gain ($37,450 – $35,000) is taxed at the lowest 0% tax rate. The rest is taxed at 15%.

Tax on $35,000 (using the tax table for Single taxpayers)	$ 4,793
Plus $2,450 × 0%	0
Plus ($15,000 – $2,450) × 15%	1,883
Tax liability on $50,000	$ 6,676

i

Net capital gains from the sale of Section 1202 qualified small business stock (¶1006) and from the sale of collectibles are taxed at a higher 28% rate for taxpayers in the 28% or higher tax brackets. Collectibles include any work of art, rugs, antiques, gemstones, stamp collections and coin collections. Those interested in learning more about how gains and losses from these assets fit into the netting process should refer to the Instructions to Schedule D (Form 1040).

Net Capital Losses

When capital losses exceed capital gains, the excess is a net capital loss. Each year, individual taxpayers can use up to $3,000 of net capital losses to offset ordinary income ($1,500 for married taxpayers who file as married filing separately (MFS)). Ordinary income is income taxed at the taxpayer's regular (ordinary) tax rate. Examples of ordinary income include wages, interest, dividends, and net profit from a business.

Any net capital loss in excess of $3,000 ($1,500 for MFS) can be carried forward indefinitely. Should the netting process produce both a net short-term and a net long-term capital loss, taxpayers first use up their net short-term capital loss, and then their net long-term capital loss. For individual taxpayers, any unused long-term capital loss is carried over to the next year to offset next year's long-term capital gains. Any unused short-term capital loss is carried over to the next year to offset next year's short-term capital gains.

EXAMPLE 13

In 2015, Moe sold three capital assets that produced a $4,000 short-term gain, a $13,000 short-term capital loss, and a $2,000 long-term capital loss. Moe is married, but files as married filing separately.

Short-Term	Long-Term
$ 4,000	($2,000)
(13,000)	
($ 9,000)	($2,000)

Moe's capital losses exceed capital gains by $11,000. He uses $1,500 (limit for MFS) of the net short-term capital loss to offset ordinary income on his 2015 tax return. Moe carries over to 2016 a $7,500 short-term capital loss ($9,000 – $1,500) and a $2,000 long-term capital loss.

EXAMPLE 14

Heather is single. In 2015, she sells three capital assets that produce a $5,000 short-term gain, a $1,000 long-term gain, and a $4,000 long-term capital loss. Heather has a $6,000 short-term capital loss carryover and a $2,000 long-term capital loss carryover from 2014. She nets these amounts against her 2015 capital gains and losses as shown below.

	Short-Term	Long-Term
carryover	($6,000)	($2,000)
	5,000	1,000
		(4,000)
	($1,000)	($5,000)

Heather uses the $1,000 net short-term capital loss and $2,000 of the net long-term capital loss to offset ordinary income on her 2015 tax return. She carries over to 2016 a $3,000 long-term capital loss ($5,000 – $2,000).

EXAMPLE 15

Continuing with Example 14, Heather sells two capital assets in 2016. Those assets produce a $14,000 long-term capital gain and a $2,000 short-term capital loss. Heather's netting process in 2016 is as follows.

	Short-Term	Long-Term
carryover		($ 3,000)
	($2,000)	14,000
	($2,000)	$11,000
	→	(2,000)
		$ 9,000

Heather uses the $3,000 long-term capital loss carryover from 2015 to offset the $14,000 long-term capital gain generated in 2016. She then offsets the $2,000 net short-term capital loss against the net long-term capital gain. Her $9,000 net capital gain will be taxed at a reduced tax rate.

EXAMPLE 16

Same facts as in Example 15, except that instead of a $14,000 long-term capital gain in 2016, Heather incurs a $14,000 long-term capital loss. In this scenario, Heather's $3,000 long-term capital loss carryover from 2015 is added to her $14,000 long-term capital loss from 2016 to produce a total $17,000 net long-term capital loss.

	Short-Term	Long-Term
carryover		($ 3,000)
	($2,000)	(14,000)
	($2,000)	($17,000)

Since the netting within the two groups results in both a net short-term loss and a net long-term capital loss, the netting process stops. Heather uses the $2,000 short-term capital loss and $1,000 of the long-term capital loss to offset her ordinary income on her 2016 tax return. This leaves Heather with a $16,000 long-term capital loss carryover ($17,000 - $1,000) to 2017.

¶1101.04 FORM 8949 AND SCHEDULE D

Individual taxpayers report the details of their sales of capital assets on Form 8949, Sales and Other Dispositions of Capital Assets. They then transfer the totals to Schedule D (Form 1040), Capital Gains and Losses. On both Form 8949 and Schedule D, short-term capital gains and losses are reported in Part I, and long-term capital gains and losses are reported in Part II.

¶1101.05 FILLED-IN FORM 8949 AND SCHEDULE D

INFORMATION FOR SCHEDULE 11-1:

On **November 20, 2015**, Curt Stevens (single, age 40) sold **100 shares of Comco Corporation common stock** for $2,975. Curt paid a $20 commission on the sale. He purchased the stock on **June 27, 2015**, for **$750**. On **September 3, 2015**, Curt sold **100 shares of Wilcox Industries preferred stock** for $6,000. He paid a $120 commission on the sale. Curt received the stock as a gift from his father on May 8, 2009. The FMV of the stock on May 8, 2009, was $9,000. His father paid $3,192 for the stock, and the father's holding period started on February 7, 2004. The father did not pay gift tax on the transfer. Curt has a $1,000 short-term capital loss carryover from 2014.

Curt enters the information in bold on the appropriate lines of Form 8949. Form 1099-B shows that Curt's basis in the stock was not reported to the IRS. Therefore, Curt marks boxes **(B)** and **(E)** located immediately above line 1.

Line # (Form 8949, page 1)

1(d): Proceeds, **$2,955** ($2,975 – $20 selling expenses)

Line # (Form 8949, page 2)

1(b): Date acquired, **2/7/04** (donor's holding period carries over since donor's basis is used)
1(d): Proceeds, **$5,880** ($6,000 – $120 selling expenses)
1(e): Cost or other basis, **$3,192** (donor's basis carries over since donor's basis is less than the FMV of the stock at the time of the gift)

Curt finishes filling out Form 8949 by adding up the amounts reported in columns (d)–(h) and entering the totals on line 2 at the bottom of both pages of the form.

Figure 11-1: Filled-In Form 8949 (Page 1)

Form **8949**

Department of the Treasury
Internal Revenue Service

Sales and Other Dispositions of Capital Assets

▶ Information about Form 8949 and its separate instructions is at *www.irs.gov/form8949.*

▶ File with your Schedule D to list your transactions for lines 1b, 2, 3, 8b, 9, and 10 of Schedule D.

OMB No. 1545-0074

2015

Attachment Sequence No. **12A**

Name(s) shown on return	Social security number or taxpayer identification number
Curtis R. Stevens	992-84-5922

Before you check Box A, B, or C below, see whether you received any Form(s) 1099-B or substitute statement(s) from your broker. A substitute statement will have the same information as Form 1099-B. Either will show whether your basis (usually your cost) was reported to the IRS by your broker and may even tell you which box to check.

Part I **Short-Term.** Transactions involving capital assets you held 1 year or less are short term. For long-term transactions, see page 2.

Note: You may aggregate all short-term transactions reported on Form(s) 1099-B showing basis was reported to the IRS and for which no adjustments or codes are required. Enter the totals directly on Schedule D, line 1a; you aren't required to report these transactions on Form 8949 (see instructions).

You *must* check Box A, B, *or* C below. Check only one box. If more than one box applies for your short-term transactions, complete a separate Form 8949, page 1, for each applicable box. If you have more short-term transactions than will fit on this page for one or more of the boxes, complete as many forms with the same box checked as you need.

☐ **(A)** Short-term transactions reported on Form(s) 1099-B showing basis was reported to the IRS (see **Note** above)

☑ **(B)** Short-term transactions reported on Form(s) 1099-B showing basis was **not** reported to the IRS

☐ **(C)** Short-term transactions not reported to you on Form 1099-B

1 (a) Description of property (Example: 100 sh. XYZ Co.)	(b) Date acquired (Mo., day, yr.)	(c) Date sold or disposed of (Mo., day, yr.)	(d) Proceeds (sales price) (see instructions)	(e) Cost or other basis. See the **Note** below and see *Column (e)* in the separate instructions	Adjustment, if any, to gain or loss. If you enter an amount in column (g), enter a code in column (f). See the separate instructions. (f) Code(s) from instructions	(g) Amount of adjustment	(h) Gain or (loss). Subtract column (e) from column (d) and combine the result with column (g)
100 sh Comco common stk	6-27-15	11-20-15	2,955	750			2,205
2 Totals. Add the amounts in columns (d), (e), (g), and (h) (subtract negative amounts). Enter each total here and include on your Schedule D, **line 1b** (if **Box A** above is checked), **line 2** (if **Box B** above is checked), or **line 3** (if **Box C** above is checked) ▶			2,955	750			2,205

Note: If you checked Box A above but the basis reported to the IRS was incorrect, enter in column (e) the basis as reported to the IRS, and enter an adjustment in column (g) to correct the basis. See *Column (g)* in the separate instructions for how to figure the amount of the adjustment.

For Paperwork Reduction Act Notice, see your tax return instructions. Cat. No. 37768Z Form **8949** (2015)

Figure 11-1: Filled-In Form 8949 (Page 2)

Form 8949 (2015) Attachment Sequence No. **12A** Page **2**

Name(s) shown on return. Name and SSN or taxpayer identification no. not required if shown on other side	**Social security number or taxpayer identification number**
Curtis R. Stevens	**992-84-5922**

Before you check Box D, E, or F below, see whether you received any Form(s) 1099-B or substitute statement(s) from your broker. A substitute statement will have the same information as Form 1099-B. Either will show whether your basis (usually your cost) was reported to the IRS by your broker and may even tell you which box to check.

Part II **Long-Term.** Transactions involving capital assets you held more than 1 year are long term. For short-term transactions, see page 1.

Note: You may aggregate all long-term transactions reported on Form(s) 1099-B showing basis was reported to the IRS and for which no adjustments or codes are required. Enter the totals directly on Schedule D, line 8a; you aren't required to report these transactions on Form 8949 (see instructions).

You *must* check Box D, E, *or* F below. Check only one box. If more than one box applies for your long-term transactions, complete a separate Form 8949, page 2, for each applicable box. If you have more long-term transactions than will fit on this page for one or more of the boxes, complete as many forms with the same box checked as you need.

☐ **(D)** Long-term transactions reported on Form(s) 1099-B showing basis was reported to the IRS (see **Note** above)
☑ **(E)** Long-term transactions reported on Form(s) 1099-B showing basis was **not** reported to the IRS
☐ **(F)** Long-term transactions not reported to you on Form 1099-B

1 (a) Description of property (Example: 100 sh. XYZ Co.)	(b) Date acquired (Mo., day, yr.)	(c) Date sold or disposed of (Mo., day, yr.)	(d) Proceeds (sales price) (see instructions)	(e) Cost or other basis. See the **Note** below and see *Column (e)* in the separate instructions	Adjustment, if any, to gain or loss. If you enter an amount in column (g), enter a code in column (f). **See the separate instructions.** (f) Code(s) from instructions	(g) Amount of adjustment	(h) **Gain or (loss).** Subtract column (e) from column (d) and combine the result with column (g)
100 sh Wilcox Ind. pfd stk	**2-7-04**	**9-3-15**	**5,880**	**3,192**			**2,688**
2 Totals. Add the amounts in columns (d), (e), (g), and (h) (subtract negative amounts). Enter each total here and include on your Schedule D, **line 8b** (if **Box D** above is checked), **line 9** (if **Box E** above is checked), or **line 10** (if **Box F** above is checked) ▶			**5,880**	**3,192**			**2,688**

Note: If you checked Box D above but the basis reported to the IRS was incorrect, enter in column (e) the basis as reported to the IRS, and enter an adjustment in column (g) to correct the basis. See *Column (g)* in the separate instructions for how to figure the amount of the adjustment.

Form **8949** (2015)

Once Curt finishes filling out Form 8949, he transfers these totals from Form 8949 (line 2) to Schedule D. Because (just above line 1) Curtis checked boxes (B) and (E), he transfers the totals from Form 8949, page 1 (line 2) to Schedule D (line 2), and the totals from Form 8949, page 2 (line 2) to Schedule D (line 9). He then enters the $1,000 short-term capital loss carryover on Schedule D (line 6). Following the instructions on Schedule D, Curt computes his net short-term and net long-term capital gains.

Figure 11-1: Filled-In Schedule D (Page 1)

SCHEDULE D (Form 1040)

Department of the Treasury Internal Revenue Service (99)

Capital Gains and Losses

▶ Attach to Form 1040 or Form 1040NR.
▶ Information about Schedule D and its separate instructions is at *www.irs.gov/scheduled*.
▶ Use Form 8949 to list your transactions for lines 1b, 2, 3, 8b, 9, and 10.

OMB No. 1545-0074
2015
Attachment Sequence No. **12**

Name(s) shown on return: Curtis R. Stevens
Your social security number: 992-84-5922

Part I Short-Term Capital Gains and Losses—Assets Held One Year or Less

See instructions for how to figure the amounts to enter on the lines below. This form may be easier to complete if you round off cents to whole dollars.	(d) Proceeds (sales price)	(e) Cost (or other basis)	(g) Adjustments to gain or loss from Form(s) 8949, Part I, line 2, column (g)	(h) Gain or (loss) Subtract column (e) from column (d) and combine the result with column (g)
1a Totals for all short-term transactions reported on Form 1099-B for which basis was reported to the IRS and for which you have no adjustments (see instructions). However, if you choose to report all these transactions on Form 8949, leave this line blank and go to line 1b				
1b Totals for all transactions reported on Form(s) 8949 with **Box A** checked				
2 Totals for all transactions reported on Form(s) 8949 with **Box B** checked	2,955	750		2,205
3 Totals for all transactions reported on Form(s) 8949 with **Box C** checked				

4 Short-term gain from Form 6252 and short-term gain or (loss) from Forms 4684, 6781, and 8824	4	
5 Net short-term gain or (loss) from partnerships, S corporations, estates, and trusts from Schedule(s) K-1	5	
6 Short-term capital loss carryover. Enter the amount, if any, from line 8 of your **Capital Loss Carryover Worksheet** in the instructions	6	(1,000)
7 **Net short-term capital gain or (loss).** Combine lines 1a through 6 in column (h). If you have any long-term capital gains or losses, go to Part II below. Otherwise, go to Part III on the back	7	1,205

Part II Long-Term Capital Gains and Losses—Assets Held More Than One Year

See instructions for how to figure the amounts to enter on the lines below. This form may be easier to complete if you round off cents to whole dollars.	(d) Proceeds (sales price)	(e) Cost (or other basis)	(g) Adjustments to gain or loss from Form(s) 8949, Part II, line 2, column (g)	(h) Gain or (loss) Subtract column (e) from column (d) and combine the result with column (g)
8a Totals for all long-term transactions reported on Form 1099-B for which basis was reported to the IRS and for which you have no adjustments (see instructions). However, if you choose to report all these transactions on Form 8949, leave this line blank and go to line 8b				
8b Totals for all transactions reported on Form(s) 8949 with **Box D** checked				
9 Totals for all transactions reported on Form(s) 8949 with **Box E** checked	5,880	3,192		2,688
10 Totals for all transactions reported on Form(s) 8949 with **Box F** checked				

11 Gain from Form 4797, Part I; long-term gain from Forms 2439 and 6252; and long-term gain or (loss) from Forms 4684, 6781, and 8824	11	
12 Net long-term gain or (loss) from partnerships, S corporations, estates, and trusts from Schedule(s) K-1	12	
13 Capital gain distributions. See the instructions	13	
14 Long-term capital loss carryover. Enter the amount, if any, from line 13 of your **Capital Loss Carryover Worksheet** in the instructions	14	( )
15 **Net long-term capital gain or (loss).** Combine lines 8a through 14 in column (h). Then go to Part III on the back	15	2,688

For Paperwork Reduction Act Notice, see your tax return instructions. Cat. No. 11338H **Schedule D (Form 1040) 2015**

Figure 11-1: Filled-In Schedule D (Page 2)

Schedule D (Form 1040) 2015 Page **2**

Part III **Summary**

16	Combine lines 7 and 15 and enter the result	16	3,893
	• If line 16 is a **gain,** enter the amount from line 16 on Form 1040, line 13, or Form 1040NR, line 14. Then go to line 17 below. • If line 16 is a **loss,** skip lines 17 through 20 below. Then go to line 21. Also be sure to complete line 22. • If line 16 is **zero,** skip lines 17 through 21 below and enter -0- on Form 1040, line 13, or Form 1040NR, line 14. Then go to line 22.		
17	Are lines 15 and 16 **both** gains? ☑ **Yes.** Go to line 18. ☐ **No.** Skip lines 18 through 21, and go to line 22.		
18	Enter the amount, if any, from line 7 of the **28% Rate Gain Worksheet** in the instructions . . ▶	18	0
19	Enter the amount, if any, from line 18 of the **Unrecaptured Section 1250 Gain Worksheet** in the instructions . . . . ▶	19	0
20	Are lines 18 and 19 **both** zero or blank? ☑ **Yes.** Complete the **Qualified Dividends and Capital Gain Tax Worksheet** in the instructions for Form 1040, line 44 (or in the instructions for Form 1040NR, line 42). **Do not** complete lines 21 and 22 below. ☐ **No.** Complete the **Schedule D Tax Worksheet** in the instructions. **Do not** complete lines 21 and 22 below.		
21	If line 16 is a loss, enter here and on Form 1040, line 13, or Form 1040NR, line 14, the **smaller** of: • The loss on line 16 or • ($3,000), or if married filing separately, ($1,500) . . . . **Note.** When figuring which amount is smaller, treat both amounts as positive numbers.	21	( )
22	Do you have qualified dividends on Form 1040, line 9b, or Form 1040NR, line 10b? ☐ **Yes.** Complete the **Qualified Dividends and Capital Gain Tax Worksheet** in the instructions for Form 1040, line 44 (or in the instructions for Form 1040NR, line 42). ☐ **No.** Complete the rest of Form 1040 or Form 1040NR.		

Schedule D (Form 1040) 2015

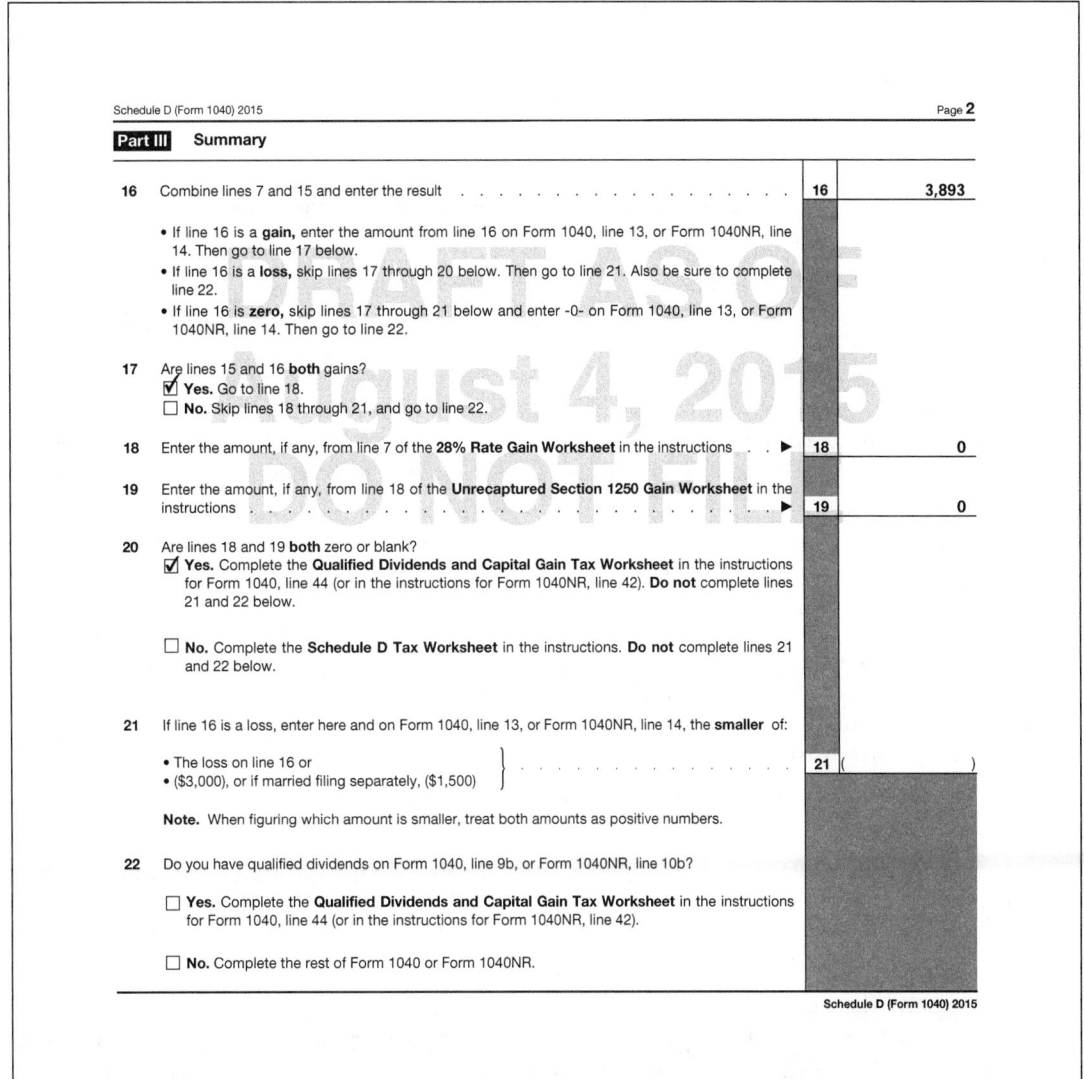

In Part III on Schedule D (line 16), taxpayers combine the net short-term capital gain or loss (line 7) and the net long-term capital gain or loss (line 15). If combining these amounts results in an overall net loss, the taxpayer enters up to $3,000 of the net loss ($1,500 if married filing separately) on Schedule D (line 21) and transfers this amount to Form 1040. When an overall net gain results, the taxpayer completes lines 17–20, which may involve completing a worksheet to compute a reduced the tax rate on net capital gain. Even if the taxpayer does not report a net capital gain, when the taxpayer reports qualified dividends on Form 1040 (line 9b), line 22 of Schedule D is answered **YES**. The taxpayer then completes the *Qualified Dividends and Capital Gain Tax Worksheet* located in the Instructions to Form 1040 to pay a reduced tax rate on the qualified dividends. This worksheet goes through a series of calculations similar to those shown earlier in the chapter in Example 12.

Because Curt reported gains on both lines 15 (net long-term capital gain) and 16 (total capital gain), Curt marks **Yes** on line 17. He then enters the amount of his capital gains taxed at no more than 28% (**$0**) and unrecaptured Section 1250 gain taxed at no more than 25% (**$0**) on lines 18 and 19, respectively. Because both lines 18 and 19 are $0 or blank, Curt answers **Yes** to line 20. It is here that he is told that he will need to complete the *Qualified Dividends and Capital Gain Tax Worksheet* to compute his tax liability.

Curt transfers the $3,893 total capital gain from Schedule D (line 16) to Form 1040 (line 13). When Curt finishes computing his $72,350 of taxable income, he determines that included in this amount is $2,688 of net capital gain (reported on Schedule D) and $500 of qualified dividends (reported on Form 1040, line 9b). Curt then completes the *Qualified Dividends and Capital Gain Tax Worksheet* to compute his tax liability. He enters this amount on Form 1040 (line 44). Using the approach from Example 12, Curt's tax liability of $13,566 is computed as follows.

Tax on $69,162* (using the tax table for Single taxpayers)	$13,088
Plus $3,188 ($2,688 + $500) × 15% (Curt is in the 25% tax bracket)	478
Tax liability on $72,350 taxable income	$13,566

*($72,350 taxable income – $2,688 net capital gain – $500 qualified dividends)

In the Instructions to Form 1040, the IRS provides a *Qualified Dividends and Capital Gain Tax Worksheet* to help taxpayers compute their tax liabilities when a reduced rate applies to qualified dividends and/or net capital gains. The process used to calculate Curt's (reduced) tax liability above is very similar to the method used in the *Qualified Dividends and Capital Gain Tax Worksheet.*

¶1101.06 SPECIAL RULES

Special rules apply to losses from worthless securities and from the sale of Section 1244 stock. Special rules also apply to gains from sales between certain related parties and from sales of subdivided real estate.

Worthless Securities

In the year securities (stocks and bonds) become worthless, the taxpayer is treated as having sold the securities for $0 on the last day of the tax year. For most taxpayers, securities are capital assets. Hence, worthless securities produce a capital loss. A long-term capital loss results if, on the last day of the tax year, the taxpayer held the securities for more than one year.

EXAMPLE 17 On April 3, 20x1, Rudy pays $10,000 for stock. On January 23, 20x2, the stock is declared worthless. Rudy is deemed to have sold the stock for $0 on December 31, 20x2. Since the period from April 4, 20x1 (the day after the purchase) until December 31, 20x2 (the "sales date") exceeds one year, Rudy recognizes a $10,000 long-term capital loss. He reports the loss in Part II on Form 8949 (line 1).

Section 1244 Stock

For most people, stock is an investment. A loss on the sale of an investment normally produces a capital loss. However, each year individuals can deduct as ordinary losses up to $50,000 ($100,000 on a joint return) of the loss on the sale, exchange, or worthlessness of *qualified small business stock* (also commonly called Section 1244 stock). Annual losses in excess of $50,000 ($100,000 on a joint return) are capital losses. Although both common and preferred stock qualify as Section 1244 stock, only the original owner of the stock qualifies for the ordinary loss treatment. To qualify as Section 1244 stock, the corporation issuing the stock must meet certain requirements. Two of the criteria are:

1. The corporation's contributed capital plus paid-in-surplus cannot exceed $1,000,000 at the time the stock is issued.
2. The corporation must be mainly an operating company rather than an investment company.

EXAMPLE 18

Paige, who is not married, sells Section 1244 stock for $17,000. Paige purchased the stock several years ago for $80,000. Her realized loss equals $63,000 ($17,000 – $80,000). Paige recognizes a $50,000 ordinary loss and a $13,000 long-term capital loss. She enters the long-term capital loss into the netting process and uses the ordinary loss to offset ordinary income such as wages, interest, and dividends. If Paige has no other capital gains or losses, only $3,000 of the $13,000 long-term capital loss can be used to offset ordinary income in the current year. Had the stock not qualified as Section 1244 stock, Paige would have recognized a $63,000 long-term capital loss.

Each year taxpayers are allowed up to $50,000 ($100,000 for MFJ) of ordinary losses from the sale of Section 1244 stock. Taxpayers whose Section 1244 stock has declined in value more than $50,000 ($100,000 for MFJ) from when they bought it should plan on selling their stock over more than one tax year to take advantage of the $50,000 ($100,000 for MFJ) of ordinary losses allowed each year.

Take, for example, Page from Example 18. If Page has sold just enough Section 1244 stock to produce a $53,000 loss, she would have been able to deduct the entire loss ($50,000 ordinary loss + $3,000 capital loss). She could then sell the rest of the stock next year, and deduct the (rest of) the loss as an ordinary loss from the sale of Section 1244 stock.

Gains from Sales Between Certain Related Parties

When individuals sell capital assets to a corporation for a gain, they should recognize a capital gain. However, for individuals who own (directly or constructively) more than 50% of the value of the corporation's outstanding stock, capital gain treatment does not apply if the property is depreciable property to the corporation. Instead, the individual recognizes ordinary income. The same rule applies to individuals who sell capital assets to a partnership in which they own (directly or constructively) more than a 50% interest. If the property is depreciable property to the partnership, the individual recognizes ordinary income. Note that this rule applies only to gains between these related parties. See Chapter 10 (¶1005) for rules disallowing losses between related parties, as well as the rules governing constructive ownership.

EXAMPLE 19

Aaron sells property to a corporation for a $10,000 gain. Aaron owns 60% of the stock in the corporation. The property is a capital asset to Aaron, but will be a depreciable asset in the hands of the corporation. Aaron recognizes $10,000 of ordinary income.

EXAMPLE 20

Same facts as in Example 19, except that Aaron owns 50% of the stock in the corporation. Because he does not own *more than* a 50% interest in the corporation's stock, Aaron recognizes a $10,000 capital gain on the sale of the property to the corporation.

EXAMPLE 21

Same facts as in Example 19, except that the property is land, and therefore is not depreciable property in the hands of the corporation. Aaron recognizes a $10,000 capital gain on the sale of the land.

Subdivided Property

Although a capital gain or loss usually results when investors sell parcels of land held for investment, special rules apply to gain (but not losses) on the sale of subdivided property. To receive capital gain treatment, taxpayers must first meet the following four conditions.

1. The taxpayer cannot be a dealer in real estate.
2. The taxpayer cannot be a corporation.
3. The taxpayer cannot make substantial improvements to the lots sold. Filling, draining, clearing, and leveling activities normally are not considered substantial improvements.
4. The taxpayer must hold the lots for at least five years before selling them. Inherited property has no minimum holding requirement.

Taxpayers who meet these four conditions recognize capital gain on the sale of all lots sold until the tax year in which they sell the sixth lot. Starting with the tax year in which the sixth lot is sold, they recognize ordinary income for up to 5% of the sales price. Gain not taxed as ordinary income is taxed as long-term capital gain. Any selling expenses first offset any ordinary income.

EXAMPLE 22

Eric bought a tract of land in 20x0. Eric, who is not a real estate dealer, subdivides the land in 20x8 and sells four lots for $12,000 each. There were no selling expenses. The adjusted basis of each lot is $9,000. Eric recognizes a $3,000 long-term capital gain on the sale of each lot ($12,000 – $9,000).

EXAMPLE 23

Continuing with Example 22, in 20x9, Eric sells two more lots for $12,000 each. There were no selling expenses. The adjusted basis of each lot is $9,000. Eric recognizes a $3,000 gain on the sale of each lot. Because Eric sells the sixth lot in 20x9, he recognizes $600 ($12,000 × 5%) of ordinary income and $2,400 ($3,000 – $600) of long-term capital gain for each lot sold in 20x9. Eric will recognize up to 5% of the sales price as ordinary income on lots sold in future years.

EXAMPLE 24

Same facts as in Example 23, except that Eric incurred $500 of selling expenses for each lot. The selling expenses reduce the recognized gain for each lot to $2,500 ($3,000 – $500). The selling expenses first offset the ordinary income. Thus, for each lot sold, Eric recognizes $100 of ordinary income ($600 – $500 selling expenses) and $2,400 of long-term capital gain ($2,500 – $100). Had the selling expenses exceeded $600, the entire recognized gain would have been long-term capital gain.

¶1101.07 OTHER WAYS OF PRODUCING CAPITAL GAINS AND LOSSES

Besides the sale or exchange of capital assets, other activities can produce capital gains and losses. These activities include nonbusiness bad debts, net casualty or theft gains on personal-use property, and certain disposals of business property.

Nonbusiness Bad Debts

Chapter 7 described the rules for deducting business bad debts (¶705.02). A nonbusiness bad debt is a bona fide debt that is not a business bad debt. A nonbusiness bad debt is reported as a short-term capital loss, regardless of how long the debt was held. This differs from business bad debts, which sole proprietors deduct on Schedule C. Also, unlike a business bad debt, taxpayers cannot deduct a nonbusiness bad debt until it becomes completely worthless.

In the year taxpayers claim a nonbusiness bad debt, they enter the name of the debtor and the words **Statement attached** on Form 8949, Part I. In the attached statement, they then include:

1. The amount of the debt and the date it was due,
2. The taxpayer's business or family relationship with the debtor,
3. The taxpayer's efforts to collect the debt, and
4. The taxpayer's reason for concluding the debt was worthless.

EXAMPLE 25

Pam made a bona fide loan of $10,000 to her friend in 20x1. In 20x3 the friend filed for bankruptcy, and Pam was told to expect $.60 on the dollar for her loan. Pam received $4,500 from bankruptcy court in 20x4. Pam recognizes a $5,500 ($10,000 – $4,500) short-term capital loss in 20x4, the year in which the $5,500 became completely worthless.

Net Personal Casualty or Theft Gains

A casualty or theft gain occurs when the insurance proceeds exceed the taxpayer's adjusted basis in the property. A casualty or theft loss occurs when the amount of the loss exceeds the insurance reimbursement. For personal-use property, the amount of the loss is measured as the *lesser of* (i) the property's adjusted basis or (ii) its decline in value (¶507).

When a person has just one personal casualty or theft during the year, the taxpayer computes the gain or loss from each property damaged or destroyed in the casualty or theft. The taxpayer then nets the gains and losses to compute a *net personal casualty or theft gain or loss.* If the result is a net gain, then all personal casualty or theft gains and losses are treated as capital gains and losses. If the result is a net loss, then the taxpayer reduces the loss by $100 and by 10% of AGI. Any remaining loss is deducted as an itemized deduction (¶507).

EXAMPLE 26

Val's home was burglarized. A family heirloom and a TV were stolen. Val's holding period in both items was long-term. Information about the items reveals the following:

	FMV Before	FMV After	Adjusted Basis	Insurance Proceeds
TV	$ 500	$0	$ 700	$ 0
Heirloom	3,000	0	1,000	2,900

Since Val did not insure the TV, the theft of the TV produces a $500 casualty or theft loss (the *lesser of* (i) $700 adjusted basis or (ii) $500 decline in value). Val insured the heirloom, which results in a $1,900 casualty or theft gain ($2,900 insurance proceeds – $1,000 adjusted basis). Val's net casualty or theft gain equals $1,400 ($1,900 – $500). Val treats the $1,400 as a long-term capital gain in the netting process since both properties had been held long-term.

When several personal casualties and thefts occur during the year, the taxpayer first computes a net gain or loss for each casualty or theft. If a single casualty or theft results in a net personal casualty or theft loss, the taxpayer reduces the loss by $100 (¶507). A net gain is not reduced by $100. The taxpayer then nets the gains and losses from the various personal casualties and thefts. If the result is an overall net gain, all personal casualty or theft gains and losses for the year are treated as capital gains and losses.

Taxpayers compute their net personal casualty or theft gain or loss on Form 4684 (Section A), Casualties and Thefts. If a net loss results, the taxpayer uses Form 4684 to support the itemized deduction for the amount of the loss that exceeds 10% of AGI. If the result is a net gain, the taxpayer transfers the personal casualty or theft gains and losses to the appropriate short-term/long-term lines on Schedule D.

¶1102 Business Gains and Losses

By definition, real and depreciable business property are not capital assets (see ¶1101.01). However, under certain conditions, disposing of real and depreciable business property held for over one year can result in long-term capital gain. (The disposal of real and depreciable business property held one year or less always produces ordinary income or loss). Real and depreciable business property held long-term is known as **Section 1231 property.** The sale, exchange, or condemnation of Section 1231 property produces a Section 1231 gain or loss. If Section 1231 gains for the year exceed Section 1231 losses, the net Section 1231 gain may be treated as long-term capital gain. If Section 1231 losses exceed Section 1231 gains, the net Section 1231 loss is treated as an ordinary loss.

EXAMPLE 27 For the year, Daniel reports a $12,000 Section 1231 gain and a $5,000 Section 1231 loss. Daniel's net Section 1231 gain equals $7,000 ($12,000 – $5,000). Daniel may be able to treat this amount as long-term capital gain in the netting process.

EXAMPLE 28 For the year, Morris reports a $10,000 Section 1231 gain and a $23,000 Section 1231 loss. Morris's net Section 1231 loss is $13,000 ($10,000 – $23,000). He deducts this amount from gross income as an ordinary loss.

¶1102.01 BUSINESS CASUALTY OR THEFT GAINS AND LOSSES

Chapter 10 presented the rules for computing business casualty or theft gains and losses (¶1009.02). At the end of the year, taxpayers sum all casualty or theft gains and losses from Section 1231 property (business property held long-term). When gains exceed losses, the excess is a *net business casualty or theft gain.* A net business casualty or theft gain is treated as a Section 1231 gain. When losses exceed gains, the difference is a *net business casualty or theft loss.* A net business casualty or theft loss is treated as an ordinary loss. Casualty or theft gains and losses from business property held short-term produce ordinary income and losses.

EXAMPLE 29 For the year, Leslie recognizes a $10,000 business casualty gain and a $4,000 business casualty loss from properties held long-term. She also recognizes a $2,000 Section 1231 loss. Leslie treats the $6,000 net business casualty or theft gain ($10,000 – $4,000) as a Section 1231 gain. Leslie's net Section 1231 gain is $4,000 ($6,000 – $2,000). She may be able to treat the $4,000 as a long-term capital gain in the netting process.

EXAMPLE 30 Demi has a $6,000 business casualty gain, a $13,000 business casualty loss, and a $5,000 Section 1231 gain. Demi's net business casualty or theft loss equals $7,000 ($6,000 – $13,000). She deducts the $7,000 from gross income as an ordinary loss. Demi may be able to treat the $5,000 net Section 1231 gain as a long-term capital gain.

Section 1231 provides taxpayers with the best of both situations: long-term capital gains for net Section 1231 gains and ordinary losses for net Section 1231 losses. Over the years, Congress identified two situations where taxpayers might take advantage of the favorable rules that govern Section 1231 property. The first situation involves the sale or exchange of depreciable property for a gain. The second situation involves Section 1231 losses.

¶1102.02 DEPRECIATION RECAPTURE

Depreciation expense is a deduction that reduces ordinary income. The tax benefit a taxpayer receives from deducting depreciation expense is equal to the amount of the deduction times the taxpayer's marginal tax rate. (The marginal tax rate is the tax imposed on the next dollar of taxable income. It is the taxpayer's "tax bracket.") When individual taxpayers sell property that generates long-term capital gain, such gain may be taxed at a rate that is lower than the taxpayer's marginal tax rate. The maximum tax rate individual taxpayers pay on net capital gain is 0%, 15%, or 20%, depending on which tax bracket the taxpayer's taxable income falls.

Because net Section 1231 gain can become long-term capital gain, depreciating property as quickly as possible increases the chance of recognizing long-term capital gain when the property is sold. This results in larger depreciation deductions (where the tax benefits are computed using the taxpayer's marginal tax rate) and possibly greater long-term capital gains (where net capital gain is taxed at a lower tax rate). Example 31 illustrates this point.

EXAMPLE 31

In March 2013, Wallace paid $20,000 for a machine that he used in his business. Wallace elected to expense the entire machine under Section 179, therefore his adjusted basis in the machine is $0 at the end of 2013. On October 12, 2015, Wallace sold the machine for $12,000, resulting in a $12,000 Section 1231 gain. If Wallace had no other Section 1231 or capital gains and losses in 2015, the entire $12,000 becomes long-term capital gain, which is taxed at a reduced rate.

Had Wallace used regular MACRS with no bonus depreciation or Section 179 expensing, he would have deducted $2,858 in 2013 ($20,000 × 14.29%), $4,898 in 2014 ($20,000 × 24.49%), and $1,749 ($20,000 × 17.49% × ½) in 2015. His adjusted basis in the machine at the time of the sale would have been $10,495 ($20,000 – $9,505) and he would have recognized a $1,505 Section 1231 gain on the sale ($12,000 – $10,495). Because Wallace has no other Section 1231 gains or losses, the $1,505 would become long-term capital gain.

In both scenarios, Wallace's overall deduction equals $8,000. In the first case, Wallace deducts $20,000 for depreciation expense but reports a $12,000 gain on the sale, which nets to $8,000. In the second case, he deducts $9,505 for depreciation expense and reports gain of $1,505, which also nets to $8,000.

If Wallace's marginal tax rate in both years is 28%. In the first case, Wallace receives a $5,600 tax benefit from the depreciation expense ($20,000 × 28%) but pays tax of $1,800 ($12,000 × 15%) on the gain from the sale. The net tax benefit equals $3,800 ($5,600 – $1,800). In the second case, Wallace's tax benefit is only $2,713 [($10,495 × 28%) – ($1,505 × 15%)]. By electing Section 179, Wallace ends up saving $1,087 in taxes ($3,800 – $2,713).

As you see from Example 31, an incentive existed for taxpayers to use the fastest depreciation method possible. To limit this opportunity, Congress introduced the concept of **depreciation recapture.** Depreciation recapture requires taxpayers to tax gains as ordinary income to the extent of "excessive depreciation." Under the Section 1245 depreciation recapture rules, gains on the disposal of depreciable personal property are taxed as ordinary income to the extent of the *lesser of* (i) the gain, or (ii) all depreciation taken. Gain not taxed as ordinary income is Section 1231 gain.

For personal property, all depreciation taken (including Section 179 expense and bonus depreciation) is subject to depreciation recapture. Even when the taxpayer uses the straight-line method to depreciate personal property, the entire amount of straight-line depreciation is subject to recapture.

EXAMPLE 32

Bonnie bought a business machine on January 3, 2013, for $20,000. Bonnie sold the machine on April 25, 2015, for $21,000. In 2013–2015, Bonnie deducted depreciation totaling $12,503. Her adjusted basis in the machine equals $7,497 ($20,000 – $12,503). Bonnie recognizes a $13,503 gain ($21,000 – $7,497), of which $12,503 is treated as ordinary income and $1,000 is treated as Section 1231 gain.

Depreciation recapture only applies to real property when an accelerated depreciation method is used to depreciate the realty. Since the only depreciation method for realty under MACRS or ADS is the straight-line method, there is no depreciation recapture on the sale of real property placed in service after 1986.

Depreciation recapture only affects gains on the disposal of depreciable Section 1231 property. Losses on the disposal of Section 1231 property are always treated as Section 1231 losses.

¶1102.03 NONRECAPTURED SECTION 1231 LOSSES

The tax treatment of Section 1231 gains and losses gives taxpayers the opportunity to treat net Section 1231 gains as long-term capital gains and net Section 1231 losses as ordinary losses. To keep taxpayers from bunching all Section 1231 gains in one year to get long-term capital gain treatment, and then bunching Section 1231 losses in the next year to deduct them as ordinary losses, Congress introduced **nonrecaptured Section 1231 losses**. Before net Section 1231 gain can become long-term capital gain, the taxpayer must look back over its past five years and compute the amount of nonrecaptured Section 1231 losses. Nonrecaptured Section 1231 losses act like depreciation recapture. That is, net Section 1231 gain is taxed as ordinary income to the extent of nonrecaptured Section 1231 losses.

In a year in which the netting process produces a net Section 1231 gain, such gain must first be taxed (recaptured) as ordinary income to the extent of the taxpayer's nonrecaptured Section 1231 losses. Taxpayers generate nonrecaptured Section 1231 losses in years in which the netting process produces net Section 1231 losses (which are treated as ordinary deductions and used to offset ordinary income). Two events reduce the amount of nonrecaptured Section 1231 losses. First, when net Section 1231 gain is taxed (recaptured) as ordinary income, nonrecaptured Section 1231 losses are reduced by the recaptured amount. Second, any amount of nonrecaptured Section 1231 losses not recaptured within five tax years is no longer considered nonrecaptured Section 1231 losses. Thus, net Section 1231 loss is treated as nonrecaptured Section 1231 loss for five tax years or until recaptured as ordinary income, whichever occurs first.

EXAMPLE 33

In 20x6, Jose has Section 1231 gains of $30,000 and Section 1231 losses of $12,000. Jose also has nonrecaptured Section 1231 losses from 20x1-20x5 of $7,000. Jose's net Section 1231 gain for 20x6 equals $18,000 ($30,000 – $12,000). He reports $7,000 of this gain as ordinary income and the rest ($18,000 – $7,000 = $11,000), as long-term capital gain. Since all nonrecaptured Section 1231 losses from 20x1-20x5 have been "recaptured" by turning Section 1231 gain from 20x6 into ordinary income, there are no nonrecaptured Section 1231 losses from 20x2-20x6 to apply against net Section 1231 gains in 20x7.

¶1102.04 UNRECAPTURED SECTION 1250 GAIN

When business real property placed in service after 1986 is sold at a gain, individual taxpayers treat the gain as Section 1231 gain. When Section 1231 gains exceed Section 1231 losses for the year (a net Section 1231 gain), such gain may be treated as long-term capital gain. However, the tax law requires that any unrecaptured Section 1250 gain be taxed at the higher 25% tax rate for individual taxpayers in the 25% or higher tax brackets.

Unrecaptured Section 1250 gain equals the *lesser of* (i) the amount of gain, or (ii) allowed or allowable depreciation on the property. (Recall from Chapter 8 (¶801) that the adjusted basis of property must be reduced by the *greater of* depreciation "allowed or allowable." This refers to depreciation that is deducted or that which the taxpayer is entitled to deduct.) Unrecaptured Section 1250 gain applies only to real property sold at a gain. It does not apply to realty sold at a loss. It also applies only to individual taxpayers, not corporations.

EXAMPLE 34

Everett sold residential realty during 2015 for $400,000. Everett paid $520,000 for the building in 2005. Depreciation taken on the building from 2005–2015 totaled $193,818. Thus, Everett's adjusted basis in the building is $326,182 ($520,000 – $193,818). His recognized gain is $73,818 ($400,000 – $326,182). Everett's unrecaptured Section 1250 gain equals $73,818 (*lesser of* (i) the $73,818 gain, or (ii) $193,818 depreciation taken).

EXAMPLE 35

Same facts as in Example 34, except that Everett sold the property for $600,000. Unrecaptured Section 1250 gain equals $193,818 (*lesser of* (i) the $273,818 gain ($600,000 – $326,182), or (ii) $193,818 depreciation taken). When Everett goes to transfer net Section 1231 gain to long-term capital gain in the netting process, he will report the first $193,818 of the net gain as 25% long-term gain and the rest ($80,000) as long-term gain taxed at the lower (0%, 15%, or 20%) rate.

Taxpayers with unrecaptured Section 1250 gain report this gain in the netting process between the short-term and long-term columns. When unrecaptured Section 1250 gain exists, netting of gains and losses is done as follows.

1. If the amount in the 15% long-term column (which represents gain taxed at the lower 0%, 15%, or 20% rate) is a net loss, it is used first to offset any 25% long-term gain, followed by any short-term gain. If there is no net 15% long-term loss, proceed to Step 2.
2. Use any net short-term capital loss to offset any 25% long-term gain, and then any net 15% long-term gain. The netting process is complete when only all gains or all losses remain.

EXAMPLE 36

Brook and Jerry Daniels sold several assets during 2015. Their taxable income is $168,125, which does not include any qualified dividends. The netting within the groups resulted in a $2,000 net short-term loss; a $6,000 25% long-term gain; and a $7,000 net 15% long-term gain. The netting process within and between groups is as follows.

		Long-Term	
Short-Term		**25%**	**15%**
$6,000		$6,000	$18,000
(8,000)			(11,000)
($2,000)	——→	(2,000)	$ 7,000
		$4,000	

Since there is no net 15% long-term loss, the Daniels skip Step 1. They begin the netting process between groups by offsetting the $2,000 net short-term loss against the 25% long-term gain (Step 2). This results in a $4,000 25% long-term gain and a $7,000 net 15% long-term gain. The Daniels compute their tax liability as follows.

Tax on $157,125 ($168,125 – $11,000 net capital gain)	$31,047
Plus $4,000 × 25% (the Daniels are in the 28% bracket)	1,000
Plus $7,000 × 15% (the Daniels are in the 28% bracket)	1,050
Tax liability on $168,125	$33,097

EXAMPLE 37

Kelli sold several capital assets during 2015. These assets produced a $9,000 net short-term loss; a $4,000 25% long-term gain; and a $13,000 net 15% long-term gain. Kelli files as head of household and her 2015 taxable income is $64,230 (no qualified dividends). The netting process between groups is as follows.

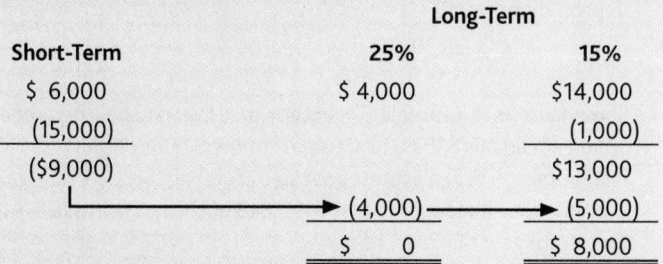

	Long-Term	
Short-Term	**25%**	**15%**
$ 6,000	$ 4,000	$14,000
(15,000)		(1,000)
($9,000) →		$13,000
	(4,000) →	(5,000)
	$ 0	$ 8,000

Because there is no net 15% long-term loss, Kelli skips Step 1. In Step 2, she uses the $9,000 net short-term loss to offset first the 25% long-term gain and then the net 15% long-term gain. Kelli is left with $8,000 net 15% long-term gain. She computes her tax liability as follows.

Tax on $56,230 ($64,230 – $8,000)	$8,379
Plus $8,000 × 15% (Kelli is in the 25% bracket)	1,200
Tax liability on $64,230	$9,579

EXAMPLE 38

Jim and Erin Stegall sold several assets during 2015. These assets produced a $6,000 net short-term loss; a $15,000 25% long-term gain; and a $2,000 net 15% long-term loss. The Stegalls file a joint return and report taxable income of $499,230 (including $2,200 of qualified dividends). The netting process between groups is as follows.

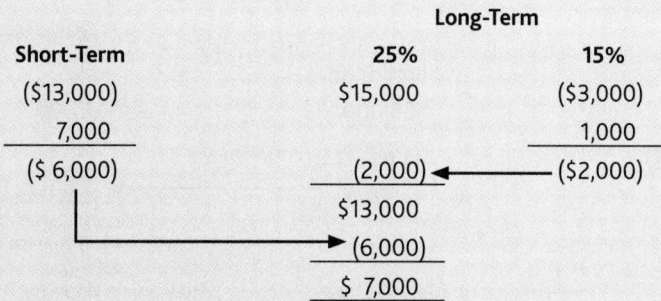

	Long-Term	
Short-Term	**25%**	**15%**
($13,000)	$15,000	($3,000)
7,000		1,000
($ 6,000)	(2,000) ←	($2,000)
	$13,000	
→	(6,000)	
	$ 7,000	

The Stegalls offset the net 15% long-term loss against the 25% gain (Step 1). They then use the short-term loss to offset more of the 25% gain (Step 2). The Stegalls are left with a $7,000 net 25% long-term capital gain. They compute their tax liability (including the reduced tax rates on the $7,000 net 25% long-term capital gain and the $2,200 of qualified dividends) as shown below.

Tax on $490,030 ($499,230 – $7,000 net gain – $2,200 qualified dividends)	$139,968
Plus $7,000 × 25% (the Stegalls are in the 39.6% bracket)	1,750
Plus $2,200 × 20% (the Stegalls are in the 39.6% bracket)	440
Tax liability on $499,230	$142,158

¶1103 Reporting Business Gains and Losses on the Tax Return

In the end, all of an individual taxpayer's recognized gains and losses appear on Form 1040. Similarly, all of a C corporation's recognized gains and losses appear on Form 1120. However, only gains and losses that appear on Schedule D, Capital Gains and Losses, receive capital gain and loss treatment. Taxpayers report the gain and loss on the sale, exchange, or condemnation of business property on Form 4797, Sales of Business Property. They report the gains and losses resulting from casualties and thefts of business property on Form 4684 (Section B), Casualties and Thefts. Net gains and losses from Form 4684 (Section B) flow through to Form 4797. Therefore, taxpayers with casualties or thefts should begin by completing Form 4684.

¶1103.01 FORM 4684 (SECTION B), CASUALTIES AND THEFTS

Taxpayers compute business casualty or theft gains and losses on Form 4684 (Section B), Casualties and Thefts. Taxpayers with more than one business casualty or theft during the year complete a separate Form 4684, Part I, for each casualty or theft. In Part II, taxpayers separate gains and losses involving Section 1231 property from gains and losses involving business property held short-term. They transfer a net business casualty or theft gain to Form 4797, Part I (line 3), and treat it as a gain from the sale of Section 1231 property. They transfer a net business casualty or theft loss to Form 4797, Part II (line 14), and deduct it as an ordinary loss. A net casualty or theft gain or loss from business property held short-term is also transferred to Form 4797, Part II (line 14), and reported as an ordinary gain or loss.

Taxpayers also use Form 4684 (Section B) to report casualty or theft gains and losses from investment property. However, the scope of this chapter is limited to business casualties or thefts. Those interested in casualty or theft gains and losses on investment property should refer to IRS Publication 547.

¶1103.02 FILLED-IN FORM 4684 (SECTION B)

INFORMATION FOR FIGURE 11-2:

On October 15, 2015, Alan Miller's laptop **computer** and color laser **printer** were stolen from his office. Alan purchased both properties on **June 4, 2014.** Before the theft, the FMV of the computer and printer were $1,500 and $1,800, respectively. The insurance company reimbursed Alan $1,000 for the computer (adjusted basis, $2,200) and $2,300 for the printer (adjusted basis, $2,000).

Line #

20A: Adjusted basis of the computer, **$2,200**
20B: Adjusted basis of the printer, **$2,000**
21A: Insurance reimbursement for the computer, **$1,000**
21B: Insurance reimbursement for the printer, **$2,300**
23A: FMV of the computer before the theft, **$1,500**
24A: FMV of the computer after the theft, **$0**
26A: Amount from line 20 since the computer was lost in a theft (see Note: below line 26), **$2,200**

Figure 11-2: Filled-In Form 4684 (Section B)

Form 4684 (2015) Attachment Sequence No. **26** Page **2**

Name(s) shown on tax return. Do not enter name and identifying number if shown on other side. **Alan J. Miller**

Identifying number **668-58-9977**

SECTION B—Business and Income-Producing Property

Part I **Casualty or Theft Gain or Loss** (Use a separate Part I for each casualty or theft.)

19 Description of properties (show type, location, and date acquired for each property). Use a separate line for each property lost or damaged from the same casualty or theft. **See instructions if claiming a loss due to a Ponzi-type investment scheme and Section C is not completed.**

Property **A** **Computer, acquired June 4, 2014**
Property **B** **Printer, acquired June 4, 2014**
Property **C**
Property **D**

		Properties A	Properties B	Properties C	Properties D
20 Cost or adjusted basis of each property	20	2,200	2,000		
21 Insurance or other reimbursement (whether or not you filed a claim). See the instructions for line 3	21	1,000	2,300		
Note: *If line 20 is **more** than line 21, skip line 22.*					
22 Gain from casualty or theft. If line 21 is **more** than line 20, enter the difference here and on line 29 or line 34, column (c), except as provided in the instructions for line 33. Also, skip lines 23 through 27 for that column. See the instructions for line 4 if line 21 includes insurance or other reimbursement you did not claim, or you received payment for your loss in a later tax year	22		300		
23 Fair market value **before** casualty or theft	23	1,500			
24 Fair market value **after** casualty or theft	24	0			
25 Subtract line 24 from line 23	25	1,500			
26 Enter the **smaller** of line 20 or line 25	26	2,200			
Note: *If the property was totally destroyed by casualty or lost from theft, enter on line 26 the amount from line 20.*					
27 Subtract line 21 from line 26. If zero or less, enter -0-	27	1,200			

28 Casualty or theft loss. Add the amounts on line 27. Enter the total here and on line 29 **or** line 34 (see instructions) **28** **1,200**

Part II **Summary of Gains and Losses** (from separate Parts I)

(a) Identify casualty or theft		(b) Losses from casualties or thefts: (i) Trade, business, rental or royalty property	(b) Losses from casualties or thefts: (ii) Income-producing and employee property		(c) Gains from casualties or thefts includible in income
Casualty or Theft of Property Held One Year or Less					
29		( )	( )		
		( )	( )		
30 Totals. Add the amounts on line 29	30	( )	( )		
31 Combine line 30, columns (b)(i) and (c). Enter the net gain or (loss) here and on Form 4797, line 14. If Form 4797 is not otherwise required, see instructions				31	
32 Enter the amount from line 30, column (b)(ii) here. Individuals, enter the amount from income-producing property on Schedule A (Form 1040), line 28, or Form 1040NR, Schedule A, line 14, and enter the amount from property used as an employee on Schedule A (Form 1040), line 23, or Form 1040NR, Schedule A, line 9. Estates and trusts, partnerships, and S corporations, see instructions				32	
Casualty or Theft of Property Held More Than One Year					
33 Casualty or theft gains from Form 4797, line 32				33	
34		(1,200)	( )		300
		( )	( )		
35 Total losses. Add amounts on line 34, columns (b)(i) and (b)(ii)	35	(1,200)	( )		
36 Total gains. Add lines 33 and 34, column (c)				36	300
37 Add amounts on line 35, columns (b)(i) and (b)(ii)				37	(1,200)
38 If the loss on line 37 is **more** than the gain on line 36:					
a Combine line 35, column (b)(i) and line 36, and enter the net gain or (loss) here. Partnerships (except electing large partnerships) and S corporations, see the note below. All others, enter this amount on Form 4797, line 14. If Form 4797 is not otherwise required, see instructions				38a	(900)
b Enter the amount from line 35, column (b)(ii) here. Individuals, enter the amount from income-producing property on Schedule A (Form 1040), line 28, or Form 1040NR, Schedule A, line 14, and enter the amount from property used as an employee on Schedule A (Form 1040), line 23, or Form 1040NR, Schedule A, line 9. Estates and trusts, enter on the "Other deductions" line of your tax return. Partnerships (except electing large partnerships) and S corporations, see the note below. Electing large partnerships, enter on Form 1065-B, Part II, line 11				38b	
39 If the loss on line 37 is **less** than or **equal** to the gain on line 36, combine lines 36 and 37 and enter here. Partnerships (except electing large partnerships), see the note below. All others, enter this amount on Form 4797, line 3				39	

Note: *Partnerships, enter the amount from line 38a, 38b, or line 39 on Form 1065, Schedule K, line 11. S corporations, enter the amount from line 38a or 38b on Form 1120S, Schedule K, line 10.*

Form **4684** (2015)

Alan's computer and printer were completely lost as a result of the theft. Thus, he enters the $2,200 adjusted basis of the computer on line 26A to measure his theft loss from the computer. Because the $1,000 insurance reimbursement he received for the computer is less than the adjusted basis, Alan reports a $1,200 casualty or theft loss from the computer on line 27A. Following the instructions on line 28, he enters this amount in Part II (line 34(b)(i)) to show loss as coming from property held for more than one year.

In regards to the printer, the $2,300 insurance reimbursement Alan received for his loss exceeds his $2,000 adjusted basis in the printer. Thus, he reports a $300 casualty or theft gain on the printer on line 22B. Following the instructions from line 22, he then enters this amount on line 34(c) to show the gain as coming from property held long-term. Alan then completes the rest of Part II to arrive at a $900 net business casualty or theft loss deduction on line 38a. Following the instructions for line 38a, Alan transfers this amount to Form 4797 (line 14), where it will be added to his other ordinary losses.

¶1103.03 FORM 4797

Taxpayers use Form 4797, Sales of Business Property, to report gains and losses from the sale, exchange, or condemnation of business property. Form 4797 consists of three parts. Part I summarizes Section 1231 gains and losses. Part II summarizes ordinary gains and losses. Part III separates the gain from the sale or exchange of property subject to depreciation recapture between ordinary income and Section 1231 gain.

Part I

In Part I, taxpayers report gains and losses from Section 1231 property not subject to depreciation recapture. Also included in Part I are net business casualty gains from Form 4684 and Section 1231 gains from the sale of depreciable property reported on Form 4797, Part III. After entering all Section 1231 gains and losses in Part I, taxpayers compute their net Section 1231 gain or loss (line 7). They transfer a net Section 1231 loss to Part II (line 11) so that it can be treated as an ordinary loss. A net Section 1231 gain is first reduced by the nonrecaptured net Section 1231 losses from the past five years (line 8), and the rest is reported as a long-term capital gain on Schedule D. Taxpayers report the recaptured gain (from Part I (line 8)) as ordinary income in Part II (line 12).

Part II

Taxpayers report gains and losses from the sale, exchange, or condemnation of business property held one year or less in Part II (line 10). Taxpayers also report in Part II (line 14) net business casualty or theft losses and casualty or theft gains and losses from business property held short-term. Net Section 1231 losses and recaptured Section 1231 gains from Part I also appear in Part II. After netting the ordinary gains and losses, individual taxpayers transfer the net amount to Form 1040 (line 14).

Part III

The concept of depreciation recapture was introduced earlier in the chapter (see ¶1102.02). The recapture where gain is taxed as ordinary income to the extent of the *accumulated depreciation taken* is referred to as **Section 1245 recapture**. Section 1245 applies to tangible personal property sold for a gain. Taxpayers report property subject to Section 1245 depreciation recapture on Form 4797, Part III. On Form 4797 (lines 19-25), taxpayers provide information about the depreciable property sold and calculate their depreciation recapture.

Also in Part III, total gains from the disposition of property subject to recapture are separated between amounts recaptured as ordinary income (line 31) and Section 1231 gain (line 32). Taxpayers report the ordinary income on Part II (line 13) and the Section 1231 gain on Part I (line 6).

¶1103.04 FILLED-IN FORM 4797

INFORMATION FOR FIGURE 11-3:

On **July 3, 2012**, Jan Gordon placed in service **equipment** costing $36,000. On **May 10, 2015**, she sold the equipment for $15,000. Depreciation taken on the equipment was $26,361. On **January 3, 2015**, Jan sold **land** used in her business for **$22,800**. Commissions paid on the sale were $1,000. Jan bought the land on **February 5, 1978**, for $14,000.

In 2015, the government notified Jan that land she held for investment was to be condemned. Jan paid **$33,200** for the land on **March 5, 1983**. She received **$30,200** from the government for the land on **May 2, 2015**. Jan has $2,500 of nonrecaptured Section 1231 losses from the past five years. Jan enters the information in bold to the appropriate lines on Form 4797 and follows the instructions on the form.

Line #

1: Gross proceeds from the sale or exchange of real estate reported on Forms 1099-B or 1099-S and included on lines 2, 10, and 20, **$53,000** ($22,800 + $30,200). The proceeds on the sale of the equipment (line 20) is not included since equipment is not real estate.
2(f): Cost or other basis plus improvements and expenses of sale, **$15,000** ($14,000 + $1,000)
8: Nonrecaptured net section 1231 losses from prior years, **$2,500**
12: Gain from line 8, **$2,500** (gain from Part I taxed as ordinary income due to nonrecaptured net Section 1231 losses from the past five years)
20: Gross sales price for the equipment, **$15,000**
21: Cost or other basis plus expenses of sale for the equipment, **$36,000**
22: Depreciation allowed or allowable, **$26,361**

Jan transfers the $2,300 of net Section 1231 gain (from Form 4797, line 9) to the long-term capital gain section of Schedule D (line 11). She transfers the $7,861 of ordinary income (from Form 4797, line 18b) to Form 1040 (line 14).

Figure 11-3: Filled-In Form 4797 (Page 1)

Form **4797**

Department of the Treasury
Internal Revenue Service

Sales of Business Property
(Also Involuntary Conversions and Recapture Amounts Under Sections 179 and 280F(b)(2))
▶ Attach to your tax return.
▶ Information about Form 4797 and its separate instructions is at *www.irs.gov/form4797.*

OMB No. 1545-0184
2015
Attachment Sequence No. **27**

Name(s) shown on return	Identifying number
Janice A. Gordon	271-57-2696

1	Enter the gross proceeds from sales or exchanges reported to you for 2015 on Form(s) 1099-B or 1099-S (or substitute statement) that you are including on line 2, 10, or 20 (see instructions)	1	53,000

Part I **Sales or Exchanges of Property Used in a Trade or Business and Involuntary Conversions From Other Than Casualty or Theft—Most Property Held More Than 1 Year** (see instructions)

2 (a) Description of property	(b) Date acquired (mo., day, yr.)	(c) Date sold (mo., day, yr.)	(d) Gross sales price	(e) Depreciation allowed or allowable since acquisition	(f) Cost or other basis, plus improvements and expense of sale	(g) Gain or (loss) Subtract (f) from the sum of (d) and (e)
Land	2-5-78	1-3-15	22,800		15,000	7,800
Land (involuntary conversion)	3-5-83	5-2-15	30,200		33,200	(3,000)

3	Gain, if any, from Form 4684, line 39	3	
4	Section 1231 gain from installment sales from Form 6252, line 26 or 37	4	
5	Section 1231 gain or (loss) from like-kind exchanges from Form 8824	5	
6	Gain, if any, from line 32, from other than casualty or theft	6	0
7	Combine lines 2 through 6. Enter the gain or (loss) here and on the appropriate line as follows:	7	4,800
	Partnerships (except electing large partnerships) and S corporations. Report the gain or (loss) following the instructions for Form 1065, Schedule K, line 10, or Form 1120S, Schedule K, line 9. Skip lines 8, 9, 11, and 12 below. **Individuals, partners, S corporation shareholders, and all others.** If line 7 is zero or a loss, enter the amount from line 7 on line 11 below and skip lines 8 and 9. If line 7 is a gain and you did not have any prior year section 1231 losses, or they were recaptured in an earlier year, enter the gain from line 7 as a long-term capital gain on the Schedule D filed with your return and skip lines 8, 9, 11, and 12 below.		
8	Nonrecaptured net section 1231 losses from prior years (see instructions)	8	2,500
9	Subtract line 8 from line 7. If zero or less, enter -0-. If line 9 is zero, enter the gain from line 7 on line 12 below. If line 9 is more than zero, enter the amount from line 8 on line 12 below and enter the gain from line 9 as a long-term capital gain on the Schedule D filed with your return (see instructions)	9	2,300

Part II **Ordinary Gains and Losses** (see instructions)

10 Ordinary gains and losses not included on lines 11 through 16 (include property held 1 year or less):

11	Loss, if any, from line 7	11	( )
12	Gain, if any, from line 7 or amount from line 8, if applicable	12	2,500
13	Gain, if any, from line 31	13	5,361
14	Net gain or (loss) from Form 4684, lines 31 and 38a	14	
15	Ordinary gain from installment sales from Form 6252, line 25 or 36	15	
16	Ordinary gain or (loss) from like-kind exchanges from Form 8824	16	
17	Combine lines 10 through 16	17	7,861
18	For all except individual returns, enter the amount from line 17 on the appropriate line of your return and skip lines a and b below. For individual returns, complete lines a and b below:		
a	If the loss on line 11 includes a loss from Form 4684, line 35, column (b)(ii), enter that part of the loss here. Enter the part of the loss from income-producing property on Schedule A (Form 1040), line 28, and the part of the loss from property used as an employee on Schedule A (Form 1040), line 23. Identify as from "Form 4797, line 18a." See instructions	18a	
b	Redetermine the gain or (loss) on line 17 excluding the loss, if any, on line 18a. Enter here and on Form 1040, line 14	18b	7,861

For Paperwork Reduction Act Notice, see separate instructions. Cat. No. 13086I Form **4797** (2015)

Figure 11-3: Filled-In Form 4797 (Page 2)

Form 4797 (2015) Page **2**

Part III Gain From Disposition of Property Under Sections 1245, 1250, 1252, 1254, and 1255 (see instructions)

19 (a) Description of section 1245, 1250, 1252, 1254, or 1255 property:	(b) Date acquired (mo., day, yr.)	(c) Date sold (mo., day, yr.)
A Equipment	7-3-12	5-10-15
B		
C		
D		

These columns relate to the properties on lines 19A through 19D. ▶		Property A	Property B	Property C	Property D
20 Gross sales price (**Note:** *See line 1 before completing.*)	20	15,000			
21 Cost or other basis plus expense of sale	21	36,000			
22 Depreciation (or depletion) allowed or allowable	22	26,361			
23 Adjusted basis. Subtract line 22 from line 21	23	9,639			
24 Total gain. Subtract line 23 from line 20	24	5,361			
25 **If section 1245 property:**					
a Depreciation allowed or allowable from line 22	25a	26,361			
b Enter the **smaller** of line 24 or 25a	25b	5,361			
26 **If section 1250 property:** If straight line depreciation was used, enter -0- on line 26g, except for a corporation subject to section 291.					
a Additional depreciation after 1975 (see instructions)	26a				
b Applicable percentage multiplied by the **smaller** of line 24 or line 26a (see instructions)	26b				
c Subtract line 26a from line 24. If residential rental property **or** line 24 is not more than line 26a, skip lines 26d and 26e	26c				
d Additional depreciation after 1969 and before 1976	26d				
e Enter the **smaller** of line 26c or 26d	26e				
f Section 291 amount (corporations only)	26f				
g Add lines 26b, 26e, and 26f	26g				
27 **If section 1252 property:** Skip this section if you did not dispose of farmland or if this form is being completed for a partnership (other than an electing large partnership).					
a Soil, water, and land clearing expenses	27a				
b Line 27a multiplied by applicable percentage (see instructions)	27b				
c Enter the **smaller** of line 24 or 27b	27c				
28 **If section 1254 property:**					
a Intangible drilling and development costs, expenditures for development of mines and other natural deposits, mining exploration costs, and depletion (see instructions)	28a				
b Enter the **smaller** of line 24 or 28a	28b				
29 **If section 1255 property:**					
a Applicable percentage of payments excluded from income under section 126 (see instructions)	29a				
b Enter the **smaller** of line 24 or 29a (see instructions)	29b				

Summary of Part III Gains. Complete property columns A through D through line 29b before going to line 30.

30 Total gains for all properties. Add property columns A through D, line 24	30	5,361
31 Add property columns A through D, lines 25b, 26g, 27c, 28b, and 29b. Enter here and on line 13	31	5,361
32 Subtract line 31 from line 30. Enter the portion from casualty or theft on Form 4684, line 33. Enter the portion from other than casualty or theft on Form 4797, line 6	32	0

Part IV Recapture Amounts Under Sections 179 and 280F(b)(2) When Business Use Drops to 50% or Less (see instructions)

		(a) Section 179	(b) Section 280F(b)(2)
33 Section 179 expense deduction or depreciation allowable in prior years	33		
34 Recomputed depreciation (see instructions)	34		
35 Recapture amount. Subtract line 34 from line 33. See the instructions for where to report	35		

Form **4797** (2015)

¶1104 Installment Sales

When property is sold, the seller may collect the sales price in full at the time of sale. Alternatively, the sales price may be collected over a number of months or years. If the full sales price is collected in the year of sale, recognized gain or loss is reported in that year. When collections extend beyond the year of sale, any gain (but not loss) may be recognized on the installment method. The installment method allows taxpayers to report the gain (and pay the related taxes) as they collect payments on the installment obligation.

To use the installment sales method, at least one payment must be received in the tax year following the year of the sale. Taxpayers, however, may elect out of using the installment method. They make this election by reporting the entire gain in the year of sale. The election must be made before the due date of the return (including extensions) for the year of the sale.

The installment method is intended for casual sales of personal and real property. Thus, it cannot be used by dealers. A dealer is someone who regularly sells personal or real property in the ordinary course of a trade or business. The installment method cannot be used to report gain from the sale of publicly traded stock or securities.

¶1104.01 COMPUTING INSTALLMENT GAIN

The amount of gain that must be reported in a given tax year is computed as follows:

Gain recognized = payments received × (gross profit ÷ contract price)

Payments Received

As payments on the sales price are collected, a portion of the profit is reported (recognized). Payments include cash and property the seller receives. Payments do not include notes or other obligations the seller receives from the buyer.

Gross Profit

Gross profit equals the amount realized less the adjusted basis of the property. Gross profit is the amount of gain that would be recognized in the year of sale if the installment method were not used. The amount realized includes cash and other property received. It also includes notes received from the buyer or mortgages the buyer assumes. It does not include any interest to be received from the transaction.

EXAMPLE 39

In 20x1, Ellen sells land held for investment and receives $18,000. Ellen paid $11,200 for the land and over the years spent $1,400 on landscaping. Ellen's gross profit of $5,400 is determined as follows.

Amount realized		$18,000
Less adjusted basis		
Cost	$11,200	
Improvements	1,400	(12,600)
Gross profit		$ 5,400

Contract Price

The gross profit ratio is gross profit divided by the contract price. The contract price is the amount realized less mortgages the buyer assumes. It is usually the sum of the principal payments. It does not include interest that the seller expects to receive.

Taxpayers compute the current year's recognized gain by multiplying the amounts received on the principal during the year by the gross profit ratio. In Example 39, Ellen's gross profit ratio equals 30% [$5,400 (gross profit) ÷ $18,000 (contract price)]. Keep in mind that payments on notes normally include interest as well as principal. Interest received by individuals is ordinary income reported on Schedule B.

EXAMPLE 40

Assume the same facts as in Example 39, except that the purchaser gives Ellen a $4,000 down payment plus an interest-bearing note for the rest ($14,000). From this note, $12,000 of principal is due in 20x1, and $2,000 is due in 20x2. If the notes are paid when due, Ellen reports the gain as follows. She reports the interest income from the note on Schedule B.

20x1	($4,000 + $12,000) × 30% =	$4,800
20x2	$2,000 × 30% =	600
Total		$5,400

A special rule applies to the sale of nondepreciable property to a related party, which includes the taxpayer's descendant, ancestor, sibling, or spouse. If nondepreciable property is sold to a related party in an installment sale *and* the related party sells the property within two years of the sale, the rest of the installment gain is taxable to the seller in the year that the related party sells the property. Thus, the subsequent sale by a related party accelerates the gain reported by the original seller.

EXAMPLE 41

On March 1, 20x1, Lucy sells land to her sister for $220,000. She accepts $20,000 down and a note that calls for four annual payments of $50,000, plus interest. The first installment is due on March 1, 20x2. Lucy paid $165,000 for the land several years ago. She realizes gross profit of $55,000 on the sale.

Amount realized	$220,000
Less adjusted basis	(165,000)
Gross profit	$ 55,000

Lucy's gross profit ratio equals 25% ($55,000 gross profit ÷ $220,000 contract price). She will report the $55,000 gain from the sale as follows.

Year	Amount	
20x1	$20,000 × 25% =	$ 5,000
20x2	$50,000 × 25% =	12,500
20x3	$50,000 × 25% =	12,500
20x4	$50,000 × 25% =	12,500
20x5	$50,000 × 25% =	12,500
Total		$55,000

EXAMPLE 42

Same facts as in Example 41, except that on January 25, 20x3 the sister sells the land. Because the sister sold the land within two years of March 1, 20x1, Lucy reports the $55,000 gain from the sale as follows.

Year	Amount	
20x1	$20,000 × 25% =	$ 5,000
20x2	$50,000 × 25% =	12,500
20x3	rest of the gain	37,500
Total		$55,000

EXAMPLE 43

Same facts as in Example 42, except that the sister sells the land on July 25, 20x3. Since the sale occurred after more than two years, the timing of the gain reported by Lucy is the same as in Example 41.

¶1104.02 DEPRECIATION RECAPTURE

If property sold as an installment sale is subject to depreciation recapture, the recapture must be recognized as ordinary income in the year of the sale, regardless of the payments received during the year. The gain reported in the first year as depreciation recapture reduces gross profit used in computing the gross profit ratio. Likewise, it reduces the amount of each installment gain to be included in income as capital gain or Section 1231 gain.

EXAMPLE 44

Jamar sells depreciable personal property for $180,000. He accepts five equal installments of $36,000 plus interest. Jamar realizes gross profit of $120,000 on the sale.

Amount realized		$180,000
Less adjusted basis		
Cost	$90,000	
Accumulated depreciation	(30,000)	(60,000)
Gross profit		$120,000

Gain on the sale of personal property is recaptured as ordinary income to the extent of depreciation taken on the property. Thus, Jamar recognizes the $30,000 of accumulated depreciation as ordinary income in the year of the sale. He also recognizes a portion of each year's receipts as Section 1231 gain. This amount is computed by reducing Jamar's gross profit by $30,000 and recalculating the gross profit ratio.

Income Recognized in Year 1	
Ordinary income (depreciation recapture)	$ 30,000
Recompute the gross profit ratio:	
($120,000 – $30,000) ÷ $180,000 = 50% gross profit ratio	
Section 1231 gain reportable in Year 1 (50% × $36,000)	18,000
Total gain recognized in Year 1	$ 48,000

Income Recognized in Years 2-5	
Section 1231 gain (50% × $36,000 = $18,000 × 4 years)	72,000
Total gain recognized over five years	$120,000

11

Name:
Section:
Date:

QUESTIONS AND PROBLEMS

1. **Capital Assets.** (Obj. 1) Indicate which of the following are capital assets.

Item	*Answer*
a. House occupied as a residence by the owner	
b. Delivery truck used in a contractor's business	
c. Corporate stocks owned by a doctor	
d. Valuable jewelry held for sale by Jones Jewelers	
e. Land held for investment by an accountant	
f. Automobile used for personal purposes by the owner	
g. Business suits worn only to work	
h. House used strictly as a summer residence	
i. Musical copyright owned by the composer	

2. **Capital Gains and Losses.** (Obj. 2)

a. Distinguish between long-term capital gain and short-term capital gain for capital assets acquired January 10, 2014.

b. If an individual has gains and losses from the sale of stocks and other investments, what form or schedule is used to support the capital gain or loss reported on Form 1040?

3. **Holding Period.** (Obj. 2) State the time when the holding period begins on capital assets acquired by the following methods:

a. Capital asset acquired by gift, if sold at a gain

b. Capital asset acquired by gift, if sold at a loss (assume the fair market value (FMV) of the property was less than the donor's basis at the time of the gift)

c. Property inherited from a decedent dying in 2015

4. **Capital Gains and Losses.** (Obj. 2) For each of the following cases, determine whether the gain would be taxed as short-term capital gain, long-term capital gain taxed at 20%, long-term capital gain taxed at 15%, or long-term capital gain taxed at 0%. Assume the taxpayer files as single and this is the only capital asset sold during the year.

a. Stock held for four years is sold for a $3,000 gain; taxable income is $25,000.

b. Stock held for eight months is sold for a $3,000 gain; taxable income is $52,000.

c. Stock held for four years is sold for a $2,000 gain; taxable income is $77,000.

d. Stock held for four years is sold for a $4,000 gain; taxable income is $480,000.

e. Stock held four months is sold for a $4,000 gain; taxable income is $410,000.

5. **Netting Capital Gains and Losses.** (Obj. 3) In each of the following cases, use the netting process between groups to determine the taxpayer's net capital gain and the tax rate paid on such gain.

   a. A $2,000 loss on the sale of a capital asset held six months; a $9,000 gain on the sale of a capital asset held for three years. The taxpayer is in the 35% tax bracket.

   b. Same as Part a., except that the taxpayer is in the 15% tax bracket.

   c. A $6,000 gain on the sale of a capital asset held nine months; a $5,000 gain on the sale of a capital asset held four years. The taxpayer is in the 28% tax bracket.

   d. Same as Part c., except that the taxpayer is in the 10% tax bracket.

   e. Same as in Part c., except that the taxpayer is in the 39.6% tax bracket.

6. **Capital Gains Tax.** (Obj. 4) During 2015, Earl, a single taxpayer, sells two capital assets. The first results in a $4,000 short-term capital gain. The second results in a $9,500 long-term capital gain. Earl's AGI without taking these two gains into consideration is $71,284 (no qualified dividends). Earl deducts the standard deduction and one personal exemption. Compute Earl's 2015 income tax liability.

7. **Capital Gains Tax.** (Obj. 4) During 2015, Angie sells two capital assets. The first results in a $4,000 short-term capital loss. The second results in a $7,500 long-term capital gain. Angie's AGI without taking these gains and losses into consideration is $44,235 (no qualified dividends). She files as head of household and deducts the standard deduction. She claims her two children as dependents. Compute Angie's 2015 income tax liability.

8. **Capital Gains Tax.** (Obj. 4) During 2015, Taylor sells two capital assets. The first results in a $9,000 short-term capital gain. The second results in a $2,600 long-term capital loss. Taylor's AGI without taking these gains and losses into consideration is $125,444 (no qualified dividends). Taylor files as a qualifying widow(er) and deducts the standard deduction. He claims his son as a dependent. Compute Taylor's 2015 income tax liability.

9. **Capital Gains Tax.** (Obj. 4) In March of 2015, Shirley sold stock of the Wingate Corporation for $15,000. Shirley had acquired the stock three years earlier at a cost of $11,600. Exclusive of this gain she expects to have a taxable income of $36,000 (after deductions and exemptions) for the year. Shirley files as single. She has no qualified dividends. In December 2015, Shirley thought about selling stock of the Roberts Printing Company, which she acquired on January 15, 2014, for $18,000. It has since declined in value to $13,000.

   a. Compute Shirley's total tax liability for 2015, assuming she does not sell the Roberts stock in 2015.

   b. Compute Shirley's total tax liability for 2015, assuming she sells the Roberts stock for $13,000 in 2015. What amount of tax savings would result from the sale?

10. **Capital Losses.** (Obj. 3) Compute the capital loss deduction that can be claimed in 2015 for each of the following individual taxpayers. Also, compute the capital loss carryover to 2016 by type (short-term, long-term) of loss. If none, insert *None.* Taxpayers A and B file as single. Taxpayer C files as head of household. Taxpayer D is a married couple filing a joint tax return. Taxpayer E is a married person who is filing a separate tax return from her spouse.

Gains and Losses	*A*	*B*	*C*	*D*	*E*
Short-term capital gains	$ 900	$ 800	$ 0	$ 400	$ 3,200
Short-term capital losses	(6,200)	(1,200)	(400)	(2,400)	(8,600)
Long-term capital gains	800	2,200	800	1,600	1,400
Long-term capital losses	(600)	(800)	(1,150)	(4,200)	(2,600)
Capital loss deduction in 2015	$_____	$_____	$_____	$_____	$_____
Short-term loss carryover to 2016	$_____	$_____	$_____	$_____	$_____
Long-term loss carryover to 2016	$_____	$_____	$_____	$_____	$_____

11. **Stock Sales.** (Obj. 2) A taxpayer is considering selling 100 shares of stock. The current market price is $7,500. Which shares should the taxpayer instruct the broker to sell, and what are the tax consequences of this selection if the taxpayer owned the following shares in the company?

Certificate Number	*Date Acquired*	*Number of Shares*	*Cost*
CR642	4-11-07	300	$15,000
DO111	9-10-11	100	9,000
EA002	8-13-04	100	6,000

12. **Worthless Securities.** (Obj. 2) On July 17, 2014, Martina paid $15,000 for 4,500 shares of stock in ABC corporation. On December 29, 2014, the stock was trading for $.03 a share. On January 6, 2015 Martina's stockbroker let her know that the stock was worthless. Discuss the tax consequences of the ABC stock on Martina's 2014 and 2015 tax returns.

13. **Section 1244 Stock.** (Obj. 2)

a. Hale sells 1,000 shares of his Section 1244 stock ("small business corporation" stock) at a loss of $200,000. If Hale and his wife file a joint return, how will this loss be treated on the tax return?

b. If Hale were single, how would he treat the loss on his tax return?

c. How might Hale have better planned for the sale of his Section 1244 stock?

14. **Subdivided Realty.** (Obj. 2) Juan, an investor, subdivided an unimproved tract of land that he acquired 20 years ago. In 2015, he sold four lots for $10,000 each. The basis of each lot is $2,000, and the selling expenses are $400 per lot.

a. What is the gain or loss on these transactions, and how will it be taxed?

b. Assuming that Juan sells five more lots in 2016 at the same price with selling expenses of $400 per lot, what will be the gain or loss, and how will it be taxed?

15. **Subdivided Realty.** (Obj. 2) Barbie, a real estate dealer, purchased two lots for $12,000 each in May 2006. On August 30, 2015, Barbie sold the tracts of land for $20,000 each. Compute the gain and describe how it will be treated on the tax return.

16. **Bad Debts.** (Obj. 2) Rita loaned her brother, Richard, $7,500 on February 14, 2014. The loan represents a bona fide loan. Richard filed for bankruptcy in 2015, and Rita learned that she could expect to receive only $.70 on the dollar on the personal loan that she had made to him. On May 17, 2016, Rita received a final settlement of $4,000.

a. How much loss can Rita deduct in 2015?

b. How much loss can Rita deduct in 2016?

c. How will this loss be treated on Rita's tax return?

17. **Section 1231 and Capital Gains and Losses.** (Obj. 3) Use the following information to answer Parts a. through c.

	Period Property Was Held	*Amount of Gain or Loss*
Nonbusiness bad debt	Three years	($2,600)
Sale of equipment used in business	Two months	(1,500)
Sale of equipment used in business	Two years	(3,000)
Sale of corporate stock	Five years	2,500
Sale of land used in business	Four years	5,000

a. What, if any, is the amount of net short-term capital loss?

b. What, if any, is the amount of net Section 1231 gain or (loss)?

c. What, if any, is the ordinary loss deduction?

18. Nonbusiness Casualty or Theft Gains and Losses. (Obj. 3) Blake's home was burglarized. Artwork purchased six years ago and a brand new Plasma TV were stolen. Blake had no other nonbusiness casualties or thefts during the year. Based on the information provided below about the theft, describe the tax consequences on Blake's tax return.

	FMV Before	*Adjusted Basis*	*Insurance Proceeds*
Artwork	$10,000	$5,500	$9,500
Plasma TV	1,200	2,000	1,000

19. Business Casualty or Theft Gains and Loss. (Obj. 3) S.R.W. Inc. had an expensive sculpture stolen from the lobby of its offices. The sculpture was insured, and S.R.W. realized an $80,000 gain from the theft. This was S.R.W.'s only casualty or theft for the year.

a. Discuss the tax consequences of this theft on S.R.W.'s tax return if S.R.W. has $100,000 of Section 1231 gains.

b. Same as in Part a., except that S.R.W. has $100,000 of Section 1231 losses.

20. Nonrecaptured Section 1231 Losses. (Obj. 5) Explain the concept of nonrecaptured Section 1231 losses and their impact a taxpayer's netting process.

21. Sale of Business Property. (Obj. 5) Carlotta purchased computer equipment for her business in 2012 for $60,000. In 2015, she sold the computer equipment for $35,000. Depreciation information follows:

Regular (accelerated) MACRS deduction claimed	$51,360
Straight-line depreciation would have been	$24,000

What is Carlotta's gain or loss on the sale of the computers, and how will it be treated?

22. **Unrecaptured Section 1250 Gain.** (Obj. 2) Victor purchased a warehouse in 2003 for $1,000,000. He sold the warehouse in July of 2015 for $1,200,000. Victor deducted $309,524 of depreciation during the period when he owned the building. How will this transaction be reported on the tax return? How will the gain on this transaction be taxed?

23. **Sale of Business Property.** (Obj. 7) In 2015, Virginia Banks (SSN 364-25-8153) had the following transactions involving property used in her manufacturing business.

- Machinery purchased for $50,000 on August 6, 2012 was sold on April 6, 2015 for $22,000. Total depreciation taken on the machine was $31,258.
- Land used in Virginia's business was sold for $23,000 on June 6, 2015. The land was purchased for $16,000 on May 3, 2003.
- A small tool shed was destroyed by fire during 2015. The loss was not covered by insurance. The shed had been used for several years and had an adjusted basis of $2,500 at the time of the fire. The loss was initially reported on Form 4684. (Enter loss on Form 4797 [line 14]).
- A warehouse purchased for $50,000 on August 10, 2006, was condemned by the city in order to acquire the land upon which it stood so that the state could build a new highway. Virginia was paid $45,000 for the building on May 1, 2015. Depreciation taken on the building was $10,897.
- Virginia received $36,000 for the condemned land. The land had a basis of $30,000.

Virginia will not reinvest any of the proceeds from the condemned land or building in qualified replacement property and wants to report the gain on her 2015 return. Virginia's nonrecaptured net Section 1231 losses the previous five years are $3,500. Prepare Form 4797, Sales of Business Property, using the blank form provided.

24. **Installment Sales.** (Obj. 6) Yvonne, a consulting engineer and cash basis taxpayer, decided to close her office and go back to college and study business. One of her business assets was a used car that she had purchased in 2013 for $15,000. She still owed $5,000 on the car when she sold it for $10,600 on June 10, 2015. The buyer agreed to assume the $5,000 note. Further, the buyer agreed to pay $1,600 as a down payment and pay $2,000 (plus 12% interest) on June 10, 2016, and $2,000 (plus 12% interest on the remaining balance) on June 10, 2017. Under the MACRS rules, Yvonne had correctly taken $9,240 of depreciation on the automobile. Assume that Yvonne has no other liabilities.

a. What is the realized gain to Yvonne on the sale of the automobile?

b. If the realized gain is reported on the installment basis, how much and what type of gain will Yvonne report as income in 2015, 2016, and 2017?

c. How much interest income will Yvonne report in 2016 and 2017?

(Use for Problem 23.)

Form **4797**

Department of the Treasury
Internal Revenue Service

Sales of Business Property

(Also Involuntary Conversions and Recapture Amounts Under Sections 179 and 280F(b)(2))

▶ Attach to your tax return.

▶ Information about Form 4797 and its separate instructions is at *www.irs.gov/form4797.*

OMB No. 1545-0184

2015

Attachment Sequence No. **27**

Name(s) shown on return	**Identifying number**

1	Enter the gross proceeds from sales or exchanges reported to you for 2015 on Form(s) 1099-B or 1099-S (or substitute statement) that you are including on line 2, 10, or 20 (see instructions)	1	

Part I **Sales or Exchanges of Property Used in a Trade or Business and Involuntary Conversions From Other Than Casualty or Theft—Most Property Held More Than 1 Year** (see instructions)

2	**(a)** Description of property	**(b)** Date acquired (mo., day, yr.)	**(c)** Date sold (mo., day, yr.)	**(d)** Gross sales price	**(e)** Depreciation allowed or allowable since acquisition	**(f)** Cost or other basis, plus improvements and expense of sale	**(g) Gain or (loss)** Subtract (f) from the sum of (d) and (e)

3	Gain, if any, from Form 4684, line 39	3	
4	Section 1231 gain from installment sales from Form 6252, line 26 or 37	4	
5	Section 1231 gain or (loss) from like-kind exchanges from Form 8824	5	
6	Gain, if any, from line 32, from other than casualty or theft.	6	
7	Combine lines 2 through 6. Enter the gain or (loss) here and on the appropriate line as follows:	7	
	Partnerships (except electing large partnerships) and S corporations. Report the gain or (loss) following the instructions for Form 1065, Schedule K, line 10, or Form 1120S, Schedule K, line 9. Skip lines 8, 9, 11, and 12 below. **Individuals, partners, S corporation shareholders, and all others.** If line 7 is zero or a loss, enter the amount from line 7 on line 11 below and skip lines 8 and 9. If line 7 is a gain and you did not have any prior year section 1231 losses, or they were recaptured in an earlier year, enter the gain from line 7 as a long-term capital gain on the Schedule D filed with your return and skip lines 8, 9, 11, and 12 below.		
8	Nonrecaptured net section 1231 losses from prior years (see instructions)	8	
9	Subtract line 8 from line 7. If zero or less, enter -0-. If line 9 is zero, enter the gain from line 7 on line 12 below. If line 9 is more than zero, enter the amount from line 8 on line 12 below and enter the gain from line 9 as a long-term capital gain on the Schedule D filed with your return (see instructions)	9	

Part II **Ordinary Gains and Losses** (see instructions)

10 Ordinary gains and losses not included on lines 11 through 16 (include property held 1 year or less):

11	Loss, if any, from line 7	11	( )
12	Gain, if any, from line 7 or amount from line 8, if applicable	12	
13	Gain, if any, from line 31	13	
14	Net gain or (loss) from Form 4684, lines 31 and 38a	14	
15	Ordinary gain from installment sales from Form 6252, line 25 or 36	15	
16	Ordinary gain or (loss) from like-kind exchanges from Form 8824.	16	
17	Combine lines 10 through 16	17	
18	For all except individual returns, enter the amount from line 17 on the appropriate line of your return and skip lines a and b below. For individual returns, complete lines a and b below:		
a	If the loss on line 11 includes a loss from Form 4684, line 35, column (b)(ii), enter that part of the loss here. Enter the part of the loss from income-producing property on Schedule A (Form 1040), line 28, and the part of the loss from property used as an employee on Schedule A (Form 1040), line 23. Identify as from "Form 4797, line 18a." See instructions . .	18a	
b	Redetermine the gain or (loss) on line 17 excluding the loss, if any, on line 18a. Enter here and on Form 1040, line 14	18b	

For Paperwork Reduction Act Notice, see separate instructions. Cat. No. 13086I Form **4797** (2015)

(Use for Problem 23.)

Form 4797 (2015) Page **2**

Part III **Gain From Disposition of Property Under Sections 1245, 1250, 1252, 1254, and 1255** (see instructions)

19 **(a)** Description of section 1245, 1250, 1252, 1254, or 1255 property:	**(b)** Date acquired (mo., day, yr.)	**(c)** Date sold (mo., day, yr.)
A		
B		
C		
D		

These columns relate to the properties on lines 19A through 19D. ▶		Property A	Property B	Property C	Property D
20 Gross sales price (**Note:** *See line 1 before completing.*)	20				
21 Cost or other basis plus expense of sale	21				
22 Depreciation (or depletion) allowed or allowable	22				
23 Adjusted basis. Subtract line 22 from line 21	23				
24 Total gain. Subtract line 23 from line 20	24				
25 **If section 1245 property:**					
a Depreciation allowed or allowable from line 22	25a				
b Enter the **smaller** of line 24 or 25a	25b				
26 **If section 1250 property:** If straight line depreciation was used, enter -0- on line 26g, except for a corporation subject to section 291.					
a Additional depreciation after 1975 (see instructions)	26a				
b Applicable percentage multiplied by the **smaller** of line 24 or line 26a (see instructions)	26b				
c Subtract line 26a from line 24. If residential rental property **or** line 24 is not more than line 26a, skip lines 26d and 26e	26c				
d Additional depreciation after 1969 and before 1976	26d				
e Enter the **smaller** of line 26c or 26d	26e				
f Section 291 amount (corporations only)	26f				
g Add lines 26b, 26e, and 26f	26g				
27 **If section 1252 property:** Skip this section if you did not dispose of farmland or if this form is being completed for a partnership (other than an electing large partnership).					
a Soil, water, and land clearing expenses	27a				
b Line 27a multiplied by applicable percentage (see instructions)	27b				
c Enter the **smaller** of line 24 or 27b	27c				
28 **If section 1254 property:**					
a Intangible drilling and development costs, expenditures for development of mines and other natural deposits, mining exploration costs, and depletion (see instructions)	28a				
b Enter the **smaller** of line 24 or 28a	28b				
29 **If section 1255 property:**					
a Applicable percentage of payments excluded from income under section 126 (see instructions)	29a				
b Enter the **smaller** of line 24 or 29a (see instructions)	29b				

Summary of Part III Gains. Complete property columns A through D through line 29b before going to line 30.

30 Total gains for all properties. Add property columns A through D, line 24	30	
31 Add property columns A through D, lines 25b, 26g, 27c, 28b, and 29b. Enter here and on line 13	31	
32 Subtract line 31 from line 30. Enter the portion from casualty or theft on Form 4684, line 33. Enter the portion from other than casualty or theft on Form 4797, line 6	32	

Part IV **Recapture Amounts Under Sections 179 and 280F(b)(2) When Business Use Drops to 50% or Less** (see instructions)

		(a) Section 179	(b) Section 280F(b)(2)
33 Section 179 expense deduction or depreciation allowable in prior years	33		
34 Recomputed depreciation (see instructions)	34		
35 Recapture amount. Subtract line 34 from line 33. See the instructions for where to report	35		

Form **4797** (2015)

25. **Installment Sales.** (Obj. 6) Tyka sold depreciable personal property for $70,000 on August 4, 2015. The buyer agreed to pay $10,000 at the time of sale and $20,000 on August 4 in each of the next three years. In addition, interest at the current market rate will be paid on the remaining installment balance. Tyka bought the property several years ago for $43,000. Depreciation totaling $18,000 was taken on the property.

a. Compute the total gain from the sale.

b. How much gain and what type of gain must be reported in the year of sale?

c. How much gain and what type of gain must be reported in each of the next three years?

26. **Internet Problem: Researching IRS Publication 537.** (Obj. 6)

During 2015, Leo, a cash basis taxpayer, sold land at a gain to an unrelated party. Leo received part of the proceeds in 2015 and will receive the rest of the proceeds in 2016 and 2017. Leo is fairly sure he would like to elect out of the installment sales method and has asked for advice on how to accomplish this. He also wants to know if he elects out of the installment method whether he can later change his mind and use the installment method to report the gain on the sale.

Go to the IRS website. Locate IRS Publication 537. Print out a copy of the page where the answer to Leo's questions can be found. Underline or highlight the pertinent information. Prepare a brief discussion of the answer to Leo's questions.

See Appendix A for instructions on use of the IRS website.

27. **Business Entity Problem.** (Obj. 2) This problem is designed for those using the "business entity" approach. **The solution may require information from Chapter 14.**

Kenya Corporation had the following capital gains and losses for the year. Discuss how these gains and losses affect Kenya Corporation's taxable income.

Short-term capital gain	$36,000
Short-term capital loss	15,000
Long-term capital gain	16,000
Long-term capital loss	42,000

COMPREHENSIVE PROBLEMS

28. (Obj. 2) On November 10, 2015, Bev sold residential realty for $300,000. Bev purchased the realty on August 5, 2007, for $275,000. She depreciated the property over 27.5 years using the straight-line method. Compute Bev's Section 1231 gain and the amount of her unrecaptured Section 1250 gain.

29. Form 8949 and Schedule D. (Obj. 7)

a. Michael L. (SSN 374-47-7774) and Joyce A. (SSN 642-81-9982) Sea, both age 38, file a joint tax return. They sold the following investments during the year. All sales were reported to the Seas on Form 1099-B. None showed the Seas' basis.

Description	*Date Acquired*	*Adjusted Basis*	*Date Sold*	*Sales Price*
20 shares Red Corp.	7-1-11	$1,661	12-6-15	$2,311
50 shares Lee Corp.	9-15-11	5,820	11-14-15	4,320
60 shares Alf Corp.	6-10-14	850	10-15-15	715
100 shares RST Corp.	5-10-95	4,600	8-8-15	2,430
$1,000 bond, TF Co.	5-5-15	800	10-15-15	900

The Seas carried over a $260 short-term capital loss and a $2,500 long-term capital loss from 2014. The Seas report taxable wages of $51,920. From this amount $1,840 was withheld for federal income taxes. The Seas's only other item of gross income during the year was $1,200 of dividend income, which includes $850 of qualified dividends.

Prepare the Seas' 2015 tax return. Neither want $3 to go to the Presidential election campaign fund. Use the approach from Examples 10-12 to compute the Seas' tax. The Seas live at 1319 Mayfair Drive, Champaign, IL 61821. They claim one dependent, their 13-year-old son, Tad (SSN 629-43-7881). The Seas get full health care coverage through Michael's work. The Seas sign their return on April 15, 2016.

b. Ellen B. Ryan (SSN 392-40-6811) is unmarried with no dependents. Ellen lives at 1840 S. 200 West, Reno, Nevada 89434. She is 34 years old. During the year, she sold common stock in the following companies. All stock sales were reported to Ellen on Form 1099-B. None showed Ellen's basis.

Description	*Date Acquired*	*Adjusted Basis*	*Date Sold*	*Sales Price*
400 shares Gable Co.	8-9-14	$5,175	5-11-15	$ 6,345
127 shares Tolano Corp.	3-10-14	3,929	7-15-15	3,556
690 shares Radian, Inc.	1-19-09	6,570	11-27-15	11,844

Ellen carried over a $3,500 long-term capital loss from 2014. Her taxable wages were $61,893 in 2015. Her employer withheld $7,630 for federal income taxes. Ellen also had $650 of taxable interest and $540 of tax-exempt interest. Ellen wants $3 to go to the Presidential campaign fund.

Prepare Ellen's 2015 tax return that she signs on April 11, 2016. Use the approach from Examples 10-12 to compute Ellen's tax. Ellen gets full health care coverage through her work.

(Use for Problem 29.)

Form **1040** Department of the Treasury—Internal Revenue Service (99) **U.S. Individual Income Tax Return** **2015** OMB No. 1545-0074 IRS Use Only—Do not write or staple in this space.

For the year Jan. 1–Dec. 31, 2015, or other tax year beginning , 2015, ending , 20 See separate instructions.

Your first name and initial	Last name	Your social security number
If a joint return, spouse's first name and initial	Last name	Spouse's social security number
Home address (number and street). If you have a P.O. box, see instructions.	Apt. no.	▲ Make sure the SSN(s) above and on line 6c are correct.
City, town or post office, state, and ZIP code. If you have a foreign address, also complete spaces below (see instructions).		**Presidential Election Campaign** Check here if you, or your spouse if filing jointly, want $3 to go to this fund. Checking a box below will not change your tax or refund. ☐ You ☐ Spouse
Foreign country name	Foreign province/state/county	Foreign postal code

Filing Status

Check only one box.

1 ☐ Single
2 ☐ Married filing jointly (even if only one had income)
3 ☐ Married filing separately. Enter spouse's SSN above and full name here. ▶
4 ☐ Head of household (with qualifying person). (See instructions.) If the qualifying person is a child but not your dependent, enter this child's name here. ▶
5 ☐ Qualifying widow(er) with dependent child

Exemptions

6a ☐ **Yourself.** If someone can claim you as a dependent, **do not** check box 6a . . . . .
b ☐ **Spouse** . . . .

Boxes checked on 6a and 6b

c **Dependents:**

(1) First name Last name	(2) Dependent's social security number	(3) Dependent's relationship to you	(4) ✓ if child under age 17 qualifying for child tax credit (see instructions)
			☐
			☐
			☐
			☐

If more than four dependents, see instructions and check here ▶☐

No. of children on 6c who:
• lived with you
• did not live with you due to divorce or separation (see instructions)

Dependents on 6c not entered above

d Total number of exemptions claimed . . . . Add numbers on lines above ▶

Income

Attach Form(s) W-2 here. Also attach Forms W-2G and 1099-R if tax was withheld.

If you did not get a W-2, see instructions.

7	Wages, salaries, tips, etc. Attach Form(s) W-2		7
8a	**Taxable** interest. Attach Schedule B if required		8a
b	**Tax-exempt** interest. **Do not** include on line 8a	8b	
9a	Ordinary dividends. Attach Schedule B if required		9a
b	Qualified dividends	9b	
10	Taxable refunds, credits, or offsets of state and local income taxes		10
11	Alimony received		11
12	Business income or (loss). Attach Schedule C or C-EZ		12
13	Capital gain or (loss). Attach Schedule D if required. If not required, check here ▶ ☐		13
14	Other gains or (losses). Attach Form 4797		14
15a	IRA distributions	15a	b Taxable amount 15b
16a	Pensions and annuities	16a	b Taxable amount 16b
17	Rental real estate, royalties, partnerships, S corporations, trusts, etc. Attach Schedule E		17
18	Farm income or (loss). Attach Schedule F		18
19	Unemployment compensation		19
20a	Social security benefits	20a	b Taxable amount 20b
21	Other income. List type and amount		21
22	Combine the amounts in the far right column for lines 7 through 21. This is your **total income** ▶		22

Adjusted Gross Income

23	Reserved	23	
24	Certain business expenses of reservists, performing artists, and fee-basis government officials. Attach Form 2106 or 2106-EZ	24	
25	Health savings account deduction. Attach Form 8889	25	
26	Moving expenses. Attach Form 3903	26	
27	Deductible part of self-employment tax. Attach Schedule SE	27	
28	Self-employed SEP, SIMPLE, and qualified plans	28	
29	Self-employed health insurance deduction	29	
30	Penalty on early withdrawal of savings	30	
31a	Alimony paid **b** Recipient's SSN ▶	31a	
32	IRA deduction	32	
33	Student loan interest deduction	33	
34	Reserved	34	
35	Domestic production activities deduction. Attach Form 8903	35	
36	Add lines 23 through 35		36
37	Subtract line 36 from line 22. This is your **adjusted gross income** ▶		37

For Disclosure, Privacy Act, and Paperwork Reduction Act Notice, see separate instructions. Cat. No. 11320B Form **1040** (2015)

(Use for Problem 29.)

Form 1040 (2015) Page **2**

Tax and Credits

38	Amount from line 37 (adjusted gross income)	38	
39a	Check if: ☐ **You** were born before January 2, 1951, ☐ Blind. ☐ **Spouse** was born before January 2, 1951, ☐ Blind. } **Total boxes checked ▶ 39a** ☐		
b	If your spouse itemizes on a separate return or you were a dual-status alien, check here ▶ 39b☐		
40	**Itemized deductions** (from Schedule A) **or** your **standard deduction** (see left margin)	40	
41	Subtract line 40 from line 38	41	
42	**Exemptions.** If line 38 is $154,950 or less, multiply $4,000 by the number on line 6d. Otherwise, see instructions	42	
43	**Taxable income.** Subtract line 42 from line 41. If line 42 is more than line 41, enter -0-	43	
44	**Tax** (see instructions). Check if any from: **a** ☐ Form(s) 8814 **b** ☐ Form 4972 **c** ☐	44	
45	**Alternative minimum tax** (see instructions). Attach Form 6251	45	
46	Excess advance premium tax credit repayment. Attach Form 8962	46	
47	Add lines 44, 45, and 46 ▶	47	
48	Foreign tax credit. Attach Form 1116 if required	48	
49	Credit for child and dependent care expenses. Attach Form 2441	49	
50	Education credits from Form 8863, line 19	50	
51	Retirement savings contributions credit. Attach Form 8880	51	
52	Child tax credit. Attach Schedule 8812, if required	52	
53	Residential energy credit. Attach Form 5695	53	
54	Other credits from Form: **a** ☐ 3800 **b** ☐ 8801 **c** ☐	54	
55	Add lines 48 through 54. These are your **total credits**	55	
56	Subtract line 55 from line 47. If line 55 is more than line 47, enter -0- ▶	56	

Standard Deduction for—
- People who check any box on line 39a or 39b **or** who can be claimed as a dependent, see instructions.
- All others:

Single or Married filing separately, $6,300

Married filing jointly or Qualifying widow(er), $12,600

Head of household, $9,250

Other Taxes

57	Self-employment tax. Attach Schedule SE	57	
58	Unreported social security and Medicare tax from Form: **a** ☐ 4137 **b** ☐ 8919	58	
59	Additional tax on IRAs, other qualified retirement plans, etc. Attach Form 5329 if required	59	
60a	Household employment taxes from Schedule H	60a	
b	First-time homebuyer credit repayment. Attach Form 5405 if required	60b	
61	Health care: individual responsibility (see instructions) Full-year coverage ☐	61	
62	Taxes from: **a** ☐ Form 8959 **b** ☐ Form 8960 **c** ☐ Instructions; enter code(s)	62	
63	Add lines 56 through 62. This is your **total tax** ▶	63	

Payments

If you have a qualifying child, attach Schedule EIC.

64	Federal income tax withheld from Forms W-2 and 1099	64	
65	2015 estimated tax payments and amount applied from 2014 return	65	
66a	**Earned income credit (EIC)**	66a	
b	Nontaxable combat pay election 66b		
67	Additional child tax credit. Attach Schedule 8812	67	
68	American opportunity credit from Form 8863, line 8	68	
69	Net premium tax credit. Attach Form 8962	69	
70	Amount paid with request for extension to file	70	
71	Excess social security and tier 1 RRTA tax withheld	71	
72	Credit for federal tax on fuels. Attach Form 4136	72	
73	Credits from Form: **a** ☐ 2439 **b** Reserved **c** ☐ 8885 **d** ☐	73	
74	Add lines 64, 65, 66a, and 67 through 73. These are your **total payments** ▶	74	

Refund

75	If line 74 is more than line 63, subtract line 63 from line 74. This is the amount you **overpaid**	75	
76a	Amount of line 75 you want **refunded to you.** If Form 8888 is attached, check here ▶ ☐	76a	
▶ b	Routing number ▶ **c** Type: ☐ Checking ☐ Savings		
▶ d	Account number		
77	Amount of line 75 you want **applied to your 2016 estimated tax** ▶ 77		

Direct deposit? See instructions.

Amount You Owe

78	**Amount you owe.** Subtract line 74 from line 63. For details on how to pay, see instructions ▶	78	
79	Estimated tax penalty (see instructions) 79		

Third Party Designee

Do you want to allow another person to discuss this return with the IRS (see instructions)? ☐ **Yes.** Complete below. ☐ **No**

Designee's name ▶ Phone no. ▶ Personal identification number (PIN) ▶

Sign Here

Joint return? See instructions. Keep a copy for your records.

Under penalties of perjury, I declare that I have examined this return and accompanying schedules and statements, and to the best of my knowledge and belief, they are true, correct, and complete. Declaration of preparer (other than taxpayer) is based on all information of which preparer has any knowledge.

Your signature	Date	Your occupation	Daytime phone number
Spouse's signature. If a joint return, **both** must sign.	Date	Spouse's occupation	If the IRS sent you an Identity Protection PIN, enter it here (see inst.)

Paid Preparer Use Only

Print/Type preparer's name	Preparer's signature	Date	Check ☐ if self-employed	PTIN
Firm's name ▶			Firm's EIN ▶	
Firm's address ▶			Phone no.	

www.irs.gov/form1040 Form **1040** (2015)

(Use for Problem 29.)

SCHEDULE D (Form 1040)

Department of the Treasury
Internal Revenue Service (99)

Capital Gains and Losses

▶ Attach to Form 1040 or Form 1040NR.
▶ Information about Schedule D and its separate instructions is at *www.irs.gov/scheduled*.
▶ Use Form 8949 to list your transactions for lines 1b, 2, 3, 8b, 9, and 10.

OMB No. 1545-0074
2015
Attachment Sequence No. **12**

Name(s) shown on return	**Your social security number**

Part I **Short-Term Capital Gains and Losses—Assets Held One Year or Less**

See instructions for how to figure the amounts to enter on the lines below. This form may be easier to complete if you round off cents to whole dollars.	(d) Proceeds (sales price)	(e) Cost (or other basis)	(g) Adjustments to gain or loss from Form(s) 8949, Part I, line 2, column (g)	(h) Gain or (loss) Subtract column (e) from column (d) and combine the result with column (g)
1a Totals for all short-term transactions reported on Form 1099-B for which basis was reported to the IRS and for which you have no adjustments (see instructions). However, if you choose to report all these transactions on Form 8949, leave this line blank and go to line 1b .				
1b Totals for all transactions reported on Form(s) 8949 with **Box A** checked				
2 Totals for all transactions reported on Form(s) 8949 with **Box B** checked				
3 Totals for all transactions reported on Form(s) 8949 with **Box C** checked				

4 Short-term gain from Form 6252 and short-term gain or (loss) from Forms 4684, 6781, and 8824 .	**4**	
5 Net short-term gain or (loss) from partnerships, S corporations, estates, and trusts from Schedule(s) K-1	**5**	
6 Short-term capital loss carryover. Enter the amount, if any, from line 8 of your **Capital Loss Carryover Worksheet** in the instructions	**6**	( )
7 **Net short-term capital gain or (loss).** Combine lines 1a through 6 in column (h). If you have any long-term capital gains or losses, go to Part II below. Otherwise, go to Part III on the back	**7**	

Part II **Long-Term Capital Gains and Losses—Assets Held More Than One Year**

See instructions for how to figure the amounts to enter on the lines below. This form may be easier to complete if you round off cents to whole dollars.	(d) Proceeds (sales price)	(e) Cost (or other basis)	(g) Adjustments to gain or loss from Form(s) 8949, Part II, line 2, column (g)	(h) Gain or (loss) Subtract column (e) from column (d) and combine the result with column (g)
8a Totals for all long-term transactions reported on Form 1099-B for which basis was reported to the IRS and for which you have no adjustments (see instructions). However, if you choose to report all these transactions on Form 8949, leave this line blank and go to line 8b .				
8b Totals for all transactions reported on Form(s) 8949 with **Box D** checked				
9 Totals for all transactions reported on Form(s) 8949 with **Box E** checked				
10 Totals for all transactions reported on Form(s) 8949 with **Box F** checked.				

11 Gain from Form 4797, Part I; long-term gain from Forms 2439 and 6252; and long-term gain or (loss) from Forms 4684, 6781, and 8824	**11**	
12 Net long-term gain or (loss) from partnerships, S corporations, estates, and trusts from Schedule(s) K-1	**12**	
13 Capital gain distributions. See the instructions	**13**	
14 Long-term capital loss carryover. Enter the amount, if any, from line 13 of your **Capital Loss Carryover Worksheet** in the instructions	**14**	( )
15 **Net long-term capital gain or (loss).** Combine lines 8a through 14 in column (h). Then go to Part III on the back	**15**	

For Paperwork Reduction Act Notice, see your tax return instructions. Cat. No. 11338H **Schedule D (Form 1040) 2015**

(Use for Problem 29.)

Schedule D (Form 1040) 2015 Page **2**

Part III **Summary**

16 Combine lines 7 and 15 and enter the result **16**

• If line 16 is a **gain,** enter the amount from line 16 on Form 1040, line 13, or Form 1040NR, line 14. Then go to line 17 below.

• If line 16 is a **loss,** skip lines 17 through 20 below. Then go to line 21. Also be sure to complete line 22.

• If line 16 is **zero,** skip lines 17 through 21 below and enter -0- on Form 1040, line 13, or Form 1040NR, line 14. Then go to line 22.

17 Are lines 15 and 16 **both** gains?

☐ **Yes.** Go to line 18.

☐ **No.** Skip lines 18 through 21, and go to line 22.

18 Enter the amount, if any, from line 7 of the **28% Rate Gain Worksheet** in the instructions . . ▶ **18**

19 Enter the amount, if any, from line 18 of the **Unrecaptured Section 1250 Gain Worksheet** in the instructions . . . . ▶ **19**

20 Are lines 18 and 19 **both** zero or blank?

☐ **Yes.** Complete the **Qualified Dividends and Capital Gain Tax Worksheet** in the instructions for Form 1040, line 44 (or in the instructions for Form 1040NR, line 42). **Do not** complete lines 21 and 22 below.

☐ **No.** Complete the **Schedule D Tax Worksheet** in the instructions. **Do not** complete lines 21 and 22 below.

21 If line 16 is a loss, enter here and on Form 1040, line 13, or Form 1040NR, line 14, the **smaller** of:

• The loss on line 16 or
• ($3,000), or if married filing separately, ($1,500) . . . . **21** ( )

Note. When figuring which amount is smaller, treat both amounts as positive numbers.

22 Do you have qualified dividends on Form 1040, line 9b, or Form 1040NR, line 10b?

☐ **Yes.** Complete the **Qualified Dividends and Capital Gain Tax Worksheet** in the instructions for Form 1040, line 44 (or in the instructions for Form 1040NR, line 42).

☐ **No.** Complete the rest of Form 1040 or Form 1040NR.

Schedule D (Form 1040) 2015

(Use for Problem 29.)

Form **8949**
Department of the Treasury
Internal Revenue Service

Sales and Other Dispositions of Capital Assets

▶ Information about Form 8949 and its separate instructions is at *www.irs.gov/form8949.*
▶ File with your Schedule D to list your transactions for lines 1b, 2, 3, 8b, 9, and 10 of Schedule D.

OMB No. 1545-0074
2015
Attachment Sequence No. **12A**

Name(s) shown on return | **Social security number or taxpayer identification number**

Before you check Box A, B, or C below, see whether you received any Form(s) 1099-B or substitute statement(s) from your broker. A substitute statement will have the same information as Form 1099-B. Either will show whether your basis (usually your cost) was reported to the IRS by your broker and may even tell you which box to check.

Part I **Short-Term.** Transactions involving capital assets you held 1 year or less are short term. For long-term transactions, see page 2.

Note: You may aggregate all short-term transactions reported on Form(s) 1099-B showing basis was reported to the IRS and for which no adjustments or codes are required. Enter the totals directly on Schedule D, line 1a; you aren't required to report these transactions on Form 8949 (see instructions).

You *must* check Box A, B, *or* C below. Check only one box. If more than one box applies for your short-term transactions, complete a separate Form 8949, page 1, for each applicable box. If you have more short-term transactions than will fit on this page for one or more of the boxes, complete as many forms with the same box checked as you need.

☐ **(A)** Short-term transactions reported on Form(s) 1099-B showing basis was reported to the IRS (see **Note** above)
☐ **(B)** Short-term transactions reported on Form(s) 1099-B showing basis was **not** reported to the IRS
☐ **(C)** Short-term transactions not reported to you on Form 1099-B

1 (a) Description of property (Example: 100 sh. XYZ Co.)	(b) Date acquired (Mo., day, yr.)	(c) Date sold or disposed of (Mo., day, yr.)	(d) Proceeds (sales price) (see instructions)	(e) Cost or other basis. See the **Note** below and see *Column (e)* in the separate instructions	**Adjustment, if any, to gain or loss.** If you enter an amount in column (g), enter a code in column (f). **See the separate instructions.** (f) Code(s) from instructions	(g) Amount of adjustment	(h) **Gain or (loss).** Subtract column (e) from column (d) and combine the result with column (g)
2 Totals. Add the amounts in columns (d), (e), (g), and (h) (subtract negative amounts). Enter each total here and include on your Schedule D, **line 1b** (if **Box A** above is checked), **line 2** (if **Box B** above is checked), or **line 3** (if **Box C** above is checked) ▶							

Note: If you checked Box A above but the basis reported to the IRS was incorrect, enter in column (e) the basis as reported to the IRS, and enter an adjustment in column (g) to correct the basis. See *Column (g)* in the separate instructions for how to figure the amount of the adjustment.

For Paperwork Reduction Act Notice, see your tax return instructions. Cat. No. 37768Z Form **8949** (2015)

(Use for Problem 29.)

Form 8949 (2015) Attachment Sequence No. **12A** Page **2**

Name(s) shown on return. Name and SSN or taxpayer identification no. not required if shown on other side | **Social security number or taxpayer identification number**

Before you check Box D, E, or F below, see whether you received any Form(s) 1099-B or substitute statement(s) from your broker. A substitute statement will have the same information as Form 1099-B. Either will show whether your basis (usually your cost) was reported to the IRS by your broker and may even tell you which box to check.

Part II **Long-Term.** Transactions involving capital assets you held more than 1 year are long term. For short-term transactions, see page 1.

Note: You may aggregate all long-term transactions reported on Form(s) 1099-B showing basis was reported to the IRS and for which no adjustments or codes are required. Enter the totals directly on Schedule D, line 8a; you aren't required to report these transactions on Form 8949 (see instructions).

You *must* check Box D, E, *or* F below. Check only one box. If more than one box applies for your long-term transactions, complete a separate Form 8949, page 2, for each applicable box. If you have more long-term transactions than will fit on this page for one or more of the boxes, complete as many forms with the same box checked as you need.

☐ **(D)** Long-term transactions reported on Form(s) 1099-B showing basis was reported to the IRS (see **Note** above)
☐ **(E)** Long-term transactions reported on Form(s) 1099-B showing basis was **not** reported to the IRS
☐ **(F)** Long-term transactions not reported to you on Form 1099-B

1 (a) Description of property (Example: 100 sh. XYZ Co.)	(b) Date acquired (Mo., day, yr.)	(c) Date sold or disposed of (Mo., day, yr.)	(d) Proceeds (sales price) (see instructions)	(e) Cost or other basis. See the **Note** below and see *Column (e)* in the separate instructions	**Adjustment, if any, to gain or loss.** If you enter an amount in column (g), enter a code in column (f). **See the separate instructions.** (f) Code(s) from instructions	(g) Amount of adjustment	(h) **Gain or (loss).** Subtract column (e) from column (d) and combine the result with column (g)
2 Totals. Add the amounts in columns (d), (e), (g), and (h) (subtract negative amounts). Enter each total here and include on your Schedule D, **line 8b** (if **Box D** above is checked), **line 9** (if **Box E** above is checked), or **line 10** (if **Box F** above is checked) ►							

Note: If you checked Box D above but the basis reported to the IRS was incorrect, enter in column (e) the basis as reported to the IRS, and enter an adjustment in column (g) to correct the basis. See *Column (g)* in the separate instructions for how to figure the amount of the adjustment.

Form **8949** (2015)

Chapter

12

NOLs, AMT, and Business Tax Credits

CHAPTER CONTENTS

LEARNING OBJECTIVES

After completing Chapter 12, you should be able to:

1. Compute a taxpayer's current year net operating loss and advise taxpayers as to their options on how to utilize the loss.
2. Understand how the alternative minimum tax affects a taxpayer's total tax liability and compute a taxpayer's alternative minimum tax.
3. Describe a variety of tax credits available to businesses through the general business credit and compute the amount of tax credit for each of these credits.
4. Complete Form 6251.

CHAPTER OVERVIEW

This chapter begins with the discussion of the net operating loss rules. These rules allow taxpayers to use certain losses generated in one tax year against income from prior and future tax years. The discussion then shifts to the alternative minimum tax, which is a second tax system that attempts to raise additional tax revenues from taxpayers who pay too little tax under the regular income tax system which has been the focus of the textbook thus far. The chapter concludes with a discussion of tax credits available to business owners and landlords of real property.

¶1201 Net Operating Loss (NOL)

A special rule applies when individual business owners and C corporations report a loss in one year and profits in other years. It would be unfair if business profits were always taxed, but no tax relief was available when the business suffered a loss. The net operating loss (NOL) provisions allow business losses to offset income from other tax years. An NOL generated in 2015 offsets taxable income of the two previous years (2013, 2014). Any remaining loss is carried forward to offset income in the next 20 years (2016-2035).

¶1201.01 CALCULATING NOL

An NOL is not the same as negative taxable income on Form 1040. In computing the NOL, individuals make the following adjustments to negative taxable income.

1. The exemption deduction (personal and dependency) is added back.
2. Nonbusiness capital losses in excess of nonbusiness capital gains are added back. Nonbusiness capital gains and losses arise from transactions involving nonbusiness property (for example, investment property).
3. The NOL carryover of a preceding or later tax year is added back.
4. Nonbusiness deductions in excess of nonbusiness income are added back. Nonbusiness deductions include all itemized deductions except casualty and theft losses. For individuals who do not itemize, their standard deduction is a nonbusiness deduction. Nonbusiness income comes from sources other than the taxpayer's business. Examples include interest, dividends, and net gains from the sale of nonbusiness property. Salaries, net gains from the sale of business property, and rental income are treated as business income.

EXAMPLE 1

Chris and Dana Bosky are married and file a joint tax return. Chris operates a business that generated $120,000 of gross revenues and $150,000 of operating expenses during 2015. The Boskys report a negative taxable income of $30,200.

Salary		$ 15,000
Business loss ($120,000 – $150,000)		(30,000)
Net business capital gains		3,000
Net nonbusiness capital gains		4,000
Interest income		1,500
AGI		($ 6,500)
Less itemized deductions:		
Mortgage interest and real estate taxes	$9,500	
Casualty loss	6,200	(15,700)
Less exemption deduction		(8,000)
Taxable income (loss)		($30,200)

Using this information, the Boskys' $18,200 NOL is computed:

Taxable loss			($30,200)
Add back:			
Exemption deduction		$8,000	
Net nonbusiness deductions	$9,500		
Nonbusiness income ($4,000 + $1,500)	(5,500)	4,000	12,000
NOL			($18,200)

¶1201.02 NOL DEDUCTION

Once computed, an NOL is carried back two years, and then carried forward 20 years. When an NOL is carried back to a prior tax year, the taxpayer completes and files Form 1045, Application for Tentative Refund, to recompute the taxpayer's tax liability in the carryback year. Alternatively, taxpayers can elect to forgo the carryback and carry forward an NOL 20 years. When carried over to another year, an individual taxpayer treats an NOL deduction as a *deduction for* AGI. On the tax return, an NOL carried forward is entered as a negative amount on Form 1040 (line 21). The taxpayer then writes "NOL" and the amount of the NOL on the dotted line after the words "Other income. List type and amount."

From Example 1, the Boskys could complete Form 1045 to apply the NOL to their 2013 taxable income and recompute their 2013 tax liability. The difference between the Boskys' original tax liability and the recomputed tax liability would be refunded to them. Alternatively, the Boskys could elect to forgo the carryback and report the $18,200 as a negative amount on the "Other income" line on their 2016 tax return.

Taxpayers elect to forego the carryback period by attaching a statement to the tax return that produced the NOL. Once made, the election to forego the carryback of an NOL is final. When a 2015 tax return showing an NOL is filed without such a statement, the IRS assumes the taxpayer is carrying back the NOL to the 2013 tax year.

¶1202 Alternative Minimum Tax (AMT)

The tax law contains many exclusions, deductions, and other tax breaks that allow taxpayers to reduce their tax liabilities. Some individuals with higher incomes use these tax benefits so much that they paid little or no income tax. As a result, Congress enacted an alternative minimum tax (AMT). The AMT works with the regular income tax in an attempt to ensure that taxpayers with higher total incomes pay some amount of income tax. The AMT operates as a completely separate tax system. If subject to the AMT, the taxpayer will pay the AMT plus the regular income tax. Below is the formula for computing the AMT.

	Regular taxable income before the exemption deduction
+	Standard deduction (if used)
+	NOL deduction (if any)
+	Tax preferences and positive adjustments
–	Negative adjustments
=	Alternative minimum taxable income (AMTI)
–	AMT exemption
=	Amount subject to tax (AMT Base)
×	AMT tax rate
=	Tentative minimum tax
–	Regular income tax
=	AMT (if a positive amount)

¶1202.01 PREFERENCES AND ADJUSTMENTS

Alternative minimum taxable income (AMTI) is regular taxable income before the exemption deduction, and then modified by the standard deduction (if used), preferences, and adjustments. Preferences and adjustments allow taxpayers to receive large exclusions and deductions in computing regular taxable income. The AMT calculation reduces the benefits of these tax incentives by limiting the exclusions or the amounts currently deductible. The amounts disallowed for AMT are added back to regular taxable income in computing AMTI.

Preference items are always added back to regular taxable income in computing AMTI. Thus, preferences increase income subject to AMT. Adjustments, on the other hand, can be positive or negative. Adjustments generally arise from timing differences. **Timing differences** occur when a deduction is allowed in computing taxable income in a year before it is allowed in computing AMTI. Thus, adjustments tend to be positive in the first years to which they apply (when the deduction allowed in computing taxable income is greater) and become negative in later years when they reverse (when the deduction allowed in computing AMTI is greater). Negative adjustments are subtracted from regular taxable income when computing AMTI.

Several adjustments and preferences used in computing AMT relate to the calculation of depreciation expense, passive losses, or tax-exempt and excluded income.

Depreciation Expense

The regular income tax system allows taxpayers to immediately expense (Section 179) and/or use an accelerated method (200% declining balance and bonus depreciation in years it is allowed) to depreciate tangible personal property. The AMT system also allows Section 179 expensing and bonus depreciation (in years bonus depreciation is allowed), but can require slower depreciation methods or longer recovery periods. Two common depreciation adjustments are:

1. **Depreciation of real property.** AMT requires that real property placed in service between 1987 and 1998 be depreciated using straight-line depreciation over 40 years. MACRS depreciates real property over 27.5, 31.5, or 39 years using the straight-line method (¶803.01). The difference in the amount of depreciation expense between these two systems is the AMT adjustment. There is no AMT depreciation adjustment for real property placed in service after 1998.
2. **Depreciation of personal property.** AMT uses the 150% declining balance (DB) method over the longer alternative depreciation system (ADS) lives. (See ¶802.04 for a discussion of ADS lives.) For computing regular taxable income, both the 200% DB and straight-line methods are allowed (¶802). The difference in the amount of depreciation expense between these two systems is an adjustment for AMT. However, no AMT adjustment is required for personal property on which bonus depreciation was taken.

EXAMPLE 2 In 1992, Nadia and Tim Orlean paid $430,000 for a ski villa in Aspen, Colorado that they use solely as rental property. They depreciate the villa using MACRS (straight-line over 27.5 years). Each year they deduct $15,636 ($430,000 ÷ 27.5) of depreciation against their rental income when computing taxable income. For purposes of computing AMTI, depreciation allowed is $10,750 ($430,000 ÷ 40). Thus, during the years that MACRS is deducted in computing the Orleans' taxable income, they must add back to taxable income the $4,886 excess ($15,636 – $10,750) to compute AMTI. After the property is fully depreciated under MACRS, the Orleans can continue to take depreciation deductions when computing AMTI. This will result in a negative adjustment to taxable income in those years. Negative adjustments are subtracted from regular taxable income when computing AMTI.

EXAMPLE 3

Same facts as in Example 2, except that the Orleans bought the villa in 2002. For real property placed in service after 1998, there is no difference in the depreciation rules for computing taxable income and AMTI. Thus, no AMT adjustment is needed.

EXAMPLE 4

In 2015, a taxpayer buys used business property that cost $30,000. The half-year convention applies to the property. The recovery period is five years for regular income tax purposes. It is eight years for AMT. Depreciation for regular income tax (200% DB over 5 years) is $6,000 in year 1 ($30,000 × 20%). AMT depreciation (150% DB over 8 years) is $2,813 ($30,000 × 1/8 × 150% × ½). The $3,187 difference ($6,000 – $2,813) is added back to taxable income in computing AMTI in year 1.

Passive Losses

Neither the regular tax nor the AMT system allows for passive losses in excess of passive income to be deducted in the year they occur. Such losses carry forward and offset passive income in future years. Any losses carried forward are deducted in full when the taxpayer disposes of the entire interest in the activity (¶905.04).

While the loss recognition for both tax calculations is deferred, the amount of the loss to be deferred will usually differ. The difference occurs because the loss for AMT purposes is determined using all required AMT tax adjustments rather than the regular income tax deductions. For example, MACRS depreciates residential realty over 27.5 years using the straight-line method. For AMT, this property is depreciated over 40 years if it was placed in service before 1999. Because this difference affects the amount of passive loss carryover for regular tax versus AMT, it will affect the amount of the recognized gain when the property is sold as well as the passive loss deduction allowed.

Tax-Exempt and Excluded Income

Three other items of income may result in adjustments for AMT. First, AMTI includes interest from "specified private activity bonds" (a type of municipal bond). In computing taxable income, all municipal bond interest is exempt from gross income (¶401.06). Thus, interest from specified private activity bonds is added to taxable income in computing AMTI. Second, when exercising an incentive stock option, the excess of the fair market value (FMV) of the stock over the exercise price is income for purposes of computing AMT. Exercising an incentive stock option does not affect regular taxable income. Thus, the excess is added to taxable income in computing AMTI. Third, 7% of the excluded gain on the sale of Section 1202 small business stock is a preference item. This amount is added to taxable income to compute AMTI (recall that sometimes only a portion of the realized gain on the sale of Section 1202 stock is taxed, see ¶1006.)

The tax law allows taxpayers to earn tax-free interest income when they invest in state and local government (municipal) bonds under the assumption that the bond proceeds would be used for various government projects. However, sometimes municipalities issue bonds and then loan the proceeds to private parties, or alternatively, they raise funds to construct facilities to be used for private projects. Bonds of this nature are called "private activity bonds." The interest from private activity bonds issued after August 7, 1986 and before January 1, 2009, or after 2010, is tax-exempt from regular taxable income, but taxable for purposes of computing AMTI. Such bonds are known as specified private activity bonds. Interest from specified private activity bonds is a preference item for purposes of computing AMT.

EXAMPLE 5

Ellie owns a specified private activity bond. During the current year, the bond pays interest totaling $2,850. All interest from state and local government bonds is excluded from gross income under the regular income tax system (¶401.06). However, interest from specified private activity bonds is not an exclusion under the AMT system. Thus, in computing AMTI, Ellie adds back $2,850 to taxable income.

EXAMPLE 6

Cam paid $60 a share for 1,000 shares of stock under an incentive stock option program at work. At the time, the stock was selling for $85 a share. The excess of the value of the stock over the amount paid for the stock is excluded from Cam's gross income under the regular income tax system. However, no such exclusion is allowed in the AMT system. Thus, Cam must add back to taxable income the $25,000 excess (($85 – $60) × 1,000 shares) to taxable income when computing AMTI.

EXAMPLE 7

Lucas realized a $30,000 gain on the sale of Section 1202 stock. Under the regular income tax system, 50% of this gain is excluded from gross income (¶1006). In computing his AMTI, Lucas adds back to taxable income 7% of the $15,000 excluded gain, or $1,050.

¶1202.02 AMT ITEMIZED DEDUCTIONS

The AMTI calculation disallows the standard deduction for taxpayers who do not itemize. For taxpayers who itemize, computing AMTI requires an adjustment to regular taxable income for certain types of itemized deductions.

Taxes and Miscellaneous Deductions

All taxes deducted on Schedule A must be added back in computing AMTI. Any state income tax refunds included in regular taxable income are not included in AMTI, and therefore must be subtracted from taxable income in computing AMTI. Also, any miscellaneous itemized deductions in excess of 2% AGI are added back when computing AMTI.

EXAMPLE 8

Kyle's itemized deductions exceed the standard deduction amount. Included in his itemized deductions are $4,740 of real estate taxes and $2,350 for state and local income taxes. Also included are $240 of miscellaneous itemized deductions in excess of 2% AGI. In computing AMTI, Kyle must add back to taxable income the $7,090 deducted for taxes and the $240 of miscellaneous deductions on Schedule A.

Medical Expenses

Only medical expenses that exceed 10% of AGI may be deducted for purposes of computing AMTI. In computing regular taxable income through 2016, taxpayers age 65 and older can deduct medical expenses in excess of 7.5% of AGI (¶503). These taxpayers recompute the medical expense deduction using a 10% AGI floor. They then add back to regular taxable income the difference between the medical expense deduction in excess of 7.5% AGI and the recomputed medical expense deduction using 10% AGI.

EXAMPLE 9

Rose, age 66, has $10,000 of unreimbursed medical expenses and AGI of $120,000. When computing her itemized deductions, Rose deducts $1,000 of medical expenses ($10,000 – (7.5% × $120,000)). When computing AMTI, she only can deduct medical expenses in excess of $12,000 (10% × $120,000). Since no medical expense deduction would be allowed in computing AMTI, Rose must add back $1,000 to taxable income when computing AMTI.

Interest

In computing regular taxable income, the interest on home equity loans up to $100,000 ($50,000 for MFS) is deductible, regardless of how the proceeds are used. In computing AMTI, the interest on home equity loans is deductible only if the loan proceeds were used to acquire or substantially improve the taxpayer's main home or second home. Thus, the interest on home equity loans when the proceeds are used for other purposes is not deductible under the AMT system. Such interest would be added back to taxable income when computing AMTI.

Investment interest is deductible for both regular tax and the AMT to the extent of net investment income. However, the amount of the interest deduction may vary because the amount of net investment income may not be the same for both regular tax and AMT.

EXAMPLE 10

Trey and Rita Smith deducted $9,600 of home equity interest on Schedule A. They used the proceeds from the $100,000 home equity loan to remodel their kitchen and master bath in their main home. The interest on the first $100,000 of home equity loans is deductible in computing taxable income under the regular income tax system. Because the proceeds from the loan were used to buy or improve their main home, the deduction is also allowed for purposes of computing AMTI. Thus, no adjustment to taxable income is necessary in computing AMTI.

EXAMPLE 11

Same facts as in Example 10, except that the Smiths used the proceeds to pay off their credit card debt, buy a new car, and take a vacation. The interest is no longer deductible for purposes of computing AMT. Thus, in computing AMTI, the Smiths must add back the $9,600 to their taxable income.

¶1202.03 AMT EXEMPTION

No deduction for personal and dependency exemptions is allowed in computing AMTI. Instead, a (larger) AMT exemption is intended to keep most lower- and middle-income taxpayers from being subject to the AMT. The exemption varies by taxpayer filing status, but starts to be phased out once AMTI reaches a certain level. The phase-out is 25% of AMTI above that threshold amount. Figure 12-1 shows, for each filing status, the exemption amount for 2015 and the phase-out calculation for the AMT exemption.

Figure 12-1: AMT Exemption

	Exemption Amount	Phase-Out Calculation
MFJ and qualifying widow(er)	$83,400	25% × (AMTI – $158,900)
Single and head of household	53,600	25% × (AMTI – $119,200)
Married filing separately	41,700	25% × (AMTI – $79,450)

EXAMPLE 12

Jess files a separate tax return from his wife. During 2015, Jess's AMTI is $99,000. He computes his AMT exemption as follows.

Initial AMT exemption for MFS		$41,700
AMTI	$99,000	
Less AMTI threshold for MFS	(79,450)	
Excess	$19,550	
Phase-out percentage	× 25%	(4,888)
AMT exemption		$36,812

EXAMPLE 13

Rocky and Randi Kane file a joint tax return. Their 2015 AMTI is $282,403. The Kanes compute their AMT exemption as follows.

Initial AMT exemption for MFJ		$83,400
AMTI	$282,403	
Less AMTI threshold for MFJ	(158,900)	
Excess	$123,503	
Phase-out percentage	× 25%	(30,876)
AMT exemption		$52,524

¶1202.04 AMT RATES AND CREDITS

Tax Rate

A two-tiered rate schedule is used to compute the AMT. The tax rate on the first $185,400 of AMTI in excess of the allowable exemption is 26% ($92,700 for MFS). A 28% rate applies to the excess. The AMT rates do not apply to net capital gain and qualified dividends. These amounts remain taxed at the taxpayer's lower 0%, 15%, or 20% tax rate (¶1101.03).

EXAMPLE 14

Continuing with Example 13, the Kanes subtract their AMT exemption from AMTI to arrive at their AMT base ($282,403 – $52,524 = $229,879). The Kane's tentative minimum tax equals $60,658 [($185,400 × 26%) + (($229,879 – $185,400) × 28%)]. If this amount exceeds their regular income tax liability, the excess is the Kanes' AMT.

Minimum Tax Credit

The portion of the AMT caused by timing differences creates a minimum tax credit in future years when the regular tax exceeds the taxpayer's tentative minimum tax. This credit can reduce the regular tax liability only in future years and may be carried forward until used. Its purpose is to help avoid double taxing of those adjustments resulting from timing differences. Those interested in learning more about the minimum tax credit should refer to the instructions to Form 8801, Credit for Prior Year Minimum Tax—Individuals, Estates, and Trusts.

¶1202.05 CALCULATING AMT

EXAMPLE 15

Jeffrey Q. Lang (single, age 47) calculates his regular tax liability for 2015 as follows.

Salary			$95,000
Rental income		$ 6,000	
Rental expenses:			
Depreciation—real property	$2,400		
Depreciation—personal property	600		
Interest expense	5,000		
Property taxes	800		
Other expenses	200	(9,000)	
Net rental loss (active participation)			(3,000)
Short-term capital gain on the sale of stock			5,000
Adjusted gross income			$97,000
Less itemized deductions:			
Charitable contributions		$20,600	
Home mortgage interest		14,400	
Home equity loan interest (proceeds used to buy a boat)		7,450	
Real estate taxes		4,400	(46,850)
Less deduction exemption			(4,000)
Taxable income			$46,150
Regular tax liability (using the 2015 Tax Table)			$ 7,338

Jeffrey used accelerated MACRS to compute depreciation. Had he depreciated the property using the AMT depreciation rules, he would have deducted $2,200 for the real property and $450 for the personal property. Jeffrey received $41,500 in tax-exempt interest from specified private activity bonds he bought in 2004. He also paid $30,000 for $50,000 of stock through an incentive stock option plan set up by his employer. Using this information, Jeffrey's AMT is $11,229, computed as follows.

Regular taxable income		$ 46,150
Add: (1) Excess depreciation		
Real property ($2,400 – $2,200)	$ 200	
Personal property ($600 – $450)	150	350
(2) Disallowed itemized deductions:		
Home equity loan interest	$ 7,450	
Real estate taxes	4,400	11,850
(3) Exemption deduction		4,000
(4) Private activity bond interest		41,500
(5) Stock option ($50,000 – $30,000)		20,000
AMTI		$123,850
Less AMT exemption (single filing status)	$53,600	
Phase-out ($123,850 – $119,200) × .25	(1,163)	(52,437)
AMT base		$ 71,413
AMT rate (on up to $185,400 of AMT base)		× 26%
Tentative minimum tax		$ 18,567
Less regular income tax		(7,338)
AMT		$ 11,229

¶1202.06 FILLED-IN FORM 6251

INFORMATION FOR FIGURE 12-2:

Jeffrey Q. Lang from Example 15, enters the amounts shown in bold on the appropriate lines of Form 6251. He then enters his AMT on Form 1040, page 2, where it becomes part of his 2015 total income tax liability.

Line #

1: Amount from Form 1040, line 41, **$50,150** ($97,000 AGI – $46,850 itemized deductions)
3: Taxes from Schedule A, line 9, **$4,400**
4: Home mortgage interest adjustment, **$7,450** (home equity loan interest)
12: Specified private activity bond interest, **$41,500**
14: Adjustment for exercise of incentive stock options, **$20,000**
18: Post-1986 depreciation adjustment, **$350** ($200 + $150)
29: Exemption amount, **$52,437**
34: Regular income tax from Form 1040, line 44, **$7,338**

The IRS offers taxpayers an "Alternative Minimum Tax (AMT) Assistant for Individuals." By answering a few simple questions about items reported on the tax return, the IRS program will perform a series of calculations and then inform taxpayers whether or not they will be subject to AMT. This program can be found by entering "AMT assistant" in the search box on the IRS website. See Appendix A for information on accessing the IRS website.

The AMT exemption, AMTI thresholds for reducing the exemption, and threshold where the 28% AMT rate is applied, are all indexed annually for inflation (see ¶202).

¶1203 General Business Credit

Chapter 2 introduced the personal tax credits available to individual taxpayers. This chapter focuses on the more common tax credits available to businesses, which includes sole proprietorships, corporations and partnerships.

After all other nonrefundable credits have been offset against the taxpayer's income tax liability, taxpayers may claim the general business credit. This nonrefundable credit is equal to the sum of several separately computed tax credits. While some credits are beyond the scope of this textbook, the remaining sections examine the following business credits:

1. Rehabilitation credit (part of the Investment credit)—Form 3468
2. Disabled access credit—Form 8826
3. Credit for small employer health insurance premiums—Form 8941
4. Credit for employer-provided childcare facilities and services—Form 8882
5. Credit for small employer pension plan startup costs—Form 8881
6. Work opportunity credit—Form 5884
7. Empowerment zone employment credit—Form 8844
8. New markets credit—Form 8874

Figure 12-2: Filled-In Form 6251

Form **6251** — Department of the Treasury, Internal Revenue Service (99)

Alternative Minimum Tax—Individuals

▶ Information about Form 6251 and its separate instructions is at *www.irs.gov/form6251*.
▶ Attach to Form 1040 or Form 1040NR.

OMB No. 1545-0074 — **2015** — Attachment Sequence No. 32

Name(s) shown on Form 1040 or Form 1040NR: **Jeffrey Q. Lang** — Your social security number: **357-41-3101**

Part I Alternative Minimum Taxable Income (See instructions for how to complete each line.)

1	If filing Schedule A (Form 1040), enter the amount from Form 1040, line 41, and go to line 2. Otherwise, enter the amount from Form 1040, line 38, and go to line 7. (If less than zero, enter as a negative amount.)	1	50,150
2	Medical and dental. If you or your spouse was 65 or older, enter the **smaller** of Schedule A (Form 1040), line 4, **or** 2.5% (.025) of Form 1040, line 38. If zero or less, enter -0-	2	
3	Taxes from Schedule A (Form 1040), line 9	3	4,400
4	Enter the home mortgage interest adjustment, if any, from line 6 of the worksheet in the instructions for this line	4	7,450
5	Miscellaneous deductions from Schedule A (Form 1040), line 27	5	
6	If Form 1040, line 38, is $154,950 or less, enter -0-. Otherwise, see instructions	6	( )
7	Tax refund from Form 1040, line 10 or line 21	7	( )
8	Investment interest expense (difference between regular tax and AMT)	8	
9	Depletion (difference between regular tax and AMT)	9	
10	Net operating loss deduction from Form 1040, line 21. Enter as a positive amount	10	
11	Alternative tax net operating loss deduction	11	( )
12	Interest from specified private activity bonds exempt from the regular tax	12	41,500
13	Qualified small business stock, see instructions	13	
14	Exercise of incentive stock options (excess of AMT income over regular tax income)	14	20,000
15	Estates and trusts (amount from Schedule K-1 (Form 1041), box 12, code A)	15	
16	Electing large partnerships (amount from Schedule K-1 (Form 1065-B), box 6)	16	
17	Disposition of property (difference between AMT and regular tax gain or loss)	17	
18	Depreciation on assets placed in service after 1986 (difference between regular tax and AMT)	18	350
19	Passive activities (difference between AMT and regular tax income or loss)	19	
20	Loss limitations (difference between AMT and regular tax income or loss)	20	
21	Circulation costs (difference between regular tax and AMT)	21	
22	Long-term contracts (difference between AMT and regular tax income)	22	
23	Mining costs (difference between regular tax and AMT)	23	
24	Research and experimental costs (difference between regular tax and AMT)	24	
25	Income from certain installment sales before January 1, 1987	25	( )
26	Intangible drilling costs preference	26	
27	Other adjustments, including income-based related adjustments	27	
28	**Alternative minimum taxable income.** Combine lines 1 through 27. (If married filing separately and line 28 is more than $246,250, see instructions.)	28	123,850

Part II Alternative Minimum Tax (AMT)

29 Exemption. (If you were under age 24 at the end of 2015, see instructions.)

IF your filing status is . . .	**AND line 28 is not over . . .**	**THEN enter on line 29 . . .**
Single or head of household	$119,200	$53,600
Married filing jointly or qualifying widow(er)	158,900	83,400
Married filing separately	79,450	41,700

If line 28 is **over** the amount shown above for your filing status, see instructions. — **29: 52,437**

30	Subtract line 29 from line 28. If more than zero, go to line 31. If zero or less, enter -0- here and on lines 31, 33, and 35, and go to line 34	30	71,413
31	• If you are filing Form 2555 or 2555-EZ, see instructions for the amount to enter. • If you reported capital gain distributions directly on Form 1040, line 13; you reported qualified dividends on Form 1040, line 9b; **or** you had a gain on both lines 15 and 16 of Schedule D (Form 1040) (as refigured for the AMT, if necessary), complete Part III on the back and enter the amount from line 64 here. • **All others:** If line 30 is $185,400 or less ($92,700 or less if married filing separately), multiply line 30 by 26% (.26). Otherwise, multiply line 30 by 28% (.28) and subtract $3,708 ($1,854 if married filing separately) from the result.	31	18,567
32	Alternative minimum tax foreign tax credit (see instructions)	32	
33	Tentative minimum tax. Subtract line 32 from line 31	33	18,567
34	Add Form 1040, line 44 (minus any tax from Form 4972), and Form 1040, line 46. Subtract from the result any foreign tax credit from Form 1040, line 48. If you used Schedule J to figure your tax on Form 1040, line 44, refigure that tax without using Schedule J before completing this line (see instructions)	34	7,338
35	**AMT.** Subtract line 34 from line 33. If zero or less, enter -0-. Enter here and on Form 1040, line 45	35	11,229

For Paperwork Reduction Act Notice, see your tax return instructions. Cat. No. 13600G Form **6251** (2015)

Any part of the general business credit not used in the current tax year is carried back to the previous tax year. Any remaining unused credit is then carried forward and combined with business credits generated in that year. The unused credit is carried forward until it is used up or the 20-year carryover period expires. In each carryforward year, the oldest credit is used first, but only after the current year's credit is used. This minimizes the possible expiration of any unused general business credit.

¶1203.01 REHABILITATION CREDIT

The purpose behind the rehabilitation credit is to encourage businesses to stay in economically distressed areas and to preserve historic structures. The credit equals a percentage of the costs incurred in substantially rehabilitating qualified buildings and certified historic structures. A building is substantially rehabilitated when the rehabilitation costs during a 24-month period exceed the *greater of* (i) the building's adjusted basis before rehabilitation, or (ii) $5,000. Once the substantial rehabilitation test has been met, all costs to rehabilitate the property (including those before and after the 24-month period) qualify for the credit. The percentage used in computing the credit is as follows:

Type of Property Credit	Credit
Certified historic structures (both nonresidential and residential)	20%
Buildings originally placed in service before 1936	10%

When taxpayers make capital expenditures to property, they normally increase their basis in the property by such costs. However, taxpayers must reduce their basis by the amount of the rehabilitation credit. This keeps them from taking depreciation deductions on the portion of the cost of the building that is taken as a tax credit.

EXAMPLE 16 Davy pays $50,000 for a certified historic structure. Over the next 18 months, he spends $60,000 to rehabilitate the structure. Davy qualifies for the rehabilitation credit since the $60,000 spent to rehabilitate the structure exceeds $50,000 (the *greater of* (i) the $50,000 adjusted basis in the building before rehabilitation, or (ii) $5,000). Davy's rehabilitation credit equals $12,000 ($60,000 × 20%). His basis in the building increases by $48,000 ($60,000 – $12,000) to $98,000 ($50,000 + $48,000). Davy uses MACRS or ADS to depreciate the $98,000 basis in the building (¶803).

Taxpayers that dispose of the property within five years of taking the rehabilitation credit must recapture 20% of the credit taken for each year shy of five years. Any recaptured amount is added to the taxpayer's tax liability and to the adjusted basis of the building. For example, if Davy (from Example 16) were to sell the property after two years, he would be required to recapture (increase his tax liability by) 60% of the credit, or $7,200 ($12,000 × 60%). The amount of the recapture is 20% for each of the three years Davy is shy of holding the property for five years. Davy would increase his basis in the property by the $7,200 of recaptured credit.

¶1203.02 DISABLED ACCESS CREDIT

This nonrefundable credit provides an incentive to small businesses to make their buildings more accessible to disabled persons. The credit equals 50% of the eligible expenditures for the year that exceed $250 but do not exceed $10,250. Thus, the maximum credit is $5,000 [50% × ($10,250 – $250)]. A business qualifies for the credit if it satisfies one of the following criteria in the previous tax year:

1. The business did not have gross receipts in excess of $1 million, or
2. The business did not employ more than 30 full-time employees.

EXAMPLE 17 In the current tax year, Harvey Enterprises pays to install ramps to allow disabled persons easier access to its building. The building was first placed in service in 1982. Last year Harvey reported gross receipts of $1.2 million and employed 30 full-time workers. Harvey qualifies for the disabled access credit because it did not employ more than 30 full-time workers in the previous tax year. To qualify for the disabled access credit, a business must only satisfy one of the two criteria listed.

EXAMPLE 18 In the current tax year, Bruce Industries pays to make improvements to its office building to make it more accessible to disabled persons. The building was first placed in service in 1983. Last year Bruce reported gross receipts of $900,000 and had 35 full-time employees. Bruce qualifies for the disabled access credit because its gross receipts did not exceed $1 million.

Eligible expenditures include amounts paid to remove barriers on buildings first placed in service before November 6, 1990 that prevent businesses from being accessible to, or usable by, disabled persons. Also included are amounts paid to buy or modify equipment used by disabled persons. Other eligible expenditures include amounts paid for qualified interpreters and audio devices that help hearing-impaired persons. Likewise, amounts paid for qualified readers and other devices that help make visual materials available to visually-impaired persons are also eligible for the credit. Taxpayers claiming the disabled assess credit increase the depreciable basis of the building by the amounts spent and then reduce it by the amount of the credit.

EXAMPLE 19 Alana owns a small business that she reports on Schedule C. During the year Alana pays $8,500 to make her office building more accessible to disabled persons. The building was placed in service in 1987. Alana's disabled access credit equals $4,125 [50% × ($8,500 – $250)]. Alana's basis in the building increases by $4,375 ($8,500 – $4,125). She uses the straight-line method to depreciate the $4,375 over 39 (MACRS, ¶803.01) or 40 years (ADS, ¶803.02).

¶1203.03 CREDIT FOR SMALL EMPLOYER HEALTH INSURANCE PREMIUMS

A tax credit for small employers who pay health insurance premiums on behalf of their employees was enacted as part of the Patient Protection and Affordable Care Act (ACA), commonly called Obamacare. This credit was intended to help small businesses afford the cost of providing health insurance for their employees. From 2010-2013, qualified small business employers could take a credit for up to 35% of the premiums they paid in providing health care insurance for their employees. The rate used for small tax-exempt employers (such as charities) was 25%.

To qualify for the credit, employers were required to pay at least half of the costs associated with providing health care coverage for each of their employees. The full credit was available to employers with ten or fewer full-time equivalent (FTE) employees whose annual wages did not exceed a certain threshold. The credit began being phased-out once the number of FTE employees exceeded 10 or employees' annual wages exceeded the threshold amount. The credit was not available to sole proprietors, and certain partners and S corporation shareholders.

Beginning in 2014, the ACA made a few changes to the credit. The maximum credit increased to 50% of the premiums paid (35% for small tax-exempt employers). However, only premiums paid on behalf of employees enrolled in a qualified health plan (QHP) offered through the Small Business Health Options Program (SHOP) Marketplace now qualify for the credit. Furthermore, this (potentially larger) credit is only available for two consecutive years (with 2014 being the first possible year), regardless of whether the employer had taken the credit during 2010-2013.

An employer's number of FTE employees is determined by dividing the total hours of service for its employees during the year (but not more than 2,080 hours for any employee) by 2,080. If the result is not a whole number, then the number of FTE employees does not include the fraction. For example, if the FTE formula results in an employer having 6.2 employees, then the employer is deemed to have six FTE employees.

EXAMPLE 20 Cole Company has seven FTE employees. Average wages paid to its FTE employees are $24,000. During 2014, Cole paid health insurance premiums totaling $63,000 on behalf of its employees. This amount was 75% of the total cost of each employee's premiums for a QHP offered through the SHOP Marketplace. Cole qualified for the full small employer health insurance credit of $31,500 ($63,000 × 50%). If Cole remains eligible to take the credit, 2015 will be the last year Cole will qualify for the credit (under the new two consecutive year rule).

For 2015, employers whose FTE employees' averages wages exceed $25,800 must reduce their credit by 4% for each $1,000 (or portion thereof) that exceeds $25,800.

EXAMPLE 21 Continuing with Example 20, in 2015 Cole pays $63,000 in premiums and its employees' average wages are $30,370. Since average wages exceed $25,800, Cole must reduce its credit by 20% ($4,570 excess/$1,000 = 4.57, which rounds to 5. 5 × 4% = 20%). Its 2015 small employer health insurance credit equals $25,200 ($31,500 – ($31,500 × 20%)).

Employers with more than 10 FTE employees must reduce their credit by 6.667% for each FTE employee over 10. The IRS provides tables to help employers compute their reduced credit.

EXAMPLE 22 Same facts as in Example 21, except that the $63,000 covers Cole's 12 FTE employees and Cole's average wages are $25,000. Since the number of FTE employees exceeds 10, Cole must reduce its credit by 13.334% (6.667% × 2 excess FTE employees). Cole's tax credit would be $27,300 ($31,500 – ($31,500 × 13.334%)).

Starting in 2014, only premiums paid on behalf of employees enrolled in a QHP offered through the SHOP Marketplace qualify for the credit. Those interested in learning more about QHPs offered through the SHOP Marketplace can find this information by visiting *www.HealthCare.gov*.

¶1203.04 CREDIT FOR EMPLOYER-PROVIDED CHILDCARE FACILITIES AND SERVICES

Employers can take a tax credit for providing childcare to their employees. The amount of the credit is the *sum of* (i) 25% of qualified childcare expenses plus (ii) 10% of qualified childcare resources or referral expenses. The maximum credit allowed each year is $150,000.

Qualified childcare expenses include amounts paid to acquire or construct property used as part of a qualified childcare facility. It also includes costs incurred to operate a qualified childcare facility and amounts paid to a qualified childcare facility that provides childcare services to employees. **Qualified childcare resource and referral expenses** are amounts paid under a contract to provide childcare resource and referral services to an employee. However, these services cannot discriminate in favor of key or highly-paid employees (as defined in ¶401.03).

EXAMPLE 23

In 2006, Harvey started a qualified childcare program for his employees. During 2015, he pays $7,000 in qualified childcare expenses and $1,000 in qualified childcare resource and referral expenses. Harvey's employer-provided childcare credit is $1,850 ([$7,000 × 25%] + [$1,000 × 10%]). He includes this amount as part of the General Business Credit when he prepares his 2015 tax return.

Employers are allowed a tax credit equal to 25% of the amounts paid to buy or construct a childcare facility (subject to an annual credit limit of $150,000). Employers reduce their basis in the building by any amounts taken as a credit. However, if within 10 years of taking the credit, the facility is no longer used to provide childcare services for employees, some of the credit must be recaptured (added to the taxpayer's tax liability). The amount recaptured is 100% in years 1-3, and is gradually reduced to 10% by years 9 and 10. The amount recaptured is then added to the employer's adjusted basis in the building. This concept (of calculating basis and recapture) is similar to that which was described earlier in the chapter for the rehabilitation credit (see Example 16 in ¶1203.01).

¶1203.05 CREDIT FOR SMALL EMPLOYER PENSION PLAN STARTUP COSTS

Certain employers can take a tax credit equal to 50% of qualified startup costs when they establish a new defined benefit plan, defined contribution plan (including a 401(k) plan), SIMPLE plan, or SEP plan for their employees. The new pension plan must cover at least one employee who is not a highly-paid employee (as defined in ¶401.03). The tax credit is limited to $500 in each of the first three years the pension plan is offered. **Qualified startup costs** include amounts paid to establish or administer the new plan, as well as amounts paid to educate employees about retirement planning. Only employers that employed 100 or fewer employees earning at least $5,000 in the prior year can claim to this credit. Furthermore, the credit is available only to employers that have not maintained a qualified plan during any of the previous three tax years.

¶1203.06 WORK OPPORTUNITY TAX CREDIT (WOTC)

For many years, the work opportunity tax credit (WOTC) provided employers with a tax credit for hiring workers from one of a number of targeted groups. Over the years the WOTC has been allowed to expire, only to be renewed. The most recent version of the WOTC expired at the end of 2014. However, since the calculation of the WOTC is based on first-year (and in one instance, second-year) wages, eligible workers hired during 2014 may qualify employers for the WOTC in 2015. For these reasons, a discussion of the credit is included in this chapter.

At the time this textbook was sent to the printer, Congress had not passed legislation to reinstate the WOTC for any worker hired after December 31, 2014. Thus, the EXAMPLES and QUESTIONS AND PROBLEMS included in the chapter all involve workers hired prior to January 1, 2015.

The federal government has identified nine targeted groups of individuals who may face challenges in finding work. To encourage employers to hire members from these targeted groups, Congress enacted the WOTC. The nine targeted groups of qualified workers included:

1. A member of a family receiving Temporary Assistance for Needy Families (TANF)
2. Qualified food stamp (SNAP) recipients
3. Qualified ex-felons
4. Designated community residents
5. Qualified social security recipients
6. Disabled persons with vocational rehabilitation referrals
7. Qualified summer youth employees

8. Qualified veterans
9. Long-term family assistance program recipients

Designated community residents are persons between the ages of 18 and 39 who live in federally-designated rural renewal counties or empowerment zones (discussed later in the chapter at ¶1203.07). **Qualified summer youth employees** are 16- and 17-year-olds that live in a federally-designated empowerment zone, and work for the employer between May 1 and September 15. Only wages paid to summer youth employees during these 4½ months while living in a designated empowerment zone can be used to compute the WOTC. Also, any person hired who is a relative, former employee, or person owning a majority interest in the company, cannot be a qualified worker, even if that person is a member of a targeted group.

Computing the Credit

The WOTC for a qualified worker equals a percentage of the *lesser of* (i) the worker's first-year wages, or (ii) a specified amount, which varies depending on the type of worker. The full 40% credit is available for new hires who work at least 400 hours for the employer during their first year. A reduced credit of 25% is allowed for those who work at least 120 hours during their first year, but do not meet the 400-hour threshold. No credit is allowed for any person working less than 120 hours during their first year.

For qualified workers from the first six targeted groups, the maximum first-year wages that can be used in computing the WOTC is $6,000. For qualified summer youth employees, the maximum is $3,000. If the employee's first 12 months of employment spans over two of the employer's tax years, the employer can take the credit over two tax years.

Type of Qualified Worker	Maximum First-Year Wages	Maximum Credit
From one of the first six targeted groups: worked ≥ 120 hours, but < 400 hours	$6,000	$1,500
From one of the first six targeted groups: worked ≥ 400 hours	6,000	2,400
Qualified summer youth employees: worked ≥ 120 hours, but < 400 hours	3,000	750
Qualified summer youth employees: worked ≥ 400 hours	3,000	1,200

EXAMPLE 24

Late in 2014, Ranger Company hired Tanner, a qualified ex-felon. Tanner worked 180 hours for Ranger during his first year. Tanner's first-year wages were $2,700 ($1,700 paid in 2014; $1,000 paid in 2015). Since Tanner worked at least 120 hours, but less than 400 hours during his first year, Ranger uses the reduced 25% rate to compute the WOTC. Ranger's 2014 WOTC is $425 (25% × $1,700 first-year wages paid in 2014). The first $6,000 of qualified first-year wages can be used in computing the WOTC. Thus, Ranger's 2015 WOTC is $250 (25% × $1,000).

Qualified veterans are one of the nine targeted groups. They include three types of veterans of the U.S. Armed Forces. The first type is a veteran who was unemployed for at least four weeks during the one-year period leading up to the date of hire. The Internal Revenue Code (Code) refers to these veterans as "returning heroes." The second type is an unemployed veteran with service-related disabilities. For these veterans (whom the Code refers to as "wounded warriors"), there is no minimum length of unemployment required prior to their being hired. The third type includes veterans receiving food stamps.

The maximum first-year wages that can be used in computing the WOTC for qualified veterans depends on the type of veteran hired. For veterans receiving food stamps, the maximum first-year wages is $6,000. The same $6,000 applies to returning heroes who had been unemployed for less than six months (but at least four weeks) during the one year period leading up to the date they are hired. For returning heroes who had been unemployed for at least six months during that same one year period, the maximum wages increase to $14,000.

When hiring a wounded warrior who had been unemployed for less than six months during the year leading up to the hire date, up to $12,000 of first-year wages can be used in computing the WOTC. This amount doubles (to $24,000) for wounded warriors who had been unemployed for at least six months during that same one year period. The following table summarizes the maximum first-year wages and maximum credit allowed for the various types of qualified veterans.

Type of Veteran	Length of Unemployment	Maximum First-Year Wages	Maximum Credit
Food stamp recipient	not applicable	$ 6,000	$2,400
Returning hero	≥ 4 weeks, but < 6 months	6,000	2,400
Returning hero	≥ 6 months	14,000	5,600
Wounded warrior	< 6 months	12,000	4,800
Wounded warrior	≥ 6 months	24,000	9,600

EXAMPLE 25

On June 22, 2014, Estes, Inc. hired a veteran who had been unemployed for the past year. First-year wages were $21,000, of which $11,200 were paid in 2014. Estes' 2014 WOTC is $4,480 (40% × $11,200 first year wages paid in 2014). Its 2015 WOTC is $1,120 [40% × ($14,000 maximum wages – $11,200 wages paid in 2014)].

EXAMPLE 26

On July 9, 2014, Brent hired Demi, a veteran with service-related disabilities. In the year leading up to her hire date, Demi had been unemployed for three weeks. Demi's first-year wages were $15,000, of which $7,700 was paid in 2014 and $7,300 were paid in 2015. Although Demi was unemployed for only three weeks leading up to her hire date, the minimum of four weeks of unemployment does not apply to veterans with service-related disabilities (wounded warriors). The WOTC is 40% of up to $12,000 of first-year wages paid to a wounded warrior who was unemployed less than six months leading up to the hire date. Thus, Brent's 2014 WOTC equals $3,080 (40% × $7,700). His 2015 WOTC equals $1,720 (40% × $4,300). The $4,300 used in computing the 2015 WOTC represents qualified first-year wages paid in 2015 ($12,000 maximum first-year wages – $7,700 wages paid in 2014).

EXAMPLE 27

On March 19, 2014, Anthem Company hired Eugene, a veteran with service-related disabilities. In the year leading up to his hire date, Eugene had been unemployed for two years. Eugene's first-year wages were $20,000, of which $17,000 was paid in 2014 and $3,000 were paid in 2015. Anthem's 2014 WOTC equals $6,800 (40% × $17,000). Its 2015 WOTC equals $1,200 (40% × $3,000). The $3,000 used in computing the 2015 WOTC represents first-year wages paid in 2015, since first-year wages did not exceed the $24,000 maximum that can be used to compute the WOTC for hiring a wounded warrior who was unemployed for at least six months leading up to the hire date.

EXAMPLE 28

On September 4, 2014, Watney, Inc. hired a veteran with a service-related disability who had been unemployed for the last nine months. First-year wages were $28,000, of which $9,000 were paid in 2014. Watney's 2014 WOTC equals $3,600 (40% × $9,000 first year wages paid in 2014). Its 2015 WOTC equals $6,000 [40% × ($24,000 maximum first-year wages– $9,000 first-year wages paid in 2014)].

EXAMPLE 29

On October 6, 2014, Grant hired a veteran who had been receiving food stamps. First-year wages were $18,000, of which $7,000 were paid in 2014. Grant's 2014 WOTC equals $2,400 (40% × $6,000 maximum first-year wages). Since the maximum $6,000 of first-year wages were paid in 2014, Grant's 2015 WOTC for this worker is $0.

Enhanced Credit for Long-Term Family Assistance Recipients

An enhanced credit is allowed for employers that hire long-term family assistance recipients. For members of this targeted group, the amount of the credit equals 40% of up to $10,000 of first-year wages, plus 50% of up to $10,000 of second-year wages. Thus, the maximum credit for wages paid to these workers is $9,000 [($10,000 × 40%) + ($10,000 × 50%)]. If the employee's first two years of employment spans over three of the employer's tax years, the employer can take the credit over three tax years.

EXAMPLE 30

On July 29, 2014, Devry, Inc. hired Dana, a qualified long-term family assistance recipient. First-year wages paid to Dana were $9,800 of which $3,000 were paid during 2014. The rest ($6,800) were paid during 2015. Second-year wages were $10,250, of which $4,500 were paid in 2015. The rest ($5,750) were paid in 2016. Devry's WOTC for 2014–2016 is as follows.

2014 WOTC	
$3,000 qualified first-year wages × 40%	$1,200
2015 WOTC	
$6,800 qualified first-year wages × 40%	$2,720
$4,500 qualified second-year wages × 50%	2,250
	$4,970
2016 WOTC	
$5,500 ($10,000 maximum) qualified second-year wages × 50%	$2,750

Employers that claim the WOTC reduce their wage expense deduction by the amount of the credit. For example, Devry (in Example 30) would reduce its 2015 wage expense deduction by $4,970.

¶1203.07 EMPOWERMENT ZONE EMPLOYMENT CREDIT

Another tax credit that has been allowed to expire in the past, only to be reinstated at a later date, is the empowerment zone employment credit. Although this credit expired at the end of 2014, many believe it will be reenacted sometime late in 2015 or early in 2016. Thus, a full discussion of the credit is included in the discussion that follows.

At the time this textbook was sent to the printer, the empowerment zone employment credit had not been reinstated. Accordingly, the EXAMPLES and QUESTIONS AND PROBLEMS included in the chapter all involve workers hired prior to January 1, 2015.

Empowerment zones are areas in the U.S. that the federal government has designated as being in need of revitalization. A list of the rural and urban empowerment zones can be found in the instructions to Form 8844, Empowerment Zone Employment Credit. To encourage employers to locate their businesses in empowerment zones, the tax laws allow employers to take a 20% tax credit on the first $15,000 of wages paid to eligible workers. Only wages paid to workers who live within an empowerment zone and work primarily within the empowerment zone where the employer's business is located can be used in computing this credit. The $15,000 limit on qualified wages is reduced by any wages used in computing the WOTC for a qualified worker who is a member of one of the targeted groups listed in ¶1203.06. Taxpayers claiming this credit must reduce their wage expense deduction by the amount of the credit taken on their tax returns.

Only wages paid during the calendar year that ends within the employer's tax year qualify for the annual credit. Thus, if the employer uses a June 1 – May 31 fiscal year, qualified wages paid or incurred during the 2014 calendar year are used in computing the employer's empowerment zone employment credit for the year ending on May 31, 2015, since the last day in 2014 falls within this fiscal year (June 1, 2014 – May 31, 2015).

EXAMPLE 31 Tony's business is located in a designated empowerment zone. Tony uses a calendar tax year. During 2014, Tony hired two people who live in an empowerment zone. Neither person belongs to one of the nine WOTC targeted groups. During 2014, one employee was paid wages of $12,000. The other was paid wages of $17,000. Tony's 2014 empowerment zone credit was $5,400 [20% × ($12,000 + $15,000 maximum wages)].

EXAMPLE 32 Same as Example 31, except that the second worker was a qualified food stamp recipient. Tony reduces the $15,000 maximum wages by the $6,000 used in computing the WOTC. Tony's empowerment zone credit would have been reduced to $4,200 [20% × ($12,000 + ($15,000 – $6,000))].

¶1203.08 NEW MARKETS CREDIT

The new markets tax credit was first enacted in 2000. Its objective was to spur revitalization efforts in low-income and impoverished areas in the U.S. The total credit was 39% of the taxpayer's investment, spread out over seven years. The new markets tax credit expired at the end of 2014. However, this credit has been allowed to expire in the past, only to be retroactively enacted. Many believe that this credit will once again be retroactively extended for 2015. For this reason, coupled with the fact that the credit is taken over a period of seven years, a complete discussion of the credit is included in the discussion that follows.

At the time this textbook was sent to the printer, Congress had not reinstated the new markets credit. Accordingly, the EXAMPLES and QUESTIONS AND PROBLEMS included in the chapter all involve investments in qualified CDEs made prior to January 1, 2015.

Taxpayers that invest in a qualified community development entity may be entitled to a new markets credit. A **qualified community development entity (qualified CDE)** is a domestic corporation or partnership whose primary mission is serving, or providing investment capital for, low-income communities or low-income persons. A qualified CDE must be certified as such by the federal government. During its first six years, a qualified CDE must use at least 85% of the cash it raises to make qualified low-income community investments. After the sixth year, it need only use 75% of its cash towards low-income community investments.

An equity investment in a qualified CDE is an investment in the stock of a qualified CDE (in the case of a corporation) or an investment in a capital interest of a qualified CDE (in the case of a partnership). Cash must be used to pay for the investment. However, taxpayers can borrow to get the cash needed to buy the CDE investment. The new markets credit equals a percentage times the amount invested in a qualified CDE. The percentage is 5% for the first three years. It increases to 6% for the next four years. Amounts claimed as a credit reduce the taxpayer's basis in the investment.

If at any time during the 7-year period in which the new markets credit is available, (1) the investment ceases to be a qualified CDE, (2) the taxpayer's investment is redeemed by the qualified CDE, or (3) the CDE fails to make qualified low-income community investments, the recapture rules apply. This would result in the taxpayer's taxes being increased by the amount the taxpayer's general business credit would have been reduced had there been no new markets credit.

EXAMPLE 33

On October 5, 2013, Creekside Corporation paid $200,000 for a qualified equity investment in a CDE. Creekside uses the calendar year. Its 2013 new markets credit was $10,000 (5% × $200,000). Creekside is entitled to another $10,000 credit on each of its 2014 and 2015 tax returns. It will be entitled to a $12,000 (6% × $200,000) credit on each of its 2016–2019 tax returns. Creekside reduces its $200,000 initial basis in the CDE by the amounts it claims for the new markets credit.

EXAMPLE 34

Continuing with Example 33, assume that in 2016, Creekside's investment is no longer a qualified CDE. Also assume that from 2013-2015, Creekside had reduced its tax liability (via the general business credit) by $30,000 for the new markets credit ($10,000 each year). Since Creekside received a $30,000 tax benefit from the new markets credit, it increases its 2016 tax liability (and basis in the CDE) by $30,000.

12

Name:
Section:
Date:

QUESTIONS AND PROBLEMS

1. **Net Operating Loss (NOL).** (Obj. 1)

   a. What is meant by an NOL?

   b. Can an individual who does not operate a business have an NOL? Explain.

   c. For what taxable years may an NOL created in 2015 be used as a deduction for AGI?

2. **Net Operating Loss.** (Obj. 1)

   a. What types of adjustments must be made in order to convert negative taxable income into an NOL?

   b. Carlos (single) reports on his 2015 tax return negative taxable income of $38,300. Included in this amount is business income of $70,000 and business deductions of $98,000. Carlos took the standard deduction and claimed one personal exemption. Compute Carlos's 2015 NOL assuming that no other adjustments are necessary.

   c. What would be the amount of the NOL if, in Part b., Carlos's gross income included net nonbusiness long-term capital gains of $10,000 and business income of $60,000?

3. **Net Operating Loss (NOL).** (Obj. 1) Robin, a single taxpayer, has opened his own law office. The following summarizes the items included in Robin's 2015 negative taxable income. Compute Robin's NOL.

Business income	$54,500	
Dividends and interest	2,300	
Long-term capital gain (nonbusiness income)	1,800	
Total income		$58,600
Business deductions	$58,800	
Itemized deductions (includes a $400 theft loss)	8,670	
Exemption deduction	4,000	
Total deductions		(71,470)
(Negative) taxable income		($12,870)

4. **AMT.** (Obj. 2) Explain how the alternative minimum tax (AMT) is computed under the AMT system, and how this calculation differs from the calculation of taxable income under the regular income tax system.

5. **AMT.** (Obj. 2)

   a. How must depreciation expense for real and personal property be determined in computing the alternative minimum tax (AMT)?

   b. Explain the types of adjustments and preference items that must be added to or subtracted from regular taxable income in order to compute AMTI.

6. **AMT.** (Obj. 2) A couple paid $295,000 for a villa in Florida. The villa is used solely as rental property. They depreciate the villa using the straight-line method over 27.5 years.

   a. Compute the couple's 2015 AMT adjustment if the condo was purchased in 1994.

   b. Same as in Part a., except that they purchased the condo in 2004.

7. **AMT.** (Obj. 4) James M. (SSN 346-57-4657) and Tammy S. (SSN 465-46-3647) Livingston prepared a joint income tax return for 2015 and claimed their four children as dependents. Their regular taxable income and tax liability were computed as follows:

Salaries	$ 90,000
Schedule C net profit	84,000
Nonqualified dividend income	4,700
Interest income	2,350
Adjusted gross income	$181,050
Itemized deductions	(23,000)
	$158,050
Personal exemptions	(24,000)
Taxable income	$134,050
Tax liability	$ 25,100

The Livingstons received $25,000 of tax-exempt interest from specified private activity bonds purchased in 2005. In computing taxable income, the Livingstons took $7,000 depreciation on Schedule C, using the MACRS 200% declining balance method on property with a five-year class life. AMT allows $5,500 of depreciation for the same property. Itemized deductions include charitable contributions of $9,000, state and local property taxes of $6,712, casualty losses of $775 (after the 10% AGI floor), state income taxes of $4,513, and miscellaneous itemized deductions of $2,000 (after the 2% AGI floor). Complete Form 6251 for the Livingstons.

8. **General Business Tax Credit.** (Obj. 3)

a. Which credits discussed in the chapter are combined into the general business credit?

b. What option is available to taxpayers who are unable to use all of the general business credit from their tax liability in the current year?

c. When the general business credit is carried to other tax years, in what year order are the carryover credits used? If general business credits from more than one year are carried over, in what order are they used?

(Use for Problem 7.)

Form **6251**

Department of the Treasury
Internal Revenue Service (99)

Alternative Minimum Tax—Individuals

▶ Information about Form 6251 and its separate instructions is at *www.irs.gov/form6251.*
▶ Attach to Form 1040 or Form 1040NR.

OMB No. 1545-0074
2015
Attachment Sequence No. **32**

Name(s) shown on Form 1040 or Form 1040NR | **Your social security number**

Part I Alternative Minimum Taxable Income (See instructions for how to complete each line.)

1	If filing Schedule A (Form 1040), enter the amount from Form 1040, line 41, and go to line 2. Otherwise, enter the amount from Form 1040, line 38, and go to line 7. (If less than zero, enter as a negative amount.)	1	
2	Medical and dental. If you or your spouse was 65 or older, enter the **smaller** of Schedule A (Form 1040), line 4, **or** 2.5% (.025) of Form 1040, line 38. If zero or less, enter -0-	2	
3	Taxes from Schedule A (Form 1040), line 9	3	
4	Enter the home mortgage interest adjustment, if any, from line 6 of the worksheet in the instructions for this line	4	
5	Miscellaneous deductions from Schedule A (Form 1040), line 27	5	
6	If Form 1040, line 38, is $154,950 or less, enter -0-. Otherwise, see instructions	6	( )
7	Tax refund from Form 1040, line 10 or line 21	7	( )
8	Investment interest expense (difference between regular tax and AMT)	8	
9	Depletion (difference between regular tax and AMT)	9	
10	Net operating loss deduction from Form 1040, line 21. Enter as a positive amount	10	
11	Alternative tax net operating loss deduction	11	( )
12	Interest from specified private activity bonds exempt from the regular tax	12	
13	Qualified small business stock, see instructions	13	
14	Exercise of incentive stock options (excess of AMT income over regular tax income)	14	
15	Estates and trusts (amount from Schedule K-1 (Form 1041), box 12, code A)	15	
16	Electing large partnerships (amount from Schedule K-1 (Form 1065-B), box 6)	16	
17	Disposition of property (difference between AMT and regular tax gain or loss)	17	
18	Depreciation on assets placed in service after 1986 (difference between regular tax and AMT)	18	
19	Passive activities (difference between AMT and regular tax income or loss)	19	
20	Loss limitations (difference between AMT and regular tax income or loss)	20	
21	Circulation costs (difference between regular tax and AMT)	21	
22	Long-term contracts (difference between AMT and regular tax income)	22	
23	Mining costs (difference between regular tax and AMT)	23	
24	Research and experimental costs (difference between regular tax and AMT)	24	
25	Income from certain installment sales before January 1, 1987	25	( )
26	Intangible drilling costs preference	26	
27	Other adjustments, including income-based related adjustments	27	
28	**Alternative minimum taxable income.** Combine lines 1 through 27. (If married filing separately and line 28 is more than $246,250, see instructions.)	28	

Part II Alternative Minimum Tax (AMT)

29 Exemption. (If you were under age 24 at the end of 2015, see instructions.)

IF your filing status is . . .	**AND line 28 is not over . . .**	**THEN enter on line 29 . . .**
Single or head of household	$119,200	$53,600
Married filing jointly or qualifying widow(er)	158,900	83,400
Married filing separately	79,450	41,700

If line 28 is **over** the amount shown above for your filing status, see instructions. | 29 |

30	Subtract line 29 from line 28. If more than zero, go to line 31. If zero or less, enter -0- here and on lines 31, 33, and 35, and go to line 34	30	
31	• If you are filing Form 2555 or 2555-EZ, see instructions for the amount to enter. • If you reported capital gain distributions directly on Form 1040, line 13; you reported qualified dividends on Form 1040, line 9b; **or** you had a gain on both lines 15 and 16 of Schedule D (Form 1040) (as refigured for the AMT, if necessary), complete Part III on the back and enter the amount from line 64 here. • **All others:** If line 30 is $185,400 or less ($92,700 or less if married filing separately), multiply line 30 by 26% (.26). Otherwise, multiply line 30 by 28% (.28) and subtract $3,708 ($1,854 if married filing separately) from the result.	31	
32	Alternative minimum tax foreign tax credit (see instructions)	32	
33	Tentative minimum tax. Subtract line 32 from line 31	33	
34	Add Form 1040, line 44 (minus any tax from Form 4972), and Form 1040, line 46. Subtract from the result any foreign tax credit from Form 1040, line 48. If you used Schedule J to figure your tax on Form 1040, line 44, refigure that tax without using Schedule J before completing this line (see instructions)	34	
35	**AMT.** Subtract line 34 from line 33. If zero or less, enter -0-. Enter here and on Form 1040, line 45	35	

For Paperwork Reduction Act Notice, see your tax return instructions. Cat. No. 13600G Form **6251** (2015)

9. **Rehabilitation Credit.** (Obj. 3) In 2014, Harriet purchased an office building that had originally been placed in service in 1932. Harriet paid $100,000 for the building, and over the next 15 months, she spent an additional $150,000 to rehabilitate it.

   a. Compute Harriet's rehabilitation credit.

   b. Compute Harriet's basis in the building for depreciation purposes if she elects to take the rehabilitation credit.

   c. How would your answers to Parts a. and b. differ if the building were a certified historic structure?

10. **Disabled Access Credit.** (Obj. 3)

    a. Can a company with $5,000,000 in gross receipts qualify for the disabled access credit? Explain.

    b. Can a company with 40 full-time employees qualify for the disabled access credit? Explain.

    c. What is the maximum disabled access credit?

11. **Credit for Small Employer Health Insurance Premiums.** (Obj. 3) In 2015, Wainrite Company paid 80% of the total costs of each employee's premiums for a qualified health plan (QHP) offered through the SHOP Marketplace. The annual health care premiums for each employee are $12,000. All of Wainrite's employees work full-time.

    a. Compute Wainrite's small employer health insurance credit if it has 8 full-time employees and average wages are $22,300.

    b. Same as in Part a., except that average wages are $28,650.

c. Same as in Part a., except the Wainrite has 14 full-time employees.

12. **Credit for Employer-Provided Childcare Facilities and Services.** (Obj. 3) In 2011, Sarah started a qualified childcare program for her employees. During 2015, she paid $8,000 in qualified childcare expenditures and $12,000 in qualified childcare resource and referral expenses. Compute Sarah's 2015 employer-provided childcare credit.

13. **Credit for Small Employer Pension Plan Startup Costs.** (Obj. 3) Certain employers are entitled to a tax credit for costs associated with establishing a new pension plan for their employees.

    a. Which employers qualify for this credit?

    b. Are there restrictions on the types of pension plans that are eligible for this credit?

    c. How is the credit computed? For how many years can the credit be taken?

14. **Work Opportunity Tax Credit (WOTC).** (Obj. 3) During 2014, Albacross, Inc. hired Dana, Ed, and Finn, each of whom are designated community residents. During their first year, Dana worked 1,600 hours; Ed worked 300 hours, and Finn worked 115 hours. First-year wages are as follows: Dana, $19,000; Ed, $4,400; and Finn, $2,300. Of these wages, $4,000, $3,000, and $2,000, respectively, were paid in 2014. Compute Albacross's 2015 WOTC and discuss its impact on Albacross's 2015 wage expense deduction.

15. **Work Opportunity Tax Credit (WOTC).** (Obj. 3) In August of 2014, Arthur Co. hired Jan, who is a long-term family assistance program recipient. Jan's qualified first-year and second-year wages were $9,000 and $11,500, respectively. Of her $9,000 of first-year wages, $3,200 were paid in 2014, and $5,800 in 2015. Of the $11,500 of second-year wages, $4,400 were paid in 2015 and $7,100 were paid in 2016. Compute Arthur's 2015 and 2016 WOTC.

16. **Work Opportunity Tax Credit (WOTC).** (Obj. 3) On June 8, 2014, Teresa hired a veteran with service-related disabilities. First-year wages were $22,000, of which $10,000 were paid in 2014. Compute Teresa's 2015 WOTC assuming the veteran had been unemployed for two years prior to his hire date.

17. **Work Opportunity Tax Credit (WOTC).** (Obj. 3) During 2014, Hopkins, Inc. hired three veterans, Abe, Bob, and Carl. All three were unemployed veterans with service-related disabilities. Abe had been out of work for 16 weeks, Bob for 16 months, and Carl for three weeks. Total first-year wages, together with the amount of first-year wages paid during 2014 and 2015, are shown below. Using this information, compute Hopkins' 2015 WOTC.

	Total First Year Wages	*Paid in 2014*	*Paid in 2015*
Abe	$25,000	$ 4,000	$21,000
Bob	20,000	17,000	3,000
Carl	16,000	7,000	9,000

18. **Work Opportunity Tax Credit (WOTC).** (Obj. 3) During 2014, Jay hired two veterans, Dave and Earl. During the one year period prior to their hiring, Dave had been unemployed for eight months, and Earl had been unemployed for two weeks. Neither veteran had a service-related disability, but Earl had been receiving food stamps at the time he was hired. Both workers were paid $12,000 in first year wages, of which $4,600 was paid during 2014. Compute Jay's 2015 WOTC.

19. **Empowerment Zone Employment Credit.** (Obj. 3) Ambly Inc. is located in a qualified empowerment zone. During 2014, Ambly hired two people who live in the empowerment zone. Wages paid in 2014 to these two employees were $13,500 and $17,000, respectively. Neither worker was from one of the targeted groups for purposes of the WOTC. Compute the amount of Ambly's empowerment zone employment credit for its fiscal year ending July 31, 2015.

20. **Empowerment Zone Employment Credit.** (Obj. 3) During 2014, Tango, Inc. (a calendar year taxpayer) paid $18,000 of qualified wages to Reba, of which $13,000 were paid in 2014 and the rest were paid in 2015. Reba works at Tango's factory located in the empowerment zone where she also lives. In which tax year(s) would Tango be entitled to claim the empowerment zone employment credit, and compute the amount of the credit.

21. New Markets Credit. (Obj. 3)

a. What types of investments are eligible for the new markets credit?

b. How is the new markets credit computed, and to which years is it available?

22. New Markets Credit. (Obj. 3) On January 1, 2014, a taxpayer paid $350,000 for an investment in a qualified community development equity (CDE).

a. Calculate the taxpayer's new markets credit for 2014-2017.

b. Describe what happens if on February 10, 2018, the taxpayer's investment no longer qualifies as a CDE.

23. Internet Problem: Researching Instructions to Form 8882. (Obj. 3)

The employer-provided childcare credit allows a tax credit for 25% of qualified childcare expenses, which includes amounts paid to a qualified childcare facility that provides childcare services to employees.

Go to the IRS website and locate Form 8882, Employer-Provided Childcare Facilities and Services Credit. Find the information immediately following the form that describes what constitutes a qualified childcare facility. Print out that page.

See Appendix A for instructions on use of the IRS website.

24. Business Entity Problem: This problem is designed for those using the "business entity" approach. **The solution may require information from Chapters 14–16.**

a. Budget Corporation has a net operating loss (NOL) of $150,000. What may the corporation do with this loss?

b. If the business was operated as a partnership, how would the loss be treated?

c. If Budget was an S corporation, how would the loss be treated?

COMPREHENSIVE PROBLEM

25. (Obj. 4) Theodore R. Langley (SSN 556-89-8227) lives at 118 Oxford Ave., Oak Park, IL 60725. In 2015, he has the following income and deductions.

Income:	
Salary	$105,000
State of Iowa (specified private activity bonds bought in 1997)	20,000
Interest from Bank of America	10,600
Deductions:	
Cash contributions to the American Red Cross	$ 4,000
Home mortgage interest	21,520
Real estate taxes	6,850
State income taxes withheld	4,820
State income taxes paid when filing his 2014 taxes	395

In addition to the above, Ted had federal income taxes withheld of $22,908 during the year. He also paid $25,000 for $47,000 worth of stock through an incentive stock option plan at work. Ted is divorced and claims his 15-year-old daughter, Teresa Langley (SSN 882-94-6648), as a dependent. Teresa lived with her father 10 months during the year.

Based on this information, prepare Ted's 2015 tax return, including Form 6251 to compute his AMT. Through his employer, Ted purchases health care insurance for himself and Teresa that complies with the ACA mandate. Ted does not want to contribute $3 to the Presidential election campaign fund. He does not have a foreign bank account nor did he receive a distribution from a foreign trust. Ted is a bank manager. He signs his return on April 15, 2016.

(Use for Problem 25.)

Form **1040** Department of the Treasury—Internal Revenue Service (99)
U.S. Individual Income Tax Return **2015** OMB No. 1545-0074 IRS Use Only—Do not write or staple in this space.

For the year Jan. 1–Dec. 31, 2015, or other tax year beginning , 2015, ending , 20 See separate instructions.

Your first name and initial	Last name	**Your social security number**
If a joint return, spouse's first name and initial	Last name	**Spouse's social security number**
Home address (number and street). If you have a P.O. box, see instructions.	Apt. no.	▲ Make sure the SSN(s) above and on line 6c are correct.
City, town or post office, state, and ZIP code. If you have a foreign address, also complete spaces below (see instructions).		**Presidential Election Campaign**
Foreign country name	Foreign province/state/county · Foreign postal code	Check here if you, or your spouse if filing jointly, want $3 to go to this fund. Checking a box below will not change your tax or refund. ☐ You ☐ Spouse

Filing Status

Check only one box.

1 ☐ Single
2 ☐ Married filing jointly (even if only one had income)
3 ☐ Married filing separately. Enter spouse's SSN above and full name here.
4 ☐ Head of household (with qualifying person). (See instructions.) If the qualifying person is a child but not your dependent, enter this child's name here.
5 ☐ Qualifying widow(er) with dependent child

Exemptions

6a ☐ **Yourself.** If someone can claim you as a dependent, **do not** check box 6a
b ☐ **Spouse**

Boxes checked on 6a and 6b

c **Dependents:** (1) First name Last name	(2) Dependent's social security number	(3) Dependent's relationship to you	(4) ✓ if child under age 17 qualifying for child tax credit (see instructions)
			☐
			☐
			☐
			☐

If more than four dependents, see instructions and check here ▶☐

No. of children on 6c who:
• lived with you
• did not live with you due to divorce or separation (see instructions)
Dependents on 6c not entered above

d Total number of exemptions claimed

Add numbers on lines above ▶

Income

Attach Form(s) W-2 here. Also attach Forms W-2G and 1099-R if tax was withheld.

If you did not get a W-2, see instructions.

7	Wages, salaries, tips, etc. Attach Form(s) W-2	7
8a	**Taxable** interest. Attach Schedule B if required	8a
b	**Tax-exempt** interest. **Do not** include on line 8a — 8b	
9a	Ordinary dividends. Attach Schedule B if required	9a
b	Qualified dividends — 9b	
10	Taxable refunds, credits, or offsets of state and local income taxes	10
11	Alimony received	11
12	Business income or (loss). Attach Schedule C or C-EZ	12
13	Capital gain or (loss). Attach Schedule D if required. If not required, check here ▶ ☐	13
14	Other gains or (losses). Attach Form 4797	14
15a	IRA distributions — 15a — b Taxable amount	15b
16a	Pensions and annuities — 16a — b Taxable amount	16b
17	Rental real estate, royalties, partnerships, S corporations, trusts, etc. Attach Schedule E	17
18	Farm income or (loss). Attach Schedule F	18
19	Unemployment compensation	19
20a	Social security benefits — 20a — b Taxable amount	20b
21	Other income. List type and amount	21
22	Combine the amounts in the far right column for lines 7 through 21. This is your **total income** ▶	22

Adjusted Gross Income

23	Reserved	23
24	Certain business expenses of reservists, performing artists, and fee-basis government officials. Attach Form 2106 or 2106-EZ	24
25	Health savings account deduction. Attach Form 8889	25
26	Moving expenses. Attach Form 3903	26
27	Deductible part of self-employment tax. Attach Schedule SE	27
28	Self-employed SEP, SIMPLE, and qualified plans	28
29	Self-employed health insurance deduction	29
30	Penalty on early withdrawal of savings	30
31a	Alimony paid b Recipient's SSN ▶	31a
32	IRA deduction	32
33	Student loan interest deduction	33
34	Reserved	34
35	Domestic production activities deduction. Attach Form 8903	35
36	Add lines 23 through 35	36
37	Subtract line 36 from line 22. This is your **adjusted gross income** ▶	37

For Disclosure, Privacy Act, and Paperwork Reduction Act Notice, see separate instructions. Cat. No. 11320B Form **1040** (2015)

(Use for Problem 25.)

Form 1040 (2015) Page **2**

Tax and Credits

38	Amount from line 37 (adjusted gross income)		38	
39a	Check if: ☐ **You** were born before January 2, 1951, ☐ Blind. ☐ **Spouse** was born before January 2, 1951, ☐ Blind. } **Total boxes checked** ▶ 39a			
b	If your spouse itemizes on a separate return or you were a dual-status alien, check here ▶ 39b☐			
40	**Itemized deductions** (from Schedule A) **or** your **standard deduction** (see left margin)		40	
41	Subtract line 40 from line 38		41	
42	**Exemptions.** If line 38 is $154,950 or less, multiply $4,000 by the number on line 6d. Otherwise, see instructions		42	
43	**Taxable income.** Subtract line 42 from line 41. If line 42 is more than line 41, enter -0-		43	
44	**Tax** (see instructions). Check if any from: **a** ☐ Form(s) 8814 **b** ☐ Form 4972 **c** ☐ ______		44	
45	**Alternative minimum tax** (see instructions). Attach Form 6251		45	
46	Excess advance premium tax credit repayment. Attach Form 8962		46	
47	Add lines 44, 45, and 46 ▶		47	
48	Foreign tax credit. Attach Form 1116 if required	48		
49	Credit for child and dependent care expenses. Attach Form 2441	49		
50	Education credits from Form 8863, line 19	50		
51	Retirement savings contributions credit. Attach Form 8880	51		
52	Child tax credit. Attach Schedule 8812, if required	52		
53	Residential energy credit. Attach Form 5695	53		
54	Other credits from Form: **a** ☐ 3800 **b** ☐ 8801 **c** ☐ ______	54		
55	Add lines 48 through 54. These are your **total credits**		55	
56	Subtract line 55 from line 47. If line 55 is more than line 47, enter -0- ▶		56	

Standard Deduction for—
- People who check any box on line 39a or 39b **or** who can be claimed as a dependent, see instructions.
- All others:

Single or Married filing separately, $6,300

Married filing jointly or Qualifying widow(er), $12,600

Head of household, $9,250

Other Taxes

57	Self-employment tax. Attach Schedule SE	57	
58	Unreported social security and Medicare tax from Form: **a** ☐ 4137 **b** ☐ 8919	58	
59	Additional tax on IRAs, other qualified retirement plans, etc. Attach Form 5329 if required	59	
60a	Household employment taxes from Schedule H	60a	
b	First-time homebuyer credit repayment. Attach Form 5405 if required	60b	
61	Health care: individual responsibility (see instructions) Full-year coverage ☐	61	
62	Taxes from: **a** ☐ Form 8959 **b** ☐ Form 8960 **c** ☐ Instructions; enter code(s) ______	62	
63	Add lines 56 through 62. This is your **total tax** ▶	63	

Payments

64	Federal income tax withheld from Forms W-2 and 1099	64			
65	2015 estimated tax payments and amount applied from 2014 return	65			
66a	**Earned income credit (EIC)**	66a			
b	Nontaxable combat pay election 66b				
67	Additional child tax credit. Attach Schedule 8812	67			
68	American opportunity credit from Form 8863, line 8	68			
69	Net premium tax credit. Attach Form 8962	69			
70	Amount paid with request for extension to file	70			
71	Excess social security and tier 1 RRTA tax withheld	71			
72	Credit for federal tax on fuels. Attach Form 4136	72			
73	Credits from Form: **a** ☐ 2439 **b** ■ Reserved **c** ☐ 8885 **d** ☐	73			
74	Add lines 64, 65, 66a, and 67 through 73. These are your **total payments** ▶			74	

If you have a qualifying child, attach Schedule EIC.

Refund

75	If line 74 is more than line 63, subtract line 63 from line 74. This is the amount you **overpaid**	75	
76a	Amount of line 75 you want **refunded to you.** If Form 8888 is attached, check here ▶☐	76a	
▶ b	Routing number ______ ▶ **c** Type: ☐ Checking ☐ Savings		
▶ d	Account number ______		
77	Amount of line 75 you want **applied to your 2016 estimated tax** ▶ 77		

Direct deposit? See instructions.

Amount You Owe

78	**Amount you owe.** Subtract line 74 from line 63. For details on how to pay, see instructions ▶	78	
79	Estimated tax penalty (see instructions) 79		

Third Party Designee

Do you want to allow another person to discuss this return with the IRS (see instructions)? ☐ **Yes.** Complete below. ☐ **No**

Designee's name ▶ Phone no. ▶ Personal identification number (PIN) ▶

Sign Here

Under penalties of perjury, I declare that I have examined this return and accompanying schedules and statements, and to the best of my knowledge and belief, they are true, correct, and complete. Declaration of preparer (other than taxpayer) is based on all information of which preparer has any knowledge.

Your signature	Date	Your occupation	Daytime phone number
Spouse's signature. If a joint return, **both** must sign.	Date	Spouse's occupation	If the IRS sent you an Identity Protection PIN, enter it here (see inst.)

Joint return? See instructions. Keep a copy for your records.

Paid Preparer Use Only

Print/Type preparer's name	Preparer's signature	Date	Check ☐ if self-employed	PTIN
Firm's name ▶			Firm's EIN ▶	
Firm's address ▶			Phone no.	

www.irs.gov/form1040 Form **1040** (2015)

(Use for Problem 25.)

SCHEDULE A (Form 1040)

Department of the Treasury Internal Revenue Service (99)

Itemized Deductions

▶ Information about Schedule A and its separate instructions is at *www.irs.gov/schedulea.*
▶ Attach to Form 1040.

OMB No. 1545-0074

2015

Attachment Sequence No. **07**

Name(s) shown on Form 1040 | **Your social security number**

Medical and Dental Expenses		**Caution.** Do not include expenses reimbursed or paid by others.		
	1	Medical and dental expenses (see instructions)	1	
	2	Enter amount from Form 1040, line 38 [2]		
	3	Multiply line 2 by 10% (.10). But if either you or your spouse was born before January 2, 1951, multiply line 2 by 7.5% (.075) instead	3	
	4	Subtract line 3 from line 1. If line 3 is more than line 1, enter -0-		4
Taxes You Paid	5	State and local		
		a ☐ Income taxes b ■ Reserved }	5	
	6	Real estate taxes (see instructions)	6	
	7	Personal property taxes	7	
	8	Other taxes. List type and amount ▶	8	
	9	Add lines 5 through 8		9
Interest You Paid **Note.** Your mortgage interest deduction may be limited (see instructions).	10	Home mortgage interest and points reported to you on Form 1098	10	
	11	Home mortgage interest not reported to you on Form 1098. If paid to the person from whom you bought the home, see instructions and show that person's name, identifying no., and address ▶	11	
	12	Points not reported to you on Form 1098. See instructions for special rules	12	
	13	Reserved	13	
	14	Investment interest. Attach Form 4952 if required. (See instructions.)	14	
	15	Add lines 10 through 14		15
Gifts to Charity If you made a gift and got a benefit for it, see instructions.	16	Gifts by cash or check. If you made any gift of $250 or more, see instructions.	16	
	17	Other than by cash or check. If any gift of $250 or more, see instructions. You **must** attach Form 8283 if over $500 . . .	17	
	18	Carryover from prior year	18	
	19	Add lines 16 through 18		19
Casualty and Theft Losses	20	Casualty or theft loss(es). Attach Form 4684. (See instructions.)		20
Job Expenses and Certain Miscellaneous Deductions	21	Unreimbursed employee expenses—job travel, union dues, job education, etc. Attach Form 2106 or 2106-EZ if required. (See instructions.) ▶	21	
	22	Tax preparation fees	22	
	23	Other expenses—investment, safe deposit box, etc. List type and amount ▶	23	
	24	Add lines 21 through 23	24	
	25	Enter amount from Form 1040, line 38 [25]		
	26	Multiply line 25 by 2% (.02)	26	
	27	Subtract line 26 from line 24. If line 26 is more than line 24, enter -0-		27
Other Miscellaneous Deductions	28	Other—from list in instructions. List type and amount ▶		28
Total Itemized Deductions	29	Is Form 1040, line 38, over $154,950? ☐ **No.** Your deduction is not limited. Add the amounts in the far right column for lines 4 through 28. Also, enter this amount on Form 1040, line 40. ☐ **Yes.** Your deduction may be limited. See the Itemized Deductions Worksheet in the instructions to figure the amount to enter.		29
	30	If you elect to itemize deductions even though they are less than your standard deduction, check here . . . . ▶ ☐		

For Paperwork Reduction Act Notice, see Form 1040 instructions. Cat. No. 17145C **Schedule A (Form 1040) 2015**

(Use for Problem 25.)

SCHEDULE B (Form 1040A or 1040)
Department of the Treasury Internal Revenue Service (99)

Interest and Ordinary Dividends

► Attach to Form 1040A or 1040.
► Information about Schedule B and its instructions is at *www.irs.gov/scheduleb.*

OMB No. 1545-0074
2015
Attachment Sequence No. 08

Name(s) shown on return | Your social security number

				Amount
Part I Interest (See instructions on back and the instructions for Form 1040A, or Form 1040, line 8a.) **Note:** If you received a Form 1099-INT, Form 1099-OID, or substitute statement from a brokerage firm, list the firm's name as the payer and enter the total interest shown on that form.	1	List name of payer. If any interest is from a seller-financed mortgage and the buyer used the property as a personal residence, see instructions on back and list this interest first. Also, show that buyer's social security number and address ►	1	
	2	Add the amounts on line 1	2	
	3	Excludable interest on series EE and I U.S. savings bonds issued after 1989. Attach Form 8815	3	
	4	Subtract line 3 from line 2. Enter the result here and on Form 1040A, or Form 1040, line 8a ►	4	

Note: If line 4 is over $1,500, you must complete Part III.

				Amount
Part II Ordinary Dividends (See instructions on back and the instructions for Form 1040A, or Form 1040, line 9a.) **Note:** If you received a Form 1099-DIV or substitute statement from a brokerage firm, list the firm's name as the payer and enter the ordinary dividends shown on that form.	5	List name of payer ►	5	
	6	Add the amounts on line 5. Enter the total here and on Form 1040A, or Form 1040, line 9a ►	6	

Note: If line 6 is over $1,500, you must complete Part III.

			Yes	No
Part III Foreign Accounts and Trusts (See instructions on back.)		You must complete this part if you **(a)** had over $1,500 of taxable interest or ordinary dividends; **(b)** had a foreign account; or **(c)** received a distribution from, or were a grantor of, or a transferor to, a foreign trust.		
	7a	At any time during 2015, did you have a financial interest in or signature authority over a financial account (such as a bank account, securities account, or brokerage account) located in a foreign country? See instructions		
		If "Yes," are you required to file FinCEN Form 114, Report of Foreign Bank and Financial Accounts (FBAR), to report that financial interest or signature authority? See FinCEN Form 114 and its instructions for filing requirements and exceptions to those requirements		
	b	If you are required to file FinCEN Form 114, enter the name of the foreign country where the financial account is located ►		
	8	During 2015, did you receive a distribution from, or were you the grantor of, or transferor to, a foreign trust? If "Yes," you may have to file Form 3520. See instructions on back		

For Paperwork Reduction Act Notice, see your tax return instructions. Cat. No. 17146N **Schedule B (Form 1040A or 1040) 2015**

(Use for Problem 25.)

Form **6251**

Department of the Treasury
Internal Revenue Service (99)

Alternative Minimum Tax—Individuals

▶ Information about Form 6251 and its separate instructions is at *www.irs.gov/form6251.*
▶ Attach to Form 1040 or Form 1040NR.

OMB No. 1545-0074

2015

Attachment Sequence No. **32**

Name(s) shown on Form 1040 or Form 1040NR | **Your social security number**

Part I Alternative Minimum Taxable Income (See instructions for how to complete each line.)

1	If filing Schedule A (Form 1040), enter the amount from Form 1040, line 41, and go to line 2. Otherwise, enter the amount from Form 1040, line 38, and go to line 7. (If less than zero, enter as a negative amount.)	1	
2	Medical and dental. If you or your spouse was 65 or older, enter the **smaller** of Schedule A (Form 1040), line 4, **or** 2.5% (.025) of Form 1040, line 38. If zero or less, enter -0-	2	
3	Taxes from Schedule A (Form 1040), line 9	3	
4	Enter the home mortgage interest adjustment, if any, from line 6 of the worksheet in the instructions for this line	4	
5	Miscellaneous deductions from Schedule A (Form 1040), line 27	5	
6	If Form 1040, line 38, is $154,950 or less, enter -0-. Otherwise, see instructions	6	( )
7	Tax refund from Form 1040, line 10 or line 21	7	( )
8	Investment interest expense (difference between regular tax and AMT)	8	
9	Depletion (difference between regular tax and AMT)	9	
10	Net operating loss deduction from Form 1040, line 21. Enter as a positive amount	10	
11	Alternative tax net operating loss deduction	11	( )
12	Interest from specified private activity bonds exempt from the regular tax	12	
13	Qualified small business stock, see instructions	13	
14	Exercise of incentive stock options (excess of AMT income over regular tax income)	14	
15	Estates and trusts (amount from Schedule K-1 (Form 1041), box 12, code A)	15	
16	Electing large partnerships (amount from Schedule K-1 (Form 1065-B), box 6)	16	
17	Disposition of property (difference between AMT and regular tax gain or loss)	17	
18	Depreciation on assets placed in service after 1986 (difference between regular tax and AMT)	18	
19	Passive activities (difference between AMT and regular tax income or loss)	19	
20	Loss limitations (difference between AMT and regular tax income or loss)	20	
21	Circulation costs (difference between regular tax and AMT)	21	
22	Long-term contracts (difference between AMT and regular tax income)	22	
23	Mining costs (difference between regular tax and AMT)	23	
24	Research and experimental costs (difference between regular tax and AMT)	24	
25	Income from certain installment sales before January 1, 1987	25	( )
26	Intangible drilling costs preference	26	
27	Other adjustments, including income-based related adjustments	27	
28	**Alternative minimum taxable income.** Combine lines 1 through 27. (If married filing separately and line 28 is more than $246,250, see instructions.)	28	

Part II Alternative Minimum Tax (AMT)

29 Exemption. (If you were under age 24 at the end of 2015, see instructions.)

IF your filing status is . . .	**AND line 28 is not over . . .**	**THEN enter on line 29 . . .**
Single or head of household	$119,200	$53,600
Married filing jointly or qualifying widow(er)	158,900	83,400
Married filing separately	79,450	41,700

If line 28 is **over** the amount shown above for your filing status, see instructions. — 29

30	Subtract line 29 from line 28. If more than zero, go to line 31. If zero or less, enter -0- here and on lines 31, 33, and 35, and go to line 34	30	
31	• If you are filing Form 2555 or 2555-EZ, see instructions for the amount to enter. • If you reported capital gain distributions directly on Form 1040, line 13; you reported qualified dividends on Form 1040, line 9b; **or** you had a gain on both lines 15 and 16 of Schedule D (Form 1040) (as refigured for the AMT, if necessary), complete Part III on the back and enter the amount from line 64 here. • **All others:** If line 30 is $185,400 or less ($92,700 or less if married filing separately), multiply line 30 by 26% (.26). Otherwise, multiply line 30 by 28% (.28) and subtract $3,708 ($1,854 if married filing separately) from the result.	31	
32	Alternative minimum tax foreign tax credit (see instructions)	32	
33	Tentative minimum tax. Subtract line 32 from line 31	33	
34	Add Form 1040, line 44 (minus any tax from Form 4972), and Form 1040, line 46. Subtract from the result any foreign tax credit from Form 1040, line 48. If you used Schedule J to figure your tax on Form 1040, line 44, refigure that tax without using Schedule J before completing this line (see instructions)	34	
35	**AMT.** Subtract line 34 from line 33. If zero or less, enter -0-. Enter here and on Form 1040, line 45	35	

For Paperwork Reduction Act Notice, see your tax return instructions. Cat. No. 13600G Form **6251** (2015)

CUMULATIVE PROBLEM (CHAPTERS 8-12)

In February 2011, Hainey paid $140,000 for a certified historic structure ($30,000 allocated to the land). During the next 14 months, Hainey spent $150,000 to rehabilitate the building. The building was placed in service as Hainey's office building on May 4, 2012. Hainey took the rehabilitation credit in that year and used MACRS to depreciate the remaining basis in the building. On July 19, 2015, he sold the building. His amount realized from the sale was $295,000, with $35,000 allocated to the land. Compute the realized and recognized gain on the sale of the building. Be sure to discuss the nature of the gain and how it is treated in the netting process.

CUMULATIVE PROBLEM (CHAPTERS 1–12)

Jerry R. (age 52, SSN 367-83-9403) and Janet K. (age 48, SSN 361-73-4098) Apps file a joint return. They reside at 410 E. Vernon Avenue, Carlock, Illinois 61725-1287. Use the following information to prepare the Appses' tax return. Use the approach shown in Examples 10-12 in Chapter 11 to compute the Appses' tax liability (¶1101.03). They both elect to have $3 to go to the Presidential election campaign fund and file their return on April 10, 2016.

The Appses' household includes David A. Apps, their 12-year-old son (SSN 965-26-4381), and Edwin R. Apps (SSN 157-43-2587), Jerry's 78-year-old father. Janet and Jerry provide over half of the support of both David and Edwin. David has no income of his own; Edwin received $4,500 in nontaxable social security benefits during the year.

Jerry works as a carpenter. The information on his Form W-2 is shown below. Jerry is an active participate in his employer's 401(k) plan. Through his employer, Jerry purchases health care insurance for his family that complies with the ACA mandate.

Taxable wages	$52,000
Social security and Medicare tax withheld	3,978
Federal income tax withheld	4,970
State income tax withheld	2,490

Janet owns and operates J&J Networking. The principal business code is 454390. Janet has no employer ID number. She uses the accrual basis in her business and the cost method for valuing the inventory. No changes have been made in the inventory system. Janet operated her business for all 12 months and has an office in her home that she uses exclusively and regularly for business. Janet materially participates in the business. Information relating to her business operation is as follows.

Gross receipts	$60,950
Returns and allowances	900
Beginning inventory	2,700
Purchases	28,625
Ending inventory	3,825

Expenses:			
Advertising	$ 400	Office expense	$ 80
Bank service charges	24	Supplies	310
Contribution to SIMPLE plan	10,000	Travel	1,035
Commissions	3,200	Meals and entertainment	490
Depreciation on equipment placed in service in 2014	1,700	Business seminars	1,000
		Other business taxes	560
Dues and publications	220	Miscellaneous expenses	35
Insurance (business)	650	Postage expense	110

In addition to the above expenses, Janet uses her personal car in her business. She keeps good records of her business mileage and uses the standard mileage method. The car was first used in the business on May 1, 2012. During 2015 Janet drove 7,631 miles, of which 1,174 were driven for business. The rest were personal miles.

Information related to the Appses' home:

Total area of home	1,800 square feet
Area used for business	180 square feet
FMV of home, for purposes of Form 8829, line 36	$240,000
Adjusted basis of home, for purposes of Form 8829, line 36	195,000
Value of land, Form 8829, line 37	20,000
Year the home office was first placed in service	1991
Mortgage interest	$6,250
Real estate taxes	2,400
Homeowner's insurance	680
Utilities	3,200

The Appses own a four-unit apartment building that they actively manage. They paid $150,000 for the building in 1994. Of this amount, $25,000 was allocated to the land. The Appses use MACRS to depreciate the building, which is located at 19 Sunset Road in Carlock, IL 60501. All units were rented for the entire year. Information on the apartments is shown below.

Rental revenue	$33,600
Rental expenses:	
Real estate taxes	$ 4,800
Utilities	1,780
Insurance	1,550
Cleaning and maintenance	5,200
Legal and professional fees	125
Mortgage interest	7,200
Repairs	827
Supplies	325

The Appses had other income consisting of the following. Neither Jerry nor Janet had any interest in a foreign trust or bank account.

Interest from Champion Savings	$2,750
Interest on bonds from the State of Illinois	930
Qualified dividends from General Morris Corporation	425
Qualified dividends from Eagle Corporation	150
Qualified dividends from Roper Corporation	650

The Appses have a $4,950 long-term capital loss carryover from 2014. They also sold the following shares of common stock during 2015. No cost basis was provided on any of the Form 1099-Bs.

Number of Shares	*Company*	*Date Acquired*	*Cost*	*Date Sold*	*Sales Price*
100	Roper Corp.	5-1-09	$5,000	6-12-15	$7,500
50	Fastco Corp.	2-14-15	3,250	7-20-15	2,950
200	Eagle Corp.	3-16-11	6,200	8-10-15	8,100
100	South Corp.	3-14-14	1,500	1-24-15	6,500

A summary of the receipts for payments the Appses made during the year includes:

Medical expenses (unreimbursed):

	Jerry	*Janet*	*David*	*Edwin*	*Total*
Prescription medicines	$ 50	$ 200	$ 25	$1,000	$1,275
Doctor bills	60	500	30	200	790
Dentist bills	150	40	200	0	390
Hospital bills	0	1,800	0	2,100	3,900
Transportation	8	72	24	16	120
Eyeglasses	0	122	125	0	247
Over-the-counter medicine	0	50	30	70	150

Taxes:	
Sales tax	$1,200
Balance due on 2014 state income tax return	25
Balance due on 2014 federal income tax return	725
Real estate taxes	2,400

Interest:	
Mortgage interest	$6,250
Credit card interest	975

Cash contributions:	
Church	$2,300
United Way	250
Presidential election campaign	50

In addition to the cash contributions, the Appses donated five shares of S&W common stock to their church on July 30. The stock had been purchased on December 15, 2013, for $2,200. The fair market value of the stock on July 30 was $6,000.

Janet and Jerry each contribute the maximum amount allowed for 2015 to their respective (traditional) IRAs. They also make the following other payments during the year:

Rental of safe deposit box for securities	$ 120
Tax preparation fee (2014 Form 1040)	524
Jerry's union dues	1,200
Automobile registration	150

(Use for Cumulative Problem.)

Form **1040** Department of the Treasury—Internal Revenue Service (99)
U.S. Individual Income Tax Return **2015** OMB No. 1545-0074 IRS Use Only—Do not write or staple in this space.

For the year Jan. 1–Dec. 31, 2015, or other tax year beginning , 2015, ending , 20 See separate instructions.

Your first name and initial	Last name	Your social security number
If a joint return, spouse's first name and initial	Last name	Spouse's social security number
Home address (number and street). If you have a P.O. box, see instructions.	Apt. no.	▲ Make sure the SSN(s) above and on line 6c are correct.
City, town or post office, state, and ZIP code. If you have a foreign address, also complete spaces below (see instructions).		**Presidential Election Campaign** Check here if you, or your spouse if filing jointly, want $3 to go to this fund. Checking a box below will not change your tax or refund. ☐ You ☐ Spouse
Foreign country name	Foreign province/state/county	Foreign postal code

Filing Status

Check only one box.

1 ☐ Single
2 ☐ Married filing jointly (even if only one had income)
3 ☐ Married filing separately. Enter spouse's SSN above and full name here.
4 ☐ Head of household (with qualifying person). (See instructions.) If the qualifying person is a child but not your dependent, enter this child's name here.
5 ☐ Qualifying widow(er) with dependent child

Exemptions

6a ☐ **Yourself.** If someone can claim you as a dependent, **do not** check box 6a . . . . .
b ☐ **Spouse** . . . .
} **Boxes checked on 6a and 6b**

c **Dependents:**

(1) First name Last name	(2) Dependent's social security number	(3) Dependent's relationship to you	(4) ✓ if child under age 17 qualifying for child tax credit (see instructions)
			☐
			☐
			☐
			☐

If more than four dependents, see instructions and check here ▶ ☐

d Total number of exemptions claimed . . . .

No. of children on 6c who:
• **lived with you**
• **did not live with you due to divorce or separation (see instructions)**
Dependents on 6c not entered above
Add numbers on lines above ▶

Income

Attach Form(s) W-2 here. Also attach Forms W-2G and 1099-R if tax was withheld.

If you did not get a W-2, see instructions.

7	Wages, salaries, tips, etc. Attach Form(s) W-2		7
8a	**Taxable** interest. Attach Schedule B if required		8a
b	**Tax-exempt** interest. **Do not** include on line 8a	8b	
9a	Ordinary dividends. Attach Schedule B if required		9a
b	Qualified dividends	9b	
10	Taxable refunds, credits, or offsets of state and local income taxes		10
11	Alimony received		11
12	Business income or (loss). Attach Schedule C or C-EZ		12
13	Capital gain or (loss). Attach Schedule D if required. If not required, check here ▶ ☐		13
14	Other gains or (losses). Attach Form 4797		14
15a	IRA distributions	15a	b Taxable amount 15b
16a	Pensions and annuities	16a	b Taxable amount 16b
17	Rental real estate, royalties, partnerships, S corporations, trusts, etc. Attach Schedule E		17
18	Farm income or (loss). Attach Schedule F		18
19	Unemployment compensation		19
20a	Social security benefits	20a	b Taxable amount 20b
21	Other income. List type and amount		21
22	Combine the amounts in the far right column for lines 7 through 21. This is your **total income** ▶		22

Adjusted Gross Income

23	Reserved	23	
24	Certain business expenses of reservists, performing artists, and fee-basis government officials. Attach Form 2106 or 2106-EZ	24	
25	Health savings account deduction. Attach Form 8889	25	
26	Moving expenses. Attach Form 3903	26	
27	Deductible part of self-employment tax. Attach Schedule SE	27	
28	Self-employed SEP, SIMPLE, and qualified plans	28	
29	Self-employed health insurance deduction	29	
30	Penalty on early withdrawal of savings	30	
31a	Alimony paid b Recipient's SSN ▶	31a	
32	IRA deduction	32	
33	Student loan interest deduction	33	
34	Reserved	34	
35	Domestic production activities deduction. Attach Form 8903	35	
36	Add lines 23 through 35		36
37	Subtract line 36 from line 22. This is your **adjusted gross income** ▶		37

For Disclosure, Privacy Act, and Paperwork Reduction Act Notice, see separate instructions. Cat. No. 11320B Form **1040** (2015)

(Use for Cumulative Problem.)

Form 1040 (2015) Page **2**

Tax and Credits

38	Amount from line 37 (adjusted gross income)	38	
39a	Check if: ☐ **You** were born before January 2, 1951, ☐ Blind. ☐ **Spouse** was born before January 2, 1951, ☐ Blind. **Total boxes checked ▶ 39a** ☐		
b	If your spouse itemizes on a separate return or you were a dual-status alien, check here ▶ 39b ☐		
40	**Itemized deductions** (from Schedule A) **or** your **standard deduction** (see left margin)	40	
41	Subtract line 40 from line 38	41	
42	**Exemptions.** If line 38 is $154,950 or less, multiply $4,000 by the number on line 6d. Otherwise, see instructions	42	
43	**Taxable income.** Subtract line 42 from line 41. If line 42 is more than line 41, enter -0-	43	
44	**Tax** (see instructions). Check if any from: **a** ☐ Form(s) 8814 **b** ☐ Form 4972 **c** ☐	44	
45	**Alternative minimum tax** (see instructions). Attach Form 6251	45	
46	Excess advance premium tax credit repayment. Attach Form 8962	46	
47	Add lines 44, 45, and 46 ▶	47	
48	Foreign tax credit. Attach Form 1116 if required	48	
49	Credit for child and dependent care expenses. Attach Form 2441	49	
50	Education credits from Form 8863, line 19	50	
51	Retirement savings contributions credit. Attach Form 8880	51	
52	Child tax credit. Attach Schedule 8812, if required	52	
53	Residential energy credit. Attach Form 5695	53	
54	Other credits from Form: **a** ☐ 3800 **b** ☐ 8801 **c** ☐	54	
55	Add lines 48 through 54. These are your **total credits**	55	
56	Subtract line 55 from line 47. If line 55 is more than line 47, enter -0- ▶	56	

Standard Deduction for—
- People who check any box on line 39a or 39b **or** who can be claimed as a dependent, see instructions.
- All others:

Single or Married filing separately, $6,300

Married filing jointly or Qualifying widow(er), $12,600

Head of household, $9,250

Other Taxes

57	Self-employment tax. Attach Schedule SE	57	
58	Unreported social security and Medicare tax from Form: **a** ☐ 4137 **b** ☐ 8919	58	
59	Additional tax on IRAs, other qualified retirement plans, etc. Attach Form 5329 if required	59	
60a	Household employment taxes from Schedule H	60a	
b	First-time homebuyer credit repayment. Attach Form 5405 if required	60b	
61	Health care: individual responsibility (see instructions) Full-year coverage ☐	61	
62	Taxes from: **a** ☐ Form 8959 **b** ☐ Form 8960 **c** ☐ Instructions; enter code(s)	62	
63	Add lines 56 through 62. This is your **total tax** ▶	63	

Payments

If you have a qualifying child, attach Schedule EIC.

64	Federal income tax withheld from Forms W-2 and 1099	64	
65	2015 estimated tax payments and amount applied from 2014 return	65	
66a	**Earned income credit (EIC)**	66a	
b	Nontaxable combat pay election 66b		
67	Additional child tax credit. Attach Schedule 8812	67	
68	American opportunity credit from Form 8863, line 8	68	
69	Net premium tax credit. Attach Form 8962	69	
70	Amount paid with request for extension to file	70	
71	Excess social security and tier 1 RRTA tax withheld	71	
72	Credit for federal tax on fuels. Attach Form 4136	72	
73	Credits from Form: **a** ☐ 2439 **b** Reserved **c** ☐ 8885 **d** ☐	73	
74	Add lines 64, 65, 66a, and 67 through 73. These are your **total payments** ▶	74	

Refund

75	If line 74 is more than line 63, subtract line 63 from line 74. This is the amount you **overpaid**	75	
76a	Amount of line 75 you want **refunded to you.** If Form 8888 is attached, check here ▶ ☐	76a	
▶ b	Routing number ▶ **c** Type: ☐ Checking ☐ Savings		
▶ d	Account number		
77	Amount of line 75 you want **applied to your 2016 estimated tax** ▶	77	

Direct deposit? See instructions.

Amount You Owe

78	**Amount you owe.** Subtract line 74 from line 63. For details on how to pay, see instructions ▶	78	
79	Estimated tax penalty (see instructions)	79	

Third Party Designee

Do you want to allow another person to discuss this return with the IRS (see instructions)? ☐ **Yes.** Complete below. ☐ **No**

Designee's name ▶ Phone no. ▶ Personal identification number (PIN) ▶

Sign Here

Under penalties of perjury, I declare that I have examined this return and accompanying schedules and statements, and to the best of my knowledge and belief, they are true, correct, and complete. Declaration of preparer (other than taxpayer) is based on all information of which preparer has any knowledge.

Joint return? See instructions. Keep a copy for your records.

Your signature	Date	Your occupation	Daytime phone number
Spouse's signature. If a joint return, **both** must sign.	Date	Spouse's occupation	If the IRS sent you an Identity Protection PIN, enter it here (see inst.)

Paid Preparer Use Only

Print/Type preparer's name	Preparer's signature	Date	Check ☐ if self-employed	PTIN
Firm's name ▶			Firm's EIN ▶	
Firm's address ▶			Phone no.	

www.irs.gov/form1040 Form **1040** (2015)

(Use for Cumulative Problem.)

SCHEDULE A (Form 1040)

Department of the Treasury
Internal Revenue Service (99)

Itemized Deductions

▶ Information about Schedule A and its separate instructions is at *www.irs.gov/schedulea*.
▶ Attach to Form 1040.

OMB No. 1545-0074
2015
Attachment Sequence No. **07**

Name(s) shown on Form 1040 | **Your social security number**

Medical and Dental Expenses		**Caution.** Do not include expenses reimbursed or paid by others.		
	1	Medical and dental expenses (see instructions)	1	
	2	Enter amount from Form 1040, line 38 [2]		
	3	Multiply line 2 by 10% (.10). But if either you or your spouse was born before January 2, 1951, multiply line 2 by 7.5% (.075) instead	3	
	4	Subtract line 3 from line 1. If line 3 is more than line 1, enter -0-		4
Taxes You Paid	5	State and local		
		a ☐ Income taxes b ■ Reserved	5	
	6	Real estate taxes (see instructions)	6	
	7	Personal property taxes	7	
	8	Other taxes. List type and amount ▶	8	
	9	Add lines 5 through 8		9
Interest You Paid **Note.** Your mortgage interest deduction may be limited (see instructions).	10	Home mortgage interest and points reported to you on Form 1098	10	
	11	Home mortgage interest not reported to you on Form 1098. If paid to the person from whom you bought the home, see instructions and show that person's name, identifying no., and address ▶	11	
	12	Points not reported to you on Form 1098. See instructions for special rules	12	
	13	Reserved	13	
	14	Investment interest. Attach Form 4952 if required. (See instructions.)	14	
	15	Add lines 10 through 14		15
Gifts to Charity If you made a gift and got a benefit for it, see instructions.	16	Gifts by cash or check. If you made any gift of $250 or more, see instructions	16	
	17	Other than by cash or check. If any gift of $250 or more, see instructions. You **must** attach Form 8283 if over $500	17	
	18	Carryover from prior year	18	
	19	Add lines 16 through 18		19
Casualty and Theft Losses	20	Casualty or theft loss(es). Attach Form 4684. (See instructions.)		20
Job Expenses and Certain Miscellaneous Deductions	21	Unreimbursed employee expenses—job travel, union dues, job education, etc. Attach Form 2106 or 2106-EZ if required. (See instructions.) ▶	21	
	22	Tax preparation fees	22	
	23	Other expenses—investment, safe deposit box, etc. List type and amount ▶	23	
	24	Add lines 21 through 23	24	
	25	Enter amount from Form 1040, line 38 [25]		
	26	Multiply line 25 by 2% (.02)	26	
	27	Subtract line 26 from line 24. If line 26 is more than line 24, enter -0-		27
Other Miscellaneous Deductions	28	Other—from list in instructions. List type and amount ▶		28
Total Itemized Deductions	29	Is Form 1040, line 38, over $154,950? ☐ **No.** Your deduction is not limited. Add the amounts in the far right column for lines 4 through 28. Also, enter this amount on Form 1040, line 40. ☐ **Yes.** Your deduction may be limited. See the Itemized Deductions Worksheet in the instructions to figure the amount to enter.		29
	30	If you elect to itemize deductions even though they are less than your standard deduction, check here ▶ ☐		

For Paperwork Reduction Act Notice, see Form 1040 instructions. Cat. No. 17145C **Schedule A (Form 1040) 2015**

(Use for Cumulative Problem.)

SCHEDULE B (Form 1040A or 1040)
Department of the Treasury Internal Revenue Service (99)

Interest and Ordinary Dividends

▶ Attach to Form 1040A or 1040.
▶ Information about Schedule B and its instructions is at *www.irs.gov/scheduleb*.

OMB No. 1545-0074
2015
Attachment Sequence No. 08

Name(s) shown on return | Your social security number

Part I Interest

(See instructions on back and the instructions for Form 1040A, or Form 1040, line 8a.)

Note: If you received a Form 1099-INT, Form 1099-OID, or substitute statement from a brokerage firm, list the firm's name as the payer and enter the total interest shown on that form.

			Amount
1	List name of payer. If any interest is from a seller-financed mortgage and the buyer used the property as a personal residence, see instructions on back and list this interest first. Also, show that buyer's social security number and address ▶	1	
2	Add the amounts on line 1	2	
3	Excludable interest on series EE and I U.S. savings bonds issued after 1989. Attach Form 8815	3	
4	Subtract line 3 from line 2. Enter the result here and on Form 1040A, or Form 1040, line 8a ▶	4	

Note: If line 4 is over $1,500, you must complete Part III.

Part II Ordinary Dividends

(See instructions on back and the instructions for Form 1040A, or Form 1040, line 9a.)

Note: If you received a Form 1099-DIV or substitute statement from a brokerage firm, list the firm's name as the payer and enter the ordinary dividends shown on that form.

			Amount
5	List name of payer ▶	5	
6	Add the amounts on line 5. Enter the total here and on Form 1040A, or Form 1040, line 9a ▶	6	

Note: If line 6 is over $1,500, you must complete Part III.

Part III Foreign Accounts and Trusts

(See instructions on back.)

You must complete this part if you **(a)** had over $1,500 of taxable interest or ordinary dividends; **(b)** had a foreign account; or **(c)** received a distribution from, or were a grantor of, or a transferor to, a foreign trust.

		Yes	No
7a	At any time during 2015, did you have a financial interest in or signature authority over a financial account (such as a bank account, securities account, or brokerage account) located in a foreign country? See instructions		
	If "Yes," are you required to file FinCEN Form 114, Report of Foreign Bank and Financial Accounts (FBAR), to report that financial interest or signature authority? See FinCEN Form 114 and its instructions for filing requirements and exceptions to those requirements		
b	If you are required to file FinCEN Form 114, enter the name of the foreign country where the financial account is located ▶		
8	During 2015, did you receive a distribution from, or were you the grantor of, or transferor to, a foreign trust? If "Yes," you may have to file Form 3520. See instructions on back		

For Paperwork Reduction Act Notice, see your tax return instructions. Cat. No. 17146N **Schedule B (Form 1040A or 1040) 2015**

(Use for Cumulative Problem.)

SCHEDULE C (Form 1040)

Department of the Treasury
Internal Revenue Service (99)

Profit or Loss From Business

(Sole Proprietorship)

▶ Information about Schedule C and its separate instructions is at *www.irs.gov/schedulec.*

▶ Attach to Form 1040, 1040NR, or 1041; partnerships generally must file Form 1065.

OMB No. 1545-0074

2015

Attachment Sequence No. **09**

Name of proprietor | **Social security number (SSN)**

A Principal business or profession, including product or service (see instructions) | **B Enter code from instructions** ▶

C Business name. If no separate business name, leave blank. | **D Employer ID number (EIN),** (see instr.)

E Business address (including suite or room no.) ▶

City, town or post office, state, and ZIP code

F Accounting method: **(1)** ☐ Cash **(2)** ☐ Accrual **(3)** ☐ Other (specify) ▶

G Did you "materially participate" in the operation of this business during 2015? If "No," see instructions for limit on losses . ☐ **Yes** ☐ **No**

H If you started or acquired this business during 2015, check here . . . ▶ ☐

I Did you make any payments in 2015 that would require you to file Form(s) 1099? (see instructions) . . . ☐ **Yes** ☐ **No**

J If "Yes," did you or will you file required Forms 1099? . . . ☐ **Yes** ☐ **No**

Part I Income

1	Gross receipts or sales. See instructions for line 1 and check the box if this income was reported to you on Form W-2 and the "Statutory employee" box on that form was checked . . . ▶ ☐	1	
2	Returns and allowances . . .	2	
3	Subtract line 2 from line 1 . . .	3	
4	Cost of goods sold (from line 42) . . .	4	
5	**Gross profit.** Subtract line 4 from line 3 . . .	5	
6	Other income, including federal and state gasoline or fuel tax credit or refund (see instructions) . . .	6	
7	**Gross income.** Add lines 5 and 6 . . . ▶	7	

Part II **Expenses.** Enter expenses for business use of your home **only** on line 30.

8	Advertising . . .	8		18	Office expense (see instructions)	18	
9	Car and truck expenses (see instructions) . . .	9		19	Pension and profit-sharing plans .	19	
				20	Rent or lease (see instructions):		
10	Commissions and fees .	10		a	Vehicles, machinery, and equipment	20a	
11	Contract labor (see instructions)	11		b	Other business property . . .	20b	
12	Depletion . . .	12		21	Repairs and maintenance . . .	21	
13	Depreciation and section 179 expense deduction (not included in Part III) (see instructions) . . .	13		22	Supplies (not included in Part III) .	22	
				23	Taxes and licenses . . .	23	
				24	Travel, meals, and entertainment:		
14	Employee benefit programs (other than on line 19) . .	14		a	Travel . . .	24a	
15	Insurance (other than health)	15		b	Deductible meals and entertainment (see instructions) .	24b	
16	Interest:			25	Utilities . . .	25	
a	Mortgage (paid to banks, etc.)	16a		26	Wages (less employment credits) .	26	
b	Other . . .	16b		27a	Other expenses (from line 48) . .	27a	
17	Legal and professional services	17		b	**Reserved for future use** . . .	27b	

28	**Total expenses** before expenses for business use of home. Add lines 8 through 27a . . . ▶	28	
29	Tentative profit or (loss). Subtract line 28 from line 7 . . .	29	
30	Expenses for business use of your home. Do not report these expenses elsewhere. Attach Form 8829 unless using the simplified method (see instructions). **Simplified method filers only:** enter the total square footage of: (a) your home: ______ and (b) the part of your home used for business: ______ . Use the Simplified Method Worksheet in the instructions to figure the amount to enter on line 30 . . .	30	
31	**Net profit or (loss).** Subtract line 30 from line 29. • If a profit, enter on both **Form 1040, line 12** (or **Form 1040NR, line 13**) and on **Schedule SE, line 2.** (If you checked the box on line 1, see instructions). Estates and trusts, enter on **Form 1041, line 3.** • If a loss, you **must** go to line 32.	31	

32 If you have a loss, check the box that describes your investment in this activity (see instructions).

• If you checked 32a, enter the loss on both **Form 1040, line 12,** (or **Form 1040NR, line 13**) and on **Schedule SE, line 2.** (If you checked the box on line 1, see the line 31 instructions). Estates and trusts, enter on **Form 1041, line 3.**

• If you checked 32b, you **must** attach **Form 6198.** Your loss may be limited.

32a ☐ All investment is at risk.
32b ☐ Some investment is not at risk.

For Paperwork Reduction Act Notice, see the separate instructions. Cat. No. 11334P **Schedule C (Form 1040) 2015**

(Use for Cumulative Problem.)

Schedule C (Form 1040) 2015 Page **2**

Part III **Cost of Goods Sold** (see instructions)

33	Method(s) used to value closing inventory: **a** ☐ Cost **b** ☐ Lower of cost or market **c** ☐ Other (attach explanation)		
34	Was there any change in determining quantities, costs, or valuations between opening and closing inventory? If "Yes," attach explanation ☐ **Yes** ☐ **No**		
35	Inventory at beginning of year. If different from last year's closing inventory, attach explanation	35	
36	Purchases less cost of items withdrawn for personal use	36	
37	Cost of labor. Do not include any amounts paid to yourself	37	
38	Materials and supplies	38	
39	Other costs	39	
40	Add lines 35 through 39	40	
41	Inventory at end of year	41	
42	**Cost of goods sold.** Subtract line 41 from line 40. Enter the result here and on line 4	42	

Part IV **Information on Your Vehicle.** Complete this part **only** if you are claiming car or truck expenses on line 9 and are not required to file Form 4562 for this business. See the instructions for line 13 to find out if you must file Form 4562.

43 When did you place your vehicle in service for business purposes? (month, day, year) ▶ ____ / ____ / ____

44 Of the total number of miles you drove your vehicle during 2015, enter the number of miles you used your vehicle for:

a Business ________ **b** Commuting (see instructions) ________ **c** Other ________

45 Was your vehicle available for personal use during off-duty hours? ☐ **Yes** ☐ **No**

46 Do you (or your spouse) have another vehicle available for personal use? ☐ **Yes** ☐ **No**

47a Do you have evidence to support your deduction? ☐ **Yes** ☐ **No**

b If "Yes," is the evidence written? ☐ **Yes** ☐ **No**

Part V **Other Expenses.** List below business expenses not included on lines 8–26 or line 30.

48 Total other expenses. Enter here and on line 27a	48	

Schedule C (Form 1040) 2015

(Use for Cumulative Problem.)

SCHEDULE D (Form 1040)

Department of the Treasury
Internal Revenue Service (99)

Capital Gains and Losses

▶ Attach to Form 1040 or Form 1040NR.
▶ Information about Schedule D and its separate instructions is at *www.irs.gov/scheduled*.
▶ Use Form 8949 to list your transactions for lines 1b, 2, 3, 8b, 9, and 10.

OMB No. 1545-0074
2015
Attachment Sequence No. 12

Name(s) shown on return	Your social security number

Part I **Short-Term Capital Gains and Losses—Assets Held One Year or Less**

See instructions for how to figure the amounts to enter on the lines below. This form may be easier to complete if you round off cents to whole dollars.	(d) Proceeds (sales price)	(e) Cost (or other basis)	(g) Adjustments to gain or loss from Form(s) 8949, Part I, line 2, column (g)	(h) Gain or (loss) Subtract column (e) from column (d) and combine the result with column (g)
1a Totals for all short-term transactions reported on Form 1099-B for which basis was reported to the IRS and for which you have no adjustments (see instructions). However, if you choose to report all these transactions on Form 8949, leave this line blank and go to line 1b .				
1b Totals for all transactions reported on Form(s) 8949 with **Box A** checked				
2 Totals for all transactions reported on Form(s) 8949 with **Box B** checked				
3 Totals for all transactions reported on Form(s) 8949 with **Box C** checked				

4 Short-term gain from Form 6252 and short-term gain or (loss) from Forms 4684, 6781, and 8824 .	**4**	
5 Net short-term gain or (loss) from partnerships, S corporations, estates, and trusts from Schedule(s) K-1	**5**	
6 Short-term capital loss carryover. Enter the amount, if any, from line 8 of your **Capital Loss Carryover Worksheet** in the instructions	**6**	( )
7 **Net short-term capital gain or (loss).** Combine lines 1a through 6 in column (h). If you have any long-term capital gains or losses, go to Part II below. Otherwise, go to Part III on the back	**7**	

Part II **Long-Term Capital Gains and Losses—Assets Held More Than One Year**

See instructions for how to figure the amounts to enter on the lines below. This form may be easier to complete if you round off cents to whole dollars.	(d) Proceeds (sales price)	(e) Cost (or other basis)	(g) Adjustments to gain or loss from Form(s) 8949, Part II, line 2, column (g)	(h) Gain or (loss) Subtract column (e) from column (d) and combine the result with column (g)
8a Totals for all long-term transactions reported on Form 1099-B for which basis was reported to the IRS and for which you have no adjustments (see instructions). However, if you choose to report all these transactions on Form 8949, leave this line blank and go to line 8b .				
8b Totals for all transactions reported on Form(s) 8949 with **Box D** checked				
9 Totals for all transactions reported on Form(s) 8949 with **Box E** checked				
10 Totals for all transactions reported on Form(s) 8949 with **Box F** checked.				

11 Gain from Form 4797, Part I; long-term gain from Forms 2439 and 6252; and long-term gain or (loss) from Forms 4684, 6781, and 8824	**11**	
12 Net long-term gain or (loss) from partnerships, S corporations, estates, and trusts from Schedule(s) K-1	**12**	
13 Capital gain distributions. See the instructions	**13**	
14 Long-term capital loss carryover. Enter the amount, if any, from line 13 of your **Capital Loss Carryover Worksheet** in the instructions	**14**	( )
15 **Net long-term capital gain or (loss).** Combine lines 8a through 14 in column (h). Then go to Part III on the back	**15**	

For Paperwork Reduction Act Notice, see your tax return instructions. Cat. No. 11338H **Schedule D (Form 1040) 2015**

(Use for Cumulative Problem.)

Schedule D (Form 1040) 2015 Page **2**

Part III **Summary**

16 Combine lines 7 and 15 and enter the result **16**

- If line 16 is a **gain,** enter the amount from line 16 on Form 1040, line 13, or Form 1040NR, line 14. Then go to line 17 below.
- If line 16 is a **loss,** skip lines 17 through 20 below. Then go to line 21. Also be sure to complete line 22.
- If line 16 is **zero,** skip lines 17 through 21 below and enter -0- on Form 1040, line 13, or Form 1040NR, line 14. Then go to line 22.

17 Are lines 15 and 16 **both** gains?
☐ **Yes.** Go to line 18.
☐ **No.** Skip lines 18 through 21, and go to line 22.

18 Enter the amount, if any, from line 7 of the **28% Rate Gain Worksheet** in the instructions . . ▶ **18**

19 Enter the amount, if any, from line 18 of the **Unrecaptured Section 1250 Gain Worksheet** in the instructions . . . . ▶ **19**

20 Are lines 18 and 19 **both** zero or blank?
☐ **Yes.** Complete the **Qualified Dividends and Capital Gain Tax Worksheet** in the instructions for Form 1040, line 44 (or in the instructions for Form 1040NR, line 42). **Do not** complete lines 21 and 22 below.

☐ **No.** Complete the **Schedule D Tax Worksheet** in the instructions. **Do not** complete lines 21 and 22 below.

21 If line 16 is a loss, enter here and on Form 1040, line 13, or Form 1040NR, line 14, the **smaller** of:

- The loss on line 16 or
- ($3,000), or if married filing separately, ($1,500) } . . . . **21** ( )

Note. When figuring which amount is smaller, treat both amounts as positive numbers.

22 Do you have qualified dividends on Form 1040, line 9b, or Form 1040NR, line 10b?

☐ **Yes.** Complete the **Qualified Dividends and Capital Gain Tax Worksheet** in the instructions for Form 1040, line 44 (or in the instructions for Form 1040NR, line 42).

☐ **No.** Complete the rest of Form 1040 or Form 1040NR.

Schedule D (Form 1040) 2015

(Use for Cumulative Problem.)

Form **8949**

Department of the Treasury
Internal Revenue Service

Sales and Other Dispositions of Capital Assets

▶ Information about Form 8949 and its separate instructions is at *www.irs.gov/form8949.*

▶ File with your Schedule D to list your transactions for lines 1b, 2, 3, 8b, 9, and 10 of Schedule D.

OMB No. 1545-0074

2015

Attachment Sequence No. **12A**

Name(s) shown on return	Social security number or taxpayer identification number

Before you check Box A, B, or C below, see whether you received any Form(s) 1099-B or substitute statement(s) from your broker. A substitute statement will have the same information as Form 1099-B. Either will show whether your basis (usually your cost) was reported to the IRS by your broker and may even tell you which box to check.

Part I **Short-Term.** Transactions involving capital assets you held 1 year or less are short term. For long-term transactions, see page 2.

Note: You may aggregate all short-term transactions reported on Form(s) 1099-B showing basis was reported to the IRS and for which no adjustments or codes are required. Enter the totals directly on Schedule D, line 1a; you aren't required to report these transactions on Form 8949 (see instructions).

You *must* check Box A, B, *or* C below. Check only one box. If more than one box applies for your short-term transactions, complete a separate Form 8949, page 1, for each applicable box. If you have more short-term transactions than will fit on this page for one or more of the boxes, complete as many forms with the same box checked as you need.

☐ **(A)** Short-term transactions reported on Form(s) 1099-B showing basis was reported to the IRS (see **Note** above)

☐ **(B)** Short-term transactions reported on Form(s) 1099-B showing basis was **not** reported to the IRS

☐ **(C)** Short-term transactions not reported to you on Form 1099-B

1 **(a)** Description of property (Example: 100 sh. XYZ Co.)	**(b)** Date acquired (Mo., day, yr.)	**(c)** Date sold or disposed of (Mo., day, yr.)	**(d)** Proceeds (sales price) (see instructions)	**(e)** Cost or other basis. See the **Note** below and see *Column (e)* in the separate instructions	**Adjustment, if any, to gain or loss.** If you enter an amount in column (g), enter a code in column (f). **See the separate instructions.** **(f)** Code(s) from instructions	**(g)** Amount of adjustment	**(h)** **Gain or (loss).** Subtract column (e) from column (d) and combine the result with column (g)
2 Totals. Add the amounts in columns (d), (e), (g), and (h) (subtract negative amounts). Enter each total here and include on your Schedule D, **line 1b** (if **Box A** above is checked), **line 2** (if **Box B** above is checked), or **line 3** (if **Box C** above is checked) ▶							

Note: If you checked Box A above but the basis reported to the IRS was incorrect, enter in column (e) the basis as reported to the IRS, and enter an adjustment in column (g) to correct the basis. See *Column (g)* in the separate instructions for how to figure the amount of the adjustment.

For Paperwork Reduction Act Notice, see your tax return instructions. Cat. No. 37768Z Form **8949** (2015)

(Use for Cumulative Problem.)

Form 8949 (2015) Attachment Sequence No. **12A** Page **2**

Name(s) shown on return. Name and SSN or taxpayer identification no. not required if shown on other side	**Social security number or taxpayer identification number**

Before you check Box D, E, or F below, see whether you received any Form(s) 1099-B or substitute statement(s) from your broker. A substitute statement will have the same information as Form 1099-B. Either will show whether your basis (usually your cost) was reported to the IRS by your broker and may even tell you which box to check.

Part II **Long-Term.** Transactions involving capital assets you held more than 1 year are long term. For short-term transactions, see page 1.

Note: You may aggregate all long-term transactions reported on Form(s) 1099-B showing basis was reported to the IRS and for which no adjustments or codes are required. Enter the totals directly on Schedule D, line 8a; you aren't required to report these transactions on Form 8949 (see instructions).

You *must* check Box D, E, *or* F below. Check only one box. If more than one box applies for your long-term transactions, complete a separate Form 8949, page 2, for each applicable box. If you have more long-term transactions than will fit on this page for one or more of the boxes, complete as many forms with the same box checked as you need.

☐ **(D)** Long-term transactions reported on Form(s) 1099-B showing basis was reported to the IRS (see **Note** above)

☐ **(E)** Long-term transactions reported on Form(s) 1099-B showing basis was **not** reported to the IRS

☐ **(F)** Long-term transactions not reported to you on Form 1099-B

1 (a) Description of property (Example: 100 sh. XYZ Co.)	(b) Date acquired (Mo., day, yr.)	(c) Date sold or disposed of (Mo., day, yr.)	(d) Proceeds (sales price) (see instructions)	(e) Cost or other basis. See the **Note** below and see *Column (e)* in the separate instructions	**Adjustment, if any, to gain or loss.** If you enter an amount in column (g), enter a code in column (f). **See the separate instructions.** (f) Code(s) from instructions	(g) Amount of adjustment	(h) **Gain or (loss).** Subtract column (e) from column (d) and combine the result with column (g)
2 Totals. Add the amounts in columns (d), (e), (g), and (h) (subtract negative amounts). Enter each total here and include on your Schedule D, **line 8b** (if **Box D** above is checked), **line 9** (if **Box E** above is checked), or **line 10** (if **Box F** above is checked) ▶							

Note: If you checked Box D above but the basis reported to the IRS was incorrect, enter in column (e) the basis as reported to the IRS, and enter an adjustment in column (g) to correct the basis. See *Column (g)* in the separate instructions for how to figure the amount of the adjustment.

Form **8949** (2015)

(Use for Cumulative Problem.)

SCHEDULE E (Form 1040)
Department of the Treasury
Internal Revenue Service (99)

Supplemental Income and Loss

(From rental real estate, royalties, partnerships, S corporations, estates, trusts, REMICs, etc.)

▶ Attach to Form 1040, 1040NR, or Form 1041.

▶ Information about Schedule E and its separate instructions is at *www.irs.gov/schedulee.*

OMB No. 1545-0074
2015
Attachment Sequence No. **13**

Name(s) shown on return | **Your social security number**

Part I **Income or Loss From Rental Real Estate and Royalties** **Note:** If you are in the business of renting personal property, use **Schedule C** or **C-EZ** (see instructions). If you are an individual, report farm rental income or loss from **Form 4835** on page 2, line 40.

A Did you make any payments in 2015 that would require you to file Form(s) 1099? (see instructions) ☐ Yes ☐ No

B If "Yes," did you or will you file required Forms 1099? ☐ Yes ☐ No

1a	Physical address of each property (street, city, state, ZIP code)
A	
B	
C	

1b	Type of Property (from list below)	**2** For each rental real estate property listed above, report the number of fair rental and personal use days. Check the **QJV** box only if you meet the requirements to file as a qualified joint venture. See instructions.		**Fair Rental Days**	**Personal Use Days**	**QJV**
A			**A**			☐
B			**B**			☐
C			**C**			☐

Type of Property:
1 Single Family Residence 3 Vacation/Short-Term Rental 5 Land 7 Self-Rental
2 Multi-Family Residence 4 Commercial 6 Royalties 8 Other (describe)

Income:	**Properties:**		**A**	**B**	**C**
3	Rents received	**3**			
4	Royalties received	**4**			
Expenses:					
5	Advertising	**5**			
6	Auto and travel (see instructions)	**6**			
7	Cleaning and maintenance	**7**			
8	Commissions	**8**			
9	Insurance	**9**			
10	Legal and other professional fees	**10**			
11	Management fees	**11**			
12	Mortgage interest paid to banks, etc. (see instructions)	**12**			
13	Other interest	**13**			
14	Repairs	**14**			
15	Supplies	**15**			
16	Taxes	**16**			
17	Utilities	**17**			
18	Depreciation expense or depletion	**18**			
19	Other (list) ▶	**19**			
20	Total expenses. Add lines 5 through 19	**20**			
21	Subtract line 20 from line 3 (rents) and/or 4 (royalties). If result is a (loss), see instructions to find out if you must file **Form 6198**	**21**			
22	Deductible rental real estate loss after limitation, if any, on **Form 8582** (see instructions)	**22**	( )	( )	( )

23a	Total of all amounts reported on line 3 for all rental properties	**23a**	
b	Total of all amounts reported on line 4 for all royalty properties	**23b**	
c	Total of all amounts reported on line 12 for all properties	**23c**	
d	Total of all amounts reported on line 18 for all properties	**23d**	
e	Total of all amounts reported on line 20 for all properties	**23e**	
24	**Income.** Add positive amounts shown on line 21. **Do not** include any losses	**24**	
25	**Losses.** Add royalty losses from line 21 and rental real estate losses from line 22. Enter total losses here	**25**	( )
26	**Total rental real estate and royalty income or (loss).** Combine lines 24 and 25. Enter the result here. If Parts II, III, IV, and line 40 on page 2 do not apply to you, also enter this amount on Form 1040, line 17, or Form 1040NR, line 18. Otherwise, include this amount in the total on line 41 on page 2	**26**	

For Paperwork Reduction Act Notice, see the separate instructions. Cat. No. 11344L **Schedule E (Form 1040) 2015**

(Use for Cumulative Problem.)

SCHEDULE SE (Form 1040)

Department of the Treasury
Internal Revenue Service (99)

Self-Employment Tax

▶ Information about Schedule SE and its separate instructions is at *www.irs.gov/schedulese.*

▶ **Attach to Form 1040 or Form 1040NR.**

OMB No. 1545-0074

2015

Attachment Sequence No. **17**

Name of person with **self-employment** income (as shown on Form 1040 or Form 1040NR)	Social security number of person with **self-employment** income ▶

Before you begin: To determine if you must file Schedule SE, see the instructions.

May I Use Short Schedule SE or Must I Use Long Schedule SE?

Note. Use this flowchart **only if** you must file Schedule SE. If unsure, see *Who Must File Schedule SE* in the instructions.

Did you receive wages or tips in 2015?

- No → Are you a minister, member of a religious order, or Christian Science practitioner who received IRS approval **not** to be taxed on earnings from these sources, **but** you owe self-employment tax on other earnings?
  - Yes → You must use Long Schedule SE on page 2
  - No → Are you using one of the optional methods to figure your net earnings (see instructions)?
    - Yes → You must use Long Schedule SE on page 2
    - No → Did you receive church employee income (see instructions) reported on Form W-2 of $108.28 or more?
      - Yes → You must use Long Schedule SE on page 2
      - No → **You may use Short Schedule SE below**
- Yes → Was the total of your wages and tips subject to social security or railroad retirement (tier 1) tax **plus** your net earnings from self-employment more than $118,500?
  - Yes → You must use Long Schedule SE on page 2
  - No → Did you receive tips subject to social security or Medicare tax that you **did not** report to your employer?
    - Yes → You must use Long Schedule SE on page 2
    - No → Did you report any wages on Form 8919, Uncollected Social Security and Medicare Tax on Wages?
      - Yes → **You must use Long Schedule SE on page 2**
      - No → Are you a minister, member of a religious order, or Christian Science practitioner … (see above)

Section A—Short Schedule SE. Caution. Read above to see if you can use Short Schedule SE.

1a	Net farm profit or (loss) from Schedule F, line 34, and farm partnerships, Schedule K-1 (Form 1065), box 14, code A	**1a**	
b	If you received social security retirement or disability benefits, enter the amount of Conservation Reserve Program payments included on Schedule F, line 4b, or listed on Schedule K-1 (Form 1065), box 20, code Z	**1b**	( )
2	Net profit or (loss) from Schedule C, line 31; Schedule C-EZ, line 3; Schedule K-1 (Form 1065), box 14, code A (other than farming); and Schedule K-1 (Form 1065-B), box 9, code J1. Ministers and members of religious orders, see instructions for types of income to report on this line. See instructions for other income to report	**2**	
3	Combine lines 1a, 1b, and 2	**3**	
4	Multiply line 3 by 92.35% (.9235). If less than $400, you do not owe self-employment tax; **do not** file this schedule unless you have an amount on line 1b . . . . ▶	**4**	
	Note. If line 4 is less than $400 due to Conservation Reserve Program payments on line 1b, see instructions.		
5	**Self-employment tax.** If the amount on line 4 is: • $118,500 or less, multiply line 4 by 15.3% (.153). Enter the result here and on **Form 1040, line 57,** or **Form 1040NR, line 55** • More than $118,500, multiply line 4 by 2.9% (.029). Then, add $14,694 to the result. Enter the total here and on **Form 1040, line 57,** or **Form 1040NR, line 55**	**5**	
6	**Deduction for one-half of self-employment tax.** Multiply line 5 by 50% (.50). Enter the result here and on **Form 1040, line 27,** or **Form 1040NR, line 27** **6**		

For Paperwork Reduction Act Notice, see your tax return instructions. Cat. No. 11358Z **Schedule SE (Form 1040) 2015**

(Use for Cumulative Problem.)

Form **4562** — Department of the Treasury, Internal Revenue Service (99)

Depreciation and Amortization

(Including Information on Listed Property)

▶ Attach to your tax return.

▶ Information about Form 4562 and its separate instructions is at *www.irs.gov/form4562.*

OMB No. 1545-0172 — 2015 — Attachment Sequence No. 179

Name(s) shown on return	Business or activity to which this form relates	Identifying number

Part I Election To Expense Certain Property Under Section 179

Note: If you have any listed property, complete Part V before you complete Part I.

1	Maximum amount (see instructions)	1	
2	Total cost of section 179 property placed in service (see instructions)	2	
3	Threshold cost of section 179 property before reduction in limitation (see instructions)	3	
4	Reduction in limitation. Subtract line 3 from line 2. If zero or less, enter -0-	4	
5	Dollar limitation for tax year. Subtract line 4 from line 1. If zero or less, enter -0-. If married filing separately, see instructions	5	

6	(a) Description of property	(b) Cost (business use only)	(c) Elected cost

7	Listed property. Enter the amount from line 29	7	
8	Total elected cost of section 179 property. Add amounts in column (c), lines 6 and 7	8	
9	Tentative deduction. Enter the **smaller** of line 5 or line 8	9	
10	Carryover of disallowed deduction from line 13 of your 2014 Form 4562	10	
11	Business income limitation. Enter the smaller of business income (not less than zero) or line 5 (see instructions)	11	
12	Section 179 expense deduction. Add lines 9 and 10, but do not enter more than line 11	12	
13	Carryover of disallowed deduction to 2016. Add lines 9 and 10, less line 12 ▶	13	

Note: Do not use Part II or Part III below for listed property. Instead, use Part V.

Part II Special Depreciation Allowance and Other Depreciation (Do not include listed property.) (See instructions.)

14	Special depreciation allowance for qualified property (other than listed property) placed in service during the tax year (see instructions)	14	
15	Property subject to section 168(f)(1) election	15	
16	Other depreciation (including ACRS)	16	

Part III MACRS Depreciation (Do not include listed property.) (See instructions.)

Section A

17	MACRS deductions for assets placed in service in tax years beginning before 2015	17	
18	If you are electing to group any assets placed in service during the tax year into one or more general asset accounts, check here ▶ ☐		

Section B—Assets Placed in Service During 2015 Tax Year Using the General Depreciation System

(a) Classification of property	(b) Month and year placed in service	(c) Basis for depreciation (business/investment use only—see instructions)	(d) Recovery period	(e) Convention	(f) Method	(g) Depreciation deduction
19a 3-year property						
b 5-year property						
c 7-year property						
d 10-year property						
e 15-year property						
f 20-year property						
g 25-year property			25 yrs.		S/L	
h Residential rental property			27.5 yrs.	MM	S/L	
			27.5 yrs.	MM	S/L	
i Nonresidential real property			39 yrs.	MM	S/L	
				MM	S/L	

Section C—Assets Placed in Service During 2015 Tax Year Using the Alternative Depreciation System

20a Class life					S/L	
b 12-year			12 yrs.		S/L	
c 40-year			40 yrs.	MM	S/L	

Part IV Summary (See instructions.)

21	Listed property. Enter amount from line 28	21	
22	**Total.** Add amounts from line 12, lines 14 through 17, lines 19 and 20 in column (g), and line 21. Enter here and on the appropriate lines of your return. Partnerships and S corporations—see instructions	22	
23	For assets shown above and placed in service during the current year, enter the portion of the basis attributable to section 263A costs	23	

For Paperwork Reduction Act Notice, see separate instructions. Cat. No. 12906N Form **4562** (2015)

(Use for Cumulative Problem.)

Form 4562 (2015) Page **2**

Part V **Listed Property** (Include automobiles, certain other vehicles, certain aircraft, certain computers, and property used for entertainment, recreation, or amusement.)

Note: For any vehicle for which you are using the standard mileage rate or deducting lease expense, complete **only** 24a, 24b, columns (a) through (c) of Section A, all of Section B, and Section C if applicable.

Section A—Depreciation and Other Information (Caution: See the instructions for limits for passenger automobiles.**)**

24a Do you have evidence to support the business/investment use claimed? ☐ **Yes** ☐ **No** **24b** If "Yes," is the evidence written? ☐ **Yes** ☐ **No**

(a) Type of property (list vehicles first)	(b) Date placed in service	(c) Business/ investment use percentage	(d) Cost or other basis	(e) Basis for depreciation (business/investment use only)	(f) Recovery period	(g) Method/ Convention	(h) Depreciation deduction	(i) Elected section 179 cost
25 Special depreciation allowance for qualified listed property placed in service during the tax year and used more than 50% in a qualified business use (see instructions) .						25		
26 Property used more than 50% in a qualified business use:								
		%						
		%						
		%						
27 Property used 50% or less in a qualified business use:								
		%				S/L –		
		%				S/L –		
		%				S/L –		
28 Add amounts in column (h), lines 25 through 27. Enter here and on line 21, page 1 .						28		
29 Add amounts in column (i), line 26. Enter here and on line 7, page 1							29	

Section B—Information on Use of Vehicles

Complete this section for vehicles used by a sole proprietor, partner, or other "more than 5% owner," or related person. If you provided vehicles to your employees, first answer the questions in Section C to see if you meet an exception to completing this section for those vehicles.

	(a) Vehicle 1		(b) Vehicle 2		(c) Vehicle 3		(d) Vehicle 4		(e) Vehicle 5		(f) Vehicle 6	
30 Total business/investment miles driven during the year (**do not** include commuting miles) .												
31 Total commuting miles driven during the year												
32 Total other personal (noncommuting) miles driven												
33 Total miles driven during the year. Add lines 30 through 32												
	Yes	**No**	**Yes**	**No**	**Yes**	**No**	**Yes**	**No**	**Yes**	**No**	**Yes**	**No**
34 Was the vehicle available for personal use during off-duty hours?												
35 Was the vehicle used primarily by a more than 5% owner or related person? . .												
36 Is another vehicle available for personal use?												

Section C—Questions for Employers Who Provide Vehicles for Use by Their Employees

Answer these questions to determine if you meet an exception to completing Section B for vehicles used by employees who **are not** more than 5% owners or related persons (see instructions).

	Yes	**No**
37 Do you maintain a written policy statement that prohibits all personal use of vehicles, including commuting, by your employees?		
38 Do you maintain a written policy statement that prohibits personal use of vehicles, except commuting, by your employees? See the instructions for vehicles used by corporate officers, directors, or 1% or more owners . .		
39 Do you treat all use of vehicles by employees as personal use?		
40 Do you provide more than five vehicles to your employees, obtain information from your employees about the use of the vehicles, and retain the information received?		
41 Do you meet the requirements concerning qualified automobile demonstration use? (See instructions.) . . .		

Note: If your answer to 37, 38, 39, 40, or 41 is "Yes," do not complete Section B for the covered vehicles.

Part VI **Amortization**

(a) Description of costs	(b) Date amortization begins	(c) Amortizable amount	(d) Code section	(e) Amortization period or percentage	(f) Amortization for this year
42 Amortization of costs that begins during your 2015 tax year (see instructions):					
43 Amortization of costs that began before your 2015 tax year				43	
44 **Total.** Add amounts in column (f). See the instructions for where to report				44	

Form **4562** (2015)

(Use for Cumulative Problem.)

Form **8829**

Department of the Treasury
Internal Revenue Service (99)

Expenses for Business Use of Your Home

▶ File only with Schedule C (Form 1040). Use a separate Form 8829 for each home you used for business during the year.

▶ Information about Form 8829 and its separate instructions is at *www.irs.gov/form8829*.

OMB No. 1545-0074

2015

Attachment Sequence No. **176**

Name(s) of proprietor(s)	Your social security number

Part I Part of Your Home Used for Business

1	Area used regularly and exclusively for business, regularly for daycare, or for storage of inventory or product samples (see instructions)			1	
2	Total area of home			2	
3	Divide line 1 by line 2. Enter the result as a percentage			3	%
	For daycare facilities not used exclusively for business, go to line 4. All others, go to line 7.				
4	Multiply days used for daycare during year by hours used per day	4	hr.		
5	Total hours available for use during the year (365 days x 24 hours) (see instructions)	5	8,760 hr.		
6	Divide line 4 by line 5. Enter the result as a decimal amount	6			
7	Business percentage. For daycare facilities not used exclusively for business, multiply line 6 by line 3 (enter the result as a percentage). All others, enter the amount from line 3 ▶			7	%

Part II Figure Your Allowable Deduction

			(a) Direct expenses	(b) Indirect expenses		
8	Enter the amount from Schedule C, line 29, **plus** any gain derived from the business use of your home, **minus** any loss from the trade or business not derived from the business use of your home (see instructions)				8	
	See instructions for columns (a) and (b) before completing lines 9–21.					
9	Casualty losses (see instructions)	9				
10	Deductible mortgage interest (see instructions)	10				
11	Real estate taxes (see instructions)	11				
12	Add lines 9, 10, and 11	12				
13	Multiply line 12, column (b) by line 7			13		
14	Add line 12, column (a) and line 13				14	
15	Subtract line 14 from line 8. If zero or less, enter -0-				15	
16	Excess mortgage interest (see instructions)	16				
17	Insurance	17				
18	Rent	18				
19	Repairs and maintenance	19				
20	Utilities	20				
21	Other expenses (see instructions)	21				
22	Add lines 16 through 21	22				
23	Multiply line 22, column (b) by line 7			23		
24	Carryover of prior year operating expenses (see instructions)			24		
25	Add line 22, column (a), line 23, and line 24				25	
26	Allowable operating expenses. Enter the **smaller** of line 15 or line 25				26	
27	Limit on excess casualty losses and depreciation. Subtract line 26 from line 15				27	
28	Excess casualty losses (see instructions)			28		
29	Depreciation of your home from line 41 below			29		
30	Carryover of prior year excess casualty losses and depreciation (see instructions)			30		
31	Add lines 28 through 30				31	
32	Allowable excess casualty losses and depreciation. Enter the **smaller** of line 27 or line 31				32	
33	Add lines 14, 26, and 32				33	
34	Casualty loss portion, if any, from lines 14 and 32. Carry amount to **Form 4684** (see instructions)				34	
35	**Allowable expenses for business use of your home.** Subtract line 34 from line 33. Enter here and on Schedule C, line 30. If your home was used for more than one business, see instructions ▶				35	

Part III Depreciation of Your Home

36	Enter the **smaller** of your home's adjusted basis or its fair market value (see instructions)	36	
37	Value of land included on line 36	37	
38	Basis of building. Subtract line 37 from line 36	38	
39	Business basis of building. Multiply line 38 by line 7	39	
40	Depreciation percentage (see instructions)	40	%
41	Depreciation allowable (see instructions). Multiply line 39 by line 40. Enter here and on line 29 above	41	

Part IV Carryover of Unallowed Expenses to 2016

42	Operating expenses. Subtract line 26 from line 25. If less than zero, enter -0-	42	
43	Excess casualty losses and depreciation. Subtract line 32 from line 31. If less than zero, enter -0-	43	

For Paperwork Reduction Act Notice, see your tax return instructions. Cat. No. 13232M Form **8829** (2015)

Chapter

13

Payroll Taxes and Tax Compliance

CHAPTER CONTENTS

LEARNING OBJECTIVES

After completing Chapter 13, you should be able to:

1. Understand an employer's responsibilities for withholding income and payroll taxes from their employees' pay.
2. Describe how and when employers pay their employment taxes.
3. Compute a taxpayer's minimum required amount of tax prepayments for the year, and understand what happens when the minimum prepayments are not made.
4. Understand the audit and appeals processes and discuss taxpayer rights and tax preparers' responsibilities when completing and filing income tax returns.
5. Describe the various penalties that affect taxpayers and tax preparers who fail to comply with the tax laws.
6. Prepare the various forms introduced in this chapter, including Form W-2, Form W-3, Form W-4, Form 941, and Form 1040X.

CHAPTER OVERVIEW

On January 1, 1943, the income of most wage earners became subject to *pay-as-you-go* withholding. Under this system, the government collects tax revenue by having the payer withhold taxes before distributing the income. This gives the government a steady cash flow and reduces tax collection problems. Withholding also lessens the cash burdens of taxpayers when they file their tax returns. When taxpayers do not have enough taxes withheld on their behalf during the year, they may be charged an underpayment penalty. Taxpayers can avoid this penalty by making quarterly estimated payments to cover the shortfall. This chapter provides background information about the tax withholding system and the estimated payment process.

The remainder of the chapter focuses on a variety of topics that relate to the tax compliance process. Included in this discussion are penalties assessed to taxpayers and tax preparers who do not abide by the tax laws. The chapter also describes the audit and appeals process that taxpayers may face when the IRS questions an item or items reported on the taxpayer's tax return. The chapter concludes with the discussion of filing an amended return. Taxpayers file an amended return when they discover an error or errors on a previously filed tax return.

¶1301 The Withholding System

Under the pay-as-you-go system, employers withhold taxes from employees' wages that approximate their employees' tax liabilities. Employers send in these withholdings to the government. To credit withholdings to the proper taxpayer accounts, the employer and each employee must have an identification number.

¶1301.01 IDENTIFICATION NUMBERS

The IRS uses computer programs to process withholding data and taxpayers' tax returns. Taxpayer identification numbers (TINs) provide the means to link related data. Taxpayers must report their TIN on tax returns they file with the IRS. Individual taxpayers use their social security number (SSN) as their TIN. Businesses use an employer identification number (EIN).

Individuals

Individuals who need a SSN apply for one by filing Form SS-5, Application for a Social Security Card. Individuals can get Form SS-5 from any social security office or from the Social Security administration website (www.ssa.gov). All U.S. citizens, including infants, should obtain a SSN. This allows them to be claimed as a dependent on another's tax return. Also, taxpayers must provide a SSN for each qualifying child in order to claim the child tax credit for that child (¶204.07).

Businesses

Employers put their EIN on payroll tax reporting forms, tax returns, and other government reports. Employers can get an EIN by calling the IRS or by filing Form SS-4, Application for Employer Identification Number, with the IRS online, by fax, or through the mail.

¶1301.02 WITHHOLDING FROM INCOME

For employees, withholding is based on the employee's gross (taxable) pay. From this amount, an employer withholds income (federal, state, and local) and payroll taxes (social security and Medicare taxes).

¶1301.03 WITHHOLDING ALLOWANCE CERTIFICATE

Form W-4, Employee's Withholding Allowance Certificate, is the focal point of the income tax withholding system. The amount of income tax withheld from an employee's gross pay depends on the employee's filing status and the number of withholding allowances the employee claims on Form W-4. The more allowances claimed, the less tax withheld. Employees receive withholding allowances for the personal and dependency exemptions they expect to claim in the current tax year. They also receive withholding allowances for anticipated deductions and credits.

Employers request a Form W-4 from each employee. If an employee fails to furnish Form W-4, the employer withholds the maximum amount of taxes allowed for single taxpayers claiming zero allowances. Thus, married employees must complete Form W-4 to take advantage of the lower withholding rates that apply to married taxpayers. Form W-4 has four sections.

1. Personal Allowances Worksheet
2. Employee's Withholding Allowance Certificate
3. Deductions and Adjustments Worksheet
4. Two-Earners/Multiple Jobs Worksheet

Personal Withholding Allowances

On the Personal Allowances Worksheet, employees enter whole numbers for personal withholding allowances (lines A through G). Single employees with more than one job, but no dependents, claim only one total withholding allowance. They should claim this allowance with the employer that pays them the highest wage. They should claim zero withholding allowances on the Form W-4 that they file with their other employers. Figure 13-1 describes the calculation of the withholding allowance on the Personal Allowances Worksheet for 2015.

An employee with more than one job may want to request that an additional amount be withheld from each paycheck if combined wages exceed $50,000. This helps ensure that the employee will not be underwithheld for the year. Likewise, if the employee is married and both spouses work, each spouse may want to have additional amounts withheld from their respective paychecks when their combined wages exceed $20,000. Alternatively, they could ask their respective employers to withhold taxes at the single rate. They do this by marking an **X** in the box on the Form W-4 (line 3), "Married, but withhold at higher Single rate."

Figure 13-1: Personal Allowances Worksheet

A. One exemption allowance for the employee, as long as the employee is not claimed as a dependent on someone else's tax return.

B. One additional exemption allowance for employees who are:
   1. Single and have only one job;
   2. Married, have one job, and their spouse does not work; or
   3. Married and their spouse's wages plus their second job wages do not exceed $1,500.

C. One exemption for the employee's spouse. However, the IRS recommends that married employees who have more than one job, or have spouses who work, claim a zero spousal allowance. This may avoid having too little withheld for the year.

D. One exemption for each dependent the employee will claim.

E. One exemption if the employee files as head of household.

F. One exemption if the employee has at least $2,000 of child or dependent care expenses and plans to claim the child and dependent care credit.

G. Additional exemptions for employees who plan to claim the child tax credit.
   - For single employees, two exemptions are allowed for each eligible child if total income is expected to be less than $65,000. However, subtract 1 from this total if the employee has two to four eligible children. Subtract 2 from the total if the employee has more than four eligible children. If total income is expected to be between $65,000 and $84,000, one exemption is allowed for each eligible child.
   - For married employees, two exemptions are allowed for each eligible child if total income is expected to be less than $100,000. However, subtract 1 from this total if the employee has two to four eligible children. Subtract 2 from the total if the employee has more than four eligible children. If total income is expected to be between $100,000 and $119,000, one exemption is allowed for each eligible child.

Married couples with dependents can choose how to divide their withholding allowances among their employers. If the husband claims withholding allowances for a particular child on his Form W-4, the wife should not claim an allowance for that same child. If both spouses claim a withholding allowance for the same child, the couple may end up not having enough taxes withheld for the year. This, in turn, could result in underpayment penalties (see ¶1307.03).

Employee's Withholding Allowance Certificate

Employees enter their name, address, and SSN on lines 1 and 2 of the Employee's Withholding Allowance Certificate. On line 3, employees designate whether they want their withholdings based on the single or married rates. Higher withholding rates apply to unmarried employees. Married taxpayers wanting additional amounts withheld have the option of checking the last box, marked "Married, but withhold at higher Single rate."

Employees enter their total number of allowances on line 5 of the Certificate. This number is determined after the employee completes all of the applicable worksheets provided on Form W-4. On line 6, employees can designate additional amounts they want withheld from each paycheck. Employees with earnings from self-employment or other forms of nonwage income often can avoid making quarterly estimated payments by having additional amounts withheld from their paychecks.

Employees wanting to claim exemption from withholding for the year state their desire by writing "Exempt" on line 7 of the Certificate. Only certain employees can claim exemption from withholding. These requirements are discussed later in the chapter (¶1301.06). Once employees finish completing all of the lines on the Employee's Withholding Allowance Certificate, they sign and date it. They then clip the bottom portion of Form W-4 (page 1) and give it to their employer. They keep the top portion of Form W-4 (page 1) and all of Form W-4 (page 2) for their records.

Deductions and Adjustments Worksheet

The Deduction and Adjustments Worksheet helps employees compute additional allowances based on their expected itemized deductions and other adjustments to income. Every $4,000 of net reductions in 2015 results in one additional withholding allowance.

To complete the Deductions and Adjustments Worksheet, employees first estimate their itemized deductions for the year and enter this amount on line 1. They then enter their basic standard deduction on line 2, and subtract that amount from the amount they entered on line 1. The excess of estimated itemized deductions (line 1) over the basic standard deduction (line 2) is entered on line 3. If the basic standard deduction exceeds the estimate of itemized deductions, $0 is entered on line 3. Employees then estimate their adjustments to income (deductions for AGI reported on page 1 of the tax return) and add to this amount any additional standard deduction they are entitled to. Employees report the sum of these two amounts on line 4 of the worksheet. Next, employees add up the amounts from lines 3 and 4 and enter the total on line 5. This amount represents employees' total reductions for the year.

On line 6, employees enter their estimate of nonwage income for the year. Nonwage income includes taxable types of income such as interest, dividends, capital gains, and net rental income. Employees' nonwage income from line 6 is then subtracted from the total reductions reported on line 5. This difference is entered on line 7 and represents employees' net reductions for the year. A negative net reduction results in no additional withholding allowances. A positive net reduction is divided by $4,000. After dropping any fraction, the whole number that is left is entered on line 8 of the worksheet. For example, if dividing the positive net reduction reported on line 7 by $4,000 equals 2.03, the whole number "2" would be entered on line 8. Likewise, the same "2" would be entered if the resulting fraction were 2.98.

The final step in completing the Deductions and Adjustments Worksheet is to enter on line 9 the number of allowances from Personal Allowances Worksheet (line H). The sum of lines 8 and 9 is then entered on line 10. Employees not required to complete the Two-Earners/Multiple Jobs Worksheet use the number from line 10 as their total withholding allowances. They do this by entering that number on the Employee's Withholding Allowance Certificate (line 5). Employees who use the Two-Earners/Multiple Jobs Worksheet complete that worksheet to determine their total withholding allowances they can claim on the Employee's Withholding Allowance Certificate.

Two-Earners/Multiple Jobs Worksheet

Employees who are married and whose spouses also work complete the Two-Earners/Multiple Jobs Worksheet when the couple's combined earnings exceed $20,000. The same rule applies to unmarried employees with more than one job and combined earnings in excess of $50,000. The goal of this worksheet is to compute additional amounts employees should have withheld. The extra withholding helps employees avoid being underwithheld for the year.

¶1301.04 FILLED-IN FORM W-4

INFORMATION FOR FIGURE 13-2:

Jerry J. Page starts a new job in January, 2015. Jerry completes Form W-4 for his new employer. He expects to file a joint tax return for 2015 with his wife Belle. For 2015 Jerry expects to earn $46,000; Belle expects to earn $35,000. The Pages provide all the support for their three children, who have no income. All three are qualifying children for purposes of claiming the child tax credit. The Pages decide that Jerry will claim all withholding allowances for the children. The Pages estimate that they will pay or receive the following amounts during 2015.

Deductible IRA payment for Belle	$3,000
Deductible IRA payment for Jerry	5,000
Child and dependent care expenses	2,300
Taxable interest and dividend income	750
Itemized deductions	15,050

Line # (Personal Allowances Worksheet, page 1)

A: Enter **1** because Jerry cannot be claimed as someone else's dependent
B: Jerry leaves this line blank because his spouse works and her wages exceed $1,500
C: The Pages choose to enter **-0-** because both spouses work
D: Enter **3** for the Pages' three dependents that the couple has agreed that Jerry will claim on his W-4
F: Enter **1** because the Pages expect to have at least $2,000 of childcare expenses and plan to claim the child and dependent care credit
G: Enter **5**. The Pages expect their total income to be less than $100,000. Because they have two to four eligible children, they subtract 1 from 6 (2 for each eligible child × 3 eligible children) to get 5.

Line # (Employee's Withholding Allowance Certificate, page 1)

3: Jerry checks the box next to "Married" because Belle has amounts withheld from her wages and the Pages do not need to have taxes withheld using the (higher) Single rate
5: Total number of allowances from line 3 of the Two-Earners/Multiple Jobs Worksheet, **9**

Line # (Deductions and Adjustments Worksheet, page 2)

1: Estimate of itemized deductions, **$15,050**
2: **$12,600** basic standard deduction for MFJ
4: Estimate of adjustments to income, **$8,000** ($3,000 + $5,000 IRA deductions)
6: Nonwage income, **$750**
8: $9,700 ÷ $4,000 = **2** after the fraction is dropped

Line # (Two-Earners/Multiple Jobs Worksheet, page 2)

1: Number from line 10 of the Deduction and Adjustments Worksheet, **12**
2: Number from Table 1 that applies to $35,000 is 5, but since MFJ and the wages from the highest paying job do not exceed $65,000, Jerry is instructed to enter no more than **3**.

Figure 13-2: Filled-In Form W-4 (Page 1)

Form W-4 (2015)

Purpose. Complete Form W-4 so that your employer can withhold the correct federal income tax from your pay. Consider completing a new Form W-4 each year and when your personal or financial situation changes.

Exemption from withholding. If you are exempt, complete **only** lines 1, 2, 3, 4, and 7 and sign the form to validate it. Your exemption for 2015 expires February 16, 2016. See Pub. 505, Tax Withholding and Estimated Tax.

Note. If another person can claim you as a dependent on his or her tax return, you cannot claim exemption from withholding if your income exceeds $1,050 and includes more than $350 of unearned income (for example, interest and dividends).

Exceptions. An employee may be able to claim exemption from withholding even if the employee is a dependent, if the employee:

- Is age 65 or older,
- Is blind, or
- Will claim adjustments to income; tax credits; or itemized deductions, on his or her tax return.

The exceptions do not apply to supplemental wages greater than $1,000,000.

Basic instructions. If you are not exempt, complete the **Personal Allowances Worksheet** below. The worksheets on page 2 further adjust your withholding allowances based on itemized deductions, certain credits, adjustments to income, or two-earners/multiple jobs situations.

Complete all worksheets that apply. However, you may claim fewer (or zero) allowances. For regular wages, withholding must be based on allowances you claimed and may not be a flat amount or percentage of wages.

Head of household. Generally, you can claim head of household filing status on your tax return only if you are unmarried and pay more than 50% of the costs of keeping up a home for yourself and your dependent(s) or other qualifying individuals. See Pub. 501, Exemptions, Standard Deduction, and Filing Information, for information.

Tax credits. You can take projected tax credits into account in figuring your allowable number of withholding allowances. Credits for child or dependent care expenses and the child tax credit may be claimed using the **Personal Allowances Worksheet** below. See Pub. 505 for information on converting your other credits into withholding allowances.

Nonwage income. If you have a large amount of nonwage income, such as interest or dividends, consider making estimated tax payments using Form 1040-ES, Estimated Tax for Individuals. Otherwise, you may owe additional tax. If you have pension or annuity income, see Pub. 505 to find out if you should adjust your withholding on Form W-4 or W-4P.

Two earners or multiple jobs. If you have a working spouse or more than one job, figure the total number of allowances you are entitled to claim on all jobs using worksheets from only one Form W-4. Your withholding usually will be most accurate when all allowances are claimed on the Form W-4 for the highest paying job and zero allowances are claimed on the others. See Pub. 505 for details.

Nonresident alien. If you are a nonresident alien, see Notice 1392, Supplemental Form W-4 Instructions for Nonresident Aliens, before completing this form.

Check your withholding. After your Form W-4 takes effect, use Pub. 505 to see how the amount you are having withheld compares to your projected total tax for 2015. See Pub. 505, especially if your earnings exceed $130,000 (Single) or $180,000 (Married).

Future developments. Information about any future developments affecting Form W-4 (such as legislation enacted after we release it) will be posted at *www.irs.gov/w4.*

Personal Allowances Worksheet (Keep for your records.)

A Enter "1" for **yourself** if no one else can claim you as a dependent . . . . . **A** 1

B Enter "1" if:
- You are single and have only one job; or
- You are married, have only one job, and your spouse does not work; or
- Your wages from a second job or your spouse's wages (or the total of both) are $1,500 or less.

. . . **B** ____

C Enter "1" for your **spouse.** But, you may choose to enter "-0-" if you are married and have either a working spouse or more than one job. (Entering "-0-" may help you avoid having too little tax withheld.) . . . . . **C** 0

D Enter number of **dependents** (other than your spouse or yourself) you will claim on your tax return . . . . . **D** 3

E Enter "1" if you will file as **head of household** on your tax return (see conditions under **Head of household** above) . . **E** ____

F Enter "1" if you have at least $2,000 of **child or dependent care expenses** for which you plan to claim a credit . . . **F** 1
(**Note.** Do **not** include child support payments. See Pub. 503, Child and Dependent Care Expenses, for details.)

G **Child Tax Credit** (including additional child tax credit). See Pub. 972, Child Tax Credit, for more information.
- If your total income will be less than $65,000 ($100,000 if married), enter "2" for each eligible child; then **less** "1" if you have two to four eligible children or **less** "2" if you have five or more eligible children.
- If your total income will be between $65,000 and $84,000 ($100,000 and $119,000 if married), enter "1" for each eligible child . . . **G** 5

H Add lines A through G and enter total here. (**Note.** This may be different from the number of exemptions you claim on your tax return.) ▶ **H** 10

For accuracy, **complete all worksheets that apply.**
- If you plan to **itemize** or **claim adjustments to income** and want to reduce your withholding, see the **Deductions and Adjustments Worksheet** on page 2.
- If you are **single and have more than one job** or are **married and you and your spouse both work** and the combined earnings from all jobs exceed $50,000 ($20,000 if married), see the **Two-Earners/Multiple Jobs Worksheet** on page 2 to avoid having too little tax withheld.
- If **neither** of the above situations applies, **stop here** and enter the number from line H on line 5 of Form W-4 below.

Separate here and give Form W-4 to your employer. Keep the top part for your records.

Form **W-4** — **Employee's Withholding Allowance Certificate** — OMB No. 1545-0074 — **2015**

Department of the Treasury Internal Revenue Service

▶ **Whether you are entitled to claim a certain number of allowances or exemption from withholding is subject to review by the IRS. Your employer may be required to send a copy of this form to the IRS.**

1 Your first name and middle initial	Last name	2 Your social security number
Jerry J.	Page	432-16-8410

Home address (number and street or rural route): 1222 West Center Avenue

3 ☐ Single ☑ Married ☐ Married, but withhold at higher Single rate.
Note. If married, but legally separated, or spouse is a nonresident alien, check the "Single" box.

City or town, state, and ZIP code: San Diego, CA 91344-8135

4 **If your last name differs from that shown on your social security card, check here. You must call 1-800-772-1213 for a replacement card.** ▶ ☐

5 Total number of allowances you are claiming (from line **H** above **or** from the applicable worksheet on page 2) **5** 9

6 Additional amount, if any, you want withheld from each paycheck . . . . . **6** $

7 I claim exemption from withholding for 2015, and I certify that I meet **both** of the following conditions for exemption.
- Last year I had a right to a refund of **all** federal income tax withheld because I had **no** tax liability, **and**
- This year I expect a refund of **all** federal income tax withheld because I expect to have **no** tax liability.

If you meet both conditions, write "Exempt" here . . . . . ▶ **7**

Under penalties of perjury, I declare that I have examined this certificate and, to the best of my knowledge and belief, it is true, correct, and complete.

Employee's signature
(This form is not valid unless you sign it.) ▶ *Jerry J. Page* **Date** ▶ *1-15-15*

8 Employer's name and address (Employer: Complete lines 8 and 10 only if sending to the IRS.)	9 Office code (optional)	10 Employer identification number (EIN)

For Privacy Act and Paperwork Reduction Act Notice, see page 2. Cat. No. 10220Q Form **W-4** (2015)

Figure 13-2: Filled-In Form W-4 (Page 2)

Form W-4 (2015) Page **2**

Deductions and Adjustments Worksheet

Note. Use this worksheet *only* if you plan to itemize deductions or claim certain credits or adjustments to income.

1	Enter an estimate of your 2015 itemized deductions. These include qualifying home mortgage interest, charitable contributions, state and local taxes, medical expenses in excess of 10% (7.5% if either you or your spouse was born before January 2, 1951) of your income, and miscellaneous deductions. For 2015, you may have to reduce your itemized deductions if your income is over $309,900 and you are married filing jointly or are a qualifying widow(er); $284,050 if you are head of household; $258,250 if you are single and not head of household or a qualifying widow(er); or $154,950 if you are married filing separately. See Pub. 505 for details	1	$ 15,050
2	Enter: { $12,600 if married filing jointly or qualifying widow(er); $9,250 if head of household; $6,300 if single or married filing separately }	2	$ 12,600
3	**Subtract** line 2 from line 1. If zero or less, enter "-0-"	3	$ 2,450
4	Enter an estimate of your 2015 adjustments to income and any additional standard deduction (see Pub. 505)	4	$ 8,000
5	**Add** lines 3 and 4 and enter the total. (Include any amount for credits from the *Converting Credits to Withholding Allowances for 2015 Form W-4* worksheet in Pub. 505.)	5	$ 10,450
6	Enter an estimate of your 2015 nonwage income (such as dividends or interest)	6	$ 750
7	**Subtract** line 6 from line 5. If zero or less, enter "-0-"	7	$ 9,700
8	**Divide** the amount on line 7 by $4,000 and enter the result here. Drop any fraction	8	2
9	Enter the number from the **Personal Allowances Worksheet,** line H, page 1	9	10
10	**Add** lines 8 and 9 and enter the total here. If you plan to use the **Two-Earners/Multiple Jobs Worksheet,** also enter this total on line 1 below. Otherwise, **stop here** and enter this total on Form W-4, line 5, page 1	10	12

Two-Earners/Multiple Jobs Worksheet (See *Two earners or multiple jobs* on page 1.)

Note. Use this worksheet *only* if the instructions under line H on page 1 direct you here.

1	Enter the number from line H, page 1 (or from line 10 above if you used the **Deductions and Adjustments Worksheet**)	1	12
2	Find the number in **Table 1** below that applies to the **LOWEST** paying job and enter it here. **However,** if you are married filing jointly and wages from the highest paying job are $65,000 or less, do not enter more than "3"	2	3
3	If line 1 is **more than or equal to** line 2, subtract line 2 from line 1. Enter the result here (if zero, enter "-0-") and on Form W-4, line 5, page 1. **Do not** use the rest of this worksheet	3	9

Note. If line 1 is **less than** line 2, enter "-0-" on Form W-4, line 5, page 1. Complete lines 4 through 9 below to figure the additional withholding amount necessary to avoid a year-end tax bill.

4	Enter the number from line 2 of this worksheet . . . . 4 ______		
5	Enter the number from line 1 of this worksheet . . . . 5 ______		
6	**Subtract** line 5 from line 4	6	
7	Find the amount in **Table 2** below that applies to the **HIGHEST** paying job and enter it here	7	$
8	**Multiply** line 7 by line 6 and enter the result here. This is the additional annual withholding needed . .	8	$
9	Divide line 8 by the number of pay periods remaining in 2015. For example, divide by 25 if you are paid every two weeks and you complete this form on a date in January when there are 25 pay periods remaining in 2015. Enter the result here and on Form W-4, line 6, page 1. This is the additional amount to be withheld from each paycheck	9	$

Table 1

Married Filing Jointly		All Others	
If wages from **LOWEST** paying job are—	Enter on line 2 above	If wages from **LOWEST** paying job are—	Enter on line 2 above
$0 - $6,000	0	$0 - $8,000	0
6,001 - 13,000	1	8,001 - 17,000	1
13,001 - 24,000	2	17,001 - 26,000	2
24,001 - 26,000	3	26,001 - 34,000	3
26,001 - 34,000	4	34,001 - 44,000	4
34,001 - 44,000	5	44,001 - 75,000	5
44,001 - 50,000	6	75,001 - 85,000	6
50,001 - 65,000	7	85,001 - 110,000	7
65,001 - 75,000	8	110,001 - 125,000	8
75,001 - 80,000	9	125,001 - 140,000	9
80,001 - 100,000	10	140,001 and over	10
100,001 - 115,000	11		
115,001 - 130,000	12		
130,001 - 140,000	13		
140,001 - 150,000	14		
150,001 and over	15		

Table 2

Married Filing Jointly		All Others	
If wages from **HIGHEST** paying job are—	Enter on line 7 above	If wages from **HIGHEST** paying job are—	Enter on line 7 above
$0 - $75,000	$600	$0 - $38,000	$600
75,001 - 135,000	1,000	38,001 - 83,000	1,000
135,001 - 205,000	1,120	83,001 - 180,000	1,120
205,001 - 360,000	1,320	180,001 - 395,000	1,320
360,001 - 405,000	1,400	395,001 and over	1,580
405,001 and over	1,580		

¶1301.05 CHANGING WITHHOLDING ALLOWANCES

Employees are not required to file a new Form W-4 with their employer each year. However, the employee should make sure that the form on file reflects the proper number of allowances for the year. While the IRS does not assess penalties for being overwithheld, it does assess a penalty for being underwithheld. Therefore, when an employee's withholding allowances decrease, a new Form W-4 should be filed within ten days of the changing event (such as divorce). When an employee's withholding allowances increase, the employee can file a new Form W-4 or leave the old Form W-4 in effect. When a continuing employee files an updated Form W-4, the employer places it in effect at the beginning of the next payroll period or 30 days after an employer receives the new Form W-4, whichever is later.

The death of a spouse or dependent in the current year does not change an employee's withholding allowances. However, an employee should file a new Form W-4 by December 1 to ensure that it becomes effective at the start of the next tax year. For the two years after a spouse's death, qualifying widows(ers) who have a dependent son or daughter living with them can use the married filing jointly tax rates and standard deduction (¶112.03). However, the qualifying widow(er) cannot claim a withholding allowance for the deceased spouse. A qualifying widow(er) should take this into consideration when completing a new Form W-4.

¶1301.06 EXEMPTION FROM WITHHOLDING

Certain employees can claim exemption from federal income tax withholding on Form W-4. However, the employer must still withhold social security and Medicare taxes on the employee's wages. The provision to claim exemption from withholding of federal income taxes helps people who work for a short period of time or earn small amounts. Without this provision, employers would withhold taxes from employees with no tax liability. If an employer does withhold taxes, the employee would need to file a tax return just to get back the amounts withheld.

To claim exemption from withholding in 2015, an employee must have had no federal income tax liability in 2014. Furthermore, the employee must not expect to owe any federal income taxes for 2015. Also, dependents under the age of 65 who have income in excess of $1,050 that includes more than $350 of unearned income cannot claim an exemption from withholding for 2015.

The exemption from withholding for a given year expires on February 15 of the next year. Employees who wish to continue a withholding exemption for the next year must file a new Form W-4 by February 15. Also, employees must revoke their exemption within 10 days of an event that causes them to no longer qualify as exempt.

EXAMPLE 1

Marisa's parents claim her as a dependent. She has never filed a tax return. Marisa is in the process of filling out her first W-4. She expects her wages for the year to be about $1,500. She has no other sources of taxable income. Thus, her standard deduction will reduce Marisa's taxable income to $0. Marisa can claim exemption from withholding for the current year. She can do this because (1) she has no unearned income, (2) she had no federal income tax liability in the previous year, and (3) she does not expect to owe taxes in the current year.

EXAMPLE 2

Same facts as in Example 1, except that Marisa will earn about $500 of taxable interest from bonds given to her by her parents. Because Marisa's income exceeds $1,050 and more than $350 of that amount comes from unearned sources, Marisa cannot claim exemption from withholding. Any amounts her employer withholds in excess of her tax liability can be refunded to her when she files her tax return.

¶1302 FICA Taxes

FICA is a payroll tax that consists of old age, survivors, and disability insurance (OASDI) and hospital insurance (HI). On Form W-2, the IRS calls the OASDI portion the **social security tax.** It calls the HI portion the **Medicare tax.** The government assesses FICA taxes on employers and employees. Each employer withholds the employee's share of FICA from the employee's wages. The employer then adds to this amount its portion of FICA taxes and remits both the employer and employee amounts to the government.

¶1302.01 SOCIAL SECURITY TAXES

The amount of FICA employers are required to withhold is set by law. In 2015, employers withhold 6.2% of the first $118,500 of each employee's social security (OASDI) wages. When an employee works for more than one employer during the year, it is possible that the employee may end up paying too much OASDI taxes. In 2015, the maximum OASDI tax an employee is required to pay is $7,347 ($118,500 × 6.2%). Employers match the amount of social security taxes they withhold from their employees' pay. They then deposit both their and their employees' shares to the IRS using the rules described later in the chapter at ¶1305.01.

If the employee ends up paying more than this amount because of FICA being withheld from multiple employers, the employee claims the excess amount withheld as an additional tax payment on his or her tax return. However, when a single employer mistakenly withholds too much OASDI taxes, the employee asks the employer to return the excess. Employees cannot recover excess withholding on their tax returns when the overwithholding is due to employer error. On a joint return, each spouse determines their withheld OASDI taxes separately. Then, each spouse determines if too much withholding took place by subtracting the tax withheld from the OASDI maximum for the year.

EXAMPLE 3

Forms W-2 for Ellie and Morton Levy report the OASDI information shown below. Because Ellie works for only one employer, her withheld OASDI tax is limited to $7,347. The Levys enter Morton's excess OASDI withholdings of $1,333 ($8,680 – $7,347) in the Payments section on their tax return.

Employee	Total Social Security Wages Paid in 2015	OASDI Tax Withheld
Ellie Levy:		
Melville Dye Co.	$140,000	$7,347
Morton Levy:		
Step Mfg. Co.	$80,000	$4,960
United Corp.	60,000	3,720
	$140,000	$8,680

¶1302.02 MEDICARE TAXES

The second part of FICA is the Medicare tax. For unmarried taxpayers (including those who file as qualifying widow(er)), a 1.45% tax rate applies to the first $200,000 of Medicare earnings. A 2.35% rate (1.45% + .9% additional Medicare tax) applies to Medicare earnings in excess of that amount. For married taxpayers who file MFJ, the 2.35% tax rate applies once the couple's combined Medicare earnings exceed $250,000. For married taxpayers who file MFS, the higher tax rate applies to the taxpayer's Medicare earnings in excess of $125,000. Medicare earnings include an employee's Medicare wages. They also include net earnings from self-employment, which is 92.35% of a sole proprietor's profit reported on Schedule C (¶706). [However, recall that through the self-employment tax, sole proprietors have paid the 1.45% employee share of Medicare taxes. Thus, any excess Medicare earnings that come from net earnings from self-employment is subject to only the .9% additional Medicare tax.]

The tax laws require employers to withhold 1.45% of the first $200,000 of each employee's Medicare wages, and 2.35% on Medicare wages in excess of $200,000. This rule applies to all employees, regardless of whether the employee is married or employed elsewhere (or self-employed) during the year. Consequently, it is possible that an employee's Medicare taxes withheld will not be the same as the employee's actual Medicare tax liability.

Employees who end up having too much Medicare tax withheld report the excess as a tax payment when they file their income tax returns. Taxpayers whose Medicare tax liability exceeds the amount of Medicare tax withheld during the year complete Form 8959, Additional Medicare Tax, to compute the amount they owe. They then report this amount as an additional tax in the "Other Taxes" section of their tax returns.

EXAMPLE 4

Mark and Teresa Holm file a joint return. Mark's Medicare wages are $230,000; Teresa's are $90,000. Since Mark's employer will withhold 1.45% on the first $200,000 of wages, and 2.35% on the $30,000 in excess of $200,000, Mark's Medicare tax withheld for the year is $3,605 (($200,000 × 1.45%) + ($30,000 × 2.35%)). Teresa's Medicare tax withheld equals $1,305 ($90,000 × 1.45%). As a couple, they have a total of $4,910 of Medicare taxes withheld for the year ($3,605 + $1,305).

The Holms' Medicare tax liability for the year is $5,270 (($250,000 × 1.45%) + ($70,000 Medicare wages in excess of $250,000 × 2.35%)). Since this amount exceeds the $4,910 they had withheld from their pay, the Holms will need to attach a completed Form 8959 to their tax return and report the $360 difference ($5,270 – $4,910) as an additional tax on Form 1040, page 2.

EXAMPLE 5

Ryan and Rita Spaulding file a joint tax return. Both work full-time. Their Medicare wages are $212,000 and $22,000, respectively. Since Ryan's Medicare wages exceed $200,000, his employer will withhold 1.45% on his first $200,000 of Medicare wages and 2.35% on the $12,000 of Medicare wages in excess of $200,000. Rita's employer will withhold Medicare taxes at the 1.45% rate on her entire Medicare wages. The Spauldings' total Medicare tax withholdings for the year are $3,501 [(($200,000 + $22,000) × 1.45%) + ($12,000 × 2.35%)]. However, the Spauldings' combined Medicare wages do not exceed $250,000. Thus, their Medicare tax liability is only $3,393 ($234,000 × 1.45%). The Spauldings will report the $108 ($3,501 – $3,393) of overwithheld Medicare taxes in the Payments section of Form 1040, page 2.

The additional .9% Medicare tax only applies to employees. For each of their employees, the employer's share of the Medicare tax is 1.45% of the employee's Medicare wages. As with social security taxes, the employer deposits both the employer and employee shares of the Medicare taxes with the IRS in accordance with the rules described in ¶1305.01.

¶1302.03 SPECIAL FICA SITUATIONS

Not all wages nor are all employees subject to FICA taxes. For example, nontaxable fringe benefits are not subject to FICA taxes (see ¶401.03 for a discussion of fringe benefits). Section 15 of IRS Publication 15, *(Circular E) Employer's Tax Guide*, provides a complete list of the types of fringe benefits and other types of payments exempt from FICA taxes. Some of the more common types of wages exempt from FICA taxes are included in the discussion that follows.

Family Employees of a Business

Wages paid to a spouse who works for the taxpayer's business are subject to FICA taxes (and withholding). However, wages paid to the taxpayer's child who is under the age of 18 are not subject to FICA taxes if the taxpayer's business is operated as either a sole proprietorship or a partnership in which each partner is the child's parent. Once the child turns 18, the child's wages become subject to FICA tax withholding (and employer matching).

Household Employees

Household employees are workers who provide domestic services in the taxpayer's private home. These workers include housekeepers, babysitters, private nurses, gardeners, and nannies. Normally, household employees who are paid $1,900 or more during 2015 are subject to FICA tax withholding (and employer matching). However, wages paid to any person who is under the age of 18 at any point during the year are exempt from FICA taxes (age 21 if the domestic worker is the taxpayer's child). Also, wages paid to the taxpayer's spouse or parent for domestic services are exempt from FICA taxes.

Employers of household workers whose wages are subject to FICA taxes report both the amounts they withheld from their employees' pay, plus their matching share of FICA taxes, on their Form 1040. Schedule H (Form 1040), Household Employment Taxes, supports the amount reported in the "Other Taxes" section of Form 1040, page 2.

¶1302.04 PENALTY FOR FAILURE TO COLLECT OR DEPOSIT TAXES

The IRS has the power to assess a 100% penalty against employers who fail to collect or deposit FICA taxes. The 100% penalty only applies to the employees' share of FICA taxes (amounts withheld from employees' pay). It does not apply to the employer's share of FICA taxes. The IRS can assess the penalty against employers who willfully try to avoid withholding income and payroll taxes by classifying employees as independent contractors. (Independent contractors are treated as self-employed workers, and as such, pay self-employment taxes on their net earnings from self-employment, as discussed in ¶706.) The IRS also can assess the penalty on any person responsible for an employer's tax withholdings when that person has the authority to decide which creditors receive payment when a shortage of funds exists.

¶1303 Reporting to Employees and the Government

In January, employers prepare a Form W-2, Wage and Tax Statement, for each employee. Thus, in January 2016, employers prepare a 2015 Form W-2 for each employee. Form W-2 shows an employee's taxable wages and tips; wages and tips subject to OASDI and tips subject to Medicare tax withholding; Federal income taxes withheld; and amounts withheld for OASDI and Medicare taxes. Form W-2 also reports an employee's pension plan contributions, state and local income taxes withheld, as well as other items.

¶1303.01 DISTRIBUTION OF FORMS W-2

Employers prepare six copies of Form W-2 for each employee. These copies are named Copy A, B, C, D, 1, and 2. Employers send Copy A to the Social Security Administration before March 1. If applicable, they file Copy 1 with the proper state or local government agency. Employers send Copies B, C, and 2 to each employee before February 1. The employer holds on to Copy D.

When employment ends before the close of a calendar year, employers still send former employees their copies of Form W-2 by January 31 of the next year. Former employees can request a Form W-2 before this date. When requested, employers must give former employees their W-2 by the later of 30 days after the request or 30 days after the last wage payment. Employees attach a copy of their W-2s to each tax return they file. They keep one copy for their records.

¶1303.02 FORM W-2

Copy A of Form W-2 is read by a machine. Therefore, it must be typed and free of erasures, whiteouts, and strikeovers. The employer should make all dollar entries without dollar signs or commas, but with decimal points (00000.00). The rest of this section describes the information reported on Form W-2. Not all boxes are covered since many are self-explanatory. For a full description of all boxes on Form W-2, see the *Instructions for Form W-2,* which can be found on the IRS website.

Box 12

Employers complete this box to report up to four items of information. For each item, a code and the dollar amount are listed. Examples of items reported in this box include:

- Taxable amounts for providing the employee with more than $50,000 of group life insurance (Code C)
- Employee pre-tax contributions to a 401(k) or SIMPLE 401(k) plan (Code D)
- Employee pre-tax contributions to a SEP (Code F)
- Reimbursements received from a nonaccountable reimbursement plan (Code L)
- Nontaxable moving expense reimbursements (Code P)
- Employee pre-tax contributions to a SIMPLE plan not part of a 401(k) plan (Code S)
- Amounts received under an adoption assistance program (Code T)

Statutory Employee, Retirement Plan, Third-Party Sick Pay (Box 13)

Employers place an **X** in the proper square (box 13) to identify one of three situations.

Statutory Employee. Employers withhold FICA taxes, but not federal income taxes, from statutory employees' wages. **Statutory employees** include certain employees from one of four occupation groups. Group 1 includes drivers who are agents of the employer or those who deliver laundry, dry-cleaning, and food products (other than milk) to customers and who are paid on commission. Group 2 includes full-time life insurance salespersons. Group 3 includes workers who work from home using materials provided by and returned to the employer. Group 4 includes traveling or city salespersons who take orders on behalf of the employer. To qualify as a statutory employee, group members must also meet other tests that are beyond the scope of this discussion.

Retirement Plan. Employers check this square to identify the employee as an active participant in the employer's retirement plan. Recall from Chapter 4 that limits may apply to the deduction for IRA contributions for taxpayers who are active participants in an employer's qualified retirement plan (¶402.11).

Third-Party Sick Pay. Employers check this square only if the payer is a third-party sick pay provider filing Form W-2 for an insured's employee.

Other (Box 14)

Employers use this box to provide any other information they feel is necessary to their employees. Each amount is labeled by its type. Items that may be listed include union dues, health insurance premiums paid by the employee, nontaxable income, after-tax contributions to retirement plans, and educational assistance payments.

¶1303.03 FILLED-IN FORM W-2

INFORMATION FOR FIGURE 13-3:

Harriett R. Shawver works for Anderson, Berger, and Green (ABG). From Harriett's **$43,500** of wages, ABG withheld **$7,356** for federal; **$2,039** for state; **$2,697** ($43,500 × 6.2%) for social security (OASDI); and **$630.75** ($43,500 × 1.45%) for Medicare taxes. These amounts (no dollar signs or commas) appear on Harriett's W-2.

Figure 13-3: Filled-In Form W-2

a Employee's social security number: 364-74-6550 — OMB No. 1545-0008 — Safe, accurate, FAST! Use IRS e-file — Visit the IRS website at www.irs.gov/efile

b Employer identification number (EIN) 92-0446587	1 Wages, tips, other compensation 43500.00	2 Federal income tax withheld 7356.00
c Employer's name, address, and ZIP code Anderson, Berger, and Green 2700 South Park Avenue Milwaukee, WI 53202-2645	3 Social security wages 43500.00	4 Social security tax withheld 2697.00
	5 Medicare wages and tips 43500.00	6 Medicare tax withheld 630.75
	7 Social security tips	8 Allocated tips
d Control number	9	10 Dependent care benefits
e Employee's first name and initial Last name Suff. Harriett R. Shawver 2123 Fairmount Milwaukee, WI 53209-3695	11 Nonqualified plans	12a See instructions for box 12
	13 Statutory employee ☐ Retirement plan ☐ Third-party sick pay ☐	12b
	14 Other	12c
f Employee's address and ZIP code		12d

15 State	Employer's state ID number	16 State wages, tips, etc.	17 State income tax	18 Local wages, tips, etc.	19 Local income tax	20 Locality name
WI	104693	43500.00	2039.00			

Form **W-2** Wage and Tax Statement **2015** Department of the Treasury—Internal Revenue Service

Copy B—To Be Filed With Employee's FEDERAL Tax Return.
This information is being furnished to the Internal Revenue Service.

¶1303.04 FORM W-3

Employers send to the Social Security Administration Copy A of Form W-2 for all employees along with Form W-3, Transmittal of Wage and Tax Statements. If filing paper forms, the due date is February 28. If filing these forms electronically, the due date is March 31. Electronic filing is required for those filing 250 or more Forms W-2. When completing Form W-3, employers type all data entries, omitting dollar signs and commas, but using decimal points and zeros to show cents (00000.00). The amounts on Form W-3 represent the totals from all the amounts on all Copies A of Forms W-2 attached. The actual person who completes Form W-3 signs it, certifying the correctness and completeness of it and of the accompanying Forms W-2.

This section describes the data contained on Form W-3. However, it does not cover every box, since most boxes contain clear descriptive headings. The instructions for Form W-3 (available on the IRS website) describe the data needs for all boxes. (See Appendix A for instructions on how to use the IRS website.)

Control Number (Box a)

Employers can assign their own control number or leave the box blank.

Kind of Payer (Box b)

Employers check one of the following types of Form W-2 they are filing. Employers with more than one type of Form W-2 file a separate Form W-3 for each type.

1. *941.* Check this square when filing Form 941 and no other group applies.
2. *Military.* Check this square when sending Forms W-2 for members of the U.S. armed forces.
3. *943.* Check this square when filing Forms 943 for agricultural employees. Employers of agricultural and nonagricultural workers prepare and submit a separate Form W-3.
4. *944.* Check this square when filing Form 944, Employer's Annual Federal Tax Return, and no other category (except "Third-party sick pay") applies.
5. *CT-1.* Check this square when sending Forms W-2 for employees under the Railroad Retirement Tax Act.
6. *Hshld. emp.* Check this square when sending Forms W-2 for household workers. Employers of household workers and nonhousehold workers prepare and submit a separate Form W-3 with each group of Forms W-2.
7. *Medicare gov't. emp.* Check this box for government and local agency employees subject to the 1.45% Medicare tax.

Total Number of Forms W-2 (Box c)

Employers enter the number of Forms W-2 they are sending with Form W-3. However, voided forms are excluded from the count.

Establishment Number (Box d)

Employers enter a four-digit number to identify separate establishments of their business. For each establishment, employers file a separate Form W-3 with related Forms W-2. They file a separate Form W-3 even though each establishment has the same EIN.

Employer's State I.D. Number (Box 15)

A state in which an employer does business may assign a state I.D. number. Employers enter the two letter abbreviation for the state's I.D. number in the space provided in box 15.

¶1303.05 FILLED-IN FORM W-3

INFORMATION FOR FIGURE 13-4:

Martinez Enterprises, Inc., sends two Forms W-2 (Copy A) to the Social Security Administration with Form W-3. The wages for the two employees total **$87,560**. For both employees, social security and Medicare wages were the same as overall wages. Federal income tax withheld for the two employees was **$13,518.40**. Social security and Medicare taxes withheld were **$5,428.72** and **$1,269.62**, respectively. Since Florida does not have a state income tax, lines 15–19 are blank.

Figure 13-4: Filled-In Form W-3

DO NOT STAPLE

33333 | a Control number | For Official Use Only ► OMB No. 1545-0008

b Kind of Payer (Check one): 941 [X] Military [ ] 943 [ ] 944 [ ] CT-1 [ ] Hshld. emp. [ ] Medicare govt. emp. [ ]

Kind of Employer (Check one): None apply [X] 501c non-govt. [ ] State/local non-501c [ ] State/local 501c [ ] Federal govt. [ ]

Third-party sick pay (Check if applicable) [ ]

c Total number of Forms W-2: 2

d Establishment number

e Employer identification number (EIN): 91-0118224

f Employer's name: Martinez Enterprises, Inc.

64 Bay Road
Miami, FL 33139-5670

g Employer's address and ZIP code

h Other EIN used this year

1 Wages, tips, other compensation: 87560.00

2 Federal income tax withheld: 13518.40

3 Social security wages: 87560.00

4 Social security tax withheld: 5428.72

5 Medicare wages and tips: 87560.00

6 Medicare tax withheld: 1269.62

7 Social security tips

8 Allocated tips

9

10 Dependent care benefits

11 Nonqualified plans

12a Deferred compensation

13 For third-party sick pay use only

12b

14 Income tax withheld by payer of third-party sick pay

15 State | Employer's state ID number

16 State wages, tips, etc.

17 State income tax

18 Local wages, tips, etc.

19 Local income tax

Employer's contact person: Edward L. Martinez

Employer's telephone number: (305) 555-3544

For Official Use Only

Employer's fax number: (305) 555-3545

Employer's email address: elmartinez@martinezenterprises.com

Under penalties of perjury, I declare that I have examined this return and accompanying documents and, to the best of my knowledge and belief, they are true, correct, and complete.

Signature ► *Edward L. Martinez* Title ► President Date ► 1-30-2016

Form **W-3** Transmittal of Wage and Tax Statements 2015

Department of the Treasury Internal Revenue Service

Send this entire page with the entire Copy A page of Form(s) W-2 to the Social Security Administration (SSA).
Photocopies are not acceptable. Do not send Form W-3 if you filed electronically with the SSA.
Do not send any payment (cash, checks, money orders, etc.) with Forms W-2 and W-3.

¶1304 Unemployment Taxes

In conjunction with state unemployment systems, the Federal Unemployment Tax Act (FUTA) makes payments to workers who have lost their jobs. The funding for the unemployment compensation comes solely from employers. Employers do not withhold any amounts from employees for this tax. Most employers pay taxes into both the state and federal unemployment systems.

¶1304.01 RATE AND BASE

Employers pay unemployment tax on the first $7,000 of each employee's taxable wages for the calendar year. For 2015, the FUTA tax rate is 6%. However, employers who make timely deposits for the amounts owed to their state's unemployment fund may be able to reduce their FUTA rate to .6%. When computing the employer's FUTA taxes, wages paid to statutory employees or any wages paid to the taxpayer's spouse, parent, or child under the age of 21, are not included. Also not included are wages paid to household employees who were not paid $1,000 or more during any quarter in the current or preceding calendar years.

Employers normally must file their FUTA tax returns by January 31 of the next year. They do this by completing and filing Form 940, Employer's Annual Federal Unemployment (FUTA) Tax Return. However, employers that deposit their FUTA taxes on a timely basis during the year have until February 10th to file their FUTA tax return.

¶1304.02 DEPOSITING FUTA TAXES

Employers deposit FUTA taxes when their debt exceeds $500. The FUTA tax is due on the last day of the month that follows the end of a quarter. When an employer's FUTA debt for any quarter does not exceed $500, the FUTA debt carries over to the next quarter. Employers with a fourth-quarter FUTA tax of $500 or less can either pay the tax when they file their FUTA return or make a deposit. If the fourth-quarter FUTA tax exceeds $500, they deposit the tax by January 31. Making a timely deposit extends the due date for filing Form 940 until February 10. When a deposit date falls on a Saturday, Sunday, or legal holiday, the deposit is timely if made by the next business banking day.

FUTA Tax Deposit Due Dates

Quarter Ending	Due Date
March 31	April 30
June 30	July 31
September 30	October 31
December 31	January 31

EXAMPLE 6

The Bucket Company's quarterly FUTA taxes for 2015 are: first, $235; second, $250; third, $245; and fourth, $200. No deposits are needed for the first and second quarters since the cumulative debt does not exceed $500 until the third quarter. Bucket must deposit $730 ($235 + $250 + $245) by November 2, 2015 (since October 31, 2015 falls on a Saturday). For the fourth quarter, Bucket must deposit the tax by February 1, 2016 (since January 31, 2016 falls on a Sunday). If Bucket makes timely deposits of its 2015 FUTA taxes, the due date for its FUTA tax return is extended to February 10, 2016.

¶1305 Federal Tax Deposit System

Most depositors of employment taxes must use the Treasury's electronic funds tax payment system to make their deposits.

Employment Taxes: What's Included?

- Federal income and FICA taxes withheld from employees
- Employer's share of FICA taxes
- Federal taxes withheld from pensions, annuities, and some deferred income
- Federal taxes withheld under the backup withholding rules

¶1305.01 DEPOSIT FREQUENCY

Employers make deposits using either a monthly or semiweekly deposit schedule. The schedule used depends on the total taxes the employer reported in the lookback period.

Lookback Period

Each employer's lookback period is the 12-month period ending on June 30 of the prior year. For 2015, the lookback period runs from July 1, 2013 through June 30, 2014. The employment taxes reported on the four Forms 941, Employer's QUARTERLY Federal Tax Return, filed during the lookback period are used to determine the employer's deposit schedule. If an employer did not exist during the lookback period, the IRS treats the employer as having zero tax accumulations.

Monthly Depositors

When total employment tax accumulations for an employer's lookback period are $50,000 or less, the employer deposits its employment taxes monthly. Monthly depositors deposit each month's employment taxes by the 15th day of the next month.

EXAMPLE 7

For the 12-month period ending June 30, 2014, Kirkwall Enterprises reported taxes on Form 941 totaling $47,000. Since this amount does not exceed $50,000, Kirkwall deposits its monthly employment taxes on the 15th day of the following month. Thus, its payroll taxes for the month of January would be deposited on February 15. Its taxes for February would be due by March 15. By making timely deposits of its employment taxes, Kirkwall will be allowed to extend the deadline for filing Form 941 by 10 days (see ¶1306.01).

Semiweekly Depositors

When total employment tax accumulations for an employer's lookback period exceed $50,000, the employer makes semiweekly deposits. Semiweekly depositors deposit their employment taxes on Wednesdays and Fridays. Wednesday deposits include tax accumulations for payrolls paid on the previous Wednesday, Thursday, and Friday. Friday deposits include tax accumulations for payrolls paid on the previous Saturday, Sunday, Monday, and Tuesday.

Semiweekly Depositors

Deposit Day	Deposit for Payrolls Paid
Wednesday	Previous Wednesday - Friday
Friday	Previous Saturday - Tuesday

EXAMPLE 8

Continuing with Example 7, for the 12-month period ending on June 30, 2015, Kirkwall's taxes reported on Form 941 total $53,000. Since this amount exceeds $50,000, Kirkwall will be required to make semiweekly deposits during 2016. On Wednesdays, Kirkwall deposits the taxes related to the payrolls paid on Wednesday, Thursday or Friday of the previous week. Then on Fridays, Kirkwall deposits the taxes related to the payrolls paid on the previous Saturday - Tuesday.

Semiweekly depositors make two deposits when the end of a calendar quarter does not fall on the employer's payday. They make one deposit for the last day(s) in the quarter just ended. They make another deposit for the starting day(s) in the new quarter. Employers must make the deposits by the next regular deposit date.

EXAMPLE 9

Elite Corporation is a semiweekly depositor. Elite pays its employees every Friday. One of its payroll periods ends on June 24. The next payroll period ends on July 1 and the one after that ends on July 8. Elite normally deposits its payroll taxes on the Wednesday following its Friday payday. During the current year, the second quarter ends on Thursday, June 30. Thus, the end of the quarter does not coincide with the end of its payroll period. The taxes for the payroll period ending on Friday, June 24 would be deposited on Wednesday, June 29. Elite then must deposit the payroll taxes related to the period June 25 through June 30. It does this on the normal deposit date for Thursday payroll periods – the following Wednesday (July 6). It deposits the taxes for the short payroll period of July 1 on the following Wednesday (July 6).

EXAMPLE 10

Same facts as in Example 9, except that Elite pays its employees once a month on the last day of each month. Although Elite is a semiweekly depositor, it makes only one deposit for the month of June. If June 30 falls on Thursday, Elite makes the deposit the next Wednesday, July 6.

One-Day Rule

Whenever an employer's employment tax deposits reach $100,000 during a deposit period, the one-day rule applies. This rule requires the employer to deposit employment taxes by the close of the next business day. This rule applies to both monthly and semiweekly depositors. Furthermore, once this event occurs for monthly depositors, they switch to being semiweekly depositors for the rest of the current calendar year and for the next calendar year. After that, the lookback period will determine whether the employer makes monthly or semiweekly deposits.

Semiweekly depositors determine whether they fall under the one-day rule by examining their employment tax accumulations since the last deposit date. They use Wednesday - Friday or Saturday - Tuesday for their examination period. On the day their accumulations reach $100,000, they meet the test for the one-day rule. Monthly depositors can determine if they fall under the one-day rule by examining their accumulations in the current month. They fall under the one-day rule on the day their accumulations reach $100,000. Once the employer deposits the employment taxes, the counting of accumulations starts over again at zero.

EXAMPLE 11

Cambry Company, a monthly depositor, has four payroll periods during the month. The first payroll period accumulates $40,000 of employment taxes. The second has $50,000 of employment taxes, for an accumulation of $90,000 ($40,000 + $50,000). The third payroll period involves $30,000 of payroll taxes. As of the end of the third payroll period, Cambry has accumulated employment taxes of $120,000 ($90,000 + $30,000). Cambry must deposit the $120,000 the next business day. Cambry becomes a semiweekly depositor, and will remain a semiweekly depositor for the rest of the current calendar year and all of the next calendar year. If Cambry's fourth payroll period for the month ends on a Saturday, as a semiweekly depositor, Cambry deposits its employment taxes by the following Friday.

Weekends and Holidays

When a deposit date falls on a Saturday, Sunday, or other depository holiday, the deposit is timely if made by the next business banking day.

EXAMPLE 12

RSV deposits employment taxes monthly. For April 20x1, RSV accumulates $10,000 of employment taxes. RSV normally would deposit these taxes by May 15, 20x1. However, in 20x1, May 15 falls on a Sunday. Thus, RSV must deposit the taxes by Monday, May 16, 20x1, the next banking day.

$2,500 Rule

A special deposit rule applies when the tax accumulations for a quarter do not reach $2,500. No deposits are necessary, and the employer may send the taxes in with Form 941.

EXAMPLE 13

A corporation's tax accumulations for the third quarter of 20x1 total $2,460. Since the total accumulations are less than $2,500, the corporation can send in the $2,460 when it files its third quarter Form 941. The due date for this return is November 30, 20x1 (or the next banking day if November 30 falls on a weekend or holiday).

Safe Harbor/De Minimis Rule

An employer satisfies its deposit requirement if the undeposited amount (shortfall) does not exceed the *larger of* (i) $100, or (ii) 2% of the required deposit. **Shortfall** means the required deposit amount less the amount deposited before the end of a deposit date. To use this rule, employers must deposit unplanned shortfalls before the end of their make-up date.

The shortfall make-up date for monthly depositors falls on the due date of the quarterly Form 941 for the period in which the shortfall occurs. The employer sends in the shortfall amount when it files its Form 941 or deposits the shortfall by the due date for filing Form 941.

A different shortfall make-up date applies to semiweekly and one-day depositors. For these employers, the shortfall must be deposited by the first Wednesday or Friday (whichever is earlier) that falls after the 14th of the month following the month of the shortfall. However, if the quarterly due date of a Form 941 falls before the shortfall make-up date, the shortfall deposit must take place by the earlier Form 941 due date.

EXAMPLE 14

Romano Company, a semiweekly depositor, has a shortfall for September 2015. Romano's make-up period ends on the first Wednesday or Friday after October 14. Since October 14, 2015, falls on a Wednesday, the first Wednesday or Friday after that date would be Friday, October 16, 2015.

EXAMPLE 15

Same facts as in Example 14, except that Romano's shortfall occurs on October 11, 2015. Normally, Romano would be required to deposit the shortfall by Wednesday, November 18 (the first Wednesday or Friday after November 14). However, Romano's third-quarter Form 941 is due on October 31. Thus, Romano must deposit the shortfall by November 2, 2015 (since October 31, 2015 falls on a Saturday).

A flowchart of the employment tax deposit rules appears in Figure 13-5. It shows how the rules separate employment tax depositors by frequency of deposits.

¶1306 Employer's Quarterly Report

Most employers that withhold income taxes or owe FICA taxes, file a quarterly Form 941, Employer's QUARTERLY Federal Tax Return. Seasonal employers that do not pay wages in a quarter do not file a Form 941 for that quarter. On every Form 941 that seasonal employers file, they place an **X** in the seasonal employer box (line 16).

All depositors complete both pages of Form 941. Semiweekly depositors also complete Schedule B (Form 941), Report of Tax Liability for Semiweekly Schedule Depositors, and attach it to Form 941.

¶1306.01 FILING THE QUARTERLY REPORT

Employers must file Form 941 by the last day of the month that follows the close of a calendar quarter. For example, for the quarter ending September 30, 20x1, employers must file a Form 941 by October 31, 20x1. If the due date falls on a weekend or legal holiday, the return would be due the next business day. Employers that deposit all "941 taxes" before the required due dates get an additional ten days to file Form 941. Thus, if the employer deposits its 941 taxes for the quarter by the required due dates, Form 941 for the quarter ending December 31, 20x1, would be due by February 10, 20x2. Employers cannot use Form 941 to report taxes from more than one calendar quarter. Instead, each quarter must be reported separately.

Figure 13-5: Summary of the Employment Tax Deposit Rules

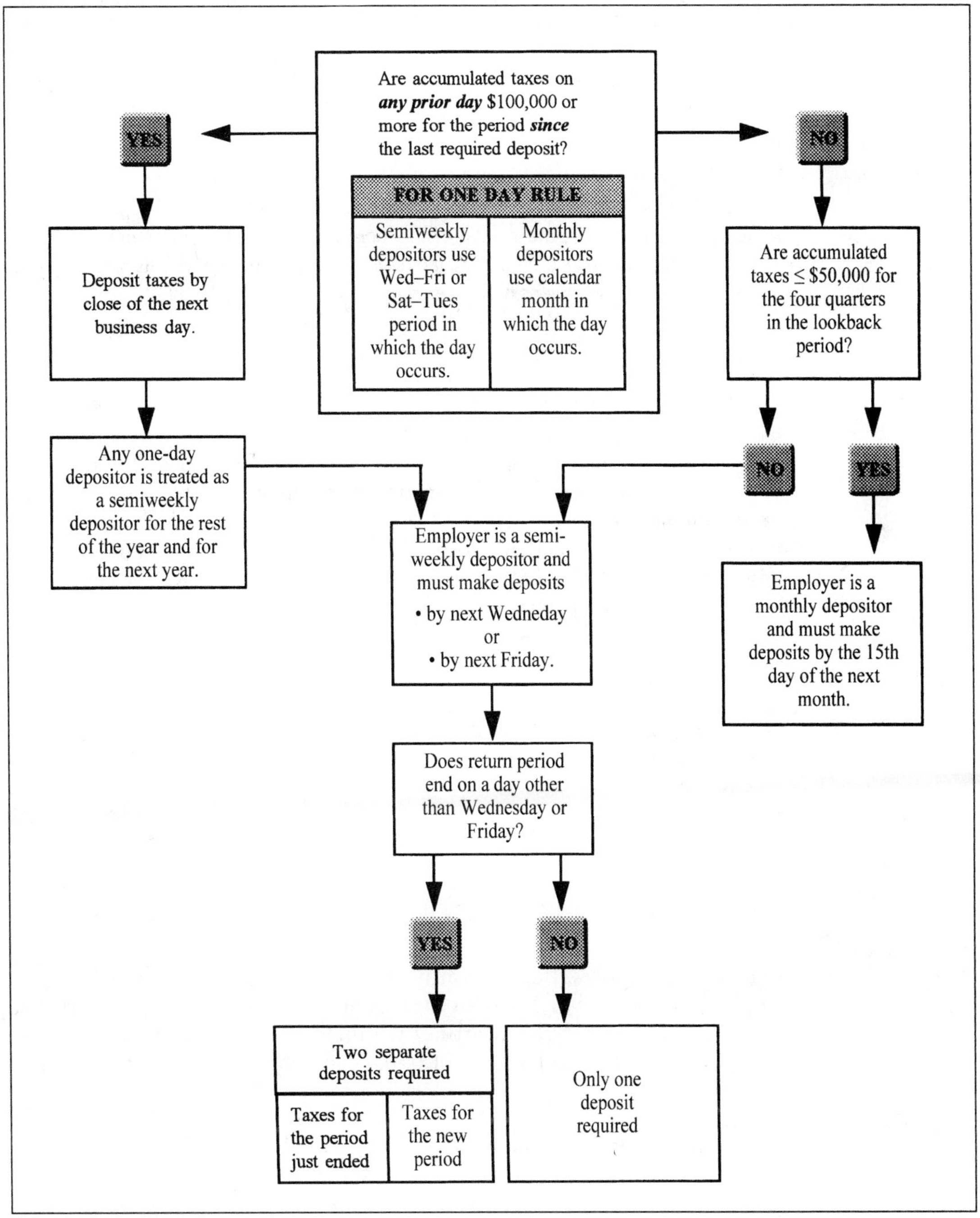

EXAMPLE 16

Betz, Inc., which uses the calendar year, withholds employment taxes from its employees' wages. Betz deposits its employees' withheld taxes plus Betz's share of employment taxes on a timely basis throughout 20x1. These actions allow Betz until May 10, 20x1 to file its first quarter Form 941 (the normal due date is April 30). It has until August 10, 20x1 to file Form 941 for the second quarter, and until November 10, 20x1 to file the third quarter Form 941. The due date for Betz's Form 941 for the fourth quarter is February 10, 20x2. If any of these days falls on a weekend or legal holiday, the return would be due the next business day.

EXAMPLE 17

Same facts as in Example 16, except that Betz fails to deposit its employment taxes on time. The due dates for filing Form 941 are the last day of the month that follows the close of the calendar quarter. This would be April 30, July 31, October 31 and January 31. If any of these days falls on a weekend or legal holiday, the return would be due the next business day.

Adjusting for Overwithholding or Underwithholding

Employers that find an error in withheld income or FICA taxes for an earlier quarter of the same year correct it on Form 941 for the quarter in which the error is discovered. For every correction (adjustment), employers attach a statement explaining and identifying the earlier return with the error(s). Employers that withhold *less* than the correct amount of tax from wages deduct the amounts underwithheld from future wages. When employers withhold *more* than the correct amount, they can repay the excess to the proper employees in any quarter of the same year.

Final Returns

When an employer goes out of business, the employer marks an **X** in the box on line 15 and in the space provided, enters the final date wages were paid.

¶1306.02 FILLED-IN FORM 941

INFORMATION FOR FIGURE 13-6:

Martinez Enterprises, Inc. (a monthly depositor), reports combined wages for withholding and employment taxes of $22,396 for the first quarter ($6,172.61 in January, $6,714.90 in February, and $9,508.49 in March). Martinez withheld $3,369.49 in federal income taxes from its two employees ($928.31 in January, $1,010.41 in February, and $1,430.77 in March).

Line #

1: Number of employees, **2**
2: Wages, tips, and other compensation, **$22,396**
3: Federal income tax withheld from amounts reported on line 2, **$3,369.49**
14: Month 1 liability, **$1,872.71** [($6,172.61 × .124) + ($6,172.61 × .029) + $928.31]
Month 2 liability, **$2,037.79** [($6,714.90 × .124) + ($6,714.90 × .029) + $1,010.41]
Month 3 liability, **$2,885.57** [($9,508.49 × .124) + ($9,508.49 × .029) + $1,430.77]

Figure 13-6: Filled-In Form 941 (Page 1)

Form **941 for 2015: Employer's QUARTERLY Federal Tax Return** 950114
(Rev. January 2015) Department of the Treasury — Internal Revenue Service OMB No. 1545-0029

Employer identification number (EIN) 9 1 – 0 1 1 8 2 2 4

Name (*not your trade name*) Martinez Enterprises, Inc.

Trade name (*if any*)

Address 64 Bay Road
Number Street Suite or room number

Miami FL 33139
City State ZIP code

Foreign country name Foreign province/county Foreign postal code

Report for this Quarter of 2015
(Check one.)

[X] **1:** January, February, March
[ ] **2:** April, May, June
[ ] **3:** July, August, September
[ ] **4:** October, November, December

Instructions and prior year forms are available at *www.irs.gov/form941.*

Read the separate instructions before you complete Form 941. Type or print within the boxes.

Part 1: Answer these questions for this quarter.

1	**Number of employees who received wages, tips, or other compensation for the pay period including:** *Mar. 12* **(Quarter 1),** *June 12* **(Quarter 2),** *Sept. 12* **(Quarter 3), or** *Dec. 12* **(Quarter 4)**	1	2
2	**Wages, tips, and other compensation**	2	22,396 . 00
3	**Federal income tax withheld from wages, tips, and other compensation**	3	3,369 . 49
4	**If no wages, tips, and other compensation are subject to social security or Medicare tax**		[ ] **Check and go to line 6.**

		Column 1		Column 2
5a	**Taxable social security wages**	22,396 . 00	× .124 =	2,777 . 10
5b	**Taxable social security tips**	.	× .124 =	.
5c	**Taxable Medicare wages & tips**	22,396 . 00	× .029 =	649 . 48
5d	**Taxable wages & tips subject to Additional Medicare Tax withholding**	.	× .009 =	.

5e	**Add Column 2 from lines 5a, 5b, 5c, and 5d**	5e	3,426 . 58
5f	**Section 3121(q) Notice and Demand—Tax due on unreported tips** (see instructions)	5f	.
6	**Total taxes before adjustments.** Add lines 3, 5e, and 5f	6	6,796 . 07
7	**Current quarter's adjustment for fractions of cents**	7	.
8	**Current quarter's adjustment for sick pay**	8	.
9	**Current quarter's adjustments for tips and group-term life insurance**	9	.
10	**Total taxes after adjustments.** Combine lines 6 through 9	10	6,796 . 07
11	**Total deposits for this quarter, including overpayment applied from a prior quarter and overpayments applied from Form 941-X, 941-X (PR), 944-X, 944-X (PR), or 944-X (SP) filed in the current quarter**	11	6,796 . 07
12	**Balance due.** If line 10 is more than line 11, enter the difference and see instructions	12	0 .
13	**Overpayment.** If line 11 is more than line 10, enter the difference .		Check one: [ ] Apply to next return. [ ] Send a refund.

▶ **You MUST complete both pages of Form 941 and SIGN it.** Next ■▶

For Privacy Act and Paperwork Reduction Act Notice, see the back of the Payment Voucher. Cat. No. 17001Z Form **941** (Rev. 1-2015)

Figure 13-6: Filled-In Form 941 (Page 2)

950214

Name (not your trade name)	Employer identification number (EIN)
Martinez Enterprises, Inc.	91-0118224

Part 2: Tell us about your deposit schedule and tax liability for this quarter.

If you are unsure about whether you are a monthly schedule depositor or a semiweekly schedule depositor, see Pub. 15 (Circular E), section 11.

14 Check one: ☐ **Line 10 on this return is less than $2,500 or line 10 on the return for the prior quarter was less than $2,500, and you did not incur a $100,000 next-day deposit obligation during the current quarter.** If line 10 for the prior quarter was less than $2,500 but line 10 on this return is $100,000 or more, you must provide a record of your federal tax liability. If you are a monthly schedule depositor, complete the deposit schedule below; if you are a semiweekly schedule depositor, attach Schedule B (Form 941). Go to Part 3.

☒ **You were a monthly schedule depositor for the entire quarter.** Enter your tax liability for each month and total liability for the quarter, then go to Part 3.

Tax liability: Month 1	1,872 . 71
Month 2	2,037 . 79
Month 3	2,885 . 57
Total liability for quarter	6,796 . 07

Total must equal line 10.

☐ **You were a semiweekly schedule depositor for any part of this quarter.** Complete Schedule B (Form 941), Report of Tax Liability for Semiweekly Schedule Depositors, and attach it to Form 941.

Part 3: Tell us about your business. If a question does NOT apply to your business, leave it blank.

15 If your business has closed or you stopped paying wages . . . . ☐ Check here, and

enter the final date you paid wages / / .

16 If you are a seasonal employer and you do not have to file a return for every quarter of the year . . ☐ Check here.

Part 4: May we speak with your third-party designee?

Do you want to allow an employee, a paid tax preparer, or another person to discuss this return with the IRS? See the instructions for details.

☐ Yes. Designee's name and phone number

Select a 5-digit Personal Identification Number (PIN) to use when talking to the IRS.

☐ No.

Part 5: Sign here. You MUST complete both pages of Form 941 and SIGN it.

Under penalties of perjury, I declare that I have examined this return, including accompanying schedules and statements, and to the best of my knowledge and belief, it is true, correct, and complete. Declaration of preparer (other than taxpayer) is based on all information of which preparer has any knowledge.

✗ **Sign your name here** *Edward L. Martinez*

Print your name here: Edward L. Martinez

Print your title here: President

Date 4/26/15

Best daytime phone (305) 555-3544

Paid Preparer Use Only

Check if you are self-employed . . . ☐

Preparer's name		PTIN	
Preparer's signature		Date	/ /
Firm's name (or yours if self-employed)		EIN	
Address		Phone	
City	State	ZIP code	

Page **2** Form **941** (Rev. 1-2015)

¶1307 Estimated Taxes

Wage earners pay taxes on their wages through the payroll withholding system. Taxpayers with income from sources other than wages (self-employment profits, interest, dividends, etc.) estimate their taxes and make quarterly payments directly to the IRS. For 2015, quarterly tax payment due dates fall on April 15, 2015; June 15, 2015; September 15, 2015; and January 15, 2016. For 2016, quarterly tax payment due dates fall on April 15, 2016; June 15, 2016; September 15, 2016; and January 17, 2017.

> When April 15 falls on a Sunday, normally the due date would be Monday, April 16. However, April 16 is Emancipation Day, which is a holiday in Washington, D.C. Thus, the due date would be extended to Tuesday, April 17.

¶1307.01 WHO MUST MAKE ESTIMATED PAYMENTS?

When individual taxpayers' estimated unpaid tax for the year equals or exceeds $1,000, they usually must make estimated tax payments. Unpaid taxes include income tax (which includes the alternative minimum tax) and self-employment taxes. It also includes any Medicare tax liability not covered through Medicare tax withholdings from employees' wages (see ¶1302.02). Employees do not need to make estimated payments in 2015 unless their tax withholdings and credits for 2015 fall below the *lesser of* (i) 90% of the tax on their 2015 tax return, or (ii) 100% of the tax on their 2014 tax return (110% for taxpayers whose 2014 AGI exceeded $150,000 ($75,000 for MFS)). Likewise, they do not need to make estimated payments in 2016 unless their tax withholdings and credits for 2016 fall below the *lesser of* (i) 90% of the tax on their 2016 tax return, or (ii) 100% of the tax on their 2015 tax return (110% for taxpayers whose 2015 AGI exceeded $150,000 ($75,000 for MFS)).

EXAMPLE 18 Tracy's AGI for 2015 was $62,500; her federal tax liability was $5,530. Tracy expects her 2016 tax liability to be $8,000. Tracy does not need to make estimated payments in 2016 unless her employer withholds less than $5,530 from her pay during the year. This amount is the *lesser of* (i) $7,200 ($8,000 × 90%), or (ii) $5,530 (100% of her 2015 tax liability).

EXAMPLE 19 Dora's AGI for 2015 was $162,500; her federal tax liability was $15,553. Dora expects her 2016 tax liability to be $18,000. Dora will not need to make estimated payments in 2016 unless her employer withholds less than $16,200 from her pay during the year. This amount is the *lesser of* (i) $16,200 ($18,000 × 90%), or (ii) $17,108 (110% of her $15,553 tax liability for 2015).

EXAMPLE 20 Same facts as in Example 19, except that Dora expects her 2016 tax liability to be $24,000. Dora will not need to make estimated payments in 2016 unless her employer withholds less than $17,108 from her pay during the year. This amount is the *lesser of* (i) $21,600 ($24,000 × 90%), or (ii) $17,108 (110% of her $15,553 tax liability for 2015).

Estimated Tax Worksheet

The IRS provides a worksheet to help taxpayers calculate their estimated tax. The difference between their total estimated tax, net of estimated credits and their employer's withholdings, represents the estimated unpaid tax. Taxpayers can pay this amount in four equal installments.

¶1307.02 FILLED-IN ESTIMATED TAX WORKSHEET

INFORMATION FOR FIGURE 13-7:

Early in 2015, Audrey McGrath (single, age 25) estimates her 2015 withholdings will be $2,600 and her AGI will be $42,873, as shown below. Audrey has no dependents and uses the standard deduction. Her 2014 income taxes were $3,950. By completing the Estimated Tax Worksheet in Figure 13-7, Audrey determines she will need to make four quarterly payments of $338 in 2015.

Salary	$31,600
Net rentals from apartment building	9,600
Net income from business	1,800
Total income	$43,000
Less deduction for employer's share of self-employment tax	(127)
AGI	$42,873

Figure 13-7: Filled-In Estimated Tax Worksheet

1.	AGI (estimate in 2015)		42,873
2.	Larger of: Estimated itemized deductions	0	
	Standard deduction (for Single in 2015)	6,300	6,300
3.	Subtract line 2 from line 1		36,573
4.	Exemption deduction (in 2015)		4,000
5.	Subtract line 4 from line 3. 2015 ESTIMATED TAXABLE INCOME		32,573
6.	Tax on amount on line 5 (using the 2015 Tax Rate Schedule for Single)		4,425
7.	Tax on Accumulation Distributions of Trusts	0	
	Tax on Lump-Sum Distributions	0	0
8.	Add lines 6 and 7		4,425
9.	Nonrefundable credits		0
10.	Subtract line 9 from line 8		4,425
11.	Self-employment tax ($1,800 × 92.35% × 15.3%)		254
12.	Other taxes (early distribution penalty and AMT tax)		0
13a.	Add lines 10 through 12		4,679
13b.	Earned income credit and other refundable credits		0
13c.	Subtract line 13b from line 13a. 2015 ESTIMATED TAX LIABILITY		4,679
14a.	90% of 2015 ESTIMATED TAX LIABILITY	4,211	
14b.	100% of tax from 2014 tax return	3,950	
14c.	Smaller of line 14a or 14b. REQUIRED PAYMENTS TO AVOID PENALTY		3,950
15.	Income taxes withheld and other prepayments		2,600
16.	Subtract line 15 from 14c		1,350
17.	Enter ¼ of line 16 ($1,350 ÷ 4), rounded up. QUARTERLY ESTIMATED PAYMENTS		338

Joint Estimated Tax Payments

A husband and wife can make joint estimated tax payments. Making a joint payment or separate payments does not commit the couple to filing a joint tax return. When a husband and wife make joint payments but file separate income tax returns, they can divide the estimated taxes as they choose. A couple separated under a decree of divorce or separate maintenance cannot make joint estimated tax payments.

EXAMPLE 21

Britney and Caleb Stonewell make joint estimated payments during 2015 that total $25,000. The Stonewells decide to file separate tax returns for 2015. They are free to split up the $25,000 amongst themselves. Thus, if Britney's tax withholdings are large enough to cover her tax liability, Caleb can apply the entire $25,000 against his 2015 tax liability. However, if it turns out that Britney's withholdings are less than her tax liability by $4,000, the couple can choose to apply $4,000 of their joint estimated payments against Britney's tax liability. The remaining $21,000 would then be taken on Caleb's separate tax return.

¶1307.03 PAYMENT OF ESTIMATED TAX

Taxpayers who make estimated tax payments mail their payment, along with their completed Form 1040ES voucher, to their regional IRS Service Center. For calendar year taxpayers, the vouchers and payments are due April 15, June 15, and September 15 of the current year, and January 15 of the next year. If the due date falls on a weekend or a legal holiday, the voucher and payment are due the next business day.

Prior-Year Overpayments

If a taxpayer's tax return for the year results in overpayment of taxes, the taxpayer can either choose to receive a refund, or apply the overpayment to any estimated tax due the next year. The taxpayer can use the overpayment either to reduce each subsequent installment until the overpayment is used up or to reduce each installment equally.

EXAMPLE 22

Betty overpaid her 2015 taxes by $1,600. Betty estimates her 2016 tax payments and withholding will be as follows.

Estimated tax for 2016	$ 18,200
Less estimated income tax withholding during the year	(12,600)
Estimated unpaid tax	$ 5,600

Because Betty's 2016 withholdings are expected to be less than her tax liability for the year, she should make estimated payments to avoid an underpayment penalty. Her quarterly installment payments are $1,400 ($5,600 ÷ 4). If Betty elects to apply her 2015 overpayment to her 2016 taxes, she will not need to pay the first installment, since the $1,400 first installment falls below last year's $1,600 overpayment. When the second installment comes due on June 15, 2016, Betty will pay $1,200 (second quarter installment of $1,400 less the remaining $200 from her last year's overpayment). Betty would then pay the full $1,400 quarterly estimate with her third and fourth installments.

Alternatively, Betty could elect to apply the overpayment evenly against each installment. If she chooses to do this, Betty divides last year's overpayment by the number of installments ($1,600 ÷ 4) and applies this amount to each installment. Betty would pay four installments of $1,000 each ($1,400 – $400).

Underpayment of Estimated Tax

No underpayment penalty will be assessed when the amount of tax due after withholding is less than $1,000. Taxpayers who expect to owe $1,000 or more after withholdings should make timely estimated tax payments. As mentioned previously in the chapter, one way to avoid the underpayment penalty is to make four equal payments that total 90% of the taxpayer's current year tax liability. A second way to avoid the penalty is to make four equal payments that total 100% of the taxpayer's prior year tax liability (110% for taxpayers whose AGI in the previous year exceeded $150,000 [$75,000 for married filing separately]). A third way to avoid the underpayment penalty is to make estimated payments based on 90% of the current year's annualized tax liability. The calculations required in annualizing taxable income and tax liability are rather involved and beyond the scope of this textbook. Those interested in learning more about the annualized method for making estimated payments should refer to IRS Publication 505.

Sometimes taxpayers need to make estimated payments, but also have wages subject to withholding. In calculating the amount of each estimated payment, wages are treated as occurring evenly throughout the year. Thus, taxpayers who work only part of the year and have $2,000 withheld from their wages will be treated as having had the $2,000 withheld evenly throughout the year.

EXAMPLE 23

On October 1, 2015, Wesley estimates that his tax liability for 2015 will be $15,000. In 2014, Wesley's AGI was $160,000 and his tax liability was $22,000. Thus, to avoid underpayment penalties, Wesley needs to have prepaid $13,500 for 2015. This amount is the *lesser of* (i) 90% of his 2015 tax liability ($15,000 × 90% = $13,500), or (ii) 110% of his 2014 tax liability ($22,000 × 110% = $24,200). Wesley's employer has been withholding $1,000 a month. Thus, Wesley is on target to have a total of $12,000 withheld during 2015. If Wesley does nothing, he will be subject to an underpayment penalty for the $1,500 deficiency ($13,500 required prepayments – $12,000 withheld from his wages). If Wesley decides to make an estimated payment for the fourth quarter to make up the $1,500 deficit, he will still be subject to penalties for not having paid enough during the first three quarters. However, if Wesley files a new W-4 with his employer and has an additional $1,500 withheld through the end of the year, he will avoid any underpayment penalties. His employer will have withheld a total of $13,500 during the year, which will be treated as having been paid evenly throughout the year.

Determining the Penalty Amount

Individual taxpayers determine the amount of their underpayment penalty on Form 2210, Underpayment of Estimated Tax by Individuals. Taxpayers enter their penalty for underpayment of estimated taxes on Form 1040 (line 79). This penalty amount is then added to any other amounts due the government. Taxpayers may choose not to file Form 2210 and instead have the IRS calculate the penalty and bill them.

The IRS adjusts the underpayment penalty rate quarterly. The rate equals the short-term federal interest rate plus 3%. Although the penalty looks like interest expense, it is a penalty, and as such, taxpayers cannot deduct it.

¶1308 Tax Penalties

When taxpayers fail to file a tax return or fail to pay the proper amount of tax, a penalty is assessed. Other actions may also invoke a penalty. Tax penalties are generally based on the amount of tax due on the tax return (tax liability in excess of credits and prepayments). Having a "reasonable cause" for not complying with the law may keep the taxpayer from owing a penalty (see ¶1308.01).

April 15th is the tax filing deadline for individual taxpayers. It is the deadline for both filing their income tax return as well as for paying any taxes owed. Taxpayers that file their tax returns on time but do not pay all the taxes they owe by April 15 will pay a late payment penalty. The **late payment penalty** is equal to one-half of 1% (.5%) of the taxes owed for each month, or part of a month, that the tax remains unpaid. The maximum late payment penalty is 25% of the taxes owed. For persons who file their tax returns by the due date, the one-half of 1% rate is reduced to one-quarter of 1% for any month in which an installment agreement is in effect.

Persons who owe taxes and do not file a tax return by the deadline (including extensions) will be charged a **late filing penalty**. This penalty is 5% of the taxes owed for each month, or part of a month, that the tax return is late. When filed more than 60 days late, the minimum late filing penalty is the *lesser of* $135 or 100% of the taxes owed. The maximum penalty is 25% of the taxes owed.

EXAMPLE 24 Agnes files her tax return on April 15. Agnes pays $500 of the $2,500 balance due when she files her return. She pays her tax balance on October 1, 5½ months after it was due. Agnes' late payment penalty is $60 ($2,000 × .5% × 6 months late).

EXAMPLE 25 Ike failed to file his tax return by the April 15 deadline and forgot to file for an extension. On June 3, he filed his tax return and paid the $500 taxes due with his return. Since Ike filed his return within 60 days of the deadline, his late filing penalty is $50 ($500 × 5% × 2 months late).

EXAMPLE 26 Same facts as in Example 25, except that Ike filed his tax return on July 3. Normally, Ike's late filing penalty would be $75 ($500 × 5% × 3 months late). However, since he filed his return more than 60 days late, his minimum late filing penalty is $135 (the *lesser of* (i) $135, or (ii) the $500 taxes owed). Since this amount exceeds what would normally be his late filing penalty ($75), Ike must pay the $135 minimum penalty.

Type of Penalty	Amount of Penalty
Failure to pay	.5% of the amount due for each full and partial month that the payment is late, up to 25%
Failure to file	5% of the amount due for each full and partial month that the return is late, up to 25%
Negligence or substantial understatement of income tax	20% of the tax due
Substantial misstatement of valuation	40% of the tax due
Fraud	15% for each full and partial month, up to 75% of the tax due
Frivolous return filing	$500

¶1308.01 REASONABLE CAUSE

Taxpayers may avoid a penalty if failure to comply was due to reasonable cause and not willful neglect. The IRS lists the following circumstances as reasonable causes for failing to comply with the tax laws. Other reasonable causes may exist. The IRS judges each case on its merits.

- Death or serious illness
- Unavoidable absence
- Destruction of certain facilities or records

- Timely mailing
- Wrong filing place
- Reliance on a competent tax advisor
- Unobtainable records
- IRS office visit in which an IRS employee was unable to be seen for reasons beyond the taxpayer's control
- Erroneous IRS information

¶1309 Information Returns

Information returns play an important part in the IRS computerized taxpayer compliance program. Persons and organizations making specific types of payments must report them to the IRS and the taxpayer. Taxpayers must then report these amounts on their income tax returns. This reporting process makes it possible for the IRS to determine whether taxpayers have reported the correct amounts on their tax returns. The taxpayer's identification number (social security number (SSN) for individuals; employer identification number (EIN) for businesses), shown on both the information return and the income tax return, is the basis for comparing reported data. Taxpayers do not attach information returns to the tax return unless Federal income tax has been withheld by the payer. They should, however, retain copies for their records.

Common Information Returns

Form 1098, Mortgage Interest Statement

Form 1099-B, Proceeds from Broker and Barter Exchange Transactions

Form 1099-DIV, Dividends and Distributions

Form 1099-INT, Interest Income

Form 1099-G, Certain Government Payments

Form 1099-MISC, Miscellaneous Income

Form 1099-R, Distributions from Pensions, Annuities, Retirement or Profit-Sharing Plans, IRAs, Insurance Contracts, Etc.

Form 1099-S, Proceeds from Real Estate Transactions

Form 5498, IRA Contribution Information

Form 8027, Employer's Annual Information Return of Tip Income and Allocated Tips

¶1309.01 IRS COMPARISONS

The IRS routinely examines the amounts reported on information returns filed by the payers of interest, dividends, and other types of payments. It compares these amounts to those reported by taxpayers on their income tax returns. Taxpayers should report all amounts received on their returns as separate items. When taxpayers detect an error on an information return, they should ask the payer to correct the mistake and issue them a corrected information return.

The computer may detect a difference between the amounts reported on the information returns and the amounts reported by the taxpayer. It may then generate a deficiency notice that will require an explanation by the taxpayer. The differences may be easily explained by the taxpayer with no penalty assessed. However, much time and effort can be saved if the taxpayer carefully reports the amounts as shown on the information returns.

¶1309.02 PENALTY FOR FAILURE TO FILE INFORMATION RETURNS

A penalty applies for filing late, incorrect, or incomplete information returns with the IRS. Most information returns are due by February 28. The deadline is extended to March 31 for returns filed electronically. The following penalty structure applies.

1. Any reporting failure corrected within 30 days after the due date—$50 per return, with a yearly maximum of $500,000 ($175,000 for small businesses)
2. Any reporting failure corrected after the 30-day period but by August 1—$100 per return, with a yearly maximum of $1.5 million ($500,000 for small businesses)
3. Any reporting failure corrected after August 1—$250 per return, with a yearly maximum of $3 million ($1 million for small businesses)

For purposes of these penalties, "small businesses" are those having average annual gross receipts of $5 million or less for the last three years.

EXAMPLE 27

On July 15, 2016, Kane Company realized it failed to file 300 Forms 1099-MISC to independent contractors who did work for the company during 2015. Kane corrected the error on July 20, 2016. Kane's penalty for filing a late information return is $30,000 (300 × $100 per return penalty because the error was corrected by August 1).

EXAMPLE 28

On March 31, 2016, Carnes, Inc. electronically filed 1,000 information returns. On August 20, 2016, Carnes realized that 600 of those returns contained incorrect information, and immediately corrected its mistake. Carnes's penalty for filing incorrect information returns is $150,000 (600 incorrect returns × $250 per return penalty because the error was not corrected by August 1).

August 1 is about when the IRS begins processing information returns. Thus, filing a return after August 1 is the same as not filing one at all. For this reason, higher penalties are imposed on information returns filed after August 1.

The IRS imposes a penalty of $50 for each failure to provide certain specified information, such as social security and other taxpayer identification numbers. The maximum penalty is $100,000 a year. No penalty applies if it can be shown that the reporting failure was due to reasonable cause and not to willful neglect. Also, a penalty waiver is available when only a small number of returns contain incomplete or incorrect information. To apply, correction of the errors must take place by August 1. The waiver limits the benefits to the *greater of*:

1. Ten returns, or
2. One-half of 1% of the total number of information returns required to be filed.

¶1310 The Audit Process

When returns reach the IRS, a computer makes an initial check for math or clerical errors. The IRS corrects these errors and sends a notice of the correction to the taxpayer. It either requests payment for additional tax or encloses a refund for an overpayment. The types of errors include:

- A math error shown on the return
- Incorrect use of an IRS table
- Inconsistent entries on the return
- Omission of information necessary to backup an amount shown on the return
- Entry of a deduction or credit item that exceeds a statutory limit based on information appearing on the return

Returns most in need of examination are identified by computer, using math formulas developed by the IRS to single out returns most likely to contain errors. The system focuses on those returns that stand the best chance of producing enough additional tax revenue to justify an audit. Examples of factors that could affect a return's selection for audit include:

- Large amounts of gross income
- Self-employed taxpayers with high incomes and large deductions
- Cash businesses (e.g., restaurants, businesses that provide services)
- Excessive itemized deductions relative to income level
- Claims for large refunds
- Disagreement between reported income and information returns (e.g., Form 1099, Form W-2)
- A large increase in dependents claimed
- A major decrease in rental income
- Informant information
- Prior tax deficiencies

Returns containing minor items that need clarification go to the audit division for correction by correspondence. Such returns may contain questionable charitable contributions or medical expenses, as an example.

Returns having the greatest audit possibility are sent to the district audit division to be examined. Within the district audit division, there are two types of audits. One is the **office audit**, which usually takes place in an IRS office and is limited in scope. A short discussion may be all that is needed to clear up any questions that arise during an office audit. The other is the **field audit**, which normally takes place on the taxpayer's premises. This is typically a much more extensive audit involving a number of major issues.

¶1310.01 BURDEN OF PROOF

Historically, the burden of proof for most tax disputes has rested with the taxpayer. During the mid-1980s, the IRS came under scrutiny for the way taxpayers were being treated during the audit process. Congress responded by enacting tax laws that shift the burden of proof to the IRS in court proceedings over factual issues when:

1. The taxpayer has provided the IRS with relevant, credible evidence,
2. The taxpayer has complied with the IRS's substantiation and record-keeping requirements, and
3. The taxpayer has maintained proper records and cooperates with any reasonable IRS request for witnesses, information, documents, meetings, and interviews.

To illustrate these rules, take a situation where the taxpayer uses the standard mileage method to deduct automobile expenses on Schedule C. As discussed in Chapter 7, the tax laws require that the taxpayer maintain written evidence to support the number of business miles driven during the year. Thus, if the taxpayer provides the IRS with the mileage log used to record the number of business miles driven during the tax year in question, the burden of proving that the deduction is not valid rests with the IRS.

In addition to the situations Congress recently added, the IRS has the burden of proof whenever it (1) uses statistics to reconstruct the taxpayer's income, (2) assesses the taxpayer with a penalty or other addition to tax, or (3) accuses the taxpayer of fraud with intent to evade taxes. The IRS also has the burden of proof in certain cases that involve hobby losses (¶603.01) and in cases that involve the accumulated earnings tax for C corporations.

¶1310.02 THE APPEALS PROCESS

After the completion of an audit, the taxpayer will receive a report of the findings, along with a 30-day-letter describing the taxpayer's rights to appeal the findings. A taxpayer who does not agree with the findings may file an appeal. The taxpayer has a right to request a meeting with the examining officer to work out their differences. This request should be made within 15 days from the date of the letter. Taxpayers not wanting to meet with the examining officer have 30 days to either start the formal appeal process or make arrangements to pay the tax.

An *Appeals Office* headed by a Regional Director of Appeals is established in each Internal Revenue Service region. Each office has the authority to fully settle cases. When the amount involved does not exceed $2,500, the taxpayer will be granted an Appeals Office conference merely by requesting it. However, when the amount exceeds $2,500, an Appeals Office conference is available only to taxpayers who file a written protest stating the facts upon which the appeal is based.

If the taxpayer and the Appeals Office cannot agree on the issues in dispute, the taxpayer will receive a 90-*day deficiency notice*. This letter must be mailed to the taxpayer within three years of the date that the income tax return was filed. The taxpayer may petition for a judicial review with one of three trial courts. The taxpayer may file a petition with the Tax Court within 90 days after the deficiency notice is mailed. The taxpayer may also file a petition with the district court or U.S. Court of Claims to have the case heard. After 90 days have lapsed, the taxpayer's only avenues for a judicial review are with the district court or U.S. Court of Claims.

Either the taxpayer or the IRS can petition the Circuit Court of Appeals to review the trial court's decision. Final disposition of the case may be taken to the United States Supreme Court. The Supreme Court will hear only those cases it chooses to review. All of these steps may take years. However, final assessment of the tax due from a taxpayer may not be made until the case is closed. The IRS Commissioner then has 60 days from the final decision to make an assessment of the tax.

¶1311 Taxpayer Rights

Taxpayers have the right to plan their business and personal affairs so they will pay the least amount of tax due under the law. They also have the right to be treated fairly, professionally, promptly, and courteously by the IRS. The law entitles taxpayers to information and IRS assistance in complying with the tax laws. The IRS provides a wide variety of informational materials, educational programs, and tax assistance programs to aid people in understanding and complying with the tax laws. IRS Publication 910, *Guide to Free Tax Services*, is a catalog of free IRS services and publications.

Taxpayers who need a copy of a prior year tax return may receive it by completing Form 4506, Request for Copy or Transcript of Tax Form. This form is sent to the IRS along with a small fee. If only certain information is needed, such as reported income from a prior year, the taxpayer may get this information for free. To receive this information, the taxpayer should write, visit, or call an IRS office.

Special assistance programs are available to people who cannot resolve their tax problems through normal channels. Help is also available to those whose tax problems cause significant hardship (that is, the inability to provide necessities).

People who have a complaint about the IRS may write to the district director or the service center director for their area. Additional information on taxpayer rights may be found in IRS Publication 1, *Your Rights as a Taxpayer.*

¶1312 Tax Preparers' Responsibilities

Currently, over one-half of all tax returns are prepared by someone other than the taxpayer. The tax laws consider anyone receiving pay in exchange for preparing an income tax return as an **income tax return preparer.** In the tax law, there are standards that must be adhered to by all income tax return preparers. Penalties that may be assessed for failing to adhere to these standards include the following. For each of the first four penalties listed, the maximum annual penalty is $25,000.

1. A $50 penalty each time the tax preparer fails to sign the tax return as a paid preparer.
2. A $50 penalty each time the tax preparer fails to provide the taxpayer with a copy of his or her tax return.
3. A $50 penalty each time the tax preparer fails to keep a copy of the taxpayer's tax return.
4. A $50 penalty each time the tax preparer fails to furnish a required identification number.
5. A $100 penalty each time the tax preparer fails to exercise due diligence with respect to determining a taxpayer's eligibility for (or the amount of) the earned income credit.
6. A $500 penalty each time the tax preparer improperly endorses a taxpayer's refund check.

In addition, the following penalties rules apply in situations where the underpayment of tax exceeds the *greater of* (i) 10% of the required tax to be shown on the tax return, or (ii) $5,000.

1. A penalty equal to the *greater of* (1) $1,000 or (ii) 50% of the income derived (or to be derived) from preparing the return will be assessed if the tax preparer allows an unrealistic position to be taken on the tax return. An **unrealistic position** is one that, if challenged by the IRS, does not have a greater-than-50-percent chance of being upheld by the courts. Tax preparers can avoid this penalty if there is a reasonable basis for taking the position and the position is disclosed on the return.
2. A penalty equal to the *greater of* (1) $5,000 or (ii) 50% of the income derived (or to be derived) from preparing the return will be assessed if the taxpayer intentionally disregards the rules or regulations, or willfully understates the taxpayer's tax liability.

Attorneys and certified public accountants (CPAs) who prepare tax returns have met certain educational standards, passed a standardized exam, and met specific experience requirements that allow them to be licensed to practice in their respective professions. Enrolled agents, while not having met the level of education or experience that is required of CPAs and attorneys, have passed an IRS exam and have been granted the authority to represent taxpayers before the IRS. Other paid preparers can receive compensation for their services, but are not allowed to communicate with the IRS on behalf of their clients.

The IRS imposes additional standards for professional tax preparers. Failure to adhere to these standards may result in penalties being assessed, including disbarment from practicing before the IRS. Those interested in learning more about the additional standards for professional tax preparers should refer to IRS Circular 230, which can be obtained from the IRS website. (See Appendix A for instructions on how to access the IRS website.)

Paid tax preparers must provide the IRS with their preparer tax identification number (PTIN) in the designated area where they sign the tax return. Paid tax preparers include anyone who prepares all or substantially all of a federal tax return. There is a small fee to get a PTIN, and the IRS requires that PTINs be renewed each year. Failing to provide a valid PTIN on the tax return will result in a $50 penalty per return, with a maximum $25,000 penalty per calendar year.

Tax preparers other than attorneys, CPAs, and enrolled agents had until the end of 2013 to pass a competency test in order to keep their PTIN. They also are now required to complete a set number of hours of continuing education (CE) each year. For the 2016 filing season, the number of required CE hours is 18. These rules do not apply to attorneys, CPAs and enrolled agents, as these groups have their own (more stringent) competency and CPE rules.

¶1313 Amended Returns

Individuals file Form 1040X, Amended U.S. Individual Income Tax Return, to correct mistakes made on their originally filed tax returns. Typical mistakes taxpayers may need to correct include incorrect use of filing status, or failing to report the correct amount of income, deductions, or tax credits. Taxpayers generally have three years from when they filed their original tax return to file an amended return. Taxpayers who file their tax return before the original due date are considered to have filed their tax return on April 15.

EXAMPLE 29 Joan filed an extension to file her 2013 tax return, giving her until October 15, 2014 (six months longer, see ¶208) to file her 2013 return. Joan files her return on July 16, 2014. Joan has until July 16, 2017 (three years after filing her return) to file an amended tax return for 2013.

EXAMPLE 30 Ami filed her 2014 return on March 29, 2015. For purpose of filing an amended return, Ami is considered to have filed her return on April 15, 2015. Thus, she has until April 15, 2018 to file an amended tax return for 2014.

¶1313.01 FILLED-IN FORM 1040X

INFORMATION FOR FIGURE 13-8:

Stephan and Sarah Martin failed to claim a **$650** contribution made on July 15, 2014 to the General Hospital, Peoria, Illinois, a qualifying charity. Accordingly, they amend their Form 1040 for 2014 and claim a refund by filing a Form 1040X on **November 30, 2015.** They enter the information shown in bold and follow the instructions on Form 1040X to compute their refund due. The Martins provide the reason they are filing Form 1040X in Part III of the form. They also attach both the originally filed and revised Schedule A to their amended return.

Line #

1: Adjusted gross income, **$89,094**
2A: Itemized deductions, originally reported, **$15,200**
2B: Net change, **$650** ($15,850 – $15,200). Change explained in Part III.
2C: Itemized deductions, **$15,850** ($15,200 originally reported + $650)
4: Exemptions, **$11,700** ($3,900 exemption amount for 2014 × 3)
6A: Tax on $62,194, **$8,419** (from the 2014 **Tax Table**)
6C: Tax on $61,544, **$8,321** (from the 2014 **Tax Table**)
10: Other taxes, **$4,177** (self-employment tax on net profits from Sarah's business)
12: Federal income withheld, **$3,856**
13: Estimated payments, **$6,500**
16: Amount paid with original return, **$2,240**

Figure 13-8: Filled-In Form 1040X (Page 1)

Form **1040X** (Rev. December 2015)

Department of the Treasury—Internal Revenue Service

Amended U.S. Individual Income Tax Return

▶ Information about Form 1040X and its separate instructions is at *www.irs.gov/form1040x*.

OMB No. 1545-0074

This return is for calendar year ☐ 2015 ☑ 2014 ☐ 2013 ☐ 2012

Other year. Enter one: calendar year **or** fiscal year (month and year ended):

Your first name and initial	Last name	Your social security number
Stephan M.	Martin	471 91 0419
If a joint return, spouse's first name and initial	Last name	Spouse's social security number
Sarah J.	Martin	916 38 2124
Current home address (number and street). If you have a P.O. box, see instructions.	Apt. no.	Your phone number
2886 Linwood Court		309-555-0846
City, town or post office, state, and ZIP code. If you have a foreign address, also complete spaces below (see instructions).		
Peoria, IL 61064-5414		
Foreign country name	Foreign province/state/county	Foreign postal code

Amended return filing status. You **must** check one box even if you are not changing your filing status. ***Caution.*** *In general, you cannot change your filing status from joint to separate returns after the due date.*

☐ Single ☐ Married filing separately
☐ Qualifying widow(er) ☐ Head of household (If the qualifying person is a child but not your dependent, see instructions.)
☑ Married filing jointly

Full-year coverage. If all members of your household have full-year minimal essential health care coverage, check "Yes." Otherwise, check "No." (See instructions.) ☑ Yes ☐ No

Use Part III on the back to explain any changes		A. Original amount or as previously adjusted (see instructions)	B. Net change—amount of increase or (decrease)—explain in Part III	C. Correct amount
Income and Deductions				
1 Adjusted gross income. If net operating loss (NOL) carryback is included, check here ▶☐	1	89,094		89,094
2 Itemized deductions or standard deduction	2	15,200	650	15,850
3 Subtract line 2 from line 1	3	73,894	(650)	73,244
4 Exemptions. **If changing, complete Part I on page 2 and enter the amount from line 29**	4	11,700		11,700
5 Taxable income. Subtract line 4 from line 3	5	62,194	(650)	61,544
Tax Liability				
6 Tax. Enter method(s) used to figure tax (see instructions): Tax Table	6	8,419	(98)	8,321
7 Credits. If general business credit carryback is included, check here ▶☐	7			
8 Subtract line 7 from line 6. If the result is zero or less, enter -0-	8	8,419	(98)	8,321
9 Health care: individual responsibility (see instructions)	9			
10 Other taxes	10	4,177		4,177
11 Total tax. Add lines 8, 9, and 10	11	12,596	(98)	12,498
Payments				
12 Federal income tax withheld and excess social security and tier 1 RRTA tax withheld (**if changing**, see instructions)	12	3,856		3,856
13 Estimated tax payments, including amount applied from prior year's return	13	6,500		6,500
14 Earned income credit (EIC)	14			
15 Refundable credits from: ☐Schedule 8812 Form(s) ☐2439 ☐4136 ☐8801 ☐8863 ☐8885 ☐8962 or ☐other (specify):	15			
16 Total amount paid with request for extension of time to file, tax paid with original return, and additional tax paid after return was filed	16			2,240
17 Total payments. Add lines 12 through 16	17			12,596
Refund or Amount You Owe ***(Note. Allow up to 16 weeks for Form 1040X to be processed.)***				
18 Overpayment, if any, as shown on original return or as previously adjusted by the IRS	18			
19 Subtract line 18 from line 17 (If less than zero, see instructions)	19			12,596
20 **Amount you owe.** If line 11, column C, is more than line 19, enter the difference	20			
21 If line 11, column C, is less than line 19, enter the difference. This is the amount **overpaid** on this return	21			98
22 Amount of line 21 you want **refunded to you**	22			98
23 Amount of line 21 you want **applied to your (enter year): estimated tax**	23			

Complete and sign this form on Page 2.

For Paperwork Reduction Act Notice, see instructions. Cat. No. 11360L Form **1040X** (Rev. 12-2014)

Figure 13-8: Filled-In Form 1040X (Page 2)

Form 1040X (Rev. 12-2015) Page **2**

Part I Exemptions

Complete this part **only** if you are increasing or decreasing the number of exemptions (personal and dependents) claimed on line 6d of the return you are amending.

See *Form 1040 or Form 1040A instructions and Form 1040X instructions.*		A. Original number of exemptions or amount reported or as previously adjusted	B. Net change	C. Correct number or amount
24 Yourself and spouse. ***Caution.*** *If someone can claim you as a dependent, you cannot claim an exemption for yourself*	24			
25 Your dependent children who lived with you	25			
26 Your dependent children who did not live with you due to divorce or separation	26			
27 Other dependents	27			
28 Total number of exemptions. Add lines 24 through 27	28			
29 Multiply the number of exemptions claimed on line 28 by the exemption amount shown in the instructions for line 29 for the year you are amending. Enter the result here and on line 4 on page 1 of this form. .	29			

30 List **ALL** dependents (children and others) claimed on this amended return. If more than 4 dependents, see instructions.

(a) First name	Last name	**(b)** Dependent's social security number	**(c)** Dependent's relationship to you	**(d)** Check box if qualifying child for child tax credit (see instructions)
				☐
				☐
				☐
				☐

Part II Presidential Election Campaign Fund

Checking below will not increase your tax or reduce your refund.

☐ Check here if you did not previously want $3 to go to the fund, but now do.

☐ Check here if this is a joint return and your spouse did not previously want $3 to go to the fund, but now does.

Part III Explanation of changes. In the space provided below, tell us why you are filing Form 1040X.

▶ Attach any supporting documents and new or changed forms and schedules.

A $650 contribution paid to General Hospital (Peoria, IL) on July 15, 2014 was omitted in error from Schedule A (line 15) on the originally filed tax return. This amount is included on Form 1040X (line 2, column C.) A copy of both the originally filed Schedule A and the revised Schedule A are attached to this amended return.

Sign Here

Remember to keep a copy of this form for your records.

Under penalties of perjury, I declare that I have filed an original return and that I have examined this amended return, including accompanying schedules and statements, and to the best of my knowledge and belief, this amended return is true, correct, and complete. Declaration of preparer (other than taxpayer) is based on all information about which the preparer has any knowledge.

▶ *Stephan M. Martin* — Your signature | *11-30-15* — Date | ▶ *Sarah J. Martin* — Spouse's signature. If a joint return, **both** must sign. | *11-30-15* — Date

Paid Preparer Use Only

▶ Preparer's signature | Date | Firm's name (or yours if self-employed)

Print/type preparer's name | Firm's address and ZIP code

PTIN | ☐ Check if self-employed | Phone number | EIN

For forms and publications, visit IRS.gov. Form **1040X** (Rev. 12-2014)

13

Name:
Section:
Date:

QUESTIONS AND PROBLEMS

1. **Withholding Allowances.** (Obj. 1)

   a. How do employees claim withholding allowances?

   b. If employees do not give their employer a completed and signed Form W-4, Employee's Withholding Allowance Certificate, what withholding action must the employer take?

   c. If a taxpayer holds more than one job, can the taxpayer claim withholding allowances with more than one employer?

2. **Withholding Rules.** (Obj. 1) What tax withholding action, if any, must a taxpayer take for each of the following situations?

   a. Withholding allowances decrease.

   b. Withholding allowances increase.

   c. The employee's dependent dies on July 23 of the current year.

3. Withholding Rules. (Obj. 1)

a. An employee files a Form W-4 on June 10, 2015, claiming to be exempt from withholding. For what period does the exempt status apply?

b. Does an exemption from withholding that an employee claims on Form W-4 apply to both FICA taxes and federal income taxes?

4. Withholding Allowances. (Obj. 1) On the basis of the information given, how many total withholding allowances can be claimed for 2015 by each of the following taxpayers A-D? Identify the type of each withholding allowance claimed.

A: A single taxpayer, age 12, is claimed as a dependent on his parents' return. The taxpayer will earn $800 in wages during the year and receive dividends of $50.

B: A single taxpayer, age 20, is not claimed as a dependent on another return. The taxpayer will have earned income of $18,500 and interest income of $150. The taxpayer uses the standard deduction and has no adjustments to income.

C: A married couple files jointly. The couple claim four dependent children (ages 3 to 16). The taxpayer has two jobs, and the spouse has one job. The taxpayer's total wages are $79,500, and the spouse's wages are $20,500. Dividend income equals $400. No adjustments to income exist. Childcare expenses are $1,200, and expected itemized deductions are $17,200.

D: A single taxpayer has one dependent (age 9) and files as head of household. The taxpayer will earn $44,600 from one job. Expected interest income is $200. The taxpayer has no adjustments to income. Childcare expenses are $3,200, and expected itemized deductions are $7,000.

Taxpayer	*Number of Withholding Allowances*	*Type of Withholding Allowances*
A	________	________________
B	________	________________
C	________	________________
D	________	________________

5. **Form W-4.** (Obj. 6) Married taxpayers, Ethel P. (SSN 448-47-4747) and Irving J. Mead, file a joint return. They reside at 1001 West Wind Plaza, Fox Lake, Wisconsin 53933-4611. Both are 42 years of age. They have one dependent child, Jean, age 14.

   On November 15, 2015, the Meads became aware that their income tax for 2015 will be underpaid. Ethel decides to file a new Form W-4, Employee's Withholding Allowance Certificate, to change the number of withholding allowances to ensure more appropriate withholding in the future. Ethel will not claim an allowance for Irving but will claim Jean. The Meads' estimated income and deductions is as follows.

Wages: Ethel: Axel Maintenance Company	$36,000
Beta Corporation	8,000
Total gross wages—Ethel	$44,000
Irving: Readers' Specialty Store	14,500
Total gross wages	$58,500
Dividend income—Ethel	1,316
Interest income—Irving	1,034
Total	$60,850

   The Meads estimate that their itemized deductions will be $16,550. In addition, they anticipate the following "deductions for AGI" and "other payments."

IRA contributions	$4,000
Fees for Mary Jean's school textbooks	216
Contributions to political party	320
Total	$4,536

   Complete the 2015 Form W-4 that Ethel files with her employer, Axel Maintenance Company. Ethel signs and dates the form on November 18, 2015. Also prepare the necessary Form W-4 worksheets to determine the total number of withholding allowances. Use the form and worksheet provided on the pages that follow.

6. **FICA Taxes.** (Obj. 1) Discuss employers' FICA withholding responsibilities and how they differ (if at all) from employees' FICA tax liabilities.

(Use for Problem 5.)

Form W-4 (2015)

Purpose. Complete Form W-4 so that your employer can withhold the correct federal income tax from your pay. Consider completing a new Form W-4 each year and when your personal or financial situation changes.

Exemption from withholding. If you are exempt, complete **only** lines 1, 2, 3, 4, and 7 and sign the form to validate it. Your exemption for 2015 expires February 16, 2016. See Pub. 505, Tax Withholding and Estimated Tax.

Note. If another person can claim you as a dependent on his or her tax return, you cannot claim exemption from withholding if your income exceeds $1,050 and includes more than $350 of unearned income (for example, interest and dividends).

Exceptions. An employee may be able to claim exemption from withholding even if the employee is a dependent, if the employee:

- Is age 65 or older,
- Is blind, or
- Will claim adjustments to income; tax credits; or itemized deductions, on his or her tax return.

The exceptions do not apply to supplemental wages greater than $1,000,000.

Basic instructions. If you are not exempt, complete the **Personal Allowances Worksheet** below. The worksheets on page 2 further adjust your withholding allowances based on itemized deductions, certain credits, adjustments to income, or two-earners/multiple jobs situations.

Complete all worksheets that apply. However, you may claim fewer (or zero) allowances. For regular wages, withholding must be based on allowances you claimed and may not be a flat amount or percentage of wages.

Head of household. Generally, you can claim head of household filing status on your tax return only if you are unmarried and pay more than 50% of the costs of keeping up a home for yourself and your dependent(s) or other qualifying individuals. See Pub. 501, Exemptions, Standard Deduction, and Filing Information, for information.

Tax credits. You can take projected tax credits into account in figuring your allowable number of withholding allowances. Credits for child or dependent care expenses and the child tax credit may be claimed using the **Personal Allowances Worksheet** below. See Pub. 505 for information on converting your other credits into withholding allowances.

Nonwage income. If you have a large amount of nonwage income, such as interest or dividends, consider making estimated tax payments using Form 1040-ES, Estimated Tax for Individuals. Otherwise, you may owe additional tax. If you have pension or annuity income, see Pub. 505 to find out if you should adjust your withholding on Form W-4 or W-4P.

Two earners or multiple jobs. If you have a working spouse or more than one job, figure the total number of allowances you are entitled to claim on all jobs using worksheets from only one Form W-4. Your withholding usually will be most accurate when all allowances are claimed on the Form W-4 for the highest paying job and zero allowances are claimed on the others. See Pub. 505 for details.

Nonresident alien. If you are a nonresident alien, see Notice 1392, Supplemental Form W-4 Instructions for Nonresident Aliens, before completing this form.

Check your withholding. After your Form W-4 takes effect, use Pub. 505 to see how the amount you are having withheld compares to your projected total tax for 2015. See Pub. 505, especially if your earnings exceed $130,000 (Single) or $180,000 (Married).

Future developments. Information about any future developments affecting Form W-4 (such as legislation enacted after we release it) will be posted at *www.irs.gov/w4*.

Personal Allowances Worksheet (Keep for your records.)

A Enter "1" for **yourself** if no one else can claim you as a dependent . . . . **A** ______

B Enter "1" if:
- You are single and have only one job; or
- You are married, have only one job, and your spouse does not work; or
- Your wages from a second job or your spouse's wages (or the total of both) are $1,500 or less.

. . . **B** ______

C Enter "1" for your **spouse.** But, you may choose to enter "-0-" if you are married and have either a working spouse or more than one job. (Entering "-0-" may help you avoid having too little tax withheld.) . . . . **C** ______

D Enter number of **dependents** (other than your spouse or yourself) you will claim on your tax return . . . . **D** ______

E Enter "1" if you will file as **head of household** on your tax return (see conditions under **Head of household** above) . . **E** ______

F Enter "1" if you have at least $2,000 of **child or dependent care expenses** for which you plan to claim a credit . . . **F** ______
(**Note.** Do **not** include child support payments. See Pub. 503, Child and Dependent Care Expenses, for details.)

G **Child Tax Credit** (including additional child tax credit). See Pub. 972, Child Tax Credit, for more information.
- If your total income will be less than $65,000 ($100,000 if married), enter "2" for each eligible child; then **less** "1" if you have two to four eligible children or **less** "2" if you have five or more eligible children.
- If your total income will be between $65,000 and $84,000 ($100,000 and $119,000 if married), enter "1" for each eligible child . . . **G** ______

H Add lines A through G and enter total here. (**Note.** This may be different from the number of exemptions you claim on your tax return.) ▶ **H** ______

For accuracy, **complete all worksheets that apply.**
- If you plan to **itemize** or **claim adjustments to income** and want to reduce your withholding, see the **Deductions and Adjustments Worksheet** on page 2.
- If you are **single and have more than one job** or are **married and you and your spouse both work** and the combined earnings from all jobs exceed $50,000 ($20,000 if married), see the **Two-Earners/Multiple Jobs Worksheet** on page 2 to avoid having too little tax withheld.
- If **neither** of the above situations applies, **stop here** and enter the number from line H on line 5 of Form W-4 below.

---------- **Separate here and give Form W-4 to your employer. Keep the top part for your records.** ----------

Form **W-4**
Department of the Treasury
Internal Revenue Service

Employee's Withholding Allowance Certificate

▶ **Whether you are entitled to claim a certain number of allowances or exemption from withholding is subject to review by the IRS. Your employer may be required to send a copy of this form to the IRS.**

OMB No. 1545-0074
2015

1 Your first name and middle initial	Last name	**2 Your social security number**
Home address (number and street or rural route)		**3** ☐ Single ☐ Married ☐ Married, but withhold at higher Single rate. **Note.** If married, but legally separated, or spouse is a nonresident alien, check the "Single" box.
City or town, state, and ZIP code		**4 If your last name differs from that shown on your social security card, check here. You must call 1-800-772-1213 for a replacement card.** ▶ ☐

5 Total number of allowances you are claiming (from line **H** above **or** from the applicable worksheet on page 2) **5** ______

6 Additional amount, if any, you want withheld from each paycheck . . . . **6** $ ______

7 I claim exemption from withholding for 2015, and I certify that I meet **both** of the following conditions for exemption.
- Last year I had a right to a refund of **all** federal income tax withheld because I had **no** tax liability, **and**
- This year I expect a refund of **all** federal income tax withheld because I expect to have **no** tax liability.

If you meet both conditions, write "Exempt" here . . . . ▶ **7** ______

Under penalties of perjury, I declare that I have examined this certificate and, to the best of my knowledge and belief, it is true, correct, and complete.

Employee's signature
(This form is not valid unless you sign it.) ▶ **Date** ▶

8 Employer's name and address (Employer: Complete lines 8 and 10 only if sending to the IRS.)	**9** Office code (optional)	**10** Employer identification number (EIN)

For Privacy Act and Paperwork Reduction Act Notice, see page 2. Cat. No. 10220Q Form **W-4** (2015)

(Use for Problem 5.)

Form W-4 (2015) Page **2**

Deductions and Adjustments Worksheet

Note. Use this worksheet *only* if you plan to itemize deductions or claim certain credits or adjustments to income.

1	Enter an estimate of your 2015 itemized deductions. These include qualifying home mortgage interest, charitable contributions, state and local taxes, medical expenses in excess of 10% (7.5% if either you or your spouse was born before January 2, 1951) of your income, and miscellaneous deductions. For 2015, you may have to reduce your itemized deductions if your income is over $309,900 and you are married filing jointly or are a qualifying widow(er); $284,050 if you are head of household; $258,250 if you are single and not head of household or a qualifying widow(er); or $154,950 if you are married filing separately. See Pub. 505 for details	1	$
2	Enter: { $12,600 if married filing jointly or qualifying widow(er); $9,250 if head of household; $6,300 if single or married filing separately }	2	$
3	**Subtract** line 2 from line 1. If zero or less, enter "-0-"	3	$
4	Enter an estimate of your 2015 adjustments to income and any additional standard deduction (see Pub. 505)	4	$
5	**Add** lines 3 and 4 and enter the total. (Include any amount for credits from the *Converting Credits to Withholding Allowances for 2015 Form W-4* worksheet in Pub. 505.)	5	$
6	Enter an estimate of your 2015 nonwage income (such as dividends or interest)	6	$
7	**Subtract** line 6 from line 5. If zero or less, enter "-0-"	7	$
8	**Divide** the amount on line 7 by $4,000 and enter the result here. Drop any fraction	8	
9	Enter the number from the **Personal Allowances Worksheet,** line H, page 1	9	
10	**Add** lines 8 and 9 and enter the total here. If you plan to use the **Two-Earners/Multiple Jobs Worksheet,** also enter this total on line 1 below. Otherwise, **stop here** and enter this total on Form W-4, line 5, page 1	10	

Two-Earners/Multiple Jobs Worksheet (See *Two earners or multiple jobs* on page 1.)

Note. Use this worksheet *only* if the instructions under line H on page 1 direct you here.

1	Enter the number from line H, page 1 (or from line 10 above if you used the **Deductions and Adjustments Worksheet**)	1	
2	Find the number in **Table 1** below that applies to the **LOWEST** paying job and enter it here. **However,** if you are married filing jointly and wages from the highest paying job are $65,000 or less, do not enter more than "3"	2	
3	If line 1 is **more than or equal to** line 2, subtract line 2 from line 1. Enter the result here (if zero, enter "-0-") and on Form W-4, line 5, page 1. **Do not** use the rest of this worksheet	3	

Note. If line 1 is **less than** line 2, enter "-0-" on Form W-4, line 5, page 1. Complete lines 4 through 9 below to figure the additional withholding amount necessary to avoid a year-end tax bill.

4	Enter the number from line 2 of this worksheet . . . . 4 ______		
5	Enter the number from line 1 of this worksheet . . . . 5 ______		
6	**Subtract** line 5 from line 4	6	
7	Find the amount in **Table 2** below that applies to the **HIGHEST** paying job and enter it here	7	$
8	**Multiply** line 7 by line 6 and enter the result here. This is the additional annual withholding needed . .	8	$
9	Divide line 8 by the number of pay periods remaining in 2015. For example, divide by 25 if you are paid every two weeks and you complete this form on a date in January when there are 25 pay periods remaining in 2015. Enter the result here and on Form W-4, line 6, page 1. This is the additional amount to be withheld from each paycheck	9	$

Table 1

Married Filing Jointly		All Others	
If wages from **LOWEST** paying job are—	Enter on line 2 above	If wages from **LOWEST** paying job are—	Enter on line 2 above
$0 - $6,000	0	$0 - $8,000	0
6,001 - 13,000	1	8,001 - 17,000	1
13,001 - 24,000	2	17,001 - 26,000	2
24,001 - 26,000	3	26,001 - 34,000	3
26,001 - 34,000	4	34,001 - 44,000	4
34,001 - 44,000	5	44,001 - 75,000	5
44,001 - 50,000	6	75,001 - 85,000	6
50,001 - 65,000	7	85,001 - 110,000	7
65,001 - 75,000	8	110,001 - 125,000	8
75,001 - 80,000	9	125,001 - 140,000	9
80,001 - 100,000	10	140,001 and over	10
100,001 - 115,000	11		
115,001 - 130,000	12		
130,001 - 140,000	13		
140,001 - 150,000	14		
150,001 and over	15		

Table 2

Married Filing Jointly		All Others	
If wages from **HIGHEST** paying job are—	Enter on line 7 above	If wages from **HIGHEST** paying job are—	Enter on line 7 above
$0 - $75,000	$600	$0 - $38,000	$600
75,001 - 135,000	1,000	38,001 - 83,000	1,000
135,001 - 205,000	1,120	83,001 - 180,000	1,120
205,001 - 360,000	1,320	180,001 - 395,000	1,320
360,001 - 405,000	1,400	395,001 and over	1,580
405,001 and over	1,580		

Privacy Act and Paperwork Reduction Act Notice. We ask for the information on this form to carry out the Internal Revenue laws of the United States. Internal Revenue Code sections 3402(f)(2) and 6109 and their regulations require you to provide this information; your employer uses it to determine your federal income tax withholding. Failure to provide a properly completed form will result in your being treated as a single person who claims no withholding allowances; providing fraudulent information may subject you to penalties. Routine uses of this information include giving it to the Department of Justice for civil and criminal litigation; to cities, states, the District of Columbia, and U.S. commonwealths and possessions for use in administering their tax laws; and to the Department of Health and Human Services for use in the National Directory of New Hires. We may also disclose this information to other countries under a tax treaty, to federal and state agencies to enforce federal nontax criminal laws, or to federal law enforcement and intelligence agencies to combat terrorism.

You are not required to provide the information requested on a form that is subject to the Paperwork Reduction Act unless the form displays a valid OMB control number. Books or records relating to a form or its instructions must be retained as long as their contents may become material in the administration of any Internal Revenue law. Generally, tax returns and return information are confidential, as required by Code section 6103.

The average time and expenses required to complete and file this form will vary depending on individual circumstances. For estimated averages, see the instructions for your income tax return.

If you have suggestions for making this form simpler, we would be happy to hear from you. See the instructions for your income tax return.

7. **FICA Taxes.** (Obj. 1) For each of the following scenarios, compute the amount of each employee's Medicare taxes owed (to be refunded) that they report on their respective tax returns.

   a. Mia, a single taxpayer, works for two employers during the year. Medicare wages at her jobs are $85,000 and $150,000, respectively.

   b. Shawn, a single taxpayer, works for two employers during the year. Medicare wages at his jobs are $215,000 and $35,000, respectively.

   c. Ron and Patty Simone file a joint tax return. Both Ron and Patty work full-time. Their Medicare wages are $210,000 and $120,000, respectively.

   d. Same as in Part c., except that Patty's wages are $20,000 (instead of $120,000).

8. **Form W-2.** (Obj. 6)

   a. By what date must an employer file Copy A of an employee's Form W-2 with the Social Security Administration?

   b. By what date must an employer give an employee Copies B and C of the employee's Form W-2?

9. **Form W-2.** (Obj. 6) Examine a Form W-2, Wage and Tax Statement. Explain the special meaning of *Statutory employee* in box 13.

10. Form W-2. (Obj. 6) Speedy Department Store (EIN is 04-0450523) is located at 2706 Bluff Drive, Boston, Massachusetts 02101-3214. Prepare the 2015 Form W-2, Wage and Tax Statement, for Susan W. Jenkins, a married employee with no dependents. The following data was taken from Speedy's payroll records:

Susan W. Jenkins (SSN 331-06-4821)	
214 Northup Street, Boston, Massachusetts 02112-1415	
Total wages paid (before payroll deductions)	$45,000.00
Social security tax withheld	Calculate
Medicare tax withheld	Calculate
Federal income tax withheld	6,552.00
State income tax withheld	1,125.75
Employer's state I.D. number	25703

a Employee's social security number	OMB No. 1545-0008 Safe, accurate, FAST! Use IRS e-file	Visit the IRS website at www.irs.gov/efile
b Employer identification number (EIN)	1 Wages, tips, other compensation	2 Federal income tax withheld
c Employer's name, address, and ZIP code	3 Social security wages	4 Social security tax withheld
	5 Medicare wages and tips	6 Medicare tax withheld
	7 Social security tips	8 Allocated tips
d Control number	9	10 Dependent care benefits
e Employee's first name and initial Last name Suff.	11 Nonqualified plans	12a See instructions for box 12 Code
	13 Statutory employee / Retirement plan / Third-party sick pay	12b Code
	14 Other	12c Code
f Employee's address and ZIP code		12d Code

15 State Employer's state ID number	16 State wages, tips, etc.	17 State income tax	18 Local wages, tips, etc.	19 Local income tax	20 Locality name

Form **W-2** Wage and Tax Statement **2015** Department of the Treasury—Internal Revenue Service

Copy B—To Be Filed With Employee's FEDERAL Tax Return.
This information is being furnished to the Internal Revenue Service.

11. Form W-3. (Obj. 6)

a. What documents does an employer transmit with Form W-3 when filing it with the Social Security Administration?

b. By what date must an employer file these documents?

12. Form W-3. (Obj. 6) Golden Door Company (EIN 39–0630726), 1906 North Avenue, Reno, Nevada 23431, withheld income and social security taxes from each of its 28 employees during 2015. Golden's telephone number is (619) 438–2444. In 2016 it prepared and sent to each employee a separate Form W-2. All wages paid to employees total $225,250. Total federal income taxes withheld from employees were $36,250. Total social security and Medicare wages equaled $209,850. No employee's wages exceeded $118,500 during 2015. Prepare the company's Form W-3, Transmittal of Wage and Tax Statements. Golden Door is a 941 payer. If no entry applies to the box, leave it blank. Have Marsha A. Golden, president of Golden, sign the form on January 21, 2016.

DO NOT STAPLE

33333	a Control number	For Official Use Only ▶ OMB No. 1545-0008	
b Kind of Payer (Check one): 941 ☐ Military ☐ 943 ☐ 944 ☐ CT-1 ☐ Hshld. emp. ☐ Medicare govt. emp. ☐		Kind of Employer (Check one): None apply ☐ 501c non-govt. ☐ State/local non-501c ☐ State/local 501c ☐ Federal govt. ☐	Third-party sick pay (Check if applicable) ☐
c Total number of Forms W-2	d Establishment number	1 Wages, tips, other compensation	2 Federal income tax withheld
e Employer identification number (EIN)		3 Social security wages	4 Social security tax withheld
f Employer's name		5 Medicare wages and tips	6 Medicare tax withheld
		7 Social security tips	8 Allocated tips
		9	10 Dependent care benefits
g Employer's address and ZIP code		11 Nonqualified plans	12a Deferred compensation
h Other EIN used this year		13 For third-party sick pay use only	12b
15 State Employer's state ID number		14 Income tax withheld by payer of third-party sick pay	
16 State wages, tips, etc.	17 State income tax	18 Local wages, tips, etc.	19 Local income tax
Employer's contact person		Employer's telephone number	For Official Use Only
Employer's fax number		Employer's email address	

Under penalties of perjury, I declare that I have examined this return and accompanying documents and, to the best of my knowledge and belief, they are true, correct, and complete.

Signature ▶ Title ▶ Date ▶

Form **W-3** Transmittal of Wage and Tax Statements 2015 Department of the Treasury Internal Revenue Service

Send this entire page with the entire Copy A page of Form(s) W-2 to the Social Security Administration (SSA).
Photocopies are not acceptable. Do not send Form W-3 if you filed electronically with the SSA.
Do not send any payment (cash, checks, money orders, etc.) with Forms W-2 and W-3.

13. FUTA Withholdings. (Obj. 1)

a. Should employers withhold FUTA taxes from employees? Explain.

b. When must an employer deposit FUTA taxes?

14. Lookback Period. (Obj. 2) Describe the lookback period and discuss its significance for purposes of determining an employer's deposit frequency.

15. Deposit Dates. (Obj. 2) For each of the following situations, determine the employer's required deposit date.

a. A monthly depositor whose payroll period ends on Friday, October 28.

b. A semiweekly depositor whose payroll period ends on Wednesday, April 12.

c. A semiweekly depositor whose payroll period ends on Friday, December 28.

d. A monthly depositor whose payroll period ends on Tuesday, May 15.

16. Form 941. (Obj. 6) During the third quarter of 2015, the Fillmore Restaurant (EIN 93-0530660) located at 244 North Second Street, Fillmore, New York 14735-0022, withheld income and social security taxes from its five employees. It withheld income taxes of $3,117 from employees' wages and tips of $15,570. In addition, Fillmore withheld $912.95 of social security taxes on $14,725 of social security wages, and $52.39 of social security taxes on $845 of social security tips. It also withheld $225.77 of Medicare taxes on $15,570 of Medicare wages. During the quarter, Fillmore electronically deposited income and employment taxes as follows: August 15, $1,833.52; September 15, $1,790.26; October 15, $1,875.43. Data for quarterly wages and reported tips of employees is as follows:

Name	*Total Wages*	*Social Security Wages*	*Taxable Tips Reported*
Barker, J. R.	$ 7,025	$ 7,025	$315
Duwe, H. K.	3,000	3,000	180
Miller, M. M.	2,000	2,000	120
Pressman, R. M.	1,200	1,200	125
Smathers, H. H.	1,500	1,500	105
	$14,725	$14,725	$845

Prepare the third quarter Form 941, Employer's QUARTERLY Federal Tax Return, for the Fillmore Restaurant, using the blank form provided on the pages that follow. Fillmore filed Form 941 and M. L. Wright, President, signed it on October 25, 2015.

(Use for Problem 16.)

Form **941 for 2015: Employer's QUARTERLY Federal Tax Return** 950114
(Rev. January 2015) Department of the Treasury — Internal Revenue Service OMB No. 1545-0029

Employer identification number (EIN) ☐☐ – ☐☐☐☐☐☐☐

Name (*not your trade name*)

Trade name (*if any*)

Address
Number Street Suite or room number
City State ZIP code
Foreign country name Foreign province/county Foreign postal code

Report for this Quarter of 2015
(Check one.)

☐ **1:** January, February, March
☐ **2:** April, May, June
☐ **3:** July, August, September
☐ **4:** October, November, December

Instructions and prior year forms are available at *www.irs.gov/form941.*

Read the separate instructions before you complete Form 941. Type or print within the boxes.

Part 1: Answer these questions for this quarter.

1	**Number of employees who received wages, tips, or other compensation for the pay period including: *Mar. 12* (Quarter 1), *June 12* (Quarter 2), *Sept. 12* (Quarter 3), or *Dec. 12* (Quarter 4)**	1	
2	**Wages, tips, and other compensation**	2	.
3	**Federal income tax withheld from wages, tips, and other compensation**	3	.
4	**If no wages, tips, and other compensation are subject to social security or Medicare tax**		☐ **Check and go to line 6.**

		Column 1		Column 2
5a	**Taxable social security wages**	.	× .124 =	.
5b	**Taxable social security tips**	.	× .124 =	.
5c	**Taxable Medicare wages & tips**	.	× .029 =	.
5d	**Taxable wages & tips subject to Additional Medicare Tax withholding**	.	× .009 =	.

5e	**Add Column 2 from lines 5a, 5b, 5c, and 5d**	5e	.
5f	**Section 3121(q) Notice and Demand—Tax due on unreported tips** (see instructions)	5f	.
6	**Total taxes before adjustments.** Add lines 3, 5e, and 5f	6	.
7	**Current quarter's adjustment for fractions of cents**	7	.
8	**Current quarter's adjustment for sick pay**	8	.
9	**Current quarter's adjustments for tips and group-term life insurance**	9	.
10	**Total taxes after adjustments.** Combine lines 6 through 9	10	.
11	**Total deposits for this quarter, including overpayment applied from a prior quarter and overpayments applied from Form 941-X, 941-X (PR), 944-X, 944-X (PR), or 944-X (SP) filed in the current quarter**	11	.
12	**Balance due.** If line 10 is more than line 11, enter the difference and see instructions	12	.
13	**Overpayment.** If line 11 is more than line 10, enter the difference	.	Check one: ☐ Apply to next return. ☐ Send a refund.

► **You MUST complete both pages of Form 941 and SIGN it.** Next ■►

For Privacy Act and Paperwork Reduction Act Notice, see the back of the Payment Voucher. Cat. No. 17001Z Form **941** (Rev. 1-2015)

(Use for Problem 16.)

950214

Name (not your trade name)	Employer identification number (EIN)

Part 2: Tell us about your deposit schedule and tax liability for this quarter.

If you are unsure about whether you are a monthly schedule depositor or a semiweekly schedule depositor, see Pub. 15 (Circular E), section 11.

14 Check one: ☐ **Line 10 on this return is less than $2,500 or line 10 on the return for the prior quarter was less than $2,500, and you did not incur a $100,000 next-day deposit obligation during the current quarter.** If line 10 for the prior quarter was less than $2,500 but line 10 on this return is $100,000 or more, you must provide a record of your federal tax liability. If you are a monthly schedule depositor, complete the deposit schedule below; if you are a semiweekly schedule depositor, attach Schedule B (Form 941). Go to Part 3.

☐ **You were a monthly schedule depositor for the entire quarter.** Enter your tax liability for each month and total liability for the quarter, then go to Part 3.

Tax liability: Month 1 ______ .

Month 2 ______ .

Month 3 ______ .

Total liability for quarter ______ . **Total must equal line 10.**

☐ **You were a semiweekly schedule depositor for any part of this quarter.** Complete Schedule B (Form 941), Report of Tax Liability for Semiweekly Schedule Depositors, and attach it to Form 941.

Part 3: Tell us about your business. If a question does NOT apply to your business, leave it blank.

15 If your business has closed or you stopped paying wages . . . . ☐ Check here, and

enter the final date you paid wages ___ / ___ / ___ .

16 If you are a seasonal employer and you do not have to file a return for every quarter of the year . . ☐ Check here.

Part 4: May we speak with your third-party designee?

Do you want to allow an employee, a paid tax preparer, or another person to discuss this return with the IRS? See the instructions for details.

☐ Yes. Designee's name and phone number ______ ______

Select a 5-digit Personal Identification Number (PIN) to use when talking to the IRS. ☐☐☐☐☐

☐ No.

Part 5: Sign here. You MUST complete both pages of Form 941 and SIGN it.

Under penalties of perjury, I declare that I have examined this return, including accompanying schedules and statements, and to the best of my knowledge and belief, it is true, correct, and complete. Declaration of preparer (other than taxpayer) is based on all information of which preparer has any knowledge.

X **Sign your name here** ______

Print your name here ______

Print your title here ______

Date ___ / ___ / ___

Best daytime phone ______

Paid Preparer Use Only Check if you are self-employed . . . ☐

Preparer's name		PTIN	
Preparer's signature		Date	/ /
Firm's name (or yours if self-employed)		EIN	
Address		Phone	
City	State	ZIP code	

17. **Form 941.** (Obj. 2)

a. When must employers file Form 941?

b. Can employers combine data from different quarters on one Form 941 as long as the combined period does not exceed three months?

18. **Estimated Taxes.** (Obj. 3) Indicate whether or not the following individuals are required to pay an estimated tax for 2016. (Check either the "*Yes*" or the "*No*" column.)

	Yes	*No*
a. Single taxpayer with income derived solely from wages subject to withholding expected to equal $12,000. Estimated unpaid tax expected to be $250.	____	____
b. Married couple with husband's income derived solely from wages subject to withholding expected to equal $21,500. Spouse does not receive wages. Estimated unpaid tax expected to be $400.	____	____
c. Qualifying widower with income derived from wages subject to withholding expected to equal $24,500. Income from other sources not subject to withholding expected to total $5,000. Estimated unpaid tax expected to be $1,200.	____	____
d. Married couple with husband's income derived solely from wages subject to withholding expected to equal $11,000. Spouse expects to receive dividend income totaling $22,000. Estimated unpaid tax expected to be $1,550.	____	____

19. **Estimated Taxes.** (Obj. 3) What steps can an unmarried taxpayer with AGI in 2015 of $75,000 take to avoid a penalty for underpayment of estimated taxes in 2016?

20. **Estimated Taxes.** (Obj. 3) What steps can a married couple with AGI of $200,000 in 2015 take to avoid the penalty for underpayment of estimated taxes in 2016?

21. Estimated Taxes. (Obj. 3) George Lewis works part-time and operates a business as a sole proprietorship on the side. For 2015, he estimates that his AGI (before consideration of the deduction for the employer's (½) share of the self-employment tax) will be $44,650. Included in this amount is wages of $19,250, net profits from his business of $25,000, and $400 of interest income. George is single and has no dependents. He estimates that his itemized deductions for the year will be $9,500, and that his employer will withhold $3,200 in federal income taxes. George's 2014 tax liability was $6,930. Using this information, complete the Estimated Tax Worksheet below to compute the amount George will be required to make in quarterly estimated payments if he wants to avoid any underpayment penalty for 2015.

1	Estimated AGI		________
2	Larger of:		
	Estimated itemized deductions	________	
	Standard deduction	________	________
3	Subtract line 2 from line 1		________
4	Exemption deduction		________
5	Subtract line 4 from line 3		________
	ESTIMATED TAXABLE INCOME		
6	Tax on amount on line 5		________
	(using the tax rate schedule)		
7	Tax on Accumulation Distributions of Trusts	________	
	Tax on Lump-Sum Distributions	________	
8	Add lines 6 and 7		________
9	Nonrefundable credits		________
10	Subtract line 9 from line 8		________
11	Self-employment tax	________	
12	Other taxes	________	________
13a	Add lines 10 through 12		________
13b	Refundable credits		________
13c	Subtract line 13b from line 13a		
	TOTAL ESTIMATED TAX LIABILITY		________
14a	90% of ESTIMATED TAX LIABILITY	________	
14b	100% of prior year's tax liability	________	
14c	Enter the smaller of line 14a or 14b		
	REQUIRED PAYMENTS TO AVOID PENALTY		________
15	Income taxes withheld and other prepayments		________
16	Subtract line 15 from 14c		________
17	Enter ¼ of line 16, rounded up to nearest whole dollar		________
	ESTIMATED QUARTERLY PAYMENT		________

22. **Penalties.** (Obj. 5) Suzy files her tax return on April 1. Her return shows a balance due of $1,000. Suzy encloses a check payable to the Department of the Treasury in the amount of $700. Compute Suzy's late payment penalty if she pays the rest of the balance due ($300) on August 31.

23. **Penalties.** (Obj. 5) Tim failed to file his tax return on April 15 and forgot to file for an extension. He files his tax return on December 27 and encloses a check for the $11,000 balance due reported on his return.

    a. Compute Tim's late filing penalty.

    b. How, if at all, would your answer to part a. change if Tim were able to file his tax return (and pay the amount owed) by July 15?

24. **Audits and Penalties.** (Objs. 4 and 5) Answer each question in the space provided.

    a. What is the monthly penalty for failure to file a tax return? __________

    b. What is the monthly penalty for late payment of taxes? __________

    c. What is the penalty for filing a frivolous return? __________

    d. What is the penalty for failing to provide an information return? __________

    e. What is the penalty assessed on a tax preparer for failing to provide a copy of the tax return to the taxpayer? __________

    f. Within the district audit division, there are two types of audits. One is the field audit. What is the other? __________

    g. After receiving a 30-day letter, how long does the taxpayer have to request a conference with the examining officer? __________

    h. After a tax return is filed, how many years does the IRS have to issue a 90-day deficiency notice? __________

25. **Preparer Responsibilities.** (Obj. 4) What penalty does the IRS impose on a tax preparer that intentionally disregards the rules and regulations, or willfully understates the taxpayer's tax liability?

26. Form 1040X. (Obj. 6) Eight months after filing their 2015 tax return with the IRS Center in Memphis, Tennessee, Jack L. (SSN 347-47-5784) and Judith K. (SSN 457-58-4758) Keith of 1618 Redford Lane, Kingsport, Tennessee 37664-3322, they realize they forgot to report their contribution of 20 shares of stock in the ABC Corporation that they made to their church on November 7, 2015. The Keiths purchased the stock for $1,200 on August 6, 2004. Its FMV on November 7, 2015 was $2,000.

The Keiths filed a joint return and claimed one dependent. Information from the 2015 Form 1040 that had been filed includes:

AGI (no qualified dividends or net capital gain)	$96,000
Itemized deductions	24,370
Taxable income	59,630
Total tax liability	8,021
Child tax credit	1,000
Federal income tax withheld	6,600
Amount paid with original return	421

The Keiths have not been advised that their 2015 income tax return is under audit. Prepare an Amended U.S. Individual Income Tax Return, Form 1040X, for the Keiths. They file the amended return on December 6, 2016.

27. Internet Problem: Researching IRS Publication 926. (Obj. 1)

Brad and Carol Thomas made an agreement with a neighbor's child to care for their lawn. The neighbor's son, Tad, takes care of the lawns of others in the neighborhood. Tad provides all of his own machinery, tools and necessary supplies. During 2015 the Thomases pay Tad $2,400 for various lawn care services. Since this amount exceeds $1,900, they are worried that they might be required to report Tad as a household employee and be required to withhold employment taxes.

Go to the IRS website. Locate IRS Publication 926, *Household Employer's Tax Guide*, and use it to answer the Thomases' question. Print out a copy of the page where you find the answer. Underline or highlight the pertinent information. Comment on what you believe to be the answer to the Thomases' question.

See Appendix A for instructions on how to access the IRS website.

28. Business Entity Problem. (Obj. 3) This problem is designed for those using the "business entity" approach. **The solution may require information from Chapter 14.**

a. Sunset Corporation had taxable income of $300,000 last year. To avoid underpayment penalties for the current year, what amount of estimated taxes must the company deposit during the year?

b. If the corporation had taxable income of $3,000,000 last year, what amount of estimated taxes must be deposited in the current year to avoid an underpayment penalty?

(Use for Problem 26.)

Form **1040X** (Rev. December 2015)

Department of the Treasury—Internal Revenue Service

Amended U.S. Individual Income Tax Return

▶ **Information about Form 1040X and its separate instructions is at *www.irs.gov/form1040x*.**

OMB No. 1545-0074

This return is for calendar year ☐ 2015 ☐ 2014 ☐ 2013 ☐ 2012

Other year. Enter one: calendar year **or** fiscal year (month and year ended):

Your first name and initial	Last name		**Your social security number**
If a joint return, spouse's first name and initial	Last name		**Spouse's social security number**
Current home address (number and street). If you have a P.O. box, see instructions.		Apt. no.	Your phone number
City, town or post office, state, and ZIP code. If you have a foreign address, also complete spaces below (see instructions).			
Foreign country name	Foreign province/state/county		Foreign postal code

Amended return filing status. You **must** check one box even if you are not changing your filing status. ***Caution.*** *In general, you cannot change your filing status from joint to separate returns after the due date.*

☐ Single ☐ Married filing separately
☐ Qualifying widow(er) ☐ Head of household (If the qualifying person is a child but not your dependent, see instructions.)
☐ Married filing jointly

Full-year coverage. If all members of your household have full-year minimal essential health care coverage, check "Yes." Otherwise, check "No." (See instructions.) ☐ Yes ☐ No

Use Part III on the back to explain any changes		**A. Original amount** or as previously adjusted (see instructions)	**B. Net change—** amount of increase or (decrease)—explain in Part III	**C. Correct amount**
Income and Deductions				
1 Adjusted gross income. If net operating loss (NOL) carryback is included, check here . . . . ▶☐	**1**			
2 Itemized deductions or standard deduction	**2**			
3 Subtract line 2 from line 1	**3**			
4 Exemptions. **If changing, complete Part I on page 2 and enter the amount from line 29**	**4**			
5 Taxable income. Subtract line 4 from line 3	**5**			
Tax Liability				
6 Tax. Enter method(s) used to figure tax (see instructions):	**6**			
7 Credits. If general business credit carryback is included, check here . . . . ▶☐	**7**			
8 Subtract line 7 from line 6. If the result is zero or less, enter -0- . . .	**8**			
9 Health care: individual responsibility (see instructions)	**9**			
10 Other taxes	**10**			
11 Total tax. Add lines 8, 9, and 10	**11**			
Payments				
12 Federal income tax withheld and excess social security and tier 1 RRTA tax withheld (**if changing**, see instructions)	**12**			
13 Estimated tax payments, including amount applied from prior year's return	**13**			
14 Earned income credit (EIC)	**14**			
15 Refundable credits from: ☐Schedule 8812 Form(s) ☐2439 ☐4136 ☐8801 ☐8863 ☐8885 ☐8962 or ☐other (specify):	**15**			
16 Total amount paid with request for extension of time to file, tax paid with original return, and additional tax paid after return was filed			**16**	
17 Total payments. Add lines 12 through 16			**17**	
Refund or Amount You Owe *(Note. Allow up to 16 weeks for Form 1040X to be processed.)*				
18 Overpayment, if any, as shown on original return or as previously adjusted by the IRS			**18**	
19 Subtract line 18 from line 17 (If less than zero, see instructions)			**19**	
20 **Amount you owe.** If line 11, column C, is more than line 19, enter the difference			**20**	
21 If line 11, column C, is less than line 19, enter the difference. This is the amount **overpaid** on this return			**21**	
22 Amount of line 21 you want **refunded to you**			**22**	
23 Amount of line 21 you want **applied to your (enter year):** **estimated tax** . **23**				

Complete and sign this form on Page 2.

For Paperwork Reduction Act Notice, see instructions. Cat. No. 11360L Form **1040X** (Rev. 12-2014)

(Use for Problem 26.)

Form 1040X (Rev. 12-2015) Page **2**

Part I **Exemptions**

Complete this part **only** if you are increasing or decreasing the number of exemptions (personal and dependents) claimed on line 6d of the return you are amending.

See *Form 1040 or Form 1040A instructions and Form 1040X instructions.*		A. Original number of exemptions or amount reported or as previously adjusted	B. Net change	C. Correct number or amount
24 Yourself and spouse. ***Caution.*** *If someone can claim you as a dependent, you cannot claim an exemption for yourself*	**24**			
25 Your dependent children who lived with you	**25**			
26 Your dependent children who did not live with you due to divorce or separation	**26**			
27 Other dependents	**27**			
28 Total number of exemptions. Add lines 24 through 27	**28**			
29 Multiply the number of exemptions claimed on line 28 by the exemption amount shown in the instructions for line 29 for the year you are amending. Enter the result here and on line 4 on page 1 of this form. .	**29**			

30 List **ALL** dependents (children and others) claimed on this amended return. If more than 4 dependents, see instructions.

(a) First name	Last name	**(b)** Dependent's social security number	**(c)** Dependent's relationship to you	**(d)** Check box if qualifying child for child tax credit (see instructions)
				☐
				☐
				☐
				☐

Part II **Presidential Election Campaign Fund**

Checking below will not increase your tax or reduce your refund.

☐ Check here if you did not previously want $3 to go to the fund, but now do.

☐ Check here if this is a joint return and your spouse did not previously want $3 to go to the fund, but now does.

Part III **Explanation of changes.** In the space provided below, tell us why you are filing Form 1040X.

▶ Attach any supporting documents and new or changed forms and schedules.

Sign Here

Remember to keep a copy of this form for your records.

Under penalties of perjury, I declare that I have filed an original return and that I have examined this amended return, including accompanying schedules and statements, and to the best of my knowledge and belief, this amended return is true, correct, and complete. Declaration of preparer (other than taxpayer) is based on all information about which the preparer has any knowledge.

▶ Your signature Date

▶ Spouse's signature. If a joint return, **both** must sign. Date

Paid Preparer Use Only

▶ Preparer's signature Date

Firm's name (or yours if self-employed)

Print/type preparer's name

Firm's address and ZIP code

☐ Check if self-employed

PTIN

Phone number

EIN

For forms and publications, visit IRS.gov. Form **1040X** (Rev. 12-2014)

Chapter

14

C Corporations

CHAPTER CONTENTS

LEARNING OBJECTIVES

After completing Chapter 14, you should be able to:

1. Understand the tax consequences to both the shareholders and the corporation when shareholders contribute cash and noncash property to a corporation in exchange for stock in the corporation.
2. Calculate a corporation's taxable income.
3. Compute a corporation's tax liability.
4. Describe the tax consequences of distributions to both the corporation and the shareholders.
5. Prepare Form 1120.

CHAPTER OVERVIEW

The sole proprietorship is the most common form of business ownership. Chapter 7 focused on the taxation of income arising from sole proprietorship operations. Partnerships and corporations are also popular ownership structures that are available to carry out business activities. Business owners must weigh the advantages and disadvantages of each when choosing the best entity from which to conduct their business operations. The impact of income taxation on each of these business entities plays a major role in this important choice.

A business organized as a corporation is a separate legal and taxable entity. The corporation exists outside of its owners (shareholders), and it must pay a tax on its income. Such companies are called C corporations. The name comes from the location (Subchapter C) in the Internal Revenue Code where the tax rules specific to this type of entity can be found. However, Congress created another tax entity, called an S corporation, which has features of both a corporation and a partnership. As the name suggests, the tax laws specific to S corporations are located in Subchapter S of the Internal Revenue Code. The tax rules specific to C corporations are the focus of this chapter. Partnerships are the focus of Chapter 15. S corporations are covered in Chapter 16.

¶1401 The Nature of C Corporations

A business organized as a corporation qualifies as a separate tax entity and pays tax on corporate taxable income. Historically, a business was treated and taxed as a corporation if it had the following corporate traits.

1. Business associates
2. A purpose to carry on a business and divide the profits
3. Continuity of life
4. Centralized management
5. Limited liability
6. Free transferability of ownership interests

Since partnerships and corporations have these first two traits in common, the Internal Revenue Service (IRS) and the courts focused on the last four to distinguish entities. To help avoid disputes in this area, the tax laws now allow businesses to choose which type of entity they wish to be taxed as. This choice is commonly known as the "check-the-box" rules. Thus, when a business is formed, the owners can choose the business's tax status without regard to the extent of its corporate traits. Corporations that pay tax on their taxable income are commonly called "C corporations" or "regular corporations." These corporations are the focus of this chapter. S corporations are a special type of corporation. They are discussed in Chapter 16.

¶1401.01 FORMING A CORPORATION

The owners of a corporation are called shareholders (or stockholders). The owners are called this because they possess shares of stock in the corporation. They get these shares in exchange for cash, property and/or services that they transfer to the corporation. This exchange can be done at the time the corporation is formed, or at a later date, when the corporation is in need of more funds (called capital). Once the transfer is complete, the investors and the corporation must determine their respective bases in the property they acquire. When investors exchange cash for shares of stock in the corporation, neither party realizes gain or loss on the exchange. Each investor's basis in the stock is the amount of cash they transfer to the corporation. These rules are the same as for any other cash purchase.

When investors transfer noncash property to a corporation solely in exchange for stock in the corporation, each investor realizes gain or loss equal to the difference between the fair market value (FMV) of the stock and the investor's adjusted basis in the property transferred to the corporation. However, if after the exchange, the transferring investors own at least 80 percent of the corporation's stock, then under the general rule, neither the investors nor the corporation recognize any gain or loss. Under these conditions, the investor's basis in the stock received is usually the amount of cash plus the investor's basis in the property transferred to the corporation. The investor's adjusted basis in the property becomes the corporation's basis in the property.

Fair market value (FMV) is the price that a willing buyer will pay and a willing seller will accept. FMV assumes that neither the buyer nor the seller must buy or sell. It also assumes that the buyer and the seller have reasonable knowledge of all necessary facts. In the absence of an actual sale or exchange, FMV can be determined by an expert appraisal or other supporting evidence.

EXAMPLE 1

Dana and Penny form a DP corporation. Dana transfers land worth $160,000 (adjusted basis of $190,000) in exchange for 50% of the stock in DP. Penny transfers $40,000 cash and a building worth $120,000 (adjusted basis of $105,000) in exchange for 50% of the stock in DP. No other property was transferred. Both parties receive stock valued at $160,000 (same as the value of the property each party transferred to the corporation).

As a result of the exchange, Dana realizes a $30,000 loss ($160,000 FMV of the stock received – $190,000 adjusted basis in the land). Penny realizes a $15,000 gain ($160,000 amount realized – $40,000 cash – $105,000 adjusted basis in the building). Since after the transfer, Dana and Penny own at least 80% of DP's stock, neither Dana, Penny, nor DP recognize gain or loss from the exchange.

Dana's basis in her shares of DP stock equals $190,000 (same as her adjusted basis in the land). Penny's basis in her shares equals $145,000 ($40,000 cash + her $105,000 basis in the building). The three parties' respective basis in the property received from the exchange is as follows:

Dana's basis in the stock	$190,000	DP's basis in the cash	$ 40,000
		DP's basis in the land	190,000
Penny's basis in the stock	$145,000	DP's basis in the building	105,000
			$335,000

The formula for calculating realized gains and losses is the same as that discussed in ¶1001. Realized gain or loss reflects the economic tax consequences of the transfer. Recognized gain or loss is the amount of realized gain or loss taxpayers report on their tax returns (see ¶1003).

In Example 1, the investors contributed business or investment property solely in exchange for stock in the corporation. When an investor transfers personal-use property to the corporation, both the investor's basis in the stock received and the corporation's basis in the property transferred is equal to the *lesser of* (i) the investor's basis in the property, or (ii) the FMV of the property transferred to the corporation. Take, as an example, an investor who transfers his personal truck to his 100% owned corporation, solely in return for more shares of stock in the corporation. At the time of the transfer, the FMV of the truck was $22,000, and the investor's adjusted basis in the truck was $37,000. In this example, the investor's basis in the stock received from the exchange would be $22,000 (the *lesser of* (i) the investor's $37,000 basis, or (ii) the $22,000 FMV of the truck). This same $22,000 would be the corporation's basis in the truck.

The general rule (nonrecognition of gain or loss, and carryover of basis) only applies when (1) after the transfer, the transferring investors own at least 80 percent of the corporation's stock, and (2) the only property the investors receive in return, is stock in the corporation. If the corporation transfers other property (called "boot", as described in ¶1007.02), the investor recognizes gain equal to the *lesser of* (i) the realized gain, or (ii) the FMV of the boot received. When an investor receives boot from the corporation, the investor's basis in the stock is decreased by the value of the boot received, and increased by any recognized gain. Any gain recognized by the investor also increases the corporation's basis in the property it received from that investor. Realized losses are never recognized when a transferring investor receives boot from the corporation. However, the value of any boot received by an investor realizing a loss, still reduces the investor's basis in the stock received.

EXAMPLE 2

Tyler and Mike own 100% of TM stock. Tyler transfers equipment worth $100,000 (adjusted basis of $75,000) in exchange for $100,000 worth of TM stock. Mike transfers land worth $125,000 (adjusted basis of $105,000) in exchange for $25,000 cash and $100,000 worth of TM stock. Tyler realizes a $25,000 gain ($100,000 FMV of the stock received – $75,000 adjusted basis in the equipment). Mike realizes a $20,000 gain ($125,000 FMV of the stock and cash received – $105,000 adjusted basis in the land).

After the exchange, the transferring investors (Tyler and Mike) own at least 80% of TM's stock. Since Tyler did not receive any boot, he does not recognize gain. Thus, his basis in the stock he received is $75,000 (same as his adjusted basis in the equipment). Mike, however, received $25,000 of boot as part of the exchange. Therefore, Mike recognizes $20,000 gain (*lesser of* (i) $25,000 realized gain, or (ii) $20,000 boot received). Mike's basis in the stock he received equals $100,000 ($105,000 basis in the land – $25,000 FMV of the boot received + $20,000 recognized gain). TM's basis in the equipment is $75,000 (same as Tyler's basis in the equipment). Its basis in the land is $125,000 (Mike's $105,000 adjusted basis + $20,000 Mike's recognized gain). After the exchange, the basis of properties owned by the three parties is:

Tyler's basis in the stock	$ 75,000	TM's basis in the equipment	$ 75,000
		TM's basis in the land	125,000
Mike's basis in the cash	$ 25,000		$200,000
Mike's basis in the stock	100,000		
	$125,000		

EXAMPLE 3

Same facts as in Example 2, except that Mike's basis in the land was $140,000. In this scenario, nothing changes with respect to Tyler or TM's basis in the equipment. However, Mike now realizes a $15,000 loss on the exchange ($125,000 FMV of property received – $140,000 adjusted basis in the land). Mike does not recognize any of this loss, since receipt of boot does not affect losses on these types of transfers. Thus, Mike's basis in the stock equals $115,000 ($140,000 basis in the land – $25,000 FMV of the boot received + $0 recognized gain). TM's basis in the land is now $140,000 (Mike's $140,000 adjusted basis + $0 recognized gain). Thus, after the exchange, the basis of the property owned by the three parties is:

Tyler's basis in the stock	$ 75,000	TM's basis in the equipment	$ 75,000
		TM's basis in the land	140,000
Mike's basis in the cash	$ 25,000		$215,000
Mike's basis in the stock	115,000		
	$140,000		

Although boot used in the above example involved cash, boot can take on other forms. Any property transferred back to an investor that is not the corporation's stock is treated as boot. For example, if the corporation transfers back to the investor its holdings of stock in another corporation, the FMV of the other corporation's stock is treated as boot. Also, when an investor transfers mortgaged property to a corporation, the assumption of debt by the corporation is treated as boot given to the investor who transferred the property. In situations where the amount of debt assumed exceeds the investor's basis in the transferred property, the investor recognizes gain to the extent of the excess, even if the excess exceeds the investor's realized gain. As you can see, the tax consequences of transfers boot that involve the assumption of debt can become quite complex, and thus, are beyond the scope of this introduction to corporate taxation.

When an investor(s) transfers property to a corporation solely in exchange for stock, and after the transfer, the transferring investors own less than 80 percent of the corporation's stock, then the investor(s) recognizes gain or loss on the transfer for the difference between the FMV of the stock and the adjusted basis of the property transferred to the corporation. The investor's basis in the stock and the corporation's basis in the property received is decreased by any recognized loss and increased by any recognized gain.

EXAMPLE 4

Stu transfers machinery worth $20,000 (adjusted basis of $0) in exchange for $20,000 of stock in a corporation. After the transfer, Stu owns 15% of the corporation's stock. Because Stu (the only transferring investor) owns less than 80% of the stock after the exchange, he realizes and recognizes a $20,000 gain ($20,000 FMV of the stock received – $0 adjusted basis in the machinery). His basis in the stock is $20,000 ($0 adjusted basis in the machinery + $20,000 recognized gain). Likewise, the corporation's basis in the machinery is $20,000.

When shareholders perform services in exchange for the corporation's stock, they recognize income equal to the FMV of the stock received. This amount also becomes their basis in the shares of the stock they receive.

EXAMPLE 5

Victor performs services in exchange for 1,000 shares of stock in a corporation. At the time the services were performed, the stock was worth $15 a share. Victor includes the $15,000 ($15 × 1,000 shares) in gross income. This becomes his basis in the 1,000 shares of stock.

Stock basis is used to compute the shareholder's gain or loss when the stock is sold. It is also used to determine the tax consequences when the corporation makes distributions to its shareholders (discussed later in the chapter at ¶1405). Thus, it is important that shareholders understand how to compute their stock basis.

¶1402 Corporate Taxable Income

For the most part, corporations compute their taxable income the same as individuals compute their business profit or loss (Chapter 7). However, gains and loss from disposing of property are included in the calculation of a corporation's taxable income. (Recall that these items were not part of the calculation of profits on Schedule C, but were part of the calculation of AGI). Most of the rules governing income and business deductions apply to both individuals and corporations. One major difference between corporations and individuals concerns the treatment of nonbusiness deductions. Although individuals may deduct certain personal expenditures as itemized deductions, corporations have no personal expenses. Thus, corporations do not use the concept of adjusted gross income (AGI) because they have no deductions from AGI (no standard deduction, itemized deductions, or exemption deduction). Furthermore, corporations have different limits on capital losses and charitable contributions. They also are taxed on only a portion of the dividends that they receive. These differences are covered in more detail later in the chapter at ¶1402.04, ¶1402.05, and ¶1402.06.

¶1402.01 ACCOUNTING METHODS

A corporation must select an accounting method for determining its taxable income. Most corporations use the accrual method of accounting. With the **accrual method**, corporations report income when it is earned, regardless of when the cash is received. Also, they deduct expenses when they are incurred, regardless of when they are paid.

Besides the accrual method, the other accounting options available to certain corporations are the cash and hybrid methods. With the **cash method**, income is taxable when received, and expenses are deductible when paid. The **hybrid method** combines cash and accrual methods. Here, the accrual method is used to compute gross profit from the sale of inventory and the cash method is used for all other income and deductions.

The types of corporations permitted to use the cash method are limited. Farming and personal service corporations may use the cash method. All other corporations must have average gross receipts for the last three years of $5 million or less. Even for these corporations, the tax law requires that they use the accrual method to compute gross profit from the sale of inventory.

¶1402.02 ACCOUNTING PERIODS

Corporations normally use a 12-month year to report their taxable income. A C corporation may choose to use a calendar year or a fiscal year. A fiscal year is any 12-month period that ends on the last day of a month other than December. For example, a corporation may use a tax year of July 1 to June 30 as its fiscal tax year.

Another tax year option that corporations may choose is a 52-53 week year. Corporations select this tax year when they want their tax year to end on the same day of the week each year. The day may be either the last one occurring in the last month of their tax year or the one occurring closest to their normal year-end.

EXAMPLE 6 Carolina Corporation closes its tax year on the last Friday in December each year. In 20x0, the last Friday falls on December 29. In 20x1, it falls on December 28, and in 20x2, it falls on December 26. Thus, Carolina's 52-53 week tax year for 20x1 runs from December 30, 20x0 to December 28, 20x1. Its tax year for 20x2 runs from December 29, 20x1 until December 26, 20x2.

Short Tax Year

Corporations can have a tax year shorter than 12 months in three situations. The first is in the year in which the corporation is formed. The second generally occurs in the last year of the corporation's operations. The third is when a corporation changes its tax year.

All taxpayers must get permission from the IRS to change their tax year. Corporations do this by filing Form 1128, Application to Adopt, Change, or Retain a Tax Year. When taxpayers change their tax year, they file a short-period return that covers the period between the close of their old tax year and the start of their new tax year.

EXAMPLE 7 A newly formed corporation selects a September 30 year-end. The corporation begins operations on May 16, 20x1. For the fiscal year ending September 30, 20x1, the corporation files a short period return for the period May 16, 20x1 – September 30, 20x1. Its fiscal year ending on September 30, 20x2 includes the activities of the corporation from October 1, 20x1 – September 30, 20x2.

EXAMPLE 8 A corporation that has a calendar year-end decides that an October 31 year-end more closely reflects the end of its annual business cycle. On June 1, 20x3, the corporation completes Form 1128 and files it with the IRS. The corporation receives permission from the IRS to change its tax year effective October 31, 20x3. The corporation files a tax return for the short period that runs from January 1, 20x3 – October 31, 20x3. Its next tax return will be for the fiscal year November 1, 20x3 – October 31, 20x4.

¶1402.03 CORPORATE TAXABLE INCOME FORMULA

Corporations compute their taxable income as gross income less business expenses. However, some specific deductions require special computations and therefore cannot be grouped with other business expenses. These include (1) the charitable contribution (CC) deduction, (2) the dividends received deduction (DRD), (3) the domestic production activities (DPA) deduction, (4) net operating loss (NOL) carrybacks, and (5) short-term capital loss (STCL) carrybacks. The formula for computing corporate taxable income is:

	Gross income
–	Deductions (all but CC, DRD, DPA, NOL carryback, STCL carryback)
=	Taxable income used to compute CC deduction
–	Charitable contribution (CC) deduction
=	Taxable income used to compute DRD
–	Dividends received deduction (DRD)
=	Taxable income before DPA deduction and carrybacks
–	DPA deduction
–	NOL carryback
–	STCL carryback
=	Taxable income

¶1402.04 INCOME ITEMS

Typically, the same Code provisions determine the tax status of income items for individual taxpayers and corporations. However, in some cases additional rules apply.

Gross Profit from Sales

Net sales are gross sales less sales returns and allowances. Net sales minus cost of goods sold equals **gross profit from sales**. Corporations can deduct *sales discounts* directly from sales or treat them as a business expense.

For many businesses, inventories are a material factor in producing gross sales. Inventories include raw materials, supplies, work in process, and finished goods. Businesses that produce goods for sale include all production costs in inventories. These costs include direct materials, direct labor, as well as direct and indirect overhead. The term for this process is **full costing**. To compute **cost of goods sold**, the taxpayer adds beginning inventories, labor, and overhead. It then subtracts ending inventories, as shown below. This formula is the same one sole proprietors use to report their cost of goods sold on Schedule C (Part III), see ¶705.05.

Beginning inventories	$100,956
Add: Purchases	207,858
Labor	74,807
Other costs	30,529
Total inventory available for sale	$414,150
Less: Ending inventories	(90,283)
Cost of goods sold	$323,867

Capital Gains and Losses

Corporations report the sale of capital assets on Schedule D (Form 1120). Unlike individuals, corporations do not get a reduced tax rate on net capital gains. Corporations must include the full amount of capital gains in their regular taxable income. Corporations record capital gains separately from other income because their capital losses can be deducted only against capital gains. Any capital losses in excess of capital gains are carried back three years and forward five years to offset capital gains in those years.

Corporations treat all capital loss carryovers as short-term capital losses. They first use capital losses arising in the current year, followed by carryover capital losses in a first-created, first-used order. Corporations that cannot use their capital losses within the carryover period lose the tax benefit of the losses.

EXAMPLE 9

McCann, Inc. has the following capital gains and losses during the 20x3.

Short-term capital gain	$18,000
Short-term capital loss	(14,000)
Long-term capital gain	13,000
Long-term capital loss	(22,000)

McCann begins the process by offsetting short-term capital losses against short-term capital gains. It then offsets long-term capital losses against long-term capital gains. This results in a $4,000 net short-term gain and a $9,000 net long-term loss. McCann uses $4,000 of the net long-term capital loss to offset its net short-term capital gain. This is the same netting process that is described in ¶1101.03.

Short-Term	**Long-Term**
$18,000	$ 13,000
(14,000)	(22,000)
$ 4,000	($ 9,000)
(4,000) ←	┘
$0	

McCann must carry back $5,000 of its capital losses ($9,000 – $4,000 used in 20x3) to 20x0 (its third preceding tax year). These losses will be treated as short-term capital losses when the netting process for 20x0 is redone. Any losses not used in 20x0 are carried forward to 20x1 and then 20x2. If McCann cannot use up all of the capital losses in those carryback years, it carries forward any remaining amount as a short-term capital loss to 20x4 – 20x8 (for a total of five carryforward years).

EXAMPLE 10

Continuing with Example 9, assume that McCann, Inc. had the following capital gains and losses during 20x0.

Short-Term	**Long-Term**
$12,000	$ 7,000
(3,000)	(5,000)
$ 9,000	$ 2,000

When the $5,000 excess capital loss from 20x3 is carried back to 20x0 as a short-term capital loss, the (redone) netting process from 20x0 looks like this.

	Short-Term	**Long-Term**
Carryback from 20x3	($ 5,000)	
	12,000	$ 7,000
	(3,000)	(5,000)
	$ 4,000	$ 2,000

When McCann adds the $5,000 short-term capital loss to the netting process, its taxable income is reduced by $5,000 ($11,000 overall net gain reported originally vs. $6,000 overall net gain as recomputed). McCann files for a refund of the taxes paid on the $5,000 of capital gain by filing Form 1139, Corporation Application for Tentative Refund. If McCann's marginal tax rate in 20x0 was 35%, then the IRS will refund McCann $1,750 ($5,000 × 35%), which represents the overpaid taxes for that year.

¶1402.05 BUSINESS DEDUCTIONS

Many corporate deductions are the same as those taken by sole proprietors (see Chapter 7). However, differences do exist. These differences are described in the discussions that follow.

Compensation

Corporations deduct payments for personal services as compensation when they pass three tests: (1) the payments represent an ordinary and necessary expense of the business, (2) the payments represent a reasonable amount for services received, and (3) the corporation pays or accrues the amount in the current tax year under its method of accounting. The deduction on the tax return for salaries and wages equals paid or accrued compensation less any tax credits (like the work opportunity tax credit, see ¶1203.06) taken on the return.

For publicly held corporations (those whose stock is publicly traded), a special rule limits the deduction for salaries paid to the Chief Executive Officer (CEO) and the other four most highly paid officers. Unless the corporation can justify paying a higher amount, the deduction for each of these officers cannot exceed $1 million, even though all compensation paid is taxable to the officer. While there is no definite rule for determining reasonable compensation, guidelines do exist. The main guideline looks at what similar organizations pay for similar services. Other guidelines include local living costs, as well as the officer's skills and degree of responsibility.

EXAMPLE 11

Easton Corporation pays its CEO $1.5 million in 20x1. Easton cannot justify why the $1 million limit should not be imposed. Although Easton can pay its CEO $1.5 million, it can only deduct $1 million on its 20x1 tax return. The CEO is taxed on the full $1.5 of compensation received.

Bad Debts

Most taxpayers, including corporations, can only use the direct write-off method for bad debts. An exception exists for certain financial institutions. These institutions use the reserve method of accounting (the method used in financial reporting).

EXAMPLE 12

In August of 20x0, an accrual basis, calendar year corporation sold merchandise on account for $1,000. The corporation included the proceeds from the sale in its 20x0 gross income. On June 15, 20x1, the accounts receivable becomes worthless. Since the corporation recognized the income from the sale in 20x0, it takes a $1,000 bad debt deduction in 20x1. It is important to note that the corporation must be able to specifically identify which accounts receivable became worthless before it can take a bad debt deduction. This is known as the "direct write-off method."

Organizational and Start-Up Costs

The Internal Revenue Code (Code) allows corporations to deduct up to $5,000 of organizational costs for the tax year in which business operations begin. The $5,000 amount is reduced by $1 for each dollar of organizational costs that exceed $50,000. Thus, no current deduction is allowed to corporations that incur over $55,000 in organizational costs. Any costs not currently expensed may be written off (amortized) over a 180-month period using the straight-line method. The amortization period starts in the month in which the corporation begins operations.

Organizational costs include any costs related to the creation of the corporation that are chargeable to a capital account. These costs include (1) legal expenses for setting up the corporation, (2) costs of incorporation charged by the state government, (3) necessary accounting services, (4) expenses of temporary directors, and (5) costs of organizational meetings. Organizational expenditures do not include the costs of issuing or selling stocks or other securities, or costs associated with transferring assets to the corporation. Instead, these costs simply reduce the amount of paid-in capital.

EXAMPLE 13

Branis Corporation incurs $53,500 of organizational costs. Branis uses a calendar year-end and began its operations on November 1, 20x1. Since the organizational costs exceed $50,000, Branis can elect to expense only $1,500 ($5,000 – $3,500) in 20x1. It can then elect to amortize the remaining $52,000 ($53,500 – $1,500) over 180 months beginning on November 1, 20x1.

Start-up costs are costs that normally would be currently deductible if they had been incurred during the operations of an existing business. They often include costs incurred to investigate entering into or acquiring a new active trade or business. Like organizational costs, businesses can deduct up to $5,000 of start-up costs. However, the $5,000 is reduced by the amount by which the start-up costs exceed $50,000. The rest may be amortized evenly over 180 months starting with the month in which the business begins. The rules that apply to start-up costs are available to all types of businesses, including sole proprietorships, C corporations, partnerships, and S corporations.

EXAMPLE 14

Addison, Inc. uses a calendar year-end. During 20x1 it incurred $53,000 of start-up costs. Addison acquired the business on May 2, 20x1. Since the start-up costs exceed $50,000, Addison can elect to expense $2,000 in 20x1 ($5,000 – $3,000 excess over $50,000). Addison can amortize the remaining $51,000 over 180 months beginning in May 20x1.

Taxpayers can elect out of amortizing their organizational and start-up costs. These taxpayers would instead capitalize their costs to an asset account, which would be used to offset the amount realized on the sale of the business.

Passive Losses

The passive loss limitations rules (discussed at ¶905) do not apply to most corporations. However, closely-held corporations (over 50% of its stock owned by five or fewer individuals) and personal service corporations (discussed in ¶1403.03) are subject to the passive loss rules.

¶1402.06 SPECIAL DEDUCTIONS

The deductions for corporations, for the most part, are treated the same as business deductions for other business entities. Nevertheless, some deductions for corporations receive special treatment. When introducing the corporation's taxable income formula in ¶1402.03, these special deductions were listed separately. The discussion that follows describes each of these special deductions.

Charitable Contributions

Like individuals, corporations can deduct contributions they make to charitable organizations. However, the deduction cannot exceed 10% of the corporation's taxable income before certain items. These items include the deductions for charitable contributions, dividends received, domestic production activities, NOL carrybacks, and capital loss carrybacks. Any contributions made in excess of the 10% taxable income limit are carried over for five years. Like capital losses, amounts carried over are used on a first-made, first-used basis. If the corporation does not have enough taxable income in the carryover period to use the carried over contributions, the deduction is lost.

EXAMPLE 15

During 20x1, a corporation makes cash contributions of $20,000 to various charitable organizations. The corporation has taxable income of $180,000 before deducting any charitable contributions (CCs), dividends received deduction (DRD), domestic production activities (DPA) deduction, or any capital loss or net operating loss (NOL) carrybacks. The corporation's charitable deduction for 20x1 is $18,000.

Taxable income used to compute the CC deduction	$180,000
	× 10%
Maximum charitable contribution deduction	$ 18,000

Cash contributions made during 20x1	$20,000
Less corporate limitation	(18,000)
Charitable contribution carryover to 20x2	$ 2,000

Sometimes, a corporation donates appreciated property to a public charity. The corporation figures the amount of the contribution in the same manner as individuals (see ¶506). Thus, when a corporation donates ordinary income property to a charity, it deducts its adjusted basis in the property.

An enhanced charitable contribution deduction is allowed for C corporations that donate food inventory to qualified charities that provide care for the ill, the needy, or infants. The enhanced deduction equals the taxpayer's basis in the inventory plus one-half of the excess of the inventory's FMV over the taxpayer's basis. However, the deduction is limited to twice the taxpayer's basis in the inventory. Thus, if a corporation with inventory having a basis of $650 and valued at $1,000, were to donate it to a qualified charity that cares for infants, the corporation's deduction would equal $825 ($650 + ½ × ($1,000 – $650)).

A corporation deducts a contribution in the year it transfers property or cash to a charity. A corporation using the accrual method of accounting, however, can choose to take the deduction in the year it makes the accrual (pledge). To take the deduction in the accrual year, the accrual basis corporation must pay the contribution within 2½ months after the close of its tax year.

Dividends Received Deduction

Corporations get a deduction for a certain amount of the dividends they receive. The deduction lessens or avoids triple taxation of the profits of corporations. Triple taxation occurs when a corporation distributes its after-tax profits to corporate shareholders. These corporate shareholders normally would pay taxes on the dividends before they distribute their profits to their shareholders (who also pay taxes on the dividends they receive). The amount of the dividends received deduction (DRD) depends on the corporation's percentage of stock ownership in the corporation paying the dividend.

Percentage Owned	DRD Percentage
Less than 20%	70%
From 20% to less than 80%	80%
From 80% to 100%	100%

EXAMPLE 16

Delta Corporation owns 60% of the total value and outstanding shares of stock in Epsilon Corporation. During the year, Epsilon pays a $100,000 dividend to Delta. Delta includes the $100,000 of dividends in income and takes a $80,000 DRD ($100,000 × 80%). Thus, the net amount of dividends taxed to Delta is $20,000 ($100,000 – $80,000).

For corporations whose ownership is at least 80%, the DRD is always 100% of the dividends received. A reduced DRD may apply to corporations whose ownership is less than 80%. Corporations with less than 80% ownership are required to apply the DRD percentage to taxable income (after deducting charitable contributions but before any capital loss or NOL carrybacks or the DPA deduction). Normally for these corporations, the DRD is computed as the *lesser of* (i) the DRD percentage times dividends received, or (ii) the DRD percentage times taxable income (as defined above). However, if deducting an amount equal to the DRD percentage times the dividends received results in an NOL for the year, then the rule limiting the deduction to the DRD times taxable income does not apply. In these situations, the corporation's DRD equals the DRD percentage times the dividends received.

Computing the DRD when ownership is less than 80%

Step 1	Multiply the appropriate DRD percentage times the dividends received.
Step 2	Multiply the DRD percentage by the corporation's taxable income after deducting charitable contributions but before any loss carrybacks or the DPA deduction.
Step 3	Subtract the result from Step 1 from the corporation's taxable income used in Step 2. If a loss results (NOL), then use the amount from Step 1 as the corporation's DRD. If the result is a positive amount, then use the *lesser of* Step 1 or Step 2 as the DRD.

EXAMPLE 17 Same facts as in Example 16, except that Delta's taxable income after the charitable contribution deduction but before any loss carrybacks or DPA deduction is $90,000. If Delta were to deduct an $80,000 DRD based on dividends received ($100,000 × 80%), a positive amount results ($90,000 – $80,000 = $10,000 taxable income). Thus, Delta computes its DRD as the *lesser of* (i) $80,000 (80% of $100,000 dividends received), or (ii) $72,000 (80% × $90,000 taxable income). Delta's DRD is $72,000.

EXAMPLE 18 Same facts as in Example 16, except that Delta's taxable income after the charitable contribution deduction but before any loss carrybacks or DPA deduction is $70,000. Now when Delta deducts an $80,000 DRD based on dividends received, an NOL results ($70,000 – $80,000 = $10,000 NOL). Thus, the DRD based on taxable income does not apply and Delta's DRD is $80,000 (80% × $100,000 dividends received).

EXAMPLE 19 Beta Corporation owns 80% of the total value and outstanding shares of stock in Alpha Corporation. During the year, Alpha pays a $50,000 dividend to Beta. Beta's taxable income after the charitable contribution deduction, but before any loss carrybacks or DPA deduction, is $60,000. (This amount includes the $50,000 of dividend income from Beta). Because Beta's ownership percentage is at least 80%, its DRD percentage is 100%. After subtracting the $50,000 DRD ($50,000 × 100%), Beta reports taxable income of $40,000. For corporations whose ownership is at least 80%, the DRD is always 100% of the dividends received, regardless of whether the DRD produces an NOL.

Net Operating Loss (NOL)

When a corporation's deductions exceed its income, the corporation may suffer a net loss for the year. A corporation needs to make only one adjustment to its taxable income in determining its NOL for the current year. It must add back any NOL carryovers from prior years that were deducted in computing the current year NOL. Like individuals, corporations carry their NOLs back 2 years and forward 20. They too have the option of electing to forego the carryback and just carry forward the NOL.

In computing taxable income for the current year, a corporation deducts any NOL or capital loss carryforwards from gross income. NOL and capital loss carrybacks are NOLs and capital losses that occurred in a future tax year. Thus, NOL and capital loss carrybacks are considered special deductions because these deductions are not known at the time the corporation computes current year taxable income. Corporations must file amended returns for prior years when using NOL or capital loss carrybacks.

EXAMPLE 20

Cougar Corporation has the following income and deductions in 2015. Included in gross sales is $110,000 of qualified production activities income (used to compute Cougar's domestic production activities (DPA) deduction, see discussion at ¶402.14).

Gross sales	$600,000
Long-term capital gains	25,000
Dividend income (18% ownership in the stock)	40,000
Interest income	10,000
Cost of goods sold	400,000
Other business expenses	60,000
Charitable contributions	22,000
Short-term capital loss carryover	15,000

Cougar computes its 2015 taxable income as follows. It carries forward a $2,000 charitable contribution to 2016 ($22,000 – $20,000).

Gross income [1]	$660,000
Less deductions [2]	(460,000)
Taxable income for computing CC deduction	$200,000
Less charitable contribution deduction [3]	(20,000)
Taxable income for figuring DRD	$180,000
Less DRD[4]	(28,000)
Taxable income for figuring DPA deduction	$152,000
Less DPA deduction [5]	(9,900)
Taxable income	$142,100

[1] $600,000 + ($25,000 capital gains – $15,000 capital losses) + $40,000 + $10,000
[2] $400,000 + $60,000
[3] $200,000 × 10%
[4] *lesser of* (i) 70% × $40,000 dividends received or (ii) 70% × $180,000, since Cougar's 18% ownership in the stock is less than 80%
[5] 9% × *lesser of* $110,000 QPAI or $152,000 TI after CC and DRD (see ¶402.14)

EXAMPLE 21

Continuing with Example 20, assume that in 2017 Cougar suffers an $80,000 NOL, which it carries back two years to 2015. Carrybacks are deducted last, so Cougar's (recomputed) 2015 taxable income is $62,100 ($142,100 – $80,000). Cougar recomputes its tax liability using $62,100 of recomputed taxable income and asks the IRS for a refund of the difference between that amount and the amount of taxes it owed based on $142,100 of taxable income.

¶1403 Corporate Tax Returns and Tax Rates

Every C corporation must file a tax return, regardless of the amount of its taxable income or loss. Once the corporation computes its taxable income, it applies the appropriate corporate tax rate. Both individual and corporate tax rates are **progressive**, which means the rates increase as taxable income increases. However, the corporate tax brackets are not indexed for inflation; whereas the individual tax brackets are indexed each year. The next sections describe the corporate tax return and its tax rates.

¶1403.01 CORPORATE TAX RETURN

C corporations use Form 1120, U.S. Corporation Income Tax Return, to report their taxable income (loss). Form 1120 has five pages. A completed Form 1120 is shown in Figure 14-2 (¶1403.04).

Due Date

The due date for most corporate income tax returns falls on the 15th of the third month after the corporation's year ends. This includes domestic corporations and foreign corporations with a U.S. place of business. Foreign corporations that do business in the U.S., but do not have a U.S. place of business have until the 15th day of the sixth month to file their U.S. tax returns. When a due date falls on a Saturday, Sunday, or legal holiday, the due date is the next business day.

A corporation that cannot file its tax return by the due date can request an automatic six-month extension to file its return by filing Form 7004 by the due date of its tax return (¶208). As with all extensions, filing this form only extends the due date for filing the tax return. It does not extend the payment of taxes owed. Taxpayers that do not pay the taxes they owe by the original due date of their tax return are subject to interest and penalties.

EXAMPLE 22 Amel, Inc. (a calendar year corporation) normally must file its tax return by March 15. If Amel is unable to file its return on time, it can file Form 7004 with the IRS by March 15. Amel will then have until September 15 (six more months) to file its tax return. Amel must, however, pay any taxes it owes when it files the extension, or else the unpaid taxes will be subject to interest and penalty. Should September 15 fall on a Saturday, Sunday or legal holiday, the deadline for filing a timely return with an extension would be the next business day.

EXAMPLE 23 Same facts as in Example 22, except that Amel uses a fiscal year that ends on March 31. Amel's due date for filing its tax return is June 15. This is 2½ months after the end of Amel's March 31 fiscal year-end. If Amel files a timely extension, its tax return deadline would be extended to December 15 (six months after June 15). If either of these deadlines falls on a weekend or legal holiday, the due date would be the next business day.

¶1403.02 CORPORATE TAX RATES

The tax rate structure for corporations is progressive. However, at higher income levels, the benefits from the lower tax rates are phased out. Once the phase-out stops, the rates stay flat (same rate for all taxable income). Other than professional service corporations (described later), all regular C corporations compute their tax using the following tax rate structure.

Taxable Income	Corporate Tax Rate
$0–$50,000	15%
$50,001–$75,000	25
$75,001–$100,000	34
$100,001–$335,000	39
$335,001–$10,000,000	34
$10,000,001–$15,000,000	35
$15,000,001–$18,333,333	38
Over $18,333,333	35

Rate Structure and Tax Calculation

For corporations with taxable income at or below $75,000, Congress set the rates low (15% and 25%) to stimulate growth. The Code phases out the benefits of the low rates by adding an additional 5% tax on taxable income between $100,001 and $335,000 (39% rather than 34%). When taxable income reaches $335,000, the government has recovered all lower-rate benefits. The amount of these benefits equals $11,750 [((34% – 15%) × $50,000) + ((34% – 25%) × $25,000)]. This is the same amount produced by the 5% surtax. [($335,000 – $100,000) × 5% = $11,750]. The tax rate then becomes a flat rate of 34% for incomes up to $10 million.

EXAMPLE 24

XYZ corporation, a calendar year corporation, has taxable income of $900,000. The computations for XYZ's income tax of $306,000 follow. Notice that XYZ's tax is the same that would be computed using a flat rate of 34% (34% × $900,000 = $306,000).

	Income Tax
15% × $50,000	$ 7,500
25% × $25,000	6,250
34% × $25,000	8,500
39% × $235,000	91,650
34% × $565,000	192,100
Tax liability	$306,000

A similar phase-out takes place for corporations whose taxable income exceeds $15,000,000. This phase-out eliminates the 1% lower tax benefit (35% vs. 34%) on incomes below $10 million ($10,000,000 × 1% = $100,000 benefit). Between $15,000,000 and $18,333,333, the Code increases the 35% rate by 3 percentage points. This rate increase produces additional revenues of $100,000 (3% × $3,333,333). For corporations with taxable incomes in excess of $18,333,333, a flat 35% tax rate applies to all taxable income.

¶1403.03 PERSONAL SERVICE CORPORATIONS

Personal service corporations (PSC) are corporations whose shareholders and employees provide professional services for a fee. Doctors, dentists, lawyers, architects, accountants, and other professionals organize as PSCs. These corporations provide the owners with several tax and nontax benefits. However, they also have some tax restrictions. For example, PSCs generally may only use a calendar year as a tax year. Also, the tax rate on PSCs is a flat rate of 35% on all taxable income. This high flat rate is intended to encourage the PSC to pay out its net earnings to its shareholder-employees as salaries. These salaries are then deducted by the PSC, and taxed to the shareholder-employee using the individual tax rates.

¶1403.04 FILLED-IN FORM 1120

INFORMATION FOR FIGURE 14-2:

Globe Manufacturing Company (EIN **86-0694770**, located at **2468 E. Van Buren, Phoenix, AZ 85019-2468**) was incorporated on **January 3, 2000**. Globe has always been on the accrual method of accounting and uses the cost method for valuing inventory of **electronic components** that it **manufactures.** Globe has over 100 shareholders. It made estimated payments of $4,000 during the year and paid out $16,446 in cash dividends.

The income and expense information for preparing Globe Manufacturing's Form 1120 comes from the Income Statement in Figure 14-1. The filled-in Form 1120 for Globe Manufacturing appears in Figure 14-2. The balance sheet information appears on Schedule L and is not provided elsewhere.

Figure 14-1: Income Statement for Globe Manufacturing

Globe Manufacturing Company
Income Statement
For Year Ended December 31, 2015

Revenue:		
Net sales (after subtracting $3,197 of goods returned)		$528,072
Interest income ($1,650 from municipal bonds)		2,559
Dividend income, 55% stock ownership ($1,750 domestic, $235 foreign)		1,985
Gross rent		500
Total revenues		$533,116
Less Expenses:		
Advertising	$ 17,500	
Bad debts written off during the year	1,960	
Charitable contributions	5,200	
Compensation of (sole) officer	80,000	
Cost of goods sold (COGS) other than depreciation	293,338	
Depreciation ($30,529 related to COGS)	36,744	
Insurance expense	2,270	
Interest expense	2,580	
Maintenance	3,140	
Other employee salaries	52,047	
Office supplies	163	
Taxes and licenses	8,200	
Utilities expense	1,087	(504,229)
Net income before federal income taxes		$ 28,887
Less income tax		(4,333)
Net income per books		$ 24,554

Line # (Form 1120, Page 1)

D: Total assets, **$428,944** (source: Schedule L, line 15(d))
1a: Gross receipts or sales, **$531,269** ($528,072 net sales + $3,197 returns)
1b: Returns and allowances, **$3,197**
2: Cost of goods sold (source: Form 1125-A), **$323,867** ($293,338 + $30,529 depreciation related to COGS)
5: Interest, **$909** ($2,559 total interest – $1,650 tax-exempt interest)
19: Charitable contributions, **$3,244** [10% × ($207,599 total income reported on line 11 minus $175,162 (total deductions through line 27 other than the charitable contribution deduction on line 19 and the DPA deduction on line 25)]
20: Depreciation not claimed on Form 1125-A (COGS), **$6,215** ($36,744 – $30,529)
25: DPA deduction, **$2,627** [9% × $29,193 (lesser of $29,193 TI before DPA deduction or $71,400 qualified production activity income (provided by the company), not to exceed 50% of $10,129 W-2 wages from domestic manufacturing activities (provided by the company))]. See ¶402.14.
26: Other deductions, **$3,520** ($2,270 insurance + $163 supplies + $1,087 utilities)

Line # (Form 1120, Schedule C)

2(a): Dividends from 20%-or-more-owned domestic corporations, **$1,750**
13(a): Dividends from foreign corporations, **$235**

Line # (Form 1120, Schedule J)

2: Income tax, **$3,775** ($25,166 taxable income × 15% tax rate)
13: 2015 estimated tax payments, **$4,000** (source: given)

Line # (Form 1120, Schedule K)

1b: Check box for Accrual method of accounting
2a: Business activity code no., **3670** (source: Instructions for Form 1120)
3-18: Mark **No**
9: Tax-exempt interest, **$1,650** (source: income statement)
10: Number of shareholders at the end of the year, leave blank since more than 100
12: NOL carryover, **$0** (source: no NOL in prior years)
13: Because Globe Manufacturing answers "No" (its total receipts and total assets are not both less than $250,000), Globe is required to complete Schedules L, M-1, and M-2. Had Globe answered "Yes", it would have been required to enter the amount of cash distributions made during the year on the line provided.

Line # (Form 1120, Schedule M-1)

5b: Charitable contributions recorded on the books not deducted on the return, **$1,956** ($5,200 – $3,244 deducted on Form 1120, line 19)
7: Tax-exempt interest recorded on books this year not included on this return, **$1,650**
8b: Deductions on this return not charged against book income, **DPA deduction, $2,627** (source: Form 1120, line 25)

Line # (Form 1120, Schedule M-2)

1: Balance in unappropriated retained earnings at beginning of the year, **$44,708** (source: Schedule L, line 25(b))
5a: Cash distributions, **$16,446** (source: given)

Figure 14-2: Filled-In Form 1120 (Page 1)

Form **1120** Department of the Treasury Internal Revenue Service

U.S. Corporation Income Tax Return

For calendar year 2015 or tax year beginning ________, 2015, ending ________, 20 ____

▶ Information about Form 1120 and its separate instructions is at *www.irs.gov/form1120.*

OMB No. 1545-0123 — **2015**

A Check if: 1a Consolidated return (attach Form 851) ☐ b Life/nonlife consolidated return ☐ 2 Personal holding co. (attach Sch. PH) ☐ 3 Personal service corp. (see instructions) ☐ 4 Schedule M-3 attached ☐	**TYPE OR PRINT** Name: Globe Manufacturing Company; Number, street, and room or suite no. If a P.O. box, see instructions.: 2468 E. Van Buren; City or town, state, or province, country, and ZIP or foreign postal code: Phoenix, AZ 85019-2468	**B Employer identification number** 86-0694770; **C** Date incorporated 1-3-2000; **D** Total assets (see instructions) $ 428,944

E Check if: (1) ☐ Initial return (2) ☐ Final return (3) ☐ Name change (4) ☐ Address change

Income	1a	Gross receipts or sales	1a	531,269		
	b	Returns and allowances	1b	3,197		
	c	Balance. Subtract line 1b from line 1a			1c	528,072
	2	Cost of goods sold (attach Form 1125-A)			2	323,867
	3	Gross profit. Subtract line 2 from line 1c			3	204,205
	4	Dividends (Schedule C, line 19)			4	1,985
	5	Interest			5	909
	6	Gross rents			6	500
	7	Gross royalties			7	
	8	Capital gain net income (attach Schedule D (Form 1120))			8	
	9	Net gain or (loss) from Form 4797, Part II, line 17 (attach Form 4797)			9	
	10	Other income (see instructions—attach statement)			10	
	11	**Total income.** Add lines 3 through 10 ▶			11	207,599
Deductions (See instructions for limitations on deductions.)	12	Compensation of officers (see instructions—attach Form 1125-E) ▶			12	80,000
	13	Salaries and wages (less employment credits)			13	52,047
	14	Repairs and maintenance			14	3,140
	15	Bad debts			15	1,960
	16	Rents			16	
	17	Taxes and licenses			17	8,200
	18	Interest			18	2,580
	19	Charitable contributions			19	3,244
	20	Depreciation from Form 4562 not claimed on Form 1125-A or elsewhere on return (attach Form 4562)			20	6,215
	21	Depletion			21	
	22	Advertising			22	17,500
	23	Pension, profit-sharing, etc., plans			23	
	24	Employee benefit programs			24	
	25	Domestic production activities deduction (attach Form 8903)			25	2,627
	26	Other deductions (attach statement)			26	3,520
	27	**Total deductions.** Add lines 12 through 26 ▶			27	181,033
	28	Taxable income before net operating loss deduction and special deductions. Subtract line 27 from line 11.			28	26,566
	29a	Net operating loss deduction (see instructions)	29a			
	b	Special deductions (Schedule C, line 20)	29b	1,400		
	c	Add lines 29a and 29b			29c	1,400
Tax, Refundable Credits, and Payments	30	**Taxable income.** Subtract line 29c from line 28 (see instructions)			30	25,166
	31	Total tax (Schedule J, Part I, line 11)			31	3,775
	32	Total payments and refundable credits (Schedule J, Part II, line 21)			32	4,000
	33	Estimated tax penalty (see instructions). Check if Form 2220 is attached ▶ ☐			33	
	34	**Amount owed.** If line 32 is smaller than the total of lines 31 and 33, enter amount owed			34	
	35	**Overpayment.** If line 32 is larger than the total of lines 31 and 33, enter amount overpaid			35	225
	36	Enter amount from line 35 you want: **Credited to 2016 estimated tax ▶**		Refunded ▶	36	225

Sign Here — Under penalties of perjury, I declare that I have examined this return, including accompanying schedules and statements, and to the best of my knowledge and belief, it is true, correct, and complete. Declaration of preparer (other than taxpayer) is based on all information of which preparer has any knowledge.

Perry Mason | 3-12-16 | President

Signature of officer | Date | Title

May the IRS discuss this return with the preparer shown below (see instructions)? ☐ Yes ☐ No

Paid Preparer Use Only				
Print/Type preparer's name	Preparer's signature	Date	Check ☐ if self-employed	PTIN
Firm's name ▶			Firm's EIN ▶	
Firm's address ▶			Phone no.	

For Paperwork Reduction Act Notice, see separate instructions. Cat. No. 11450Q Form **1120** (2015)

Figure 14-2: Filled-In Form 1120 (Page 2)

Form 1120 (2015) Page 2

Schedule C **Dividends and Special Deductions** (see instructions)	**(a)** Dividends received	**(b)** %	**(c)** Special deductions **(a)** × **(b)**
1 Dividends from less-than-20%-owned domestic corporations (other than debt-financed stock)		70	
2 Dividends from 20%-or-more-owned domestic corporations (other than debt-financed stock)	1,750	80	1,400
3 Dividends on debt-financed stock of domestic and foreign corporations		see instructions	
4 Dividends on certain preferred stock of less-than-20%-owned public utilities		42	
5 Dividends on certain preferred stock of 20%-or-more-owned public utilities		48	
6 Dividends from less-than-20%-owned foreign corporations and certain FSCs		70	
7 Dividends from 20%-or-more-owned foreign corporations and certain FSCs		80	
8 Dividends from wholly owned foreign subsidiaries		100	
9 **Total.** Add lines 1 through 8. See instructions for limitation			1,400
10 Dividends from domestic corporations received by a small business investment company operating under the Small Business Investment Act of 1958		100	
11 Dividends from affiliated group members		100	
12 Dividends from certain FSCs		100	
13 Dividends from foreign corporations not included on lines 3, 6, 7, 8, 11, or 12	235		
14 Income from controlled foreign corporations under subpart F (attach Form(s) 5471)			
15 Foreign dividend gross-up			
16 IC-DISC and former DISC dividends not included on lines 1, 2, or 3			
17 Other dividends			
18 Deduction for dividends paid on certain preferred stock of public utilities			
19 **Total dividends.** Add lines 1 through 17. Enter here and on page 1, line 4 ►	1,985		
20 **Total special deductions.** Add lines 9, 10, 11, 12, and 18. Enter here and on page 1, line 29b ►			1,400

Form **1120** (2015)

Figure 14-2: Filled-In Form 1120 (Page 3)

Form 1120 (2015) Page **3**

Schedule J **Tax Computation and Payment** (see instructions)

Part I–Tax Computation

1	Check if the corporation is a member of a controlled group (attach Schedule O (Form 1120)) ▶ ☐				
2	Income tax. Check if a qualified personal service corporation (see instructions) ▶ ☐			2	3,775
3	Alternative minimum tax (attach Form 4626)			3	
4	Add lines 2 and 3			4	3,775
5a	Foreign tax credit (attach Form 1118)	5a			
b	Credit from Form 8834 (see instructions)	5b			
c	General business credit (attach Form 3800)	5c			
d	Credit for prior year minimum tax (attach Form 8827)	5d			
e	Bond credits from Form 8912	5e			
6	**Total credits.** Add lines 5a through 5e			6	0
7	Subtract line 6 from line 4			7	3,775
8	Personal holding company tax (attach Schedule PH (Form 1120))			8	
9a	Recapture of investment credit (attach Form 4255)	9a			
b	Recapture of low-income housing credit (attach Form 8611)	9b			
c	Interest due under the look-back method—completed long-term contracts (attach Form 8697)	9c			
d	Interest due under the look-back method—income forecast method (attach Form 8866)	9d			
e	Alternative tax on qualifying shipping activities (attach Form 8902)	9e			
f	Other (see instructions—attach statement)	9f			
10	**Total.** Add lines 9a through 9f			10	0
11	**Total tax.** Add lines 7, 8, and 10. Enter here and on page 1, line 31			11	3,775

Part II–Payments and Refundable Credits

12	2014 overpayment credited to 2015			12	
13	2015 estimated tax payments			13	4,000
14	2015 refund applied for on Form 4466			14	( )
15	Combine lines 12, 13, and 14			15	4,000
16	Tax deposited with Form 7004			16	
17	Withholding (see instructions)			17	
18	**Total payments.** Add lines 15, 16, and 17			18	4,000
19	Refundable credits from:				
a	Form 2439	19a			
b	Form 4136	19b			
c	Form 8827, line 8c	19c			
d	Other (attach statement—see instructions)	19d			
20	**Total credits.** Add lines 19a through 19d			20	0
21	**Total payments and credits.** Add lines 18 and 20. Enter here and on page 1, line 32			21	4,000

Schedule K **Other Information** (see instructions)

		Yes	No
1	Check accounting method: a ☐ Cash b ☑ Accrual c ☐ Other (specify) ▶		
2	See the instructions and enter the:		
a	Business activity code no. ▶ 3670		
b	Business activity ▶ Manufacturing		
c	Product or service ▶ Electronic components		
3	Is the corporation a subsidiary in an affiliated group or a parent-subsidiary controlled group? If "Yes," enter name and EIN of the parent corporation ▶		✓
4	At the end of the tax year:		
a	Did any foreign or domestic corporation, partnership (including any entity treated as a partnership), trust, or tax-exempt organization own directly 20% or more, or own, directly or indirectly, 50% or more of the total voting power of all classes of the corporation's stock entitled to vote? If "Yes," complete Part I of Schedule G (Form 1120) (attach Schedule G)		✓
b	Did any individual or estate own directly 20% or more, or own, directly or indirectly, 50% or more of the total voting power of all classes of the corporation's stock entitled to vote? If "Yes," complete Part II of Schedule G (Form 1120) (attach Schedule G)		✓

Form **1120** (2015)

Figure 14-2: Filled-In Form 1120 (Page 4)

Form 1120 (2015) Page **4**

Schedule K **Other Information** *continued* (see instructions)

		Yes	No
5	At the end of the tax year, did the corporation:		
a	Own directly 20% or more, or own, directly or indirectly, 50% or more of the total voting power of all classes of stock entitled to vote of any foreign or domestic corporation not included on **Form 851,** Affiliations Schedule? For rules of constructive ownership, see instructions. If "Yes," complete (i) through (iv) below.		✓

(i) Name of Corporation	(ii) Employer Identification Number (if any)	(iii) Country of Incorporation	(iv) Percentage Owned in Voting Stock

		Yes	No
b	Own directly an interest of 20% or more, or own, directly or indirectly, an interest of 50% or more in any foreign or domestic partnership (including an entity treated as a partnership) or in the beneficial interest of a trust? For rules of constructive ownership, see instructions. If "Yes," complete (i) through (iv) below.		✓

(i) Name of Entity	(ii) Employer Identification Number (if any)	(iii) Country of Organization	(iv) Maximum Percentage Owned in Profit, Loss, or Capital

		Yes	No
6	During this tax year, did the corporation pay dividends (other than stock dividends and distributions in exchange for stock) in excess of the corporation's current and accumulated earnings and profits? (See sections 301 and 316.) If "Yes," file **Form 5452,** Corporate Report of Nondividend Distributions. If this is a consolidated return, answer here for the parent corporation and on Form 851 for each subsidiary.		✓
7	At any time during the tax year, did one foreign person own, directly or indirectly, at least 25% of **(a)** the total voting power of all classes of the corporation's stock entitled to vote or **(b)** the total value of all classes of the corporation's stock? For rules of attribution, see section 318. If "Yes," enter: **(i)** Percentage owned ▶ ________ and **(ii)** Owner's country ▶ ________ **(c)** The corporation may have to file **Form 5472,** Information Return of a 25% Foreign-Owned U.S. Corporation or a Foreign Corporation Engaged in a U.S. Trade or Business. Enter the number of Forms 5472 attached ▶ ________		✓
8	Check this box if the corporation issued publicly offered debt instruments with original issue discount ▶ ☐ If checked, the corporation may have to file **Form 8281,** Information Return for Publicly Offered Original Issue Discount Instruments.		
9	Enter the amount of tax-exempt interest received or accrued during the tax year ▶ $ 1,650		
10	Enter the number of shareholders at the end of the tax year (if 100 or fewer) ▶ ________		
11	If the corporation has an NOL for the tax year and is electing to forego the carryback period, check here ▶ ☐ If the corporation is filing a consolidated return, the statement required by Regulations section 1.1502-21(b)(3) must be attached or the election will not be valid.		
12	Enter the available NOL carryover from prior tax years (do not reduce it by any deduction on line 29a.) ▶ $ 0		
13	Are the corporation's total receipts (page 1, line 1a, plus lines 4 through 10) for the tax year **and** its total assets at the end of the tax year less than $250,000? If "Yes," the corporation is not required to complete Schedules L, M-1, and M-2. Instead, enter the total amount of cash distributions and the book value of property distributions (other than cash) made during the tax year ▶ $ ________		✓
14	Is the corporation required to file Schedule UTP (Form 1120), Uncertain Tax Position Statement (see instructions)? If "Yes," complete and attach Schedule UTP.		✓
15a	Did the corporation make any payments in 2015 that would require it to file Form(s) 1099?		✓
b	If "Yes," did or will the corporation file required Forms 1099?		
16	During this tax year, did the corporation have an 80% or more change in ownership, including a change due to redemption of its own stock?		✓
17	During or subsequent to this tax year, but before the filing of this return, did the corporation dispose of more than 65% (by value) of its assets in a taxable, non-taxable, or tax deferred transaction?		✓
18	Did the corporation receive assets in a section 351 transfer in which any of the transferred assets had a fair market basis or fair market value of more than $1 million?		✓

Form **1120** (2015)

Figure 14-2: Filled-In Form 1120 (Page 5)

Form 1120 (2015) Page **5**

Schedule L **Balance Sheets per Books**

	Assets	Beginning of tax year (a)	(b)	End of tax year (c)	(d)
1	Cash		12,572		48,678
2a	Trade notes and accounts receivable	51,524		60,719	
b	Less allowance for bad debts	(4,589)	46,935	(4,589)	56,130
3	Inventories		100,956		90,283
4	U.S. government obligations		3,000		3,000
5	Tax-exempt securities (see instructions)		949		4,678
6	Other current assets (attach statement)				
7	Loans to shareholders				
8	Mortgage and real estate loans				
9	Other investments (attach statement)		18,100		30,000
10a	Buildings and other depreciable assets	200,001		220,500	
b	Less accumulated depreciation	(16,401)	183,600	(53,175)	167,325
11a	Depletable assets				
b	Less accumulated depletion	( )		( )	
12	Land (net of any amortization)		3,650		28,850
13a	Intangible assets (amortizable only)				
b	Less accumulated amortization	( )		( )	
14	Other assets (attach statement)				
15	Total assets		369,762		428,944
	Liabilities and Shareholders' Equity				
16	Accounts payable		14,184		16,452
17	Mortgages, notes, bonds payable in less than 1 year		2,000		
18	Other current liabilities (attach statement)		10,640		1,840
19	Loans from shareholders				
20	Mortgages, notes, bonds payable in 1 year or more		100,000		100,000
21	Other liabilities (attach statement)		8,230		12,836
22	Capital stock: a Preferred stock	45,000		45,000	
	b Common stock	125,000	170,000	180,000	225,000
23	Additional paid-in capital		20,000		20,000
24	Retained earnings—Appropriated (attach statement)				
25	Retained earnings—Unappropriated		44,708		52,816
26	Adjustments to shareholders' equity (attach statement)				
27	Less cost of treasury stock		( )		( )
28	Total liabilities and shareholders' equity		369,762		428,944

Schedule M-1 **Reconciliation of Income (Loss) per Books With Income per Return**

Note: The corporation may be required to file Schedule M-3 (see instructions).

1	Net income (loss) per books	24,554	7	Income recorded on books this year not included on this return (itemize): Tax-exempt interest $ 1,650	1,650
2	Federal income tax per books	4,333			
3	Excess of capital losses over capital gains				
4	Income subject to tax not recorded on books this year (itemize):		8	Deductions on this return not charged against book income this year (itemize):	
5	Expenses recorded on books this year not deducted on this return (itemize):		a	Depreciation $	
a	Depreciation $		b	Charitable contributions $	
b	Charitable contributions $ 1,956			DPA deduction, $2,627	2,627
c	Travel and entertainment $	1,956	9	Add lines 7 and 8	4,277
6	Add lines 1 through 5	30,843	10	Income (page 1, line 28)—line 6 less line 9	26,566

Schedule M-2 **Analysis of Unappropriated Retained Earnings per Books (Line 25, Schedule L)**

1	Balance at beginning of year	44,708	5	Distributions: a Cash	16,446
2	Net income (loss) per books	24,554		b Stock	
3	Other increases (itemize):			c Property	
			6	Other decreases (itemize):	
			7	Add lines 5 and 6	16,446
4	Add lines 1, 2, and 3	69,262	8	Balance at end of year (line 4 less line 7)	52,816

Form **1120** (2015)

Form 1120 Schedules M-1 and M-2

Corporations with total receipts during the year and total assets at the end of the year of $250,000 or more must complete Schedules L, M-1 and M-2. (Total receipts are the sum of line 1c plus lines 4 through 10 on page 1, Form 1120.) The changes to retained earnings during the year are explained in Schedule M-2. On Schedule M-1, net income (loss) per books is reconciled with the amount reported on Form 1120, line 28 (taxable income before any NOL or DRD). For Globe Manufacturing in Figure 14-2, differences between book net income and taxable income before NOL and DRD include:

- The deduction for federal income taxes (deducted on the income statement, but not deductible in computing taxable income)
- Charitable contributions limited on the tax return by 10% of taxable income
- Tax-exempt interest (included on the income statement, but not taxable)
- Domestic production activities deduction (deductible on the tax return, but not a deduction reported on the income statement)

However, other differences may exist. For example, differences between net income and taxable income that may be reported on Schedule M-1 may result from:

- Differences in methods used to compute depreciation expense
- Amounts spent on travel, meals and entertainment that are not deductible on the tax return (for example, 50% of meals and entertainment)
- Differences in methods used to compute bad debt expense
- Charitable contributions carried over from a prior tax year that are deducted on the tax return in the current year

¶1404 Credits, Special Taxes, and Prepayments

¶1404.01 TAX CREDITS

Like individuals, corporations may offset their tax liabilities with available tax credits. Most of the credits available to corporations are also available to other businesses (see ¶1203). However, corporations cannot use the personal tax credits available to individuals, such as the earned income credit, child tax credit, or child and dependent care credit.

¶1404.02 SPECIAL TAXES

Besides the regular income tax, corporations may be subject to the accumulated earnings tax, the personal holding company tax, and the alternative minimum tax (AMT). The first two taxes are penalty taxes on undistributed earnings. The AMT, on the other hand, is an alternative method of computing taxable income and income taxes. Careful tax planning can eliminate the need to pay these additional taxes. Discussion of these taxes is beyond the scope of this textbook.

¶1404.03 ESTIMATED TAX PAYMENTS

Corporations that expect their tax liability (after tax credits) to be $500 or more must make estimated tax payments. These payments are due in equal quarterly installments by the 15th day of the fourth, sixth, ninth, and twelfth months of the corporation's tax year. If the due date falls on a weekend or a legal holiday, the payment is due the next business day. For corporations using the calendar year, the payment due dates are April 15, June 15, September 15, and December 15.

Penalty for Underpayment of Estimated Tax: Small Corporations

Failure to pay the minimum amount due at each installment date results in an underpayment penalty. The IRS considers the estimated tax underpaid if a quarterly payment is less than 25% of the minimum amount due for the year. For small corporations, this amount is 25% of the *lesser of* (i) 100% of the total tax liability (after tax credits) shown on the current year's return or (ii) 100% of the total tax liability (after tax credits) for the preceding year. A small corporation is a corporation whose taxable income before any NOL or capital loss carryback is less than $1 million for each of the last three tax years.

Estimated Payment Requirements: Large Corporations

For large corporations, the minimum amount due each quarter is 25% of the current year's total tax liability (after tax credits). Large corporations cannot avoid underpayment penalties by making their estimated payments based on last year's taxes. A large corporation has a taxable income before any NOL or capital loss carrybacks of $1 million or more in any of its last three preceding tax years.

¶1405 Corporate Distributions

Shareholders receiving corporate distributions may have taxable dividends, tax-free returns of capital, or capital gain. A distribution may be subject to all three treatments. Determining the nature of a distribution takes place at the corporate level. However, the final taxability of a distribution may depend on shareholder circumstances.

¶1405.01 TAXABLE DIVIDENDS

Unless affected parties provide contrary evidence, corporate distributions receive ordinary dividend treatment. Shareholders include in gross income the full amount of any ordinary dividends received. When the distribution involves property, the property's FMV at the distribution date determines the amount of the dividend received. Technically, dividends receive ordinary income treatment only if the company has earnings and profits to cover the distribution amount. Shareholders treat distributions in excess of E&P as a tax-free recovery of their basis in the stock (see ¶1401.01 for discussion of how a shareholder's basis is determined). After shareholders recover their basis, any additional distribution is taxed as capital gain.

EXAMPLE 25

PDQ had $90,000 of E&P at the end of the current year. On the last day of the year, PDQ distributed $120,000 to its three shareholders Xandra, Yang, and Zack ($40,000 to each shareholder). It was PDQ's only distribution for the year. Immediately before the distribution, the shareholders had the following basis in their stock: Xandra—$0, Yang—$8,000, and Zack—$60,000. The tax consequences of the distribution are as follows:

	Xandra	Yang	Zack
Amount of the distribution	$40,000	$40,000	$40,000
From E&P (dividend income)	(30,000)	(30,000)	(30,000)
Not from E&P	$10,000	$10,000	$10,000
Return of capital (basis reduced)	(0)	(8,000)	(10,000)
Capital gain	$10,000	$2,000	$0

As this summary shows, each shareholder recognizes $30,000 of dividend income. In addition, Xandra and Yang recognize capital gain ($10,000 and $2,000, respectively). After the distribution, Xandra and Yang each have a $0 stock basis. Zack's basis in the stock is $50,000 ($60,000 – $10,000 return of capital).

¶1405.02 EARNINGS AND PROFITS

The Code does not specifically define earnings and profits (E&P). Consequently, many people compare E&P with retained earnings. While similarities exist, there are numerous differences, which causes much confusion. Corporate directors may think they can distribute cash or other property tax free when the corporation has zero retained earnings. However, this would be wrong.

If the corporation has E&P, some portion of the distribution will be a dividend. Basically, transactions that increase a corporation's ability to pay a dividend increase E&P. Transactions that decrease a corporation's ability to pay a dividend decrease E&P. Consider the following examples. When a corporation receives tax-exempt interest, the interest is not taxed. However, E&P is increased by the interest received because the interest can serve as a source for dividend distributions. In contrast, the deduction for charitable contributions is limited to 10% of taxable income. When the actual contribution exceeds this limitation, E&P is decreased by the full contribution because the company has reduced its ability to pay a dividend by the full amount given to the charity. Also, while there is no definition of E&P, the law may require the use of certain accounting methods in some situations. For example, there are various acceptable methods by which to calculate depreciation expense for the tax return. However, the Alternative Depreciation System (¶802.04, ¶803.02) is required to calculate depreciation expense for purposes of E&P.

¶1405.03 DISTRIBUTIONS OF PROPERTY

Corporate distributions may involve either cash or property. For distributions of property, FMV determines the amount of the distribution. Corporations recognize a gain when they distribute appreciated property. E&P increases as a result of the gain, and E&P decreases by the FMV of the property distributed. Corporations do not recognize a loss when they distribute property where the FMV is less than its basis. The basis of the property shareholders receive is its FMV.

EXAMPLE 26 CQ corporation distributes appreciated land to its sole shareholder. The FMV of the land was $50,000. CQ's basis in the land was $10,000. Prior to the distribution, CQ's E&P was $100,000. CQ recognizes $40,000 gain on the distribution ($50,000 FMV – $10,000 basis). The gain increases CQ's E&P to $140,000 ($100,000 + $40,000). Thus, the entire $50,000 distribution is treated as a dividend (coming from E&P). After the distribution, CQ's E&P is $90,000 ($140,000 – $50,000).

EXAMPLE 27 At the end of the year, TLC distributes land (FMV of $10,000) with an adjusted basis of $4,000 to its only shareholder. TLC had no E&P before the distribution. As a result of the distribution, TLC reports gain of $6,000 ($10,000 – $4,000). This causes TLC's E&P to increase to $6,000 ($0 + $6,000). The shareholder receives a distribution equal to the FMV of the land. However, only $6,000 is a dividend (amount of E&P). The remaining portion of the distribution ($4,000) is a return of capital or capital gain, depending on the shareholder's basis in the stock. TLC's E&P is reduced to $0 after the distribution.

EXAMPLE 28 Same facts as in Example 27, except that the adjusted basis of the property is $24,000. As a result of the distribution, TLC reports no gain or loss. The shareholder still receives a distribution equal to the FMV of the land ($10,000). However, with no E&P, the entire $10,000 distribution is a return of capital or capital gain, depending on the shareholder's basis in the stock.

i As you can see from Example 28, C corporations should avoid distributing property where the FMV is less than the corporation's adjusted basis in the property.

14

Name:

Section:

Date:

QUESTIONS AND PROBLEMS

1. **Corporate Tax Status.** (Obj. 1) How do the tax laws determine whether a business should be taxed as a C corporation?

2. **Forming a Corporation.** (Obj. 1) Betty forms a corporation by transferring land worth $100,000 for 100% of the stock in the corporation. Betty paid $30,000 for the land.

   a. How much gain or loss do Betty and the corporation recognize on the transfer?

   b. What is Betty's basis in her shares of stock in the corporation?

   c. What is the corporation's basis in the land?

3. **Forming a Corporation.** (Obj. 1) Daniel forms a corporation by transferring land worth $50,000 for 100% of the stock in the corporation. Daniel paid $60,000 for the land.

   a. How much gain or loss do Daniel and the corporation recognize on the transfer?

   b. What is Daniel's basis in his shares of stock in the corporation?

   c. What is the corporation's basis in the land?

4. **Shareholder's Basis.** (Obj. 1) Jeannie is not currently a shareholder in ABC corporation. Jeannie contributes $20,000 cash and equipment worth $30,000 in exchange for 25% of the stock in ABC. Jeannie's basis in the equipment is $7,000. No other transfers were made at this time.

   a. How much gain or loss do Jeannie and the corporation recognize on the transfer?

   b. What is Jeannie's basis in the stock?

   c. What is the corporation's basis in the equipment?

5. **Forming a Corporation and Shareholder's Basis.** (Obj. 1) Toby contributes $60,000 cash in exchange for stock in the corporation. Keith contributes land worth $70,000 (basis of $55,000) in exchange for $10,000 cash and $60,000 worth of stock in the corporation. After the transfer, Toby and Keith own 100% of the corporation.

   a. How much gain or loss do Toby, Keith, and the corporation recognize on the transfer?

   b. What is Toby's basis in the stock?

   c. What is Keith's basis in the stock?

   d. What is the corporation's basis in the land?

   e. How, if at all, would your answers to parts a. through d. change if Keith's basis in the land were $66,000 (instead of $55,000)?

   f. How, if at all, would your answers to parts a. through d. change if Keith's basis in the land were $81,000 (instead of $55,000)?

6. **Forming a Corporation.** (Obj. 1) Howard and Todd form a corporation. Howard contributes $25,000 cash in exchange for 1,000 shares of stock. Todd performs services worth $25,000 in exchange for 1,000 shares of stock.

   a. How much gain or loss do Howard, Todd, and the corporation recognize on the transfer?

   b. What is Howard's basis in his shares of stock in the corporation?

   c. What is Todd's basis in his shares of stock in the corporation?

7. **Corporation Taxable Income.** (Obj. 2)

   a. What is the difference in the tax treatment of corporate taxable income and business profits reported on Schedule C of a sole proprietor?

   b. Explain why corporations do not compute AGI.

8. **Accounting Periods.** (Obj. 2) What is a short year return and when would a corporation have one?

9. **Accounting Periods.** (Obj. 2)

   a. Explain the difference between a calendar year, a fiscal year, and a 52-53 week tax year. Why might a corporation want to use a 52-53 week tax year?

   b. If a corporation wants to change its tax year from October 31 to July 31, what must it do?

10. Corporate Capital Gains and Losses. (Obj. 2)

a. How does the tax treatment of net capital gain differ between individual and corporate taxpayers?

b. How does the tax treatment of net capital losses differ between individual and corporate taxpayers?

11. Corporation Taxable Income. (Obj. 2)

a. For the current year, Wish Corporation had ordinary income from operations of $80,000, a net long-term capital gain of $17,000, and a net short-term capital loss of $7,000. Compute Wish's taxable income for the year.

b. For the current year, BB Corporation had net income from operations of $65,000 and a net long-term capital loss of $9,000. It also had a net short-term capital gain of $7,000. Compute BB's taxable income for the year.

c. For the current year, before considering capital loss carryovers, Adam Corporation had a net long-term capital loss of $8,000 and a net short-term capital loss of $3,000. Its net capital loss carryover from last year was $2,000. How much is Adam's capital loss carryover to the next tax year, and what is its nature (long-term or short-term)?

12. Corporate Taxable Income. (Obj. 2) A corporation pays its Chief Executive Office (CEO) $2 million during the year. Discuss the tax implications of the CEO's salary both to the corporation and the CEO.

13. Bad Debts. (Obj. 2) A corporation properly uses the reserve method to deduct bad debts on the financial statements (as it is the only method allowed under Generally Accepted Accounting Principles). Does an accrual basis corporation use this method to deduct bad debts the corporate income tax return? Explain.

14. **Bad Debts.** (Obj. 2) HST uses the accrual method of reporting for income taxes. It is a retail hardware store. On average, 1% of its gross sales on account ($500,000 for the current year) become uncollectible. During the year, HST actually wrote off $4,700 of accounts receivable that were uncollectible. What is HST's deduction for bad debts on its tax return?

15. **Organizational Costs.** (Obj. 2) At formation, a corporation incurs the following costs: legal services to obtain a corporate charter, $1,000; state incorporation fees, $700; and costs related to issuing common stock, $3,000. How quickly will the corporation be allowed to deduct these costs?

16. **Organizational Costs.** (Obj. 2) In the process of incorporating a business, ABC corporation incurs organizational costs. ABC was incorporated on June 8, 2015. It officially began business on September 2, 2015. It uses a calendar year-end. The officers have asked that ABC take the maximum deduction as allowed under the tax law.

    a. How much can ABC deduct in 2015 if the total organizational costs are $45,000?

    b. How much can ABC deduct in 2015 if the total organizational costs are $52,000?

    c. How much can ABC deduct in 2015 if the total organizational costs are $75,000?

17. **Start-Up Costs.** (Obj. 2) DEF corporation uses a calendar year-end. DEF incurs start-up costs prior to the beginning of its business operations. DEF's business began on March 1, 2015.

    a. How much can DEF deduct in 2015 and 2016 if the total start-up costs are $35,000?

    b. How much can DEF deduct in 2015 and 2016 if the total start-up costs are $51,200?

    c. How much can DEF deduct in 2015 and 2016 if the total start-up costs are $85,000?

18. Charitable Contributions. (Obj. 2) How is the charitable contribution limitation for a C corporation computed and how are excess charitable contributions treated?

19. Charitable Contributions. (Obj. 2) Regal, Inc. reported the following for the year.

Gross income includable on the tax return	$115,000
Allowable business deductions, not including charitable contributions	90,000
Contributions to qualified charitable organizations	2,750
Dividends received from domestic corporations (30% ownership and included in the $115,000 gross income amount)	2,000

a. What is Regal's charitable contribution deduction for the current year?

b. What is the amount of taxable income for the current year?

c. What is Regal's charitable contribution deduction carryover, if any?

20. Charitable Contributions. (Obj. 2) A corporation has taxable income of $107,000 after all deductions except the charitable contribution deduction, dividends received deduction, domestic production activities deduction and loss carryforwards. The corporation contributed $30,000 to a qualified charity during the year. Compute the current year charitable contribution deduction and discuss what happens to any excess contribution.

21. Charitable Contributions. (Obj. 2) A calendar year corporation donates food inventory to a qualified charity that cares for the needy. The inventory is valued at $70,000; the corporation's basis in the inventory is $55,000. Compute the corporation's charitable contribution for this donation.

22. Charitable Contributions. (Obj. 2) An accrual basis corporation reports the following income and expenses for 2015. The corporation does not manufacture the merchandise that is sells, and therefore is not entitled to the domestic production activities deduction.

Gross sales and receipts	$700,000
Returns and allowances	12,000
Cost of goods sold	330,000
Interest received	20,000
Rent expense	55,000
Wage expense	140,000
Charitable contributions	12,000
Other operating expenses	75,000
Depreciation expense	15,000

a. Compute the corporation's taxable income for the 2015 tax year.

b. What is the amount of the corporation's charitable contribution carryover (if any)? To which tax years can the corporation carry over this excess?

23. Dividends Received Deduction. (Obj. 2) Treeline Industries receives a $50,000 dividend from a corporation in which it owns 35% of the stock. Treeline's revenues (not including the dividends) and operating expenses for the year are $400,000 and $375,000, respectively. Other than the dividends received deduction, these are the only items of revenue and expense.

a. Compute Treeline's taxable income.

b. How, if at all, would your answer to Part a. change if Treeline owned 10% of the stock in the corporation?

c. How, if at all, would your answer to Part a. change if Treeline's revenues were $370,000 (instead of $400,000), but it continued to own 35% of the corporation's stock?

24. Dividends Received Deduction. (Obj. 2) Express Corporation receives a $120,000 dividend from a corporation in which it owns 55% of the stock. Express's revenues (not including the dividends) and operating expenses for the year are $370,000 and $390,000, respectively. These are the only items of revenue and expense.

a. Compute Express's taxable income.

b. How, if at all, would your answer to Part a. change if Express owned 90% of the stock in the corporation?

25. Filing Deadlines. (Obj. 3) For each of the following corporations, determine the deadline for filing the corporate income tax return.

a. The original due date for a corporation with a calendar year-end.

b. The extended due date for a calendar year corporation that files Form 7004 prior to the original filing deadline.

c. The original due date for a corporation with a May 31 year-end.

d. The extended due date for corporation with a July 31 year-end that files Form 7004 prior to the original filing deadline.

e. The original due date for a corporation with an August 31 year-end.

f. The extended due date for a corporation with an October 31 year-end that files Form 7004 prior to the original filing deadline.

(Use for Problem 30.)

Form **1120** Department of the Treasury Internal Revenue Service

U.S. Corporation Income Tax Return

For calendar year 2015 or tax year beginning ________, 2015, ending ________, 20 ___

▶ Information about Form 1120 and its separate instructions is at *www.irs.gov/form1120.*

OMB No. 1545-0123 **2015**

A Check if:
1a Consolidated return (attach Form 851) ☐
b Life/nonlife consolidated return ☐
2 Personal holding co. (attach Sch. PH) ☐
3 Personal service corp. (see instructions) ☐
4 Schedule M-3 attached ☐

TYPE OR PRINT
Name
Number, street, and room or suite no. If a P.O. box, see instructions.
City or town, state, or province, country, and ZIP or foreign postal code

B Employer identification number
C Date incorporated
D Total assets (see instructions) $

E Check if: **(1)** ☐ Initial return **(2)** ☐ Final return **(3)** ☐ Name change **(4)** ☐ Address change

Income	1a	Gross receipts or sales	1a	
	b	Returns and allowances	1b	
	c	Balance. Subtract line 1b from line 1a	1c	
	2	Cost of goods sold (attach Form 1125-A)	2	
	3	Gross profit. Subtract line 2 from line 1c	3	
	4	Dividends (Schedule C, line 19)	4	
	5	Interest	5	
	6	Gross rents	6	
	7	Gross royalties	7	
	8	Capital gain net income (attach Schedule D (Form 1120))	8	
	9	Net gain or (loss) from Form 4797, Part II, line 17 (attach Form 4797)	9	
	10	Other income (see instructions—attach statement)	10	
	11	**Total income.** Add lines 3 through 10 ▶	11	
Deductions (See instructions for limitations on deductions.)	12	Compensation of officers (see instructions—attach Form 1125-E) ▶	12	
	13	Salaries and wages (less employment credits)	13	
	14	Repairs and maintenance	14	
	15	Bad debts	15	
	16	Rents	16	
	17	Taxes and licenses	17	
	18	Interest	18	
	19	Charitable contributions	19	
	20	Depreciation from Form 4562 not claimed on Form 1125-A or elsewhere on return (attach Form 4562)	20	
	21	Depletion	21	
	22	Advertising	22	
	23	Pension, profit-sharing, etc., plans	23	
	24	Employee benefit programs	24	
	25	Domestic production activities deduction (attach Form 8903)	25	
	26	Other deductions (attach statement)	26	
	27	**Total deductions.** Add lines 12 through 26 ▶	27	
	28	Taxable income before net operating loss deduction and special deductions. Subtract line 27 from line 11	28	
	29a	Net operating loss deduction (see instructions)	29a	
	b	Special deductions (Schedule C, line 20)	29b	
	c	Add lines 29a and 29b	29c	
Tax, Refundable Credits, and Payments	30	**Taxable income.** Subtract line 29c from line 28 (see instructions)	30	
	31	Total tax (Schedule J, Part I, line 11)	31	
	32	Total payments and refundable credits (Schedule J, Part II, line 21)	32	
	33	Estimated tax penalty (see instructions). Check if Form 2220 is attached ▶ ☐	33	
	34	**Amount owed.** If line 32 is smaller than the total of lines 31 and 33, enter amount owed	34	
	35	**Overpayment.** If line 32 is larger than the total of lines 31 and 33, enter amount overpaid	35	
	36	Enter amount from line 35 you want: **Credited to 2016 estimated tax ▶** **Refunded ▶**	36	

Sign Here
Under penalties of perjury, I declare that I have examined this return, including accompanying schedules and statements, and to the best of my knowledge and belief, it is true, correct, and complete. Declaration of preparer (other than taxpayer) is based on all information of which preparer has any knowledge.

▶ Signature of officer | Date | ▶ Title

May the IRS discuss this return with the preparer shown below (see instructions)? ☐ **Yes** ☐ **No**

Paid Preparer Use Only

Print/Type preparer's name	Preparer's signature	Date	Check ☐ if self-employed	PTIN
Firm's name ▶			Firm's EIN ▶	
Firm's address ▶			Phone no.	

For Paperwork Reduction Act Notice, see separate instructions. Cat. No. 11450Q Form **1120** (2015)

(Use for Problem 30.)

Form 1120 (2015) Page 2

Schedule C **Dividends and Special Deductions** (see instructions)

		(a) Dividends received	(b) %	(c) Special deductions (a) × (b)
1	Dividends from less-than-20%-owned domestic corporations (other than debt-financed stock)		70	
2	Dividends from 20%-or-more-owned domestic corporations (other than debt-financed stock)		80	
3	Dividends on debt-financed stock of domestic and foreign corporations		see instructions	
4	Dividends on certain preferred stock of less-than-20%-owned public utilities		42	
5	Dividends on certain preferred stock of 20%-or-more-owned public utilities		48	
6	Dividends from less-than-20%-owned foreign corporations and certain FSCs		70	
7	Dividends from 20%-or-more-owned foreign corporations and certain FSCs		80	
8	Dividends from wholly owned foreign subsidiaries		100	
9	**Total.** Add lines 1 through 8. See instructions for limitation			
10	Dividends from domestic corporations received by a small business investment company operating under the Small Business Investment Act of 1958		100	
11	Dividends from affiliated group members		100	
12	Dividends from certain FSCs		100	
13	Dividends from foreign corporations not included on lines 3, 6, 7, 8, 11, or 12			
14	Income from controlled foreign corporations under subpart F (attach Form(s) 5471)			
15	Foreign dividend gross-up			
16	IC-DISC and former DISC dividends not included on lines 1, 2, or 3			
17	Other dividends			
18	Deduction for dividends paid on certain preferred stock of public utilities			
19	**Total dividends.** Add lines 1 through 17. Enter here and on page 1, line 4 ▶			
20	**Total special deductions.** Add lines 9, 10, 11, 12, and 18. Enter here and on page 1, line 29b ▶			

Form **1120** (2015)

(Use for Problem 30.)

Form 1120 (2015) Page 3

Schedule J **Tax Computation and Payment** (see instructions)

Part I–Tax Computation

1	Check if the corporation is a member of a controlled group (attach Schedule O (Form 1120)) ▶ ☐				
2	Income tax. Check if a qualified personal service corporation (see instructions) ▶ ☐			2	
3	Alternative minimum tax (attach Form 4626)			3	
4	Add lines 2 and 3			4	
5a	Foreign tax credit (attach Form 1118)	5a			
b	Credit from Form 8834 (see instructions)	5b			
c	General business credit (attach Form 3800)	5c			
d	Credit for prior year minimum tax (attach Form 8827)	5d			
e	Bond credits from Form 8912	5e			
6	**Total credits.** Add lines 5a through 5e			6	
7	Subtract line 6 from line 4			7	
8	Personal holding company tax (attach Schedule PH (Form 1120))			8	
9a	Recapture of investment credit (attach Form 4255)	9a			
b	Recapture of low-income housing credit (attach Form 8611)	9b			
c	Interest due under the look-back method—completed long-term contracts (attach Form 8697)	9c			
d	Interest due under the look-back method—income forecast method (attach Form 8866)	9d			
e	Alternative tax on qualifying shipping activities (attach Form 8902)	9e			
f	Other (see instructions—attach statement)	9f			
10	**Total.** Add lines 9a through 9f			10	
11	**Total tax.** Add lines 7, 8, and 10. Enter here and on page 1, line 31			11	

Part II–Payments and Refundable Credits

12	2014 overpayment credited to 2015			12	
13	2015 estimated tax payments			13	
14	2015 refund applied for on Form 4466			14	( )
15	Combine lines 12, 13, and 14			15	
16	Tax deposited with Form 7004			16	
17	Withholding (see instructions)			17	
18	**Total payments.** Add lines 15, 16, and 17			18	
19	Refundable credits from:				
a	Form 2439	19a			
b	Form 4136	19b			
c	Form 8827, line 8c	19c			
d	Other (attach statement—see instructions)	19d			
20	**Total credits.** Add lines 19a through 19d			20	
21	**Total payments and credits.** Add lines 18 and 20. Enter here and on page 1, line 32			21	

Schedule K **Other Information** (see instructions)

		Yes	No
1	Check accounting method: a ☐ Cash b ☐ Accrual c ☐ Other (specify) ▶		
2	See the instructions and enter the:		
a	Business activity code no. ▶		
b	Business activity ▶		
c	Product or service ▶		
3	Is the corporation a subsidiary in an affiliated group or a parent-subsidiary controlled group? If "Yes," enter name and EIN of the parent corporation ▶		
4	At the end of the tax year:		
a	Did any foreign or domestic corporation, partnership (including any entity treated as a partnership), trust, or tax-exempt organization own directly 20% or more, or own, directly or indirectly, 50% or more of the total voting power of all classes of the corporation's stock entitled to vote? If "Yes," complete Part I of Schedule G (Form 1120) (attach Schedule G)		
b	Did any individual or estate own directly 20% or more, or own, directly or indirectly, 50% or more of the total voting power of all classes of the corporation's stock entitled to vote? If "Yes," complete Part II of Schedule G (Form 1120) (attach Schedule G)		

Form **1120** (2015)

(Use for Problem 30.)

Form 1120 (2015) Page **4**

Schedule K **Other Information** *continued* (see instructions)

		Yes	No
5	At the end of the tax year, did the corporation:		
a	Own directly 20% or more, or own, directly or indirectly, 50% or more of the total voting power of all classes of stock entitled to vote of any foreign or domestic corporation not included on **Form 851,** Affiliations Schedule? For rules of constructive ownership, see instructions. If "Yes," complete (i) through (iv) below.		

(i) Name of Corporation	**(ii)** Employer Identification Number (if any)	**(iii)** Country of Incorporation	**(iv)** Percentage Owned in Voting Stock

		Yes	No
b	Own directly an interest of 20% or more, or own, directly or indirectly, an interest of 50% or more in any foreign or domestic partnership (including an entity treated as a partnership) or in the beneficial interest of a trust? For rules of constructive ownership, see instructions. If "Yes," complete (i) through (iv) below.		

(i) Name of Entity	**(ii)** Employer Identification Number (if any)	**(iii)** Country of Organization	**(iv)** Maximum Percentage Owned in Profit, Loss, or Capital

		Yes	No
6	During this tax year, did the corporation pay dividends (other than stock dividends and distributions in exchange for stock) in excess of the corporation's current and accumulated earnings and profits? (See sections 301 and 316.)		
	If "Yes," file **Form 5452,** Corporate Report of Nondividend Distributions. If this is a consolidated return, answer here for the parent corporation and on Form 851 for each subsidiary.		
7	At any time during the tax year, did one foreign person own, directly or indirectly, at least 25% of **(a)** the total voting power of all classes of the corporation's stock entitled to vote or **(b)** the total value of all classes of the corporation's stock?		
	For rules of attribution, see section 318. If "Yes," enter: **(i)** Percentage owned ▶ ________ and **(ii)** Owner's country ▶ ________		
	(c) The corporation may have to file **Form 5472,** Information Return of a 25% Foreign-Owned U.S. Corporation or a Foreign Corporation Engaged in a U.S. Trade or Business. Enter the number of Forms 5472 attached ▶ ________		
8	Check this box if the corporation issued publicly offered debt instruments with original issue discount . . . . ▶ ☐		
	If checked, the corporation may have to file **Form 8281,** Information Return for Publicly Offered Original Issue Discount Instruments.		
9	Enter the amount of tax-exempt interest received or accrued during the tax year ▶ $ ________		
10	Enter the number of shareholders at the end of the tax year (if 100 or fewer) ▶ ________		
11	If the corporation has an NOL for the tax year and is electing to forego the carryback period, check here . . . . . . ▶ ☐		
	If the corporation is filing a consolidated return, the statement required by Regulations section 1.1502-21(b)(3) must be attached or the election will not be valid.		
12	Enter the available NOL carryover from prior tax years (do not reduce it by any deduction on line 29a.) ▶ $ ________		
13	Are the corporation's total receipts (page 1, line 1a, plus lines 4 through 10) for the tax year **and** its total assets at the end of the tax year less than $250,000?		
	If "Yes," the corporation is not required to complete Schedules L, M-1, and M-2. Instead, enter the total amount of cash distributions and the book value of property distributions (other than cash) made during the tax year ▶ $ ________		
14	Is the corporation required to file Schedule UTP (Form 1120), Uncertain Tax Position Statement (see instructions)?		
	If "Yes," complete and attach Schedule UTP.		
15a	Did the corporation make any payments in 2015 that would require it to file Form(s) 1099?		
b	If "Yes," did or will the corporation file required Forms 1099?		
16	During this tax year, did the corporation have an 80% or more change in ownership, including a change due to redemption of its own stock?		
17	During or subsequent to this tax year, but before the filing of this return, did the corporation dispose of more than 65% (by value) of its assets in a taxable, non-taxable, or tax deferred transaction?		
18	Did the corporation receive assets in a section 351 transfer in which any of the transferred assets had a fair market basis or fair market value of more than $1 million?		

Form **1120** (2015)

(Use for Problem 30.)

Form 1120 (2015) Page **5**

Schedule L **Balance Sheets per Books**

	Assets	Beginning of tax year (a)	(b)	End of tax year (c)	(d)
1	Cash				
2a	Trade notes and accounts receivable				
b	Less allowance for bad debts	( )		( )	
3	Inventories				
4	U.S. government obligations				
5	Tax-exempt securities (see instructions)				
6	Other current assets (attach statement)				
7	Loans to shareholders				
8	Mortgage and real estate loans				
9	Other investments (attach statement)				
10a	Buildings and other depreciable assets				
b	Less accumulated depreciation	( )		( )	
11a	Depletable assets				
b	Less accumulated depletion	( )		( )	
12	Land (net of any amortization)				
13a	Intangible assets (amortizable only)				
b	Less accumulated amortization	( )		( )	
14	Other assets (attach statement)				
15	Total assets				
	Liabilities and Shareholders' Equity				
16	Accounts payable				
17	Mortgages, notes, bonds payable in less than 1 year				
18	Other current liabilities (attach statement)				
19	Loans from shareholders				
20	Mortgages, notes, bonds payable in 1 year or more				
21	Other liabilities (attach statement)				
22	Capital stock: **a** Preferred stock				
	b Common stock				
23	Additional paid-in capital				
24	Retained earnings—Appropriated (attach statement)				
25	Retained earnings—Unappropriated				
26	Adjustments to shareholders' equity (attach statement)				
27	Less cost of treasury stock		( )		( )
28	Total liabilities and shareholders' equity				

Schedule M-1 **Reconciliation of Income (Loss) per Books With Income per Return**

Note: The corporation may be required to file Schedule M-3 (see instructions).

1	Net income (loss) per books		7	Income recorded on books this year not included on this return (itemize):	
2	Federal income tax per books			Tax-exempt interest $	
3	Excess of capital losses over capital gains				
4	Income subject to tax not recorded on books this year (itemize):				
5	Expenses recorded on books this year not deducted on this return (itemize):		8	Deductions on this return not charged against book income this year (itemize):	
a	Depreciation $		a	Depreciation $	
b	Charitable contributions $		b	Charitable contributions $	
c	Travel and entertainment $				
			9	Add lines 7 and 8	
6	Add lines 1 through 5		10	Income (page 1, line 28)—line 6 less line 9	

Schedule M-2 **Analysis of Unappropriated Retained Earnings per Books (Line 25, Schedule L)**

1	Balance at beginning of year		5	Distributions: **a** Cash	
2	Net income (loss) per books			**b** Stock	
3	Other increases (itemize):			**c** Property	
			6	Other decreases (itemize):	
			7	Add lines 5 and 6	
4	Add lines 1, 2, and 3		8	Balance at end of year (line 4 less line 7)	

Form **1120** (2015)

Chapter

15

Partnerships

CHAPTER CONTENTS

LEARNING OBJECTIVES

After completing Chapter 15, you should be able to:

1. Understand the tax characteristics of partnerships, including the selection of a year-end and how they are formed (along with the tax consequences).
2. Distinguish between ordinary income and separately stated items, explain the need for separately stated items, and compute ordinary income.
3. Compute a partner's distributive share of partnership items, including how partners treat payments made to them from the partnership for services rendered.
4. Compute a partner's basis and understand its impact on the partner's ability to deduct losses and its impact on how distributions are treated.
5. Prepare the tax forms introduced in this chapter, including Form 1065 and Schedule K-1 (Form 1065).

CHAPTER OVERVIEW

Partnerships and S corporations are separate legal entities. However, neither is responsible for the income taxes on the business's profits. Instead, the results of all of the business's activities belong to the owners, who report their respective shares of the business activities on their own income tax returns. This results in only one level of tax being levied on the entity's profits. Partnerships and S corporations file informational tax returns at the end of each tax year. These returns tell the IRS the total income, deductions, gains, losses and credits generated by the business during the year. These returns also tell the IRS and each owner the share of each item that belongs to each of the owners. For this reason, partnerships and S corporations are often called flow-through entities.

This chapter focuses on partnership taxation. It looks at the tax aspects from the standpoint of the partnership and its partners. S corporations are the focus of Chapter 16.

¶1501 The Nature of Partnerships

A partnership is an association of two or more persons (or other entities) that conducts business with an intent to share profits or losses. A partnership does not include a joint undertaking merely to share expenses. Thus, if two neighbors dig a ditch merely to drain surface water from their respective properties, they do not create a partnership. However, if they actively carry on a business and divide the profits, they have created a partnership and become partners.

Each person contributing property or services to the partnership receives an ownership interest. Each person then becomes a partner. Partners can be individuals, corporations, estates, other partnerships, or trusts.

A partner's interest in a partnership can be a profits-only interest or a capital and profits interest. The distinction lies in whether the partner will share in the partnership assets should the partnership go out of business. When a partner contributes property or services to the partnership in exchange for the right to share future profits and losses and to receive assets from the partnership should the entity go out of business, the partner is said to acquire a **capital and profits interest** in the partnership. If, on the other hand, the partner renders services to the partnership in exchange solely for the right to share in future profits and losses of the partnership, the partner's interest is a **profits-only interest**.

Partnerships can be formed as either general or limited partnerships. In a general partnership, all of the partners are general partners. A **general partner** is fully liable for the debts and actions of the partnership. A limited partnership has limited partner(s) and at least one general partner. A **limited partner** is liable for the debts and actions of the partnership only to the extent of the partner's basis in the partnership interest plus any amounts the partnership owes the limited partner.

¶1502 Partnership Tax Returns

In a partnership, the partners, not the partnership, are responsible for the income taxes on the partnership's profits. All items of partnership income and loss pass through to the partners, where they appear on the partners' own tax returns. Partners must pay taxes on their respective shares of partnership income regardless of whether they receive distributions from the partnership.

Every partnership doing business within the United States files the informational return Form 1065, U.S. Return of Partnership Income. The return reports the partnership's revenues and expenses. It also provides each partner's share of all partnership items. The return is due by the 15th day of the fourth month after the end of the partnership's tax year. For a calendar year partnership, the due date is April 15. A partnership may receive an automatic five-month extension for filing its return by submitting Form 7004, Application for Automatic Extension of Time To File Certain Business Income Tax, Information, and Other Returns. This form must be filed by the due date for the original return. The Internal Revenue Code (Code) imposes a penalty on the partnership (not the partners) when it fails to file Form 1065 in a timely manner. For each month that the failure continues (not to exceed 12 months), the penalty equals $195 times the number of persons who were partners at any time during the year.

Form 1065 consists of five pages. Page 1 provides general information about the partnership and shows the calculation of ordinary income. Schedule B appears on pages 2 and 3. It is here that other information about the partnership is provided. Schedule K is found on page 4. All items that must be separately stated are listed on Schedule K. Finally, page 5 contains the book balance sheet (Schedule L), reconciliation of book and tax income (Schedule M-1) and an analysis of the partners' capital account (Schedule M-2).

A Schedule K-1 (Form 1065) is completed for each person who was a partner at any time during the year. All Schedules K-1 are attached to and filed with Form 1065, and the partnership furnishes the partners with a copy of their respective Schedule K-1. Failure to furnish a timely Schedule K-1 to a partner results in a $100 penalty for each failure. Thus, if a partnership with 150 partners fails to timely furnish Schedules K-1 to its partners, the partnership will be assessed a $15,000 penalty ($100 penalty × 150 partners). If the failure to furnish this information is found to be intentional, the $100 penalty increases to $250.

A partnership does not need to be taxed as a flow through entity. Instead, it can choose to be taxed as a corporation. This is done by having the business "check the box" to be taxed as a corporation on its first income tax return (see discussion at ¶1401). When this election is made, the rules discussed in Chapter 14 apply to both the business and its owners.

¶1502.01 YEAR TO REPORT PARTNERSHIP INCOME

Partners are taxed on their shares of partnership items in their tax year that includes the last day of the partnership's tax year. Partners include these partnership items on their tax returns in that year.

EXAMPLE 1 Amber uses a calendar tax year. Amber is a partner in ABC partnership that uses a January 31 fiscal tax year. Amber reports her share of partnership items for the fiscal year February 1, 20x1 – January 31, 20x2 on her 20x2 tax return (Amber's tax year that includes January 31, 20x2). Because of this rule, the income ABC earns for the 11 months from February 1, 20x1 – December 31, 20x1 is not taxed until Amber files her 20x2 tax return. This is known as an 11-month deferral.

¶1502.02 REQUIRED TAX YEAR

To prevent partners from deferring partnership income into the next year (like Amber did for 11 months in Example 1), Congress passed rules to limit a partnership's choice of tax years it can use. The partnership must select the same tax year as the majority of its partners. Majority partners own, in total, more than 50% of capital and profits. Because most individual partners use a calendar year, most partnerships also use the calendar year. However, if there is not a majority of partners with the same tax year, the partnership must select the same tax year as all of its principal partners. A principal partner is a partner that owns at least 5% of capital or profits. Partnerships unable to determine a tax year using these rules must adopt a tax year that results in the least aggregate deferral of income. The method used to determine the tax year with the least aggregate deferral of income is complex, and beyond the scope of this discussion.

EXAMPLE 2 Partners A and B contribute property to form AB partnership in exchange for a 70% and 30% interest in capital and profits, respectively. Partner A uses a June 30 year-end; Partner B uses the calendar year-end. Since Partner A is a majority partner, AB's required tax year is a June 30 fiscal year.

EXAMPLE 3 ABC partnership is formed when partners A, B and C contribute property in exchange for a 40%, 30%, and 30% interest in capital and profits, respectively. Partner A uses a June 30 year-end. Partners B and C use a calendar year-end. Since Partners B and C together own a majority interest in the partnership, ABC's required tax year is the calendar year.

EXAMPLE 4 Same facts as in Example 3, except that Partner C's year-end is October 31. In this example, no group of partners owns a majority interest in the partnership. Also, the principal partners (A, B, and C) do not all have the same year-end. Thus, ABC's required tax year must be determined using the least aggregate deferral of income method.

EXAMPLE 5

D and E each own 25% of DE partnership. The remaining 50% is owned by 20 other partners, each of whom has less than a 5% partnership interest. D and E both have a June 30 year-end. The other 20 partners all use a calendar year-end. Since no group of partners having the same year-end owns more than a 50% interest in capital and profits, the partnership's required tax year is not determined by the majority interest rule. However, D and E are the only principal partners, and since all principal partners share the same tax year, DE's required tax year is June 30.

Exceptions to the Required Tax Year Rule

Two exceptions allow a partnership to use a tax year other than its required tax year. The first permits a partnership to select a tax year based on the partnership's natural business year. A natural business year is one in which at least 25% of gross receipts are received in the last two months of a 12-month period for three consecutive years. Thus, the natural business year exception may be adopted only by partnerships that have been in existence for at least three years. The second exception allows partnerships to select a tax year that provides no more than a three-month deferral for its partners. Thus, a partnership with a calendar year as its required tax year could select a tax year ending the last day of September, October, or November. The partnership makes the election by filing Form 8716, Election To Have a Tax Year Other Than a Required Tax Year. This election requires partnerships to make tax deposits approximating the amount of tax deferral due to the difference in the partnership and the partners' tax years. These tax deposits eliminate any tax benefits the partners get by being able to defer reporting the income from the partnership. Treasury Regulations provide details regarding the computation of the required tax deposits.

EXAMPLE 6

Continuing with Example 5, DE's required tax year is June 30. The partnership can elect to use a March 31, April 30 or May 31 year-end as long as it agrees to make tax deposits equal to the estimated taxes the partners would owe on the profits generated during the deferral months.

Change in Tax Year

A partnership wanting to change its tax year must first get permission from the IRS. Partnerships make the request on Form 1128, Application to Adopt, Change, or Retain a Tax Year. A partnership receiving permission to change its tax year files a short-year tax return in the year of change. This return covers the period from its prior year-end to its new year-end.

EXAMPLE 7

A change from a fiscal year ending March 31 to the calendar year ending December 31 requires a short-year return. The short-year return covers the nine-month period of April 1 to December 31.

Changes in partnership membership or in the relative interests among the partners can terminate the partnership. Normally, the following events will not terminate the partnership tax year: death of a partner, addition of a partner, or a shift of a partial interest in the firm among partners. In these situations, the partnership tax year closes with respect to a partner whose entire partnership interest terminates, but it does not close the tax year for the other partners.

However, when the cumulative effect of any events during a 12-month period causes at least a 50% change in ownership, the partnership tax year does close. The partnership tax year also closes when the partnership ceases to carry on any business. When a partnership tax year closes, all of the partners must recognize their shares of income/loss items at the time of closing.

¶1502.03 REPORTING PARTNERSHIP INCOME AND DEDUCTIONS

A partnership is not a taxable entity. A partnership *passes through* income and expenses to each of its partners. This pass-through treatment is an application of the **conduit principle**. Many partnership income and expense items receive special tax treatment on the partners' own tax returns. For example, net capital gain is taxed differently to individual and corporate taxpayers (compare discussions at ¶1101.03 and ¶1402.04). Also, different limitations on charitable contributions apply to these two types of taxpayers (compare discussions at ¶506.04 and ¶1402.06). Accordingly, the partnership must report these types of items separately on its tax return. Any items that do not require separate reporting are passed through to the partners as ordinary income or loss from partnership operations.

¶1502.04 SEPARATELY STATED ITEMS

Form 1065, Schedule K, is where separately stated items are listed. Each partner receives a Schedule K-1 (Form 1065), which shows that partner's share of ordinary income and each separately stated item. The following sections present the more common separately stated items.

Examples of Separately Stated Items

- Rental income
- Interest income from investments
- Dividend income
- Royalty income
- Net short-term capital gains and losses
- Net long-term capital gains and losses
- Other investment income
- Net Section 1231 gains and losses
- Charitable contributions
- Section 179 deductions
- Investment expenses
- Credits and recaptures of the credits
- Guaranteed payments*
- AMT adjustments and preferences
- Foreign taxes
- Tax-exempt income
- Nondeductible expenses
- Personal expenses paid for the partners

*Deducted in total in computing ordinary income but separately stated for each partner (see ¶1502.05)

Income Items

Rental income, interest, dividends, royalties, and gains (losses) from the sale of capital assets or business properties (Section 1231 assets) are separately stated on Schedules K and K-1. The partnership files Form 4797 to report and summarize any gains (losses) from the sale of business properties. Schedule D (Form 1065) supports the calculation of the partnership's long-term or short-term capital gains and losses. Partners add each separately stated item reported on their Schedule K-1 to other similar items they have personally. For example, an individual partner's share of partnership capital gains and losses is reported on the partner's own Schedule D (Form 1040). Similarly, partners report their shares of gains and losses from the sale of partnership business properties with their other business gains and losses on their own Form 4797.

Even though state and local (municipal) bond interest is exempt from federal income taxes, it may be subject to state income tax. Also, individuals must report tax-exempt interest on their tax returns. For these reasons, tax-exempt interest is reported on Schedules K and K-1 as a separately stated item.

Deduction Items

Relatively few deductions are separately stated on Schedules K and K-1. The partnership deducts most expenses in the calculation of ordinary income (¶1502.05). Three more common separately stated deductions include Section 179 expense, deductions related to portfolio (investment) income, and charitable contributions.

You may recall from Chapter 8 that Section 179 allows the immediate expensing of certain property purchased in the current year. The partnership decides whether or not to take the Section 179 deduction. The dollar amount and placed in service limits (¶802.05) apply at both the partnership level and again at the partner level. The partners add their distributive shares of this deduction to the amounts they have from other businesses in determining their own Section 179 deduction amount.

Individual taxpayers deduct investment interest expense to the extent of their net investment income (¶505.04). In addition, higher-income taxpayers may be subject to a 3.8% net investment income (NII) tax (¶315). Net investment income equals taxable investment income less deductible investment expenses. Individual taxpayers deduct investment expenses as itemized deductions (¶603). Thus, any partnership item affecting the calculation of NII must be separately stated.

Charitable contributions are not business expenses for individual taxpayers. Therefore, the partnership does not claim them as a deduction in computing ordinary income. Instead, the partnership lists the total amount of charitable contributions on Schedule K. Individual partners add their shares of each contribution to their personal contributions and show the total as an itemized deduction on Schedule A (¶506).

Net Operating Losses (NOLs)

A net operating loss (NOL) generally equals the excess of allowable deductions over taxable gross income in any tax year. A NOL from a trade or business may be carried back to the two preceding tax years and then forward to the next 20 years (¶1201). A partnership, however, does not carry over its losses to other partnership tax years. Instead, the partners report their shares of the partnership's losses on their own returns as deductions from gross income. The partnership allocates income and losses to partners only for that portion of the year that the partner is a member of the partnership. Partners cannot be allocated losses for the period before they joined the partnership.

When partners deduct losses, they reduce their basis in the partnership interest. However, basis cannot be reduced below zero. Any disallowed losses remain available to the partners in future years. When the basis increases, they can then deduct some or all of the suspended loss. Partners' basis is discussed in greater detail later in the chapter at ¶1503.01.

EXAMPLE 8 At the beginning of 20x1, Monroe has a 40% partnership interest with a basis of $16,000. During 20x1, the partnership has an ordinary loss of $60,000. Monroe's share of the loss is $24,000 ($60,000 × 40%). However, Monroe can only deduct $16,000 (to the extent of his basis). His basis in the partnership interest is reduced to $0. The $8,000 ($24,000 – $16,000) of the loss not deductible in 20x1 carries forward to future tax years. Monroe will be able to deduct his suspended loss when he establishes a positive partnership basis.

Foreign Taxes

Partnerships engaging in business activities outside the United States may pay income taxes to foreign countries. Such taxes receive special treatment on the tax return of an individual, and therefore, are separately stated. Individual partners report their shares of these foreign income taxes on their own tax returns, either as an itemized deduction (¶504.04), or as a tax credit (¶204.01).

Credits

Since partnerships do not pay income tax, they do not take tax credits. The benefits of any credits pass through to the partners as separately stated items. The partnership makes any elections necessary to qualify for the credits. The partners claim the benefits on their own returns to the extent they meet the limitations that apply to the credits.

¶1502.05 PARTNERSHIP ORDINARY INCOME

When completing the partnership tax return, all income and expense items must be divided between separately stated items and ordinary items. The items not requiring separate statement are combined on Form 1065, page 1 and result in the ordinary income or loss for the partnership. Ordinary income generally consists of the receipts from the partnership's principal business activity. Thus, the gross profits from the sales of products or services are ordinary income. Any other income that is ordinary when passed-through to the partners is ordinary income for this purpose. Items such as gains from the sale of business property held short-term, depreciation recapture (¶1102.02), and interest received on accounts receivables fall into this category.

From total (ordinary) income, the partnership subtracts out all nonseparately stated deductions. The partnership reports this difference on its tax return as ordinary business income (loss).

Calculating Ordinary Income

Gross receipts or gross sales		$xx
Less: Returns and allowances		(xx)
Less: Cost of goods sold from Form 1125-A		(xx)
Gross profit		$xx
Ordinary income (loss) from other entities		xx
Net ordinary gain (loss) from Form 4797		xx
Other income (loss)		xx
Total income (loss)		$xx
Less: Nonseparately stated expenses	$xx	
Guaranteed payments to partners	xx	(xx)
Ordinary business income (loss)		$xx

Guaranteed Payments to Partners

Partnership agreements frequently provide that some or all partners receive payments as compensation. These payments recognize the varying skills and amounts of time partners devote to partnership business. Also, partners may receive a stated rate of interest on the amount of capital that each has invested in the partnership.

The partnership generally deducts these guaranteed payments in computing partnership ordinary income. To be deductible, the payments must be reasonable in amount and determined without regard to partnership income. Guaranteed payments to partners are deducted to arrive at ordinary income and are taxable to the partner that receives them. The partnership reports guaranteed payments separately on Schedule K-1s for the partners that receive them.

Although partners may receive payments for providing services, they are not considered employees. Therefore, the guaranteed payments are not subject to withholding of social security (OASDI), Medicare, or income taxes. Instead, guaranteed payments are subject to self-employment taxes. The partners report guaranteed payments they receive as nonpassive income on Form 1040, Schedule E, Supplemental Income and Loss. The partnership can deduct salaries and wages paid to spouses or other members of a partner's family, provided they are reasonable in amount. Any unreasonable portion is considered a payment to the related partner.

EXAMPLE 9

Dave and Bob are equal general partners in a law firm that uses a calendar year. Dave and Bob receive monthly guaranteed payments of $3,000 and $2,500, respectively. Prior to deducting the guaranteed payments, the partnership has ordinary income of $146,000. After deducting the guaranteed payments ($36,000 to Dave ($3,000 × 12); $30,000 to Bob ($2,500 × 12)), the partnership's ordinary income is $80,000 ($146,000 – $36,000 – $30,000).

On his tax return, Dave will report $76,000 in income from the partnership. This includes $36,000 for his guaranteed payments and $40,000 for his share of partnership income ($80,000 × 50%). Both of these amounts will be subject to self-employment tax (as well as income tax). On his tax return, Bob will report $70,000 of income from the partnership ($30,000 guaranteed payments + $40,000 partnership ordinary income). Again, the entire $70,000 will be subject to self-employment tax (as well as income tax).

Partners are not employees of the partnership. Thus, there are no taxes withheld on their earnings. Instead, partners must make estimated payments large enough to cover both income and self-employment taxes on their shares of partnership income. See ¶1307 for a discussion of estimated tax payments.

¶1502.06 DEDUCTIONS NOT APPLICABLE TO PARTNERSHIPS

Partnerships do not include any nonbusiness deductions in the computation of ordinary income. There is no exemption deduction, standard deduction, or deduction for any personal expenses. These deductions apply solely to individuals. Personal expenses of a partner paid directly by the partnership are treated as withdrawals by the partner. They are not included in the calculation of partnership income. Withdrawals (distributions) are generally treated as tax-free reductions in the partner's investment. Usually, partners only pay taxes on partnership income, not distributions. The tax consequences of partnership distributions are discussed later in the chapter at ¶1503.02.

¶1502.07 FILLED-IN FORM 1065

INFORMATION FOR FIGURE 15-2:

Sarah Morton (SSN 294-65-8321) and Doug Baker are both active partners in **M&B Partnership (EIN 56-0464077)**. M&B is a general partnership that has been in existence since **July 1, 2000**. The offices of M&B are located at **524 Southside, Raleigh, NC 27610-4241**. M&B uses the **accrual method** of reporting for its **sporting goods business** (business code number **5941**). Sarah is the designated tax matters partner. She lives at **418 N. Elm Street, Raleigh, NC 27604-1470**. Under their partnership agreement, each partner is paid guaranteed payments of $1,600 per month. They share the remaining profits and losses equally. Of these profits, $7,000 was distributed in cash to Sarah. No distributions (other than his guaranteed payments) were made to Doug during the year.

The primary information for preparing Form 1065 comes from the information shown in Figure 15-1. The filled-in Form 1065 for M&B Partnership appears in Figure 15-2. On April 15, 2016, Sarah Morton signs and dates Form 1065 as a general partner of M&B. Although total assets and total gross receipts are not large enough to require completion of Item F on page 1, or Schedules L, M-1 and M-2, these schedules are completed in Figure 15-2 for illustration purposes. Depreciation expense is the same for book and tax purposes.

Figure 15-1: M&B Partnership Financial Statements

M&B Partnership
Income Statement
For Year Ended December 31, 2015

Sales	$216,410
Less: Sales returns and allowances	(3,502)
Net sales	$212,908
Less: Cost of goods sold (see schedule)	(106,754)
Gross profit on sales	$106,154
Less: Operating expenses (see schedule)	(87,622)
Operating income	$ 18,532
Interest income (business, $145; investment $1,100; tax-exempt, $50)	1,295
Qualified dividend income	1,700
Less: Interest expense	(253)
Less: Charitable contributions	(426)
Net income	$ 20,848

Schedule of Cost of Goods Sold

Inventory at beginning of year		$ 34,969
Purchases	$105,867	
Less: Purchases returns and allowances	(775)	
Less: Purchase discounts	(1,003)	
Net purchases		104,089
Merchandise available for sale		$139,058
Less: Inventory at end of year		(32,304)
Cost of goods sold		$106,754

Schedule of Operating Expenses
For Year Ended December 31, 2015

General and Administrative Expenses:		Selling Expenses:	
Sarah Morton, salary	$19,200	Sales salaries	$20,000
Doug Baker, salary	19,200	Advertising	1,164
Payroll taxes	4,378	Depreciation	1,400
Rent	5,400	Store supplies	492
Automobile	999	Miscellaneous	242
Utilities	1,345	Total selling expenses	$23,298
Bad debts (direct write-off method)	750		
Insurance	571	Total operating expenses	$87,622
Travel	673		
Office supplies	408		
Office salaries	11,250		
Depreciation	150		
Total G&A expenses	$64,324		

Line # (Form 1065, page 1)

F: Total assets, **$78,340** (source: Schedule L, line 14(d))
Because M&B answers "Yes" to Question 6 on Schedule B (Form 1065), it is not required to complete Item F on page 1 of Form 1065 (see instructions in Question 6). Item F is completed here for illustration purposes.
H: Accounting method, mark box **(2)**
I: Number of Schedules K-1, **2** (Sarah Morton, Doug Baker)
7: Other income, **$145** (business interest)
9: Salaries and wages, **$31,250** ($20,000 sales salaries + $11,250 office salaries)
10: Guaranteed payments to partners, **$38,400** ($19,200 + $19,200)
16a: Depreciation, **$1,550** ($1,400 + $150)
20: Other deductions, **$5,894** ($1,164 advertising expense + $999 automobile expense + $1,345 utilities expense + $571 insurance expense + $673 travel expense + $492 store supplies + $408 office supplies + $242 miscellaneous selling expense)

Line # (Form 1065, pages 2 and 3, Schedule B)

1: Type of entity, mark box **(a)** for Domestic general partnership
2-5: mark **No**
6: mark **Yes** since all four conditions are met
7-12: mark **No**
14-18: mark **No**
19: Number of Form(s) 5471 attached to the return, **0**
20: Number of partners that are foreign governments, **0**

Line # (Form 1065, page 4, Schedule K)

1: Ordinary business income (loss), **$18,424** (source: Form 1065 (page 1), line 22)
4: Guaranteed payments to partners, **$38,400** ($19,200 + $19,200)
5: Interest income, **$1,100** (taxable portfolio interest income)
14a: Net earnings from self-employment, **$56,824** ($18,424 ordinary income + $38,400 guaranteed payments)
18a: Tax-exempt interest income **$50** (source: Income Statement, included as part of Interest income)
20a: Investment income **$2,800** ($1,100 taxable interest income + $1,700 dividend income)

Line # (Analysis of Net Income (Loss), Form 1065, page 5)

1: Net income (loss), **$59,198** (following the instructions on line 1, this amount is $18,424 + $38,400 + $1,100 + $1,700 – $426)

Line # (Form 1065, Schedule M-2)

1: Beginning partners' capital account balance, **$55,472** (source: Schedule L, line 21(b))
3: Net income (loss) per books, **$20,848** (source: Income Statement and Schedule M-1, line 1)
6a: Cash distributions, **$7,000** (source: given)

Figure 15-2: Filled-In Form 1065 (Page 1)

Form **1065** — Department of the Treasury, Internal Revenue Service

U.S. Return of Partnership Income

For calendar year 2015, or tax year beginning ________, 2015, ending ________, 20____.

▶ Information about Form 1065 and its separate instructions is at *www.irs.gov/form1065.*

OMB No. 1545-0123 — **2015**

A Principal business activity: Retail	Type or Print	Name of partnership: M&B Partnership	D Employer identification number: 56-0464077
B Principal product or service: Sporting goods		Number, street, and room or suite no. If a P.O. box, see the instructions.: 524 Southside	E Date business started: 7-1-2000
C Business code number: 5941		City or town, state or province, country, and ZIP or foreign postal code: Raleigh, NC 27610-4241	F Total assets (see the instructions): $ 78,340

G Check applicable boxes: (1) ☐ Initial return (2) ☐ Final return (3) ☐ Name change (4) ☐ Address change (5) ☐ Amended return (6) ☐ Technical termination - also check (1) or (2)

H Check accounting method: (1) ☐ Cash (2) ☑ Accrual (3) ☐ Other (specify) ▶

I Number of Schedules K-1. Attach one for each person who was a partner at any time during the tax year ▶ 2

J Check if Schedules C and M-3 are attached . . . ☐

Caution. *Include **only** trade or business income and expenses on lines 1a through 22 below. See the instructions for more information.*

Income	1a	Gross receipts or sales	1a	216,410		
	b	Returns and allowances	1b	3,502		
	c	Balance. Subtract line 1b from line 1a			1c	212,908
	2	Cost of goods sold (attach Form 1125-A)			2	106,754
	3	Gross profit. Subtract line 2 from line 1c			3	106,154
	4	Ordinary income (loss) from other partnerships, estates, and trusts (attach statement)			4	
	5	Net farm profit (loss) (attach Schedule F (Form 1040))			5	
	6	Net gain (loss) from Form 4797, Part II, line 17 (attach Form 4797)			6	
	7	Other income (loss) (attach statement)			7	145
	8	**Total income (loss).** Combine lines 3 through 7			8	106,299
Deductions (see the instructions for limitations)	9	Salaries and wages (other than to partners) (less employment credits)			9	31,250
	10	Guaranteed payments to partners			10	38,400
	11	Repairs and maintenance			11	
	12	Bad debts			12	750
	13	Rent			13	5,400
	14	Taxes and licenses			14	4,378
	15	Interest			15	253
	16a	Depreciation (if required, attach Form 4562)	16a	1,550		
	b	Less depreciation reported on Form 1125-A and elsewhere on return	16b		16c	1,550
	17	Depletion **(Do not deduct oil and gas depletion.)**			17	
	18	Retirement plans, etc.			18	
	19	Employee benefit programs			19	
	20	Other deductions (attach statement)			20	5,894
	21	**Total deductions.** Add the amounts shown in the far right column for lines 9 through 20			21	87,875
	22	**Ordinary business income (loss).** Subtract line 21 from line 8			22	18,424

Sign Here

Under penalties of perjury, I declare that I have examined this return, including accompanying schedules and statements, and to the best of my knowledge and belief, it is true, correct, and complete. Declaration of preparer (other than general partner or limited liability company member manager) is based on all information of which preparer has any knowledge.

▶ Sarah Morton — Signature of general partner or limited liability company member manager ▶ 4-15-16 — Date

May the IRS discuss this return with the preparer shown below (see instructions)? ☐ Yes ☐ No

Paid Preparer Use Only

Print/Type preparer's name	Preparer's signature	Date	Check ☐ if self-employed	PTIN
Firm's name ▶			Firm's EIN ▶	
Firm's address ▶			Phone no.	

For Paperwork Reduction Act Notice, see separate instructions. Cat. No. 11390Z Form **1065** (2015)

Figure 15-2: Filled-In Form 1065 (Page 2)

Form 1065 (2015) Page **2**

Schedule B Other Information

		Yes	No
1	What type of entity is filing this return? Check the applicable box:		
a	☑ Domestic general partnership **b** ☐ Domestic limited partnership		
c	☐ Domestic limited liability company **d** ☐ Domestic limited liability partnership		
e	☐ Foreign partnership **f** ☐ Other ▶		
2	At any time during the tax year, was any partner in the partnership a disregarded entity, a partnership (including an entity treated as a partnership), a trust, an S corporation, an estate (other than an estate of a deceased partner), or a nominee or similar person?		✓
3	At the end of the tax year:		
a	Did any foreign or domestic corporation, partnership (including any entity treated as a partnership), trust, or tax-exempt organization, or any foreign government own, directly or indirectly, an interest of 50% or more in the profit, loss, or capital of the partnership? For rules of constructive ownership, see instructions. If "Yes," attach Schedule B-1, Information on Partners Owning 50% or More of the Partnership		✓
b	Did any individual or estate own, directly or indirectly, an interest of 50% or more in the profit, loss, or capital of the partnership? For rules of constructive ownership, see instructions. If "Yes," attach Schedule B-1, Information on Partners Owning 50% or More of the Partnership		✓
4	At the end of the tax year, did the partnership:		
a	Own directly 20% or more, or own, directly or indirectly, 50% or more of the total voting power of all classes of stock entitled to vote of any foreign or domestic corporation? For rules of constructive ownership, see instructions. If "Yes," complete (i) through (iv) below		✓

(i) Name of Corporation	**(ii)** Employer Identification Number (if any)	**(iii)** Country of Incorporation	**(iv)** Percentage Owned in Voting Stock

		Yes	No
b	Own directly an interest of 20% or more, or own, directly or indirectly, an interest of 50% or more in the profit, loss, or capital in any foreign or domestic partnership (including an entity treated as a partnership) or in the beneficial interest of a trust? For rules of constructive ownership, see instructions. If "Yes," complete (i) through (v) below		✓

(i) Name of Entity	**(ii)** Employer Identification Number (if any)	**(iii)** Type of Entity	**(iv)** Country of Organization	**(v)** Maximum Percentage Owned in Profit, Loss, or Capital

		Yes	No
5	Did the partnership file Form 8893, Election of Partnership Level Tax Treatment, or an election statement under section 6231(a)(1)(B)(ii) for partnership-level tax treatment, that is in effect for this tax year? See Form 8893 for more details		✓
6	Does the partnership satisfy **all four** of the following conditions?		
a	The partnership's total receipts for the tax year were less than $250,000.		
b	The partnership's total assets at the end of the tax year were less than $1 million.		
c	Schedules K-1 are filed with the return and furnished to the partners on or before the due date (including extensions) for the partnership return.		
d	The partnership is not filing and is not required to file Schedule M-3	✓	
	If "Yes," the partnership is not required to complete Schedules L, M-1, and M-2; Item F on page 1 of Form 1065; or Item L on Schedule K-1.		
7	Is this partnership a publicly traded partnership as defined in section 469(k)(2)?		✓
8	During the tax year, did the partnership have any debt that was cancelled, was forgiven, or had the terms modified so as to reduce the principal amount of the debt?		✓
9	Has this partnership filed, or is it required to file, Form 8918, Material Advisor Disclosure Statement, to provide information on any reportable transaction?		✓
10	At any time during calendar year 2015, did the partnership have an interest in or a signature or other authority over a financial account in a foreign country (such as a bank account, securities account, or other financial account)? See the instructions for exceptions and filing requirements for FinCEN Form 114, Report of Foreign Bank and Financial Accounts (FBAR). If "Yes," enter the name of the foreign country. ▶		✓

Form **1065** (2015)

Figure 15-2: Filled-In Form 1065 (Page 3)

Form 1065 (2015) Page **3**

Schedule B **Other Information *(continued)***

		Yes	No
11	At any time during the tax year, did the partnership receive a distribution from, or was it the grantor of, or transferor to, a foreign trust? If "Yes," the partnership may have to file Form 3520, Annual Return To Report Transactions With Foreign Trusts and Receipt of Certain Foreign Gifts. See instructions		✓
12a	Is the partnership making, or had it previously made (and not revoked), a section 754 election? . . . . See instructions for details regarding a section 754 election.		✓
b	Did the partnership make for this tax year an optional basis adjustment under section 743(b) or 734(b)? If "Yes," attach a statement showing the computation and allocation of the basis adjustment. See instructions		✓
c	Is the partnership required to adjust the basis of partnership assets under section 743(b) or 734(b) because of a substantial built-in loss (as defined under section 743(d)) or substantial basis reduction (as defined under section 734(d))? If "Yes," attach a statement showing the computation and allocation of the basis adjustment. See instructions		✓
13	like-kind exchange or contributed such property to another entity (other than disregarded entities wholly Check this box if, during the current or prior tax year, the partnership distributed any property received in a owned by the partnership throughout the tax year) . . . . ▶ ☐		
14	At any time during the tax year, did the partnership distribute to any partner a tenancy-in-common or other undivided interest in partnership property?		✓
15	If the partnership is required to file Form 8858, Information Return of U.S. Persons With Respect To Foreign Disregarded Entities, enter the number of Forms 8858 attached. See instructions ▶		
16	Does the partnership have any foreign partners? If "Yes," enter the number of Forms 8805, Foreign Partner's Information Statement of Section 1446 Withholding Tax, filed for this partnership. ▶		✓
17	Enter the number of Forms 8865, Return of U.S. Persons With Respect to Certain Foreign Partnerships, attached to this return. ▶		
18a	Did you make any payments in 2015 that would require you to file Form(s) 1099? See instructions		✓
b	If "Yes," did you or will you file required Form(s) 1099?		✓
19	Enter the number of Form(s) 5471, Information Return of U.S. Persons With Respect To Certain Foreign Corporations, attached to this return. ▶ **0**		
20	Enter the number of partners that are foreign governments under section 892. ▶ **0**		

Designation of Tax Matters Partner (see instructions)

Enter below the general partner or member-manager designated as the tax matters partner (TMP) for the tax year of this return:

Name of designated TMP ▶	**Sarah Morton**	Identifying number of TMP ▶	**294-65-8321**
If the TMP is an entity, name of TMP representative ▶		Phone number of TMP ▶	
Address of designated TMP ▶	**418 N. Elm Street, Raleigh, NC 27604-1470**		

Form **1065** (2015)

Figure 15-2: Filled-In Form 1065 (Page 4)

Form 1065 (2015) Page **4**

Section	Line	Schedule K — Partners' Distributive Share Items		Line	Total amount
Income (Loss)	1	Ordinary business income (loss) (page 1, line 22)		1	18,424
	2	Net rental real estate income (loss) (attach Form 8825)		2	
	3a	Other gross rental income (loss)	3a		
	b	Expenses from other rental activities (attach statement)	3b		
	c	Other net rental income (loss). Subtract line 3b from line 3a		3c	
	4	Guaranteed payments		4	38,400
	5	Interest income		5	1,100
	6	Dividends: a Ordinary dividends		6a	1,700
		b Qualified dividends	6b 1,700		
	7	Royalties		7	
	8	Net short-term capital gain (loss) (attach Schedule D (Form 1065))		8	
	9a	Net long-term capital gain (loss) (attach Schedule D (Form 1065))		9a	
	b	Collectibles (28%) gain (loss)	9b		
	c	Unrecaptured section 1250 gain (attach statement)	9c		
	10	Net section 1231 gain (loss) (attach Form 4797)		10	
	11	Other income (loss) (see instructions) Type ▶		11	
Deductions	12	Section 179 deduction (attach Form 4562)		12	
	13a	Contributions		13a	426
	b	Investment interest expense		13b	
	c	Section 59(e)(2) expenditures: (1) Type ▶ (2) Amount ▶		13c(2)	
	d	Other deductions (see instructions) Type ▶		13d	
Self-Employment	14a	Net earnings (loss) from self-employment		14a	56,824
	b	Gross farming or fishing income		14b	
	c	Gross nonfarm income		14c	
Credits	15a	Low-income housing credit (section 42(j)(5))		15a	
	b	Low-income housing credit (other)		15b	
	c	Qualified rehabilitation expenditures (rental real estate) (attach Form 3468, if applicable)		15c	
	d	Other rental real estate credits (see instructions) Type ▶		15d	
	e	Other rental credits (see instructions) Type ▶		15e	
	f	Other credits (see instructions) Type ▶		15f	
Foreign Transactions	16a	Name of country or U.S. possession ▶			
	b	Gross income from all sources		16b	
	c	Gross income sourced at partner level		16c	
		Foreign gross income sourced at partnership level			
	d	Passive category ▶ e General category ▶ f Other ▶		16f	
		Deductions allocated and apportioned at partner level			
	g	Interest expense ▶ h Other ▶		16h	
		Deductions allocated and apportioned at partnership level to foreign source income			
	i	Passive category ▶ j General category ▶ k Other ▶		16k	
	l	Total foreign taxes (check one): ▶ Paid ☐ Accrued ☐		16l	
	m	Reduction in taxes available for credit (attach statement)		16m	
	n	Other foreign tax information (attach statement)			
Alternative Minimum Tax (AMT) Items	17a	Post-1986 depreciation adjustment		17a	
	b	Adjusted gain or loss		17b	
	c	Depletion (other than oil and gas)		17c	
	d	Oil, gas, and geothermal properties—gross income		17d	
	e	Oil, gas, and geothermal properties—deductions		17e	
	f	Other AMT items (attach statement)		17f	
Other Information	18a	Tax-exempt interest income		18a	50
	b	Other tax-exempt income		18b	
	c	Nondeductible expenses		18c	
	19a	Distributions of cash and marketable securities		19a	7,000
	b	Distributions of other property		19b	
	20a	Investment income		20a	2,800
	b	Investment expenses		20b	
	c	Other items and amounts (attach statement)			

Form **1065** (2015)

Figure 15-2: Filled-In Form 1065 (Page 5)

Form 1065 (2015) Page **5**

Analysis of Net Income (Loss)

1	Net income (loss). Combine Schedule K, lines 1 through 11. From the result, subtract the sum of Schedule K, lines 12 through 13d, and 16l					1	59,198
2	Analysis by partner type:	(i) Corporate	(ii) Individual (active)	(iii) Individual (passive)	(iv) Partnership	(v) Exempt Organization	(vi) Nominee/Other
a	General partners		59,198				
b	Limited partners						

Schedule L — Balance Sheets per Books

		Beginning of tax year (a)	(b)	End of tax year (c)	(d)
1	Cash		4,816		17,347
2a	Trade notes and accounts receivable	10,415		11,918	
b	Less allowance for bad debts	600	9,815	720	11,198
3	Inventories		34,969		32,304
4	U.S. government obligations				
5	Tax-exempt securities				
6	Other current assets (attach statement)				
7a	Loans to partners (or persons related to partners)				
b	Mortgage and real estate loans				
8	Other investments (attach statement)		9,465		9,465
9a	Buildings and other depreciable assets	11,900		11,900	
b	Less accumulated depreciation	3,850	8,050	5,400	6,500
10a	Depletable assets				
b	Less accumulated depletion				
11	Land (net of any amortization)				
12a	Intangible assets (amortizable only)				
b	Less accumulated amortization				
13	Other assets (attach statement)		1,475		1,526
14	Total assets		68,590		78,340
	Liabilities and Capital				
15	Accounts payable		7,639		8,623
16	Mortgages, notes, bonds payable in less than 1 year		5,000		
17	Other current liabilities (attach statement)		479		397
18	All nonrecourse loans				
19a	Loans from partners (or persons related to partners)				
b	Mortgages, notes, bonds payable in 1 year or more				
20	Other liabilities (attach statement)				
21	Partners' capital accounts		55,472		69,320
22	Total liabilities and capital		68,590		78,340

Schedule M-1 — Reconciliation of Income (Loss) per Books With Income (Loss) per Return

Note. The partnership may be required to file Schedule M-3 (see instructions).

1	Net income (loss) per books	20,848	6	Income recorded on books this year not included on Schedule K, lines 1 through 11 (itemize):	
2	Income included on Schedule K, lines 1, 2, 3c, 5, 6a, 7, 8, 9a, 10, and 11, not recorded on books this year (itemize):		a	Tax-exempt interest $ 50	50
3	Guaranteed payments (other than health insurance)	38,400	7	Deductions included on Schedule K, lines 1 through 13d, and 16l, not charged against book income this year (itemize):	
4	Expenses recorded on books this year not included on Schedule K, lines 1 through 13d, and 16l (itemize):		a	Depreciation $	
a	Depreciation $		8	Add lines 6 and 7	50
b	Travel and entertainment $		9	Income (loss) (Analysis of Net Income (Loss), line 1). Subtract line 8 from line 5	59,198
5	Add lines 1 through 4	59,248			

Schedule M-2 — Analysis of Partners' Capital Accounts

1	Balance at beginning of year	55,472	6	Distributions: a Cash	7,000
2	Capital contributed: a Cash			b Property	
	b Property		7	Other decreases (itemize):	
3	Net income (loss) per books	20,848			
4	Other increases (itemize):		8	Add lines 6 and 7	7,000
5	Add lines 1 through 4	76,320	9	Balance at end of year. Subtract line 8 from line 5	69,320

Form **1065** (2015)

¶1502.08 SCHEDULE K ITEMS

Those items of partnership income and expense not included in the calculation of ordinary income are separately stated items. Since the partnership is not a tax-paying entity, its credits are also separately stated. Schedule K provides a summary of these items as well as the partnership's ordinary income or loss.

Income Items

The income items requiring separate statement are those that receive special treatment or have limitations imposed at the partner level (see ¶1502.04). The partners combine their shares of the partnership income items with their own income items and then apply the special treatment or limitations. The resulting amounts appear on the partner's tax return.

Deductions

Most partnership expenses are incurred in the production of ordinary income. Therefore, there are only a few separately stated deductions. The expense items that must be separately stated on Schedule K include:

1. Section 179 deduction
2. Deductions related to portfolio income
3. AMT adjustments and preferences
4. Nondeductible expenses
5. Charitable contributions

As previously noted, charitable contributions are not deductible by the partnership in computing ordinary income. Rather, the partnership informs each partner on Schedule K-1 of the partner's share of contributions subject to the 50%, 30%, and 20% limitations. Individual partners combine their shares with their personal contributions and claim these as itemized deductions (¶506.04). Corporate partners combine their shares of the partnership contributions with their own and apply the 10% taxable income limit (¶1402.06).

¶1502.09 OTHER SCHEDULES

A partnership is only required to complete Schedules L, M-1, and M-2 if it answers "No" to question 6 on Schedule B. This question asks whether each of the following four conditions have been met. Thus, if any of the following conditions are not met, the partnership must complete Schedules L, M-1, and M-2, as well as Item F (total assets) on page 1 of Form 1065.

1. The partnership's total receipts for the year were less than $250,000;
2. The partnership's total assets at the end of the year were less than $1 million;
3. Schedules K-1 are filed with the return and given to the partners on or before the due date (including extensions) for the partnership return; and
4. The partnership is not filing and is not required to file Schedule M-3.

Schedule L

Schedule L shows the balance sheet at the beginning and end of the tax year. Some items require supporting schedules, such as other assets and other liabilities. The amounts on Schedule L should agree with the books of the partnership, regardless of whether the accounts are kept in accordance with income tax law. Figure 15-2 shows the balance sheet for M&B Partnership.

Schedule M-1

Schedule M-1, Reconciliation of Income (Loss) per Books With Income (Loss) per Return, reconciles the financial net income (loss) with the income (loss) reported on the Analysis of Net Income (Loss), line 1 (found at the top of Form 1065, page 5). This amount includes ordinary income from page 1 plus separately stated income and deductions reported on Schedule K. Income and expenses appearing on the books but not on the tax return are disclosed in Schedule M-1. Also, income and expenses appearing on Form 1065 but not included in financial net income (loss) are reconciling items shown on Schedule M-1. The amount on Schedule M-1 (line 9) is also the amount on line 1 in the "Analysis of Net Income (Loss)" section found at the top of page 5 (Form 1065).

Most Schedule M-1 reconciliations tend to be more complex than the one in Figure 15-2. Other reconciling items include differences in book and tax depreciation, and differences in computing bad debt expense.

Schedule M-2

Schedule M-2, Analysis of Partners' Capital Accounts, reconciles the beginning capital accounts balance to the ending balance. The beginning and ending balances appear on the balance sheets in Schedule L (line 21). The amounts in Schedule M-2 should agree with the partnership's books. The partnership attaches a statement to Form 1065 to explain any differences.

Schedule K-1 (Form 1065)

The partnership prepares a Schedule K-1, Partner's Share of Income, Deductions, Credits, etc., for each partner. This schedule informs the partners of their respective share of the items reported on Schedule K. The line numbers on the Schedule K and Schedule K-1 are coordinated to make transferring the information easier. For example, guaranteed payments appear on line 4 of both Schedule K and Schedule K-1.

¶1502.10 FILLED-IN SCHEDULE K-1 (FORM 1065)

INFORMATION FOR FIGURE 15-3:

Figure 15-3 shows Schedule K-1 for one partner of M&B Partnership. Since Doug's Schedule K-1 would resemble Sarah's, only Sarah's K-1 is shown here.

Line #

K: Partner's share of recourse liabilities at the end of the year, **$4,510** (as a general partner, Sarah is responsible for 50% of the partnership's $9,020 of total liabilities)

L: Beginning capital account balance, **$27,736** (source: last year's ending balance)
Current year increase or decrease, **$10,424** ($20,848 book net income × 50%)
Because M&B answered "Yes" to Question 6 on Schedule B of Form 1065, M&B is not required to complete Item L on Schedule K-1. Item L is completed here for illustration purposes.

1: Ordinary business income (loss), **$9,212** ($18,424 × 50%)

4: Guaranteed payments to partners, **$19,200** ($1,600 × 12 months)

5: Interest income, **$550** ($1,100 × 50%)

6: Dividends (both ordinary and qualified), **$850** ($1,700 × 50%)

13: Charitable contributions, **$213** ($426 × 50%; contributions subject to the 50% AGI limit are designated Code "A" according to the instructions for Schedule K-1)

14: Self-employment earnings, **$28,412** ($9,212 from line 1 + $19,200 from line 4)

18: Tax-exempt income, **$25** ($50 × 50%) – Designated Code "A" in the instructions
19: Distributions, **$7,000** (provided) – Cash distributions are designated Code "A"
20: Investment income, **$1,400** ($2,800 × 50%) – Designated Code "A" in the instructions

Figure 15-3: Filled-In Schedule K-1 (Form 1065)

651113

☐ Final K-1 ☐ Amended K-1 OMB No. 1545-0123

Schedule K-1 (Form 1065) **2015**

Department of the Treasury
Internal Revenue Service

For calendar year 2015, or tax year beginning ________, 2015 ending ________, 20____

Partner's Share of Income, Deductions, Credits, etc. ▶ See back of form and separate instructions.

Part I Information About the Partnership

A Partnership's employer identification number
56-0464077

B Partnership's name, address, city, state, and ZIP code
M&B Partnership
524 Southside
Raleigh, NC 27610-4241

C IRS Center where partnership filed return
Cincinnati, OH

D ☐ Check if this is a publicly traded partnership (PTP)

Part II Information About the Partner

E Partner's identifying number
294-65-8321

F Partner's name, address, city, state, and ZIP code
Sarah Morton
418 N. Elm Street
Raleigh, NC 27604-1470

G ☒ General partner or LLC member-manager ☐ Limited partner or other LLC member

H ☒ Domestic partner ☐ Foreign partner

I1 What type of entity is this partner? **Individual**

I2 If this partner is a retirement plan (IRA/SEP/Keogh/etc.), check here ☐

J Partner's share of profit, loss, and capital (see instructions):

	Beginning	Ending
Profit	50 %	50 %
Loss	50 %	50 %
Capital	50 %	50 %

K Partner's share of liabilities at year end:

Nonrecourse	$ 0
Qualified nonrecourse financing	$
Recourse	$ 4,510

L Partner's capital account analysis:

Beginning capital account	$ 27,736
Capital contributed during the year	$
Current year increase (decrease)	$ 10,424
Withdrawals & distributions	$ (7,000)
Ending capital account	$ 31,160

☐ Tax basis ☐ GAAP ☒ Section 704(b) book
☐ Other (explain)

M Did the partner contribute property with a built-in gain or loss?
☐ Yes ☒ No
If "Yes," attach statement (see instructions)

Part III Partner's Share of Current Year Income, Deductions, Credits, and Other Items

1	Ordinary business income (loss)	9,212
2	Net rental real estate income (loss)	
3	Other net rental income (loss)	
4	Guaranteed payments	19,200
5	Interest income	550
6a	Ordinary dividends	850
6b	Qualified dividends	850
7	Royalties	
8	Net short-term capital gain (loss)	
9a	Net long-term capital gain (loss)	
9b	Collectibles (28%) gain (loss)	
9c	Unrecaptured section 1250 gain	
10	Net section 1231 gain (loss)	
11	Other income (loss)	555
12	Section 179 deduction	
13	Other deductions	A Charitable contrib., 213
14	Self-employment earnings (loss)	28,412
15	Credits	
16	Foreign transactions	
17	Alternative minimum tax (AMT) items	
18	Tax-exempt income and nondeductible expenses	A 25
19	Distributions	A 7,000
20	Other information	A Investment inc., 1,400

*See attached statement for additional information.

For IRS Use Only

For Paperwork Reduction Act Notice, see Instructions for Form 1065. IRS.gov/form1065 Cat. No. 11394R **Schedule K-1 (Form 1065) 2015**

¶1503 Transactions Between Partnerships and Partners

A unique aspect to operating a business as a partnership versus a C corporation is that the profits of a partnership are only taxed once. This is accomplished, in part, by having the partnership file informational tax return, Form 1065, to report the activities of the business and allocate those activities amongst the partners (on Schedule K-1). These allocated amounts are then reported on the partners' income tax returns. Keeping with the concept of single level of taxation, the tax laws allow partners to make tax-free withdrawals of both the contributions they made to the partnership plus their shares of previously taxed profits. However, if the partnership distributes cash to a partner in excess of these amounts, the partner is taxed on the excess. Thus, it is important to understand how partners keep track of their basis in a partnership interest to ensure a single layer of taxation of partnership profits.

¶1503.01 FACTORS AFFECTING BASIS

When a partnership is formed, the partners contribute cash, other property, or services to the partnership. Under the general rule, neither the partners nor the partnership recognize gain or loss on the transfer of property to a partnership in exchange for an interest in the partnership. This rule applies both upon formation of a partnership, as well as to later transfers. The tax law does not require an 80% or more collective ownership for partnership transfers, like it does for C corporations (see discussion at ¶1401.01). The partner's basis includes the amount of cash plus the partner's basis in assets contributed to the partnership. The partnership's basis in contributed property is the same as that of the contributing partner.

EXAMPLE 10 Fran and Meg form FM partnership. Fran contributes land worth $50,000 ($65,000 basis) in exchange for a 50% partnership interest. Meg contributes $30,000 cash and equipment worth $20,000 ($3,000 basis) in exchange for a 50% partnership interest. Fran's basis in FM is $65,000 (same as her basis in the land). Meg's basis in FM is $33,000 ($30,000 cash + her $3,000 basis in the equipment). FM's basis in the assets it acquires is: cash, $30,000; land, $65,000; equipment, $3,000.

When a partner performs services to a partnership in exchange for a partnership interest, the partner recognizes ordinary income equal to the fair market value (FMV) of the partnership interest. This amount becomes the partner's initial basis in the partnership interest received.

EXAMPLE 11 Mel performs services for EFO partnership. In return, Mel acquires a 10% partnership interest in EFO, valued at $12,000. Mel includes the $12,000 in gross income. This amount becomes his initial basis in EFO partnership.

The above discussion involved transfers of cash, other property, or services to a partnership in exchange for an interest in the partnership. The tax consequences of transfers involving mortgaged property (where the debt attached to the property is assumed by the partnership); as well as transfers from the partnership of property other than an interest in the partnership can be more complex. Hence, the scope of this discussion is limited to transfers to a partnership of cash, other property, or services solely in exchange for a partnership interest.

To ensure a single level of taxation on partnership activities, partners adjust their basis to reflect their respective shares of partnership activities reported to them on Schedule K-1 (Form 1065). Partners increase their partnership basis by their allocated shares of ordinary income and separately stated income. This includes tax-exempt income, which is reported separately on Schedule K-1. Making these adjustments ensures that the taxable activities of the partnership are taxed only one time, and that tax-exempt income is never taxed. Examples 12 and 13 show how the adjustments to a partner's basis work to ensure income from the partnership is only taxed once.

EXAMPLE 12

Bree and Kate form BK partnership by each contributing $50,000 cash in exchange for a 50% interest in BK. Each partner's initial basis in BK is $50,000. BK uses the cash to invest in taxable bonds (face value of $100,000). During the first year, the bonds pay $6,000 of interest. BK reports $6,000 as taxable interest on Form 1065 (Schedule K). BK then reports $3,000 of interest income on each partner's Schedule K-1. Bree and Kate each report the $3,000 of taxable interest on their respective income tax returns.

At the end of the first year, BK's only assets are the $6,000 of cash plus the $100,000 bond. The value of BK to a third party should be $106,000 (assuming the value of the bonds is still $100,000). Thus, the value of each partner's interest in BK, is one-half of this amount, or $53,000. If the partners do not increase their basis by the $3,000 of taxable interest, then should a partner sell her interest in BK, she would recognize a $3,000 capital gain ($53,000 FMV – $50,000 basis). Accordingly, the partner would be taxed a second time on the interest from the bonds -- once when the interest income is reported on the partner's return, and a second time when the gain is taxed to the partner. To keep this from happening, a partner's basis is increased for the partner's share of ordinary income and separately stated income items.

EXAMPLE 13

Same facts as in Example 12, except that BK invests the $100,000 in tax-exempt bonds that pay $6,000 of interest during the first year. BK reports the $6,000 as tax-exempt interest on Schedule K. Each partner is allocated $3,000 of tax-exempt interest on Schedule K-1, but neither is taxed on this income. However, as in Example 12, at the end of the first year, BK still has assets valued at $106,000 ($6,000 cash + $100,000 bond). Once again, if the partners do not increase their basis by the tax-exempt interest allocated to them, they will be taxed on this amount when they go to sell their partnership interests ($53,000 FMV – $50,000 basis = $3,000 gain). Accordingly, each partner's basis also must be adjusted upwards for the nontaxable income allocated to the partner. This ensures that the partner is never taxed on tax-exempt income.

Partners decrease their basis by their allocated share of ordinary loss, as well as any separately stated items of expense or loss (including nondeductible expenditures). These adjustments ensure that the partners only get a tax break for tax deductions one time, and that no tax benefit comes from nondeductible expenditures the partnership makes. Example 14 shows how the adjustments to a partner's basis work to ensure the partners only benefit one time from deductions and losses generated by partnership activities.

EXAMPLE 14

Karl and Joey form KJ partnership by each contributing $50,000 in exchange for a 50% interest in KJ. Each partner's initial basis in KJ is $50,000. During the first year of operations, KJ incurs a $20,000 ordinary loss, which is allocated to the partners on Schedule K-1. Thus, each partner deducts one-half of the loss, or $10,000, on his personal income tax return. This, in turn, reduces each partner's AGI by $10,000.

At the end of the first year, KJ's value should be less due to the loss incurred during the first year of operations. Assuming the decline in value is the same as the $20,000 ordinary loss, KJ's value at the end of the first year would be $80,000. If Karl and Joey do not adjust their basis downward for their allocated losses, when they go to sell their respective partnership interests, the higher basis will result in each partner recognizing a $10,000 loss ($40,000 FMV – $50,000 basis). This loss would allow the partner to benefit twice from the partnership's first year operating loss. To keep this from happening, the tax laws require that a partner's basis be reduced for the partner's share of all losses and expense items. This includes both deductible and nondeductible expenditures.

Another aspect of partnerships that distinguish them from corporations is that general partners are personally liable for the debts of the partnership (¶1501). In contrast, shareholders are only liable to the extent of their stock basis. Because the general partners are personally liable for the debts of the partnership, they are at risk to the extent of their share of partnership debt. For example, if a partnership's debt increases by $20,000 during the year, a 15% general partner's amount at risk would increase by $3,000 (15% × $20,000). Likewise, if a partnership's debt decreases by $5,000, a 50% general partner's amount at risk would decrease by $2,500 (50% × $5,000). By adjusting a partner's basis at the end of the year by the change in the partner's share of partnership debt during the year ensures that the partner's basis reflects the partner's amount at risk with respect to their investment in the partnership. For more on the at-risk rules, see ¶904.

Limited partners are not liable for the general debts of the partnership. Instead, they are only at-risk to the extent of their investment (basis) in their partnership interest. They do, however, increase their partnership basis by amounts owed to them by the partnership.

EXAMPLE 15

Leon and Joyce are partners in LJ general partnership. They share profits and losses 40% and 60%, respectively. Leon's basis is $20,000; Joyce's basis is $30,000. LJ takes on $10,000 more of debt. Leon's basis increases to $24,000 [$20,000 + ($10,000 × 40%)]. Joyce's basis increases to $36,000 [$30,000 + ($10,000 × 60%)].

Adjustments to Partner's Basis

In summary, partners adjust their basis in the partnership by the following:

1. Their allocated share of ordinary income (loss)
2. Their allocated share of all separately stated items
3. Contributions they make to the partnership
4. Distributions (withdrawals) from the partnership
5. Their proper share of changes to the partnership's debt

A partner's basis can never be reduced below zero. Any losses allocated to a partner that are in excess of a partner's basis carry over to the future when the partner gets a positive basis. This can be done when the partner makes another contribution to the partnership, or when the partner is allocated income (either taxable or tax-exempt) from the partnership. When computing a partner's basis, all items that increase basis are taken into account before taking into account items that decrease the partner's basis.

EXAMPLE 16

At the beginning of the year, Marshall's basis in his 20% interest in L&M partnership is $23,000. During the year, L&M reports an ordinary loss of $61,000, tax-exempt interest of $5,000, and $25,000 of Section 179 expense. Also during the year, L&M's debt increased by $14,000. Marshall first increases his basis in L&M by $3,800 for his share of L&M's income and increase in partnership debt (($5,000 + $14,000) × 20%). After this adjustment, Marshall's basis in his L&M partnership interest is $26,800 ($23,000 + $3,800 positive adjustments). Marshall's negative adjustments for the year total $17,200 (($61,000 + $25,000) × 20%). Since Marshall has enough basis to cover his negative adjustments, he can deduct the entire amount of his share of the partnership loss and Section 179 on his personal tax return. Marshall's basis in his L&M partnership interest at the end of the year is $9,600 ($26,800 – $17,200).

EXAMPLE 17

At the beginning of the year, Eve's basis in her 35% interest in DEF partnership is $6,000. During the year, DEF reports an ordinary loss of $40,000 and dividend income of $6,000. Also during the year, DEF's debt increased by $10,000. Eve first increases her basis in DEF by $5,600 for her share of DEF income and increase in partnership debt (($6,000 + $10,000) × 35%). After this adjustment, Eve's basis in her partnership interest is $11,600 ($6,000 + $5,600). Eve's negative adjustments for the year are $14,000 ($40,000 × 35%). Since this amount is greater than Eve's basis in DEF, she will only be able to deduct $11,600 of the partnership losses on her tax return. She carries over the $2,400 excess ($14,000 – $11,600 allowed under the basis rules). Eve will deduct this loss in the year she produces enough positive basis in her partnership interest to absorb the loss. Eve's basis in DEF at the end of the year is $0 ($11,600 – $11,600 of allowed losses).

¶1503.02 PARTNERSHIP DISTRIBUTIONS

Partnerships can make current or liquidating distributions. A **liquidating distribution** is one made to a partner who is exiting (being bought out of) the partnership. In a liquidating distribution, it is possible for the exiting partner to recognize gain or loss. A **current distribution** is any distribution that is not a liquidating distribution. Most distributions are current distributions, and are the focus of the discussion in this textbook.

Most distributions are tax free to the partners. In a current distribution, partners are simply withdrawing their contributions or previously taxed profits from the partnership. Distributions of money or property decrease partners' bases in their partnership interests, but never below zero. Distributions of cash in excess of the partner's basis result in capital gain to the partner. The partner's basis in the partnership interest decreases by the adjusted basis of the property distributed. The basis of the property received by the partner is usually the same as it was in the hands of the partnership.

EXAMPLE 18 A partnership purchases stock in 20x1 for $5,000. In 20x3, the partnership distributes the stock (now worth $23,000) to the partners. Although a 50% partner with a partnership basis of $50,000 receives stock with a market value of $11,500 ($23,000 × 50%), he takes a $2,500 basis in the stock ($5,000 × 50%). His partnership basis is reduced to $47,500 ($50,000 – $2,500). No gain is recognized until the partner sells his stock.

When a partnership distributes both cash and property to one of its partners, the tax laws treat the cash as having been distributed first, followed by the property (at its adjusted basis to the partnership). If the partner's basis in the partnership is less than the partnership's basis in the property distributed, then the partner's basis (after reducing it for any cash distributions) becomes the partner's basis in the distributed property.

EXAMPLE 19 M&M partnership distributes $10,000 cash and land worth $20,000 (adjusted basis of $5,000) to one of its partners, Marcia. Marcia's basis in her interest in M&M is $18,000 immediately before the distribution. In determining the tax consequences of the distribution, the cash is distributed first. Since Marcia's $18,000 basis in M&M is greater than the $10,000 cash distributed, Marcia is not taxed on the cash distribution, and she reduces her basis in M&M to $8,000 ($18,000 – $10,000). Next, the land is distributed at its adjusted basis to M&M. Since Marcia's remaining basis exceeds M&M's $5,000 basis in the land, Marcia takes a $5,000 basis in the land, and reduces her basis in M&M to $3,000 ($8,000 – $5,000).

EXAMPLE 20 Same facts as in Example 19, except that M&M's basis in the land is $15,000. Once again, the cash is distributed first (tax-free), and Marcia's basis in M&M is reduced to $8,000. However, now M&M's $15,000 basis in the land is greater than Marcia's remaining basis. Since Marcia's basis in M&M cannot be reduced below zero, her $8,000 remaining basis in M&M becomes her basis in the land. Marcia's basis in M&M is reduced to $0, and neither Marcia nor M&M recognize gain or loss on the distribution.

EXAMPLE 21 Same facts as in Example 19, except that M&M's cash distribution is $25,000. Since the cash distributed exceeds Marcia's basis in M&M, Marcia is taxed on the $7,000 excess ($25,000 – $18,000), and her basis in M&M is reduced to $0. When the land is distributed, Marcia's $0 basis in the partnership becomes her basis in the land. Neither party recognizes gain or loss on the distribution of the land (Marcia still recognizes $7,000 capital gain from the cash distribution).

Cash distributions in excess of a partner's basis are taxable to the partner. In contrast, property distributions are tax-free to the partner, even when the partner's basis in the partnership is less than the partnership's adjusted basis in the property distributed (as shown in Examples 20 and 21). Hence, the tax laws that allow cash distributions to be considered as having been distributed prior to any property reduces the chance that the partner will recognize gain on the distribution.

¶1504 Limited Liability Companies and Partnerships

Limited liability companies (LLCs) are a popular form of business ownership. All states have laws recognizing this form of business. LLCs provide the owners with the limited personal liability features of a corporation, but the flow through aspects of a partnership for tax purposes. Form 1065, Schedule B, now recognizes limited liability companies as one of the partnership forms along with general partnerships and limited partnerships. The major advantage of the LLC form of partnership over the general and limited partnerships is the limited liability. With a general partnership, all partners become personally liable for the debts of the partnership. Even with a limited partnership, there must be at least one general partner personally liable for the debts of the partnership. For limited partners to retain their limited liability, they cannot participate in the management of the partnership. The LLC grants personal limited liability for **all** of its owners and still allows each owner to participate in the management of the business. Thus, the LLC combines the corporate legal benefits of limited liability with the partnership tax benefits of a single level of tax.

While an LLC is a formal corporation for state legal purposes, a limited liability partnership (LLP) is a partnership for state legal and income tax purposes. Therefore, most LLPs avoid state taxes placed on corporations, such as franchise taxes. Yet the most important difference between LLCs and LLPs is in the owners' liability. LLC owners have the corporate benefit of limited liability. LLP owners, on the other hand, are liable for commercial debt and for their own malpractice and torts. However, they are not liable for the malpractice or torts of their partners. For this reason, most of the national and regional CPA firms have reorganized as LLPs. Changing from a general partnership to a LLP is not a taxable event. It is considered a continuation of the same partnership in most cases. Nevertheless, an LLP must register with the state to place the liability limitation on public record. The benefits of limited liability with the tax treatment as partnerships make LLCs and LLPs very popular business forms for doing business today.

15

Name:
Section:
Date:

QUESTIONS AND PROBLEMS

1. **Partnership Characteristics.** (Obj. 1)

   a. Which tax form do partnerships use?

   b. Do partnerships withhold income taxes on guaranteed payments made to partners?

   c. An LLC is what type of tax entity?

   d. What is the extended due date for a calendar year partnership?

   e. What is the original due date for the tax return of a fiscal year partnership with an April 30 year-end?

2. **Partnership Tax Year.** (Obj. 1) ABCD partnership consists of four partners, A, B, C, and D. Each partner's year-end along with their ownership percentage of capital and profits is shown below. Determine ABCD's required tax year.

Partner	*Year-End*	*Percentage*
A	June 30	47%
B	May 31	3%
C	May 31	3%
D	June 30	47%
		100%

3. **Partnership Tax Year.** (Obj. 1) EFGH partnership consists of four partners, E, F, G, and H. Each partner's year-end along with their ownership percentage of capital and profits is shown below. Determine EFGH's required tax year.

Partner	*Year-End*	*Percentage*
E	June 30	48%
F	October 31	4%
G	December 31	24%
H	December 31	24%
		100%

4. **Partnership Activities.** (Obj. 2) Indicate how each of the following items is reported on the partnership tax return by placing a check mark in the appropriate column.

Item	*Ordinary Income*	*Separately Stated*
a. Rent received from rental property	________	________
b. Short-term loss on the sale of a capital asset	________	________
c. Dividends received from a U.S. corporation	________	________
d. Contribution to the Red Cross	________	________
e. Guaranteed payments to partners	________	________
f. Section 179 expense	________	________
g. Interest expense on a business loan	________	________
h. Annual business license	________	________
i. Interest income from a municipal bond	________	________
j. Property taxes on partnership assets	________	________

5. **Partner's Distributive Share.** (Obj. 3) Helen is a member of a partnership that reports ordinary income of $68,000 for the current taxable year. Helen's distributive share of the partnership income is $34,000, of which she withdrew $18,000 during the year. Compute the amount Helen should report as income from the partnership when preparing her personal income tax return for the year.

6. **Partnership Income.** (Obj. 2) Which of the following are separately stated partnership items?

a. Business bad debts
b. Foreign taxes paid
c. Tax-exempt interest
d. Guaranteed payments
e. Net Section 1231 loss
f. Depreciation recapture
g. Interest income from business activities

7. **Partnership Charitable Contributions.** (Obj. 2) Leona and Calley operate a placement service as partners, sharing profits and losses equally. During the current calendar year, the partnership contributes $3,000 to Calley's alma mater, State University. The partnership treats this contribution as an expense in computing its $47,500 profit from operations.

a. Is the partnership entitled to treat the contribution to State University as a deduction from ordinary income in the partnership return?

b. What is each partner's distributive share of ordinary income from the partnership?

c. Can each partner claim a deduction on her personal income tax return for the contribution the partnership made to State University? If so, how much?

8. **Guaranteed Payments.** (Obj. 2) What are guaranteed payments to partners and how are they treated by the partnership and the partner?

9. **Guaranteed Payments and Allocation of Partnership Income.** (Obj. 3) ABC partnership provides for "salaries" (guaranteed payments) of $70,000, $64,000, and $60,000 for partners A, B, and C, respectively. After the guaranteed payments are deducted, the partnership agreement calls for sharing of profits and losses as follows: A – 40%; B – 35%; and C – 25%.

   a. If partnership profits before the guaranteed payments are $120,000, what amount of income from the partnership should each partner report on his or her own personal income tax return?

   b. How would your answer to Part a. change if partnership profits before guaranteed payments were $220,000 (instead of $120,000)?

10. **Partnership Income.** (Obj. 3) Fred and Ken are general partners in a business sharing profits and losses 60% and 40%, respectively. The partnership uses a calendar year. Ken files his individual return on the basis of the calendar year. The partnership's ordinary income for the year is $140,000 (after deducting partners' guaranteed payments). During the year, each partner received a guaranteed payment of $8,000 per month. Compute the amount of partnership income Ken should report on his personal income tax return. How much of this amount is subject to self-employment tax?

11. **Partner's Basis.** (Objs. 1 and 4) Nikki and Nancy form N&N partnership. Nikki contributes $40,000 cash and a building worth $70,000 ($58,000 adjusted basis) in exchange for a 50% interest in N&N. Nancy contributes $10,000 and land worth $100,000 (basis of $120,000) in exchange for a 50% interest in N&N.

    a. How much gain or loss do Nikki, Nancy, and N&N recognize from the transfer?

    b. What is Nikki's basis in her partnership interest?

    c. What is Nancy's basis in her partnership interest?

    d. What is N&N's basis in the assets it acquired on the transfer?

12. **Partner's Basis.** (Objs. 1 and 4) Paul and Kyle form PK partnership. Paul contributes land worth $100,000 ($75,000) in exchange for a 50% interest in PK. Kyle contributes $23,000 cash, his personal automobile worth $17,000 (basis of $32,000), and machinery worth $60,000 (basis of $37,000) in exchange for a 50% interest in PK.

    a. How much gain or loss do Paul, Kyle, and PK recognize from the transfer?

    b. What is Paul's basis in his partnership interest?

    c. What is Kyle's basis in his partnership interest?

    d. What is PK's basis in the assets it acquired on the transfer?

13. **Partner's Basis.** (Objs. 1 and 4) Brett performs services for ABC partnership. In return, Brett receives a 25% interest in ABC. At the time of the transfer, the assets of ABC are valued at $200,000.

    a. How much gain or loss do Brett and ABC recognize from the transfer?

    b. What is Brett's basis in his partnership interest?

14. **Partner's Basis.** (Obj. 4) At the beginning of the year, Robin's basis in her 25% interest in R&B partnership is $4,000. That year, on Schedule K, R&B reports an ordinary loss of $36,000, taxable interest of $4,500, tax-exempt interest of $3,000, and Section 179 expense of $25,000. During the year, R&B's debt increased by $42,000. Discuss the tax consequences of these partnership activities on Robin's personal income tax return, and compute her basis in R&B partnership at the end of the year.

15. **Partner's Basis.** (Obj. 4) At the beginning of the year, Bruce's basis in his 40% interest in B&R partnership is $11,000. That year, on Schedule K, B&R reports ordinary income of $6,000, dividend income of $12,400, and charitable contributions of $16,000. During the year, B&R's debt decreased by $25,000. Discuss the tax consequences of these partnership activities on Bruce's personal income tax return, and compute his basis in B&R partnership at the end of the year.

16. **Distributions.** (Obj. 4) AB partnership distributes $52,000 to one of its partners, Alice.

    a. What are the tax consequences of the distribution if Alice's basis in AB partnership is $45,000 immediately before the distribution?

    b. How, if at all, would your answer to Part a. change if Alice's basis was $60,000 (instead of $45,000)?

17. **Distributions.** (Obj. 4) AJ partnership distributes $10,000 cash and a building worth $80,000 (adjusted basis of $66,000) to one of its partners, Joe.

    a. What are the tax consequences of the distribution if Joe's basis in AJ partnership is $46,000 immediately before the distribution?

    b. How, if at all, would your answer to Part a. change if Joe's basis in AJ partnership was $90,000 (instead of $46,000)?

    c. How, if at all, would your answer to Part a. change if the cash distribution was $50,000 (instead of $10,000)?

18. Distributions. (Obj. 4) PJ partnership distributes $6,000 cash and land worth $50,000 (adjusted basis of $56,000) to one of its partners, Patrick.

a. What are the tax consequences of the distribution if Patrick's basis in PJ partnership is $80,000 immediately before the distribution?

b. How, if at all, would your answer to Part a. change if the cash distribution was $60,000 (instead of $6,000)?

c. How, if at all, would your answer to Part a. change if the cash distribution was $85,000 (instead of $6,000)?

19. Form 1065. (Obj. 5) On January 3, 2015, Ellen Elvers (SSN 299-84-1945) and Jack Ford form Elvers and Ford general partnership (EIN 31-0960341). Elvers and Ford operate a business that sells various types of merchandise (business code 5963) at 1425 Tyron Street, Charlotte, North Carolina 28201. To form the partnership, Ellen contributes $24,000; Jack contributes $16,000. The agreement provides that Ellen will participate in the partnership on a full-time basis and Jack on a part-time basis. The agreement further provides that Ellen and Jack will receive guaranteed annual payments of $34,000 and $18,000, respectively. The remaining profits go 60% to Ellen and 40% to Jack.

Prepare Form 1065 and Schedule K-1 (Form 1065) for Ellen Elvers. Ellen is the Designated Tax Matters Partner. Her address is 1609 Amber Way, Charlotte, NC 28201. Ellen signs the partnership return on April 10, 2016. The partnership tax return will be filed with the IRS Center in Cincinnati, Ohio. Although the partnership is not required to complete Schedules L, M-1, M-2, or Item F on Form 1065 (page 1), complete these items for Elvers and Ford partnership.

The trial balance that follows was prepared as of December 31 after all necessary adjustments. Merchandise inventory is an exception. Total purchases of inventory during the year were $162,700. The ending balance in inventory was $22,000. Also, the partners' capital accounts do not reflect the partners' distributive shares of income and loss for the year. The accounts for the partners' "Drawings" represent withdrawals in addition to their respective guaranteed payments. Net income per books (Schedule M-1, line 1) is $23,990.

The partnership uses the accrual method of accounting. Worthless accounts totaling to $800 were written off directly to bad debt expense during the year. The partnership calculates depreciation using (accelerated) MACRS. The equipment was the only personal property purchased during 2015. The partnership does not elect Section 179. Book depreciation is reported on the trial balance. Book depreciation is based on a different method than MACRS. Charitable contributions are subject to the 50% limitation. On October 3, 2015, 50 shares of common stock in ZMT Corporation were sold for $2,900. The stock was purchased for $1,700 on March 29, 2015. For purposes of preparing Form 1065, assume that Form 4562 and Schedule D have been properly prepared.

ELVERS AND FORD
Trial Balance
December 31, 2015

Account	*Debit*	*Credit*
Cash	$ 11,017	
Accounts and notes receivable	17,550	
Equipment (purchased January 4, 2015)	28,000	
Accumulated depreciation-equipment		$ 5,000
Prepaid assets	900	
Long-term notes payable (to banks)		5,000
Accounts payable		8,797
Other accrued current liabilities		1,880
Ellen Elvers, Capital		24,000
Ellen Elvers, Drawing	2,000	
Jack Ford, Capital		16,000
Jack Ford, Drawing	3,200	
Sales		260,500
Sales returns and allowances	3,000	
Gain on sale of stock		1,200
Purchases	162,700	
Interest expense (business related)	300	
Partners' salaries	52,000	
Office and store salaries	14,300	
Rent expense	6,500	
Office expense	3,000	
Depreciation expense	5,000	
Property taxes on business property	383	
Payroll taxes	4,052	
Delivery expense	2,010	
Bad debt expense	800	
Store expenses	2,600	
Advertising expense	2,705	
Taxable interest income		200
Charitable contributions	560	
Total	$322,577	$322,577

(Use for Problem 19.)

Form **1065** — Department of the Treasury, Internal Revenue Service

U.S. Return of Partnership Income

For calendar year 2015, or tax year beginning ________, 2015, ending ________, 20____.

▶ Information about Form 1065 and its separate instructions is at *www.irs.gov/form1065*.

OMB No. 1545-0123 — **2015**

A Principal business activity	Type or Print — Name of partnership	D Employer identification number
B Principal product or service	Number, street, and room or suite no. If a P.O. box, see the instructions.	E Date business started
C Business code number	City or town, state or province, country, and ZIP or foreign postal code	F Total assets (see the instructions) $

G Check applicable boxes: (1) ☐ Initial return (2) ☐ Final return (3) ☐ Name change (4) ☐ Address change (5) ☐ Amended return (6) ☐ Technical termination - also check (1) or (2)

H Check accounting method: (1) ☐ Cash (2) ☐ Accrual (3) ☐ Other (specify) ▶

I Number of Schedules K-1. Attach one for each person who was a partner at any time during the tax year ▶

J Check if Schedules C and M-3 are attached ☐

Caution. *Include **only** trade or business income and expenses on lines 1a through 22 below. See the instructions for more information.*

Income

1a	Gross receipts or sales	1a	
b	Returns and allowances	1b	
c	Balance. Subtract line 1b from line 1a		1c
2	Cost of goods sold (attach Form 1125-A)		2
3	Gross profit. Subtract line 2 from line 1c		3
4	Ordinary income (loss) from other partnerships, estates, and trusts (attach statement)		4
5	Net farm profit (loss) (attach Schedule F (Form 1040))		5
6	Net gain (loss) from Form 4797, Part II, line 17 (attach Form 4797)		6
7	Other income (loss) (attach statement)		7
8	**Total income (loss).** Combine lines 3 through 7		8

Deductions (see the instructions for limitations)

9	Salaries and wages (other than to partners) (less employment credits)		9
10	Guaranteed payments to partners		10
11	Repairs and maintenance		11
12	Bad debts		12
13	Rent		13
14	Taxes and licenses		14
15	Interest		15
16a	Depreciation (if required, attach Form 4562)	16a	
b	Less depreciation reported on Form 1125-A and elsewhere on return	16b	16c
17	Depletion **(Do not deduct oil and gas depletion.)**		17
18	Retirement plans, etc.		18
19	Employee benefit programs		19
20	Other deductions (attach statement)		20
21	**Total deductions.** Add the amounts shown in the far right column for lines 9 through 20.		21
22	**Ordinary business income (loss).** Subtract line 21 from line 8		22

Sign Here

Under penalties of perjury, I declare that I have examined this return, including accompanying schedules and statements, and to the best of my knowledge and belief, it is true, correct, and complete. Declaration of preparer (other than general partner or limited liability company member manager) is based on all information of which preparer has any knowledge.

▶ Signature of general partner or limited liability company member manager ▶ Date

May the IRS discuss this return with the preparer shown below (see instructions)? ☐ **Yes** ☐ **No**

Paid Preparer Use Only

Print/Type preparer's name	Preparer's signature	Date	Check ☐ if self-employed	PTIN
Firm's name ▶			Firm's EIN ▶	
Firm's address ▶			Phone no.	

For Paperwork Reduction Act Notice, see separate instructions. Cat. No. 11390Z Form **1065** (2015)

(Use for Problem 19.)

Form 1065 (2015) Page **2**

Schedule B Other Information

		Yes	No
1	What type of entity is filing this return? Check the applicable box:		
a	☐ Domestic general partnership **b** ☐ Domestic limited partnership		
c	☐ Domestic limited liability company **d** ☐ Domestic limited liability partnership		
e	☐ Foreign partnership **f** ☐ Other ▶		
2	At any time during the tax year, was any partner in the partnership a disregarded entity, a partnership (including an entity treated as a partnership), a trust, an S corporation, an estate (other than an estate of a deceased partner), or a nominee or similar person?		
3	At the end of the tax year:		
a	Did any foreign or domestic corporation, partnership (including any entity treated as a partnership), trust, or tax-exempt organization, or any foreign government own, directly or indirectly, an interest of 50% or more in the profit, loss, or capital of the partnership? For rules of constructive ownership, see instructions. If "Yes," attach Schedule B-1, Information on Partners Owning 50% or More of the Partnership		
b	Did any individual or estate own, directly or indirectly, an interest of 50% or more in the profit, loss, or capital of the partnership? For rules of constructive ownership, see instructions. If "Yes," attach Schedule B-1, Information on Partners Owning 50% or More of the Partnership		
4	At the end of the tax year, did the partnership:		
a	Own directly 20% or more, or own, directly or indirectly, 50% or more of the total voting power of all classes of stock entitled to vote of any foreign or domestic corporation? For rules of constructive ownership, see instructions. If "Yes," complete (i) through (iv) below		

(i) Name of Corporation	**(ii)** Employer Identification Number (if any)	**(iii)** Country of Incorporation	**(iv)** Percentage Owned in Voting Stock

b	Own directly an interest of 20% or more, or own, directly or indirectly, an interest of 50% or more in the profit, loss, or capital in any foreign or domestic partnership (including an entity treated as a partnership) or in the beneficial interest of a trust? For rules of constructive ownership, see instructions. If "Yes," complete (i) through (v) below		

(i) Name of Entity	**(ii)** Employer Identification Number (if any)	**(iii)** Type of Entity	**(iv)** Country of Organization	**(v)** Maximum Percentage Owned in Profit, Loss, or Capital

		Yes	No
5	Did the partnership file Form 8893, Election of Partnership Level Tax Treatment, or an election statement under section 6231(a)(1)(B)(ii) for partnership-level tax treatment, that is in effect for this tax year? See Form 8893 for more details		
6	Does the partnership satisfy **all four** of the following conditions?		
a	The partnership's total receipts for the tax year were less than $250,000.		
b	The partnership's total assets at the end of the tax year were less than $1 million.		
c	Schedules K-1 are filed with the return and furnished to the partners on or before the due date (including extensions) for the partnership return.		
d	The partnership is not filing and is not required to file Schedule M-3		
	If "Yes," the partnership is not required to complete Schedules L, M-1, and M-2; Item F on page 1 of Form 1065; or Item L on Schedule K-1.		
7	Is this partnership a publicly traded partnership as defined in section 469(k)(2)?		
8	During the tax year, did the partnership have any debt that was cancelled, was forgiven, or had the terms modified so as to reduce the principal amount of the debt?		
9	Has this partnership filed, or is it required to file, Form 8918, Material Advisor Disclosure Statement, to provide information on any reportable transaction?		
10	At any time during calendar year 2015, did the partnership have an interest in or a signature or other authority over a financial account in a foreign country (such as a bank account, securities account, or other financial account)? See the instructions for exceptions and filing requirements for FinCEN Form 114, Report of Foreign Bank and Financial Accounts (FBAR). If "Yes," enter the name of the foreign country. ▶		

Form **1065** (2015)

(Use for Problem 19.)

Form 1065 (2015) Page **3**

Schedule B **Other Information *(continued)***

		Yes	No
11	At any time during the tax year, did the partnership receive a distribution from, or was it the grantor of, or transferor to, a foreign trust? If "Yes," the partnership may have to file Form 3520, Annual Return To Report Transactions With Foreign Trusts and Receipt of Certain Foreign Gifts. See instructions		
12a	Is the partnership making, or had it previously made (and not revoked), a section 754 election? . . . . . . See instructions for details regarding a section 754 election.		
b	Did the partnership make for this tax year an optional basis adjustment under section 743(b) or 734(b)? If "Yes," attach a statement showing the computation and allocation of the basis adjustment. See instructions		
c	Is the partnership required to adjust the basis of partnership assets under section 743(b) or 734(b) because of a substantial built-in loss (as defined under section 743(d)) or substantial basis reduction (as defined under section 734(d))? If "Yes," attach a statement showing the computation and allocation of the basis adjustment. See instructions		
13	like-kind exchange or contributed such property to another entity (other than disregarded entities wholly Check this box if, during the current or prior tax year, the partnership distributed any property received in a owned by the partnership throughout the tax year) . . . . ▶ ☐		
14	At any time during the tax year, did the partnership distribute to any partner a tenancy-in-common or other undivided interest in partnership property?		
15	If the partnership is required to file Form 8858, Information Return of U.S. Persons With Respect To Foreign Disregarded Entities, enter the number of Forms 8858 attached. See instructions ▶		
16	Does the partnership have any foreign partners? If "Yes," enter the number of Forms 8805, Foreign Partner's Information Statement of Section 1446 Withholding Tax, filed for this partnership. ▶		
17	Enter the number of Forms 8865, Return of U.S. Persons With Respect to Certain Foreign Partnerships, attached to this return. ▶		
18a	Did you make any payments in 2015 that would require you to file Form(s) 1099? See instructions		
b	If "Yes," did you or will you file required Form(s) 1099?		
19	Enter the number of Form(s) 5471, Information Return of U.S. Persons With Respect To Certain Foreign Corporations, attached to this return. ▶		
20	Enter the number of partners that are foreign governments under section 892. ▶		

Designation of Tax Matters Partner (see instructions)

Enter below the general partner or member-manager designated as the tax matters partner (TMP) for the tax year of this return:

Name of designated TMP ▶		Identifying number of TMP ▶	
If the TMP is an entity, name of TMP representative ▶		Phone number of TMP ▶	
Address of designated TMP ▶			

Form **1065** (2015)

(Use for Problem 19.)

Form 1065 (2015) Page **4**

Schedule K		Partners' Distributive Share Items		Total amount
Income (Loss)	1	Ordinary business income (loss) (page 1, line 22)	1	
	2	Net rental real estate income (loss) (attach Form 8825)	2	
	3a	Other gross rental income (loss) . . . 3a		
	b	Expenses from other rental activities (attach statement) 3b		
	c	Other net rental income (loss). Subtract line 3b from line 3a	3c	
	4	Guaranteed payments	4	
	5	Interest income	5	
	6	Dividends: a Ordinary dividends	6a	
		b Qualified dividends . . . 6b		
	7	Royalties	7	
	8	Net short-term capital gain (loss) (attach Schedule D (Form 1065))	8	
	9a	Net long-term capital gain (loss) (attach Schedule D (Form 1065))	9a	
	b	Collectibles (28%) gain (loss) . . . 9b		
	c	Unrecaptured section 1250 gain (attach statement) 9c		
	10	Net section 1231 gain (loss) (attach Form 4797)	10	
	11	Other income (loss) (see instructions) Type ▶	11	
Deductions	12	Section 179 deduction (attach Form 4562)	12	
	13a	Contributions	13a	
	b	Investment interest expense	13b	
	c	Section 59(e)(2) expenditures: (1) Type ▶ (2) Amount ▶	13c(2)	
	d	Other deductions (see instructions) Type ▶	13d	
Self-Employment	14a	Net earnings (loss) from self-employment	14a	
	b	Gross farming or fishing income	14b	
	c	Gross nonfarm income	14c	
Credits	15a	Low-income housing credit (section 42(j)(5))	15a	
	b	Low-income housing credit (other)	15b	
	c	Qualified rehabilitation expenditures (rental real estate) (attach Form 3468, if applicable)	15c	
	d	Other rental real estate credits (see instructions) Type ▶	15d	
	e	Other rental credits (see instructions) Type ▶	15e	
	f	Other credits (see instructions) Type ▶	15f	
Foreign Transactions	16a	Name of country or U.S. possession ▶		
	b	Gross income from all sources	16b	
	c	Gross income sourced at partner level	16c	
		Foreign gross income sourced at partnership level		
	d	Passive category ▶ e General category ▶ f Other ▶	16f	
		Deductions allocated and apportioned at partner level		
	g	Interest expense ▶ h Other ▶	16h	
		Deductions allocated and apportioned at partnership level to foreign source income		
	i	Passive category ▶ j General category ▶ k Other ▶	16k	
	l	Total foreign taxes (check one): ▶ Paid ☐ Accrued ☐	16l	
	m	Reduction in taxes available for credit (attach statement)	16m	
	n	Other foreign tax information (attach statement)		
Alternative Minimum Tax (AMT) Items	17a	Post-1986 depreciation adjustment	17a	
	b	Adjusted gain or loss	17b	
	c	Depletion (other than oil and gas)	17c	
	d	Oil, gas, and geothermal properties—gross income	17d	
	e	Oil, gas, and geothermal properties—deductions	17e	
	f	Other AMT items (attach statement)	17f	
Other Information	18a	Tax-exempt interest income	18a	
	b	Other tax-exempt income	18b	
	c	Nondeductible expenses	18c	
	19a	Distributions of cash and marketable securities	19a	
	b	Distributions of other property	19b	
	20a	Investment income	20a	
	b	Investment expenses	20b	
	c	Other items and amounts (attach statement)		

Form **1065** (2015)

(Use for Problem 19.)

Form 1065 (2015) Page **5**

Analysis of Net Income (Loss)

1	Net income (loss). Combine Schedule K, lines 1 through 11. From the result, subtract the sum of Schedule K, lines 12 through 13d, and 16l					**1**	
2	Analysis by partner type:	**(i)** Corporate	**(ii)** Individual (active)	**(iii)** Individual (passive)	**(iv)** Partnership	**(v)** Exempt Organization	**(vi)** Nominee/Other
a	General partners						
b	Limited partners						

Schedule L — Balance Sheets per Books

		Beginning of tax year (a)	Beginning of tax year (b)	End of tax year (c)	End of tax year (d)
1	Cash				
2a	Trade notes and accounts receivable				
b	Less allowance for bad debts				
3	Inventories				
4	U.S. government obligations				
5	Tax-exempt securities				
6	Other current assets (attach statement)				
7a	Loans to partners (or persons related to partners)				
b	Mortgage and real estate loans				
8	Other investments (attach statement)				
9a	Buildings and other depreciable assets				
b	Less accumulated depreciation				
10a	Depletable assets				
b	Less accumulated depletion				
11	Land (net of any amortization)				
12a	Intangible assets (amortizable only)				
b	Less accumulated amortization				
13	Other assets (attach statement)				
14	Total assets				
	Liabilities and Capital				
15	Accounts payable				
16	Mortgages, notes, bonds payable in less than 1 year				
17	Other current liabilities (attach statement)				
18	All nonrecourse loans				
19a	Loans from partners (or persons related to partners)				
b	Mortgages, notes, bonds payable in 1 year or more				
20	Other liabilities (attach statement)				
21	Partners' capital accounts				
22	Total liabilities and capital				

Schedule M-1 — Reconciliation of Income (Loss) per Books With Income (Loss) per Return

Note. The partnership may be required to file Schedule M-3 (see instructions).

1	Net income (loss) per books		**6**	Income recorded on books this year not included on Schedule K, lines 1 through 11 (itemize):	
2	Income included on Schedule K, lines 1, 2, 3c, 5, 6a, 7, 8, 9a, 10, and 11, not recorded on books this year (itemize):		**a**	Tax-exempt interest $	
3	Guaranteed payments (other than health insurance)		**7**	Deductions included on Schedule K, lines 1 through 13d, and 16l, not charged against book income this year (itemize):	
4	Expenses recorded on books this year not included on Schedule K, lines 1 through 13d, and 16l (itemize):		**a**	Depreciation $	
a	Depreciation $		**8**	Add lines 6 and 7	
b	Travel and entertainment $		**9**	Income (loss) (Analysis of Net Income (Loss), line 1). Subtract line 8 from line 5	
5	Add lines 1 through 4				

Schedule M-2 — Analysis of Partners' Capital Accounts

1	Balance at beginning of year		**6**	Distributions: **a** Cash	
2	Capital contributed: **a** Cash			**b** Property	
	b Property		**7**	Other decreases (itemize):	
3	Net income (loss) per books				
4	Other increases (itemize):		**8**	Add lines 6 and 7	
5	Add lines 1 through 4		**9**	Balance at end of year. Subtract line 8 from line 5	

Form **1065** (2015)

(Use for Problem 19.)

651113

☐ Final K-1 ☐ Amended K-1 OMB No. 1545-0123

Schedule K-1 (Form 1065) **2015**

Department of the Treasury
Internal Revenue Service

For calendar year 2015, or tax year beginning ________, 2015 ending ________, 20____

Partner's Share of Income, Deductions, Credits, etc. ▶ **See back of form and separate instructions.**

Part I Information About the Partnership

A Partnership's employer identification number

B Partnership's name, address, city, state, and ZIP code

C IRS Center where partnership filed return

D ☐ Check if this is a publicly traded partnership (PTP)

Part II Information About the Partner

E Partner's identifying number

F Partner's name, address, city, state, and ZIP code

G ☐ General partner or LLC member-manager ☐ Limited partner or other LLC member

H ☐ Domestic partner ☐ Foreign partner

I1 What type of entity is this partner? ________

I2 If this partner is a retirement plan (IRA/SEP/Keogh/etc.), check here . . . ☐

J Partner's share of profit, loss, and capital (see instructions):

	Beginning	Ending
Profit	%	%
Loss	%	%
Capital	%	%

K Partner's share of liabilities at year end:

Nonrecourse . . . . $ ________
Qualified nonrecourse financing . $ ________
Recourse . . . . $ ________

L Partner's capital account analysis:

Beginning capital account . . . $ ________
Capital contributed during the year $ ________
Current year increase (decrease) . $ ________
Withdrawals & distributions . . . $ (________)
Ending capital account . . . . $ ________

☐ Tax basis ☐ GAAP ☐ Section 704(b) book
☐ Other (explain)

M Did the partner contribute property with a built-in gain or loss?
☐ **Yes** ☐ **No**
If "Yes," attach statement (see instructions)

Part III Partner's Share of Current Year Income, Deductions, Credits, and Other Items

1	Ordinary business income (loss)	15	Credits
2	Net rental real estate income (loss)		
3	Other net rental income (loss)	16	Foreign transactions
4	Guaranteed payments		
5	Interest income		
6a	Ordinary dividends		
6b	Qualified dividends		
7	Royalties		
8	Net short-term capital gain (loss)		
9a	Net long-term capital gain (loss)	17	Alternative minimum tax (AMT) items
9b	Collectibles (28%) gain (loss)		
9c	Unrecaptured section 1250 gain		
10	Net section 1231 gain (loss)	18	Tax-exempt income and nondeductible expenses
11	Other income (loss)		
		19	Distributions
12	Section 179 deduction		
13	Other deductions	20	Other information
14	Self-employment earnings (loss)		

*See attached statement for additional information.

For IRS Use Only

For Paperwork Reduction Act Notice, see Instructions for Form 1065. IRS.gov/form1065 Cat. No. 11394R **Schedule K-1 (Form 1065) 2015**

Chapter

16

S Corporations

CHAPTER CONTENTS

LEARNING OBJECTIVES

After completing Chapter 16, you should be able to:

1. Understand the tax characteristics of S corporations, including the selection of a year-end, how they are formed and terminated (along with the tax consequences), and the eligibility requirements.
2. Distinguish between ordinary income and separately stated items, explain the need for separately stated items, and compute ordinary income.
3. Compute a shareholder's pro rata share of S corporation items, including how owners should treat payments made to them from the business for services rendered.
4. Compute an S corporation shareholder's basis and understand its impact on the shareholder's ability to deduct losses and its impact on how distributions are treated.
5. Prepare the tax forms introduced in this chapter, including Form 1120S and Schedule K-1 (Form 1120S).

CHAPTER OVERVIEW

Partnerships and S corporations are both flow-through entities. Although partnerships and S corporations share some common traits, S corporations have some corporate traits as well. For one, like a (regular) C corporation, the owners of an S corporation are shareholders. In contrast, the owners of a partnership are partners. Thus, shareholders of an S corporation have the same protection from the debts of the corporation that shareholders in a C corporation have. This chapter examines the tax aspects of S corporations both from the standpoint of the corporation and its shareholders.

¶1601 The Nature of S Corporations

When a corporation elects S corporation status, the shareholders, not the corporation, are responsible for the income taxes. The shareholders include their pro rata shares of the corporation's taxable income on their personal tax returns. This happens regardless of whether the corporation makes cash distributions to the shareholders. The corporation files an information return similar to a partnership's tax return. Hence, the conduit concept of passing through income, deductions, and credits to the owners applies to S corporations and partnerships.

Even though an S corporation generally pays no income tax, it is in all other respects a corporation under state law and must act accordingly. This means that the owners can choose the S corporation form of organization for nontax reasons (like limited liability) and still benefit from the single level of taxing income. It should be noted that some states do not recognize S corporation status in filing a corporate tax return. In these states, the corporation must file a state corporate tax return and pay a state corporate income tax.

¶1602 S Corporation Status

A corporation must qualify as a small business corporation before it can elect S corporation status. The term "**small business corporation**" may seem misleading because the law does not limit the size of the corporation. Rather, it limits the types of corporations that qualify for S status, as well as the types and number of shareholders an S corporation can have.

¶1602.01 REQUIREMENTS

A corporation must have certain traits to qualify as a small business corporation. First, it must be a domestic corporation. Second, it can only have one class of stock. Third, it cannot have more than 100 shareholders; and finally, it can only have certain types of shareholders.

Domestic Corporation

An S corporation must be a U.S. or U.S. territory corporation. Certain U.S. corporations cannot elect S corporation status. These corporations include Domestic International Sales Corporations, financial institutions, insurance companies, and corporations taking the Puerto Rico or possessions tax credit.

One Class of Stock

A small business corporation can only have one class of stock outstanding. One class of stock means that the outstanding shares of the corporation must have identical rights in both the distribution of profits and the liquidation of corporate assets. The articles of incorporation, other binding agreements, and state law determine whether all outstanding shares have identical rights. The tax laws, however, allow for differences in the voting rights within the one class of stock.

EXAMPLE 1

A corporation's articles of incorporation allow the corporation to issue both common and preferred stock. However, the corporation currently only has common shares outstanding. The preferred shares had been issued in the past, but no shares are outstanding at this time. The corporation currently has only one class of stock outstanding. Thus, it passes the one class of stock test.

EXAMPLE 2

All of the outstanding shares of common stock in a corporation give the owners the same rights to distribution and liquidation proceeds. However, some shares give the owner the right to vote on corporate matters, while others do not. Because all shares have the same distribution and liquidation rights, the corporation will be considered to have only one class of stock, even though some shares are voting and others are nonvoting.

Number of Shareholders

A small business corporation may have up to 100 shareholders. Family members are treated as one shareholder for purposes of counting the number of shareholders. "Family members" include a common ancestor and all lineal descendants within six generations of that common ancestor, as well as the spouses and former spouses of these individuals. Thus, the S corporation can actually have more than 100 shareholders when some of the shareholders are family members. All other shareholders (i.e., those who are not family members) are counted separately, even if they own the stock jointly with someone else. Finally, when a voting trust holds stock in an S corporation, each "non-family" beneficiary of the trust, not the trust itself, counts as a shareholder for purposes of the 100 shareholder limit.

EXAMPLE 3

Lou and Marge Carter own stock in an S corporation. Lou's father, as well as the Carters' six children and nine grandchildren also own stock in the S corporation. These 18 individuals are treated as one shareholder for purposes of the 100 shareholder limit because they all have a common ancestor (Lou's father) and the family members are within six generations of one another.

EXAMPLE 4

Jan and her best friend own stock in an S corporation as joint tenants. Jan and her friend are treated as two shareholders for purposes the 100 shareholder limit.

EXAMPLE 5

John and Mary, a married couple, each own shares in an S corporation. The corporation has 100 shareholders, counting John and Mary as one shareholder under the "family member" rule. If John and Mary divorce and each retain shares in the S corporation, the corporation would still have 100 shareholders, since former spouses count as family members.

Shareholder Type Limitation

Shareholders in an S corporation must be individuals (other than nonresident aliens), estates, and certain trusts. Partnerships, C corporations, and other S corporations cannot be shareholders in an S corporation. If these business entities were allowed to be owners, the 100-shareholder limit could easily be avoided. Trusts that can be shareholders include (1) a trust owned by one individual, (2) voting trusts, and (3) a "qualified S corporation trust." A voting trust is a trust set up to combine the voting rights of its beneficiaries. A qualified S corporation trust owns stock in one or more S corporations and distributes all of its income to only one qualified individual.

¶1602.02 ELECTION

A corporation meeting the four requirements discussed in ¶1602.01 may make an S election with the consent of all its shareholders. The corporation makes the election by filing Form 2553, Election by a Small Business Corporation.

Timing of Election

An election to become an S corporation always becomes effective at the beginning of the corporation's tax year. To have the election apply to the corporation's current tax year, the corporation must file Form 2553 during the prior tax year or within the first 2½ months of the current year. Also, the corporation must meet the requirements for S status from the beginning of the current year and must continue meeting the requirements in order to maintain its S election. An election filed after the 15th day of the third month applies to the following tax year.

EXAMPLE 6

On March 1, 20x1, a calendar year C corporation files Form 2553 with the IRS to elect S corporation status. Because the election is filed by March 15, it normally would be effective retroactive to January 1, 20x1. However, if during any time from January 1, 20x1 and March 1, 20x1, the corporation failed to qualify as a small business corporation, then its election would not be effective until January 1, 20x2.

Only existing corporations can elect S status. Thus, deciding when a corporation comes into existence is important. This is especially true when determining the 2½-month election period. The election period begins in the month the corporation comes into existence. A corporation begins to exist when it (1) begins conducting business transactions, (2) acquires assets, or (3) first issues stock.

EXAMPLE 7

On November 11, 20x1, a corporation comes into existence. The corporation has until 2½ months after November 11, 20x1 to file its S election if it wants to file as an S corporation in its first tax year (assuming it qualifies as a small business corporation).

Shareholder Consent

All shareholders must consent to the S corporation election. This includes any former shareholders who owned stock in the year the election is effective, but prior to the filing of Form 2553. If a former shareholder will not agree to the election (but all current shareholders will), then the election will become effective on the first day of the next tax year. A shareholder's consent is binding and may be withdrawn only by following certain prescribed procedures.

EXAMPLE 8

On January 1, 20x1, Karen owned stock in X Corporation (a calendar year taxpayer). She sells the stock on February 10, 20x1. On March 1, 20x1, all current X Corporation shareholders elect to be an S corporation effective January 1, 20x1. In order for the election to be valid, Karen must consent to the election, even though she is no longer a shareholder on March 1, 20x1. Karen's consent is necessary because she will report on her 20x1 tax return her share of income from January 1, 20x1, to February 10, 20x1, while she owned stock in X Corporation. If Karen does not consent to the S election, the election will become effective on January 1, 20x2.

Shareholders execute a consent by providing all of the required information on Form 2553. Shareholders may also consent by signing a separate consent statement, which should be attached to Form 2553. The separate consent should furnish the following information:

1. The name, address, and taxpayer identification number of the corporation,
2. The name, address, and taxpayer identification number of the shareholder,
3. The number of shares owned by the shareholder and the dates on which the stock was acquired, and
4. The day and month of the end of the shareholder's tax year.

Each co-owner, tenant by entirety, tenant in common, and joint tenant must consent to the S election. This means that each family member must consent, even though they are treated as one shareholder. The legal representative or guardian may consent for a minor shareholder. The executor or administrator of an estate makes the consent for the estate. The consent of a qualified trust holding stock must be made by each person who is treated as a shareholder. Extensions of time to file a consent may be granted under certain circumstances.

¶1602.03 TERMINATION

An S corporation election may be terminated either voluntarily or automatically upon the occurrence of certain events.

Voluntary Termination

To voluntarily terminate S corporation status, shareholders owning more than 50% of the shares must consent to end the S status. The corporation then files a statement to this effect with the IRS office where it had previously filed its election. If a timely filed revocation specifies an effective date, the revocation will be effective on that date. From that date forward, the corporation is taxed as a (regular) C corporation. Thus, even though an election to become an S corporation must be effective on the first day of a tax year, a termination may be effective before the end of the regular tax year. When no specific termination date is given, a revocation filed within the first 2½ months of the corporation's tax year is retroactive to the first day of the tax year. When filed after the first 2½ months, the revocation is effective on the first day of the following tax year.

EXAMPLE 9

On March 15, 20x1, a calendar year S corporation files a statement with the IRS to revoke its S election. If the statement does not specify a future date on which the revocation is to take effect, the corporation's S status will be revoked retroactively to January 1, 20x1.

EXAMPLE 10

Same facts as in Example 9, except that the corporation files the statement to revoke its S election on March 18, 20x1. If the statement does not specify a future date on which the revocation is to take effect, the corporation's S status will be revoked effective January 1, 20x2.

To elect S status, the tax law requires that all affected shareholders consent to the election. To revoke an S election, only a majority of the corporation's shareholders must provide their consent.

Automatic Termination

S corporation status automatically terminates upon the occurrence of one of the following events:

1. The corporation fails to remain a small business corporation.
2. The corporation that has earnings and profits (E&P) carried over from when it was a regular C corporation generates passive investment income in excess of 25% of its gross receipts for three consecutive years. (Thus, if the corporation was always an S corporation or was once a C corporation but has no E&P, passive investment income cannot trigger automatic termination).

When an S corporation no longer qualifies as a small business corporation, the S status terminates as of the date on which the disqualifying event occurs. As a result, the day before the terminating event is the last day for the S corporation, and the day of termination becomes the first day of C corporation status. When the S status terminates because of prolonged excessive passive income, the termination is effective beginning with the first day of the next tax year.

EXAMPLE 11 An S corporation has been operating on a calendar year basis for the last few years with 100 shareholders. On July 21, 20x1, one of the shareholders dies, with his shares passing equally to his wife and best friend on that date. Having no common ancestor, the wife and best friend count as two shareholders. Thus, the status as an S corporation automatically terminates on July 21, 20x1. The S corporation must file a return for the period January 1, 20x1, through July 20, 20x1. On July 21, 20x1, the corporation becomes a C corporation for the remainder of the year ending December 31, 20x1. All income (loss) and separately stated items are prorated between the S corporation tax return and the C corporation tax return on a daily basis.

Reelection

Generally, if an election terminates (either voluntarily or automatically), the corporation may not reelect S status for five years. However, the IRS may allow an earlier election when violations of the S corporation requirements were minor. If the S corporation election was inadvertently terminated, the IRS may even waive termination when the corporation promptly corrects the violation.

¶1603 S Corporation Tax Returns

An S corporation files an annual informational tax return, Form 1120S, U.S. Income Tax Return for an S Corporation. It is due on the 15th day of the third month after the end of the corporation's tax year. For a calendar year corporation (C or S corporation), the return is due March 15. As with a C corporation, an S corporation receives an automatic six-month extension of time to file its return when it completes and files Form 7004 by the due date for the original return. The Internal Revenue Code (Code) imposes a penalty on the S corporation (not the shareholders) when it fails to file Form 1120S in a timely manner. The monthly penalty (imposed for up to 12 months) is $195 times the number of persons who were shareholders at any time during the year. This is the same penalty that is imposed on partnerships that fail to file a timely tax return (¶1502).

The character of all items of income, deductions, losses, and credits passes through from the corporation to the shareholders in a manner similar to partnerships. The shareholders receive a Schedule K-1 (Form 1120S) that reports their shares of the ordinary income and each separately stated item. The tax law requires companies to furnish this information to owners no later than the filing due date for Form 1120S. The S corporation is assessed a penalty of $100 for each Schedule K-1 not provided to its shareholders in a timely manner. Thus, if an S corporation with 120 shareholders fails to timely furnish Schedules K-1 to its shareholders, the corporation will be assessed a $12,000 penalty ($100 penalty × 120 shareholders). If the failure to furnish this information is found to be intentional, the $100 penalty increases to $250. This penalty is the same penalty imposed on a partnership that fails to furnish timely Schedules K-1 (Form 1065) to each of its partners (¶1502). The information reported on Form 1120S and Schedule K-1 (Form 1120S) is explained in greater detail later in the chapter in ¶1603.06 and ¶1603.07, respectively.

¶1603.01 TAX YEAR

S corporations must have the same tax year as the shareholders owning more than 50% of the stock. Since most S corporation shareholders are individuals, this is generally a calendar year. However, exceptions may apply. One exception involves the natural business year. In a natural business year, 25% of gross receipts are received in the last two months of the fiscal year for three years in a row. A second exception allows an S corporation to elect a tax year that provides no more than a three-month deferral for its shareholders. This is known as a Section 444 election. These two exceptions are the same two exceptions to the required tax year rule for partnerships. See ¶1502.02 for further discussion of these exceptions and for more on the Section 444 election.

EXAMPLE 12

The shareholders of an S corporation have a calendar tax year. If allowed, they would prefer the S corporation to have a January 31 year-end. This would allow the income earned from February 1, 20x1, to January 31, 20x2, to be taxable on the shareholders' 20x2 tax returns. This would result in an 11-month tax deferral. The tax law, however, requires S corporations have a calendar year-end unless they can meet requirements for one of the exceptions to the required tax year rule.

¶1603.02 REPORTING INCOME AND DEDUCTIONS

When completing Form 1120S, it is necessary to divide the S corporation's tax items into two categories: (1) separately stated items and (2) ordinary items. The ordinary items not separately stated comprise ordinary income or loss. As with partnerships, the separately stated items and ordinary income (loss) pass through to the shareholders, who report them on their personal income tax returns.

Separately Stated Items

As discussed in Chapter 15, separately stated items are income, deductions, and tax credits that have the possibility of affecting shareholders' tax returns differently. The most common separately stated items for S corporations are the same as the items separately stated for partnerships (see discussion at ¶1502.04). These items appear on Form 1120S, Schedule K, Shareholders' Pro Rata Share Items. Schedule K-1 (Form 1120S) provides each shareholder's share of separately stated items.

Examples of Separately Stated Items

- Charitable contributions
- Net short-term and long-term capital gains (losses)
- Tax-exempt income
- Investment income (interest, dividends)
- Nondeductible expenses
- Section 179 expense deduction
- Investment expenses
- Net Section 1231 gains (losses)
- Personal expenses paid for the shareholder's benefit
- Foreign taxes
- Tax credits
- Tax preferences and adjustments related to AMT activities
- Net income (loss) from rental real estate activities

Ordinary Income or Loss

Ordinary income (loss) is generally the net result of the S corporation's trade or business activities. It includes all items of income or deductions that are not separately stated. These tend to be the same items used in determining partnership ordinary income (see discussion at ¶1502.05). The resulting amount of ordinary income (loss) passes through to the shareholders along with the separately stated items on the Schedule K-1 (Form 1120S). A copy of each shareholder's Schedule K-1 is attached to the S corporation's Form 1120S. A copy is also given to the shareholder. The shareholders include taxable items from their Schedules K-1 on their own income tax returns. For example, the shareholder's pro rata share of an S corporation's ordinary income (loss) appears on the shareholder's Form 1040, Schedule E.

In general partnerships, limited liability companies, and sole proprietorships, FICA taxes (self-employment taxes) apply to all ordinary income passing to the owners. However, in S corporations, FICA taxes apply only to designated salaries, and the corporation is responsible for sending in the FICA taxes to the government. Recall that FICA is shared by the employee and the employer (¶1302.01). No FICA taxes are paid on the S corporation's ordinary income, which flows through to the owners.

Deductions Not Allowed

Like partnerships, certain individual deductions are not available to S corporations, such as the standard deduction, itemized deductions, and the deduction for personal and dependency exemptions. S corporations also cannot take certain deductions available to regular taxable C corporations. The most notable of these deductions is the dividends received deduction.

¶1603.03 ALLOCATION OF TAX ITEMS TO SHAREHOLDERS

A shareholder's share of S corporation income, deductions, losses, and credits is determined on a per-share-per-day basis. The S corporation allocates an equal amount of each item to each share on a per-day basis for the corporation's tax year. The per-share-per-day amount is multiplied by the number of shares the shareholder owned each day of the year. The shareholders' personal tax returns include their allocated yearly totals for each of the S corporation tax items.

EXAMPLE 13 On January 1, 20x1, the 30,000 shares of stock outstanding in a calendar year S corporation are owned equally by Greene, White, and Brown. On October 19, 20x1, Brown sells his 10,000 shares to Black. During 20x1, the corporation earns $150,000 of ordinary taxable income and $90,000 of long-term capital gains. Since Greene and White own their respective one-third interests for the entire year, each reports one-third of the ordinary income ($50,000) and one-third of the capital gains ($30,000) on their 20x1 tax returns. However, because neither Brown nor Black owned their shares for the entire tax year, their pro rata share of the corporation's ordinary income and long-term capital gain must be determined on a per-share, per-day basis.

Brown owned 10,000 shares from January 1 through October 19, a total of 292 days. Black owned 10,000 shares for 73 days (from October 20 through December 31). Brown's pro rata share of ordinary income and capital gain equal $40,000 ($50,000 × 292/365) and $24,000 ($30,000 × 292/365), respectively. Similarly, Black's pro rata share of these items equals $10,000 ($50,000 × 73/365) and $6,000 ($30,000 × 73/365), respectively. These prorated amounts are reported on each shareholder's respective Schedule K-1.

¶1603.04 UTILIZING LOSSES

S corporation shareholders may deduct their pro rata share of losses to the extent of their basis in the S corporation stock. Thus, losses cannot reduce the owner's basis below zero. A partner's basis includes the partner's share of all partnership liabilities. In contrast, the S corporation's general liabilities are not part of the S shareholder's basis because of the limited liability feature that comes with having corporate status. The only time the corporation's debt increases an S corporation shareholder's basis is when the shareholder has loaned amounts directly to the corporation. Thus, a partner generally has a larger basis for utilizing losses than would an S shareholder. Disallowed losses carry forward and are deductible when the shareholder has sufficient basis to cover the losses.

EXAMPLE 14

Swift (an S corporation) has five shareholders, each owning 100 shares and each having a $25,000 basis in the stock. Each shareholder materially participates in the operations of Swift. For 20x1, Swift reports an operating loss of $75,000. Each shareholder's pro rata share of the loss ($15,000) is deductible on the shareholder's individual tax return because it does not reduce any shareholder's basis below zero. After the $15,000 loss, each shareholder's basis in his or her Swift shares is $10,000 ($25,000 – $15,000).

EXAMPLE 15

Chang owns a 30% interest in Inco, an S corporation. At the end of 20x1, Chang's basis in Inco stock is $15,000 and she has $12,000 of loans outstanding to Inco. The corporation reports an operating loss for 20x1 of $120,000, of which Chang's 30% share is $36,000. Chang deducts $27,000 of the total loss ($15,000 stock basis + $12,000 loan basis) on her personal tax return. The remaining $9,000 loss ($36,000 – $27,000) carries over to 20x2 and later years to be offset against future positive stock basis.

When the lack of basis limits the shareholder's deductibility of losses, an allocation of the allowed loss among the various items is necessary. The allocation percentage equals each loss item divided by the shareholder's total losses for the year. The portion of each item disallowed carries forward.

EXAMPLE 16

Ike has a $20,000 basis in his 40% ownership in an S corporation. Ike's 40% share of the corporation's ordinary loss and capital loss is $24,000 and $8,000, respectively. His pro rata share of total losses equal $32,000 ($24,000 + $8,000). Ike can deduct $20,000 of losses (an amount equal to his basis). More specifically, he deducts $15,000 of ordinary income ($20,000 × $24,000/$32,000) on his tax return and includes $5,000 of capital loss in his netting process ($20,000 × $8,000/$32,000). Ike carries forward to future years a total loss of $12,000. The carryover loss consists of an ordinary loss deduction of $9,000 ($24,000 – $15,000) and a capital loss deduction of $3,000 ($8,000 – $5,000)

i

In addition to the basis loss limitation rules described above, S corporation shareholders are also subject to the at-risk (¶904) and passive loss (¶905) rules.

When an S corporation election terminates, any disallowed loss can be deducted as long as the shareholders restore their stock basis sufficiently to cover their losses. The basis must be restored by the *later of* the following two dates:

1. One year after the effective date of termination or the due date of the last S corporation tax return, whichever is later, or
2. 120 days after a determination that the corporation's election had terminated for a previous year.

¶1603.05 FORM 1120S

Form 1120S is set up very much like the partnership tax return. Form 1120S consists of five pages. On page 1, the S corporation provides general information about itself and computes its ordinary income. On page 2 of Form 1120S, the corporation provides other information about itself on Schedule B. Schedule K begins on page 3 and concludes at the top of page 4. Like with the partnership tax return, Schedule K reports the corporation's ordinary income (or loss) plus all separately stated items. Page 4 also reports the corporation's balance sheet on Schedule L. Finally, page 5 concludes with Schedules M-1 (reconciliation of book income and tax income), and M-2 (analysis of the accumulated adjustment account and other capital accounts).

As with partnerships, the calculation of ordinary income on page 1 includes all items of income and expense that are treated and taxed the same for all taxpayers. These items are not subject to any limitations that would be unique to any one taxpayer. The calculation of ordinary income for S corporations is essentially the same as that for partnerships, with one important exception. In Chapter 15, you learned that partners could not be employees of the partnership. Thus, payments that resemble "salaries" paid to partners are called guaranteed payments (see ¶1502.05). These amounts are deducted in the calculation of the partnership's ordinary income. With respect to an S corporation, all shareholders working for the S corporation are considered employees, and payments to shareholders in exchange for services they perform are deducted as wages. Thus, an S corporation does not make guaranteed payments.

Schedule K Items

The S corporation's ordinary business income (loss) from Form 1120S, page 1 (line 21) is also reported on Schedule K, Shareholders' Pro Rata Share Items. Income and expense items not part of ordinary income as well as tax credits, are separately stated and reported on Schedule K. The S corporation uses the amounts found on the Schedule K to make its per-share-per-day allocations to its shareholders. These are reported to each shareholder on a separate Schedule K-1. The shareholders combine their Schedule K-1 items with their other income, expense, and credit items. The resulting amounts appear on the shareholders' own income tax returns.

Schedule L

Schedule L, Balance Sheets per Books, contains a beginning and ending balance sheet for the S corporation. The amounts shown should agree with the corporation's regular books or records. Thus, they typically are not reported on a tax basis. An S corporation is required to complete Schedule L only when its total assets at the end of the year or total receipts for the year are $250,000 or more (see instructions below question 10 on Form 1120S, page 2, Section B).

Schedule M-1

Schedule M-1, Reconciliation of Income (Loss) per Books With Income (Loss) per Return, is completed if total assets at year-end or total receipts for the year are $250,000 or more (see instructions below question 10 on Form 1120S, page 2, Section B). This schedule accounts for all differences between book (financial) income and the income reported on the tax return. The tax return income includes ordinary income (loss) plus the separately stated items found on Schedule K. Any items included in book income, but not on Form 1120S or vice versa, are reconciling items on Schedule M-1. The most common reconciling items on Schedule M-1 are depreciation; travel and entertainment expenses; and tax-exempt items.

Schedule M-2

Schedule M-2, Analysis of Accumulated Adjustments Account, Other Adjustments Account, and Shareholders' Undistributed Taxable Income Previously Taxed, shows the changes in the equity accounts for the income and deductions reported on Form 1120S. Column (a) provides the changes in the accumulated adjustments account (AAA) for the year (described later in the chapter at ¶1604.02). The ending balance becomes the beginning balance of Schedule M-2 (line 1), column (a) for the next year. Column (b), Other Adjustments Account, is for an analysis of other items, such as tax-exempt income and related expenses, not used in computing AAA. Column (c) on Schedule M-2 lists the amount of undistributed taxable income previously included in shareholders' income tax returns. Only corporations electing S status before 1983 use column (c).

¶1603.06 FILLED-IN FORM 1120S

INFORMATION FOR FIGURE 16-2:

Kendall Management Company is a cash basis management service business that provides consulting services to its clients. Kendall was a regular C corporation prior to it S status election on **January 15, 2004** (EIN **52-1739257**; business activity code number **7389**). Originally formed on **October 1, 1989**, Kendall is located at **731 Delhi Road, Atlanta, GA 30307. Tax Consultants, Inc.** prepares Kendall's Form 1120S. **Virginia Kendall, President**, signs the tax return for the corporation on **March 1, 2016**.

The amounts reported on Schedule L come from Kendall's balance sheet using its set of books and records. Kendall's accumulated earnings and profits at the end of the year is $56,900. Its beginning balance in the AAA account is $25,800. During the year, Kendall distributed a total of $30,000 to its shareholders out of AAA. Kendall had six shareholders during the year. The remaining information for preparing Form 1120S comes from the income statement found in Figure 16-1.

Line # (Form 1120S, page 1)

F: Total assets, **$225,650** (source: Schedule L, line 15, column d)
I: Number of shareholders, **6** (source: given)
18: Employee benefits program, **$7,300** (employee health insurance)
19: Other deductions, **$4,500** ($1,000 insurance + $800 supplies + $2,700 utilities)

Line # (Form 1120S, Schedule B)

1: Accounting method, check box **a** (source: cash basis taxpayer)
2a: Business activity, **Management services** (source: given)
2b: Product or service, **Consulting** (source: given)
9: Year-end balance in accumulated earnings and profits, **$56,900** (source: provided by company)
10: Check box for **Yes**, since both total receipts and total assets are less than $250,000

Line # (Form 1120S, Schedule K)

4: Interest income, **$720** (source: taxable interest reported on the Income Statement)
5a: Ordinary dividends, **$2,000** (source: total dividends reported on the Income Statement)
5b: Qualified dividends, **$1,250** (source: Income Statement)
8a: Net long-term capital gain, **$10,480** (source: Schedule D (Form 1120S), line 13)
12a: Charitable contributions, **$7,000** (source: Income Statement)
16a: Tax-exempt interest, **$1,100** (source: Income Statement)
17a: Investment income, **$2,720** ($720 taxable interest + $2,000 dividend income)
18: Income/loss reconciliation, **$46,200** ($40,000 + $720 + $2,000 + $10,480 – $7,000)

Line # (Form 1120S, Schedule M-1)

1: Net income (loss) per books, **$47,300** (source: Net income form the Income Statement)
5a: Tax-exempt interest, **$1,100** (source: Income Statement and Schedule K, line 16a)

Line # (Form 1120S, Schedule M-2)

1(a): Beginning balance Accumulated adjustments account, **$25,800** (source: last year's ending balance)
1(b): Beginning balance Other adjustments account, **$1,000** (source: last year's ending balance)
3(a): Other additions to AAA, **$13,200** ($720 taxable interest + $2,000 ordinary dividends + $10,480 capital gain)
3(b): Other additions to Other adjustments account, **$1,100** (tax-exempt interest)
5(a): Other reductions, **$7,000** (charitable contributions)
7(a): Distributions, **$30,000** (source: given)

Figure 16-1: Kendall Management 2015 Income Statement

Income:	
Receipts from services	$165,350
Interest income (taxable, $720; tax-exempt, $1,100)	1,820
Dividend income (qualified dividends, $1,250)	2,000
Gain on sale of stock	10,480
Total income	$179,650
Expenses:	
Advertising	$ 7,700
Bad debts (direct write-off method)	400
Charitable contributions	7,000
Depreciation (book and tax depreciation)	1,700
Employee health insurance	7,300
Insurance expense	1,000
Maintenance and repairs	1,200
Officers' salaries	70,000
Other employee salaries	21,550
Office supplies	800
Payroll taxes	5,000
Retirement plan contributions	6,000
Utilities	2,700
Total expenses	$132,350
Net Income	$ 47,300

Figure 16-2: Filled-In Form 1120S (Page 1)

Form **1120S** | Department of the Treasury Internal Revenue Service

U.S. Income Tax Return for an S Corporation

▶ **Do not file this form unless the corporation has filed or is attaching Form 2553 to elect to be an S corporation.**

▶ **Information about Form 1120S and its separate instructions is at *www.irs.gov/form1120s.***

OMB No. 1545-0123 | **2015**

For calendar year 2015 or tax year beginning , 2015, ending , 20

A S election effective date: **1-15-2004**	TYPE OR PRINT	Name: **Kendall Management Company**	**D** Employer identification number: **52-1739257**
B Business activity code number (see instructions): **7389**		Number, street, and room or suite no. If a P.O. box, see instructions.: **731 Delhi Road**	**E** Date incorporated: **10-1-89**
C Check if Sch. M-3 attached ☐		City or town, state or province, country, and ZIP or foreign postal code: **Atlanta, GA 30307**	**F** Total assets (see instructions): $ **225,650**

G Is the corporation electing to be an S corporation beginning with this tax year? ☐ Yes ☑ No If "Yes," attach Form 2553 if not already filed

H Check if: **(1)** ☐ Final return **(2)** ☐ Name change **(3)** ☐ Address change **(4)** ☐ Amended return **(5)** ☐ S election termination or revocation

I Enter the number of shareholders who were shareholders during any part of the tax year . . . ▶ **6**

Caution: Include **only** trade or business income and expenses on lines 1a through 21. See the instructions for more information.

Income	1a	Gross receipts or sales	1a	165,350		
	b	Returns and allowances	1b			
	c	Balance. Subtract line 1b from line 1a			1c	165,350
	2	Cost of goods sold (attach Form 1125-A)			2	
	3	Gross profit. Subtract line 2 from line 1c			3	165,350
	4	Net gain (loss) from Form 4797, line 17 (attach Form 4797)			4	
	5	Other income (loss) (see instructions—attach statement)			5	
	6	**Total income (loss).** Add lines 3 through 5 ▶			6	165,350
Deductions (see instructions for limitations)	7	Compensation of officers (see instructions—attach Form 1125-E)			7	70,000
	8	Salaries and wages (less employment credits)			8	21,550
	9	Repairs and maintenance			9	1,200
	10	Bad debts			10	400
	11	Rents			11	
	12	Taxes and licenses			12	5,000
	13	Interest			13	
	14	Depreciation not claimed on Form 1125-A or elsewhere on return (attach Form 4562)			14	1,700
	15	Depletion **(Do not deduct oil and gas depletion.)**			15	
	16	Advertising			16	7,700
	17	Pension, profit-sharing, etc., plans			17	6,000
	18	Employee benefit programs			18	7,300
	19	Other deductions (attach statement)			19	4,500
	20	**Total deductions.** Add lines 7 through 19 ▶			20	125,350
	21	**Ordinary business income (loss).** Subtract line 20 from line 6			21	40,000
Tax and Payments	22a	Excess net passive income or LIFO recapture tax (see instructions)	22a			
	b	Tax from Schedule D (Form 1120S)	22b			
	c	Add lines 22a and 22b (see instructions for additional taxes)			22c	0
	23a	2015 estimated tax payments and 2014 overpayment credited to 2015	23a			
	b	Tax deposited with Form 7004	23b			
	c	Credit for federal tax paid on fuels (attach Form 4136)	23c			
	d	Add lines 23a through 23c			23d	0
	24	Estimated tax penalty (see instructions). Check if Form 2220 is attached ▶ ☐			24	
	25	**Amount owed.** If line 23d is smaller than the total of lines 22c and 24, enter amount owed			25	0
	26	**Overpayment.** If line 23d is larger than the total of lines 22c and 24, enter amount overpaid			26	
	27	Enter amount from line 26 **Credited to 2016 estimated tax** ▶		**Refunded** ▶	27	

Sign Here

Under penalties of perjury, I declare that I have examined this return, including accompanying schedules and statements, and to the best of my knowledge and belief, it is true, correct, and complete. Declaration of preparer (other than taxpayer) is based on all information of which preparer has any knowledge.

Signature of officer	Date	Title	May the IRS discuss this return with the preparer shown below (see instructions)?
Virginia Kendall	3-1-16	**President**	☐ Yes ☐ No

Paid Preparer Use Only

Print/Type preparer's name	Preparer's signature	Date	Check ☐ if self-employed	PTIN
John Downs	*John Downs*	2-28-16		**89-512334**
Firm's name ▶ **Tax Consultants, Inc.**			Firm's EIN ▶	**61-9077665**
Firm's address ▶ **12 Peachtree Street, Atlanta GA 30337**			Phone no.	

For Paperwork Reduction Act Notice, see separate instructions. Cat. No. 11510H Form **1120S** (2015)

Figure 16-2: Filled-In Form 1120S (Page 2)

Form 1120S (2015) Page **2**

Schedule B **Other Information** (see instructions)

		Yes	No
1	Check accounting method: a ☑ Cash b ☐ Accrual c ☐ Other (specify) ▶		
2	See the instructions and enter the: a Business activity ▶ **Management Services** b Product or service ▶ **Consulting**		
3	At any time during the tax year, was any shareholder of the corporation a disregarded entity, a trust, an estate, or a nominee or similar person? If "Yes," attach Schedule B-1, Information on Certain Shareholders of an S Corporation		✓
4	At the end of the tax year, did the corporation:		
a	Own directly 20% or more, or own, directly or indirectly, 50% or more of the total stock issued and outstanding of any foreign or domestic corporation? For rules of constructive ownership, see instructions. If "Yes," complete (i) through (v) below		✓

(i) Name of Corporation	(ii) Employer Identification Number (if any)	(iii) Country of Incorporation	(iv) Percentage of Stock Owned	(v) If Percentage in (iv) is 100%, Enter the Date (if any) a Qualified Subchapter S Subsidiary Election Was Made

		Yes	No
b	Own directly an interest of 20% or more, or own, directly or indirectly, an interest of 50% or more in the profit, loss, or capital in any foreign or domestic partnership (including an entity treated as a partnership) or in the beneficial interest of a trust? For rules of constructive ownership, see instructions. If "Yes," complete (i) through (v) below		✓

(i) Name of Entity	(ii) Employer Identification Number (if any)	(iii) Type of Entity	(iv) Country of Organization	(v) Maximum Percentage Owned in Profit, Loss, or Capital

		Yes	No
5a	At the end of the tax year, did the corporation have any outstanding shares of restricted stock? If "Yes," complete lines (i) and (ii) below. (i) Total shares of restricted stock ▶ (ii) Total shares of non-restricted stock ▶		✓
b	At the end of the tax year, did the corporation have any outstanding stock options, warrants, or similar instruments? If "Yes," complete lines (i) and (ii) below. (i) Total shares of stock outstanding at the end of the tax year ▶ (ii) Total shares of stock outstanding if all instruments were executed ▶		✓
6	Has this corporation filed, or is it required to file, **Form 8918,** Material Advisor Disclosure Statement, to provide information on any reportable transaction?		✓
7	Check this box if the corporation issued publicly offered debt instruments with original issue discount ▶ ☐ If checked, the corporation may have to file **Form 8281,** Information Return for Publicly Offered Original Issue Discount Instruments.		
8	If the corporation: **(a)** was a C corporation before it elected to be an S corporation **or** the corporation acquired an asset with a basis determined by reference to the basis of the asset (or the basis of any other property) in the hands of a C corporation **and (b)** has net unrealized built-in gain in excess of the net recognized built-in gain from prior years, enter the net unrealized built-in gain reduced by net recognized built-in gain from prior years (see instructions) ▶ $		
9	Enter the accumulated earnings and profits of the corporation at the end of the tax year. $ **56,900**		
10	Does the corporation satisfy **both** of the following conditions?		
a	The corporation's total receipts (see instructions) for the tax year were less than $250,000		
b	The corporation's total assets at the end of the tax year were less than $250,000. If "Yes," the corporation is not required to complete Schedules L and M-1.	✓	
11	During the tax year, did the corporation have any non-shareholder debt that was canceled, was forgiven, or had the terms modified so as to reduce the principal amount of the debt? If "Yes," enter the amount of principal reduction $		✓
12	During the tax year, was a qualified subchapter S subsidiary election terminated or revoked? If "Yes," see instructions		✓
13a	Did the corporation make any payments in 2015 that would require it to file Form(s) 1099?		✓
b	If "Yes," did the corporation file or will it file required Forms 1099?		

Form **1120S** (2015)

Figure 16-2: Filled-In Form 1120S (Page 3)

Form 1120S (2015) Page **3**

Schedule K		Shareholders' Pro Rata Share Items		Total amount
Income (Loss)	1	Ordinary business income (loss) (page 1, line 21)	1	40,000
	2	Net rental real estate income (loss) (attach Form 8825)	2	
	3a	Other gross rental income (loss) — 3a		
	b	Expenses from other rental activities (attach statement) — 3b		
	c	Other net rental income (loss). Subtract line 3b from line 3a	3c	
	4	Interest income	4	720
	5	Dividends: a Ordinary dividends	5a	2,000
		b Qualified dividends — 5b 1,250		
	6	Royalties	6	
	7	Net short-term capital gain (loss) (attach Schedule D (Form 1120S))	7	
	8a	Net long-term capital gain (loss) (attach Schedule D (Form 1120S))	8a	10,480
	b	Collectibles (28%) gain (loss) — 8b		
	c	Unrecaptured section 1250 gain (attach statement) — 8c		
	9	Net section 1231 gain (loss) (attach Form 4797)	9	
	10	Other income (loss) (see instructions) Type ▶	10	
Deductions	11	Section 179 deduction (attach Form 4562)	11	
	12a	Charitable contributions	12a	7,000
	b	Investment interest expense	12b	
	c	Section 59(e)(2) expenditures (1) Type ▶ (2) Amount ▶	12c(2)	
	d	Other deductions (see instructions) Type ▶	12d	
Credits	13a	Low-income housing credit (section 42(j)(5))	13a	
	b	Low-income housing credit (other)	13b	
	c	Qualified rehabilitation expenditures (rental real estate) (attach Form 3468, if applicable)	13c	
	d	Other rental real estate credits (see instructions) Type ▶	13d	
	e	Other rental credits (see instructions) Type ▶	13e	
	f	Biofuel producer credit (attach Form 6478)	13f	
	g	Other credits (see instructions) Type ▶	13g	
Foreign Transactions	14a	Name of country or U.S. possession ▶		
	b	Gross income from all sources	14b	
	c	Gross income sourced at shareholder level	14c	
		Foreign gross income sourced at corporate level		
	d	Passive category	14d	
	e	General category	14e	
	f	Other (attach statement)	14f	
		Deductions allocated and apportioned at shareholder level		
	g	Interest expense	14g	
	h	Other	14h	
		Deductions allocated and apportioned at corporate level to foreign source income		
	i	Passive category	14i	
	j	General category	14j	
	k	Other (attach statement)	14k	
		Other information		
	l	Total foreign taxes (check one): ▶ ☐ Paid ☐ Accrued	14l	
	m	Reduction in taxes available for credit (attach statement)	14m	
	n	Other foreign tax information (attach statement)		
Alternative Minimum Tax (AMT) Items	15a	Post-1986 depreciation adjustment	15a	
	b	Adjusted gain or loss	15b	
	c	Depletion (other than oil and gas)	15c	
	d	Oil, gas, and geothermal properties—gross income	15d	
	e	Oil, gas, and geothermal properties—deductions	15e	
	f	Other AMT items (attach statement)	15f	
Items Affecting Shareholder Basis	16a	Tax-exempt interest income	16a	1,100
	b	Other tax-exempt income	16b	
	c	Nondeductible expenses	16c	
	d	Distributions (attach statement if required) (see instructions)	16d	
	e	Repayment of loans from shareholders	16e	

Form **1120S** (2015)

Figure 16-2: Filled-In Form 1120S (Page 4)

Form 1120S (2015) Page **4**

Schedule K — Shareholders' Pro Rata Share Items (continued)

				Total amount
Other Information	17a	Investment income	17a	2,720
	b	Investment expenses	17b	
	c	Dividend distributions paid from accumulated earnings and profits	17c	
	d	Other items and amounts (attach statement)		
Reconciliation	18	**Income/loss reconciliation.** Combine the amounts on lines 1 through 10 in the far right column. From the result, subtract the sum of the amounts on lines 11 through 12d and 14l	18	46,200

Schedule L — Balance Sheets per Books

		Beginning of tax year (a)	Beginning of tax year (b)	End of tax year (c)	End of tax year (d)
	Assets				
1	Cash		14,000		18,000
2a	Trade notes and accounts receivable	18,000		21,600	
b	Less allowance for bad debts	( )	18,000	( )	21,600
3	Inventories				
4	U.S. government obligations				
5	Tax-exempt securities (see instructions)				
6	Other current assets (attach statement)		25,650		33,000
7	Loans to shareholders				
8	Mortgage and real estate loans				
9	Other investments (attach statement)		100,000		111,400
10a	Buildings and other depreciable assets	53,550		53,550	
b	Less accumulated depreciation	(10,200)	43,350	(11,900)	41,650
11a	Depletable assets				
b	Less accumulated depletion	( )		( )	
12	Land (net of any amortization)				
13a	Intangible assets (amortizable only)				
b	Less accumulated amortization	( )		( )	
14	Other assets (attach statement)				
15	Total assets		201,000		225,650
	Liabilities and Shareholders' Equity				
16	Accounts payable		6,400		10,150
17	Mortgages, notes, bonds payable in less than 1 year				
18	Other current liabilities (attach statement)				
19	Loans from shareholders				
20	Mortgages, notes, bonds payable in 1 year or more				20,900
21	Other liabilities (attach statement)				
22	Capital stock		40,000		40,000
23	Additional paid-in capital		100,000		100,000
24	Retained earnings		54,600		54,600
25	Adjustments to shareholders' equity (attach statement)				
26	Less cost of treasury stock		( )		( )
27	Total liabilities and shareholders' equity		201,000		225,650

Form **1120S** (2015)

Figure 16-2: Filled-In Form 1120S (Page 5)

Form 1120S (2015) Page **5**

Schedule M-1 **Reconciliation of Income (Loss) per Books With Income (Loss) per Return**
Note: The corporation may be required to file Schedule M-3 (see instructions)

1 Net income (loss) per books	47,300	5 Income recorded on books this year not included on Schedule K, lines 1 through 10 (itemize): a Tax-exempt interest $ 1,100	1,100
2 Income included on Schedule K, lines 1, 2, 3c, 4, 5a, 6, 7, 8a, 9, and 10, not recorded on books this year (itemize)			
3 Expenses recorded on books this year not included on Schedule K, lines 1 through 12 and 14l (itemize): a Depreciation $ b Travel and entertainment $		6 Deductions included on Schedule K, lines 1 through 12 and 14l, not charged against book income this year (itemize): a Depreciation $	
		7 Add lines 5 and 6	1,100
4 Add lines 1 through 3	47,300	8 Income (loss) (Schedule K, line 18). Line 4 less line 7	46,200

Schedule M-2 **Analysis of Accumulated Adjustments Account, Other Adjustments Account, and Shareholders' Undistributed Taxable Income Previously Taxed** (see instructions)

	(a) Accumulated adjustments account	(b) Other adjustments account	(c) Shareholders' undistributed taxable income previously taxed
1 Balance at beginning of tax year	25,800	1,000	
2 Ordinary income from page 1, line 21	40,000		
3 Other additions	13,200	1,100	
4 Loss from page 1, line 21	( )		
5 Other reductions	(7,000)	( )	
6 Combine lines 1 through 5	72,000	2,100	
7 Distributions other than dividend distributions	30,000		
8 Balance at end of tax year. Subtract line 7 from line 6	42,000	2,100	

Form **1120S** (2015)

¶1603.07 FILLED-IN SCHEDULE K-1 (FORM 1120S)

INFORMATION FOR FIGURE 16-3:

Virginia Kendall **(SSN 421-63-8045)** owns 30% of the corporation's stock. Virginia's address is **4524 Peachtree Drive, Atlanta, GA 30307.**

Line #

- C: IRS Center where corporation filed return, **Cincinnati, OH**
- F: Shareholder's percentage of stock ownership for tax year, **30**
- 1: Ordinary income, **$12,000** (30% × $40,000)
- 4: Interest income, **$216** (30% × $720)
- 5a: Ordinary dividends, **$600** (30% × $2,000)
- 5b: Qualified dividends, **$375** (30% × $1,250)
- 8a: Net long-term capital gain, **$3,144** (30% × $10,480)
- 12: Charitable contributions, **$2,100** (30% × $7,000) – Designated with a code **A** from the instructions to Schedule K-1
- 16: Tax-exempt interest, **$330** (30% × $1,100) – Designated with a code **A** from the instructions to Schedule K-1
- 17: Investment income, **$816** (30% × ($720 + $2,000)) – Designated with a code **A** from the instructions to Schedule K-1

Figure 16-3: Filled-In Schedule K-1 (Form 1120S)

671113

☐ Final K-1 ☐ Amended K-1 OMB No. 1545-0123

Schedule K-1 (Form 1120S) **2015**
Department of the Treasury
Internal Revenue Service

For calendar year 2015, or tax year beginning ________, 2015 ending ________, 20____

Shareholder's Share of Income, Deductions, Credits, etc. ► See back of form and separate instructions.

Part I Information About the Corporation

A Corporation's employer identification number
52-1739257

B Corporation's name, address, city, state, and ZIP code
Kendall Management Company
731 Delhi Road
Atlanta, GA 30307

C IRS Center where corporation filed return
Cincinnati, OH

Part II Information About the Shareholder

D Shareholder's identifying number
421-63-8045

E Shareholder's name, address, city, state, and ZIP code
Virginia Kendall
4524 Peachtree Drive
Atlanta, GA 30307

F Shareholder's percentage of stock ownership for tax year . . . . **30** %

For IRS Use Only

Part III Shareholder's Share of Current Year Income, Deductions, Credits, and Other Items

1	Ordinary business income (loss)	**12,000**
2	Net rental real estate income (loss)	
3	Other net rental income (loss)	
4	Interest income	**216**
5a	Ordinary dividends	**600**
5b	Qualified dividends	**375**
6	Royalties	
7	Net short-term capital gain (loss)	
8a	Net long-term capital gain (loss)	**3,144**
8b	Collectibles (28%) gain (loss)	
8c	Unrecaptured section 1250 gain	
9	Net section 1231 gain (loss)	
10	Other income (loss)	
11	Section 179 deduction	
12	Other deductions	
A		**Charitable cont., 2,100**
13	Credits	
14	Foreign transactions	
15	Alternative minimum tax (AMT) items	
16	Items affecting shareholder basis	
A		**Tax-exempt int., 330**
17	Other information	
A		**Investment int., 816**

* See attached statement for additional information.

For Paperwork Reduction Act Notice, see Instructions for Form 1120S. IRS.gov/form1120s Cat. No. 11520D **Schedule K-1 (Form 1120S) 2015**

¶1604 Transactions Between S Corporations and Shareholders

¶1604.01 SHAREHOLDER'S INVESTMENT (BASIS) IN STOCK

Shareholders compute their initial basis in S corporation stock using the same rules used when forming a regular C corporation (see discussion at ¶1401.01). If the requirements are met, their basis in the assets contributed to the corporation becomes the basis of their investment (stock) in the corporation. Thus, shareholders can avoid the taxation of gains or losses on forming an S corporation. When shareholders purchase their shares, their basis in the stock is its cost. Shareholders adjust their initial basis in S corporation stock by the following:

1. Ordinary income (loss)
2. Separately stated items
3. Additional contributions to the S corporation
4. Distributions from the S corporation

Ordinary income, separately stated income, and additional contributions increase the shareholder's basis in the stock. Ordinary loss, separately stated deductions or losses, and distributions reduce the shareholder's basis. Corporate liabilities generally do not affect a shareholder's basis unless the shareholder personally loans money to the corporation.

EXAMPLE 17

Jody pays $7,500 for 100 shares of S corporation stock at the beginning of the corporation's 20x1 calendar tax year. Her share of income and separately stated items of the S corporation are $1,500 of ordinary income and $300 of long-term capital gains. The corporation distributed $1,000 cash to Jody during the year. Jody's $8,300 basis in her stock on December 31, 20x1 is calculated as follows:

Amount paid for S shares	$7,500
Add: Share of ordinary income	1,500
Share of capital gains	300
Less: Distributions received	(1,000)
Basis at December 31, 20x1	$8,300

When S corporation shareholders sell stock, the taxable gain or loss cannot be determined until after the end of the corporation's tax year. The shareholders who sell shares must adjust their stock bases by their share of the S corporation's ordinary income or loss and separately stated items. This information will not be known until after the S corporation's year-end. The unknown effect at the time of sale can be lessened if the seller and the buyer agree to an adjustment of the selling price based on the year-end profit or loss results. As an alternative, the affected shareholders can agree to divide the tax year into two parts for accounting purposes. One part would be from the beginning of the year through the day of sale; the second part would be the remainder of the year. This agreement limits the income or loss of the selling shareholder to the corporation's results up to the date of sale. The shareholders who remain will share income or losses occurring after the date of sale. Even though the tax year is split into two parts for shareholder income (loss) computations, the S corporation files only one tax return for the year.

¶1604.02 DISTRIBUTIONS TO SHAREHOLDERS

Distributions from S corporations formed after 1983 are generally tax free to the shareholder. The distributions reduce the shareholder's basis in the stock, but not below zero. If the distributions exceed the shareholder's stock basis, the excess is treated as a capital gain. The tax consequences of distributions from an S corporation formed before 1984 are more complex and beyond the scope of this discussion.

The S corporation keeps track of all its income and losses in a special account called the **accumulated adjustments account,** or **AAA.** The account can have a positive or negative balance, depending on the income and losses the corporation has sustained. Distributions to shareholders reduce the AAA balance. However, distributions themselves cannot reduce the balance below zero. The distributions from AAA can be thought of as disbursing income that has already been taxed on the shareholders' personal income tax returns. When an S election terminates, shareholders can still receive tax free distributions. The payments cannot exceed the balance of AAA and must be made within an acceptable period (about one year after termination).

EXAMPLE 18

JL Corporation, formed on January 1, 20x1, elected S corporation status. Shareholders Jill and Lisa each invested $30,000, and each received 50% of the stock. JL's taxable income for 20x1 was $20,000, all ordinary income. The shareholders each received $12,000 in cash distributions during 20x1, from a total distribution of $24,000.

In 20x1, Jill and Lisa each report $10,000 of income on their individual income tax returns. The $12,000 distribution to each shareholder is tax free. The basis of the stock to each shareholder at the end of 20x1 is $28,000 ($30,000 + $10,000 – $12,000). The balance in the AAA account is zero ($20,000 income – $20,000 distribution). The distribution cannot reduce AAA below zero. Thus, $2,000 of each shareholder's distribution in 20x1 is treated as a tax-free return of capital.

Distributions from an S corporation that was previously a regular C corporation may be taxable. This occurs when an S corporation has earnings and profits (E&P) carried over from C corporation years. (See ¶1405.02 for a discussion of E&P.) Distributions are first payments out of AAA, which are tax free and reduce the shareholder's basis in the stock. To the extent that the distributions exceed AAA, they are considered to be payments out of E&P and taxed as dividends. The corporation's E&P is reduced but shareholders do not reduce their stock basis for these taxable distributions. Any distributions in excess of AAA and E&P are not taxable as long as they do not exceed the shareholder's remaining basis in the stock. Such distributions, however, reduce the shareholder's basis in the stock. Any amount the distribution in excess of AAA, E&P, and the shareholder's basis is taxed as capital gain to the shareholder.

EXAMPLE 19

KK Corporation was a regular corporation until 20x4, when an S election was made. KK carried over $5,000 of E&P from its C corporation years. In 20x4 KK has $16,000 of ordinary income, which is added to KK's AAA balance. KK distributes $30,000 to its sole shareholder, Ken, whose stock basis prior to the distribution was $40,000.

The first $16,000 of distributions comes out of AAA and is not taxable. Both Ken's basis in his stock and KK's AAA balance are reduced by $16,000. The next $5,000 comes from E&P and is a taxable dividend. No stock basis reduction results from the $5,000. The last $9,000 distributed is not taxable. Ken reduces his stock basis by the nontaxable distributions. His stock basis at the end of 20x4 is $15,000 ($40,000 – $16,000 – $9,000).

S corporations can elect to have distributions come from E&P first, thus bypassing AAA. The election requires the consent of all shareholders and is irrevocable. The reason S corporations may want to make this election is to remove all prior C corporation E&P at a time when its shareholders can most afford to pay tax the income. Further, corporations benefit from this election by removing the possibility of being subject to a special tax on excess passive investment income (beyond the scope of this discussion). Along those same lines, an S corporation with E&P and too much passive investment income runs the risk of terminating its S corporation status (see ¶1602.03).

Distributions of Property

Distributions to shareholders may be in cash or property. As with C corporations, the fair market value (FMV) of the property determines the amount of the distribution. This is the amount by which the AAA balance and the shareholder's stock basis are reduced. The shareholder's basis in the property is its FMV. If an S corporation distributes appreciated property to shareholders, the corporation recognizes gain. The amount of gain recognized is the same as if the property had been sold for its FMV. This gain then passes through to the shareholders. Both the S corporation's AAA balance and the shareholder's stock basis increase accordingly. However, the S corporation does not recognize a loss when the FMV of the property distributed is less than its corporate basis. The shareholder's basis in the property is its FMV.

EXAMPLE 20

Freda receives a distribution of property from Flint, an S corporation. Freda is the sole shareholder. Her basis in the Flint stock (prior to the distribution) is $75,000. The property Freda receives has a FMV of $30,000 and an adjusted basis to Flint of $50,000. Freda's basis in the property received is $30,000. Her basis in the Flint stock is reduced to $45,000 ($75,000 – $30,000). Flint does not recognize the $20,000 loss ($50,000 – $30,000). Flint's AAA is reduced by $30,000.

EXAMPLE 21

Same facts as in Example 20, except that the FMV of the property is $70,000 (instead of $30,000). Flint recognizes gain of $20,000 ($70,000 – $50,000) when it distributes appreciated property to its shareholder. This causes Flint's AAA to increase by $20,000. Freda reports the $20,000 of gain on her tax return when it flows through to her on the Schedule K-1 she receives from Flint. This increases her basis in the S corporation stock by $20,000. The distribution of the property will then reduce her basis in the stock by $70,000 (its FMV). After the distribution, Freda's basis in her Flint stock will be $25,000 ($75,000 + $20,000 – $70,000). Her basis in the property is $70,000.

Since neither the corporation nor the shareholder recognizes the loss, S corporations should avoid distributing property that has declined in value.

16

Name:

Section:

Date:

QUESTIONS AND PROBLEMS

1. **Comparison of Business Entities.** (Obj. 1) How is an S corporation similar to, yet different from, a partnership?

2. **Comparison of Business Entities.** (Obj. 1) How is an S corporation similar to, yet different from, a C corporation?

3. **S Corporation Eligibility Requirements.** (Obj. 1) What corporations qualify as a small business corporation?

4. **S Corporation Eligibility Requirements.** (Obj. 1) When will a corporation be treated as having one class of stock?

5. **S Corporation Eligibility Requirements.** (Obj. 1) Can a corporation that has previously issued shares of preferred stock ever qualify as a small business corporation? Explain.

6. **S Corporation Eligibility Requirements.** (Obj. 1) Discuss how a corporation that currently has 102 shareholders, one of whom is a partnership, can pass the number of shareholders test and qualify as a small business corporation.

7. **S Corporation Eligibility Requirements.** (Obj. 1) The stock of an S corporation is owned by 105 different persons. Among its shareholders are Bob, Bob's mother and Bob's two children, Bob's brother and Bob's niece. Based on these facts, how many shareholders does the corporation have for purposes of determining whether it can elect S status?

8. **S Corporation Characteristics.** (Obj. 1) Answer each of the following questions.

   a. How many shareholders may an S corporation have?

   b. What types of shareholders can an S corporation have?

9. **S Corporation Characteristics.** (Obj. 1)

   a. What are the tax advantages of S corporation status over C corporation status?

   b. What are the advantages of S corporation status over being a general partnership?

10. **Electing and Terminating S Status.** (Obj. 1)

    a. What is the period during which the shareholders of a corporation may elect S corporation status?

    b. What events automatically terminate a corporation's S status?

    c. When is the termination of S corporation status effective under voluntary termination versus under automatic termination?

11. **Electing S Corporation Status.** (Obj. 1) Sherwin Corporation is a U.S. corporation owned by 12 shareholders. All of the stock outstanding is common stock. At a regular meeting of the shareholders, all shareholders except one agreed to have the corporation become an S corporation. Can Sherwin Corporation elect S corporation status? Explain.

12. **Electing S Corporation Status.** (Obj. 1) A newly formed corporation issues its first shares of stock on June 1. On July 15, it purchases its first asset, and on August 1, it begins business operations. If the corporation wants to elect S status for its first tax year, by what date must it file a valid S election with the IRS?

13. **Terminating an S Election.** (Obj. 1) For each of the scenarios, determine whether the calendar year corporation's S status has terminated, and if so, the date the corporation starts being taxed as a C corporation.

    a. An S corporation currently has 63 shareholders. On April 4, 20x1, one of its shareholders sells his shares of stock to a partnership that has 10 partners.

    b. An S corporation currently has 100 shareholders. On October 14, 20x1, one of its shareholders sells half of his shares of stock to his sister.

    c. An S corporation currently has 35 shareholders. On February 26, 20x1, one of its shareholders dies, and his shares of stock are transferred to his estate.

    d. An S corporation currently has 97 shareholders. On August 11, 20x1, one of the shareholders sells her shares to a voting trust that has 5 beneficiaries, none of whom are related.

14. Terminating an S Election. (Obj. 1) For each of the following scenarios, determine whether the calendar year corporation's S status has terminated, and if so, the date the corporation starts being taxed as a C corporation.

a. An S corporation was previously a C corporation, but does not have any E&P carried over from its years as a C corporation. For the past three years, the corporation has generated passive investment income in excess of 25% of its gross receipts.

b. Same as in Part a., except that the C corporation had $1,000 of E&P from when it was a C corporation.

c. Same as in Part a., except that the corporation was never a C corporation.

15. Terminating an S Election. (Obj. 1) For each of the following scenarios, determine whether the calendar year corporation's S status has terminated, and if so, the date the corporation starts being taxed as a C corporation.

a. On February 1, 20x1, 75% of the shareholders consent to revoke the corporation's S election. No date specific termination date is provided.

b. Same as in Part a., except that the shareholders specify July 1, 20x1 as their desired termination date.

c. Same as in Part a., except that only 50% of the shareholders provide their consent.

d. Same as in Part a., except that the date the shareholders filed their consent is April 5, 20x1.

16. Sale of S Corporation Stock. (Obj. 4) Jordan owned a 10% interest in an S corporation for several years. The basis of his stock on January 1, 2015 is $40,000. On April 30, 2015, Jordan sells his entire interest in the S corporation for $58,000. For the calendar year 2015, the S corporation estimated that its ordinary income would be $80,000. No distributions were made in 2015 prior to the sale of Jordan's stock.

a. On April 30, 2015, the date of sale, what is the expected gain Jordan will report on his 2015 tax return as the result of the sale of his stock?

b. At year-end, the S corporation determines that its actual ordinary income for 2015 is $100,000. On the basis of this year-end knowledge, does this additional information affect Jordan's 2015 tax return? If so, how is the 2015 tax return affected, and if it is not affected, why not?

17. S Corporation Loss. (Obj. 3) The Viking Corporation, a calendar year corporation, formed and immediately elected to become an S corporation as of January 2, 2013. Brendon has owned 40% of the stock since the corporation's inception, with an original investment of $27,000. In 2013 and 2014, Viking had ordinary losses of $45,000 and $30,000, respectively. During 2015, Viking reported taxable income of $60,000, all ordinary income. During 2015, Viking made cash distributions of $40,000.

a. How does Brendon report his share of the 2013 and 2014 losses?

b. How does Brendon report his share of the 2015 ordinary income and cash distributions from Viking?

c. What is Brendon's basis in his shares of Viking stock on December 31, 2015?

18. S Corporation Income. (Obj. 3) Siegal Management Corporation has operated as an S corporation for the years 2013, 2014, and 2015. The shareholders of the corporation are Erica and Dina. They each own 200 shares of stock of the corporation, for which each paid $25,000 at the beginning of 2013. The corporation's ordinary income and cash distributions for the three years are as follows.

	2013	*2014*	*2015*
Ordinary income	$10,000	$11,000	$16,000
Cash distributions	6,000	11,000	24,000

a. How much do Erica and Dina report as income on their individual income tax returns for 2015?

b. Compute Erica and Dina's stock bases at the end of 2015.

19. S Corporation Losses. (Obj. 3) Melbourne Corporation is an S corporation with ten shareholders. Chris owns 100 shares of stock, which represents a 15% interest in the corporation. His basis for those 100 shares is $12,000. He also has loaned the corporation $4,000 to support the purchase of a special machine. For the year 2015, the corporation reports an operating loss of $120,000. In addition, the corporation made charitable contributions for the year of $10,000.

a. Explain how Chris reports his share of the S corporation's operating loss and charitable contributions.

b. What is Chris's basis in his S corporation stock at the end of 2015?

c. Compute the amount for each type of carryover to 2016. Discuss what must happen in order for Chris to be able to deduct these amounts in 2016.

20. **Accumulated Adjustments Account.** (Obj. 4) What is the accumulated adjustments account and what purpose does it serve?

21. **Shareholder's Basis in S Corporation Stock.** (Obj. 4) An S corporation (with a $3,000 balance in its AAA and no E&P) distributes $9,000 to one of its shareholders. The shareholder's basis in his shares of stock was $5,000 prior to the distribution.

    a. Is the shareholder taxed on the distribution, and if so, how?

    b. Compute the shareholder's basis in the S stock after the distribution.

22. **Shareholder's Basis in S Corporation Stock.** (Obj. 4) An S corporation (with a $5,000 balance in its AAA and $8,000 of E&P) distributes $15,000 to one of its shareholders. The shareholder's adjusted basis in his shares of stock was $12,000 prior to the distribution.

    a. Is the shareholder taxed on the distribution, and if so, how?

    b. Compute the shareholder's basis in the S stock after the distribution.

23. Form 1120S. (Obj. 5) Prince Corporation (EIN 78-2152973), an S corporation, operates as a small variety store on the accrual basis. It is located at 1701 Governors Drive, College Station, TX 77843. The company was incorporated on January 2, 1999, and elected S corporation status on the same day. The business code is 5995. John R. Prince (SSN 201-03-5064) and his wife, Joyce B. Prince (SSN 265-72-8133) each own 35% of the corporation. Together they manage the store. The remaining stock is owned by John's father. John is President; Joyce is VP and Treasurer.

At the end of the calendar year 2015, the income statement accounts, balance sheet accounts, and other information taken from the records are as follows.

Inventory, January 1, 2015 (at cost)	$ 29,500
Inventory, December 31, 2015 (at cost)	32,400
Purchases (net)	133,800
Sales revenue	246,500
Sales returns and allowances	15,900
Taxable interest income	4,650
Tax exempt interest	6,000
Depreciation expense ("book" depreciation was $7,000)	5,200
Bad debts expense ("book" bad debt expense was $1,000)	1,500
Repairs and maintenance	3,300
Interest expense (business related)	2,700
Payroll taxes	7,800
Compensation of officers	30,000
Salaries and wages	24,500
Rental of equipment	700
Charitable contributions	1,600
Advertising	1,400
Distributions made during the year	24,000
Total assets, December 31, 2015	108,700

Based on this information, the Princes have asked you to prepare the 2015 Form 1120S for Prince Corporation. The return will be filed at the IRS Center in Ogden, Utah and will be signed by John Prince on April 10, 2016. Even though it is not required, prepare Schedules M-1 and M-2. Do not prepare Schedule L. On page 4, assume that the net income per books of Schedule M-1 (line 1) is $30,350 and the beginning balance of the AAA is $42,630 (Schedule M-2 (line 1a)). The beginning balance in the Other adjustments account (Schedule M-2 (line 1b)) is $19,400. Assume that Form 1125-A showing the calculation of Cost of Goods Sold (Form 1120S, line 2) has been completed. Schedule K-1 should be prepared for Joyce's 35% share of the S corporation's items of income and deductions. John and Joyce live at 1074 Bright Leaf Square, College Station, TX 77841.

(Use for Problem 23.)

Form **1120S** Department of the Treasury Internal Revenue Service

U.S. Income Tax Return for an S Corporation

▶ **Do not file this form unless the corporation has filed or is attaching Form 2553 to elect to be an S corporation.**
▶ **Information about Form 1120S and its separate instructions is at *www.irs.gov/form1120s.***

OMB No. 1545-0123

2015

For calendar year 2015 or tax year beginning , 2015, ending , 20

	TYPE OR PRINT	
A S election effective date	Name	D Employer identification number
B Business activity code number (see instructions)	Number, street, and room or suite no. If a P.O. box, see instructions.	E Date incorporated
C Check if Sch. M-3 attached ☐	City or town, state or province, country, and ZIP or foreign postal code	F Total assets (see instructions) $

G Is the corporation electing to be an S corporation beginning with this tax year? ☐ Yes ☐ No If "Yes," attach Form 2553 if not already filed

H Check if: **(1)** ☐ Final return **(2)** ☐ Name change **(3)** ☐ Address change **(4)** ☐ Amended return **(5)** ☐ S election termination or revocation

I Enter the number of shareholders who were shareholders during any part of the tax year . . . . ▶

Caution: Include **only** trade or business income and expenses on lines 1a through 21. See the instructions for more information.

Income	1a	Gross receipts or sales	1a			
	b	Returns and allowances	1b			
	c	Balance. Subtract line 1b from line 1a			1c	
	2	Cost of goods sold (attach Form 1125-A)			2	
	3	Gross profit. Subtract line 2 from line 1c			3	
	4	Net gain (loss) from Form 4797, line 17 (attach Form 4797)			4	
	5	Other income (loss) (see instructions—attach statement)			5	
	6	**Total income (loss).** Add lines 3 through 5 ▶			6	
Deductions (see instructions for limitations)	7	Compensation of officers (see instructions—attach Form 1125-E)			7	
	8	Salaries and wages (less employment credits)			8	
	9	Repairs and maintenance			9	
	10	Bad debts			10	
	11	Rents			11	
	12	Taxes and licenses			12	
	13	Interest			13	
	14	Depreciation not claimed on Form 1125-A or elsewhere on return (attach Form 4562)			14	
	15	Depletion **(Do not deduct oil and gas depletion.)**			15	
	16	Advertising			16	
	17	Pension, profit-sharing, etc., plans			17	
	18	Employee benefit programs			18	
	19	Other deductions (attach statement)			19	
	20	**Total deductions.** Add lines 7 through 19 ▶			20	
	21	**Ordinary business income (loss).** Subtract line 20 from line 6			21	
Tax and Payments	22a	Excess net passive income or LIFO recapture tax (see instructions)	22a			
	b	Tax from Schedule D (Form 1120S)	22b			
	c	Add lines 22a and 22b (see instructions for additional taxes)			22c	
	23a	2015 estimated tax payments and 2014 overpayment credited to 2015	23a			
	b	Tax deposited with Form 7004	23b			
	c	Credit for federal tax paid on fuels (attach Form 4136)	23c			
	d	Add lines 23a through 23c			23d	
	24	Estimated tax penalty (see instructions). Check if Form 2220 is attached ▶ ☐			24	
	25	**Amount owed.** If line 23d is smaller than the total of lines 22c and 24, enter amount owed			25	
	26	**Overpayment.** If line 23d is larger than the total of lines 22c and 24, enter amount overpaid			26	
	27	Enter amount from line 26 **Credited to 2016 estimated tax ▶**		**Refunded ▶**	27	

Sign Here

Under penalties of perjury, I declare that I have examined this return, including accompanying schedules and statements, and to the best of my knowledge and belief, it is true, correct, and complete. Declaration of preparer (other than taxpayer) is based on all information of which preparer has any knowledge.

▶ Signature of officer | Date | ▶ Title

May the IRS discuss this return with the preparer shown below (see instructions)? ☐ Yes ☐ No

Paid Preparer Use Only

Print/Type preparer's name	Preparer's signature	Date	Check ☐ if self-employed	PTIN
Firm's name ▶			Firm's EIN ▶	
Firm's address ▶			Phone no.	

For Paperwork Reduction Act Notice, see separate instructions. Cat. No. 11510H Form **1120S** (2015)

(Use for Problem 23.)

Form 1120S (2015) Page 2

Schedule B Other Information (see instructions)

		Yes	No
1	Check accounting method: a ☐ Cash b ☐ Accrual c ☐ Other (specify) ▶		
2	See the instructions and enter the: a Business activity ▶ b Product or service ▶		
3	At any time during the tax year, was any shareholder of the corporation a disregarded entity, a trust, an estate, or a nominee or similar person? If "Yes," attach Schedule B-1, Information on Certain Shareholders of an S Corporation		
4	At the end of the tax year, did the corporation:		
a	Own directly 20% or more, or own, directly or indirectly, 50% or more of the total stock issued and outstanding of any foreign or domestic corporation? For rules of constructive ownership, see instructions. If "Yes," complete (i) through (v) below		

(i) Name of Corporation	(ii) Employer Identification Number (if any)	(iii) Country of Incorporation	(iv) Percentage of Stock Owned	(v) If Percentage in (iv) is 100%, Enter the Date (if any) a Qualified Subchapter S Subsidiary Election Was Made

		Yes	No
b	Own directly an interest of 20% or more, or own, directly or indirectly, an interest of 50% or more in the profit, loss, or capital in any foreign or domestic partnership (including an entity treated as a partnership) or in the beneficial interest of a trust? For rules of constructive ownership, see instructions. If "Yes," complete (i) through (v) below		

(i) Name of Entity	(ii) Employer Identification Number (if any)	(iii) Type of Entity	(iv) Country of Organization	(v) Maximum Percentage Owned in Profit, Loss, or Capital

		Yes	No
5 a	At the end of the tax year, did the corporation have any outstanding shares of restricted stock?		
	If "Yes," complete lines (i) and (ii) below.		
	(i) Total shares of restricted stock ▶		
	(ii) Total shares of non-restricted stock ▶		
b	At the end of the tax year, did the corporation have any outstanding stock options, warrants, or similar instruments?		
	If "Yes," complete lines (i) and (ii) below.		
	(i) Total shares of stock outstanding at the end of the tax year ▶		
	(ii) Total shares of stock outstanding if all instruments were executed ▶		
6	Has this corporation filed, or is it required to file, **Form 8918,** Material Advisor Disclosure Statement, to provide information on any reportable transaction?		
7	Check this box if the corporation issued publicly offered debt instruments with original issue discount ▶ ☐		
	If checked, the corporation may have to file **Form 8281,** Information Return for Publicly Offered Original Issue Discount Instruments.		
8	If the corporation: **(a)** was a C corporation before it elected to be an S corporation **or** the corporation acquired an asset with a basis determined by reference to the basis of the asset (or the basis of any other property) in the hands of a C corporation **and (b)** has net unrealized built-in gain in excess of the net recognized built-in gain from prior years, enter the net unrealized built-in gain reduced by net recognized built-in gain from prior years (see instructions) ▶ $		
9	Enter the accumulated earnings and profits of the corporation at the end of the tax year. $		
10	Does the corporation satisfy **both** of the following conditions?		
a	The corporation's total receipts (see instructions) for the tax year were less than $250,000		
b	The corporation's total assets at the end of the tax year were less than $250,000		
	If "Yes," the corporation is not required to complete Schedules L and M-1.		
11	During the tax year, did the corporation have any non-shareholder debt that was canceled, was forgiven, or had the terms modified so as to reduce the principal amount of the debt?		
	If "Yes," enter the amount of principal reduction $		
12	During the tax year, was a qualified subchapter S subsidiary election terminated or revoked? If "Yes," see instructions		
13a	Did the corporation make any payments in 2015 that would require it to file Form(s) 1099?		
b	If "Yes," did the corporation file or will it file required Forms 1099?		

Form **1120S** (2015)

(Use for Problem 23.)

Form 1120S (2015) Page **3**

Schedule K **Shareholders' Pro Rata Share Items**

					Total amount
Income (Loss)	1	Ordinary business income (loss) (page 1, line 21)		1	
	2	Net rental real estate income (loss) (attach Form 8825)		2	
	3a	Other gross rental income (loss)	3a		
	b	Expenses from other rental activities (attach statement)	3b		
	c	Other net rental income (loss). Subtract line 3b from line 3a		3c	
	4	Interest income		4	
	5	Dividends: **a** Ordinary dividends		5a	
		b Qualified dividends	5b		
	6	Royalties		6	
	7	Net short-term capital gain (loss) (attach Schedule D (Form 1120S))		7	
	8a	Net long-term capital gain (loss) (attach Schedule D (Form 1120S))		8a	
	b	Collectibles (28%) gain (loss)	8b		
	c	Unrecaptured section 1250 gain (attach statement)	8c		
	9	Net section 1231 gain (loss) (attach Form 4797)		9	
	10	Other income (loss) (see instructions) . . Type ▶		10	
Deductions	11	Section 179 deduction (attach Form 4562)		11	
	12a	Charitable contributions		12a	
	b	Investment interest expense		12b	
	c	Section 59(e)(2) expenditures **(1)** Type ▶ **(2)** Amount ▶		12c(2)	
	d	Other deductions (see instructions) . . . Type ▶		12d	
Credits	13a	Low-income housing credit (section 42(j)(5))		13a	
	b	Low-income housing credit (other)		13b	
	c	Qualified rehabilitation expenditures (rental real estate) (attach Form 3468, if applicable)		13c	
	d	Other rental real estate credits (see instructions) Type ▶		13d	
	e	Other rental credits (see instructions) . . . Type ▶		13e	
	f	Biofuel producer credit (attach Form 6478)		13f	
	g	Other credits (see instructions) . . . . . Type ▶		13g	
Foreign Transactions	14a	Name of country or U.S. possession ▶			
	b	Gross income from all sources		14b	
	c	Gross income sourced at shareholder level		14c	
		Foreign gross income sourced at corporate level			
	d	Passive category		14d	
	e	General category		14e	
	f	Other (attach statement)		14f	
		Deductions allocated and apportioned at shareholder level			
	g	Interest expense		14g	
	h	Other		14h	
		Deductions allocated and apportioned at corporate level to foreign source income			
	i	Passive category		14i	
	j	General category		14j	
	k	Other (attach statement)		14k	
		Other information			
	l	Total foreign taxes (check one): ▶ ☐ Paid ☐ Accrued		14l	
	m	Reduction in taxes available for credit (attach statement)		14m	
	n	Other foreign tax information (attach statement)			
Alternative Minimum Tax (AMT) Items	15a	Post-1986 depreciation adjustment		15a	
	b	Adjusted gain or loss		15b	
	c	Depletion (other than oil and gas)		15c	
	d	Oil, gas, and geothermal properties—gross income		15d	
	e	Oil, gas, and geothermal properties—deductions		15e	
	f	Other AMT items (attach statement)		15f	
Items Affecting Shareholder Basis	16a	Tax-exempt interest income		16a	
	b	Other tax-exempt income		16b	
	c	Nondeductible expenses		16c	
	d	Distributions (attach statement if required) (see instructions)		16d	
	e	Repayment of loans from shareholders		16e	

Form **1120S** (2015)

(Use for Problem 23.)

Form 1120S (2015) Page **4**

Schedule K **Shareholders' Pro Rata Share Items** (continued)

				Total amount
Other Information	**17a**	Investment income	**17a**	
	b	Investment expenses	**17b**	
	c	Dividend distributions paid from accumulated earnings and profits	**17c**	
	d	Other items and amounts (attach statement)		
Recon-ciliation	**18**	**Income/loss reconciliation.** Combine the amounts on lines 1 through 10 in the far right column. From the result, subtract the sum of the amounts on lines 11 through 12d and 14l	**18**	

Schedule L **Balance Sheets per Books**

		Beginning of tax year		End of tax year	
	Assets	(a)	(b)	(c)	(d)
1	Cash				
2a	Trade notes and accounts receivable				
b	Less allowance for bad debts	( )		( )	
3	Inventories				
4	U.S. government obligations				
5	Tax-exempt securities (see instructions)				
6	Other current assets (attach statement)				
7	Loans to shareholders				
8	Mortgage and real estate loans				
9	Other investments (attach statement)				
10a	Buildings and other depreciable assets				
b	Less accumulated depreciation	( )		( )	
11a	Depletable assets				
b	Less accumulated depletion	( )		( )	
12	Land (net of any amortization)				
13a	Intangible assets (amortizable only)				
b	Less accumulated amortization	( )		( )	
14	Other assets (attach statement)				
15	Total assets				
	Liabilities and Shareholders' Equity				
16	Accounts payable				
17	Mortgages, notes, bonds payable in less than 1 year				
18	Other current liabilities (attach statement)				
19	Loans from shareholders				
20	Mortgages, notes, bonds payable in 1 year or more				
21	Other liabilities (attach statement)				
22	Capital stock				
23	Additional paid-in capital				
24	Retained earnings				
25	Adjustments to shareholders' equity (attach statement)				
26	Less cost of treasury stock		( )		( )
27	Total liabilities and shareholders' equity				

Form **1120S** (2015)

(Use for Problem 23.)

Form 1120S (2015) Page **5**

Schedule M-1 **Reconciliation of Income (Loss) per Books With Income (Loss) per Return**

Note: The corporation may be required to file Schedule M-3 (see instructions)

1	Net income (loss) per books		5	Income recorded on books this year not included on Schedule K, lines 1 through 10 (itemize):	
2	Income included on Schedule K, lines 1, 2, 3c, 4, 5a, 6, 7, 8a, 9, and 10, not recorded on books this year (itemize)		a	Tax-exempt interest $	
3	Expenses recorded on books this year not included on Schedule K, lines 1 through 12 and 14l (itemize):		6	Deductions included on Schedule K, lines 1 through 12 and 14l, not charged against book income this year (itemize):	
a	Depreciation $		a	Depreciation $	
b	Travel and entertainment $				
			7	Add lines 5 and 6	
4	Add lines 1 through 3		8	Income (loss) (Schedule K, line 18). Line 4 less line 7	

Schedule M-2 **Analysis of Accumulated Adjustments Account, Other Adjustments Account, and Shareholders' Undistributed Taxable Income Previously Taxed** (see instructions)

		(a) Accumulated adjustments account	**(b)** Other adjustments account	**(c)** Shareholders' undistributed taxable income previously taxed
1	Balance at beginning of tax year			
2	Ordinary income from page 1, line 21			
3	Other additions			
4	Loss from page 1, line 21	( )		
5	Other reductions	( )	( )	
6	Combine lines 1 through 5			
7	Distributions other than dividend distributions			
8	Balance at end of tax year. Subtract line 7 from line 6			

Form **1120S** (2015)

(Use for Problem 23.)

671113

☐ Final K-1 ☐ Amended K-1 OMB No. 1545-0123

Schedule K-1
(Form 1120S) **2015**
Department of the Treasury
Internal Revenue Service

For calendar year 2015, or tax year beginning ____________, 2015 ending ____________, 20____

Shareholder's Share of Income, Deductions, Credits, etc. ▶ See back of form and separate instructions.

Part I Information About the Corporation

A Corporation's employer identification number

B Corporation's name, address, city, state, and ZIP code

C IRS Center where corporation filed return

Part II Information About the Shareholder

D Shareholder's identifying number

E Shareholder's name, address, city, state, and ZIP code

F Shareholder's percentage of stock ownership for tax year . . . . ____________ %

For IRS Use Only

Part III Shareholder's Share of Current Year Income, Deductions, Credits, and Other Items

1	Ordinary business income (loss)	**13**	Credits
2	Net rental real estate income (loss)		
3	Other net rental income (loss)		
4	Interest income		
5a	Ordinary dividends		
5b	Qualified dividends	**14**	Foreign transactions
6	Royalties		
7	Net short-term capital gain (loss)		
8a	Net long-term capital gain (loss)		
8b	Collectibles (28%) gain (loss)		
8c	Unrecaptured section 1250 gain		
9	Net section 1231 gain (loss)		
10	Other income (loss)	**15**	Alternative minimum tax (AMT) items
11	Section 179 deduction	**16**	Items affecting shareholder basis
12	Other deductions		
		17	Other information

* See attached statement for additional information.

For Paperwork Reduction Act Notice, see Instructions for Form 1120S. IRS.gov/form1120s Cat. No. 11520D **Schedule K-1 (Form 1120S) 2015**

CUMULATIVE PROBLEM (CHAPTERS 14 – 16)

Bebop, Inc. distributes investment property to its shareholders. The property was acquired five years ago and has a basis of $50,000 and a market value of $80,000.

a. How will this distribution be treated for tax purposes at both the corporate and shareholder levels if Bebop is a C corporation?

b. If Bebop, Inc. was an S corporation, how would your answer to Part a. differ?

c. If the company was a partnership, how would the distribution be treated for tax purposes at the partnership and partner levels?

Appendix

A

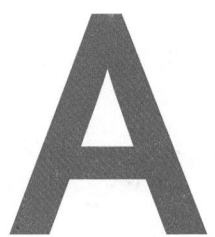

Viewing and Downloading IRS Tax Forms and Publications

In order to view IRS tax forms and publications, you must have Adobe (Acrobat Reader) installed on your computer. If you do not have Adobe Acrobat Reader on your computer, you can download a copy free from the Adobe web site: *http://get.adobe.com/reader*

- To access and download forms and IRS publications, you must first go to the IRS website: *www.irs.gov*
- This will take you to the IRS web page, titled, **IRS**. On this page you will see a series of tabs across the top of the page (see sample below). Click on the tab, **Form & Pubs**. This will take you to the **Forms & Publications** page.

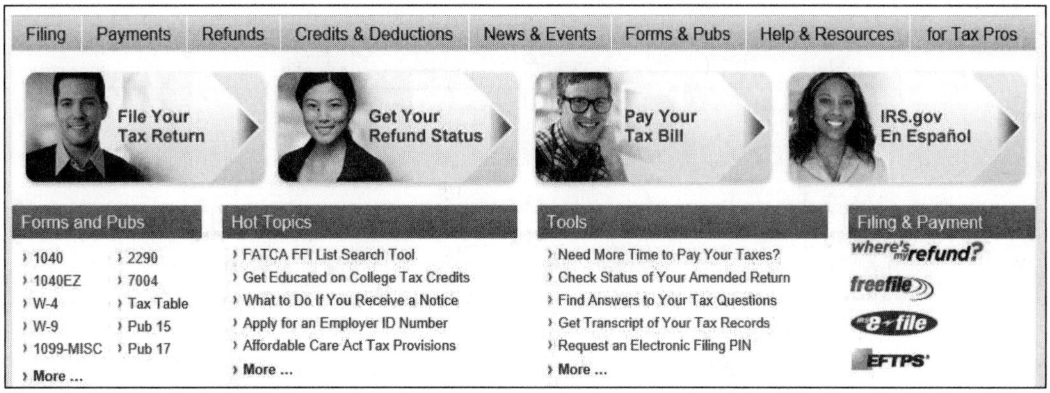

- On the **Forms & Publications** page, you will find a series of tabs (see sample below). The first one, **CURRENT**, shows a list of "Featured Forms & Publications" for individuals and businesses. Here you will find links to the forms and instructions for the more commonly requested forms and publications. If the form or publication you want is not listed, click on the button, "Find All Current Forms & Pubs," and it will take you to a page where you can search for the form or publication you are looking to find.

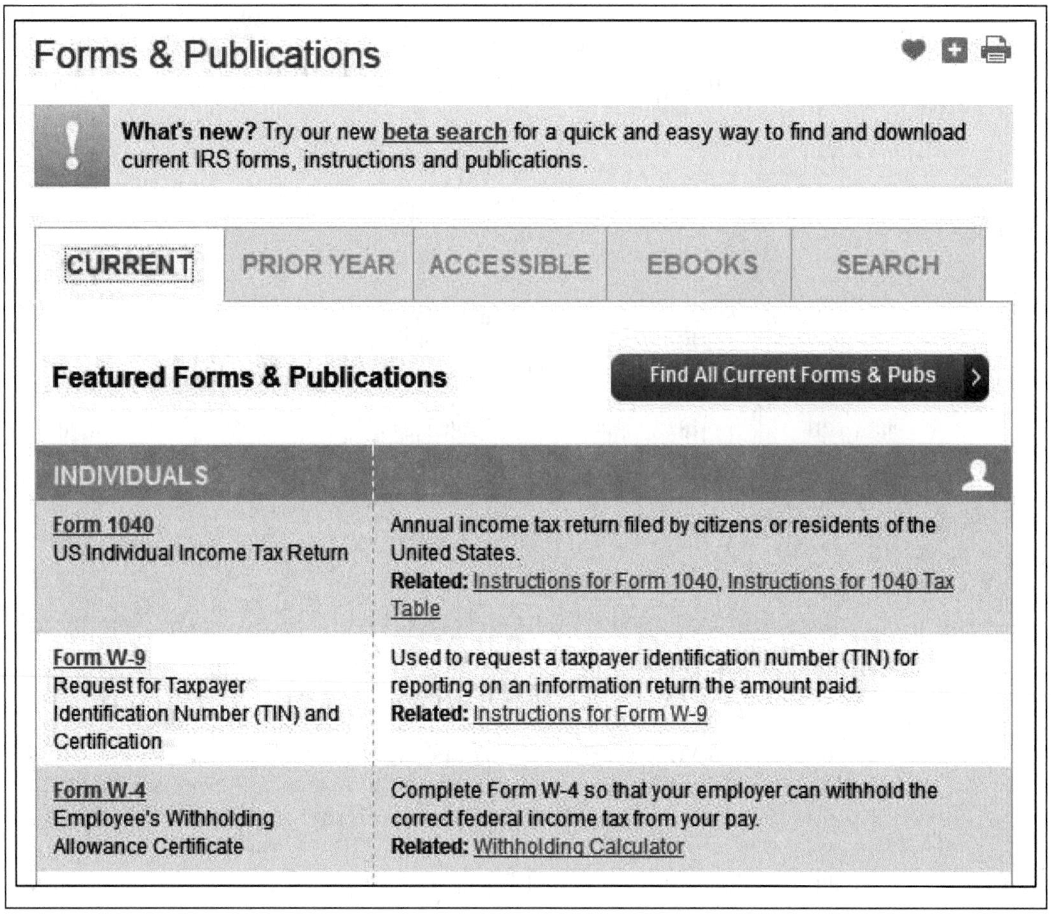

Forms & Publications

What's new? Try our new beta search for a quick and easy way to find and download current IRS forms, instructions and publications.

CURRENT | PRIOR YEAR | ACCESSIBLE | EBOOKS | SEARCH

Featured Forms & Publications

Find All Current Forms & Pubs

INDIVIDUALS	
Form 1040 US Individual Income Tax Return	Annual income tax return filed by citizens or residents of the United States. **Related:** Instructions for Form 1040, Instructions for 1040 Tax Table
Form W-9 Request for Taxpayer Identification Number (TIN) and Certification	Used to request a taxpayer identification number (TIN) for reporting on an information return the amount paid. **Related:** Instructions for Form W-9
Form W-4 Employee's Withholding Allowance Certificate	Complete Form W-4 so that your employer can withhold the correct federal income tax from your pay. **Related:** Withholding Calculator

- Once you are on the page with the list of form and publications, you can enter in a specific form number or publication number in the box to the right of the word "**Find**." For example, if you were interested in locating Form 8332, you could enter **8332** in the box (as shown below) and then click on the **Find** button. The following information would then appear.

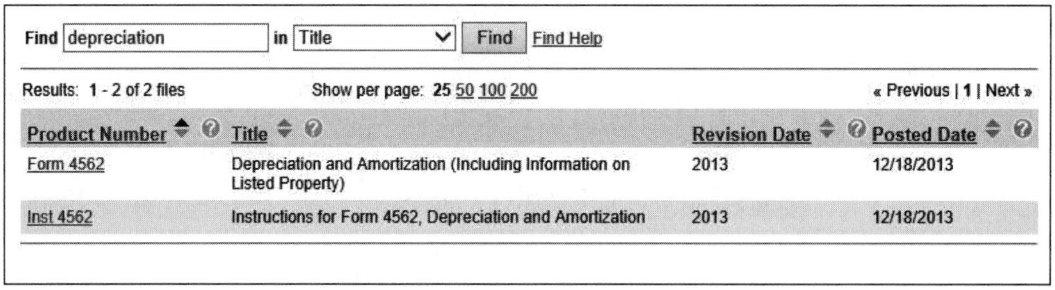

Find depreciation in Title Find Find Help

Results: 1 - 2 of 2 files Show per page: 25 50 100 200 « Previous | 1 | Next »

Product Number	Title	Revision Date	Posted Date
Form 4562	Depreciation and Amortization (Including Information on Listed Property)	2013	12/18/2013
Inst 4562	Instructions for Form 4562, Depreciation and Amortization	2013	12/18/2013

- By clicking on the link for Form 8332, you can open this form on your computer. (Depending on your browser, you may need to follow some additional instructions to be allowed to open the .pdf file). Many of the forms and schedules are available as fill-in forms, where you can type in the information you want on the form, print it out, and save it to your computer as a .pdf file for future reference. However, please note that this is not a computer program, so you still must type in the information correctly (no spell check or automatic calculations).

- The default for the search command is in the Product Number; however, you can change the search to a keyword search within the title of the document by selecting “Title” from the pull down menu. For example, if you wanted to locate a form or publication on depreciation, you would enter, **depreciation**, in the search box, pull down **Title** from the menu, and click the **Find** button. Below is a sample of what would appear. Once again, you can then click on the appropriate link to download/view the item of interest.

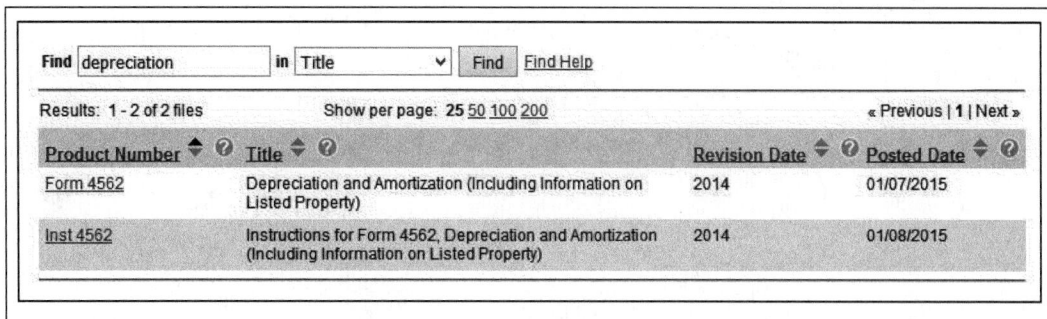

Find depreciation in Title Find Find Help

Results: 1 - 2 of 2 files Show per page: 25 50 100 200 « Previous | 1 | Next »

Product Number	Title	Revision Date	Posted Date
Form 4562	Depreciation and Amortization (Including Information on Listed Property)	2014	01/07/2015
Inst 4562	Instructions for Form 4562, Depreciation and Amortization (Including Information on Listed Property)	2014	01/08/2015

Appendix B

Selected Forms and Schedules

On the following pages you will find blank copies of selected forms and schedules that you can use to help you visualize the flow of information through the tax return, Form 1040. For example, Forms 4684 (Section B) and 4797 can be used to help visualize how gains and losses from the disposal of business assets flow through the various tax forms to end up as capital gains and losses on Schedule D. Form 8949 supports the other capital gain and loss amounts on Schedule D. Schedules A, B, C, D, and SE are common schedules used to support information reported on Form 1040.

Form **1040** Department of the Treasury—Internal Revenue Service (99)
U.S. Individual Income Tax Return **2015** OMB No. 1545-0074 IRS Use Only—Do not write or staple in this space.

For the year Jan. 1–Dec. 31, 2015, or other tax year beginning , 2015, ending , 20 | See separate instructions.

Your first name and initial	Last name	Your social security number
If a joint return, spouse's first name and initial	Last name	Spouse's social security number
Home address (number and street). If you have a P.O. box, see instructions.	Apt. no.	▲ Make sure the SSN(s) above and on line 6c are correct.
City, town or post office, state, and ZIP code. If you have a foreign address, also complete spaces below (see instructions).		**Presidential Election Campaign** Check here if you, or your spouse if filing jointly, want $3 to go to this fund. Checking a box below will not change your tax or refund. ☐ You ☐ Spouse
Foreign country name	Foreign province/state/county	Foreign postal code

Filing Status

Check only one box.

1 ☐ Single
2 ☐ Married filing jointly (even if only one had income)
3 ☐ Married filing separately. Enter spouse's SSN above and full name here.
4 ☐ Head of household (with qualifying person). (See instructions.) If the qualifying person is a child but not your dependent, enter this child's name here.
5 ☐ Qualifying widow(er) with dependent child

Exemptions

6a ☐ **Yourself.** If someone can claim you as a dependent, **do not** check box 6a
b ☐ **Spouse**

Boxes checked on 6a and 6b

c **Dependents:**

(1) First name Last name	(2) Dependent's social security number	(3) Dependent's relationship to you	(4) ✓ if child under age 17 qualifying for child tax credit (see instructions)
			☐
			☐
			☐
			☐

If more than four dependents, see instructions and check here ▶☐

No. of children on 6c who:
• lived with you
• did not live with you due to divorce or separation (see instructions)
Dependents on 6c not entered above

d Total number of exemptions claimed

Add numbers on lines above ▶

Income

Attach Form(s) W-2 here. Also attach Forms W-2G and 1099-R if tax was withheld.

If you did not get a W-2, see instructions.

7	Wages, salaries, tips, etc. Attach Form(s) W-2		7
8a	**Taxable** interest. Attach Schedule B if required		8a
b	**Tax-exempt** interest. **Do not** include on line 8a	8b	
9a	Ordinary dividends. Attach Schedule B if required		9a
b	Qualified dividends	9b	
10	Taxable refunds, credits, or offsets of state and local income taxes		10
11	Alimony received		11
12	Business income or (loss). Attach Schedule C or C-EZ		12
13	Capital gain or (loss). Attach Schedule D if required. If not required, check here ▶ ☐		13
14	Other gains or (losses). Attach Form 4797		14
15a	IRA distributions 15a	b Taxable amount	15b
16a	Pensions and annuities 16a	b Taxable amount	16b
17	Rental real estate, royalties, partnerships, S corporations, trusts, etc. Attach Schedule E		17
18	Farm income or (loss). Attach Schedule F		18
19	Unemployment compensation		19
20a	Social security benefits 20a	b Taxable amount	20b
21	Other income. List type and amount		21
22	Combine the amounts in the far right column for lines 7 through 21. This is your **total income** ▶		22

Adjusted Gross Income

23	Reserved	23	
24	Certain business expenses of reservists, performing artists, and fee-basis government officials. Attach Form 2106 or 2106-EZ	24	
25	Health savings account deduction. Attach Form 8889	25	
26	Moving expenses. Attach Form 3903	26	
27	Deductible part of self-employment tax. Attach Schedule SE	27	
28	Self-employed SEP, SIMPLE, and qualified plans	28	
29	Self-employed health insurance deduction	29	
30	Penalty on early withdrawal of savings	30	
31a	Alimony paid **b** Recipient's SSN ▶	31a	
32	IRA deduction	32	
33	Student loan interest deduction	33	
34	Reserved	34	
35	Domestic production activities deduction. Attach Form 8903	35	
36	Add lines 23 through 35		36
37	Subtract line 36 from line 22. This is your **adjusted gross income** ▶		37

For Disclosure, Privacy Act, and Paperwork Reduction Act Notice, see separate instructions. Cat. No. 11320B Form **1040** (2015)

Form 1040 (2015) Page **2**

Tax and Credits

38	Amount from line 37 (adjusted gross income)	38	
39a	Check if: ☐ **You** were born before January 2, 1951, ☐ Blind. ☐ **Spouse** was born before January 2, 1951, ☐ Blind. **Total boxes checked ▶ 39a** ☐		
b	If your spouse itemizes on a separate return or you were a dual-status alien, check here ▶ 39b☐		
40	**Itemized deductions** (from Schedule A) **or** your **standard deduction** (see left margin)	40	
41	Subtract line 40 from line 38	41	
42	**Exemptions.** If line 38 is $154,950 or less, multiply $4,000 by the number on line 6d. Otherwise, see instructions	42	
43	**Taxable income.** Subtract line 42 from line 41. If line 42 is more than line 41, enter -0-	43	
44	**Tax** (see instructions). Check if any from: **a** ☐ Form(s) 8814 **b** ☐ Form 4972 **c** ☐	44	
45	**Alternative minimum tax** (see instructions). Attach Form 6251	45	
46	Excess advance premium tax credit repayment. Attach Form 8962	46	
47	Add lines 44, 45, and 46 ▶	47	
48	Foreign tax credit. Attach Form 1116 if required	48	
49	Credit for child and dependent care expenses. Attach Form 2441	49	
50	Education credits from Form 8863, line 19	50	
51	Retirement savings contributions credit. Attach Form 8880	51	
52	Child tax credit. Attach Schedule 8812, if required	52	
53	Residential energy credit. Attach Form 5695	53	
54	Other credits from Form: **a** ☐ 3800 **b** ☐ 8801 **c** ☐	54	
55	Add lines 48 through 54. These are your **total credits**	55	
56	Subtract line 55 from line 47. If line 55 is more than line 47, enter -0- ▶	56	

Standard Deduction for—
- People who check any box on line 39a or 39b **or** who can be claimed as a dependent, see instructions.
- All others:

Single or Married filing separately, $6,300

Married filing jointly or Qualifying widow(er), $12,600

Head of household, $9,250

Other Taxes

57	Self-employment tax. Attach Schedule SE	57	
58	Unreported social security and Medicare tax from Form: **a** ☐ 4137 **b** ☐ 8919	58	
59	Additional tax on IRAs, other qualified retirement plans, etc. Attach Form 5329 if required	59	
60a	Household employment taxes from Schedule H	60a	
b	First-time homebuyer credit repayment. Attach Form 5405 if required	60b	
61	Health care: individual responsibility (see instructions) Full-year coverage ☐	61	
62	Taxes from: **a** ☐ Form 8959 **b** ☐ Form 8960 **c** ☐ Instructions; enter code(s)	62	
63	Add lines 56 through 62. This is your **total tax** ▶	63	

Payments

64	Federal income tax withheld from Forms W-2 and 1099	64	
65	2015 estimated tax payments and amount applied from 2014 return	65	
66a	**Earned income credit (EIC)**	66a	
b	Nontaxable combat pay election 66b		
67	Additional child tax credit. Attach Schedule 8812	67	
68	American opportunity credit from Form 8863, line 8	68	
69	Net premium tax credit. Attach Form 8962	69	
70	Amount paid with request for extension to file	70	
71	Excess social security and tier 1 RRTA tax withheld	71	
72	Credit for federal tax on fuels. Attach Form 4136	72	
73	Credits from Form: **a** ☐ 2439 **b** ■ Reserved **c** ☐ 8885 **d** ☐	73	
74	Add lines 64, 65, 66a, and 67 through 73. These are your **total payments** ▶	74	

If you have a qualifying child, attach Schedule EIC.

Refund

75	If line 74 is more than line 63, subtract line 63 from line 74. This is the amount you **overpaid**	75	
76a	Amount of line 75 you want **refunded to you.** If Form 8888 is attached, check here ▶☐	76a	
▶ b	Routing number ▶ **c** Type: ☐ Checking ☐ Savings		
▶ d	Account number		
77	Amount of line 75 you want **applied to your 2016 estimated tax** ▶ 77		

Direct deposit? See instructions.

Amount You Owe

78	**Amount you owe.** Subtract line 74 from line 63. For details on how to pay, see instructions ▶	78	
79	Estimated tax penalty (see instructions) 79		

Third Party Designee

Do you want to allow another person to discuss this return with the IRS (see instructions)? ☐ **Yes.** Complete below. ☐ **No**

Designee's name ▶ Phone no. ▶ Personal identification number (PIN) ▶

Sign Here

Under penalties of perjury, I declare that I have examined this return and accompanying schedules and statements, and to the best of my knowledge and belief, they are true, correct, and complete. Declaration of preparer (other than taxpayer) is based on all information of which preparer has any knowledge.

Joint return? See instructions. Keep a copy for your records.

Your signature	Date	Your occupation	Daytime phone number
Spouse's signature. If a joint return, **both** must sign.	Date	Spouse's occupation	If the IRS sent you an Identity Protection PIN, enter it here (see inst.)

Paid Preparer Use Only

Print/Type preparer's name	Preparer's signature	Date	Check ☐ if self-employed	PTIN
Firm's name ▶			Firm's EIN ▶	
Firm's address ▶			Phone no.	

www.irs.gov/form1040 Form **1040** (2015)

SCHEDULE A (Form 1040)

Department of the Treasury
Internal Revenue Service (99)

Itemized Deductions

▶ Information about Schedule A and its separate instructions is at *www.irs.gov/schedulea*.
▶ Attach to Form 1040.

OMB No. 1545-0074
2015
Attachment Sequence No. **07**

Name(s) shown on Form 1040 | **Your social security number**

Medical and Dental Expenses		**Caution.** Do not include expenses reimbursed or paid by others.		
	1	Medical and dental expenses (see instructions)	1	
	2	Enter amount from Form 1040, line 38 [2]		
	3	Multiply line 2 by 10% (.10). But if either you or your spouse was born before January 2, 1951, multiply line 2 by 7.5% (.075) instead	3	
	4	Subtract line 3 from line 1. If line 3 is more than line 1, enter -0-		4
Taxes You Paid	5	State and local		
		a ☐ Income taxes	5	
		b ■ Reserved		
	6	Real estate taxes (see instructions)	6	
	7	Personal property taxes	7	
	8	Other taxes. List type and amount ▶	8	
	9	Add lines 5 through 8		9
Interest You Paid	10	Home mortgage interest and points reported to you on Form 1098	10	
Note. Your mortgage interest deduction may be limited (see instructions).	11	Home mortgage interest not reported to you on Form 1098. If paid to the person from whom you bought the home, see instructions and show that person's name, identifying no., and address ▶	11	
	12	Points not reported to you on Form 1098. See instructions for special rules	12	
	13	Reserved	13	
	14	Investment interest. Attach Form 4952 if required. (See instructions.)	14	
	15	Add lines 10 through 14		15
Gifts to Charity	16	Gifts by cash or check. If you made any gift of $250 or more, see instructions	16	
If you made a gift and got a benefit for it, see instructions.	17	Other than by cash or check. If any gift of $250 or more, see instructions. You **must** attach Form 8283 if over $500	17	
	18	Carryover from prior year	18	
	19	Add lines 16 through 18		19
Casualty and Theft Losses	20	Casualty or theft loss(es). Attach Form 4684. (See instructions.)		20
Job Expenses and Certain Miscellaneous Deductions	21	Unreimbursed employee expenses—job travel, union dues, job education, etc. Attach Form 2106 or 2106-EZ if required. (See instructions.) ▶	21	
	22	Tax preparation fees	22	
	23	Other expenses—investment, safe deposit box, etc. List type and amount ▶	23	
	24	Add lines 21 through 23	24	
	25	Enter amount from Form 1040, line 38 [25]		
	26	Multiply line 25 by 2% (.02)	26	
	27	Subtract line 26 from line 24. If line 26 is more than line 24, enter -0-		27
Other Miscellaneous Deductions	28	Other—from list in instructions. List type and amount ▶		28
Total Itemized Deductions	29	Is Form 1040, line 38, over $154,950? ☐ **No.** Your deduction is not limited. Add the amounts in the far right column for lines 4 through 28. Also, enter this amount on Form 1040, line 40. ☐ **Yes.** Your deduction may be limited. See the Itemized Deductions Worksheet in the instructions to figure the amount to enter.		29
	30	If you elect to itemize deductions even though they are less than your standard deduction, check here ▶ ☐		

For Paperwork Reduction Act Notice, see Form 1040 instructions. Cat. No. 17145C **Schedule A (Form 1040) 2015**

SCHEDULE B
(Form 1040A or 1040)
Department of the Treasury
Internal Revenue Service (99)

Interest and Ordinary Dividends

▶ Attach to Form 1040A or 1040.
▶ Information about Schedule B and its instructions is at *www.irs.gov/scheduleb*.

OMB No. 1545-0074
2015
Attachment Sequence No. 08

Name(s) shown on return | Your social security number

Part I Interest

(See instructions on back and the instructions for Form 1040A, or Form 1040, line 8a.)

Note: If you received a Form 1099-INT, Form 1099-OID, or substitute statement from a brokerage firm, list the firm's name as the payer and enter the total interest shown on that form.

			Amount
1	List name of payer. If any interest is from a seller-financed mortgage and the buyer used the property as a personal residence, see instructions on back and list this interest first. Also, show that buyer's social security number and address ▶	1	
2	Add the amounts on line 1	2	
3	Excludable interest on series EE and I U.S. savings bonds issued after 1989. Attach Form 8815	3	
4	Subtract line 3 from line 2. Enter the result here and on Form 1040A, or Form 1040, line 8a . . . . ▶	4	

Note: If line 4 is over $1,500, you must complete Part III.

Part II Ordinary Dividends

(See instructions on back and the instructions for Form 1040A, or Form 1040, line 9a.)

Note: If you received a Form 1099-DIV or substitute statement from a brokerage firm, list the firm's name as the payer and enter the ordinary dividends shown on that form.

			Amount
5	List name of payer ▶	5	
6	Add the amounts on line 5. Enter the total here and on Form 1040A, or Form 1040, line 9a . . . . ▶	6	

Note: If line 6 is over $1,500, you must complete Part III.

Part III Foreign Accounts and Trusts

(See instructions on back.)

You must complete this part if you **(a)** had over $1,500 of taxable interest or ordinary dividends; **(b)** had a foreign account; or **(c)** received a distribution from, or were a grantor of, or a transferor to, a foreign trust.

		Yes	No
7a	At any time during 2015, did you have a financial interest in or signature authority over a financial account (such as a bank account, securities account, or brokerage account) located in a foreign country? See instructions		
	If "Yes," are you required to file FinCEN Form 114, Report of Foreign Bank and Financial Accounts (FBAR), to report that financial interest or signature authority? See FinCEN Form 114 and its instructions for filing requirements and exceptions to those requirements		
b	If you are required to file FinCEN Form 114, enter the name of the foreign country where the financial account is located ▶		
8	During 2015, did you receive a distribution from, or were you the grantor of, or transferor to, a foreign trust? If "Yes," you may have to file Form 3520. See instructions on back		

For Paperwork Reduction Act Notice, see your tax return instructions. Cat. No. 17146N **Schedule B (Form 1040A or 1040) 2015**

SCHEDULE C (Form 1040)
Department of the Treasury Internal Revenue Service (99)

Profit or Loss From Business
(Sole Proprietorship)

▶ **Information about Schedule C and its separate instructions is at *www.irs.gov/schedulec.***
▶ **Attach to Form 1040, 1040NR, or 1041; partnerships generally must file Form 1065.**

OMB No. 1545-0074
2015
Attachment Sequence No. **09**

Name of proprietor | **Social security number (SSN)**

A Principal business or profession, including product or service (see instructions) | **B Enter code from instructions** ▶

C Business name. If no separate business name, leave blank. | **D Employer ID number (EIN),** (see instr.)

E Business address (including suite or room no.) ▶
City, town or post office, state, and ZIP code

F Accounting method: **(1)** ☐ Cash **(2)** ☐ Accrual **(3)** ☐ Other (specify) ▶

G Did you "materially participate" in the operation of this business during 2015? If "No," see instructions for limit on losses ☐ **Yes** ☐ **No**

H If you started or acquired this business during 2015, check here ▶ ☐

I Did you make any payments in 2015 that would require you to file Form(s) 1099? (see instructions) ☐ **Yes** ☐ **No**

J If "Yes," did you or will you file required Forms 1099? ☐ **Yes** ☐ **No**

Part I Income

1	Gross receipts or sales. See instructions for line 1 and check the box if this income was reported to you on Form W-2 and the "Statutory employee" box on that form was checked ▶☐	1	
2	Returns and allowances	2	
3	Subtract line 2 from line 1	3	
4	Cost of goods sold (from line 42)	4	
5	**Gross profit.** Subtract line 4 from line 3	5	
6	Other income, including federal and state gasoline or fuel tax credit or refund (see instructions)	6	
7	**Gross income.** Add lines 5 and 6 ▶	7	

Part II Expenses. Enter expenses for business use of your home only on line 30.

8	Advertising	8		18	Office expense (see instructions)	18	
9	Car and truck expenses (see instructions)	9		19	Pension and profit-sharing plans	19	
				20	Rent or lease (see instructions):		
10	Commissions and fees	10		a	Vehicles, machinery, and equipment	20a	
11	Contract labor (see instructions)	11		b	Other business property	20b	
12	Depletion	12		21	Repairs and maintenance	21	
13	Depreciation and section 179 expense deduction (not included in Part III) (see instructions)	13		22	Supplies (not included in Part III)	22	
				23	Taxes and licenses	23	
				24	Travel, meals, and entertainment:		
14	Employee benefit programs (other than on line 19)	14		a	Travel	24a	
				b	Deductible meals and entertainment (see instructions)	24b	
15	Insurance (other than health)	15					
16	Interest:			25	Utilities	25	
a	Mortgage (paid to banks, etc.)	16a		26	Wages (less employment credits)	26	
b	Other	16b		27a	Other expenses (from line 48)	27a	
17	Legal and professional services	17		b	**Reserved for future use**	27b	

28	**Total expenses** before expenses for business use of home. Add lines 8 through 27a ▶	28	
29	Tentative profit or (loss). Subtract line 28 from line 7	29	
30	Expenses for business use of your home. Do not report these expenses elsewhere. Attach Form 8829 unless using the simplified method (see instructions). **Simplified method filers only:** enter the total square footage of: (a) your home: ______ and (b) the part of your home used for business: ______ . Use the Simplified Method Worksheet in the instructions to figure the amount to enter on line 30	30	
31	**Net profit or (loss).** Subtract line 30 from line 29. • If a profit, enter on both **Form 1040, line 12** (or **Form 1040NR, line 13**) and on **Schedule SE, line 2.** (If you checked the box on line 1, see instructions). Estates and trusts, enter on **Form 1041, line 3.** • If a loss, you **must** go to line 32.	31	

32 If you have a loss, check the box that describes your investment in this activity (see instructions).
- If you checked 32a, enter the loss on both **Form 1040, line 12,** (or **Form 1040NR, line 13**) and on **Schedule SE, line 2.** (If you checked the box on line 1, see the line 31 instructions). Estates and trusts, enter on **Form 1041, line 3.**
- If you checked 32b, you **must** attach **Form 6198.** Your loss may be limited.

32a ☐ All investment is at risk.
32b ☐ Some investment is not at risk.

For Paperwork Reduction Act Notice, see the separate instructions. Cat. No. 11334P **Schedule C (Form 1040) 2015**

Schedule C (Form 1040) 2015 Page **2**

Part III **Cost of Goods Sold** (see instructions)

33 Method(s) used to value closing inventory: **a** ☐ Cost **b** ☐ Lower of cost or market **c** ☐ Other (attach explanation)

34 Was there any change in determining quantities, costs, or valuations between opening and closing inventory? If "Yes," attach explanation . . . ☐ **Yes** ☐ **No**

35	Inventory at beginning of year. If different from last year's closing inventory, attach explanation	35	
36	Purchases less cost of items withdrawn for personal use	36	
37	Cost of labor. Do not include any amounts paid to yourself	37	
38	Materials and supplies	38	
39	Other costs	39	
40	Add lines 35 through 39	40	
41	Inventory at end of year	41	
42	**Cost of goods sold.** Subtract line 41 from line 40. Enter the result here and on line 4	42	

Part IV **Information on Your Vehicle.** Complete this part **only** if you are claiming car or truck expenses on line 9 and are not required to file Form 4562 for this business. See the instructions for line 13 to find out if you must file Form 4562.

43 When did you place your vehicle in service for business purposes? (month, day, year) ▶ / /

44 Of the total number of miles you drove your vehicle during 2015, enter the number of miles you used your vehicle for:

a Business ______ **b** Commuting (see instructions) ______ **c** Other ______

45 Was your vehicle available for personal use during off-duty hours? . . . ☐ **Yes** ☐ **No**

46 Do you (or your spouse) have another vehicle available for personal use? . . . ☐ **Yes** ☐ **No**

47a Do you have evidence to support your deduction? . . . ☐ **Yes** ☐ **No**

b If "Yes," is the evidence written? . . . ☐ **Yes** ☐ **No**

Part V **Other Expenses.** List below business expenses not included on lines 8–26 or line 30.

48 **Total other expenses.** Enter here and on line 27a	48	

Schedule C (Form 1040) 2015

SCHEDULE D (Form 1040)

Department of the Treasury
Internal Revenue Service (99)

Capital Gains and Losses

► Attach to Form 1040 or Form 1040NR.
► Information about Schedule D and its separate instructions is at *www.irs.gov/scheduled*.
► Use Form 8949 to list your transactions for lines 1b, 2, 3, 8b, 9, and 10.

OMB No. 1545-0074
2015
Attachment Sequence No. **12**

Name(s) shown on return | **Your social security number**

Part I Short-Term Capital Gains and Losses—Assets Held One Year or Less

See instructions for how to figure the amounts to enter on the lines below. This form may be easier to complete if you round off cents to whole dollars.	(d) Proceeds (sales price)	(e) Cost (or other basis)	(g) Adjustments to gain or loss from Form(s) 8949, Part I, line 2, column (g)	(h) Gain or (loss) Subtract column (e) from column (d) and combine the result with column (g)
1a Totals for all short-term transactions reported on Form 1099-B for which basis was reported to the IRS and for which you have no adjustments (see instructions). However, if you choose to report all these transactions on Form 8949, leave this line blank and go to line 1b .				
1b Totals for all transactions reported on Form(s) 8949 with **Box A** checked				
2 Totals for all transactions reported on Form(s) 8949 with **Box B** checked				
3 Totals for all transactions reported on Form(s) 8949 with **Box C** checked				

4 Short-term gain from Form 6252 and short-term gain or (loss) from Forms 4684, 6781, and 8824 .	4	
5 Net short-term gain or (loss) from partnerships, S corporations, estates, and trusts from Schedule(s) K-1	5	
6 Short-term capital loss carryover. Enter the amount, if any, from line 8 of your **Capital Loss Carryover Worksheet** in the instructions	6	( )
7 **Net short-term capital gain or (loss).** Combine lines 1a through 6 in column (h). If you have any long-term capital gains or losses, go to Part II below. Otherwise, go to Part III on the back	7	

Part II Long-Term Capital Gains and Losses—Assets Held More Than One Year

See instructions for how to figure the amounts to enter on the lines below. This form may be easier to complete if you round off cents to whole dollars.	(d) Proceeds (sales price)	(e) Cost (or other basis)	(g) Adjustments to gain or loss from Form(s) 8949, Part II, line 2, column (g)	(h) Gain or (loss) Subtract column (e) from column (d) and combine the result with column (g)
8a Totals for all long-term transactions reported on Form 1099-B for which basis was reported to the IRS and for which you have no adjustments (see instructions). However, if you choose to report all these transactions on Form 8949, leave this line blank and go to line 8b .				
8b Totals for all transactions reported on Form(s) 8949 with **Box D** checked				
9 Totals for all transactions reported on Form(s) 8949 with **Box E** checked				
10 Totals for all transactions reported on Form(s) 8949 with **Box F** checked.				

11 Gain from Form 4797, Part I; long-term gain from Forms 2439 and 6252; and long-term gain or (loss) from Forms 4684, 6781, and 8824	11	
12 Net long-term gain or (loss) from partnerships, S corporations, estates, and trusts from Schedule(s) K-1	12	
13 Capital gain distributions. See the instructions	13	
14 Long-term capital loss carryover. Enter the amount, if any, from line 13 of your **Capital Loss Carryover Worksheet** in the instructions	14	( )
15 **Net long-term capital gain or (loss).** Combine lines 8a through 14 in column (h). Then go to Part III on the back	15	

For Paperwork Reduction Act Notice, see your tax return instructions. Cat. No. 11338H **Schedule D (Form 1040) 2015**

Part III **Summary**

16 Combine lines 7 and 15 and enter the result **16**

- If line 16 is a **gain,** enter the amount from line 16 on Form 1040, line 13, or Form 1040NR, line 14. Then go to line 17 below.
- If line 16 is a **loss,** skip lines 17 through 20 below. Then go to line 21. Also be sure to complete line 22.
- If line 16 is **zero,** skip lines 17 through 21 below and enter -0- on Form 1040, line 13, or Form 1040NR, line 14. Then go to line 22.

17 Are lines 15 and 16 **both** gains?
☐ **Yes.** Go to line 18.
☐ **No.** Skip lines 18 through 21, and go to line 22.

18 Enter the amount, if any, from line 7 of the **28% Rate Gain Worksheet** in the instructions . . ▶ **18**

19 Enter the amount, if any, from line 18 of the **Unrecaptured Section 1250 Gain Worksheet** in the instructions . . . . ▶ **19**

20 Are lines 18 and 19 **both** zero or blank?
☐ **Yes.** Complete the **Qualified Dividends and Capital Gain Tax Worksheet** in the instructions for Form 1040, line 44 (or in the instructions for Form 1040NR, line 42). **Do not** complete lines 21 and 22 below.

☐ **No.** Complete the **Schedule D Tax Worksheet** in the instructions. **Do not** complete lines 21 and 22 below.

21 If line 16 is a loss, enter here and on Form 1040, line 13, or Form 1040NR, line 14, the **smaller** of:

- The loss on line 16 or
- ($3,000), or if married filing separately, ($1,500) } . . . . **21** ( )

Note. When figuring which amount is smaller, treat both amounts as positive numbers.

22 Do you have qualified dividends on Form 1040, line 9b, or Form 1040NR, line 10b?

☐ **Yes.** Complete the **Qualified Dividends and Capital Gain Tax Worksheet** in the instructions for Form 1040, line 44 (or in the instructions for Form 1040NR, line 42).

☐ **No.** Complete the rest of Form 1040 or Form 1040NR.

SCHEDULE SE (Form 1040)

Department of the Treasury
Internal Revenue Service (99)

Self-Employment Tax

▶ Information about Schedule SE and its separate instructions is at *www.irs.gov/schedulese*.

▶ Attach to Form 1040 or Form 1040NR.

OMB No. 1545-0074

2015

Attachment Sequence No. **17**

Name of person with **self-employment** income (as shown on Form 1040 or Form 1040NR)	Social security number of person with **self-employment** income ▶	

Before you begin: To determine if you must file Schedule SE, see the instructions.

May I Use Short Schedule SE or Must I Use Long Schedule SE?

Note. Use this flowchart **only if** you must file Schedule SE. If unsure, see *Who Must File Schedule SE* in the instructions.

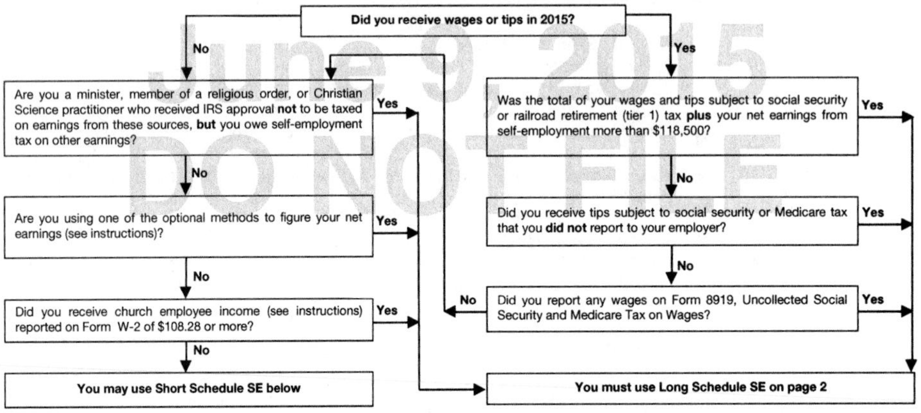
Did you receive wages or tips in 2015?
No
Yes
Are you a minister, member of a religious order, or Christian Science practitioner who received IRS approval not to be taxed on earnings from these sources, but you owe self-employment tax on other earnings?
Yes
No
Was the total of your wages and tips subject to social security or railroad retirement (tier 1) tax plus your net earnings from self-employment more than $118,500?
Yes
No
Are you using one of the optional methods to figure your net earnings (see instructions)?
Yes
No
Did you receive tips subject to social security or Medicare tax that you did not report to your employer?
Yes
No
Did you receive church employee income (see instructions) reported on Form W-2 of $108.28 or more?
Yes
No
Did you report any wages on Form 8919, Uncollected Social Security and Medicare Tax on Wages?
Yes
No
You may use Short Schedule SE below
You must use Long Schedule SE on page 2

Section A—Short Schedule SE. Caution. Read above to see if you can use Short Schedule SE.

1a	Net farm profit or (loss) from Schedule F, line 34, and farm partnerships, Schedule K-1 (Form 1065), box 14, code A	**1a**	
b	If you received social security retirement or disability benefits, enter the amount of Conservation Reserve Program payments included on Schedule F, line 4b, or listed on Schedule K-1 (Form 1065), box 20, code Z	**1b**	( )
2	Net profit or (loss) from Schedule C, line 31; Schedule C-EZ, line 3; Schedule K-1 (Form 1065), box 14, code A (other than farming); and Schedule K-1 (Form 1065-B), box 9, code J1. Ministers and members of religious orders, see instructions for types of income to report on this line. See instructions for other income to report	**2**	
3	Combine lines 1a, 1b, and 2	**3**	
4	Multiply line 3 by 92.35% (.9235). If less than $400, you do not owe self-employment tax; **do not** file this schedule unless you have an amount on line 1b . . . . ▶	**4**	
	Note. If line 4 is less than $400 due to Conservation Reserve Program payments on line 1b, see instructions.		
5	**Self-employment tax.** If the amount on line 4 is: • $118,500 or less, multiply line 4 by 15.3% (.153). Enter the result here and on **Form 1040, line 57,** or **Form 1040NR, line 55** • More than $118,500, multiply line 4 by 2.9% (.029). Then, add $14,694 to the result. Enter the total here and on **Form 1040, line 57,** or **Form 1040NR, line 55**	**5**	
6	**Deduction for one-half of self-employment tax.** Multiply line 5 by 50% (.50). Enter the result here and on **Form 1040, line 27,** or **Form 1040NR, line 27** **6**		

For Paperwork Reduction Act Notice, see your tax return instructions. Cat. No. 11358Z **Schedule SE (Form 1040) 2015**

Schedule SE (Form 1040) 2015 Attachment Sequence No. **17** Page **2**

Name of person with **self-employment** income (as shown on Form 1040 or Form 1040NR) | Social security number of person with **self-employment** income ▶

Section B—Long Schedule SE

Part I Self-Employment Tax

Note. If your only income subject to self-employment tax is **church employee income,** see instructions. Also see instructions for the definition of church employee income.

A	If you are a minister, member of a religious order, or Christian Science practitioner **and** you filed Form 4361, but you had $400 or more of **other** net earnings from self-employment, check here and continue with Part I . . . . . . ▶ ☐			
1a	Net farm profit or (loss) from Schedule F, line 34, and farm partnerships, Schedule K-1 (Form 1065), box 14, code A. **Note.** Skip lines 1a and 1b if you use the farm optional method (see instructions)	1a		
b	If you received social security retirement or disability benefits, enter the amount of Conservation Reserve Program payments included on Schedule F, line 4b, or listed on Schedule K-1 (Form 1065), box 20, code Z	1b	(	)
2	Net profit or (loss) from Schedule C, line 31; Schedule C-EZ, line 3; Schedule K-1 (Form 1065), box 14, code A (other than farming); and Schedule K-1 (Form 1065-B), box 9, code J1. Ministers and members of religious orders, see instructions for types of income to report on this line. See instructions for other income to report. **Note.** Skip this line if you use the nonfarm optional method (see instructions) . . .	2		
3	Combine lines 1a, 1b, and 2 . . .	3		
4a	If line 3 is more than zero, multiply line 3 by 92.35% (.9235). Otherwise, enter amount from line 3	4a		
	Note. If line 4a is less than $400 due to Conservation Reserve Program payments on line 1b, see instructions.			
b	If you elect one or both of the optional methods, enter the total of lines 15 and 17 here . .	4b		
c	Combine lines 4a and 4b. If less than $400, **stop;** you do not owe self-employment tax. **Exception.** If less than $400 and you had **church employee income,** enter -0- and continue ▶	4c		
5a	Enter your **church employee income** from Form W-2. See instructions for definition of church employee income . . . **5a**			
b	Multiply line 5a by 92.35% (.9235). If less than $100, enter -0- . . .	5b		
6	Add lines 4c and 5b . . .	6		
7	Maximum amount of combined wages and self-employment earnings subject to social security tax or the 6.2% portion of the 7.65% railroad retirement (tier 1) tax for 2015 . . .	7	118,500	00
8a	Total social security wages and tips (total of boxes 3 and 7 on Form(s) W-2) and railroad retirement (tier 1) compensation. If $118,500 or more, skip lines 8b through 10, and go to line 11 **8a**			
b	Unreported tips subject to social security tax (from Form 4137, line 10) **8b**			
c	Wages subject to social security tax (from Form 8919, line 10) **8c**			
d	Add lines 8a, 8b, and 8c . . .	8d		
9	Subtract line 8d from line 7. If zero or less, enter -0- here and on line 10 and go to line 11 . ▶	9		
10	Multiply the **smaller** of line 6 or line 9 by 12.4% (.124) . . .	10		
11	Multiply line 6 by 2.9% (.029) . . .	11		
12	**Self-employment tax.** Add lines 10 and 11. Enter here and on **Form 1040, line 57,** or **Form 1040NR, line 55**	12		
13	**Deduction for one-half of self-employment tax.** Multiply line 12 by 50% (.50). Enter the result here and on **Form 1040, line 27,** or **Form 1040NR, line 27** . . . **13**			

Part II Optional Methods To Figure Net Earnings (see instructions)

Farm Optional Method. You may use this method **only** if **(a)** your gross farm income[1] was not more than $7,320, **or (b)** your net farm profits[2] were less than $5,284.

14	Maximum income for optional methods . . .	14	4,880	00
15	Enter the **smaller** of: two-thirds (²/₃) of gross farm income[1] (not less than zero) **or** $4,880. Also include this amount on line 4b above . . .	15		

Nonfarm Optional Method. You may use this method **only** if **(a)** your net nonfarm profits[3] were less than $5,284 and also less than 72.189% of your gross nonfarm income,[4] **and (b)** you had net earnings from self-employment of at least $400 in 2 of the prior 3 years. **Caution.** You may use this method no more than five times.

16	Subtract line 15 from line 14 . . .	16		
17	Enter the **smaller** of: two-thirds (²/₃) of gross nonfarm income[4] (not less than zero) **or** the amount on line 16. Also include this amount on line 4b above . . .	17		

[1] From Sch. F, line 9, and Sch. K-1 (Form 1065), box 14, code B.

[2] From Sch. F, line 34, and Sch. K-1 (Form 1065), box 14, code A—minus the amount you would have entered on line 1b had you not used the optional method.

[3] From Sch. C, line 31; Sch. C-EZ, line 3; Sch. K-1 (Form 1065), box 14, code A; and Sch. K-1 (Form 1065-B), box 9, code J1.

[4] From Sch. C, line 7; Sch. C-EZ, line 1; Sch. K-1 (Form 1065), box 14, code C; and Sch. K-1 (Form 1065-B), box 9, code J2.

Schedule SE (Form 1040) 2015

Form 4684 (2015) Attachment Sequence No. **26** Page **2**

Name(s) shown on tax return. Do not enter name and identifying number if shown on other side. | **Identifying number**

SECTION B—Business and Income-Producing Property

Part I Casualty or Theft Gain or Loss (Use a separate Part I for each casualty or theft.)

19 Description of properties (show type, location, and date acquired for each property). Use a separate line for each property lost or damaged from the same casualty or theft. **See instructions if claiming a loss due to a Ponzi-type investment scheme and Section C is not completed.**

Property **A** ______

Property **B** ______

Property **C** ______

Property **D** ______

		Properties A	Properties B	Properties C	Properties D
20 Cost or adjusted basis of each property	20				
21 Insurance or other reimbursement (whether or not you filed a claim). See the instructions for line 3	21				
Note: *If line 20 is **more** than line 21, skip line 22.*					
22 Gain from casualty or theft. If line 21 is **more** than line 20, enter the difference here and on line 29 or line 34, column (c), except as provided in the instructions for line 33. Also, skip lines 23 through 27 for that column. See the instructions for line 4 if line 21 includes insurance or other reimbursement you did not claim, or you received payment for your loss in a later tax year	22				
23 Fair market value **before** casualty or theft	23				
24 Fair market value **after** casualty or theft	24				
25 Subtract line 24 from line 23	25				
26 Enter the **smaller** of line 20 or line 25	26				
Note: *If the property was totally destroyed by casualty or lost from theft, enter on line 26 the amount from line 20.*					
27 Subtract line 21 from line 26. If zero or less, enter -0-	27				

28 Casualty or theft loss. Add the amounts on line 27. Enter the total here and on line 29 **or** line 34 (see instructions) | **28** |

Part II Summary of Gains and Losses (from separate Parts I)

(a) Identify casualty or theft		(b) Losses from casualties or thefts: (i) Trade, business, rental or royalty property	(b) Losses from casualties or thefts: (ii) Income-producing and employee property	(c) Gains from casualties or thefts includible in income
Casualty or Theft of Property Held One Year or Less				
29 ______		( )	( )	
______		( )	( )	
30 Totals. Add the amounts on line 29	30	( )	( )	
31 Combine line 30, columns (b)(i) and (c). Enter the net gain or (loss) here and on Form 4797, line 14. If Form 4797 is not otherwise required, see instructions			31	
32 Enter the amount from line 30, column (b)(ii) here. Individuals, enter the amount from income-producing property on Schedule A (Form 1040), line 28, or Form 1040NR, Schedule A, line 14, and enter the amount from property used as an employee on Schedule A (Form 1040), line 23, or Form 1040NR, Schedule A, line 9. Estates and trusts, partnerships, and S corporations, see instructions			32	
Casualty or Theft of Property Held More Than One Year				
33 Casualty or theft gains from Form 4797, line 32			33	
34 ______		( )	( )	
______		( )	( )	
35 Total losses. Add amounts on line 34, columns (b)(i) and (b)(ii)	35	( )	( )	
36 Total gains. Add lines 33 and 34, column (c)			36	
37 Add amounts on line 35, columns (b)(i) and (b)(ii)			37	
38 If the loss on line 37 is **more** than the gain on line 36:				
a Combine line 35, column (b)(i) and line 36, and enter the net gain or (loss) here. Partnerships (except electing large partnerships) and S corporations, see the note below. All others, enter this amount on Form 4797, line 14. If Form 4797 is not otherwise required, see instructions			38a	
b Enter the amount from line 35, column (b)(ii) here. Individuals, enter the amount from income-producing property on Schedule A (Form 1040), line 28, or Form 1040NR, Schedule A, line 14, and enter the amount from property used as an employee on Schedule A (Form 1040), line 23, or Form 1040NR, Schedule A, line 9. Estates and trusts, enter on the "Other deductions" line of your tax return. Partnerships (except electing large partnerships) and S corporations, see the note below. Electing large partnerships, enter on Form 1065-B, Part II, line 11			38b	
39 If the loss on line 37 is **less** than or **equal** to the gain on line 36, combine lines 36 and 37 and enter here. Partnerships (except electing large partnerships), see the note below. All others, enter this amount on Form 4797, line 3			39	

Note: *Partnerships, enter the amount from line 38a, 38b, or line 39 on Form 1065, Schedule K, line 11. S corporations, enter the amount from line 38a or 38b on Form 1120S, Schedule K, line 10.*

Form **4684** (2015)

Form **4797**

Department of the Treasury
Internal Revenue Service

Sales of Business Property

(Also Involuntary Conversions and Recapture Amounts Under Sections 179 and 280F(b)(2))

▶ Attach to your tax return.
▶ Information about Form 4797 and its separate instructions is at *www.irs.gov/form4797.*

OMB No. 1545-0184
2015
Attachment Sequence No. **27**

Name(s) shown on return	**Identifying number**

1	Enter the gross proceeds from sales or exchanges reported to you for 2015 on Form(s) 1099-B or 1099-S (or substitute statement) that you are including on line 2, 10, or 20 (see instructions)	1	

Part I **Sales or Exchanges of Property Used in a Trade or Business and Involuntary Conversions From Other Than Casualty or Theft—Most Property Held More Than 1 Year** (see instructions)

2	**(a)** Description of property	**(b)** Date acquired (mo., day, yr.)	**(c)** Date sold (mo., day, yr.)	**(d)** Gross sales price	**(e)** Depreciation allowed or allowable since acquisition	**(f)** Cost or other basis, plus improvements and expense of sale	**(g) Gain or (loss)** Subtract (f) from the sum of (d) and (e)

3	Gain, if any, from Form 4684, line 39	3	
4	Section 1231 gain from installment sales from Form 6252, line 26 or 37	4	
5	Section 1231 gain or (loss) from like-kind exchanges from Form 8824	5	
6	Gain, if any, from line 32, from other than casualty or theft.	6	
7	Combine lines 2 through 6. Enter the gain or (loss) here and on the appropriate line as follows:	7	
	Partnerships (except electing large partnerships) and S corporations. Report the gain or (loss) following the instructions for Form 1065, Schedule K, line 10, or Form 1120S, Schedule K, line 9. Skip lines 8, 9, 11, and 12 below.		
	Individuals, partners, S corporation shareholders, and all others. If line 7 is zero or a loss, enter the amount from line 7 on line 11 below and skip lines 8 and 9. If line 7 is a gain and you did not have any prior year section 1231 losses, or they were recaptured in an earlier year, enter the gain from line 7 as a long-term capital gain on the Schedule D filed with your return and skip lines 8, 9, 11, and 12 below.		
8	Nonrecaptured net section 1231 losses from prior years (see instructions)	8	
9	Subtract line 8 from line 7. If zero or less, enter -0-. If line 9 is zero, enter the gain from line 7 on line 12 below. If line 9 is more than zero, enter the amount from line 8 on line 12 below and enter the gain from line 9 as a long-term capital gain on the Schedule D filed with your return (see instructions)	9	

Part II **Ordinary Gains and Losses** (see instructions)

10 Ordinary gains and losses not included on lines 11 through 16 (include property held 1 year or less):

11	Loss, if any, from line 7	11	( )
12	Gain, if any, from line 7 or amount from line 8, if applicable	12	
13	Gain, if any, from line 31	13	
14	Net gain or (loss) from Form 4684, lines 31 and 38a	14	
15	Ordinary gain from installment sales from Form 6252, line 25 or 36	15	
16	Ordinary gain or (loss) from like-kind exchanges from Form 8824.	16	
17	Combine lines 10 through 16	17	
18	For all except individual returns, enter the amount from line 17 on the appropriate line of your return and skip lines a and b below. For individual returns, complete lines a and b below:		
a	If the loss on line 11 includes a loss from Form 4684, line 35, column (b)(ii), enter that part of the loss here. Enter the part of the loss from income-producing property on Schedule A (Form 1040), line 28, and the part of the loss from property used as an employee on Schedule A (Form 1040), line 23. Identify as from "Form 4797, line 18a." See instructions . .	18a	
b	Redetermine the gain or (loss) on line 17 excluding the loss, if any, on line 18a. Enter here and on Form 1040, line 14	18b	

For Paperwork Reduction Act Notice, see separate instructions. Cat. No. 13086I Form **4797** (2015)

Form 4797 (2015) Page **2**

Part III **Gain From Disposition of Property Under Sections 1245, 1250, 1252, 1254, and 1255** (see instructions)

19	(a) Description of section 1245, 1250, 1252, 1254, or 1255 property:	(b) Date acquired (mo., day, yr.)	(c) Date sold (mo., day, yr.)
A			
B			
C			
D			

	These columns relate to the properties on lines 19A through 19D. ▶		Property A	Property B	Property C	Property D
20	Gross sales price (**Note:** *See line 1 before completing.*) .	20				
21	Cost or other basis plus expense of sale	21				
22	Depreciation (or depletion) allowed or allowable . . .	22				
23	Adjusted basis. Subtract line 22 from line 21	23				
24	Total gain. Subtract line 23 from line 20	24				
25	**If section 1245 property:**					
a	Depreciation allowed or allowable from line 22 . . .	25a				
b	Enter the **smaller** of line 24 or 25a	25b				
26	**If section 1250 property:** If straight line depreciation was used, enter -0- on line 26g, except for a corporation subject to section 291.					
a	Additional depreciation after 1975 (see instructions) .	26a				
b	Applicable percentage multiplied by the **smaller** of line 24 or line 26a (see instructions)	26b				
c	Subtract line 26a from line 24. If residential rental property **or** line 24 is not more than line 26a, skip lines 26d and 26e	26c				
d	Additional depreciation after 1969 and before 1976. .	26d				
e	Enter the **smaller** of line 26c or 26d	26e				
f	Section 291 amount (corporations only)	26f				
g	Add lines 26b, 26e, and 26f.	26g				
27	**If section 1252 property:** Skip this section if you did not dispose of farmland or if this form is being completed for a partnership (other than an electing large partnership).					
a	Soil, water, and land clearing expenses	27a				
b	Line 27a multiplied by applicable percentage (see instructions)	27b				
c	Enter the **smaller** of line 24 or 27b	27c				
28	**If section 1254 property:**					
a	Intangible drilling and development costs, expenditures for development of mines and other natural deposits, mining exploration costs, and depletion (see instructions)	28a				
b	Enter the **smaller** of line 24 or 28a	28b				
29	**If section 1255 property:**					
a	Applicable percentage of payments excluded from income under section 126 (see instructions)	29a				
b	Enter the **smaller** of line 24 or 29a (see instructions) .	29b				

Summary of Part III Gains. Complete property columns A through D through line 29b before going to line 30.

30	Total gains for all properties. Add property columns A through D, line 24	30	
31	Add property columns A through D, lines 25b, 26g, 27c, 28b, and 29b. Enter here and on line 13	31	
32	Subtract line 31 from line 30. Enter the portion from casualty or theft on Form 4684, line 33. Enter the portion from other than casualty or theft on Form 4797, line 6	32	

Part IV **Recapture Amounts Under Sections 179 and 280F(b)(2) When Business Use Drops to 50% or Less** (see instructions)

			(a) Section 179	(b) Section 280F(b)(2)
33	Section 179 expense deduction or depreciation allowable in prior years.	33		
34	Recomputed depreciation (see instructions)	34		
35	Recapture amount. Subtract line 34 from line 33. See the instructions for where to report . .	35		

Form **4797** (2015)

Form **8949**

Department of the Treasury
Internal Revenue Service

Sales and Other Dispositions of Capital Assets

▶ Information about Form 8949 and its separate instructions is at *www.irs.gov/form8949.*

▶ File with your Schedule D to list your transactions for lines 1b, 2, 3, 8b, 9, and 10 of Schedule D.

OMB No. 1545-0074

2015

Attachment Sequence No. **12A**

Name(s) shown on return | **Social security number or taxpayer identification number**

Before you check Box A, B, or C below, see whether you received any Form(s) 1099-B or substitute statement(s) from your broker. A substitute statement will have the same information as Form 1099-B. Either will show whether your basis (usually your cost) was reported to the IRS by your broker and may even tell you which box to check.

Part I **Short-Term.** Transactions involving capital assets you held 1 year or less are short term. For long-term transactions, see page 2.

Note: You may aggregate all short-term transactions reported on Form(s) 1099-B showing basis was reported to the IRS and for which no adjustments or codes are required. Enter the totals directly on Schedule D, line 1a; you aren't required to report these transactions on Form 8949 (see instructions).

You *must* check Box A, B, *or* C below. Check only one box. If more than one box applies for your short-term transactions, complete a separate Form 8949, page 1, for each applicable box. If you have more short-term transactions than will fit on this page for one or more of the boxes, complete as many forms with the same box checked as you need.

☐ **(A)** Short-term transactions reported on Form(s) 1099-B showing basis was reported to the IRS (see **Note** above)
☐ **(B)** Short-term transactions reported on Form(s) 1099-B showing basis was **not** reported to the IRS
☐ **(C)** Short-term transactions not reported to you on Form 1099-B

1 (a) Description of property (Example: 100 sh. XYZ Co.)	(b) Date acquired (Mo., day, yr.)	(c) Date sold or disposed of (Mo., day, yr.)	(d) Proceeds (sales price) (see instructions)	(e) Cost or other basis. See the **Note** below and see *Column (e)* in the separate instructions	Adjustment, if any, to gain or loss. If you enter an amount in column (g), enter a code in column (f). See the separate instructions. (f) Code(s) from instructions	(g) Amount of adjustment	(h) Gain or (loss). Subtract column (e) from column (d) and combine the result with column (g)
2 Totals. Add the amounts in columns (d), (e), (g), and (h) (subtract negative amounts). Enter each total here and include on your Schedule D, **line 1b** (if **Box A** above is checked), **line 2** (if **Box B** above is checked), or **line 3** (if **Box C** above is checked) ▶							

Note: If you checked Box A above but the basis reported to the IRS was incorrect, enter in column (e) the basis as reported to the IRS, and enter an adjustment in column (g) to correct the basis. See *Column (g)* in the separate instructions for how to figure the amount of the adjustment.

Form 8949 (2015) Attachment Sequence No. **12A** Page **2**

Name(s) shown on return. Name and SSN or taxpayer identification no. not required if shown on other side	**Social security number or taxpayer identification number**

Before you check Box D, E, or F below, see whether you received any Form(s) 1099-B or substitute statement(s) from your broker. A substitute statement will have the same information as Form 1099-B. Either will show whether your basis (usually your cost) was reported to the IRS by your broker and may even tell you which box to check.

Part II **Long-Term.** Transactions involving capital assets you held more than 1 year are long term. For short-term transactions, see page 1.

Note: You may aggregate all long-term transactions reported on Form(s) 1099-B showing basis was reported to the IRS and for which no adjustments or codes are required. Enter the totals directly on Schedule D, line 8a; you aren't required to report these transactions on Form 8949 (see instructions).

You *must* check Box D, E, *or* F below. Check only one box. If more than one box applies for your long-term transactions, complete a separate Form 8949, page 2, for each applicable box. If you have more long-term transactions than will fit on this page for one or more of the boxes, complete as many forms with the same box checked as you need.

☐ **(D)** Long-term transactions reported on Form(s) 1099-B showing basis was reported to the IRS (see **Note** above)
☐ **(E)** Long-term transactions reported on Form(s) 1099-B showing basis was **not** reported to the IRS
☐ **(F)** Long-term transactions not reported to you on Form 1099-B

1 (a) Description of property (Example: 100 sh. XYZ Co.)	(b) Date acquired (Mo., day, yr.)	(c) Date sold or disposed of (Mo., day, yr.)	(d) Proceeds (sales price) (see instructions)	(e) Cost or other basis. See the **Note** below and see *Column (e)* in the separate instructions	Adjustment, if any, to gain or loss. If you enter an amount in column (g), enter a code in column (f). **See the separate instructions.** (f) Code(s) from instructions	(g) Amount of adjustment	(h) **Gain or (loss).** Subtract column (e) from column (d) and combine the result with column (g)
2 Totals. Add the amounts in columns (d), (e), (g), and (h) (subtract negative amounts). Enter each total here and include on your Schedule D, **line 8b** (if **Box D** above is checked), **line 9** (if **Box E** above is checked), or **line 10** (if **Box F** above is checked) ▶							

Note: If you checked Box D above but the basis reported to the IRS was incorrect, enter in column (e) the basis as reported to the IRS, and enter an adjustment in column (g) to correct the basis. See *Column (g)* in the separate instructions for how to figure the amount of the adjustment.

Form **8949** (2015)

Appendix C

Applicable Figures (Used in Computing the Premium Tax Credit)

TIP *If the amount on line 5 is less than 133, your applicable figure is .0200. If the amount on line 5 is between 300 through 400, your applicable figure is .0950.*

IF Form 8962, line 5 is . . .	**ENTER** on Form 8962, line 7 . . .	**IF** Form 8962, line 5 is . . .	**ENTER** on Form 8962, line 7 . . .	**IF** Form 8962, line 5 is . . .	**ENTER** on Form 8962, line 7 . . .	**IF** Form 8962, line 5 is . . .	**ENTER** on Form 8962, line 7 . . .
less than 133	0.0200	175	0.0515	218	0.0693	261	0.0837
133	0.0300	176	0.0520	219	0.0697	262	0.0840
134	0.0306	177	0.0524	220	0.0700	263	0.0843
135	0.0312	178	0.0529	221	0.0704	264	0.0846
136	0.0318	179	0.0533	222	0.0707	265	0.0849
137	0.0324	180	0.0538	223	0.0711	266	0.0851
138	0.0329	181	0.0543	224	0.0714	267	0.0854
139	0.0335	182	0.0547	225	0.0718	268	0.0857
140	0.0341	183	0.0552	226	0.0721	269	0.0860
141	0.0347	184	0.0556	227	0.0725	270	0.0863
142	0.0353	185	0.0561	228	0.0728	271	0.0866
143	0.0359	186	0.0566	229	0.0732	272	0.0869
144	0.0365	187	0.0570	230	0.0735	273	0.0872
145	0.0371	188	0.0575	231	0.0739	274	0.0875
146	0.0376	189	0.0579	232	0.0742	275	0.0878
147	0.0382	190	0.0584	233	0.0746	276	0.0880
148	0.0388	191	0.0589	234	0.0749	277	0.0883
149	0.0394	192	0.0593	235	0.0753	278	0.0886
150	0.0400	193	0.0598	236	0.0756	279	0.0889
151	0.0405	194	0.0602	237	0.0760	280	0.0892
152	0.0409	195	0.0607	238	0.0763	281	0.0895
153	0.0414	196	0.0612	239	0.0767	282	0.0898
154	0.0418	197	0.0616	240	0.0770	283	0.0901
155	0.0423	198	0.0621	241	0.0774	284	0.0904
156	0.0428	199	0.0625	242	0.0777	285	0.0907
157	0.0432	200	0.0630	243	0.0781	286	0.0909
158	0.0437	201	0.0634	244	0.0784	287	0.0912
159	0.0441	202	0.0637	245	0.0788	288	0.0915
160	0.0446	203	0.0641	246	0.0791	289	0.0918
161	0.0451	204	0.0644	247	0.0795	290	0.0921
162	0.0455	205	0.0648	248	0.0798	291	0.0924
163	0.0460	206	0.0651	249	0.0802	292	0.0927
164	0.0464	207	0.0655	250	0.0805	293	0.0930
165	0.0469	208	0.0658	251	0.0808	294	0.0933
166	0.0474	209	0.0662	252	0.0811	295	0.0936
167	0.0478	210	0.0665	253	0.0814	296	0.0938
168	0.0483	211	0.0669	254	0.0817	297	0.0941
169	0.0487	212	0.0672	255	0.0820	298	0.0944
170	0.0492	213	0.0676	256	0.0822	299	0.0947
171	0.0497	214	0.0679	257	0.0825	300 thru 400	0.0950
172	0.0501	215	0.0683	258	0.0828		
173	0.0506	216	0.0686	259	0.0831		
174	0.0510	217	0.0690	260	0.0834		

Appendix E

Earned Income Credit Tables

2015 Earned Income Credit (EIC) Table

Caution. This is **not** a tax table.

1. To find your credit, read down the "At least - But less than" columns and find the line that includes the amount you were told to look up from your EIC Worksheet.

2. Then, go to the column that includes your filing status and the number of qualifying children you have. Enter the credit from that column on your EIC Worksheet.

Example. If your filing status is single, you have one qualifying child, and the amount you are looking up from your EIC Worksheet is $2,455, you would enter $842.

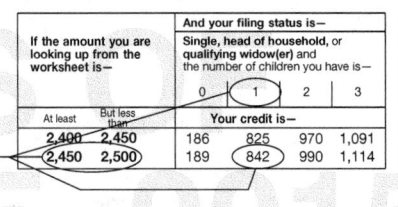

If the amount you are looking up from the worksheet is–		And your filing status is– Single, head of household, or qualifying widow(er) and the number of children you have is–			
		0	1	2	3
At least	But less than	Your credit is–			
2,400	2,450	186	825	970	1,091
2,450	2,500	189	842	990	1,114

If the amount you are looking up from the worksheet is–		And your filing status is– Single, head of household, or qualifying widow(er) and the number of children you have is–				Married filing jointly and the number of children you have is–			
		0	1	2	3	0	1	2	3
At least	But less than	Your credit is–				Your credit is–			
$1	$50	$2	$9	$10	$11	$2	$9	$10	$11
50	100	6	26	30	34	6	26	30	34
100	150	10	43	50	56	10	43	50	56
150	200	13	60	70	79	13	60	70	79
200	250	17	77	90	101	17	77	90	101
250	300	21	94	110	124	21	94	110	124
300	350	25	111	130	146	25	111	130	146
350	400	29	128	150	169	29	128	150	169
400	450	33	145	170	191	33	145	170	191
450	500	36	162	190	214	36	162	190	214
500	550	40	179	210	236	40	179	210	236
550	600	44	196	230	259	44	196	230	259
600	650	48	213	250	281	48	213	250	281
650	700	52	230	270	304	52	230	270	304
700	750	55	247	290	326	55	247	290	326
750	800	59	264	310	349	59	264	310	349
800	850	63	281	330	371	63	281	330	371
850	900	67	298	350	394	67	298	350	394
900	950	71	315	370	416	71	315	370	416
950	1,000	75	332	390	439	75	332	390	439
1,000	1,050	78	349	410	461	78	349	410	461
1,050	1,100	82	366	430	484	82	366	430	484
1,100	1,150	86	383	450	506	86	383	450	506
1,150	1,200	90	400	470	529	90	400	470	529
1,200	1,250	94	417	490	551	94	417	490	551
1,250	1,300	98	434	510	574	98	434	510	574
1,300	1,350	101	451	530	596	101	451	530	596
1,350	1,400	105	468	550	619	105	468	550	619
1,400	1,450	109	485	570	641	109	485	570	641
1,450	1,500	113	502	590	664	113	502	590	664
1,500	1,550	117	519	610	686	117	519	610	686
1,550	1,600	120	536	630	709	120	536	630	709
1,600	1,650	124	553	650	731	124	553	650	731
1,650	1,700	128	570	670	754	128	570	670	754
1,700	1,750	132	587	690	776	132	587	690	776
1,750	1,800	136	604	710	799	136	604	710	799
1,800	1,850	140	621	730	821	140	621	730	821
1,850	1,900	143	638	750	844	143	638	750	844
1,900	1,950	147	655	770	866	147	655	770	866
1,950	2,000	151	672	790	889	151	672	790	889
2,000	2,050	155	689	810	911	155	689	810	911
2,050	2,100	159	706	830	934	159	706	830	934
2,100	2,150	163	723	850	956	163	723	850	956
2,150	2,200	166	740	870	979	166	740	870	979
2,200	2,250	170	757	890	1,001	170	757	890	1,001
2,250	2,300	174	774	910	1,024	174	774	910	1,024
2,300	2,350	178	791	930	1,046	178	791	930	1,046
2,350	2,400	182	808	950	1,069	182	808	950	1,069
2,400	2,450	186	825	970	1,091	186	825	970	1,091
2,450	2,500	189	842	990	1,114	189	842	990	1,114
2,500	2,550	193	859	1,010	1,136	193	859	1,010	1,136
2,550	2,600	197	876	1,030	1,159	197	876	1,030	1,159
2,600	2,650	201	893	1,050	1,181	201	893	1,050	1,181
2,650	2,700	205	910	1,070	1,204	205	910	1,070	1,204
2,700	2,750	208	927	1,090	1,226	208	927	1,090	1,226
2,750	2,800	212	944	1,110	1,249	212	944	1,110	1,249

If the amount you are looking up from the worksheet is–		And your filing status is– Single, head of household, or qualifying widow(er) and the number of children you have is–				Married filing jointly and the number of children you have is–			
		0	1	2	3	0	1	2	3
At least	But less than	Your credit is–				Your credit is–			
2,800	2,850	216	961	1,130	1,271	216	961	1,130	1,271
2,850	2,900	220	978	1,150	1,294	220	978	1,150	1,294
2,900	2,950	224	995	1,170	1,316	224	995	1,170	1,316
2,950	3,000	228	1,012	1,190	1,339	228	1,012	1,190	1,339
3,000	3,050	231	1,029	1,210	1,361	231	1,029	1,210	1,361
3,050	3,100	235	1,046	1,230	1,384	235	1,046	1,230	1,384
3,100	3,150	239	1,063	1,250	1,406	239	1,063	1,250	1,406
3,150	3,200	243	1,080	1,270	1,429	243	1,080	1,270	1,429
3,200	3,250	247	1,097	1,290	1,451	247	1,097	1,290	1,451
3,250	3,300	251	1,114	1,310	1,474	251	1,114	1,310	1,474
3,300	3,350	254	1,131	1,330	1,496	254	1,131	1,330	1,496
3,350	3,400	258	1,148	1,350	1,519	258	1,148	1,350	1,519
3,400	3,450	262	1,165	1,370	1,541	262	1,165	1,370	1,541
3,450	3,500	266	1,182	1,390	1,564	266	1,182	1,390	1,564
3,500	3,550	270	1,199	1,410	1,586	270	1,199	1,410	1,586
3,550	3,600	273	1,216	1,430	1,609	273	1,216	1,430	1,609
3,600	3,650	277	1,233	1,450	1,631	277	1,233	1,450	1,631
3,650	3,700	281	1,250	1,470	1,654	281	1,250	1,470	1,654
3,700	3,750	285	1,267	1,490	1,676	285	1,267	1,490	1,676
3,750	3,800	289	1,284	1,510	1,699	289	1,284	1,510	1,699
3,800	3,850	293	1,301	1,530	1,721	293	1,301	1,530	1,721
3,850	3,900	296	1,318	1,550	1,744	296	1,318	1,550	1,744
3,900	3,950	300	1,335	1,570	1,766	300	1,335	1,570	1,766
3,950	4,000	304	1,352	1,590	1,789	304	1,352	1,590	1,789
4,000	4,050	308	1,369	1,610	1,811	308	1,369	1,610	1,811
4,050	4,100	312	1,386	1,630	1,834	312	1,386	1,630	1,834
4,100	4,150	316	1,403	1,650	1,856	316	1,403	1,650	1,856
4,150	4,200	319	1,420	1,670	1,879	319	1,420	1,670	1,879
4,200	4,250	323	1,437	1,690	1,901	323	1,437	1,690	1,901
4,250	4,300	327	1,454	1,710	1,924	327	1,454	1,710	1,924
4,300	4,350	331	1,471	1,730	1,946	331	1,471	1,730	1,946
4,350	4,400	335	1,488	1,750	1,969	335	1,488	1,750	1,969
4,400	4,450	339	1,505	1,770	1,991	339	1,505	1,770	1,991
4,450	4,500	342	1,522	1,790	2,014	342	1,522	1,790	2,014
4,500	4,550	346	1,539	1,810	2,036	346	1,539	1,810	2,036
4,550	4,600	350	1,556	1,830	2,059	350	1,556	1,830	2,059
4,600	4,650	354	1,573	1,850	2,081	354	1,573	1,850	2,081
4,650	4,700	358	1,590	1,870	2,104	358	1,590	1,870	2,104
4,700	4,750	361	1,607	1,890	2,126	361	1,607	1,890	2,126
4,750	4,800	365	1,624	1,910	2,149	365	1,624	1,910	2,149
4,800	4,850	369	1,641	1,930	2,171	369	1,641	1,930	2,171
4,850	4,900	373	1,658	1,950	2,194	373	1,658	1,950	2,194
4,900	4,950	377	1,675	1,970	2,216	377	1,675	1,970	2,216
4,950	5,000	381	1,692	1,990	2,239	381	1,692	1,990	2,239
5,000	5,050	384	1,709	2,010	2,261	384	1,709	2,010	2,261
5,050	5,100	388	1,726	2,030	2,284	388	1,726	2,030	2,284
5,100	5,150	392	1,743	2,050	2,306	392	1,743	2,050	2,306
5,150	5,200	396	1,760	2,070	2,329	396	1,760	2,070	2,329
5,200	5,250	400	1,777	2,090	2,351	400	1,777	2,090	2,351
5,250	5,300	404	1,794	2,110	2,374	404	1,794	2,110	2,374
5,300	5,350	407	1,811	2,130	2,396	407	1,811	2,130	2,396
5,350	5,400	411	1,828	2,150	2,419	411	1,828	2,150	2,419
5,400	5,450	415	1,845	2,170	2,441	415	1,845	2,170	2,441
5,450	5,500	419	1,862	2,190	2,464	419	1,862	2,190	2,464
5,500	5,550	423	1,879	2,210	2,486	423	1,879	2,210	2,486
5,550	5,600	426	1,896	2,230	2,509	426	1,896	2,230	2,509

Earned Income Credit (EIC) Table - *Continued* (**Caution.** This is **not** a tax table.)

If the amount you are looking up from the worksheet is–		And your filing status is– **Single, head of household,** or **qualifying widow(er)** and the number of children you have is–				**Married filing jointly** and the number of children you have is–			
		0	1	2	3	0	1	2	3
At least	But less than	Your credit is–				Your credit is–			
5,600	**5,650**	430	1,913	2,250	2,531	430	1,913	2,250	2,531
5,650	**5,700**	434	1,930	2,270	2,554	434	1,930	2,270	2,554
5,700	**5,750**	438	1,947	2,290	2,576	438	1,947	2,290	2,576
5,750	**5,800**	442	1,964	2,310	2,599	442	1,964	2,310	2,599
5,800	**5,850**	446	1,981	2,330	2,621	446	1,981	2,330	2,621
5,850	**5,900**	449	1,998	2,350	2,644	449	1,998	2,350	2,644
5,900	**5,950**	453	2,015	2,370	2,666	453	2,015	2,370	2,666
5,950	**6,000**	457	2,032	2,390	2,689	457	2,032	2,390	2,689
6,000	**6,050**	461	2,049	2,410	2,711	461	2,049	2,410	2,711
6,050	**6,100**	465	2,066	2,430	2,734	465	2,066	2,430	2,734
6,100	**6,150**	469	2,083	2,450	2,756	469	2,083	2,450	2,756
6,150	**6,200**	472	2,100	2,470	2,779	472	2,100	2,470	2,779
6,200	**6,250**	476	2,117	2,490	2,801	476	2,117	2,490	2,801
6,250	**6,300**	480	2,134	2,510	2,824	480	2,134	2,510	2,824
6,300	**6,350**	484	2,151	2,530	2,846	484	2,151	2,530	2,846
6,350	**6,400**	488	2,168	2,550	2,869	488	2,168	2,550	2,869
6,400	**6,450**	492	2,185	2,570	2,891	492	2,185	2,570	2,891
6,450	**6,500**	495	2,202	2,590	2,914	495	2,202	2,590	2,914
6,500	**6,550**	499	2,219	2,610	2,936	499	2,219	2,610	2,936
6,550	**6,600**	503	2,236	2,630	2,959	503	2,236	2,630	2,959
6,600	**6,650**	503	2,253	2,650	2,981	503	2,253	2,650	2,981
6,650	**6,700**	503	2,270	2,670	3,004	503	2,270	2,670	3,004
6,700	**6,750**	503	2,287	2,690	3,026	503	2,287	2,690	3,026
6,750	**6,800**	503	2,304	2,710	3,049	503	2,304	2,710	3,049
6,800	**6,850**	503	2,321	2,730	3,071	503	2,321	2,730	3,071
6,850	**6,900**	503	2,338	2,750	3,094	503	2,338	2,750	3,094
6,900	**6,950**	503	2,355	2,770	3,116	503	2,355	2,770	3,116
6,950	**7,000**	503	2,372	2,790	3,139	503	2,372	2,790	3,139
7,000	**7,050**	503	2,389	2,810	3,161	503	2,389	2,810	3,161
7,050	**7,100**	503	2,406	2,830	3,184	503	2,406	2,830	3,184
7,100	**7,150**	503	2,423	2,850	3,206	503	2,423	2,850	3,206
7,150	**7,200**	503	2,440	2,870	3,229	503	2,440	2,870	3,229
7,200	**7,250**	503	2,457	2,890	3,251	503	2,457	2,890	3,251
7,250	**7,300**	503	2,474	2,910	3,274	503	2,474	2,910	3,274
7,300	**7,350**	503	2,491	2,930	3,296	503	2,491	2,930	3,296
7,350	**7,400**	503	2,508	2,950	3,319	503	2,508	2,950	3,319
7,400	**7,450**	503	2,525	2,970	3,341	503	2,525	2,970	3,341
7,450	**7,500**	503	2,542	2,990	3,364	503	2,542	2,990	3,364
7,500	**7,550**	503	2,559	3,010	3,386	503	2,559	3,010	3,386
7,550	**7,600**	503	2,576	3,030	3,409	503	2,576	3,030	3,409
7,600	**7,650**	503	2,593	3,050	3,431	503	2,593	3,050	3,431
7,650	**7,700**	503	2,610	3,070	3,454	503	2,610	3,070	3,454
7,700	**7,750**	503	2,627	3,090	3,476	503	2,627	3,090	3,476
7,750	**7,800**	503	2,644	3,110	3,499	503	2,644	3,110	3,499
7,800	**7,850**	503	2,661	3,130	3,521	503	2,661	3,130	3,521
7,850	**7,900**	503	2,678	3,150	3,544	503	2,678	3,150	3,544
7,900	**7,950**	503	2,695	3,170	3,566	503	2,695	3,170	3,566
7,950	**8,000**	503	2,712	3,190	3,589	503	2,712	3,190	3,589
8,000	**8,050**	503	2,729	3,210	3,611	503	2,729	3,210	3,611
8,050	**8,100**	503	2,746	3,230	3,634	503	2,746	3,230	3,634
8,100	**8,150**	503	2,763	3,250	3,656	503	2,763	3,250	3,656
8,150	**8,200**	503	2,780	3,270	3,679	503	2,780	3,270	3,679
8,200	**8,250**	503	2,797	3,290	3,701	503	2,797	3,290	3,701
8,250	**8,300**	501	2,814	3,310	3,724	503	2,814	3,310	3,724
8,300	**8,350**	497	2,831	3,330	3,746	503	2,831	3,330	3,746
8,350	**8,400**	493	2,848	3,350	3,769	503	2,848	3,350	3,769
8,400	**8,450**	489	2,865	3,370	3,791	503	2,865	3,370	3,791
8,450	**8,500**	485	2,882	3,390	3,814	503	2,882	3,390	3,814
8,500	**8,550**	482	2,899	3,410	3,836	503	2,899	3,410	3,836
8,550	**8,600**	478	2,916	3,430	3,859	503	2,916	3,430	3,859
8,600	**8,650**	474	2,933	3,450	3,881	503	2,933	3,450	3,881
8,650	**8,700**	470	2,950	3,470	3,904	503	2,950	3,470	3,904
8,700	**8,750**	466	2,967	3,490	3,926	503	2,967	3,490	3,926
8,750	**8,800**	462	2,984	3,510	3,949	503	2,984	3,510	3,949
8,800	**8,850**	459	3,001	3,530	3,971	503	3,001	3,530	3,971
8,850	**8,900**	455	3,018	3,550	3,994	503	3,018	3,550	3,994
8,900	**8,950**	451	3,035	3,570	4,016	503	3,035	3,570	4,016
8,950	**9,000**	447	3,052	3,590	4,039	503	3,052	3,590	4,039
9,000	**9,050**	443	3,069	3,610	4,061	503	3,069	3,610	4,061
9,050	**9,100**	439	3,086	3,630	4,084	503	3,086	3,630	4,084
9,100	**9,150**	436	3,103	3,650	4,106	503	3,103	3,650	4,106
9,150	**9,200**	432	3,120	3,670	4,129	503	3,120	3,670	4,129

If the amount you are looking up from the worksheet is–		And your filing status is– **Single, head of household,** or **qualifying widow(er)** and the number of children you have is–				**Married filing jointly** and the number of children you have is–			
		0	1	2	3	0	1	2	3
At least	But less than	Your credit is–				Your credit is–			
9,200	**9,250**	428	3,137	3,690	4,151	503	3,137	3,690	4,151
9,250	**9,300**	424	3,154	3,710	4,174	503	3,154	3,710	4,174
9,300	**9,350**	420	3,171	3,730	4,196	503	3,171	3,730	4,196
9,350	**9,400**	417	3,188	3,750	4,219	503	3,188	3,750	4,219
9,400	**9,450**	413	3,205	3,770	4,241	503	3,205	3,770	4,241
9,450	**9,500**	409	3,222	3,790	4,264	503	3,222	3,790	4,264
9,500	**9,550**	405	3,239	3,810	4,286	503	3,239	3,810	4,286
9,550	**9,600**	401	3,256	3,830	4,309	503	3,256	3,830	4,309
9,600	**9,650**	397	3,273	3,850	4,331	503	3,273	3,850	4,331
9,650	**9,700**	394	3,290	3,870	4,354	503	3,290	3,870	4,354
9,700	**9,750**	390	3,307	3,890	4,376	503	3,307	3,890	4,376
9,750	**9,800**	386	3,324	3,910	4,399	503	3,324	3,910	4,399
9,800	**9,850**	382	3,341	3,930	4,421	503	3,341	3,930	4,421
9,850	**9,900**	378	3,359	3,950	4,444	503	3,359	3,950	4,444
9,900	**9,950**	374	3,359	3,970	4,466	503	3,359	3,970	4,466
9,950	**10,000**	371	3,359	3,990	4,489	503	3,359	3,990	4,489
10,000	**10,050**	367	3,359	4,010	4,511	503	3,359	4,010	4,511
10,050	**10,100**	363	3,359	4,030	4,534	503	3,359	4,030	4,534
10,100	**10,150**	359	3,359	4,050	4,556	503	3,359	4,050	4,556
10,150	**10,200**	355	3,359	4,070	4,579	503	3,359	4,070	4,579
10,200	**10,250**	352	3,359	4,090	4,601	503	3,359	4,090	4,601
10,250	**10,300**	348	3,359	4,110	4,624	503	3,359	4,110	4,624
10,300	**10,350**	344	3,359	4,130	4,646	503	3,359	4,130	4,646
10,350	**10,400**	340	3,359	4,150	4,669	503	3,359	4,150	4,669
10,400	**10,450**	336	3,359	4,170	4,691	503	3,359	4,170	4,691
10,450	**10,500**	332	3,359	4,190	4,714	503	3,359	4,190	4,714
10,500	**10,550**	329	3,359	4,210	4,736	503	3,359	4,210	4,736
10,550	**10,600**	325	3,359	4,230	4,759	503	3,359	4,230	4,759
10,600	**10,650**	321	3,359	4,250	4,781	503	3,359	4,250	4,781
10,650	**10,700**	317	3,359	4,270	4,804	503	3,359	4,270	4,804
10,700	**10,750**	313	3,359	4,290	4,826	503	3,359	4,290	4,826
10,750	**10,800**	309	3,359	4,310	4,849	503	3,359	4,310	4,849
10,800	**10,850**	306	3,359	4,330	4,871	503	3,359	4,330	4,871
10,850	**10,900**	302	3,359	4,350	4,894	503	3,359	4,350	4,894
10,900	**10,950**	298	3,359	4,370	4,916	503	3,359	4,370	4,916
10,950	**11,000**	294	3,359	4,390	4,939	503	3,359	4,390	4,939
11,000	**11,050**	290	3,359	4,410	4,961	503	3,359	4,410	4,961
11,050	**11,100**	286	3,359	4,430	4,984	503	3,359	4,430	4,984
11,100	**11,150**	283	3,359	4,450	5,006	503	3,359	4,450	5,006
11,150	**11,200**	279	3,359	4,470	5,029	503	3,359	4,470	5,029
11,200	**11,250**	275	3,359	4,490	5,051	503	3,359	4,490	5,051
11,250	**11,300**	271	3,359	4,510	5,074	503	3,359	4,510	5,074
11,300	**11,350**	267	3,359	4,530	5,096	503	3,359	4,530	5,096
11,350	**11,400**	264	3,359	4,550	5,119	503	3,359	4,550	5,119
11,400	**11,450**	260	3,359	4,570	5,141	503	3,359	4,570	5,141
11,450	**11,500**	256	3,359	4,590	5,164	503	3,359	4,590	5,164
11,500	**11,550**	252	3,359	4,610	5,186	503	3,359	4,610	5,186
11,550	**11,600**	248	3,359	4,630	5,209	503	3,359	4,630	5,209
11,600	**11,650**	244	3,359	4,650	5,231	503	3,359	4,650	5,231
11,650	**11,700**	241	3,359	4,670	5,254	503	3,359	4,670	5,254
11,700	**11,750**	237	3,359	4,690	5,276	503	3,359	4,690	5,276
11,750	**11,800**	233	3,359	4,710	5,299	503	3,359	4,710	5,299
11,800	**11,850**	229	3,359	4,730	5,321	503	3,359	4,730	5,321
11,850	**11,900**	225	3,359	4,750	5,344	503	3,359	4,750	5,344
11,900	**11,950**	221	3,359	4,770	5,366	503	3,359	4,770	5,366
11,950	**12,000**	218	3,359	4,790	5,389	503	3,359	4,790	5,389
12,000	**12,050**	214	3,359	4,810	5,411	503	3,359	4,810	5,411
12,050	**12,100**	210	3,359	4,830	5,434	503	3,359	4,830	5,434
12,100	**12,150**	206	3,359	4,850	5,456	503	3,359	4,850	5,456
12,150	**12,200**	202	3,359	4,870	5,479	503	3,359	4,870	5,479
12,200	**12,250**	199	3,359	4,890	5,501	503	3,359	4,890	5,501
12,250	**12,300**	195	3,359	4,910	5,524	503	3,359	4,910	5,524
12,300	**12,350**	191	3,359	4,930	5,546	503	3,359	4,930	5,546
12,350	**12,400**	187	3,359	4,950	5,569	503	3,359	4,950	5,569
12,400	**12,450**	183	3,359	4,970	5,591	503	3,359	4,970	5,591
12,450	**12,500**	179	3,359	4,990	5,614	503	3,359	4,990	5,614
12,500	**12,550**	176	3,359	5,010	5,636	503	3,359	5,010	5,636
12,550	**12,600**	172	3,359	5,030	5,659	503	3,359	5,030	5,659
12,600	**12,650**	168	3,359	5,050	5,681	503	3,359	5,050	5,681
12,650	**12,700**	164	3,359	5,070	5,704	503	3,359	5,070	5,704
12,700	**12,750**	160	3,359	5,090	5,726	503	3,359	5,090	5,726
12,750	**12,800**	156	3,359	5,110	5,749	503	3,359	5,110	5,749

Earned Income Credit (EIC) Table - *Continued* **(Caution.** This is **not** a tax table.)

If the amount you are looking up from the worksheet is–		And your filing status is–							
		Single, head of household, or **qualifying widow(er)** and the number of children you have is–				**Married filing jointly** and the number of children you have is–			
		0	1	2	3	0	1	2	3
At least	But less than	Your credit is–				Your credit is–			
12,800	**12,850**	153	3,359	5,130	5,771	503	3,359	5,130	5,771
12,850	**12,900**	149	3,359	5,150	5,794	503	3,359	5,150	5,794
12,900	**12,950**	145	3,359	5,170	5,816	503	3,359	5,170	5,816
12,950	**13,000**	141	3,359	5,190	5,839	503	3,359	5,190	5,839
13,000	**13,050**	137	3,359	5,210	5,861	503	3,359	5,210	5,861
13,050	**13,100**	133	3,359	5,230	5,884	503	3,359	5,230	5,884
13,100	**13,150**	130	3,359	5,250	5,906	503	3,359	5,250	5,906
13,150	**13,200**	126	3,359	5,270	5,929	503	3,359	5,270	5,929
13,200	**13,250**	122	3,359	5,290	5,951	503	3,359	5,290	5,951
13,250	**13,300**	118	3,359	5,310	5,974	503	3,359	5,310	5,974
13,300	**13,350**	114	3,359	5,330	5,996	503	3,359	5,330	5,996
13,350	**13,400**	111	3,359	5,350	6,019	503	3,359	5,350	6,019
13,400	**13,450**	107	3,359	5,370	6,041	503	3,359	5,370	6,041
13,450	**13,500**	103	3,359	5,390	6,064	503	3,359	5,390	6,064
13,500	**13,550**	99	3,359	5,410	6,086	503	3,359	5,410	6,086
13,550	**13,600**	95	3,359	5,430	6,109	503	3,359	5,430	6,109
13,600	**13,650**	91	3,359	5,450	6,131	503	3,359	5,450	6,131
13,650	**13,700**	88	3,359	5,470	6,154	503	3,359	5,470	6,154
13,700	**13,750**	84	3,359	5,490	6,176	503	3,359	5,490	6,176
13,750	**13,800**	80	3,359	5,510	6,199	501	3,359	5,510	6,199
13,800	**13,850**	76	3,359	5,530	6,221	498	3,359	5,530	6,221
13,850	**13,900**	72	3,359	5,548	6,242	494	3,359	5,548	6,242
13,900	**13,950**	68	3,359	5,548	6,242	490	3,359	5,548	6,242
13,950	**14,000**	65	3,359	5,548	6,242	486	3,359	5,548	6,242
14,000	**14,050**	61	3,359	5,548	6,242	482	3,359	5,548	6,242
14,050	**14,100**	57	3,359	5,548	6,242	479	3,359	5,548	6,242
14,100	**14,150**	53	3,359	5,548	6,242	475	3,359	5,548	6,242
14,150	**14,200**	49	3,359	5,548	6,242	471	3,359	5,548	6,242
14,200	**14,250**	46	3,359	5,548	6,242	467	3,359	5,548	6,242
14,250	**14,300**	42	3,359	5,548	6,242	463	3,359	5,548	6,242
14,300	**14,350**	38	3,359	5,548	6,242	459	3,359	5,548	6,242
14,350	**14,400**	34	3,359	5,548	6,242	456	3,359	5,548	6,242
14,400	**14,450**	30	3,359	5,548	6,242	452	3,359	5,548	6,242
14,450	**14,500**	26	3,359	5,548	6,242	448	3,359	5,548	6,242
14,500	**14,550**	23	3,359	5,548	6,242	444	3,359	5,548	6,242
14,550	**14,600**	19	3,359	5,548	6,242	440	3,359	5,548	6,242
14,600	**14,650**	15	3,359	5,548	6,242	436	3,359	5,548	6,242
14,650	**14,700**	11	3,359	5,548	6,242	433	3,359	5,548	6,242
14,700	**14,750**	7	3,359	5,548	6,242	429	3,359	5,548	6,242
14,750	**14,800**	3	3,359	5,548	6,242	425	3,359	5,548	6,242
14,800	**14,850**	*	3,359	5,548	6,242	421	3,359	5,548	6,242
14,850	**14,900**	0	3,359	5,548	6,242	417	3,359	5,548	6,242
14,900	**14,950**	0	3,359	5,548	6,242	413	3,359	5,548	6,242
14,950	**15,000**	0	3,359	5,548	6,242	410	3,359	5,548	6,242
15,000	**15,050**	0	3,359	5,548	6,242	406	3,359	5,548	6,242
15,050	**15,100**	0	3,359	5,548	6,242	402	3,359	5,548	6,242
15,100	**15,150**	0	3,359	5,548	6,242	398	3,359	5,548	6,242
15,150	**15,200**	0	3,359	5,548	6,242	394	3,359	5,548	6,242
15,200	**15,250**	0	3,359	5,548	6,242	391	3,359	5,548	6,242
15,250	**15,300**	0	3,359	5,548	6,242	387	3,359	5,548	6,242
15,300	**15,350**	0	3,359	5,548	6,242	383	3,359	5,548	6,242
15,350	**15,400**	0	3,359	5,548	6,242	379	3,359	5,548	6,242
15,400	**15,450**	0	3,359	5,548	6,242	375	3,359	5,548	6,242
15,450	**15,500**	0	3,359	5,548	6,242	371	3,359	5,548	6,242
15,500	**15,550**	0	3,359	5,548	6,242	368	3,359	5,548	6,242
15,550	**15,600**	0	3,359	5,548	6,242	364	3,359	5,548	6,242
15,600	**15,650**	0	3,359	5,548	6,242	360	3,359	5,548	6,242
15,650	**15,700**	0	3,359	5,548	6,242	356	3,359	5,548	6,242
15,700	**15,750**	0	3,359	5,548	6,242	352	3,359	5,548	6,242
15,750	**15,800**	0	3,359	5,548	6,242	348	3,359	5,548	6,242
15,800	**15,850**	0	3,359	5,548	6,242	345	3,359	5,548	6,242
15,850	**15,900**	0	3,359	5,548	6,242	341	3,359	5,548	6,242
15,900	**15,950**	0	3,359	5,548	6,242	337	3,359	5,548	6,242
15,950	**16,000**	0	3,359	5,548	6,242	333	3,359	5,548	6,242

If the amount you are looking up from the worksheet is–		And your filing status is–							
		Single, head of household, or **qualifying widow(er)** and the number of children you have is–				**Married filing jointly** and the number of children you have is–			
		0	1	2	3	0	1	2	3
At least	But less than	Your credit is–				Your credit is–			
16,000	**16,050**	0	3,359	5,548	6,242	329	3,359	5,548	6,242
16,050	**16,100**	0	3,359	5,548	6,242	326	3,359	5,548	6,242
16,100	**16,150**	0	3,359	5,548	6,242	322	3,359	5,548	6,242
16,150	**16,200**	0	3,359	5,548	6,242	318	3,359	5,548	6,242
16,200	**16,250**	0	3,359	5,548	6,242	314	3,359	5,548	6,242
16,250	**16,300**	0	3,359	5,548	6,242	310	3,359	5,548	6,242
16,300	**16,350**	0	3,359	5,548	6,242	306	3,359	5,548	6,242
16,350	**16,400**	0	3,359	5,548	6,242	303	3,359	5,548	6,242
16,400	**16,450**	0	3,359	5,548	6,242	299	3,359	5,548	6,242
16,450	**16,500**	0	3,359	5,548	6,242	295	3,359	5,548	6,242
16,500	**16,550**	0	3,359	5,548	6,242	291	3,359	5,548	6,242
16,550	**16,600**	0	3,359	5,548	6,242	287	3,359	5,548	6,242
16,600	**16,650**	0	3,359	5,548	6,242	283	3,359	5,548	6,242
16,650	**16,700**	0	3,359	5,548	6,242	280	3,359	5,548	6,242
16,700	**16,750**	0	3,359	5,548	6,242	276	3,359	5,548	6,242
16,750	**16,800**	0	3,359	5,548	6,242	272	3,359	5,548	6,242
16,800	**16,850**	0	3,359	5,548	6,242	268	3,359	5,548	6,242
16,850	**16,900**	0	3,359	5,548	6,242	264	3,359	5,548	6,242
16,900	**16,950**	0	3,359	5,548	6,242	260	3,359	5,548	6,242
16,950	**17,000**	0	3,359	5,548	6,242	257	3,359	5,548	6,242
17,000	**17,050**	0	3,359	5,548	6,242	253	3,359	5,548	6,242
17,050	**17,100**	0	3,359	5,548	6,242	249	3,359	5,548	6,242
17,100	**17,150**	0	3,359	5,548	6,242	245	3,359	5,548	6,242
17,150	**17,200**	0	3,359	5,548	6,242	241	3,359	5,548	6,242
17,200	**17,250**	0	3,359	5,548	6,242	238	3,359	5,548	6,242
17,250	**17,300**	0	3,359	5,548	6,242	234	3,359	5,548	6,242
17,300	**17,350**	0	3,359	5,548	6,242	230	3,359	5,548	6,242
17,350	**17,400**	0	3,359	5,548	6,242	226	3,359	5,548	6,242
17,400	**17,450**	0	3,359	5,548	6,242	222	3,359	5,548	6,242
17,450	**17,500**	0	3,359	5,548	6,242	218	3,359	5,548	6,242
17,500	**17,550**	0	3,359	5,548	6,242	215	3,359	5,548	6,242
17,550	**17,600**	0	3,359	5,548	6,242	211	3,359	5,548	6,242
17,600	**17,650**	0	3,359	5,548	6,242	207	3,359	5,548	6,242
17,650	**17,700**	0	3,359	5,548	6,242	203	3,359	5,548	6,242
17,700	**17,750**	0	3,359	5,548	6,242	199	3,359	5,548	6,242
17,750	**17,800**	0	3,359	5,548	6,242	195	3,359	5,548	6,242
17,800	**17,850**	0	3,359	5,548	6,242	192	3,359	5,548	6,242
17,850	**17,900**	0	3,359	5,548	6,242	188	3,359	5,548	6,242
17,900	**17,950**	0	3,359	5,548	6,242	184	3,359	5,548	6,242
17,950	**18,000**	0	3,359	5,548	6,242	180	3,359	5,548	6,242
18,000	**18,050**	0	3,359	5,548	6,242	176	3,359	5,548	6,242
18,050	**18,100**	0	3,359	5,548	6,242	173	3,359	5,548	6,242
18,100	**18,150**	0	3,359	5,548	6,242	169	3,359	5,548	6,242
18,150	**18,200**	0	3,349	5,534	6,228	165	3,359	5,548	6,242
18,200	**18,250**	0	3,341	5,524	6,217	161	3,359	5,548	6,242
18,250	**18,300**	0	3,333	5,513	6,207	157	3,359	5,548	6,242
18,300	**18,350**	0	3,325	5,503	6,196	153	3,359	5,548	6,242
18,350	**18,400**	0	3,317	5,492	6,186	150	3,359	5,548	6,242
18,400	**18,450**	0	3,309	5,482	6,175	146	3,359	5,548	6,242
18,450	**18,500**	0	3,301	5,471	6,165	142	3,359	5,548	6,242
18,500	**18,550**	0	3,293	5,461	6,154	138	3,359	5,548	6,242
18,550	**18,600**	0	3,285	5,450	6,144	134	3,359	5,548	6,242
18,600	**18,650**	0	3,277	5,440	6,133	130	3,359	5,548	6,242
18,650	**18,700**	0	3,269	5,429	6,123	127	3,359	5,548	6,242
18,700	**18,750**	0	3,261	5,418	6,112	123	3,359	5,548	6,242
18,750	**18,800**	0	3,253	5,408	6,101	119	3,359	5,548	6,242
18,800	**18,850**	0	3,245	5,397	6,091	115	3,359	5,548	6,242
18,850	**18,900**	0	3,237	5,387	6,080	111	3,359	5,548	6,242
18,900	**18,950**	0	3,229	5,376	6,070	107	3,359	5,548	6,242
18,950	**19,000**	0	3,221	5,366	6,059	104	3,359	5,548	6,242
19,000	**19,050**	0	3,213	5,355	6,049	100	3,359	5,548	6,242
19,050	**19,100**	0	3,205	5,345	6,038	96	3,359	5,548	6,242
19,100	**19,150**	0	3,197	5,334	6,028	92	3,359	5,548	6,242
19,150	**19,200**	0	3,189	5,324	6,017	88	3,359	5,548	6,242

If the amount you are looking up from the worksheet is at least $14,800 but less than $14,820, and you have no qualifying children, your credit is $1.
If the amount you are looking up from the worksheet is $14,820 or more, and you have no qualifying children, you can't take the credit.

Earned Income Credit (EIC) Table - *Continued*

(Caution. This is **not** a tax table.)

If the amount you are looking up from the worksheet is–		And your filing status is–							
		Single, head of household, or **qualifying widow(er)** and the number of children you have is–				**Married filing jointly** and the number of children you have is–			
		0	1	2	3	0	1	2	3
At least	But less than	Your credit is–				Your credit is–			
19,200	19,250	0	3,181	5,313	6,007	85	3,359	5,548	6,242
19,250	19,300	0	3,173	5,303	5,996	81	3,359	5,548	6,242
19,300	19,350	0	3,165	5,292	5,986	77	3,359	5,548	6,242
19,350	19,400	0	3,157	5,282	5,975	73	3,359	5,548	6,242
19,400	19,450	0	3,149	5,271	5,965	69	3,359	5,548	6,242
19,450	19,500	0	3,141	5,261	5,954	65	3,359	5,548	6,242
19,500	19,550	0	3,133	5,250	5,944	62	3,359	5,548	6,242
19,550	19,600	0	3,125	5,239	5,933	58	3,359	5,548	6,242
19,600	19,650	0	3,117	5,229	5,922	54	3,359	5,548	6,242
19,650	19,700	0	3,109	5,218	5,912	50	3,359	5,548	6,242
19,700	19,750	0	3,101	5,208	5,901	46	3,359	5,548	6,242
19,750	19,800	0	3,093	5,197	5,891	42	3,359	5,548	6,242
19,800	19,850	0	3,085	5,187	5,880	39	3,359	5,548	6,242
19,850	19,900	0	3,077	5,176	5,870	35	3,359	5,548	6,242
19,900	19,950	0	3,069	5,166	5,859	31	3,359	5,548	6,242
19,950	20,000	0	3,061	5,155	5,849	27	3,359	5,548	6,242
20,000	20,050	0	3,053	5,145	5,838	23	3,359	5,548	6,242
20,050	20,100	0	3,045	5,134	5,828	20	3,359	5,548	6,242
20,100	20,150	0	3,037	5,124	5,817	16	3,359	5,548	6,242
20,150	20,200	0	3,029	5,113	5,807	12	3,359	5,548	6,242
20,200	20,250	0	3,021	5,103	5,796	8	3,359	5,548	6,242
20,250	20,300	0	3,013	5,092	5,786	4	3,359	5,548	6,242
20,300	20,350	0	3,005	5,082	5,775	*	3,359	5,548	6,242
20,350	20,400	0	2,997	5,071	5,764	0	3,359	5,548	6,242
20,400	20,450	0	2,989	5,060	5,754	0	3,359	5,548	6,242
20,450	20,500	0	2,981	5,050	5,743	0	3,359	5,548	6,242
20,500	20,550	0	2,973	5,039	5,733	0	3,359	5,548	6,242
20,550	20,600	0	2,965	5,029	5,722	0	3,359	5,548	6,242
20,600	20,650	0	2,957	5,018	5,712	0	3,359	5,548	6,242
20,650	20,700	0	2,949	5,008	5,701	0	3,359	5,548	6,242
20,700	20,750	0	2,941	4,997	5,691	0	3,359	5,548	6,242
20,750	20,800	0	2,933	4,987	5,680	0	3,359	5,548	6,242
20,800	20,850	0	2,925	4,976	5,670	0	3,359	5,548	6,242
20,850	20,900	0	2,917	4,966	5,659	0	3,359	5,548	6,242
20,900	20,950	0	2,909	4,955	5,649	0	3,359	5,548	6,242
20,950	21,000	0	2,901	4,945	5,638	0	3,359	5,548	6,242
21,000	21,050	0	2,893	4,934	5,628	0	3,359	5,548	6,242
21,050	21,100	0	2,885	4,924	5,617	0	3,359	5,548	6,242
21,100	21,150	0	2,877	4,913	5,607	0	3,359	5,548	6,242
21,150	21,200	0	2,869	4,903	5,596	0	3,359	5,548	6,242
21,200	21,250	0	2,861	4,892	5,585	0	3,359	5,548	6,242
21,250	21,300	0	2,853	4,881	5,575	0	3,359	5,548	6,242
21,300	21,350	0	2,845	4,871	5,564	0	3,359	5,548	6,242
21,350	21,400	0	2,837	4,860	5,554	0	3,359	5,548	6,242
21,400	21,450	0	2,829	4,850	5,543	0	3,359	5,548	6,242
21,450	21,500	0	2,821	4,839	5,533	0	3,359	5,548	6,242
21,500	21,550	0	2,813	4,829	5,522	0	3,359	5,548	6,242
21,550	21,600	0	2,805	4,818	5,512	0	3,359	5,548	6,242
21,600	21,650	0	2,798	4,808	5,501	0	3,359	5,548	6,242
21,650	21,700	0	2,790	4,797	5,491	0	3,359	5,548	6,242
21,700	21,750	0	2,782	4,787	5,480	0	3,359	5,548	6,242
21,750	21,800	0	2,774	4,776	5,470	0	3,359	5,548	6,242
21,800	21,850	0	2,766	4,766	5,459	0	3,359	5,548	6,242
21,850	21,900	0	2,758	4,755	5,449	0	3,359	5,548	6,242
21,900	21,950	0	2,750	4,745	5,438	0	3,359	5,548	6,242
21,950	22,000	0	2,742	4,734	5,428	0	3,359	5,548	6,242
22,000	22,050	0	2,734	4,724	5,417	0	3,359	5,548	6,242
22,050	22,100	0	2,726	4,713	5,406	0	3,359	5,548	6,242
22,100	22,150	0	2,718	4,702	5,396	0	3,359	5,548	6,242
22,150	22,200	0	2,710	4,692	5,385	0	3,359	5,548	6,242
22,200	22,250	0	2,702	4,681	5,375	0	3,359	5,548	6,242
22,250	22,300	0	2,694	4,671	5,364	0	3,359	5,548	6,242
22,300	22,350	0	2,686	4,660	5,354	0	3,359	5,548	6,242
22,350	22,400	0	2,678	4,650	5,343	0	3,359	5,548	6,242
22,400	22,450	0	2,670	4,639	5,333	0	3,359	5,548	6,242
22,450	22,500	0	2,662	4,629	5,322	0	3,359	5,548	6,242
22,500	22,550	0	2,654	4,618	5,312	0	3,359	5,548	6,242
22,550	22,600	0	2,646	4,608	5,301	0	3,359	5,548	6,242
22,600	22,650	0	2,638	4,597	5,291	0	3,359	5,548	6,242
22,650	22,700	0	2,630	4,587	5,280	0	3,359	5,548	6,242
22,700	22,750	0	2,622	4,576	5,270	0	3,359	5,548	6,242
22,750	22,800	0	2,614	4,566	5,259	0	3,359	5,548	6,242
22,800	22,850	0	2,606	4,555	5,249	0	3,359	5,548	6,242
22,850	22,900	0	2,598	4,544	5,238	0	3,359	5,548	6,242
22,900	22,950	0	2,590	4,534	5,227	0	3,359	5,548	6,242
22,950	23,000	0	2,582	4,523	5,217	0	3,359	5,548	6,242
23,000	23,050	0	2,574	4,513	5,206	0	3,359	5,548	6,242
23,050	23,100	0	2,566	4,502	5,196	0	3,359	5,548	6,242
23,100	23,150	0	2,558	4,492	5,185	0	3,359	5,548	6,242
23,150	23,200	0	2,550	4,481	5,175	0	3,359	5,548	6,242
23,200	23,250	0	2,542	4,471	5,164	0	3,359	5,548	6,242
23,250	23,300	0	2,534	4,460	5,154	0	3,359	5,548	6,242
23,300	23,350	0	2,526	4,450	5,143	0	3,359	5,548	6,242
23,350	23,400	0	2,518	4,439	5,133	0	3,359	5,548	6,242
23,400	23,450	0	2,510	4,429	5,122	0	3,359	5,548	6,242
23,450	23,500	0	2,502	4,418	5,112	0	3,359	5,548	6,242
23,500	23,550	0	2,494	4,408	5,101	0	3,359	5,548	6,242
23,550	23,600	0	2,486	4,397	5,091	0	3,359	5,548	6,242
23,600	23,650	0	2,478	4,387	5,080	0	3,359	5,548	6,242
23,650	23,700	0	2,470	4,376	5,070	0	3,352	5,539	6,232
23,700	23,750	0	2,462	4,365	5,059	0	3,344	5,528	6,221
23,750	23,800	0	2,454	4,355	5,048	0	3,336	5,517	6,211
23,800	23,850	0	2,446	4,344	5,038	0	3,328	5,507	6,200
23,850	23,900	0	2,438	4,334	5,027	0	3,320	5,496	6,190
23,900	23,950	0	2,430	4,323	5,017	0	3,312	5,486	6,179
23,950	24,000	0	2,422	4,313	5,006	0	3,304	5,475	6,169
24,000	24,050	0	2,414	4,302	4,996	0	3,296	5,465	6,158
24,050	24,100	0	2,406	4,292	4,985	0	3,288	5,454	6,148
24,100	24,150	0	2,398	4,281	4,975	0	3,280	5,444	6,137
24,150	24,200	0	2,390	4,271	4,964	0	3,272	5,433	6,127
24,200	24,250	0	2,382	4,260	4,954	0	3,264	5,423	6,116
24,250	24,300	0	2,374	4,250	4,943	0	3,256	5,412	6,106
24,300	24,350	0	2,366	4,239	4,933	0	3,248	5,402	6,095
24,350	24,400	0	2,358	4,229	4,922	0	3,240	5,391	6,085
24,400	24,450	0	2,350	4,218	4,912	0	3,232	5,381	6,074
24,450	24,500	0	2,342	4,208	4,901	0	3,224	5,370	6,064
24,500	24,550	0	2,334	4,197	4,891	0	3,216	5,360	6,053
24,550	24,600	0	2,326	4,186	4,880	0	3,208	5,349	6,042
24,600	24,650	0	2,318	4,176	4,869	0	3,200	5,338	6,032
24,650	24,700	0	2,310	4,165	4,859	0	3,192	5,328	6,021
24,700	24,750	0	2,302	4,155	4,848	0	3,184	5,317	6,011
24,750	24,800	0	2,294	4,144	4,838	0	3,176	5,307	6,000
24,800	24,850	0	2,286	4,134	4,827	0	3,168	5,296	5,990
24,850	24,900	0	2,278	4,123	4,817	0	3,160	5,286	5,979
24,900	24,950	0	2,270	4,113	4,806	0	3,152	5,275	5,969
24,950	25,000	0	2,262	4,102	4,796	0	3,144	5,265	5,958
25,000	25,050	0	2,254	4,092	4,785	0	3,136	5,254	5,948
25,050	25,100	0	2,246	4,081	4,775	0	3,128	5,244	5,937
25,100	25,150	0	2,238	4,071	4,764	0	3,120	5,233	5,927
25,150	25,200	0	2,230	4,060	4,754	0	3,112	5,223	5,916
25,200	25,250	0	2,222	4,050	4,743	0	3,104	5,212	5,906
25,250	25,300	0	2,214	4,039	4,733	0	3,096	5,202	5,895
25,300	25,350	0	2,206	4,029	4,722	0	3,088	5,191	5,885
25,350	25,400	0	2,198	4,018	4,711	0	3,080	5,181	5,874
25,400	25,450	0	2,190	4,007	4,701	0	3,072	5,170	5,863
25,450	25,500	0	2,182	3,997	4,690	0	3,064	5,159	5,853
25,500	25,550	0	2,174	3,986	4,680	0	3,056	5,149	5,842
25,550	25,600	0	2,166	3,976	4,669	0	3,048	5,138	5,832

* If the amount you are looking up from the worksheet is at least $20,300 but less than $20,330, and you have no qualifying children, your credit is $1.
If the amount you are looking up from the worksheet is $20,330 or more, and you have no qualifying children, you can't take the credit.

Earned Income Credit (EIC) Table - *Continued* (**Caution.** This is **not** a tax table.)

If the amount you are looking up from the worksheet is–		And your filing status is– **Single, head of household,** or **qualifying widow(er)** and the number of children you have is–				**Married filing jointly** and the number of children you have is–			
		0	1	2	3	0	1	2	3
At least	But less than	Your credit is–				Your credit is–			
25,600	25,650	0	2,158	3,965	4,659	0	3,040	5,128	5,821
25,650	25,700	0	2,150	3,955	4,648	0	3,032	5,117	5,811
25,700	25,750	0	2,142	3,944	4,638	0	3,024	5,107	5,800
25,750	25,800	0	2,134	3,934	4,627	0	3,016	5,096	5,790
25,800	25,850	0	2,126	3,923	4,617	0	3,008	5,086	5,779
25,850	25,900	0	2,118	3,913	4,606	0	3,000	5,075	5,769
25,900	25,950	0	2,110	3,902	4,596	0	2,992	5,065	5,758
25,950	26,000	0	2,102	3,892	4,585	0	2,984	5,054	5,748
26,000	26,050	0	2,094	3,881	4,575	0	2,976	5,044	5,737
26,050	26,100	0	2,086	3,871	4,564	0	2,968	5,033	5,727
26,100	26,150	0	2,078	3,860	4,554	0	2,960	5,023	5,716
26,150	26,200	0	2,070	3,850	4,543	0	2,953	5,012	5,706
26,200	26,250	0	2,062	3,839	4,532	0	2,945	5,001	5,695
26,250	26,300	0	2,054	3,828	4,522	0	2,937	4,991	5,684
26,300	26,350	0	2,046	3,818	4,511	0	2,929	4,980	5,674
26,350	26,400	0	2,038	3,807	4,501	0	2,921	4,970	5,663
26,400	26,450	0	2,030	3,797	4,490	0	2,913	4,959	5,653
26,450	26,500	0	2,022	3,786	4,480	0	2,905	4,949	5,642
26,500	26,550	0	2,014	3,776	4,469	0	2,897	4,938	5,632
26,550	26,600	0	2,006	3,765	4,459	0	2,889	4,928	5,621
26,600	26,650	0	1,999	3,755	4,448	0	2,881	4,917	5,611
26,650	26,700	0	1,991	3,744	4,438	0	2,873	4,907	5,600
26,700	26,750	0	1,983	3,734	4,427	0	2,865	4,896	5,590
26,750	26,800	0	1,975	3,723	4,417	0	2,857	4,886	5,579
26,800	26,850	0	1,967	3,713	4,406	0	2,849	4,875	5,569
26,850	26,900	0	1,959	3,702	4,396	0	2,841	4,865	5,558
26,900	26,950	0	1,951	3,692	4,385	0	2,833	4,854	5,548
26,950	27,000	0	1,943	3,681	4,375	0	2,825	4,844	5,537
27,000	27,050	0	1,935	3,671	4,364	0	2,817	4,833	5,527
27,050	27,100	0	1,927	3,660	4,353	0	2,809	4,822	5,516
27,100	27,150	0	1,919	3,649	4,343	0	2,801	4,812	5,505
27,150	27,200	0	1,911	3,639	4,332	0	2,793	4,801	5,495
27,200	27,250	0	1,903	3,628	4,322	0	2,785	4,791	5,484
27,250	27,300	0	1,895	3,618	4,311	0	2,777	4,780	5,474
27,300	27,350	0	1,887	3,607	4,301	0	2,769	4,770	5,463
27,350	27,400	0	1,879	3,597	4,290	0	2,761	4,759	5,453
27,400	27,450	0	1,871	3,586	4,280	0	2,753	4,749	5,442
27,450	27,500	0	1,863	3,576	4,269	0	2,745	4,738	5,432
27,500	27,550	0	1,855	3,565	4,259	0	2,737	4,728	5,421
27,550	27,600	0	1,847	3,555	4,248	0	2,729	4,717	5,411
27,600	27,650	0	1,839	3,544	4,238	0	2,721	4,707	5,400
27,650	27,700	0	1,831	3,534	4,227	0	2,713	4,696	5,390
27,700	27,750	0	1,823	3,523	4,217	0	2,705	4,686	5,379
27,750	27,800	0	1,815	3,513	4,206	0	2,697	4,675	5,369
27,800	27,850	0	1,807	3,502	4,196	0	2,689	4,665	5,358
27,850	27,900	0	1,799	3,491	4,185	0	2,681	4,654	5,348
27,900	27,950	0	1,791	3,481	4,174	0	2,673	4,643	5,337
27,950	28,000	0	1,783	3,470	4,164	0	2,665	4,633	5,326
28,000	28,050	0	1,775	3,460	4,153	0	2,657	4,622	5,316
28,050	28,100	0	1,767	3,449	4,143	0	2,649	4,612	5,305
28,100	28,150	0	1,759	3,439	4,132	0	2,641	4,601	5,295
28,150	28,200	0	1,751	3,428	4,122	0	2,633	4,591	5,284
28,200	28,250	0	1,743	3,418	4,111	0	2,625	4,580	5,274
28,250	28,300	0	1,735	3,407	4,101	0	2,617	4,570	5,263
28,300	28,350	0	1,727	3,397	4,090	0	2,609	4,559	5,253
28,350	28,400	0	1,719	3,386	4,080	0	2,601	4,549	5,242
28,400	28,450	0	1,711	3,376	4,069	0	2,593	4,538	5,232
28,450	28,500	0	1,703	3,365	4,059	0	2,585	4,528	5,221
28,500	28,550	0	1,695	3,355	4,048	0	2,577	4,517	5,211
28,550	28,600	0	1,687	3,344	4,038	0	2,569	4,507	5,200
28,600	28,650	0	1,679	3,334	4,027	0	2,561	4,496	5,190
28,650	28,700	0	1,671	3,323	4,017	0	2,553	4,486	5,179
28,700	28,750	0	1,663	3,312	4,006	0	2,545	4,475	5,168
28,750	28,800	0	1,655	3,302	3,995	0	2,537	4,464	5,158
28,800	28,850	0	1,647	3,291	3,985	0	2,529	4,454	5,147
28,850	28,900	0	1,639	3,281	3,974	0	2,521	4,443	5,137
28,900	28,950	0	1,631	3,270	3,964	0	2,513	4,433	5,126
28,950	29,000	0	1,623	3,260	3,953	0	2,505	4,422	5,116
29,000	29,050	0	1,615	3,249	3,943	0	2,497	4,412	5,105
29,050	29,100	0	1,607	3,239	3,932	0	2,489	4,401	5,095
29,100	29,150	0	1,599	3,228	3,922	0	2,481	4,391	5,084
29,150	29,200	0	1,591	3,218	3,911	0	2,473	4,380	5,074
29,200	29,250	0	1,583	3,207	3,901	0	2,465	4,370	5,063
29,250	29,300	0	1,575	3,197	3,890	0	2,457	4,359	5,053
29,300	29,350	0	1,567	3,186	3,880	0	2,449	4,349	5,042
29,350	29,400	0	1,559	3,176	3,869	0	2,441	4,338	5,032
29,400	29,450	0	1,551	3,165	3,859	0	2,433	4,328	5,021
29,450	29,500	0	1,543	3,155	3,848	0	2,425	4,317	5,011
29,500	29,550	0	1,535	3,144	3,838	0	2,417	4,307	5,000
29,550	29,600	0	1,527	3,133	3,827	0	2,409	4,296	4,989
29,600	29,650	0	1,519	3,123	3,816	0	2,401	4,285	4,979
29,650	29,700	0	1,511	3,112	3,806	0	2,393	4,275	4,968
29,700	29,750	0	1,503	3,102	3,795	0	2,385	4,264	4,958
29,750	29,800	0	1,495	3,091	3,785	0	2,377	4,254	4,947
29,800	29,850	0	1,487	3,081	3,774	0	2,369	4,243	4,937
29,850	29,900	0	1,479	3,070	3,764	0	2,361	4,233	4,926
29,900	29,950	0	1,471	3,060	3,753	0	2,353	4,222	4,916
29,950	30,000	0	1,463	3,049	3,743	0	2,345	4,212	4,905
30,000	30,050	0	1,455	3,039	3,732	0	2,337	4,201	4,895
30,050	30,100	0	1,447	3,028	3,722	0	2,329	4,191	4,884
30,100	30,150	0	1,439	3,018	3,711	0	2,321	4,180	4,874
30,150	30,200	0	1,431	3,007	3,701	0	2,313	4,170	4,863
30,200	30,250	0	1,423	2,997	3,690	0	2,305	4,159	4,853
30,250	30,300	0	1,415	2,986	3,680	0	2,297	4,149	4,842
30,300	30,350	0	1,407	2,976	3,669	0	2,289	4,138	4,832
30,350	30,400	0	1,399	2,965	3,658	0	2,281	4,128	4,821
30,400	30,450	0	1,391	2,954	3,648	0	2,273	4,117	4,810
30,450	30,500	0	1,383	2,944	3,637	0	2,265	4,106	4,800
30,500	30,550	0	1,375	2,933	3,627	0	2,257	4,096	4,789
30,550	30,600	0	1,367	2,923	3,616	0	2,249	4,085	4,779
30,600	30,650	0	1,359	2,912	3,606	0	2,241	4,075	4,768
30,650	30,700	0	1,351	2,902	3,595	0	2,233	4,064	4,758
30,700	30,750	0	1,343	2,891	3,585	0	2,225	4,054	4,747
30,750	30,800	0	1,335	2,881	3,574	0	2,217	4,043	4,737
30,800	30,850	0	1,327	2,870	3,564	0	2,209	4,033	4,726
30,850	30,900	0	1,319	2,860	3,553	0	2,201	4,022	4,716
30,900	30,950	0	1,311	2,849	3,543	0	2,193	4,012	4,705
30,950	31,000	0	1,303	2,839	3,532	0	2,185	4,001	4,695
31,000	31,050	0	1,295	2,828	3,522	0	2,177	3,991	4,684
31,050	31,100	0	1,287	2,818	3,511	0	2,169	3,980	4,674
31,100	31,150	0	1,279	2,807	3,501	0	2,161	3,970	4,663
31,150	31,200	0	1,271	2,797	3,490	0	2,154	3,959	4,653
31,200	31,250	0	1,263	2,786	3,479	0	2,146	3,948	4,642
31,250	31,300	0	1,255	2,775	3,469	0	2,138	3,938	4,631
31,300	31,350	0	1,247	2,765	3,458	0	2,130	3,927	4,621
31,350	31,400	0	1,239	2,754	3,448	0	2,122	3,917	4,610
31,400	31,450	0	1,231	2,744	3,437	0	2,114	3,906	4,600
31,450	31,500	0	1,223	2,733	3,427	0	2,106	3,896	4,589
31,500	31,550	0	1,215	2,723	3,416	0	2,098	3,885	4,579
31,550	31,600	0	1,207	2,712	3,406	0	2,090	3,875	4,568
31,600	31,650	0	1,200	2,702	3,395	0	2,082	3,864	4,558
31,650	31,700	0	1,192	2,691	3,385	0	2,074	3,854	4,547
31,700	31,750	0	1,184	2,681	3,374	0	2,066	3,843	4,537
31,750	31,800	0	1,176	2,670	3,364	0	2,058	3,833	4,526
31,800	31,850	0	1,168	2,660	3,353	0	2,050	3,822	4,516
31,850	31,900	0	1,160	2,649	3,343	0	2,042	3,812	4,505
31,900	31,950	0	1,152	2,639	3,332	0	2,034	3,801	4,495
31,950	32,000	0	1,144	2,628	3,322	0	2,026	3,791	4,484
32,000	32,050	0	1,136	2,618	3,311	0	2,018	3,780	4,474
32,050	32,100	0	1,128	2,607	3,300	0	2,010	3,769	4,463
32,100	32,150	0	1,120	2,596	3,290	0	2,002	3,759	4,452
32,150	32,200	0	1,112	2,586	3,279	0	1,994	3,748	4,442
32,200	32,250	0	1,104	2,575	3,269	0	1,986	3,738	4,431
32,250	32,300	0	1,096	2,565	3,258	0	1,978	3,727	4,421
32,300	32,350	0	1,088	2,554	3,248	0	1,970	3,717	4,410
32,350	32,400	0	1,080	2,544	3,237	0	1,962	3,706	4,400
32,400	32,450	0	1,072	2,533	3,227	0	1,954	3,696	4,389
32,450	32,500	0	1,064	2,523	3,216	0	1,946	3,685	4,379
32,500	32,550	0	1,056	2,512	3,206	0	1,938	3,675	4,368
32,550	32,600	0	1,048	2,502	3,195	0	1,930	3,664	4,358
32,600	32,650	0	1,040	2,491	3,185	0	1,922	3,654	4,347
32,650	32,700	0	1,032	2,481	3,174	0	1,914	3,643	4,337
32,700	32,750	0	1,024	2,470	3,164	0	1,906	3,633	4,326
32,750	32,800	0	1,016	2,460	3,153	0	1,898	3,622	4,316

Earned Income Credit (EIC) Table - *Continued* (**Caution.** This is **not** a tax table.)

If the amount you are looking up from the worksheet is–		And your filing status is– Single, head of household, or qualifying widow(er) and the number of children you have is–				Married filing jointly and the number of children you have is–			
At least	But less than	0	1	2	3	0	1	2	3
		Your credit is–				Your credit is–			
32,800	32,850	0	1,008	2,449	3,143	0	1,890	3,612	4,305
32,850	32,900	0	1,000	2,438	3,132	0	1,882	3,601	4,295
32,900	32,950	0	992	2,428	3,121	0	1,874	3,590	4,284
32,950	33,000	0	984	2,417	3,111	0	1,866	3,580	4,273
33,000	33,050	0	976	2,407	3,100	0	1,858	3,569	4,263
33,050	33,100	0	968	2,396	3,090	0	1,850	3,559	4,252
33,100	33,150	0	960	2,386	3,079	0	1,842	3,548	4,242
33,150	33,200	0	952	2,375	3,069	0	1,834	3,538	4,231
33,200	33,250	0	944	2,365	3,058	0	1,826	3,527	4,221
33,250	33,300	0	936	2,354	3,048	0	1,818	3,517	4,210
33,300	33,350	0	928	2,344	3,037	0	1,810	3,506	4,200
33,350	33,400	0	920	2,333	3,027	0	1,802	3,496	4,189
33,400	33,450	0	912	2,323	3,016	0	1,794	3,485	4,179
33,450	33,500	0	904	2,312	3,006	0	1,786	3,475	4,168
33,500	33,550	0	896	2,302	2,995	0	1,778	3,464	4,158
33,550	33,600	0	888	2,291	2,985	0	1,770	3,454	4,147
33,600	33,650	0	880	2,281	2,974	0	1,762	3,443	4,137
33,650	33,700	0	872	2,270	2,964	0	1,754	3,433	4,126
33,700	33,750	0	864	2,259	2,953	0	1,746	3,422	4,115
33,750	33,800	0	856	2,249	2,942	0	1,738	3,411	4,105
33,800	33,850	0	848	2,238	2,932	0	1,730	3,401	4,094
33,850	33,900	0	840	2,228	2,921	0	1,722	3,390	4,084
33,900	33,950	0	832	2,217	2,911	0	1,714	3,380	4,073
33,950	34,000	0	824	2,207	2,900	0	1,706	3,369	4,063
34,000	34,050	0	816	2,196	2,890	0	1,698	3,359	4,052
34,050	34,100	0	808	2,186	2,879	0	1,690	3,348	4,042
34,100	34,150	0	800	2,175	2,869	0	1,682	3,338	4,031
34,150	34,200	0	792	2,165	2,858	0	1,674	3,327	4,021
34,200	34,250	0	784	2,154	2,848	0	1,666	3,317	4,010
34,250	34,300	0	776	2,144	2,837	0	1,658	3,306	4,000
34,300	34,350	0	768	2,133	2,827	0	1,650	3,296	3,989
34,350	34,400	0	760	2,123	2,816	0	1,642	3,285	3,979
34,400	34,450	0	752	2,112	2,806	0	1,634	3,275	3,968
34,450	34,500	0	744	2,102	2,795	0	1,626	3,264	3,958
34,500	34,550	0	736	2,091	2,785	0	1,618	3,254	3,947
34,550	34,600	0	728	2,080	2,774	0	1,610	3,243	3,936
34,600	34,650	0	720	2,070	2,763	0	1,602	3,232	3,926
34,650	34,700	0	712	2,059	2,753	0	1,594	3,222	3,915
34,700	34,750	0	704	2,049	2,742	0	1,586	3,211	3,905
34,750	34,800	0	696	2,038	2,732	0	1,578	3,201	3,894
34,800	34,850	0	688	2,028	2,721	0	1,570	3,190	3,884
34,850	34,900	0	680	2,017	2,711	0	1,562	3,180	3,873
34,900	34,950	0	672	2,007	2,700	0	1,554	3,169	3,863
34,950	35,000	0	664	1,996	2,690	0	1,546	3,159	3,852
35,000	35,050	0	656	1,986	2,679	0	1,538	3,148	3,842
35,050	35,100	0	648	1,975	2,669	0	1,530	3,138	3,831
35,100	35,150	0	640	1,965	2,658	0	1,522	3,127	3,821
35,150	35,200	0	632	1,954	2,648	0	1,514	3,117	3,810
35,200	35,250	0	624	1,944	2,637	0	1,506	3,106	3,800
35,250	35,300	0	616	1,933	2,627	0	1,498	3,096	3,789
35,300	35,350	0	608	1,923	2,616	0	1,490	3,085	3,779
35,350	35,400	0	600	1,912	2,605	0	1,482	3,075	3,768
35,400	35,450	0	592	1,901	2,595	0	1,474	3,064	3,757
35,450	35,500	0	584	1,891	2,584	0	1,466	3,053	3,747
35,500	35,550	0	576	1,880	2,574	0	1,458	3,043	3,736
35,550	35,600	0	568	1,870	2,563	0	1,450	3,032	3,726
35,600	35,650	0	560	1,859	2,553	0	1,442	3,022	3,715
35,650	35,700	0	552	1,849	2,542	0	1,434	3,011	3,705
35,700	35,750	0	544	1,838	2,532	0	1,426	3,001	3,694
35,750	35,800	0	536	1,828	2,521	0	1,418	2,990	3,684
35,800	35,850	0	528	1,817	2,511	0	1,410	2,980	3,673
35,850	35,900	0	520	1,807	2,500	0	1,402	2,969	3,663
35,900	35,950	0	512	1,796	2,490	0	1,394	2,959	3,652
35,950	36,000	0	504	1,786	2,479	0	1,386	2,948	3,642
36,000	36,050	0	496	1,775	2,469	0	1,378	2,938	3,631
36,050	36,100	0	488	1,765	2,458	0	1,370	2,927	3,621
36,100	36,150	0	480	1,754	2,448	0	1,362	2,917	3,610
36,150	36,200	0	472	1,744	2,437	0	1,355	2,906	3,600
36,200	36,250	0	464	1,733	2,426	0	1,347	2,895	3,589
36,250	36,300	0	456	1,722	2,416	0	1,339	2,885	3,578
36,300	36,350	0	448	1,712	2,405	0	1,331	2,874	3,568
36,350	36,400	0	440	1,701	2,395	0	1,323	2,864	3,557
36,400	36,450	0	432	1,691	2,384	0	1,315	2,853	3,547
36,450	36,500	0	424	1,680	2,374	0	1,307	2,843	3,536
36,500	36,550	0	416	1,670	2,363	0	1,299	2,832	3,526
36,550	36,600	0	408	1,659	2,353	0	1,291	2,822	3,515
36,600	36,650	0	401	1,649	2,342	0	1,283	2,811	3,505
36,650	36,700	0	393	1,638	2,332	0	1,275	2,801	3,494
36,700	36,750	0	385	1,628	2,321	0	1,267	2,790	3,484
36,750	36,800	0	377	1,617	2,311	0	1,259	2,780	3,473
36,800	36,850	0	369	1,607	2,300	0	1,251	2,769	3,463
36,850	36,900	0	361	1,596	2,290	0	1,243	2,759	3,452
36,900	36,950	0	353	1,586	2,279	0	1,235	2,748	3,442
36,950	37,000	0	345	1,575	2,269	0	1,227	2,738	3,431
37,000	37,050	0	337	1,565	2,258	0	1,219	2,727	3,421
37,050	37,100	0	329	1,554	2,247	0	1,211	2,716	3,410
37,100	37,150	0	321	1,543	2,237	0	1,203	2,706	3,399
37,150	37,200	0	313	1,533	2,226	0	1,195	2,695	3,389
37,200	37,250	0	305	1,522	2,216	0	1,187	2,685	3,378
37,250	37,300	0	297	1,512	2,205	0	1,179	2,674	3,368
37,300	37,350	0	289	1,501	2,195	0	1,171	2,664	3,357
37,350	37,400	0	281	1,491	2,184	0	1,163	2,653	3,347
37,400	37,450	0	273	1,480	2,174	0	1,155	2,643	3,336
37,450	37,500	0	265	1,470	2,163	0	1,147	2,632	3,326
37,500	37,550	0	257	1,459	2,153	0	1,139	2,622	3,315
37,550	37,600	0	249	1,449	2,142	0	1,131	2,611	3,305
37,600	37,650	0	241	1,438	2,132	0	1,123	2,601	3,294
37,650	37,700	0	233	1,428	2,121	0	1,115	2,590	3,284
37,700	37,750	0	225	1,417	2,111	0	1,107	2,580	3,273
37,750	37,800	0	217	1,407	2,100	0	1,099	2,569	3,263
37,800	37,850	0	209	1,396	2,090	0	1,091	2,559	3,252
37,850	37,900	0	201	1,385	2,079	0	1,083	2,548	3,242
37,900	37,950	0	193	1,375	2,068	0	1,075	2,537	3,231
37,950	38,000	0	185	1,364	2,058	0	1,067	2,527	3,220
38,000	38,050	0	177	1,354	2,047	0	1,059	2,516	3,210
38,050	38,100	0	169	1,343	2,037	0	1,051	2,506	3,199
38,100	38,150	0	161	1,333	2,026	0	1,043	2,495	3,189
38,150	38,200	0	153	1,322	2,016	0	1,035	2,485	3,178
38,200	38,250	0	145	1,312	2,005	0	1,027	2,474	3,168
38,250	38,300	0	137	1,301	1,995	0	1,019	2,464	3,157
38,300	38,350	0	129	1,291	1,984	0	1,011	2,453	3,147
38,350	38,400	0	121	1,280	1,974	0	1,003	2,443	3,136
38,400	38,450	0	113	1,270	1,963	0	995	2,432	3,126
38,450	38,500	0	105	1,259	1,953	0	987	2,422	3,115
38,500	38,550	0	97	1,249	1,942	0	979	2,411	3,105
38,550	38,600	0	89	1,238	1,932	0	971	2,401	3,094
38,600	38,650	0	81	1,228	1,921	0	963	2,390	3,084
38,650	38,700	0	73	1,217	1,911	0	955	2,380	3,073
38,700	38,750	0	65	1,206	1,900	0	947	2,369	3,062
38,750	38,800	0	57	1,196	1,889	0	939	2,358	3,052
38,800	38,850	0	49	1,185	1,879	0	931	2,348	3,041
38,850	38,900	0	41	1,175	1,868	0	923	2,337	3,031
38,900	38,950	0	33	1,164	1,858	0	915	2,327	3,020
38,950	39,000	0	25	1,154	1,847	0	907	2,316	3,010
39,000	39,050	0	17	1,143	1,837	0	899	2,306	2,999
39,050	39,100	0	9	1,133	1,826	0	891	2,295	2,989
39,100	39,150	0	*	1,122	1,816	0	883	2,285	2,978
39,150	39,200	0	0	1,112	1,805	0	875	2,274	2,968

* If the amount you are looking up from the worksheet is at least $39,100 but less than $39,131, and you have one qualifying child, your credit is $3. If the amount you are looking up from the worksheet is $39,131 or more, and you have one qualifying child, you can't take the credit.

Earned Income Credit (EIC) Table - *Continued* (**Caution.** This is **not** a tax table.)

If the amount you are looking up from the worksheet is–		And your filing status is– **Single, head of household,** or **qualifying widow(er)** and the number of children you have is–				**Married filing jointly** and the number of children you have is–			
		0	1	2	3	0	1	2	3
At least	But less than	Your credit is–				Your credit is–			
39,200	39,250	0	0	1,101	1,795	0	867	2,264	2,957
39,250	39,300	0	0	1,091	1,784	0	859	2,253	2,947
39,300	39,350	0	0	1,080	1,774	0	851	2,243	2,936
39,350	39,400	0	0	1,070	1,763	0	843	2,232	2,926
39,400	39,450	0	0	1,059	1,753	0	835	2,222	2,915
39,450	39,500	0	0	1,049	1,742	0	827	2,211	2,905
39,500	39,550	0	0	1,038	1,732	0	819	2,201	2,894
39,550	39,600	0	0	1,027	1,721	0	811	2,190	2,883
39,600	39,650	0	0	1,017	1,710	0	803	2,179	2,873
39,650	39,700	0	0	1,006	1,700	0	795	2,169	2,862
39,700	39,750	0	0	996	1,689	0	787	2,158	2,852
39,750	39,800	0	0	985	1,679	0	779	2,148	2,841
39,800	39,850	0	0	975	1,668	0	771	2,137	2,831
39,850	39,900	0	0	964	1,658	0	763	2,127	2,820
39,900	39,950	0	0	954	1,647	0	755	2,116	2,810
39,950	40,000	0	0	943	1,637	0	747	2,106	2,799
40,000	40,050	0	0	933	1,626	0	739	2,095	2,789
40,050	40,100	0	0	922	1,616	0	731	2,085	2,778
40,100	40,150	0	0	912	1,605	0	723	2,074	2,768
40,150	40,200	0	0	901	1,595	0	715	2,064	2,757
40,200	40,250	0	0	891	1,584	0	707	2,053	2,747
40,250	40,300	0	0	880	1,574	0	699	2,043	2,736
40,300	40,350	0	0	870	1,563	0	691	2,032	2,726
40,350	40,400	0	0	859	1,552	0	683	2,022	2,715
40,400	40,450	0	0	848	1,542	0	675	2,011	2,704
40,450	40,500	0	0	838	1,531	0	667	2,000	2,694
40,500	40,550	0	0	827	1,521	0	659	1,990	2,683
40,550	40,600	0	0	817	1,510	0	651	1,979	2,673
40,600	40,650	0	0	806	1,500	0	643	1,969	2,662
40,650	40,700	0	0	796	1,489	0	635	1,958	2,652
40,700	40,750	0	0	785	1,479	0	627	1,948	2,641
40,750	40,800	0	0	775	1,468	0	619	1,937	2,631
40,800	40,850	0	0	764	1,458	0	611	1,927	2,620
40,850	40,900	0	0	754	1,447	0	603	1,916	2,610
40,900	40,950	0	0	743	1,437	0	595	1,906	2,599
40,950	41,000	0	0	733	1,426	0	587	1,895	2,589
41,000	41,050	0	0	722	1,416	0	579	1,885	2,578
41,050	41,100	0	0	712	1,405	0	571	1,874	2,568
41,100	41,150	0	0	701	1,395	0	563	1,864	2,557
41,150	41,200	0	0	691	1,384	0	556	1,853	2,547
41,200	41,250	0	0	680	1,373	0	548	1,842	2,536
41,250	41,300	0	0	669	1,363	0	540	1,832	2,525
41,300	41,350	0	0	659	1,352	0	532	1,821	2,515
41,350	41,400	0	0	648	1,342	0	524	1,811	2,504
41,400	41,450	0	0	638	1,331	0	516	1,800	2,494
41,450	41,500	0	0	627	1,321	0	508	1,790	2,483
41,500	41,550	0	0	617	1,310	0	500	1,779	2,473
41,550	41,600	0	0	606	1,300	0	492	1,769	2,462
41,600	41,650	0	0	596	1,289	0	484	1,758	2,452
41,650	41,700	0	0	585	1,279	0	476	1,748	2,441
41,700	41,750	0	0	575	1,268	0	468	1,737	2,431
41,750	41,800	0	0	564	1,258	0	460	1,727	2,420
41,800	41,850	0	0	554	1,247	0	452	1,716	2,410
41,850	41,900	0	0	543	1,237	0	444	1,706	2,399
41,900	41,950	0	0	533	1,226	0	436	1,695	2,389
41,950	42,000	0	0	522	1,216	0	428	1,685	2,378
42,000	42,050	0	0	512	1,205	0	420	1,674	2,368
42,050	42,100	0	0	501	1,194	0	412	1,663	2,357
42,100	42,150	0	0	490	1,184	0	404	1,653	2,346
42,150	42,200	0	0	480	1,173	0	396	1,642	2,336
42,200	42,250	0	0	469	1,163	0	388	1,632	2,325
42,250	42,300	0	0	459	1,152	0	380	1,621	2,315
42,300	42,350	0	0	448	1,142	0	372	1,611	2,304
42,350	42,400	0	0	438	1,131	0	364	1,600	2,294
42,400	42,450	0	0	427	1,121	0	356	1,590	2,283
42,450	42,500	0	0	417	1,110	0	348	1,579	2,273
42,500	42,550	0	0	406	1,100	0	340	1,569	2,262
42,550	42,600	0	0	396	1,089	0	332	1,558	2,252
42,600	42,650	0	0	385	1,079	0	324	1,548	2,241
42,650	42,700	0	0	375	1,068	0	316	1,537	2,231
42,700	42,750	0	0	364	1,058	0	308	1,527	2,220
42,750	42,800	0	0	354	1,047	0	300	1,516	2,210
42,800	42,850	0	0	343	1,037	0	292	1,506	2,199
42,850	42,900	0	0	332	1,026	0	284	1,495	2,189
42,900	42,950	0	0	322	1,015	0	276	1,484	2,178
42,950	43,000	0	0	311	1,005	0	268	1,474	2,167
43,000	43,050	0	0	301	994	0	260	1,463	2,157
43,050	43,100	0	0	290	984	0	252	1,453	2,146
43,100	43,150	0	0	280	973	0	244	1,442	2,136
43,150	43,200	0	0	269	963	0	236	1,432	2,125
43,200	43,250	0	0	259	952	0	228	1,421	2,115
43,250	43,300	0	0	248	942	0	220	1,411	2,104
43,300	43,350	0	0	238	931	0	212	1,400	2,094
43,350	43,400	0	0	227	921	0	204	1,390	2,083
43,400	43,450	0	0	217	910	0	196	1,379	2,073
43,450	43,500	0	0	206	900	0	188	1,369	2,062
43,500	43,550	0	0	196	889	0	180	1,358	2,052
43,550	43,600	0	0	185	879	0	172	1,348	2,041
43,600	43,650	0	0	175	868	0	164	1,337	2,031
43,650	43,700	0	0	164	858	0	156	1,327	2,020
43,700	43,750	0	0	153	847	0	148	1,316	2,009
43,750	43,800	0	0	143	836	0	140	1,305	1,999
43,800	43,850	0	0	132	826	0	132	1,295	1,988
43,850	43,900	0	0	122	815	0	124	1,284	1,978
43,900	43,950	0	0	111	805	0	116	1,274	1,967
43,950	44,000	0	0	101	794	0	108	1,263	1,957
44,000	44,050	0	0	90	784	0	100	1,253	1,946
44,050	44,100	0	0	80	773	0	92	1,242	1,936
44,100	44,150	0	0	69	763	0	84	1,232	1,925
44,150	44,200	0	0	59	752	0	76	1,221	1,915
44,200	44,250	0	0	48	742	0	68	1,211	1,904
44,250	44,300	0	0	38	731	0	60	1,200	1,894
44,300	44,350	0	0	27	721	0	52	1,190	1,883
44,350	44,400	0	0	17	710	0	44	1,179	1,873
44,400	44,450	0	0	6	700	0	36	1,169	1,862
44,450	44,500	0	0	0	689	0	28	1,158	1,852
44,500	44,550	0	0	0	679	0	20	1,148	1,841
44,550	44,600	0	0	0	668	0	12	1,137	1,830
44,600	44,650	0	0	0	657	0	4	1,126	1,820
44,650	44,700	0	0	0	647	0	0	1,116	1,809
44,700	44,750	0	0	0	636	0	0	1,105	1,799
44,750	44,800	0	0	0	626	0	0	1,095	1,788
44,800	44,850	0	0	0	615	0	0	1,084	1,778
44,850	44,900	0	0	0	605	0	0	1,074	1,767
44,900	44,950	0	0	0	594	0	0	1,063	1,757
44,950	45,000	0	0	0	584	0	0	1,053	1,746
45,000	45,050	0	0	0	573	0	0	1,042	1,736
45,050	45,100	0	0	0	563	0	0	1,032	1,725
45,100	45,150	0	0	0	552	0	0	1,021	1,715
45,150	45,200	0	0	0	542	0	0	1,011	1,704
45,200	45,250	0	0	0	531	0	0	1,000	1,694
45,250	45,300	0	0	0	521	0	0	990	1,683
45,300	45,350	0	0	0	510	0	0	979	1,673
45,350	45,400	0	0	0	499	0	0	969	1,662
45,400	45,450	0	0	0	489	0	0	958	1,651
45,450	45,500	0	0	0	478	0	0	947	1,641
45,500	45,550	0	0	0	468	0	0	937	1,630
45,550	45,600	0	0	0	457	0	0	926	1,620
45,600	45,650	0	0	0	447	0	0	916	1,609
45,650	45,700	0	0	0	436	0	0	905	1,599
45,700	45,750	0	0	0	426	0	0	895	1,588
45,750	45,800	0	0	0	415	0	0	884	1,578
45,800	45,850	0	0	0	405	0	0	874	1,567
45,850	45,900	0	0	0	394	0	0	863	1,557
45,900	45,950	0	0	0	384	0	0	853	1,546
45,950	46,000	0	0	0	373	0	0	842	1,536
46,000	46,050	0	0	0	363	0	0	832	1,525
46,050	46,100	0	0	0	352	0	0	821	1,515
46,100	46,150	0	0	0	342	0	0	811	1,504
46,150	46,200	0	0	0	331	0	0	800	1,494
46,200	46,250	0	0	0	320	0	0	789	1,483
46,250	46,300	0	0	0	310	0	0	779	1,472
46,300	46,350	0	0	0	299	0	0	768	1,462
46,350	46,400	0	0	0	289	0	0	758	1,451

Earned Income Credit (EIC) Table - *Continued*

(Caution. This is **not** a tax table.)

If the amount you are looking up from the worksheet is–		And your filing status is– Single, head of household, or qualifying widow(er) and the number of children you have is–				Married filing jointly and the number of children you have is–			
		0	1	2	3	0	1	2	3
At least	But less than	Your credit is–				Your credit is–			
46,400	46,450	0	0	0	278	0	0	747	1,441
46,450	46,500	0	0	0	268	0	0	737	1,430
46,500	46,550	0	0	0	257	0	0	726	1,420
46,550	46,600	0	0	0	247	0	0	716	1,409
46,600	46,650	0	0	0	236	0	0	705	1,399
46,650	46,700	0	0	0	226	0	0	695	1,388
46,700	46,750	0	0	0	215	0	0	684	1,378
46,750	46,800	0	0	0	205	0	0	674	1,367
46,800	46,850	0	0	0	194	0	0	663	1,357
46,850	46,900	0	0	0	184	0	0	653	1,346
46,900	46,950	0	0	0	173	0	0	642	1,336
46,950	47,000	0	0	0	163	0	0	632	1,325
47,000	47,050	0	0	0	152	0	0	621	1,315
47,050	47,100	0	0	0	141	0	0	610	1,304
47,100	47,150	0	0	0	131	0	0	600	1,293
47,150	47,200	0	0	0	120	0	0	589	1,283
47,200	47,250	0	0	0	110	0	0	579	1,272
47,250	47,300	0	0	0	99	0	0	568	1,262
47,300	47,350	0	0	0	89	0	0	558	1,251
47,350	47,400	0	0	0	78	0	0	547	1,241
47,400	47,450	0	0	0	68	0	0	537	1,230
47,450	47,500	0	0	0	57	0	0	526	1,220
47,500	47,550	0	0	0	47	0	0	516	1,209
47,550	47,600	0	0	0	36	0	0	505	1,199
47,600	47,650	0	0	0	26	0	0	495	1,188
47,650	47,700	0	0	0	15	0	0	484	1,178
47,700	47,750	0	0	0	*	0	0	474	1,167
47,750	47,800	0	0	0	0	0	0	463	1,157
47,800	47,850	0	0	0	0	0	0	453	1,146
47,850	47,900	0	0	0	0	0	0	442	1,136
47,900	47,950	0	0	0	0	0	0	431	1,125
47,950	48,000	0	0	0	0	0	0	421	1,114
48,000	48,050	0	0	0	0	0	0	410	1,104
48,050	48,100	0	0	0	0	0	0	400	1,093
48,100	48,150	0	0	0	0	0	0	389	1,083
48,150	48,200	0	0	0	0	0	0	379	1,072
48,200	48,250	0	0	0	0	0	0	368	1,062
48,250	48,300	0	0	0	0	0	0	358	1,051
48,300	48,350	0	0	0	0	0	0	347	1,041
48,350	48,400	0	0	0	0	0	0	337	1,030
48,400	48,450	0	0	0	0	0	0	326	1,020
48,450	48,500	0	0	0	0	0	0	316	1,009
48,500	48,550	0	0	0	0	0	0	305	999
48,550	48,600	0	0	0	0	0	0	295	988
48,600	48,650	0	0	0	0	0	0	284	978
48,650	48,700	0	0	0	0	0	0	274	967
48,700	48,750	0	0	0	0	0	0	263	956
48,750	48,800	0	0	0	0	0	0	252	946
48,800	48,850	0	0	0	0	0	0	242	935
48,850	48,900	0	0	0	0	0	0	231	925
48,900	48,950	0	0	0	0	0	0	221	914
48,950	49,000	0	0	0	0	0	0	210	904
49,000	49,050	0	0	0	0	0	0	200	893
49,050	49,100	0	0	0	0	0	0	189	883
49,100	49,150	0	0	0	0	0	0	179	872
49,150	49,200	0	0	0	0	0	0	168	862
49,200	49,250	0	0	0	0	0	0	158	851
49,250	49,300	0	0	0	0	0	0	147	841
49,300	49,350	0	0	0	0	0	0	137	830
49,350	49,400	0	0	0	0	0	0	126	820
49,400	49,450	0	0	0	0	0	0	116	809
49,450	49,500	0	0	0	0	0	0	105	799
49,500	49,550	0	0	0	0	0	0	95	788
49,550	49,600	0	0	0	0	0	0	84	777
49,600	49,650	0	0	0	0	0	0	73	767
49,650	49,700	0	0	0	0	0	0	63	756
49,700	49,750	0	0	0	0	0	0	52	746
49,750	49,800	0	0	0	0	0	0	42	735
49,800	49,850	0	0	0	0	0	0	31	725
49,850	49,900	0	0	0	0	0	0	21	714
49,900	49,950	0	0	0	0	0	0	10	704
49,950	50,000	0	0	0	0	0	0	**	693
50,000	50,050	0	0	0	0	0	0	0	683
50,050	50,100	0	0	0	0	0	0	0	672
50,100	50,150	0	0	0	0	0	0	0	662
50,150	50,200	0	0	0	0	0	0	0	651
50,200	50,250	0	0	0	0	0	0	0	641
50,250	50,300	0	0	0	0	0	0	0	630
50,300	50,350	0	0	0	0	0	0	0	620
50,350	50,400	0	0	0	0	0	0	0	609
50,400	50,450	0	0	0	0	0	0	0	598
50,450	50,500	0	0	0	0	0	0	0	588
50,500	50,550	0	0	0	0	0	0	0	577
50,550	50,600	0	0	0	0	0	0	0	567
50,600	50,650	0	0	0	0	0	0	0	556
50,650	50,700	0	0	0	0	0	0	0	546
50,700	50,750	0	0	0	0	0	0	0	535
50,750	50,800	0	0	0	0	0	0	0	525
50,800	50,850	0	0	0	0	0	0	0	514
50,850	50,900	0	0	0	0	0	0	0	504
50,900	50,950	0	0	0	0	0	0	0	493
50,950	51,000	0	0	0	0	0	0	0	483
51,000	51,050	0	0	0	0	0	0	0	472
51,050	51,100	0	0	0	0	0	0	0	462
51,100	51,150	0	0	0	0	0	0	0	451
51,150	51,200	0	0	0	0	0	0	0	441
51,200	51,250	0	0	0	0	0	0	0	430
51,250	51,300	0	0	0	0	0	0	0	419
51,300	51,350	0	0	0	0	0	0	0	409
51,350	51,400	0	0	0	0	0	0	0	398
51,400	51,450	0	0	0	0	0	0	0	388
51,450	51,500	0	0	0	0	0	0	0	377
51,500	51,550	0	0	0	0	0	0	0	367
51,550	51,600	0	0	0	0	0	0	0	356
51,600	51,650	0	0	0	0	0	0	0	346
51,650	51,700	0	0	0	0	0	0	0	335
51,700	51,750	0	0	0	0	0	0	0	325
51,750	51,800	0	0	0	0	0	0	0	314
51,800	51,850	0	0	0	0	0	0	0	304
51,850	51,900	0	0	0	0	0	0	0	293
51,900	51,950	0	0	0	0	0	0	0	283
51,950	52,000	0	0	0	0	0	0	0	272
52,000	52,050	0	0	0	0	0	0	0	262
52,050	52,100	0	0	0	0	0	0	0	251
52,100	52,150	0	0	0	0	0	0	0	240
52,150	52,200	0	0	0	0	0	0	0	230
52,200	52,250	0	0	0	0	0	0	0	219
52,250	52,300	0	0	0	0	0	0	0	209
52,300	52,350	0	0	0	0	0	0	0	198
52,350	52,400	0	0	0	0	0	0	0	188
52,400	52,450	0	0	0	0	0	0	0	177
52,450	52,500	0	0	0	0	0	0	0	167
52,500	52,550	0	0	0	0	0	0	0	156
52,550	52,600	0	0	0	0	0	0	0	146
52,600	52,650	0	0	0	0	0	0	0	135
52,650	52,700	0	0	0	0	0	0	0	125
52,700	52,750	0	0	0	0	0	0	0	114
52,750	52,800	0	0	0	0	0	0	0	104

* If the amount you are looking up from the worksheet is at least $47,700 but less than $47,747, and you have three qualifying children, your credit is $5.

If the amount you are looking up from the worksheet is $47,747 or more, and you have three qualifying children, you can't take the credit.

** If the amount you are looking up from the worksheet is at least $49,950 but less than $49,974, and you have two qualifying children, your credit is $2.

If the amount you are looking up from the worksheet is $49,974 or more, and you have two qualifying children, you can't take the credit.

Earned Income Credit (EIC) Table - *Continued* (**Caution.** This is **not** a tax table.)

If the amount you are looking up from the worksheet is–		And your filing status is– **Single, head of household,** or **qualifying widow(er)** and the number of children you have is–				**Married filing jointly** and the number of children you have is–			
At least	But less than	0	1	2	3	0	1	2	3
		Your credit is–				Your credit is–			
52,800	52,850	0	0	0	0	0	0	0	93
52,850	52,900	0	0	0	0	0	0	0	83
52,900	52,950	0	0	0	0	0	0	0	72
52,950	53,000	0	0	0	0	0	0	0	61
53,000	53,050	0	0	0	0	0	0	0	51
53,050	53,100	0	0	0	0	0	0	0	40
53,100	53,150	0	0	0	0	0	0	0	30
53,150	53,200	0	0	0	0	0	0	0	19
53,200	53,250	0	0	0	0	0	0	0	9
53,250	53,267	0	0	0	0	0	0	0	2

Appendix T

Tax Tables

2015 Tax Table

CAUTION *See the instructions for line 44 to see if you must use the Tax Table below to figure your tax.*

Example. Mr. and Mrs. Brown are filing a joint return. Their taxable income on Form 1040, line 43, is $25,300. First, they find the $25,300-25,350 taxable income line. Next, they find the column for married filing jointly and read down the column. The amount shown where the taxable income line and filing status column meet is $2,876. This is the tax amount they should enter on Form 1040, line 44.

Sample Table

At Least	But Less Than	Single	Married filing jointly*	Married filing sepa-rately	Head of a house-hold
		Your tax is—			
25,200	**25,250**	3,323	2,861	3,323	3,126
25,250	**25,300**	3,330	2,869	3,330	3,134
25,300	**25,350**	3,338	(2,876)	3,338	3,141
25,350	**25,400**	3,345	2,884	3,345	3,149

If line 43 (taxable income) is—		And you are—			
At least	But less than	Single	Married filing jointly *	Married filing sepa-rately	Head of a house-hold
		Your tax is—			
0	**5**	0	0	0	0
5	**15**	1	1	1	1
15	**25**	2	2	2	2
25	**50**	4	4	4	4
50	**75**	6	6	6	6
75	**100**	9	9	9	9
100	**125**	11	11	11	11
125	**150**	14	14	14	14
150	**175**	16	16	16	16
175	**200**	19	19	19	19
200	**225**	21	21	21	21
225	**250**	24	24	24	24
250	**275**	26	26	26	26
275	**300**	29	29	29	29
300	**325**	31	31	31	31
325	**350**	34	34	34	34
350	**375**	36	36	36	36
375	**400**	39	39	39	39
400	**425**	41	41	41	41
425	**450**	44	44	44	44
450	**475**	46	46	46	46
475	**500**	49	49	49	49
500	**525**	51	51	51	51
525	**550**	54	54	54	54
550	**575**	56	56	56	56
575	**600**	59	59	59	59
600	**625**	61	61	61	61
625	**650**	64	64	64	64
650	**675**	66	66	66	66
675	**700**	69	69	69	69
700	**725**	71	71	71	71
725	**750**	74	74	74	74
750	**775**	76	76	76	76
775	**800**	79	79	79	79
800	**825**	81	81	81	81
825	**850**	84	84	84	84
850	**875**	86	86	86	86
875	**900**	89	89	89	89
900	**925**	91	91	91	91
925	**950**	94	94	94	94
950	**975**	96	96	96	96
975	**1,000**	99	99	99	99

If line 43 (taxable income) is—		And you are—			
At least	But less than	Single	Married filing jointly *	Married filing sepa-rately	Head of a house-hold
		Your tax is—			
1,000					
1,000	**1,025**	101	101	101	101
1,025	**1,050**	104	104	104	104
1,050	**1,075**	106	106	106	106
1,075	**1,100**	109	109	109	109
1,100	**1,125**	111	111	111	111
1,125	**1,150**	114	114	114	114
1,150	**1,175**	116	116	116	116
1,175	**1,200**	119	119	119	119
1,200	**1,225**	121	121	121	121
1,225	**1,250**	124	124	124	124
1,250	**1,275**	126	126	126	126
1,275	**1,300**	129	129	129	129
1,300	**1,325**	131	131	131	131
1,325	**1,350**	134	134	134	134
1,350	**1,375**	136	136	136	136
1,375	**1,400**	139	139	139	139
1,400	**1,425**	141	141	141	141
1,425	**1,450**	144	144	144	144
1,450	**1,475**	146	146	146	146
1,475	**1,500**	149	149	149	149
1,500	**1,525**	151	151	151	151
1,525	**1,550**	154	154	154	154
1,550	**1,575**	156	156	156	156
1,575	**1,600**	159	159	159	159
1,600	**1,625**	161	161	161	161
1,625	**1,650**	164	164	164	164
1,650	**1,675**	166	166	166	166
1,675	**1,700**	169	169	169	169
1,700	**1,725**	171	171	171	171
1,725	**1,750**	174	174	174	174
1,750	**1,775**	176	176	176	176
1,775	**1,800**	179	179	179	179
1,800	**1,825**	181	181	181	181
1,825	**1,850**	184	184	184	184
1,850	**1,875**	186	186	186	186
1,875	**1,900**	189	189	189	189
1,900	**1,925**	191	191	191	191
1,925	**1,950**	194	194	194	194
1,950	**1,975**	196	196	196	196
1,975	**2,000**	199	199	199	199

If line 43 (taxable income) is—		And you are—			
At least	But less than	Single	Married filing jointly *	Married filing sepa-rately	Head of a house-hold
		Your tax is—			
2,000					
2,000	**2,025**	201	201	201	201
2,025	**2,050**	204	204	204	204
2,050	**2,075**	206	206	206	206
2,075	**2,100**	209	209	209	209
2,100	**2,125**	211	211	211	211
2,125	**2,150**	214	214	214	214
2,150	**2,175**	216	216	216	216
2,175	**2,200**	219	219	219	219
2,200	**2,225**	221	221	221	221
2,225	**2,250**	224	224	224	224
2,250	**2,275**	226	226	226	226
2,275	**2,300**	229	229	229	229
2,300	**2,325**	231	231	231	231
2,325	**2,350**	234	234	234	234
2,350	**2,375**	236	236	236	236
2,375	**2,400**	239	239	239	239
2,400	**2,425**	241	241	241	241
2,425	**2,450**	244	244	244	244
2,450	**2,475**	246	246	246	246
2,475	**2,500**	249	249	249	249
2,500	**2,525**	251	251	251	251
2,525	**2,550**	254	254	254	254
2,550	**2,575**	256	256	256	256
2,575	**2,600**	259	259	259	259
2,600	**2,625**	261	261	261	261
2,625	**2,650**	264	264	264	264
2,650	**2,675**	266	266	266	266
2,675	**2,700**	269	269	269	269
2,700	**2,725**	271	271	271	271
2,725	**2,750**	274	274	274	274
2,750	**2,775**	276	276	276	276
2,775	**2,800**	279	279	279	279
2,800	**2,825**	281	281	281	281
2,825	**2,850**	284	284	284	284
2,850	**2,875**	286	286	286	286
2,875	**2,900**	289	289	289	289
2,900	**2,925**	291	291	291	291
2,925	**2,950**	294	294	294	294
2,950	**2,975**	296	296	296	296
2,975	**3,000**	299	299	299	299

* This column must also be used by a qualifying widow(er).

2015 Tax Table — *Continued*

3,000

If line 43 (taxable income) is— At least	But less than	And you are— Single	Married filing jointly *	Married filing separately	Head of a household
		Your tax is—			
3,000	3,050	303	303	303	303
3,050	3,100	308	308	308	308
3,100	3,150	313	313	313	313
3,150	3,200	318	318	318	318
3,200	3,250	323	323	323	323
3,250	3,300	328	328	328	328
3,300	3,350	333	333	333	333
3,350	3,400	338	338	338	338
3,400	3,450	343	343	343	343
3,450	3,500	348	348	348	348
3,500	3,550	353	353	353	353
3,550	3,600	358	358	358	358
3,600	3,650	363	363	363	363
3,650	3,700	368	368	368	368
3,700	3,750	373	373	373	373
3,750	3,800	378	378	378	378
3,800	3,850	383	383	383	383
3,850	3,900	388	388	388	388
3,900	3,950	393	393	393	393
3,950	4,000	398	398	398	398

4,000

At least	But less than	Single	Married filing jointly *	Married filing separately	Head of a household
4,000	4,050	403	403	403	403
4,050	4,100	408	408	408	408
4,100	4,150	413	413	413	413
4,150	4,200	418	418	418	418
4,200	4,250	423	423	423	423
4,250	4,300	428	428	428	428
4,300	4,350	433	433	433	433
4,350	4,400	438	438	438	438
4,400	4,450	443	443	443	443
4,450	4,500	448	448	448	448
4,500	4,550	453	453	453	453
4,550	4,600	458	458	458	458
4,600	4,650	463	463	463	463
4,650	4,700	468	468	468	468
4,700	4,750	473	473	473	473
4,750	4,800	478	478	478	478
4,800	4,850	483	483	483	483
4,850	4,900	488	488	488	488
4,900	4,950	493	493	493	493
4,950	5,000	498	498	498	498

5,000

At least	But less than	Single	Married filing jointly *	Married filing separately	Head of a household
5,000	5,050	503	503	503	503
5,050	5,100	508	508	508	508
5,100	5,150	513	513	513	513
5,150	5,200	518	518	518	518
5,200	5,250	523	523	523	523
5,250	5,300	528	528	528	528
5,300	5,350	533	533	533	533
5,350	5,400	538	538	538	538
5,400	5,450	543	543	543	543
5,450	5,500	548	548	548	548
5,500	5,550	553	553	553	553
5,550	5,600	558	558	558	558
5,600	5,650	563	563	563	563
5,650	5,700	568	568	568	568
5,700	5,750	573	573	573	573
5,750	5,800	578	578	578	578
5,800	5,850	583	583	583	583
5,850	5,900	588	588	588	588
5,900	5,950	593	593	593	593
5,950	6,000	598	598	598	598

6,000

At least	But less than	Single	Married filing jointly *	Married filing separately	Head of a household
6,000	6,050	603	603	603	603
6,050	6,100	608	608	608	608
6,100	6,150	613	613	613	613
6,150	6,200	618	618	618	618
6,200	6,250	623	623	623	623
6,250	6,300	628	628	628	628
6,300	6,350	633	633	633	633
6,350	6,400	638	638	638	638
6,400	6,450	643	643	643	643
6,450	6,500	648	648	648	648
6,500	6,550	653	653	653	653
6,550	6,600	658	658	658	658
6,600	6,650	663	663	663	663
6,650	6,700	668	668	668	668
6,700	6,750	673	673	673	673
6,750	6,800	678	678	678	678
6,800	6,850	683	683	683	683
6,850	6,900	688	688	688	688
6,900	6,950	693	693	693	693
6,950	7,000	698	698	698	698

7,000

At least	But less than	Single	Married filing jointly *	Married filing separately	Head of a household
7,000	7,050	703	703	703	703
7,050	7,100	708	708	708	708
7,100	7,150	713	713	713	713
7,150	7,200	718	718	718	718
7,200	7,250	723	723	723	723
7,250	7,300	728	728	728	728
7,300	7,350	733	733	733	733
7,350	7,400	738	738	738	738
7,400	7,450	743	743	743	743
7,450	7,500	748	748	748	748
7,500	7,550	753	753	753	753
7,550	7,600	758	758	758	758
7,600	7,650	763	763	763	763
7,650	7,700	768	768	768	768
7,700	7,750	773	773	773	773
7,750	7,800	778	778	778	778
7,800	7,850	783	783	783	783
7,850	7,900	788	788	788	788
7,900	7,950	793	793	793	793
7,950	8,000	798	798	798	798

8,000

At least	But less than	Single	Married filing jointly *	Married filing separately	Head of a household
8,000	8,050	803	803	803	803
8,050	8,100	808	808	808	808
8,100	8,150	813	813	813	813
8,150	8,200	818	818	818	818
8,200	8,250	823	823	823	823
8,250	8,300	828	828	828	828
8,300	8,350	833	833	833	833
8,350	8,400	838	838	838	838
8,400	8,450	843	843	843	843
8,450	8,500	848	848	848	848
8,500	8,550	853	853	853	853
8,550	8,600	858	858	858	858
8,600	8,650	863	863	863	863
8,650	8,700	868	868	868	868
8,700	8,750	873	873	873	873
8,750	8,800	878	878	878	878
8,800	8,850	883	883	883	883
8,850	8,900	888	888	888	888
8,900	8,950	893	893	893	893
8,950	9,000	898	898	898	898

9,000

At least	But less than	Single	Married filing jointly *	Married filing separately	Head of a household
9,000	9,050	903	903	903	903
9,050	9,100	908	908	908	908
9,100	9,150	913	913	913	913
9,150	9,200	918	918	918	918
9,200	9,250	923	923	923	923
9,250	9,300	930	928	930	928
9,300	9,350	938	933	938	933
9,350	9,400	945	938	945	938
9,400	9,450	953	943	953	943
9,450	9,500	960	948	960	948
9,500	9,550	968	953	968	953
9,550	9,600	975	958	975	958
9,600	9,650	983	963	983	963
9,650	9,700	990	968	990	968
9,700	9,750	998	973	998	973
9,750	9,800	1,005	978	1,005	978
9,800	9,850	1,013	983	1,013	983
9,850	9,900	1,020	988	1,020	988
9,900	9,950	1,028	993	1,028	993
9,950	10,000	1,035	998	1,035	998

10,000

At least	But less than	Single	Married filing jointly *	Married filing separately	Head of a household
10,000	10,050	1,043	1,003	1,043	1,003
10,050	10,100	1,050	1,008	1,050	1,008
10,100	10,150	1,058	1,013	1,058	1,013
10,150	10,200	1,065	1,018	1,065	1,018
10,200	10,250	1,073	1,023	1,073	1,023
10,250	10,300	1,080	1,028	1,080	1,028
10,300	10,350	1,088	1,033	1,088	1,033
10,350	10,400	1,095	1,038	1,095	1,038
10,400	10,450	1,103	1,043	1,103	1,043
10,450	10,500	1,110	1,048	1,110	1,048
10,500	10,550	1,118	1,053	1,118	1,053
10,550	10,600	1,125	1,058	1,125	1,058
10,600	10,650	1,133	1,063	1,133	1,063
10,650	10,700	1,140	1,068	1,140	1,068
10,700	10,750	1,148	1,073	1,148	1,073
10,750	10,800	1,155	1,078	1,155	1,078
10,800	10,850	1,163	1,083	1,163	1,083
10,850	10,900	1,170	1,088	1,170	1,088
10,900	10,950	1,178	1,093	1,178	1,093
10,950	11,000	1,185	1,098	1,185	1,098

11,000

At least	But less than	Single	Married filing jointly *	Married filing separately	Head of a household
11,000	11,050	1,193	1,103	1,193	1,103
11,050	11,100	1,200	1,108	1,200	1,108
11,100	11,150	1,208	1,113	1,208	1,113
11,150	11,200	1,215	1,118	1,215	1,118
11,200	11,250	1,223	1,123	1,223	1,123
11,250	11,300	1,230	1,128	1,230	1,128
11,300	11,350	1,238	1,133	1,238	1,133
11,350	11,400	1,245	1,138	1,245	1,138
11,400	11,450	1,253	1,143	1,253	1,143
11,450	11,500	1,260	1,148	1,260	1,148
11,500	11,550	1,268	1,153	1,268	1,153
11,550	11,600	1,275	1,158	1,275	1,158
11,600	11,650	1,283	1,163	1,283	1,163
11,650	11,700	1,290	1,168	1,290	1,168
11,700	11,750	1,298	1,173	1,298	1,173
11,750	11,800	1,305	1,178	1,305	1,178
11,800	11,850	1,313	1,183	1,313	1,183
11,850	11,900	1,320	1,188	1,320	1,188
11,900	11,950	1,328	1,193	1,328	1,193
11,950	12,000	1,335	1,198	1,335	1,198

* This column must also be used by a qualifying widow(er).

2015 Tax Table — *Continued*

If line 43 (taxable income) is— At least	But less than	And you are— Single	Married filing jointly *	Married filing sepa-rately	Head of a house-hold
		Your tax is—			
12,000					
12,000	12,050	1,343	1,203	1,343	1,203
12,050	12,100	1,350	1,208	1,350	1,208
12,100	12,150	1,358	1,213	1,358	1,213
12,150	12,200	1,365	1,218	1,365	1,218
12,200	12,250	1,373	1,223	1,373	1,223
12,250	12,300	1,380	1,228	1,380	1,228
12,300	12,350	1,388	1,233	1,388	1,233
12,350	12,400	1,395	1,238	1,395	1,238
12,400	12,450	1,403	1,243	1,403	1,243
12,450	12,500	1,410	1,248	1,410	1,248
12,500	12,550	1,418	1,253	1,418	1,253
12,550	12,600	1,425	1,258	1,425	1,258
12,600	12,650	1,433	1,263	1,433	1,263
12,650	12,700	1,440	1,268	1,440	1,268
12,700	12,750	1,448	1,273	1,448	1,273
12,750	12,800	1,455	1,278	1,455	1,278
12,800	12,850	1,463	1,283	1,463	1,283
12,850	12,900	1,470	1,288	1,470	1,288
12,900	12,950	1,478	1,293	1,478	1,293
12,950	13,000	1,485	1,298	1,485	1,298
13,000					
13,000	13,050	1,493	1,303	1,493	1,303
13,050	13,100	1,500	1,308	1,500	1,308
13,100	13,150	1,508	1,313	1,508	1,313
13,150	13,200	1,515	1,318	1,515	1,319
13,200	13,250	1,523	1,323	1,523	1,326
13,250	13,300	1,530	1,328	1,530	1,334
13,300	13,350	1,538	1,333	1,538	1,341
13,350	13,400	1,545	1,338	1,545	1,349
13,400	13,450	1,553	1,343	1,553	1,356
13,450	13,500	1,560	1,348	1,560	1,364
13,500	13,550	1,568	1,353	1,568	1,371
13,550	13,600	1,575	1,358	1,575	1,379
13,600	13,650	1,583	1,363	1,583	1,386
13,650	13,700	1,590	1,368	1,590	1,394
13,700	13,750	1,598	1,373	1,598	1,401
13,750	13,800	1,605	1,378	1,605	1,409
13,800	13,850	1,613	1,383	1,613	1,416
13,850	13,900	1,620	1,388	1,620	1,424
13,900	13,950	1,628	1,393	1,628	1,431
13,950	14,000	1,635	1,398	1,635	1,439
14,000					
14,000	14,050	1,643	1,403	1,643	1,446
14,050	14,100	1,650	1,408	1,650	1,454
14,100	14,150	1,658	1,413	1,658	1,461
14,150	14,200	1,665	1,418	1,665	1,469
14,200	14,250	1,673	1,423	1,673	1,476
14,250	14,300	1,680	1,428	1,680	1,484
14,300	14,350	1,688	1,433	1,688	1,491
14,350	14,400	1,695	1,438	1,695	1,499
14,400	14,450	1,703	1,443	1,703	1,506
14,450	14,500	1,710	1,448	1,710	1,514
14,500	14,550	1,718	1,453	1,718	1,521
14,550	14,600	1,725	1,458	1,725	1,529
14,600	14,650	1,733	1,463	1,733	1,536
14,650	14,700	1,740	1,468	1,740	1,544
14,700	14,750	1,748	1,473	1,748	1,551
14,750	14,800	1,755	1,478	1,755	1,559
14,800	14,850	1,763	1,483	1,763	1,566
14,850	14,900	1,770	1,488	1,770	1,574
14,900	14,950	1,778	1,493	1,778	1,581
14,950	15,000	1,785	1,498	1,785	1,589

If line 43 (taxable income) is— At least	But less than	And you are— Single	Married filing jointly *	Married filing sepa-rately	Head of a house-hold
		Your tax is—			
15,000					
15,000	15,050	1,793	1,503	1,793	1,596
15,050	15,100	1,800	1,508	1,800	1,604
15,100	15,150	1,808	1,513	1,808	1,611
15,150	15,200	1,815	1,518	1,815	1,619
15,200	15,250	1,823	1,523	1,823	1,626
15,250	15,300	1,830	1,528	1,830	1,634
15,300	15,350	1,838	1,533	1,838	1,641
15,350	15,400	1,845	1,538	1,845	1,649
15,400	15,450	1,853	1,543	1,853	1,656
15,450	15,500	1,860	1,548	1,860	1,664
15,500	15,550	1,868	1,553	1,868	1,671
15,550	15,600	1,875	1,558	1,875	1,679
15,600	15,650	1,883	1,563	1,883	1,686
15,650	15,700	1,890	1,568	1,890	1,694
15,700	15,750	1,898	1,573	1,898	1,701
15,750	15,800	1,905	1,578	1,905	1,709
15,800	15,850	1,913	1,583	1,913	1,716
15,850	15,900	1,920	1,588	1,920	1,724
15,900	15,950	1,928	1,593	1,928	1,731
15,950	16,000	1,935	1,598	1,935	1,739
16,000					
16,000	16,050	1,943	1,603	1,943	1,746
16,050	16,100	1,950	1,608	1,950	1,754
16,100	16,150	1,958	1,613	1,958	1,761
16,150	16,200	1,965	1,618	1,965	1,769
16,200	16,250	1,973	1,623	1,973	1,776
16,250	16,300	1,980	1,628	1,980	1,784
16,300	16,350	1,988	1,633	1,988	1,791
16,350	16,400	1,995	1,638	1,995	1,799
16,400	16,450	2,003	1,643	2,003	1,806
16,450	16,500	2,010	1,648	2,010	1,814
16,500	16,550	2,018	1,653	2,018	1,821
16,550	16,600	2,025	1,658	2,025	1,829
16,600	16,650	2,033	1,663	2,033	1,836
16,650	16,700	2,040	1,668	2,040	1,844
16,700	16,750	2,048	1,673	2,048	1,851
16,750	16,800	2,055	1,678	2,055	1,859
16,800	16,850	2,063	1,683	2,063	1,866
16,850	16,900	2,070	1,688	2,070	1,874
16,900	16,950	2,078	1,693	2,078	1,881
16,950	17,000	2,085	1,698	2,085	1,889
17,000					
17,000	17,050	2,093	1,703	2,093	1,896
17,050	17,100	2,100	1,708	2,100	1,904
17,100	17,150	2,108	1,713	2,108	1,911
17,150	17,200	2,115	1,718	2,115	1,919
17,200	17,250	2,123	1,723	2,123	1,926
17,250	17,300	2,130	1,728	2,130	1,934
17,300	17,350	2,138	1,733	2,138	1,941
17,350	17,400	2,145	1,738	2,145	1,949
17,400	17,450	2,153	1,743	2,153	1,956
17,450	17,500	2,160	1,748	2,160	1,964
17,500	17,550	2,168	1,753	2,168	1,971
17,550	17,600	2,175	1,758	2,175	1,979
17,600	17,650	2,183	1,763	2,183	1,986
17,650	17,700	2,190	1,768	2,190	1,994
17,700	17,750	2,198	1,773	2,198	2,001
17,750	17,800	2,205	1,778	2,205	2,009
17,800	17,850	2,213	1,783	2,213	2,016
17,850	17,900	2,220	1,788	2,220	2,024
17,900	17,950	2,228	1,793	2,228	2,031
17,950	18,000	2,235	1,798	2,235	2,039

If line 43 (taxable income) is— At least	But less than	And you are— Single	Married filing jointly *	Married filing sepa-rately	Head of a house-hold
		Your tax is—			
18,000					
18,000	18,050	2,243	1,803	2,243	2,046
18,050	18,100	2,250	1,808	2,250	2,054
18,100	18,150	2,258	1,813	2,258	2,061
18,150	18,200	2,265	1,818	2,265	2,069
18,200	18,250	2,273	1,823	2,273	2,076
18,250	18,300	2,280	1,828	2,280	2,084
18,300	18,350	2,288	1,833	2,288	2,091
18,350	18,400	2,295	1,838	2,295	2,099
18,400	18,450	2,303	1,843	2,303	2,106
18,450	18,500	2,310	1,849	2,310	2,114
18,500	18,550	2,318	1,856	2,318	2,121
18,550	18,600	2,325	1,864	2,325	2,129
18,600	18,650	2,333	1,871	2,333	2,136
18,650	18,700	2,340	1,879	2,340	2,144
18,700	18,750	2,348	1,886	2,348	2,151
18,750	18,800	2,355	1,894	2,355	2,159
18,800	18,850	2,363	1,901	2,363	2,166
18,850	18,900	2,370	1,909	2,370	2,174
18,900	18,950	2,378	1,916	2,378	2,181
18,950	19,000	2,385	1,924	2,385	2,189
19,000					
19,000	19,050	2,393	1,931	2,393	2,196
19,050	19,100	2,400	1,939	2,400	2,204
19,100	19,150	2,408	1,946	2,408	2,211
19,150	19,200	2,415	1,954	2,415	2,219
19,200	19,250	2,423	1,961	2,423	2,226
19,250	19,300	2,430	1,969	2,430	2,234
19,300	19,350	2,438	1,976	2,438	2,241
19,350	19,400	2,445	1,984	2,445	2,249
19,400	19,450	2,453	1,991	2,453	2,256
19,450	19,500	2,460	1,999	2,460	2,264
19,500	19,550	2,468	2,006	2,468	2,271
19,550	19,600	2,475	2,014	2,475	2,279
19,600	19,650	2,483	2,021	2,483	2,286
19,650	19,700	2,490	2,029	2,490	2,294
19,700	19,750	2,498	2,036	2,498	2,301
19,750	19,800	2,505	2,044	2,505	2,309
19,800	19,850	2,513	2,051	2,513	2,316
19,850	19,900	2,520	2,059	2,520	2,324
19,900	19,950	2,528	2,066	2,528	2,331
19,950	20,000	2,535	2,074	2,535	2,339
20,000					
20,000	20,050	2,543	2,081	2,543	2,346
20,050	20,100	2,550	2,089	2,550	2,354
20,100	20,150	2,558	2,096	2,558	2,361
20,150	20,200	2,565	2,104	2,565	2,369
20,200	20,250	2,573	2,111	2,573	2,376
20,250	20,300	2,580	2,119	2,580	2,384
20,300	20,350	2,588	2,126	2,588	2,391
20,350	20,400	2,595	2,134	2,595	2,399
20,400	20,450	2,603	2,141	2,603	2,406
20,450	20,500	2,610	2,149	2,610	2,414
20,500	20,550	2,618	2,156	2,618	2,421
20,550	20,600	2,625	2,164	2,625	2,429
20,600	20,650	2,633	2,171	2,633	2,436
20,650	20,700	2,640	2,179	2,640	2,444
20,700	20,750	2,648	2,186	2,648	2,451
20,750	20,800	2,655	2,194	2,655	2,459
20,800	20,850	2,663	2,201	2,663	2,466
20,850	20,900	2,670	2,209	2,670	2,474
20,900	20,950	2,678	2,216	2,678	2,481
20,950	21,000	2,685	2,224	2,685	2,489

* This column must also be used by a qualifying widow(er).

2015 Tax Table — *Continued*

If line 43 (taxable income) is—		And you are—			
At least	But less than	Single	Married filing jointly *	Married filing sepa-rately	Head of a house-hold
		Your tax is—			
21,000					
21,000	21,050	2,693	2,231	2,693	2,496
21,050	21,100	2,700	2,239	2,700	2,504
21,100	21,150	2,708	2,246	2,708	2,511
21,150	21,200	2,715	2,254	2,715	2,519
21,200	21,250	2,723	2,261	2,723	2,526
21,250	21,300	2,730	2,269	2,730	2,534
21,300	21,350	2,738	2,276	2,738	2,541
21,350	21,400	2,745	2,284	2,745	2,549
21,400	21,450	2,753	2,291	2,753	2,556
21,450	21,500	2,760	2,299	2,760	2,564
21,500	21,550	2,768	2,306	2,768	2,571
21,550	21,600	2,775	2,314	2,775	2,579
21,600	21,650	2,783	2,321	2,783	2,586
21,650	21,700	2,790	2,329	2,790	2,594
21,700	21,750	2,798	2,336	2,798	2,601
21,750	21,800	2,805	2,344	2,805	2,609
21,800	21,850	2,813	2,351	2,813	2,616
21,850	21,900	2,820	2,359	2,820	2,624
21,900	21,950	2,828	2,366	2,828	2,631
21,950	22,000	2,835	2,374	2,835	2,639
22,000					
22,000	22,050	2,843	2,381	2,843	2,646
22,050	22,100	2,850	2,389	2,850	2,654
22,100	22,150	2,858	2,396	2,858	2,661
22,150	22,200	2,865	2,404	2,865	2,669
22,200	22,250	2,873	2,411	2,873	2,676
22,250	22,300	2,880	2,419	2,880	2,684
22,300	22,350	2,888	2,426	2,888	2,691
22,350	22,400	2,895	2,434	2,895	2,699
22,400	22,450	2,903	2,441	2,903	2,706
22,450	22,500	2,910	2,449	2,910	2,714
22,500	22,550	2,918	2,456	2,918	2,721
22,550	22,600	2,925	2,464	2,925	2,729
22,600	22,650	2,933	2,471	2,933	2,736
22,650	22,700	2,940	2,479	2,940	2,744
22,700	22,750	2,948	2,486	2,948	2,751
22,750	22,800	2,955	2,494	2,955	2,759
22,800	22,850	2,963	2,501	2,963	2,766
22,850	22,900	2,970	2,509	2,970	2,774
22,900	22,950	2,978	2,516	2,978	2,781
22,950	23,000	2,985	2,524	2,985	2,789
23,000					
23,000	23,050	2,993	2,531	2,993	2,796
23,050	23,100	3,000	2,539	3,000	2,804
23,100	23,150	3,008	2,546	3,008	2,811
23,150	23,200	3,015	2,554	3,015	2,819
23,200	23,250	3,023	2,561	3,023	2,826
23,250	23,300	3,030	2,569	3,030	2,834
23,300	23,350	3,038	2,576	3,038	2,841
23,350	23,400	3,045	2,584	3,045	2,849
23,400	23,450	3,053	2,591	3,053	2,856
23,450	23,500	3,060	2,599	3,060	2,864
23,500	23,550	3,068	2,606	3,068	2,871
23,550	23,600	3,075	2,614	3,075	2,879
23,600	23,650	3,083	2,621	3,083	2,886
23,650	23,700	3,090	2,629	3,090	2,894
23,700	23,750	3,098	2,636	3,098	2,901
23,750	23,800	3,105	2,644	3,105	2,909
23,800	23,850	3,113	2,651	3,113	2,916
23,850	23,900	3,120	2,659	3,120	2,924
23,900	23,950	3,128	2,666	3,128	2,931
23,950	24,000	3,135	2,674	3,135	2,939
24,000					
24,000	24,050	3,143	2,681	3,143	2,946
24,050	24,100	3,150	2,689	3,150	2,954
24,100	24,150	3,158	2,696	3,158	2,961
24,150	24,200	3,165	2,704	3,165	2,969
24,200	24,250	3,173	2,711	3,173	2,976
24,250	24,300	3,180	2,719	3,180	2,984
24,300	24,350	3,188	2,726	3,188	2,991
24,350	24,400	3,195	2,734	3,195	2,999
24,400	24,450	3,203	2,741	3,203	3,006
24,450	24,500	3,210	2,749	3,210	3,014
24,500	24,550	3,218	2,756	3,218	3,021
24,550	24,600	3,225	2,764	3,225	3,029
24,600	24,650	3,233	2,771	3,233	3,036
24,650	24,700	3,240	2,779	3,240	3,044
24,700	24,750	3,248	2,786	3,248	3,051
24,750	24,800	3,255	2,794	3,255	3,059
24,800	24,850	3,263	2,801	3,263	3,066
24,850	24,900	3,270	2,809	3,270	3,074
24,900	24,950	3,278	2,816	3,278	3,081
24,950	25,000	3,285	2,824	3,285	3,089
25,000					
25,000	25,050	3,293	2,831	3,293	3,096
25,050	25,100	3,300	2,839	3,300	3,104
25,100	25,150	3,308	2,846	3,308	3,111
25,150	25,200	3,315	2,854	3,315	3,119
25,200	25,250	3,323	2,861	3,323	3,126
25,250	25,300	3,330	2,869	3,330	3,134
25,300	25,350	3,338	2,876	3,338	3,141
25,350	25,400	3,345	2,884	3,345	3,149
25,400	25,450	3,353	2,891	3,353	3,156
25,450	25,500	3,360	2,899	3,360	3,164
25,500	25,550	3,368	2,906	3,368	3,171
25,550	25,600	3,375	2,914	3,375	3,179
25,600	25,650	3,383	2,921	3,383	3,186
25,650	25,700	3,390	2,929	3,390	3,194
25,700	25,750	3,398	2,936	3,398	3,201
25,750	25,800	3,405	2,944	3,405	3,209
25,800	25,850	3,413	2,951	3,413	3,216
25,850	25,900	3,420	2,959	3,420	3,224
25,900	25,950	3,428	2,966	3,428	3,231
25,950	26,000	3,435	2,974	3,435	3,239
26,000					
26,000	26,050	3,443	2,981	3,443	3,246
26,050	26,100	3,450	2,989	3,450	3,254
26,100	26,150	3,458	2,996	3,458	3,261
26,150	26,200	3,465	3,004	3,465	3,269
26,200	26,250	3,473	3,011	3,473	3,276
26,250	26,300	3,480	3,019	3,480	3,284
26,300	26,350	3,488	3,026	3,488	3,291
26,350	26,400	3,495	3,034	3,495	3,299
26,400	26,450	3,503	3,041	3,503	3,306
26,450	26,500	3,510	3,049	3,510	3,314
26,500	26,550	3,518	3,056	3,518	3,321
26,550	26,600	3,525	3,064	3,525	3,329
26,600	26,650	3,533	3,071	3,533	3,336
26,650	26,700	3,540	3,079	3,540	3,344
26,700	26,750	3,548	3,086	3,548	3,351
26,750	26,800	3,555	3,094	3,555	3,359
26,800	26,850	3,563	3,101	3,563	3,366
26,850	26,900	3,570	3,109	3,570	3,374
26,900	26,950	3,578	3,116	3,578	3,381
26,950	27,000	3,585	3,124	3,585	3,389
27,000					
27,000	27,050	3,593	3,131	3,593	3,396
27,050	27,100	3,600	3,139	3,600	3,404
27,100	27,150	3,608	3,146	3,608	3,411
27,150	27,200	3,615	3,154	3,615	3,419
27,200	27,250	3,623	3,161	3,623	3,426
27,250	27,300	3,630	3,169	3,630	3,434
27,300	27,350	3,638	3,176	3,638	3,441
27,350	27,400	3,645	3,184	3,645	3,449
27,400	27,450	3,653	3,191	3,653	3,456
27,450	27,500	3,660	3,199	3,660	3,464
27,500	27,550	3,668	3,206	3,668	3,471
27,550	27,600	3,675	3,214	3,675	3,479
27,600	27,650	3,683	3,221	3,683	3,486
27,650	27,700	3,690	3,229	3,690	3,494
27,700	27,750	3,698	3,236	3,698	3,501
27,750	27,800	3,705	3,244	3,705	3,509
27,800	27,850	3,713	3,251	3,713	3,516
27,850	27,900	3,720	3,259	3,720	3,524
27,900	27,950	3,728	3,266	3,728	3,531
27,950	28,000	3,735	3,274	3,735	3,539
28,000					
28,000	28,050	3,743	3,281	3,743	3,546
28,050	28,100	3,750	3,289	3,750	3,554
28,100	28,150	3,758	3,296	3,758	3,561
28,150	28,200	3,765	3,304	3,765	3,569
28,200	28,250	3,773	3,311	3,773	3,576
28,250	28,300	3,780	3,319	3,780	3,584
28,300	28,350	3,788	3,326	3,788	3,591
28,350	28,400	3,795	3,334	3,795	3,599
28,400	28,450	3,803	3,341	3,803	3,606
28,450	28,500	3,810	3,349	3,810	3,614
28,500	28,550	3,818	3,356	3,818	3,621
28,550	28,600	3,825	3,364	3,825	3,629
28,600	28,650	3,833	3,371	3,833	3,636
28,650	28,700	3,840	3,379	3,840	3,644
28,700	28,750	3,848	3,386	3,848	3,651
28,750	28,800	3,855	3,394	3,855	3,659
28,800	28,850	3,863	3,401	3,863	3,666
28,850	28,900	3,870	3,409	3,870	3,674
28,900	28,950	3,878	3,416	3,878	3,681
28,950	29,000	3,885	3,424	3,885	3,689
29,000					
29,000	29,050	3,893	3,431	3,893	3,696
29,050	29,100	3,900	3,439	3,900	3,704
29,100	29,150	3,908	3,446	3,908	3,711
29,150	29,200	3,915	3,454	3,915	3,719
29,200	29,250	3,923	3,461	3,923	3,726
29,250	29,300	3,930	3,469	3,930	3,734
29,300	29,350	3,938	3,476	3,938	3,741
29,350	29,400	3,945	3,484	3,945	3,749
29,400	29,450	3,953	3,491	3,953	3,756
29,450	29,500	3,960	3,499	3,960	3,764
29,500	29,550	3,968	3,506	3,968	3,771
29,550	29,600	3,975	3,514	3,975	3,779
29,600	29,650	3,983	3,521	3,983	3,786
29,650	29,700	3,990	3,529	3,990	3,794
29,700	29,750	3,998	3,536	3,998	3,801
29,750	29,800	4,005	3,544	4,005	3,809
29,800	29,850	4,013	3,551	4,013	3,816
29,850	29,900	4,020	3,559	4,020	3,824
29,900	29,950	4,028	3,566	4,028	3,831
29,950	30,000	4,035	3,574	4,035	3,839

* This column must also be used by a qualifying widow(er).

2015 Tax Table — *Continued*

If line 43 (taxable income) is—		And you are—			
At least	But less than	Single	Married filing jointly *	Married filing sepa-rately	Head of a house-hold
		Your tax is—			
30,000					
30,000	30,050	4,043	3,581	4,043	3,846
30,050	30,100	4,050	3,589	4,050	3,854
30,100	30,150	4,058	3,596	4,058	3,861
30,150	30,200	4,065	3,604	4,065	3,869
30,200	30,250	4,073	3,611	4,073	3,876
30,250	30,300	4,080	3,619	4,080	3,884
30,300	30,350	4,088	3,626	4,088	3,891
30,350	30,400	4,095	3,634	4,095	3,899
30,400	30,450	4,103	3,641	4,103	3,906
30,450	30,500	4,110	3,649	4,110	3,914
30,500	30,550	4,118	3,656	4,118	3,921
30,550	30,600	4,125	3,664	4,125	3,929
30,600	30,650	4,133	3,671	4,133	3,936
30,650	30,700	4,140	3,679	4,140	3,944
30,700	30,750	4,148	3,686	4,148	3,951
30,750	30,800	4,155	3,694	4,155	3,959
30,800	30,850	4,163	3,701	4,163	3,966
30,850	30,900	4,170	3,709	4,170	3,974
30,900	30,950	4,178	3,716	4,178	3,981
30,950	31,000	4,185	3,724	4,185	3,989
31,000					
31,000	31,050	4,193	3,731	4,193	3,996
31,050	31,100	4,200	3,739	4,200	4,004
31,100	31,150	4,208	3,746	4,208	4,011
31,150	31,200	4,215	3,754	4,215	4,019
31,200	31,250	4,223	3,761	4,223	4,026
31,250	31,300	4,230	3,769	4,230	4,034
31,300	31,350	4,238	3,776	4,238	4,041
31,350	31,400	4,245	3,784	4,245	4,049
31,400	31,450	4,253	3,791	4,253	4,056
31,450	31,500	4,260	3,799	4,260	4,064
31,500	31,550	4,268	3,806	4,268	4,071
31,550	31,600	4,275	3,814	4,275	4,079
31,600	31,650	4,283	3,821	4,283	4,086
31,650	31,700	4,290	3,829	4,290	4,094
31,700	31,750	4,298	3,836	4,298	4,101
31,750	31,800	4,305	3,844	4,305	4,109
31,800	31,850	4,313	3,851	4,313	4,116
31,850	31,900	4,320	3,859	4,320	4,124
31,900	31,950	4,328	3,866	4,328	4,131
31,950	32,000	4,335	3,874	4,335	4,139
32,000					
32,000	32,050	4,343	3,881	4,343	4,146
32,050	32,100	4,350	3,889	4,350	4,154
32,100	32,150	4,358	3,896	4,358	4,161
32,150	32,200	4,365	3,904	4,365	4,169
32,200	32,250	4,373	3,911	4,373	4,176
32,250	32,300	4,380	3,919	4,380	4,184
32,300	32,350	4,388	3,926	4,388	4,191
32,350	32,400	4,395	3,934	4,395	4,199
32,400	32,450	4,403	3,941	4,403	4,206
32,450	32,500	4,410	3,949	4,410	4,214
32,500	32,550	4,418	3,956	4,418	4,221
32,550	32,600	4,425	3,964	4,425	4,229
32,600	32,650	4,433	3,971	4,433	4,236
32,650	32,700	4,440	3,979	4,440	4,244
32,700	32,750	4,448	3,986	4,448	4,251
32,750	32,800	4,455	3,994	4,455	4,259
32,800	32,850	4,463	4,001	4,463	4,266
32,850	32,900	4,470	4,009	4,470	4,274
32,900	32,950	4,478	4,016	4,478	4,281
32,950	33,000	4,485	4,024	4,485	4,289

If line 43 (taxable income) is—		And you are—			
At least	But less than	Single	Married filing jointly *	Married filing sepa-rately	Head of a house-hold
		Your tax is—			
33,000					
33,000	33,050	4,493	4,031	4,493	4,296
33,050	33,100	4,500	4,039	4,500	4,304
33,100	33,150	4,508	4,046	4,508	4,311
33,150	33,200	4,515	4,054	4,515	4,319
33,200	33,250	4,523	4,061	4,523	4,326
33,250	33,300	4,530	4,069	4,530	4,334
33,300	33,350	4,538	4,076	4,538	4,341
33,350	33,400	4,545	4,084	4,545	4,349
33,400	33,450	4,553	4,091	4,553	4,356
33,450	33,500	4,560	4,099	4,560	4,364
33,500	33,550	4,568	4,106	4,568	4,371
33,550	33,600	4,575	4,114	4,575	4,379
33,600	33,650	4,583	4,121	4,583	4,386
33,650	33,700	4,590	4,129	4,590	4,394
33,700	33,750	4,598	4,136	4,598	4,401
33,750	33,800	4,605	4,144	4,605	4,409
33,800	33,850	4,613	4,151	4,613	4,416
33,850	33,900	4,620	4,159	4,620	4,424
33,900	33,950	4,628	4,166	4,628	4,431
33,950	34,000	4,635	4,174	4,635	4,439
34,000					
34,000	34,050	4,643	4,181	4,643	4,446
34,050	34,100	4,650	4,189	4,650	4,454
34,100	34,150	4,658	4,196	4,658	4,461
34,150	34,200	4,665	4,204	4,665	4,469
34,200	34,250	4,673	4,211	4,673	4,476
34,250	34,300	4,680	4,219	4,680	4,484
34,300	34,350	4,688	4,226	4,688	4,491
34,350	34,400	4,695	4,234	4,695	4,499
34,400	34,450	4,703	4,241	4,703	4,506
34,450	34,500	4,710	4,249	4,710	4,514
34,500	34,550	4,718	4,256	4,718	4,521
34,550	34,600	4,725	4,264	4,725	4,529
34,600	34,650	4,733	4,271	4,733	4,536
34,650	34,700	4,740	4,279	4,740	4,544
34,700	34,750	4,748	4,286	4,748	4,551
34,750	34,800	4,755	4,294	4,755	4,559
34,800	34,850	4,763	4,301	4,763	4,566
34,850	34,900	4,770	4,309	4,770	4,574
34,900	34,950	4,778	4,316	4,778	4,581
34,950	35,000	4,785	4,324	4,785	4,589
35,000					
35,000	35,050	4,793	4,331	4,793	4,596
35,050	35,100	4,800	4,339	4,800	4,604
35,100	35,150	4,808	4,346	4,808	4,611
35,150	35,200	4,815	4,354	4,815	4,619
35,200	35,250	4,823	4,361	4,823	4,626
35,250	35,300	4,830	4,369	4,830	4,634
35,300	35,350	4,838	4,376	4,838	4,641
35,350	35,400	4,845	4,384	4,845	4,649
35,400	35,450	4,853	4,391	4,853	4,656
35,450	35,500	4,860	4,399	4,860	4,664
35,500	35,550	4,868	4,406	4,868	4,671
35,550	35,600	4,875	4,414	4,875	4,679
35,600	35,650	4,883	4,421	4,883	4,686
35,650	35,700	4,890	4,429	4,890	4,694
35,700	35,750	4,898	4,436	4,898	4,701
35,750	35,800	4,905	4,444	4,905	4,709
35,800	35,850	4,913	4,451	4,913	4,716
35,850	35,900	4,920	4,459	4,920	4,724
35,900	35,950	4,928	4,466	4,928	4,731
35,950	36,000	4,935	4,474	4,935	4,739

If line 43 (taxable income) is—		And you are—			
At least	But less than	Single	Married filing jointly *	Married filing sepa-rately	Head of a house-hold
		Your tax is—			
36,000					
36,000	36,050	4,943	4,481	4,943	4,746
36,050	36,100	4,950	4,489	4,950	4,754
36,100	36,150	4,958	4,496	4,958	4,761
36,150	36,200	4,965	4,504	4,965	4,769
36,200	36,250	4,973	4,511	4,973	4,776
36,250	36,300	4,980	4,519	4,980	4,784
36,300	36,350	4,988	4,526	4,988	4,791
36,350	36,400	4,995	4,534	4,995	4,799
36,400	36,450	5,003	4,541	5,003	4,806
36,450	36,500	5,010	4,549	5,010	4,814
36,500	36,550	5,018	4,556	5,018	4,821
36,550	36,600	5,025	4,564	5,025	4,829
36,600	36,650	5,033	4,571	5,033	4,836
36,650	36,700	5,040	4,579	5,040	4,844
36,700	36,750	5,048	4,586	5,048	4,851
36,750	36,800	5,055	4,594	5,055	4,859
36,800	36,850	5,063	4,601	5,063	4,866
36,850	36,900	5,070	4,609	5,070	4,874
36,900	36,950	5,078	4,616	5,078	4,881
36,950	37,000	5,085	4,624	5,085	4,889
37,000					
37,000	37,050	5,093	4,631	5,093	4,896
37,050	37,100	5,100	4,639	5,100	4,904
37,100	37,150	5,108	4,646	5,108	4,911
37,150	37,200	5,115	4,654	5,115	4,919
37,200	37,250	5,123	4,661	5,123	4,926
37,250	37,300	5,130	4,669	5,130	4,934
37,300	37,350	5,138	4,676	5,138	4,941
37,350	37,400	5,145	4,684	5,145	4,949
37,400	37,450	5,153	4,691	5,153	4,956
37,450	37,500	5,163	4,699	5,163	4,964
37,500	37,550	5,175	4,706	5,175	4,971
37,550	37,600	5,188	4,714	5,188	4,979
37,600	37,650	5,200	4,721	5,200	4,986
37,650	37,700	5,213	4,729	5,213	4,994
37,700	37,750	5,225	4,736	5,225	5,001
37,750	37,800	5,238	4,744	5,238	5,009
37,800	37,850	5,250	4,751	5,250	5,016
37,850	37,900	5,263	4,759	5,263	5,024
37,900	37,950	5,275	4,766	5,275	5,031
37,950	38,000	5,288	4,774	5,288	5,039
38,000					
38,000	38,050	5,300	4,781	5,300	5,046
38,050	38,100	5,313	4,789	5,313	5,054
38,100	38,150	5,325	4,796	5,325	5,061
38,150	38,200	5,338	4,804	5,338	5,069
38,200	38,250	5,350	4,811	5,350	5,076
38,250	38,300	5,363	4,819	5,363	5,084
38,300	38,350	5,375	4,826	5,375	5,091
38,350	38,400	5,388	4,834	5,388	5,099
38,400	38,450	5,400	4,841	5,400	5,106
38,450	38,500	5,413	4,849	5,413	5,114
38,500	38,550	5,425	4,856	5,425	5,121
38,550	38,600	5,438	4,864	5,438	5,129
38,600	38,650	5,450	4,871	5,450	5,136
38,650	38,700	5,463	4,879	5,463	5,144
38,700	38,750	5,475	4,886	5,475	5,151
38,750	38,800	5,488	4,894	5,488	5,159
38,800	38,850	5,500	4,901	5,500	5,166
38,850	38,900	5,513	4,909	5,513	5,174
38,900	38,950	5,525	4,916	5,525	5,181
38,950	39,000	5,538	4,924	5,538	5,189

* This column must also be used by a qualifying widow(er).

2015 Tax Table — *Continued*

If line 43 (taxable income) is— At least	But less than	And you are— Single	Married filing jointly *	Married filing separately	Head of a household
		Your tax is—			
39,000					
39,000	39,050	5,550	4,931	5,550	5,196
39,050	39,100	5,563	4,939	5,563	5,204
39,100	39,150	5,575	4,946	5,575	5,211
39,150	39,200	5,588	4,954	5,588	5,219
39,200	39,250	5,600	4,961	5,600	5,226
39,250	39,300	5,613	4,969	5,613	5,234
39,300	39,350	5,625	4,976	5,625	5,241
39,350	39,400	5,638	4,984	5,638	5,249
39,400	39,450	5,650	4,991	5,650	5,256
39,450	39,500	5,663	4,999	5,663	5,264
39,500	39,550	5,675	5,006	5,675	5,271
39,550	39,600	5,688	5,014	5,688	5,279
39,600	39,650	5,700	5,021	5,700	5,286
39,650	39,700	5,713	5,029	5,713	5,294
39,700	39,750	5,725	5,036	5,725	5,301
39,750	39,800	5,738	5,044	5,738	5,309
39,800	39,850	5,750	5,051	5,750	5,316
39,850	39,900	5,763	5,059	5,763	5,324
39,900	39,950	5,775	5,066	5,775	5,331
39,950	40,000	5,788	5,074	5,788	5,339
40,000					
40,000	40,050	5,800	5,081	5,800	5,346
40,050	40,100	5,813	5,089	5,813	5,354
40,100	40,150	5,825	5,096	5,825	5,361
40,150	40,200	5,838	5,104	5,838	5,369
40,200	40,250	5,850	5,111	5,850	5,376
40,250	40,300	5,863	5,119	5,863	5,384
40,300	40,350	5,875	5,126	5,875	5,391
40,350	40,400	5,888	5,134	5,888	5,399
40,400	40,450	5,900	5,141	5,900	5,406
40,450	40,500	5,913	5,149	5,913	5,414
40,500	40,550	5,925	5,156	5,925	5,421
40,550	40,600	5,938	5,164	5,938	5,429
40,600	40,650	5,950	5,171	5,950	5,436
40,650	40,700	5,963	5,179	5,963	5,444
40,700	40,750	5,975	5,186	5,975	5,451
40,750	40,800	5,988	5,194	5,988	5,459
40,800	40,850	6,000	5,201	6,000	5,466
40,850	40,900	6,013	5,209	6,013	5,474
40,900	40,950	6,025	5,216	6,025	5,481
40,950	41,000	6,038	5,224	6,038	5,489
41,000					
41,000	41,050	6,050	5,231	6,050	5,496
41,050	41,100	6,063	5,239	6,063	5,504
41,100	41,150	6,075	5,246	6,075	5,511
41,150	41,200	6,088	5,254	6,088	5,519
41,200	41,250	6,100	5,261	6,100	5,526
41,250	41,300	6,113	5,269	6,113	5,534
41,300	41,350	6,125	5,276	6,125	5,541
41,350	41,400	6,138	5,284	6,138	5,549
41,400	41,450	6,150	5,291	6,150	5,556
41,450	41,500	6,163	5,299	6,163	5,564
41,500	41,550	6,175	5,306	6,175	5,571
41,550	41,600	6,188	5,314	6,188	5,579
41,600	41,650	6,200	5,321	6,200	5,586
41,650	41,700	6,213	5,329	6,213	5,594
41,700	41,750	6,225	5,336	6,225	5,601
41,750	41,800	6,238	5,344	6,238	5,609
41,800	41,850	6,250	5,351	6,250	5,616
41,850	41,900	6,263	5,359	6,263	5,624
41,900	41,950	6,275	5,366	6,275	5,631
41,950	42,000	6,288	5,374	6,288	5,639
42,000					
42,000	42,050	6,300	5,381	6,300	5,646
42,050	42,100	6,313	5,389	6,313	5,654
42,100	42,150	6,325	5,396	6,325	5,661
42,150	42,200	6,338	5,404	6,338	5,669
42,200	42,250	6,350	5,411	6,350	5,676
42,250	42,300	6,363	5,419	6,363	5,684
42,300	42,350	6,375	5,426	6,375	5,691
42,350	42,400	6,388	5,434	6,388	5,699
42,400	42,450	6,400	5,441	6,400	5,706
42,450	42,500	6,413	5,449	6,413	5,714
42,500	42,550	6,425	5,456	6,425	5,721
42,550	42,600	6,438	5,464	6,438	5,729
42,600	42,650	6,450	5,471	6,450	5,736
42,650	42,700	6,463	5,479	6,463	5,744
42,700	42,750	6,475	5,486	6,475	5,751
42,750	42,800	6,488	5,494	6,488	5,759
42,800	42,850	6,500	5,501	6,500	5,766
42,850	42,900	6,513	5,509	6,513	5,774
42,900	42,950	6,525	5,516	6,525	5,781
42,950	43,000	6,538	5,524	6,538	5,789
43,000					
43,000	43,050	6,550	5,531	6,550	5,796
43,050	43,100	6,563	5,539	6,563	5,804
43,100	43,150	6,575	5,546	6,575	5,811
43,150	43,200	6,588	5,554	6,588	5,819
43,200	43,250	6,600	5,561	6,600	5,826
43,250	43,300	6,613	5,569	6,613	5,834
43,300	43,350	6,625	5,576	6,625	5,841
43,350	43,400	6,638	5,584	6,638	5,849
43,400	43,450	6,650	5,591	6,650	5,856
43,450	43,500	6,663	5,599	6,663	5,864
43,500	43,550	6,675	5,606	6,675	5,871
43,550	43,600	6,688	5,614	6,688	5,879
43,600	43,650	6,700	5,621	6,700	5,886
43,650	43,700	6,713	5,629	6,713	5,894
43,700	43,750	6,725	5,636	6,725	5,901
43,750	43,800	6,738	5,644	6,738	5,909
43,800	43,850	6,750	5,651	6,750	5,916
43,850	43,900	6,763	5,659	6,763	5,924
43,900	43,950	6,775	5,666	6,775	5,931
43,950	44,000	6,788	5,674	6,788	5,939
44,000					
44,000	44,050	6,800	5,681	6,800	5,946
44,050	44,100	6,813	5,689	6,813	5,954
44,100	44,150	6,825	5,696	6,825	5,961
44,150	44,200	6,838	5,704	6,838	5,969
44,200	44,250	6,850	5,711	6,850	5,976
44,250	44,300	6,863	5,719	6,863	5,984
44,300	44,350	6,875	5,726	6,875	5,991
44,350	44,400	6,888	5,734	6,888	5,999
44,400	44,450	6,900	5,741	6,900	6,006
44,450	44,500	6,913	5,749	6,913	6,014
44,500	44,550	6,925	5,756	6,925	6,021
44,550	44,600	6,938	5,764	6,938	6,029
44,600	44,650	6,950	5,771	6,950	6,036
44,650	44,700	6,963	5,779	6,963	6,044
44,700	44,750	6,975	5,786	6,975	6,051
44,750	44,800	6,988	5,794	6,988	6,059
44,800	44,850	7,000	5,801	7,000	6,066
44,850	44,900	7,013	5,809	7,013	6,074
44,900	44,950	7,025	5,816	7,025	6,081
44,950	45,000	7,038	5,824	7,038	6,089
45,000					
45,000	45,050	7,050	5,831	7,050	6,096
45,050	45,100	7,063	5,839	7,063	6,104
45,100	45,150	7,075	5,846	7,075	6,111
45,150	45,200	7,088	5,854	7,088	6,119
45,200	45,250	7,100	5,861	7,100	6,126
45,250	45,300	7,113	5,869	7,113	6,134
45,300	45,350	7,125	5,876	7,125	6,141
45,350	45,400	7,138	5,884	7,138	6,149
45,400	45,450	7,150	5,891	7,150	6,156
45,450	45,500	7,163	5,899	7,163	6,164
45,500	45,550	7,175	5,906	7,175	6,171
45,550	45,600	7,188	5,914	7,188	6,179
45,600	45,650	7,200	5,921	7,200	6,186
45,650	45,700	7,213	5,929	7,213	6,194
45,700	45,750	7,225	5,936	7,225	6,201
45,750	45,800	7,238	5,944	7,238	6,209
45,800	45,850	7,250	5,951	7,250	6,216
45,850	45,900	7,263	5,959	7,263	6,224
45,900	45,950	7,275	5,966	7,275	6,231
45,950	46,000	7,288	5,974	7,288	6,239
46,000					
46,000	46,050	7,300	5,981	7,300	6,246
46,050	46,100	7,313	5,989	7,313	6,254
46,100	46,150	7,325	5,996	7,325	6,261
46,150	46,200	7,338	6,004	7,338	6,269
46,200	46,250	7,350	6,011	7,350	6,276
46,250	46,300	7,363	6,019	7,363	6,284
46,300	46,350	7,375	6,026	7,375	6,291
46,350	46,400	7,388	6,034	7,388	6,299
46,400	46,450	7,400	6,041	7,400	6,306
46,450	46,500	7,413	6,049	7,413	6,314
46,500	46,550	7,425	6,056	7,425	6,321
46,550	46,600	7,438	6,064	7,438	6,329
46,600	46,650	7,450	6,071	7,450	6,336
46,650	46,700	7,463	6,079	7,463	6,344
46,700	46,750	7,475	6,086	7,475	6,351
46,750	46,800	7,488	6,094	7,488	6,359
46,800	46,850	7,500	6,101	7,500	6,366
46,850	46,900	7,513	6,109	7,513	6,374
46,900	46,950	7,525	6,116	7,525	6,381
46,950	47,000	7,538	6,124	7,538	6,389
47,000					
47,000	47,050	7,550	6,131	7,550	6,396
47,050	47,100	7,563	6,139	7,563	6,404
47,100	47,150	7,575	6,146	7,575	6,411
47,150	47,200	7,588	6,154	7,588	6,419
47,200	47,250	7,600	6,161	7,600	6,426
47,250	47,300	7,613	6,169	7,613	6,434
47,300	47,350	7,625	6,176	7,625	6,441
47,350	47,400	7,638	6,184	7,638	6,449
47,400	47,450	7,650	6,191	7,650	6,456
47,450	47,500	7,663	6,199	7,663	6,464
47,500	47,550	7,675	6,206	7,675	6,471
47,550	47,600	7,688	6,214	7,688	6,479
47,600	47,650	7,700	6,221	7,700	6,486
47,650	47,700	7,713	6,229	7,713	6,494
47,700	47,750	7,725	6,236	7,725	6,501
47,750	47,800	7,738	6,244	7,738	6,509
47,800	47,850	7,750	6,251	7,750	6,516
47,850	47,900	7,763	6,259	7,763	6,524
47,900	47,950	7,775	6,266	7,775	6,531
47,950	48,000	7,788	6,274	7,788	6,539

* This column must also be used by a qualifying widow(er).

2015 Tax Table — *Continued*

If line 43 (taxable income) is—		And you are—			
At least	But less than	Single	Married filing jointly *	Married filing sepa-rately	Head of a house-hold
		Your tax is—			
48,000					
48,000	**48,050**	7,800	6,281	7,800	6,546
48,050	**48,100**	7,813	6,289	7,813	6,554
48,100	**48,150**	7,825	6,296	7,825	6,561
48,150	**48,200**	7,838	6,304	7,838	6,569
48,200	**48,250**	7,850	6,311	7,850	6,576
48,250	**48,300**	7,863	6,319	7,863	6,584
48,300	**48,350**	7,875	6,326	7,875	6,591
48,350	**48,400**	7,888	6,334	7,888	6,599
48,400	**48,450**	7,900	6,341	7,900	6,606
48,450	**48,500**	7,913	6,349	7,913	6,614
48,500	**48,550**	7,925	6,356	7,925	6,621
48,550	**48,600**	7,938	6,364	7,938	6,629
48,600	**48,650**	7,950	6,371	7,950	6,636
48,650	**48,700**	7,963	6,379	7,963	6,644
48,700	**48,750**	7,975	6,386	7,975	6,651
48,750	**48,800**	7,988	6,394	7,988	6,659
48,800	**48,850**	8,000	6,401	8,000	6,666
48,850	**48,900**	8,013	6,409	8,013	6,674
48,900	**48,950**	8,025	6,416	8,025	6,681
48,950	**49,000**	8,038	6,424	8,038	6,689
49,000					
49,000	**49,050**	8,050	6,431	8,050	6,696
49,050	**49,100**	8,063	6,439	8,063	6,704
49,100	**49,150**	8,075	6,446	8,075	6,711
49,150	**49,200**	8,088	6,454	8,088	6,719
49,200	**49,250**	8,100	6,461	8,100	6,726
49,250	**49,300**	8,113	6,469	8,113	6,734
49,300	**49,350**	8,125	6,476	8,125	6,741
49,350	**49,400**	8,138	6,484	8,138	6,749
49,400	**49,450**	8,150	6,491	8,150	6,756
49,450	**49,500**	8,163	6,499	8,163	6,764
49,500	**49,550**	8,175	6,506	8,175	6,771
49,550	**49,600**	8,188	6,514	8,188	6,779
49,600	**49,650**	8,200	6,521	8,200	6,786
49,650	**49,700**	8,213	6,529	8,213	6,794
49,700	**49,750**	8,225	6,536	8,225	6,801
49,750	**49,800**	8,238	6,544	8,238	6,809
49,800	**49,850**	8,250	6,551	8,250	6,816
49,850	**49,900**	8,263	6,559	8,263	6,824
49,900	**49,950**	8,275	6,566	8,275	6,831
49,950	**50,000**	8,288	6,574	8,288	6,839
50,000					
50,000	**50,050**	8,300	6,581	8,300	6,846
50,050	**50,100**	8,313	6,589	8,313	6,854
50,100	**50,150**	8,325	6,596	8,325	6,861
50,150	**50,200**	8,338	6,604	8,338	6,869
50,200	**50,250**	8,350	6,611	8,350	6,879
50,250	**50,300**	8,363	6,619	8,363	6,891
50,300	**50,350**	8,375	6,626	8,375	6,904
50,350	**50,400**	8,388	6,634	8,388	6,916
50,400	**50,450**	8,400	6,641	8,400	6,929
50,450	**50,500**	8,413	6,649	8,413	6,941
50,500	**50,550**	8,425	6,656	8,425	6,954
50,550	**50,600**	8,438	6,664	8,438	6,966
50,600	**50,650**	8,450	6,671	8,450	6,979
50,650	**50,700**	8,463	6,679	8,463	6,991
50,700	**50,750**	8,475	6,686	8,475	7,004
50,750	**50,800**	8,488	6,694	8,488	7,016
50,800	**50,850**	8,500	6,701	8,500	7,029
50,850	**50,900**	8,513	6,709	8,513	7,041
50,900	**50,950**	8,525	6,716	8,525	7,054
50,950	**51,000**	8,538	6,724	8,538	7,066

If line 43 (taxable income) is—		And you are—			
At least	But less than	Single	Married filing jointly *	Married filing sepa-rately	Head of a house-hold
		Your tax is—			
51,000					
51,000	**51,050**	8,550	6,731	8,550	7,079
51,050	**51,100**	8,563	6,739	8,563	7,091
51,100	**51,150**	8,575	6,746	8,575	7,104
51,150	**51,200**	8,588	6,754	8,588	7,116
51,200	**51,250**	8,600	6,761	8,600	7,129
51,250	**51,300**	8,613	6,769	8,613	7,141
51,300	**51,350**	8,625	6,776	8,625	7,154
51,350	**51,400**	8,638	6,784	8,638	7,166
51,400	**51,450**	8,650	6,791	8,650	7,179
51,450	**51,500**	8,663	6,799	8,663	7,191
51,500	**51,550**	8,675	6,806	8,675	7,204
51,550	**51,600**	8,688	6,814	8,688	7,216
51,600	**51,650**	8,700	6,821	8,700	7,229
51,650	**51,700**	8,713	6,829	8,713	7,241
51,700	**51,750**	8,725	6,836	8,725	7,254
51,750	**51,800**	8,738	6,844	8,738	7,266
51,800	**51,850**	8,750	6,851	8,750	7,279
51,850	**51,900**	8,763	6,859	8,763	7,291
51,900	**51,950**	8,775	6,866	8,775	7,304
51,950	**52,000**	8,788	6,874	8,788	7,316
52,000					
52,000	**52,050**	8,800	6,881	8,800	7,329
52,050	**52,100**	8,813	6,889	8,813	7,341
52,100	**52,150**	8,825	6,896	8,825	7,354
52,150	**52,200**	8,838	6,904	8,838	7,366
52,200	**52,250**	8,850	6,911	8,850	7,379
52,250	**52,300**	8,863	6,919	8,863	7,391
52,300	**52,350**	8,875	6,926	8,875	7,404
52,350	**52,400**	8,888	6,934	8,888	7,416
52,400	**52,450**	8,900	6,941	8,900	7,429
52,450	**52,500**	8,913	6,949	8,913	7,441
52,500	**52,550**	8,925	6,956	8,925	7,454
52,550	**52,600**	8,938	6,964	8,938	7,466
52,600	**52,650**	8,950	6,971	8,950	7,479
52,650	**52,700**	8,963	6,979	8,963	7,491
52,700	**52,750**	8,975	6,986	8,975	7,504
52,750	**52,800**	8,988	6,994	8,988	7,516
52,800	**52,850**	9,000	7,001	9,000	7,529
52,850	**52,900**	9,013	7,009	9,013	7,541
52,900	**52,950**	9,025	7,016	9,025	7,554
52,950	**53,000**	9,038	7,024	9,038	7,566
53,000					
53,000	**53,050**	9,050	7,031	9,050	7,579
53,050	**53,100**	9,063	7,039	9,063	7,591
53,100	**53,150**	9,075	7,046	9,075	7,604
53,150	**53,200**	9,088	7,054	9,088	7,616
53,200	**53,250**	9,100	7,061	9,100	7,629
53,250	**53,300**	9,113	7,069	9,113	7,641
53,300	**53,350**	9,125	7,076	9,125	7,654
53,350	**53,400**	9,138	7,084	9,138	7,666
53,400	**53,450**	9,150	7,091	9,150	7,679
53,450	**53,500**	9,163	7,099	9,163	7,691
53,500	**53,550**	9,175	7,106	9,175	7,704
53,550	**53,600**	9,188	7,114	9,188	7,716
53,600	**53,650**	9,200	7,121	9,200	7,729
53,650	**53,700**	9,213	7,129	9,213	7,741
53,700	**53,750**	9,225	7,136	9,225	7,754
53,750	**53,800**	9,238	7,144	9,238	7,766
53,800	**53,850**	9,250	7,151	9,250	7,779
53,850	**53,900**	9,263	7,159	9,263	7,791
53,900	**53,950**	9,275	7,166	9,275	7,804
53,950	**54,000**	9,288	7,174	9,288	7,816

If line 43 (taxable income) is—		And you are—			
At least	But less than	Single	Married filing jointly *	Married filing sepa-rately	Head of a house-hold
		Your tax is—			
54,000					
54,000	**54,050**	9,300	7,181	9,300	7,829
54,050	**54,100**	9,313	7,189	9,313	7,841
54,100	**54,150**	9,325	7,196	9,325	7,854
54,150	**54,200**	9,338	7,204	9,338	7,866
54,200	**54,250**	9,350	7,211	9,350	7,879
54,250	**54,300**	9,363	7,219	9,363	7,891
54,300	**54,350**	9,375	7,226	9,375	7,904
54,350	**54,400**	9,388	7,234	9,388	7,916
54,400	**54,450**	9,400	7,241	9,400	7,929
54,450	**54,500**	9,413	7,249	9,413	7,941
54,500	**54,550**	9,425	7,256	9,425	7,954
54,550	**54,600**	9,438	7,264	9,438	7,966
54,600	**54,650**	9,450	7,271	9,450	7,979
54,650	**54,700**	9,463	7,279	9,463	7,991
54,700	**54,750**	9,475	7,286	9,475	8,004
54,750	**54,800**	9,488	7,294	9,488	8,016
54,800	**54,850**	9,500	7,301	9,500	8,029
54,850	**54,900**	9,513	7,309	9,513	8,041
54,900	**54,950**	9,525	7,316	9,525	8,054
54,950	**55,000**	9,538	7,324	9,538	8,066
55,000					
55,000	**55,050**	9,550	7,331	9,550	8,079
55,050	**55,100**	9,563	7,339	9,563	8,091
55,100	**55,150**	9,575	7,346	9,575	8,104
55,150	**55,200**	9,588	7,354	9,588	8,116
55,200	**55,250**	9,600	7,361	9,600	8,129
55,250	**55,300**	9,613	7,369	9,613	8,141
55,300	**55,350**	9,625	7,376	9,625	8,154
55,350	**55,400**	9,638	7,384	9,638	8,166
55,400	**55,450**	9,650	7,391	9,650	8,179
55,450	**55,500**	9,663	7,399	9,663	8,191
55,500	**55,550**	9,675	7,406	9,675	8,204
55,550	**55,600**	9,688	7,414	9,688	8,216
55,600	**55,650**	9,700	7,421	9,700	8,229
55,650	**55,700**	9,713	7,429	9,713	8,241
55,700	**55,750**	9,725	7,436	9,725	8,254
55,750	**55,800**	9,738	7,444	9,738	8,266
55,800	**55,850**	9,750	7,451	9,750	8,279
55,850	**55,900**	9,763	7,459	9,763	8,291
55,900	**55,950**	9,775	7,466	9,775	8,304
55,950	**56,000**	9,788	7,474	9,788	8,316
56,000					
56,000	**56,050**	9,800	7,481	9,800	8,329
56,050	**56,100**	9,813	7,489	9,813	8,341
56,100	**56,150**	9,825	7,496	9,825	8,354
56,150	**56,200**	9,838	7,504	9,838	8,366
56,200	**56,250**	9,850	7,511	9,850	8,379
56,250	**56,300**	9,863	7,519	9,863	8,391
56,300	**56,350**	9,875	7,526	9,875	8,404
56,350	**56,400**	9,888	7,534	9,888	8,416
56,400	**56,450**	9,900	7,541	9,900	8,429
56,450	**56,500**	9,913	7,549	9,913	8,441
56,500	**56,550**	9,925	7,556	9,925	8,454
56,550	**56,600**	9,938	7,564	9,938	8,466
56,600	**56,650**	9,950	7,571	9,950	8,479
56,650	**56,700**	9,963	7,579	9,963	8,491
56,700	**56,750**	9,975	7,586	9,975	8,504
56,750	**56,800**	9,988	7,594	9,988	8,516
56,800	**56,850**	10,000	7,601	10,000	8,529
56,850	**56,900**	10,013	7,609	10,013	8,541
56,900	**56,950**	10,025	7,616	10,025	8,554
56,950	**57,000**	10,038	7,624	10,038	8,566

* This column must also be used by a qualifying widow(er).

2015 Tax Table — *Continued*

If line 43 (taxable income) is—		And you are—			
At least	But less than	Single	Married filing jointly *	Married filing separately	Head of a household
		Your tax is—			
57,000					
57,000	57,050	10,050	7,631	10,050	8,579
57,050	57,100	10,063	7,639	10,063	8,591
57,100	57,150	10,075	7,646	10,075	8,604
57,150	57,200	10,088	7,654	10,088	8,616
57,200	57,250	10,100	7,661	10,100	8,629
57,250	57,300	10,113	7,669	10,113	8,641
57,300	57,350	10,125	7,676	10,125	8,654
57,350	57,400	10,138	7,684	10,138	8,666
57,400	57,450	10,150	7,691	10,150	8,679
57,450	57,500	10,163	7,699	10,163	8,691
57,500	57,550	10,175	7,706	10,175	8,704
57,550	57,600	10,188	7,714	10,188	8,716
57,600	57,650	10,200	7,721	10,200	8,729
57,650	57,700	10,213	7,729	10,213	8,741
57,700	57,750	10,225	7,736	10,225	8,754
57,750	57,800	10,238	7,744	10,238	8,766
57,800	57,850	10,250	7,751	10,250	8,779
57,850	57,900	10,263	7,759	10,263	8,791
57,900	57,950	10,275	7,766	10,275	8,804
57,950	58,000	10,288	7,774	10,288	8,816
58,000					
58,000	58,050	10,300	7,781	10,300	8,829
58,050	58,100	10,313	7,789	10,313	8,841
58,100	58,150	10,325	7,796	10,325	8,854
58,150	58,200	10,338	7,804	10,338	8,866
58,200	58,250	10,350	7,811	10,350	8,879
58,250	58,300	10,363	7,819	10,363	8,891
58,300	58,350	10,375	7,826	10,375	8,904
58,350	58,400	10,388	7,834	10,388	8,916
58,400	58,450	10,400	7,841	10,400	8,929
58,450	58,500	10,413	7,849	10,413	8,941
58,500	58,550	10,425	7,856	10,425	8,954
58,550	58,600	10,438	7,864	10,438	8,966
58,600	58,650	10,450	7,871	10,450	8,979
58,650	58,700	10,463	7,879	10,463	8,991
58,700	58,750	10,475	7,886	10,475	9,004
58,750	58,800	10,488	7,894	10,488	9,016
58,800	58,850	10,500	7,901	10,500	9,029
58,850	58,900	10,513	7,909	10,513	9,041
58,900	58,950	10,525	7,916	10,525	9,054
58,950	59,000	10,538	7,924	10,538	9,066
59,000					
59,000	59,050	10,550	7,931	10,550	9,079
59,050	59,100	10,563	7,939	10,563	9,091
59,100	59,150	10,575	7,946	10,575	9,104
59,150	59,200	10,588	7,954	10,588	9,116
59,200	59,250	10,600	7,961	10,600	9,129
59,250	59,300	10,613	7,969	10,613	9,141
59,300	59,350	10,625	7,976	10,625	9,154
59,350	59,400	10,638	7,984	10,638	9,166
59,400	59,450	10,650	7,991	10,650	9,179
59,450	59,500	10,663	7,999	10,663	9,191
59,500	59,550	10,675	8,006	10,675	9,204
59,550	59,600	10,688	8,014	10,688	9,216
59,600	59,650	10,700	8,021	10,700	9,229
59,650	59,700	10,713	8,029	10,713	9,241
59,700	59,750	10,725	8,036	10,725	9,254
59,750	59,800	10,738	8,044	10,738	9,266
59,800	59,850	10,750	8,051	10,750	9,279
59,850	59,900	10,763	8,059	10,763	9,291
59,900	59,950	10,775	8,066	10,775	9,304
59,950	60,000	10,788	8,074	10,788	9,316

If line 43 (taxable income) is—		And you are—			
At least	But less than	Single	Married filing jointly *	Married filing separately	Head of a household
		Your tax is—			
60,000					
60,000	60,050	10,800	8,081	10,800	9,329
60,050	60,100	10,813	8,089	10,813	9,341
60,100	60,150	10,825	8,096	10,825	9,354
60,150	60,200	10,838	8,104	10,838	9,366
60,200	60,250	10,850	8,111	10,850	9,379
60,250	60,300	10,863	8,119	10,863	9,391
60,300	60,350	10,875	8,126	10,875	9,404
60,350	60,400	10,888	8,134	10,888	9,416
60,400	60,450	10,900	8,141	10,900	9,429
60,450	60,500	10,913	8,149	10,913	9,441
60,500	60,550	10,925	8,156	10,925	9,454
60,550	60,600	10,938	8,164	10,938	9,466
60,600	60,650	10,950	8,171	10,950	9,479
60,650	60,700	10,963	8,179	10,963	9,491
60,700	60,750	10,975	8,186	10,975	9,504
60,750	60,800	10,988	8,194	10,988	9,516
60,800	60,850	11,000	8,201	11,000	9,529
60,850	60,900	11,013	8,209	11,013	9,541
60,900	60,950	11,025	8,216	11,025	9,554
60,950	61,000	11,038	8,224	11,038	9,566
61,000					
61,000	61,050	11,050	8,231	11,050	9,579
61,050	61,100	11,063	8,239	11,063	9,591
61,100	61,150	11,075	8,246	11,075	9,604
61,150	61,200	11,088	8,254	11,088	9,616
61,200	61,250	11,100	8,261	11,100	9,629
61,250	61,300	11,113	8,269	11,113	9,641
61,300	61,350	11,125	8,276	11,125	9,654
61,350	61,400	11,138	8,284	11,138	9,666
61,400	61,450	11,150	8,291	11,150	9,679
61,450	61,500	11,163	8,299	11,163	9,691
61,500	61,550	11,175	8,306	11,175	9,704
61,550	61,600	11,188	8,314	11,188	9,716
61,600	61,650	11,200	8,321	11,200	9,729
61,650	61,700	11,213	8,329	11,213	9,741
61,700	61,750	11,225	8,336	11,225	9,754
61,750	61,800	11,238	8,344	11,238	9,766
61,800	61,850	11,250	8,351	11,250	9,779
61,850	61,900	11,263	8,359	11,263	9,791
61,900	61,950	11,275	8,366	11,275	9,804
61,950	62,000	11,288	8,374	11,288	9,816
62,000					
62,000	62,050	11,300	8,381	11,300	9,829
62,050	62,100	11,313	8,389	11,313	9,841
62,100	62,150	11,325	8,396	11,325	9,854
62,150	62,200	11,338	8,404	11,338	9,866
62,200	62,250	11,350	8,411	11,350	9,879
62,250	62,300	11,363	8,419	11,363	9,891
62,300	62,350	11,375	8,426	11,375	9,904
62,350	62,400	11,388	8,434	11,388	9,916
62,400	62,450	11,400	8,441	11,400	9,929
62,450	62,500	11,413	8,449	11,413	9,941
62,500	62,550	11,425	8,456	11,425	9,954
62,550	62,600	11,438	8,464	11,438	9,966
62,600	62,650	11,450	8,471	11,450	9,979
62,650	62,700	11,463	8,479	11,463	9,991
62,700	62,750	11,475	8,486	11,475	10,004
62,750	62,800	11,488	8,494	11,488	10,016
62,800	62,850	11,500	8,501	11,500	10,029
62,850	62,900	11,513	8,509	11,513	10,041
62,900	62,950	11,525	8,516	11,525	10,054
62,950	63,000	11,538	8,524	11,538	10,066

If line 43 (taxable income) is—		And you are—			
At least	But less than	Single	Married filing jointly *	Married filing separately	Head of a household
		Your tax is—			
63,000					
63,000	63,050	11,550	8,531	11,550	10,079
63,050	63,100	11,563	8,539	11,563	10,091
63,100	63,150	11,575	8,546	11,575	10,104
63,150	63,200	11,588	8,554	11,588	10,116
63,200	63,250	11,600	8,561	11,600	10,129
63,250	63,300	11,613	8,569	11,613	10,141
63,300	63,350	11,625	8,576	11,625	10,154
63,350	63,400	11,638	8,584	11,638	10,166
63,400	63,450	11,650	8,591	11,650	10,179
63,450	63,500	11,663	8,599	11,663	10,191
63,500	63,550	11,675	8,606	11,675	10,204
63,550	63,600	11,688	8,614	11,688	10,216
63,600	63,650	11,700	8,621	11,700	10,229
63,650	63,700	11,713	8,629	11,713	10,241
63,700	63,750	11,725	8,636	11,725	10,254
63,750	63,800	11,738	8,644	11,738	10,266
63,800	63,850	11,750	8,651	11,750	10,279
63,850	63,900	11,763	8,659	11,763	10,291
63,900	63,950	11,775	8,666	11,775	10,304
63,950	64,000	11,788	8,674	11,788	10,316
64,000					
64,000	64,050	11,800	8,681	11,800	10,329
64,050	64,100	11,813	8,689	11,813	10,341
64,100	64,150	11,825	8,696	11,825	10,354
64,150	64,200	11,838	8,704	11,838	10,366
64,200	64,250	11,850	8,711	11,850	10,379
64,250	64,300	11,863	8,719	11,863	10,391
64,300	64,350	11,875	8,726	11,875	10,404
64,350	64,400	11,888	8,734	11,888	10,416
64,400	64,450	11,900	8,741	11,900	10,429
64,450	64,500	11,913	8,749	11,913	10,441
64,500	64,550	11,925	8,756	11,925	10,454
64,550	64,600	11,938	8,764	11,938	10,466
64,600	64,650	11,950	8,771	11,950	10,479
64,650	64,700	11,963	8,779	11,963	10,491
64,700	64,750	11,975	8,786	11,975	10,504
64,750	64,800	11,988	8,794	11,988	10,516
64,800	64,850	12,000	8,801	12,000	10,529
64,850	64,900	12,013	8,809	12,013	10,541
64,900	64,950	12,025	8,816	12,025	10,554
64,950	65,000	12,038	8,824	12,038	10,566
65,000					
65,000	65,050	12,050	8,831	12,050	10,579
65,050	65,100	12,063	8,839	12,063	10,591
65,100	65,150	12,075	8,846	12,075	10,604
65,150	65,200	12,088	8,854	12,088	10,616
65,200	65,250	12,100	8,861	12,100	10,629
65,250	65,300	12,113	8,869	12,113	10,641
65,300	65,350	12,125	8,876	12,125	10,654
65,350	65,400	12,138	8,884	12,138	10,666
65,400	65,450	12,150	8,891	12,150	10,679
65,450	65,500	12,163	8,899	12,163	10,691
65,500	65,550	12,175	8,906	12,175	10,704
65,550	65,600	12,188	8,914	12,188	10,716
65,600	65,650	12,200	8,921	12,200	10,729
65,650	65,700	12,213	8,929	12,213	10,741
65,700	65,750	12,225	8,936	12,225	10,754
65,750	65,800	12,238	8,944	12,238	10,766
65,800	65,850	12,250	8,951	12,250	10,779
65,850	65,900	12,263	8,959	12,263	10,791
65,900	65,950	12,275	8,966	12,275	10,804
65,950	66,000	12,288	8,974	12,288	10,816

* This column must also be used by a qualifying widow(er).

2015 Tax Table — *Continued*

If line 43 (taxable income) is— At least	But less than	And you are— Single	Married filing jointly *	Married filing separately	Head of a household
		Your tax is—			
66,000					
66,000	66,050	12,300	8,981	12,300	10,829
66,050	66,100	12,313	8,989	12,313	10,841
66,100	66,150	12,325	8,996	12,325	10,854
66,150	66,200	12,338	9,004	12,338	10,866
66,200	66,250	12,350	9,011	12,350	10,879
66,250	66,300	12,363	9,019	12,363	10,891
66,300	66,350	12,375	9,026	12,375	10,904
66,350	66,400	12,388	9,034	12,388	10,916
66,400	66,450	12,400	9,041	12,400	10,929
66,450	66,500	12,413	9,049	12,413	10,941
66,500	66,550	12,425	9,056	12,425	10,954
66,550	66,600	12,438	9,064	12,438	10,966
66,600	66,650	12,450	9,071	12,450	10,979
66,650	66,700	12,463	9,079	12,463	10,991
66,700	66,750	12,475	9,086	12,475	11,004
66,750	66,800	12,488	9,094	12,488	11,016
66,800	66,850	12,500	9,101	12,500	11,029
66,850	66,900	12,513	9,109	12,513	11,041
66,900	66,950	12,525	9,116	12,525	11,054
66,950	67,000	12,538	9,124	12,538	11,066
67,000					
67,000	67,050	12,550	9,131	12,550	11,079
67,050	67,100	12,563	9,139	12,563	11,091
67,100	67,150	12,575	9,146	12,575	11,104
67,150	67,200	12,588	9,154	12,588	11,116
67,200	67,250	12,600	9,161	12,600	11,129
67,250	67,300	12,613	9,169	12,613	11,141
67,300	67,350	12,625	9,176	12,625	11,154
67,350	67,400	12,638	9,184	12,638	11,166
67,400	67,450	12,650	9,191	12,650	11,179
67,450	67,500	12,663	9,199	12,663	11,191
67,500	67,550	12,675	9,206	12,675	11,204
67,550	67,600	12,688	9,214	12,688	11,216
67,600	67,650	12,700	9,221	12,700	11,229
67,650	67,700	12,713	9,229	12,713	11,241
67,700	67,750	12,725	9,236	12,725	11,254
67,750	67,800	12,738	9,244	12,738	11,266
67,800	67,850	12,750	9,251	12,750	11,279
67,850	67,900	12,763	9,259	12,763	11,291
67,900	67,950	12,775	9,266	12,775	11,304
67,950	68,000	12,788	9,274	12,788	11,316
68,000					
68,000	68,050	12,800	9,281	12,800	11,329
68,050	68,100	12,813	9,289	12,813	11,341
68,100	68,150	12,825	9,296	12,825	11,354
68,150	68,200	12,838	9,304	12,838	11,366
68,200	68,250	12,850	9,311	12,850	11,379
68,250	68,300	12,863	9,319	12,863	11,391
68,300	68,350	12,875	9,326	12,875	11,404
68,350	68,400	12,888	9,334	12,888	11,416
68,400	68,450	12,900	9,341	12,900	11,429
68,450	68,500	12,913	9,349	12,913	11,441
68,500	68,550	12,925	9,356	12,925	11,454
68,550	68,600	12,938	9,364	12,938	11,466
68,600	68,650	12,950	9,371	12,950	11,479
68,650	68,700	12,963	9,379	12,963	11,491
68,700	68,750	12,975	9,386	12,975	11,504
68,750	68,800	12,988	9,394	12,988	11,516
68,800	68,850	13,000	9,401	13,000	11,529
68,850	68,900	13,013	9,409	13,013	11,541
68,900	68,950	13,025	9,416	13,025	11,554
68,950	69,000	13,038	9,424	13,038	11,566
69,000					
69,000	69,050	13,050	9,431	13,050	11,579
69,050	69,100	13,063	9,439	13,063	11,591
69,100	69,150	13,075	9,446	13,075	11,604
69,150	69,200	13,088	9,454	13,088	11,616
69,200	69,250	13,100	9,461	13,100	11,629
69,250	69,300	13,113	9,469	13,113	11,641
69,300	69,350	13,125	9,476	13,125	11,654
69,350	69,400	13,138	9,484	13,138	11,666
69,400	69,450	13,150	9,491	13,150	11,679
69,450	69,500	13,163	9,499	13,163	11,691
69,500	69,550	13,175	9,506	13,175	11,704
69,550	69,600	13,188	9,514	13,188	11,716
69,600	69,650	13,200	9,521	13,200	11,729
69,650	69,700	13,213	9,529	13,213	11,741
69,700	69,750	13,225	9,536	13,225	11,754
69,750	69,800	13,238	9,544	13,238	11,766
69,800	69,850	13,250	9,551	13,250	11,779
69,850	69,900	13,263	9,559	13,263	11,791
69,900	69,950	13,275	9,566	13,275	11,804
69,950	70,000	13,288	9,574	13,288	11,816
70,000					
70,000	70,050	13,300	9,581	13,300	11,829
70,050	70,100	13,313	9,589	13,313	11,841
70,100	70,150	13,325	9,596	13,325	11,854
70,150	70,200	13,338	9,604	13,338	11,866
70,200	70,250	13,350	9,611	13,350	11,879
70,250	70,300	13,363	9,619	13,363	11,891
70,300	70,350	13,375	9,626	13,375	11,904
70,350	70,400	13,388	9,634	13,388	11,916
70,400	70,450	13,400	9,641	13,400	11,929
70,450	70,500	13,413	9,649	13,413	11,941
70,500	70,550	13,425	9,656	13,425	11,954
70,550	70,600	13,438	9,664	13,438	11,966
70,600	70,650	13,450	9,671	13,450	11,979
70,650	70,700	13,463	9,679	13,463	11,991
70,700	70,750	13,475	9,686	13,475	12,004
70,750	70,800	13,488	9,694	13,488	12,016
70,800	70,850	13,500	9,701	13,500	12,029
70,850	70,900	13,513	9,709	13,513	12,041
70,900	70,950	13,525	9,716	13,525	12,054
70,950	71,000	13,538	9,724	13,538	12,066
71,000					
71,000	71,050	13,550	9,731	13,550	12,079
71,050	71,100	13,563	9,739	13,563	12,091
71,100	71,150	13,575	9,746	13,575	12,104
71,150	71,200	13,588	9,754	13,588	12,116
71,200	71,250	13,600	9,761	13,600	12,129
71,250	71,300	13,613	9,769	13,613	12,141
71,300	71,350	13,625	9,776	13,625	12,154
71,350	71,400	13,638	9,784	13,638	12,166
71,400	71,450	13,650	9,791	13,650	12,179
71,450	71,500	13,663	9,799	13,663	12,191
71,500	71,550	13,675	9,806	13,675	12,204
71,550	71,600	13,688	9,814	13,688	12,216
71,600	71,650	13,700	9,821	13,700	12,229
71,650	71,700	13,713	9,829	13,713	12,241
71,700	71,750	13,725	9,836	13,725	12,254
71,750	71,800	13,738	9,844	13,738	12,266
71,800	71,850	13,750	9,851	13,750	12,279
71,850	71,900	13,763	9,859	13,763	12,291
71,900	71,950	13,775	9,866	13,775	12,304
71,950	72,000	13,788	9,874	13,788	12,316
72,000					
72,000	72,050	13,800	9,881	13,800	12,329
72,050	72,100	13,813	9,889	13,813	12,341
72,100	72,150	13,825	9,896	13,825	12,354
72,150	72,200	13,838	9,904	13,838	12,366
72,200	72,250	13,850	9,911	13,850	12,379
72,250	72,300	13,863	9,919	13,863	12,391
72,300	72,350	13,875	9,926	13,875	12,404
72,350	72,400	13,888	9,934	13,888	12,416
72,400	72,450	13,900	9,941	13,900	12,429
72,450	72,500	13,913	9,949	13,913	12,441
72,500	72,550	13,925	9,956	13,925	12,454
72,550	72,600	13,938	9,964	13,938	12,466
72,600	72,650	13,950	9,971	13,950	12,479
72,650	72,700	13,963	9,979	13,963	12,491
72,700	72,750	13,975	9,986	13,975	12,504
72,750	72,800	13,988	9,994	13,988	12,516
72,800	72,850	14,000	10,001	14,000	12,529
72,850	72,900	14,013	10,009	14,013	12,541
72,900	72,950	14,025	10,016	14,025	12,554
72,950	73,000	14,038	10,024	14,038	12,566
73,000					
73,000	73,050	14,050	10,031	14,050	12,579
73,050	73,100	14,063	10,039	14,063	12,591
73,100	73,150	14,075	10,046	14,075	12,604
73,150	73,200	14,088	10,054	14,088	12,616
73,200	73,250	14,100	10,061	14,100	12,629
73,250	73,300	14,113	10,069	14,113	12,641
73,300	73,350	14,125	10,076	14,125	12,654
73,350	73,400	14,138	10,084	14,138	12,666
73,400	73,450	14,150	10,091	14,150	12,679
73,450	73,500	14,163	10,099	14,163	12,691
73,500	73,550	14,175	10,106	14,175	12,704
73,550	73,600	14,188	10,114	14,188	12,716
73,600	73,650	14,200	10,121	14,200	12,729
73,650	73,700	14,213	10,129	14,213	12,741
73,700	73,750	14,225	10,136	14,225	12,754
73,750	73,800	14,238	10,144	14,238	12,766
73,800	73,850	14,250	10,151	14,250	12,779
73,850	73,900	14,263	10,159	14,263	12,791
73,900	73,950	14,275	10,166	14,275	12,804
73,950	74,000	14,288	10,174	14,288	12,816
74,000					
74,000	74,050	14,300	10,181	14,300	12,829
74,050	74,100	14,313	10,189	14,313	12,841
74,100	74,150	14,325	10,196	14,325	12,854
74,150	74,200	14,338	10,204	14,338	12,866
74,200	74,250	14,350	10,211	14,350	12,879
74,250	74,300	14,363	10,219	14,363	12,891
74,300	74,350	14,375	10,226	14,375	12,904
74,350	74,400	14,388	10,234	14,388	12,916
74,400	74,450	14,400	10,241	14,400	12,929
74,450	74,500	14,413	10,249	14,413	12,941
74,500	74,550	14,425	10,256	14,425	12,954
74,550	74,600	14,438	10,264	14,438	12,966
74,600	74,650	14,450	10,271	14,450	12,979
74,650	74,700	14,463	10,279	14,463	12,991
74,700	74,750	14,475	10,286	14,475	13,004
74,750	74,800	14,488	10,294	14,488	13,016
74,800	74,850	14,500	10,301	14,500	13,029
74,850	74,900	14,513	10,309	14,513	13,041
74,900	74,950	14,525	10,319	14,525	13,054
74,950	75,000	14,538	10,331	14,538	13,066

* This column must also be used by a qualifying widow(er).

2015 Tax Table — *Continued*

If line 43 (taxable income) is—		And you are—			
At least	But less than	Single	Married filing jointly *	Married filing separately	Head of a household
		Your tax is—			
75,000					
75,000	75,050	14,550	10,344	14,550	13,079
75,050	75,100	14,563	10,356	14,563	13,091
75,100	75,150	14,575	10,369	14,575	13,104
75,150	75,200	14,588	10,381	14,588	13,116
75,200	75,250	14,600	10,394	14,600	13,129
75,250	75,300	14,613	10,406	14,613	13,141
75,300	75,350	14,625	10,419	14,625	13,154
75,350	75,400	14,638	10,431	14,638	13,166
75,400	75,450	14,650	10,444	14,650	13,179
75,450	75,500	14,663	10,456	14,663	13,191
75,500	75,550	14,675	10,469	14,675	13,204
75,550	75,600	14,688	10,481	14,688	13,216
75,600	75,650	14,700	10,494	14,701	13,229
75,650	75,700	14,713	10,506	14,715	13,241
75,700	75,750	14,725	10,519	14,729	13,254
75,750	75,800	14,738	10,531	14,743	13,266
75,800	75,850	14,750	10,544	14,757	13,279
75,850	75,900	14,763	10,556	14,771	13,291
75,900	75,950	14,775	10,569	14,785	13,304
75,950	76,000	14,788	10,581	14,799	13,316
76,000					
76,000	76,050	14,800	10,594	14,813	13,329
76,050	76,100	14,813	10,606	14,827	13,341
76,100	76,150	14,825	10,619	14,841	13,354
76,150	76,200	14,838	10,631	14,855	13,366
76,200	76,250	14,850	10,644	14,869	13,379
76,250	76,300	14,863	10,656	14,883	13,391
76,300	76,350	14,875	10,669	14,897	13,404
76,350	76,400	14,888	10,681	14,911	13,416
76,400	76,450	14,900	10,694	14,925	13,429
76,450	76,500	14,913	10,706	14,939	13,441
76,500	76,550	14,925	10,719	14,953	13,454
76,550	76,600	14,938	10,731	14,967	13,466
76,600	76,650	14,950	10,744	14,981	13,479
76,650	76,700	14,963	10,756	14,995	13,491
76,700	76,750	14,975	10,769	15,009	13,504
76,750	76,800	14,988	10,781	15,023	13,516
76,800	76,850	15,000	10,794	15,037	13,529
76,850	76,900	15,013	10,806	15,051	13,541
76,900	76,950	15,025	10,819	15,065	13,554
76,950	77,000	15,038	10,831	15,079	13,566
77,000					
77,000	77,050	15,050	10,844	15,093	13,579
77,050	77,100	15,063	10,856	15,107	13,591
77,100	77,150	15,075	10,869	15,121	13,604
77,150	77,200	15,088	10,881	15,135	13,616
77,200	77,250	15,100	10,894	15,149	13,629
77,250	77,300	15,113	10,906	15,163	13,641
77,300	77,350	15,125	10,919	15,177	13,654
77,350	77,400	15,138	10,931	15,191	13,666
77,400	77,450	15,150	10,944	15,205	13,679
77,450	77,500	15,163	10,956	15,219	13,691
77,500	77,550	15,175	10,969	15,233	13,704
77,550	77,600	15,188	10,981	15,247	13,716
77,600	77,650	15,200	10,994	15,261	13,729
77,650	77,700	15,213	11,006	15,275	13,741
77,700	77,750	15,225	11,019	15,289	13,754
77,750	77,800	15,238	11,031	15,303	13,766
77,800	77,850	15,250	11,044	15,317	13,779
77,850	77,900	15,263	11,056	15,331	13,791
77,900	77,950	15,275	11,069	15,345	13,804
77,950	78,000	15,288	11,081	15,359	13,816

If line 43 (taxable income) is—		And you are—			
At least	But less than	Single	Married filing jointly *	Married filing separately	Head of a household
		Your tax is—			
78,000					
78,000	78,050	15,300	11,094	15,373	13,829
78,050	78,100	15,313	11,106	15,387	13,841
78,100	78,150	15,325	11,119	15,401	13,854
78,150	78,200	15,338	11,131	15,415	13,866
78,200	78,250	15,350	11,144	15,429	13,879
78,250	78,300	15,363	11,156	15,443	13,891
78,300	78,350	15,375	11,169	15,457	13,904
78,350	78,400	15,388	11,181	15,471	13,916
78,400	78,450	15,400	11,194	15,485	13,929
78,450	78,500	15,413	11,206	15,499	13,941
78,500	78,550	15,425	11,219	15,513	13,954
78,550	78,600	15,438	11,231	15,527	13,966
78,600	78,650	15,450	11,244	15,541	13,979
78,650	78,700	15,463	11,256	15,555	13,991
78,700	78,750	15,475	11,269	15,569	14,004
78,750	78,800	15,488	11,281	15,583	14,016
78,800	78,850	15,500	11,294	15,597	14,029
78,850	78,900	15,513	11,306	15,611	14,041
78,900	78,950	15,525	11,319	15,625	14,054
78,950	79,000	15,538	11,331	15,639	14,066
79,000					
79,000	79,050	15,550	11,344	15,653	14,079
79,050	79,100	15,563	11,356	15,667	14,091
79,100	79,150	15,575	11,369	15,681	14,104
79,150	79,200	15,588	11,381	15,695	14,116
79,200	79,250	15,600	11,394	15,709	14,129
79,250	79,300	15,613	11,406	15,723	14,141
79,300	79,350	15,625	11,419	15,737	14,154
79,350	79,400	15,638	11,431	15,751	14,166
79,400	79,450	15,650	11,444	15,765	14,179
79,450	79,500	15,663	11,456	15,779	14,191
79,500	79,550	15,675	11,469	15,793	14,204
79,550	79,600	15,688	11,481	15,807	14,216
79,600	79,650	15,700	11,494	15,821	14,229
79,650	79,700	15,713	11,506	15,835	14,241
79,700	79,750	15,725	11,519	15,849	14,254
79,750	79,800	15,738	11,531	15,863	14,266
79,800	79,850	15,750	11,544	15,877	14,279
79,850	79,900	15,763	11,556	15,891	14,291
79,900	79,950	15,775	11,569	15,905	14,304
79,950	80,000	15,788	11,581	15,919	14,316
80,000					
80,000	80,050	15,800	11,594	15,933	14,329
80,050	80,100	15,813	11,606	15,947	14,341
80,100	80,150	15,825	11,619	15,961	14,354
80,150	80,200	15,838	11,631	15,975	14,366
80,200	80,250	15,850	11,644	15,989	14,379
80,250	80,300	15,863	11,656	16,003	14,391
80,300	80,350	15,875	11,669	16,017	14,404
80,350	80,400	15,888	11,681	16,031	14,416
80,400	80,450	15,900	11,694	16,045	14,429
80,450	80,500	15,913	11,706	16,059	14,441
80,500	80,550	15,925	11,719	16,073	14,454
80,550	80,600	15,938	11,731	16,087	14,466
80,600	80,650	15,950	11,744	16,101	14,479
80,650	80,700	15,963	11,756	16,115	14,491
80,700	80,750	15,975	11,769	16,129	14,504
80,750	80,800	15,988	11,781	16,143	14,516
80,800	80,850	16,000	11,794	16,157	14,529
80,850	80,900	16,013	11,806	16,171	14,541
80,900	80,950	16,025	11,819	16,185	14,554
80,950	81,000	16,038	11,831	16,199	14,566

If line 43 (taxable income) is—		And you are—			
At least	But less than	Single	Married filing jointly *	Married filing separately	Head of a household
		Your tax is—			
81,000					
81,000	81,050	16,050	11,844	16,213	14,579
81,050	81,100	16,063	11,856	16,227	14,591
81,100	81,150	16,075	11,869	16,241	14,604
81,150	81,200	16,088	11,881	16,255	14,616
81,200	81,250	16,100	11,894	16,269	14,629
81,250	81,300	16,113	11,906	16,283	14,641
81,300	81,350	16,125	11,919	16,297	14,654
81,350	81,400	16,138	11,931	16,311	14,666
81,400	81,450	16,150	11,944	16,325	14,679
81,450	81,500	16,163	11,956	16,339	14,691
81,500	81,550	16,175	11,969	16,353	14,704
81,550	81,600	16,188	11,981	16,367	14,716
81,600	81,650	16,200	11,994	16,381	14,729
81,650	81,700	16,213	12,006	16,395	14,741
81,700	81,750	16,225	12,019	16,409	14,754
81,750	81,800	16,238	12,031	16,423	14,766
81,800	81,850	16,250	12,044	16,437	14,779
81,850	81,900	16,263	12,056	16,451	14,791
81,900	81,950	16,275	12,069	16,465	14,804
81,950	82,000	16,288	12,081	16,479	14,816
82,000					
82,000	82,050	16,300	12,094	16,493	14,829
82,050	82,100	16,313	12,106	16,507	14,841
82,100	82,150	16,325	12,119	16,521	14,854
82,150	82,200	16,338	12,131	16,535	14,866
82,200	82,250	16,350	12,144	16,549	14,879
82,250	82,300	16,363	12,156	16,563	14,891
82,300	82,350	16,375	12,169	16,577	14,904
82,350	82,400	16,388	12,181	16,591	14,916
82,400	82,450	16,400	12,194	16,605	14,929
82,450	82,500	16,413	12,206	16,619	14,941
82,500	82,550	16,425	12,219	16,633	14,954
82,550	82,600	16,438	12,231	16,647	14,966
82,600	82,650	16,450	12,244	16,661	14,979
82,650	82,700	16,463	12,256	16,675	14,991
82,700	82,750	16,475	12,269	16,689	15,004
82,750	82,800	16,488	12,281	16,703	15,016
82,800	82,850	16,500	12,294	16,717	15,029
82,850	82,900	16,513	12,306	16,731	15,041
82,900	82,950	16,525	12,319	16,745	15,054
82,950	83,000	16,538	12,331	16,759	15,066
83,000					
83,000	83,050	16,550	12,344	16,773	15,079
83,050	83,100	16,563	12,356	16,787	15,091
83,100	83,150	16,575	12,369	16,801	15,104
83,150	83,200	16,588	12,381	16,815	15,116
83,200	83,250	16,600	12,394	16,829	15,129
83,250	83,300	16,613	12,406	16,843	15,141
83,300	83,350	16,625	12,419	16,857	15,154
83,350	83,400	16,638	12,431	16,871	15,166
83,400	83,450	16,650	12,444	16,885	15,179
83,450	83,500	16,663	12,456	16,899	15,191
83,500	83,550	16,675	12,469	16,913	15,204
83,550	83,600	16,688	12,481	16,927	15,216
83,600	83,650	16,700	12,494	16,941	15,229
83,650	83,700	16,713	12,506	16,955	15,241
83,700	83,750	16,725	12,519	16,969	15,254
83,750	83,800	16,738	12,531	16,983	15,266
83,800	83,850	16,750	12,544	16,997	15,279
83,850	83,900	16,763	12,556	17,011	15,291
83,900	83,950	16,775	12,569	17,025	15,304
83,950	84,000	16,788	12,581	17,039	15,316

* This column must also be used by a qualifying widow(er).

2015 Tax Table — *Continued*

If line 43 (taxable income) is— / And you are— / Your tax is—

84,000

At least	But less than	Single	Married filing jointly *	Married filing separately	Head of a household
84,000	84,050	16,800	12,594	17,053	15,329
84,050	84,100	16,813	12,606	17,067	15,341
84,100	84,150	16,825	12,619	17,081	15,354
84,150	84,200	16,838	12,631	17,095	15,366
84,200	84,250	16,850	12,644	17,109	15,379
84,250	84,300	16,863	12,656	17,123	15,391
84,300	84,350	16,875	12,669	17,137	15,404
84,350	84,400	16,888	12,681	17,151	15,416
84,400	84,450	16,900	12,694	17,165	15,429
84,450	84,500	16,913	12,706	17,179	15,441
84,500	84,550	16,925	12,719	17,193	15,454
84,550	84,600	16,938	12,731	17,207	15,466
84,600	84,650	16,950	12,744	17,221	15,479
84,650	84,700	16,963	12,756	17,235	15,491
84,700	84,750	16,975	12,769	17,249	15,504
84,750	84,800	16,988	12,781	17,263	15,516
84,800	84,850	17,000	12,794	17,277	15,529
84,850	84,900	17,013	12,806	17,291	15,541
84,900	84,950	17,025	12,819	17,305	15,554
84,950	85,000	17,038	12,831	17,319	15,566

85,000

At least	But less than	Single	Married filing jointly *	Married filing separately	Head of a household
85,000	85,050	17,050	12,844	17,333	15,579
85,050	85,100	17,063	12,856	17,347	15,591
85,100	85,150	17,075	12,869	17,361	15,604
85,150	85,200	17,088	12,881	17,375	15,616
85,200	85,250	17,100	12,894	17,389	15,629
85,250	85,300	17,113	12,906	17,403	15,641
85,300	85,350	17,125	12,919	17,417	15,654
85,350	85,400	17,138	12,931	17,431	15,666
85,400	85,450	17,150	12,944	17,445	15,679
85,450	85,500	17,163	12,956	17,459	15,691
85,500	85,550	17,175	12,969	17,473	15,704
85,550	85,600	17,188	12,981	17,487	15,716
85,600	85,650	17,200	12,994	17,501	15,729
85,650	85,700	17,213	13,006	17,515	15,741
85,700	85,750	17,225	13,019	17,529	15,754
85,750	85,800	17,238	13,031	17,543	15,766
85,800	85,850	17,250	13,044	17,557	15,779
85,850	85,900	17,263	13,056	17,571	15,791
85,900	85,950	17,275	13,069	17,585	15,804
85,950	86,000	17,288	13,081	17,599	15,816

86,000

At least	But less than	Single	Married filing jointly *	Married filing separately	Head of a household
86,000	86,050	17,300	13,094	17,613	15,829
86,050	86,100	17,313	13,106	17,627	15,841
86,100	86,150	17,325	13,119	17,641	15,854
86,150	86,200	17,338	13,131	17,655	15,866
86,200	86,250	17,350	13,144	17,669	15,879
86,250	86,300	17,363	13,156	17,683	15,891
86,300	86,350	17,375	13,169	17,697	15,904
86,350	86,400	17,388	13,181	17,711	15,916
86,400	86,450	17,400	13,194	17,725	15,929
86,450	86,500	17,413	13,206	17,739	15,941
86,500	86,550	17,425	13,219	17,753	15,954
86,550	86,600	17,438	13,231	17,767	15,966
86,600	86,650	17,450	13,244	17,781	15,979
86,650	86,700	17,463	13,256	17,795	15,991
86,700	86,750	17,475	13,269	17,809	16,004
86,750	86,800	17,488	13,281	17,823	16,016
86,800	86,850	17,500	13,294	17,837	16,029
86,850	86,900	17,513	13,306	17,851	16,041
86,900	86,950	17,525	13,319	17,865	16,054
86,950	87,000	17,538	13,331	17,879	16,066

87,000

At least	But less than	Single	Married filing jointly *	Married filing separately	Head of a household
87,000	87,050	17,550	13,344	17,893	16,079
87,050	87,100	17,563	13,356	17,907	16,091
87,100	87,150	17,575	13,369	17,921	16,104
87,150	87,200	17,588	13,381	17,935	16,116
87,200	87,250	17,600	13,394	17,949	16,129
87,250	87,300	17,613	13,406	17,963	16,141
87,300	87,350	17,625	13,419	17,977	16,154
87,350	87,400	17,638	13,431	17,991	16,166
87,400	87,450	17,650	13,444	18,005	16,179
87,450	87,500	17,663	13,456	18,019	16,191
87,500	87,550	17,675	13,469	18,033	16,204
87,550	87,600	17,688	13,481	18,047	16,216
87,600	87,650	17,700	13,494	18,061	16,229
87,650	87,700	17,713	13,506	18,075	16,241
87,700	87,750	17,725	13,519	18,089	16,254
87,750	87,800	17,738	13,531	18,103	16,266
87,800	87,850	17,750	13,544	18,117	16,279
87,850	87,900	17,763	13,556	18,131	16,291
87,900	87,950	17,775	13,569	18,145	16,304
87,950	88,000	17,788	13,581	18,159	16,316

88,000

At least	But less than	Single	Married filing jointly *	Married filing separately	Head of a household
88,000	88,050	17,800	13,594	18,173	16,329
88,050	88,100	17,813	13,606	18,187	16,341
88,100	88,150	17,825	13,619	18,201	16,354
88,150	88,200	17,838	13,631	18,215	16,366
88,200	88,250	17,850	13,644	18,229	16,379
88,250	88,300	17,863	13,656	18,243	16,391
88,300	88,350	17,875	13,669	18,257	16,404
88,350	88,400	17,888	13,681	18,271	16,416
88,400	88,450	17,900	13,694	18,285	16,429
88,450	88,500	17,913	13,706	18,299	16,441
88,500	88,550	17,925	13,719	18,313	16,454
88,550	88,600	17,938	13,731	18,327	16,466
88,600	88,650	17,950	13,744	18,341	16,479
88,650	88,700	17,963	13,756	18,355	16,491
88,700	88,750	17,975	13,769	18,369	16,504
88,750	88,800	17,988	13,781	18,383	16,516
88,800	88,850	18,000	13,794	18,397	16,529
88,850	88,900	18,013	13,806	18,411	16,541
88,900	88,950	18,025	13,819	18,425	16,554
88,950	89,000	18,038	13,831	18,439	16,566

89,000

At least	But less than	Single	Married filing jointly *	Married filing separately	Head of a household
89,000	89,050	18,050	13,844	18,453	16,579
89,050	89,100	18,063	13,856	18,467	16,591
89,100	89,150	18,075	13,869	18,481	16,604
89,150	89,200	18,088	13,881	18,495	16,616
89,200	89,250	18,100	13,894	18,509	16,629
89,250	89,300	18,113	13,906	18,523	16,641
89,300	89,350	18,125	13,919	18,537	16,654
89,350	89,400	18,138	13,931	18,551	16,666
89,400	89,450	18,150	13,944	18,565	16,679
89,450	89,500	18,163	13,956	18,579	16,691
89,500	89,550	18,175	13,969	18,593	16,704
89,550	89,600	18,188	13,981	18,607	16,716
89,600	89,650	18,200	13,994	18,621	16,729
89,650	89,700	18,213	14,006	18,635	16,741
89,700	89,750	18,225	14,019	18,649	16,754
89,750	89,800	18,238	14,031	18,663	16,766
89,800	89,850	18,250	14,044	18,677	16,779
89,850	89,900	18,263	14,056	18,691	16,791
89,900	89,950	18,275	14,069	18,705	16,804
89,950	90,000	18,288	14,081	18,719	16,816

90,000

At least	But less than	Single	Married filing jointly *	Married filing separately	Head of a household
90,000	90,050	18,300	14,094	18,733	16,829
90,050	90,100	18,313	14,106	18,747	16,841
90,100	90,150	18,325	14,119	18,761	16,854
90,150	90,200	18,338	14,131	18,775	16,866
90,200	90,250	18,350	14,144	18,789	16,879
90,250	90,300	18,363	14,156	18,803	16,891
90,300	90,350	18,375	14,169	18,817	16,904
90,350	90,400	18,388	14,181	18,831	16,916
90,400	90,450	18,400	14,194	18,845	16,929
90,450	90,500	18,413	14,206	18,859	16,941
90,500	90,550	18,425	14,219	18,873	16,954
90,550	90,600	18,438	14,231	18,887	16,966
90,600	90,650	18,450	14,244	18,901	16,979
90,650	90,700	18,463	14,256	18,915	16,991
90,700	90,750	18,475	14,269	18,929	17,004
90,750	90,800	18,488	14,281	18,943	17,016
90,800	90,850	18,502	14,294	18,957	17,029
90,850	90,900	18,516	14,306	18,971	17,041
90,900	90,950	18,530	14,319	18,985	17,054
90,950	91,000	18,544	14,331	18,999	17,066

91,000

At least	But less than	Single	Married filing jointly *	Married filing separately	Head of a household
91,000	91,050	18,558	14,344	19,013	17,079
91,050	91,100	18,572	14,356	19,027	17,091
91,100	91,150	18,586	14,369	19,041	17,104
91,150	91,200	18,600	14,381	19,055	17,116
91,200	91,250	18,614	14,394	19,069	17,129
91,250	91,300	18,628	14,406	19,083	17,141
91,300	91,350	18,642	14,419	19,097	17,154
91,350	91,400	18,656	14,431	19,111	17,166
91,400	91,450	18,670	14,444	19,125	17,179
91,450	91,500	18,684	14,456	19,139	17,191
91,500	91,550	18,698	14,469	19,153	17,204
91,550	91,600	18,712	14,481	19,167	17,216
91,600	91,650	18,726	14,494	19,181	17,229
91,650	91,700	18,740	14,506	19,195	17,241
91,700	91,750	18,754	14,519	19,209	17,254
91,750	91,800	18,768	14,531	19,223	17,266
91,800	91,850	18,782	14,544	19,237	17,279
91,850	91,900	18,796	14,556	19,251	17,291
91,900	91,950	18,810	14,569	19,265	17,304
91,950	92,000	18,824	14,581	19,279	17,316

92,000

At least	But less than	Single	Married filing jointly *	Married filing separately	Head of a household
92,000	92,050	18,838	14,594	19,293	17,329
92,050	92,100	18,852	14,606	19,307	17,341
92,100	92,150	18,866	14,619	19,321	17,354
92,150	92,200	18,880	14,631	19,335	17,366
92,200	92,250	18,894	14,644	19,349	17,379
92,250	92,300	18,908	14,656	19,363	17,391
92,300	92,350	18,922	14,669	19,377	17,404
92,350	92,400	18,936	14,681	19,391	17,416
92,400	92,450	18,950	14,694	19,405	17,429
92,450	92,500	18,964	14,706	19,419	17,441
92,500	92,550	18,978	14,719	19,433	17,454
92,550	92,600	18,992	14,731	19,447	17,466
92,600	92,650	19,006	14,744	19,461	17,479
92,650	92,700	19,020	14,756	19,475	17,491
92,700	92,750	19,034	14,769	19,489	17,504
92,750	92,800	19,048	14,781	19,503	17,516
92,800	92,850	19,062	14,794	19,517	17,529
92,850	92,900	19,076	14,806	19,531	17,541
92,900	92,950	19,090	14,819	19,545	17,554
92,950	93,000	19,104	14,831	19,559	17,566

* This column must also be used by a qualifying widow(er).

2015 Tax Table — *Continued*

If line 43 (taxable income) is—		And you are—			
At least	But less than	Single	Married filing jointly *	Married filing separately	Head of a household
		Your tax is—			
93,000					
93,000	93,050	19,118	14,844	19,573	17,579
93,050	93,100	19,132	14,856	19,587	17,591
93,100	93,150	19,146	14,869	19,601	17,604
93,150	93,200	19,160	14,881	19,615	17,616
93,200	93,250	19,174	14,894	19,629	17,629
93,250	93,300	19,188	14,906	19,643	17,641
93,300	93,350	19,202	14,919	19,657	17,654
93,350	93,400	19,216	14,931	19,671	17,666
93,400	93,450	19,230	14,944	19,685	17,679
93,450	93,500	19,244	14,956	19,699	17,691
93,500	93,550	19,258	14,969	19,713	17,704
93,550	93,600	19,272	14,981	19,727	17,716
93,600	93,650	19,286	14,994	19,741	17,729
93,650	93,700	19,300	15,006	19,755	17,741
93,700	93,750	19,314	15,019	19,769	17,754
93,750	93,800	19,328	15,031	19,783	17,766
93,800	93,850	19,342	15,044	19,797	17,779
93,850	93,900	19,356	15,056	19,811	17,791
93,900	93,950	19,370	15,069	19,825	17,804
93,950	94,000	19,384	15,081	19,839	17,816
94,000					
94,000	94,050	19,398	15,094	19,853	17,829
94,050	94,100	19,412	15,106	19,867	17,841
94,100	94,150	19,426	15,119	19,881	17,854
94,150	94,200	19,440	15,131	19,895	17,866
94,200	94,250	19,454	15,144	19,909	17,879
94,250	94,300	19,468	15,156	19,923	17,891
94,300	94,350	19,482	15,169	19,937	17,904
94,350	94,400	19,496	15,181	19,951	17,916
94,400	94,450	19,510	15,194	19,965	17,929
94,450	94,500	19,524	15,206	19,979	17,941
94,500	94,550	19,538	15,219	19,993	17,954
94,550	94,600	19,552	15,231	20,007	17,966
94,600	94,650	19,566	15,244	20,021	17,979
94,650	94,700	19,580	15,256	20,035	17,991
94,700	94,750	19,594	15,269	20,049	18,004
94,750	94,800	19,608	15,281	20,063	18,016
94,800	94,850	19,622	15,294	20,077	18,029
94,850	94,900	19,636	15,306	20,091	18,041
94,900	94,950	19,650	15,319	20,105	18,054
94,950	95,000	19,664	15,331	20,119	18,066
95,000					
95,000	95,050	19,678	15,344	20,133	18,079
95,050	95,100	19,692	15,356	20,147	18,091
95,100	95,150	19,706	15,369	20,161	18,104
95,150	95,200	19,720	15,381	20,175	18,116
95,200	95,250	19,734	15,394	20,189	18,129
95,250	95,300	19,748	15,406	20,203	18,141
95,300	95,350	19,762	15,419	20,217	18,154
95,350	95,400	19,776	15,431	20,231	18,166
95,400	95,450	19,790	15,444	20,245	18,179
95,450	95,500	19,804	15,456	20,259	18,191
95,500	95,550	19,818	15,469	20,273	18,204
95,550	95,600	19,832	15,481	20,287	18,216
95,600	95,650	19,846	15,494	20,301	18,229
95,650	95,700	19,860	15,506	20,315	18,241
95,700	95,750	19,874	15,519	20,329	18,254
95,750	95,800	19,888	15,531	20,343	18,266
95,800	95,850	19,902	15,544	20,357	18,279
95,850	95,900	19,916	15,556	20,371	18,291
95,900	95,950	19,930	15,569	20,385	18,304
95,950	96,000	19,944	15,581	20,399	18,316
96,000					
96,000	96,050	19,958	15,594	20,413	18,329
96,050	96,100	19,972	15,606	20,427	18,341
96,100	96,150	19,986	15,619	20,441	18,354
96,150	96,200	20,000	15,631	20,455	18,366
96,200	96,250	20,014	15,644	20,469	18,379
96,250	96,300	20,028	15,656	20,483	18,391
96,300	96,350	20,042	15,669	20,497	18,404
96,350	96,400	20,056	15,681	20,511	18,416
96,400	96,450	20,070	15,694	20,525	18,429
96,450	96,500	20,084	15,706	20,539	18,441
96,500	96,550	20,098	15,719	20,553	18,454
96,550	96,600	20,112	15,731	20,567	18,466
96,600	96,650	20,126	15,744	20,581	18,479
96,650	96,700	20,140	15,756	20,595	18,491
96,700	96,750	20,154	15,769	20,609	18,504
96,750	96,800	20,168	15,781	20,623	18,516
96,800	96,850	20,182	15,794	20,637	18,529
96,850	96,900	20,196	15,806	20,651	18,541
96,900	96,950	20,210	15,819	20,665	18,554
96,950	97,000	20,224	15,831	20,679	18,566
97,000					
97,000	97,050	20,238	15,844	20,693	18,579
97,050	97,100	20,252	15,856	20,707	18,591
97,100	97,150	20,266	15,869	20,721	18,604
97,150	97,200	20,280	15,881	20,735	18,616
97,200	97,250	20,294	15,894	20,749	18,629
97,250	97,300	20,308	15,906	20,763	18,641
97,300	97,350	20,322	15,919	20,777	18,654
97,350	97,400	20,336	15,931	20,791	18,666
97,400	97,450	20,350	15,944	20,805	18,679
97,450	97,500	20,364	15,956	20,819	18,691
97,500	97,550	20,378	15,969	20,833	18,704
97,550	97,600	20,392	15,981	20,847	18,716
97,600	97,650	20,406	15,994	20,861	18,729
97,650	97,700	20,420	16,006	20,875	18,741
97,700	97,750	20,434	16,019	20,889	18,754
97,750	97,800	20,448	16,031	20,903	18,766
97,800	97,850	20,462	16,044	20,917	18,779
97,850	97,900	20,476	16,056	20,931	18,791
97,900	97,950	20,490	16,069	20,945	18,804
97,950	98,000	20,504	16,081	20,959	18,816
98,000					
98,000	98,050	20,518	16,094	20,973	18,829
98,050	98,100	20,532	16,106	20,987	18,841
98,100	98,150	20,546	16,119	21,001	18,854
98,150	98,200	20,560	16,131	21,015	18,866
98,200	98,250	20,574	16,144	21,029	18,879
98,250	98,300	20,588	16,156	21,043	18,891
98,300	98,350	20,602	16,169	21,057	18,904
98,350	98,400	20,616	16,181	21,071	18,916
98,400	98,450	20,630	16,194	21,085	18,929
98,450	98,500	20,644	16,206	21,099	18,941
98,500	98,550	20,658	16,219	21,113	18,954
98,550	98,600	20,672	16,231	21,127	18,966
98,600	98,650	20,686	16,244	21,141	18,979
98,650	98,700	20,700	16,256	21,155	18,991
98,700	98,750	20,714	16,269	21,169	19,004
98,750	98,800	20,728	16,281	21,183	19,016
98,800	98,850	20,742	16,294	21,197	19,029
98,850	98,900	20,756	16,306	21,211	19,041
98,900	98,950	20,770	16,319	21,225	19,054
98,950	99,000	20,784	16,331	21,239	19,066
99,000					
99,000	99,050	20,798	16,344	21,253	19,079
99,050	99,100	20,812	16,356	21,267	19,091
99,100	99,150	20,826	16,369	21,281	19,104
99,150	99,200	20,840	16,381	21,295	19,116
99,200	99,250	20,854	16,394	21,309	19,129
99,250	99,300	20,868	16,406	21,323	19,141
99,300	99,350	20,882	16,419	21,337	19,154
99,350	99,400	20,896	16,431	21,351	19,166
99,400	99,450	20,910	16,444	21,365	19,179
99,450	99,500	20,924	16,456	21,379	19,191
99,500	99,550	20,938	16,469	21,393	19,204
99,550	99,600	20,952	16,481	21,407	19,216
99,600	99,650	20,966	16,494	21,421	19,229
99,650	99,700	20,980	16,506	21,435	19,241
99,700	99,750	20,994	16,519	21,449	19,254
99,750	99,800	21,008	16,531	21,463	19,266
99,800	99,850	21,022	16,544	21,477	19,279
99,850	99,900	21,036	16,556	21,491	19,291
99,900	99,950	21,050	16,569	21,505	19,304
99,950	100,000	21,064	16,581	21,519	19,316

$100,000 or over use the Tax Computation Worksheet

* This column must also be used by a qualifying widow(er).

Topical Index

References are to paragraph (¶) numbers

A

B

CHA

D

E

J

K

L

M

S

U

V